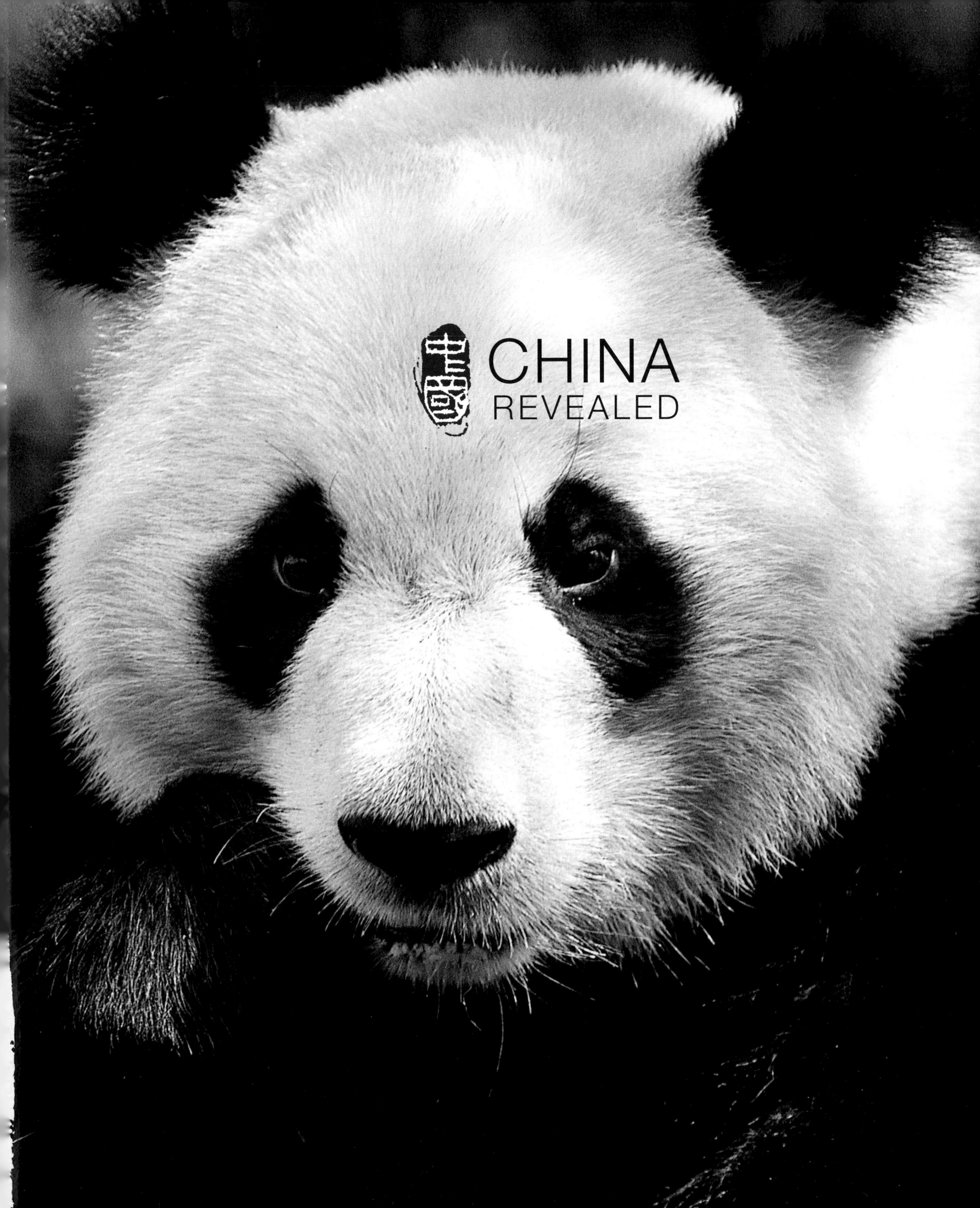

CHINA
REVEALED

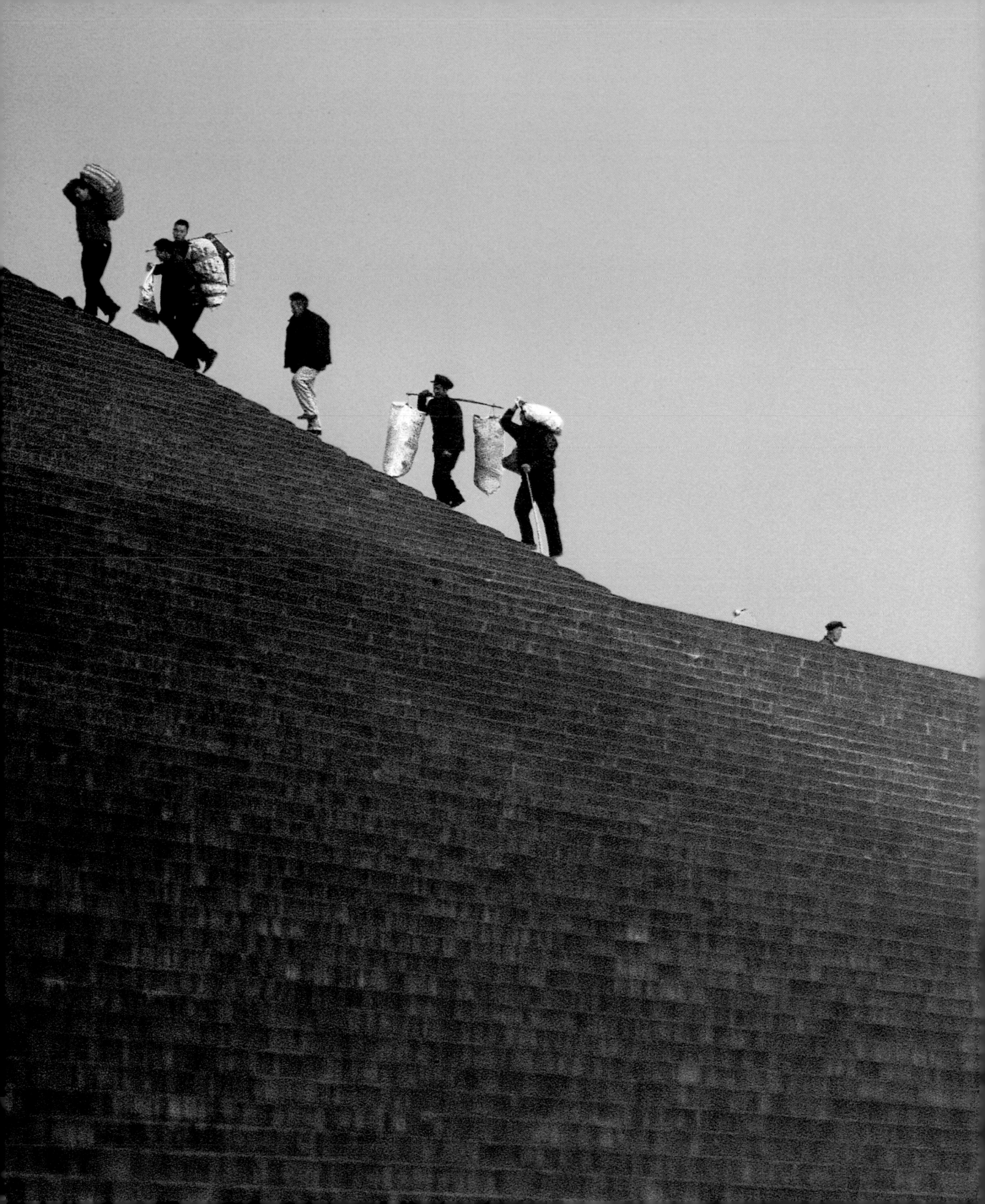

CHINA
REVEALED

AN EXTRAORDINARY JOURNEY
OF REDISCOVERY

TEXT & PHOTOGRAPHS BY
BASIL PAO

ABBEVILLE PRESS PUBLISHERS
New York London

PRODUCER/RESEARCHER (CHINA) **NINA HUANG FAN**
RESEARCHER/EDITOR **GAVIN GREENWOOD**
MANAGING EDITOR **DEBBIE WOSKA**
ART DIRECTION & DESIGN **BASIL PAO**
ASSOCIATE DESIGNER **STELLA LAI**

FIRST PUBLISHED IN GREAT BRITAIN IN 2007 BY WEIDENFELD & NICOLSON, ORION
PUBLISHING GROUP, UPPER SAINT MARTIN'S LANE, LONDON, WC2H 9EA

FIRST PUBLISHED IN THE UNITED STATES OF AMERICA IN 2007 BY ABBEVILLE PRESS
PUBLISHERS, 137 VARICK STREET, NEW YORK, NY 10013

10 9 8 7 6 5 4 3 2 1

TEXT & PHOTOGRAPHS © BASIL PAO 2007

ISBN-13: 978-0-7892-0947-4
ISBN-10: 0-7892-0947-0

CALLIGRAPHY BY ZHEUNG YAO QUN
COLOUR REPRODUCTIONS BY NEWSELE, MILAN
PRINTED AND BOUND IN ITALY BY PRINTER TRENTO

FOR BULK AND PREMIUM SALES AND FOR TEXT ADOPTION PROCEDURES, WRITE TO
CUSTOMER SERVICE MANAGER, ABBEVILLE PRESS, 137 VARICK STREET,
NEW YORK, NY 10013, OR CALL 1-800-ARTBOOK.

LIBRARY OF CONGRESS CATALOGING-IN-PUBLICATION DATA IS AVAILABLE UPON REQUEST

VISIT **ABBEVILLE PRESS** ONLINE AT: *www.abbeville.com*

[RIGHT] Li Jiang river, Guang'xi province.

[PRECEDING PAGES]
[1] Cheng'du Panda Breeding & Research Centre.
[2–3] The docks at Chao'tian'men in Chong'qing.

[FOLLOWING PAGES]
[6–7] The end of the Great Wall at Jia'yu'guan, Gan'su province.
[10–11] Snowstorm over Ta'erqin, Western Tibet.
[12–13] Khunjerab Pass, Xin'jiang.
[30–31] The Lu'sheng festival in Zhou'xi, Gui'zhou province.

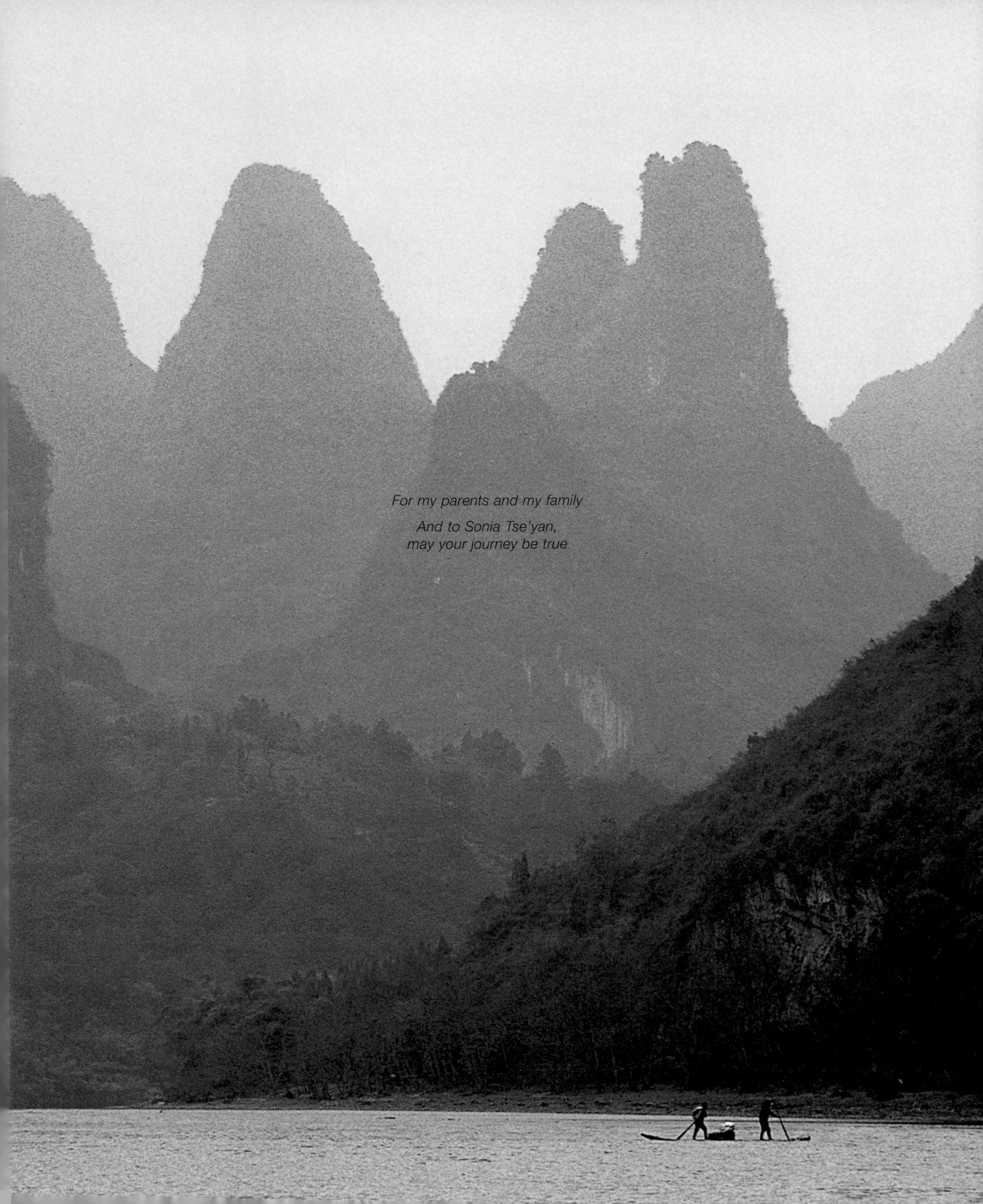

For my parents and my family

*And to Sonia Tse'yan,
may your journey be true*

CONTENTS

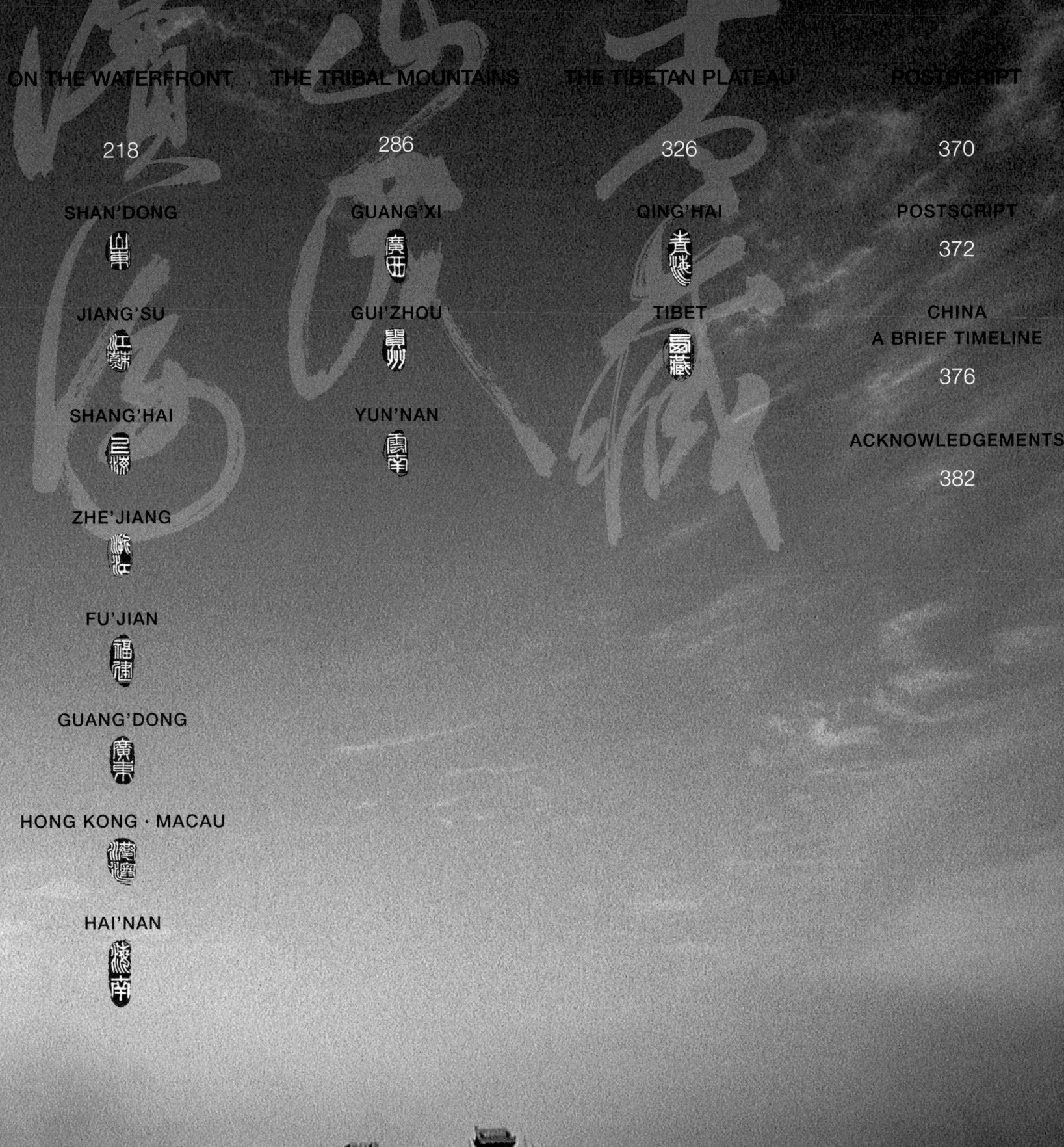

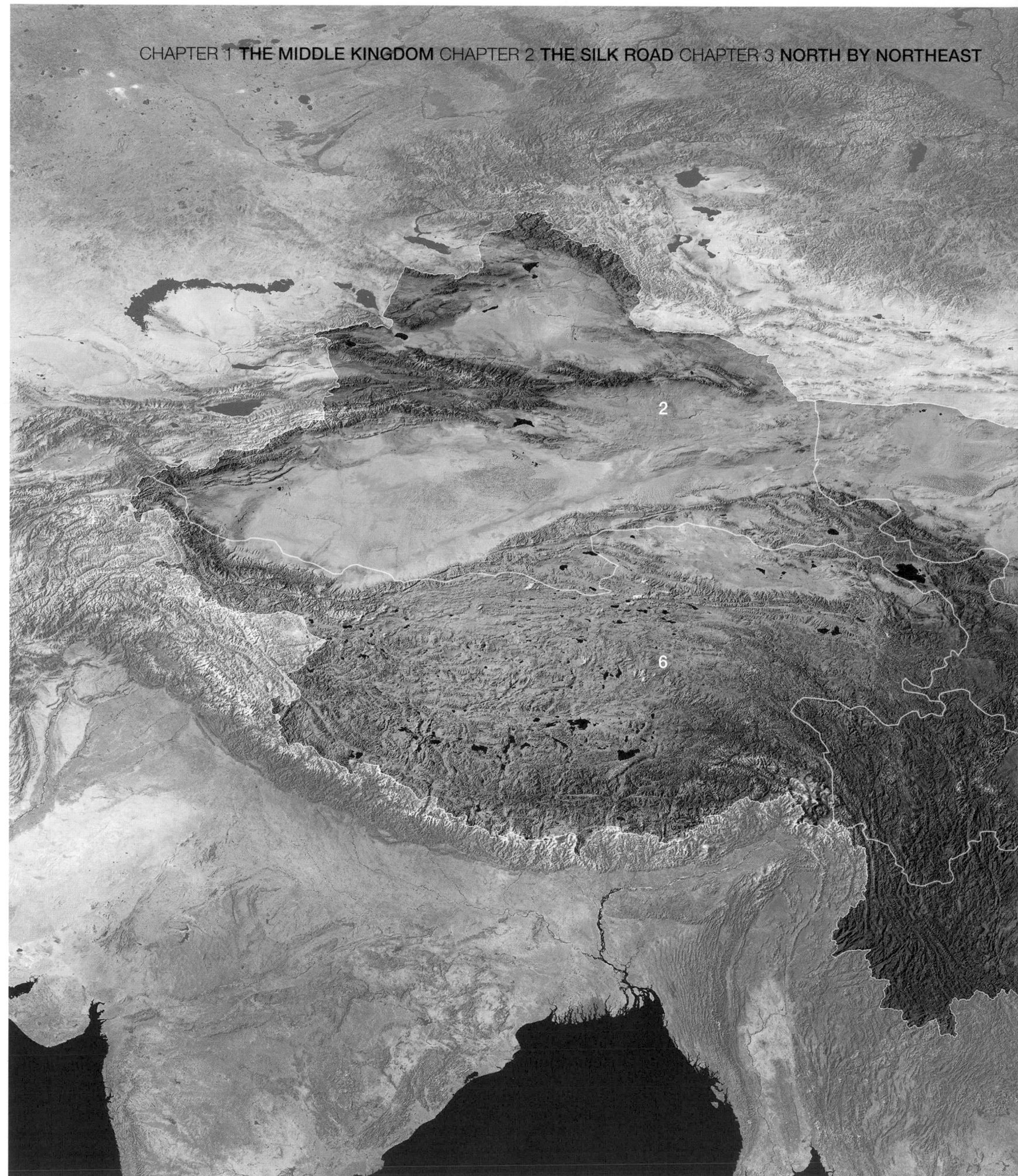

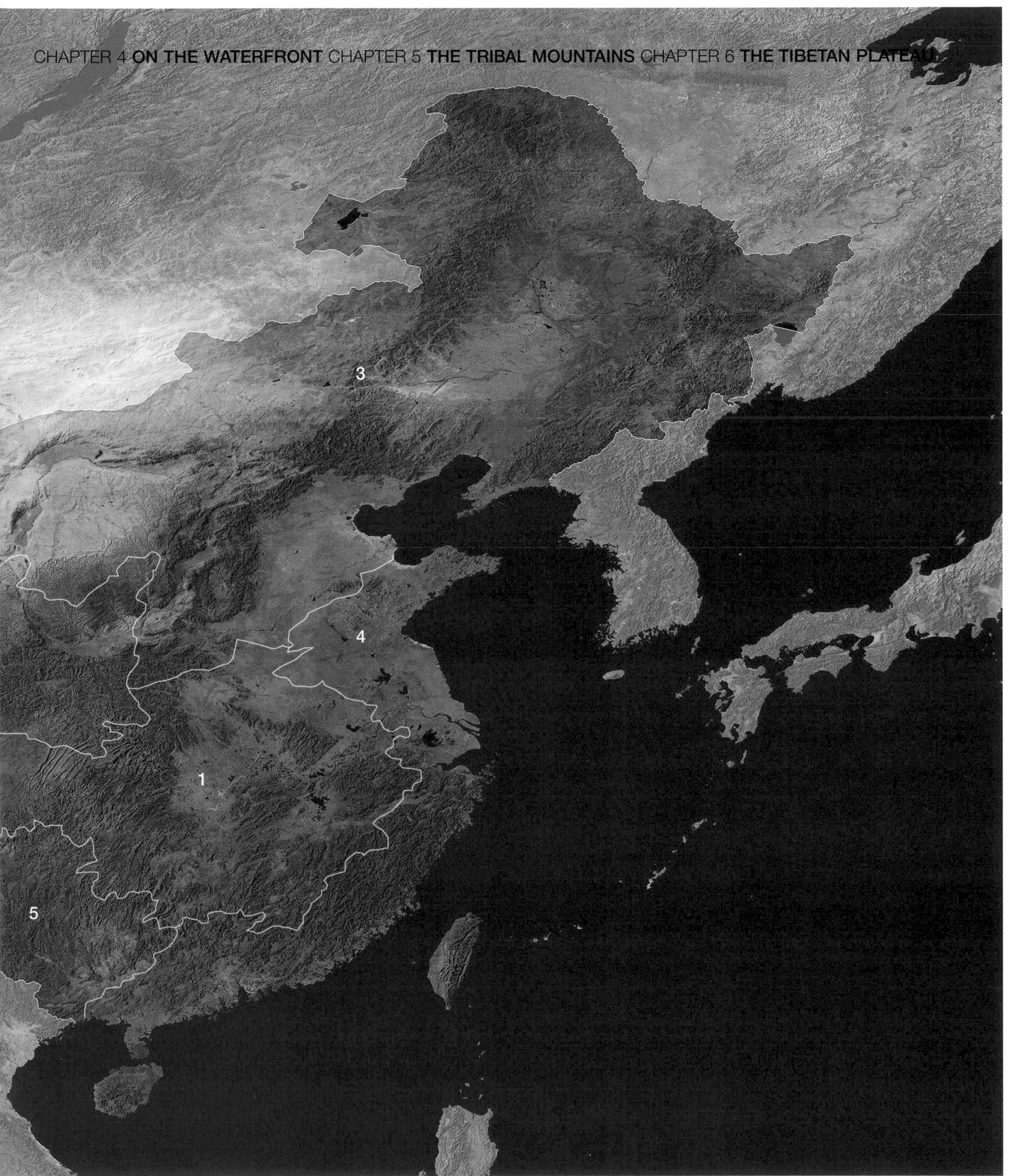

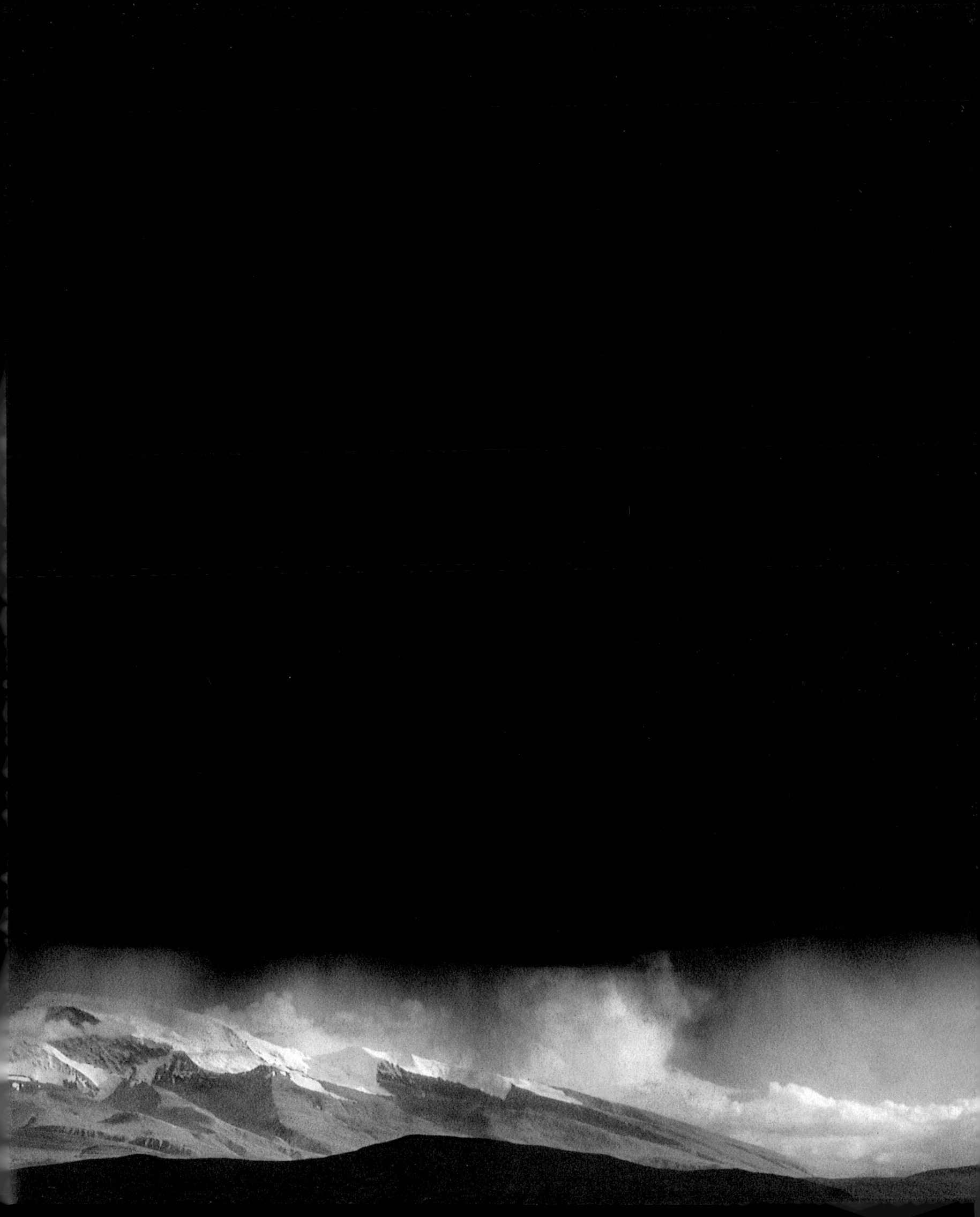

CONTEMPLATING ORCHIDS FROM A GALLOPING HORSE
OR
PUFF THE TRAGIC DRAGON

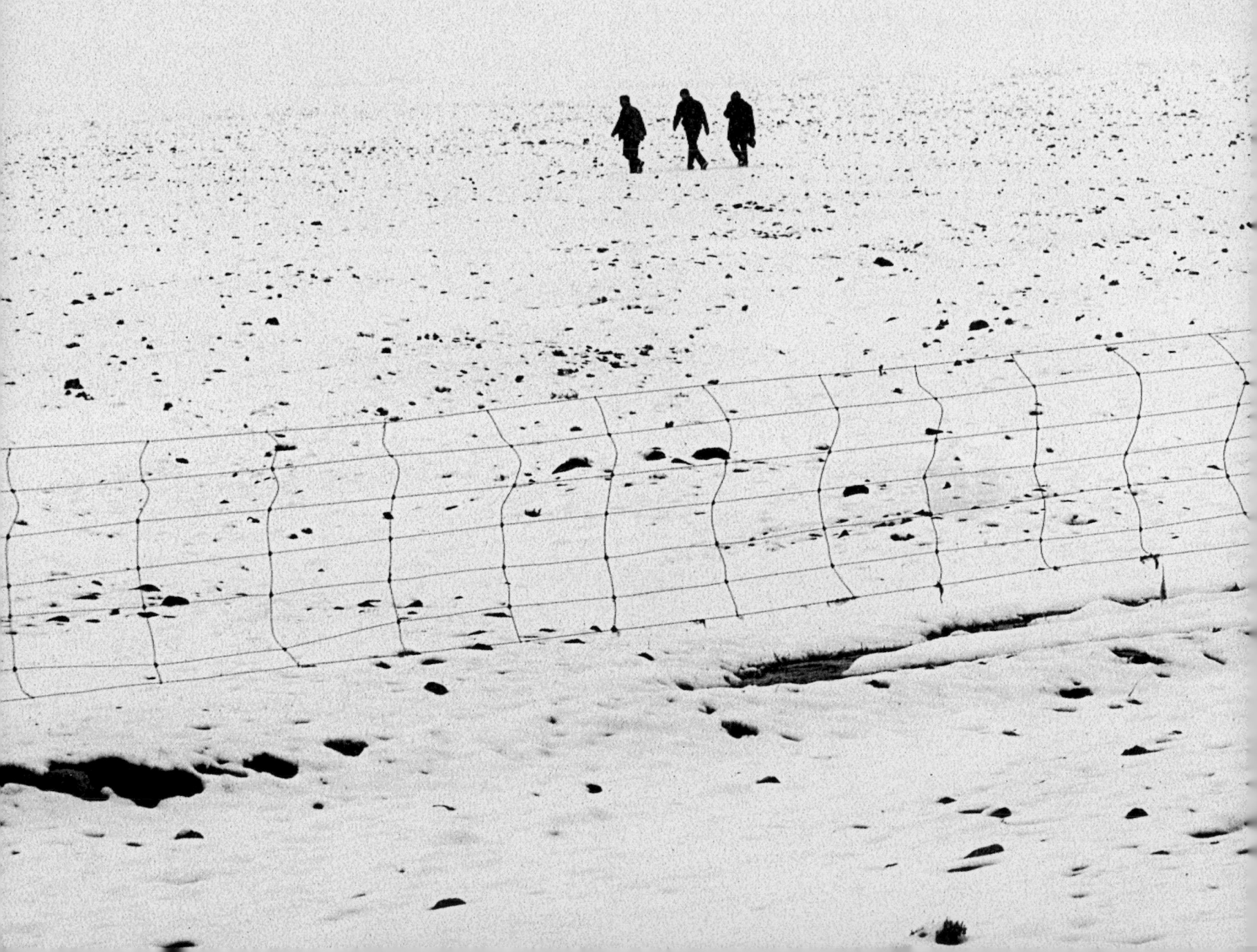

The phone rings in the dark. My eyes refuse to open. I reach out towards the unfamiliar ring, arms flailing and finding nothing but air. By the time I wake up enough to realize that I have no idea where I am and decide to let it ring, it stops. In a heartbeat it starts again, next door. Through the thin wall behind my headboard, I can't help but hear a man's voice shouting "Wei..." rather too loudly into the receiver. Suddenly I know where I am. I am in China. And judging by the density and close proximity of the smell emanating from the bathroom, I'm in a standard room of a three-star, sold as four-star, hotel in a provincial city; and the call was just another massage girl from the hotel's 'Health & Beauty Centre' offering room service to strangers in the night; just one of the thousands of such offers being made at that moment all across the country. But before I can manage to coax any more information from my jetlagged brain, a powerful memory reaches out like a claw and drags me deep into the past, that spectral zone of eternal twilight from which there is no escape...

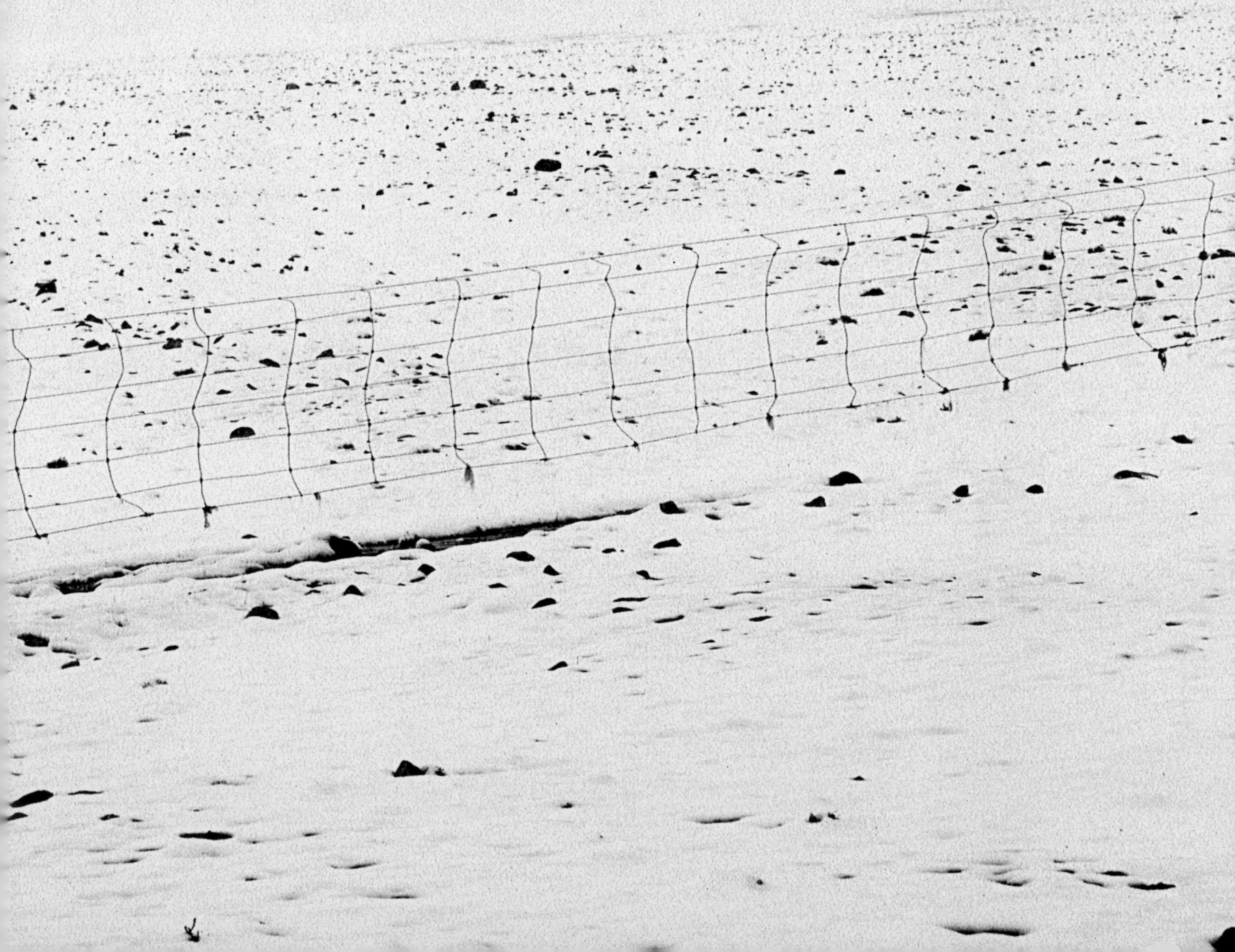

The phone rang in the dark. I opened my eyes and instinctively looked for the light on the desk by the window where, on moonlit nights, the reflection on the glass top glowed like fresh snow on the ground. But it was pitch black and the night suddenly felt colder.

The old-fashioned ring, a ghostly shadow of the one in Hitchcock's *Dial M for Murder*, echoed along the long, narrow corridor and into our room. My brother stirred on the bunk above me, while on the upper berth opposite, our 'great-uncle' tossed and turned and continued to snore. There was a tiny squeak as our parents' bedroom door opened and my father's footsteps, the leather soles of his slippers slip-sliding against the hard-wood floor like sandpaper, shifted hurriedly towards the dining room. A pause, then a click, and the fluorescent tube over the corridor flickered on and a cold green light streamed into our room through the narrow doorway. The ringing stopped and I strained to hear my father's voice as the grandfather clock chimed four times.

A flurry of footsteps, voices and shifting shadows on the walls seeped into my consciousness. I heard my father calling my mother to the phone; and my grandfather asking, "Who is it?" from his doorway opposite ours, while in the background, my grandmother coughed, gurgled and spat into the spittoon beside her bed. Then, at some point, a silhouette reached in and gently pulled our door to, and a slice of light swept across the ceiling and escaped through the closing door. The snoring from the far wall stopped abruptly, plunging the darkness into a deep silence. I remember pulling the blanket over my head in confusion and thinking only that the phone had never rung at four in the morning before. At breakfast the next day, we learned that the call was from Auntie Ida, our mother's older sister, with the news that their older brother, 'Elder Brother Chong' as he was known to the family, had 'come down' from China during the night and managed to find his way to her villa in Kowloon Tong.

Throughout the next day at school, I raked my memory for information about this uncle who had arrived unannounced, in the hours – as my grandmother believed – when spirits returned. About the only thing I was sure about was that he had lived in Canton until the night before. Everything else I knew about him floated in a murky pool of stories that flowed from our parents' collective streams of nostalgia, illustrated only by the few tiny, faded photographs of him in the family album. According to my father, who had been a fine swimmer himself in his youth, Elder Brother Chong was a rather famous volleyball player and the star of a team of talented young players who represented Hong Kong in the East Asian Games before the War. Nicknamed the 'Spike of God', he was apparently unstoppable at the net.

Our mother's stories tended to centre around her family's history, a *Gone with the Wind*-like saga of wealthy landowners whose vast fortune and holdings, stretching across South East Asia from southern Guang'dong to Hong Kong as far as Penang, ebbed and drained with the tides of war and revolution.

Judging by these stories, Elder Brother Chong was also very popular with the ladies, a well-known man-about-town with the reputation of a first-class womanizer.

Ten babies had emerged from my maternal grandmother's womb, of which eight survived; my uncle was the second, and the only son. As he was the sole heir to carry on the family line, and a thoroughly modern youth educated in western schools, who had an obvious disinclination to follow in the tradition of a 'blind and mute' (arranged) marriage, an elaborate trap was laid for him when he turned eighteen. It involved the building of a new family mansion in the ancestral village and his compulsory attendance at the all-important ceremonies surrounding the raising and blessing of the main crossbeams of the house. He was lured back to Tai Shan from Hong Kong, where he promptly found himself married to a peasant girl he had never laid eyes on before.

He dutifully took his new bride back to Hong Kong and, over the next several years, fulfilled his family obligations by producing a girl and a boy with her, but there was never any doubt in anyone's mind that they remained total strangers to each other and led separate lives. The marriage did not stop him from becoming a star athlete, nor did it prevent him from courting society ladies and romancing 'taxi-girls' in the most famous nightclubs of the Pearl River delta. Later, when his father died suddenly, some said mysteriously, somewhere on the Malay Peninsula where he was investing in a tin mine, Elder Brother Chong inherited the vast family fortune. Eventually he got heavily involved with a nightclub hostess and took her in as a concubine, and it was with her that he lived for the rest of his life.

With the passage of World War II, the Japanese invasion, the Chinese civil war and the dawn of Red China, everything – his life and that of millions of others – fell apart. Yet the image of him that our parents persisted in projecting, perpetuated perhaps as much by nostalgia as denial – a fear of facing the truth of what was happening in China – had always been of a heroic, almost mythical figure: a universally adored, fabulously wealthy and dashing young stud who made women swoon with desire on the dance floor and his opponents quake with fear on the volleyball court.

As I rang the doorbell, panting a little from running up the eight flights of stairs to our apartment, my imagination was churning with images of him rising like an eagle over the net and striking the white ball with the wrath of heaven, then on his way down, gliding gracefully like Fred Astaire across a mirrored floor with a beauty in his arms…

My mother was sitting with a group of solemn-looking women in the living room, all speaking in hushed voices as if trying not to wake a sleeping baby. I dutifully paid my respects to everyone, addressing each of them in order of seniority and by their proper titles within the family hierarchy, my mother the prompter by my side. "Say hello to your uncle…" she finally said, her eyes reaching over my head towards the dining room behind me.

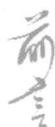

He was sitting alone at the dining table with his back to us. The first thought that entered my head was that he was smaller than I had imagined. "Big uncle," I shouted as I walked quickly towards him, raising my voice for the first time since I entered the flat. Slowly he turned his head in my general direction, but before I had a chance to see his face, his head disappeared again behind his hunched shoulders. I moved gingerly forward, and, unsure of what to do next, walked around him to the far side of the table, not daring to look at him directly. I poked my head inside the kitchen and shouted greetings to the cook and the amah before climbing onto the row of red vinyl-upholstered chairs by the windows. I worked up the courage to face him, but my eyes kept wandering from the telephone next to me to the grandfather clock overhead, hearing again the voices announcing his unexpected arrival, until finally they settled uncomfortably on his face. An unfamiliar tightness, like a claw, gripped my chest.

His hair was spiky and specked with muddy grey; his face was worn, the good bone structure now hidden under a layer of sun-hardened hide, almost black and tinged with a shroud of mouldy green. Awkward stubble left by a hasty shave framed his face and his once-handsome features were tattered by toil. He was looking down, concentrating very hard on spooning heaps of white sugar from the bowl onto a piece of soft white bread. Carefully, he folded the bread in half and put it in his mouth, taking almost the entire piece in one gulp. He looked up as he chewed, staring straight ahead into the dark corridor, his eyes blank, his face expressionless except for the mechanical motion of chewing, changing into a mild grimace only when he swallowed hard. He took another piece of white bread out of the pack, and repeated the process. As I watched him, I overheard snippets of conversation from the living room, about possible places to stay and potential work opportunities, where to take him to shop for clothes... And while his future was being decided in front of him behind his back, our uncle prepared and ate sugar sandwiches, in a world all his own, like a machine that had forgotten its purpose.

Finally, when his hand came out empty from the bread packet, he stopped and took a breath. He stared at his hands for a while, then, slowly and meticulously, began picking up the grains of sugar left on the tabletop with his thumb and forefingers, putting them into his mouth with great care, repeating the action mechanically until the table was clean. With his tongue he licked the last specks of sugar from his fingers, then, closing his mouth and eyes and with a deep sigh of relief, he let his hands fall to his sides and leaned back from the table.

Without warning, he turned and looked straight at me, or rather straight through me. What happened next I never fully understood. All I remember was falling, falling into his empty grey eyes, into a place darker and blacker and deeper and more bottomless than anything I could have imagined, and that I couldn't move, as though I had been frozen. My chest was hurting and I was struggling for breath, yet I couldn't look away; I was mesmerized by a fascination more powerful than all physical sensations.

Then he turned away, as mindlessly as he had turned towards me, and the spell slowly evaporated. It wasn't until years later that I learned all the proper names for what I had felt at that moment when our eyes met. But more importantly, that was the moment China first became 'real' for me. It was the winter of 1962, February to be exact, and I was nine years old.

It was the year the utopian folly known as the Great Leap Forward that had begun in 1958 finally came to an end. Mao had just been forced to issue a 'self-criticism' at the Meeting of the Seven Thousand, finally pushed into taking some responsibility for the failed policies that had directly led to the deaths of at least 30 million people in the course of four short years, during the greatest man-made famine in the history of mankind. For several days in that February of 1962, the Chinese government in Guangdong province threw open its gates along the Hong Kong border, and in the ensuing exodus more than 50,000 people, my uncle amongst them, successfully negotiated the barbed-wire fences to enter British territory and a new life.

Up until the moment I first met the husk that had once been the mighty 'Spike of God', and looked into his vacant eyes, 'China' had belonged purely in the realm of fantasies. My conceptions of it were based largely on the brush-and-ink world of comic books and the little history I knew came from their depictions of the classical novels such as *The Journey to the West*, *The Water Margin* and *Romance of the Three Kingdoms*. And to complete the misconceptions there were bad Cantonese movies and the period soap operas, which I listened to religiously every day on the radio in my grandparents' room. During the long hot afternoons of the summer holidays I would lie on my grandfather's bed on a cool straw mat, my eyes tight shut, listening to the radio and painting the scenes on the back of my eyelids while he sat at his desk scribbling endlessly onto stacks of lined paper that he kept in three-ringed binders. And whatever tinge of patriotism I may have felt for the 'Motherland', while living under the roof of a housing complex reserved for the families of those who served Her Majesty's Government of Hong Kong, derived from that curious but highly popular serial called *The Adventures of Uncle Chai*, about a bandit-cum-'freedom fighter' who reversed the history of World War II week after week by single-handedly defeating the Japanese invaders in Manchuria, dressed – nobody seemed to know why – like a Canadian lumberjack replete with a Daniel Boone raccoon hat and a faithful German Shepherd by his side.

As for the entity known as The People's Republic of China, my only exposure to it came from our 'great-uncle', who lived with us. He was technically, though only in his twenties and younger than him, my father's uncle, because he was my grandmother's adopted brother from another branch of her family. He was a self-professed leftist and unabashed patriot. He subscribed to *China Pictorial*, the communist party's answer to *LIFE* magazine, where I first saw heavily retouched photos of Mao, Chou, Stalin and Castro along with impossibly happy peasant women in vast fields of wheat, their cheeks rosy even in black and

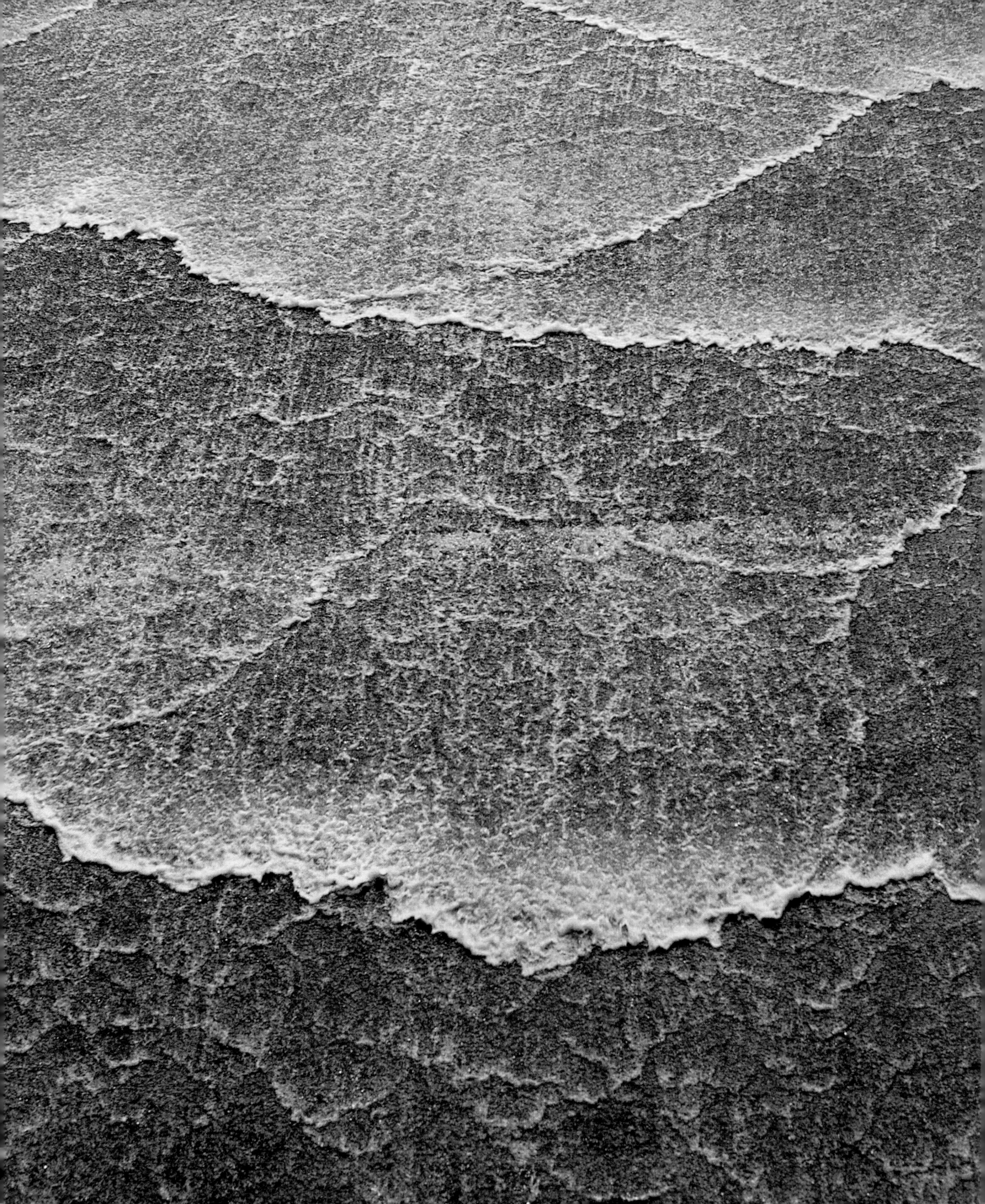

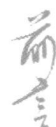

white, and improbably proud men in hard hats looking determined and heroic in front of rivers of molten steel or towering oil rigs. They were later joined by images of Ho Chi-min and North Vietnamese comrades repelling the 'Paper Tiger American Imperialist' invaders.

And the only physical contact I had with Mao's China was when we went shopping at the various 'China Products' emporiums, which specialized in cheap household goods, processed foods and everything else manufactured under the red sun. Like those crazy naked rubber dolls covered with inexplicable multi-coloured lines and dots which I only learned much later on to be acupuncture models showing meridians and pressure points. And then there were the chocolates, the nastiest-tasting cocoa products that ever passed my lips, which our 'great-uncle' insisted on buying for us, either out of patriotic duty or for some other perverse reason known only to him, for they were truly foul and he knew we hated them. At times I wondered if those chocolates may not have had something to do with my resolute drift away from the culture that supposedly ran through my veins towards the alien embrace of Da Vinci and Led Zepplin. Was the battle over cultural identity just a war of confectionaries; was it simply Cadbury versus Temple of Heaven?

All that changed the day after 'Big Uncle Chong' came to the house and had a whole loaf of sugar sandwiches. The moment I fell through his eyes into the abyss of a man whose spirit had been broken and whose soul had taken flight, the romance went out of the *Three Kingdoms* and the Monkey King came crashing down to earth in mid-flight. 'China', in all its facets, ceased to be simply a benign mystery, it was transformed instead into a fire-breathing dragon, one capable of reducing the strongest of men into an empty hulk. I never suspected that the sheer, unadulterated terror that gripped my body and turned my veins to ice that day would stay with me, but stay it did, and stayed and stayed, and silently grew.

I thought the beast had left me when I saw my uncle again a couple of weeks later at a clan dinner. He had been cleaned up and had lost that 'fresh from the grave' look. A haircut, a clean shave and a new suit made him look younger and considerably more human. And, despite the coldness and an otherworldliness that still appeared to shroud him, and though I steadfastly avoided eye contact with him (as I was to do for the rest of his life), I was no longer afraid of him and I thought I that my nightmare was over. But I could not have been more wrong, for he was only the vassal that delivered the beast, and I was a marked man. The dragon was about to become my worst friend and best enemy, a life-long companion slithering invisibly in my subconscious, silently moulding my destiny to its will, so that the harder I pushed away, the closer it drew me near, and the more I tried to ignore and turn my back on it, the more irresistible it became. Like an insatiable lover it entwined me in a suffocating embrace, and I was doomed to struggle with the conflicts between repulsion and fascination, hate and love for the beast that lived in me and stood for everything that was evil and good about China and, ultimately, about myself.

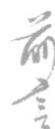

For whatever I may have tried to do or had since become, its 3,000-year-old blood ran in my veins. But for the next forty years I denied that simple truth and tried in vain to break free.

Over the next few years, as I staggered involuntarily towards puberty, the reformers, led by Liu Shao-chi and Deng Xiao-ping, pulled China back from the brink of total disaster, while Mao retreated to his various scenic villas around the country to plot his revenge. And while China was slowly recovering from the famine, the dragon slept as my body experienced a sudden spurt of growth that removed the last traces of the happy little chap they once nicknamed 'little Buddha', and left me more gawky and moody with each passing day. And my mental landscape also began to change. At first the shift to the West seemed superficial: Chinese historical comics were replaced by the hysterical antics of the Three Stooges, and Steve McQueen with his sawn-off Winchester in *Wanted Dead or Alive* on television took the place of Zhao Yun and his long spear in *Three Kingdoms* as the hero of choice, while Top 40 Hits knocked out the Cantonese soap operas on the radio. And I saw my first copies of *Playboy* magazine, smuggled into the house in a PanAm flight bag by a naughty cousin who was spending the weekend. Just exactly what my mother thought about three boys going into the bathroom together I will never know, but she never said anything.

By the time my voice broke, Mao was ready to strike. He launched the Great Proletarian Cultural Revolution in May 1966, calling upon the students of China to rise and 'struggle' against their teachers and all other authority figures. By June, all classes were suspended and a prestigious middle school in Bei'jing gave birth to the infamous name 'Red Guards'. The wholesale destruction of Chinese culture began and an entire generation of students took a summer break that lasted for ten years. High on freedom and crazed with hormones, they went about their task with the youthful exuberance typical of teenagers the world over. In August, while England was still intoxicated by the euphoria of their Football World Cup win, the headmistress of a Bei'jing girls' school was tortured to death by her students. Two weeks later on 18th August, Mao stood on top of Tian'an'men Gate and unleashed the Red Guards on a world shocked and awed by the sheer spectacle of an imminent typhoon of chaos manipulated by a malevolent ego.

The newsreel images of hundreds of thousands of devotees singing and yelling slogans and pledging undying loyalty to a frail seventy-two-year-old man brought to mind Leni Riefenstahl's classic *Triumph of the Will* – the gold standard of propaganda film-making, and where it lacked the sophistication and artistry of the Nazi production, the footage of the Red Guards Review at Tian'an'men Square made up for it with raw passion and spellbinding madness. And thanks to the new policy of the rail networks, where the ticket price to anywhere in China was a Red Guard armband, a Mao badge and a copy of Mao's *Little Red Book*, armies of Red Guards from the cities descended upon the interior and the revolution of 'Let's smash everything, including the people…' spread like wildfire into the farthest corner of the country – much to the horror of an already-terrified populace only just recovering from the 'Great Leap Backward'. And about the

time John Lennon's "the Beatles are bigger than Jesus" furore hit the U.S. and Americans were burning Beatles records, historic monuments and cultural relics, not to mention millions of ancient scrolls and precious books, were in flames all over China.

The dragon laid back and enjoyed the fireworks as the hormones exploded in my system like incendiaries in the blitz. Being unnaturally shy and a natural coward, I was girl-crazy but totally clueless. Destined never to become a predator, I settled for the role of the benign stalker instead, taking to admiring from afar the girls of St Margaret's Girls' College, an institution more renowned for its relaxed attitude towards regulation-defying short skirts than for its academic prowess. I did manage to get into the final rounds of some amateur song contest sponsored by a teenybopper magazine, playing my twelve-string guitar and singing Bob Dylan's 'The Times They Are A-Changin'. But I never got near the prizes nor the girls, and so I battled my multitude of demons in solitude.

As a dazed and confused teenager, I became stupid and reckless and experimented with self-destruction for the first time. I hung out with 'fly-boys' (the Cantonese jargon for a juvenile poser whose entire reason-for-being was based on the ducktail hairdo of Elvis and the insolent pout of James Dean in *Rebel without a Cause*). I played basketball in Triad-infested public courts that no sane person would enter voluntarily. I started gambling in class, for which I was eventually busted. My school grades went schizoid as well. I managed to maintain A's and B's in my English subjects, but scored the almost-impossible-to-get grade H for both Chinese History and Chinese Literature, which meant, in effect, that I slept through them and did absolutely nothing during the school year.

By May 1967, the Cultural Revolution was spilling over into Hong Kong in the form of industrial disputes that resulted in strikes and riots. Soon curfews were imposed and homemade bombs packed in plain brown paper bags, nicknamed 'pineapples', were going off all over town. And when a popular radio host who spoke out against the violence was assassinated by the 'lefties', blown up in his car along with his brother, fear gripped the city, and those who could afford it began sending their children abroad. That summer, my brother and my cousin were packed off to England – where Sgt Pepper ruled – and my two best friends from school went to the U.S., just in time for the Summer of Love. After they left, my life took a turn for the worse. Bombarded by violent images of a world convulsing with wars and revolutions, the beast became increasingly restless and took to coming out to play at night. Feeding on my loneliness and frustrations, it haunted my dreams until the nightmares spilled over into daylight.

Finally, with eighteen conduct points deducted, just two points shy of expulsion and barely making the grades, I went to my parents one night and asked if I could go to school in England. And though they could ill afford it, and knew full well that my father would have to take on even more film subtitle translation work at night and that the family would have to tighten their belts for a very long time, they agreed. Perhaps they had recognized the plea of a desperate soul, or maybe they saw that it was time for me to leave

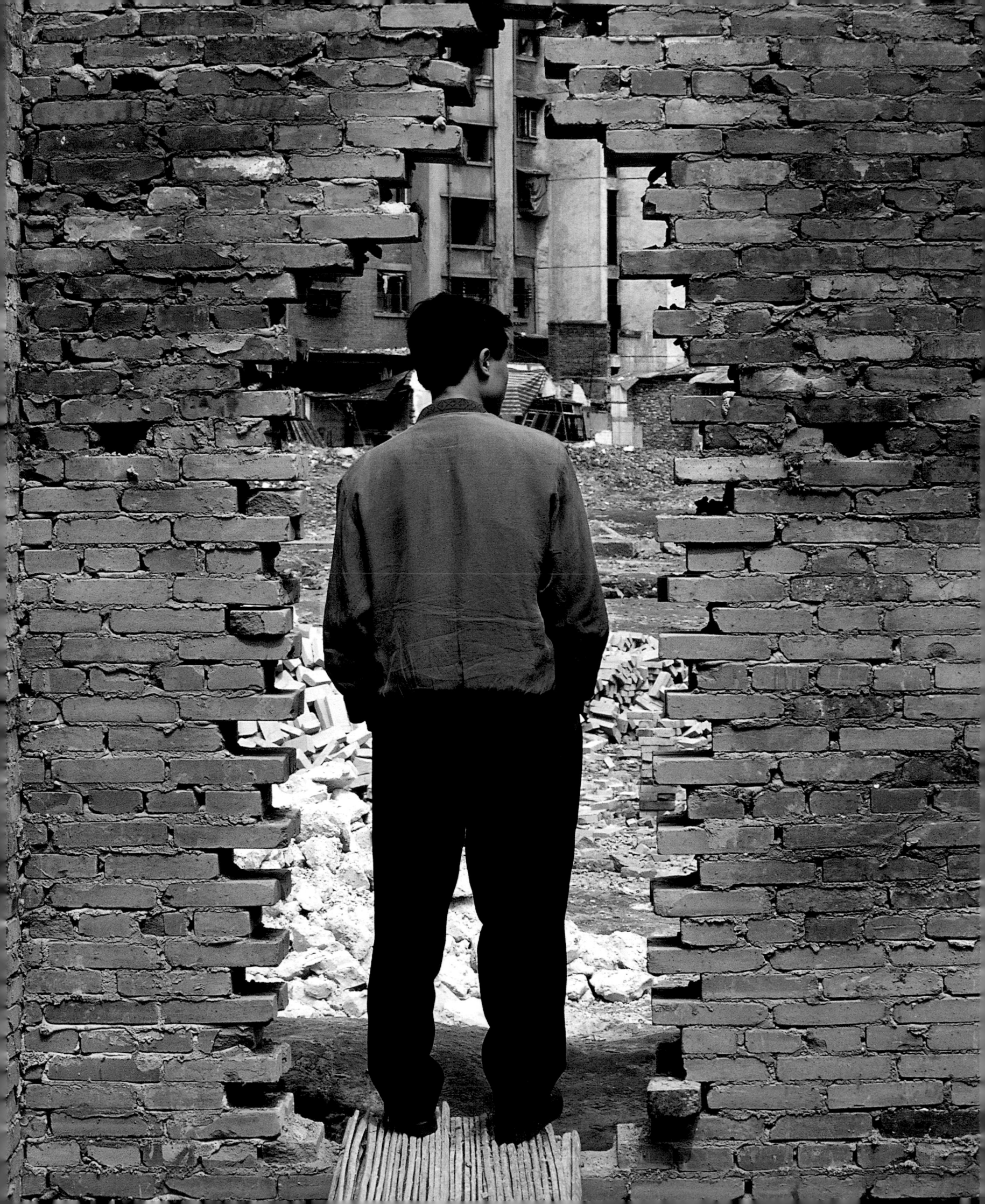

because Hong Kong's political future was becoming increasingly uncertain, but it was unconditional love that pushed them to take on the extra burden and endure the sacrifices, and for that, my heart will belong to them forever – for I shudder to think what I would have become had they said "no". As if by a miracle, I was accepted by Kingswood School in Bath, the school John Wesley had built for the children of Methodist ministers.

And soon after, one steamy, starry night, I found myself boarding a charter flight bound for Amsterdam with a connecting flight to London. My fellow passengers were mostly immigrants from the rural New Territories heading for the Chinatowns of Europe. Their carry-on luggage included a lot of pots and pans and one man was hugging his favourite wok in his arms. Someone else had fresh choi-sum from his vegetable patch, cut that very day. And I seem to remember a woman getting quite emotional when they refused to let her bring her chickens on board, but I'm not sure about that memory. What I am sure about is the excitement I felt – about my first journey on an aircraft, about flying solo for the first time, and, above all, about the new life that awaited me at the other end of the world. I was leaving the dragon behind and I was going to turn my back on China once and for all. As I entered the cabin of the Viscount Turboprop 800 I walked straight into a cosmic joke: all the seats were facing the tail of the plane, and so I flew to London backwards, with refuelling stops in Calcutta and Dubai, then a plane change in Amsterdam where most of the passengers disembarked, and thence across the English Channel to London, facing China the entire way.

But it didn't matter. Once I reached Victoria Terminal and met up with my brother and his friends, the prison break was a success, I had escaped and I was free. A huge weight had lifted and I felt elated and liberated, a feeling that by and large stayed with me through all the ups and down of the next twelve years of self-imposed exile. During which time I tried to shed my Chinese skin to become what the Americans call a 'banana' – yellow on the outside and white on the inside – for I had the misconception that the cultural baggage that I carried by being Chinese was going to hold me back, and to my eternal shame I succeeded in burying my cultural heritage to a very large extent, despite early setbacks like being nicknamed 'slits' by the school bully within the first week.

But it was also a time of tremendous personal growth, which started in the tranquil hills of Bath where I became interested in learning for the first time in my life, and ended in the skyscraper jungle of New York City and the smog-filled valleys of Los Angeles where my natural talents were valued and nurtured. I also learned important survival skills, such as how to pee into an empty Heineken can while inside your sleeping bag without cutting yourself, because Jimmy Hendrix was about to come on and there were 600,000 people who were stoned out of their skulls between you and the portable loos. There are many other tales of struggles and successes from this period but they do not belong here, for the dragon slept through most of it while I pushed China further and further into the recesses of my mind, barely

glancing back even when Mao died, the Gang of Four were arrested, and the reformers, led by Deng, were once again called upon to save the people. By that time I was in the U.S., in search of the busty blonde California beach bunny in the pink polka-dot bikini on the cover of *LIFE* magazine and the American Dream that she had inspired. There is, however, one anecdote that should be included. When I received a full scholarship during my second year at Art Center College of Design in L.A. and phoned home with the news, my mother got so excited that she dropped and broke the sugar jar. It never occurred to me to ask if it was the same jar that my uncle had made his sandwiches from.

Then, one smoggy Sunday afternoon in my one-bedroom shack up in Laurel Canyon, the thumping rhythm of a helicopter right outside the window woke the beast from its long hibernation, and by nightfall, it had poked its head out of the murky waters of my soul and called me home. The day was 16th September 1979, the year when all the comedians the world over were having a field-day with Ronald Reagan jokes, back in those days-of-innocence when nobody could actually believe that he was running for President of the United States.

I ran up the road to the top of the hill where our absent neighbours' Spanish castle stood like a watchtower overlooking the canyons all around. The sky was thick with smoke and helicopters and the air was dense with smog and just enough oxygen to fuel the flames, reeking with the stench of melting metal and the strangely intoxicating scent emanating from the row of giant eucalyptus burning below. From the top of the spur, I watched the inferno blazing across the canyons, engulfing the houses along the winding 'goat's intestines' roads that I travelled on each day to and from work. I saw that the fire was coming straight at us. And we had no water. I saw people further down the hill trying to drown the smoldering bushes and put out the sparks swirling over their crispy dry lawns with water from their swimming pools, bucket by painful bucket, I looked at the green gardening hose in my hand that was oozing less water than a baby's tinkle, and I choked back a bitter laugh. The idea of wetting down the grounds and the three-storey chateau behind me suddenly seemed a bit silly. Without warning, the fire that was burning in the bottom of the ravine 100 metres (330 feet) below shot up along the face of the canyon and a huge wall of flames erupted right in front of me. As I reeled backwards, waving the green hose impotently at the fire, the dragon rose and howled, sending an unfamiliar chill of terror through my bones.

The police came and ordered us to evacuate, and as my next-door neighbours Joey and Ritchie corralled the three dogs into the back of the pick-up, I threw my passport into my empty attaché case, grabbed my Nikon-F and a roll of film, quickly surveyed my collection of paintings on the wall, and said a silent farewell as I turned around and walked out, closing the door behind me without bothering to lock it.

We stopped halfway down the hill on the other side of the canyon, where there was a good view of our houses, and waited for the fire to round the corner and consume everything we owned and swallow our past. I put

the film in the camera, but I never got to take the picture. A Fire Department helicopter dropped its load of water into the canyon wall right next to my shack – I still have a picture from *Newsweek* of that exact moment somewhere – and that was where the fire lost its will and stopped.

By late afternoon, the police barricades had been lifted and we went home. I opened the front door and was stunned by the tranquility permeating the living room. The silence was pristine. Even the smell, or rather the absence of it, was noiseless. It was as though the room had been hermetically sealed and placed in another dimension while the flames and smoke raged all around, a small cubical of peace within a towering inferno. And the first thing I saw was the Tibetan 'thanka' I had bought from a wandering monk in the Buddhist temple in New York Chinatown the year before, and Sakamuni was smiling down at me from its centre. As twilight folded itself over the city below, I watched the neon signs and the spotlights on the giant billboards below flicker on at the mouth of Sunset Strip. The Chateau Marmont caught my eye and I found the balcony of my room where I had stayed for several months when I first came out to Hollywood from New York, and I remembered how different things had become: how much I had enjoyed what I was doing then and how much I dreaded going to work now; how good I had felt then, and how awful I was feeling now.

The dragon stirred, and emerging from a dark pool it whispered something I didn't understand. I had come to the New World in search of the American Dream and by all ordinary measures I had achieved it, but I wondered then, to paraphrase Ingmar Bergman, "What if I was actually someone else's dream and she had woken up and felt ashamed…" I knew more people, and more people knew me, than ever before, yet I had never been so desperately lonely in all my life. I had found many different versions of the beach bunny on the *LIFE* magazine cover that had first brought me there, and yet I loved no one. And when I had foolishly thought that I was surfing the crest of the big waves of Sex, Drugs and Rock'n'Roll, I was actually being crushed underfoot like a cockroach against the brass stars on the pavement of the Walk of Fame. I stared at the gap in the broken life-line on my right palm for a long time, and, as the street lamps spread an amber grid over the city of angels all the way to the Pacific Ocean, the dragon spoke again – and this time I heard him. I had come West to find myself, and I had found him at the end of a long and arduous journey only to discover that he was not really worth looking for. And at that moment I realized that my American Dream was finally over for good.

The next day, on my way to work, I saw that a neighbour's yellow Cadillac that had always greeted me as I turned the corner had been reduced to a shapeless puddle on the driveway. The destruction further down the hill was even more devastating, with the burnt and tattered palm trees giving it the feel of a North Vietnamese village after a napalm run. And by the time I reached the office in Burbank, I knew it was time to go home. Soon afterwards, I gave notice and quit my job. But it was not until the eve of the new Chinese Year of the Monkey in February 1980 that I finally boarded the 'red-eye' for New York to begin my long journey home, turning my back on Hollywood and my chosen career for good, penniless and sick at heart.

I returned to Hong Kong and settled into a modest existence on the fishing island of Cheng Chau, where the rent was cheap. And over the next ten years, I embarked on a personal excavation, an expedition into the very heart of my soul, to try to recover the pieces not yet broken by my own cultural revolution that had begun all those years ago. I dug deep and hard, devouring the Chinese classics and delving into whatever subject happened to take my fancy at any given time. From history to Taoism, feng shui to Confucius, Buddhism to architecture, I-Ching to regional cuisines, even Tang poetry and herbal medicine. I went about my rehabilitation with the same zeal that I had put into expelling the Chinese heritage from my system. Unfortunately, as I was to discover, it was much easier to stop being Chinese than it was to become Chinese, and I had done such a good job of annihilating my past that the inside of the banana got only a little yellow – with age. All I managed to accomplish was to have enough information on a given subject to have a dinner party conversation without embarrassing myself. I made forays into China to see first-hand what I had been rebelling against and I learned to speak Mandarin badly. So by the time Bertolucci's *The Last Emperor* juggernaut hit town in 1986, I had just about enough confidence and ability to confront the dragon head-on. The months that I spent on the film set in Bei'jing changed my life and my attitude towards China, and I entered at last a period of détente with the beast as I hitched a ride on the back of the film's enormous success to a new career in photography.

The dragon slept peacefully until the early morning hours of June 4th, 1989, when I stared into the electronic eye of a 27" Sony Trinitron and saw the carnage in Tian'an'men Square, and I felt again the force of the dragon in full flight. For several months afterwards, I was paralyzed with rage and crippled by a deep sense of impotence; I couldn't work and even lost my appetite for food. And I made then, in my state of anguish and despair, one of the worst decisions of my life. As I watched my baby Sonia in her sweet slumber one night, I determined that I would never teach my daughter any Chinese, for I believed passionately then as I had all those years ago, when I first turned my back on China, that language and cultural baggage came as a package deal. I thought with conviction then that China was doomed to repeat its tragic history, and I wanted her to have no part of a culture that was forever sacrificing its young at the altar of absolute power. And though my opinion on that tragedy may not have altered much over time, as Sonia has grown almost imperceptibly into a young woman I have come to regret that decision. I had no right to turn her back on China without her consent.

And though I swore never to return and routinely turned down assignments in China after that day, I found myself in the winter of 1996 on a ferry from the Korean port of Inchon with Michael Palin and his crew, arriving at dawn in Qing'dao for his *Full Circle* television series. In the intervening years, the beast had writhed and twisted even as the dust settled, until only two memories remained from the ashes of the tragedy. They were the image of the man trying to block the way of the tanks and the last line of the

Wuerhuaixi interview in *Newsweek* magazine in which the student leader said, "I feel like a rock star." That pretty much summed up the whole affair for me, it was the Rolling Stones at Altamont all over again, except this time, they were all Hells Angels.

Then, in 2003, Michael's *Himalaya* series fulfilled one of my life-long dreams by taking me to Tibet. Before we crossed into Tibet from Nepal, we filmed an audience with His Holiness the Dalai Lama at his residence in Dharamsala in India. Afterwards, he asked me if I was Tibetan, and when he realized that I was not even a little bit Tibetan, not even from the fringes of Si'chuan or Yun'nan but from Hong Kong instead, he seemed momentarily disappointed. But the sunshine of his smile quickly returned and he asked if I had been to China lately. When I explained that I had been trying my best to avoid travelling or working in China since the Tian'an'men incident, his smile faded again and his expression became serious for the first time. "That is a mistake," he said. "You must go back... Go back and educate you brothers and sisters, because they are very closed-minded. You must tell them about the rest of the world..."

And so the wheels were set in motion. And when Michael announced after the *Himalaya* journey that he was taking a year off from travelling to consider his next move, I knew the time had finally arrived for me to come to terms with the dragon once and for all. It was time for me to dive into the belly of the beast...

Wide-awake now, I hear my neighbour's doorbell ring, and through the wall I listen as he opens his door to let someone in. I find my glasses and put them on as I tumble out of bed. There is a slither of light from the crack between the curtains and I pull them open and look out onto a generic provincial Chinese city. It looks like any number of places where I have spent the night in this past year, once again looking for myself, this time in every province in China. But tonight I'm lost; not even the neon signs are giving away my location. I look at my watch: it is around midnight. Lighting a cigarette, I take a deep drag and watch the smoke swirl like mating serpents, hanging in the air for a moment before dissolving into the semi-darkness, and find myself wondering whether my dragon is enjoying the tour so far...

Whether I will ever completely overcome a lifetime of prejudices and arrive at a lasting peace with the beast remains to be seen, but in the pages that follow, I present to you the images from my tour of reconciliation, made while moving around this vast country at breakneck speed, 'contemplating orchids from a galloping horse' as the Chinese saying goes, in an attempt at recording what is left of an authentic China before globalization truly sets in and removes the last traces of what makes it so unique. It is a souvenir from a journey of redemption, and it is also my way of apologizing to my daughter, in the form of a book – for Sonia loves books – in the hope that it will spark her interest in a culture and heritage that I had so foolishly denied her, and whose blood still runs in her veins.

CHINA MAP OF THE JOURNEY

Heavenly Lake

Turpan

Akesu

Kuche

Kashgar

XINJIANG

Tashkurgan

Khunjerab Pass

TIBET

Mt.Kailash

Namtso Lake

Lake Manasorovar

Zhongba

Saga

Zhangmu

Latse

Shikatse

Lhasa

Dingri

Mt.Everest

Gyangtse

Zedang

THE JOURNEY began just after the Spring Festival celebrations for the Year of the Rooster on 18 February 2005 and continued, on and off, for the rest of the year until just before the Year of the Dog was ushered in on 29 January 2006. During which time I crisscrossed the country by road, driving for over 25,000 kilometres (15,534 miles) and flew to the more remote locations before continuing the journey by car. This map shows all the places I have visited that are represented in this book. I have left out all the other locations that I have travelled to but that are not included in the book to avoid confusion.

Editor's note The statistics in the provincial opening pages represent the latest figures available at the time of going to press.

Dunhuang

GANSU

Jiayuguan

Qinghai Lake

QINGHAI

Xining

Yushu

Binglingsi Grottos • Lanzhou **NINGXIA**

Yinchuan

INNER MONGOLIA

Manzhouli • • Haila'er

Hulun Lake •

HEILONGJIANG

Ha'erbin •

JILIN

Changchun •

LIAONING

Shenyang •

Tonghua • • Baishan

Hanging Temple

Datong • • Hanging Temple

SHANXI

Taiyuan

HEBEI

BEIJING

TIANJIN

Wuqiao • • Qinhuangdao

Dalian •

Dandong •

Yan'an •

Hukou • • Pingyao

Yuncheng •

SHAANXI

Xi'an •

Luoyang • Shaolin Temple • Kaifeng

Zhuxianzhen •

HENAN

SHANDONG

Qufu • • Mt.Taishan

Qingdao •

JIANGSU

ANHUI

Nanjing •

SHANGHAI

SICHUAN

Kangding •

Qionglai • • Chengdu

Leshan •

Dazu • **CHONGQING**

Tiger Leaping Gorge

Lugu Lake

Lijiang •

Dali •

YUNNAN

Shilin • Kunming

Jinghong • Yuanyang

Yichang •

HUBEI

Wuhan •

Mt.Huangshan

Jingdezhen •

Tunxi • Suzhou

Hangzhou •

Shaoxing •

ZHEJIANG

Fenghuang •

Shaoshan • Changsha •

HUNNAN

Nanchang •

Wuyuan •

JIANGXI

FUJIAN

Hukeng • • Hui'an

Xiamen •

GUIZHOU

Guiyang •

Kaili •

Rongjiang • Zhaoxing

Xiajiang • Sanjiang

Longsheng • Guilin

GUANGXI Yangshuo

GAUNGDONG

Kaiping • Guangzhou

Houmen • Pinghai

Zhuhai •

Dongfang • Haikou

Sanya •

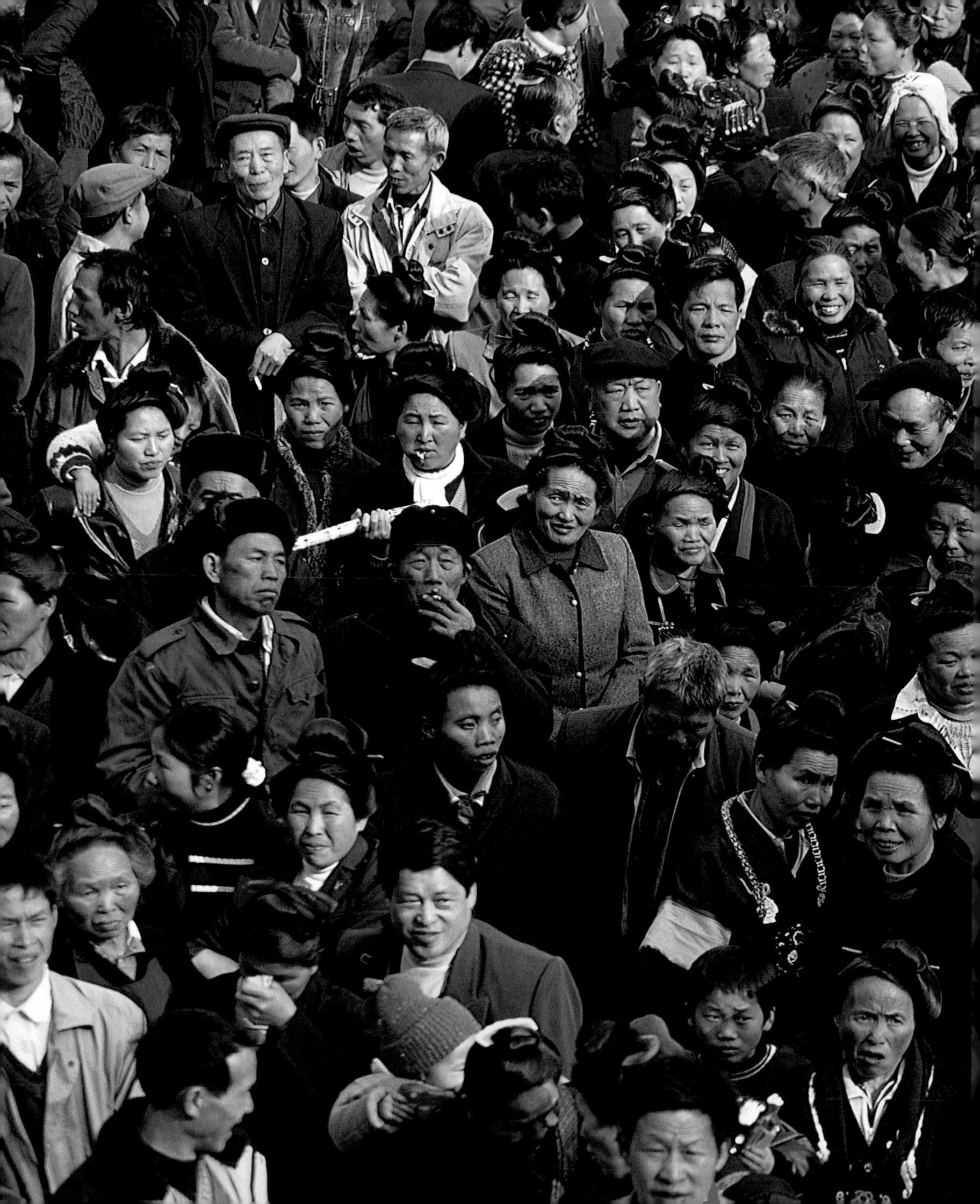

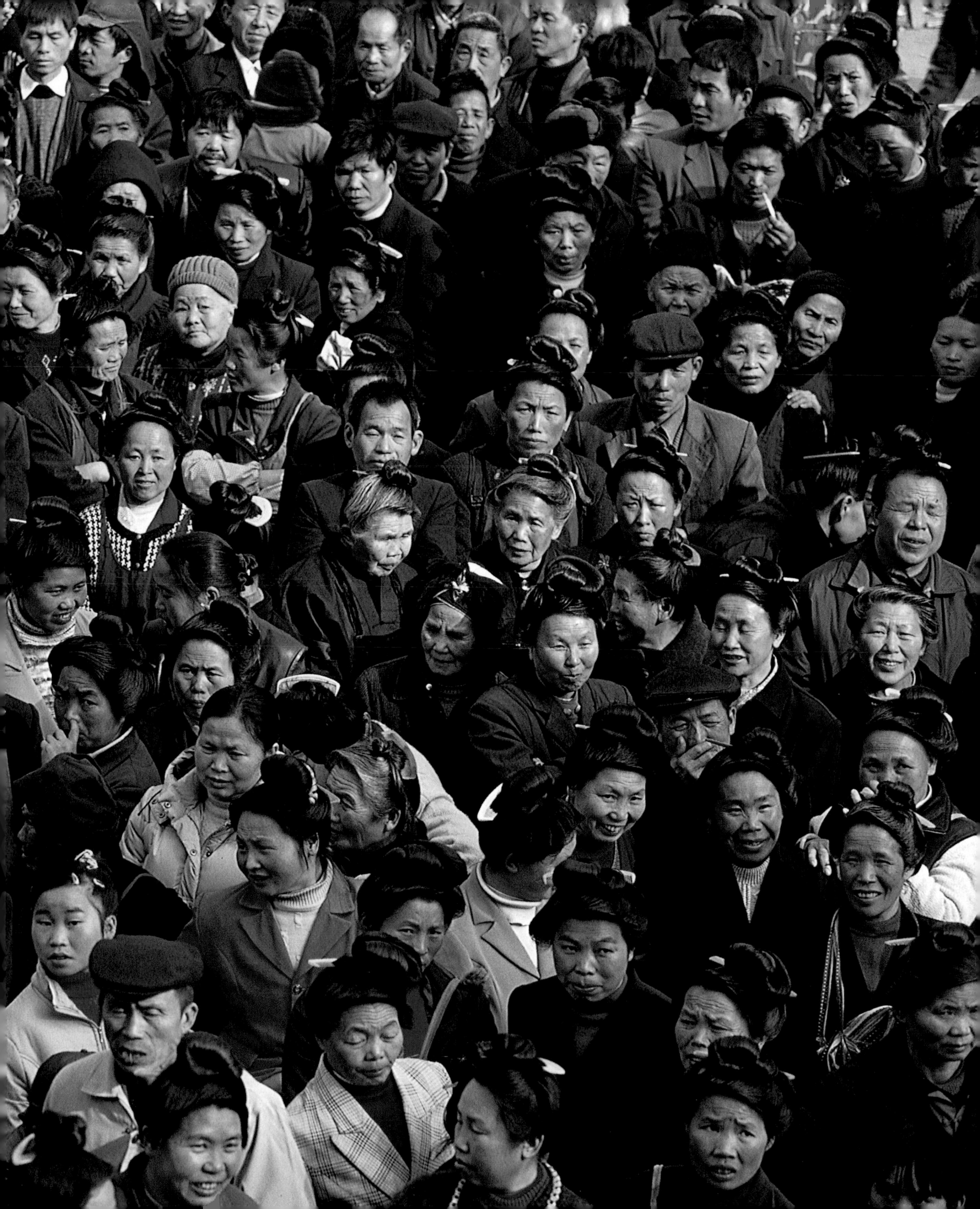

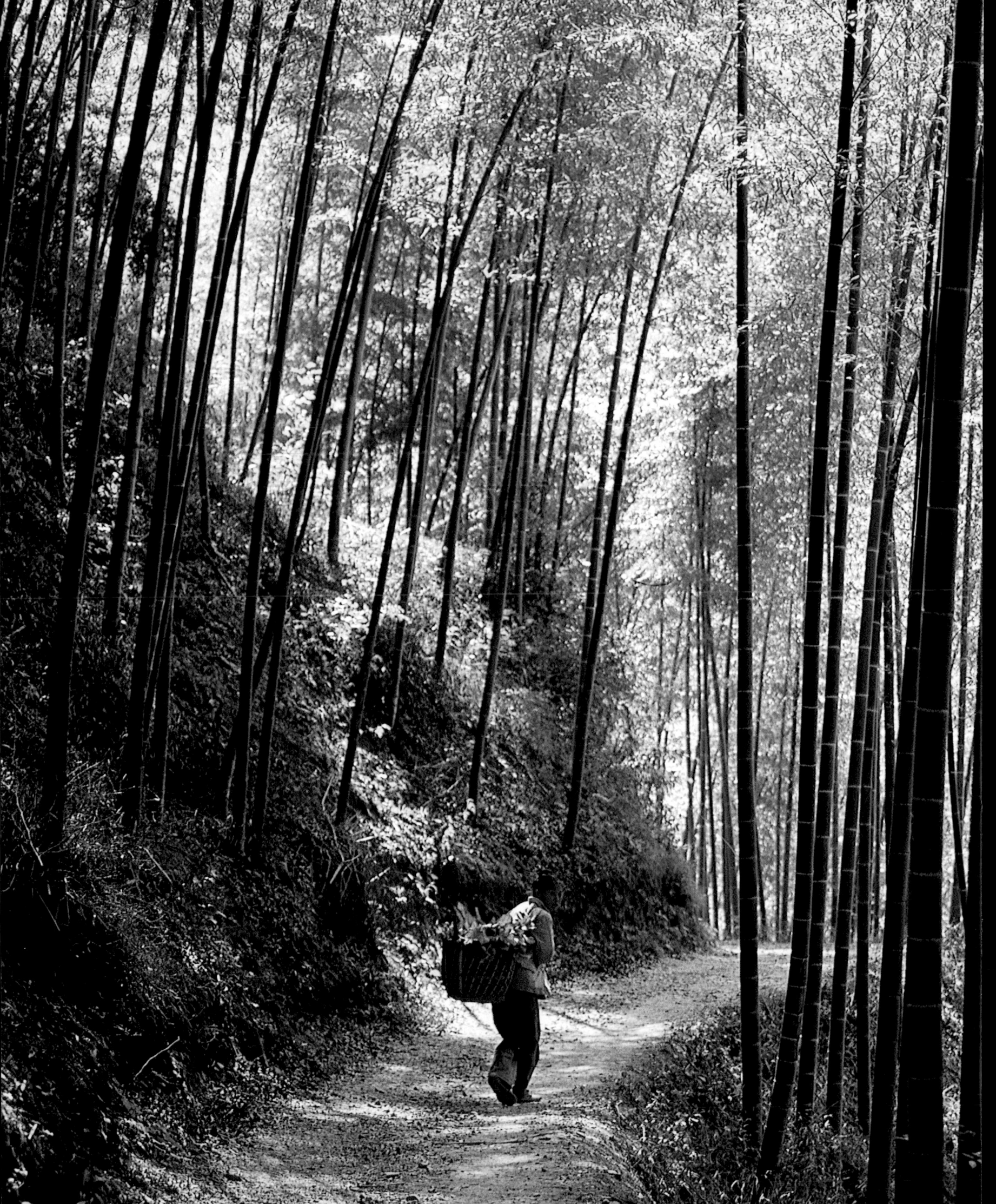

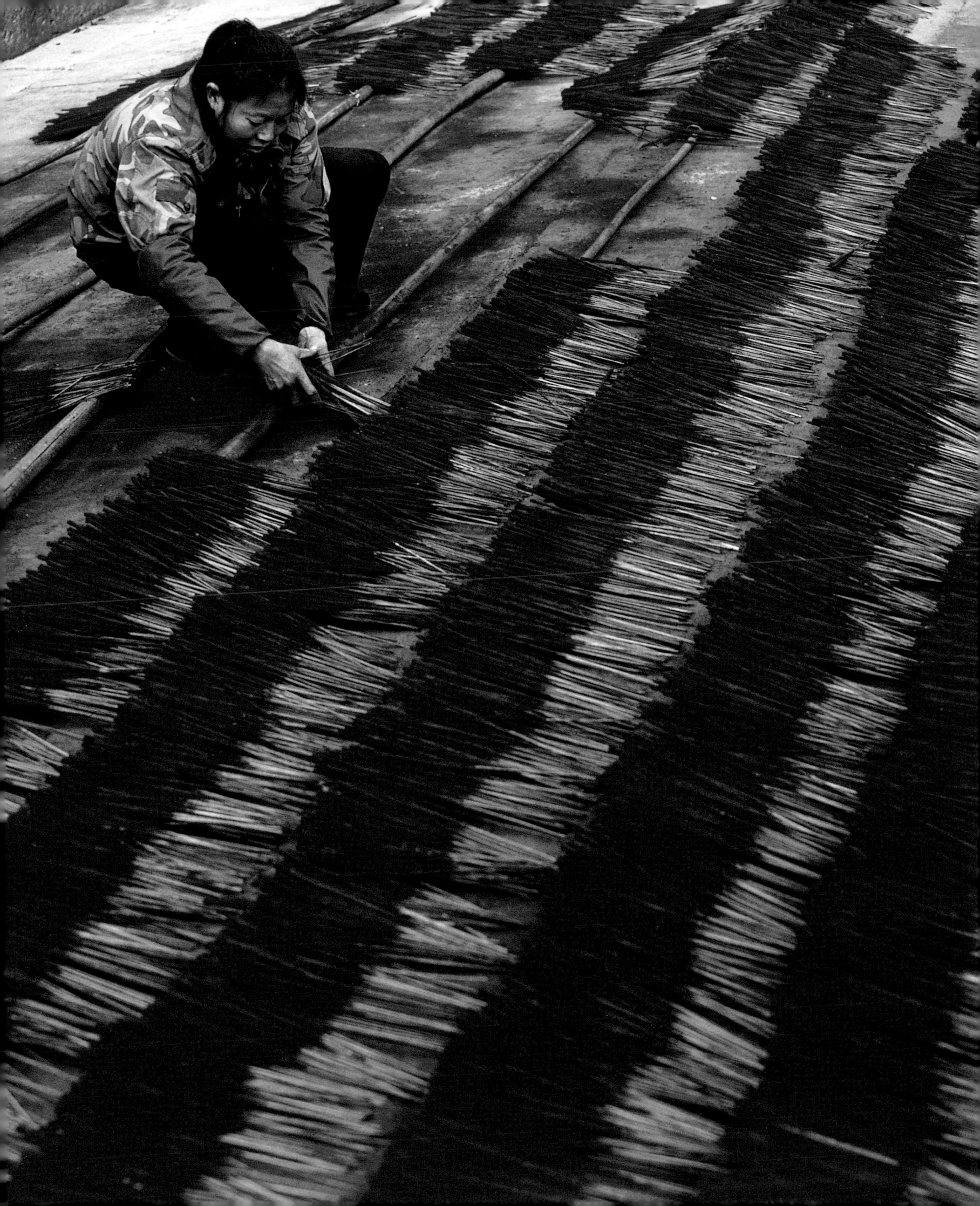

THE MIDDLE KINGDOM

The 'Kamikaze twins' are getting frisky. The sight of the faint red glow of steel dust and exhaust hanging over the bright lights of downtown Wu'han, with its unspoken promise of wine, women and karaoke in a 'Relaxation Centre', pumps a shot of adrenalin into the *Red Bull*-addled brains of my restless drivers. They laugh and giggle as the world-weary Volkswagen *Santana* lurches and jumps from side to side, and as, with a sudden burst of speed, the vehicle charges through a tiny gap between two heavily laden trucks with just inches to spare on either side, a great cry of joy erupts from the front seats. They remind me of two teenage boys in a video games parlour who have just shot down the 'alien-mother-ship'. No sooner have they laid a bet on how long it will take to get to the hotel than the brakes are violently slammed on and we screech to a grinding halt behind an epic traffic jam. The boys fall silent as we inch forward behind a trail of red tail-lights that stretch for miles ahead. Then, without warning, a gap presents itself and they cut across two lanes onto a turnoff and exit the highway into total darkness.

We have landed in a new-development zone on the outer ring road of the city: a labyrinth of half-built factory buildings where street lights have not yet been installed and the streets have no signs because they have not been named. After driving around in the dark for a long spell, turning down every deserted blind alley they can find in search of a way out, the boys finally declare that we are lost.

I had arrived in Wu'han, the Pittsburgh of China, in a mood as foul as the weather that had been dogging me during the drive from one ugly polluted city to another grey nondescript provincial capital across the Middle Kingdom, only to be told on arrival that the arrangements made months ago to photograph a steel mill had been cancelled due to new government restrictions. So by the time the boys (I have since nicknamed them Kami and Kaze) emerged from the drizzly dawn at the hotel in a beat-up car, looking like a couple of trainee hoods in a Hong Kong gangster movie, my mask of Zen-like calmness and reason had already cracked and my frustration at not having taken a good picture in a week was starting to manifest itself in strange and unpredictable ways. My dislike for Kami was almost immediate. I think it was either his sideburns or his sleazy grin. And by the time he had disingenuously explained that he had brought along his mate Kaze, a former PLA lorry driver, as navigator because he was unfamiliar with the road to the Three Gorges Dam, my loathing for the man at the wheel was complete. The 'road' in question is a series of highways and toll-roads that leaves you practically at the gates of the dam, so it was clear from the start that the boys were out for a joy ride, with party plans for the overnight stay in Yi'chang.

After a five-hour, 360-kilometre (224-mile) drive, I found myself standing on top of a viewing platform on the hill overlooking the Three Gorges Dam. A forest of enormous cranes hovered over the nearly completed dam like branches of a giant mechanical tree swaying in the breeze. Though one could argue that there is a certain terrible beauty in the sheer scale and audacity of the enterprise, the dam itself looked strangely unimpressive. The architecture is utilitarian in the extreme and lacking any of the drama or majesty that one might expect or hope for 'the world's largest hydro-electric project'. In the end, the massive barrier (2.3-kilometre/1.43-mile wide and 185-metres /607-feet high) across the Xi'ling Gorge that has transformed the central expanse of the once fast-moving Yang'tze River into the world's largest reservoir turned out to be just another great wall, albeit one capable of producing the energy equivalent of 15 nuclear power stations. It is a monument to ambition rather than inspiration; a product of the ego instead of the human heart.

[LEFT] Incense maker in Da'zu. [PRECEDING PAGES] 'Bamboo sea' in An'hui, a location for *Crouching Tiger Hidden Dragon*.

I remembered joking with my companions in 1992 during our river journey through the Yang'tze gorges, that we should start Scuba-diving tours of all the historic sites once they'd been flooded; now that it had actually happened, with everything we had seen along the riverbanks from Yi'chang to Chong'qing now under at least 135 metres (440 feet) of water, the idea didn't seem all that funny any more. As I tried to make out the workers walking along the gigantic causeway like tiny ants on the sidewalk, I knew I would need a helicopter for a dawn and a sunset run to get the shot I really wanted, and the chances of that happening were less than zero. So after dutifully driving around for several hours looking in vain for *the* shot of the dam, I decided to save the structure that has "frightened the heavens and shaken the earth" for another day and headed back to Wu'han.

Many historians have used the device of a spaceship journey over China in their introductions as a way of describing the geological features that shaped its history. In 2006, such a flight of fancy may well have revealed a giant piece of graffiti spray-painted over the entire country from the Pamirs to the tip of Manchuria that read "Country under construction. Due for completion in Spring 2008". And nowhere else was this pre-Olympics construction craze more obvious than in the seven densely populated provinces of the Middle Kingdom. Over 450 million people live in this fertile central plain along China's longest river, and wherever I went, construction crews were working overtime to complete new highways, factories, and housing estates.

From the outskirts of Chong'qing to the suburbs of the ancient capitals of Luo'yang and Kai'feng, vast tracts of farmland were being converted into industrial bases or luxury housing estates with names like American Town, Dream Town, Future City, Palm Springs and Olympic Gardens; the billboard for Blue Lake County in Cheng'du featured a *Gone with the Wind*-style southern mansion with a white horse on a diving board by a blue lake. But behind the glamorous billboards proclaiming China's love affair with the American dream were often sordid tales of collusion between local party chiefs and private developers to cheat the farmers out of their livelihood without proper compensation. During the Long March, Mao's Red Army executed hundreds of thousands of landowners along the way and redistributed the land to the farmers who tilled it. Land reform became the promise for a better future and the cornerstone for the success of the peasants' revolution. Millions more landowners have died since then but the farmers of China never saw the deeds to their land; instead, the communist government became the legal owners and party officials the landlords. These illegal or barely legal land seizures have created many angry and frustrated farmers, as the state-controlled judiciaries are often powerless or unwilling to address their grievances. According to government figures, the number of 'mass protests' (demonstrations involving more than 100 people), rose from 10,000 in 1994 to 87,000 in 2005 – a year in which 3.7 million people protested in 337 cities and 1,955 counties; a great number of them over land seizures. One particularly thorny area is the appropriation of farmland for the construction of arrow-straight toll-roads through rural areas, where the land grabs can be executed in the guise of infrastructural development, so little or no compensation is offered and the potential future profits are huge.

Through my producer's 'guang'xi' – a word that use to simply mean 'relationship' but has now taken on the connotation of 'connections with political cover' – we were loaned a car and driver by Hu'nan Television to make the journey from the provincial capital of Chang'sha to the mountain hideaway of Feng'huang. The Toyota

the journey from the provincial capital of Chang'sha to the mountain hideaway of Feng'huang. The Toyota *Landcruiser* was emblazoned with logos of the famous station, one of the most popular networks in the country. The driver was taking the opportunity to drop his wife off in Zhang'jia'jie to visit friends and family, and through their 'guang'xi', an old schoolmate who was the engineer in charge of the Zhang'jia'jie section, we managed to get onto the mostly-completed-but-not-officially-open toll-road, which shaved 4 hours off our 533-kilometre (331-mile) journey and avoided the risk of getting stuck in a landslide on the rain-soaked mountain roads. Twenty kilometres (12 miles) outside of the Zhang'jia'jie exit, great tree trunks lay across the three-lane highway, and a heated argument was taking place between a group of angry peasants and several agitated drivers in front of their blocked vehicles. I wanted to get out to take some pictures but received a resounding "No" from the husband and wife team, with a firm reminder that historically, Hu'nan is famous for its bandits. They got out and negotiated with the farmers whose fields had been 'appropriated' by the local authorities for the toll road without proper compensation. When the farmers saw the insignia on our car, they wanted to be on the evening news; my driver had to explain that we were actually not reporters but promised to let the news department know about their grievances. They exchanged phone numbers and the tree was moved just far enough to let us through before slamming back into place. As we drove away, I saw a flurry of pushing and shoving as angry drivers protested against our special treatment.

Several days later, on our return journey, we arrived at the Zhang'jia'jie entrance of the toll road accompanied by our engineer friend. We waited behind the locked gates of the unfinished toll booths as he got out of his car to talk to a group of hard-looking men in leather jackets. Calls were made and mobile phones passed around as various superiors who were probably still in bed were consulted. Finally, they reluctantly unlocked the gates and let us through. As we drove away into the early morning mist, I inadvertently looked into the eyes of one of the men in black leather and felt a chill of premonition that things were about to get ugly for the farmers. By the time we reached Chang'sha, word came through from the engineer that the local police and private 'security guards' had moved in on the protesters and there were many injuries and arrests.

Kami and Kaze have gone from being agitated to sullen, they have been on their cell phones asking their mates if *they* have any idea where we are, and harsh sounding words are exchanged between them. Suddenly, out of the darkness come three blinding flashes of light. It takes me a second to register that they are reflections of our headlamps off the fluorescent stripes on the vests of road workers. In a heavy Hu'bei accent the boys ask the three workmen for directions. We eventually get back on the highway and it is past 9pm by the time we get back to the hotel.

I stagger out of the car exhausted from yet another long and unsuccessful day, my nerves raw and my knuckles white from all the near misses on the highway. I want to yell and scream at the twins for their recklessness and incompetence, but in the end, I realize that they had been in a hurry because I had been in a hurry, and I had been in a rush because China is in a hurry. So I just bid them farewell with a vague complaint about the car not being terribly comfortable for long journeys, to which Kami gamely replies, flashing his slimy, lopsided grin, "I'll send you a different car tomorrow," before speeding out of the parking lot into a drizzly night full of wine, women and songs.

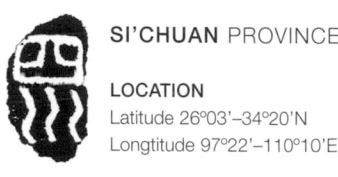

SI'CHUAN PROVINCE

LOCATION
Latitude 26°03'–34°20'N
Longtitude 97°22'–110°10'E

AREA 569,800 km² (220,000 sq miles)

GEOGRAPHY The Si'chuan Basin is ringed by the Three Gorges and the Yang'tze River in the east, the mountainous Yun'nan province to the south, the Tibetan Plateau in the west and the Qin'ling range to the north. The dominant waterway is the Yang'tze, with its tributaries the Min, Tuo and Wu rivers. The Ya'long River crosses the Western Plateau, where average elevation is 4,000 m. The Eastern Basin lies between 1,000 m and 3,000 m above sea level.

CLIMATE The Eastern Basin is has a sub-tropical monsoonal climate: high humidity with plenty of rainfall, mist and fog, and not much sunshine. Average temperature here is 25°C to 29°C in July and 3°C to 8°C in January, while the Western Plateau has a highland climate with lower temperatures, less rain, frequent fog and intense sunlight. The provincial annual average temperature is 16.5°C, with average rainfall of 1,000 mm.

POPULATION 87.24 million (end 2005)

MAJOR CITIES Cheng'du (capital), Mian'yang, Le'shan, Yi'bin, Pan'zhi'hua, Zi'gong, Nan'chong

AGRICULTURE Known as the 'Rice Bowl' of China, Si'chuan is the country's leading rice producer. Other food crops include sugar cane, potatoes, citrus fruits, wheat, corn, sugar beet, sweet potatoes and beans. This province also grows cotton, ramie, hemp, medicinal herbs, tea, oilseed and silk worms. The grazing land on the plateau supports the largest cattle and pig populations in the country.

MAIN INDUSTRIES As well as coal, iron, steel and energy production, there are light manufacturing industries for textiles, wine, electronics, machinery, building materials, metallurgy, wood and food processing, and silk – including the once world-famous Shu brocades and Ba satins.

ANNUAL PER CAPITA INCOME (2005)
Disposable income of urban residents:
RMB 8,386 (US$1,046)
Net income of rural residents:
RMB 2802.8 (US$350)

IMPORTANT HISTORICAL SITES
UNESCO World Heritage Sites include Da'zu Stone Carvings and Du'jiang'yan Irrigation System. Huang'long, Jiu'zhai'gou Valley, Mount Qin'cheng and Mount Emei scenic and historic areas, including Le'shan Giant Buddha.

FOOD Si'chuan is one of the Eight Great Cuisines of China, characterized by spicy and pungent flavours with heavy use of chili, hot red peppers and garlic. Classic dishes include hotpot, smoked duck, Kung Pao chicken, twice cooked pork and Mapo Dofu.

[RIGHT] Work underway on the Central Station of Cheng'du's metro system.

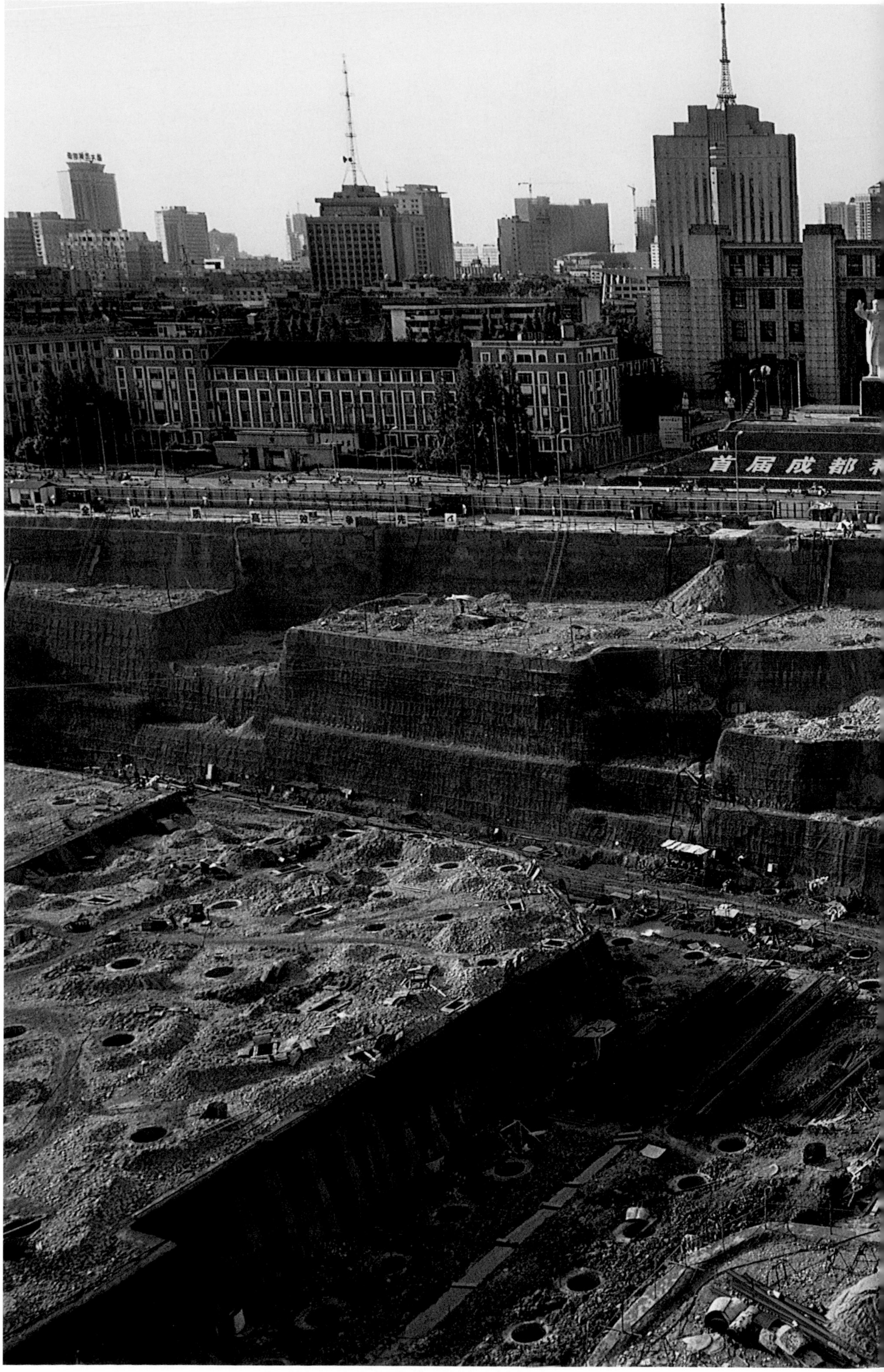

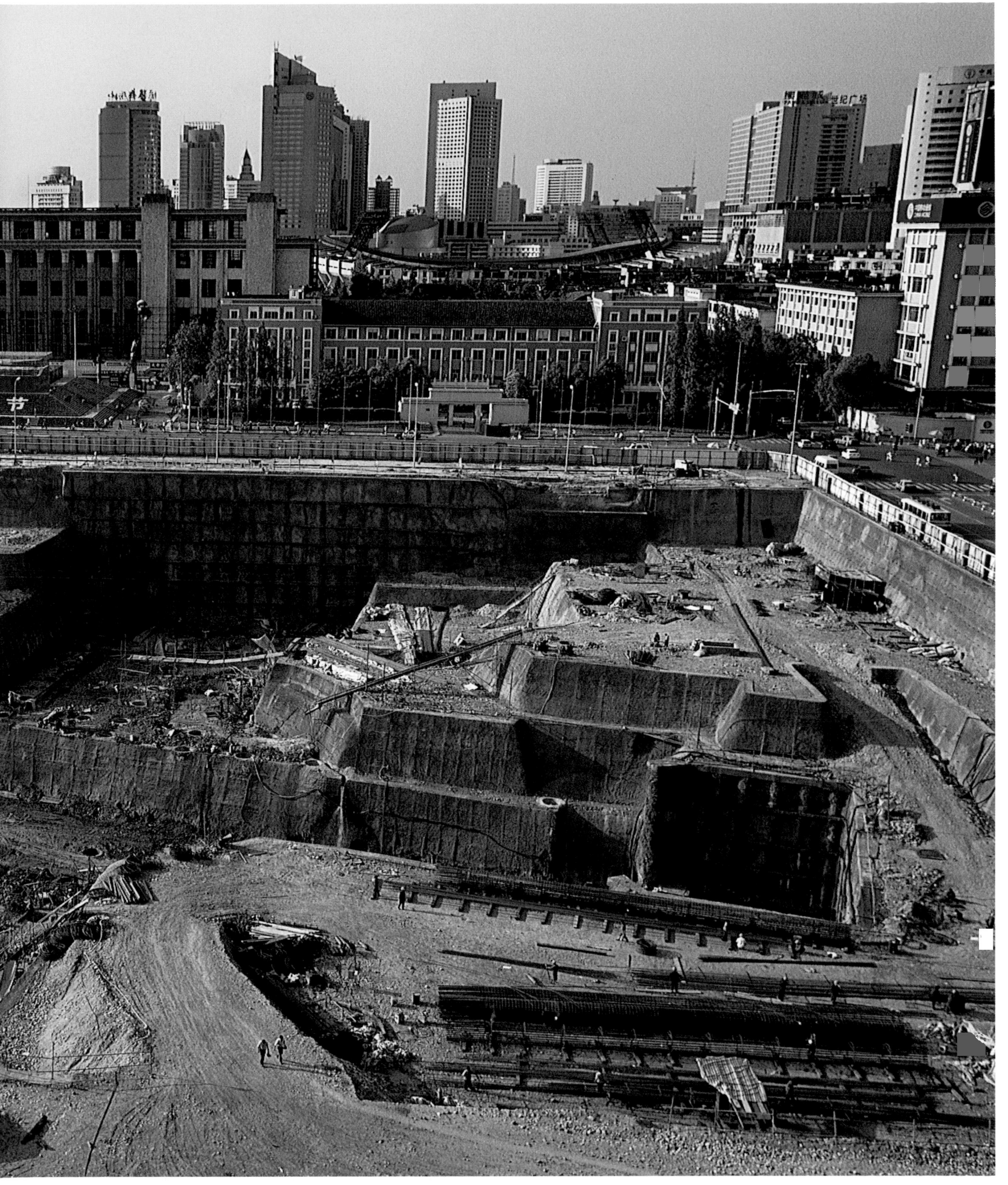

THE CHENG'DU PANDA BREEDING AND RESEARCH CENTRE

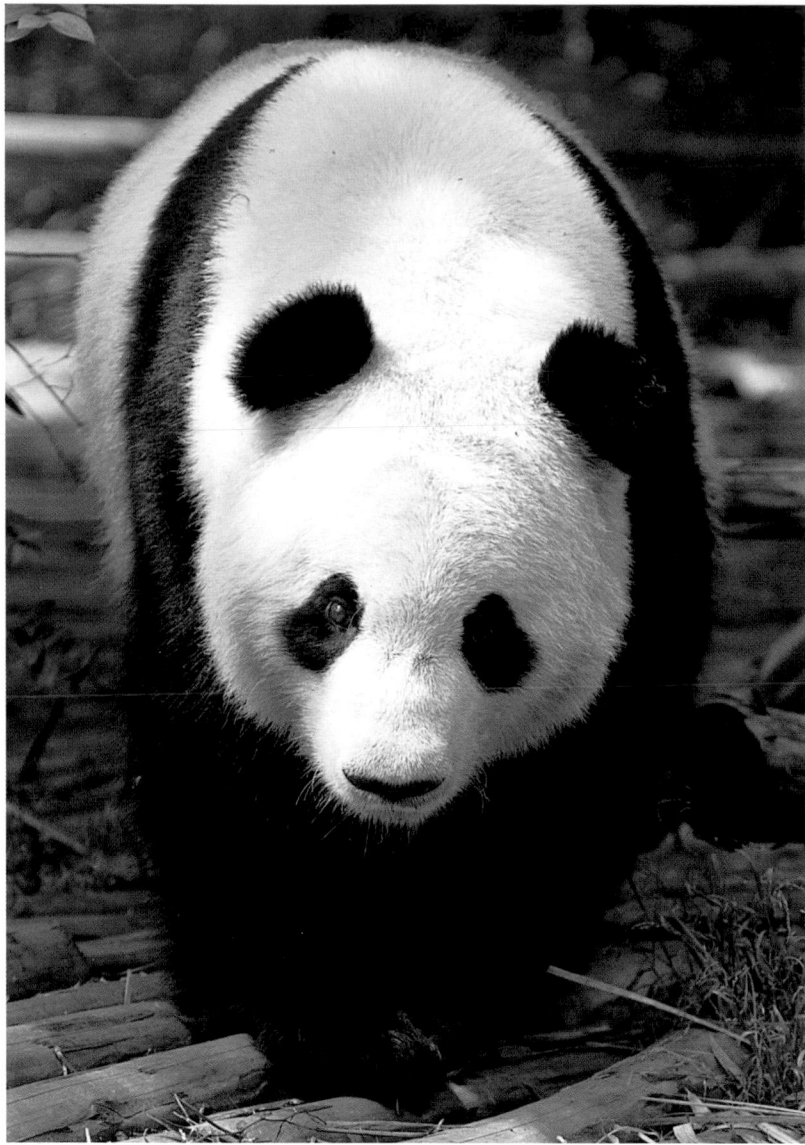

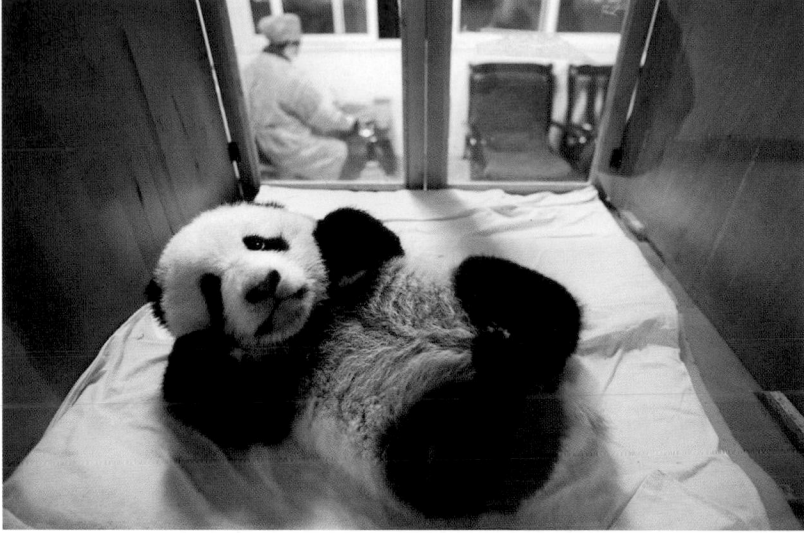

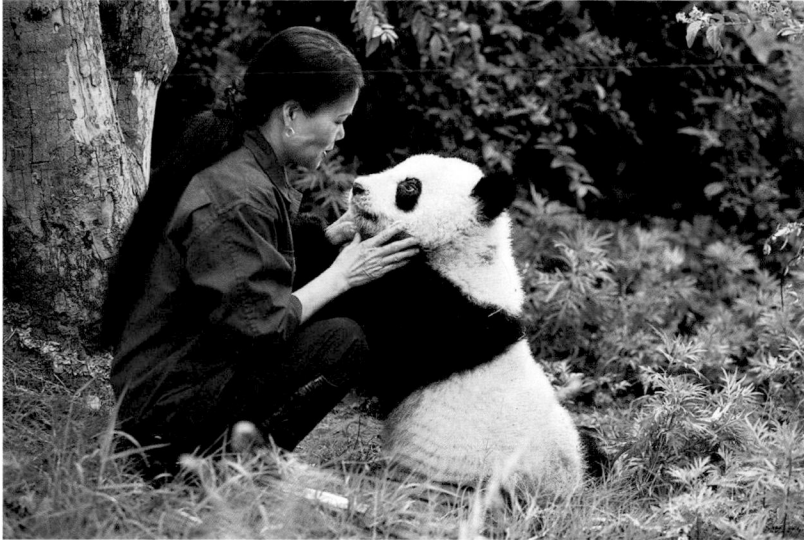

FEWER THAN 2,000 GIANT PANDAS REMAIN IN THE WORLD, and about 1,600 of them live wild in the remote mountains of northern Si'chuan that border Gan'su and Qing'hai provinces. Since the Wo'long Nature Reserve was established in 1963 to protect their natural habitat and ensure the survival of the species, the number of panda reserves in the region has grown to 40. [1] Catching even a glimpse of these shy creatures in the wild is almost impossible, but the Panda Breeding Centre a few miles outside Cheng'du offers visitors a chance to observe them at close quarters. [2] When I first visited the centre this panda cub was three months old and still living in a display room in the nursery. He gave me a fright when he suddenly barked at me like a puppy just after I took this shot. When I returned three months later I found him outside playing with two friends of his own age, [3] bonding with his keeper and [4] having a grand time on the swing.

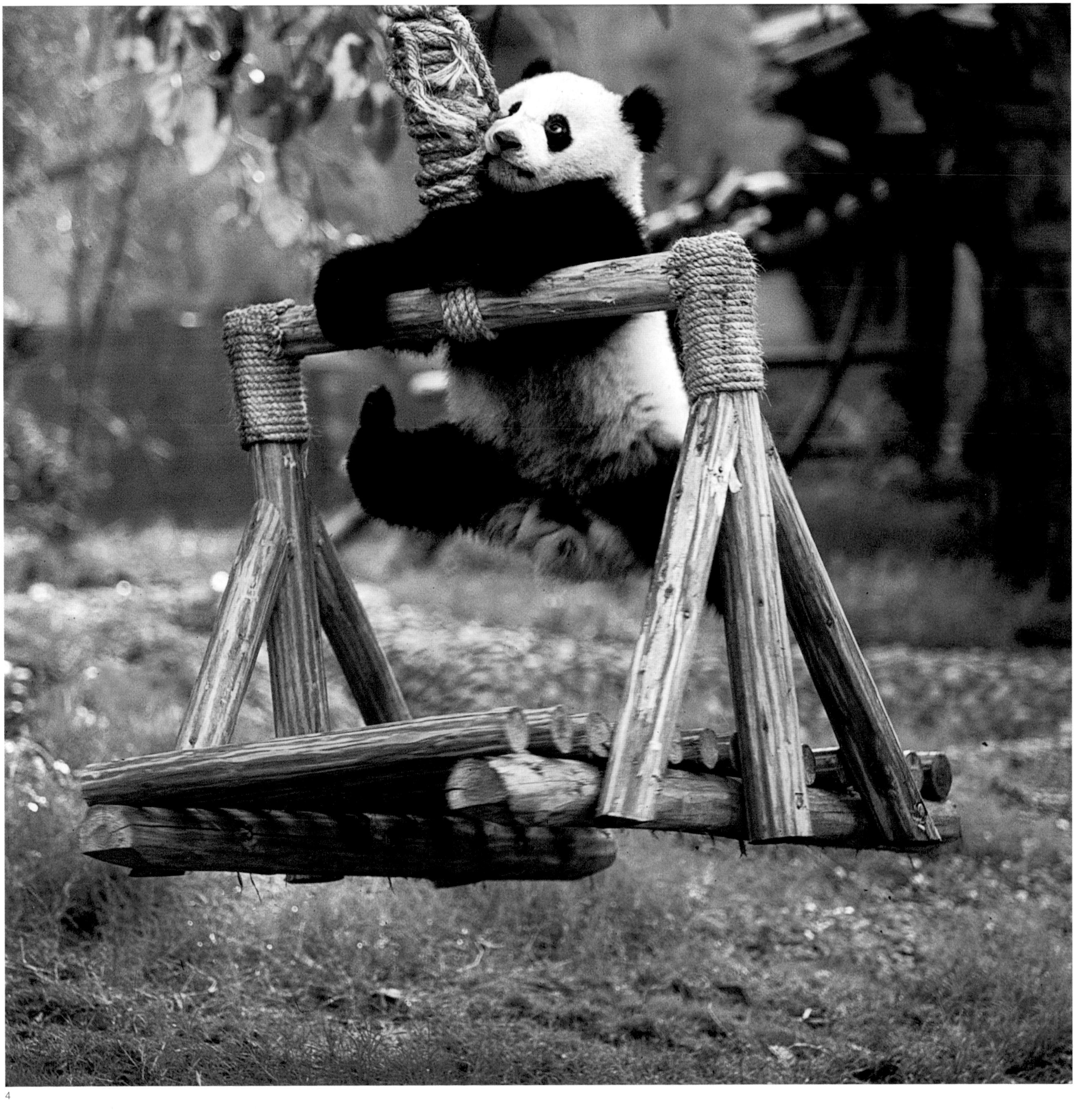

THE GRAND BUDDHA

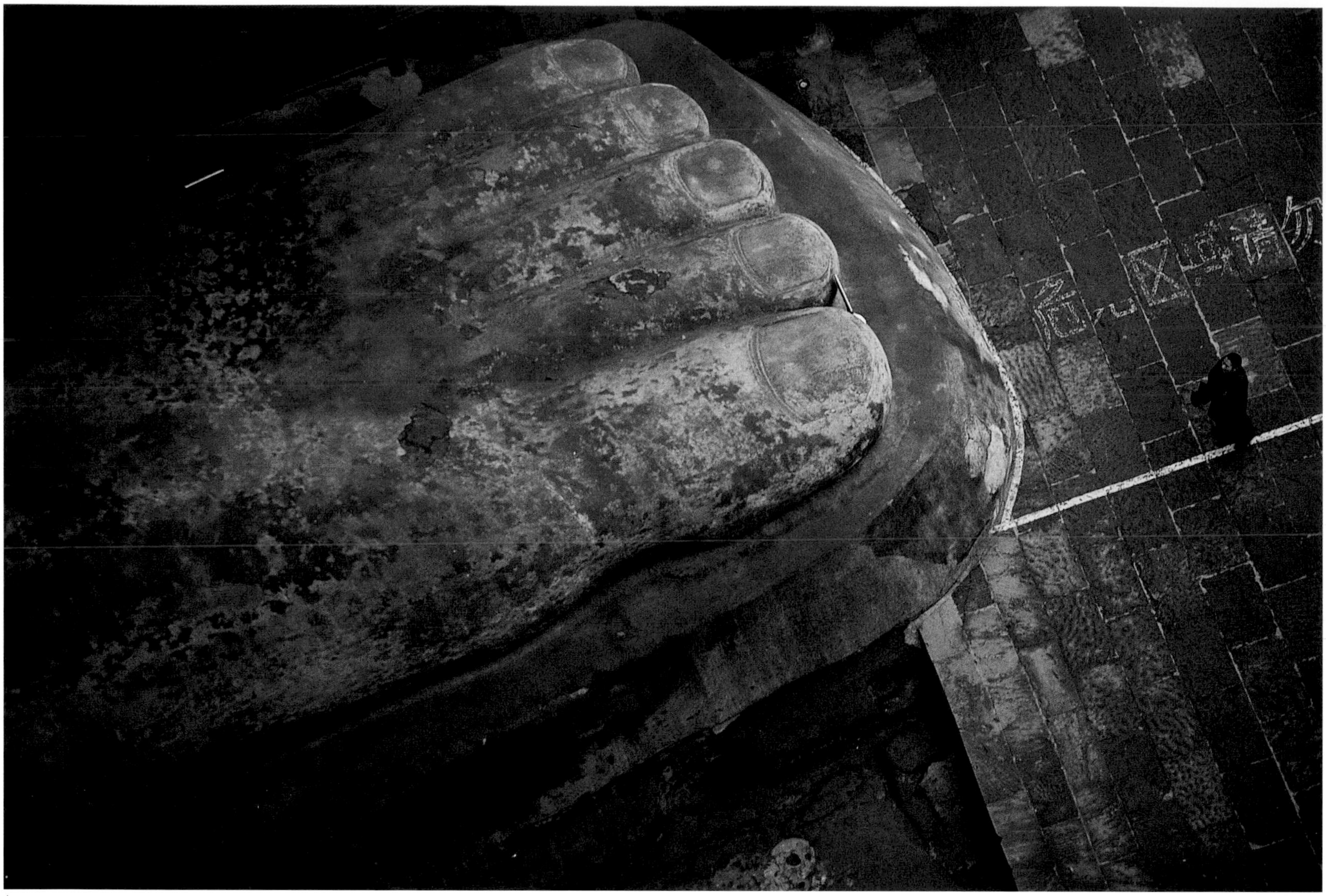

1

"THE MOUNTAIN IS A BUDDHA, AND THE BUDDHA IS A MOUNTAIN" goes a Le'shan saying describing the world's largest carved stone sculpture. [4] Situated at the confluence of the Min, Qing'yi and Da'du rivers, the Grand Buddha has been chiseled into a Ling'yun Mountain cliff face. The mountain itself resembles a reclining Buddha when viewed from the far shore. The seated Sakyamuni Buddha is 71 metres (233 feet) tall, his head is almost 15 metres (50 feet) high, the shoulders span over 28 metres (90 feet) and his toes stretch nearly 8.5 metres (28 feet). Tang Dynasty monk Hai'tong began the immense task of sculpting the Buddha in 713 CE, but died long before its completion 90 years later. It was his hope that the Buddha's presence would tame the dangerous currents where the three rivers met. As it happened, the excavated rock and soil dumped into the turbulent waters during construction did ease the treacherous rapids and fulfill the monk's hopes. [1] The Buddha's left foot. [2] A quiet winter's day and [3] chaos at the height of summer tourist season.

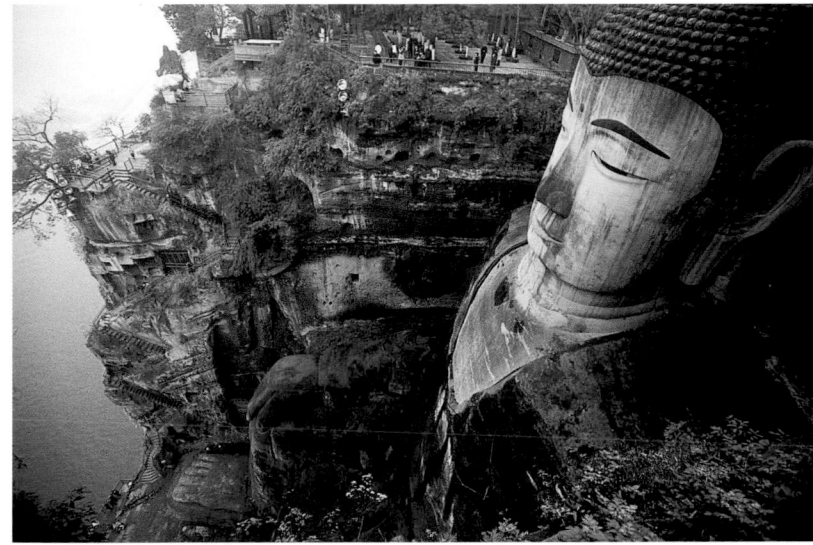

2

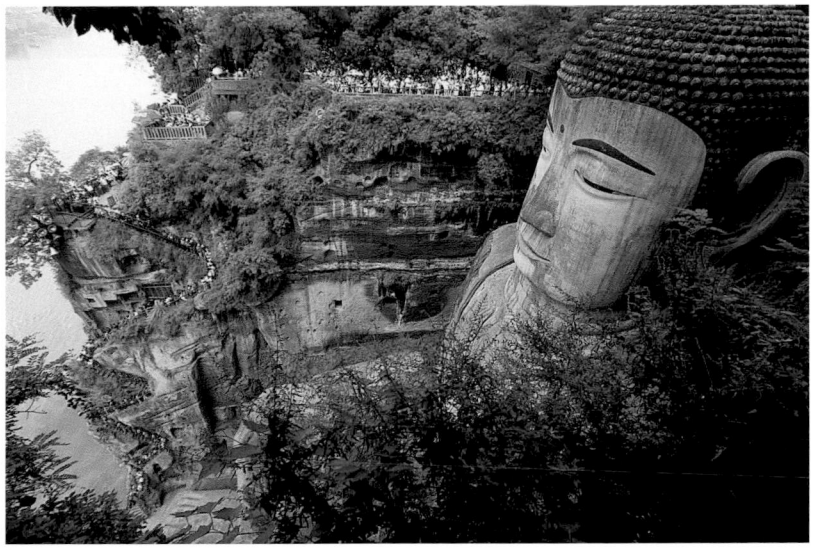

3

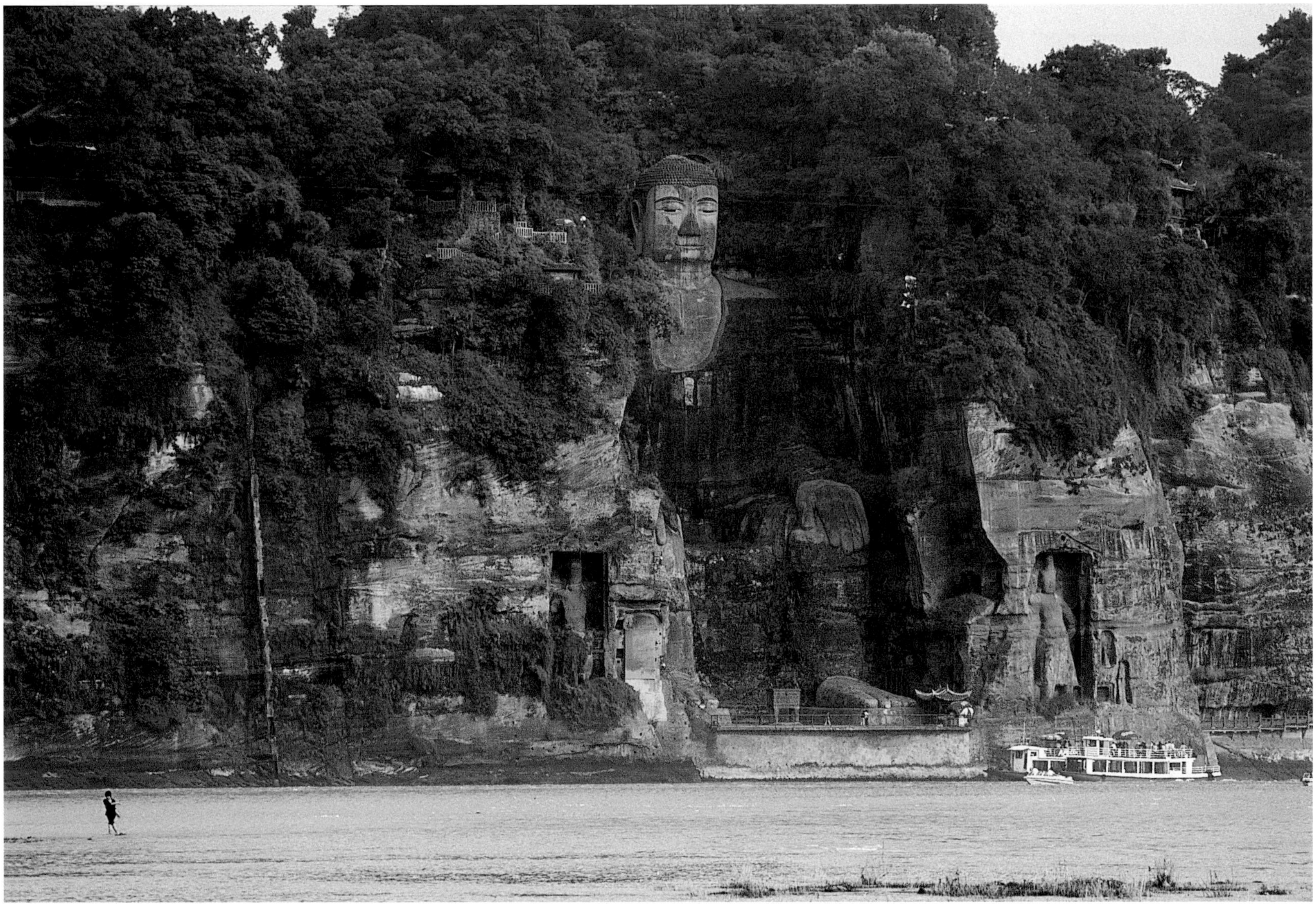

4

ROAD TO KAN'DING

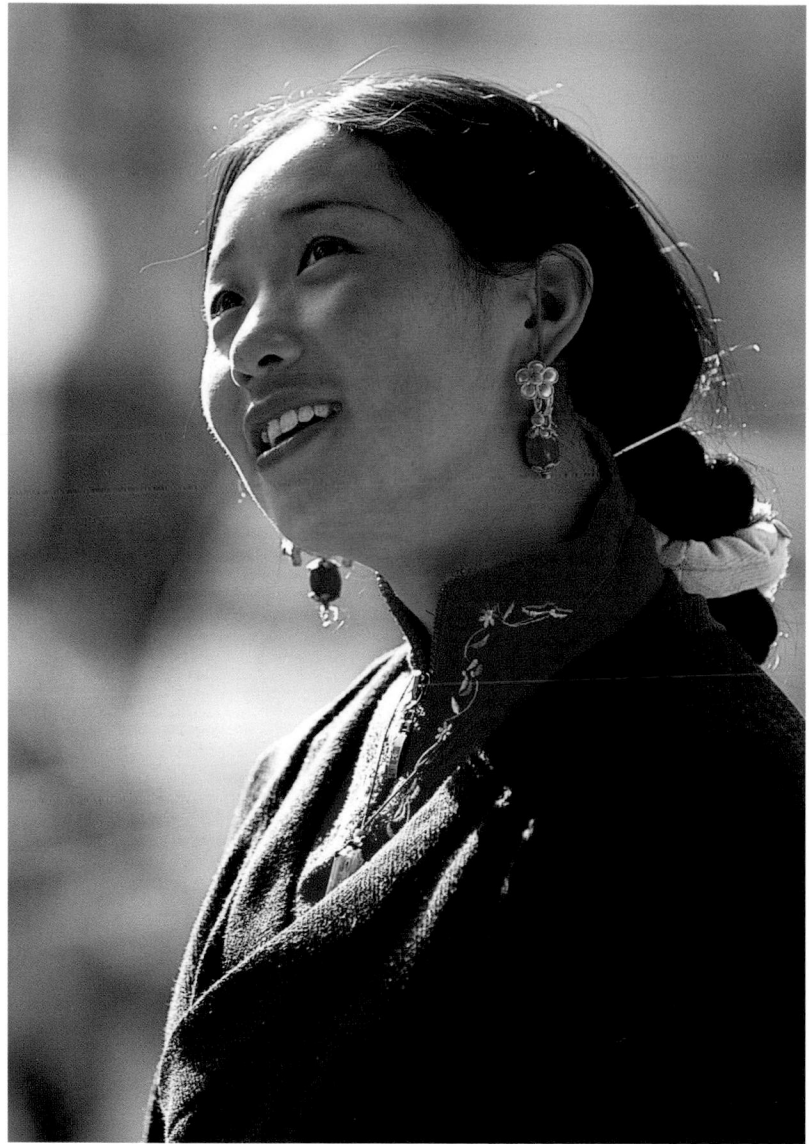

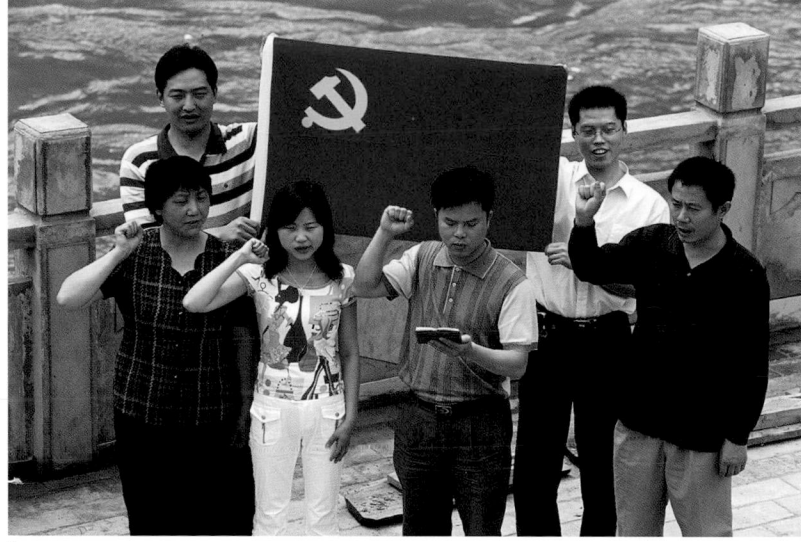

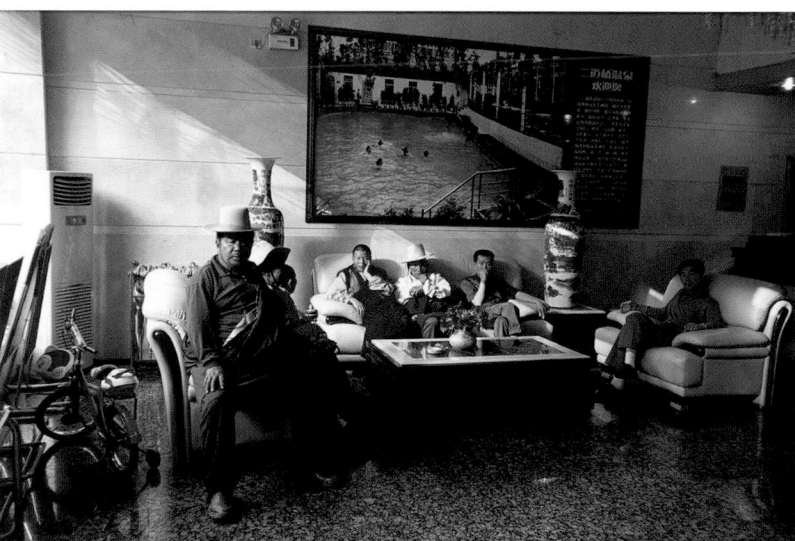

1

2

3

KANDING IS THE GATEWAY OF THE SI'CHUAN–TIBET HIGHWAY, which divides into its northern and southern routes some 70 kilometres (45 miles) outside the town. Situated on the eastern edge of the Tibetan Plateau in the Kham province of old Tibet, the city was the capital of the kingdom of Chakla and a historically important trade hub between Tibet and China. [1] A Tibetan girl and [4] a young monk shop on the main street, while [3] a party of Khambas attending the Kangding Mountain Kora Festival relax in a hotel lobby. The journey from Cheng'du took about six hours as we stopped en route to look at the Lu'ding Bridge. The 18th-century chain bridge spanning the Da'du River was the site of a legendary Red Army victory during the Long March when communist troops trapped by Kuo'min'tang forces battled their way over the partially wrecked structure. [2] Although a new biography of Mao Ze'dong disputes the veracity of the story, it made no difference to this group of young party members who passionately recited from the *Little Red Book*.

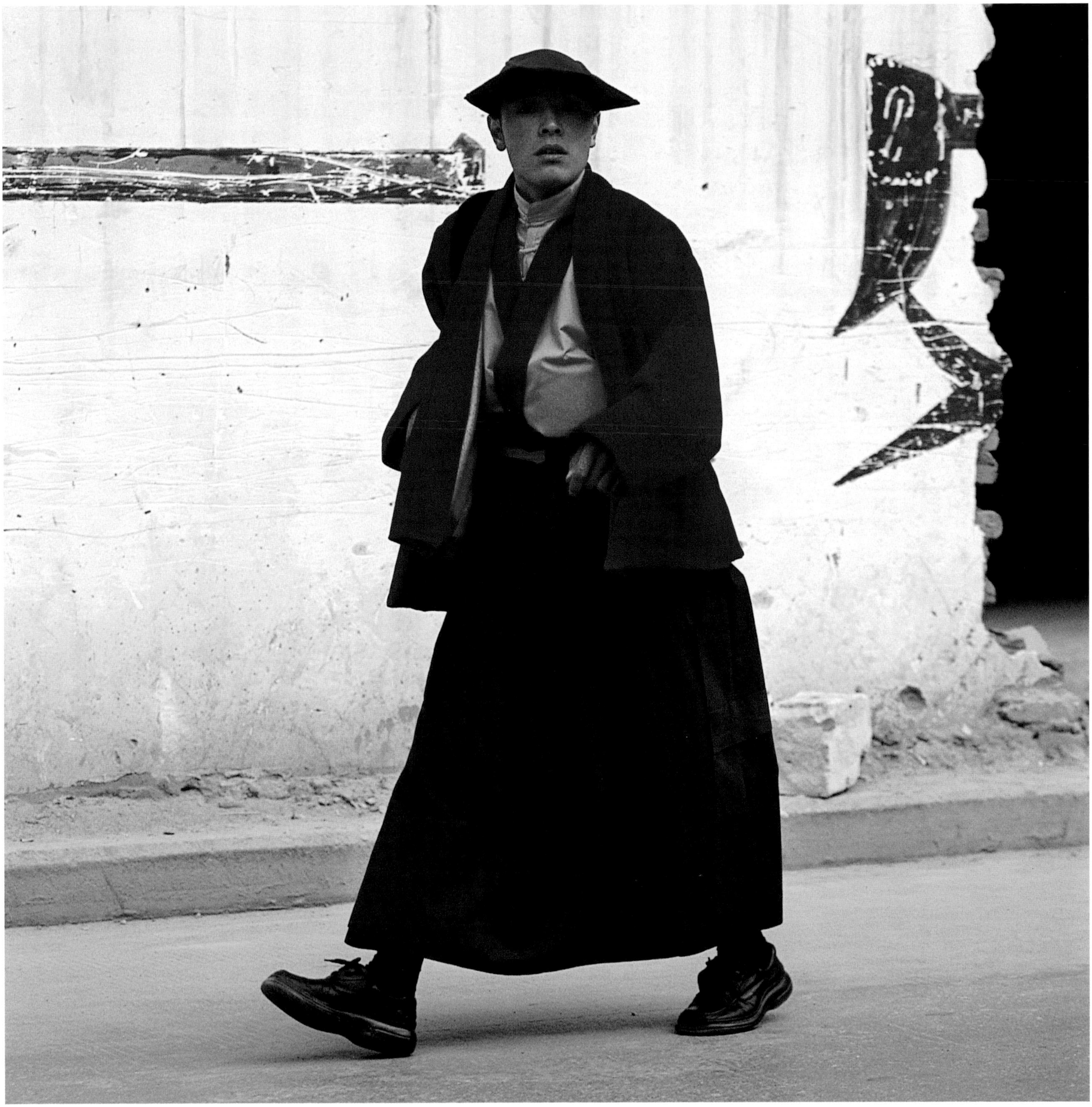

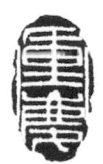

CHONG'QING
MUNICIPALITY

LOCATION
Latitude 28°10'–32°13'N
Longtitude 105°17'–110°11'E

AREA 82,400 km² (31,800 sq miles)
CITY 1,543 km² (592 sq miles)

GEOGRAPHY Located on the edge of the Yungui Plateau, Chong'qing is at the intersection of the Jia'ling River and the upper reaches of the Yang'tze. The city is built on hills and surrounded by mountains: the Daba Shan to the north, Wu Shan in the east, Wuling Shan in the southeast and Da'lou to the south. The average elevation of the city is about 500 m above sea level.

CLIMATE The climate is semi-tropical, with the two-season monsoonal variation typical of South Asia. Winters are warm and summers hot, with an early spring and short autumn. Temperatures range between 6°C and 40°C. The highest recorded temperature is 44.1°C and the lowest, -13.2°C. Dense fog and heavy air pollution restrict sunlight to a maximum of 1,200 hours a year. Annual average rainfall is between 1,000 mm and 1,400 mm.

POPULATION 27.98 million (end 2005)

MAJOR CITIES Cheng'du (capital), Mian'yang, Le'shan, Yi'bin, Pan'zhi'hua, Zi'gong, Nan'chong

AGRICULTURE Rice, maize, wheat, oranges, kale and sweet potatoes are grown here.

MAIN INDUSTRIES Chong'qing's industries include a large integrated iron and steel complex, oil and copper refineries, motor vehicle, machine, food-processing and military ammunition factories, cotton, paper and silk mills, chemical and cement plants and tanneries. Large coal and iron ore mines and a major oil field are also nearby.

ANNUAL PER CAPITA INCOME (2005)
Disposable income of urban residents:
RMB 10,240 (US$1,277)
Net income of rural residents:
RMB 2,785 (US$347)

HISTORICAL AND SCENIC SITES
Chong'qing is a major terminal for Three Gorges cruises. Local sites include the Da'zu Stone Carvings and the battlefield at Diao'yu'cheng where Mongol expansion toward the west was halted.

FOOD Chong'qing is a centre for Si'chuan cooking, one of the Eight Great Cuisines of China that makes much use of chilli, hot red peppers and garlic. Dishes include Chong'qing hotpot, camphor smoked duck, Kung Pao chicken, spicy steamed beef and shredded pork stir fried with chillies, bamboo shoots and mushrooms.

[RIGHT] A 'stickman' at the Chao'tian'men pier.

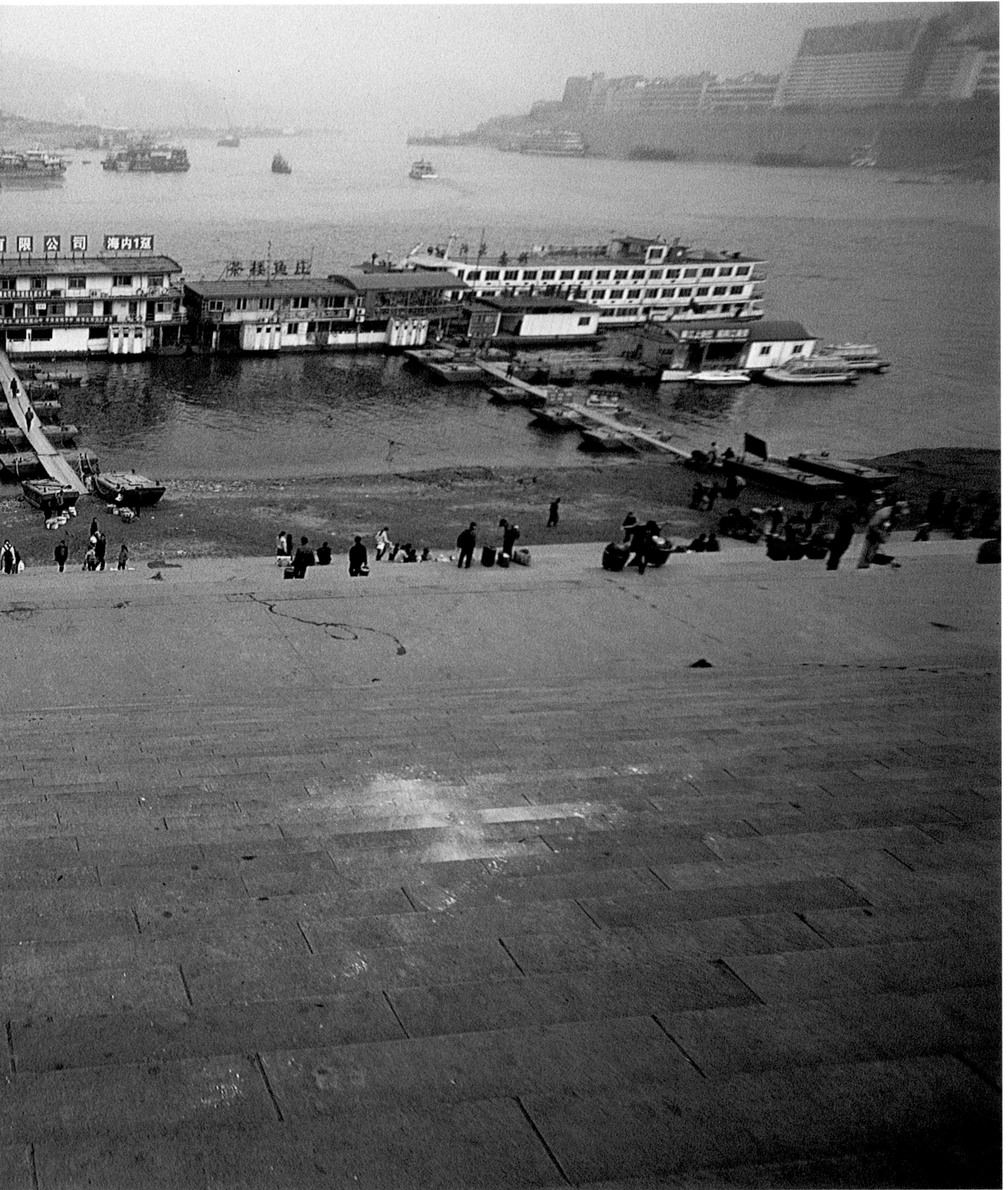

STREETS OF CHONG'QING

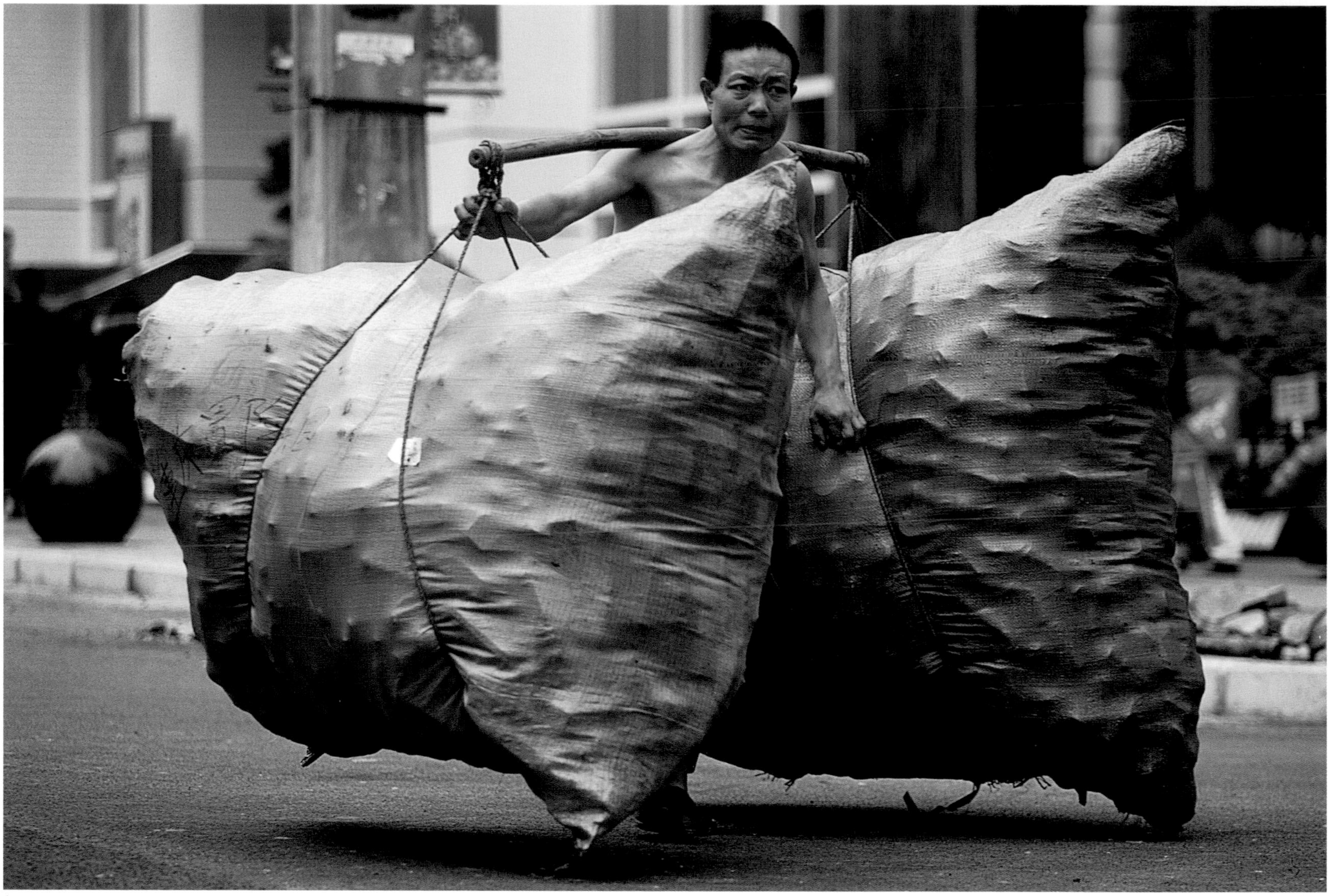

1

CHONG'QING BROKE AWAY FROM SI'CHUAN PROVINCE IN 1997 to become a municipality and, with a population of around 30 million, is now China's biggest urban centre. The bustling port city sprawling up the steep slopes of the Si'chuan Basin at the confluence of the Yang'tze and Jia'ling rivers has historically been a major transportation centre on China's longest river. Chong'qing is also the only major city in China where bicycles are a rare sight. They are replaced here by [1] the ubiquitous 'stickmen' who transport everything from vegetables to sofas suspended from their shoulder poles up and down the hilly city's steep and densely packed streets. [2] In the fast-disappearing old town, ancient hairstyling equipment still has a role. [3] Ducks and chickens from the countryside land at the piers of The Gate Facing Heaven (Chao'tian'men), the main terminal for passenger traffic on the upper reaches of Yang'tze River. [4] A 'street doctor' on the steps in the old town. [5] A baby in a traditional Sichuan 'backpack' on the platform at Chong'qing railway station.

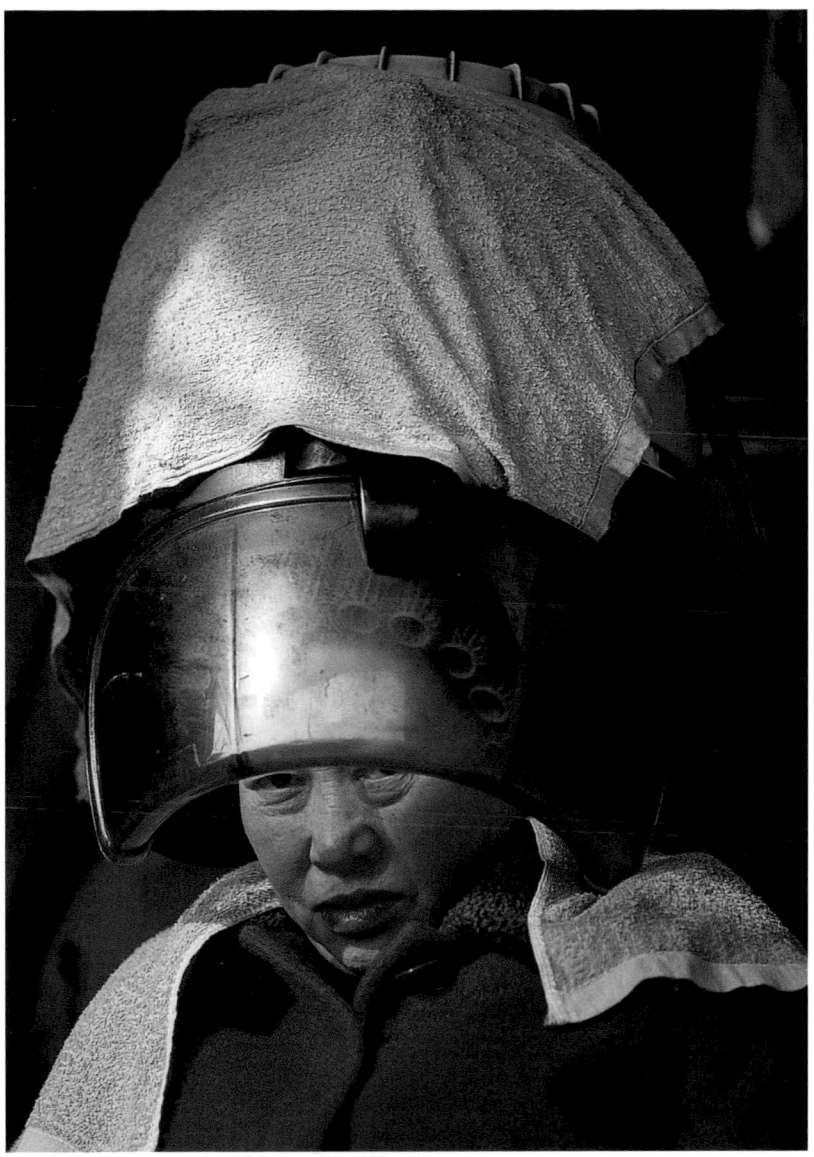

2

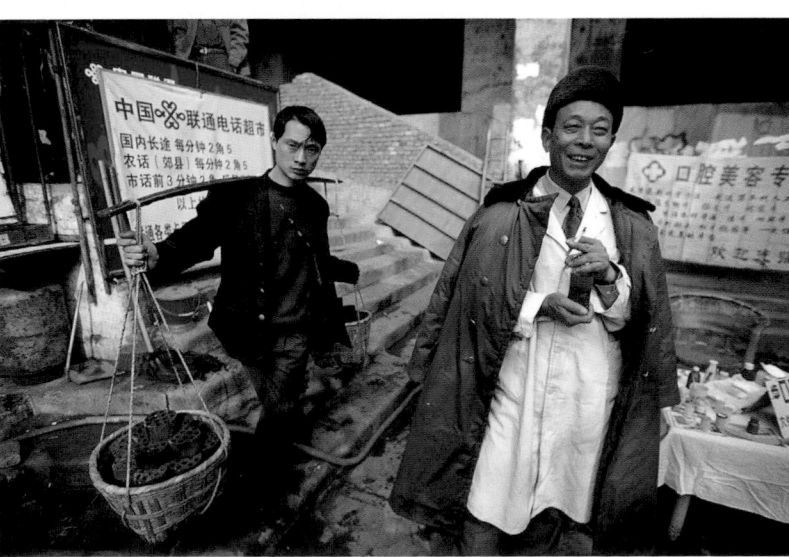

3

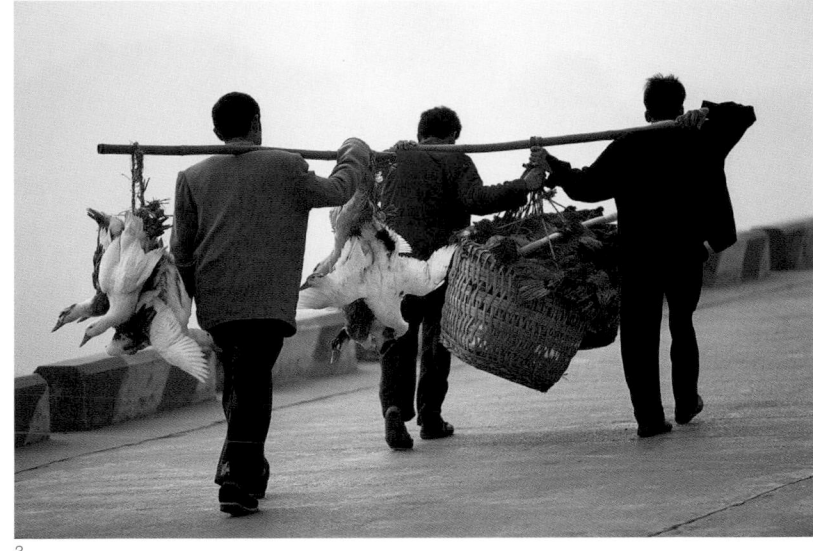

4

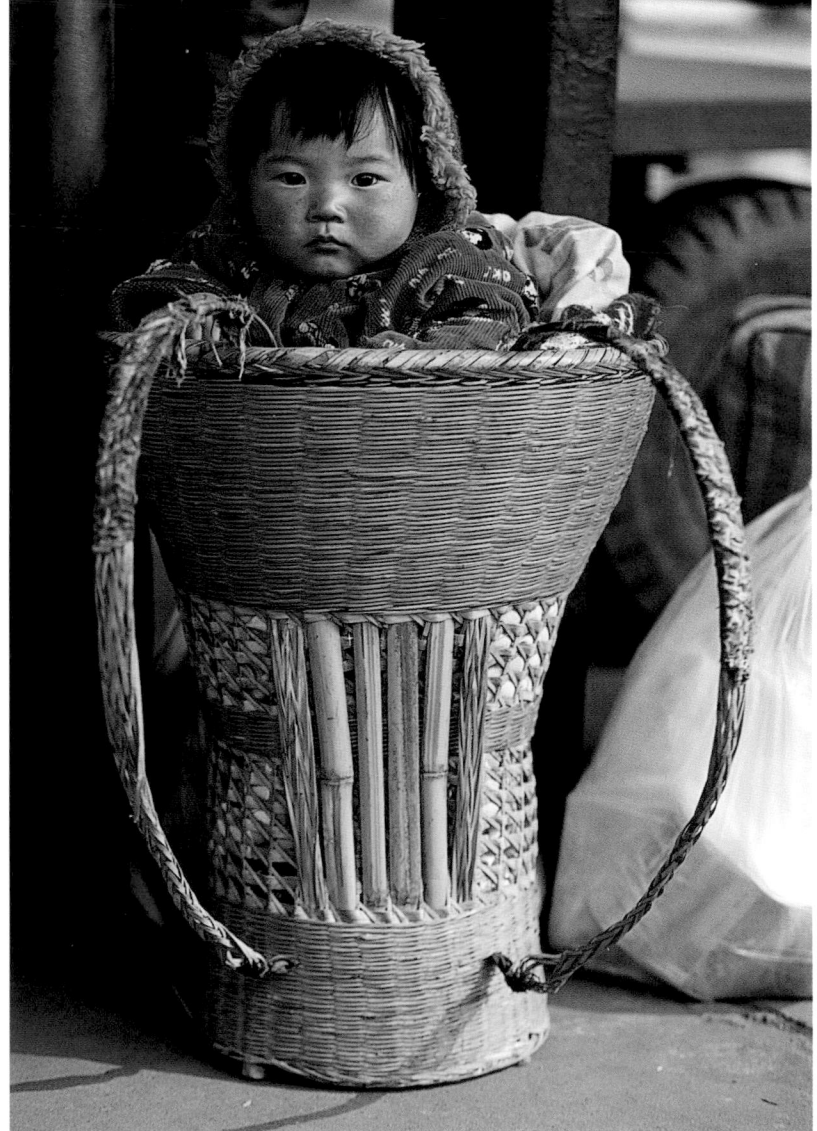

5

STREETS OF CHONG'QING

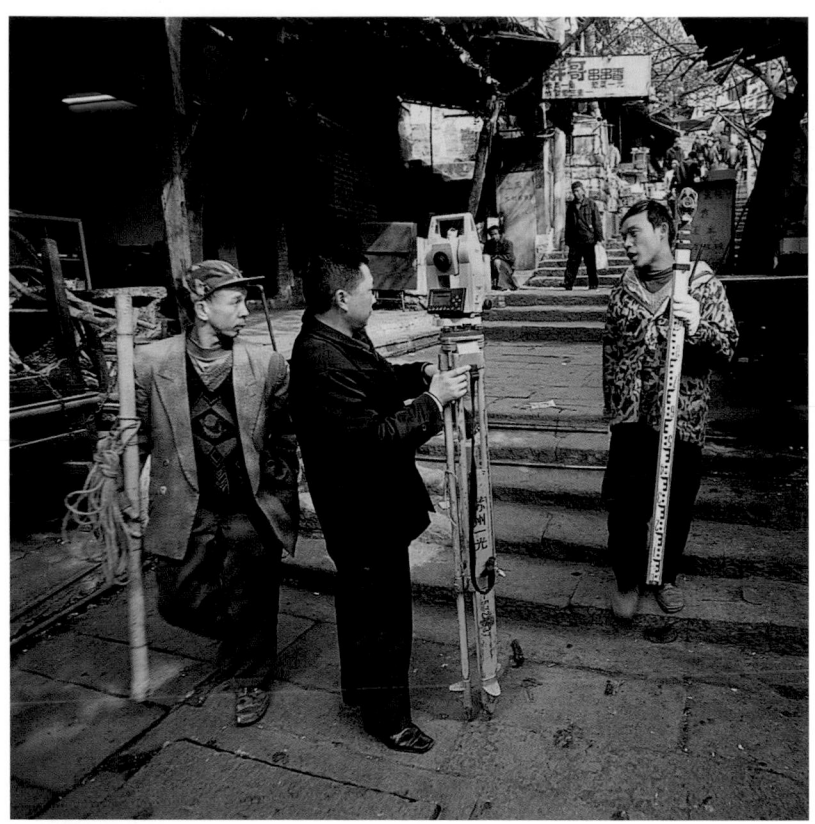

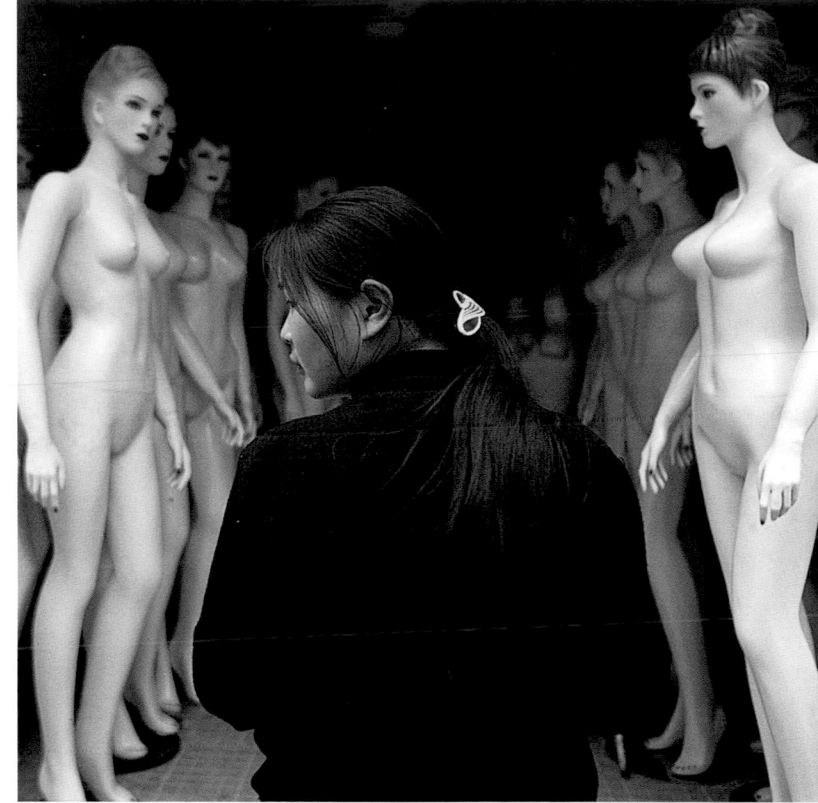

1

2

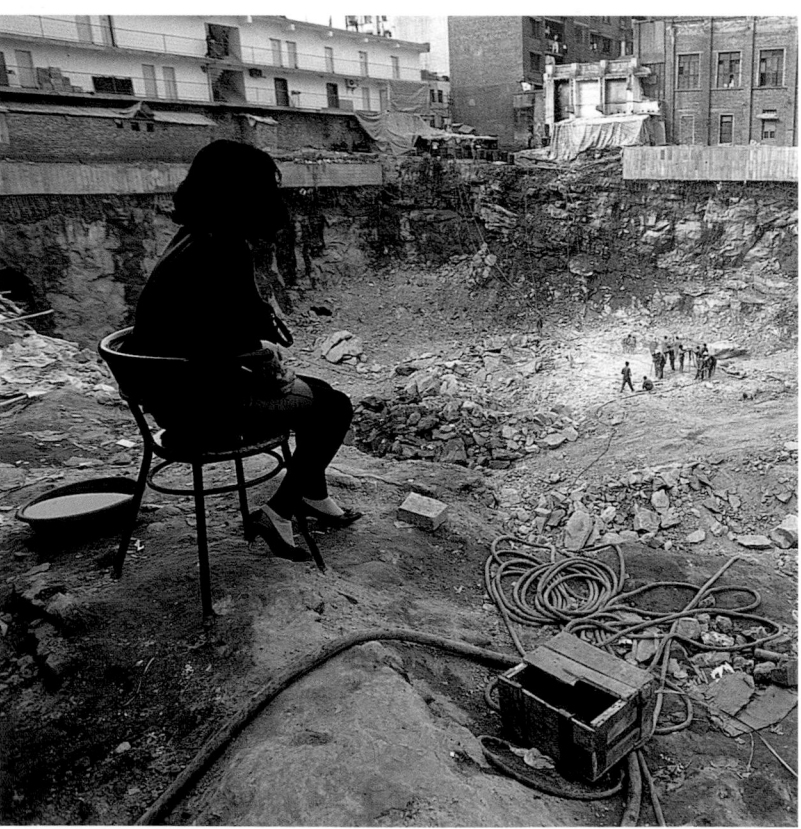

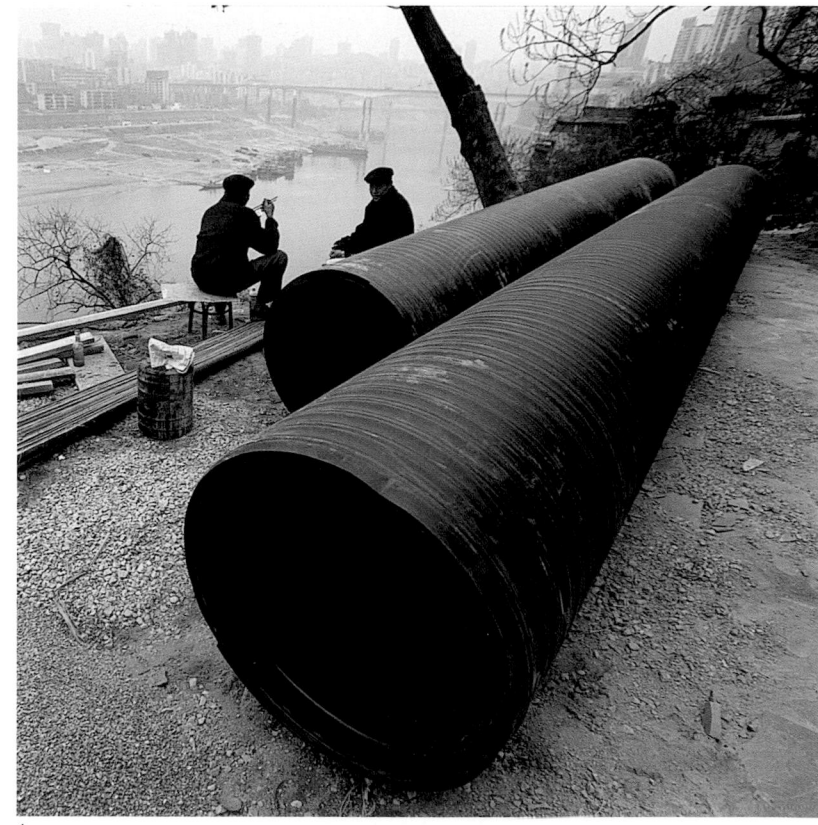

3

4

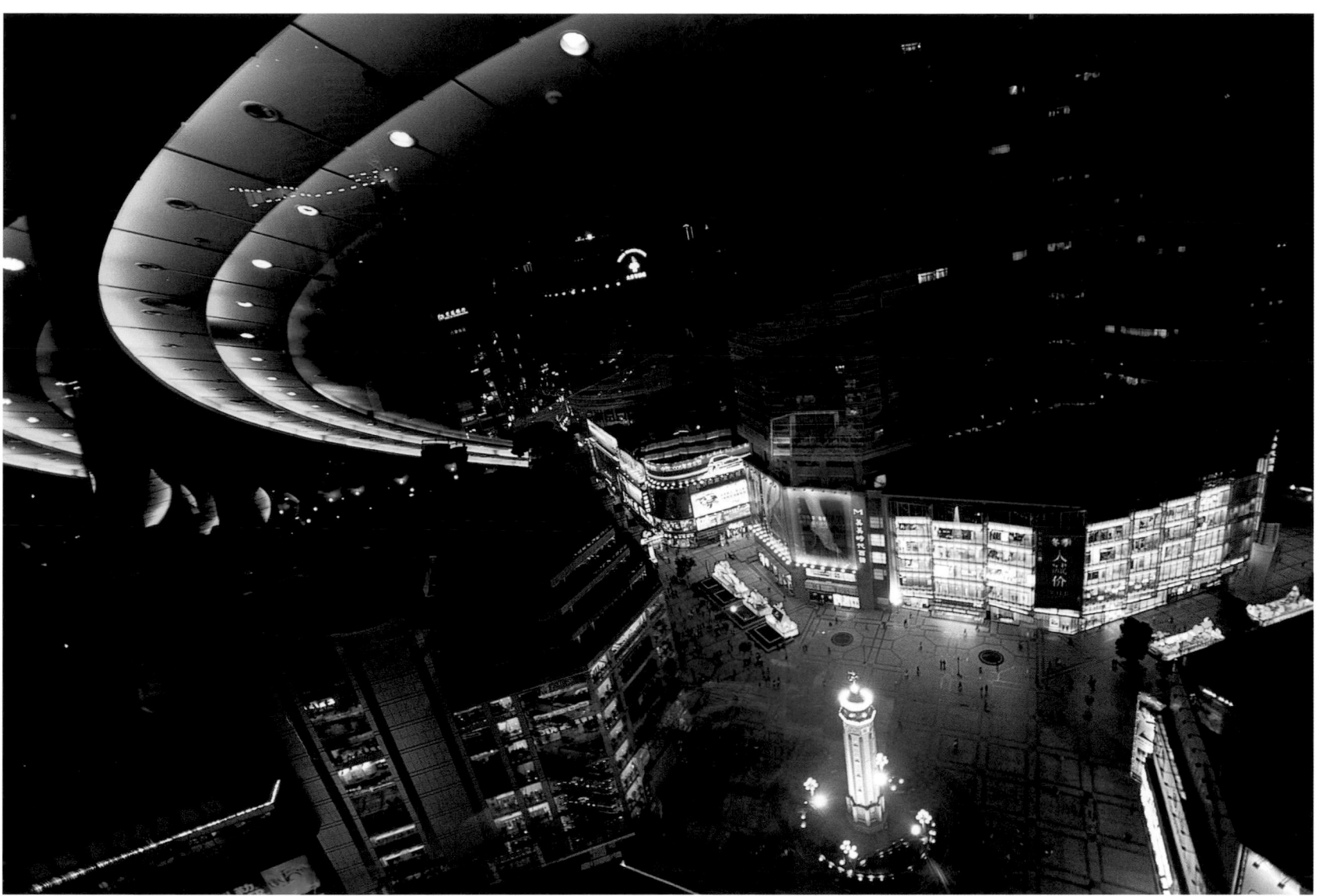

5

CHONG'QING HAS BEEN AN IMPORTANT TRANSPORTATION CENTRE for southwest China since the Qin Dynasty (221–207 BCE). The city's transformation into an industrial powerhouse did not begin until Chong'qing became the capital of Chiang Kai'shek's Kuo'min'tang government during the Second World War. As Japanese forces pressed in on all sides, entrepreneurs, professionals and refugees poured into Chong'qing from all over China. This fusion of entrepreneurial experience, technical skills and an inexhaustible pool of cheap labour jump-started the city's industrial development. [1] The presence of surveyors in the old town at the centre of the city can only mean that much of Chong'qing's original core will soon be demolished and turned into [3] a giant pit waiting to be filled by enormous skyscrapers. [2] A mannequin shop in the old town. [4] Workers take their lunch break at a riverfront construction site. [5] Looking down from the rotating restaurant on top of the shopping mall jungle in downtown Chong'qing, it is difficult to imagine that the neon-lit Liberation Monument was until quite recently the city's tallest structure.

TREASURE SUMMIT HILL

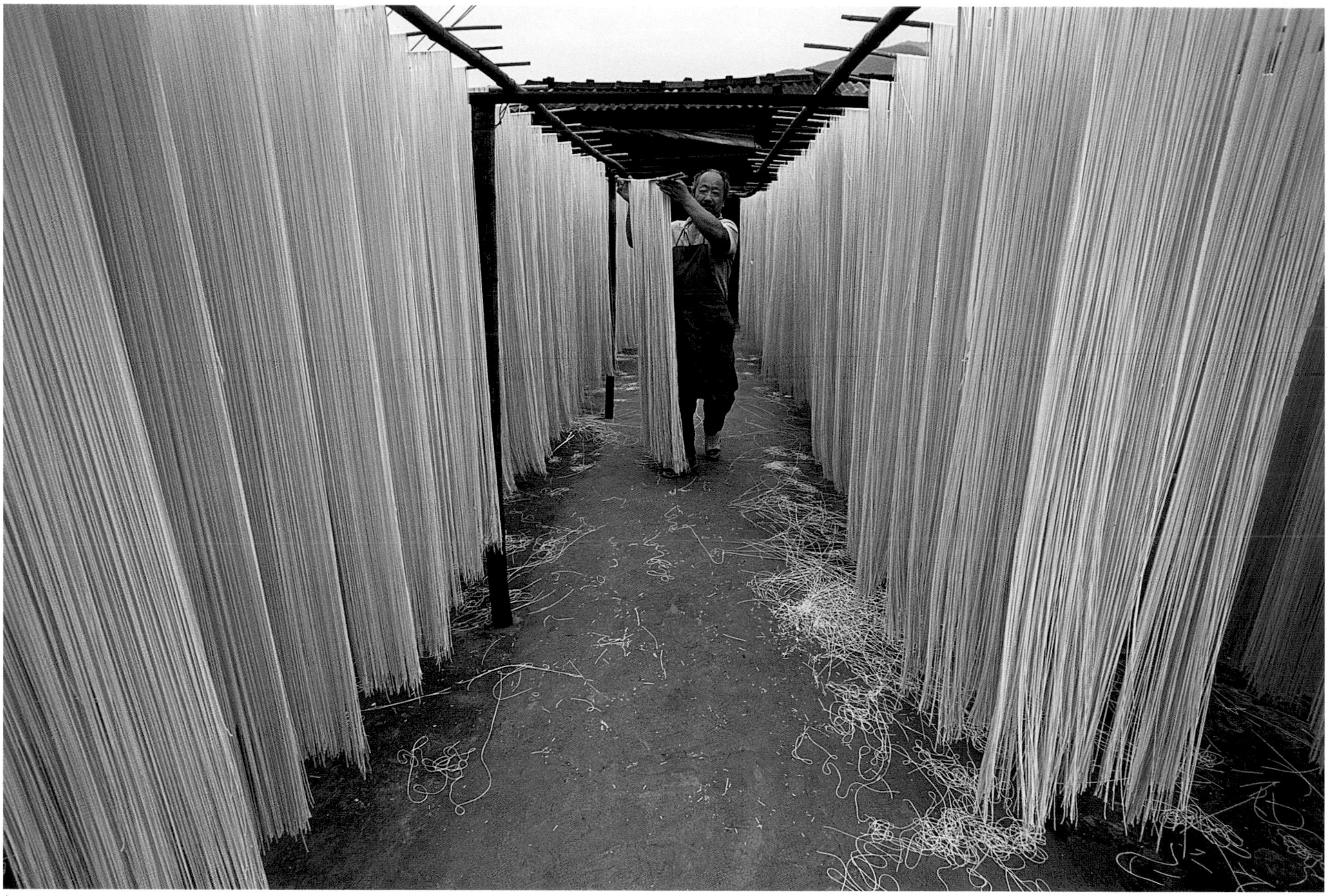

1

DA'ZU, WHICH MEANS 'ABUNDANT HARVEST' but sounds like 'big foot' in Chinese, is a county renowned for its rock carvings. More than 60,000 Buddhist, Taoist and Confucian statues and rock carvings, as well as 100,000 chiselled characters, have been carved into the region's sandstone cliff faces. Work began on these inscriptions in 650 CE, the first year of the Yong'hui reign in the Tang Dynasty. The most famous grottoes are in the Bao'ding'shan (*Treasure Summit Hill*). [2–5] The horseshoe canyon is filled with exquisite Buddhist carvings of exceptional craftsmanship on a breathtaking scale, believed to have been executed between 1179 and 1249 during the Jin and Yuan dynasties. In 1999 the Da'zu rock carvings were declared a World Cultural Heritage Site. Along the way to Da'zu, which lies to the north of the Chong'qing-Cheng'du highway, I came across [1] a small family workshop that specializes in making the traditional 'hanging noodles.' It was run by an annoying man who insisted on addressing me as 'uncle' despite being a lot older and a grandfather.

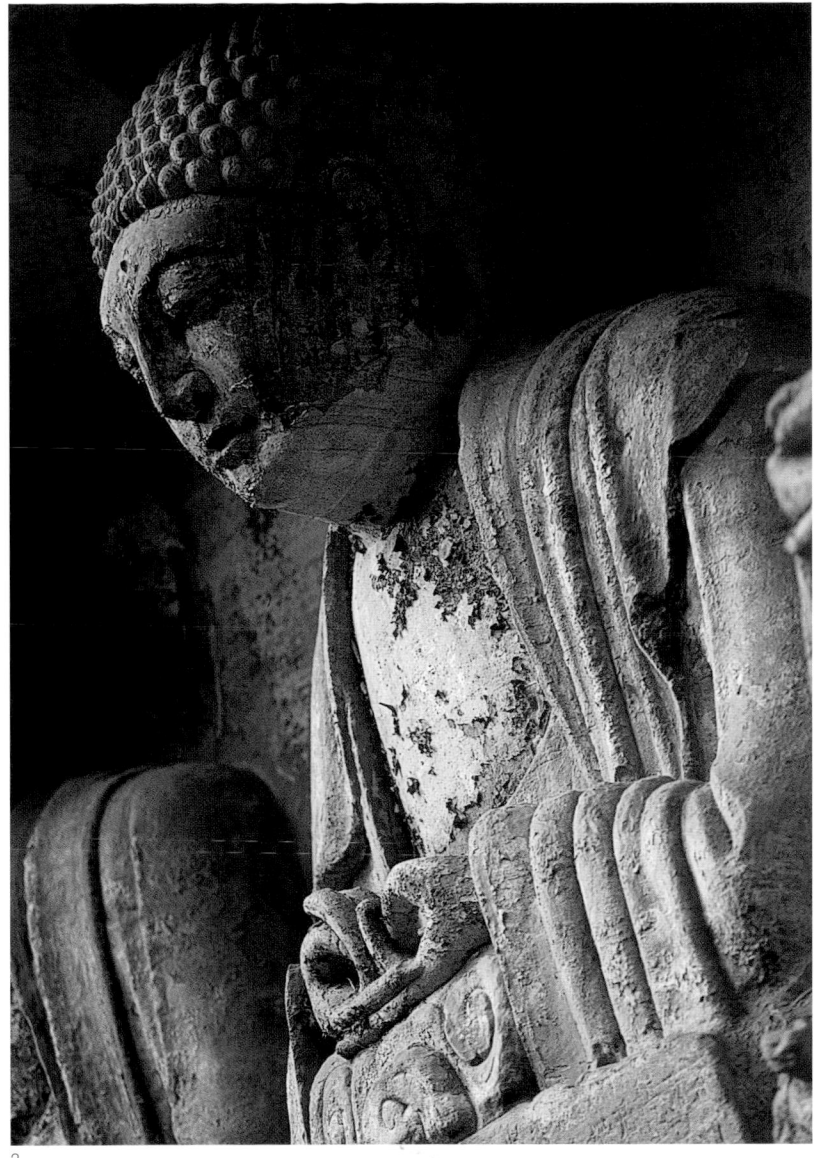

2

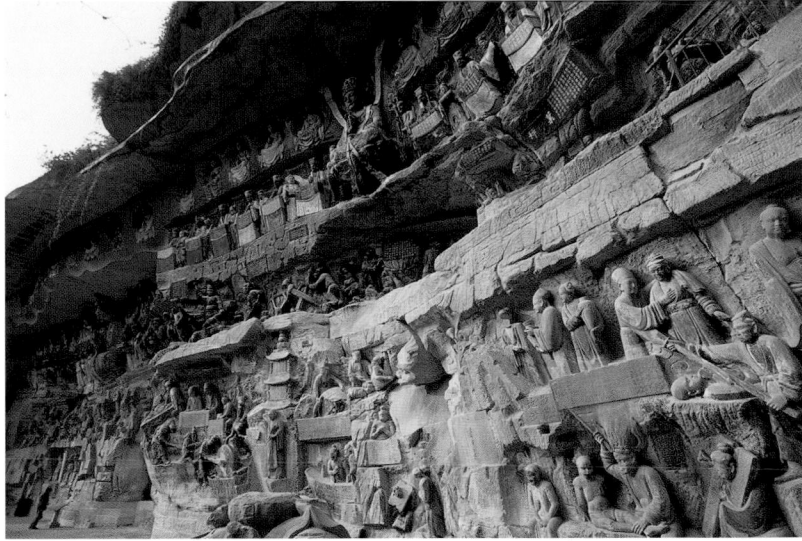

3

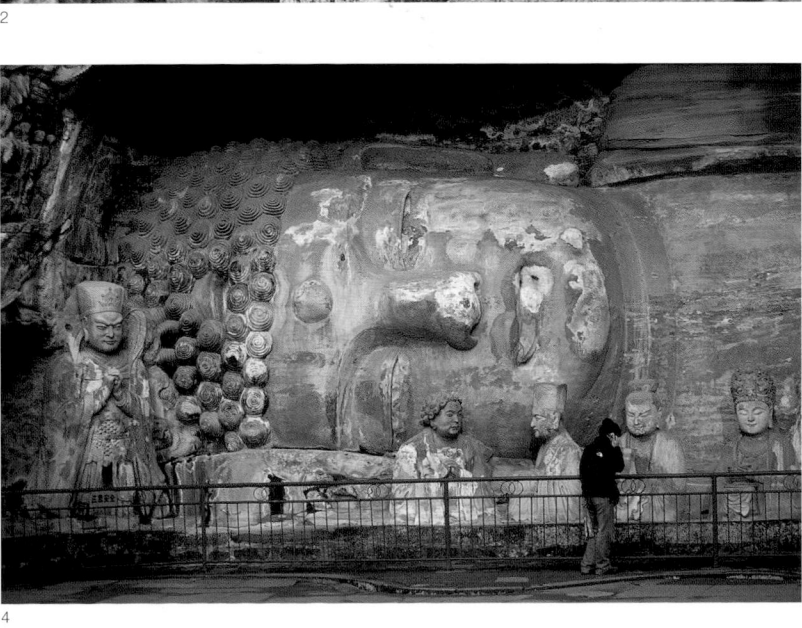

4

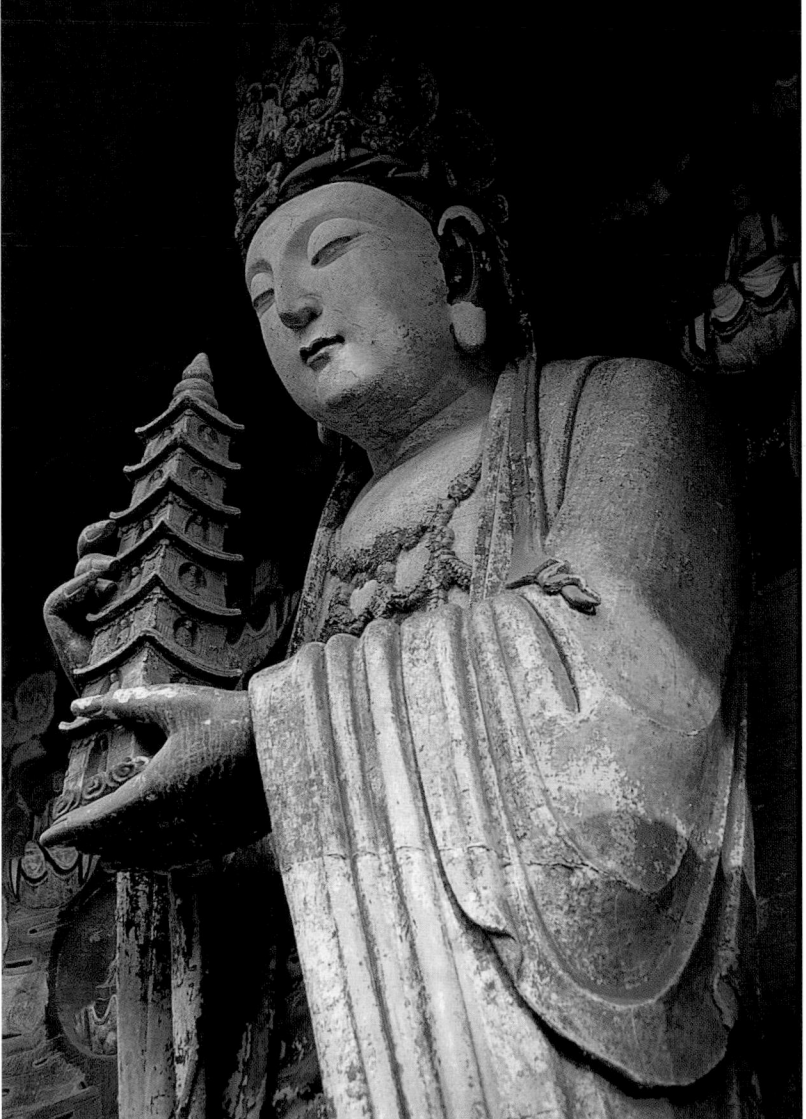

5

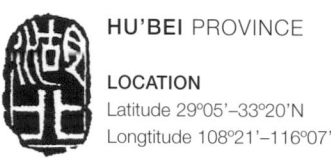

HU'BEI PROVINCE

LOCATION
Latitude 29º05'–33º20'N
Longtitude 108º21'–116º07'E

AREA 569,800 km² (220,000 sq miles)

GEOGRAPHY This is a mountainous region. The central and eastern Jian'ghan Plain accounts for only 20 per cent of the province, with the remaining landmass taken up by the ring of mountains and foothills that surround it. The west is dominated by the Wu'dang, Jing'shan, Daba and Wu Shan ranges. The Da'bie Mountains lie to the northeast, the Tongbai to the north and the Mu'fu in the southeast. The Yang'tze River enters Hu'bei from the west through the Three Gorges and the Han'shui River flows from the northwest. Average elevation ranges from 50 m to 1,000 m, with the highest point at the summit of Mount Shen'nong'jia at 3,105 m.

CLIMATE Hu'bei has a subtropical climate with distinct seasons. Average January temperatures range from 1ºC to 6ºC, reaching 24ºC to 30ºC in July. The highest recorded temperature is 41.3ºC and the lowest is -18.1ºC. Average annual rainfall is 800 mm to 1,600 mm.

POPULATION 60.31 million (end 2005)

MAJOR CITIES Wu'han (capital), Jing'zhou, Yi'chang, Shi'yan

AGRICULTURE Main food crops are rice and wheat. Cash crops include cotton, tea, oilseeds and ramie.

MAIN INDUSTRIES Main industries include vehicles, metallurgy, machinery, power generation, textiles, foodstuffs and high-technology products. The province is a major supplier of hydroelectric power, and the huge Three Gorges Dam project under construction in western Hu'bei will increase this role.

ANNUAL PER CAPITA INCOME (2005)
Disposable income of urban residents:
RMB 8,786 (US$1,096)
Net income of rural residents:
RMB 3,099 (US$387)

HISTORICAL AND SCENIC SITES Mount Wu'dang, Yellow Crane Tower, Yang'tze Three Gorges Dam Project, Shen'nong'jia Nature Reserve, Red Cliff Battlefield.

FOOD Hu'bei cuisine is noted for its freshwater fish dishes, reflecting the province's numerous lakes and major river systems. Dishes include steamed bream, boiled fish with tangerine pulp, stewed turtle and Dragon and Phoenix (eel and chicken).

[RIGHT] Medicine man on the hills over the Yang'tze Gorge.

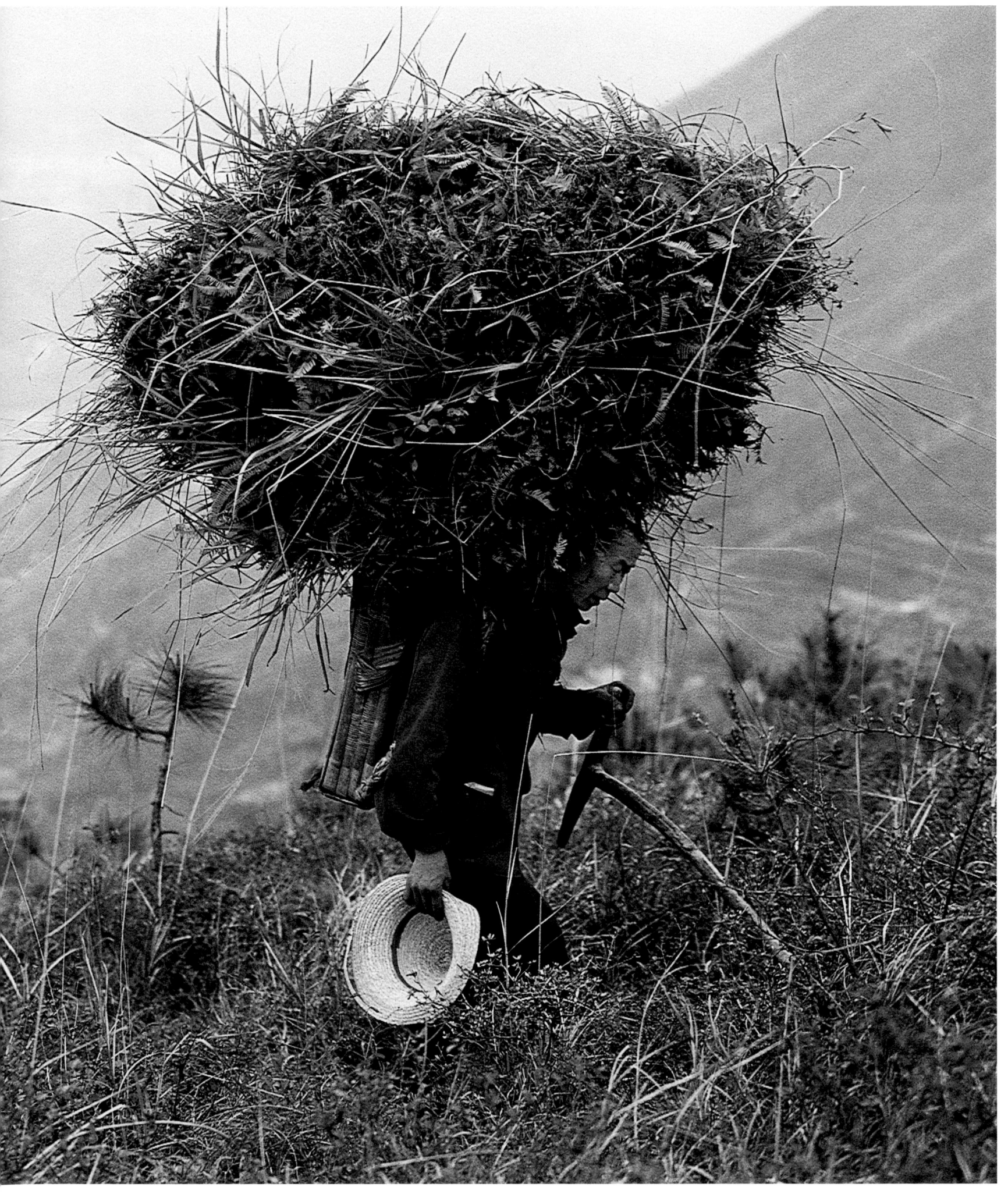

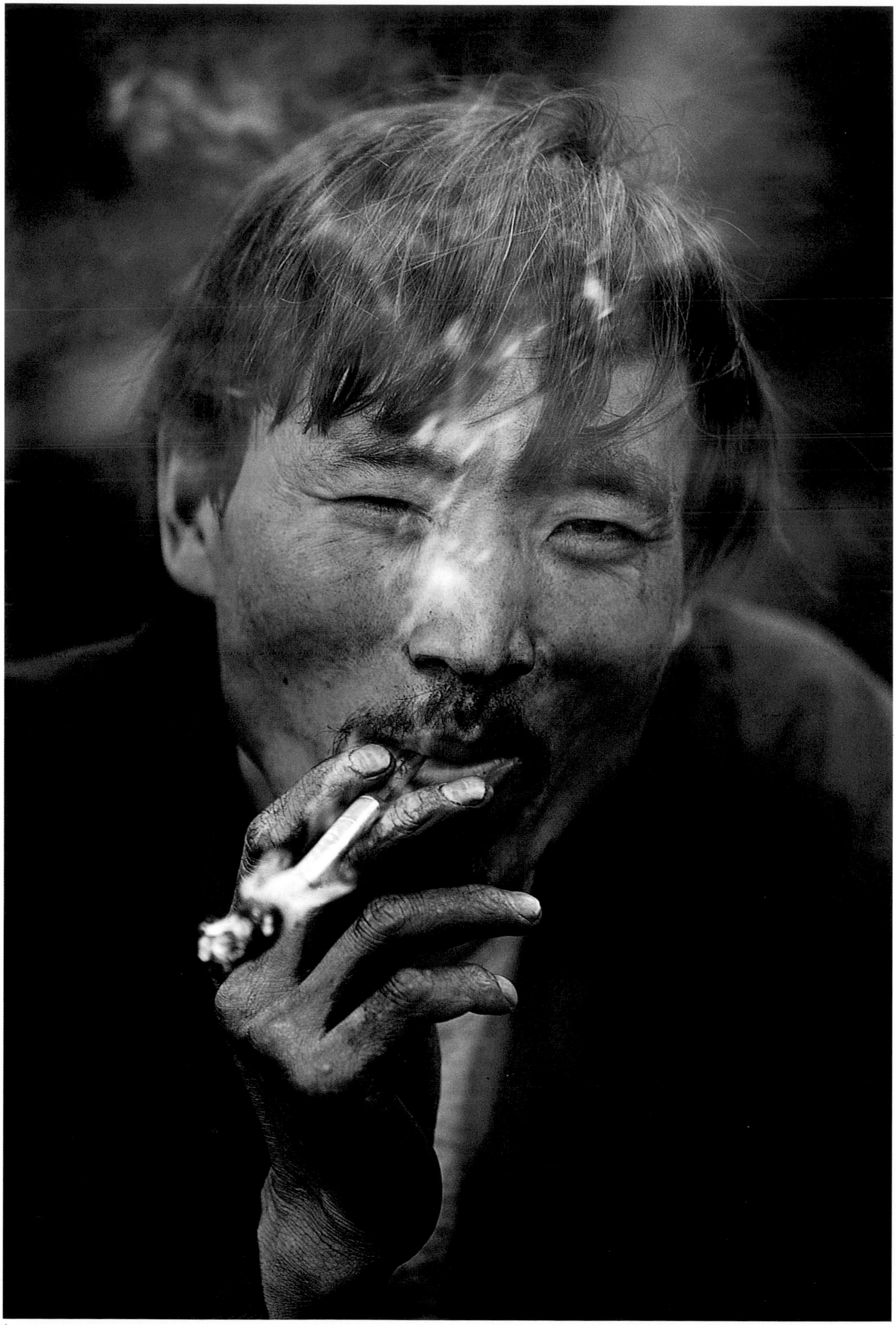

1

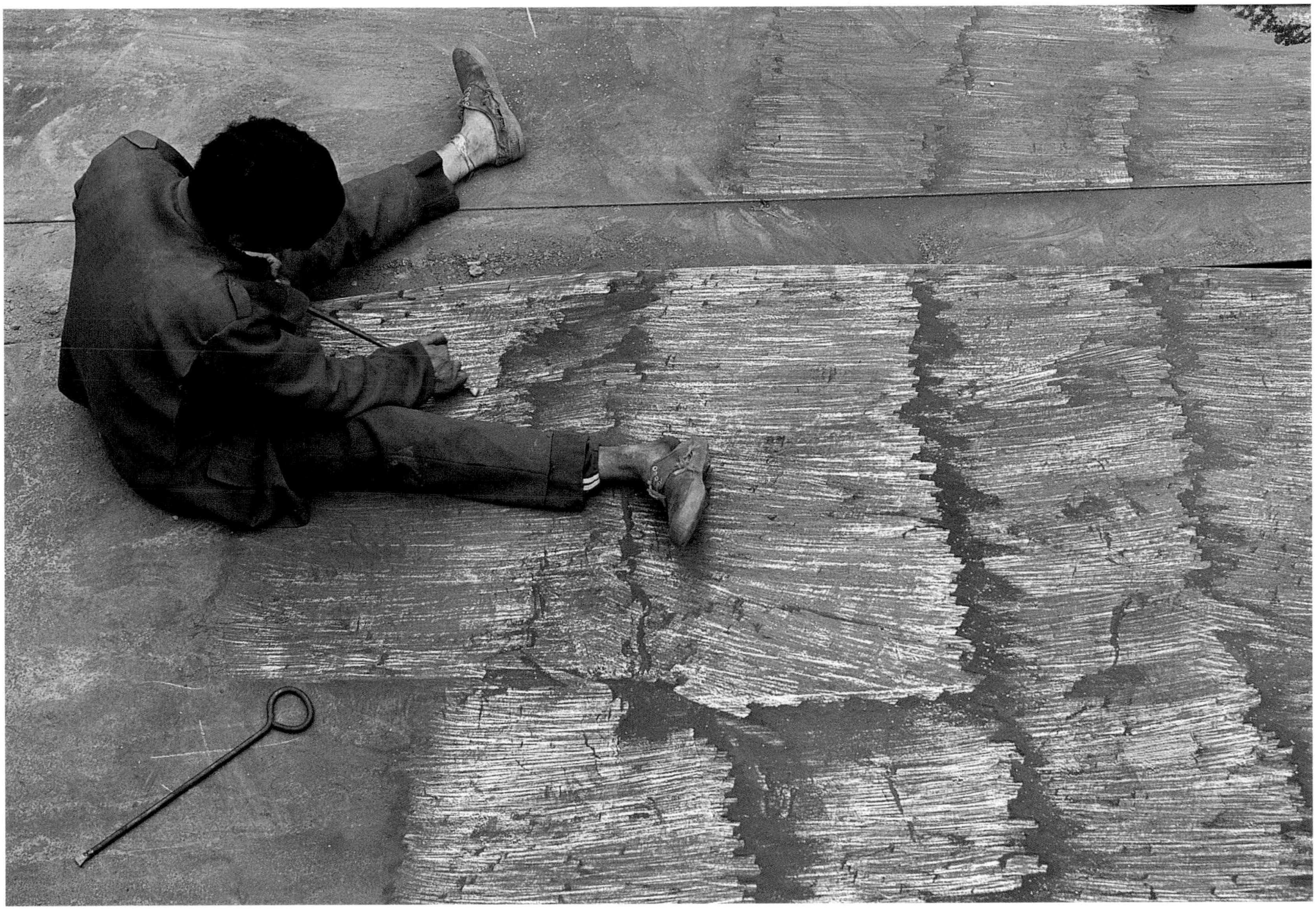

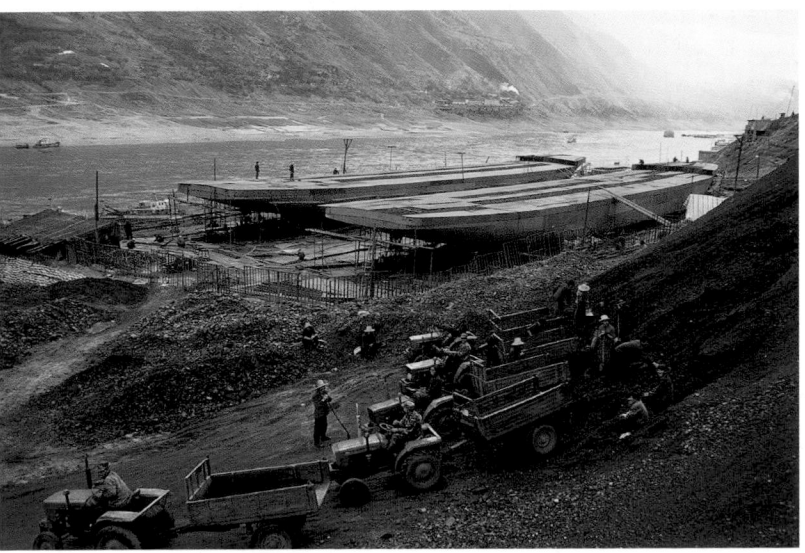

2

OLD WU'SHAN WAS A BUSTLING, NOISY LITTLE TOWN full of karaoke bars and brothels disguised as hairdressing salons. I once spent a pleasant evening there, en route from Yi'chang to Chong'qing on a Yang'tze Gorges ferry that stopped there for the night. Sitting on a red plastic stool on the filthy pavement, I drank beer, snacked on local street 'delicacies' and watched the swirl of humanity in the night market from behind my broken wooden table. The town is no longer there, and the places where I had left my footprints in the coal dust as I took these pictures in 1992 are now 135 metres (440 feet) beneath the waters of Lake Placid. This man-made reservoir is the largest on earth and was formed by the Three Gorges Dam as it stemmed the flow of the Yang'tze and flooded a huge swath of the river's valley. [1] A local labourer working a coal pile deposited by the riverbank takes a cigarette break. [3] 'Stickmen' transport the coal up the winding road in baskets to a factory. [2] A worker in the makeshift shipyard on the edge of the river strips the rust off a tanker the hard way.

3

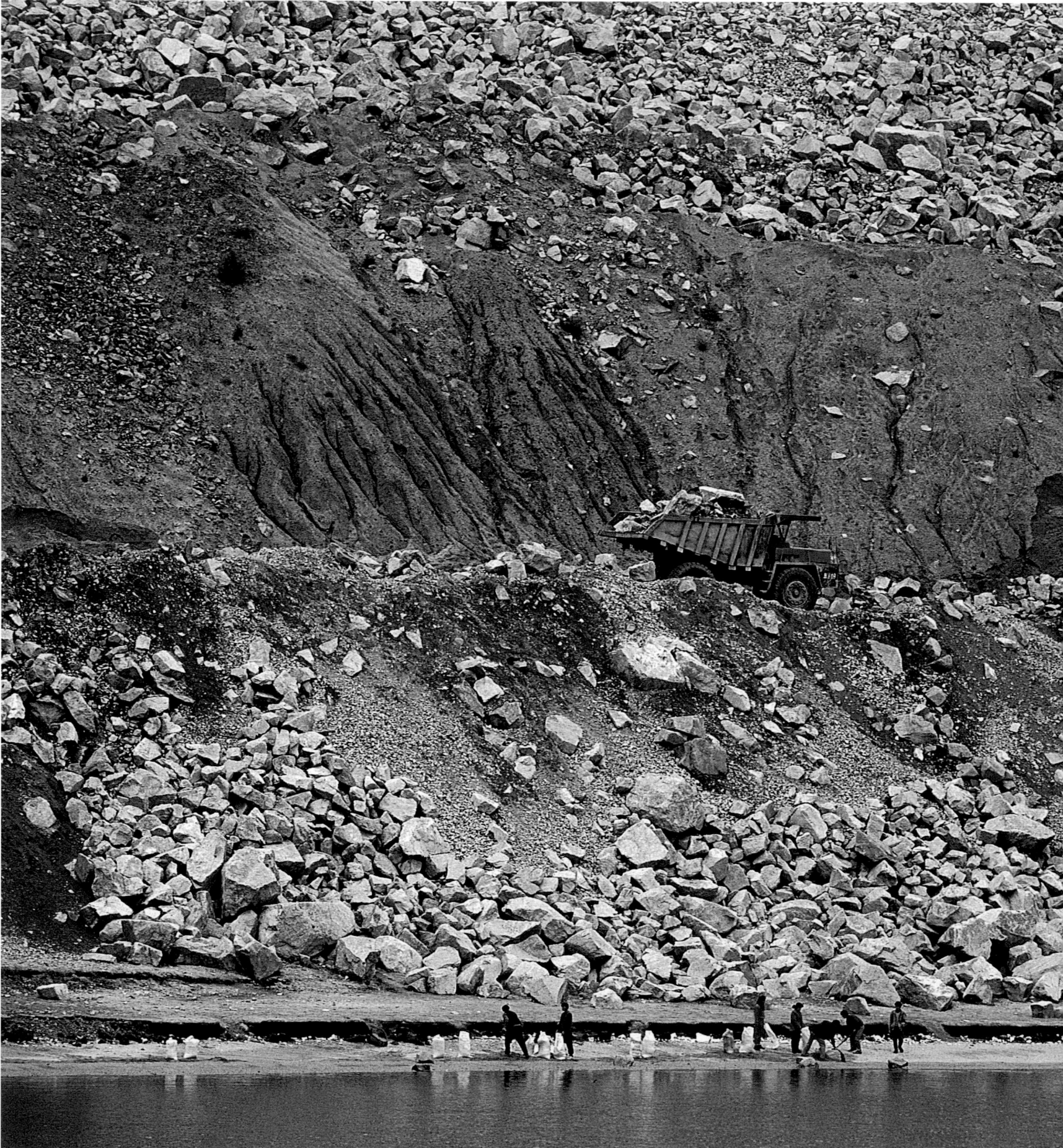

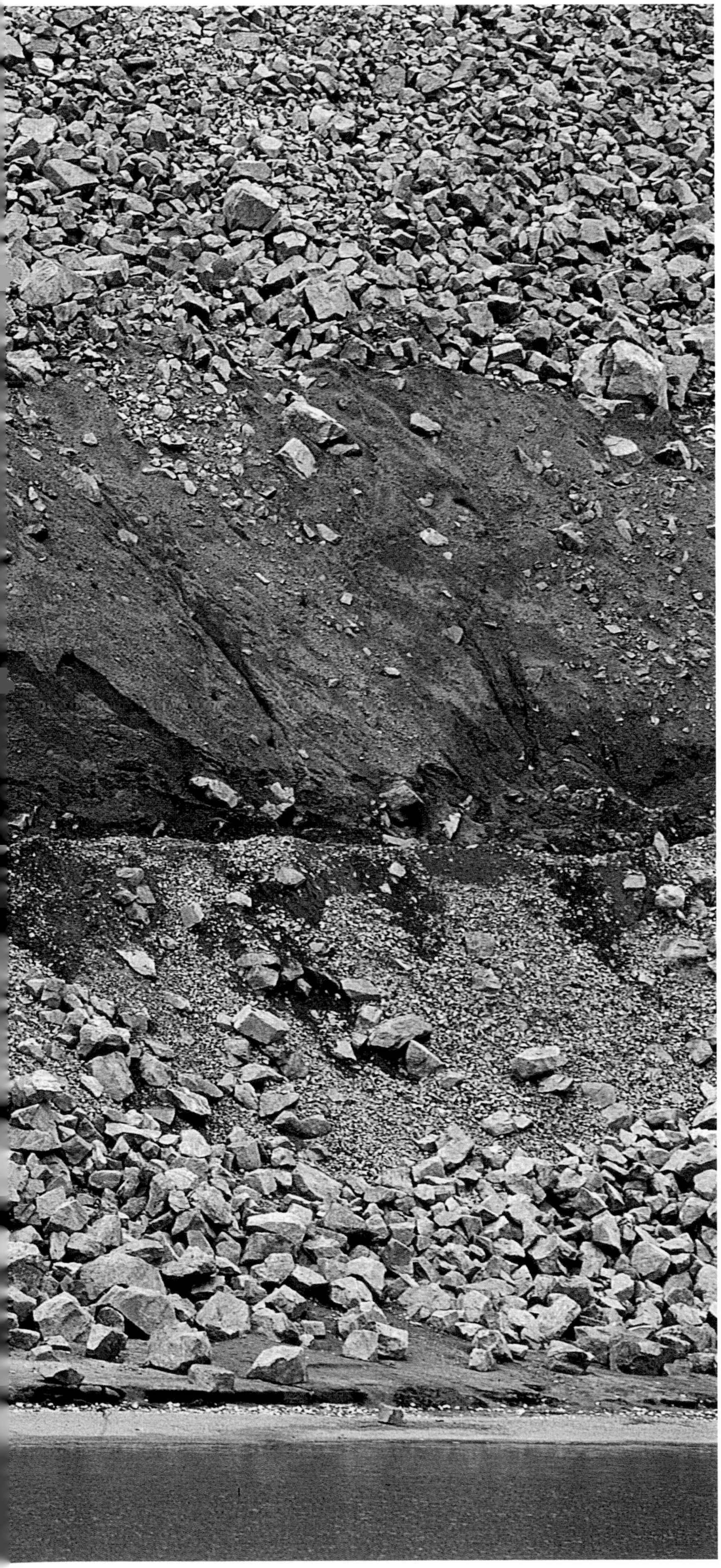

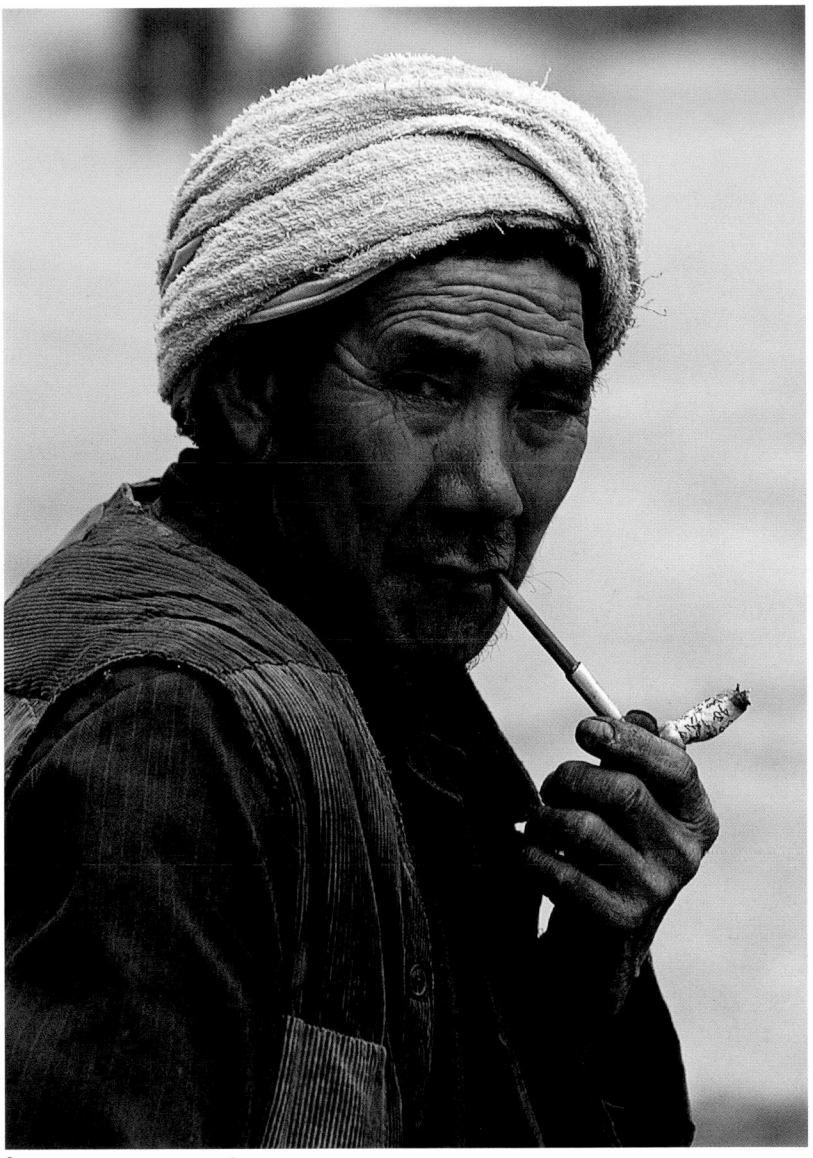

2

THE PROSPECT OF TAMING THE MERCURIAL YANG'TZE, China's longest river, has tantalized the country's rulers for centuries. Plans for the controversial Three Gorges Dam were first drawn up before the Great Leap Forward in the late 1950s, but construction work on this huge project did not begin until 1994. By October 2002 the north bank section of the dam was complete, and 14 hydroelectric turbines were generating 49 billion kw/h of electricity by the end of 2005. Construction ended in May 2006 and the entire project is expected to be fully operational in 2008. The dam forms a barrier 2.3 kilometres (1.43 miles) wide and 185 metres (607 feet) high that seals off the Xi'ling Gorge. Water level in the reservoir will reach 156 metres (512 feet), allowing 26 turbines to generate 84.7 billion kw/h of electricity annually – equivalent to the capacity of 15 nuclear power plants. Environmentalists have long questioned the wisdom of the project. One serious concern is that the reservoir, which stretches 600 kilometres (373 miles) upstream, will eventually become a festering bog as pollutants rising from the submerged mines and factories combine with the waste from the major industrial centres up river. Their voices were drowned out by the noise of construction and propaganda. [1] A quarry near the site of the dam. [2] One of the 1.3 million people displaced by the Three Gorges Dam.

THE THREE GORGES

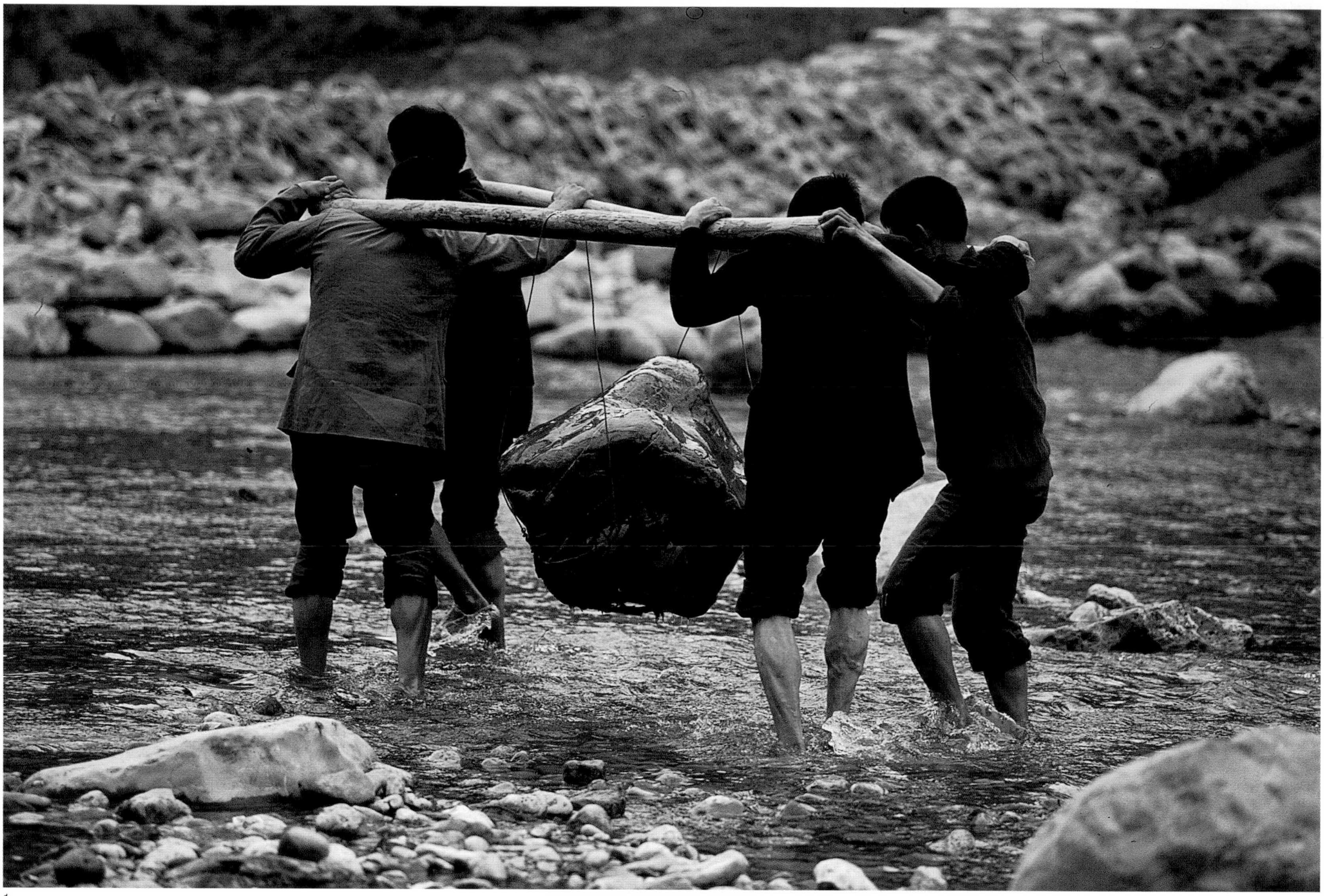

1

THERE IS NO DOUBT CHINA NEEDS CHEAP ELECTRICITY to sustain growth and bring wealth to the country's poorest provinces. However, many have questioned the ability of the Three Gorges Dam to meet those needs. Apart from environmentalists' fears over the impact of pollution on the region's ecology, engineers have long argued for a series of smaller dams that could produce similar levels of power without the potential silting problem facing the 'Mother of All Dams'. The human cost of the project is already becoming evident. A large number of the one million people displaced so far by the US$25 billion project have been reduced to poverty by massive and pervasive corruption. Huge amounts of the budget earmarked for their resettlement compensation has simply vanished. All locations in these pictures are now submerged and the people dispersed. [1] 'Stickmen' clearing boulders from rapids. The rocks are used to shore up the dykes along [2] the Dan'ning River in the 'mini' Three Gorges. [4] Contemplating the Yangtze. [3] Industrial pollution. [5] A fisherman mends his nets on the banks of Yi'chang.

THE MIDDLE KINGDOM

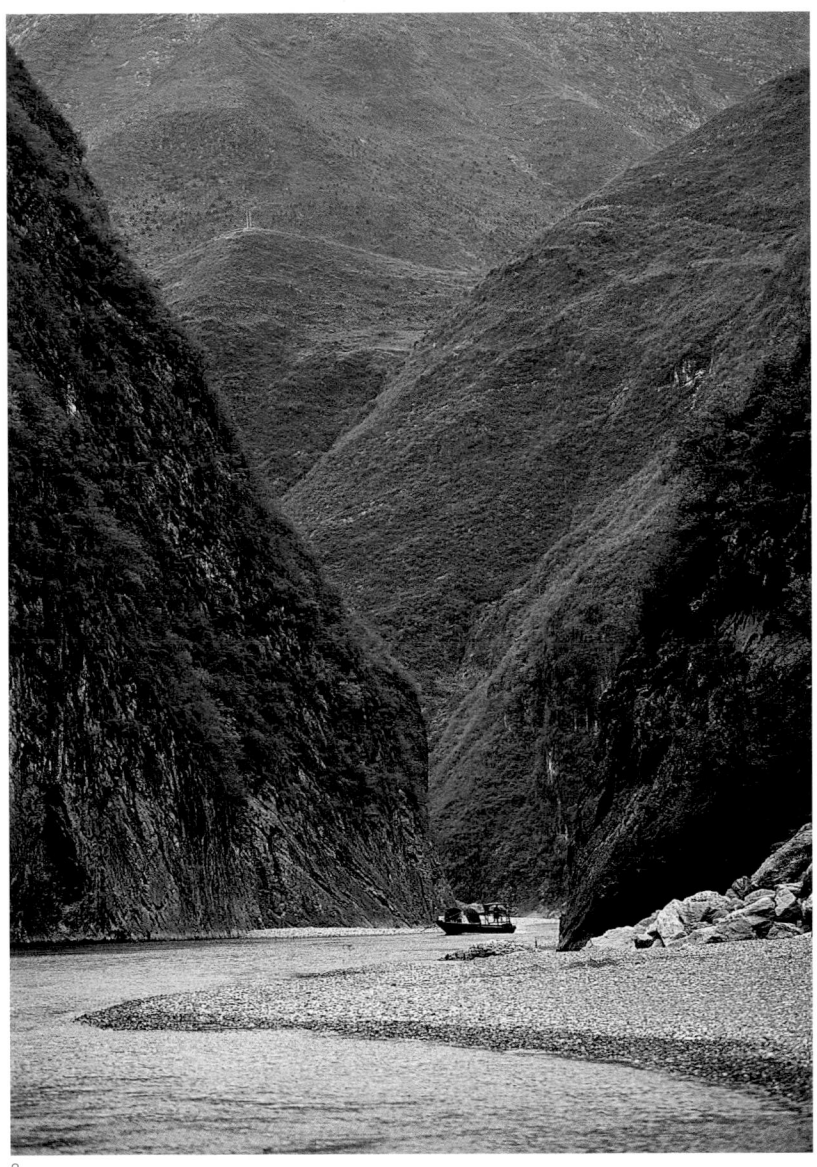

2

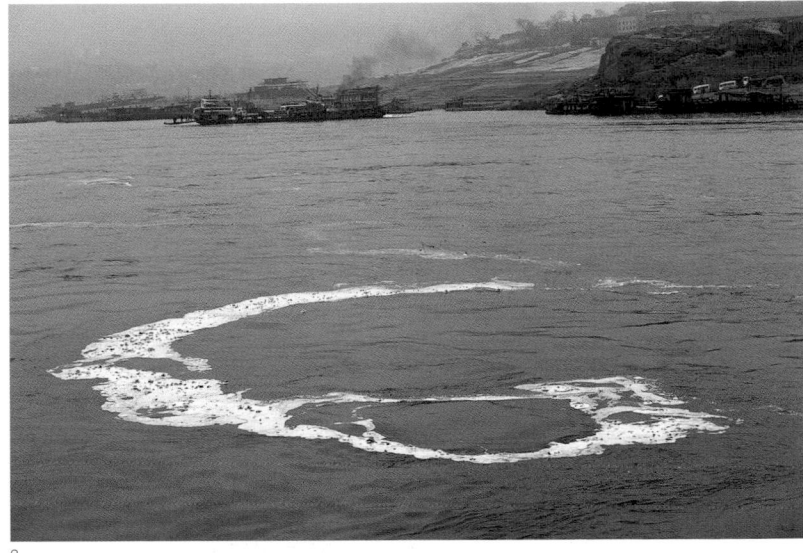

3

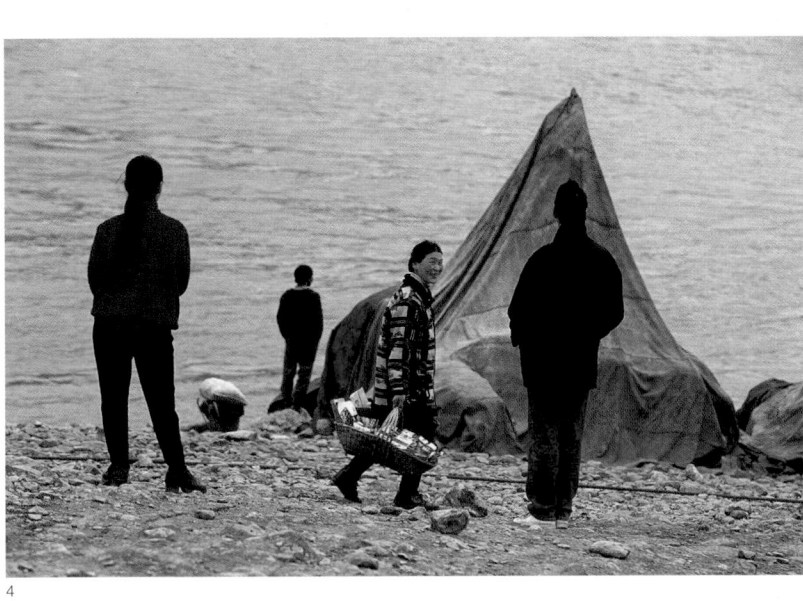

4

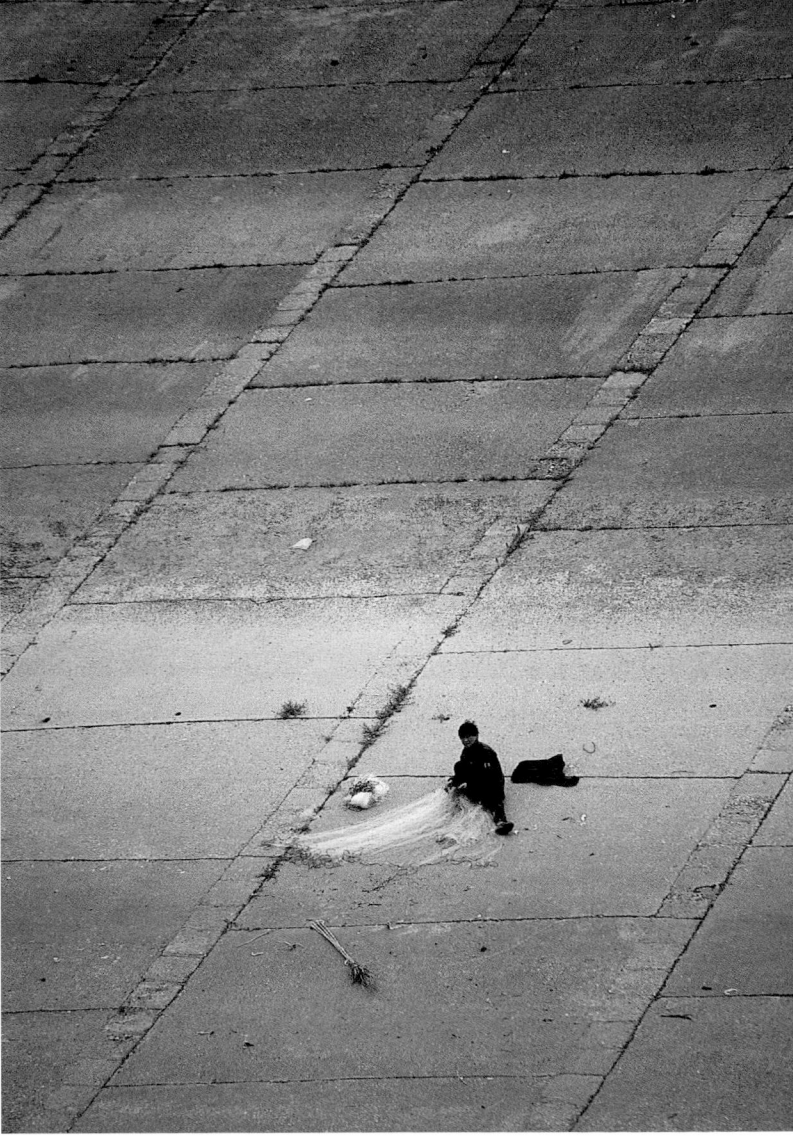

5

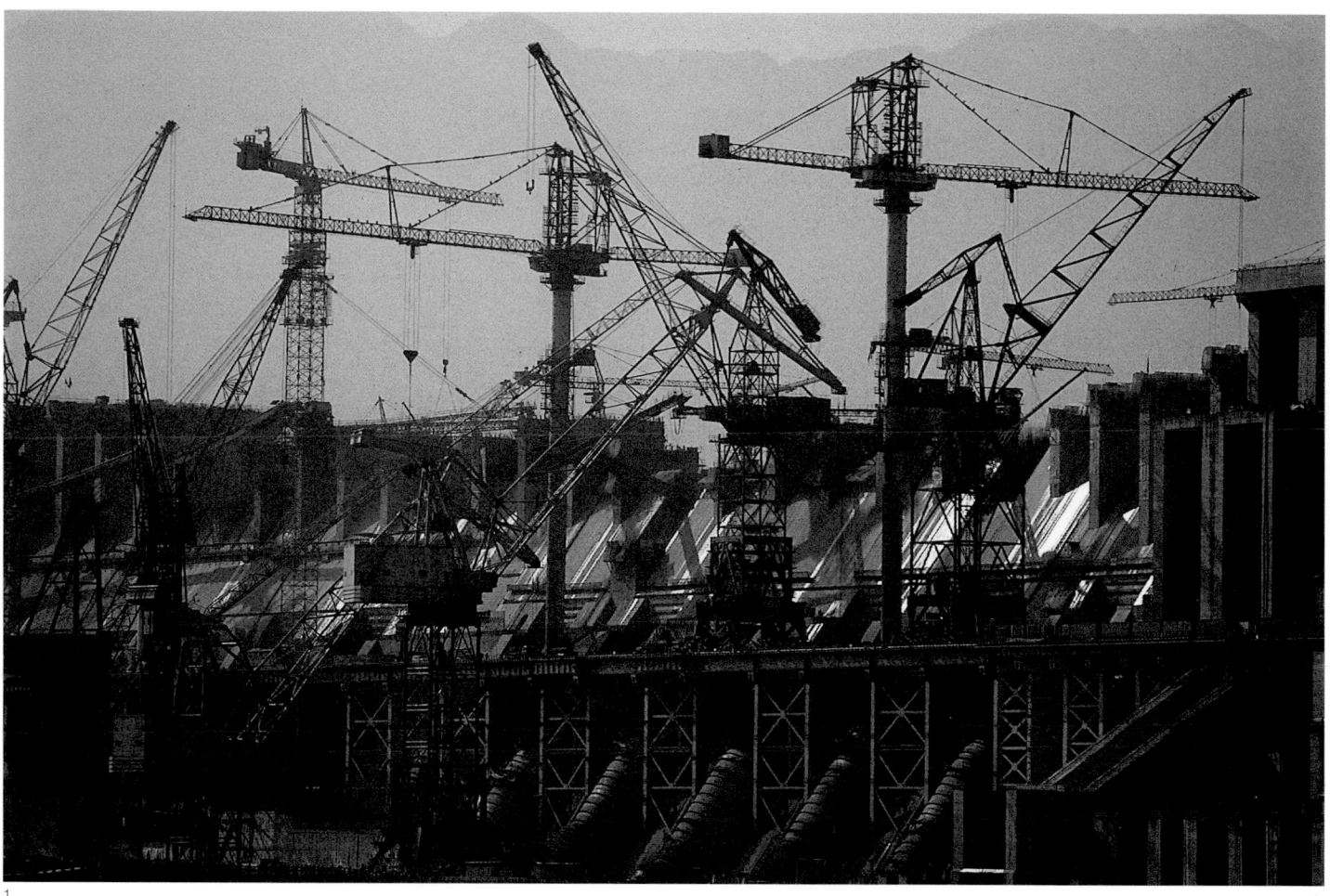

1

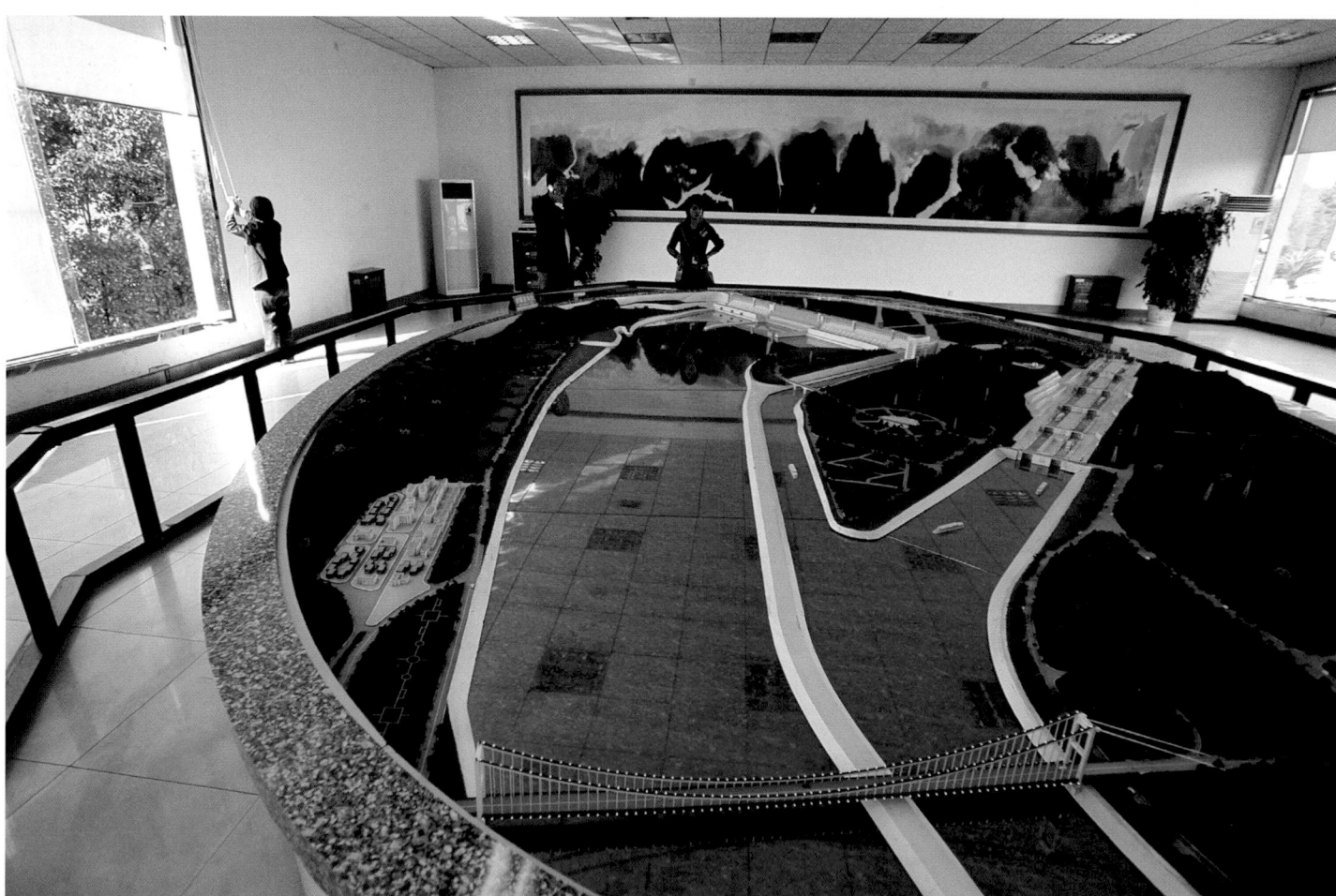

2

THE YELLOW CRANE PAVILION

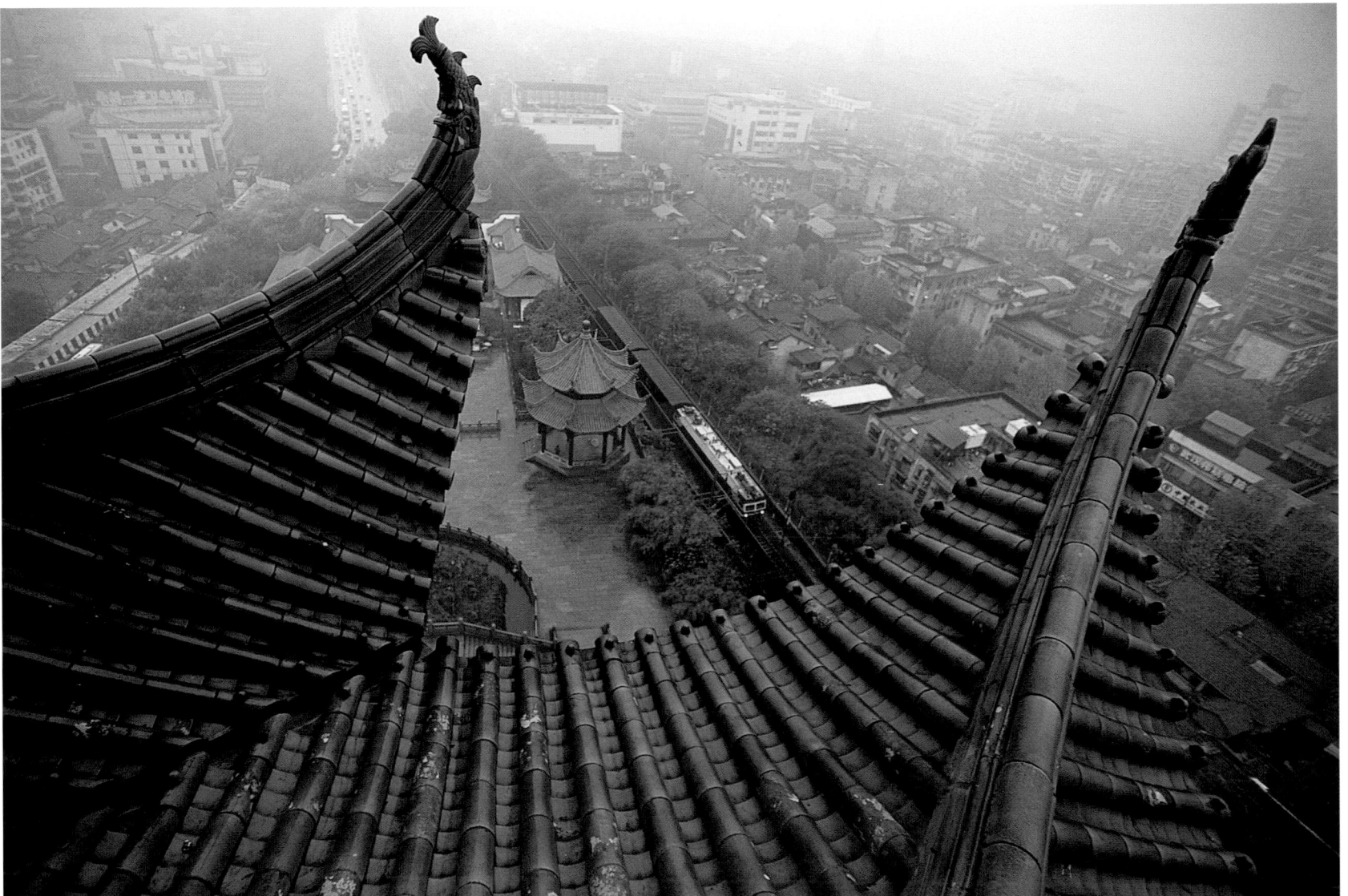

3

WU'HAN IS CHINA'S PITTSBURGH: famed for its heavy steel industry and notorious as one of the country's most polluted cities. On a truly depressing day, when grey skies laden with metallic fumes drench the city with persistent rain, it is difficult to imagine that [3] the Yellow Crane Pavilion on the south bank of the Yang'tze was once the most famous royal pleasure palace of the region. Here princes and ministers enjoyed the best views of their domain along with the best 'wine, women and song'. Tang Dynasty poet Li Bai immortalized it in his ode to loss: "My old friend bids me farewell, in the west, at Yellow Crane Pavilion. Down to Yangzh'ou he goes, amidst the flowers and mist of spring. The distant image of his lonely sail; disappears into blue emptiness. And all I see is the Long River, flowing to the edge of the sky." [1] The Three Gorges Dam nearing completion. [2] A scale-model of the 'largest hydroelectric project in history' at the site's visitor centre.

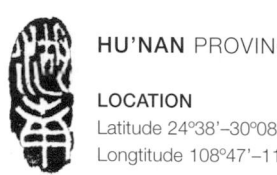

HU'NAN PROVINCE

LOCATION
Latitude 24°38'–30°08'N
Longtitude 108°47'–114°13'E

AREA 207,254 km² (80,000 sq miles)

GEOGRAPHY Half of Hu'nan is mountainous, with the remainder divided almost equally into plains, hills and river basins. The Wu'ling range lies to the northwest, the Xue'feng range to the west, the Nan'ling are to the south and the Luo'xiao to the east. The northeast is dominated by the lake systems of the Dong'ting Basin. The Xiang River traverses the province north to south, and with the smaller Yuan and Zi rivers feed Dong'ting Lake. The central south and west are characterized by the river systems floodplains or the foothills of the mountain ranges. Elevations range from 1,500 m in the mountains to below 50 m on the plains.

CLIMATE Hunan's climate is subtropical with mild winters and plenty of rainfall. January's temperatures average at 3°C to 8°C and July's range between 27°C and 30°C. The highest recorded temperature was 43°C, and the lowest, -18°C. Average annual rainfall is between 1,200 mm and 1,700 mm.

POPULATION 66.97 million (end 2004)

MAJOR CITIES Chang'sha (capital), Zhu Zhou, Heng'yang, Yue'yang

AGRICULTURE Main food crops are rice (Hu'nan is China's largest rice-producing province), corn, sweet potatoes, barley, buckwheat and citrus fruit. Cash crops include ramie, tea and rapeseed. There is also a significant freshwater fishery.

MAIN INDUSTRIES Heavy industries include aluminum smelting, iron and steel making, coal mining, oil refining and hydroelectric power production. Other industries include textiles, machine tools and handicrafts. The province is also a major manufacturer of fireworks.

ANNUAL PER CAPITA INCOME (2005)
Disposable income of urban residents:
RMB 9,524 (US$1,187)
Net income of rural residents:
RMB 3,118 (US$389)

HISTORICAL AND SCENIC SITES
Shao'shan (Mao Ze'dong's birthplace), Wu'ling'yuan (UNESCO World Heritage Site – includes Zhang'jia'jie, Suoxi Valley, Mount Tian'zi, Meng'dong River), Mount Heng'shan and Yue'yang Tower.

FOOD Hu'nan cuisine makes great use of fresh and dried chillies, garlic and a wide range of hot and sweet and sour sauces. Dishes associated with the province include orange beef, crispy duck, garlic-fried beans, steamed soft-shell turtle, Dong'ting fat fish maw and fermented bean curd.

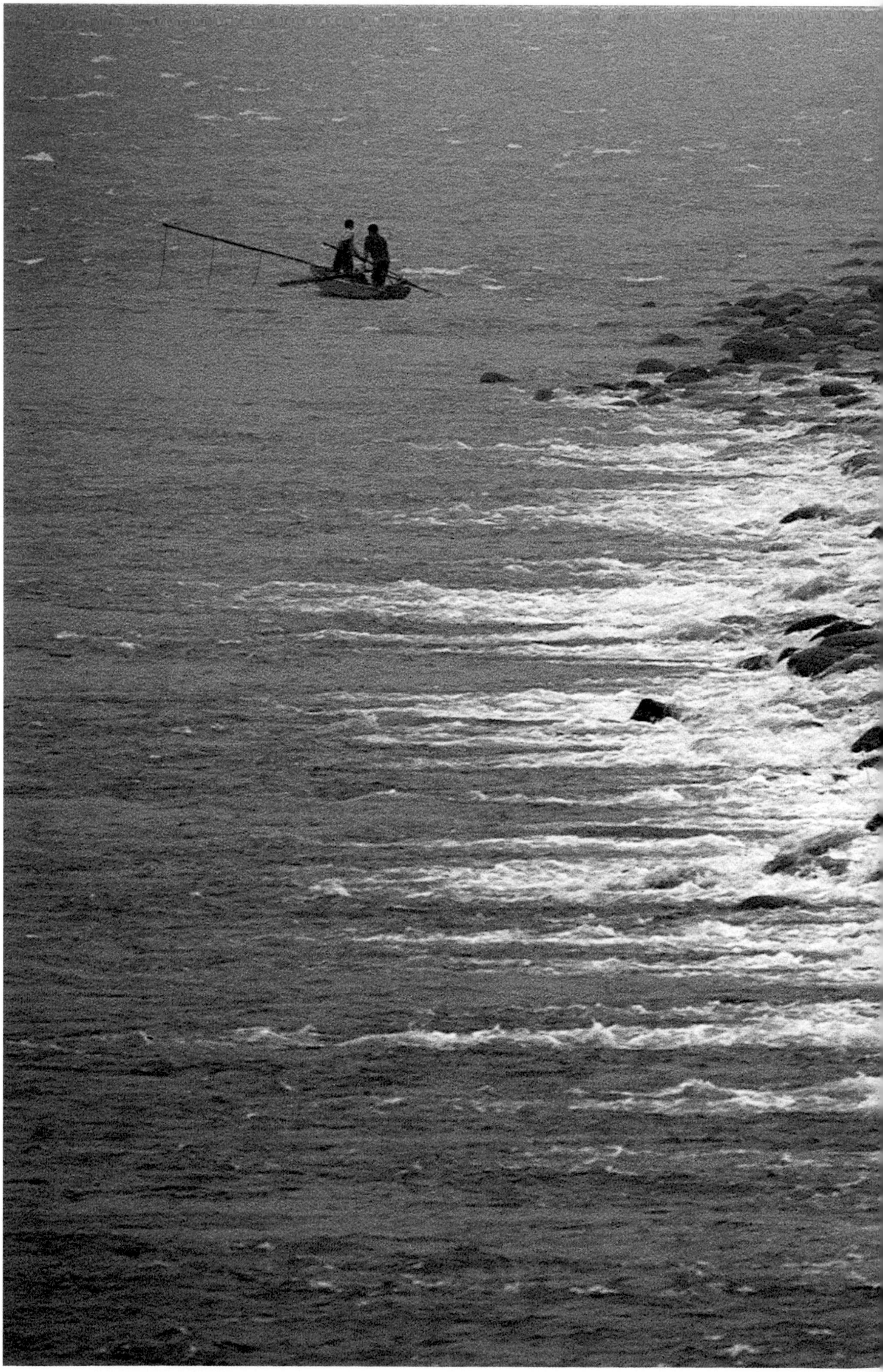

[RIGHT] The Xiang'jiang River.

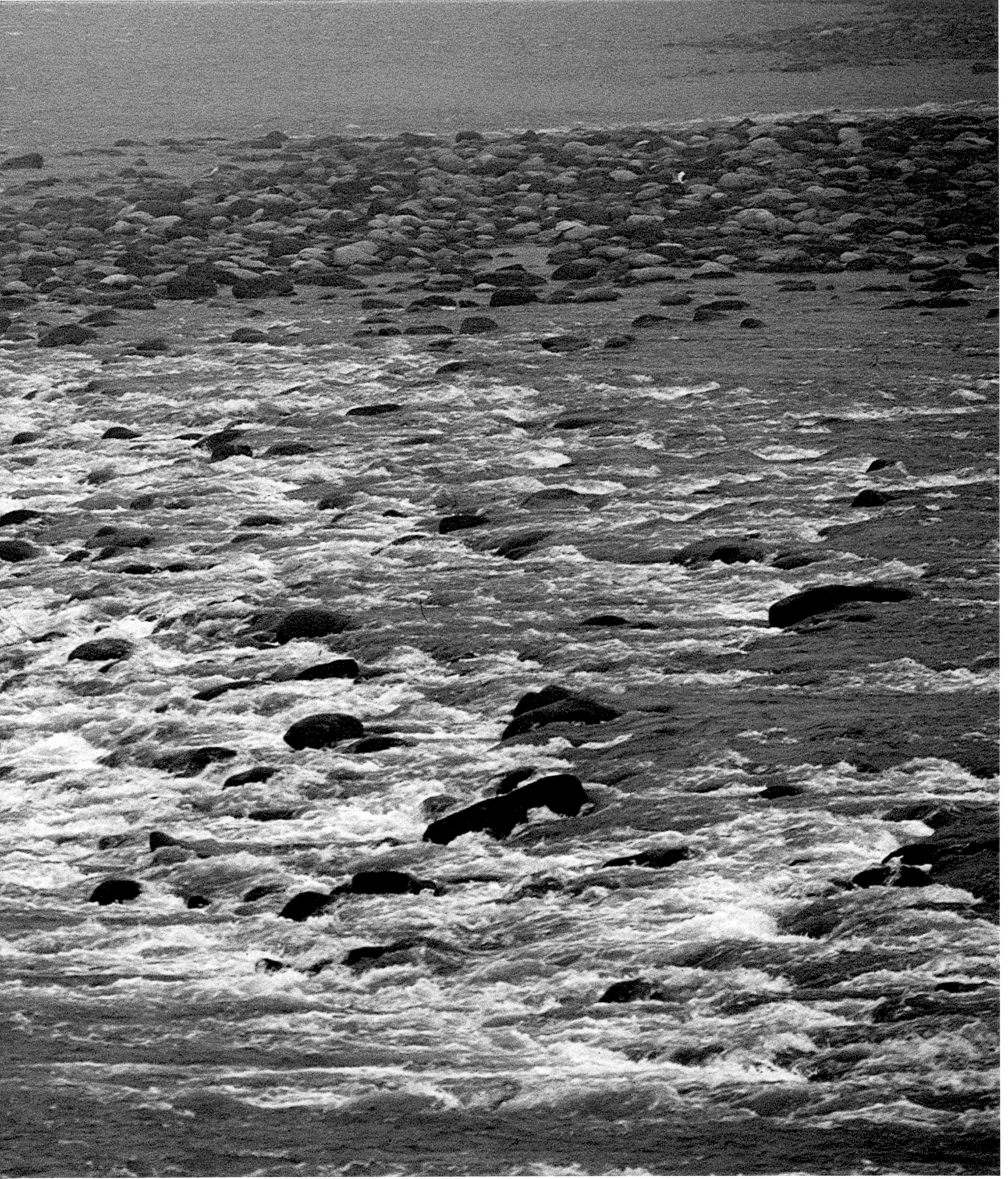

THE WALLED CITY OF PHOENIX

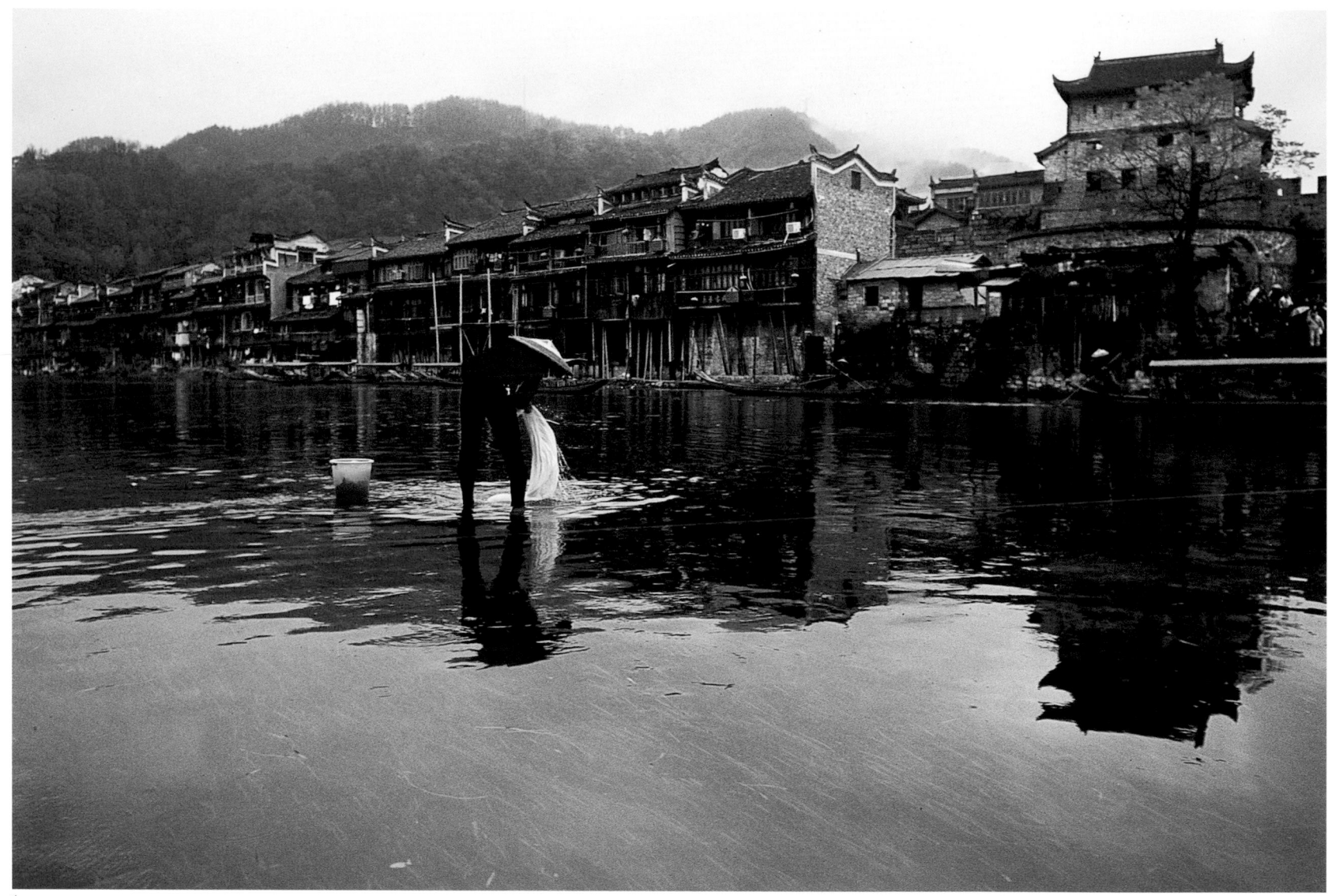

1

HU'NAN HAS ALWAYS BEEN ONE OF CHINA'S BACKWATERS. The remoteness and inaccessibility has served the province well, helping Hu'nan survive wars and the destructive excesses of the Maoist era as soldiers and ideologues hurried by to more promising regions. Feng'huang, nestling in the province's western hills, is one of the best-preserved architectural gems from the Ming and Qing dynasties. [1] A woman washes sheets in the Tuo'jiang River as it passes through Fen'huang's old town. [2] A restaurant owner adjusts her window display. [3] Painting an advertisement on the wall of a building near Shao'shan, Mao Ze'dong's birthplace. Millions of tourists make the pilgrimage to the dusty little village southwest of Chang'sha. Local officials built a massive villa at Dripping Water Cave after Mao had casually mentioned that he would like to retire there and swim in the small reservoir. The villa is one of the many 'travelling palaces' built for the Chairman's pleasure at a time when much of China was literally starving to death. Mao spent a total of 11 days in his Shao'shan retreat.

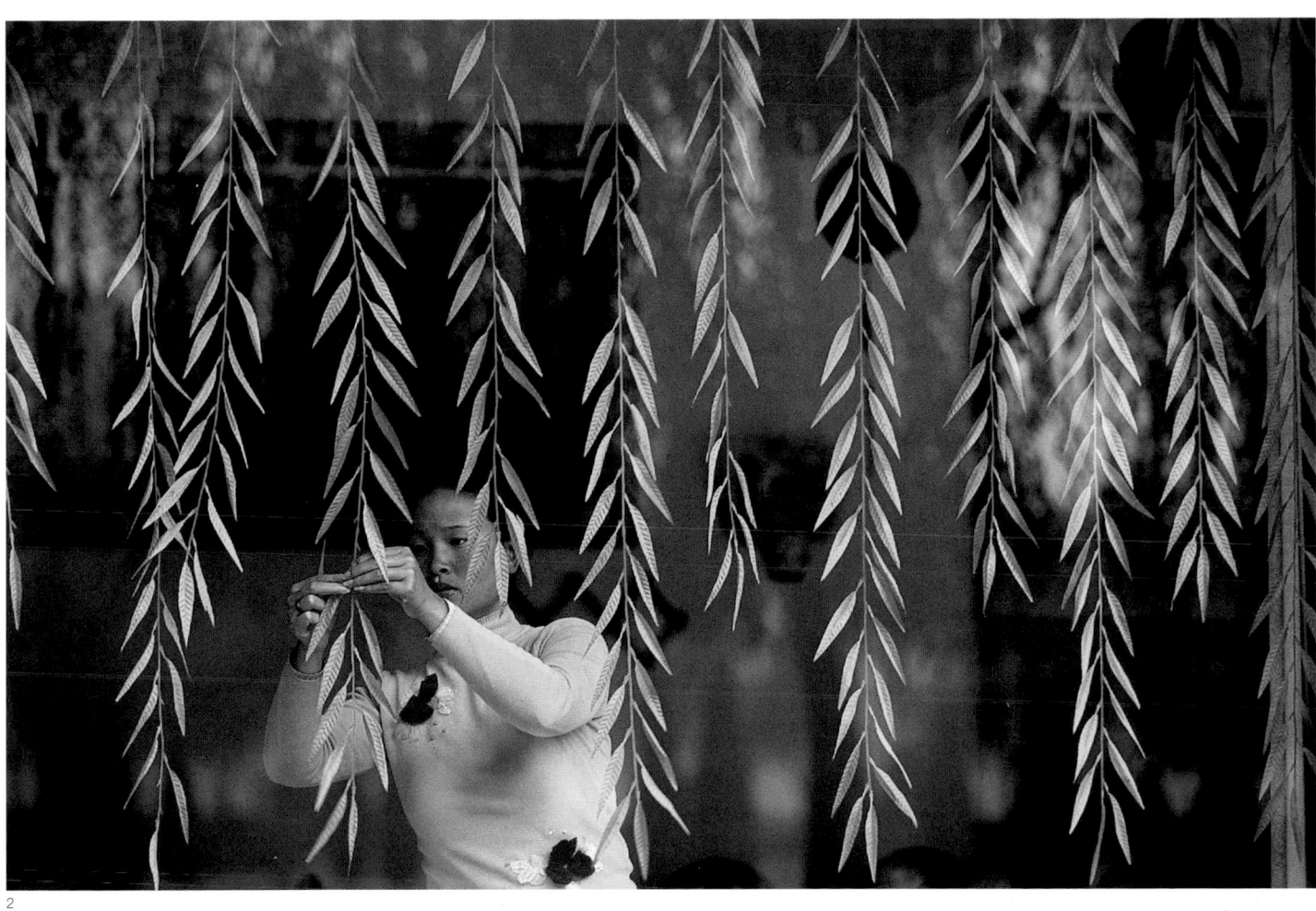

2

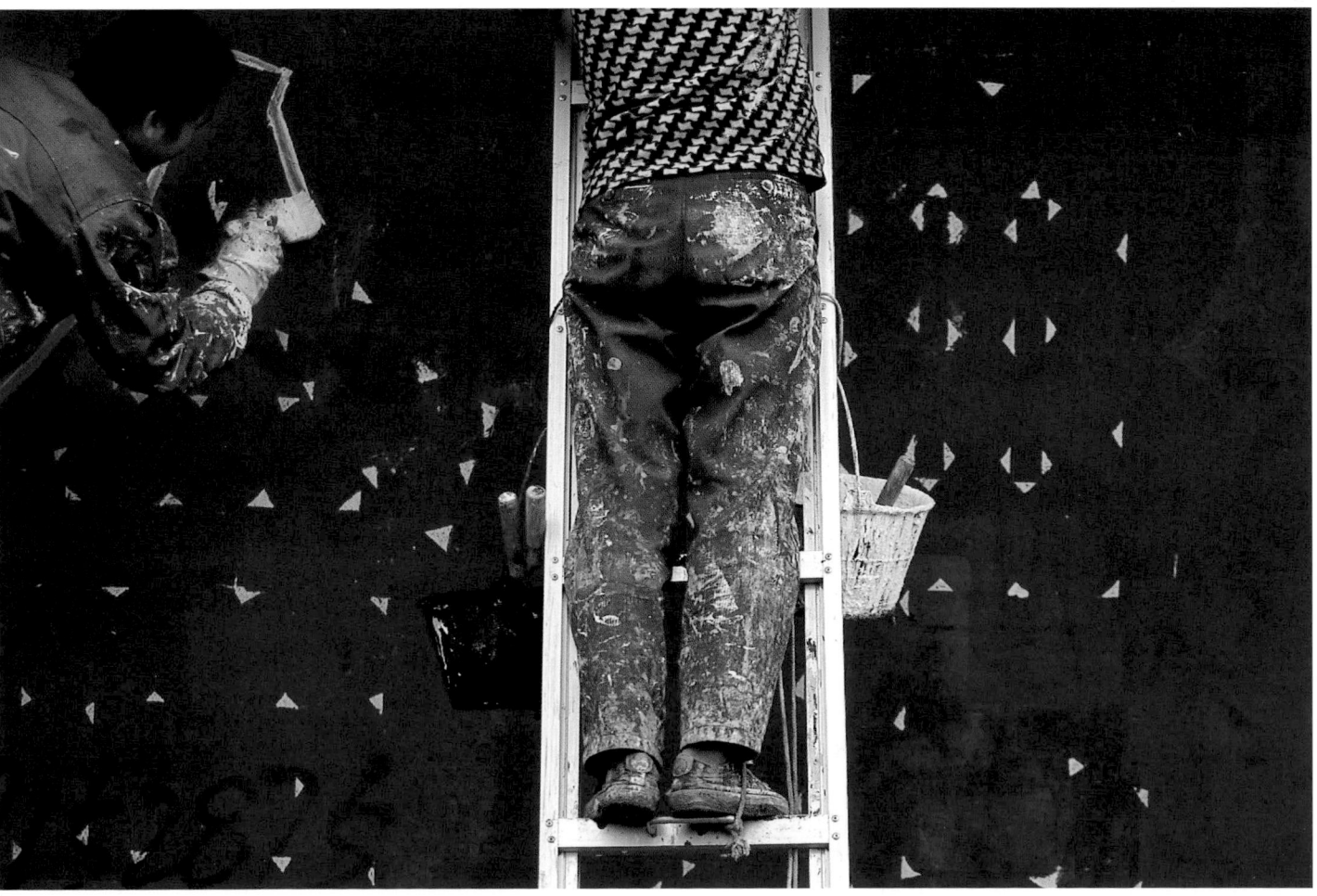

3

MAO ZE'DONG, Hunan's most famous son, was born in Shao'shan in 1893 to a middle-class landowning family. There are few figures in human history who, despite being implicated in the deaths of millions of their own subjects through direct force or due to disastrous policies, are still worshipped as demi-gods. Such is Mao's perverse genius that having willfully engineered the wholesale destruction of his country's cultural heritage, and several generations' intellectual aspirations, in the name of a questionable ideology, his actions remain a model for other aspiring revolutionaries. Efforts to deconstruct Maoist propaganda and lay bare the true and often squalid heart of Mao's legacy has had little impact on the determination of marginalized and oppressed groups around the world to emulate his example. While Peru's Maoist Shining Path guerrilla group was defeated and its leader imprisoned, Maoists in Nepal are poised to enter parliament in a position of some strength having prevailed in a protracted guerrilla campaign that cost thousands of lives. Such peasant revolutions may lack the ideological basis of Mao's communist revolt, but they can certainly recognize a successful brand. The memory of Mao's actions in China has also become warped by time. While it is impossible to imagine a 183-metre (600-foot) statue honouring Hitler or Stalin will ever be built in Germany or Russia, China's ambivalent sentiment towards Mao reverses such a maxim. Official efforts to demystify Mao's personality cult now appear to have been abandoned. Hu'nan's provincial government announced in late 2005 that in the interests of 'Red Tourism' it planned to erect a 183-metre statue of Mao (he was 1.83 metres tall) on Juzi'zhou Island in the Yang'tze River near the provincial capital of Chang'sha. By comparison, the Statue of Liberty in New York harbour is 93 metres (305 feet) from the tip of her torch to the ground. In early 2006 the Chinese government announced a 12-metre (40-foot) statute of Mao would be built near the Tibetan capital Lhasa. Other similar memorials can be expected as time erodes the harsher memories of the Maoist era with the imperatives of Chinese nationalism. 'Mao as Saviour' is also less puzzling when viewed through the historical prism of China's humiliation during the century before the communists seized power in 1949. For a longer view it may be worth recalling that since Qin Shi'huang became China's first emperor in 221 BCE, only the most ruthless tyrants have successfully ruled a united China. Under this interpretation, Mao was most certainly the last of China's great emperors. It is easy to forget the 'inner man' given his reputation as a cold-blooded megalomaniac. Even his most ardent critics will grudgingly admit Mao was a scholar of Chinese history and literature, one of modern China's greatest poets and a fine calligrapher. Such accomplishments shine brightly against the talents and abilities of most of the world's leaders today. [1] Using Mao as a sales tool, a young man tries to convince elderly villagers to part with 100 Yuan (about US$12.50) for a gravestone portrait engraved on tile. [2] [3] Scenes of Red Guards' parades in the Cultural Revolution in Bernardo Bertolucci's film *The Last Emperor*. [4] Tiananmen Gate in Bei'jing. [5] One of the largest statues of Mao is in Kashgar, in the Xin'jiang Uygur Autonomous Region. [6] Mao buttons for sale on Hong Kong's Hollywood Road. [7] Mao adorns 100 Yuan banknotes. [8] Wang An'ting's Mao Museum, the largest privately owned collection of Mao memorabilia in the world, is crammed into a small house in the backstreets of Cheng'du.

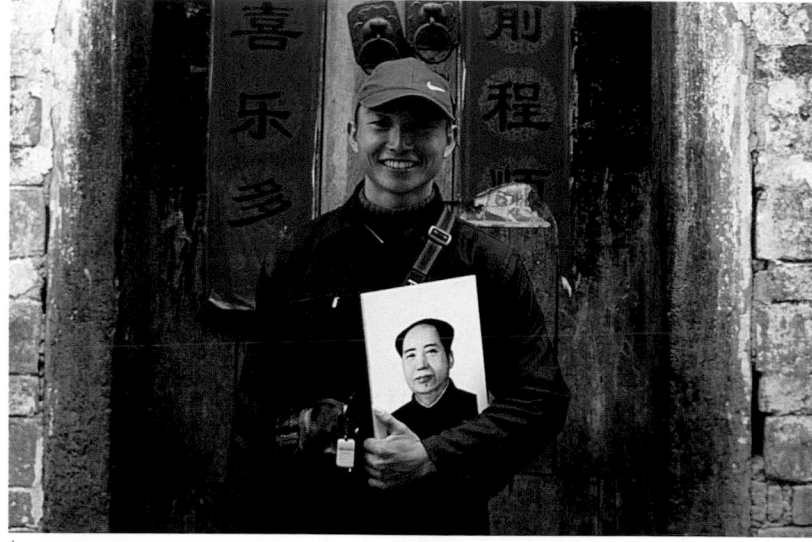

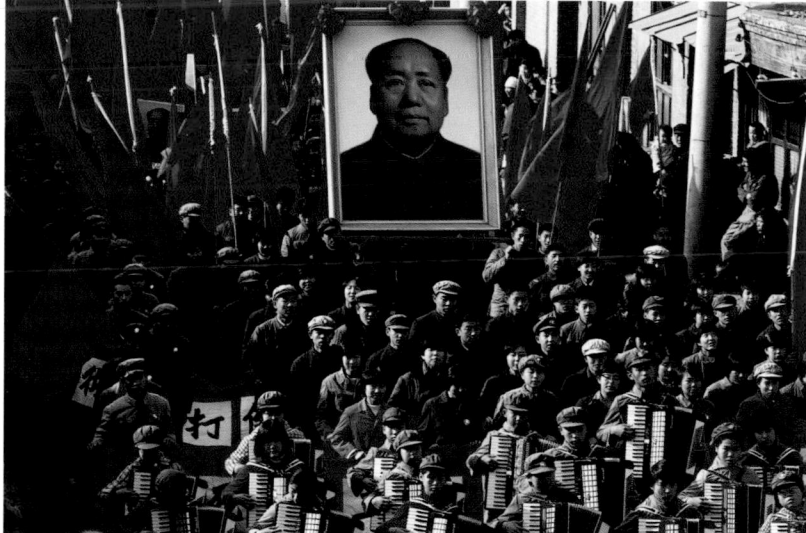

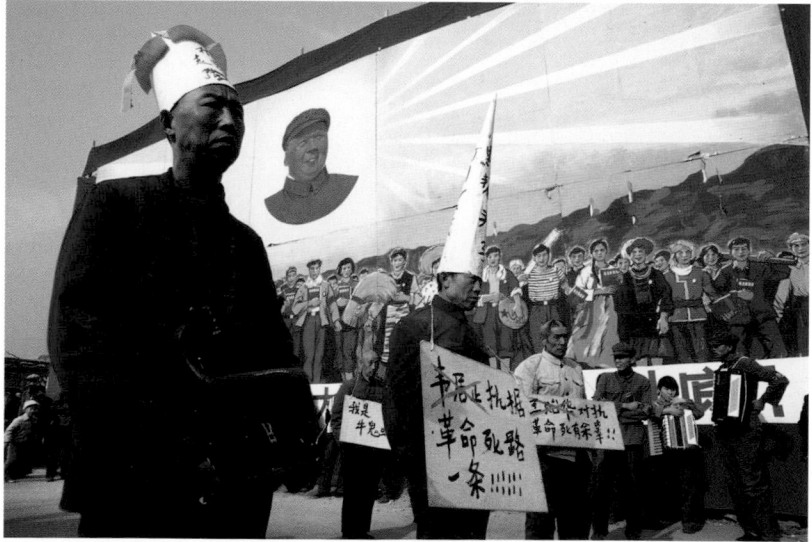

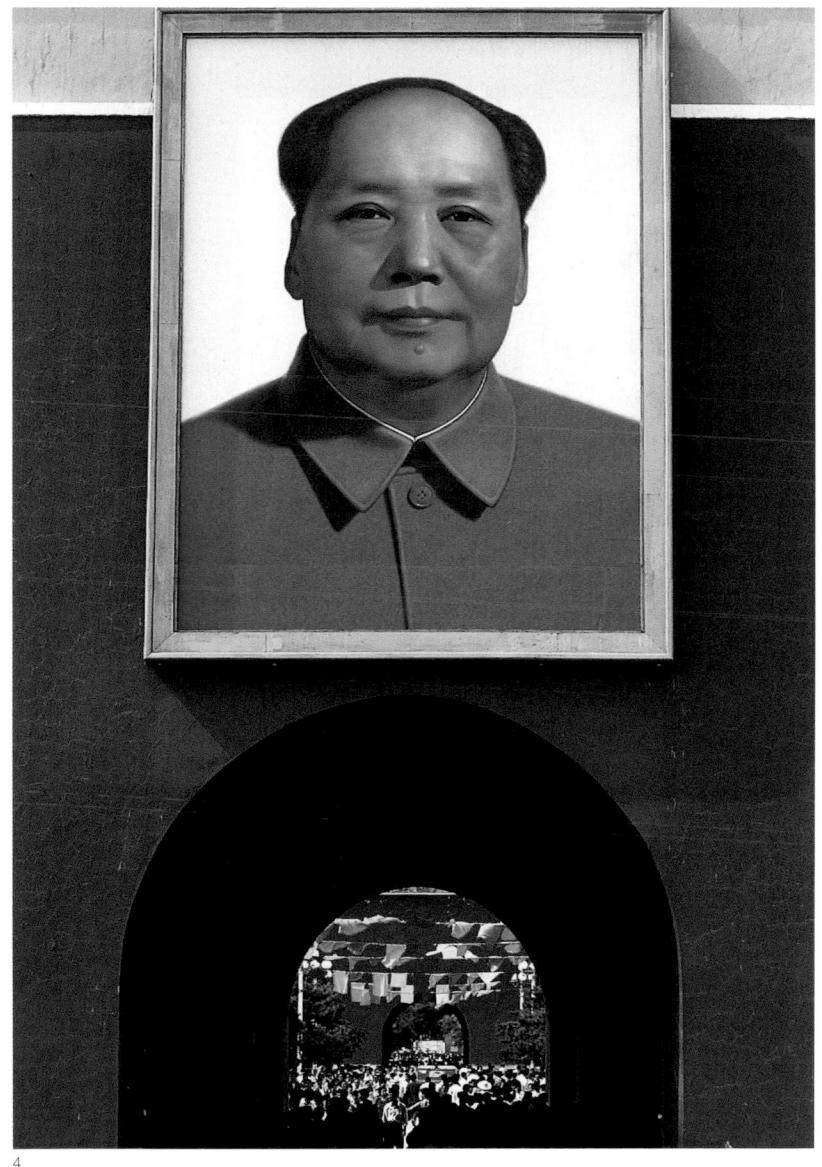

4

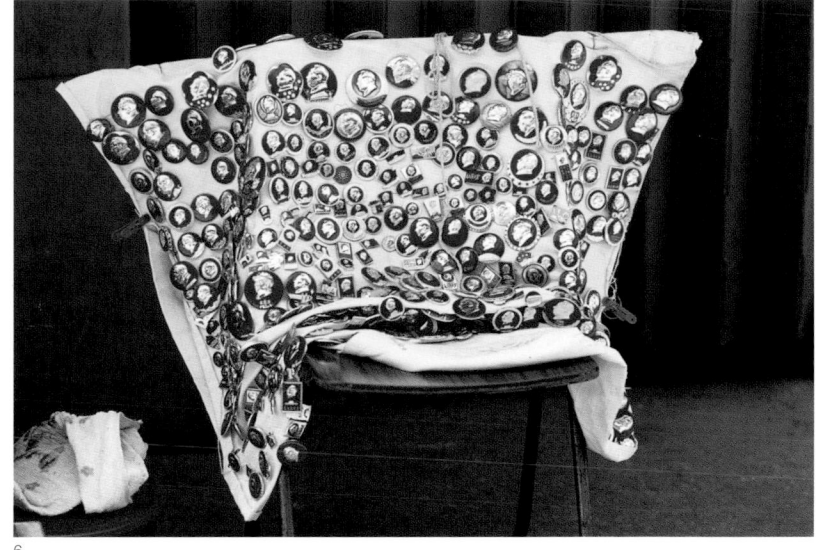

6

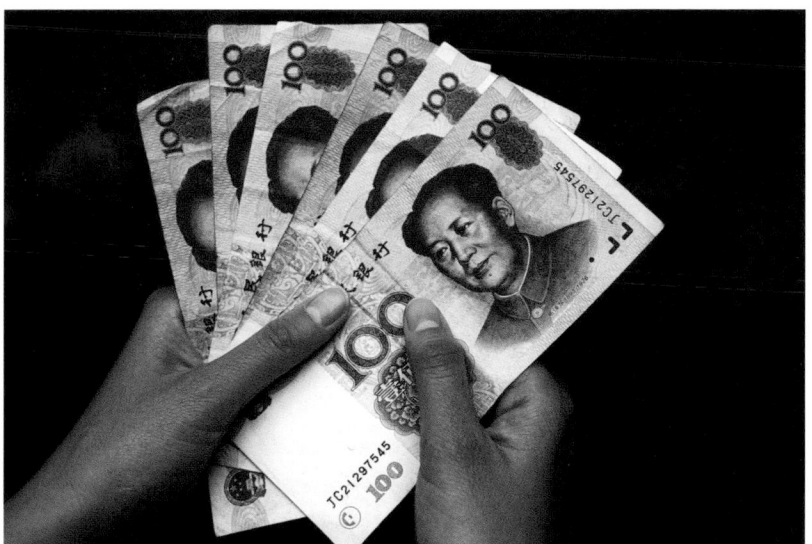

7

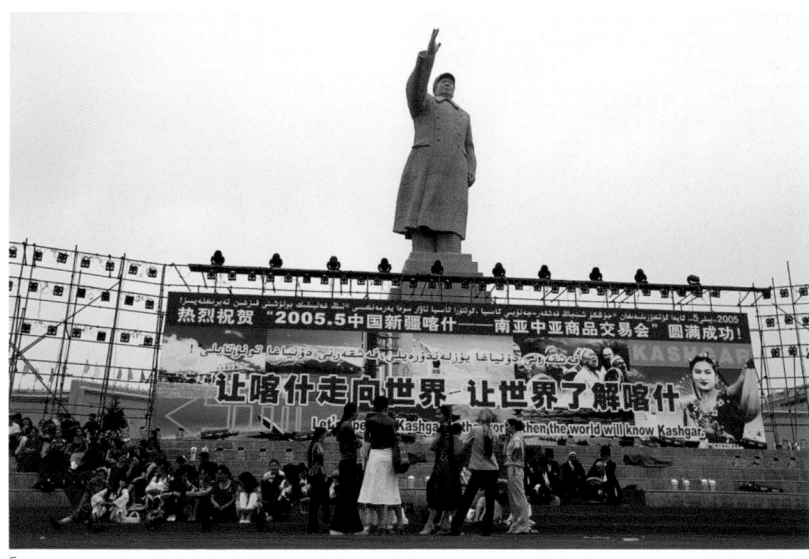

5

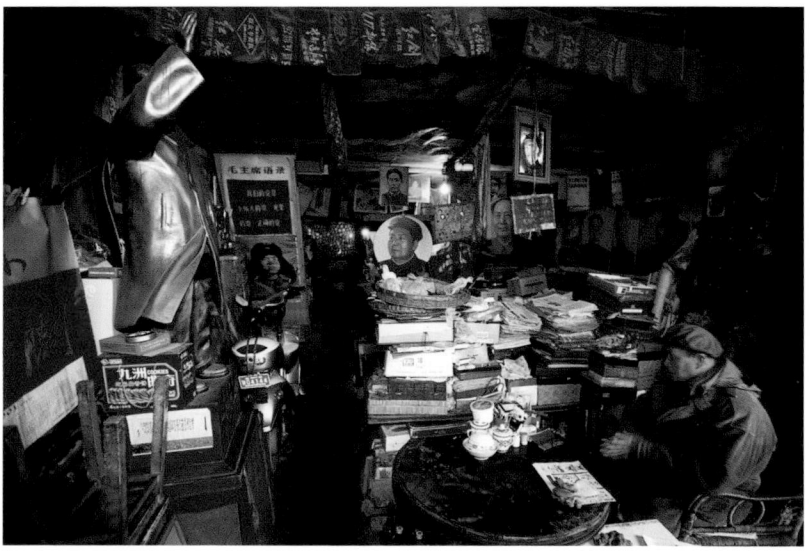

8

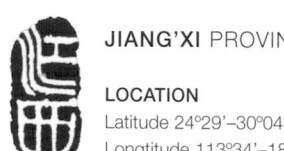

JIANG'XI PROVINCE

LOCATION
Latitude 24°29'–30°04'N
Longtitude 113°34'–18°28'E

AREA 170,940 km² (66,000 sq miles)

GEOGRAPHY Jiang'xi is almost encircled by mountains. Nearly 80 per cent of the province is either mountainous or hilly, with the remainder plains and lakes. The Gan River bisects Jiang'xi, entering Lake Po'yang – China's largest – in the north. Lake Po'yang empties into the Yang'tze River, which forms part of the province's northern border. The Mu'fu, Jiu'ling and Luo'xiao mountain ranges dominate the west, the Huai'yu and Wu'yi mountains the east and the Jiu'lian and Da'yu mountains in the south. Jiang'xi's highest point is 2,157 m at the summit of Mount Huang'gang in the Wu'yi Mountains.

CLIMATE Jiang'xi's climate is subtropical. Average January temperatures are between 3°C and 9°C, reaching 27°C to 31°C in July. The highest recorded temperature is 44.9°C, and the lowest, -18.9°C. Annual average rainfall is between 1,200 mm and 1,900 mm.

POPULATION 42.83 million (end 2005)

MAJOR CITIES Nan'chang (capital), Jiu'jiang, Ping'xiang, Jing'de'zhen, Ying'tan, Gan'zhou

AGRICULTURE Rice is the main food crop. Cash crops include cotton and rapeseed.

MAIN INDUSTRIES The province is a major mining centre, producing iron, manganese, titanium, copper, gold and silver. Asia's largest copper mine and China's main copper smelters are in Jiang'xi. Other industries include textiles, petrochemicals, processed food, printing and ceramics. Porcelain has been produced in the province for at least 1,800 years.

ANNUAL PER CAPITA INCOME (2005)
Disposable income of urban residents:
RMB 8,620 (US$1,076)
Net income of rural residents:
RMB 3,266 (US$408)

IMPORTANT HISTORICAL SITES
Mount Lu'shan National Park (UNESCO World Heritage Site), Mount Jing'gang, Mount San'qing, Mount Longhu Temple, Jing'de'zhen.

FOOD Jiang'xi cuisine is similar to those of Si'chuan and neighbouring Hu'nan in its reliance on chillies, strong flavours and sugar. The province is also noted for its pickled and fermented foods. Notable dishes include stone fish, *chukar* (partridge), *rock tripe* (lichen) and crunchy candy.

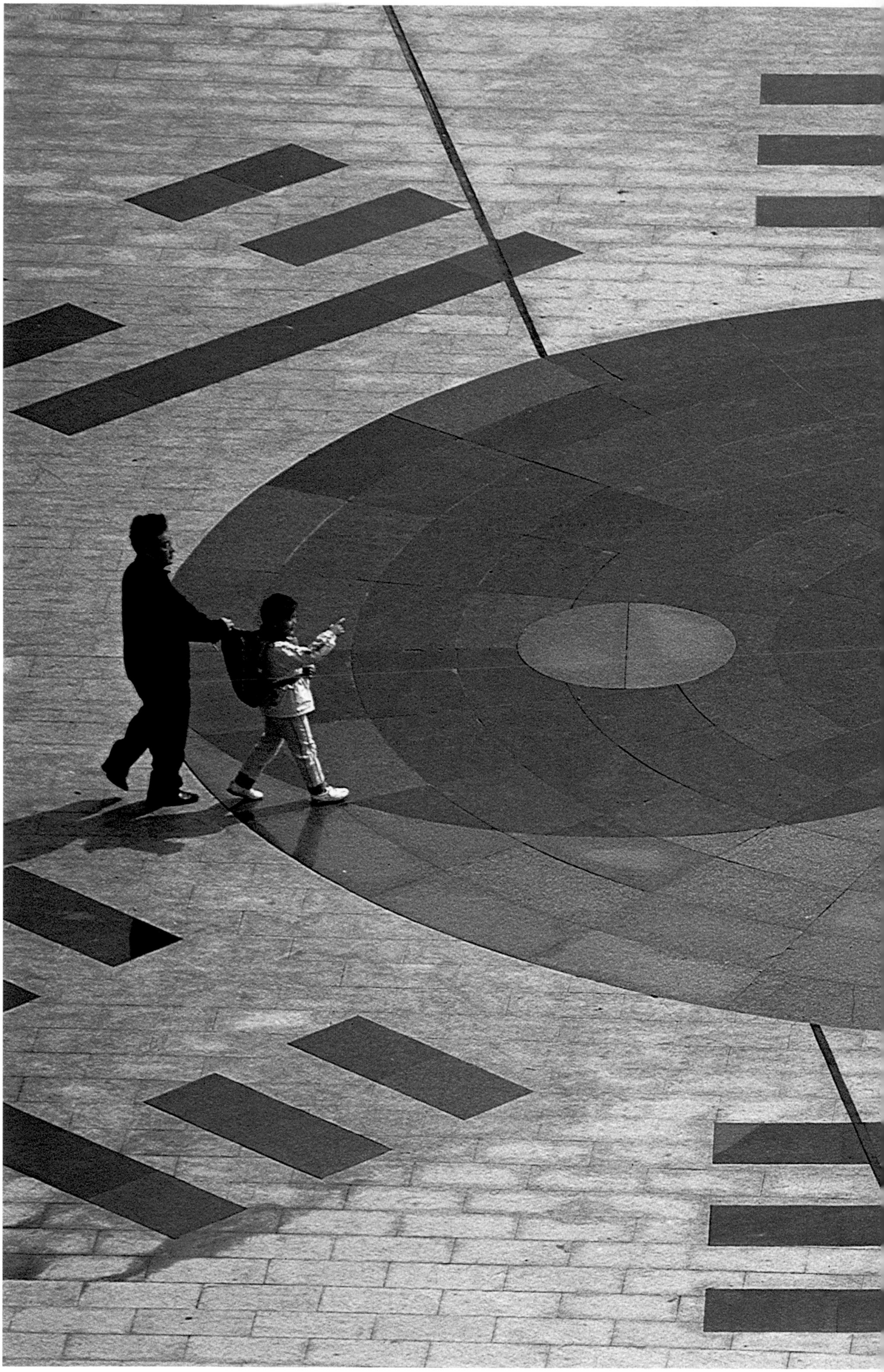

[RIGHT] The forecourt of the Teng'wang Pavilion in Nan'chang.

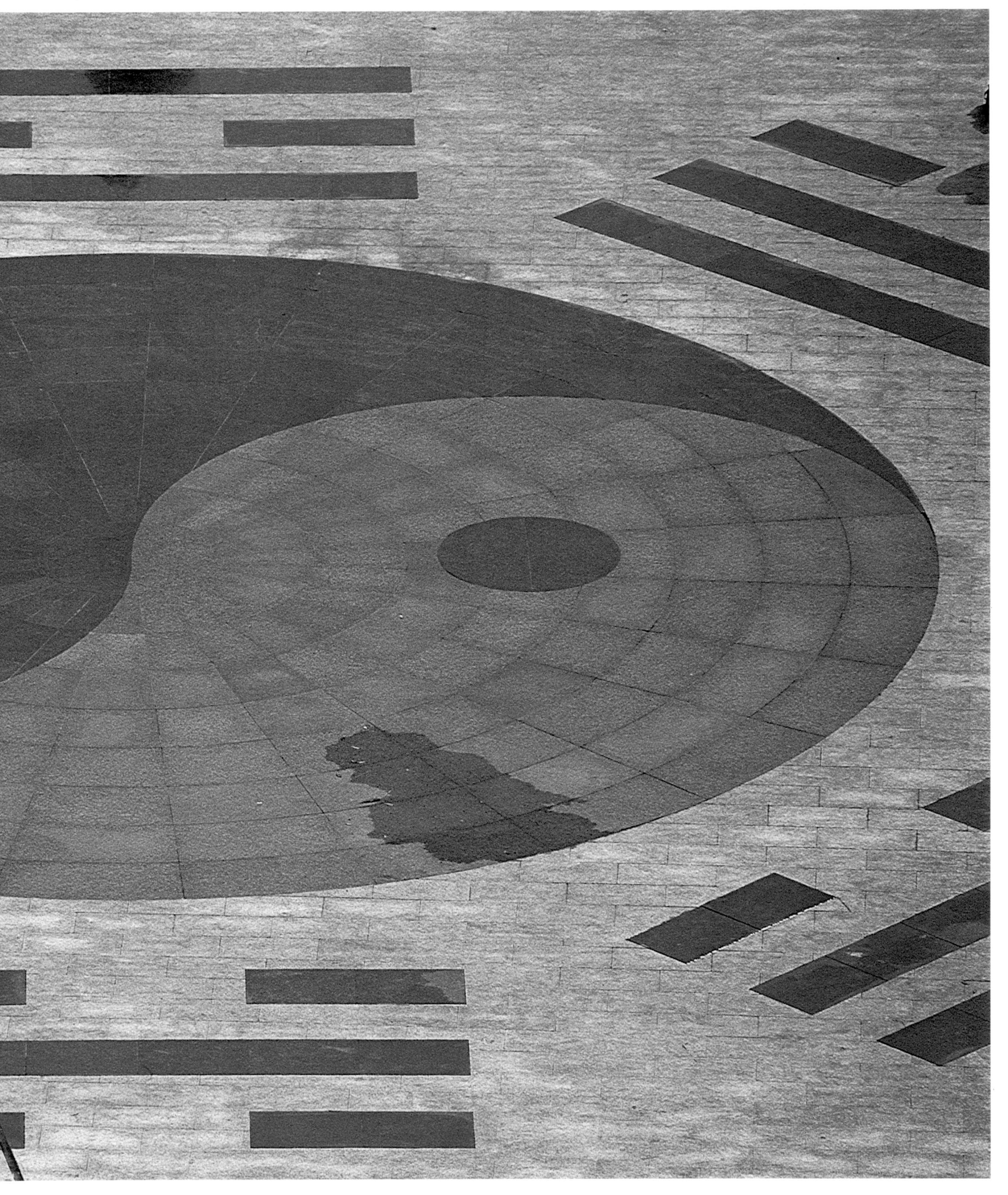

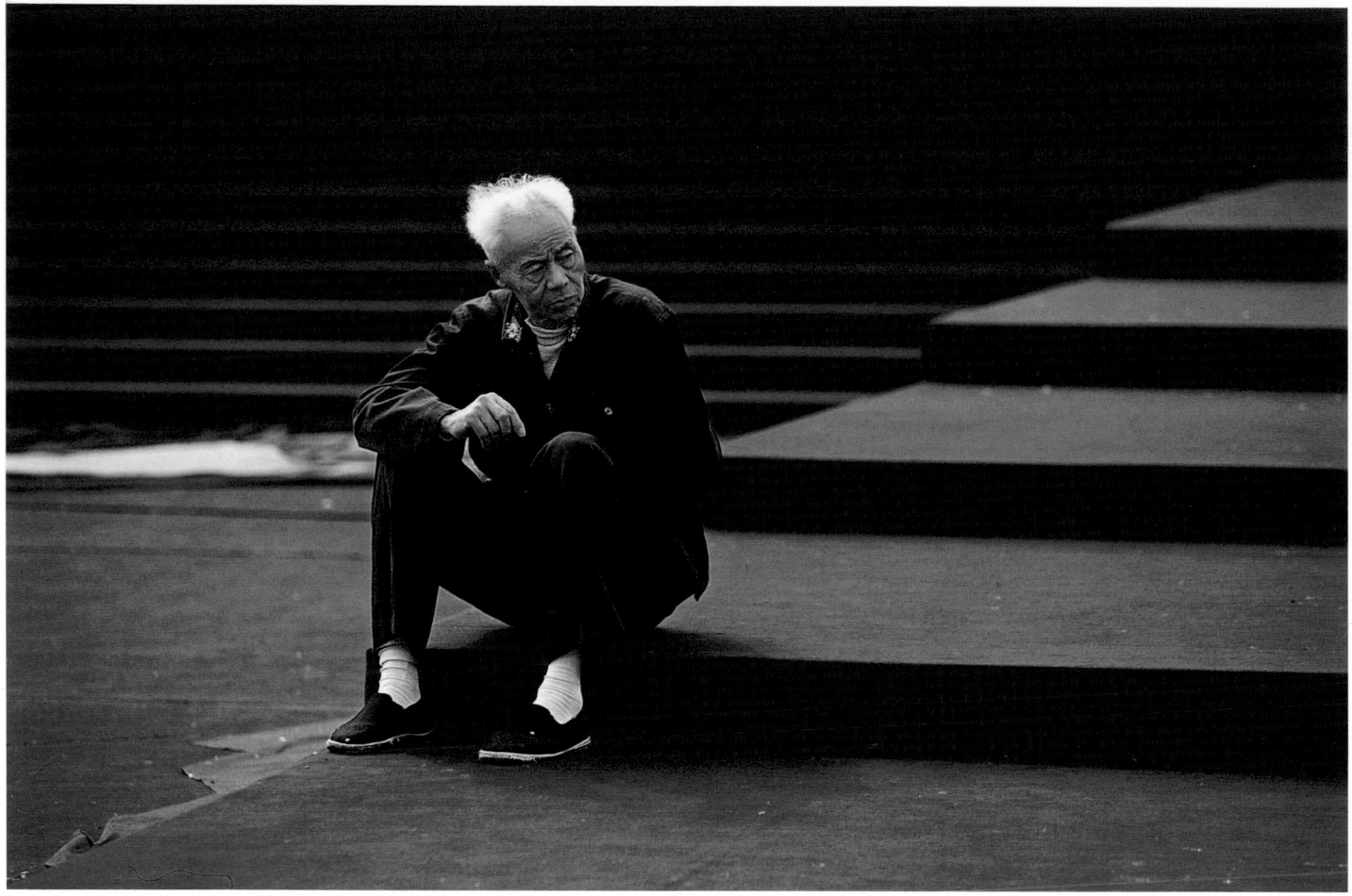

1

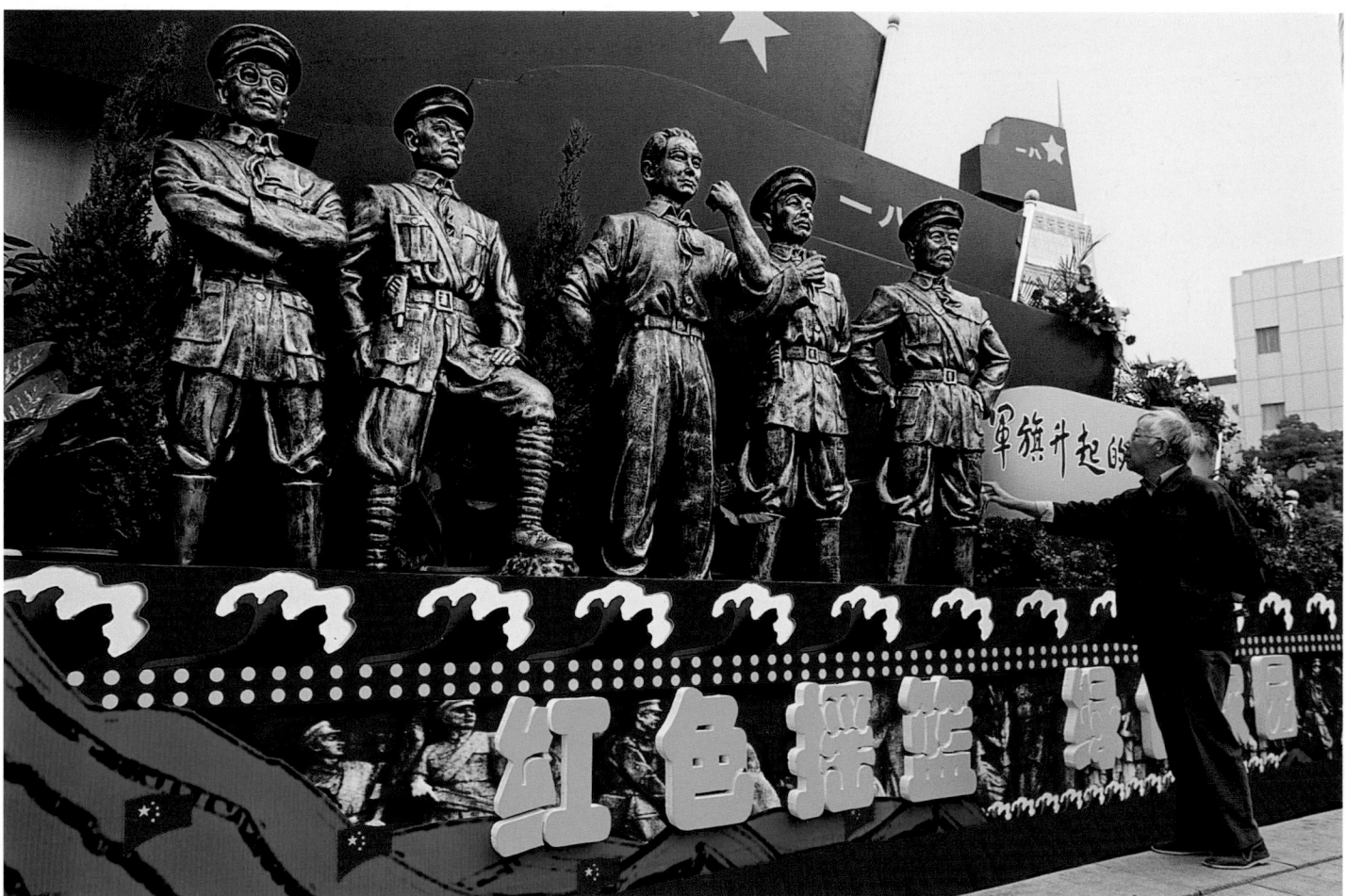

2

THE 8.1 SQUARE

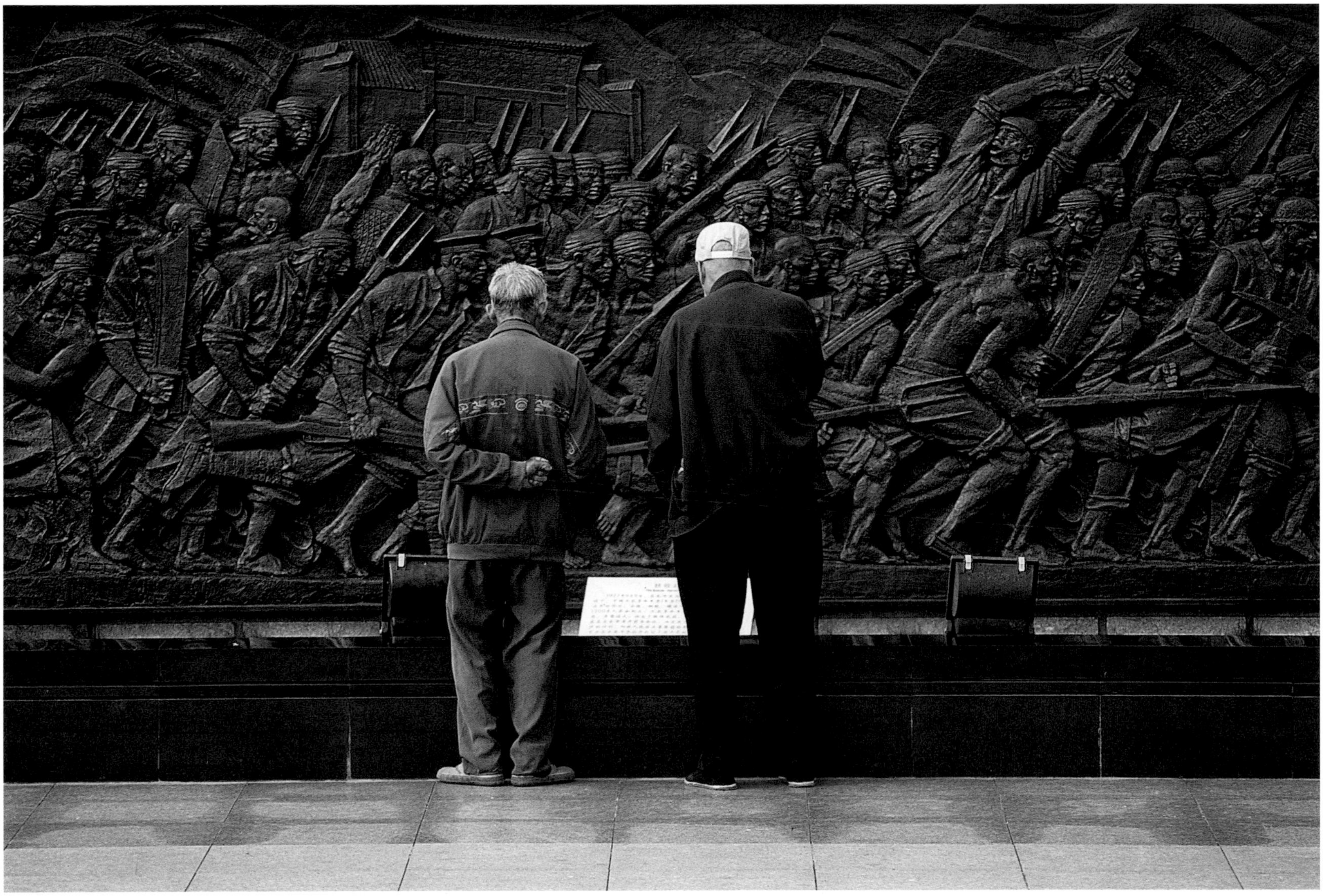

3

NAN'CHANG IS THE CAPITAL OF JIANG'XI PROVINCE and best known for the Teng'wang Pavilion, the 57-metre (187-foot) high tower on the banks of the Gan River was first built in 653 CE during the Tang Dynasty by Li Yuan'ying, the emperor's brother. It has since been destroyed and rebuilt twenty-eight times. The present structure was completed in 1989 as a replica of the Song Dynasty model. China's second largest public space, the Ba'yi (8.1) Square, features a monument commemorating the birth of the Red Army. On 1st August 1927 Zhou En'lai and other communist party leaders led the '8.1 Nan'chang Uprising' that signalled the start of the civil war with the Kuo'min'tang. The group went on to form the core of the military elite whose loyalties were traded, bought and sold in the power struggles that shaped China's fate for generations to come. [1] A man who has witnessed the emergence of a new nation. [2] One of the 'Red Tours' floats around the square featuring plastic revolutionary heroes. [3] Two old friends reminisce about the revolution.

THE MIDDLE KINGDOM

JIANG'XI WATER VILLAGES

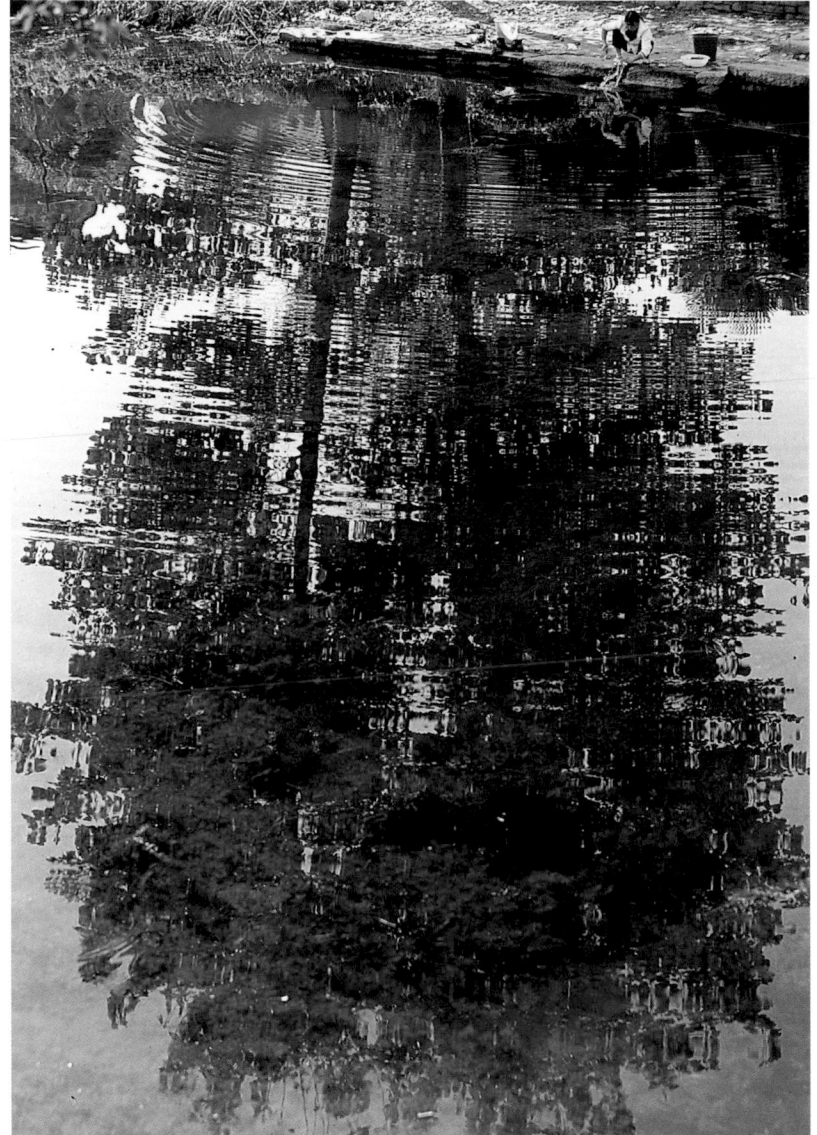

1

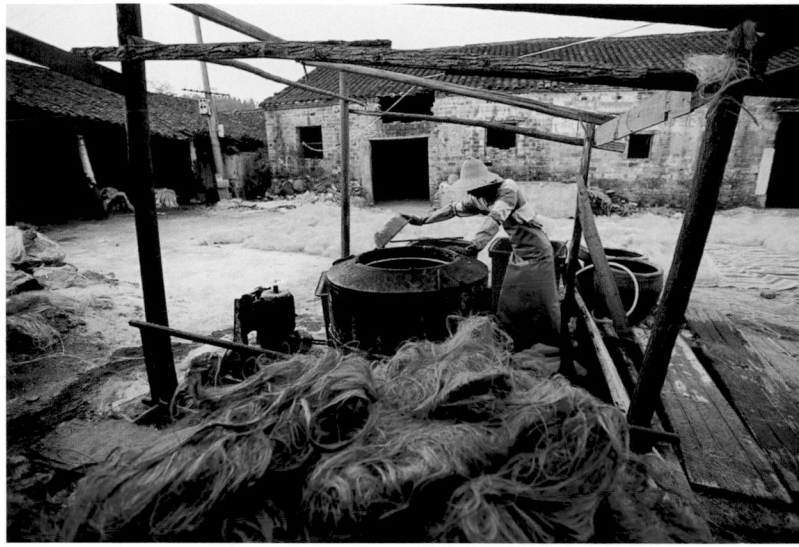

2

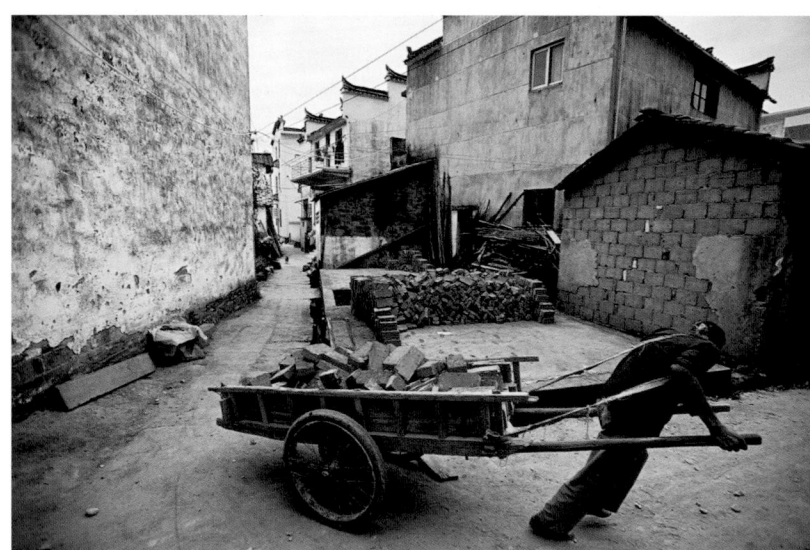

3

THE MIDDLE KINGDOM

THE VILLAGES OF WU'YUAN COUNTY in the remote and heavily forested northeastern hills of Jiang'xi are considered among the most beautiful rural communities in China. Some of these unspoiled farming villages, hidden in verdant valleys and nestled around crystal-clear streams, contain some of the best-preserved Tang Dynasty architecture in the country, dating back to mid-700 CE. In the Si'xi village, [1] local women do their washing by the river on the edge of the forest, while [4] workers bring in supplies across an elegantly simple bridge upstream. [3] A local farmer in Xiao'qi village prepares to build a house all by himself. [2] On the road between Tuo'chuan and Jing'de'zhen we came upon a stretch of fluorescent green pavement that appeared to be covered with seaweed from a radioactive ocean. It turned out that the village's cottage industry is dyeing thin strands of hemp and synthetic threads for dolls' hair, the manes of toy horses, and, presumably, any stuffed toys requiring psychedelic fur. [5] An old-fashioned mill in use outside traditional houses near Jing'de'zhen.

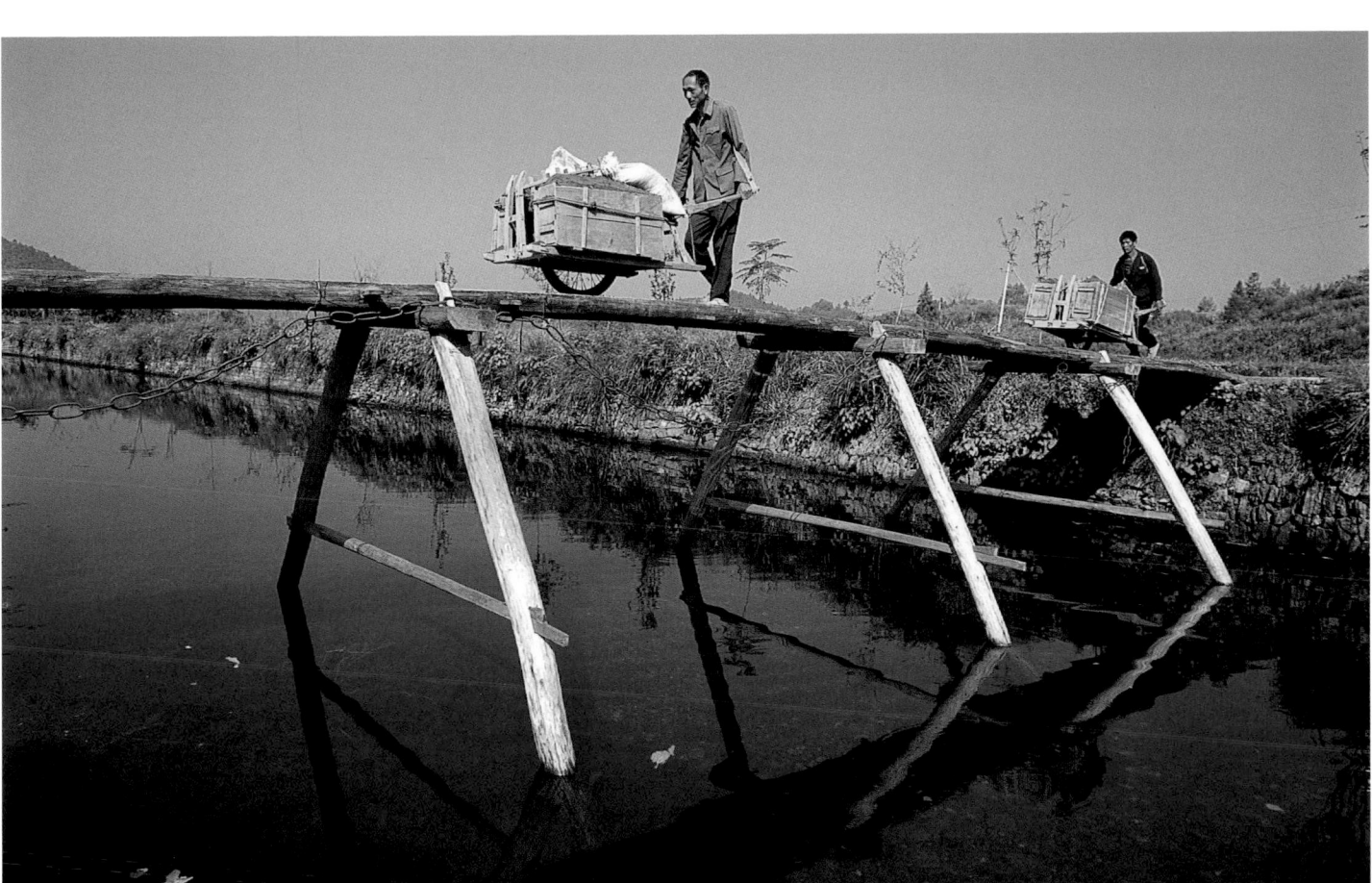

4

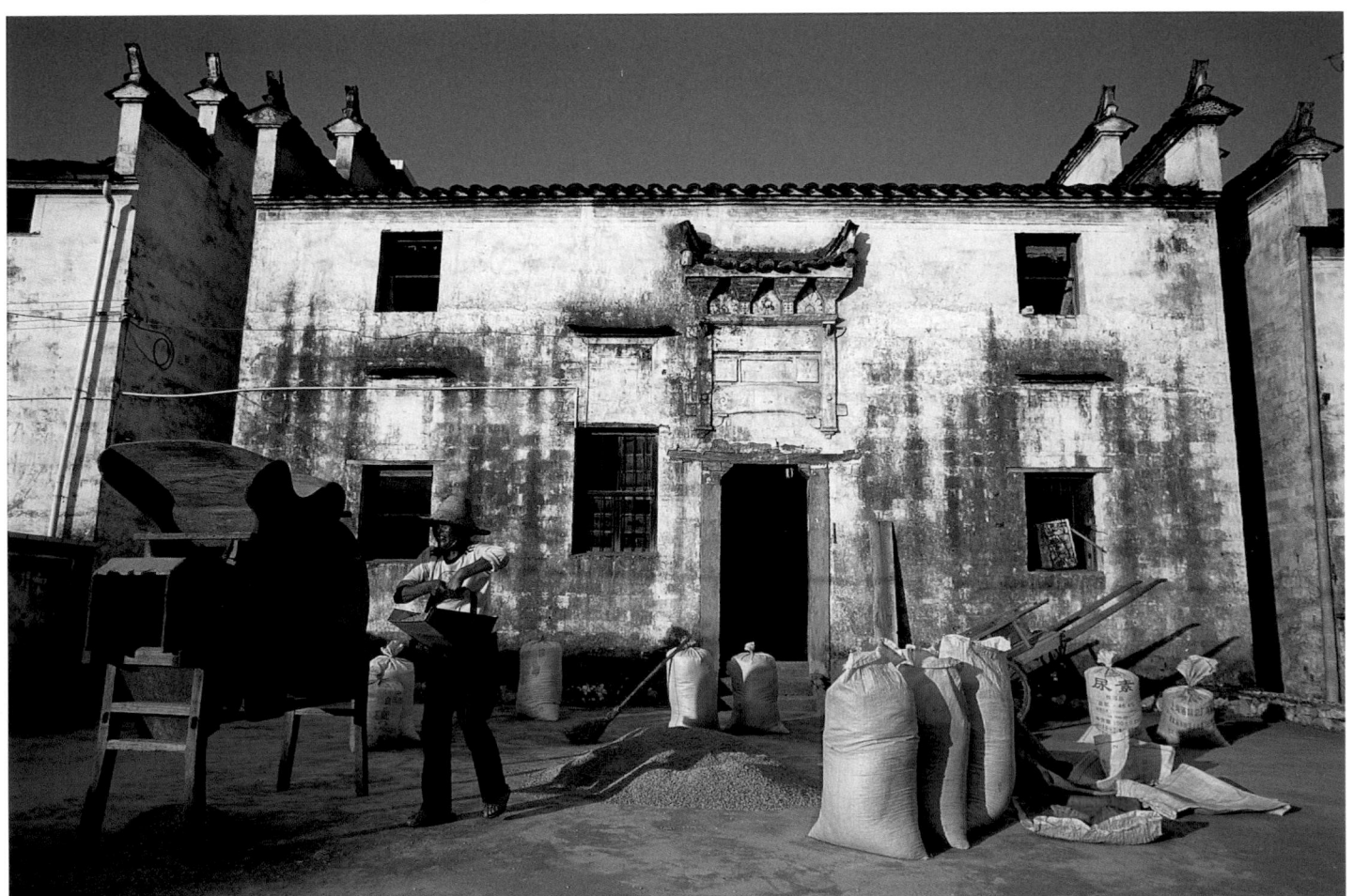

5

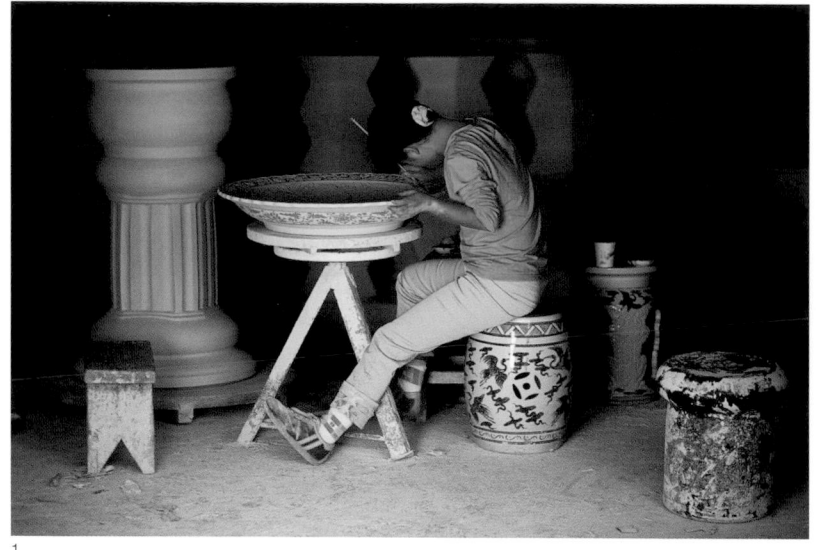

1

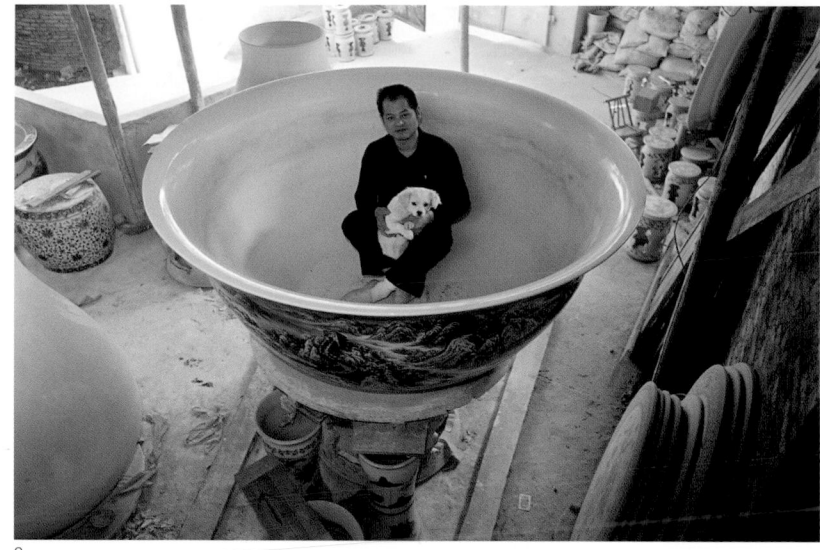

2

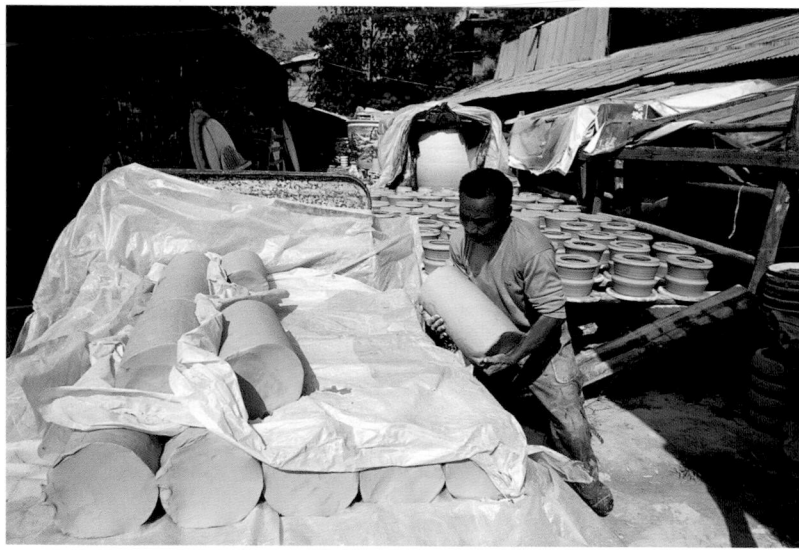

3

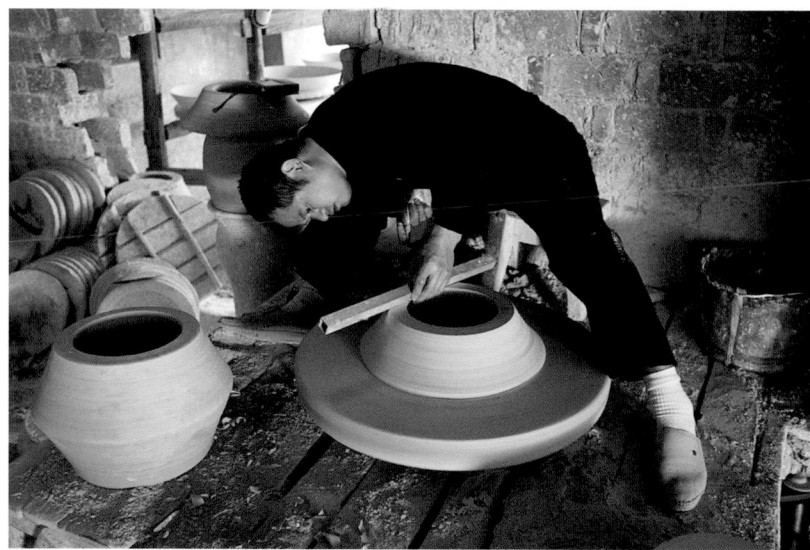

4

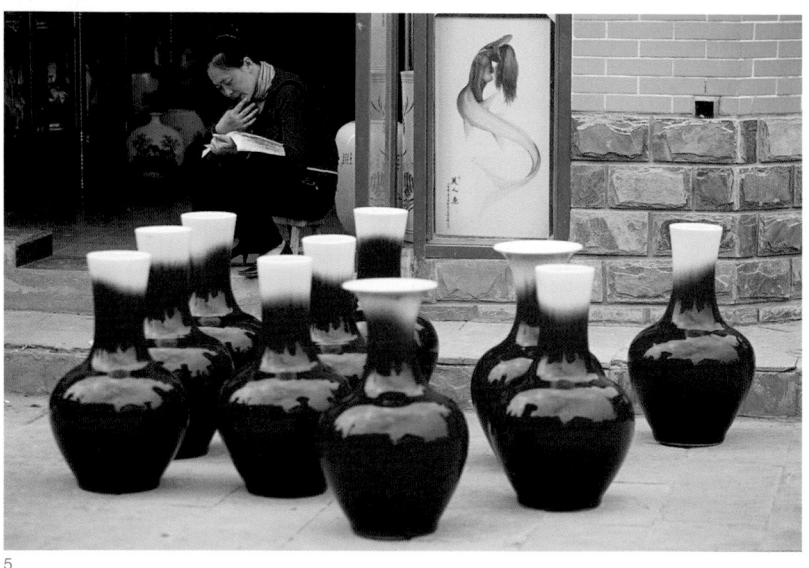

5

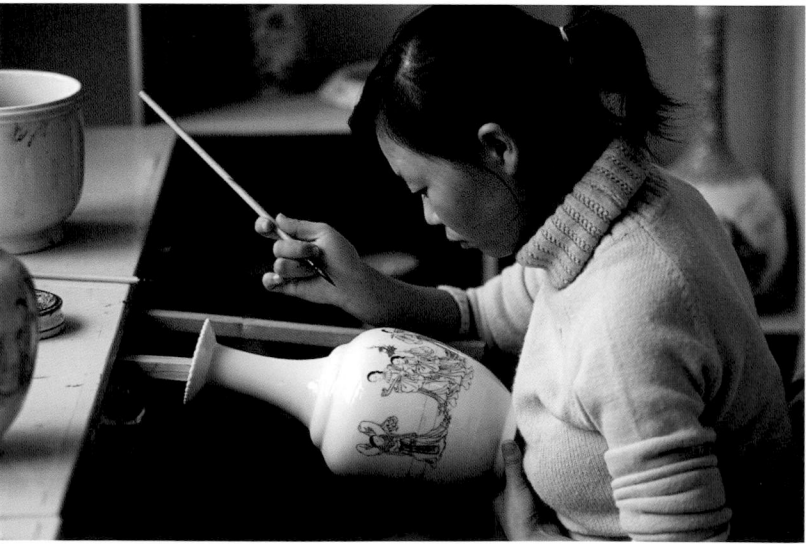

6

THE CITY OF PORCELAIN

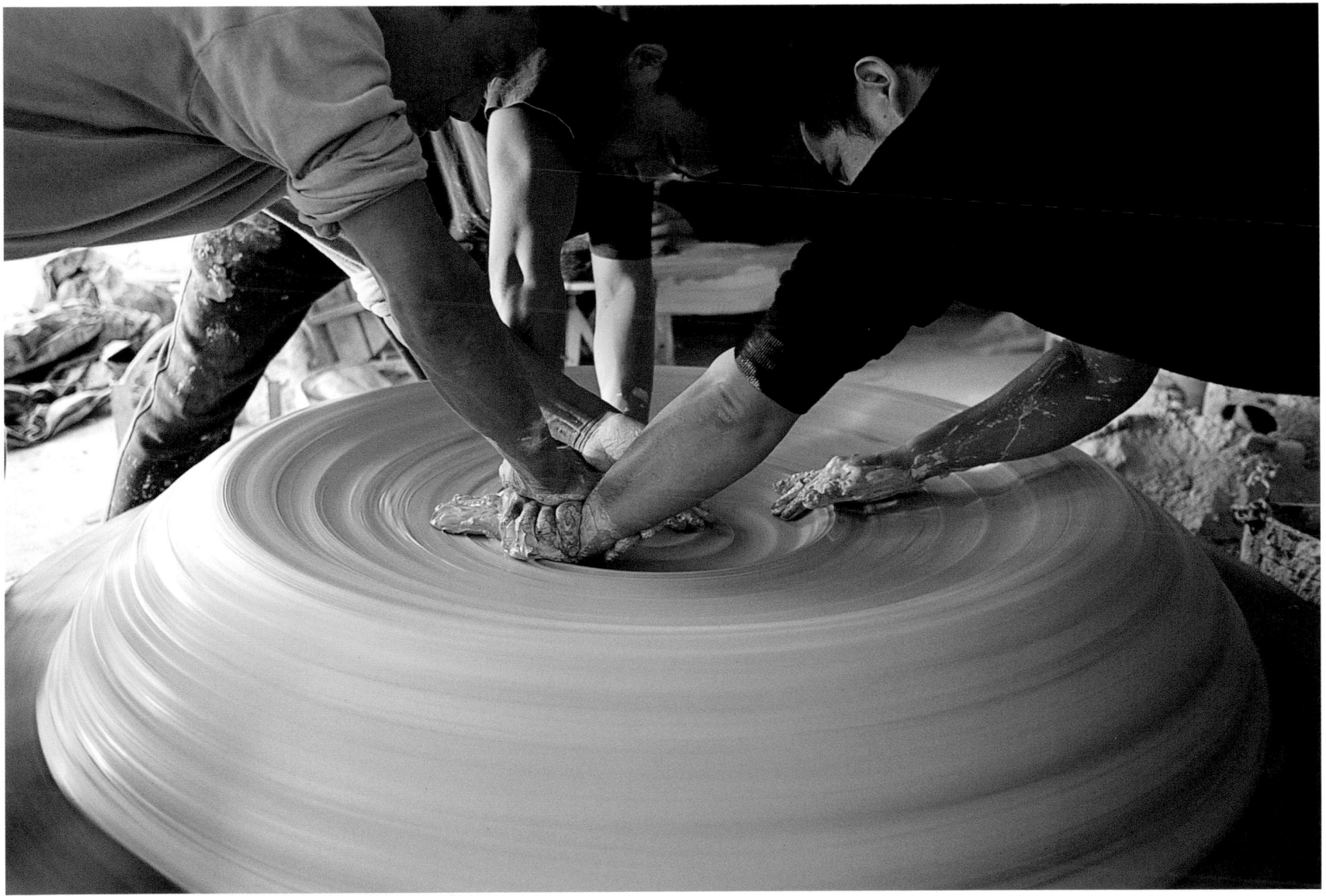

7

THE AREA AROUND THE MOUNTAIN HAMLET of Jing'de'zhen is rich in kaolin, a clay of great strength and lightness. With a plentiful supply of firewood from nearby hills, the local kilns have been firing pottery since the Han Dynasty 1,700 years ago. In 1004 CE the region's potters received a royal charter from Song Emperor Jing'de and permission to affix the seal 'Made in the Reign of Jing'de' on their work. The city took the emperor's title and the Jing'de'zhen 'brand' became synonymous with the finest Chinese porcelain. [1] [6] Decorating unfired porcelain. [2] Yu Peng'fei is the man behind (and inside) the 'Biggest Porcelain Rice Bowl in the World.' The bowl is 1.98 metres (6.5 feet) in diameter, weighs 400 kilograms (880 pounds) and is said to hold enough noodles for 1,000 people. The bowl is intended to symbolize Yu's hope that the Chinese people will always have enough food. [3] Kaolin clay being delivered to Yu's workshop. [4] Yu at work on the wheel. [5] A shop on the main street. [7] Yu's team making a giant plate.

THE MIDDLE KINGDOM

AN'HUI PROVINCE

LOCATION
Latitude 29°41'–34°38'N
Longtitude 114°51'–119°37'E

AREA 142,450 km² (55,000 sq miles)

GEOGRAPHY The Huai'he River system dominates the north-central plain. To the south, the Yang'tze River cuts through the Jiu'hua Shan and Huang Shan ranges and the Da'bie Mountains, which cover much of southwestern An'hui. The Lotus Flower Peak, at 1,873 m, is the highest point of Huang Shan, which has 30 peaks rising above 1,500 m.

CLIMATE The north is temperate with clearly defined seasons; average winter temperatures in January are between -1°C and 2°C south of the river. In July, temperatures are 27°C or above. The lowest recorded temperature is -20.6°C and the highest is 42.4°C. The 'Plum' rains fall in June and July and can cause flooding. Average annual rainfall in the province is between 800 mm and 1,800 mm.

POPULATION 65.16 million (end 2005)

MAJOR CITIES He'fei (capital), An'qing, Huang'shan City, Ma'an'shan

AGRICULTURE The main crops are wheat, sorghum, corn, soybeans and cotton. The southern half of the province is a major rice-producing region, able to harvest two annual crops. Wheat, sweet potatoes, cotton, barley and tobacco are also grown, while tea is produced in the southeast. Pigs and sheep are raised throughout the province, while An'hui's rivers and lakes sustain important freshwater fisheries.

MAIN INDUSTRIES An'hui has abundant quantities of iron and copper ores as well as coal. Four of China's leading industrial centers are in the province, which forms part of the Shang'hai Special Economic Zone. The area around He'fei is dominated by textile mills, iron and steel and machine-tool plants. Huai'nan is a major coal-mining and chemical manufacturing centre. Beng'bu produces agricultural machinery and processed food. Ma'an'shan is a major river port and industrial complex.

ANNUAL PER CAPITA INCOME (2005)
Disposable income of urban residents:
RMB 8,471 (US$1,056)
Net income of rural residents:
RMB 2,641 (US$330)

HISTORICAL AND SCENIC SITES
Xidi and Hong'chun villages from the Ming and Qing dynasties, Mount Huang'shan, Mount Jiu'hua, Mount Qi'yun and Mount Tian'zhu.

FOOD An'hui cooking is one of the Eight Great Cuisines of China. Local chefs are famed for braising and stewing, with hams and sugar often added to enhance colour and flavour. A most famous signature dish is stewed soft-shell turtle braised with ham, bamboo shoots, sausages and dried mushrooms.

[RIGHT] The Huang'shan range.

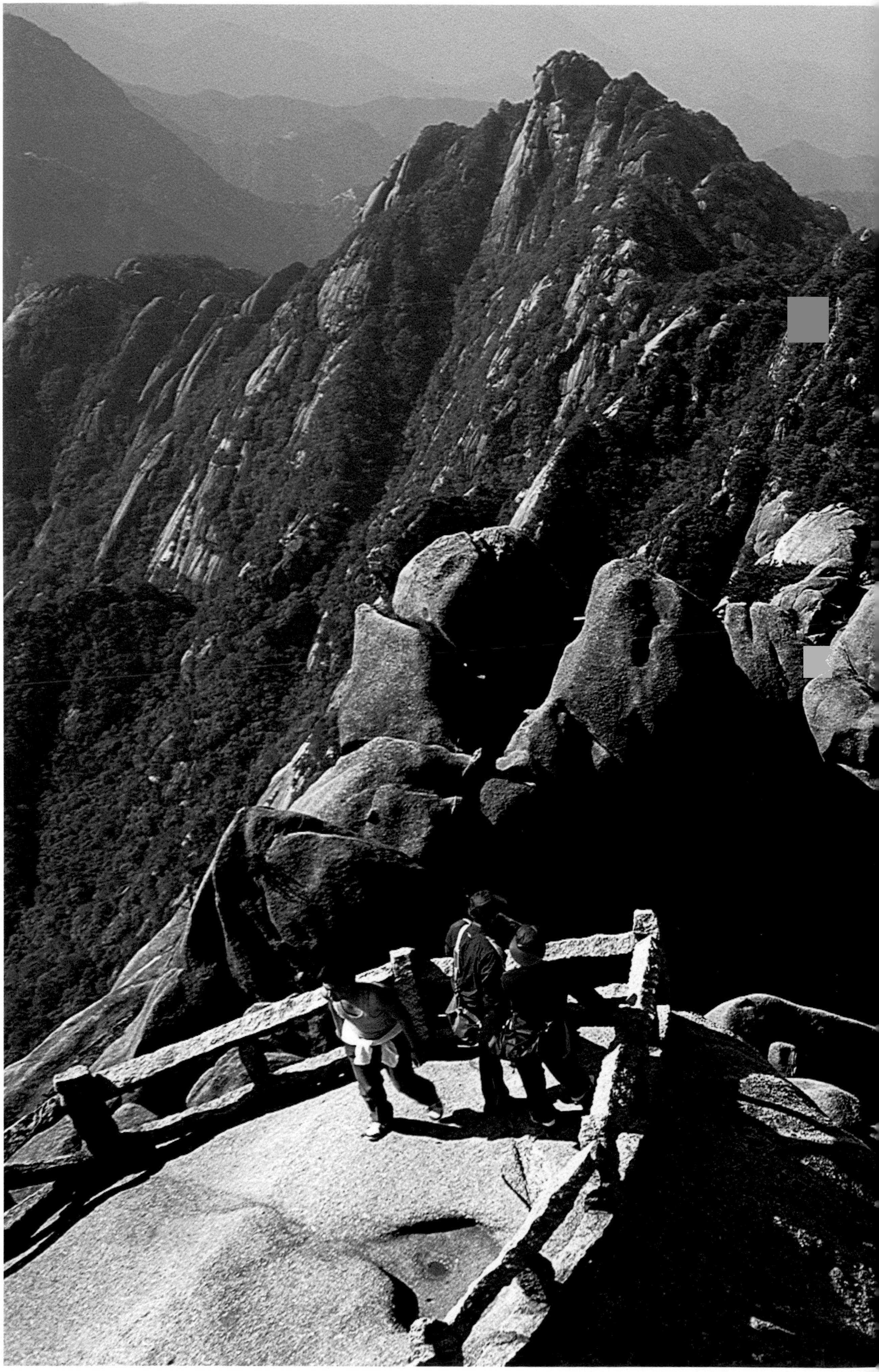

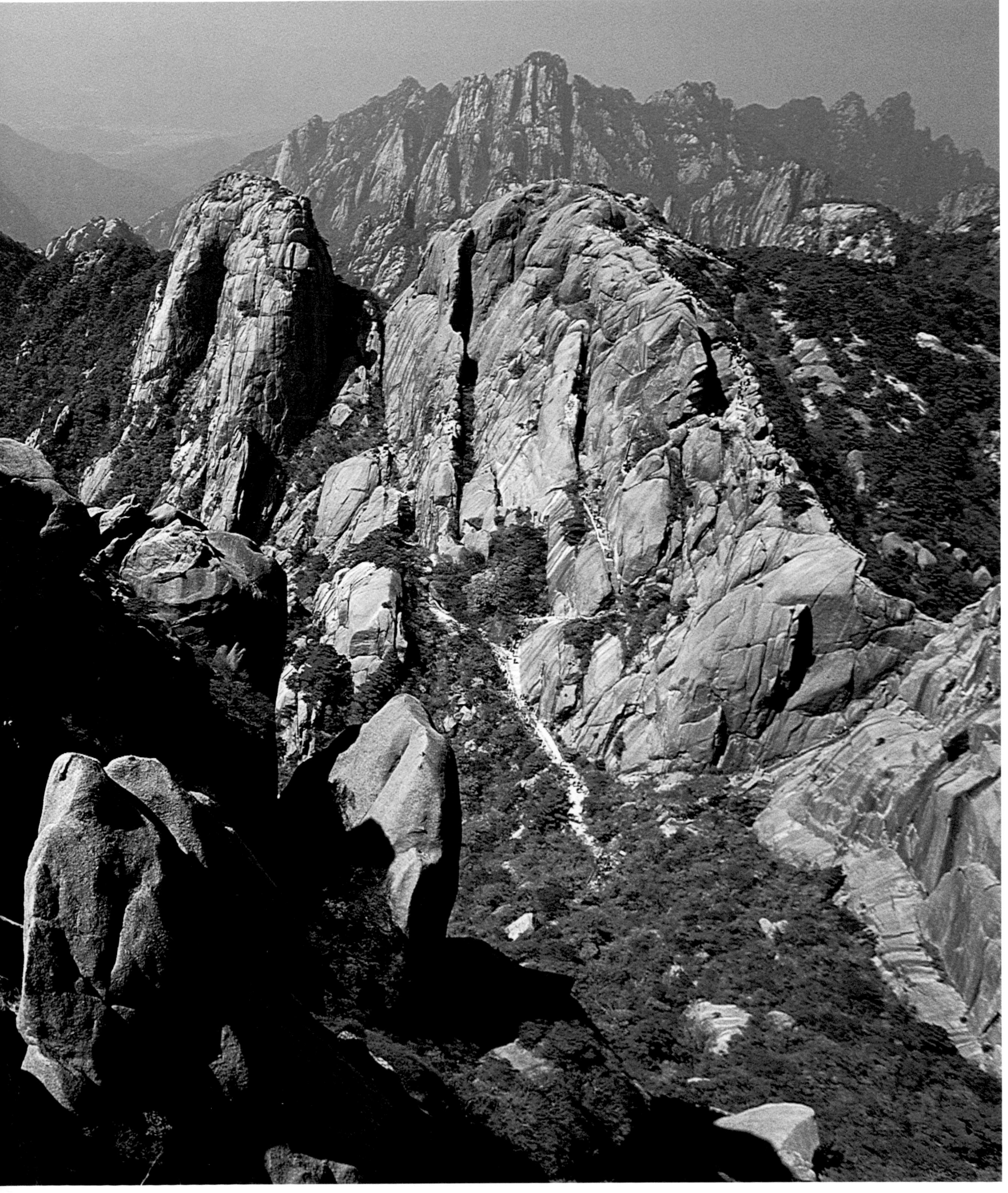

THE LOTUS PEAK

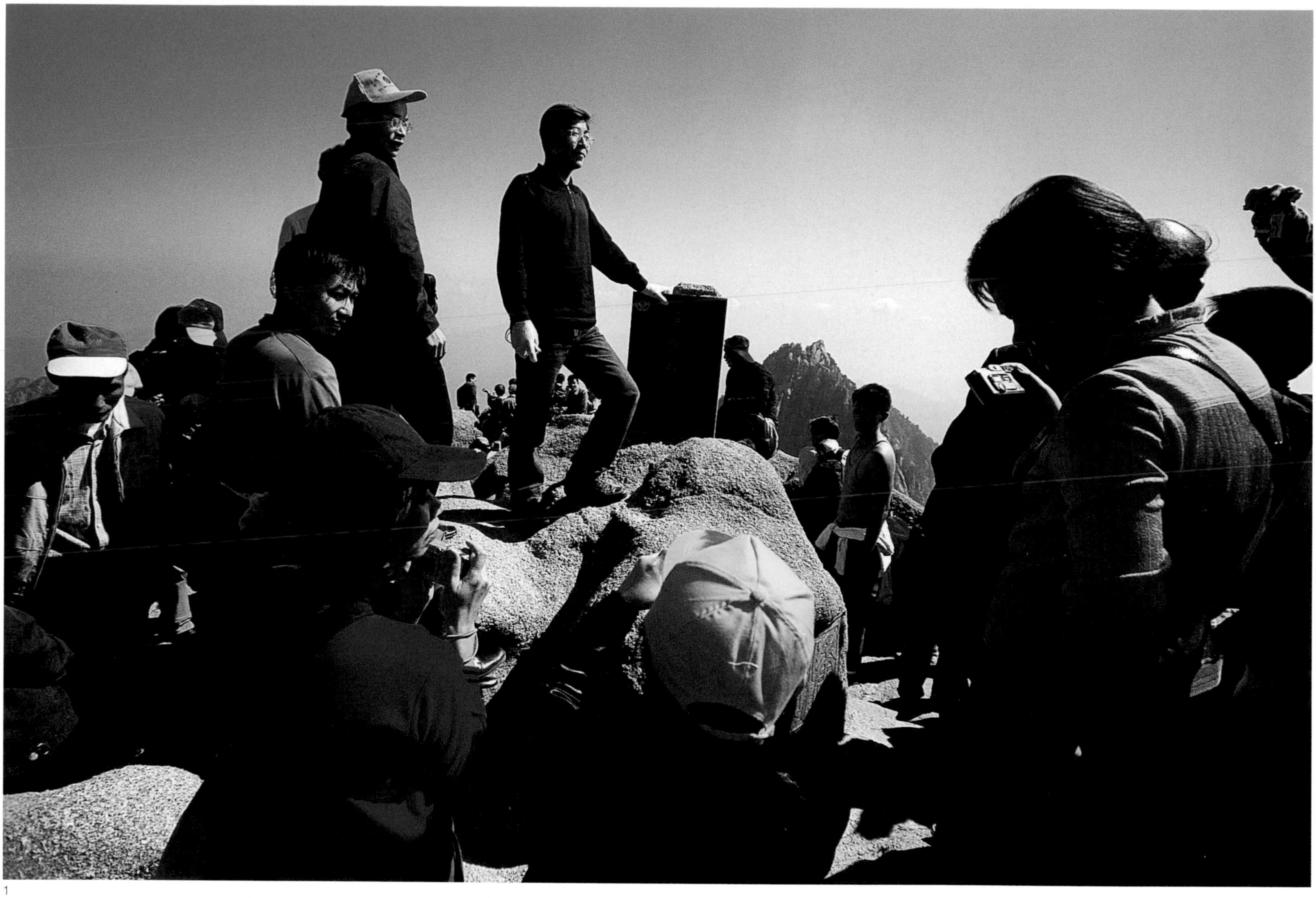

MOUNT YI'SHAN WAS RENAMED HUANG'SHAN in 747 CE as a tribute to the legendry Huang Di, the ancestor of the Chinese people, who is said to have brewed the elixir of life somewhere in the mountain fastness on the south bank of the Yang'tze River. The seventy-two mountains of the Huang'shan range have inspired poets and painters for over 1,000 years. Their trademark 'sea of clouds with islands of jutting peaks' and 'gnarly pines twisting in the wind' are much loved staples of traditional Chinese paintings. Those days of tranquil and poetic meditation have, sadly, long passed. These days a constant stream of Chinese tour groups clog the steep narrow stone steps to the peaks, yelling and screaming into the canyons in order to hear the 'echoes of their empty souls.' [1] Tourists jostling to have their picture taken next to a stone tablet that reads: "Lotus, the absolute peak of Huang'shan, 1,873 m." [2] A member of the police force charged with keeping the tourists in order. [3] Tourists being carried up to the summit by *palanquin*.

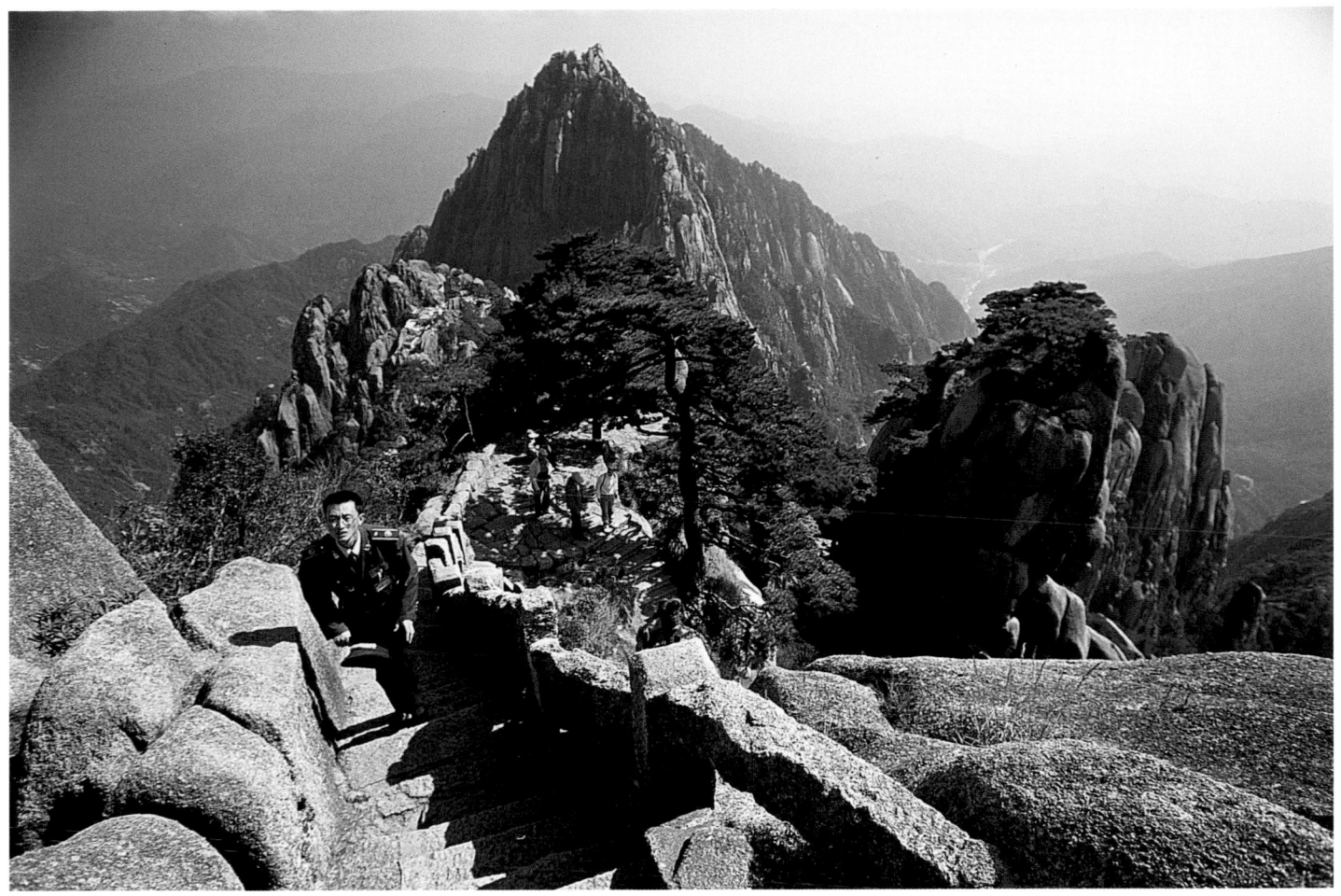

2

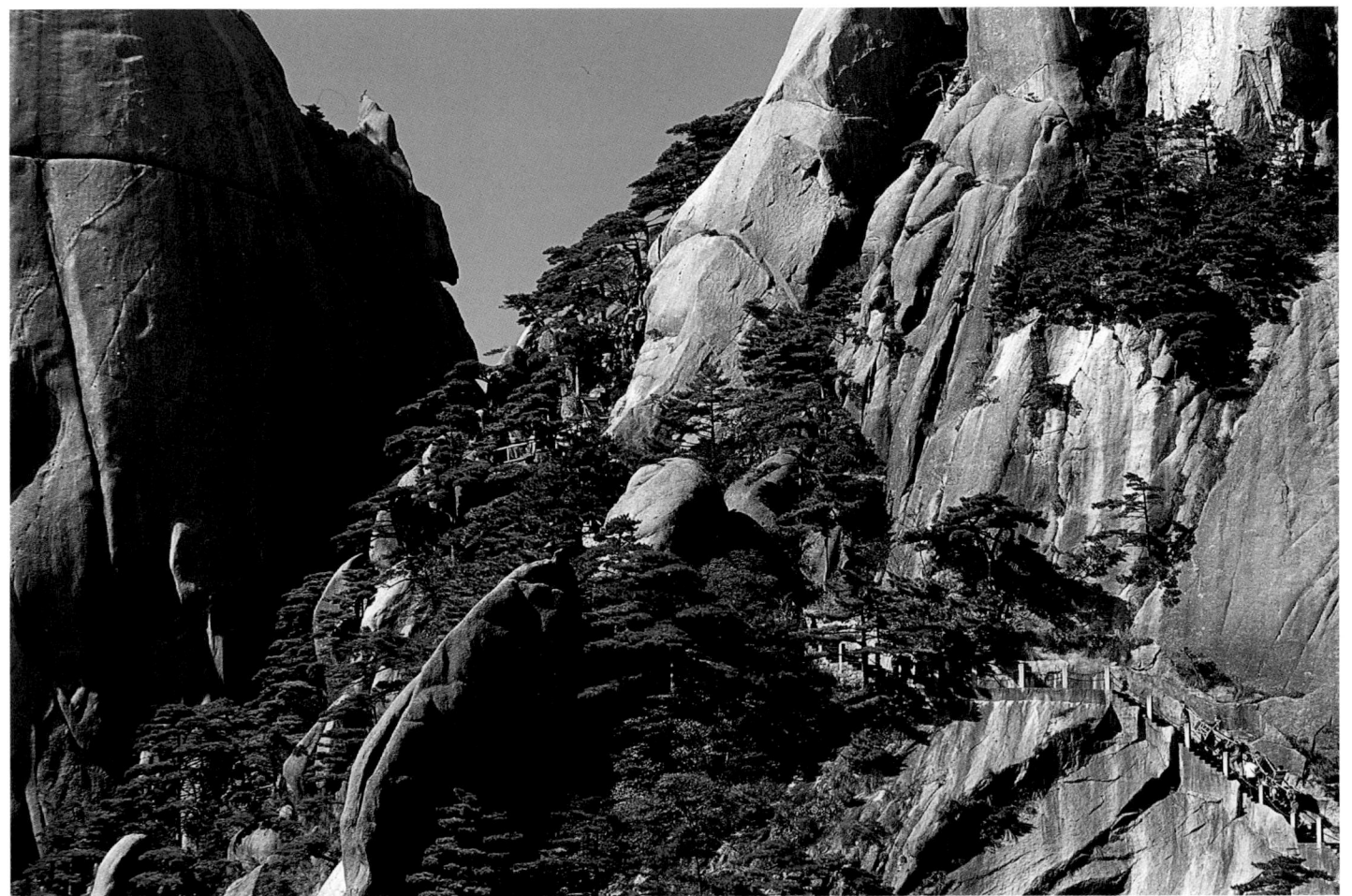

3

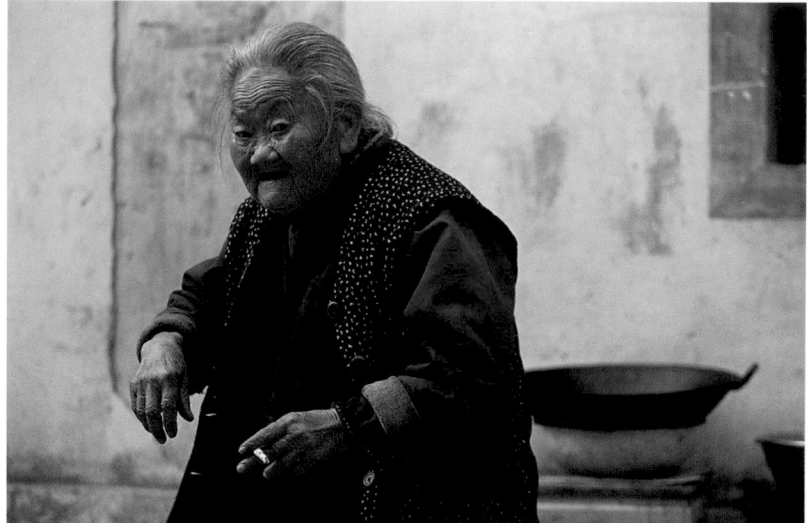

1

2

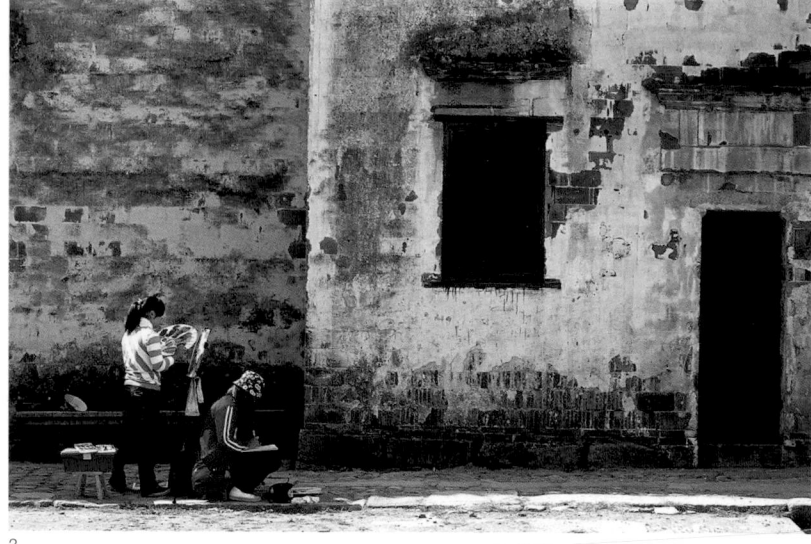

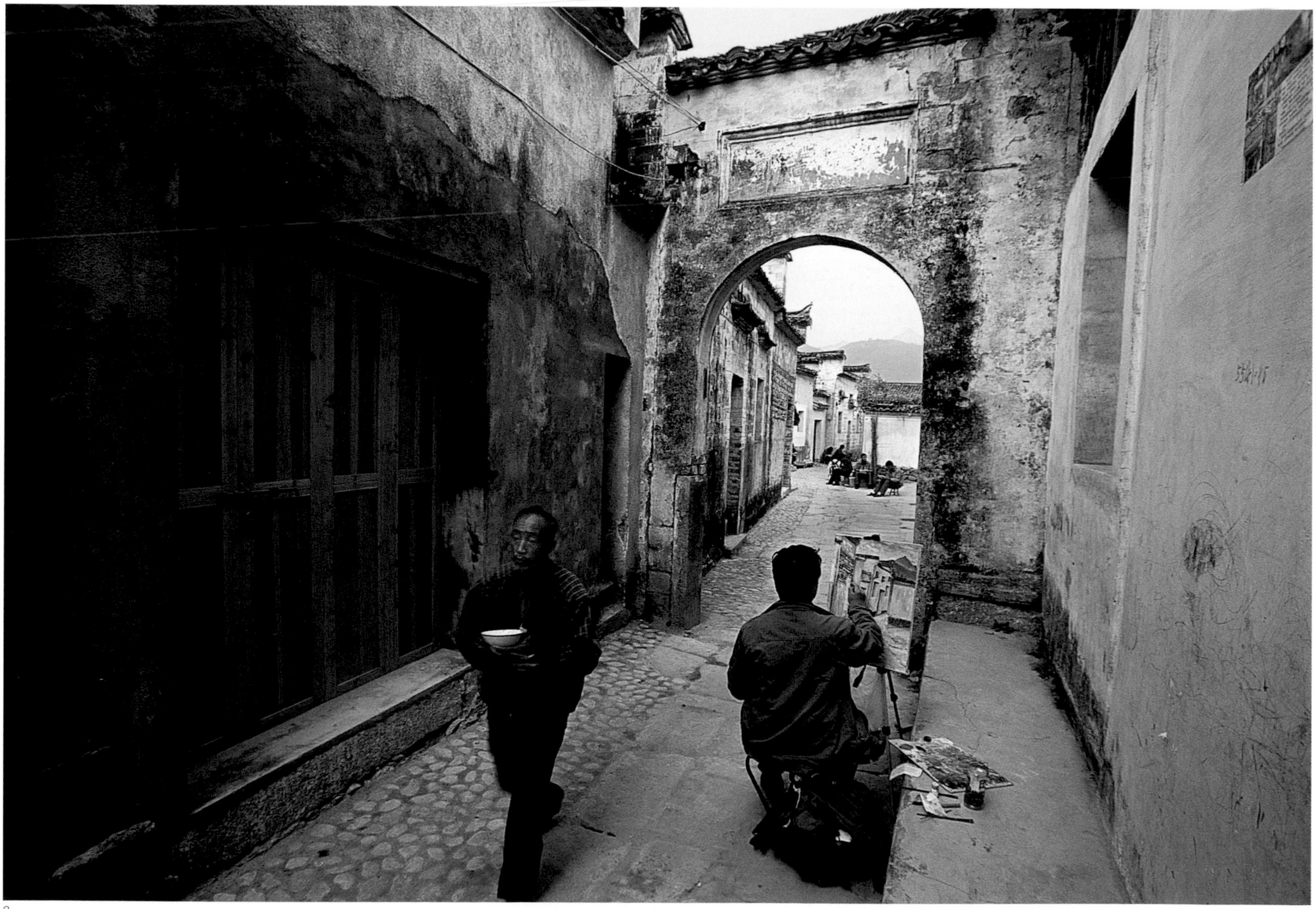

3

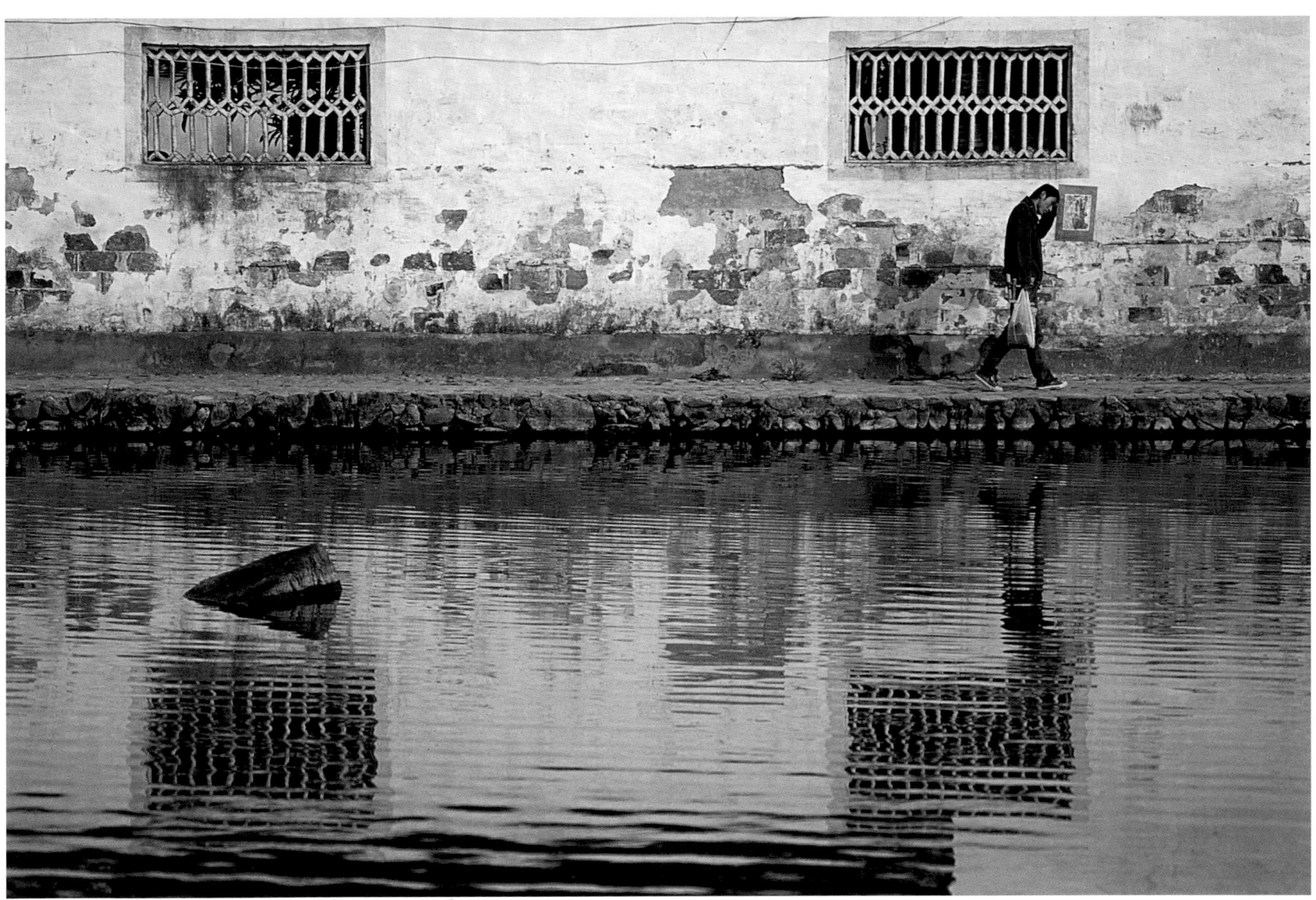

4

AN'HUI'S HONG VILLAGE is one of China's most famous beauty spots. The village's transformation from a quiet working community to a major tourist destination is a tragedy that is being repeated all across the country. A thirty-year tourism development contract was awarded to a Bei'jing company headed by the daughter of a senior official. A team of young 'public security personnel' with serious attitude problems were dispatched from Bei'jing to control access to the village, where they demanded to see admission tickets and generally intimidated tourists and villagers alike. The income went to Bei'jing, with only a tiny percentage remaining in the hands of the local inhabitants. As a result, the residents despise the tourists and in all probability those who sent the 'trainee gangsters' in. [1] A 96-year-old lady cursed me for taking her picture, but eventually calmed down after I bought her entire stock of chestnuts at wildly inflated prices. [2] [3] [4] A popular destination for school trips, art students and architecture majors, who come from all over the country to sketch the village.

HE'NAN PROVINCE

LOCATION
Latitude 31º23'–36º22'N
Longtitude 110º21'–116º39'E

AREA 160,000 km² (65,000 sq miles)

GEOGRAPHY Northern He'nan is bisected by the Huang'he (Yellow) River, marking the division between the Hai'he and Huai'he watersheds. The Tai'hang Mountains separate He'nan from Shaan'xi province in the north-west, while the Da'bie Mountains form the border with Hu'bei province in the south. The Qin'ling Mountains dominate the west, with the relatively flat North China Plain covers much of eastern and central He'nan. The mountainous regions comprise 44 per cent of the province's landmass. He'nan's terrain rises from 23 m on the plains to 2,414 m at the summit of Mount Lao'ya'cha.

CLIMATE He'nan's temperate climate gives the province four distinct seasons, characterized by hot and wet summers. Temperatures average 0ºC in January and 28ºC in July. The highest recorded temperature is 44.2ºC and the lowest is -21.7ºC. Average annual rainfall is between 570 mm and 1,120 mm.

POPULATION 97.17 million (end 2005)

MAJOR CITIES Zheng'zhou (capital), Luo'yang, Kai'feng

AGRICULTURE He'nan is a major wheat and cotton producer. Other food crops include sorghum, rice, millet, sweet potatoes, tobacco and fruit. Cash crops include oak leaf silk, sesame and peanuts.

MAIN INDUSTRIES The province's Zhong'yuan and He'nan oilfields produce significant quantities of crude oil and natural gas, providing feedstock for refineries and a petrochemical industry. Ample supplies of hydroelectric power have led to the development of heavy industries, including an aluminum smelter at San'men Gorge and chemical and vehicle plants. Other industries include textiles, domestic appliances, electronics and ceramics.

ANNUAL PER CAPITA INCOME (2005)
Disposable income of urban residents:
RMB 8,650 (US$1,078)
Cash Income of rural residents:
RMB 2,870 (US$358)

HISTORICAL AND SCENIC SITES
Three of China's seven ancient capitals, serving twenty dynasties, are located in He'nan: An'yang, Luo'yang and Kai'feng. This legacy is represented in numerous sites, including the Shao'lin Temple, Long'men Grottoes, White Horse Temple, Iron Pagoda, Dragon Pavilion and Xiang'guo Temple.

FOOD He'nan cooking is noted for its soups. This is embodied in the Luo'yang Water Table, a banquet comprising 24 soup-based dishes. Other dishes include quick-fried Yellow River carp in sweet and sour sauce with baked noodles, fried purple crisp pork, seared bean curd and sea cucumber in the shape of Lotus flowers.

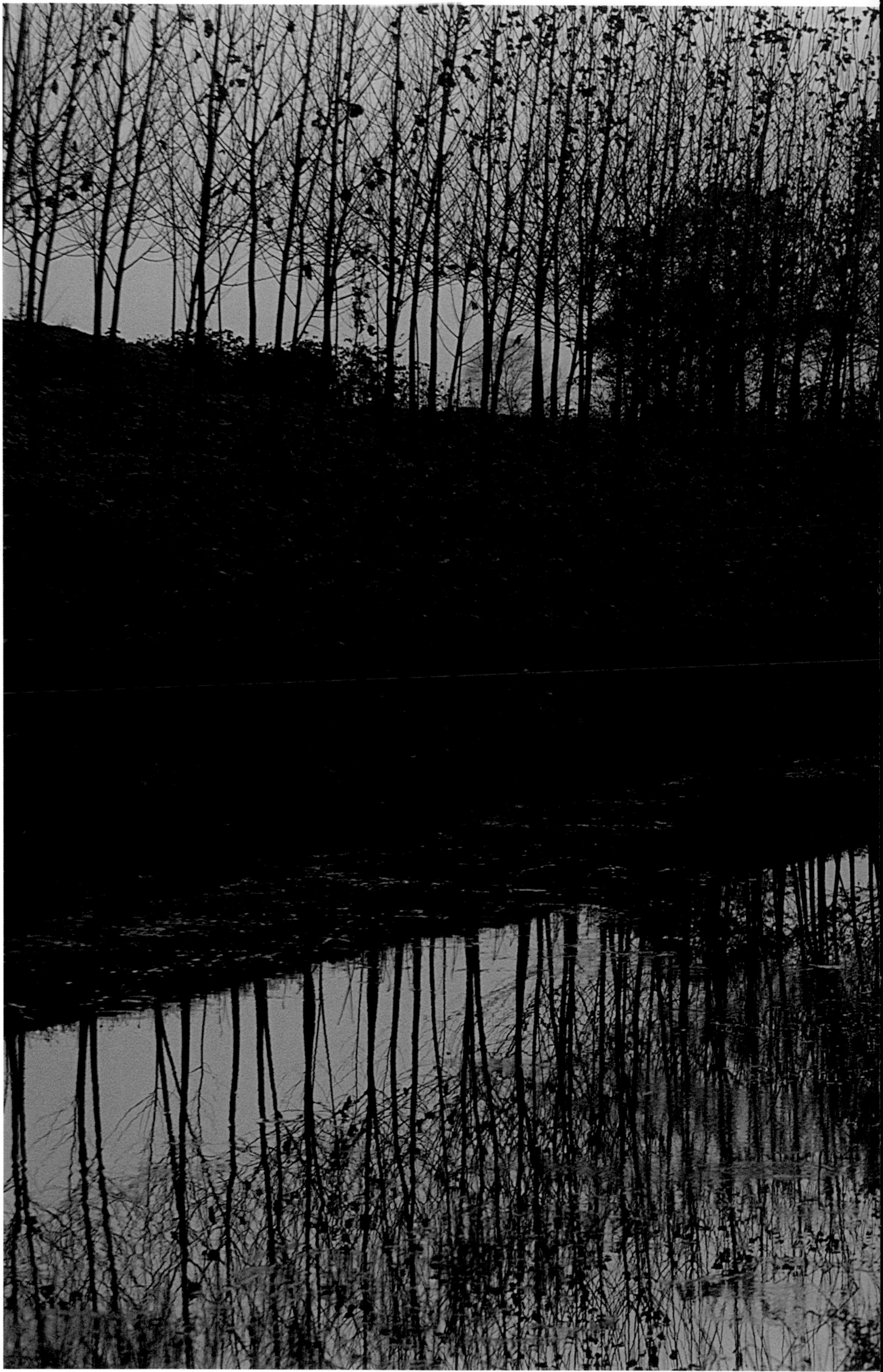

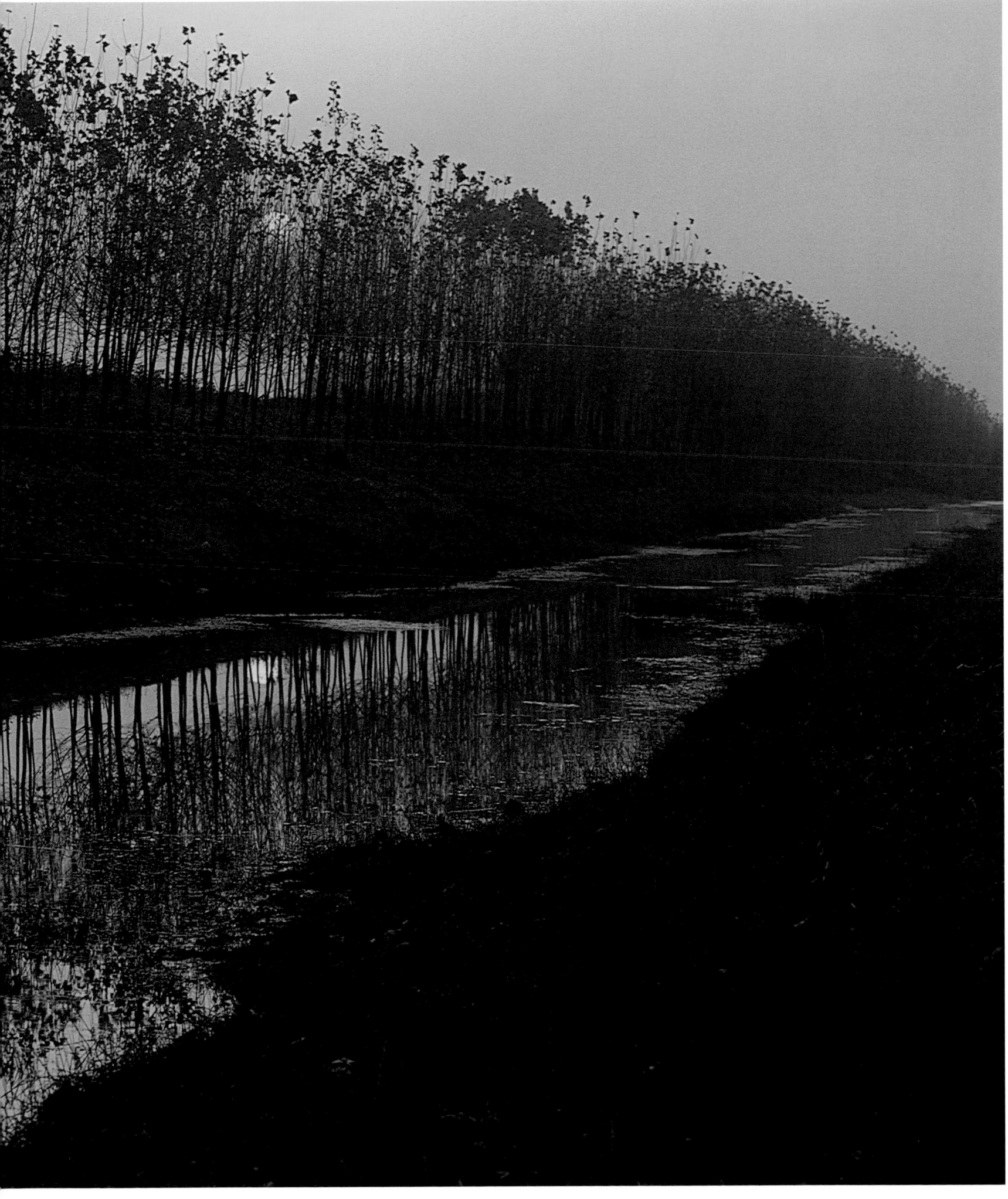

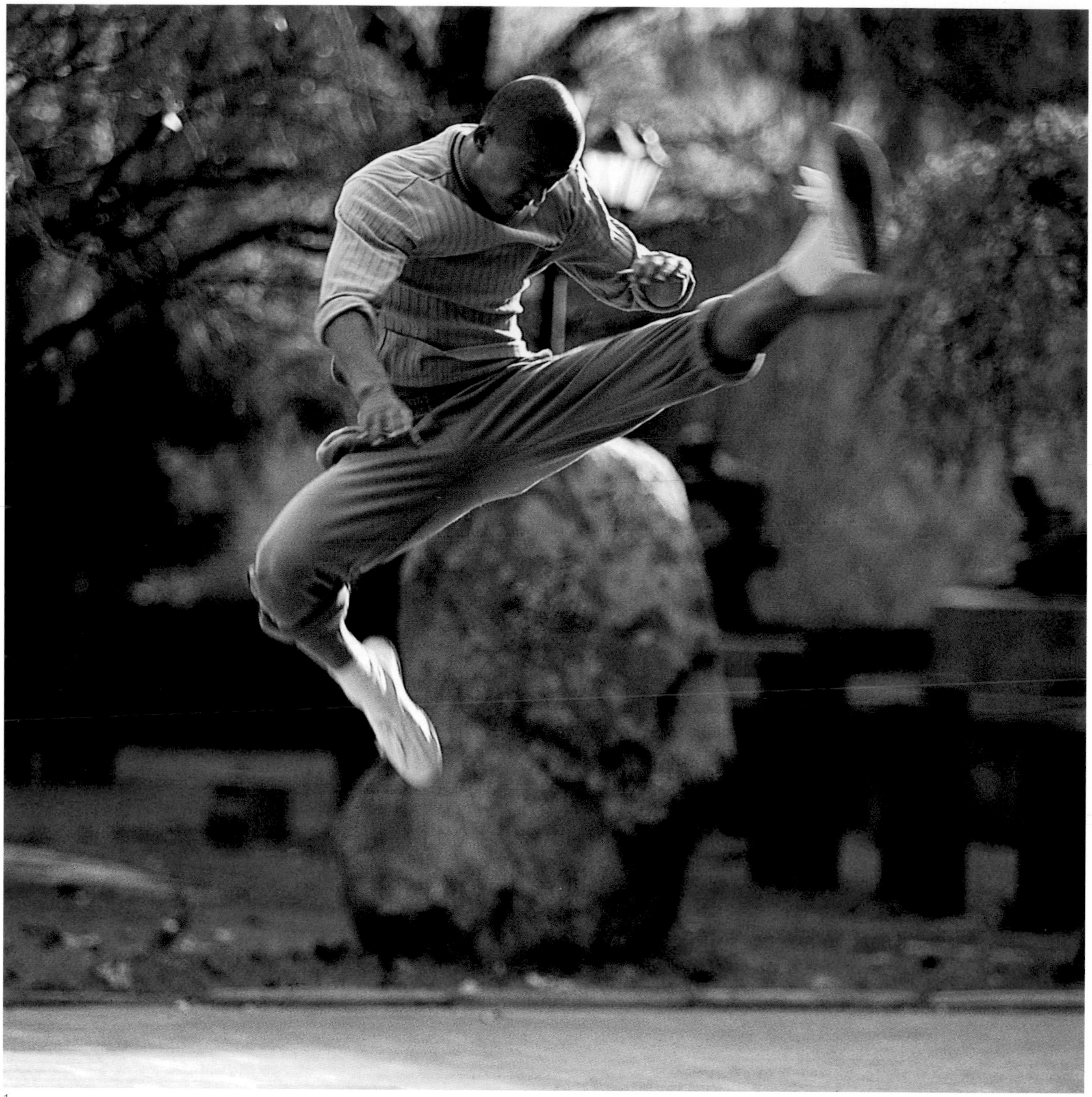

1

THE ORIGINS OF CHINA'S MOST FAMOUS MONASTERY are shrouded in Buddhist legend and martial arts mythology. Historical records, however, agree that the original Shao'lin Temple was built around 495–497 CE by order of Northern Wei Dynasty Emperor Xiao'wen for the Indian master Damo Bodhidharma, who came to China in 464 CE and later founded Zen (Chan) Buddhism. One legend recounts that when Bodhidharma discovered acolytes were unable to hold their meditation position for long periods, he developed a series of yoga-based strengthening exercises. These became the basis of Shao'lin Kung Fu, the ancestor of all subsequent schools of Chinese martial arts. [1] Although many question the lineage of the current martial monks at Shao'lin because of their association with the government, the international success of Jet Li's film *Shao'lin Monastery* and other martial arts classics have made the area a magnet for fans and kung fu a major local industry. [2] [3] In addition to the 8,000 students at the official Shao'lin Monastery Institute, more than 50 martial arts academies in the city train a further 50,000 students from all over the world. •

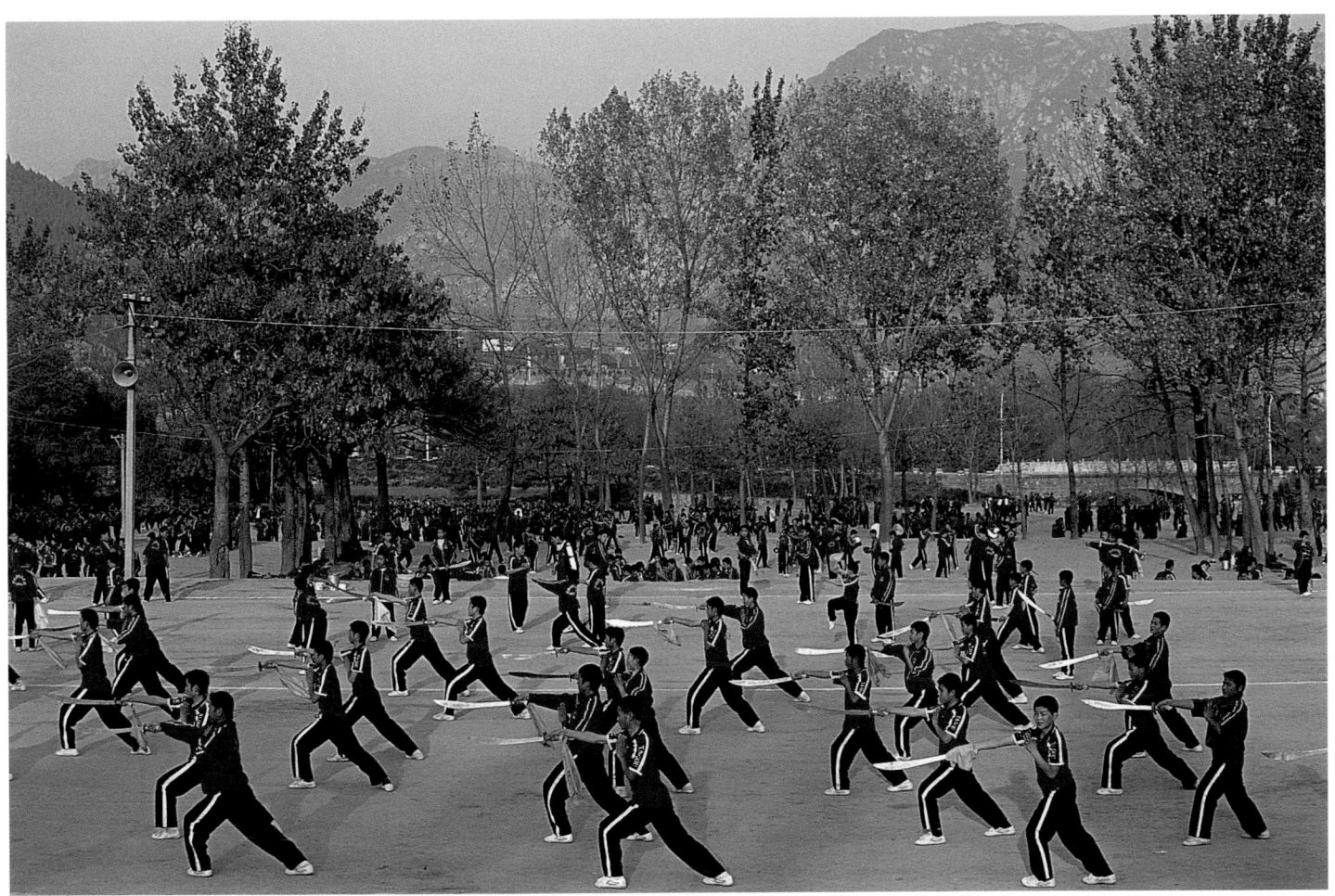

2

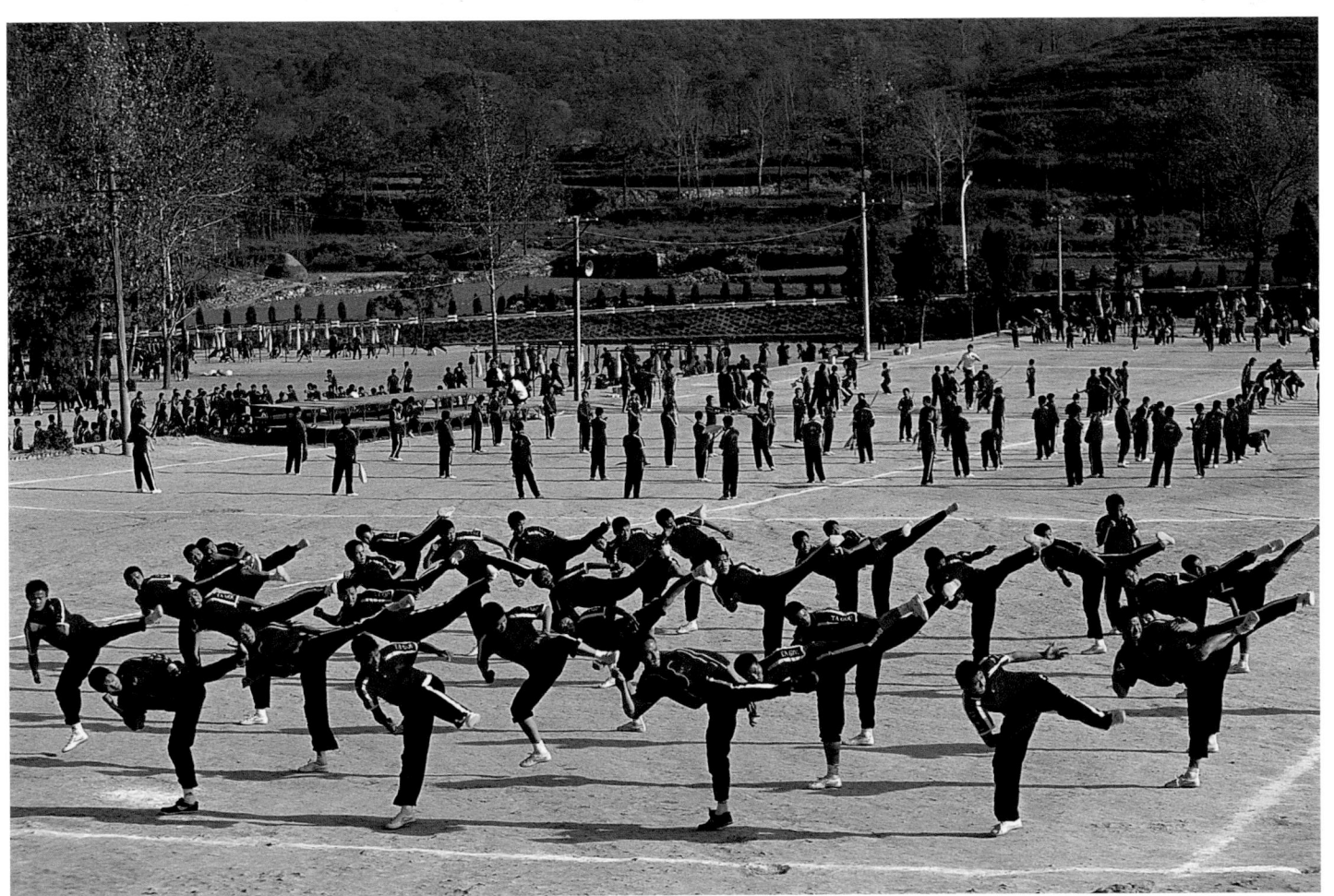

3

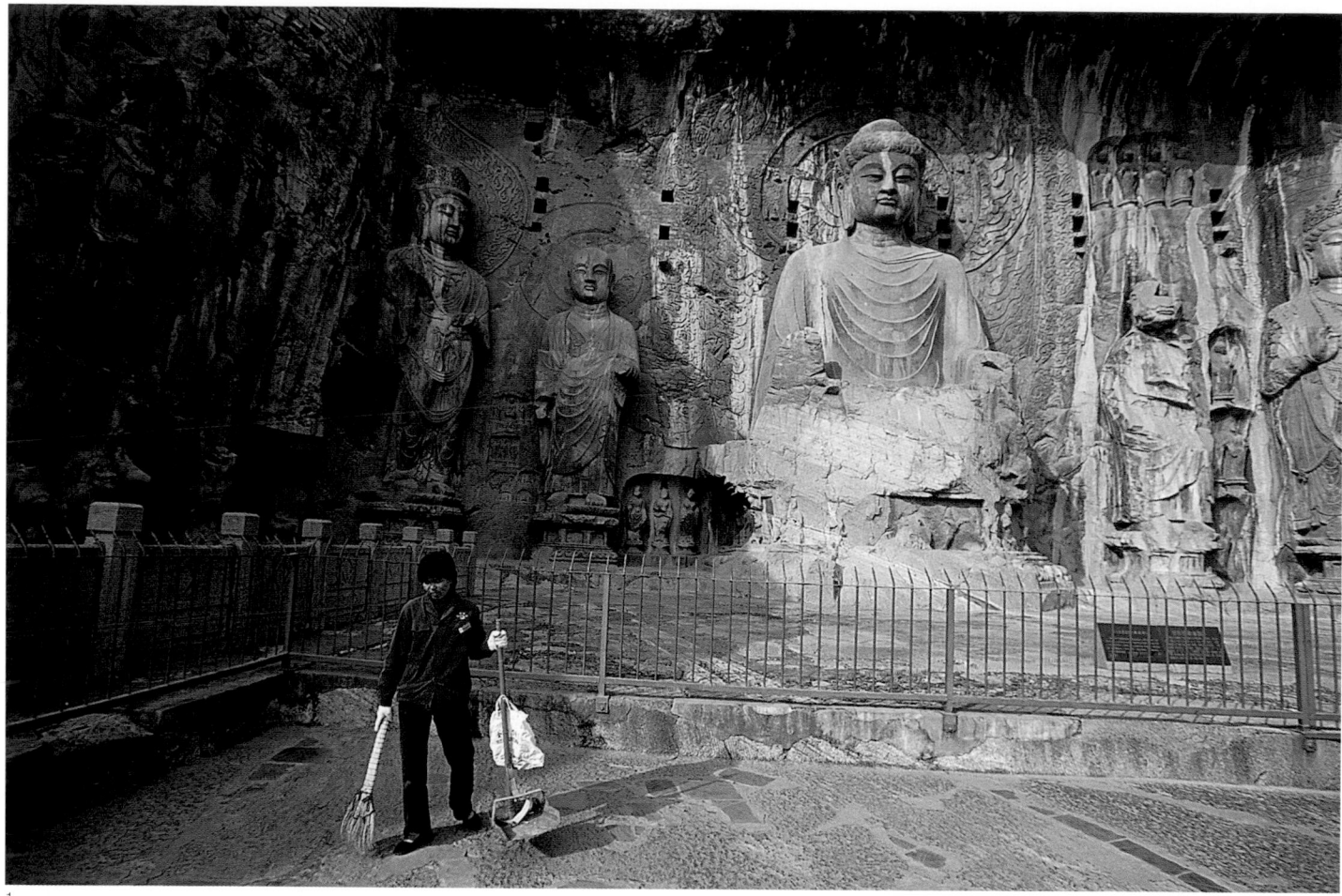

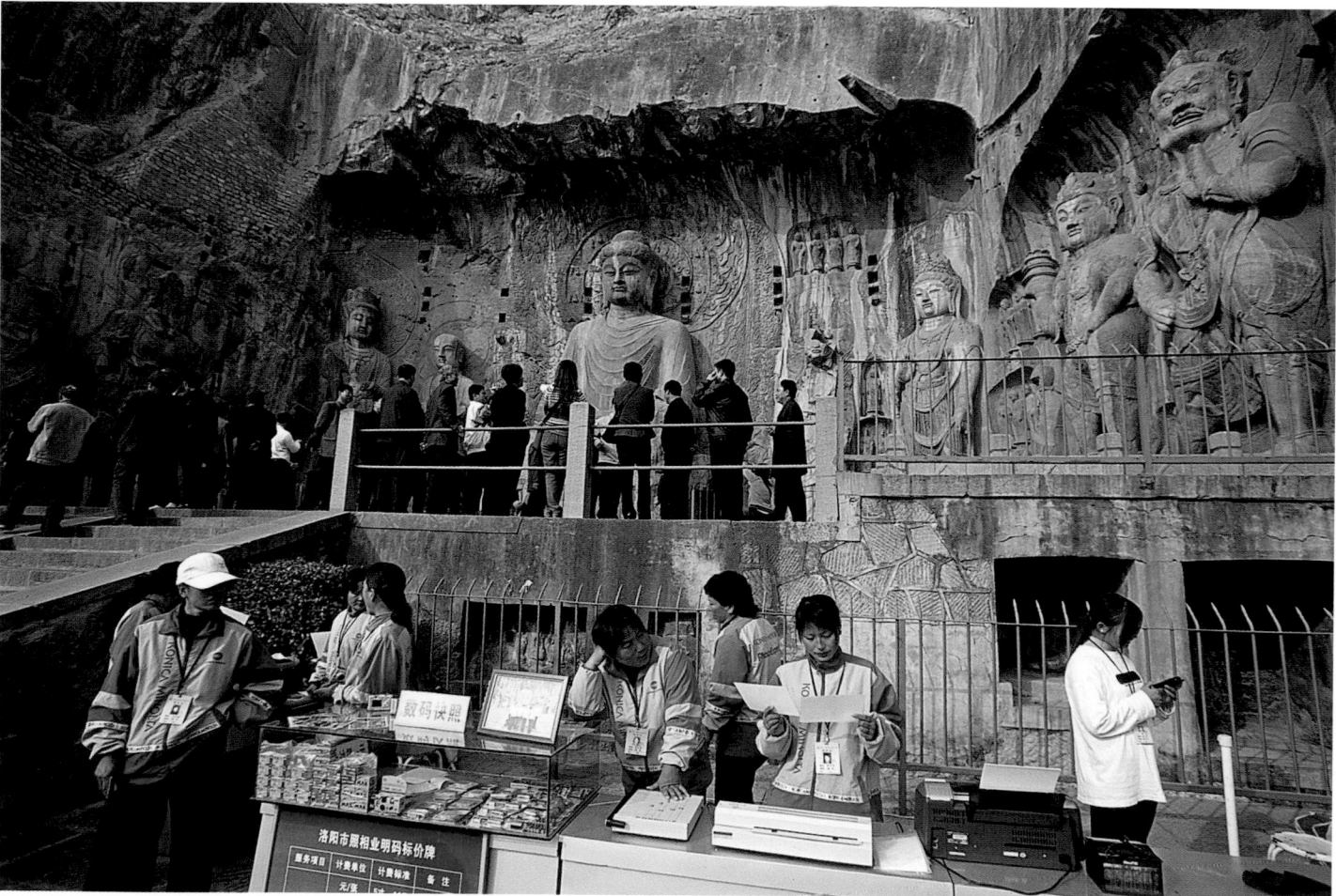

1

2

THE DRAGON GATE GROTTOES

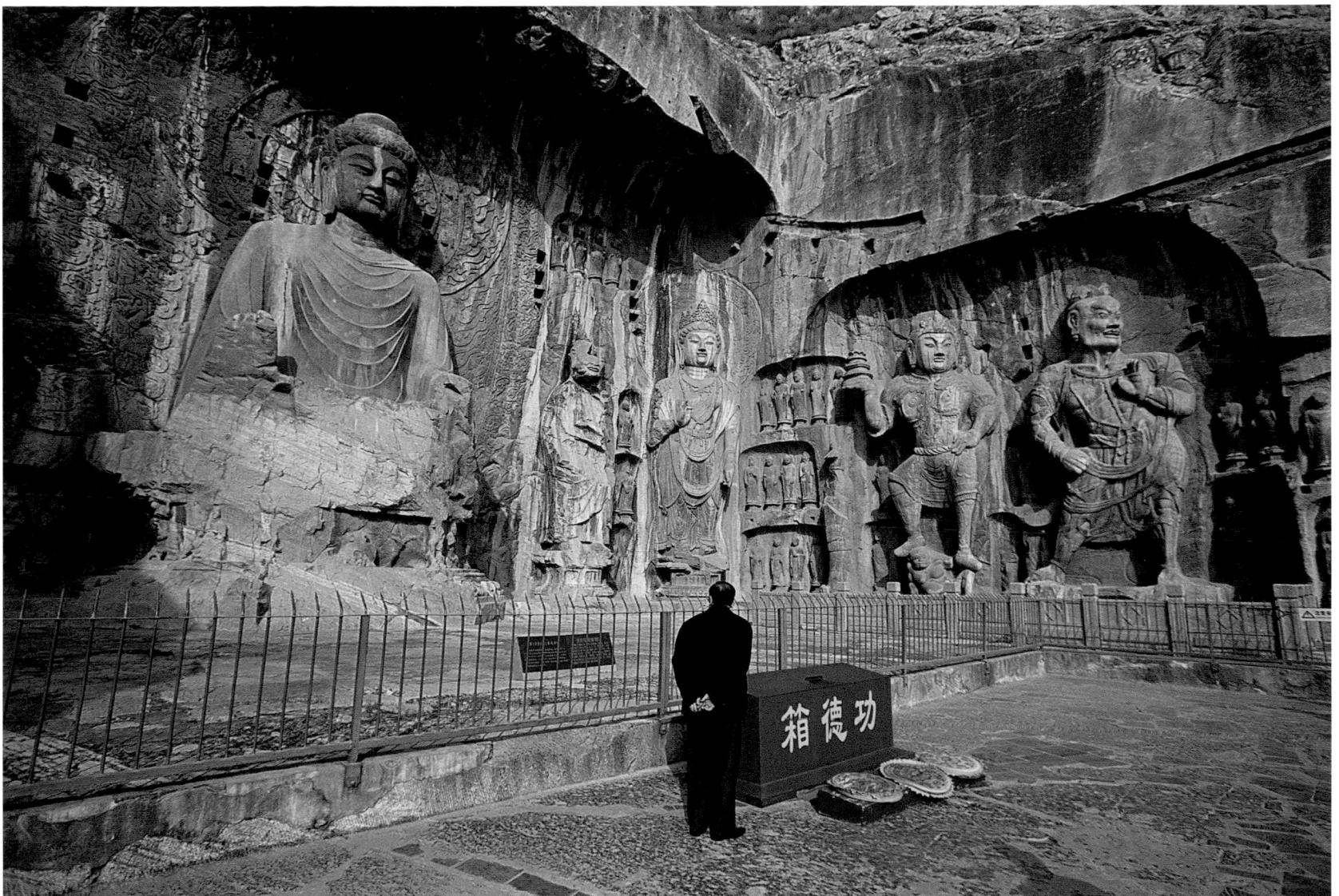

3

THE GRAND VAIROCANA BUDDHA EAVE, also known as Feng'xian (Ancestral Worship) Temple [3] is the largest and most elaborate grotto in the Long'man (Dragon Gate) complex on the banks of the Yi He River. The roof of the cave has eroded and fallen away over the centuries and the beautiful Tang Dynasty sculptures, carved into the cliff face between 672–675 CE, are now exposed to the elements. [1] The face of the magnificent 17-metre (55-foot) seated Buddha in the centre of the stone ensemble is said to be based on Empress Wu Ze'tian, the only 'female emperor in the history of China, who had commissioned the temple. The benevolence of the expression and the enigmatic smile on the Buddha's lips has prompted some art historians to call the statue the 'Mona Lisa of the East'. In a rare moment of peace, the cleaner tidies up after the tourists. [2] The digital age meets the distant past at the Dragon Gate where instant photographic prints are available to tourists at the most popular cave sites.

THE MIDDLE KINGDOM

1

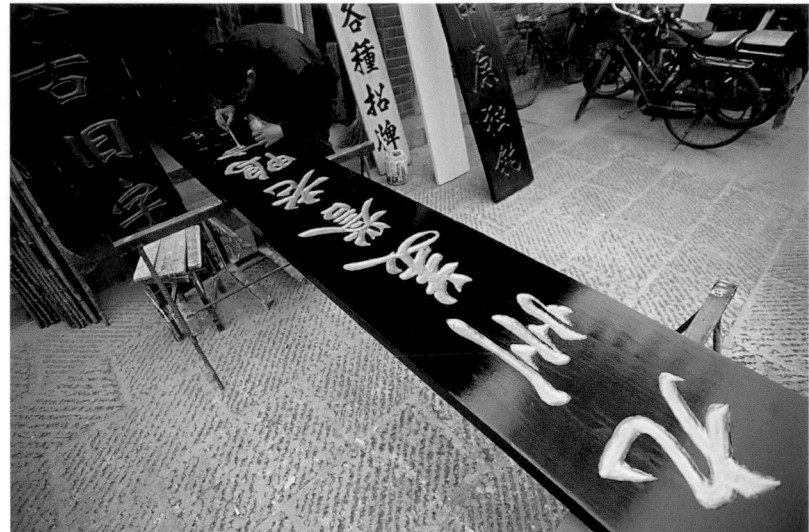

2

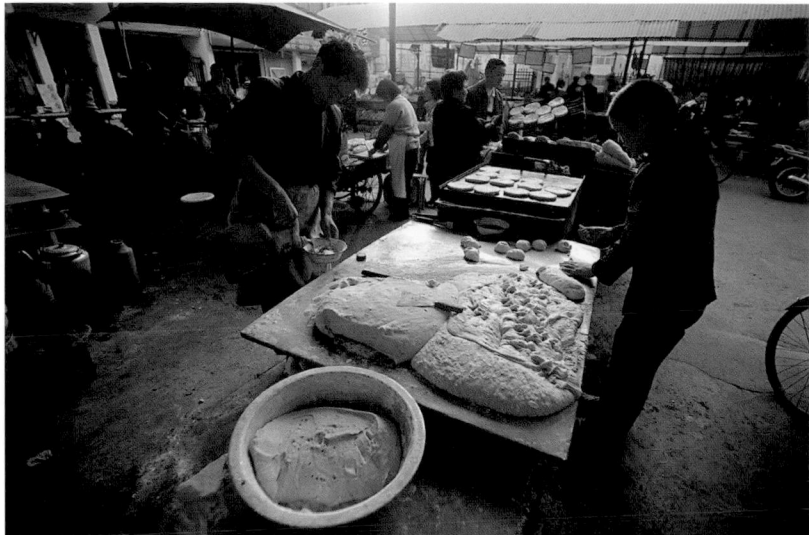

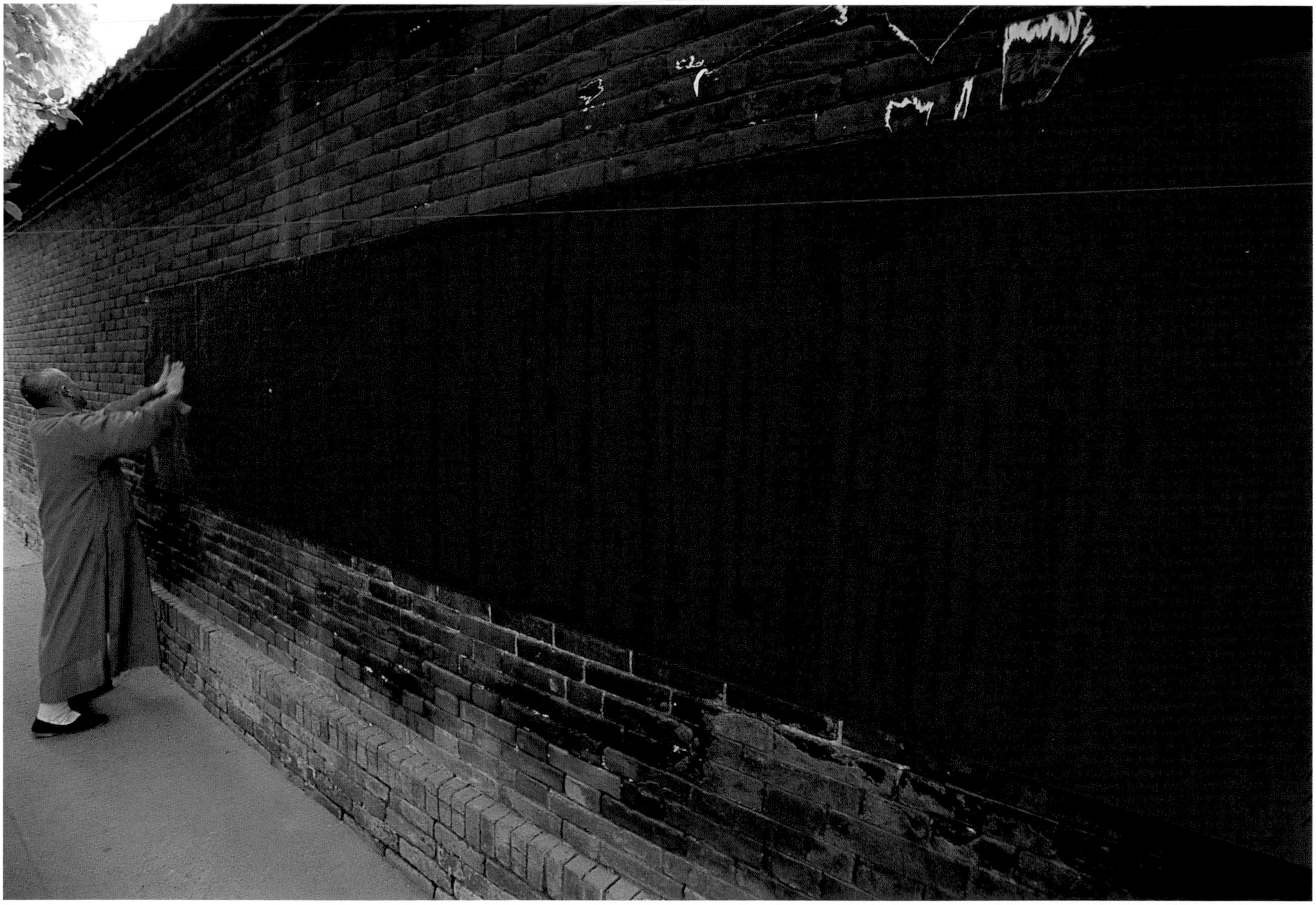

3

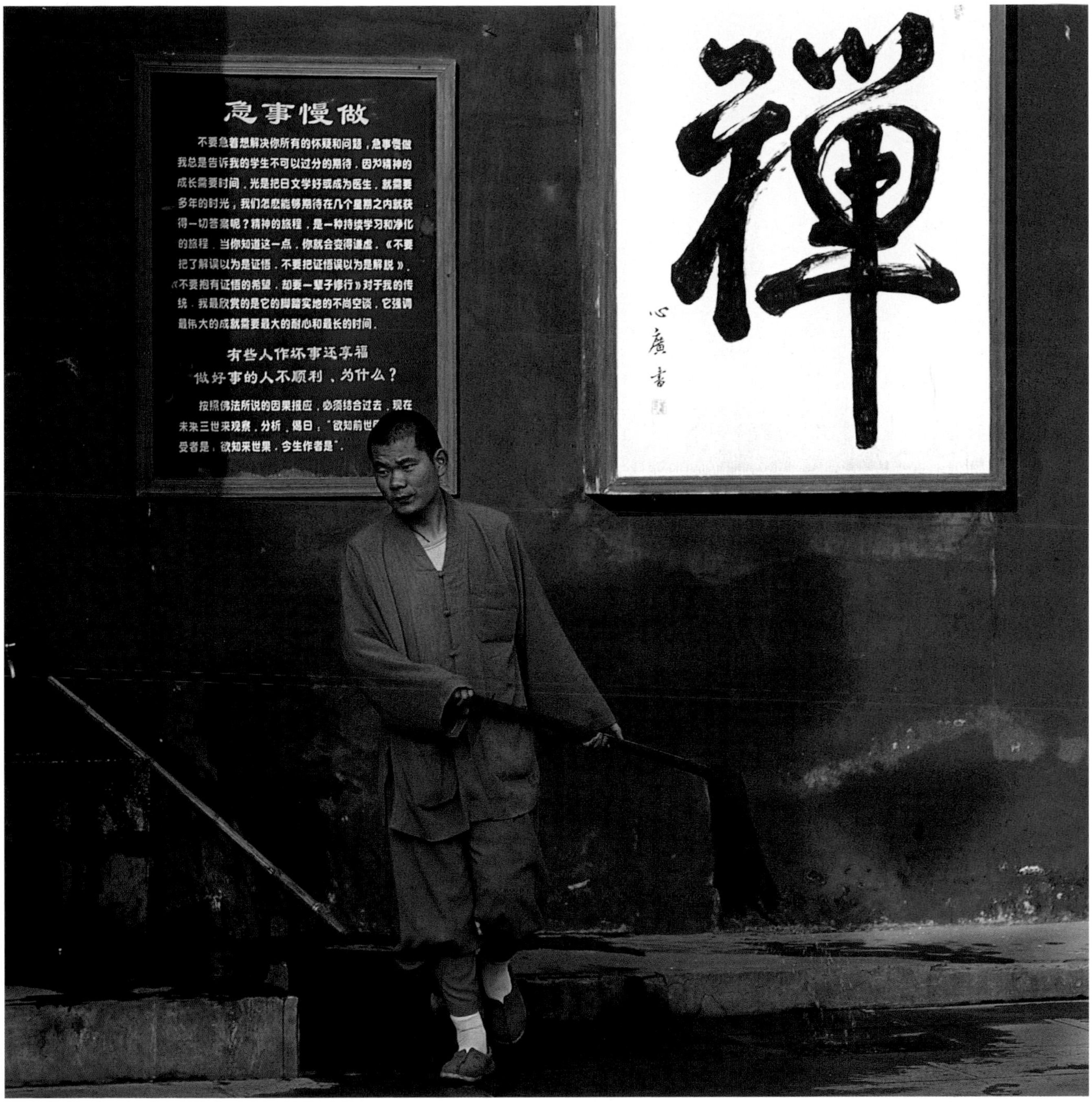

4

LUO'YANG WAS THE SECOND MOST IMPORTANT CITY of ancient China after Xi'an. The city was the capital of 13 dynasties until the 10th Century CE and contains the first Buddhist temple built on Chinese soil. It is said that at the beginning of the Eastern Han Dynasty, monks representing the emperor returned from Kandahar with two Indian masters. The emperor ordered a temple built to house the scriptures and relics carried to China by two white horses. Baima Si (White Horse Temple) is just north of Luo'yang, and is where Sanskrit scriptures were first translated into Chinese. Kai'feng is the birthplace of Hsuan Tsang, the Tang Dynasty monk who undertook the legendary pilgrimage to Central Asia and India between 629–645 CE. [1] A traditional sign painter inside Luo'yang's old walled city. [2] Breakfast at a local produce market. [3] Monks and volunteers put up posters listing pilgrims' donations at the White Horse temple. [4] A monk rinses his mop next to a giant 'Zen' inscription at the Great Xiang'guo Temple in Kai'feng.

THE MIDDLE KINGDOM

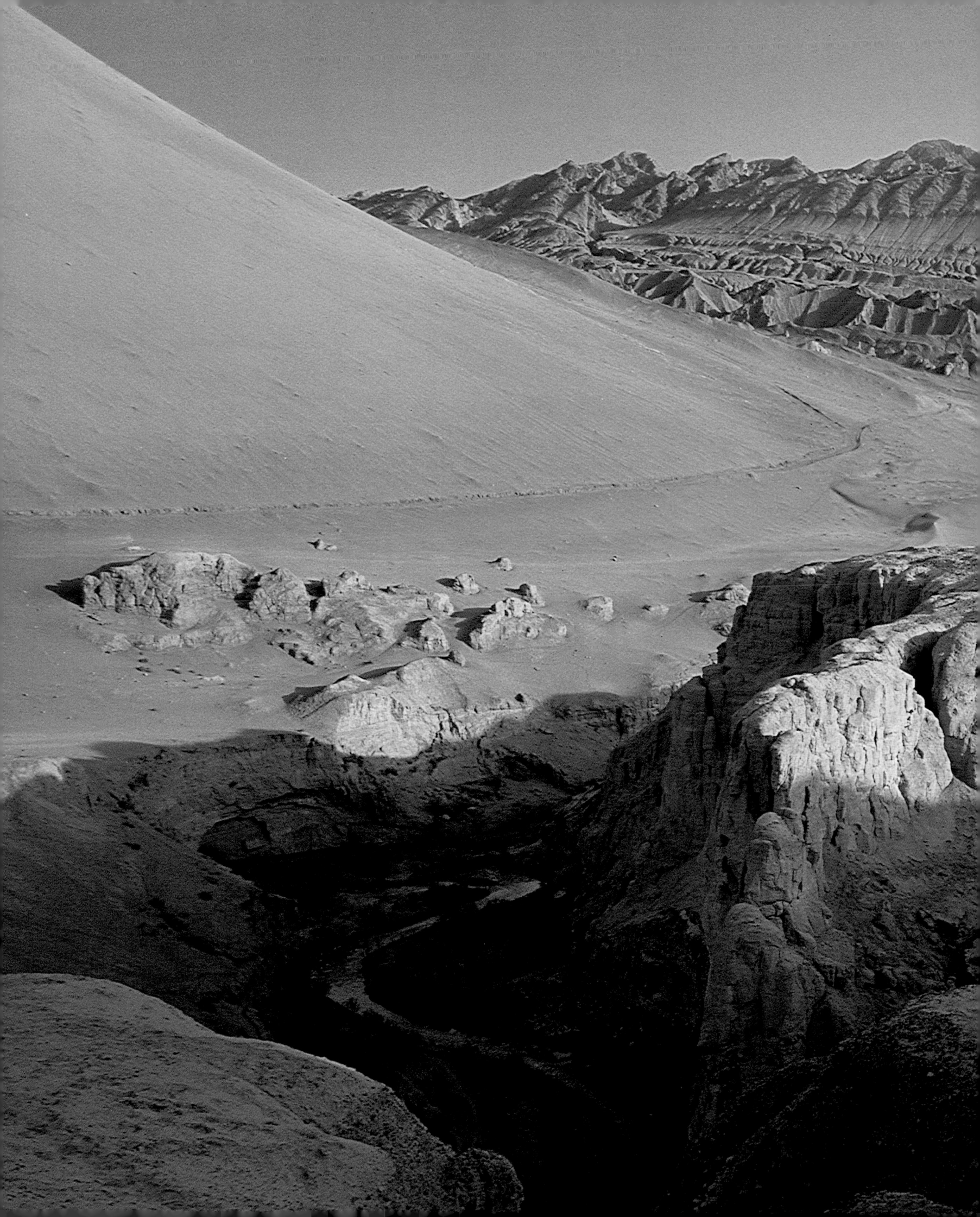

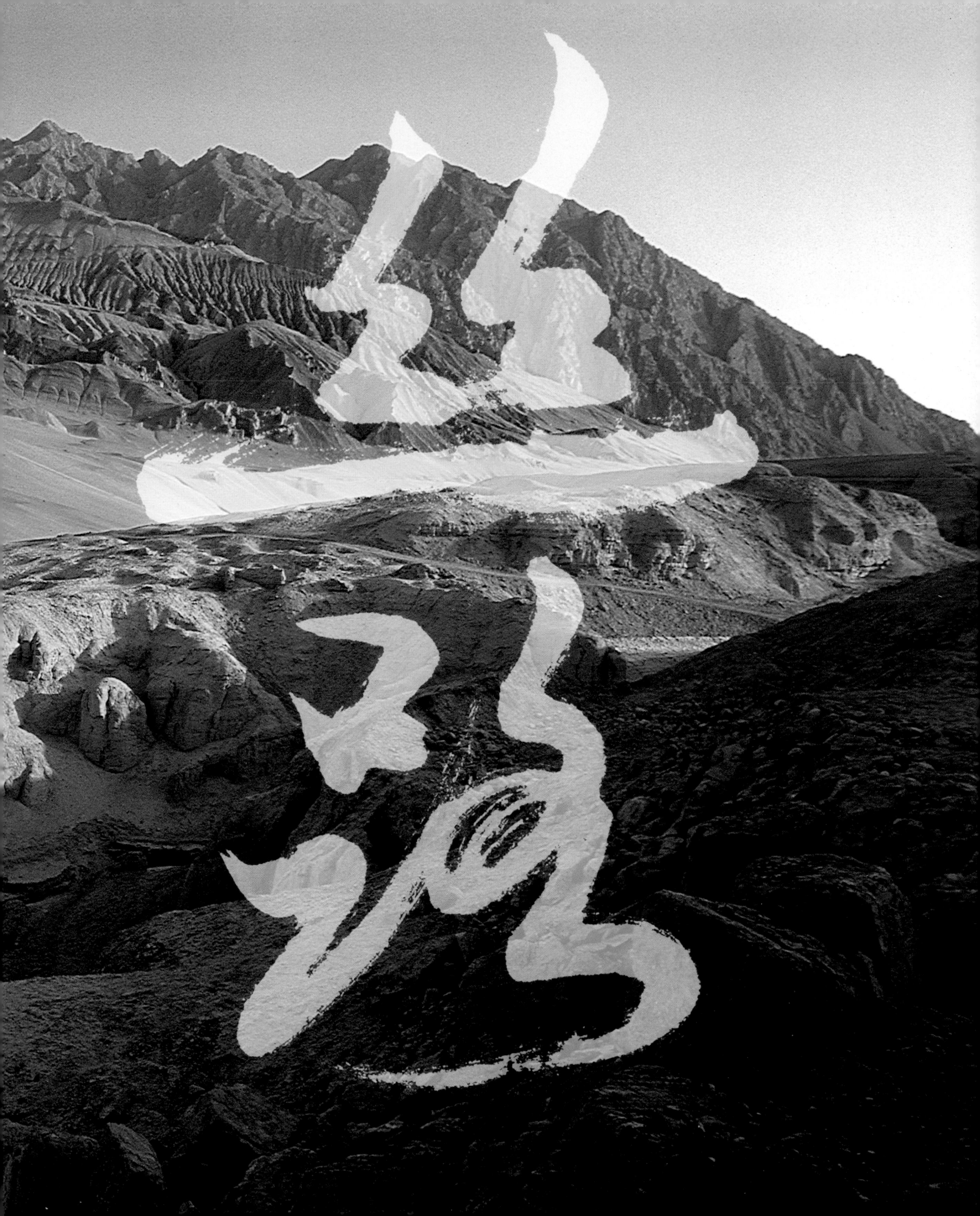

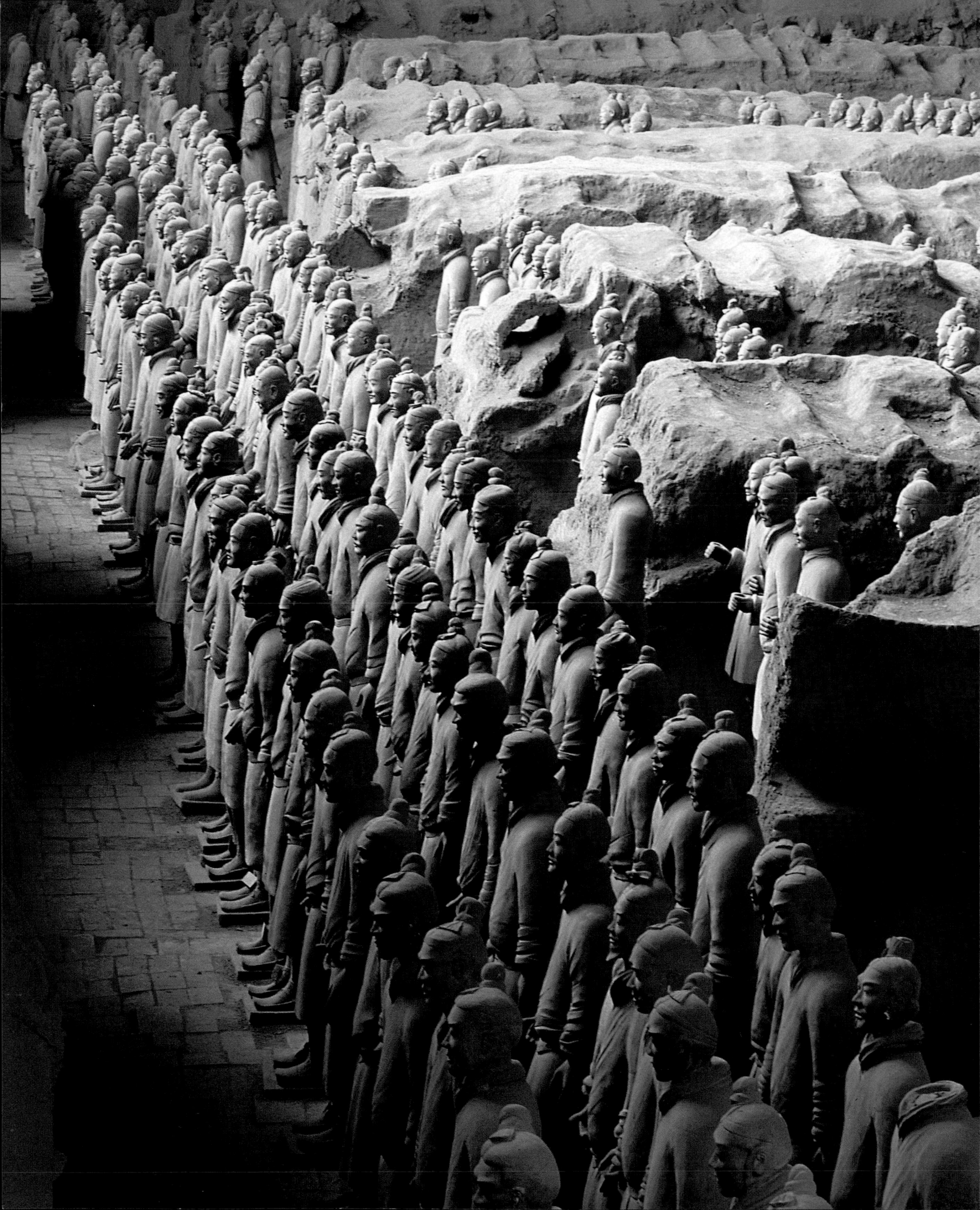

THE SILK ROAD

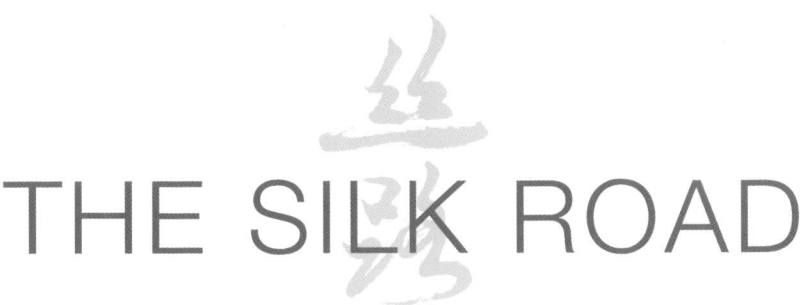

I have done some quite moronic things in my life, like white-water rafting down the Zambezi River through rapids 7.6 metres (25 feet) deep without the slightest idea how to swim, or chasing wild Afghan camels in the centre of Australia in an open 'chopper' the size of a coat hanger, piloted by a teenage Mad Max who belonged in an asylum for the lethally insane… But this latest act of idiocy is the most unforgivably dumb of all.

We are 66 kilometres (41 miles) northwest of Dun'huang, about two thirds of the way to Jade Doors Gate (Yu'men Guan), when the sandstorm hits. Our Red Flag sedan, long favoured by high officials for its sturdiness because of the extra-heavy East German chassis, swerves to one side as we drive into the storm; the driver quickly reduces speed, straightens his course, and glances back at me as if to ask whether we should go on. "How far are we?" "We're over half way…" The whole point of the current journey is to fill in the blanks from my previous outing on the Silk Road: I never had the chance then to see the ruins of the 'First Gate between Heaven and Earth', as Yu'men Guan was known in Chinese history for being the last outpost of the empire in the west and the starting point of the northern silk route that takes you to Kashgar, through Samarkand and into Persia and Europe. So I decide to press on despite the fact that we can't see anything except for the few yards of road directly in front of the windshield, illuminated by our head lamps – two beams of yellow swirling sand in a sea of grey…

My first journey across the Silk Road was on a train. I was photographing the inaugural run of the *Marco Polo Express* for *Travel & Leisure* magazine in New York. This luxury charter was China's answer to the *Orient Express*. The train was made up of East German-built, mahogany-panelled passenger carriages that once belonged to Chairman Mao's personal train, used on his inspection tours across the country. It was a 3,220-kilometre (1,996-mile) journey from Bei'jing to Urum'qi, the capital of Chinese Turkistan (Xin'jiang Uygur Autonomous Region), and from there I took a plane to Kashgar.

The first stop was Xi'an in Shaan'xi province. Formerly known as Chang'an (City of Eternal Peace), this was the first capital of China, the united nation established by Qin Shi'huang in 221 BCE. It is home to the famous Terracotta Warriors and countless other treasures that encapsulate its more or less uninterrupted history as the capital of the Chinese empire for 1,100 years. At its peak, during the Tang Dynasty between the 7th and 10th centuries – a time when the powerful and confident court threw its doors wide open to the cultural and economic influences of the known world – Xi'an was the Manhattan of its time; the largest and most sophisticated cosmopolitan city in the world. People from the Byzantine Empire, Arabia, Persia, India, the Central Asian kingdoms, Tibet, Burma, Korea and Japan were all here, trading, studying, opening restaurants and, if the murals of the period are any indication, partying – hard. It was a 'Golden Age' of East-West communication, with different cultures exchanging goods, ideas, knowledge and DNA. And this was all made possible by the network of trade routes collectively known as the Silk Road, of which Chang'an was both the starting point and the final destination.

Some of China's best poetry, art and architecture came out of the Tang period, and Buddhist scholarship made a giant leap when the 'superstar' monk Hsuan Tsang (596–664 CE) returned from his legendary 15-year pilgrimage to Gandahara (present day Pakistan/Afghanistan) and India. His journeys along both the northern and

[LEFT] The Army of Terracotta Warriors. [PRECEDING PAGES] The Flaming Mountains in Turpan.

southern silk routes inspired the Chinese allegorical classic *Journey to the West*, while his own travelogue, *The Great Tang Chronicles of the Western World*, has become a priceless historical document: filled with minute observation and the kind of exacting detail that would make a train spotter green with envy, it offers a valuable insight into the way of life of an extinct world. Hsuan Tsang was also an exceptional scholar and translator. He mastered Sanskrit during his years in the Buddhist universities in Taxila and Gandahara, and his translations of the scriptures he brought back from India marked the zenith of Chinese scholarship in the field of Buddhism – making Xi'an the beacon and transmission tower for *Mahayana* Buddhism to the rest of Asia.

The next stop was Lan'zhou, on the banks of the Yellow River; an important transport hub since the times of the Silk Road with not much to offer apart from the excellent local 'hand-pulled' noodles served in a beautiful beef broth. I made an effort to visit the museum that was supposedly the home of the most famous of Chinese bronzes, the 'Flying Horse', only to find, on display in its place of honour inside a bubble of filthy glass, a replica identical to the one I had bought in Bei'jing a few years earlier. No one in the museum could tell me where the original was being kept.

Further down the line, Jia'yu Guan (Pleasant Valley Gate), the fortress at the western tip of the Great Wall in Gan'su province, was a considerably more moving experience. I remember walking out through the western gate and far into the desert, which was strewn with sharp rocks. I looked back at the restored fortress, first built in 1372 at the beginning of the Ming Dynasty, and imagined myself a soldier in an invading army or a trader in a caravan, thinking how differently they must have felt about coming across this enormous object rising out of the empty desert like a hallucination after weeks of deprivation through the inhospitable He'xi Corridor. From here, the travellers of old, after passing through customs, would enter China by exiting through the eastern gate of the fortress, Guang'hua Men – the Gate of Enlightenment.

The sandstorm is not subsiding as I'd hoped. Instead, it's wrapping itself around the sedan like a billowing duvet, and the leather interior of our vehicle suddenly feels like a cocoon, enveloped by the unfamiliar yet almost soothing sound of millions of grains of sand brushing against glass and steel. The scene through the windows reminds me of an old sci-fi movie with primitive special effects, of a time capsule travelling through an hour-glass, gliding through the all-embracing mist towards the beginning of the Silk Road. Memories of my first major sandstorm come rushing back.

It was *Mohammed*'s birthday in 1992 and we had just spent 13 hours crossing the Nubian Desert in Sudan in a public bus. Stuck in traffic on top of a bridge in the suburbs of Khartoum, we watched in horror as a fast-moving black cloud – which had been far away on the horizon just a few minutes before – came tearing straight down the river like a UFO charging onto a runway for an emergency landing, ripping through the mud houses and tearing up the large celebration tents on either side of the river before swallowing us whole like a bat out of hell. It came in through the pane-less windows of the bus in a blast of frozen air and covered everything with a thick cake of red sand.

I remember how vulnerable and frightened I felt then as sand forced its way into every orifice despite our best efforts to cover up, and how ridiculously secure and smug I feel now, lounging in the cool comfort of a luxury sedan, sipping green tea with honey and pretending we're not in any danger at all. And I remember how fine the weather was last time I was in Dun'huang.

I rode a camel to the top of the tallest dune of the Singing Sands (Ming'sha Shan) behind the Crescent Moon Lake (Yue'ya Quan) before dawn and, watching the sun rise over the endless sweep of dunes to the west, I finally understood the significance of the Mogao Caves. For a millennium from the 4th Century, merchants had been commissioning artists and craftsman to construct temples inside the caves on the western cliff face of Ming'sha Shan and filling them with magnificent murals and statues depicting Buddhist legends. I realized then that one would definitely feel the need to seek protection from a higher power before going into those dunes, and to give thanks after coming out of them alive.

At the sight of the lonesome wooden gateway and weather-beaten fences just ahead, my mind abruptly turns from the *Marco Polo Express* to the new places I am about to see. Like the Bezeklik Thousand Buddha Caves, hidden in the rugged heart of the Flaming Mountains – the 100-kilometre (62-mile) long red sandstone range outside of Turfan, where the Monkey King had the battle of his life to save the fictional Hsuan Tsang from the clutches of the Iron-fan Princess and her beau the evil Buffalo King in *Journey to the West*. And of course, the highlight of the journey, the trip beyond Kashgar onto the Karakoram Highway and on to the no-man's-land of the Khunjerab Pass on the Pakistan border, the route that Hsuan Tsang took on his way out to India in his search for the sacred scriptures.

We sit outside the closed gates for a while, honking our horn into the storm, hoping that whoever is inside the little shack at the end of the fence can hear us. In the meantime, the gates rattle and shake in the wind. Once or twice, it looks as though the storm is going to open the gates for us. Finally, a figure emerges from the hut and, bracing himself against the wind, fights his way towards us. Our driver cracks his window a couple of inches and we can faintly hear the man asking, "What are you doing here?" "They want to see the Jade Doors Gate…" The young man grins, shaking his head in disbelief, "On a day like this? Are you sure?" He can see that we are serious when Huang-fan pulls out some bills to pay the admission. He takes the money and disappears behind the gates through a gap in the fence. After a while, the gates struggle open. We drive through and up a dirt track to the top of a small hill, stopping directly in front of a huge lump of mud-brick ruins in the vague shape of a fort. To the side is a large stone tablet proclaiming that we were looking at the 'First Gate between Heaven and Earth'. The storm seems to have subsided so I decide to take a closer look, but, as I open the door, a blast of sand hits me and I decide to leave the cameras in the car. I stagger around towards the back of the 'Number One Lump between Here and Eternity'. Once there, as it always happens in the great outdoors, anywhere in the world and for as long as I can remember, particularly at places of great historical importance or spectacular scenery, I feel an overwhelming desire to relieve myself. What happens next need not be described in too much detail; suffice to say that no sooner have I started than the sandstorm rises and kicks into top gear again and a gust practically knocks me over the edge from where I am standing. And thus, at some cost to the family jewels, a new champion for the 'Stupidest Thing I've Ever Done' title is born.

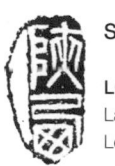

SHAAN'XI PROVINCE

LOCATION
Latitude 31°42'–39°35' N
Longtitude 105°29'–110°15' E

AREA 200,000 km² (77,220 sq miles)

GEOGRAPHY Shaan'xi is located close to China's centre. The province falls into three natural divisions running north to south. The Northern Plateau rises to around 1,500 m before dropping down to the Guan'zhong Plain, bisected by the Weihe River and its tributaries. The land then rises into the Qin'ba Mountainous Region, which includes the Qin'ling and Da'ba ranges, to reach some 3,000 m. The Qin'ling range is the major watershed of the Huang'he (Yellow) and Yang'tze rivers and represents an important geographical divide between northern and southern China.

CLIMATE Shaan'xi has a continental monsoonal climate, but with wide differences between areas north and south of the Qin'ling range. The north is cold in winter and very hot in summer. The south generally receives more rain. Temperatures in January range from -11°C to 3.5°C, rising in July to 21°C–28°C. The lowest recorded temperature is -32.7°C and the highest is 42.8°C. Annual rainfall averages between 340 mm and 1,240 mm.

POPULATION 37.2 million (end 2005)

MAJOR CITIES Xi'an (capital), Xian'yang, Yan'an

AGRICULTURE Main food crops are wheat, millet, corn, rice and fruit. Cash crops include cotton, soybeans, tea and tung oil. There is also a large livestock, notably sheep, sector.

MAIN INDUSTRIES Shaan'xi is a major coal producer and has significant reserves of natural gas. Other industries include textiles, machinery, electronics and chemicals.

ANNUAL PER CAPITA INCOME (2005)
Disposable income of urban residents:
RMB 8,272 (US$1,033)
Net income of rural residents:
RMB 2,052 (US$256)

HISTORICAL AND SCENIC SITES
Xi'an's Qin Dynasty terracotta warriors (UNESCO World Cultural Site), Xi'an Forest of Stone Tablets, Emperor Huang Di's Tomb, Wild Goose Pagoda, Famen Temple.

FOOD Shaan'xi cooking is substantial, reflecting the province's ample resources, and deceptively simple. Traditional dishes include roast piglet, *Yangrou Paomo* (steamed bun in mutton soup) with pickled garlic, innumerable types of dumplings and noodles, meat and fungus stew

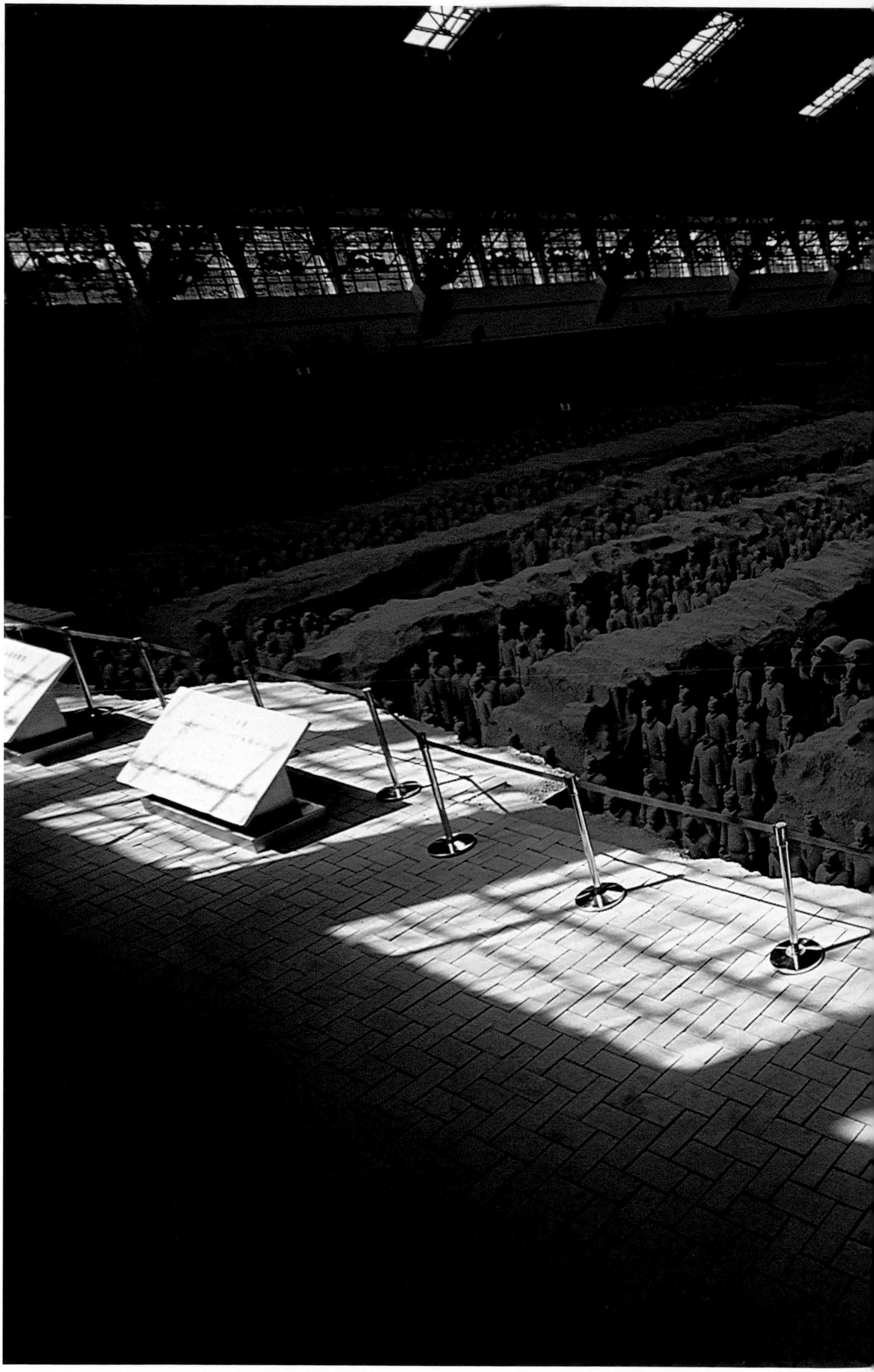

[RIGHT] Pit Number One of the Qin Shi Huang'di Mausoleum.

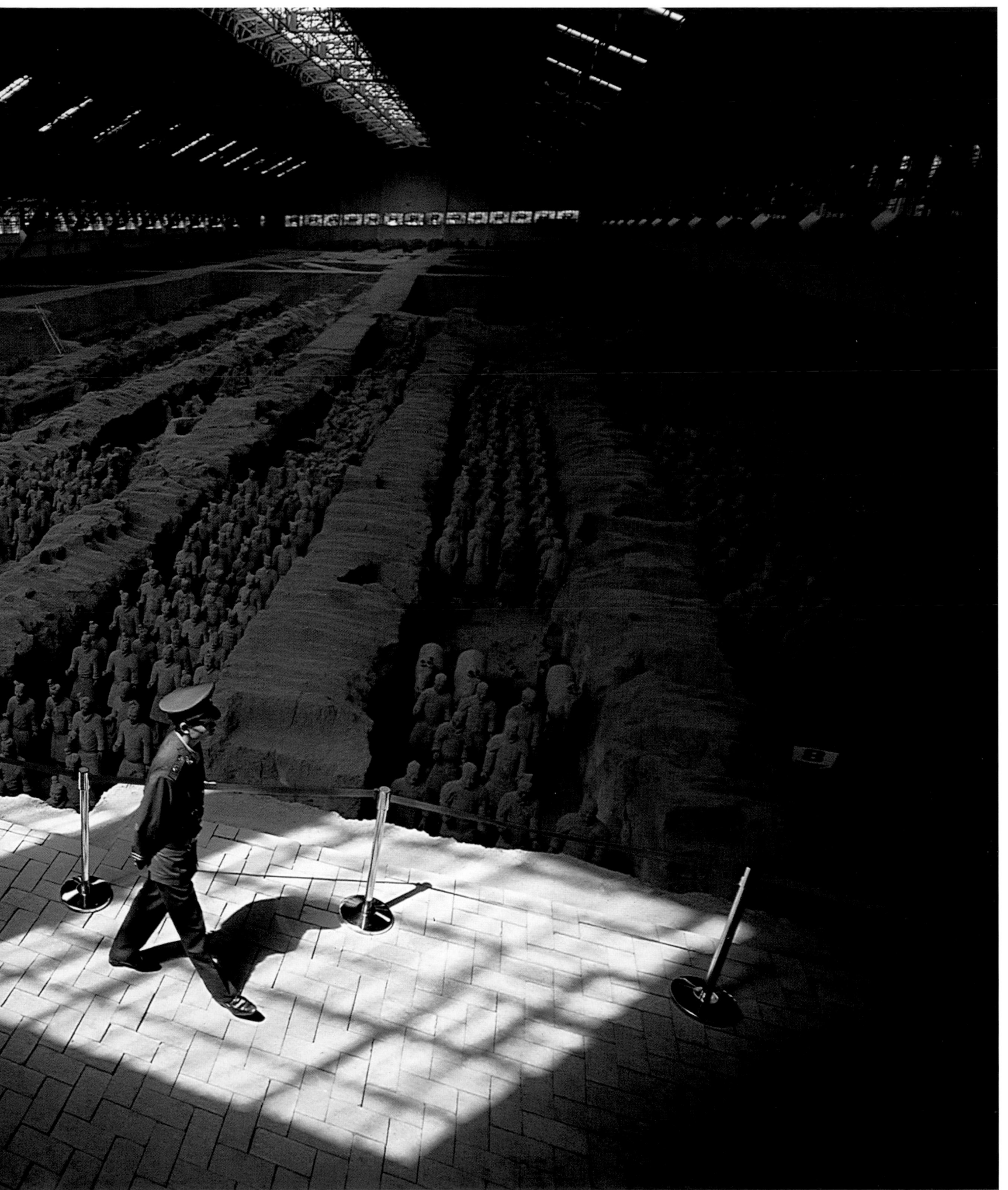

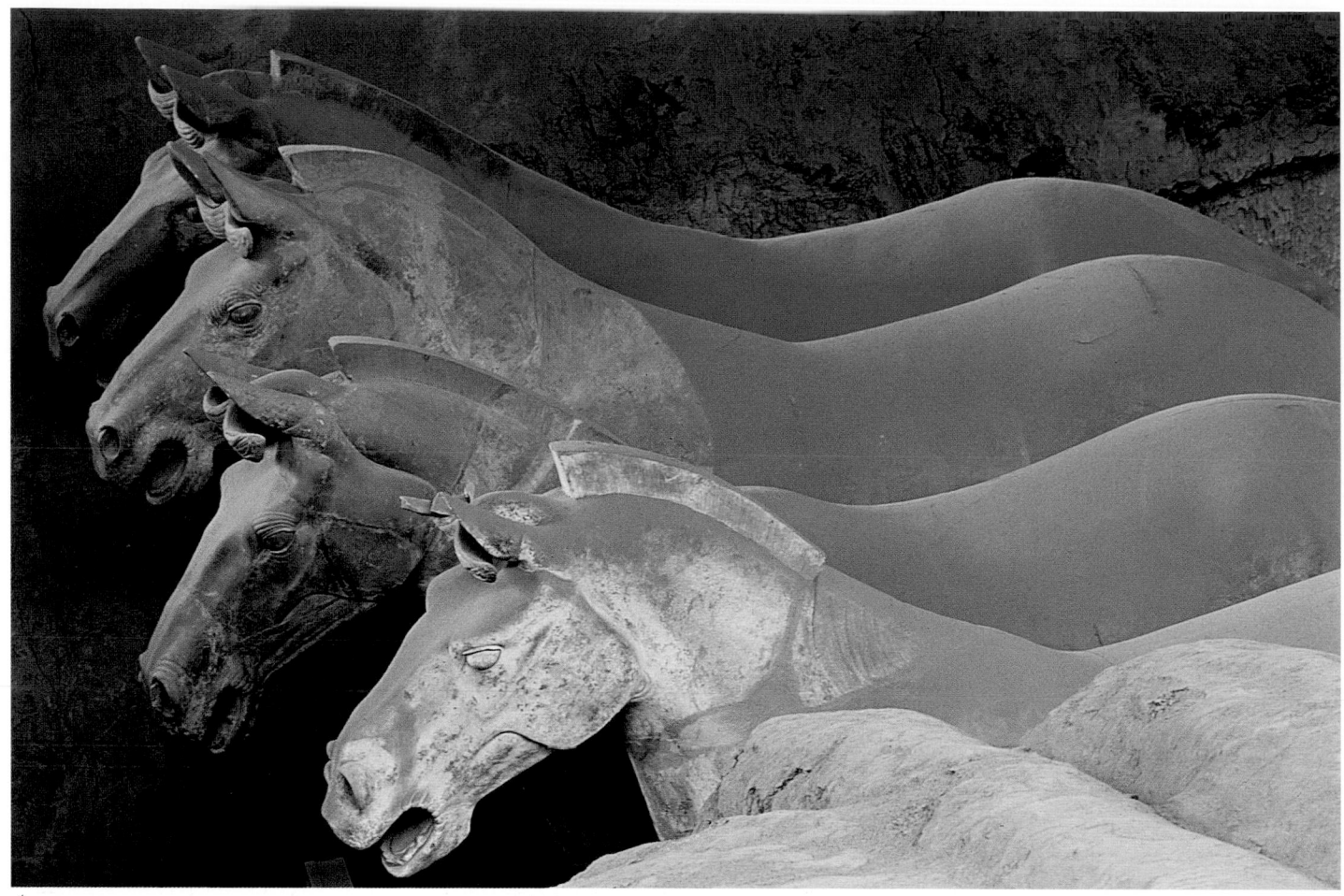

1

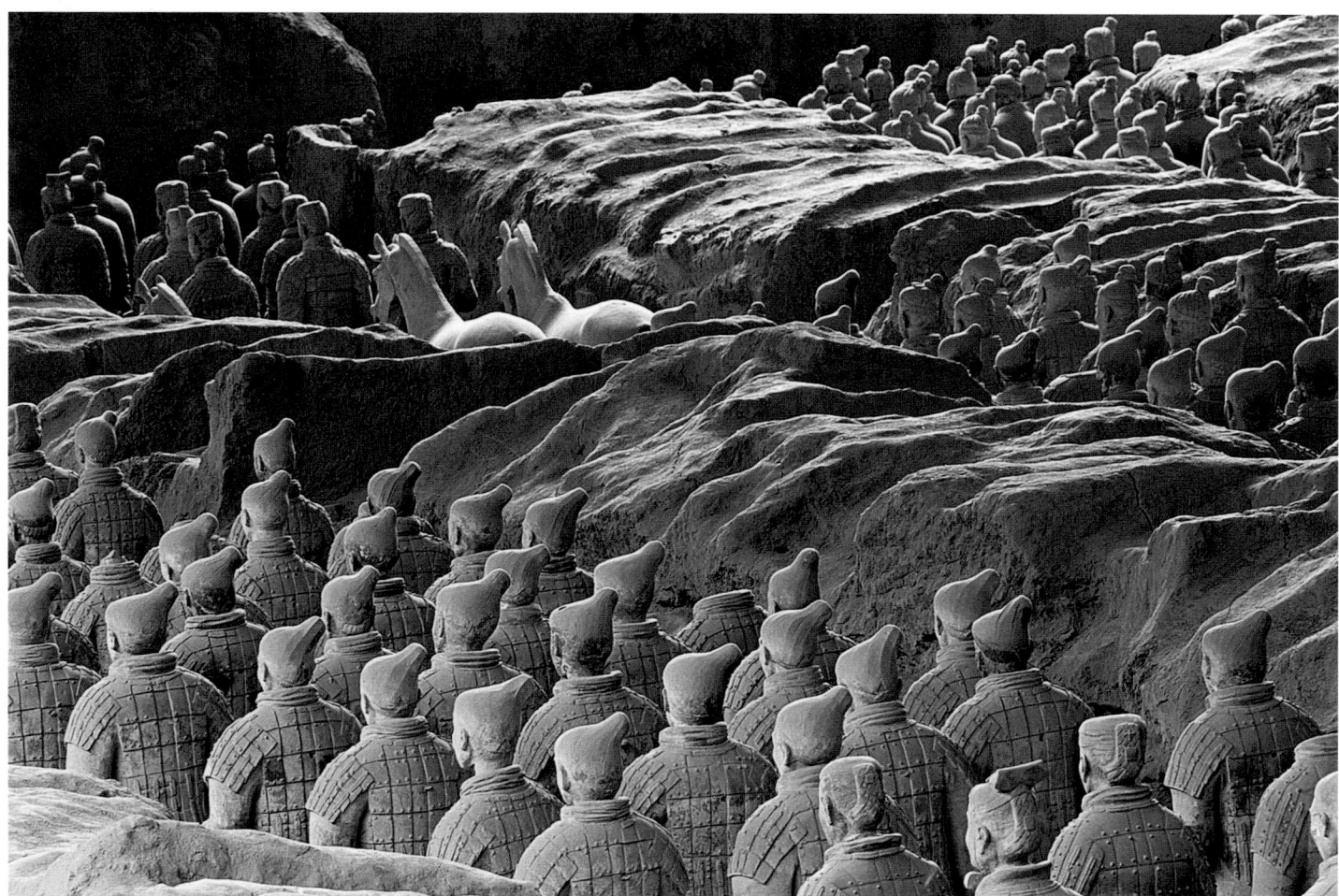

2

THE ARMY OF TERRACOTTA WARRIORS

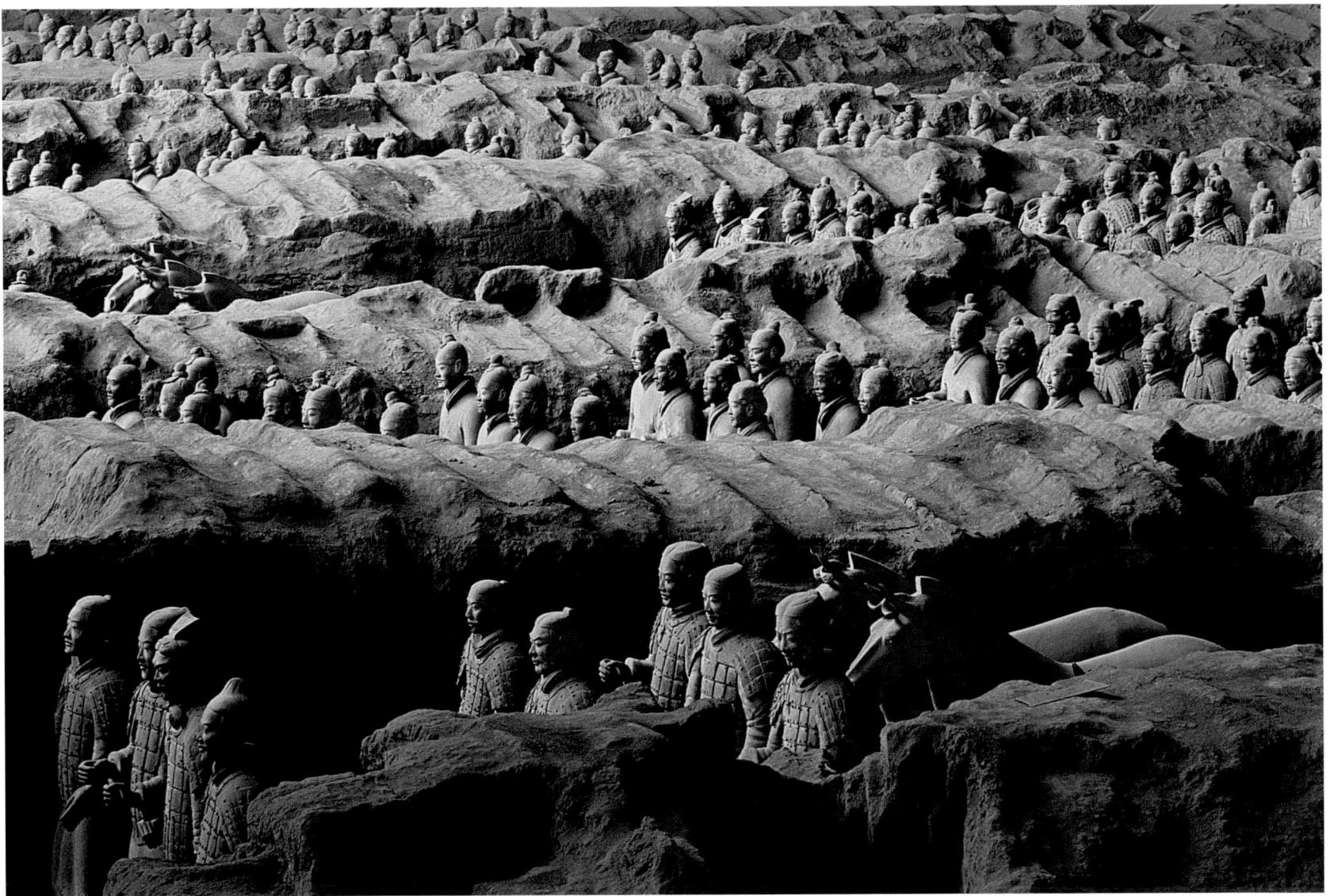

3

THE TOMB OF QIN SHI HUANG'DI, the first Emperor of China, was discovered by accident in May 1974 by local peasants digging a well in the northern foothills of Mount Li'shan, 35 kilometres (22 miles) east of Xi'an. The terracotta fragments they found started the largest archaeological excavations in China's history. Archaeologists believe the entire gravesite covers 114,260 square metres (1.2 million square feet), with only a 960-square-metre (10,300-square-foot) section excavated so far. In 246 BCE, a 13-year-old boy named Ying Zheng ascended to the throne of Qin, one of the seven Warring States vying for dominance amid the chaos that would emerge as China. By the time he died in 210 BCE he had established an administrative structure and legal system, standardized language, writing, weights, measures and money, built the Great Wall and created the Middle Kingdom. He also burned books and delighted in torturing and killing his critics. [1] [2] [3] Pit Number One of his mausoleum speaks eloquently of one visionary's megalomania and the genius of a people who had toiled under his rule.

THE SILK ROAD

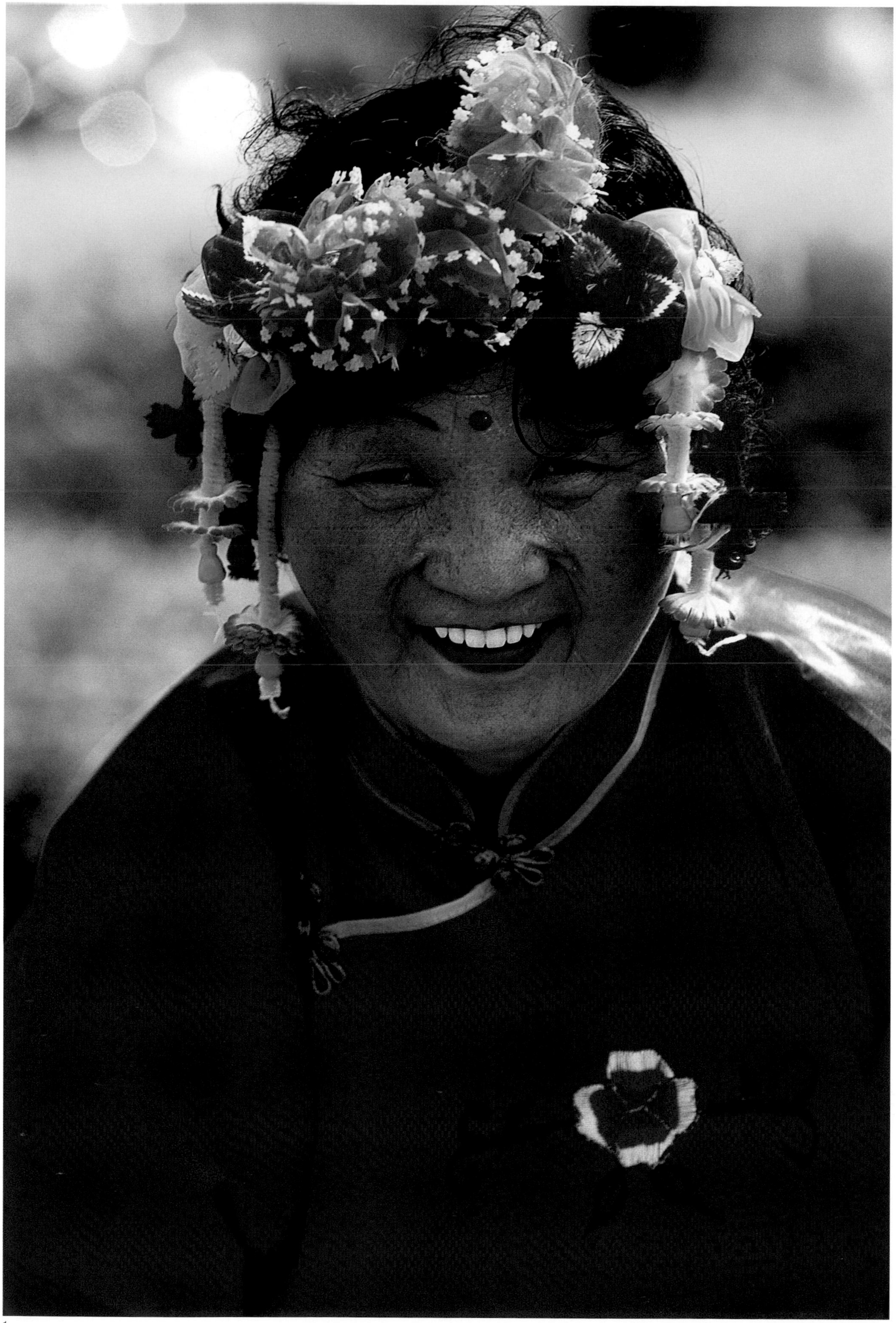

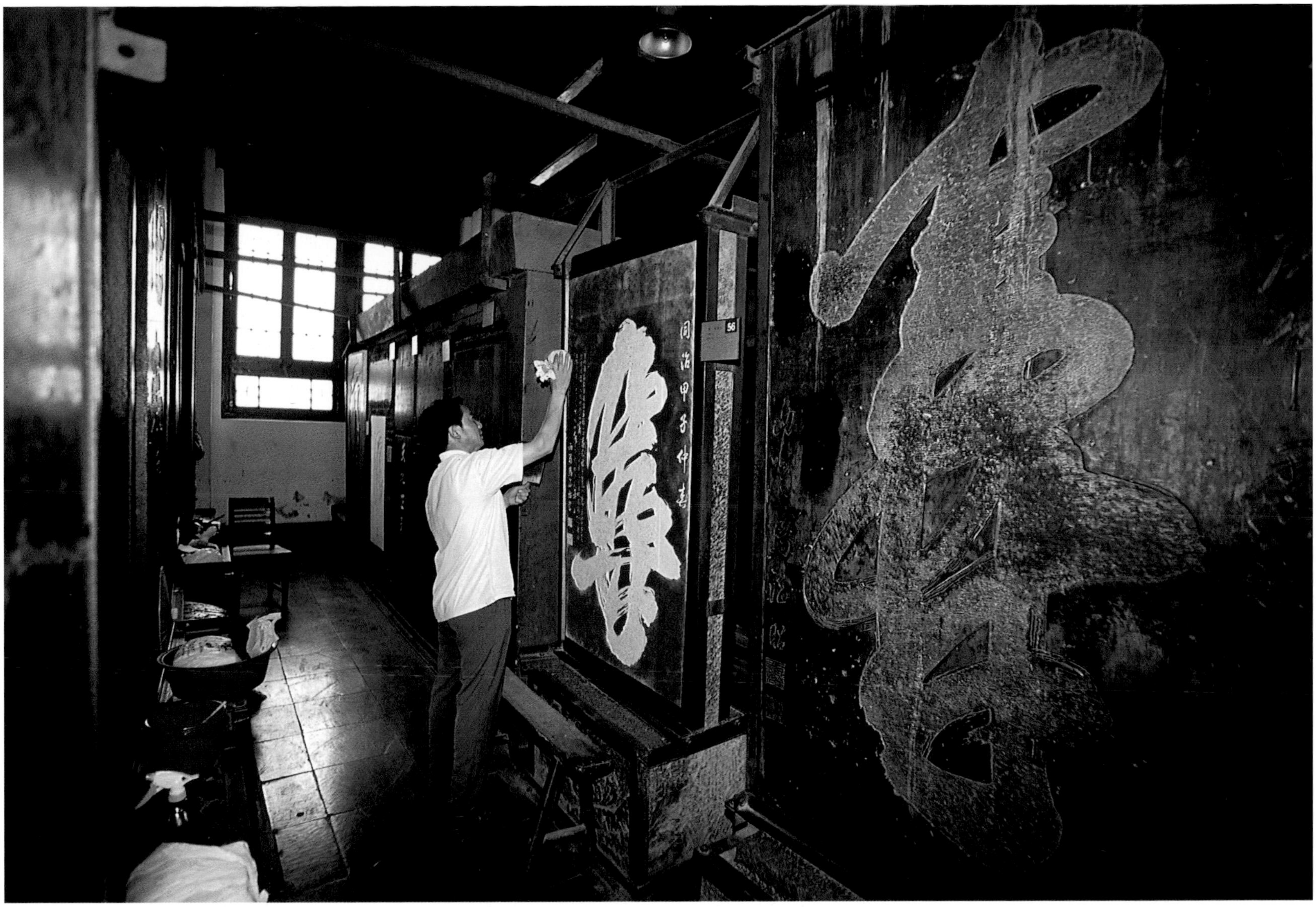

2

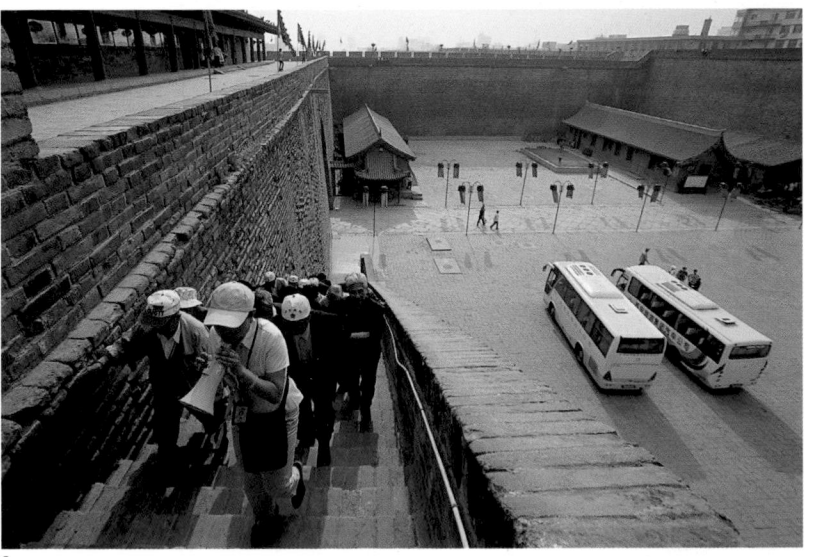

3

THE CAPITAL OF SIX DIFFERENT DYNASTIES, the city of Xi'an remained for over a thousand years in the eye of the stormy upheavals that characterized the dramatic evolution of Chinese civilization – from the rise of the Han Dynasty in 206 BCE through to the fall of the Tang Dynasty in 906 CE. At the height of the Tang Dynasty, one of the most outward-looking eras in China's history, Xi'an reached the zenith of its cultural supremacy as the eastern terminus of the Silk Road. With its gates wide open to the influences of the intellectual, technological and religious knowledge flowing freely between world powers, the city presided over an unprecedented fusion of all the diverse cultures connected by the silk routes; the impact of which continues to resonate through modern Xi'an more than a millennium later. [1] A lady from a Shaan'xi folk dancing troupe. [2] A museum technician making a stone rubbing in the Forest of Steles, where Chinese history is recorded in 2,300 carved stone tablets dating from the Han Dynasty. [3] Tourists climb the 12-metre (40-foot) high Ming city walls, built on the foundations of the Tang Dynasty's Forbidden City.

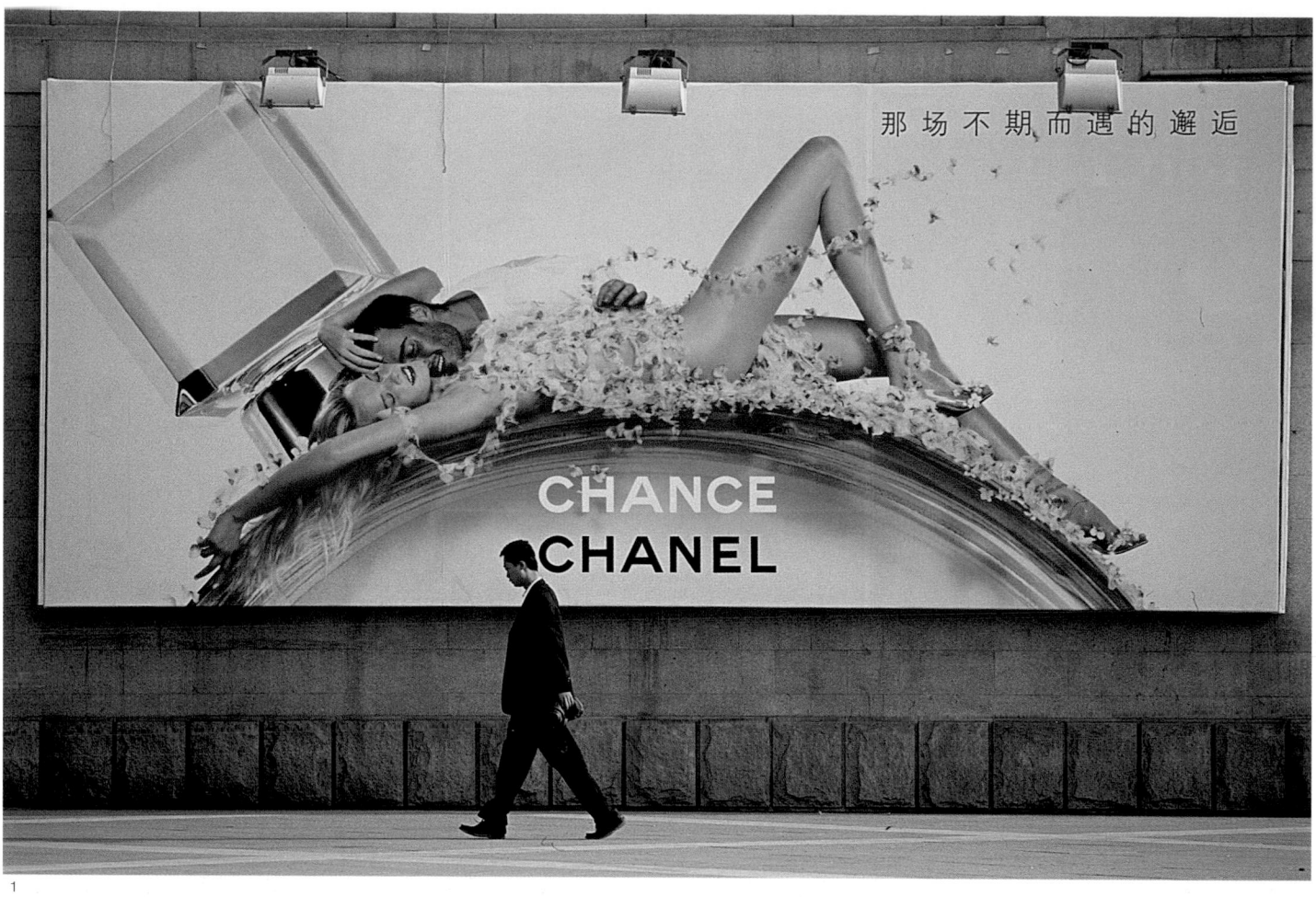

那场不期而遇的邂逅

1

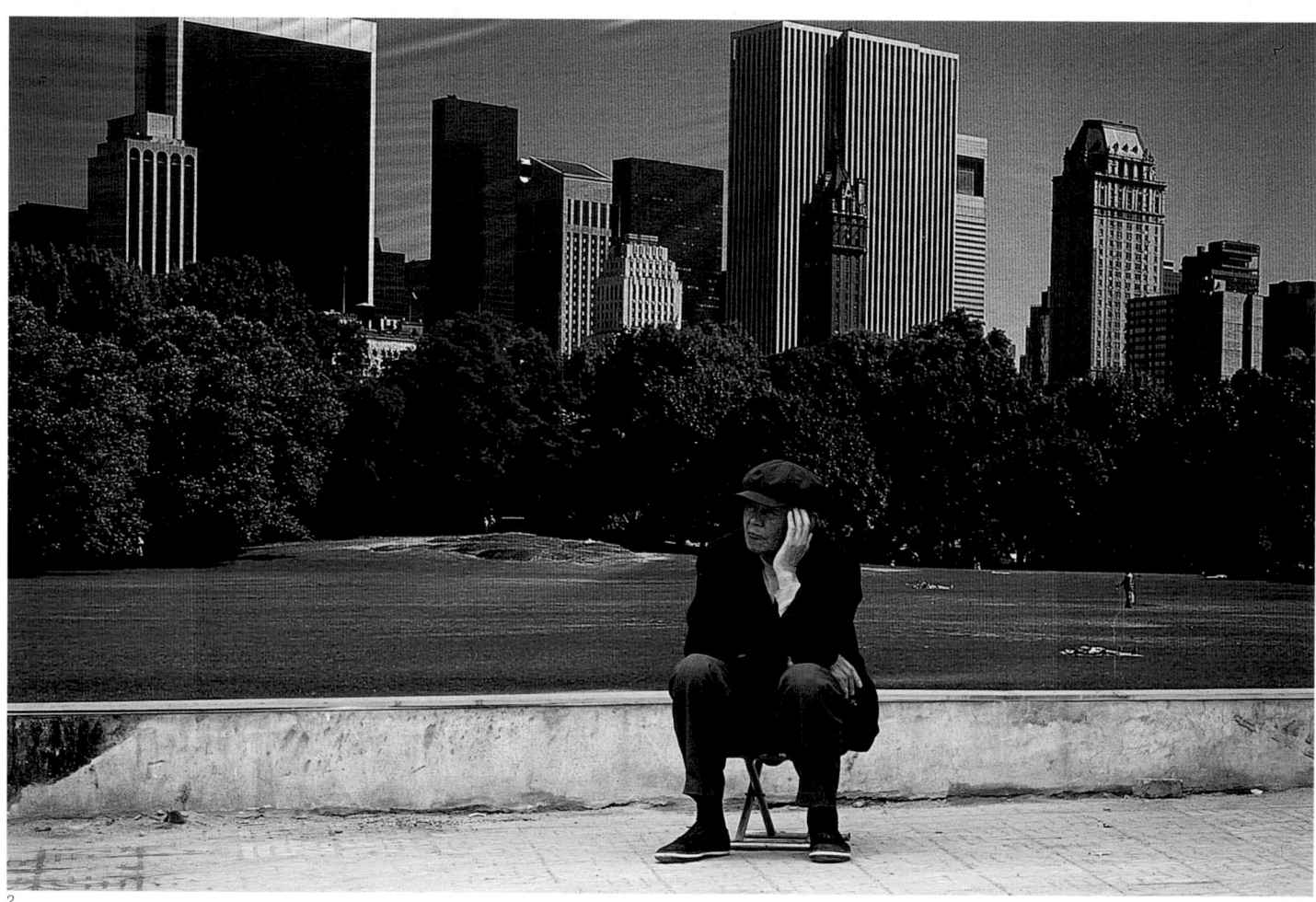

2

THE DRUM TOWER ROUNDABOUT

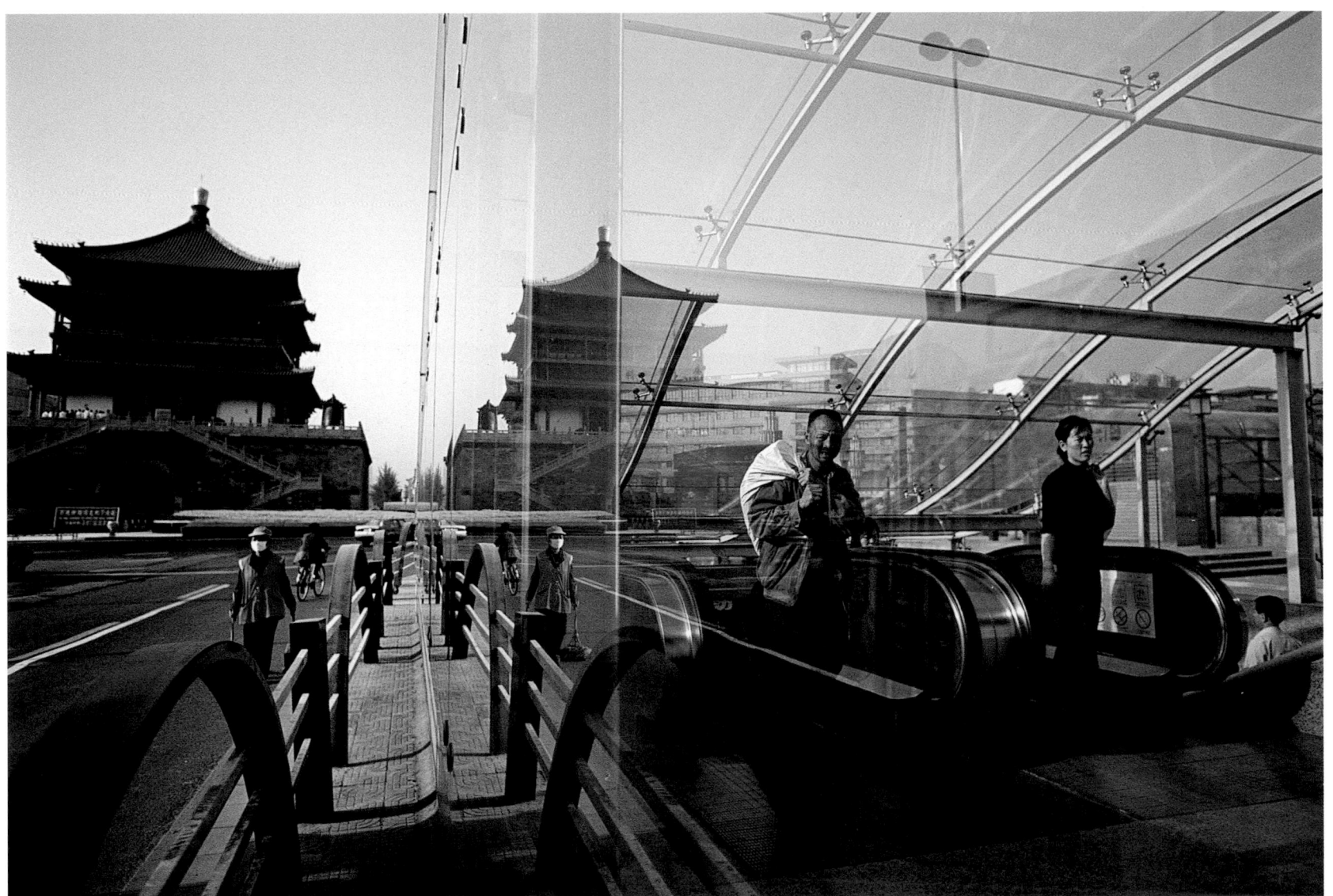

3

THE FAME OF THE TERRACOTTA ARMY overshadows Xi'an's many other treasures dating from its glory days when it was known as Chang'an – the City of Eternal Peace. In terms of quality, quantity and antiquity, Xi'an's cultural and architectural relics and remains far outstrip those of any other city in China. A local taxi driver once lamented to me that his beloved city will never have an underground mass transit system because "the whole damn place is an archeological site, and you can't dig a hole in your own yard without finding something." As I watched the downtown traffic crawling through the canyon of office towers towards [3] the Drum Tower roundabout from on top of the Ming Dynasty city gate, impressed by how well the old blended with the new, I could not help but wonder what Bei'jing would be like now if Mao had not given the order to tear down the old city walls. Some residents remain unimpressed by [1] the luxury brands and [2] the real-estate dreams that are trying to muscle their way into the landscape of their historical city.

THE SILK ROAD

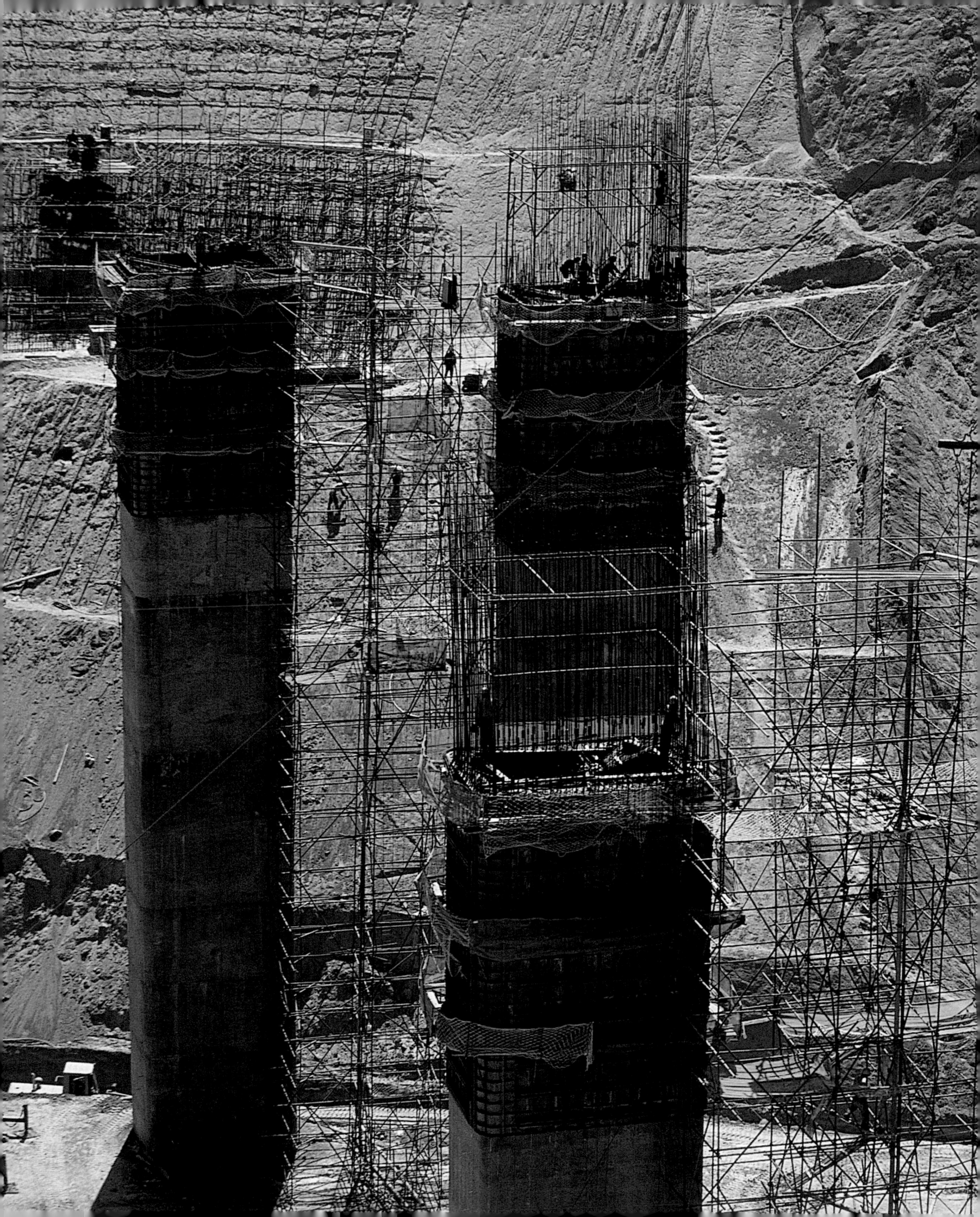

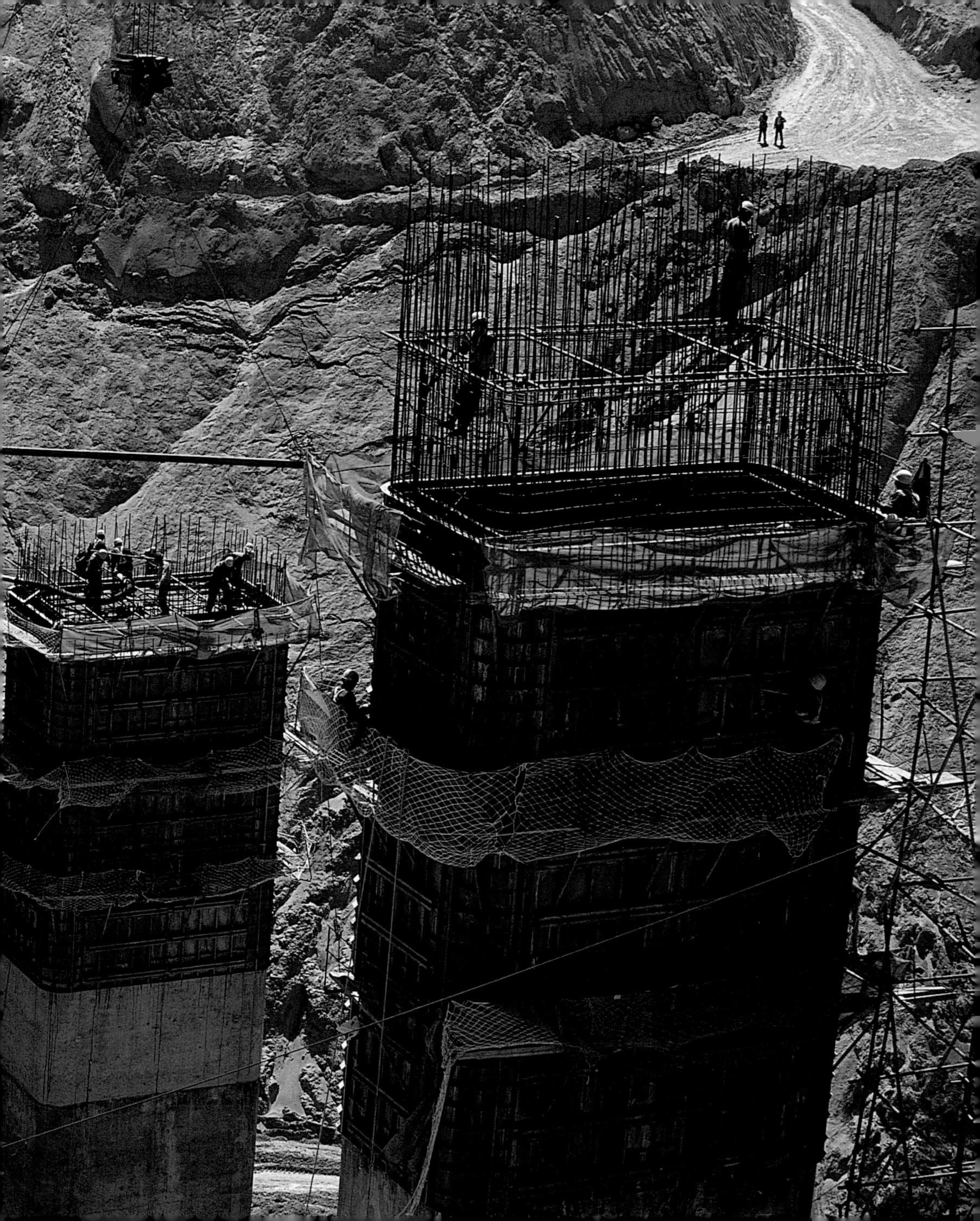

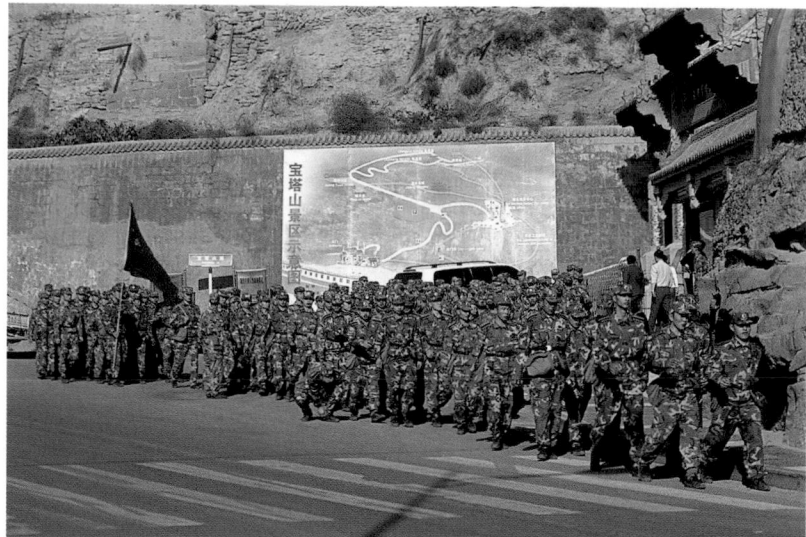

1

2

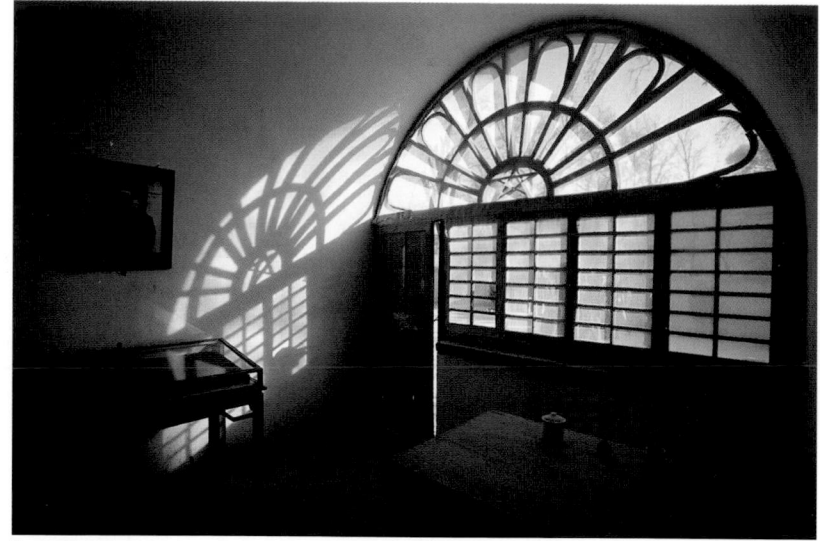

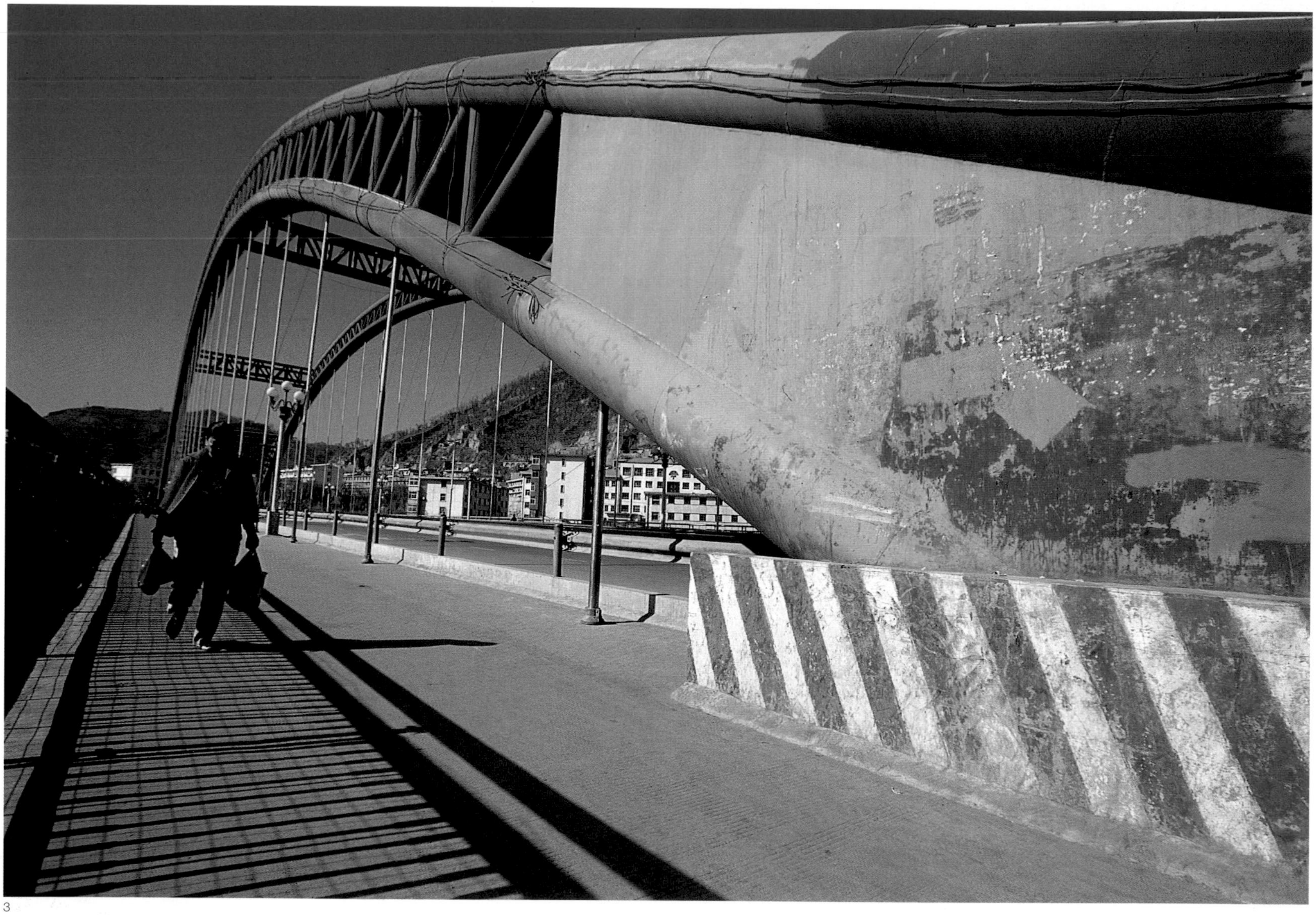

3

RED TOUR 2005

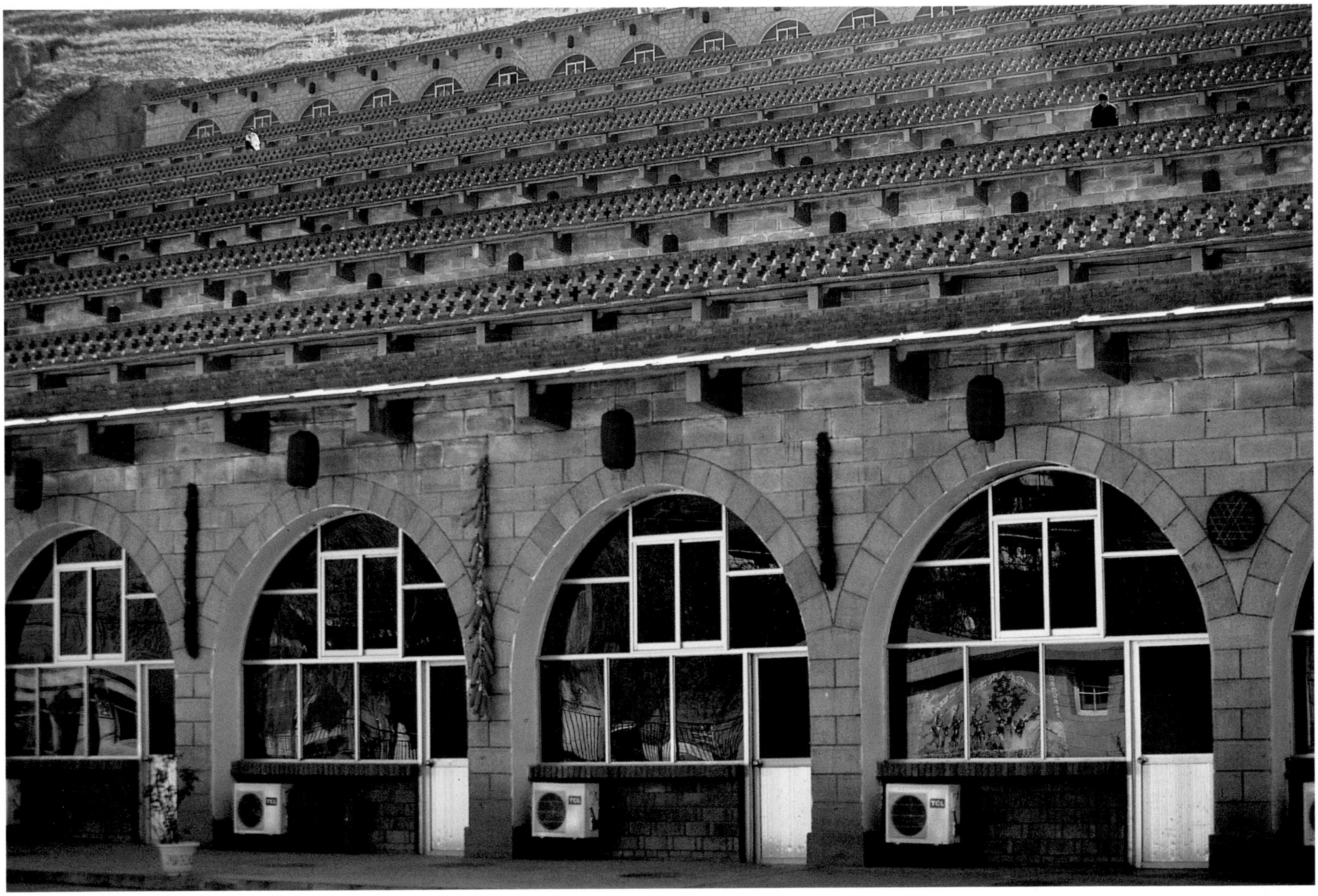

4

AS THE END OF THE LONG MARCH, Yan'an serves as the spiritual heart and key pilgrimage site for Chinese communists. The Red Army arrived here in tatters in the autumn of 1935. Of the 90,000 men and women who had left Jiang'xi a year earlier, only 20,000 survived the 8,000-kilometre (5,000-mile) epic trek across some of China's most treacherous terrain. Yan'an is the highlight in the 'Red Tour of 2005' itinerary – a campaign aimed at luring tourist dollars into China's impoverished hinterland. [1] New PLA recruits on an 'educational tour' to the Cradle of the Revolution. [2] The living room of Chairman Mao's cave dwelling at the Yang'jia'ling Revolution Headquarters Site, where he first met General George Marshall in 1946; the US unwittingly rescued the communists from the brink of defeat by trying to stop the civil war. [3]The new bridge across the Yan'he River. [4] A recently completed cave hotel in the loess hills above the city, awaiting the tide of Red tourists. [PRECEDING PAGES] A major motorway under construction over the gorges of the loess plateau.

THE SILK ROAD

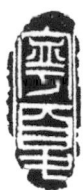

NING'XIA
HUI AUTONOMOUS REGION

LOCATION
Latitude 35°14'–39°14'N
Longtitude 104°17'–109°39'E

AREA 66,400 km² (25,637 sq miles)

GEOGRAPHY Ning'xia is dominated by the Huang'he (Yellow) River and its tributaries. The fertile Ning'xia Plain, formed by the Huang'he's alluvial deposits, bisects the region's north. The south is dominated by a loess plateau, fringed to the west by the Liu'pan range. All of the region is more than 1,000 m above sea level, with the highest point reaching 3,556 m.

CLIMATE Ning'xia has a temperate continental climate, giving long cold winters and short hot summers. Temperatures in January average between -10°C and -7°C, climbing to between 17°C and 24°C in July. The lowest recorded temperature is -32.6°C and the highest is 41.4°C. Annual rainfall ranges from 190 mm to 700 mm.

POPULATION 5.87 million (end 2004)

MAJOR CITIES Yin'chuan (capital), Tianshuibou, Shi'zui'shan, Xi'ji

AGRICULTURE The region's well-irrigated grasslands make livestock its most important agricultural sector. Rice, sorghum, beans and fruit also thrive, while the rivers produce carp and freshwater shrimp and crab.

MAIN INDUSTRIES Coal and gypsum mining, and oil and natural gas extraction, are the main heavy industries. Lighter industries include textile, paper and food processing.

ANNUAL PER CAPITA INCOME (2005)
Disposable income of urban residents:
RMB 8,093 (US$1,010)
Net income of rural residents:
RMB 2,508 (US$313)

HISTORICAL AND SCENIC SITES
Xi'xia Tomb, He'lan Shan, the 108 Dagobas, Baisikou's twin pagodas, the Great Wall.

FOOD Ning'xia cooking reflects the region's diverse cultures, and is heavily influenced by the Muslim dietary restrictions of its Hui community. Noted dishes include roast whole sheep, mutton with Wolfberries, steamed Dove fish and deep-fried dough twists.

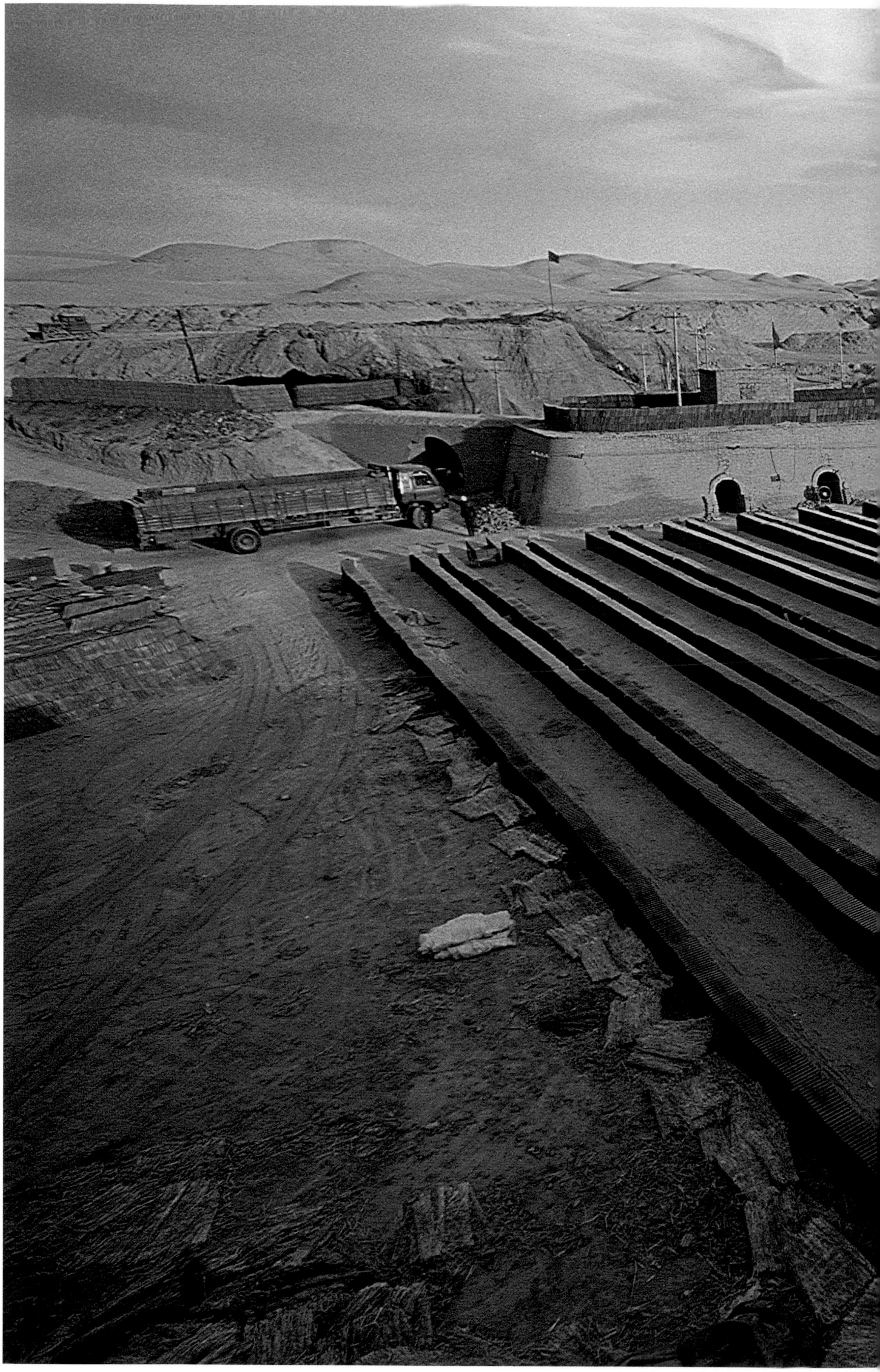

[RIGHT] A tile factory near the Ning'xia–Gan'su border at sunset.

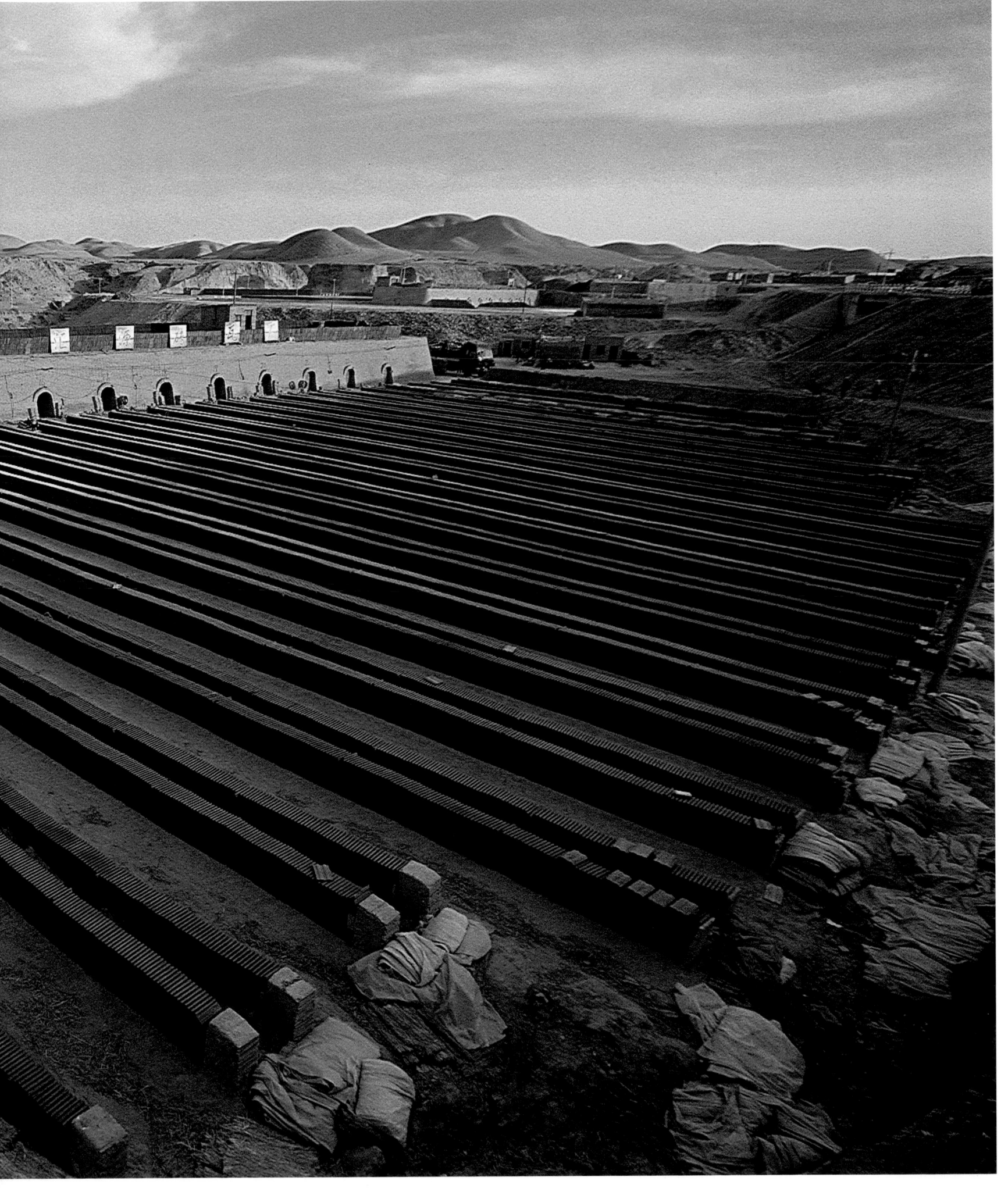

1

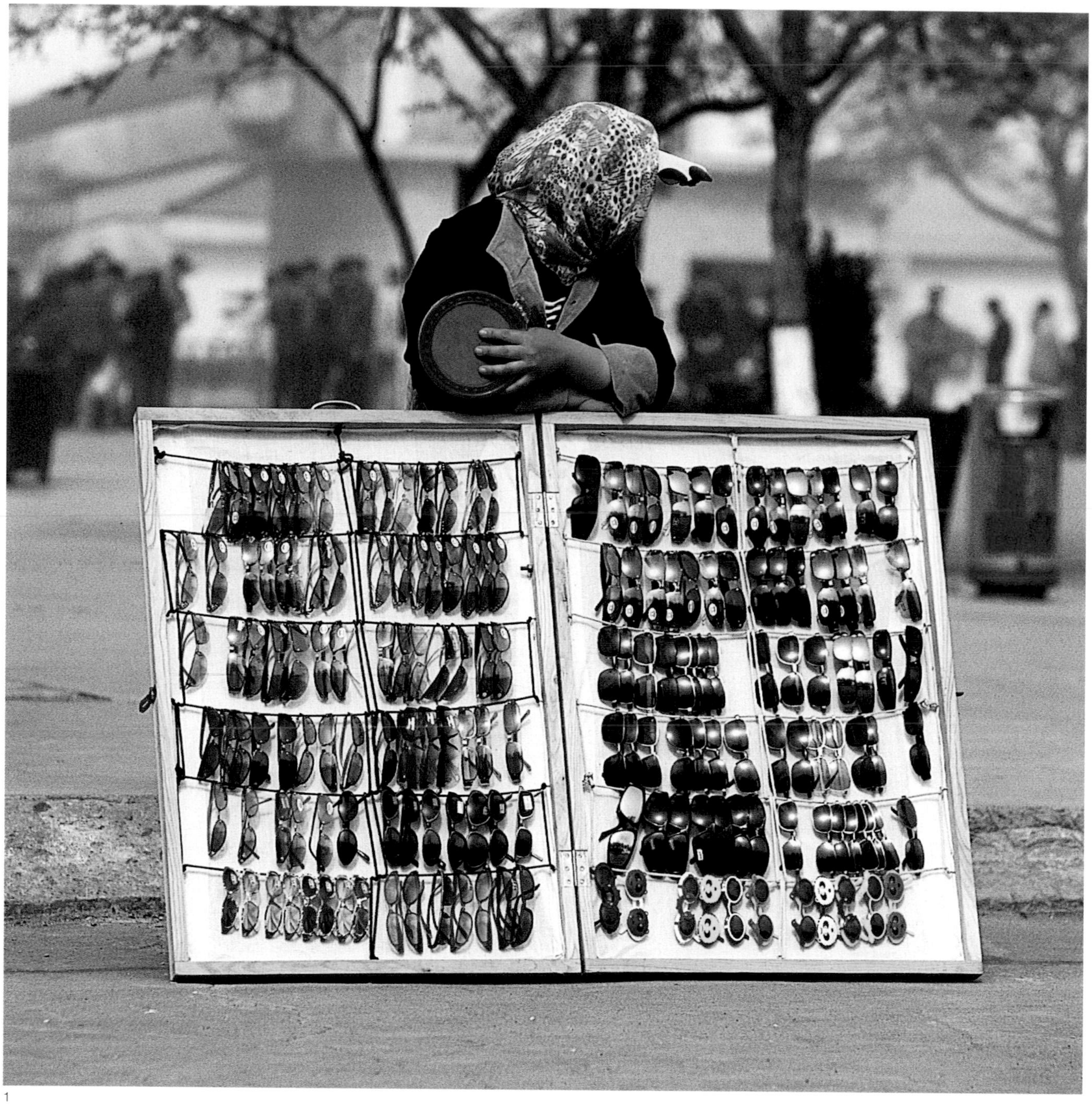

NING'XIA PROVINCE IS SHAPED LIKE AN ARMLESS TORSO with its head thrown back in agony trying to push itself up and away from the grip of Gan'su and Shaan'xi. The 'head' of the province burrows into Inner Mongolia to the north, with the Yellow River slicing east to west across its 'face' to provide abundant water in this arid region. To the northwest the He'lan'shan mountains shelter much of the province from the harsh Mongolian deserts. Or at least that's the theory. We ran into a massive sandstorm just outside the capital Yin'chuan (Silver Stream) that was blowing out of the northwest with total disregard for the principles of mountain barriers. Our inexperienced local guide completely lost her sense of direction and we drove around in circles for hours, seeking directions from anyone we could find along country roads that we could not find on the map – including [2] [3] these farmers transporting artfully stacked hay. We eventually reached [1] Sha'hu Lake, a scenic spot famous for its giant salamanders, which turned out to be just another local tourist trap.

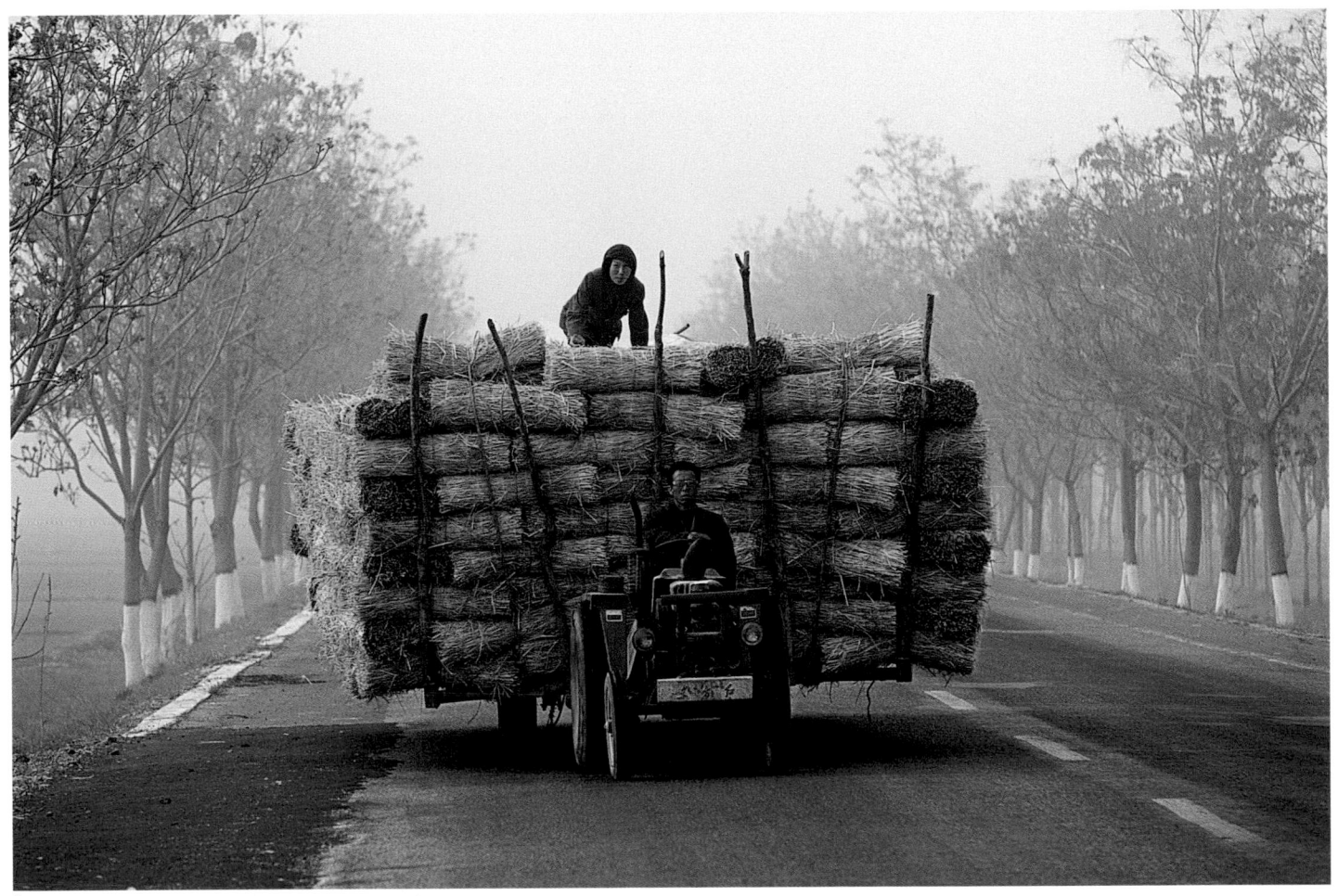

2

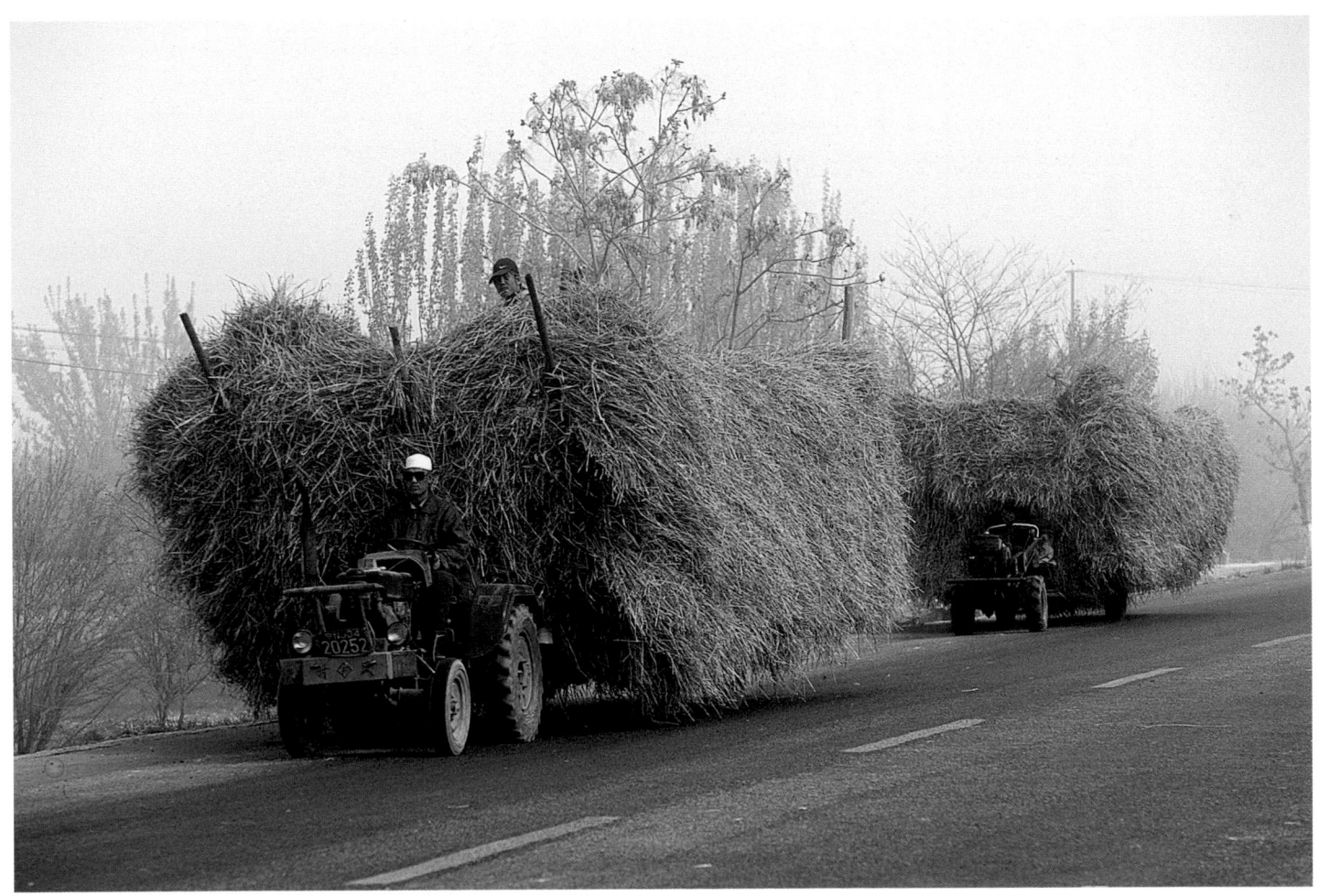

3

XI'XIA ROYAL TOMBS

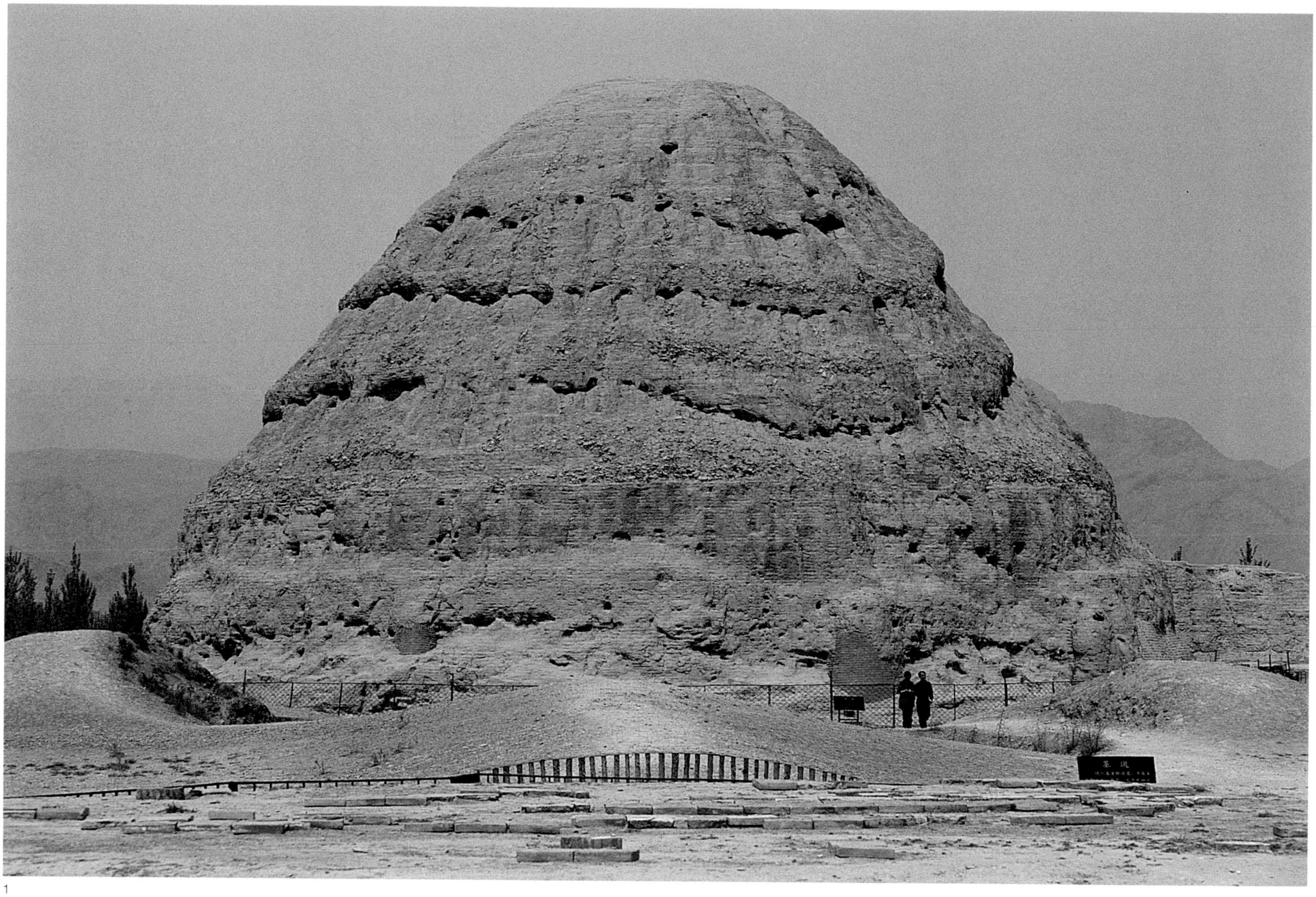

THE XI'XIA (WESTERN SUMMER) KINGDOM was founded in 1038 by Li Yuan'hao, a descendant of a lost tribe of Tibetans who had been chased off the plateau and fled north into Mongolia at the end of the 10th Century. Known as the Tan'guts to the Chinese, they were initially regarded as just another of the troublesome barbarian tribes the Great Wall was built to keep out. But the Buddhist kingdom soon proved itself to be a force to be reckoned with, growing rapidly in strength and size until eventually it occupied a territory that encompassed the present-day provinces of Shaan'xi, Ning'xia, Gan'su and a large slice of Mongolia, giving it control of the He'xi Corridor and Silk Road trade. After their defeat at the hands of the Mongols in 1237, the kingdom and its culture vanished into oblivion, leaving behind only the seventy tombs on the eastern slopes of the He'lan'shan Mountains, 35 kilometres (22 miles) northeast of Yin'chuan. [1] The tourist-minded locals call the Xi'xia royal tombs the 'Pyramids of China'. [2] A tile factory near the Ning'xia–Gan'su border.

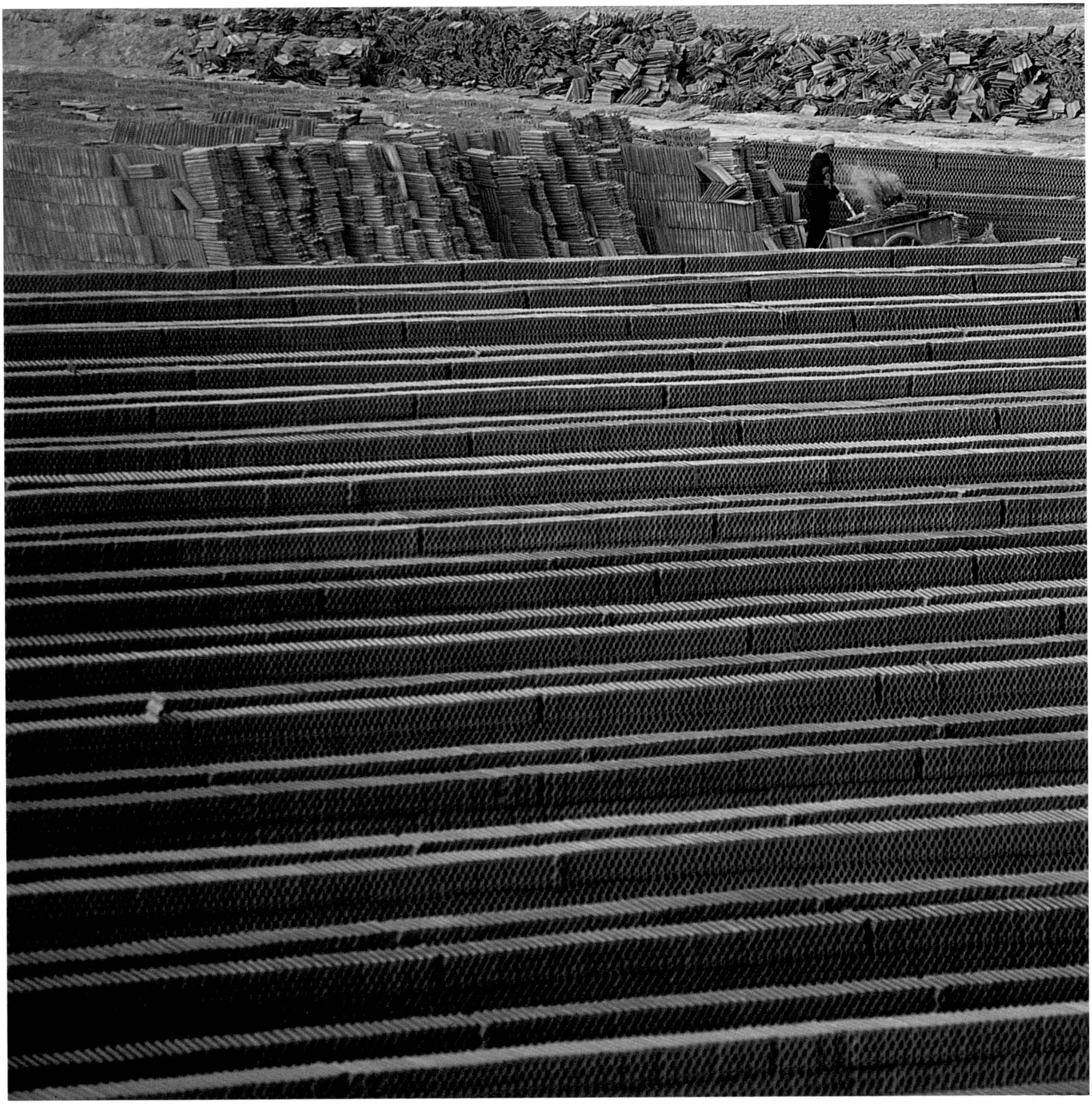

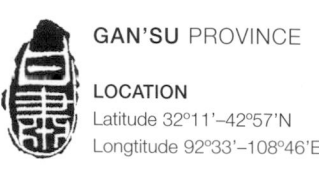

GAN'SU PROVINCE

LOCATION
Latitude 32°11'–42°57'N
Longtitude 92°33'–108°46'E

AREA 365,284 km² (141,000 sq miles)

GEOGRAPHY Gan'su is dominated by rugged mountains and deserts. The major geographic features in the province are the Huang'tu Plateau to the east, the Qi'lian Mountains and the Tibetan Plateau to the south and west and the Gobi desert to the north. Much of the province's terrain is over 1,000 m above sea level, with the peak of Qi'lian Shan (5,547 m) the highest point. The He'xi Corridor of the Silk Road passed through Gan'su, while the Huang'he (Yellow) River cuts through the south of the province.

CLIMATE Gan'su climate is caught between the temperate monsoon and the harsher characteristics of the continental weather system. Average temperatures are -14°C to 3°C in January and 22°C to 25°C in July. The highest recorded temperature is 43.6°C and the lowest is -29.1°C. Average annual rainfall is between 30 mm and 860 mm.

POPULATION 25.9445 million (end 2005)

MAJOR CITIES Lan'zhou (capital), Dun'huang, Jia'yu'guan, Wu'wei, Bai'yin, Yu'men, Zhang'ye

AGRICULTURE Cash crops include cotton, linseed oil, maize, melons, millet and wheat. Gan'su is also renowned as a source of wild herbs used in Chinese medicine.

MAIN INDUSTRIES The province's industrial base is built around mining and oil. Local mines extract antimony, chromium, cobalt, fluorite, iridium, mercury, nickel, platinum, tungsten and zinc. Lan'zhou is a heavy industrial centre with one of China's largest oil refineries while Chang'qing and Yu'men are major oil centres. There is a space-launch site near Jiu'quan and the province is thought to host elements of China's nuclear industry.

ANNUAL PER CAPITA INCOME (2005)
Disposable income of urban residents:
RMB 8,080 (US$1,008)
Net income of rural residents:
RMB 1,963 (US$245)

HISTORICAL AND SCENIC SITES
Silk Road sites include the Jia'yu'guan Pass of the Great Wall, Mogao Grottoes, Dun'huang City, Bingling Temple and Labrang Monastery.

FOOD Gan'su cuisine's most notable dishes include Lan'zhou *La'mian* (handmade noodles in a clear beef broth), Jingning roast chicken and Dun'huang *Sao'zi* noodles.

[RIGHT] The Gate of Enlightenment at Jia'yu'guan, the end of western Great Wall.

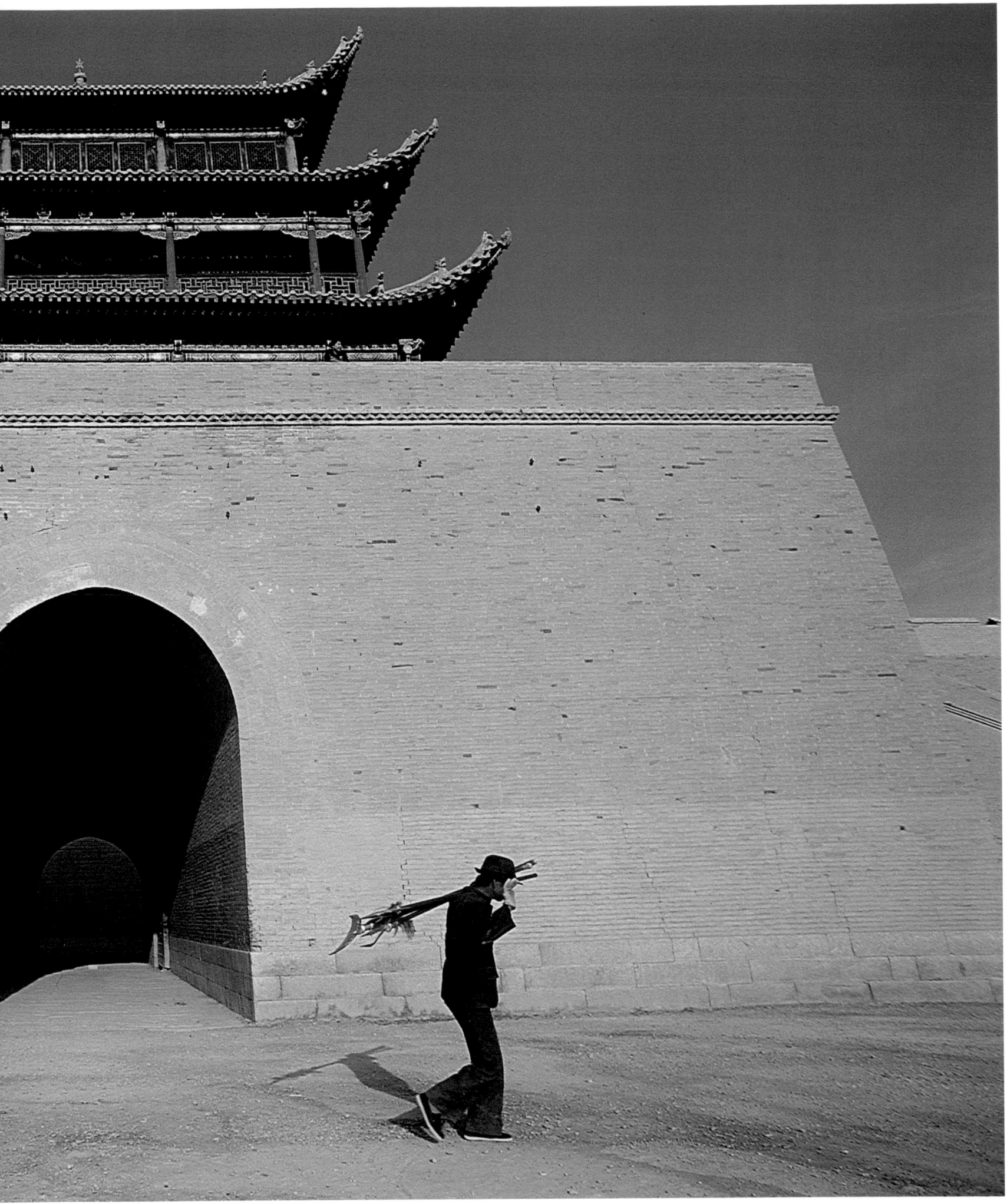

GOAT-SKIN RAFTS

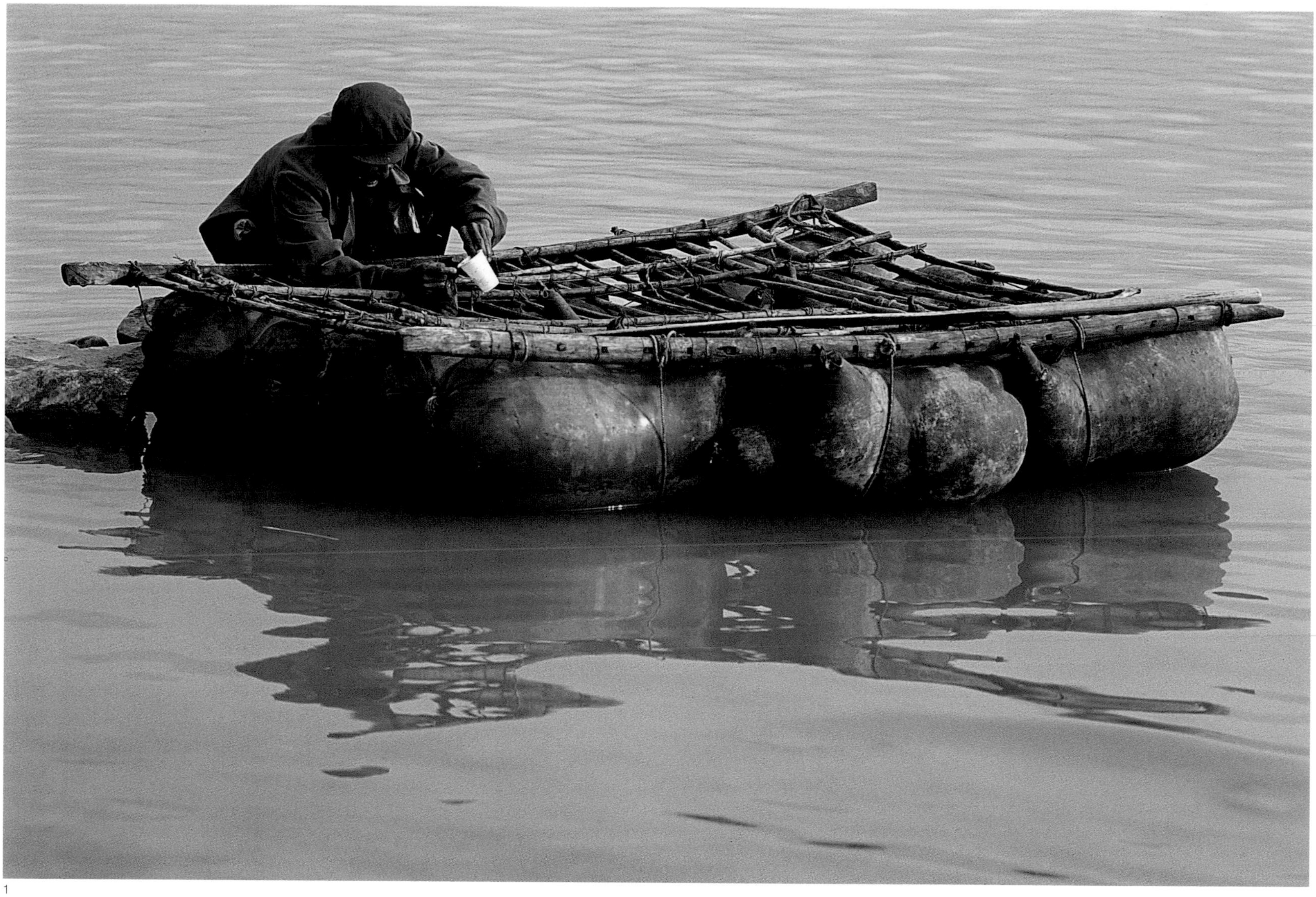

1

FOR ME, THE NAME 'LAN'ZHOU' will always be associated with just one thing: their truly excellent Beef Noodle Soup – a bowl of freshly hand-pulled noodles swimming in a steaming, delicious beef broth. But for others, the capital of Gan'su probably means a lot more. Its strategic position on the upper reaches of the Yellow River where the He'xi Corridor ends at the water's edge has made the city an important garrison since the Qin Dynasty (221–207 BCE). Lan'zhou's proximity to the southern trade routes across the Tibetan Plateau also ensured its prominence as a key transportation centre when Chinese silk became popular in the Roman Empire. [1] [2] [3] One remnant from those distant times that survives to this day is the goat-skin raft. The design of these craft is so perfect and simple, and the materials used so basic and utilitarian, that few improvements could have been made over the millennia. Though the rafts once served as a primary means of transport for goods and passengers along the Yellow River, today they are strictly a 'fairground ride' for tourists.

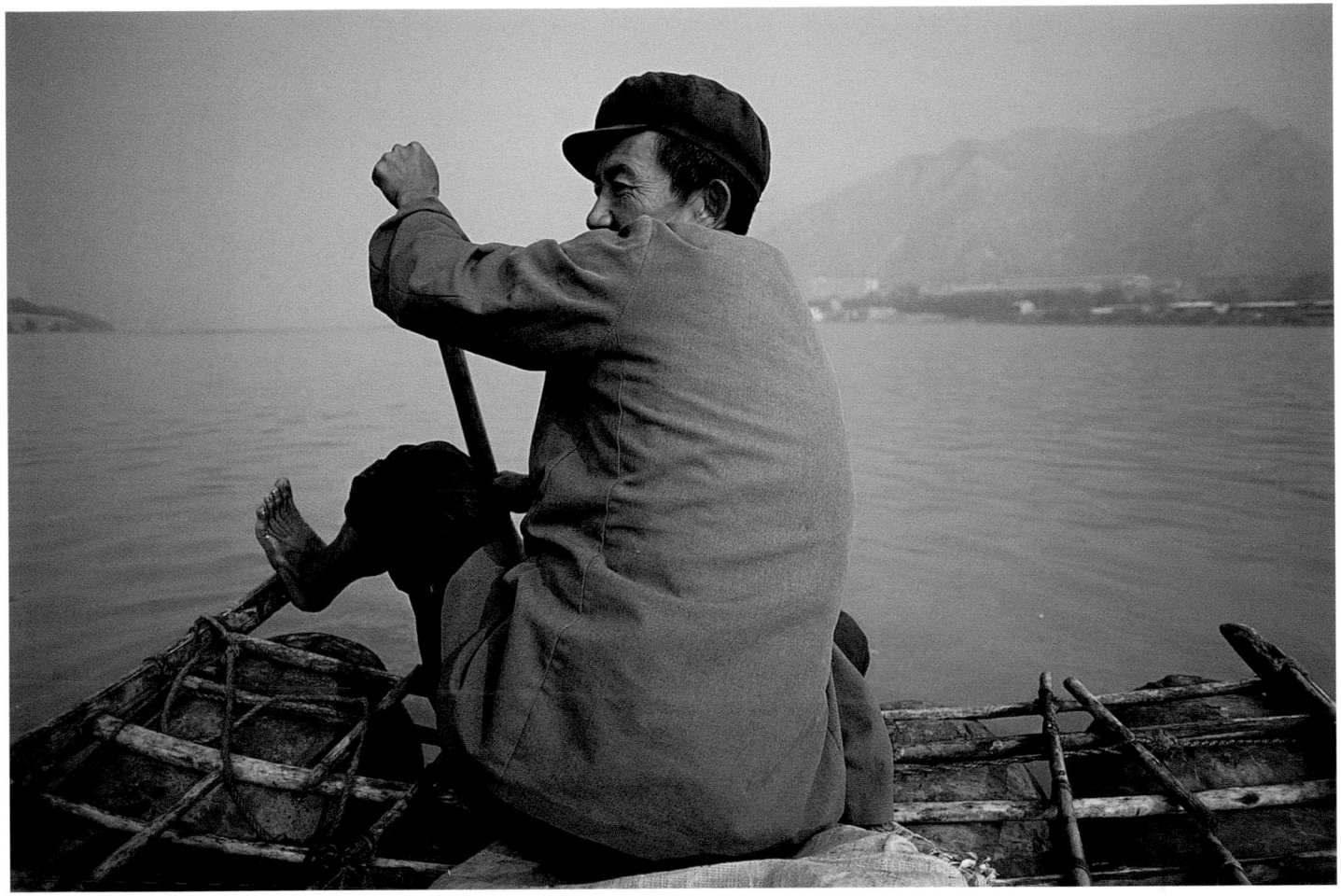

2

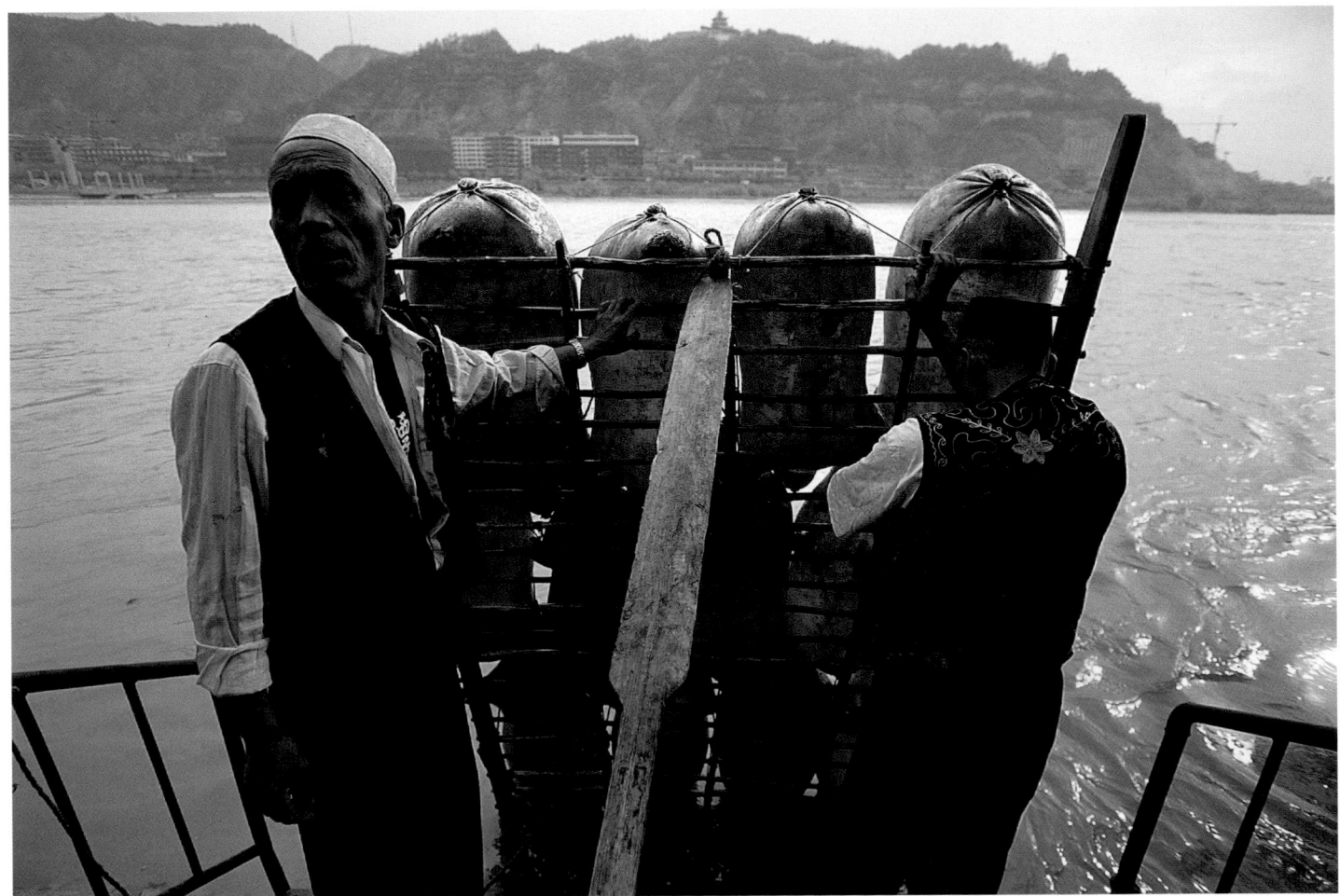

3

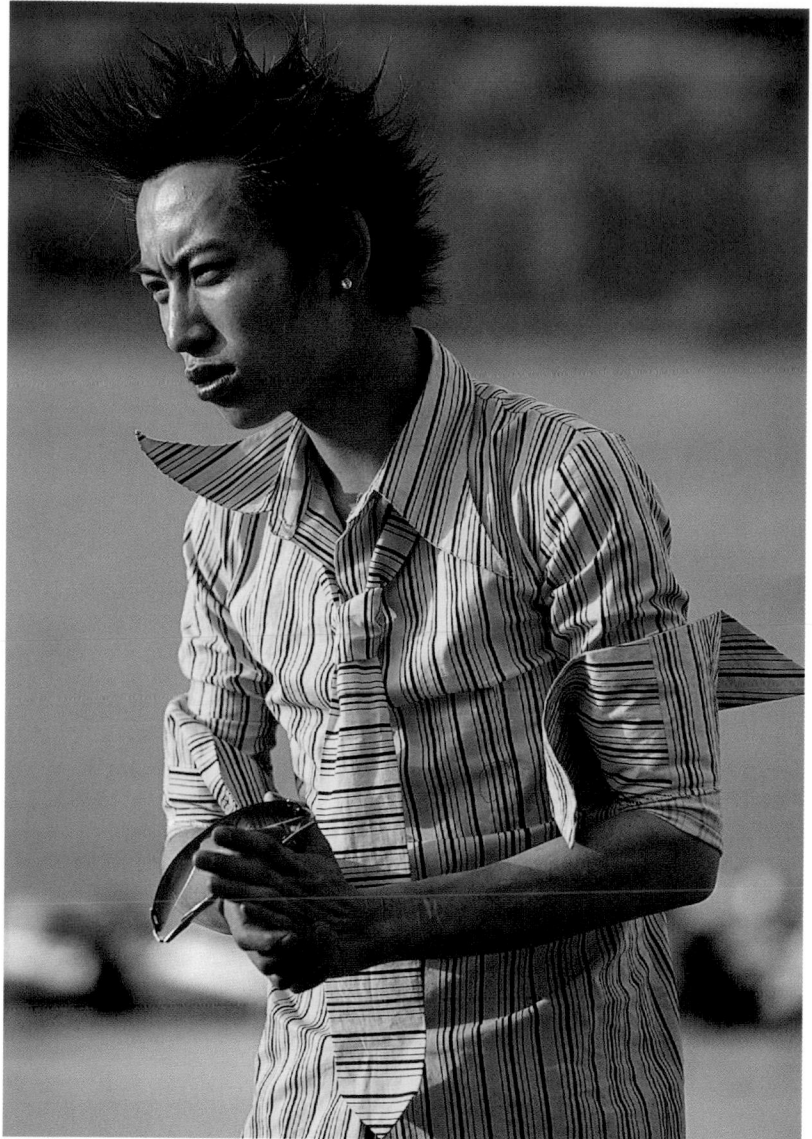

1

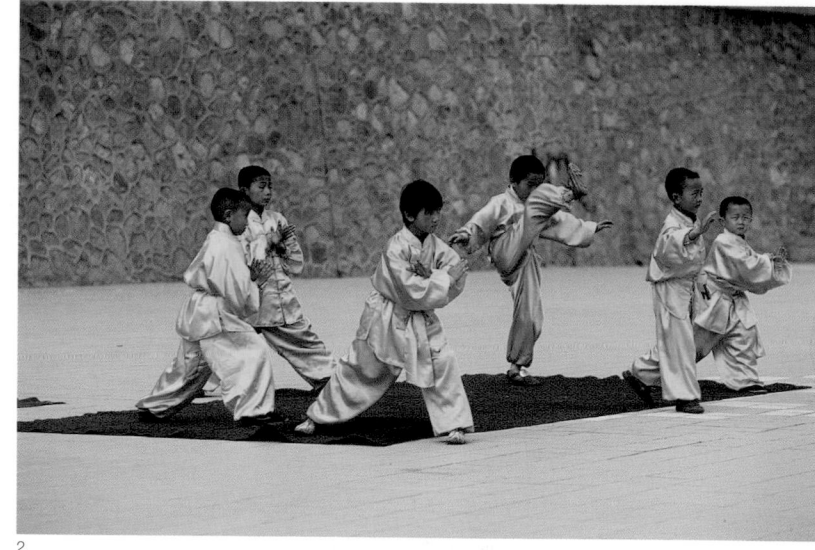

2

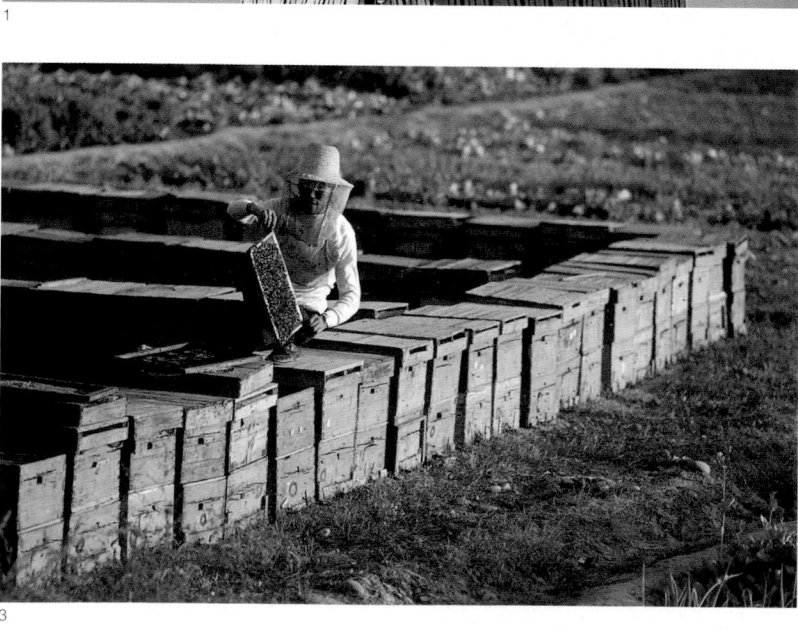

3

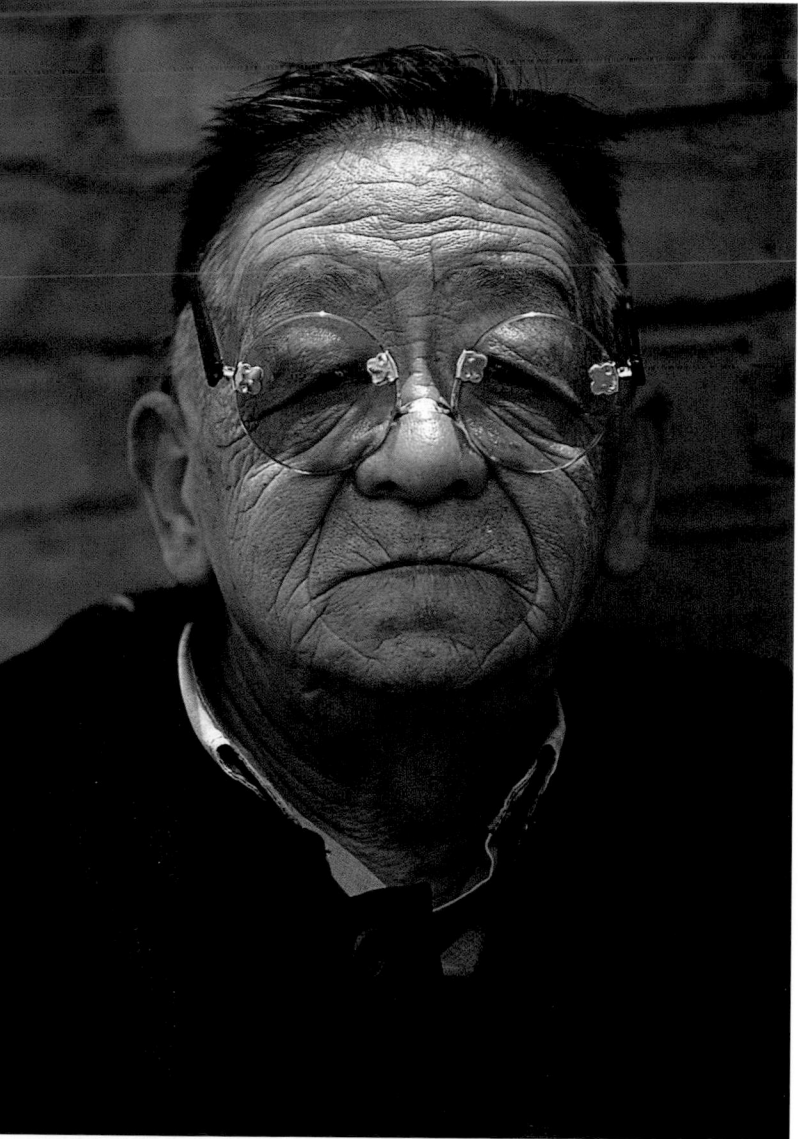

4

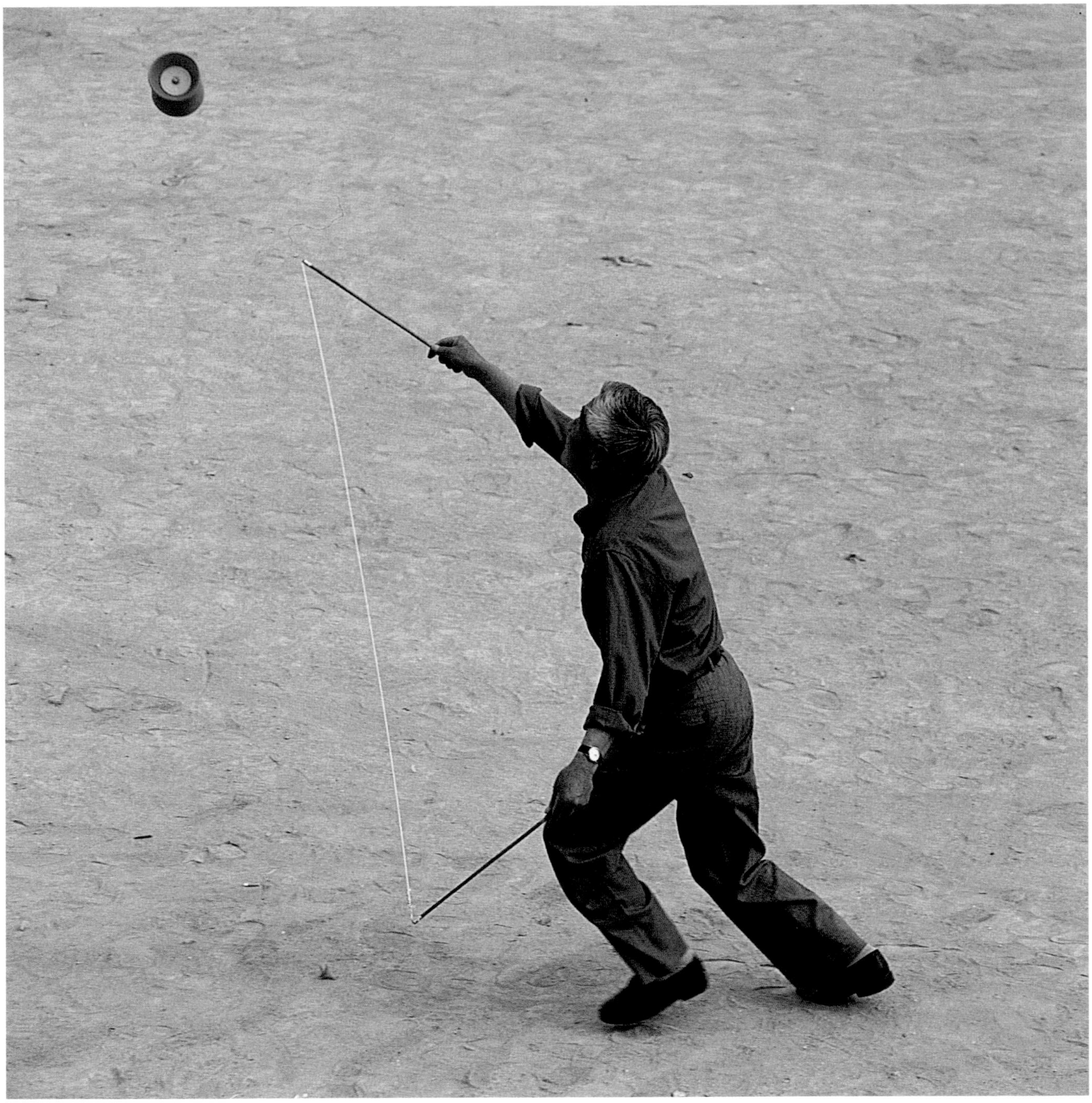

5

OVER THE CENTURIES Lan'zhou has served as a major east-west communication hub for the Silk Road and, following Khubilai Khan's conquest of China, an important link in the north-south trade routes linking South Asia, Tibet and Mongolia. This strategic crossroads city has attracted visitors from the far corners of the earth. People of every race, creed, tribe and vocation have made stopovers here on their way to somewhere else, creating, through the ages, what must be one of the most varied gene pools in China. Traces of these long-departed visitors remain etched in some of the faces on the streets of Lan'zhou. A giant motorcycle brushed past me on the crowded sidewalk before disappearing nosily into a thicket of pedestrians. Later, I saw [1] its owner and tried to guess whether he was a rock star, a gangster or a hairdresser. Meanwhile, down by the river it is [2] kung fu lessons for the children and [5] acrobatic exercises for the elderly. [3] A beekeeper in the suburbs of the city. [4] An old gentleman with Qing Dynasty spectacles.

THE SILK ROAD

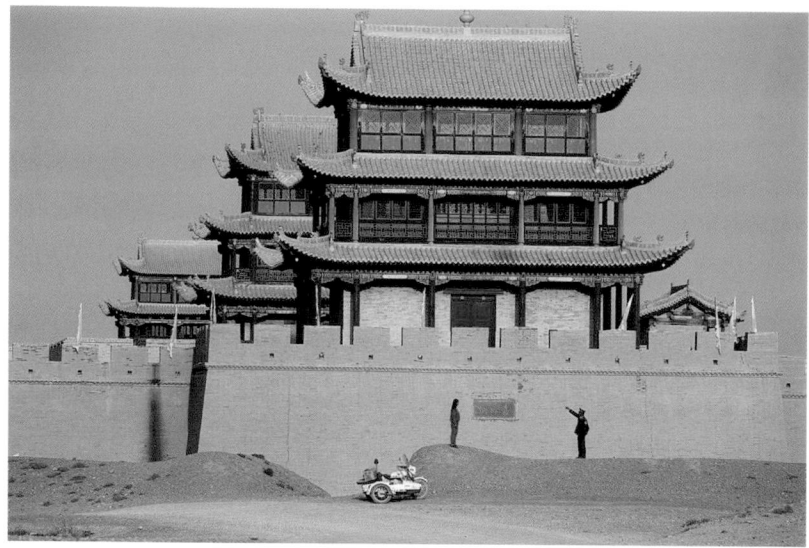

1

ALTHOUGH THE PRESENT STRUCTURE was not built until 1372, during the Ming Dynasty, the fortress of Jia'yu'guan (Barrier of the Pleasant Valley) stands at a historical site where, for centuries, garrison forts have marked the end of the Great Wall and the western frontier of the Middle Kingdom. Beyond this point, China's authority ceased and the barbarian lands began. I walked out through the western gate towards the arching sun. The pancake-flat desert stretched across a sea of jagged rocks into infinity, as waves of shimmering heat rising up from the bone-dry ground obliterated the horizon. Several hundred metres away stood a pavilion, inside which was a large black stone tablet that resembled the monolith the apes discovered in the movie 2001. From beyond the pavilion I turned to look at the fortress, and was immediately struck by the immense desolation and loneliness of the place. It was easy to imagine myself an ancient traveller in a camel caravan, and how it must have felt to leave the inhospitable empty quarters full of nothing but mirages to discover this dream-like structure rising out of the naked sands. I took refuge from the blazing sun in the pavilion to wait for the light to soften for my wide shot. I cannot remember what was carved on the stone tablet, but I do remember that it reminded me of *The Chariot Song* – Du Fu's brilliantly cinematic anti-war poem. The opening stanzas depict a scene of dust-filled chaos, with reluctant army conscripts marching off to the western frontier while their desperate families tried to block their way; all played against a beautifully drawn 'soundscape' of rumbling chariots, neighing horses and wailing women, whose "cries pierced the high heavens." The story unfolds with an old soldier's words to a passer-by, lamenting the fate of the conscript:

"We went north to guard the river shore at fifteen,
Then sent west to till the land at forty-four.
The elders had to show us how to wrap our heads when we first left,
Our hair was white when we returned, but we're off to the western front once again.
The blood spilled over the frontiers can fill an ocean,
Yet the martial Emperor's thirst for conquest remains unquenched."

[1] The western gate of Jia'yu'guan. [2] Gravesites near the Ming'sha dunes.

122

2

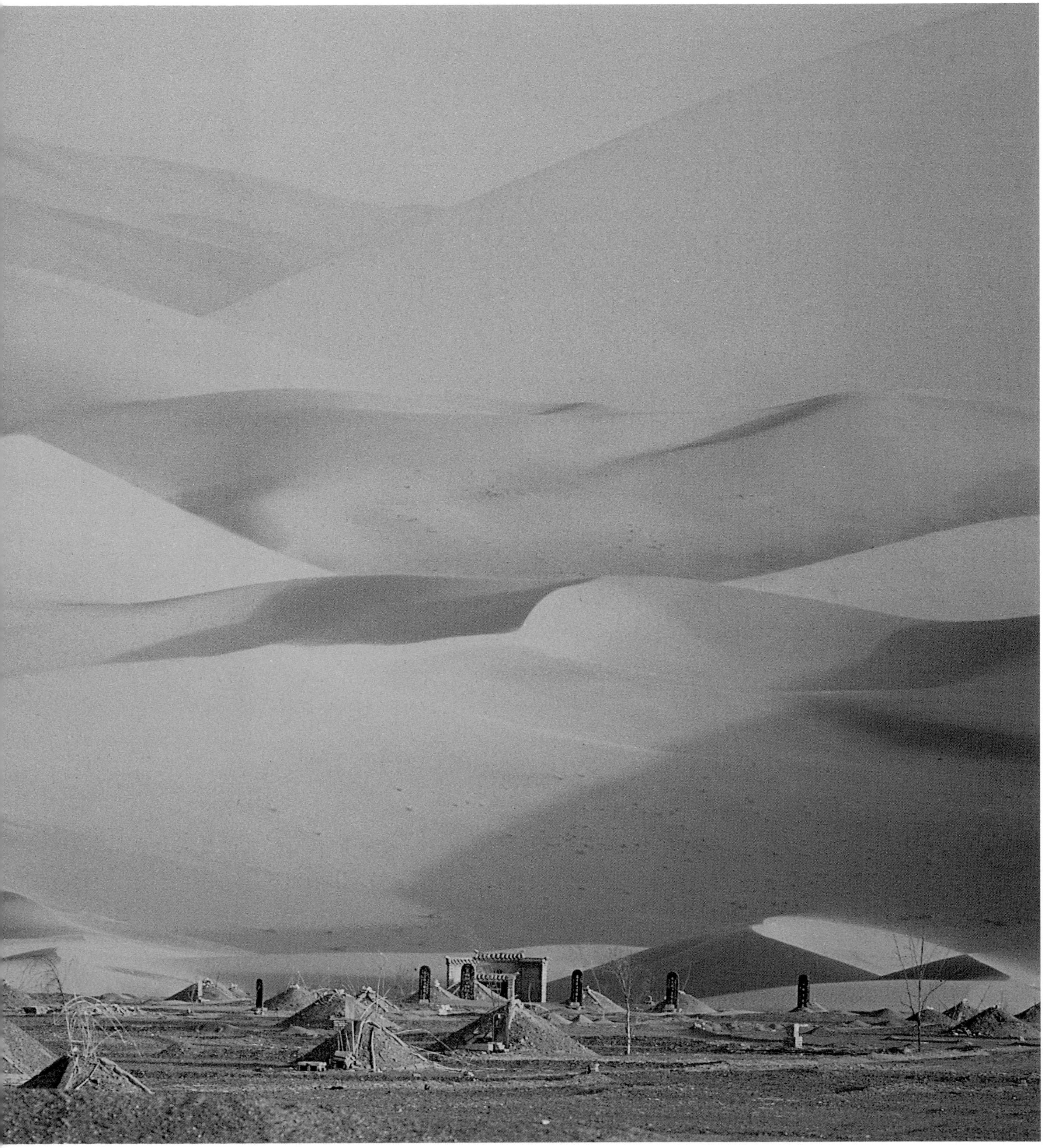

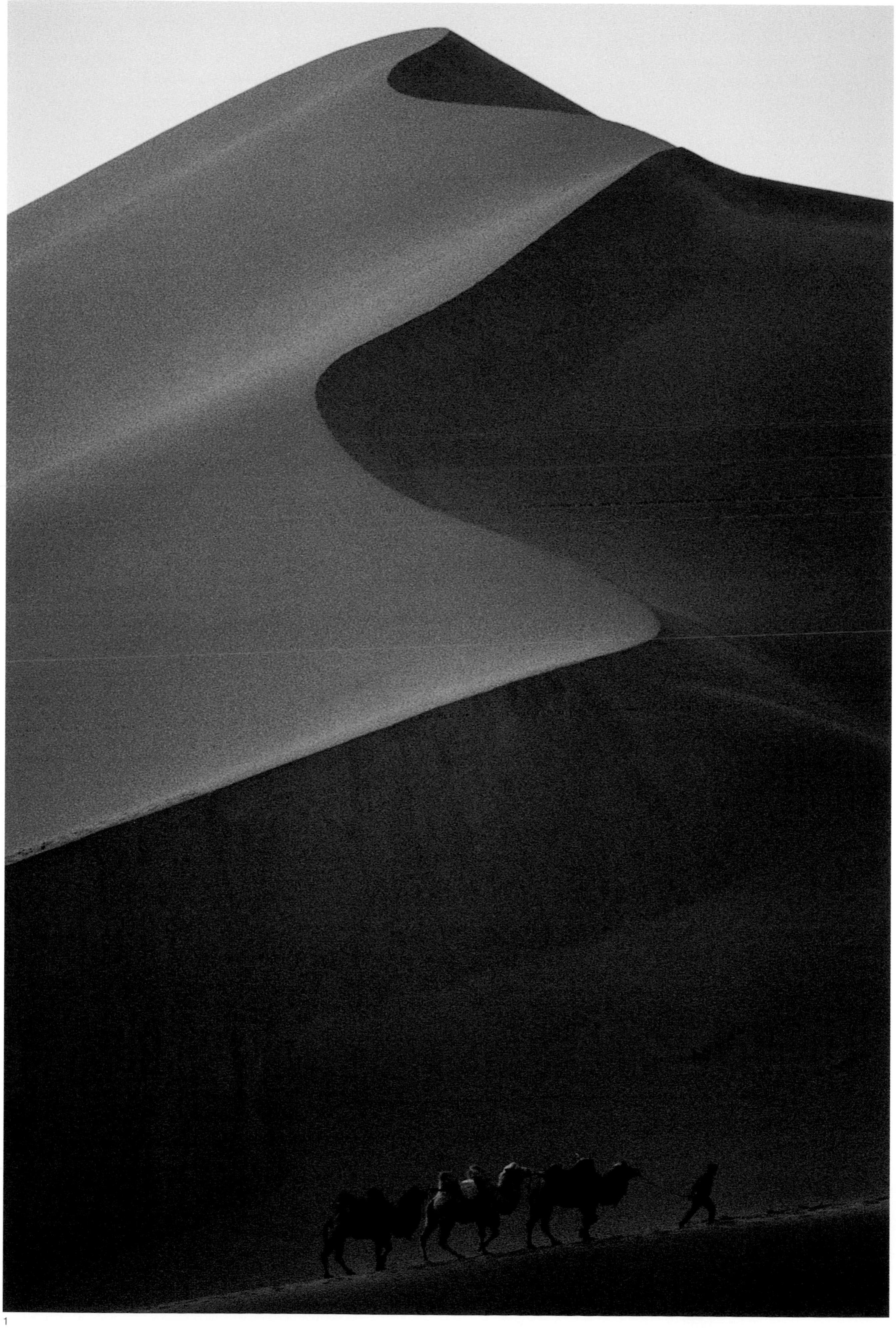

1

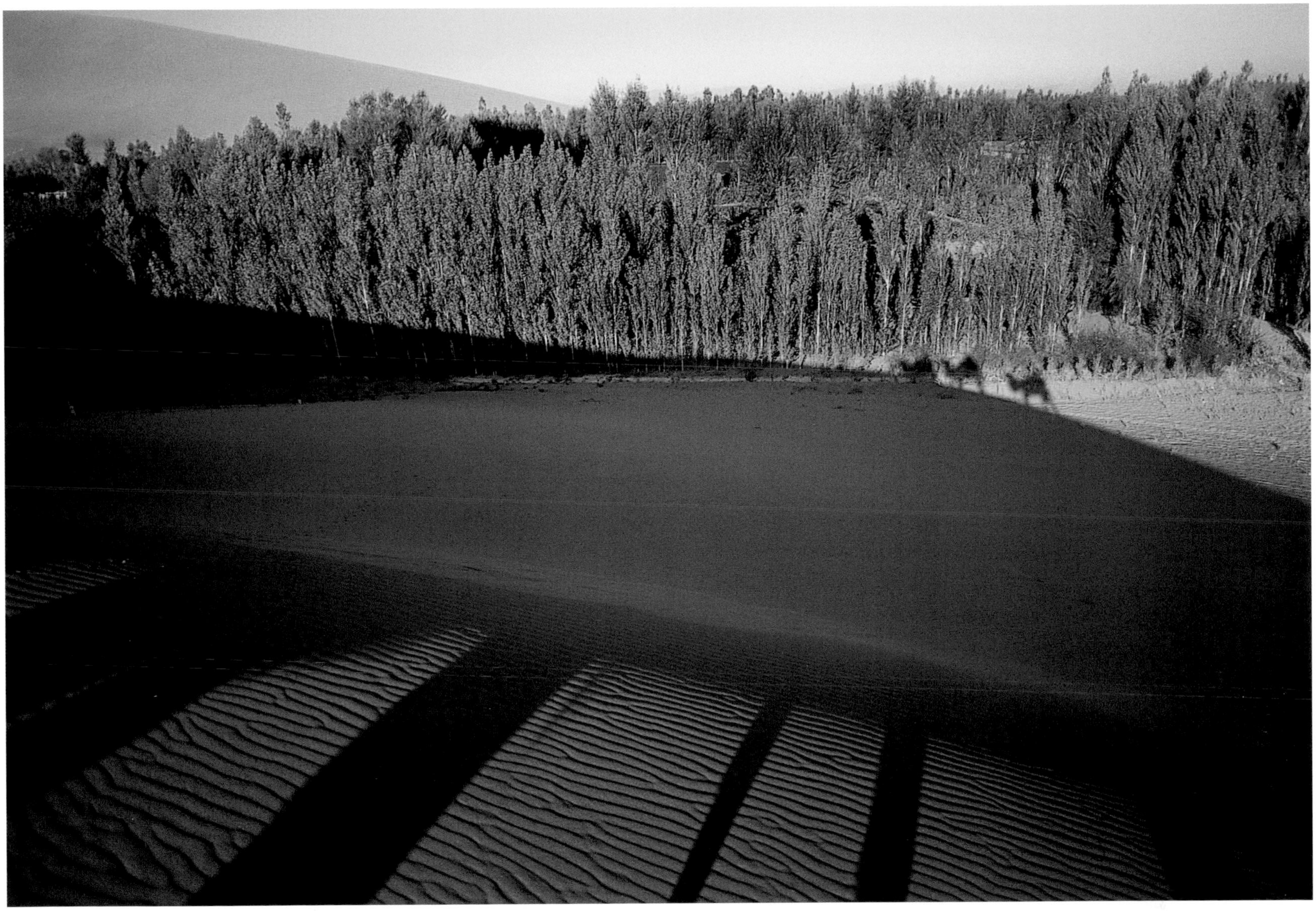

2

IN THE 1ST CENTURY BCE, Dun'huang (Blazing Beacon) was nothing more than a lonely outpost on the outer fringes of the Han Empire. But by the 4th Century CE it had become the key supply base for Silk Road caravans heading into the Gobi and Taklamakan deserts. Dun'huang was also the first great centre for Buddhism in China, with a community of over 1,500 monks. The famous Mogao grottoes began around 353 CE, when wealthy merchants seeking protection or wishing to offer thanks commissioned muralists and sculptors to decorate the cave temples hewn into the cliff face at Mingsha'shan, 25 kilometres (15 miles) from Dun'huang, by the great dunes of the Gobi. For centuries the grottos remained relatively undisturbed, while the arid desert air helped ensure their preservation, until Chinese and western 'explorers' arrived in 1900. The manuscripts, murals and statuary they found inside the Mogao caves covered every stylistic change in the arts and each philosophical shift in Buddhism between the 4th and 14th centuries. Today, 45,000 murals and 2,000 statues remain in good condition inside 500 caves. [1] [2] The great dunes around Dun'huang oasis. [3] The cliffs of Mogao.

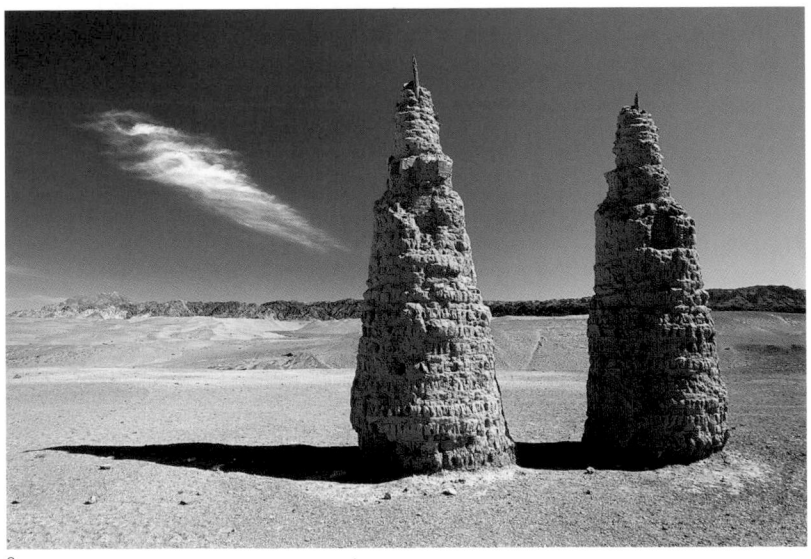

3

125

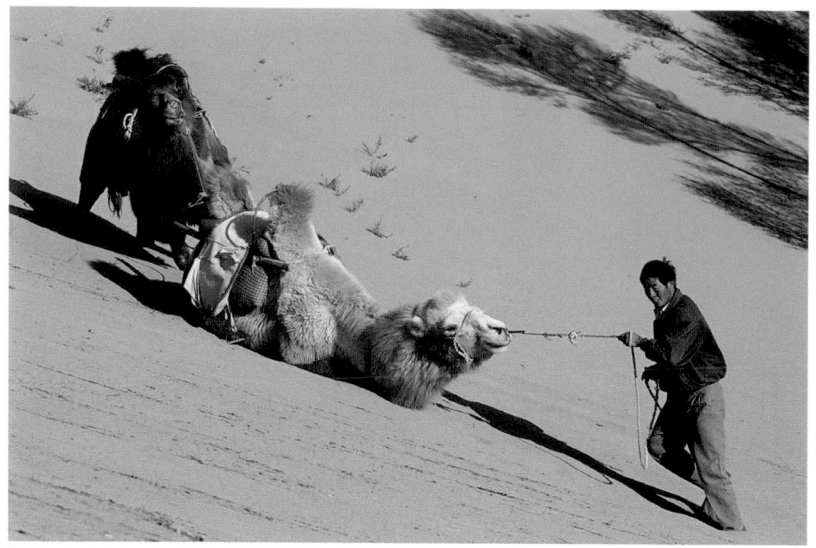

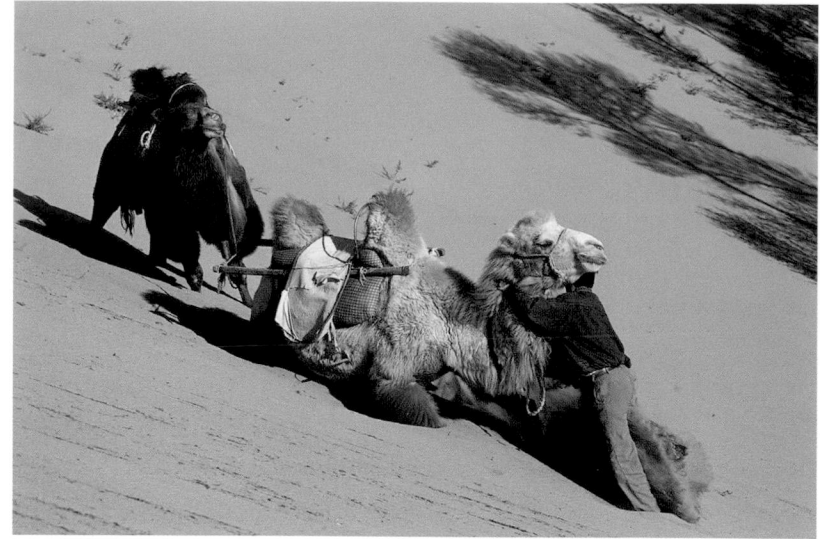

1

2

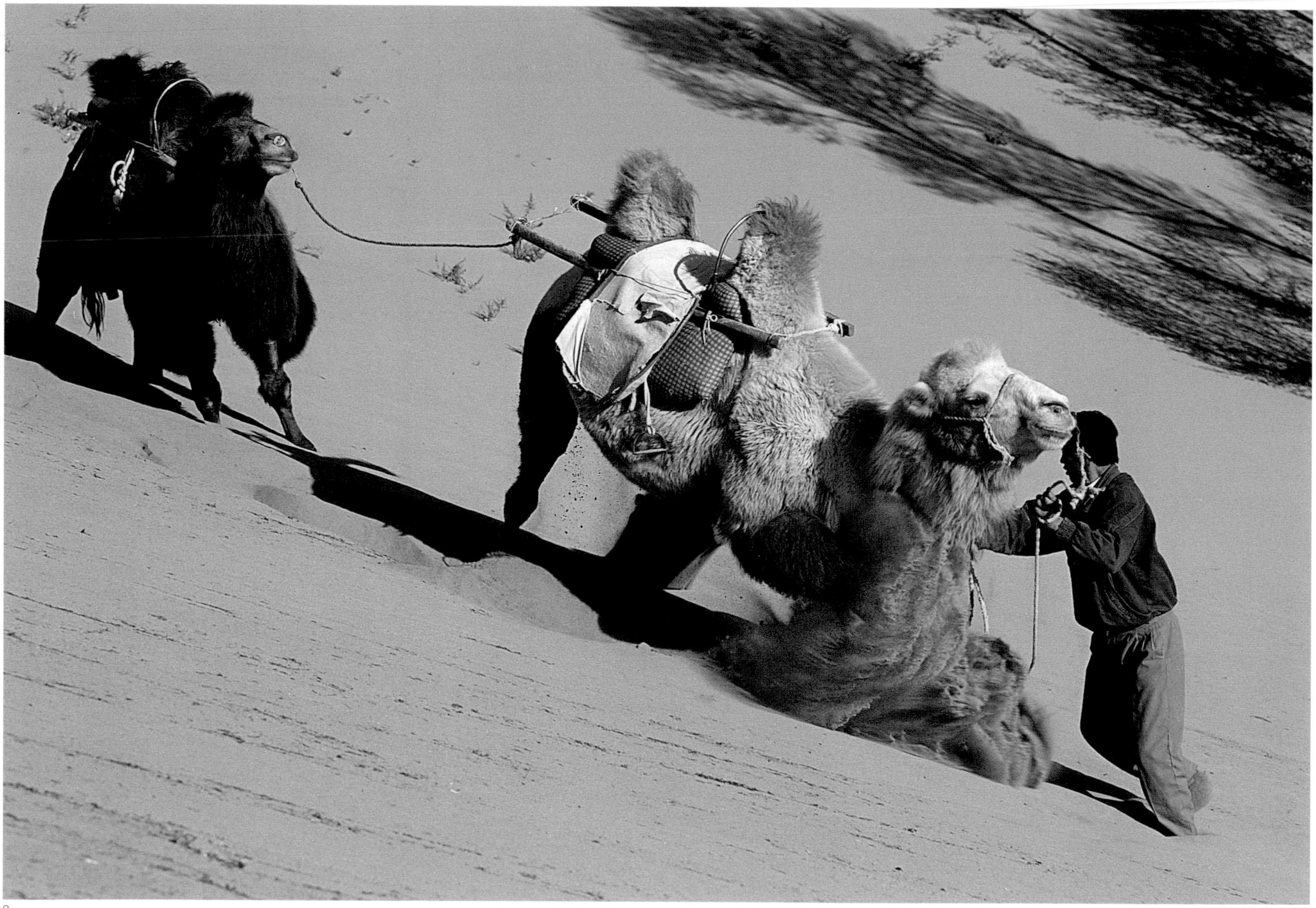

3

THE SINGING SANDS

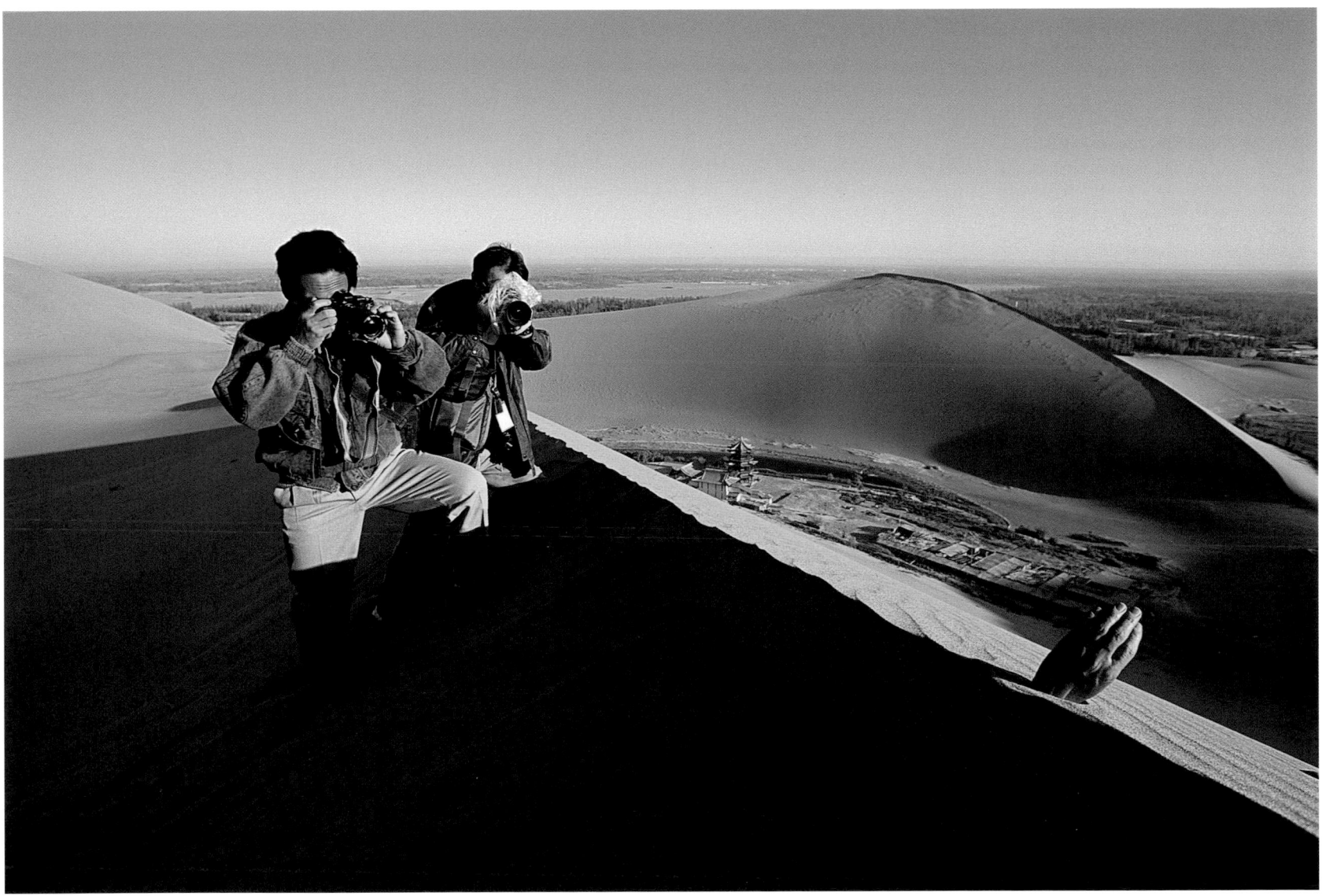

4

WE SET OFF WELL BEFORE DAWN from Dun'huang to cover the short distance to the Ming'sha (Singing Sand) dunes south of the town. The night before, two fellow passengers on the *Marco Polo Express* had asked about hitching a ride. They were doctors from Hong Kong and keen amateurs who were desperate to photograph sunrise over the dunes. I reluctantly agreed to take them. In the dark we found camel drivers to carry us to the top of the dunes in a long and freezing-cold ride through the pre-dawn frost. The views from the lip of the tallest dune were spectacular, but the sun was already too high. [4] I gazed out to the west and considered the enormity of the Gobi desert and the meaning of the caves, before turning around to find this surreal scene. I was glad I had given the doctors a ride. [1] [2] [3] We found out it was illegal to ride camels up the dunes only when the animals got stuck coming down the back way in order to avoid the guards.

THE SILK ROAD

XIN'JIANG UYGUR AUTONOMOUS REGION

LOCATION
Latitude 34.22º–49.33ºN
Longtitude 73.41º–96.18ºE

AREA 1,650,257 km² (637,000 sq miles)

GEOGRAPHY The region is characterized
by two huge basins divided and surrounded by
mountain ranges. The north is dominated
by Junggar Pendi and the Altai Mountains,
the centre by the Tien Shan range and the
south by the massive Tarim Pendi – much of
which is covered by the Taklimakan Desert.
The Tarim basis is bounded to the southeast
by the Pamir and Karakoram ranges and to
the southwest by the Himalayas. The
Taklimakan stretches into the Gobi desert to
the east. Xin'jiang's (and China's) lowest point
is 155 m below sea level and its highest peak
is 8,611 m on the Kashmir border. The region
shares international borders with Mongolia,
Russia, Kazakhstan, Kyrgyzstan, Tajikistan,
Afghanistan, Pakistan and India.

CLIMATE Xin'jiang's location in the arid and
mountainous centre of the Eurasian landmass
creates great climatic extremes. Average
temperatures in January are -20ºC in the north
and -10ºC in the south, reaching around 25ºC
in July. The lowest recorded temperature is
-51.5ºC and the highest, 49.6ºC. Average
annual rainfall rarely exceeds 150 mm.

POPULATION 19.63 million (end 2004)

MAJOR CITIES Urum'qi (capital), Hotan,
Kashgar, Korla , Ili, Turpan, Yi'ning, Hami

AGRICULTURE The river valleys support
wheat, rice, millet, sugar beet and fruit. Cash
crops include cotton and silkworms. Livestock
– notably sheep, goats, cattle and camels –
are raised on the grasslands.

MAIN INDUSTRIES The region is rich in
minerals, ranging from the huge Karamay oil
fields to coal, copper, gold, silver and other
metal ores. Heavy industries include oil
refining, iron and steel, chemicals, textiles,
sugar and cement.

ANNUAL PER CAPITA INCOME (2005)
Disposable income of urban residents:
RMB 8,100 (US$1,010)
Net income of rural residents:
RMB 2,475 (US$309)

HISTORICAL AND SCENIC SITES
Gao'chang, Bezeklik Thousand Buddha Caves,
Tianchi Lake, Kashgar Bazaar, Huo'yan Shan.

FOOD The region's food is robust and
reflects the Uygar community's Islamic faith.
Cooking revolves largely around mutton, lamb
and flour. Noted dishes include roast lamb,
stewed mutton cubes, dumplings stuffed
with mutton, mutton rice *pillau*, noodles and
nan (flatbread).

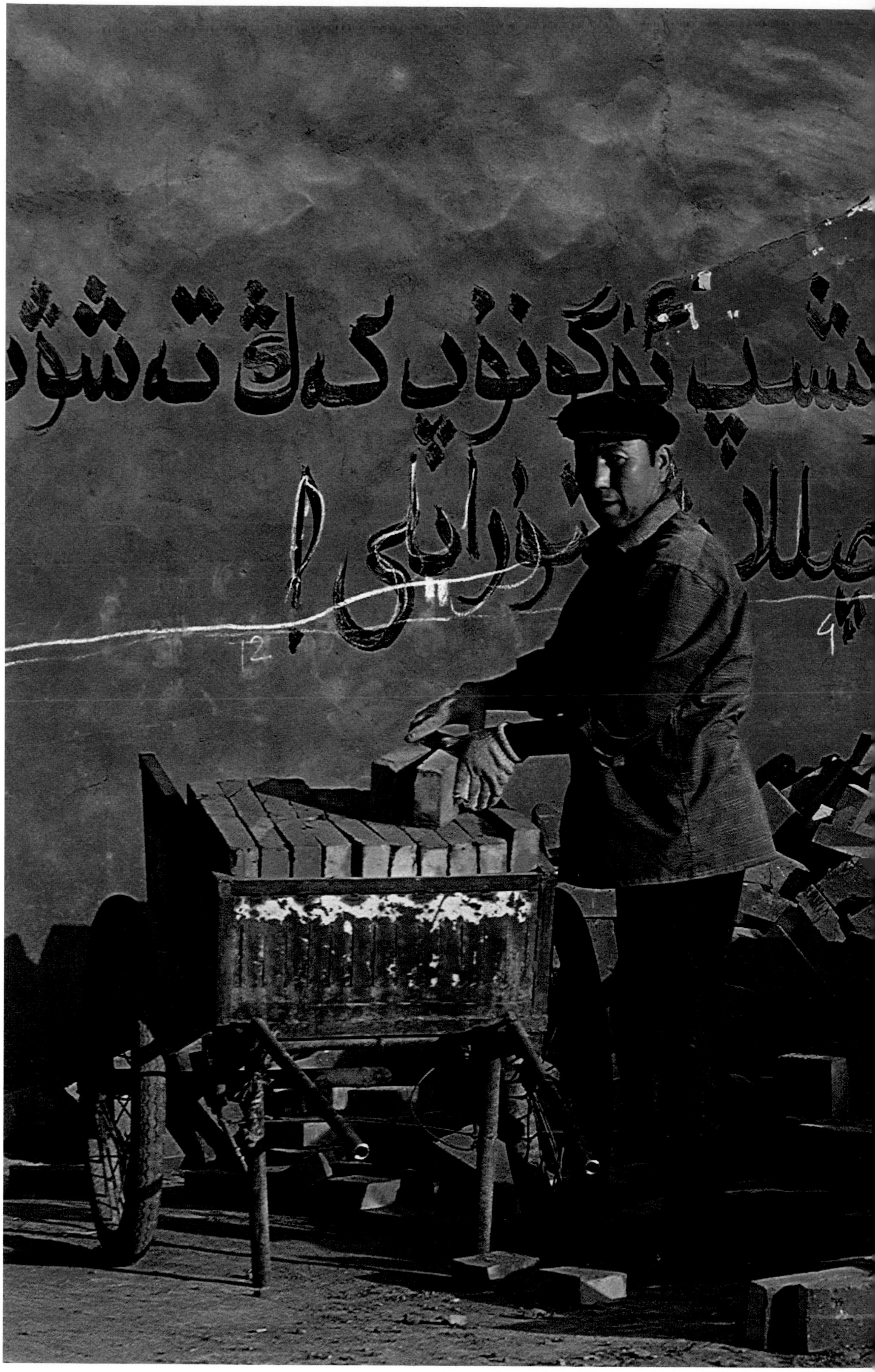

[RIGHT] Twilight in Turpan.

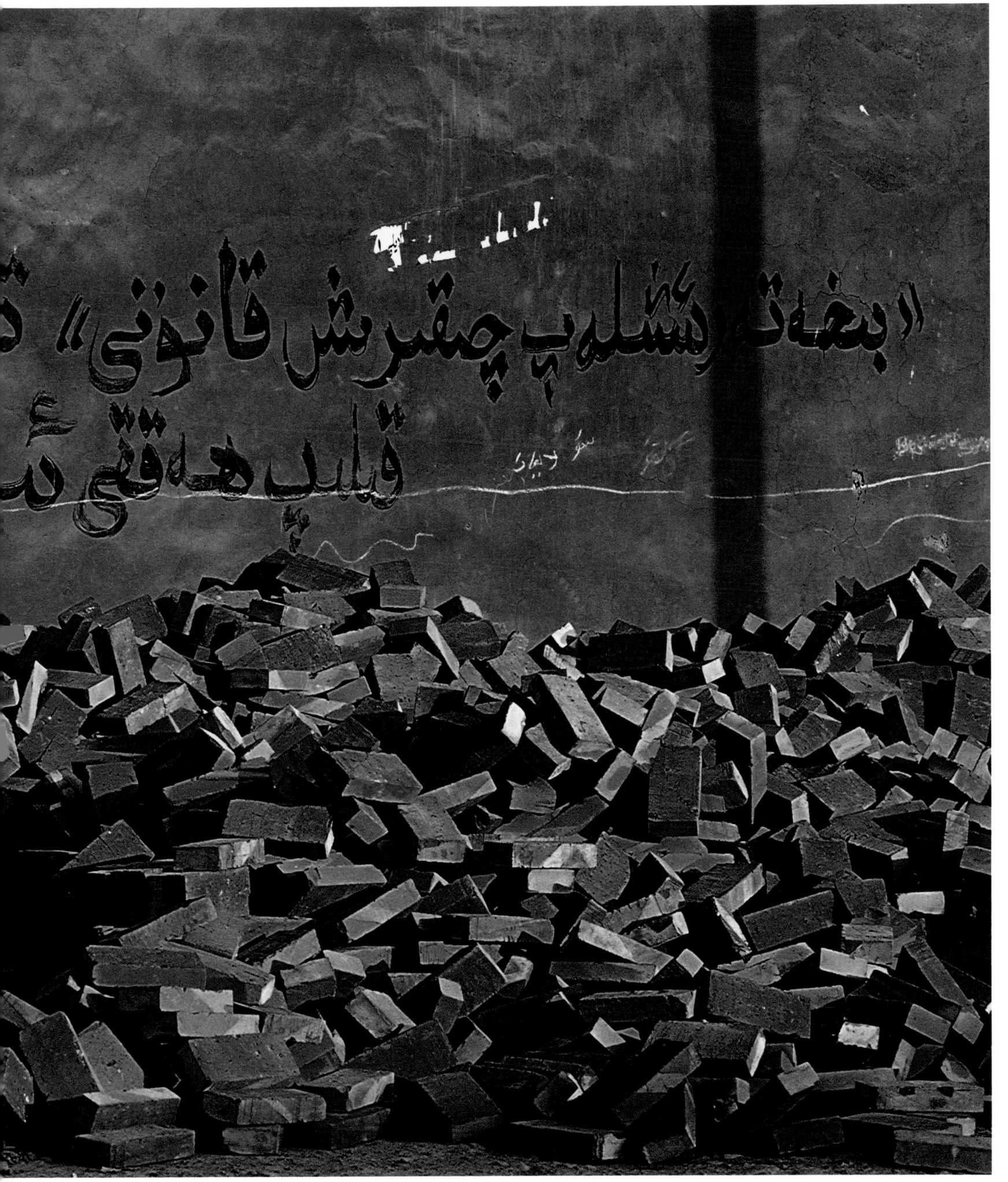

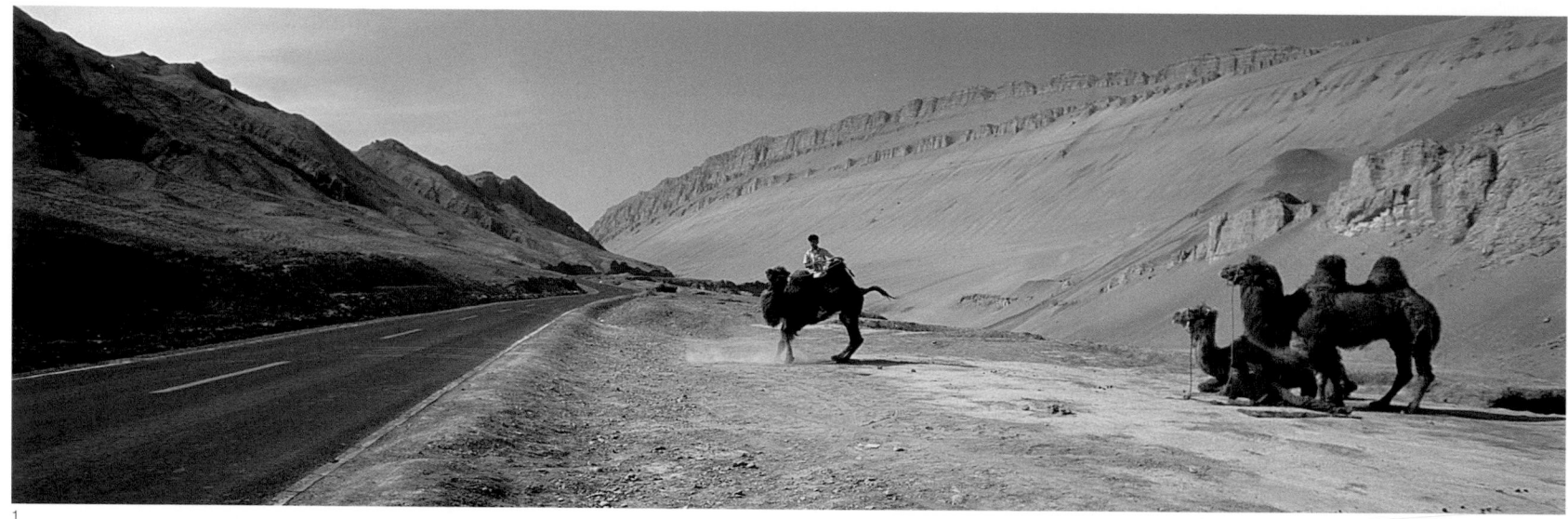

1

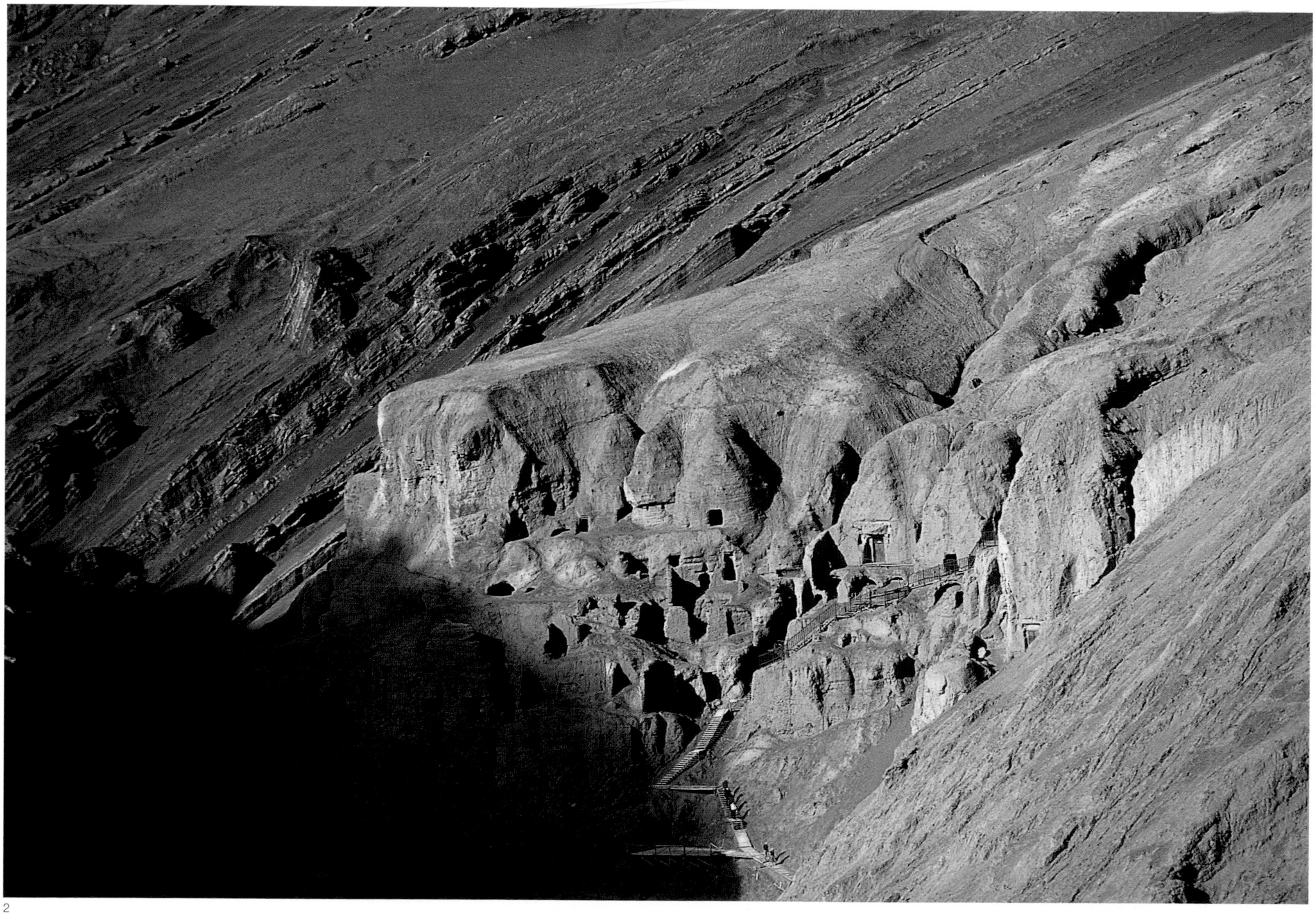

2

THE FLAMING MOUNTAINS

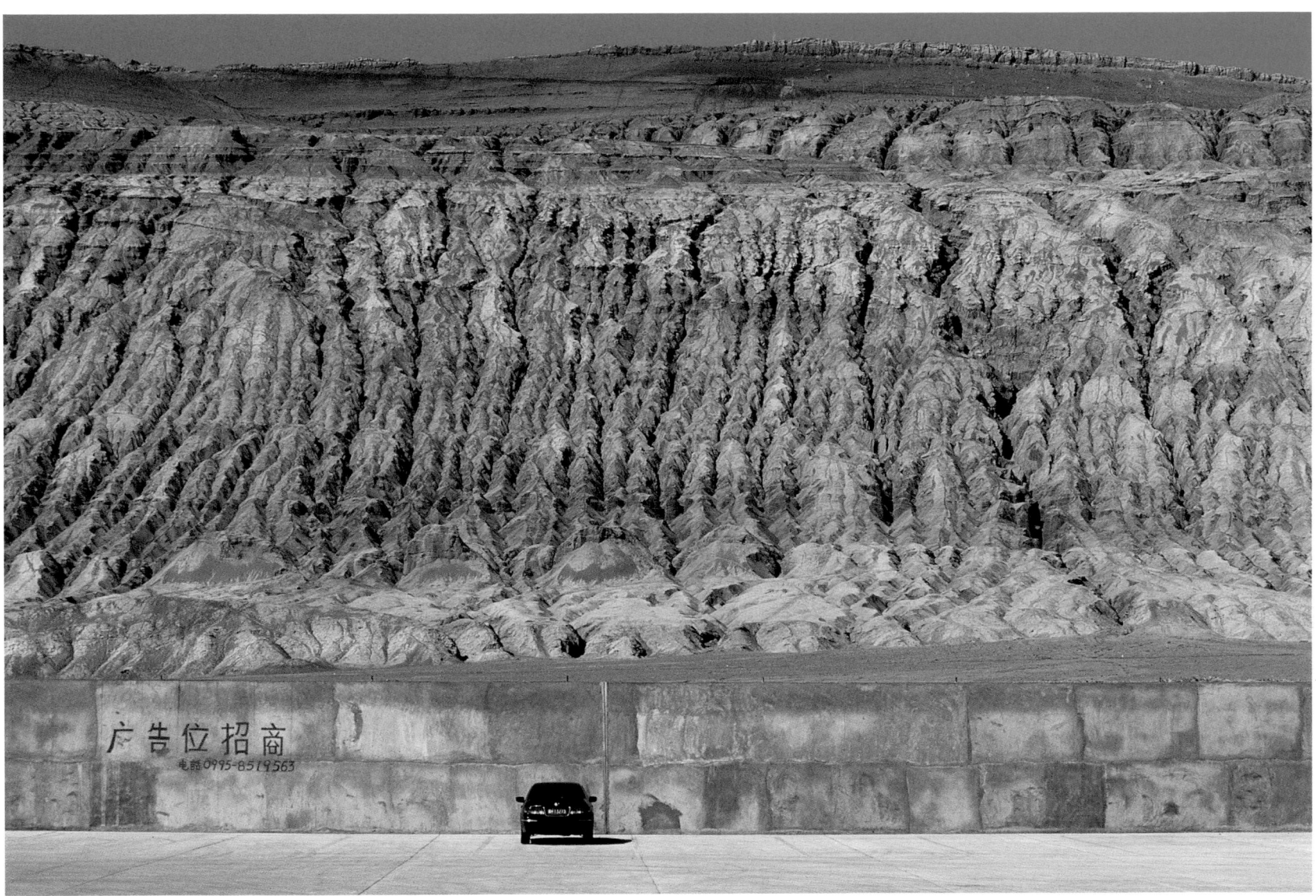

3

THE FLAMING MOUNTAINS owe their current name to Ming Dynasty novelist Wu Chen'geng, who set one of the most dramatic episodes of the *Journey to the West* here. The book, a classic Buddhist allegorical epic with more than a hint of *Star Wars*, follows the legendary 15-year pilgrimage by Tang Dynasty monk Hsuan Tsang (596–664) to Central Asia and India. The book has embedded the remote 100-kilometre (62-mile) long, 9-kilometre (5.6-mile) wide, red sandstone range on the edge of the Turpan Basin into China's collective memory. Local Uygur legends tell of a dragon emerging from deep beneath the Tien'shan Mountains to feed on local children. An Uygur warrior fought the dragon for three days and nights, finally slicing the beast into eight pieces that turned into mountains dyed scarlet by its own blood. The sword cuts became the eight valleys in the Flaming Mountains, including the famous Grape Valley. [1] Uygur children touting camel rides by the road. [2] 3rd-century Buddhist caves behind the Tuyu'gou Valley. [3] The new parking lot at the Flaming Mountain tourists centre.

THE SILK ROAD

THE TURPAN BASIN

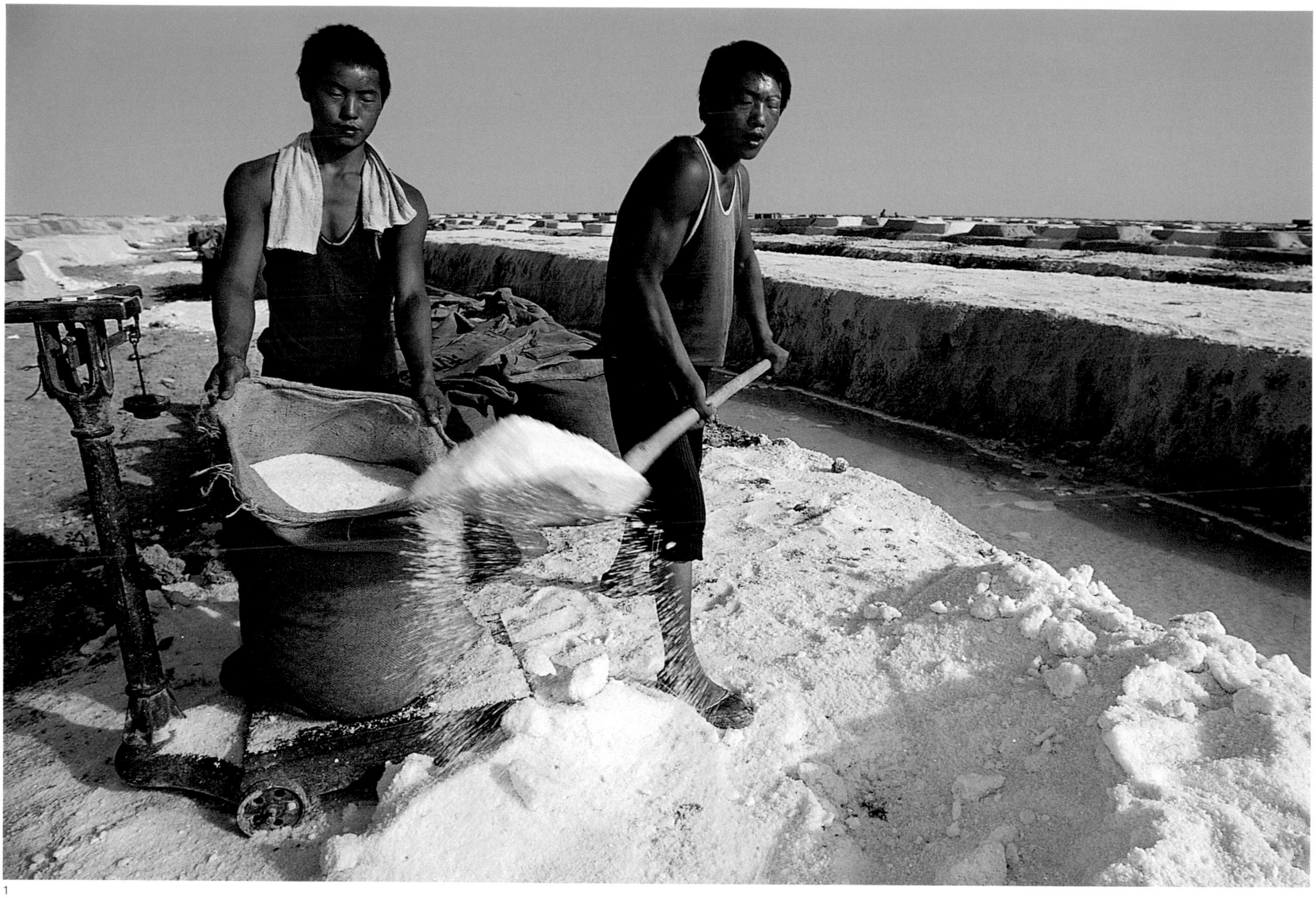

![image](full-page photograph)

1

THE OASIS SETTLEMENTS IN THE TURPAN BASIN at the southern foothills of Tien'shan (Mountains of Heaven) have rested and fed travellers on the northern Silk Road since the Han Dynasty, but the basin is perhaps better known for it climatic and geographical attributes. It is the hottest place in China (highest recorded temperature: 49.6°C) and it is 154 metres (505 feet) below sea level – the second lowest spot on earth after the Dead Sea. In the heart of the depression, 55 kilometres (35 miles) southeast of Turpan, lies [1] the salt-encrusted Moon Lake. Here, thousands of workers toil under the relentless sun producing industrial salt for the chemical industry. Some of them are political prisoners, sent here to be 're-educated through hard labour', a government policy that is unfortunately as old as the Silk Road itself. [2] Turpan is also famous for its grapes, introduced into the region 2,000 years ago. With the discovery of oil, [4] some vineyards now produce both wine and fossil fuel. [3] The reservoir below the Gao'chang ruins, originally a Tang Dynasty outpost.

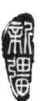

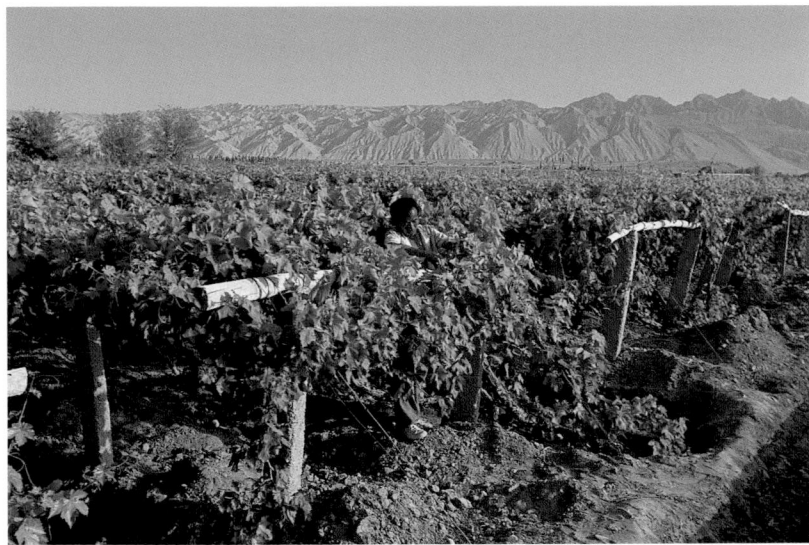

2

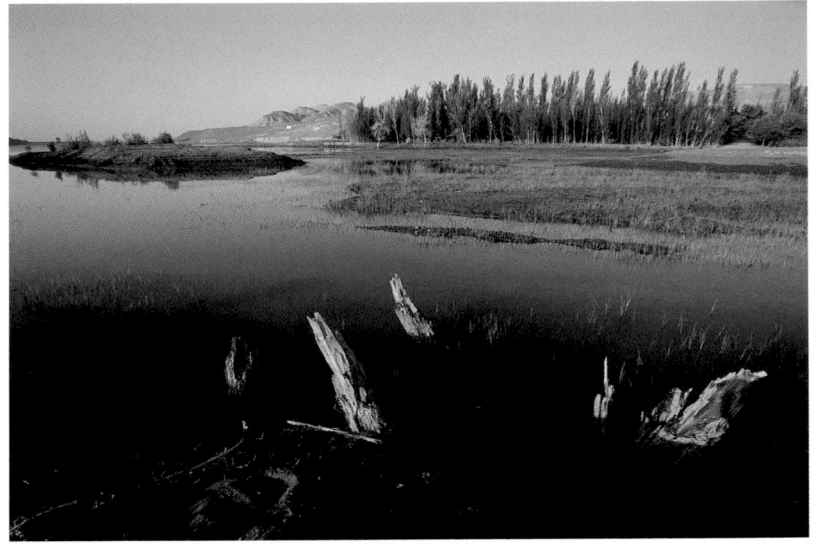

3

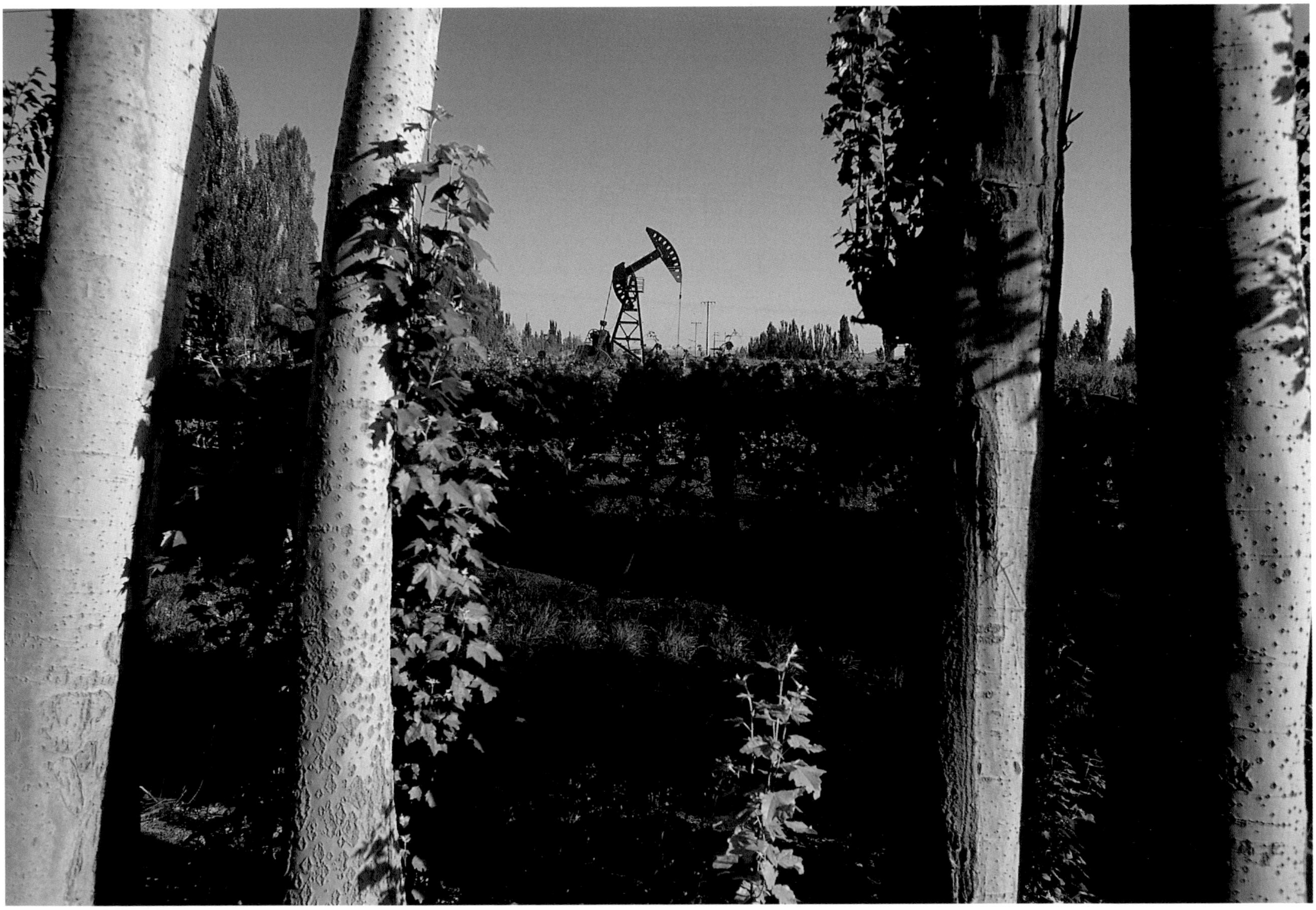

4

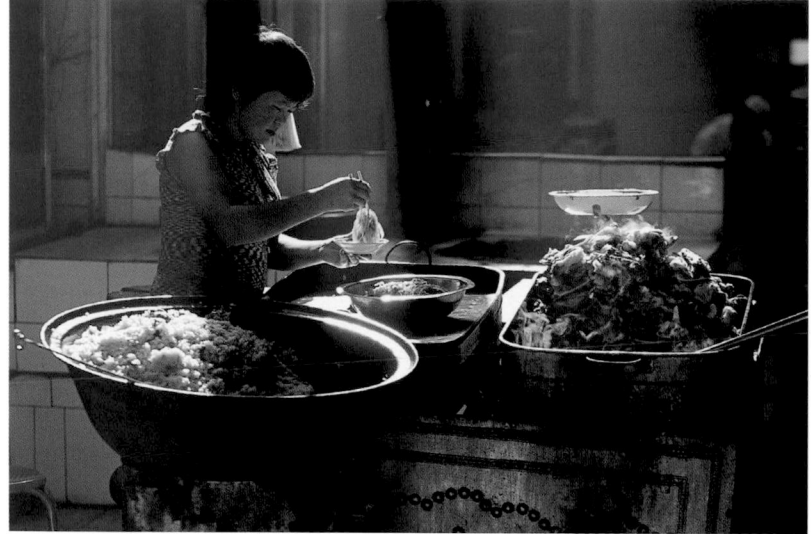

1

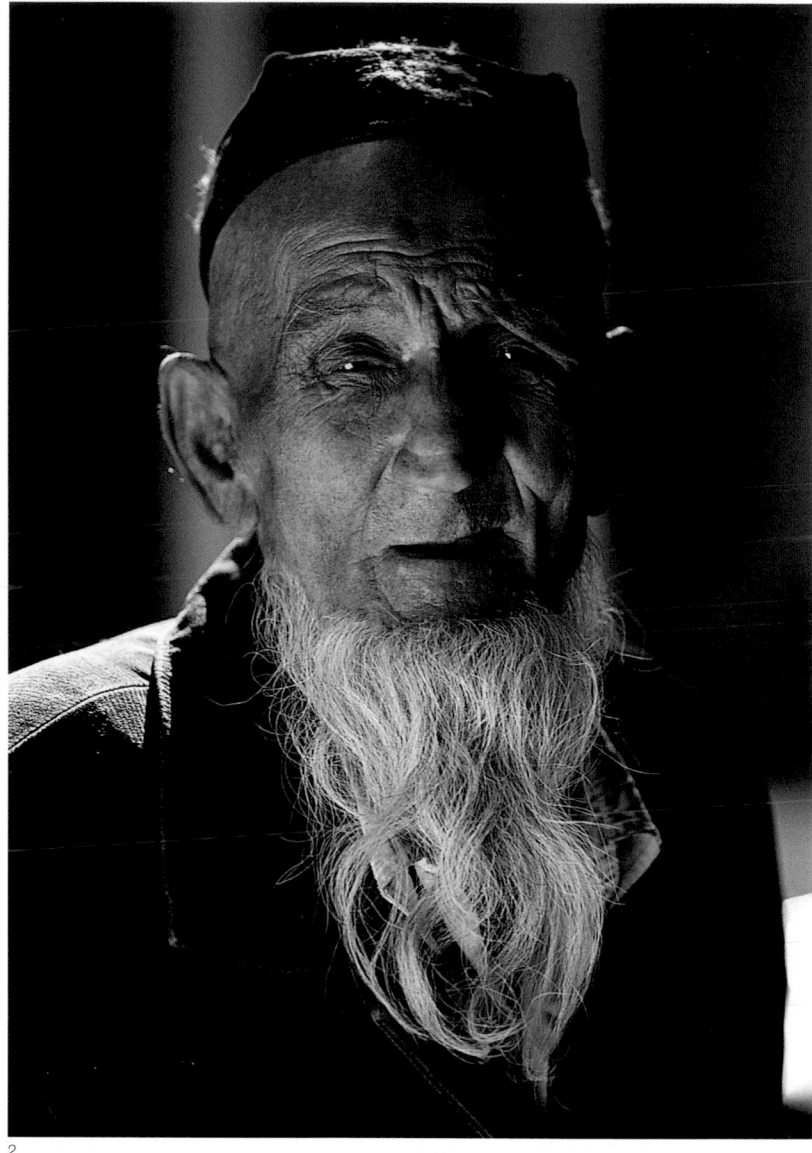

2

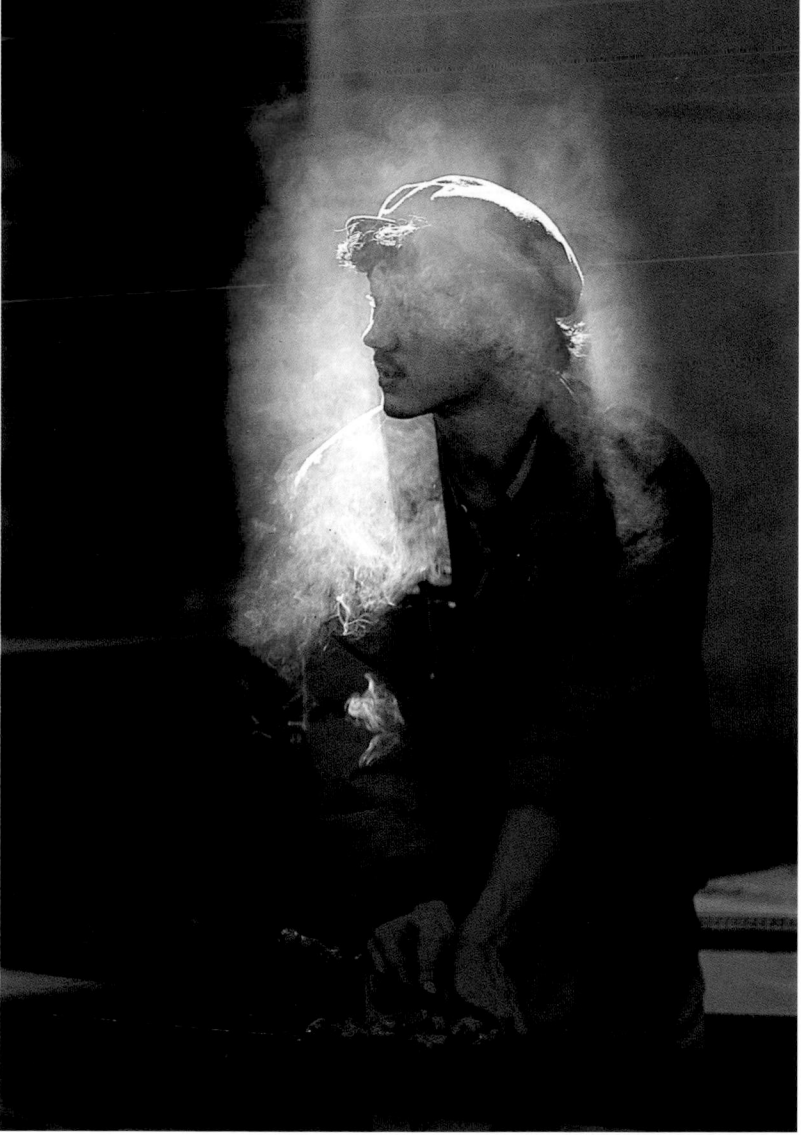

3

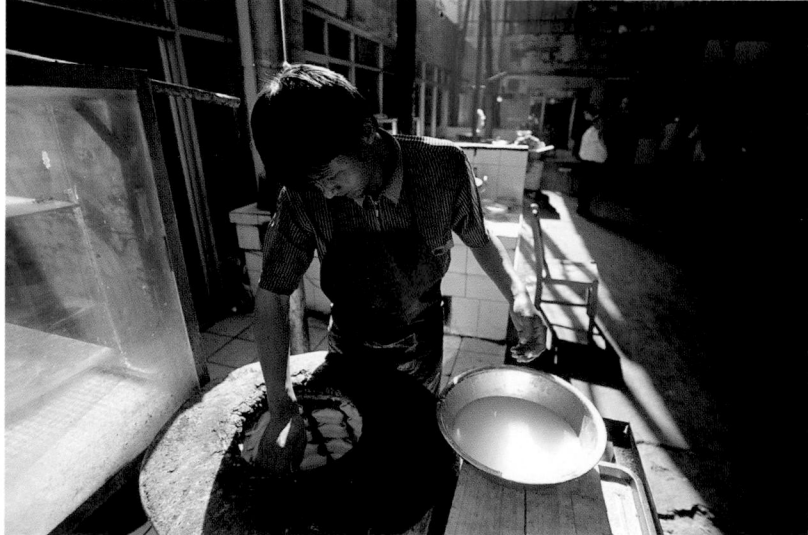

4

THE CITY OF TURPAN

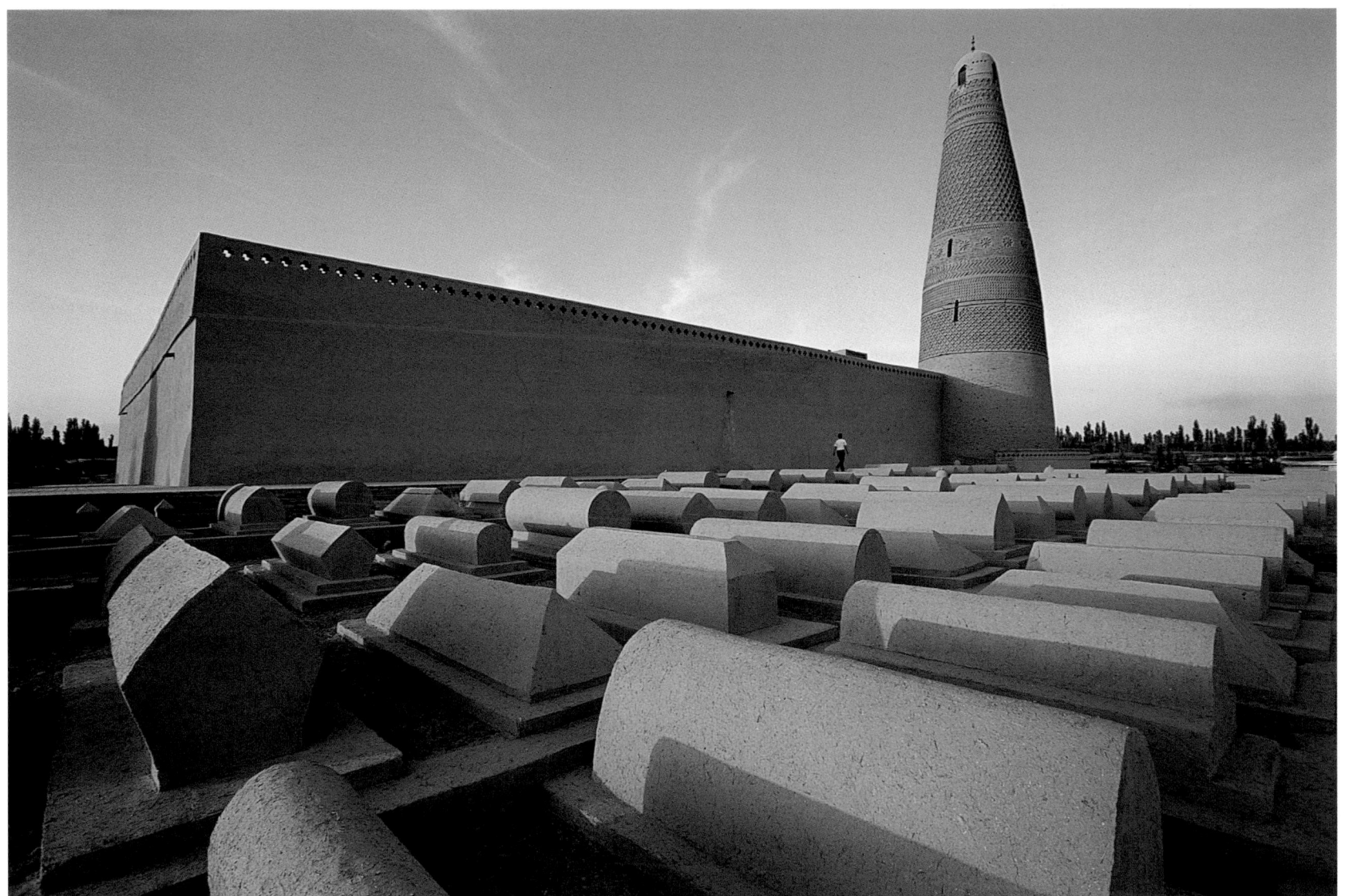

5

LIKE MOST OF THE CITIES IN CHINA'S AUTONOMOUS REGIONS from Inner Mongolia to Tibet, Turpan is dominated by functional and often hideous Soviet 'Neo-Brutalist' architecture, with one notable exception – the use of vine trellises to shade the sidewalks, which is both practical and attractive. Reminders of a more illustrious architectural past are also scattered around the city. Just to the east of Turpan [5] the Emin Minaret of the Su Gong mosque, completed in 1778, is a gem of Islamic architecture. Designed by Uygur architect Ibrahim, the 44-metre (145-foot) high tower tapers gracefully towards the sky in plain sun-dried bricks constructed in simple geometric and floral patterns. Silk Road influences are also evident at the bazaar's food court. [1] The Uygur version of the popular Persian rice dish *polo* is made with lamb here and commonly known as 'hand-grasp-rice,' referring to the preferred technique of eating with one's fingers. [2] The old gentleman is a regular at the rice shop. [3] Lamb skewers on the grill. [4] Pastries filled with lamb and onions go into a Tandoor oven.

THE SILK ROAD

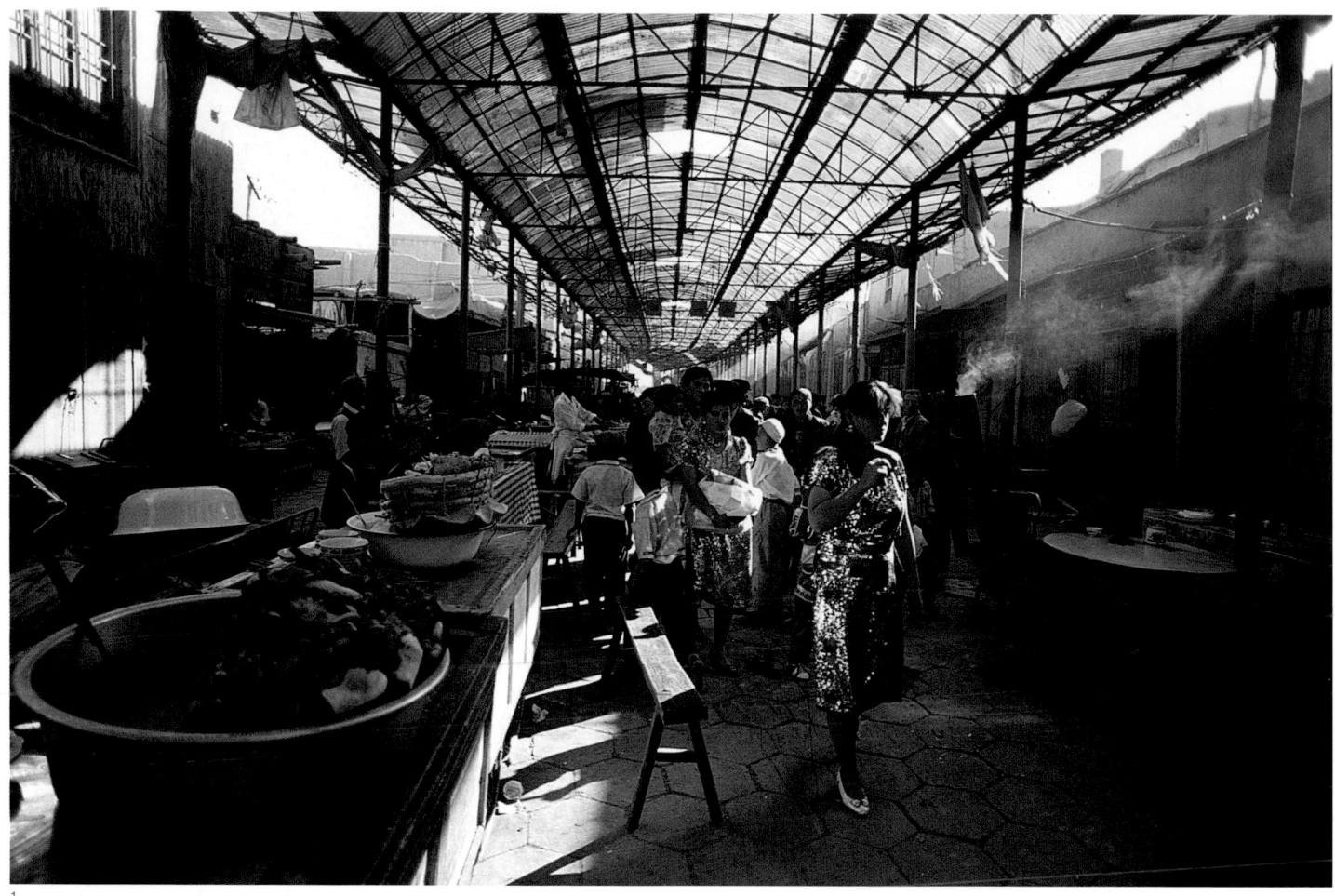

1

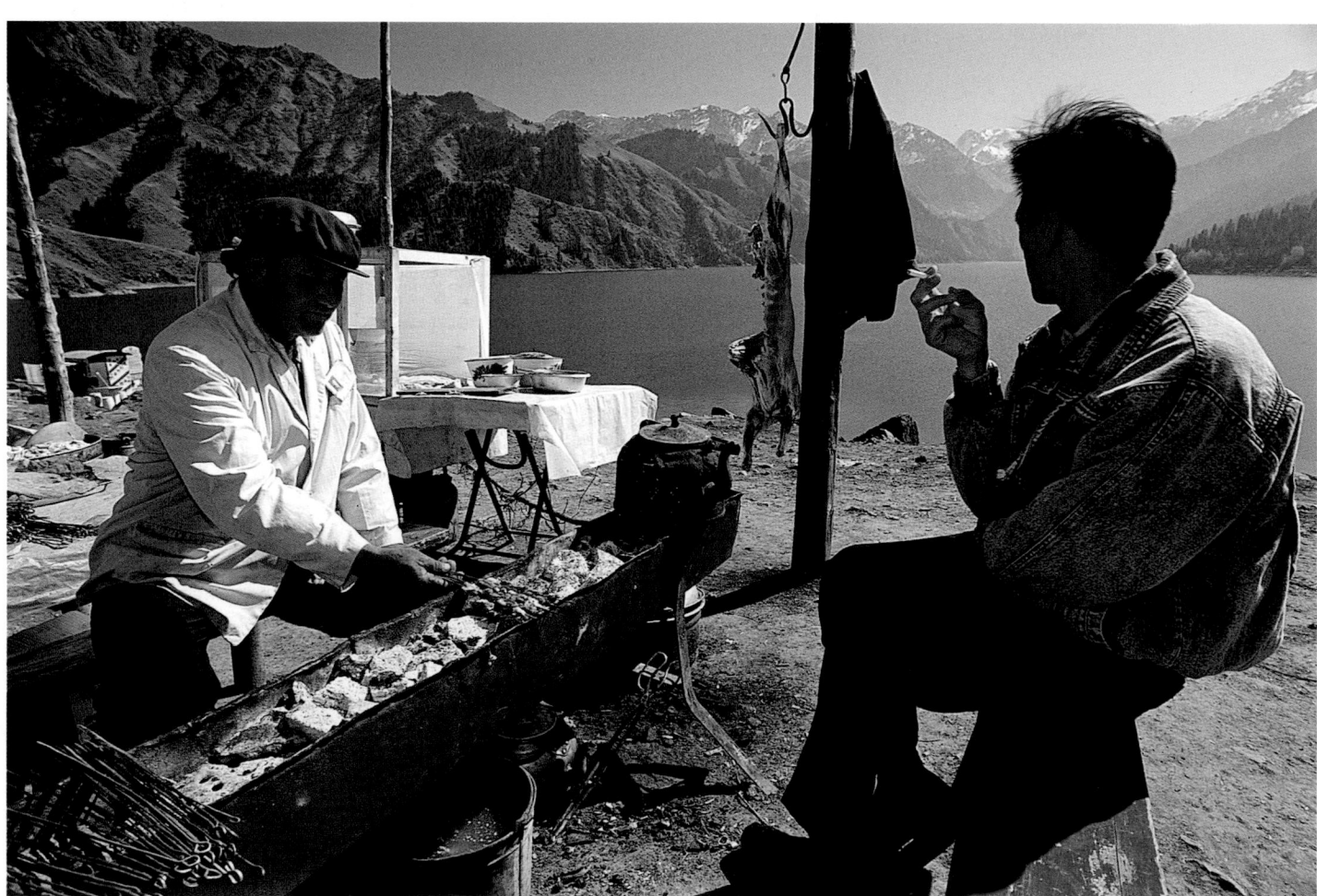

2

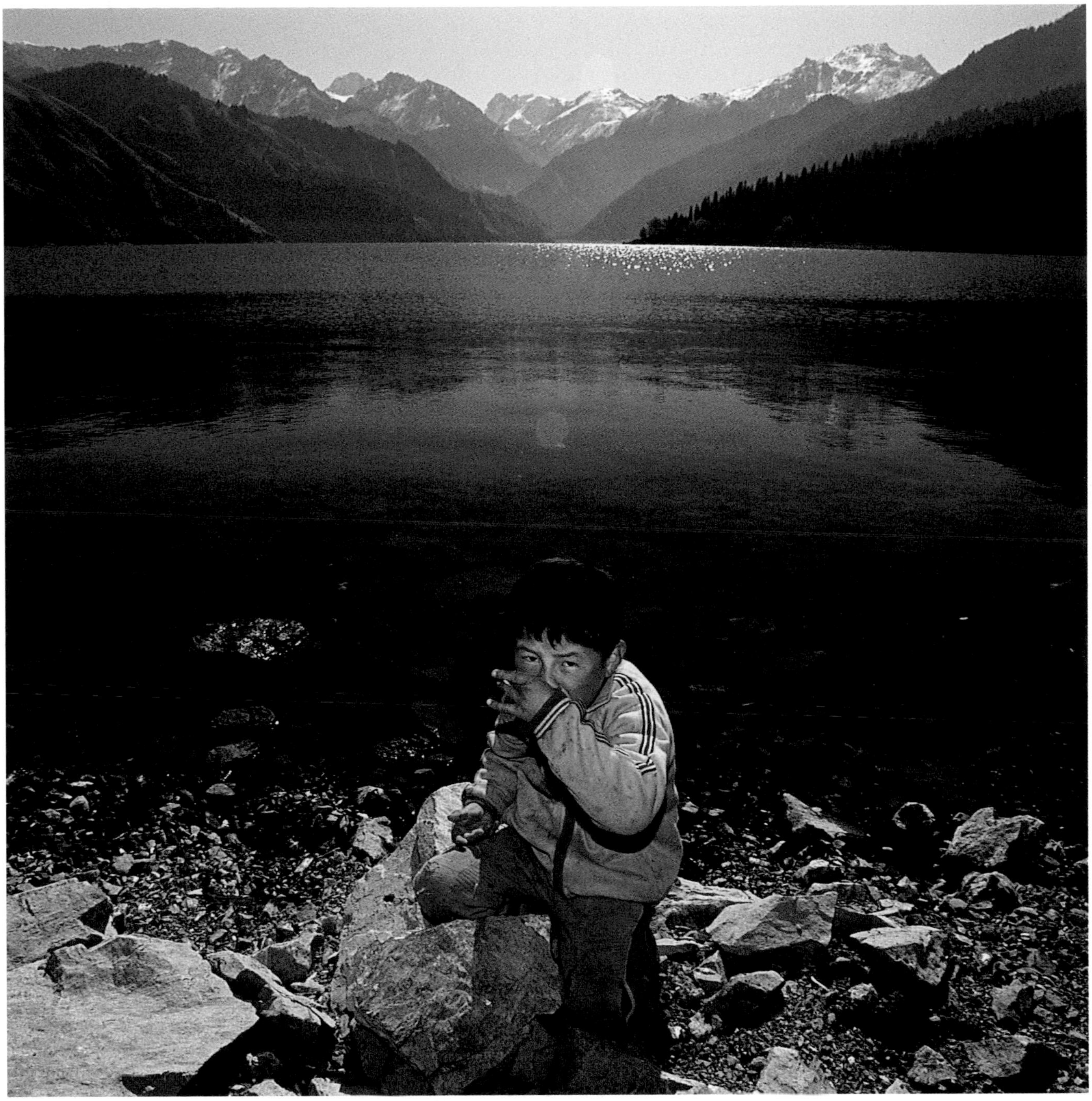

3

THE ONLY THING I REMEMBER ABOUT URUM'QI, capital of Xin'jiang Autonomous Region, is that it is the most landlocked city in the world. Urum'qi is 2,240 kilometres (1,390 miles) from the nearest sea, though [1] fish is available in the bazaar. Tian'chi (Heaven's Pond) Lake is 115 kilometres (70 miles) northeast of Urum'qi and reached by a spectacular drive through the Tian'shan (Mountains of Heaven) range. [3] This pristine azure lake ringed by snow-capped mountains is home to a rare plant species called 'Snow Lotus', which, according to kung fu novels, is a cure-all for the most extreme poisons. Some Chinese Buddhists believe that Guan'yin, the Goddess of Mercy (the Chinese incarnation of *Avalokiteshvara Bodhisattva*) resides here and they come in special tour groups to commune with the lady of the lake. Nomadic Kazakhs set up *yurts* and graze their horses on the shores of the lake in the summer months. Some offered to take me for a horseback ride, but [2] I opted for delicious lamb kebabs with a large bottle of beer by the lake instead.

THE SILK ROAD

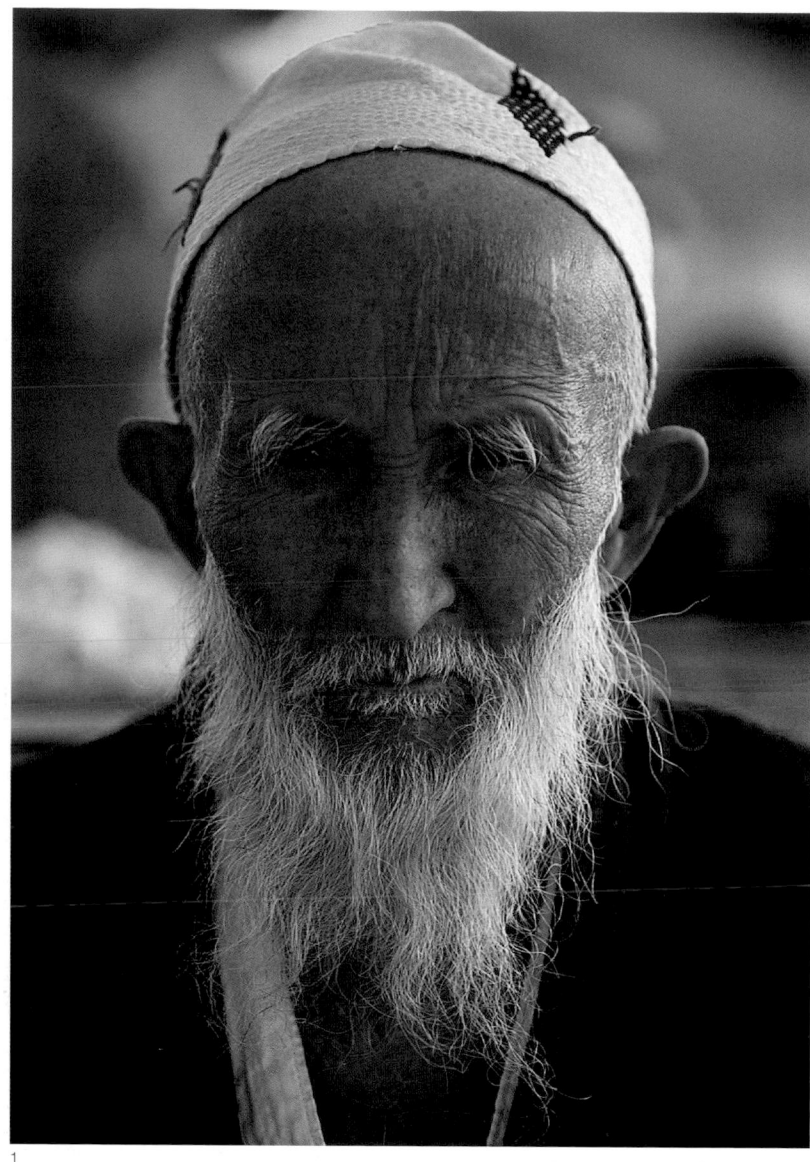

1

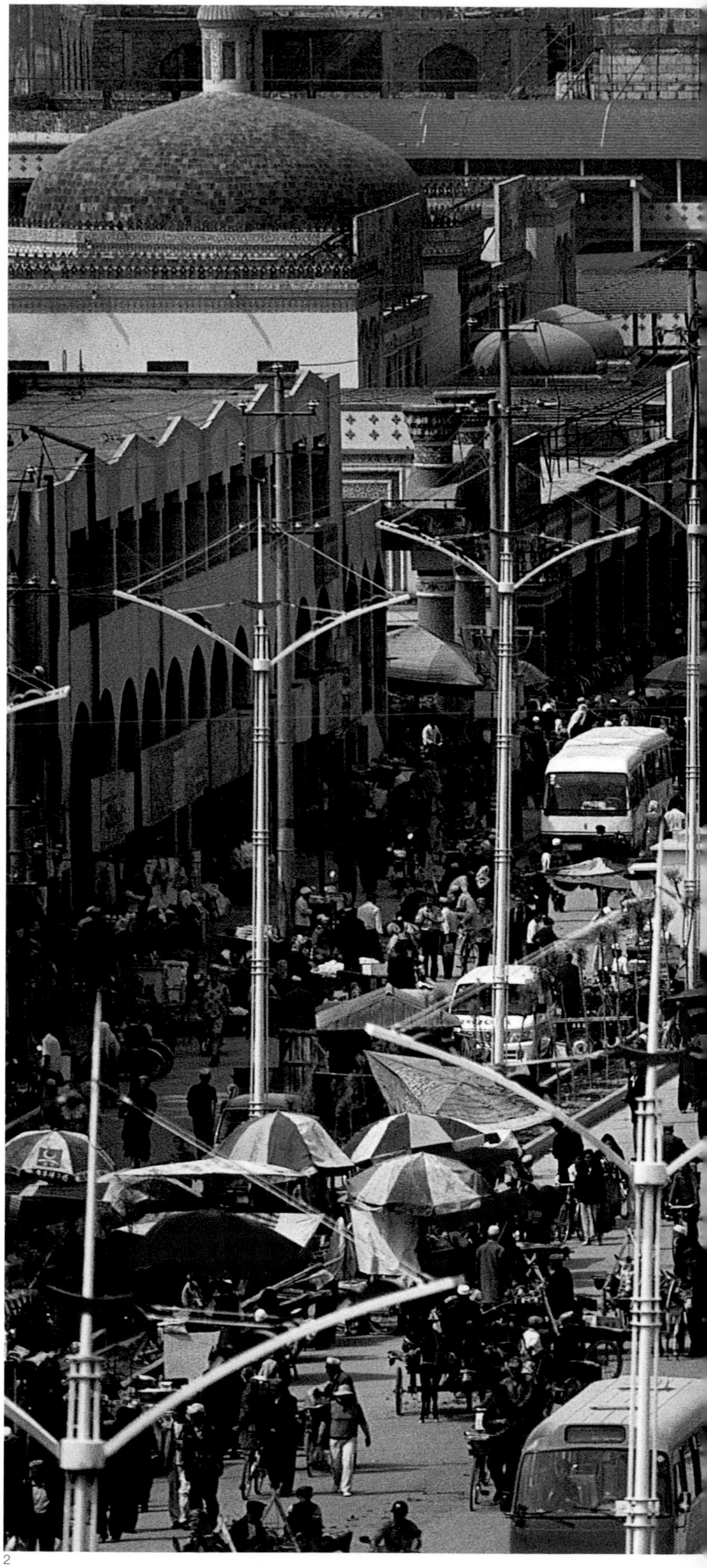

FOR OVER 2,000 YEARS, through peace, war, boom and bust, the crossroad oasis of Kashgar has been like the revolving door through which people, goods, ideas and technologies have moved between China and the West. Strategically located at the foot of the Pamir Mountains on the western edge of the Taklimakan Desert, Kashgar was the refuge for weary traders descending from the 6,000-metre (20,000-foot) mountain passes of the Karakorum and exhausted travellers emerging from the vast and unforgiving sand seas of the Gobi. In Kashgar they could thaw or chill out, exchange tales of wonder and horror, swap business intelligence, trade and re-supply before continuing the next stage of their gruelling journeys. At its peak, Kashgar was the crown jewel of the Silk Road, boasting the most famous bazaars in the world. Gunpowder, silk, noodles, paper and printing came through here on their way west. From the other direction, Buddhist masters, Gandaharan sculptors, Indian muralists, Persian metal workers, Nestorian Christians and Islamic warriors entered China through Kashgar's gates. Following centuries of decline, Kashgar's role as an entrepôt has been restored as [1] traders from across Central Asia again fill [2] the streets of the Sunday Bazaar.

2

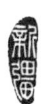

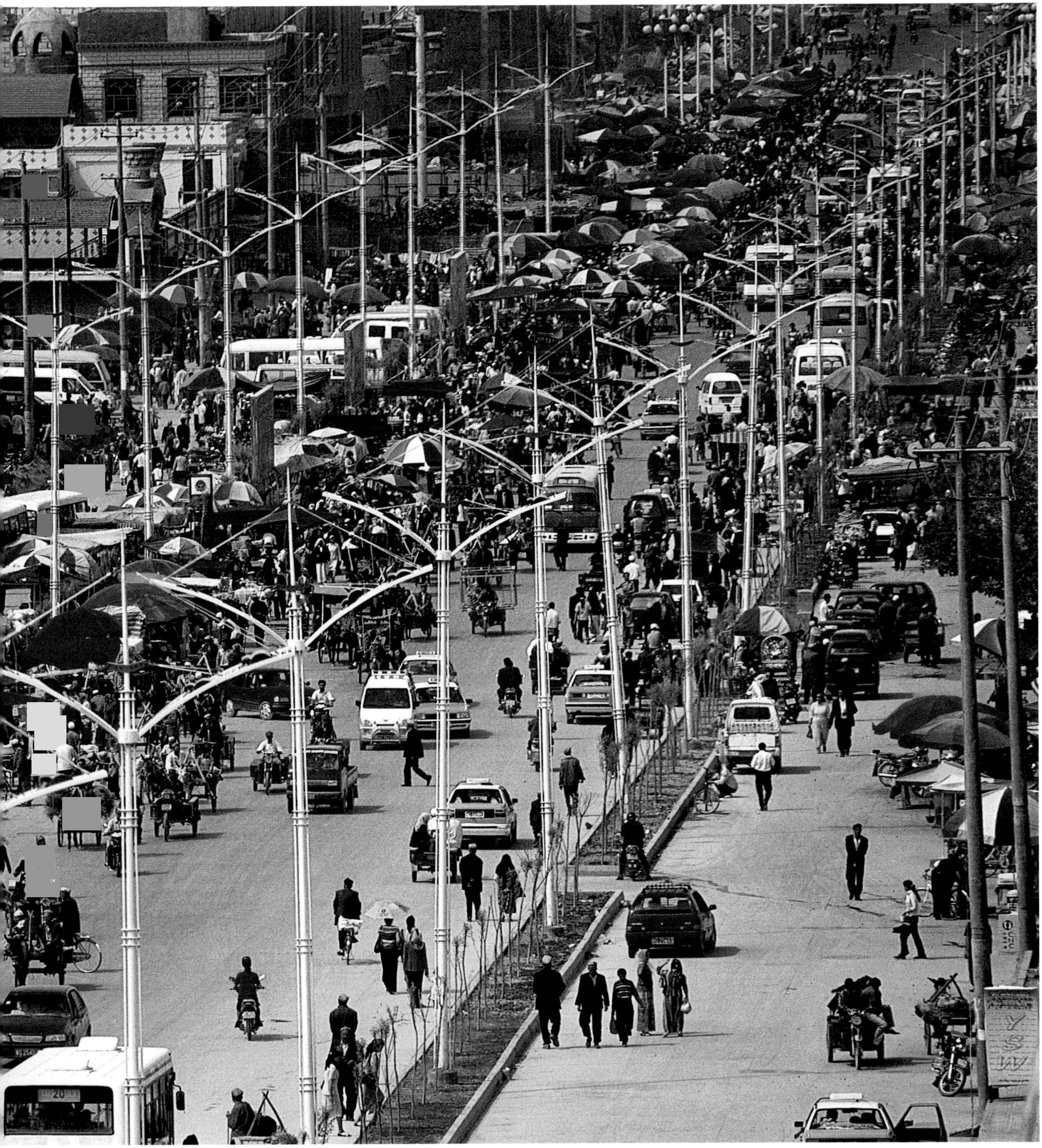

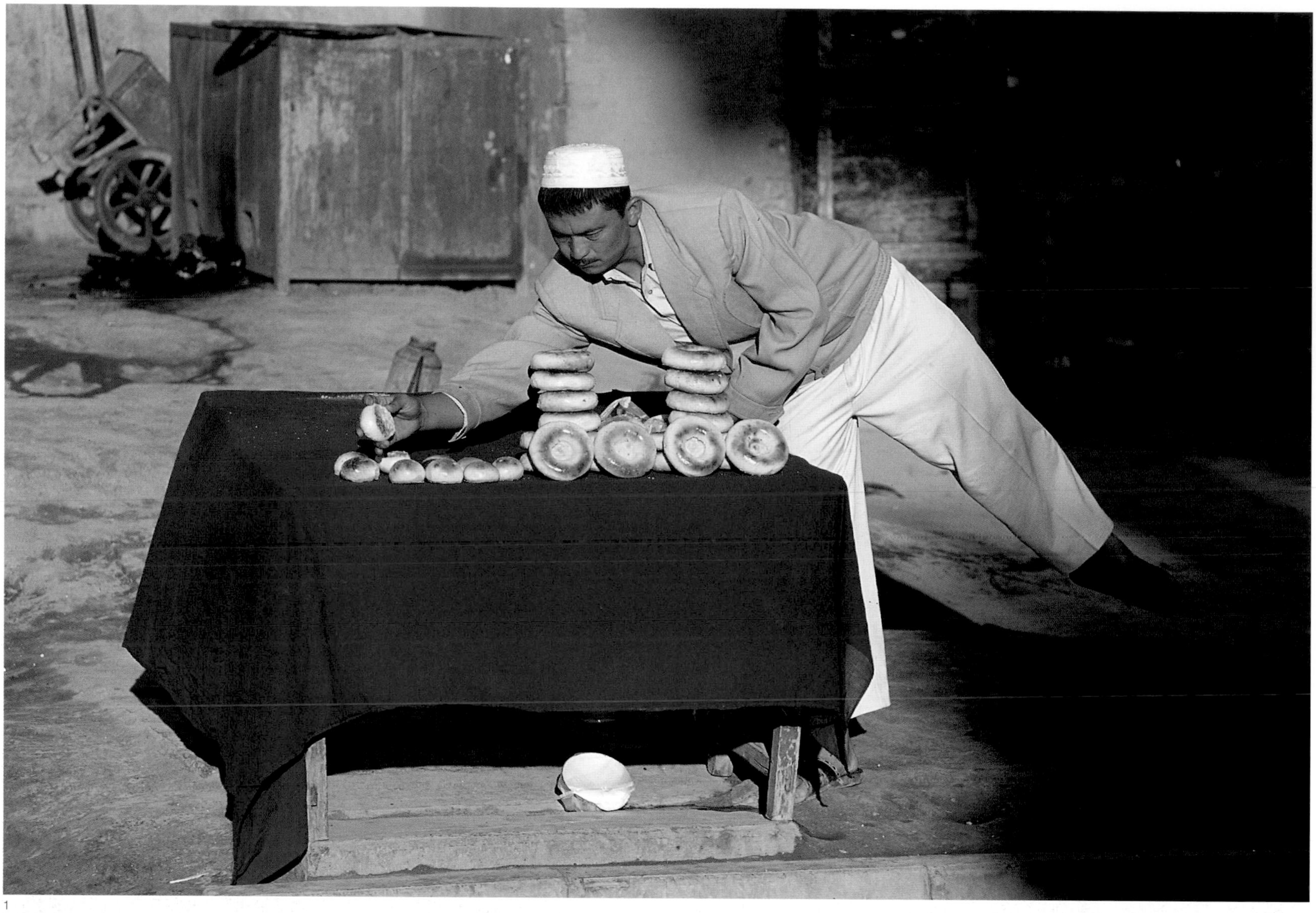

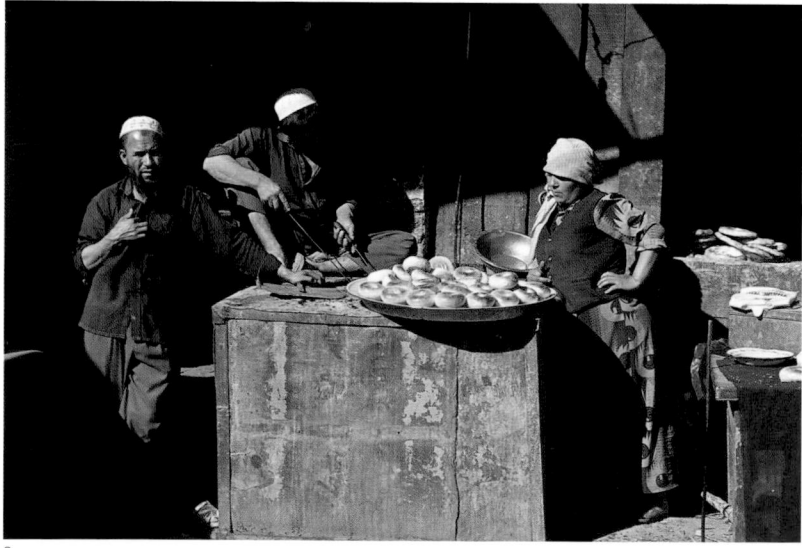

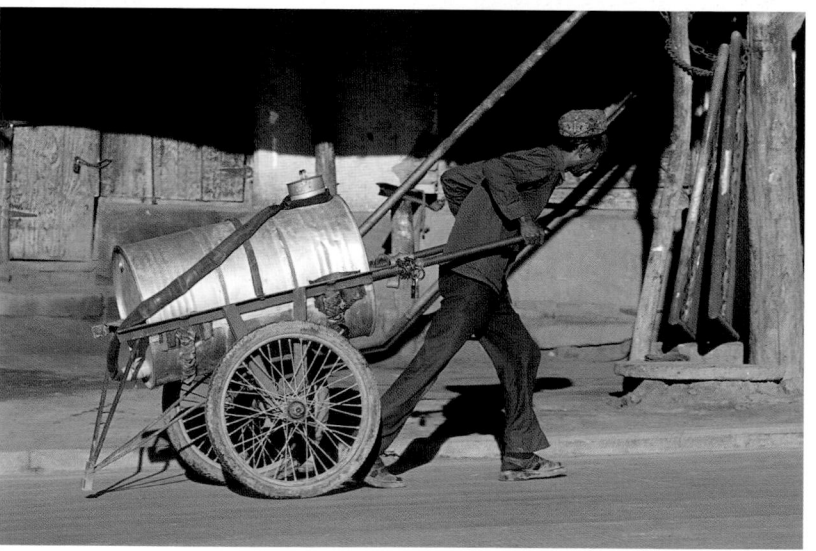

1

2

3

THE OLD TOWN

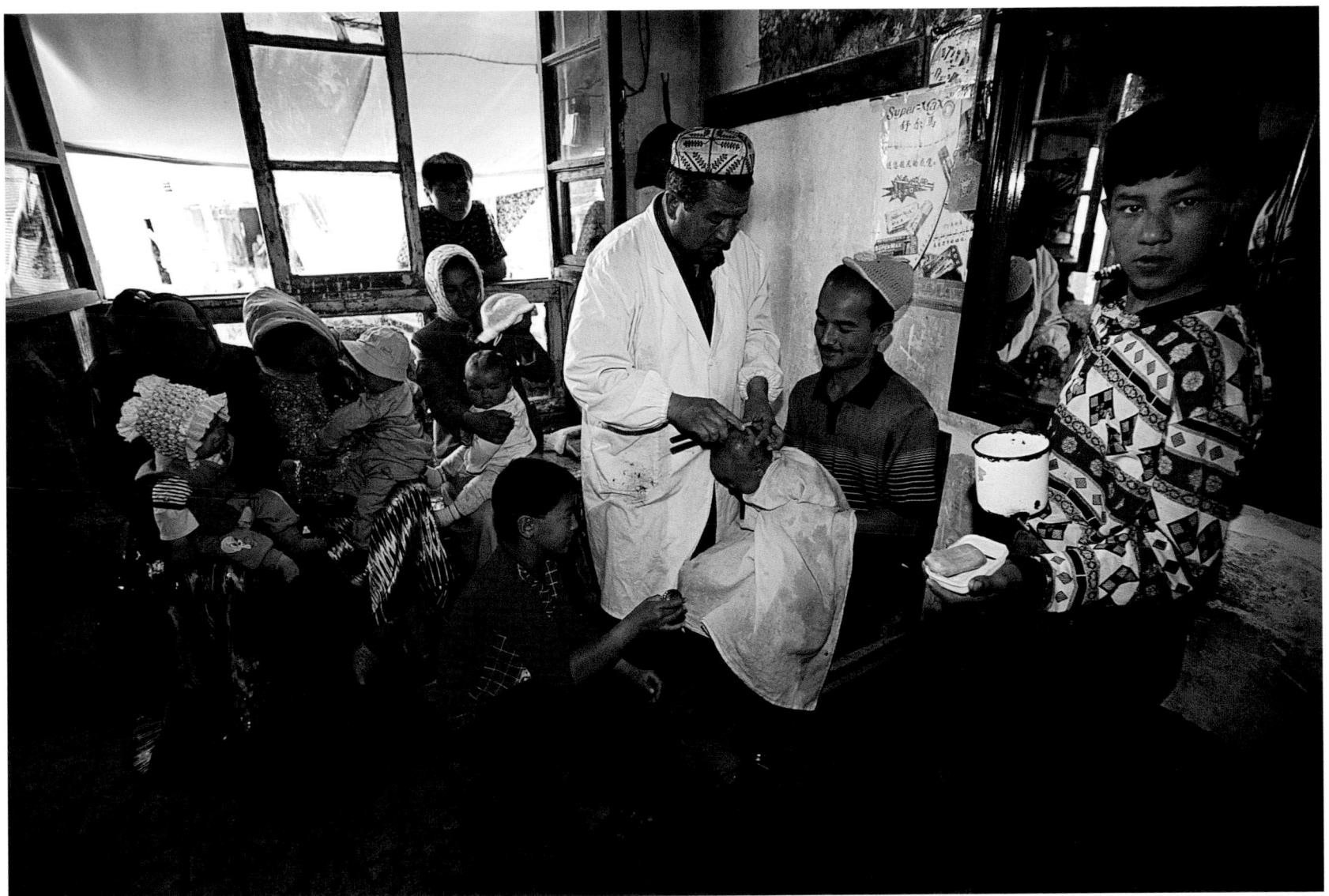

4

CHINA'S SURGING ECONOMY AND A HUGE GROWTH in demand from the 'stans' that formed the old Soviet Central Asian empire has sent traders from across the region pouring into Kashgar to buy Chinese goods. The Chinese government, whose thirst for energy grows by the hour, is meanwhile investing billions of dollars into Xi'an'jiang's infrastructure – while also eyeing their neighbour's oil and gas fields with barely concealed lust. As a result, Kashgar finds itself once again poised on the brink of history, with economists predicting its resurrection as a major player along the new 'Hi-tech Silk Road.' New air, rail and road links are ending the city's isolation, yet a stroll through what remains of the Old Town confirms that – regardless of Internet cafés and mobile phones – Kashgar will remain at heart a medieval city. [1] [2] Looks are deceptive; these 'bagels' are as hard as rock and usually eaten in small pieces soaked in goat soup. [3] The milkman on his rounds. [4] Babies' heads are shaved in the local barber shop to ward off the 'evil eye'.

THE SILK ROAD

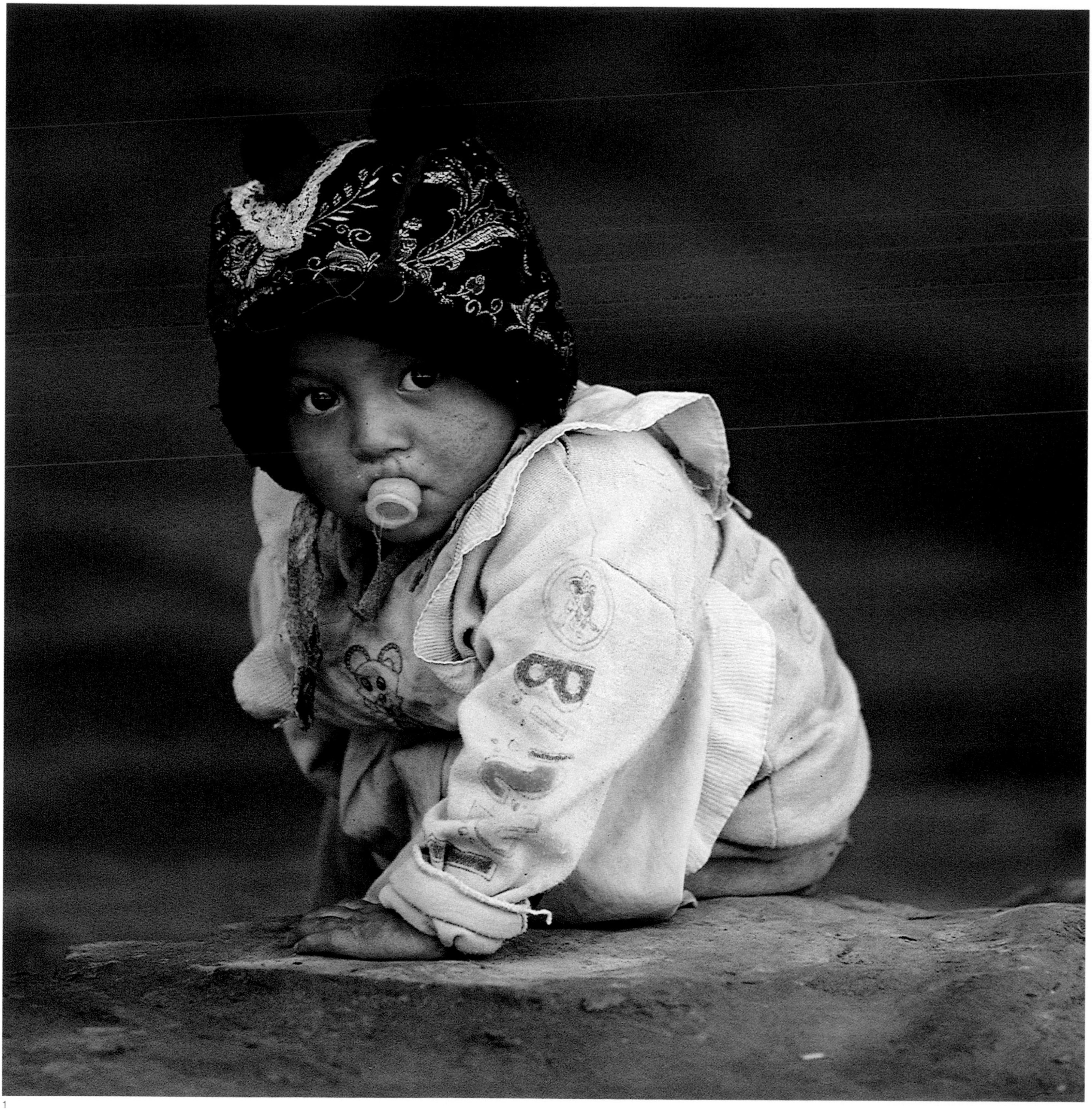

PEOPLE OF KASHGAR

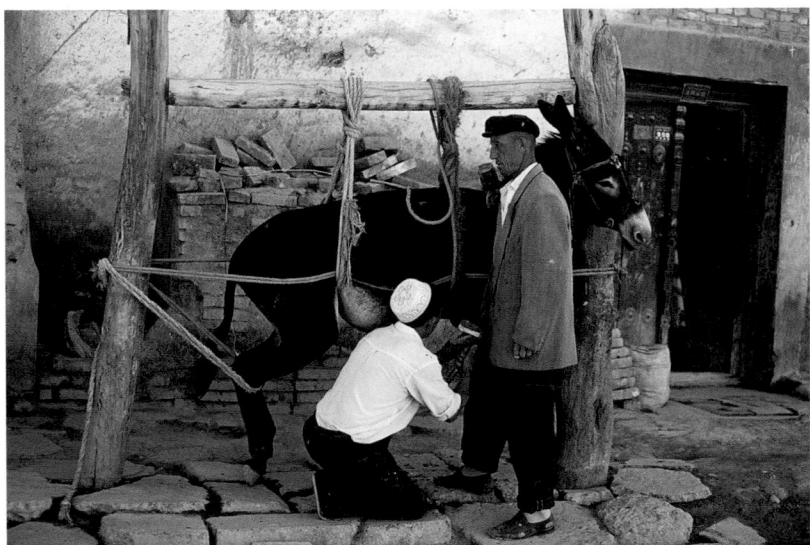

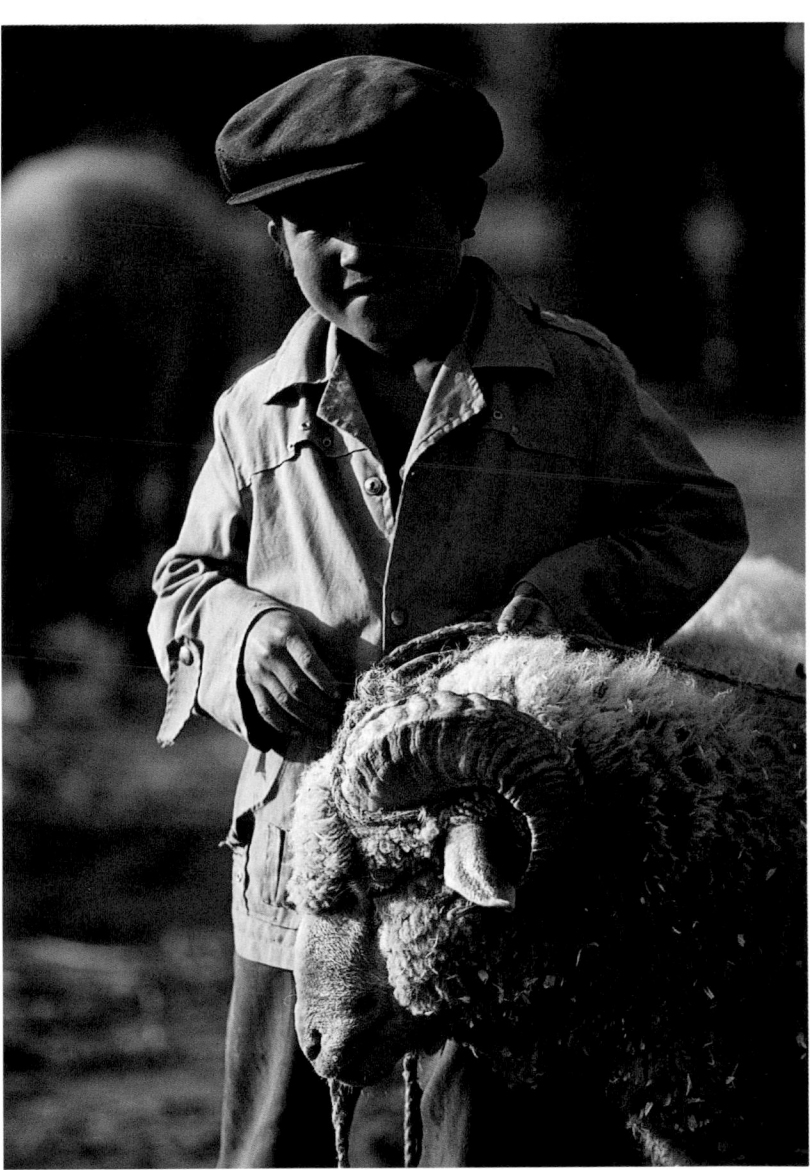

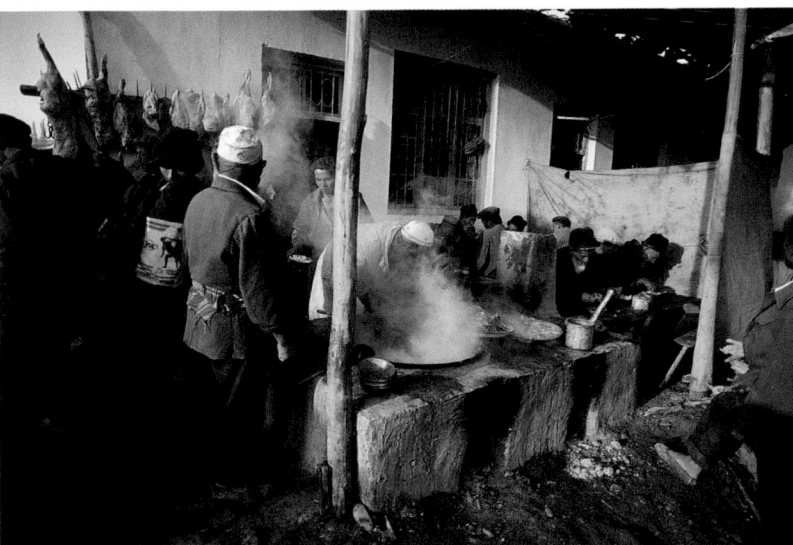

GANDAHARAN INDO-EUROPEANS ARRIVED IN KASHGAR from the Indus Valley in the 1st Century, introducing *Hinayana* Buddhism and establishing the first Buddhist kingdom in the Tarim Basin. They were followed by Han Dynasty General Ban Chao, who conquered Kashgar, subdued the kingdoms of the Silk Road and established Chinese control over the trade route that lasted almost continuously until the fall of the Tang Dynasty in 907 CE. During the 8th Century ancestors of the Uygurs, nomadic Turkic tribes from the Altai Mountains, came to dominate the basin, taking control of the Silk Road trade. At the end of the Tang Dynasty Sunni Muslim Qarlug Turkic tribes conquered Kashgar and launched jihads against all the Buddhist kingdoms. The Uygurs converted to Islam in this period. Uygurs now comprise around 90 per cent of Kashgar's 360,000 population, with the remainder drawn form Tajik, Kyrgyz, Uzbek, Mongolian and Han Chinese ethnic groups. [1] A baby at the Abakh Khoja Tomb. [2] A blacksmith in the old town. [3] Breakfast at the Sunday bazaar. [4] A boy and his ram at the livestock market.

THE SILK ROAD

LIVESTOCK MARKET AT THE SUNDAY BAZAAR

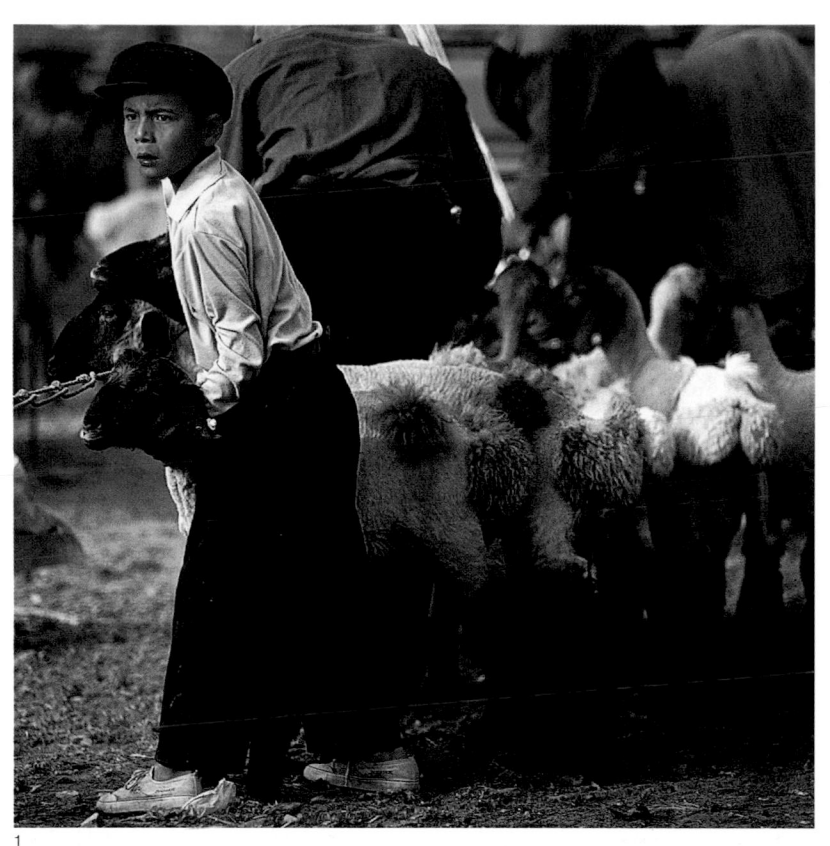

1

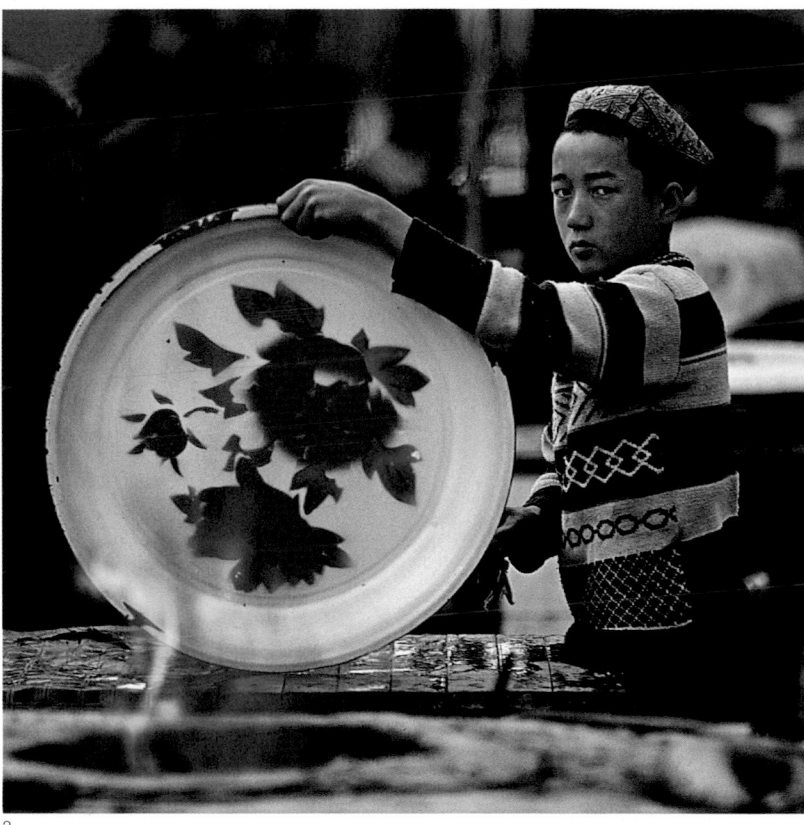

2

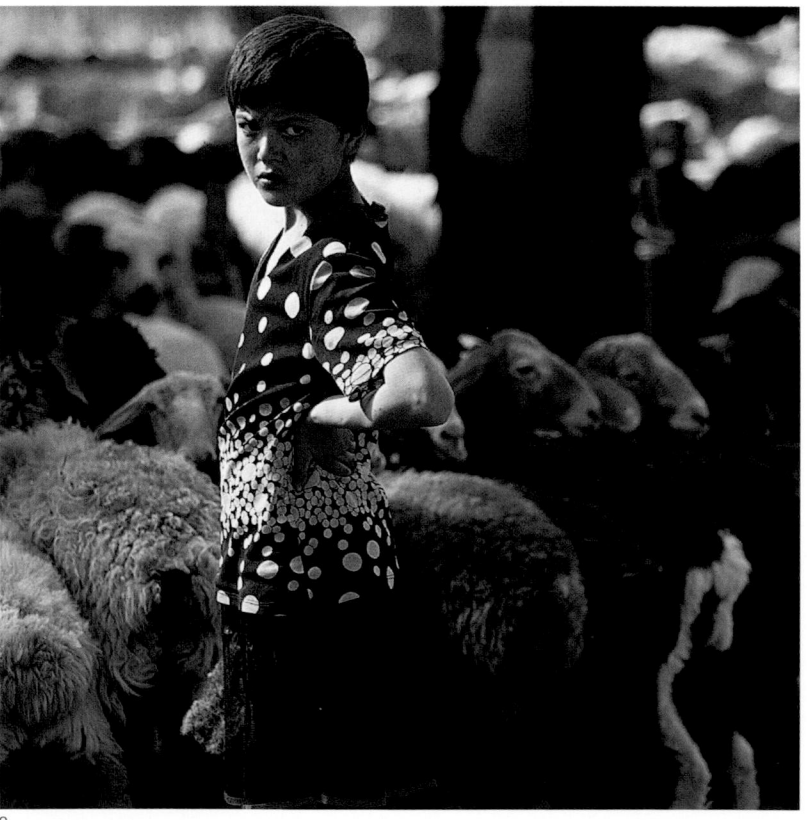

3

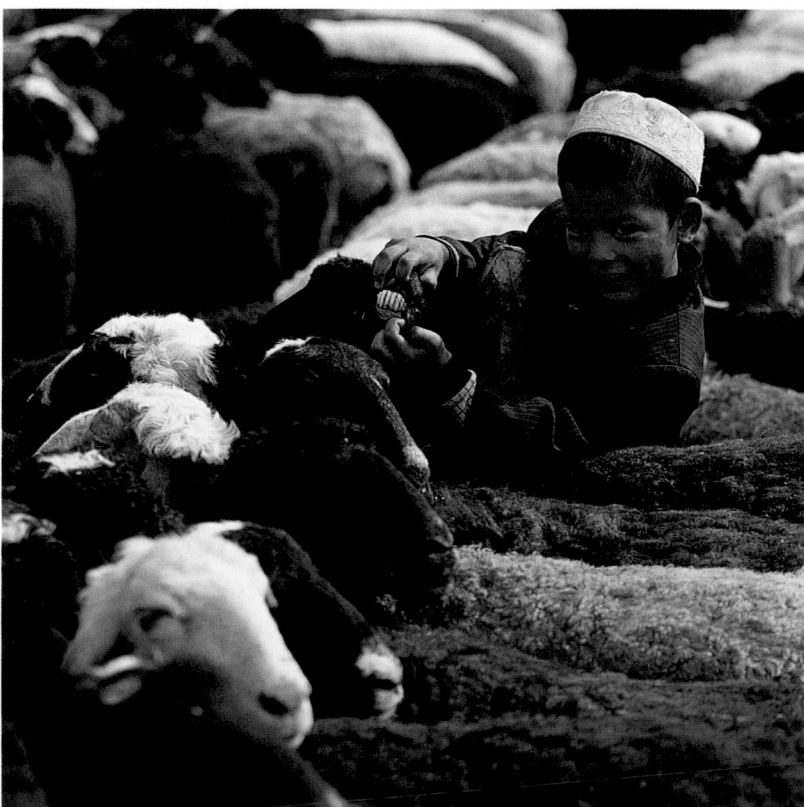

4

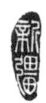

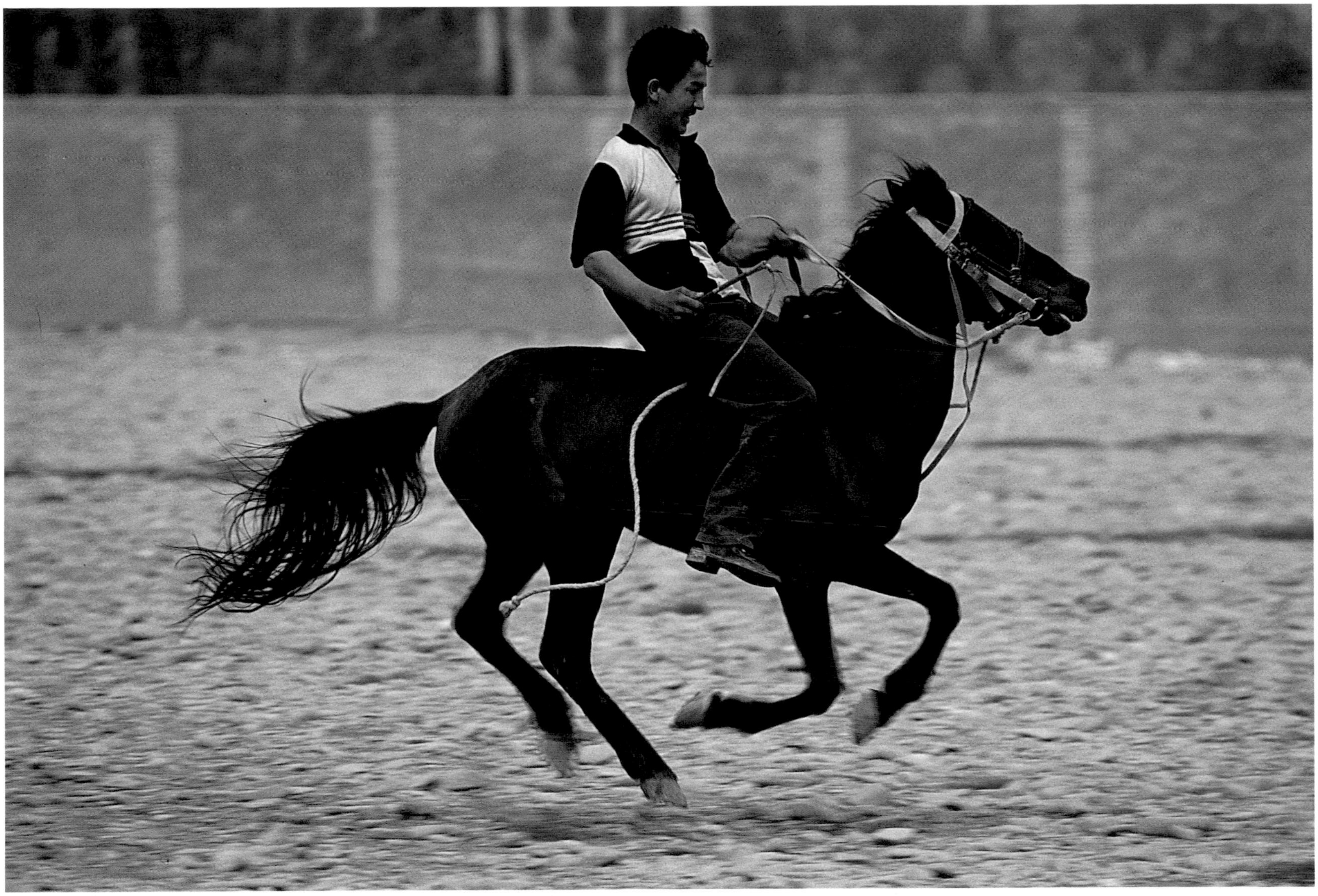

5

KASHGAR GREW UP WHERE SILK ROAD CARAVANS STOPPED TO EXCHANGE THEIR PACK ANIMALS. Camels were traded for the mules and horses needed to tackle the glacial passes over the Pamirs or the Karakorum. Horses and mules were swapped for the camels needed to cross the deserts towards Xi'an. The Sunday bazaar livestock market, now one of the region's major tourist attractions, had its origins in those distant trades. Unlike their city counterparts, most children in the countryside are put to work at an early age. The children of Kashgar, heirs to 20 centuries of tradition, spend their Sundays learning the skills they may need at the livestock bazaar. The market, far away in time from the giant Mao statue in the sterile new town, embodies the essence and excitement of Kashgar's great and long-lived history. Some may treat their duties as play, like [4] the boy learning to check the teeth of a goat. Others, however, take their tasks – whether [1] wrangling, [2] cleaning dishes, [3] standing guard or [5] 'test driving' horses for potential buyers – more seriously.

THE SILK ROAD

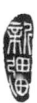

THE KARAKORUM HIGHWAY

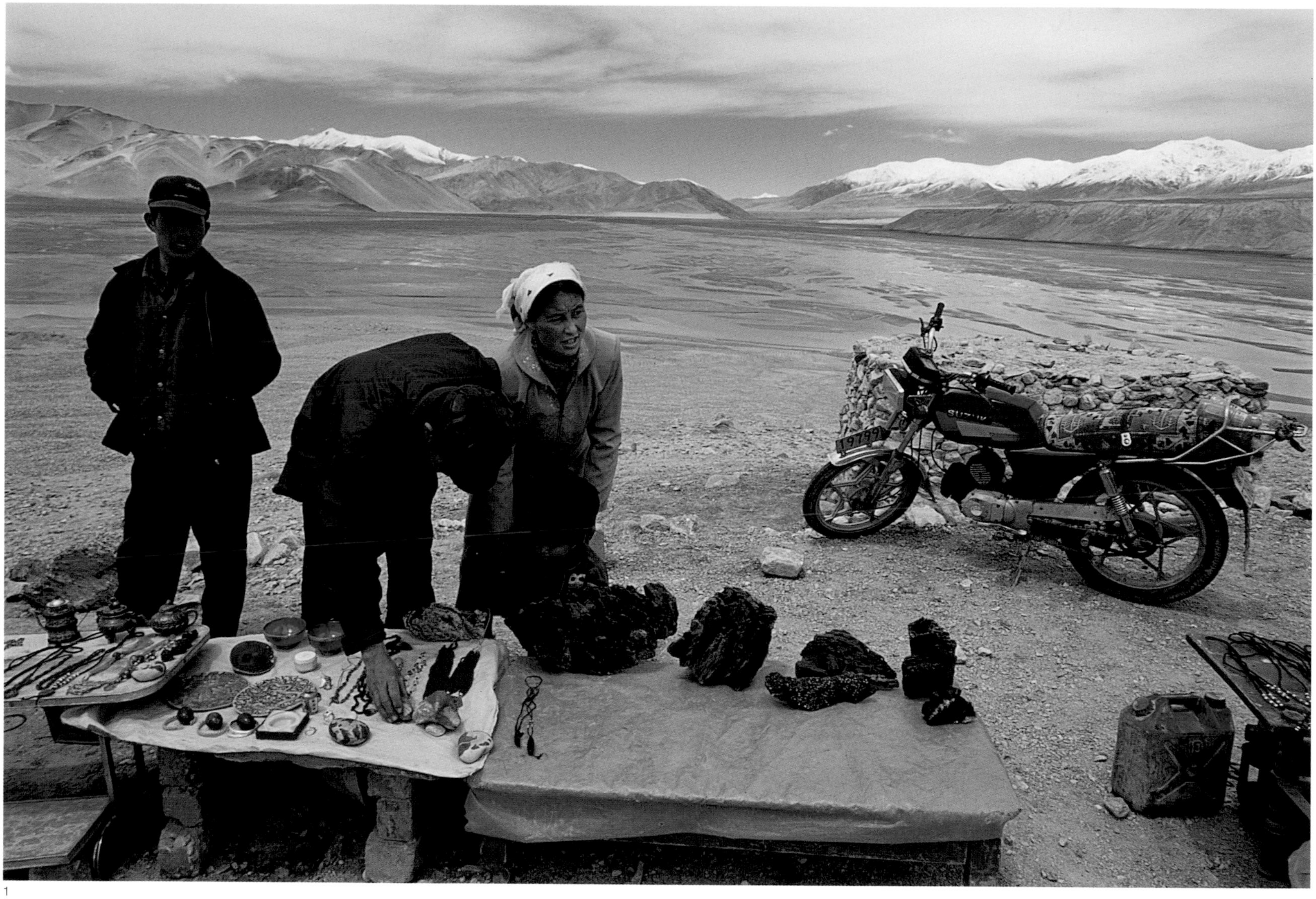

I FIRST TRAVELLED THE PAKISTAN SIDE OF THE KARAKORUM HIGHWAY in the spring of 2003. We got as far as the Hunsa Valley before *karakorum* (Turkish for 'crumbling rock') and mudslides blocked our way north to the Chinese border. Built along the ancient caravan path that Hsuan Tsang took to Swat in the 7th Century, the 1,284-kilometre (780-mile) highway linking Rawalpindi to Kashgar was literally blasted out of the granite precipices of one of world's youngest mountain ranges. The Karakorum is 'only' 55 million years old and is growing at the rate of nearly two inches (5 cm) a year. The astounding engineering feat took 20 years (1968–88) to complete and cost the lives of 400 Chinese workers. In May 2005 I set off from Kashgar heading south towards the Khunjerab Pass. While the Pakistani section of the highway consisted primarily of vertical cliffs plunging into abyssal canyons, the Xin'jiang side is surrounded by open vistas of rolling pastures fringed by towering snowcapped mountains. [1] [2] Bulungkul, a vast wetland in [3] the Ghez River Valley on the Pamir Plateau.

146

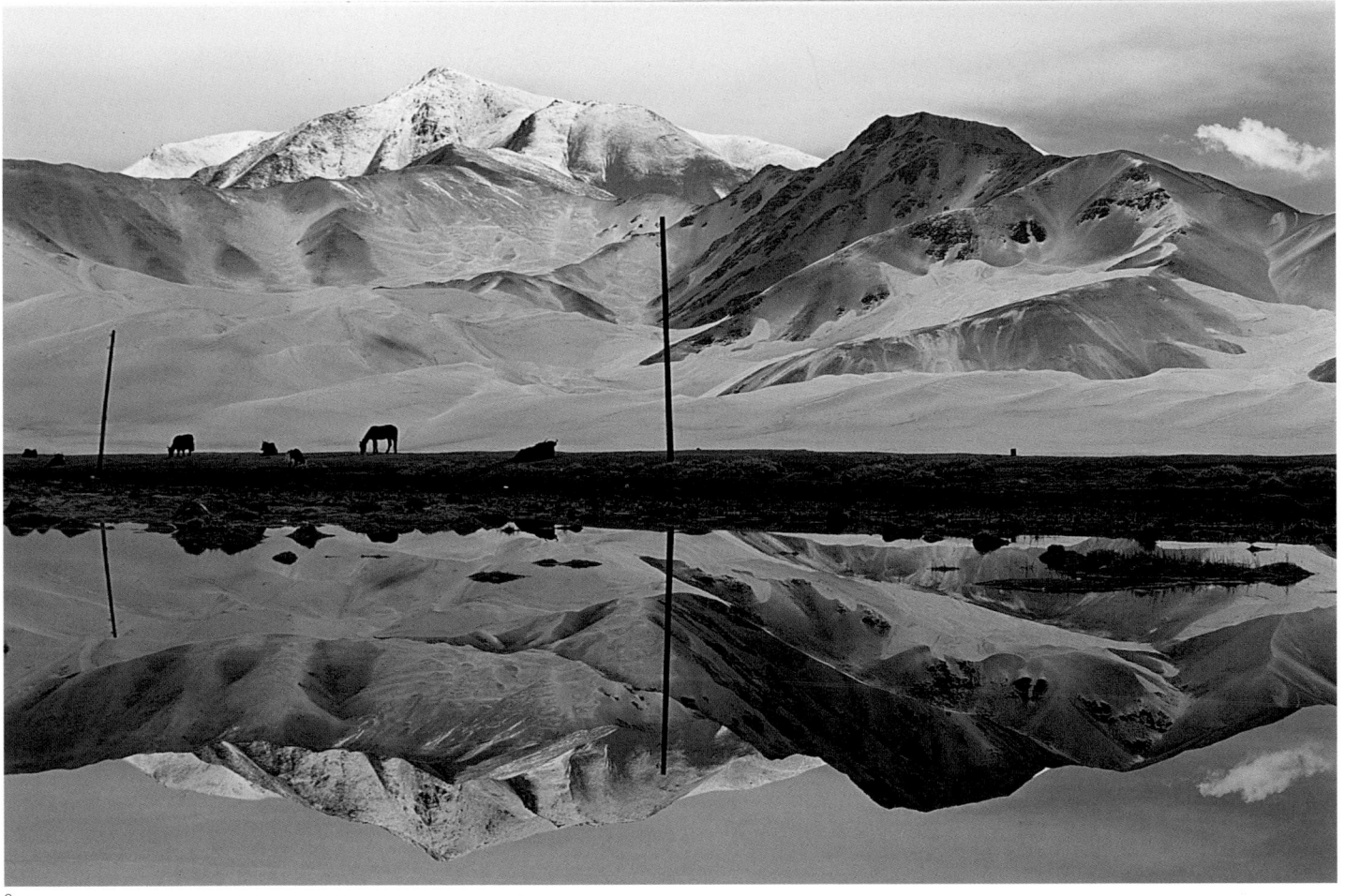

2

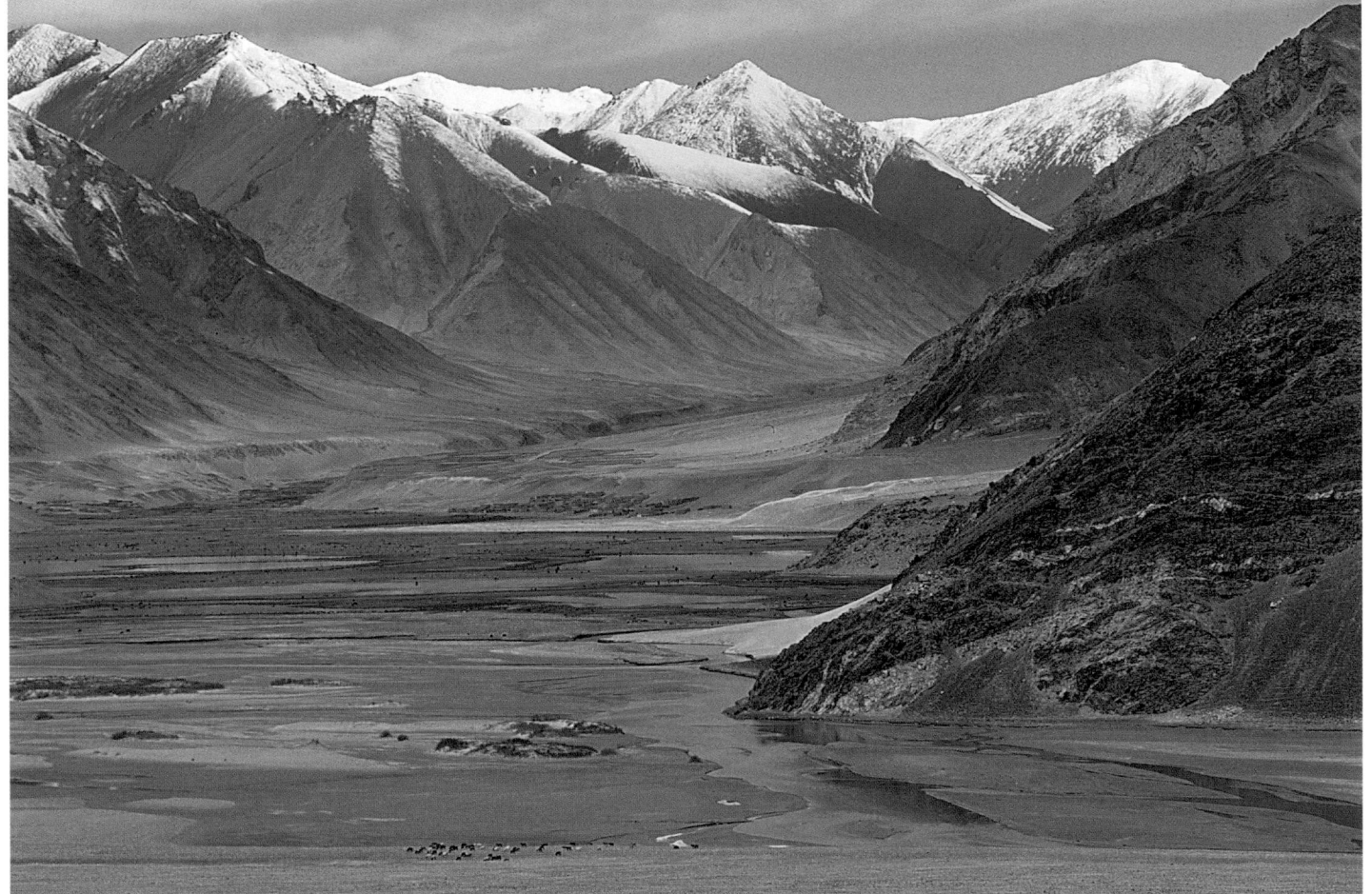

3

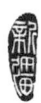

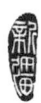

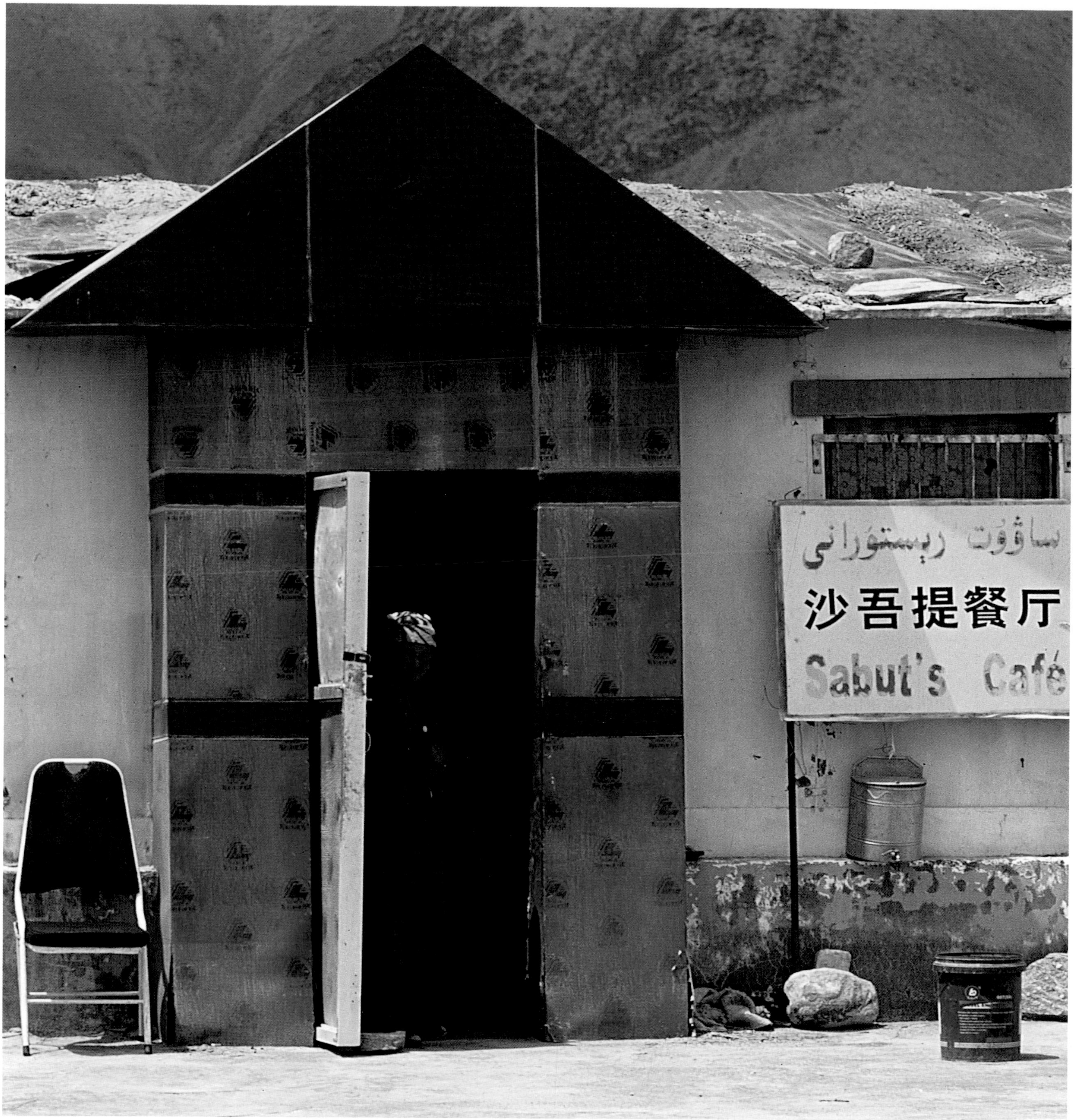

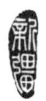

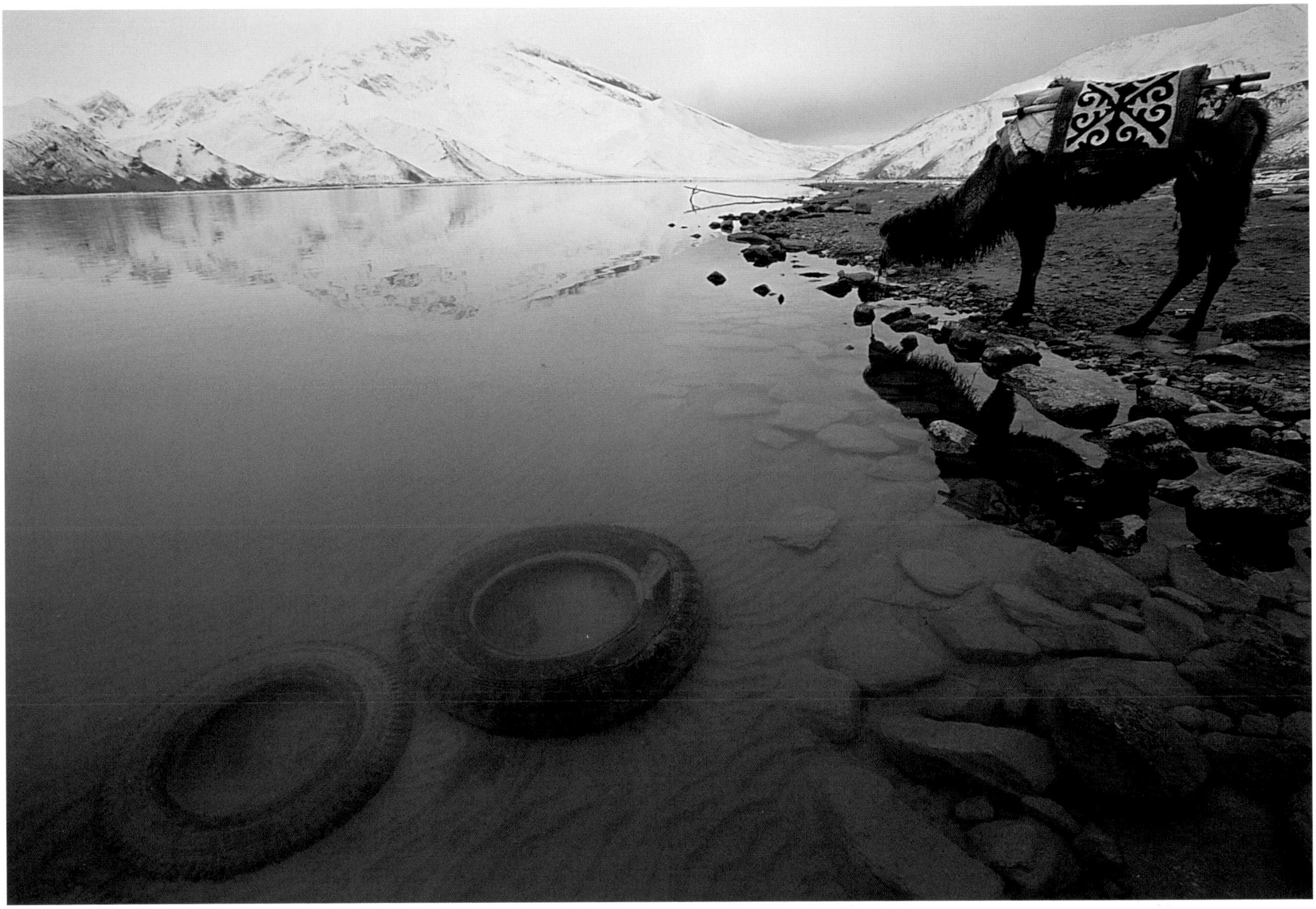

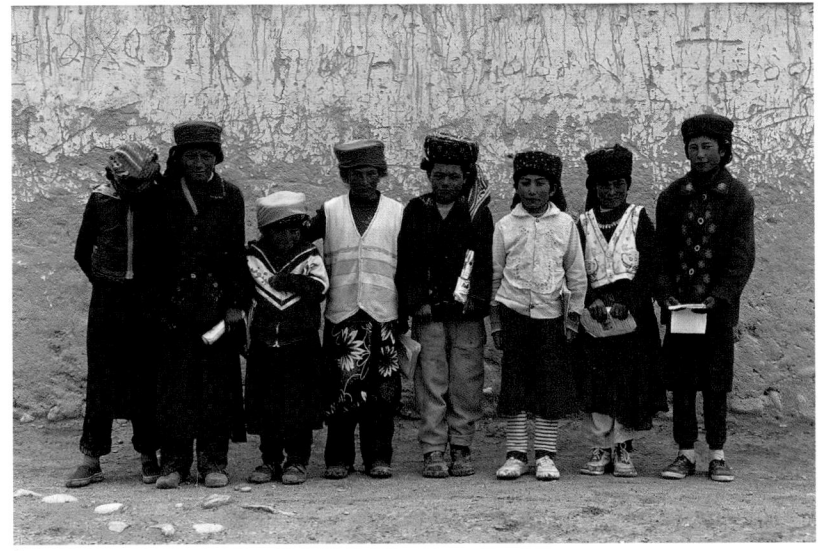

2

IT TOOK US SIX HOURS TO NEGOTIATE THE 196 KILOMETRES (122 miles) from Kashgar to Karakuli Lake at the base of the Muztagata Glacier. Karakuli, 'black sea' in Uygur, is at an altitude of 3,600 metres (11,800 feet), covers an area of about 10 square kilometres (4 square miles) and is some 30 metres (100 feet) deep in places. A tourist brochure notes that the surrounding Kongur and Muztagata mountains are "reflected on the silvery surface of the pristine water" where Tajik and Kirghiz nomads graze herds of camels, yaks and horses. An *in situ* reality check records a vicious icy wind whipping the surface of the lake into frenzy while fast-moving clouds transform the sun into a rapidly blinking heliograph. A tourist bus is parked next to a row of souvenir stands, all exhibiting the same junk that seems to follow me around China. A few tourists lean against the wind or stagger down to the lake shore, where Kara-Kirghiz touts are offering horseback and camel rides. [1] We arrived too late for lunch at Satut's Café. [2] The wind dropped after lunch and the mountain reflections reappeared in the less than pristine water. [3] Tajik school children.

3

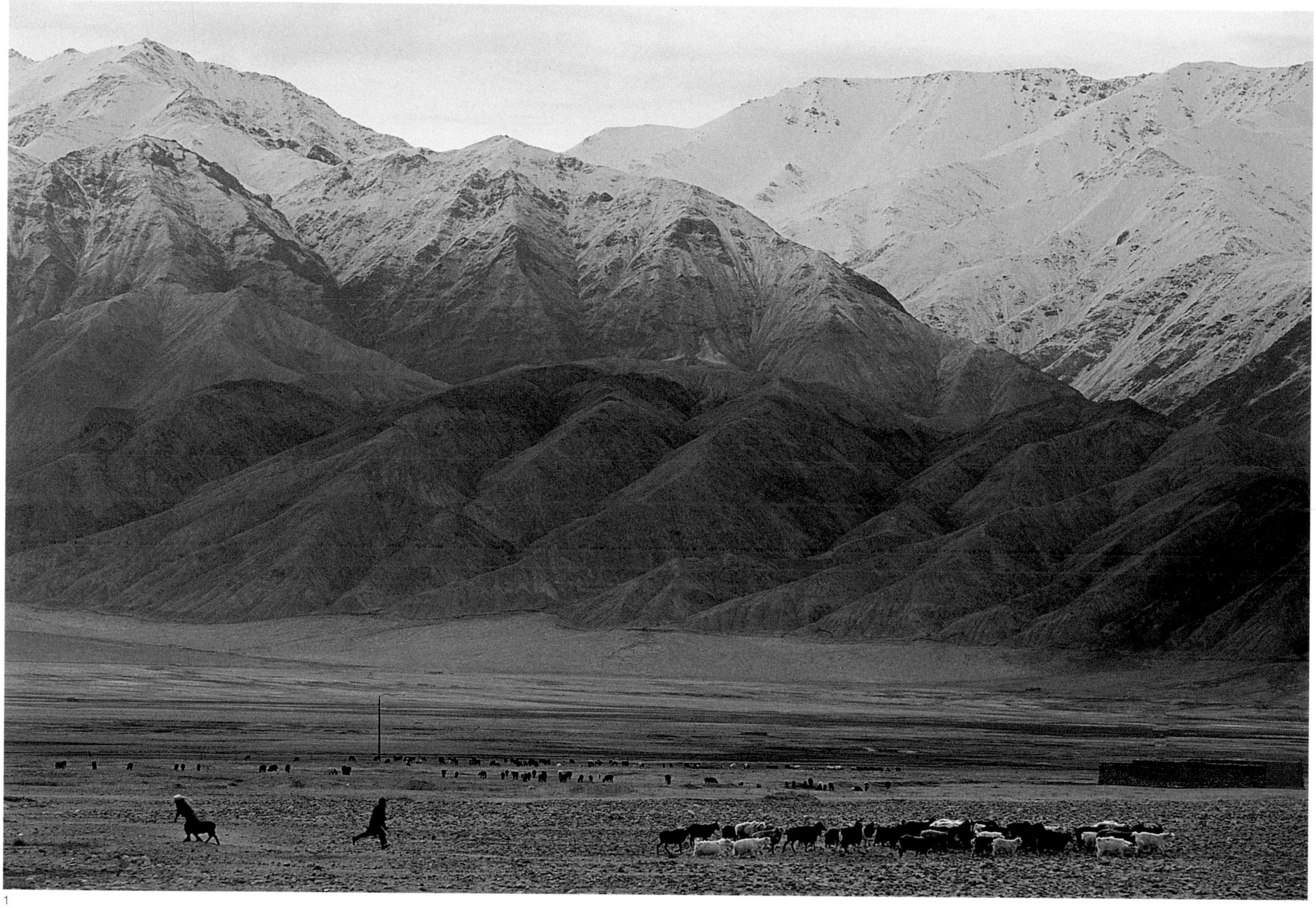

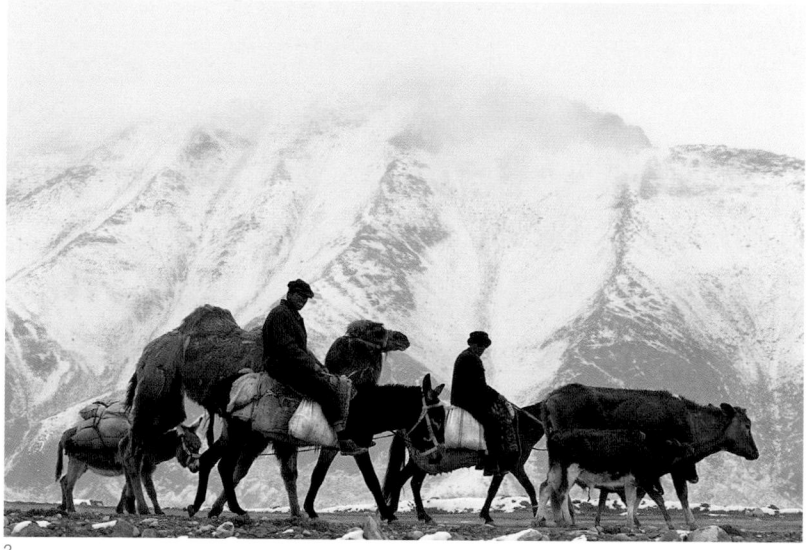

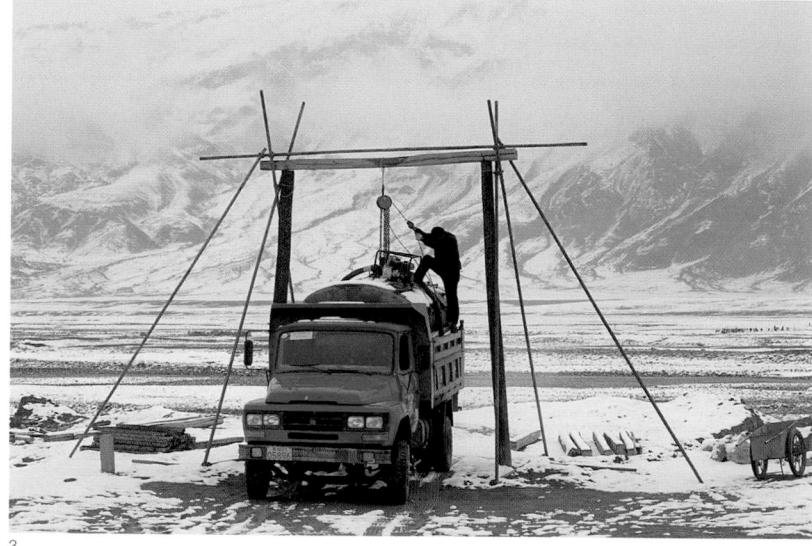

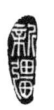

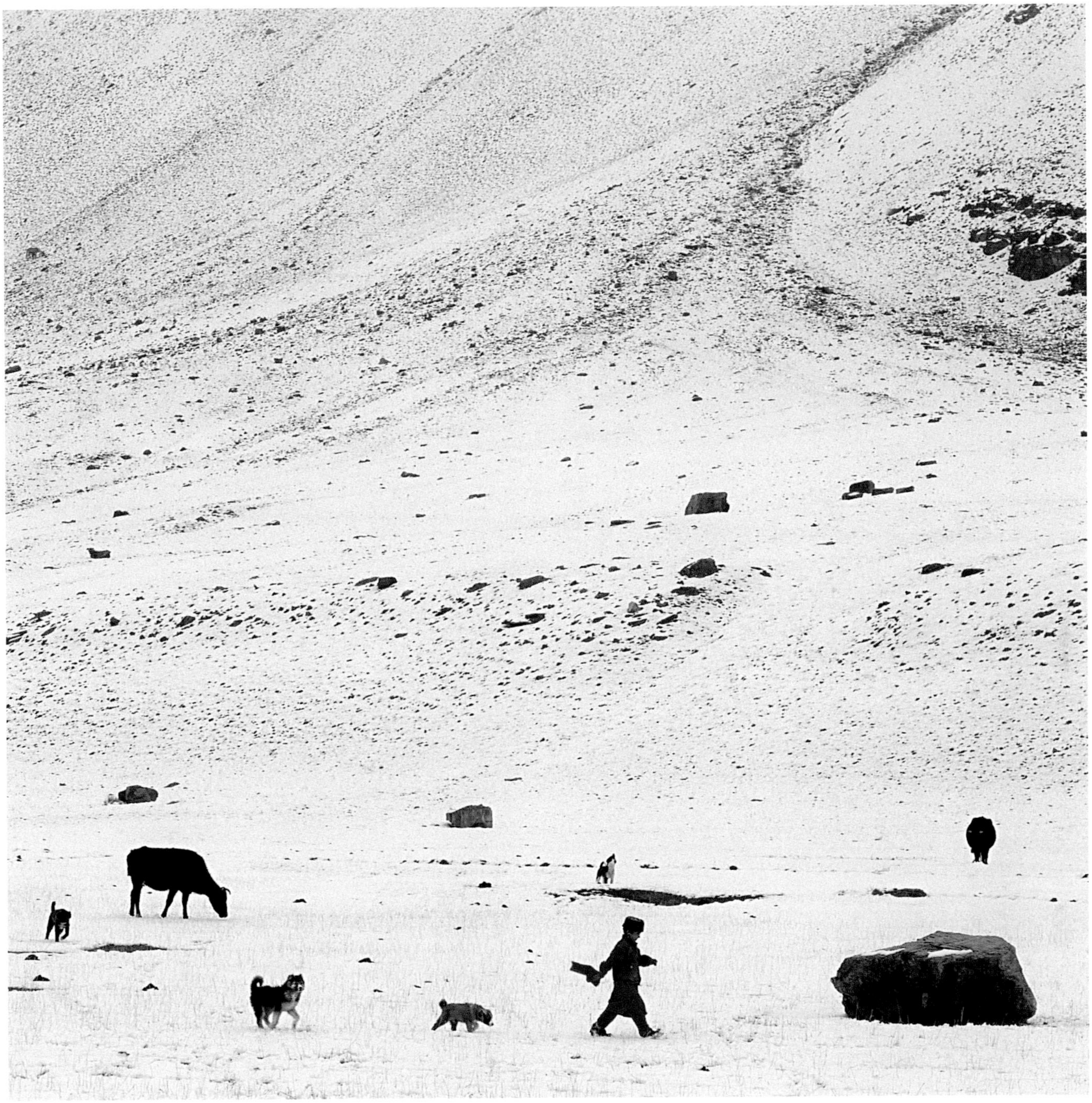

4

WE LEFT TASHKURGAN BEFORE DAWN under a slate grey sky. Thirty minutes into the six-hour journey to the summit of the 4,733-metre (15,500-foot) Khunjerab Pass and the Pakistan border-post of Sost, snowflakes began to stick on the windscreen. The storm gathered strength as we drove further into the pass. Rutted plains with a fresh dusting of snow took on the surreal appearance of vast oceans churned by white-headed waves. Only an occasional distant herd of yak or a flock of sheep grazing in the foothills of the immense cloud-shrouded mountains drew the scenery back to reality. The Khunjerab, which means 'valley of blood' and is a reference to the murderous Hunza bandits who once preyed on travellers negotiating these remote passes, was a study in monochrome relieved only by red splashes provided by the Tajik women's traditional dress. [1] A goat is separated from the flock to be taken to meet its destiny. [2] A 21st-century caravan. [3] A portable generator being unloaded at a frontier depot. [4] A Tajik boy on his way home from school.

THE SILK ROAD

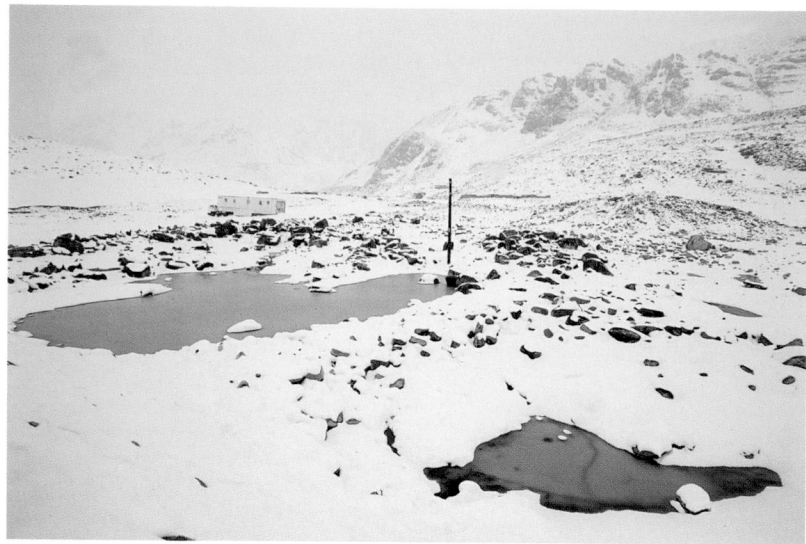

1

"Over a thousand mountains the birds have vanished,
Not a soul in sight through ten thousand paths.
In a solitary boat, an old man in straw hat and cape,
Fishes the cold river snow alone."

Cold River in the Snow by Liu Zong'yuan

THE HIGHWAY GRADUALLY EMPTIED as we drew closer to the border. Only the occasional house tucked into the shadows of the great snow-covered mountains interrupted the monotony of the silent snow. Two men in the distance rode towards us, and we stopped to take their picture. As they came nearer we made out a young man in a long PLA coat mounted on a fine-looking horse, accompanied by an older man straddling a small donkey playing 'air-guitar' with a broom. This odd couple was laughing and singing and acting as though they had enjoyed a long and convivial lunch. I then recognized the song. It was the Cantonese theme tune to a popular Hong Kong television drama from the 1990s. The snow stopped as we neared our destination, and so did the Karakorum Highway. A pile of snow-covered rubble blocked the road 'sleeping-policeman' style. It was evidently there to stop vehicles from crossing a bridge that had ceased to exist. We stretched our legs, chewing on cold, stale nan bread. The only indication that we were actually on this planet was [1] a forlorn container truck with "Chinese Customs" markings abandoned and half-buried in the snow a few hundred yards from the road. "So what can we see up there, on top of the pass?" Akbar, my guide, said there was a monument to the Karakorum Highway and a red road sign that said "China drive right" and "Pakistan drive left". I stared hard into the distance at the faint outline of the mountains and the storm swirling over them, checked my watch, and made an executive decision. We would turn back rather than go off-road to try our luck navigating uncertain tracks that ran through the shallows of icy rivers. As I turned to get back into the car I made a wish for 'third time lucky' on the Karakorum Highway.

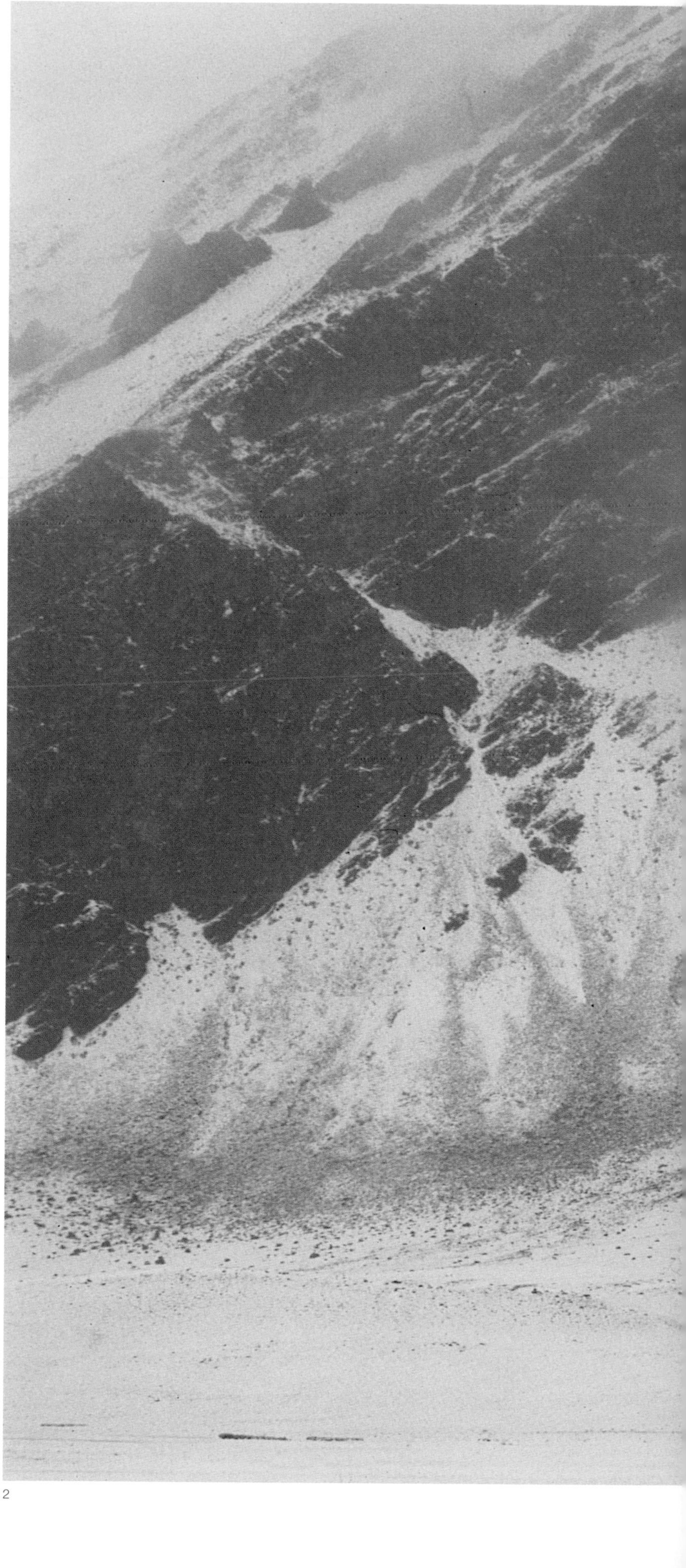

2

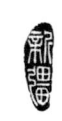

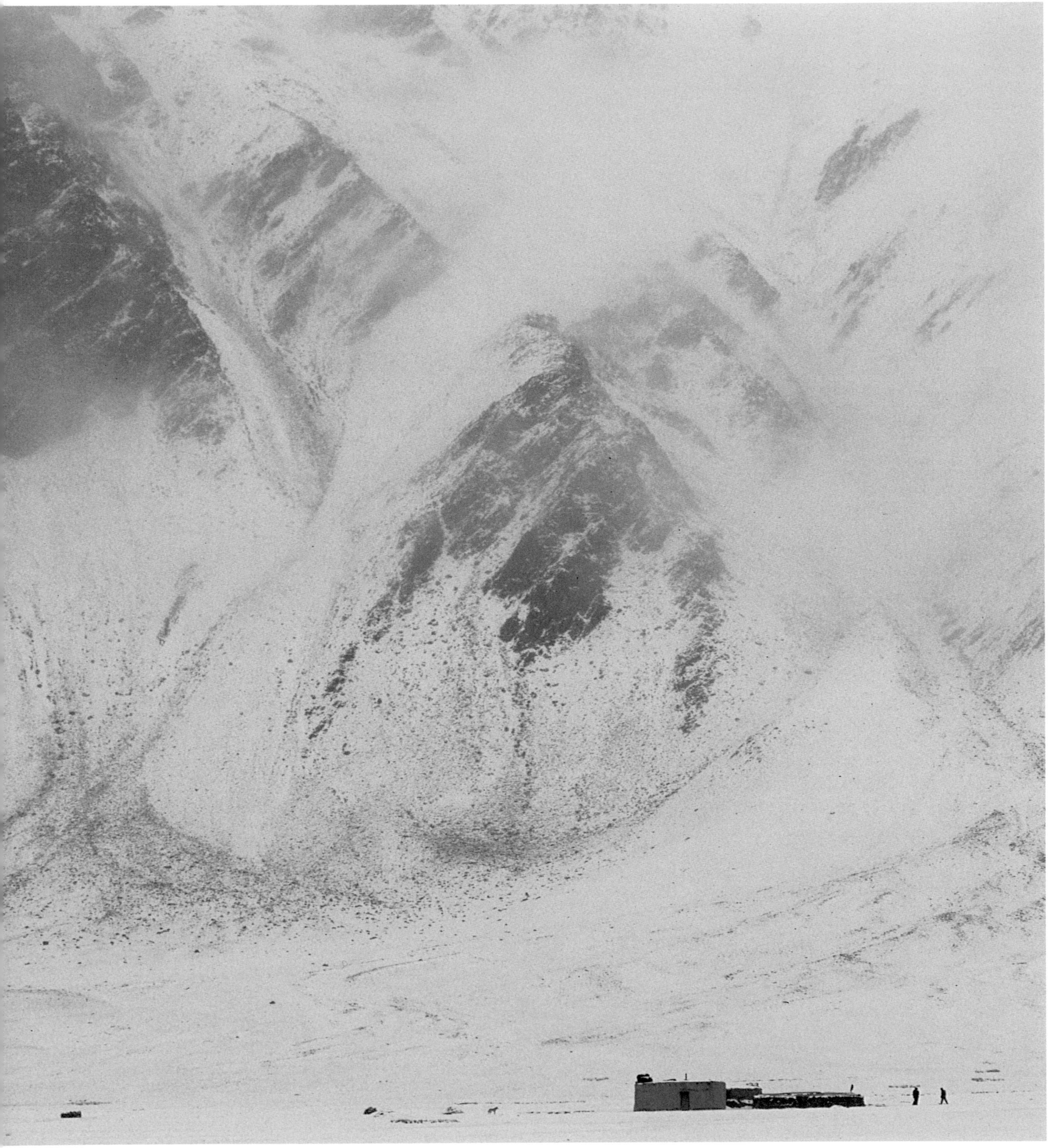

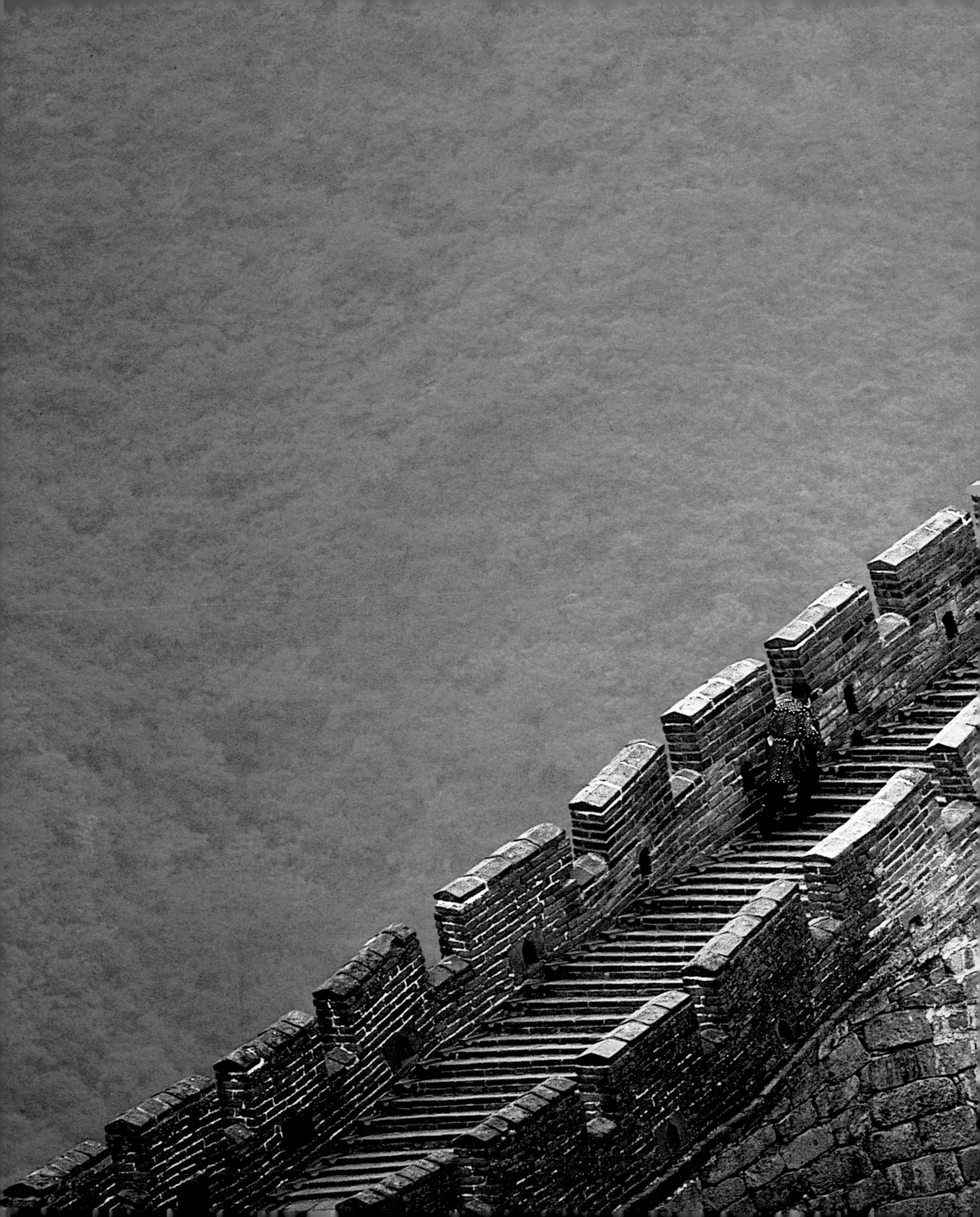

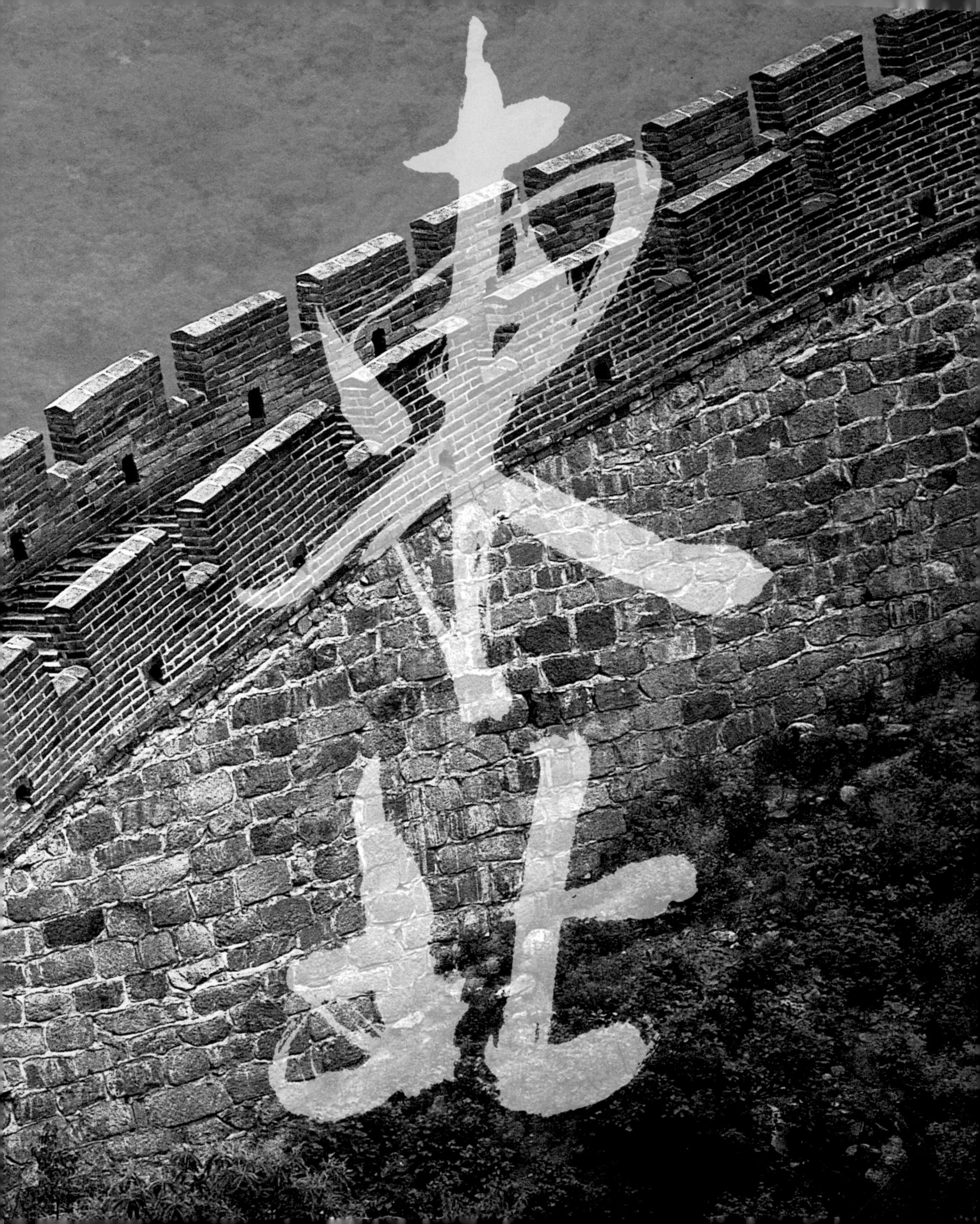

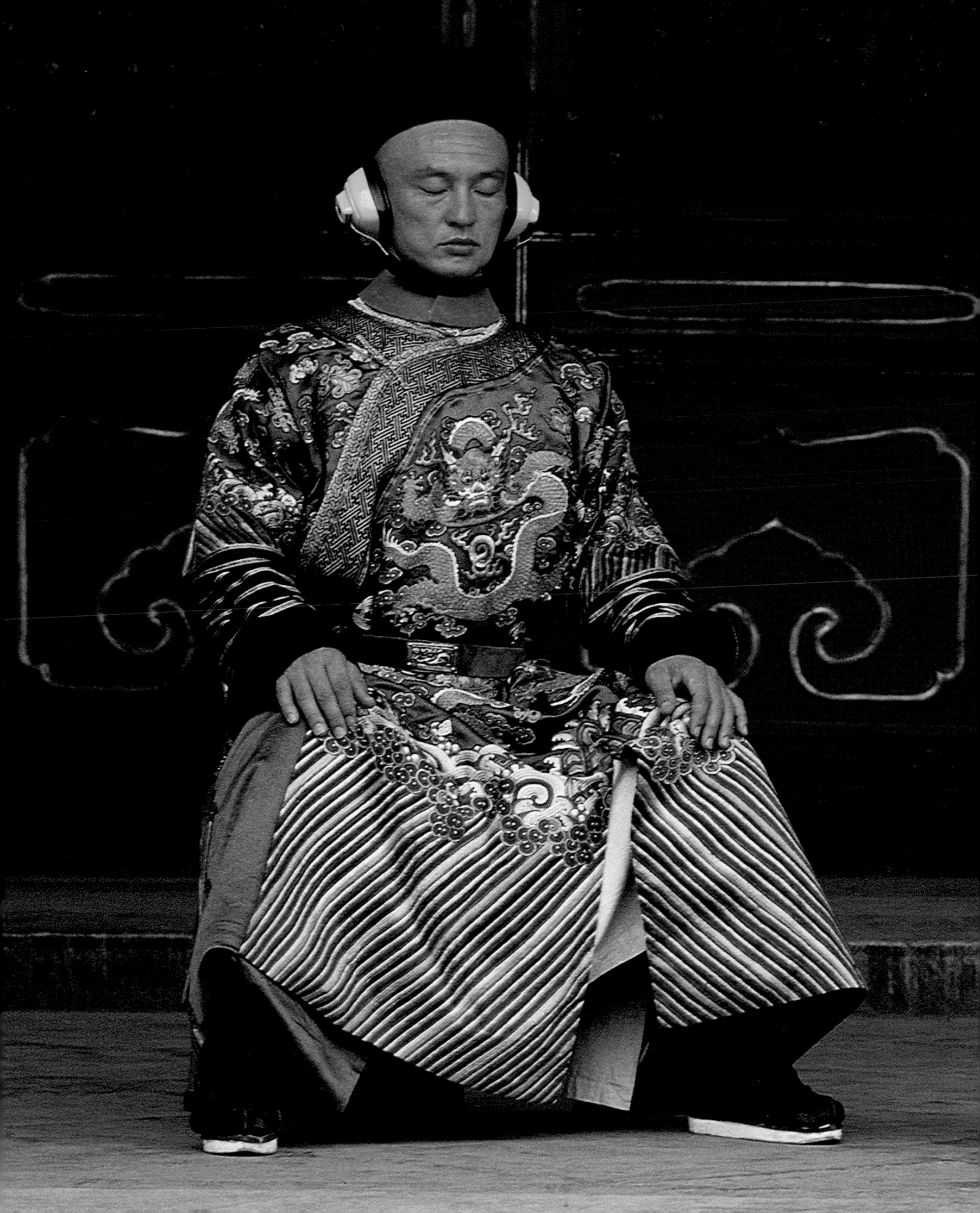

NORTH BY NORTHEAST

Driving rain whips the car with unrelenting lashes as I drift in and out of consciousness; my driver is having a hard time seeing out even though the windshield wipers are going at a manic speed. We're on our way north from Chang'chun to Ha'erbin, or is it the other way round? The endless highways are beginning to blend together…

I remember sitting alone on the Dragon throne in my knee-length under-shirt, while my heavy embroidered dragon robe was draped unceremoniously over a workbench down below. With only the middle doors opened, the vast hall was shrouded in semi-darkness in the half-light of dawn. I sat in the shadows like a ghost, watching the silhouettes of crewmembers drifting in and out through the central doorway, attending to their various tasks. And then suddenly, as though in a dream sequence, they all disappeared from view, and I found myself completely alone in the Hall of Supreme Harmony. Dawn was just breaking over the enormous empty courtyards on either side of the white marble 'Imperial Way', where on previous days, ten thousand extras in Qing imperial costumes had congregated for the filming of the coronation. And for a moment that seemed like an eternity, time stood still. I was alone in the Forbidden City.

In that cocooned fragment of time, as I sat in the place where twenty-four flesh-and-blood humans were once enthroned as the 'Son of Heaven' and 'Emperor of China', with the mandate of life and death over all beings within the realm, many strange thoughts flashed through my head. But I only remember the feeling of tremendous loneliness, a sensation that was deeper and sharper than anything I had known or have experienced since. In the far distance, in front of the Gate of Supreme Harmony, the tiny figure of a woman on a bicycle slipped into my field of vision through the open doors and I followed her long shadow gliding as though in slow motion across the vast emptiness until she disappeared behind the doorframe. In that instant, the spell was broken and a hive of activity erupted as suddenly as it had vanished. One by one the row of doors to the hall began to open, revealing gigantic reflectors of white silk being hoisted in front of a bank of lights on the terrace.

As light slowly crept up the platform, I got up and quickly descended the side steps – theatrically, so that all the people who were coming into the hall would think that I was just rehearsing a scene. Which, indeed, was the reason why I was up there in the first place, on the set of Bertolucci's *The Last Emperor*. I was rehearsing my scene, where I had to descend rapidly down the narrow side steps to chase after my two-year-old son, who had become bored with the coronation and jumped off the throne to go off and play. So up and down the platform I went, practising running down the seven steps in silk costume boots that were not exactly designed for tennis, while holding up the invisible hem of my imaginary robe so that I won't trip and fall when I made my rapid descent in front of the camera. And when my dresser had stepped out to get himself some coffee, I had decided to sit down for a rest.

The curators of the Palace Museum had reluctantly granted their permission for the *Last Emperor* crew to film in their 'Holy of the Holies' with one tricky condition, no equipment was allowed to touch the metal brick floor inside the Hall of Supreme Harmony, as the original hard tiles from Su'zhou were deemed to be irreplaceable. So production had to bring in a Steady-cam crew from Italy for the sequence and the hall had to be lit from the outside. Somewhere in that agreement must also have been a clause forbidding the crew from parking their behinds on the Dragon throne. Feeling like a naughty schoolboy who just had a cigarette behind the bicycle sheds, I walked towards the exit as nonchalantly as I could only to be surprised by a palace custodian I had come to know,

[LEFT] A moment of peace on the set of *The Last Emperor* in Bei'jing. [PRECEDING PAGES] The Great Wall at Mu'tian'yu.

in my other capacity as a lowly third assistant director. "You looked good up there, Prince Chun," he said with a friendly, knowing smile as if to say, "We both know that it's only a replica, a movie set recreated for the tourists, but you still shouldn't have done it."

This was the day when I finally got to deliver my one line in the film, the line of dialogue that distinguished me as an 'actor' as opposed to just an overdressed extra. And it is a line that they cannot cut from the film because it is one of the most famous lines in the history of the Qing Dynasty. Allegedly, during the enthronement ceremony in this very same hall in 1908, two-year-old Pu'yi, the last emperor of imperial China, became whiny and restless as the interminable rituals dragged on, and in an effort to calm him, his father the regent Prince Chun uttered the unintentionally prophetic words, "It'll all soon be over."

Little did I know then, when I uttered those words into the lens of the Steady-cam over and over again while I was down on my knees, that years later, my journey through the provinces of North by Northeast – a region that everyone from the Russians to the Japanese, the Chinese warlords, the republicans, the communists and the Soviets had fought bloody battles to control – would unintentionally echo the footsteps of my movie son. For the story of Pu'yi Aisin-Gioro was in many ways a reflection of China's own tragic history in the first half of the 20th Century.

It was his ancestors, the Jurched people, forebears of the Manchus and founders of the Jin kingdom, who first swept out of Manchuria to conquer northern China. They captured the Song Dynasty capital of Kai'feng along with the emperor and the imperial family in 1227, forcing what remained of the Song court to flee south across the Yang'tze River to Hang'zhou, where they established the Southern Song Dynasty. But the powerful Jin kingdom was soon overrun by the irresistible Mongol warriors on their way to conquering the Song Dynasty. Kubilai Khan, grandson of Genghis, established the Yuan (Beginning) Dynasty in 1279 and built a new capital *Khanbalik* (City of the Khan) in present-day Bei'jing. From then on, the Mongols ruled over the largest empire in history, ushering in an era of *Pax Mongolica* during which there was an unprecedented exchange of ideas, technology, arts and sciences, people and goods between the East and the West. A time when, according to one Turkish historian, "a young virgin carrying on her head a tray of gold could travel from the Levant to where the sun sets, from the shores of the Pacific to those of the Mediterranean, without suffering the slightest harm."

In the intervening years, through the fall of the Yuan and rise of the Ming Dynasty, Pu'yi's ancestors withdrew into their homeland in Manchuria and waited for their chance to launch another invasion. That time came in the early 1600s. The Ming (Bright) Dynasty was falling apart at the seams, Japanese pirates terrorized the coast and peasant revolts were rising up all over China; as many as 100,000 eunuchs controlled the government in the Forbidden City, and by the time they poisoned the emperor Tai'chang and seized power in 1620, the army of Nurhaci Aisin-Gioro, leader of the Manchus and founder of the Qing (Pure) Dynasty, were knocking at the gates of the Great Wall. He died during a campaign in 1626, but his son Abahai carried on his mission. However, it was his grandchild, Abahai's young son, also under the control of a prince regent, who presided over the fall of Bei'jing and became the first emperor of the Qing Dynasty in 1644.

Although China, and indeed the world, was already in turmoil by the time he ascended the throne nearly three centuries later, Pu'yi's own contribution towards the chaos through his personal actions can not be discounted.

Two decades after his abdication, and eight years after he was forcibly evicted from the Forbidden City by a 'Republican' warlord, Pu'yi became the Chief Executive of Manchu'kuo, and two years later, in 1934, was enthroned in Chang'chun as the emperor of the puppet state of Imperial Japan. The move legitimized the Japanese invasion of China that began in 1931, and marked the beginning of the full-scale assault that culminated in the occupation of Manchuria, the Liao'dong Peninsula and most of northern China; and by the end of 1937, the Yang'tze Valley, Shang'hai and Nan'jing had fallen. The Republican government fled from the invasion and abandoned their capital in Nan'jing, but, fearful of the burden of a mass exodus, they 'encouraged' the people to stay by locking the city gates and issuing one of the most shamefully hypocritical proclamations in history before they left: "All those who have blood and breath in them must feel that they wish to be broken as jade rather than remain whole as tiles." The result was the infamous Rape of Nan'jing, where over 300,000 civilians were 'broken as jade' by the Japanese army in an officially sanctioned continuous orgy of rape and murder that lasted for six weeks. Although he may have been powerless to stop them, as titular head of the nation in whose name this and countless other atrocities were committed during the war, my 'movie son' must share some moral responsibility.

The rain is showing no sign of abating, but I know that we are heading back to Chang'chun from Hei'long'jiang because I remember photographing the onion domes of the Russian Orthodox church of Santa Sophia in Haer'bin at dusk, and because the driver has said so. Anyway, the Japanese are back in Chang'chun. When I was there last week, I stayed well clear of Pu'yi's old palace and visited a couple of car factories instead; one of them is a brand new, state-of-the-art Mazda assembly line, pumping out cheap cars for the domestic Chinese market. I remember reading somewhere that ninety-nine per cent of the 1.3 billion people in China do not own a car, and if they ever reach the level of car ownership in the U.S. – about 77 cars per 100 people – there will be no room to stand. My Chinese cell phone buzzes with a text message, composed in classical couplets, "Beijing Public Security Bureau reminds you: Do not believe the rumours, do not spread the rumours, express your patriotism rationally. Do not participate in illegal demonstrations. Be helpful without creating more trouble; be patriotic without violating the law. Be a good and well-behaved citizen." This is in reference to all the demonstrations in Bei'jing recently against the Japanese government's continuing efforts to 'airbrush' over their wartime actions in China; this renewed outrage was sparked by the anti-Japanese riots that broke out after the Japanese team knocked China out of the World Cup, in a qualifying game in Bei'jing of all places.

The car slows to a crawl, a line of cars in front are changing lanes to go around what must be an accident. Two cars are parked on the fast lane, and as we drive slowly past them, I see a young peasant woman cradled in a man's arms. Her eyes are wide open with shock, and blood is leaking out from a wound in her head. Beside her, the rain is transforming the pool into a river of blood on the road. I remember all the near misses we have had on the high-speed expressways all over the country, where the local people risk their lives by taking shortcuts home across the highways that have been planted between their houses and their fields. And it reminds me of all the rivers of blood that have flowed across the black earth of this tragic region, where the line between man and beast had been repeatedly crossed in the name of war.

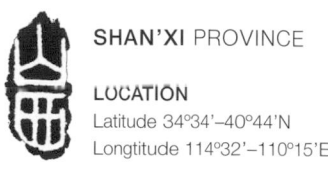

SHAN'XI PROVINCE

LOCATION
Latitude 34º34'–40º44'N
Longtitude 114º32'–110º15'E

AREA 155,400 km² (155,400 sq miles)

GEOGRAPHY Much of Shan'xi is located on a plateau, divided north to south by the course of the Fen He River. The Tai'hang Mountains rise to the east of the river and the Lü'liang Mountains to the west. Average elevation is around 1,000 m, with the highest point of 3,058 m at the summit of Mount Wutai. The Great Wall runs along much of the province's northern border with Inner Mongolia while the Huang'he River (Yellow River) demarcates the western border with Shaan'xi.

CLIMATE The province's north has a temperate monsoonal and semi-arid climate while the south has sub-tropical characteristics. Average January temperatures range from -11ºC to 4ºC, rising to 21–28ºC in July. The lowest recorded temperature is -32ºC and the highest is 40.5ºC. Average annual rainfall is between 350 mm and 700 mm – 60 per cent of it in June–August.

POPULATION 37.2 million (end 2005)

MAJOR CITIES Tai'yuan (capital), Da'tong, Yun'cheng

AGRICULTURE Main food crops include wheat, corn, sorghum, millet, barely and fruit. Cash crops include soybeans, cotton and tobacco. Livestock is also raised in the northern grasslands.

MAIN INDUSTRIES With 35 per cent of China's coal reserves in Shan'xi, the province is the country's leading coal producer. This ample source of energy is reflected in heavy industries such as power generation, smelting and other metal-based processes. The province is also major source of industrial salt.

ANNUAL PER CAPITA INCOME (2005)
Disposable income of urban residents:
RMB 8,800 (US$1,098)
Net income of rural residents:
RMB 2,800 (US$350)

HISTORICAL AND SCENIC SITES
Ping'yao, the Great Wall, Yun'gang Grottoes, Mount Wu'tai, Mount Heng'shan.

FOOD Shanxi food is in keeping with the province's dependence on meat and flour. Its cuisine is noted for its noodles, pungent vinegar and lamb. Dishes include *tounao*, or Eight-Delicacy soup, combining mutton, herbs and vegetables, naked oats steamed dough balls and *shaomai*, which is similar to haggis.

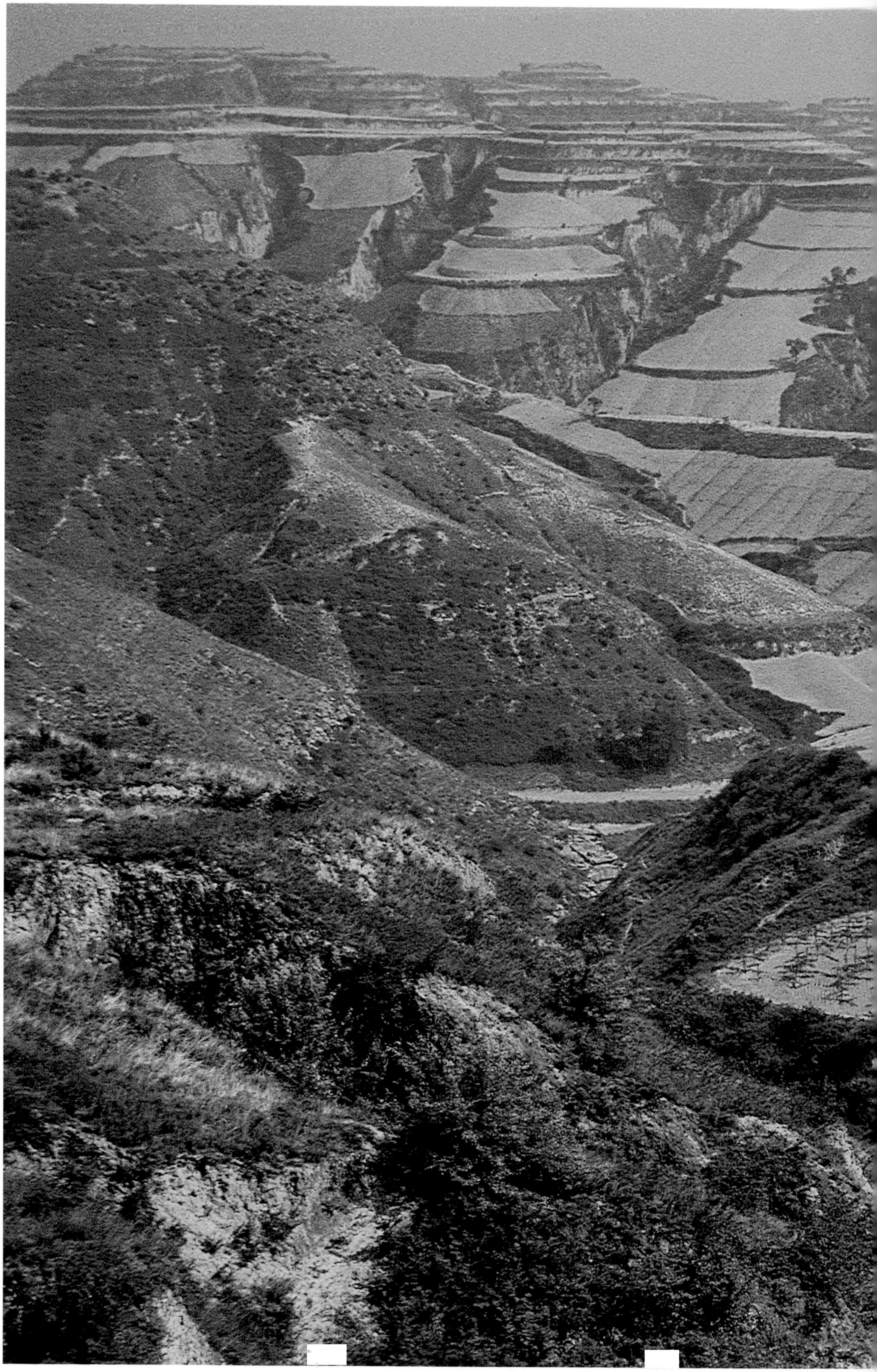

[RIGHT] The Loess Plateau.

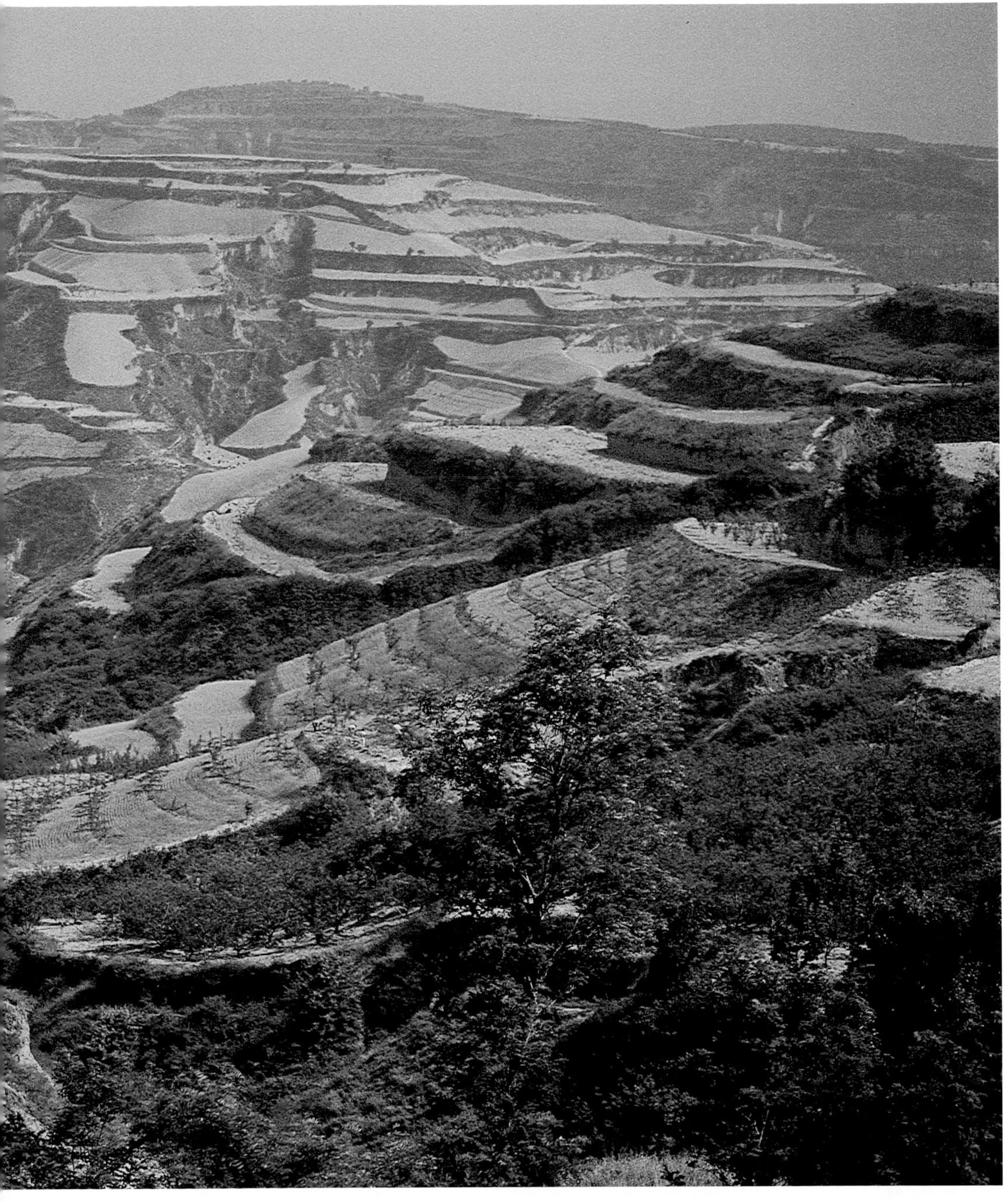

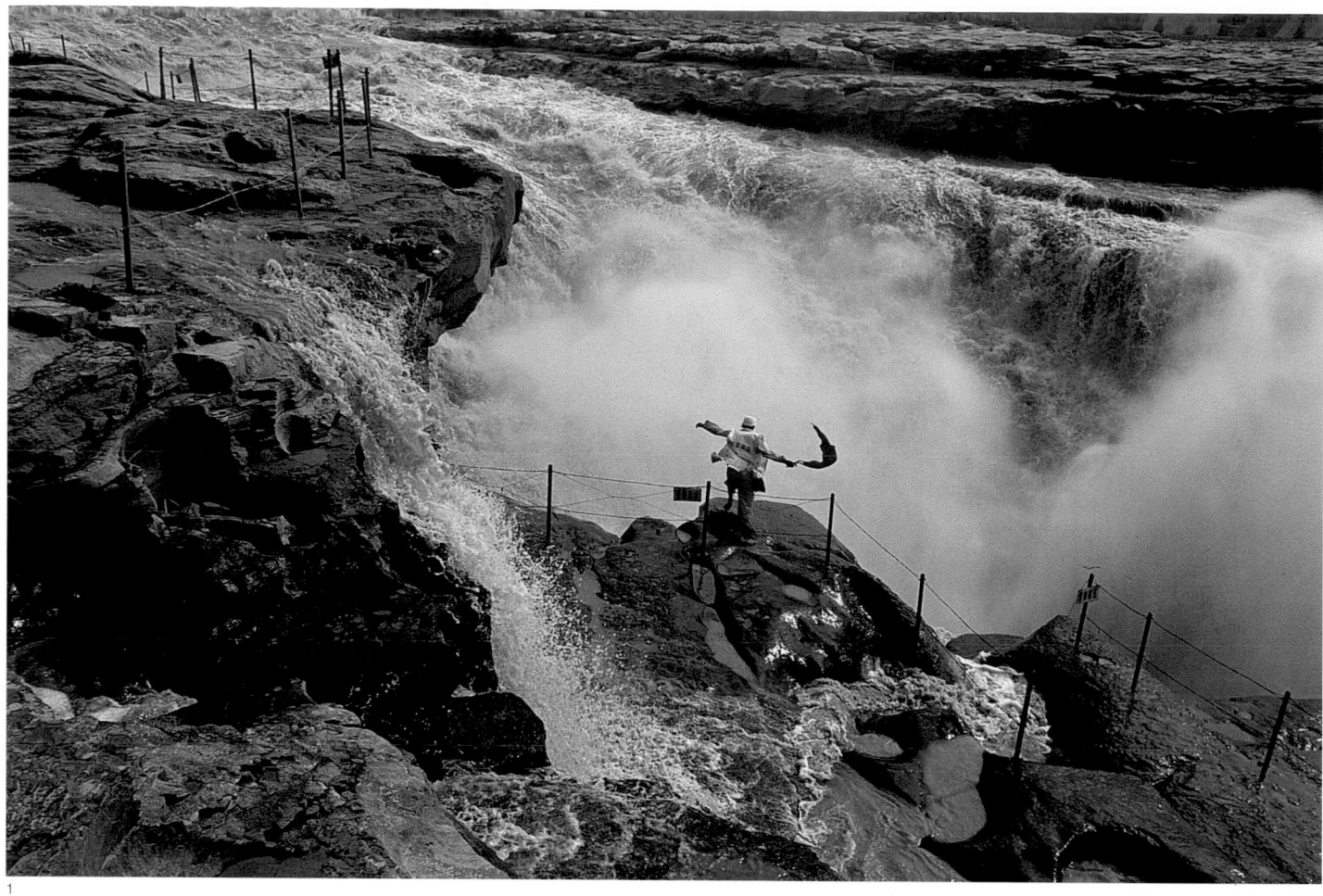

1

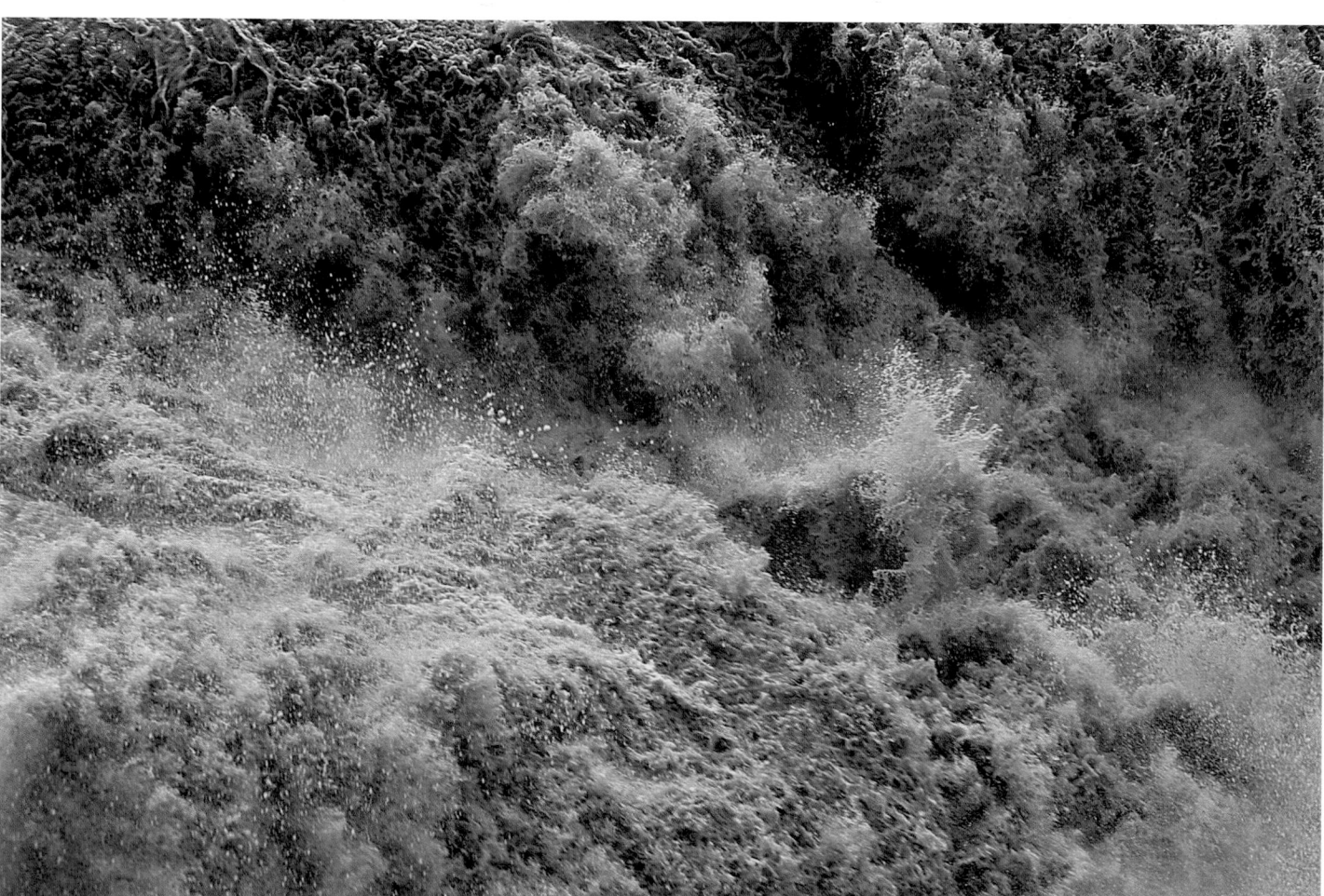

2

THE HU'KUO FALLS

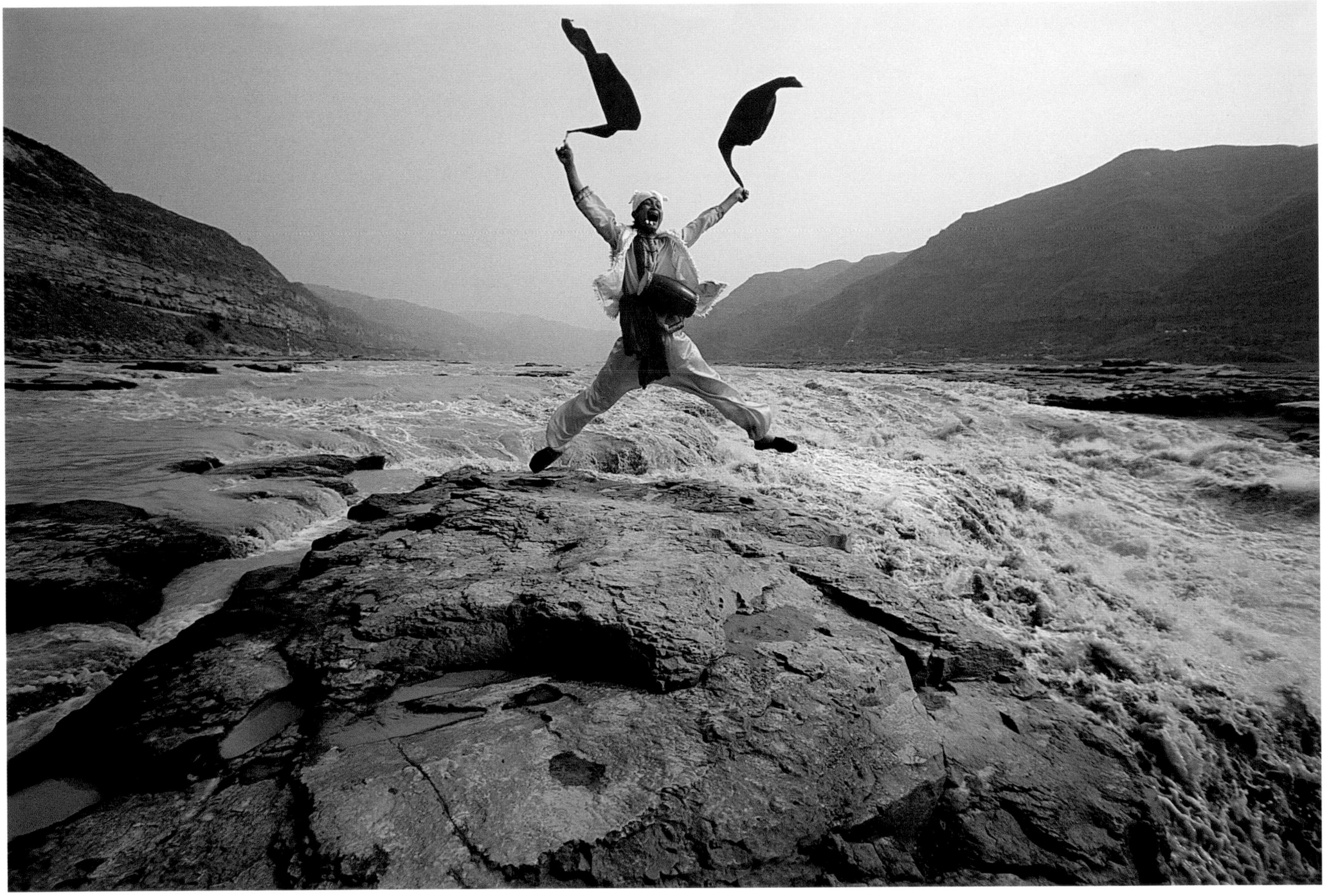

3

THE LOESS PLATEAU STRETCHES ACROSS SIX PROVINCES of northern China, from the tip of Gan'su to the outskirts of Bei'jing – an area approximately the size of France. The Yellow River leaves Inner Mongolia, moving due south around a great sweeping horseshoe bend that guides its waters – heavy with the ochre silt that gives it its name – through the mountains along the Shaan'xi–Shan'xi border. In a remote valley 50 kilometres (30 miles) east of Yi'chuan in Shan'xi province, the 250-metre (820-foot) wide river is abruptly squeezed into a 30-metre (100-foot) wide basin. The river continues to narrow until the water is pushed with incredible force into a narrow gorge and through a 10-metre (30-foot) gap. The gap is aptly named the Hu'kou (Mouth of the Teapot) and is China's second largest waterfall. [1] [3] This 19-year-old boy in traditional Ansai Drummer costume makes his living posing for tourists. I declined his offer to show me his "best moves," but he did them anyway. [2] Water rushing like "ten thousand stampeding horses" over the Hu'kou Falls.

NORTH BY NORTHEAST

THE ANCIENT CITY OF PING'YAO

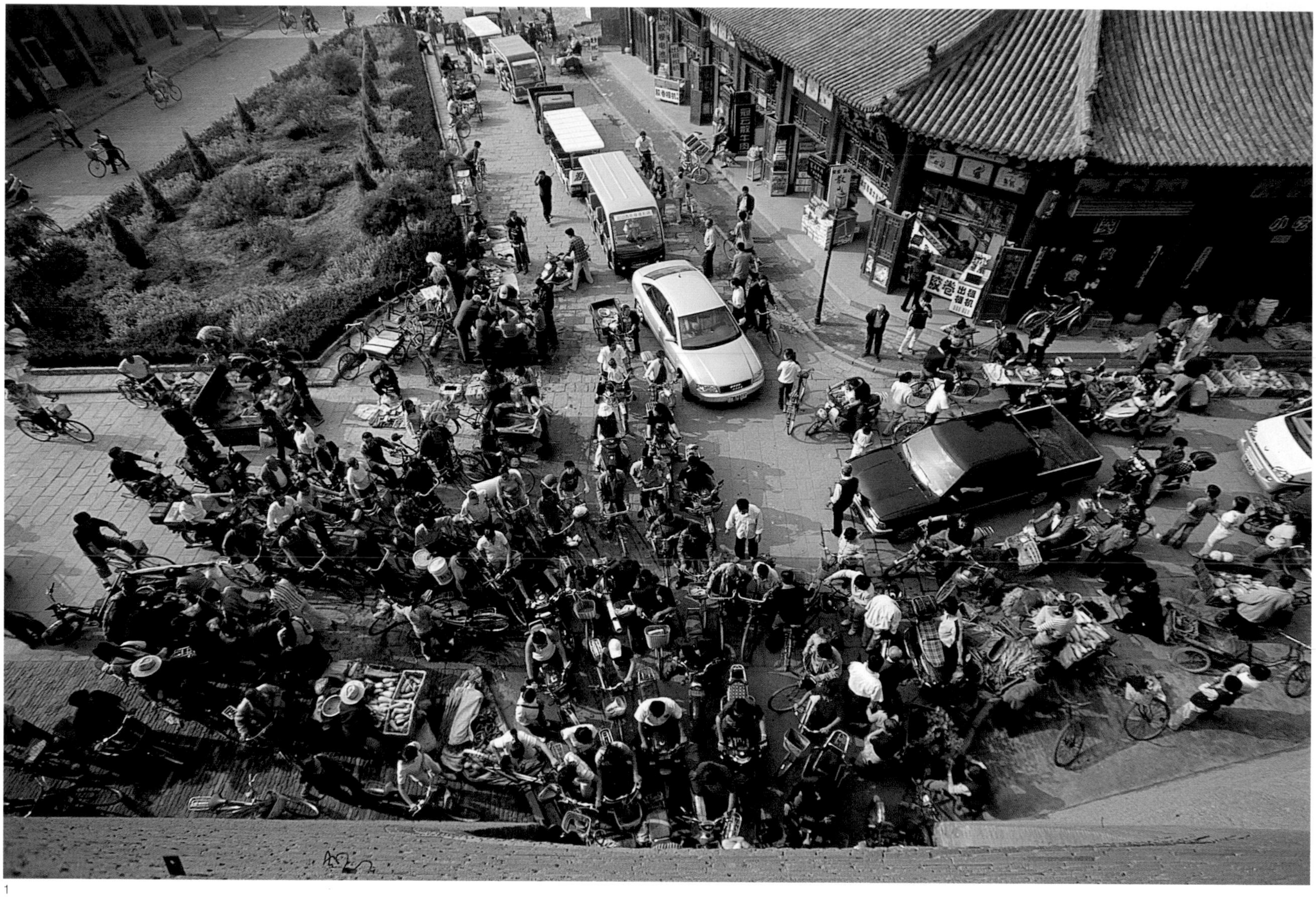

PING'YAO'S ORIGINS STRETCH BACK 2,700 YEARS to the reign of King Xuan (827–782 BCE) in the Western Zhou Dynasty. The city became an important mercantile centre in the Ming Dynasty, when the existing walls were built. At one stage during the Qing Dynasty the city was the financial and banking centre of the empire, a function not immediately apparent today. Ping'yao's design follows classic Chinese geomancy. The city gates face the cardinal points and are accessed through drawbridges over 3-metre (10-foot) wide moats. Inside, four main roads radiate out to eight smaller streets, which connect with 72 lanes containing temples and 3,797 black-brick and grey-tile houses. Ping'yao may well be the best-preserved walled city in China, but from my own experience the local residents' penchant for fleecing tourists may well backfire and kill the golden goose. [1] Morning traffic jam at the city gate. [2] A tour guide waits for her clients on top of the 6-kilometre (3-mile) long city wall. [3] A tourist café. [4] Young Mao in the courtyard of the boarding house.

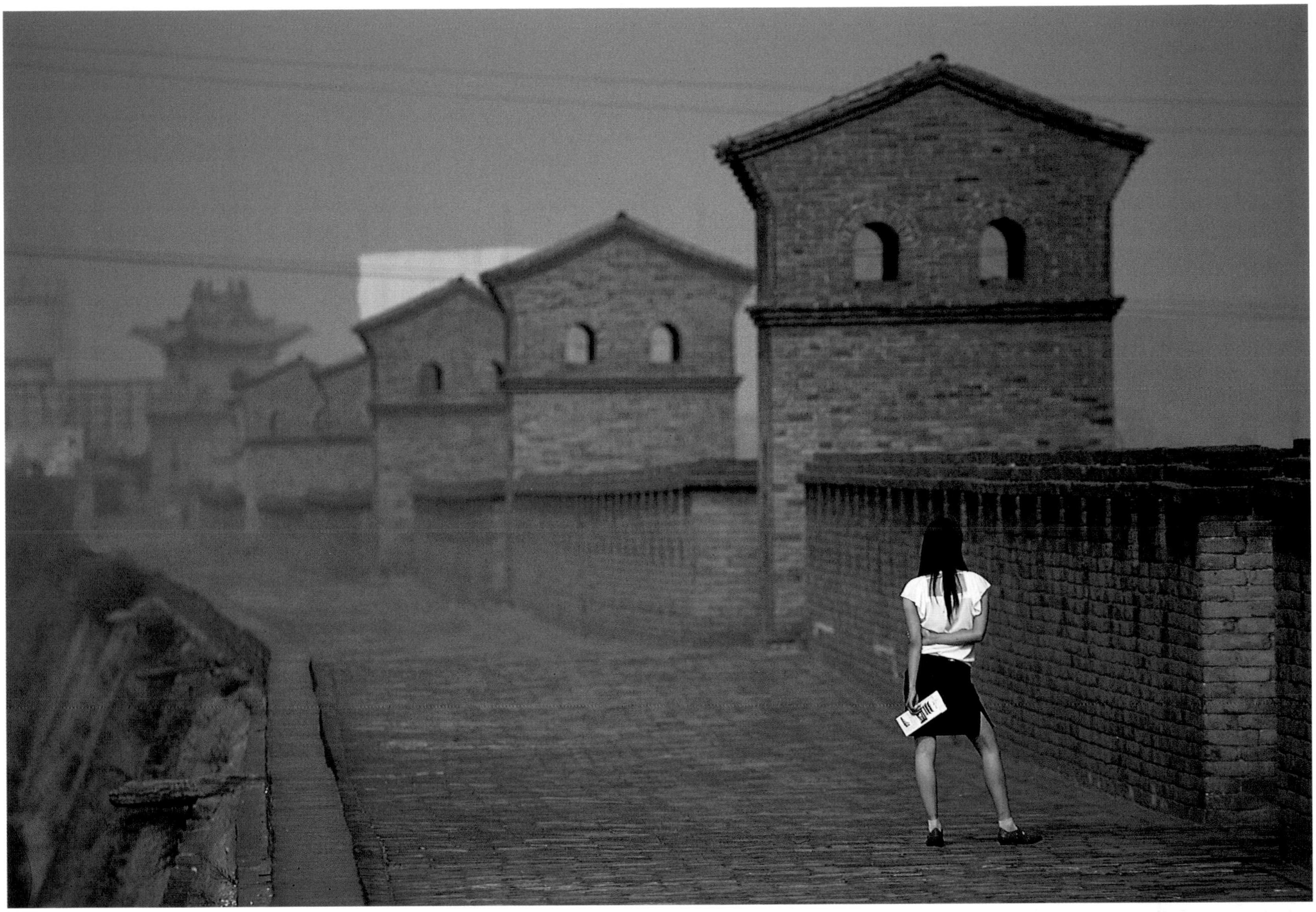

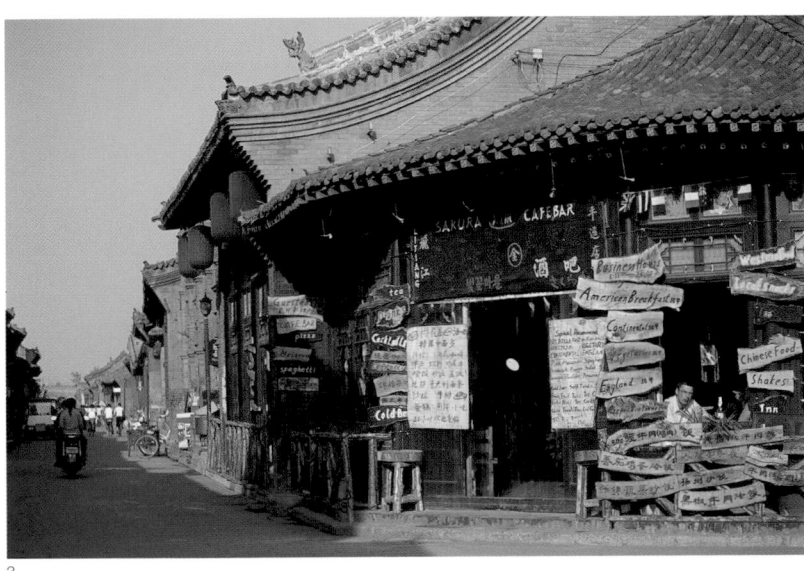

2

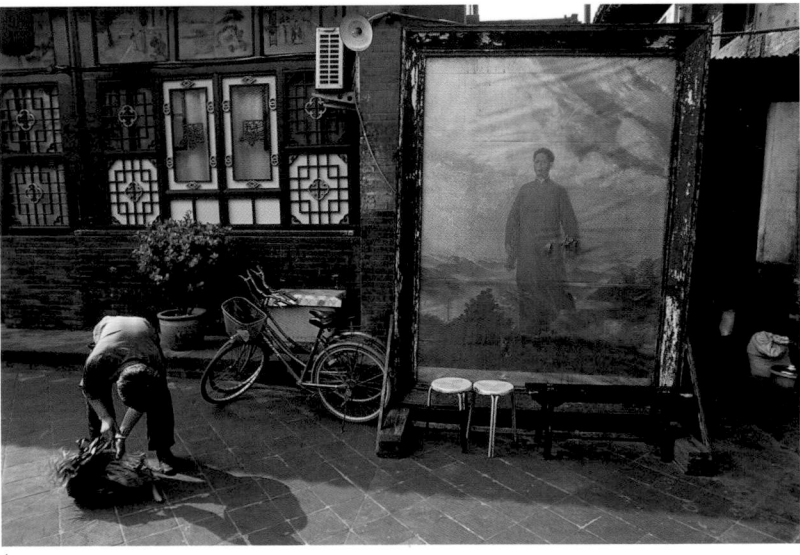

3

4

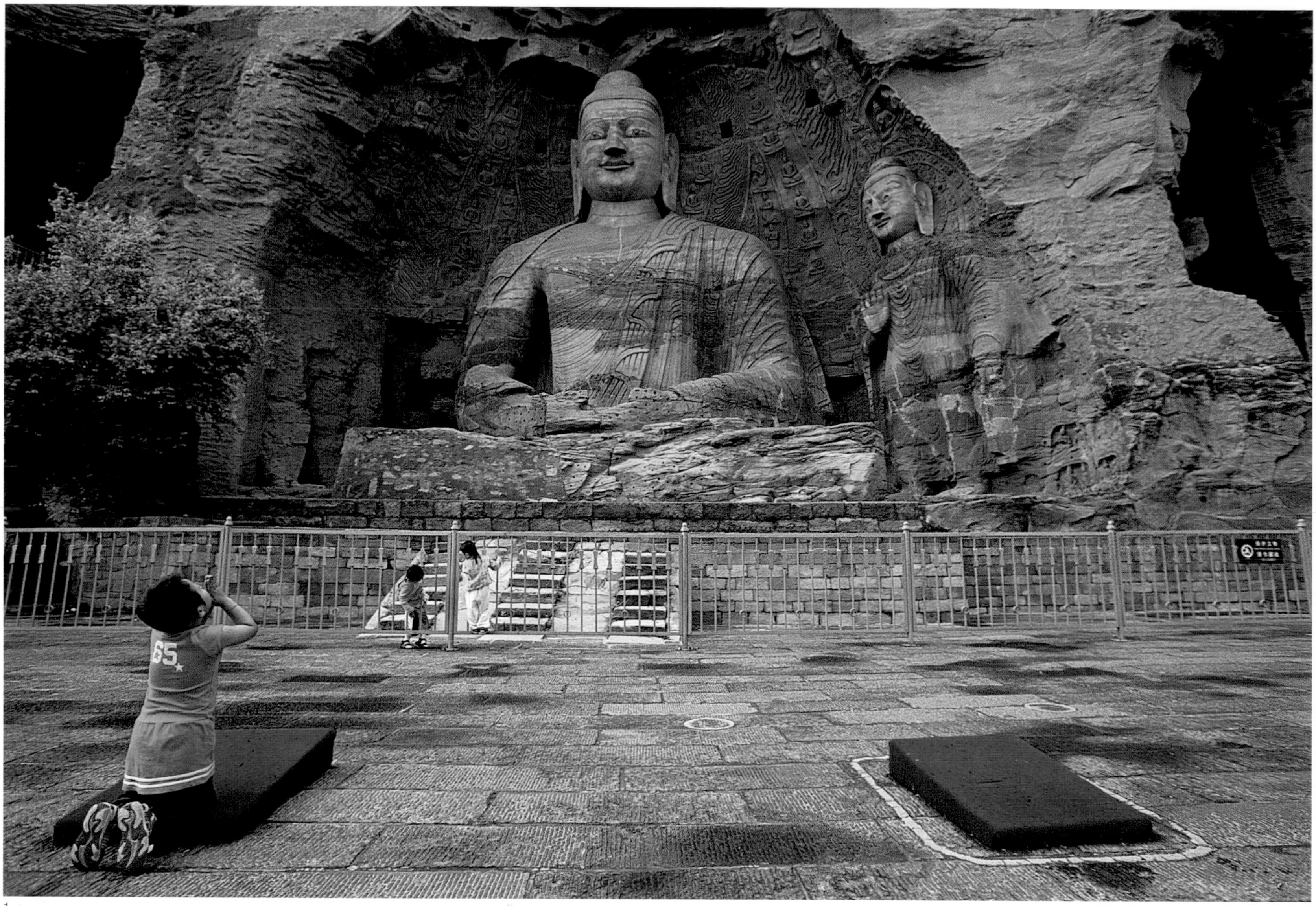

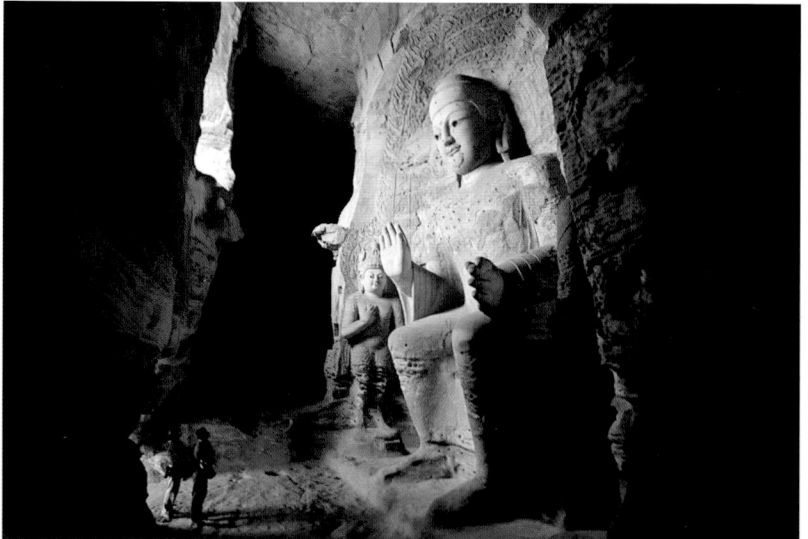

THERE WAS NO DIRECT ROAD link between Da'tong and the Yun'gang (Cloud-Ridge) Caves when I last visited the area in the mid-1970s. After negotiating the packed-dirt roads, choked full of ancient trucks belching black smoke and trailing coal dust, we were then let off by the bridge [5] over the Wu'zhou River opposite the coalmine and walked the rest of way. The coal traffic has now been diverted and a brand new highway takes you straight into a giant parking lot and souvenir shop complex. The muddy tracks that had once linked the ridge's 20 caves and the 50,000 Buddhist statues carved into its sandstone walls have been replaced by concrete paths, and railings now protect the sculptures from the tourist hordes. But the statues, the finest examples of 5th-century Buddhist sculpture, remain the same – serene and awe-inspiring. [1] The colossal 17-metre (56-foot) high seated Buddha, the emblem of the Cloud-Ridge grottoes. [2] The 14-metre (46-foot) seated Buddha is a representation of Emperor Wen'cheng, who restored Buddhism to the Northern Wei Dynasty. [3] Coalminers taking a cigarette break before going underground for the evening shift. [4] A day-shift miner heading for the showers.

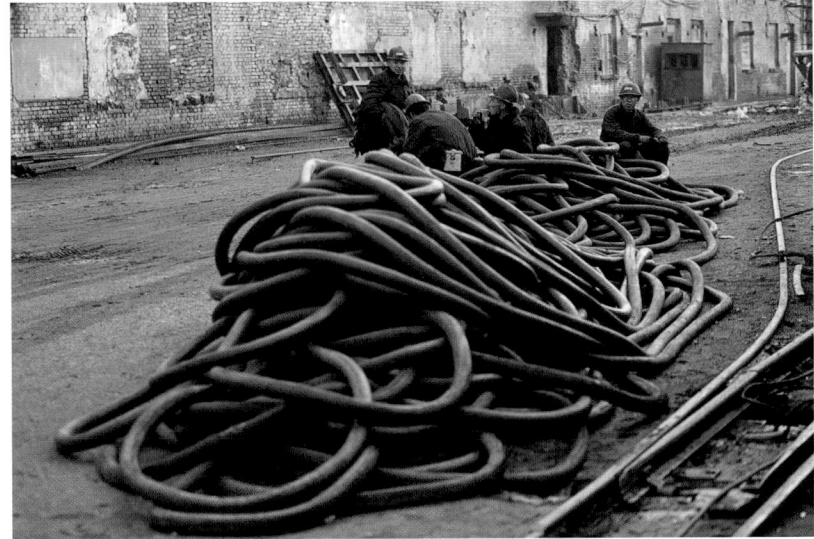

3

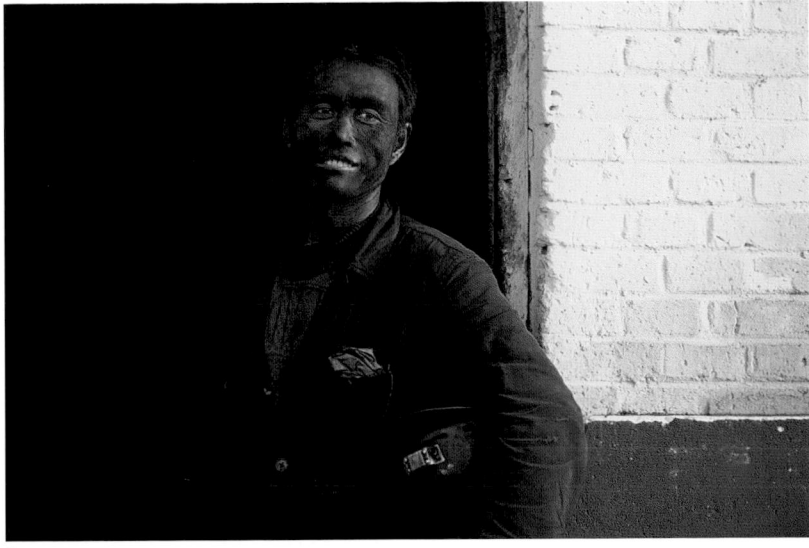

4

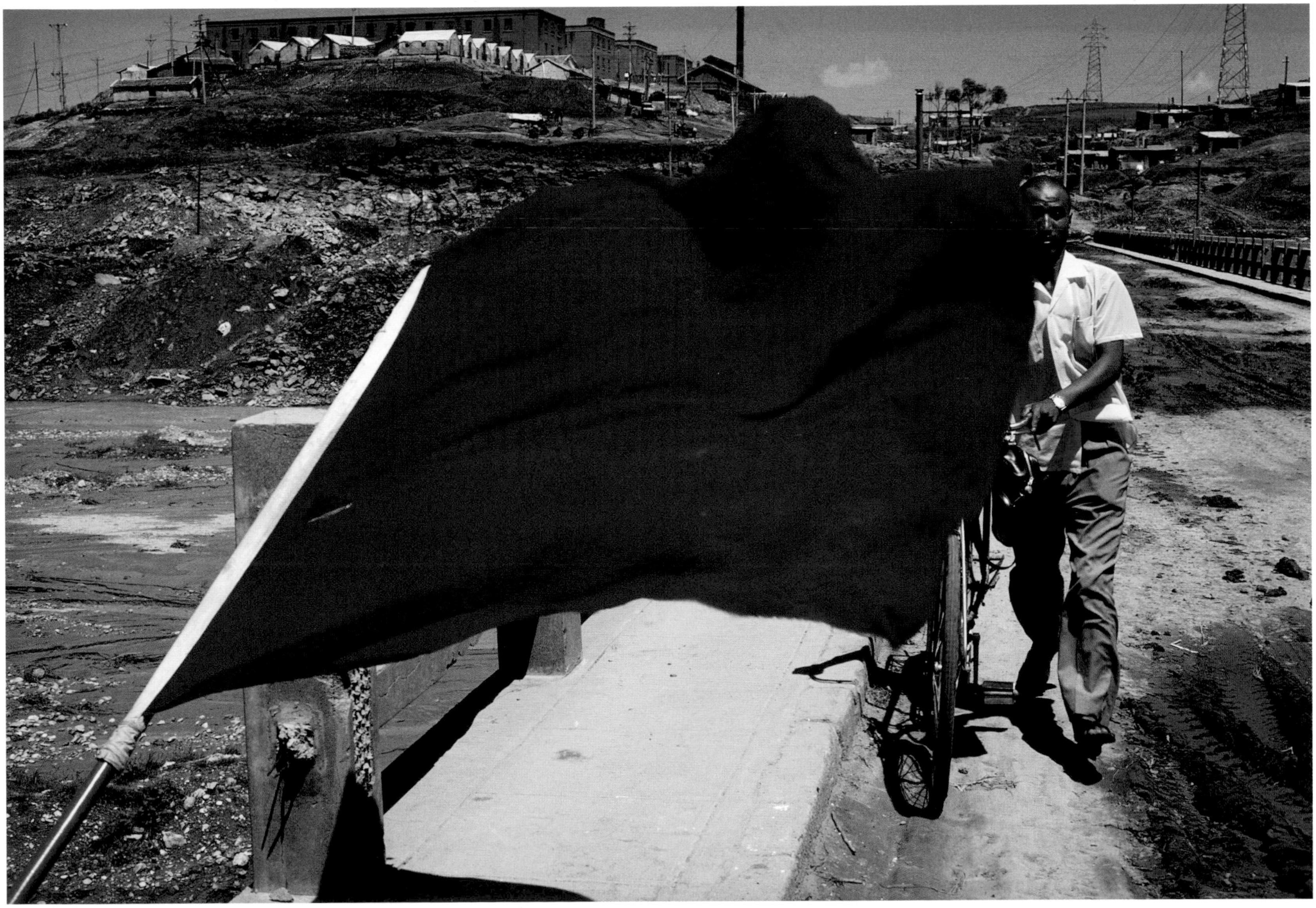

5

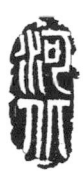

HE'BEI PROVINCE

LOCATION
Latitude 36°01'–42°37'N
Longtitude 113°4'–119°53'E

AREA 204,404 km² (78,900 sq miles)

GEOGRAPHY He'bei is bordered by the Yan Mountains to the north, the Bo'hai Sea in the east and the Tai'hang Mountains to the west, while the southeast forms part of the North China Plain. The plains, which comprise more than 40 per cent of the province, are below 50 m, while the mountains reach a height of 2,882 m on Mount Xiao'wu'tai, the highest peak in the northern mountains. The Hai'he River watershed covers much of the province's central and southern regions. The Luan'he River watershed dominates the northeast.

CLIMATE He'bei has a continental monsoon climate, giving harsh winters and hot summers. Temperatures in January range between -16°C and -3°C, climbing to 27°C in July. The highest recorded temperature is 42.7°C, and the lowest is below -30°C. The province experiences severe sandstorms in the spring and heavy rains in the summer. Average annual rainfall is between 400 mm and 800 mm.

POPULATION 60.31 million (end 2005)

MAJOR CITIES Shi'jia'zhuang (capital), Bao'ding, Tang'shan, Qin'huang'dao, Han'dan, Zhang'jia'kou

AGRICULTURE The province is China's main cotton-producing region. Other crops include wheat, maize, millet, sorghum, peanut, soybean and sesame.

MAIN INDUSTRIES He'bei is a major industrial, coal mining and oil production centre. Industries include petroleum and petrochemicals, iron and steel, textiles, engineering, ceramics and food processing.

ANNUAL PER CAPITA INCOME (2005)
Disposable income of urban residents:
RMB 9,107 (US$1,135)
Net income of rural residents:
RMB 3,481 (US$434)

HISTORICAL AND SCENIC SITES
The Great Wall, the Cheng'de Imperial Mountain Resort and its temples, the Eastern and Western Tombs of Qing Dynasty emperors, Zhao'zhou An'ji Bridge and Beidahe beach resort.

FOOD He'bei cuisine reflects the often harsh environment and scarcity of meat and green vegetables. Staples are built around wheat noodles, breads and potatoes rather than rice. He'bei specialties include Shi'jia'zhuang braised chicken, Xiao'yang mixed noodles and Song'hua pickled duck eggs.

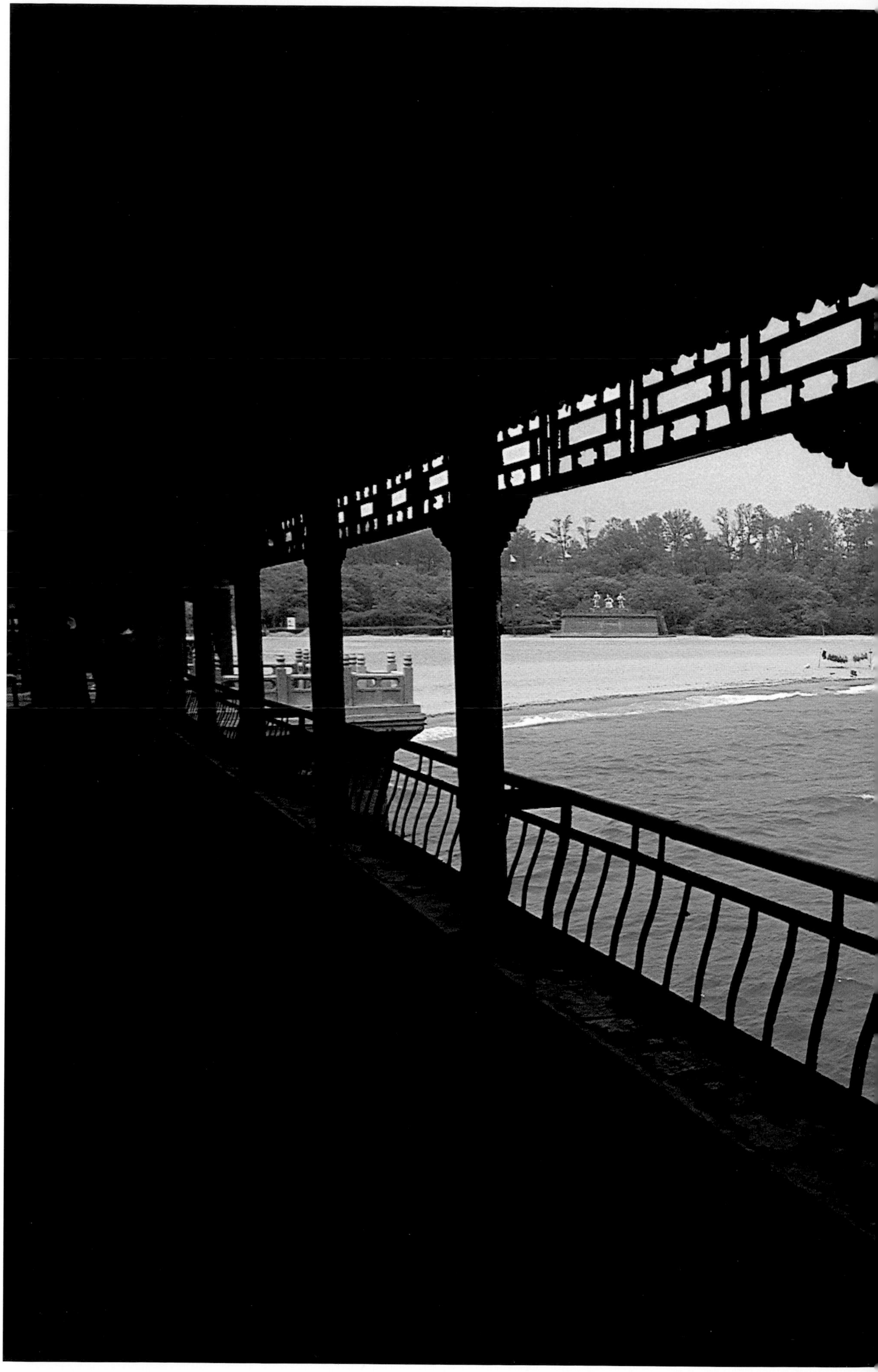

[RIGHT] The eastern end of the Great Wall.

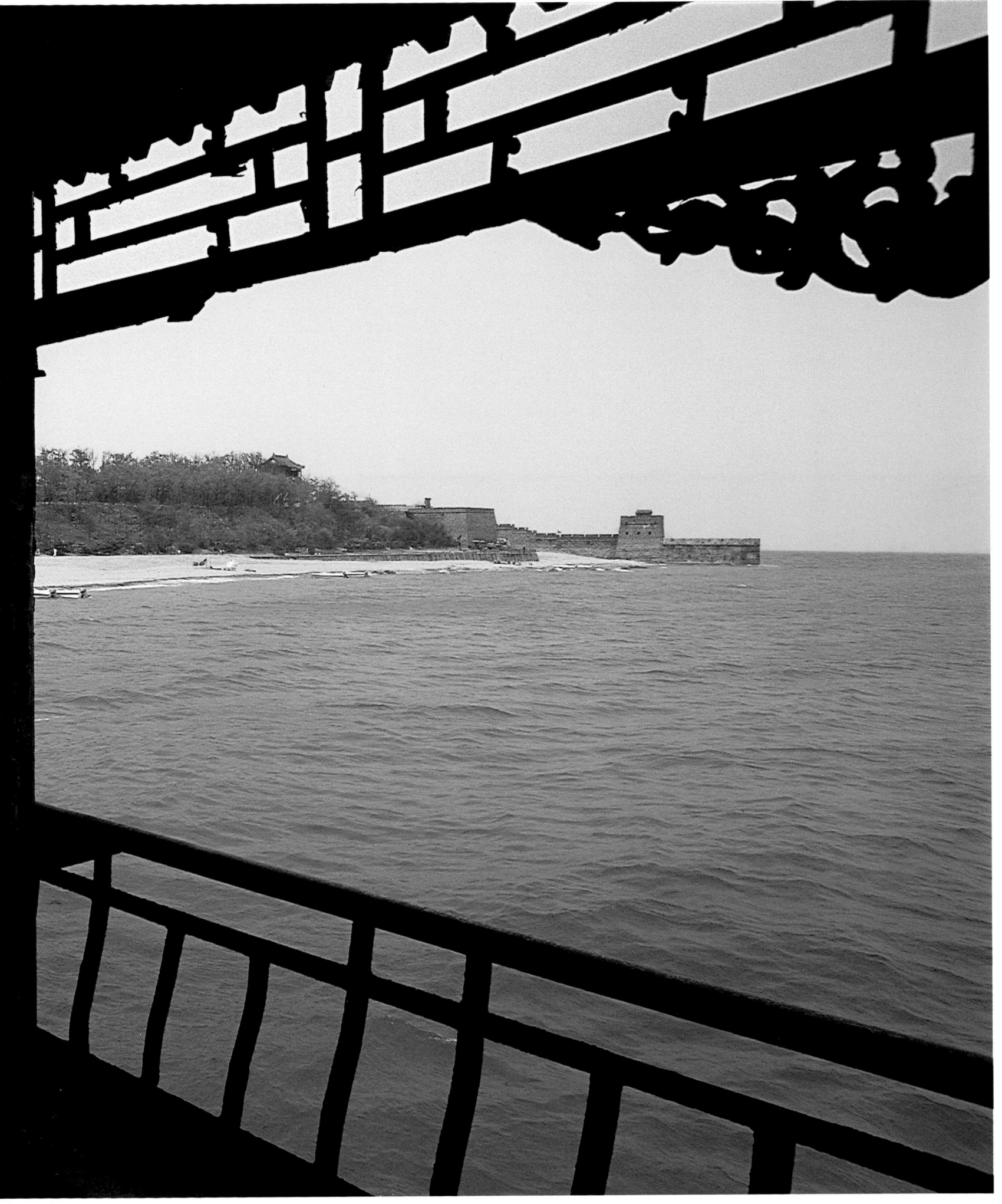

THE OLD DRAGON HEAD

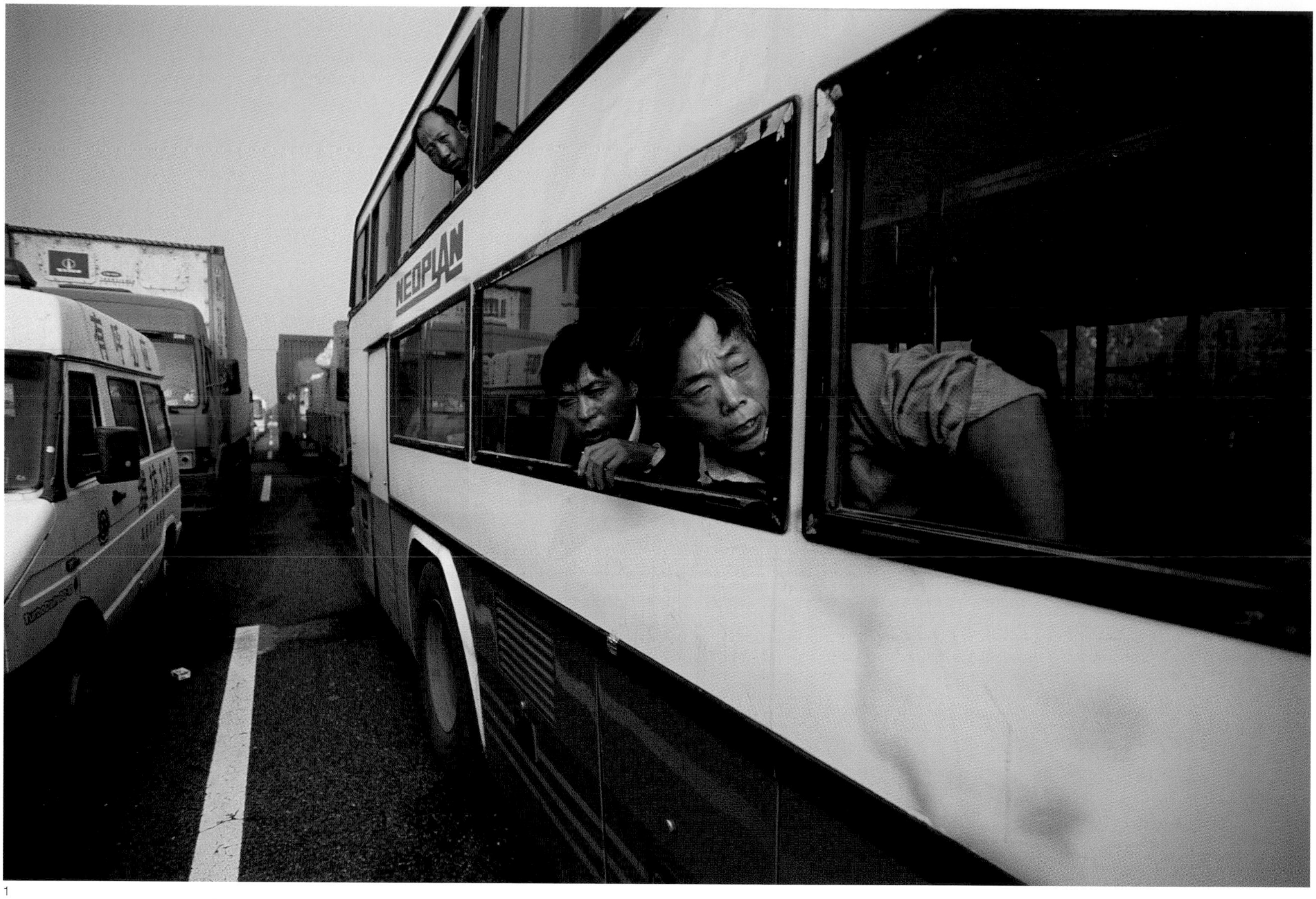

1

NORTH BY NORTHEAST

FROM THE NORTH OF BEI'JING, the Great Wall meanders over the hills of He'bei province before dropping down to the edge of the Bo'hai Sea at Shan'hai'guan (Mountain Ocean Pass). A massive fortress with 12-metre (40-foot) high walls, popularly known as the 'First Pass under Heaven,' was built in 1381 in the early years of the Ming Dynasty (1368–1644) to defend this strategic gateway to the northeast. It failed, as in 1644 the Manchu army stormed the fortress and went on conquer China. The 'Old Dragon Head' was a watchtower garrison a few miles south of Shan'hai'guan. The battlement extended for 23 metres (76 feet) into the ocean like 'a dragon drinking from the sea', and marked the eastern terminus of the Great Wall. [2] [3] The present fort is a reconstruction built in the 1980s, but the stone-carved dragon's head for which it was named is no more. [1] Heavy fog on the motorway between Bei'jing and Tian'jin meant a two-hour wait in a seemingly endless traffic jam. [4] A bored shopkeeper at the temple by the beach.

170

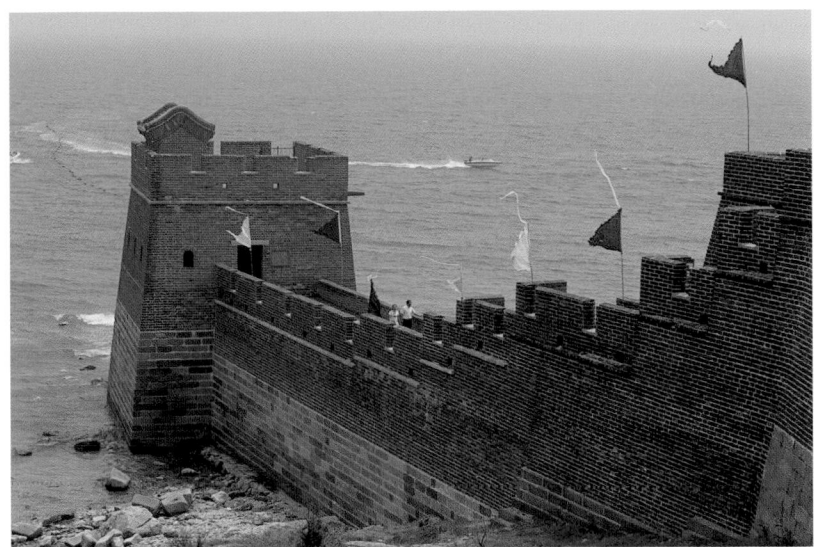

2

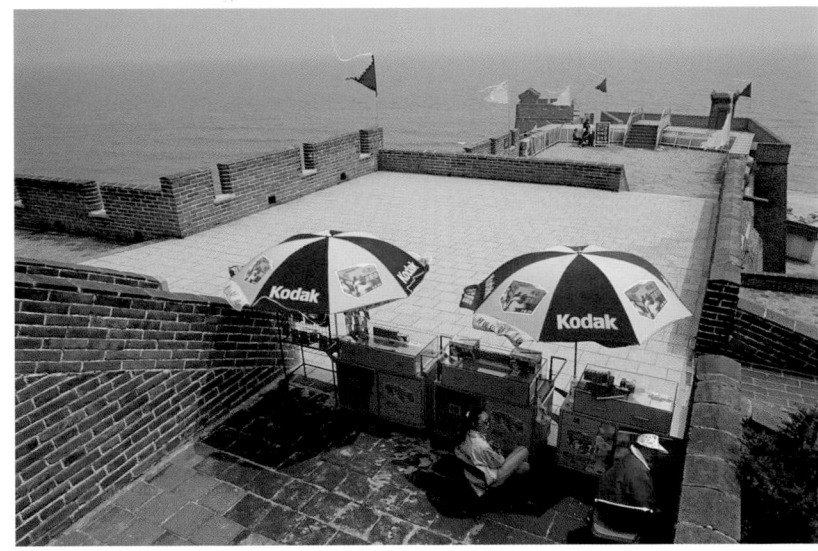

3

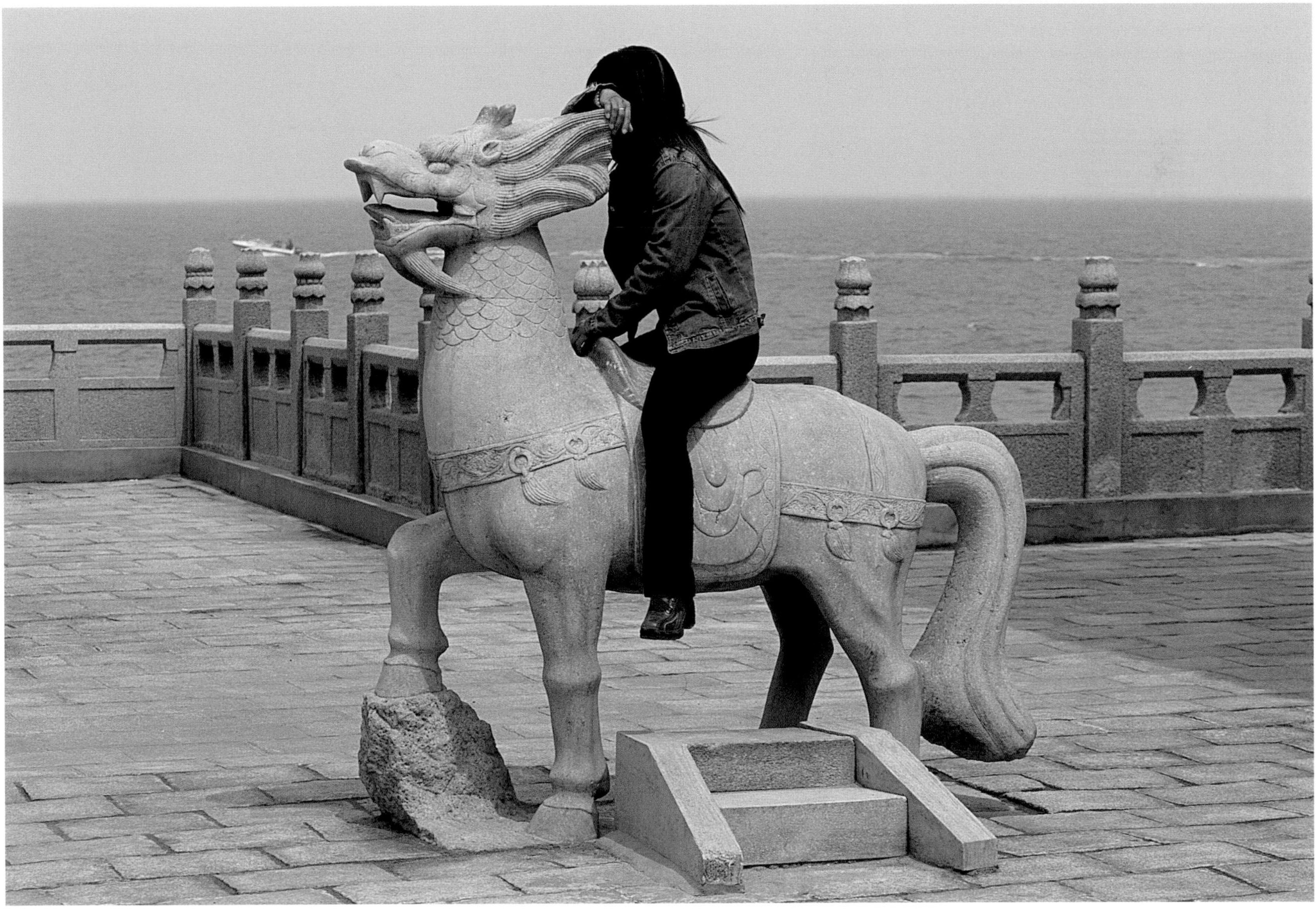

4

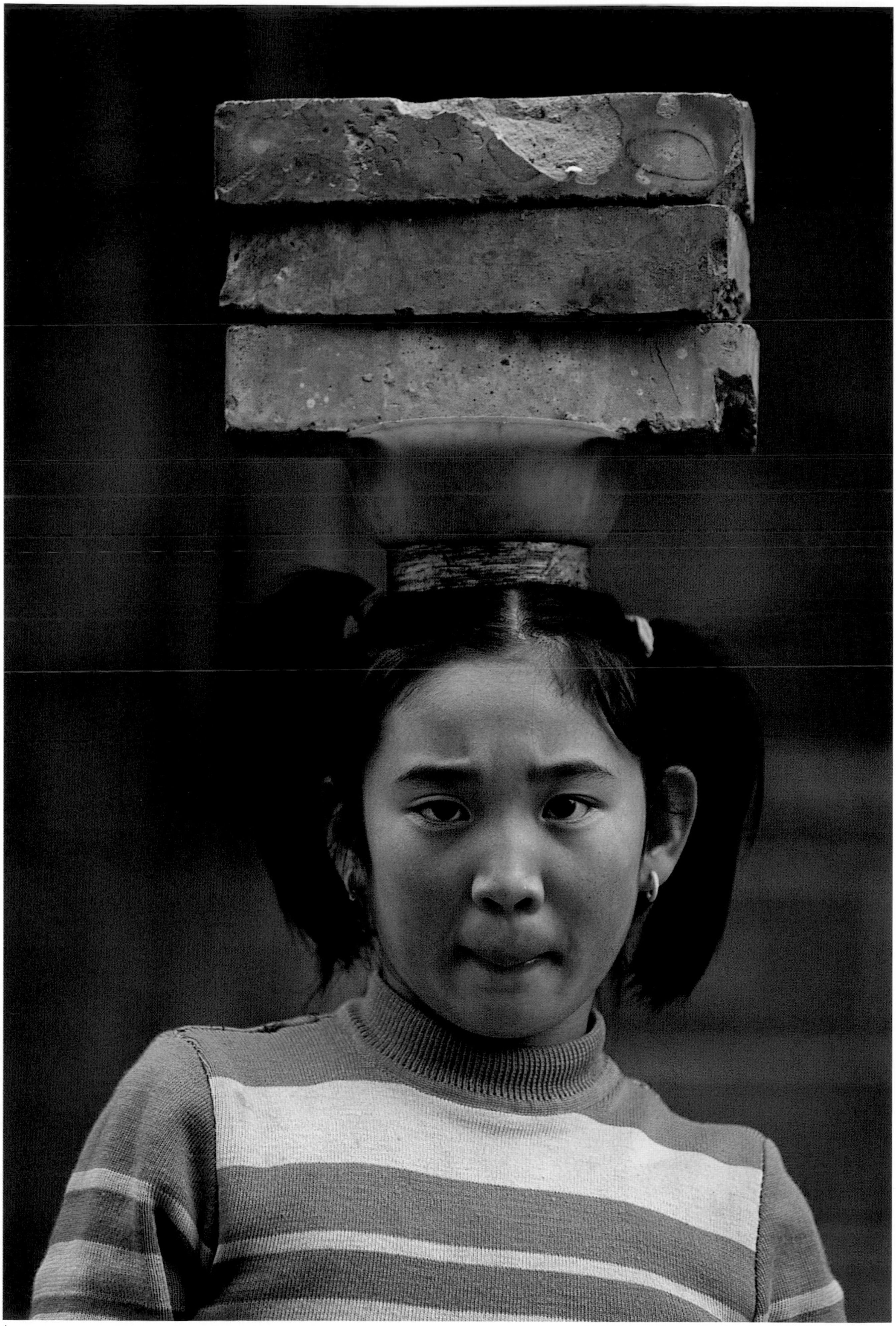

1

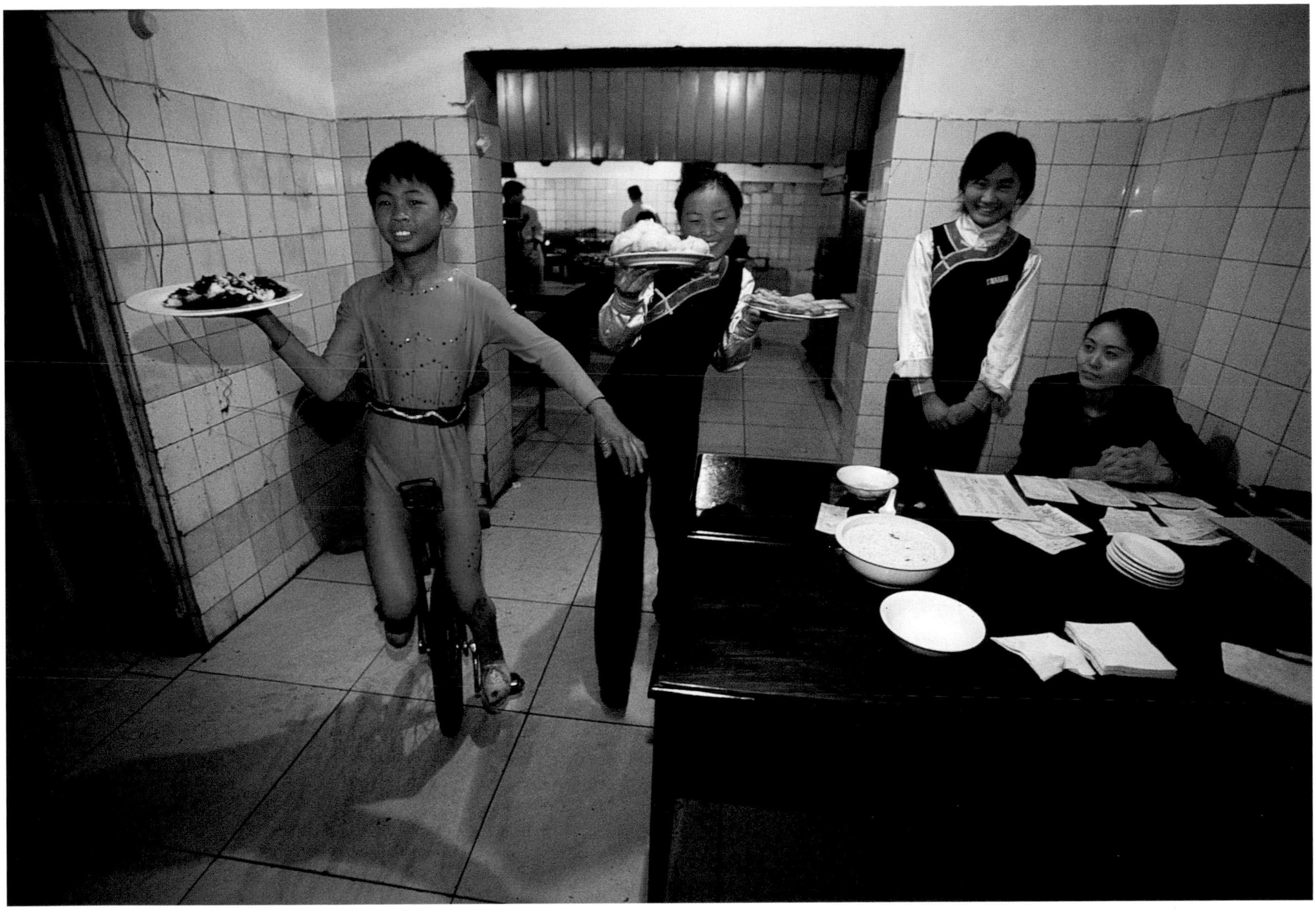

2

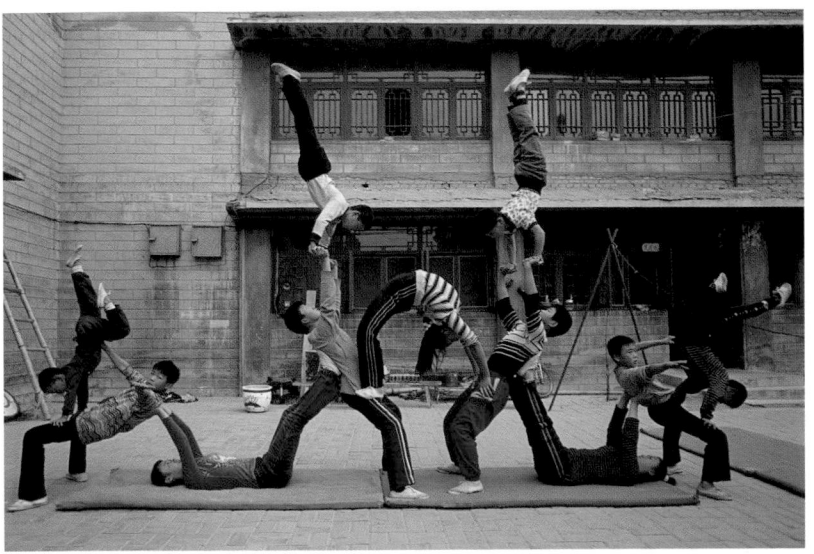

3

WITH ITS ROOTS PLANTED IN THE PEASANTRY, acrobatics is arguably China's oldest form of folk art. Displays of agility, strength and precision utilizing farm tools like hoes, rakes and ropes or such household articles as tables and chairs date back to the Warring States period (475–221 BCE). Acrobatics grew in content and sophistication through the centuries. The '100 Plays' from the Han Dynasty include music and stagecraft, while in the Tang Dynasty acrobatics moved from street corners into the Imperial Court. The victory of the 'Peasants' Revolution' in 1949 saw acrobatics finally take to the stages of grand theatres and opera houses and accorded the status of 'Art'. Wu'qiao County is known as the 'Home of Chinese Acrobatics,' where residents of all ages practice their acrobatic routines on the sidewalks. I visited the school inside The Big Acrobatic World of Wu'qiao where [1] children were being trained. [3] They put on a show for us, and though I was greatly impressed by their skills I came away with the nagging feeling the content and presentation actually hadn't evolved that much in 2,500 years. [2] Students find work as 'acrobatic waiters' at special banquets in the hotel restaurant.

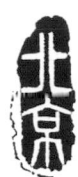

BEI'JING MUNICIPALITY

LOCATION
Latitude 39°26'N
Longtitude 115°25'–117°30'E

AREA 17,000 km² (6,564 sq miles)

GEOGRAPHY Bei'jing is situated at the northern tip of the North China Plain at an altitude of 20 m to 60 m above sea level. Major rivers flowing through the municipality include the Yong'ding and the Chaobai. Bei'jing is shielded from the deserts of northern China by the Jun'da Mountains to the northwest and the Xi'shan Mountains to the west. These ranges have a maximum elevation of 1,500 m.

CLIMATE Bei'jing's climate is harsh, characterized by hot and humid monsoonal summers and cold, dry winters caused by Siberian weather systems. Average temperatures are -7°C to -4°C in January and 25°C to 26°C in July. The lowest recorded temperature is -18.3°C; the highest, 39.5°C. Annual rainfall is around 600 mm, 75 per cent of which falls in summer. Heavy air pollution from industry and traffic, and dust storms from the deserts to the north and west of the city, are dominant features of the capital's environment.

POPULATION over 15.30 million (end 2005)

AGRICULTURE The main crops are wheat and maize. Vegetables are cultivated in market gardens close to the city to supply the capital's population.

MAIN INDUSTRIES Main industries include textiles, iron and steel, plastics, petrochemicals, railway equipment, machine tools and electronics. Increased pollution has halted new industrial development around the capital, which is now concentrating on employment opportunities in the service and government administrative sectors.

ANNUAL PER CAPITA INCOME (2005)
Disposable income of urban residents:
RMB 17,653 (US$2,200)
Net income of rural residents:
RMB 7,860 (US$980)

HISTORICAL AND SCENIC SITES
The Great Wall, Palace Museum, Summer Palace, Yuan'ming'yuan Garden, Tian'an'men Square, Temple of Heaven, Ming Tombs.

FOOD Bei'jing specialties include Peking roast duck, dishes made with medicinal roots and herbs, mutton hotpot, dumplings, sausages, quick-fried tripe, soybean milk, jellied bean curd and fried pastries.

[RIGHT] The golden roofs of the Forbidden City as seen from Prospect Hill.

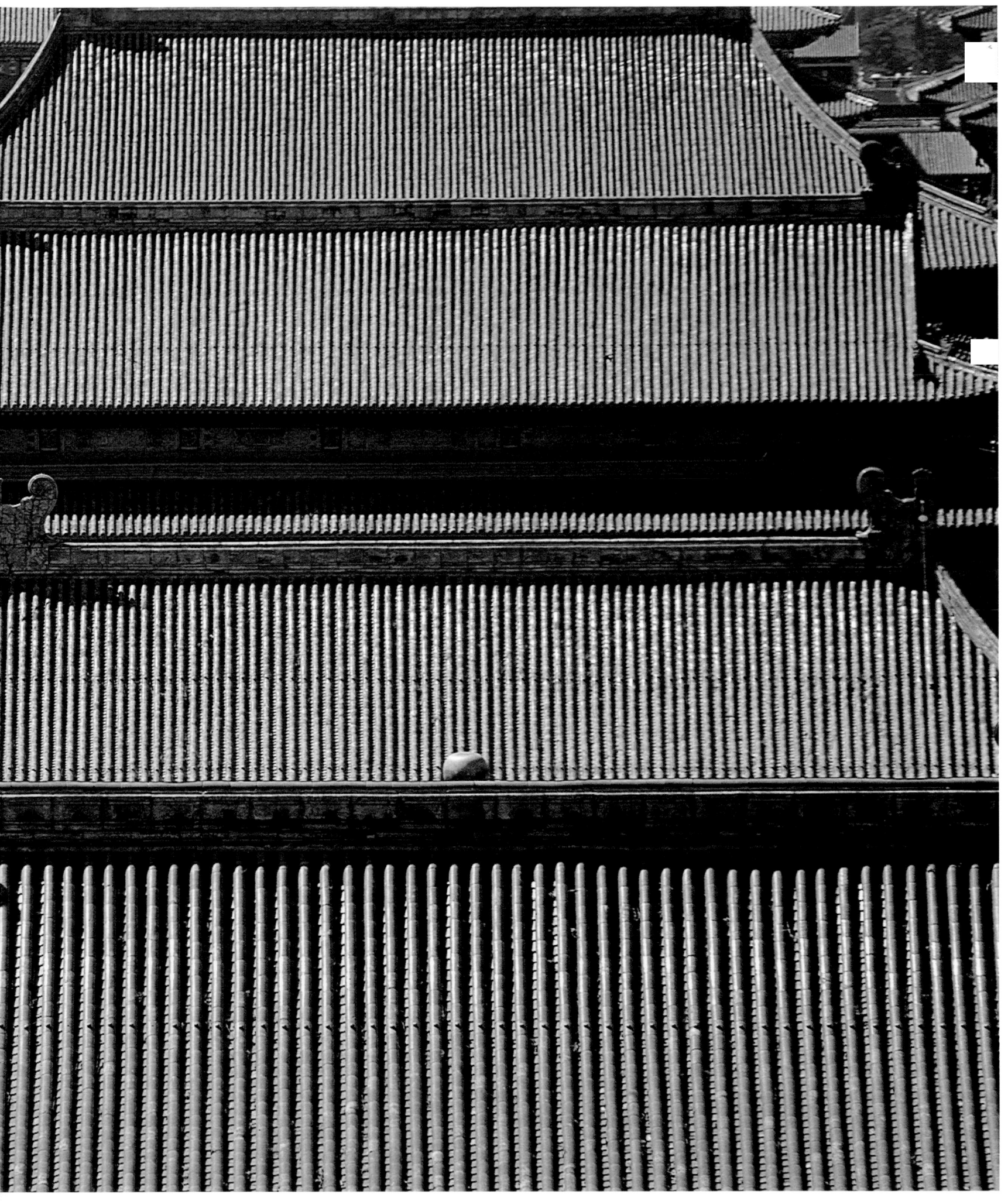

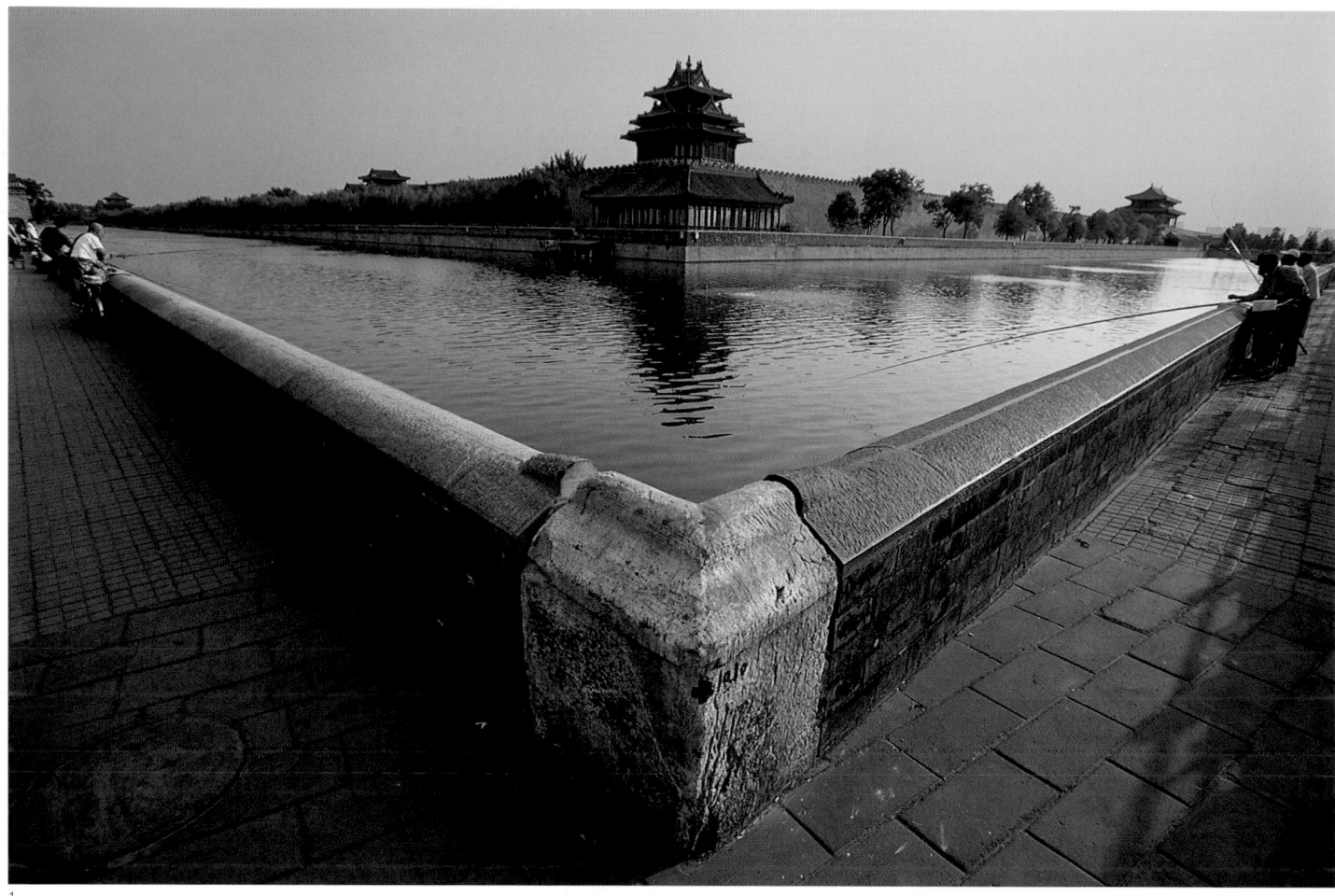

1

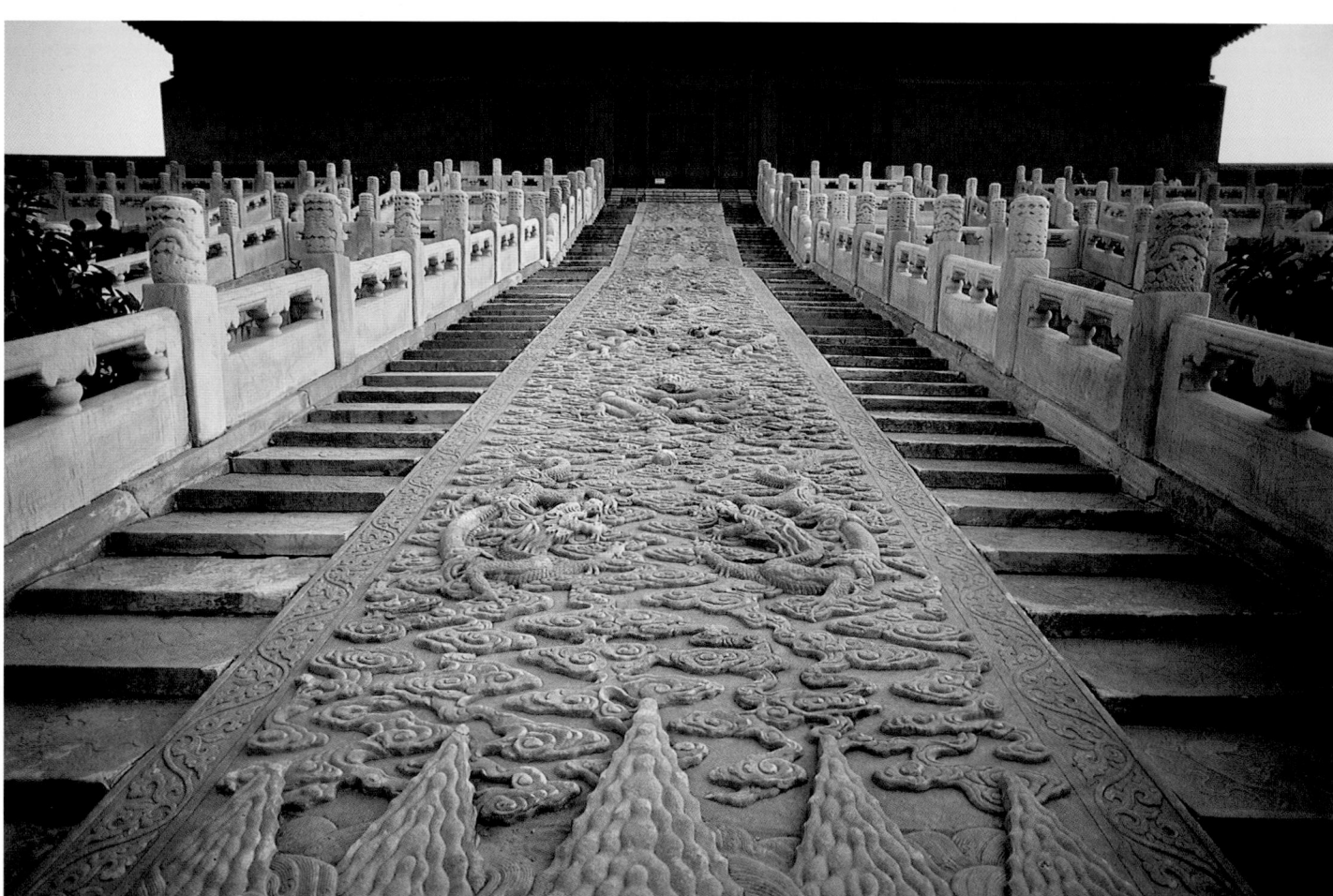

2

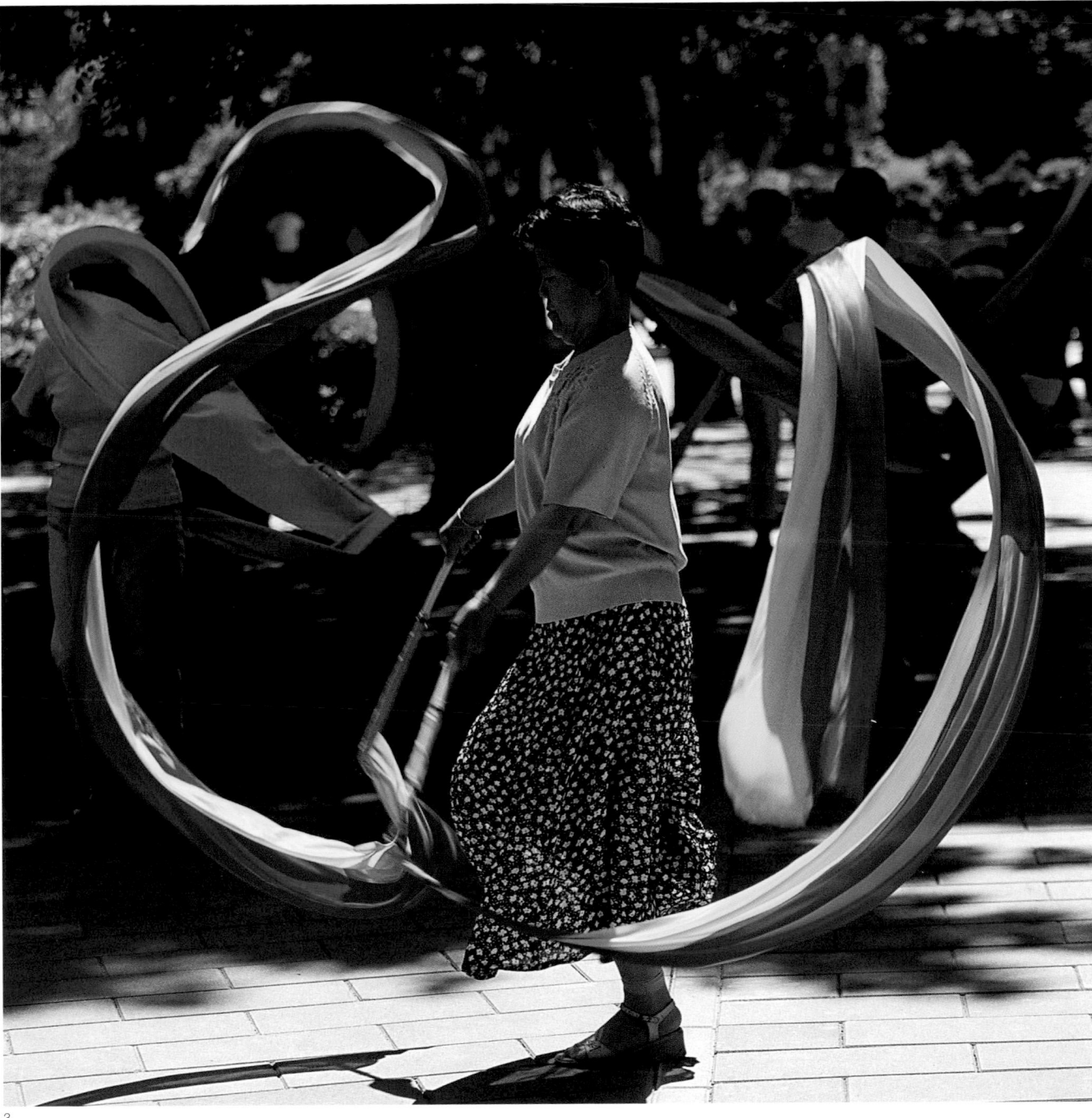

3

SINCE ITS COMPLETION DURING THE REIGN OF YONG'LE IN 1420, the Purple Forbidden City has been the seat of political power in China. Although it ceased to be the emperor's residence with the end of the Qing Dynasty in 1912, the aura of power never moved out. Today, the Chinese leadership and their families reside right next door in the walled compound of Zhong'nan'hai – the former imperial lake gardens. Up to a million workers toiled for 15 years to build the 720,000-square-metre (178-acre) walled city of 800 palaces with 8,888 rooms, only to be forbidden from entering once they had finished the job. Twenty-four emperors of the Ming (14) and Qing (10) dynasties 'ruled' from within these walls, insulated from the petty annoyances of reality – never waking from their velvet dreams until either the buildings caught on fire or angry mobs and foreign armies came crashing through the gates. [1] The palace moat around the northeast watchtower. [2] The Imperial Way leading up to the Gate of Supreme Harmony. [3] *Morning exercise in the Jing'shan (Prospect Hill) Park*

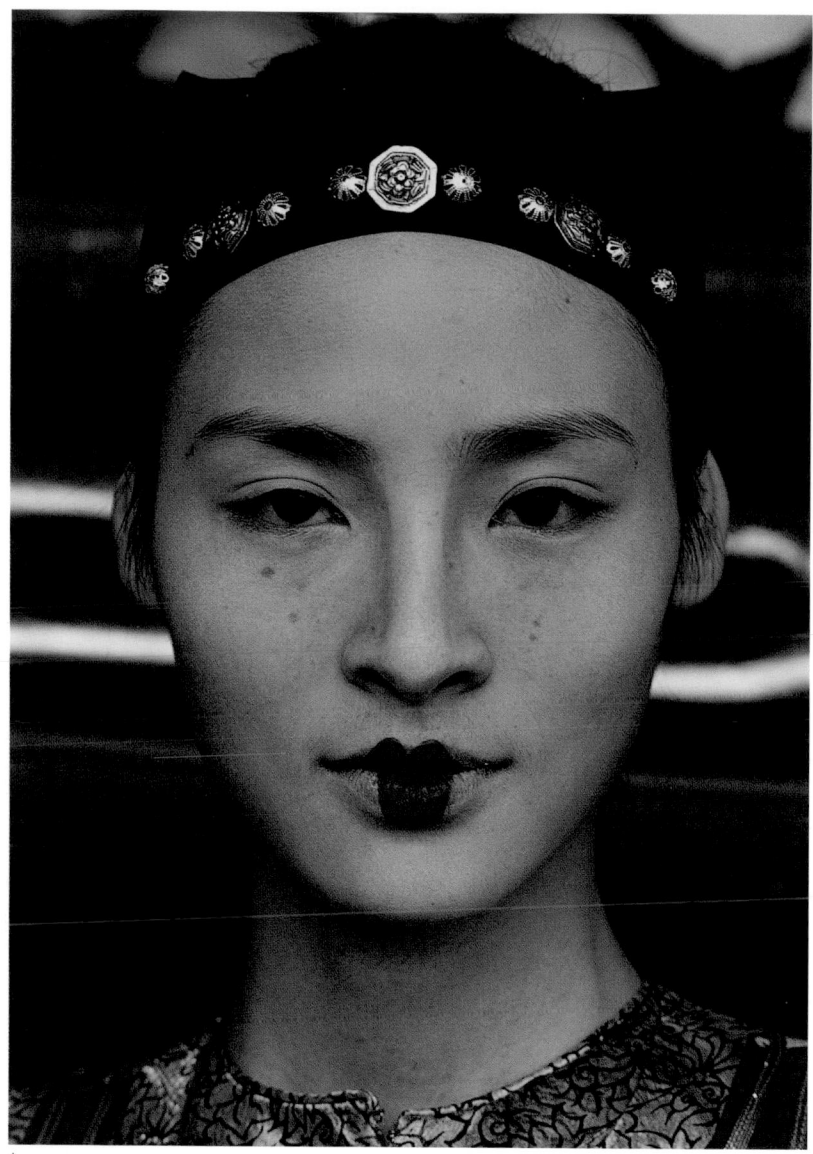

1

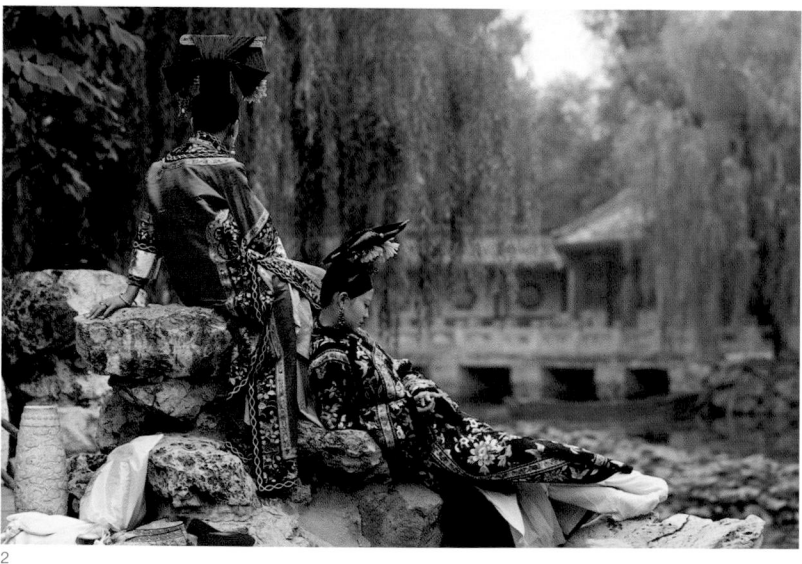

2

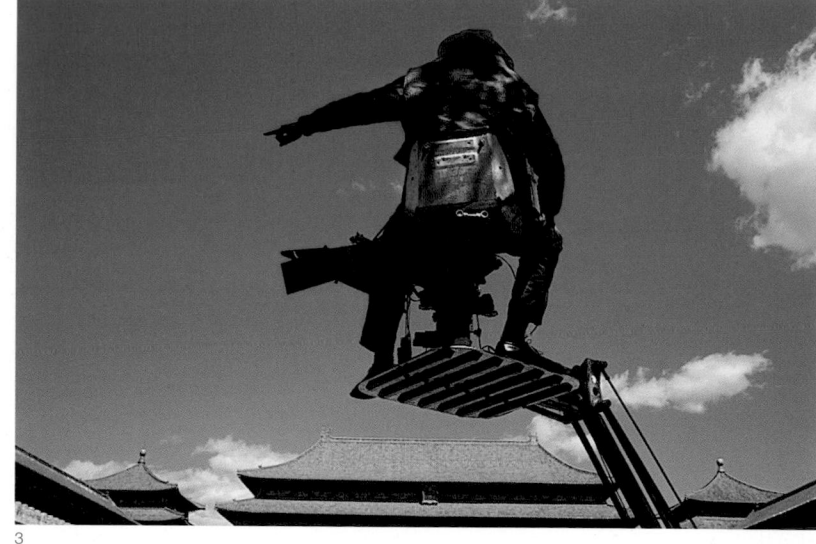

3

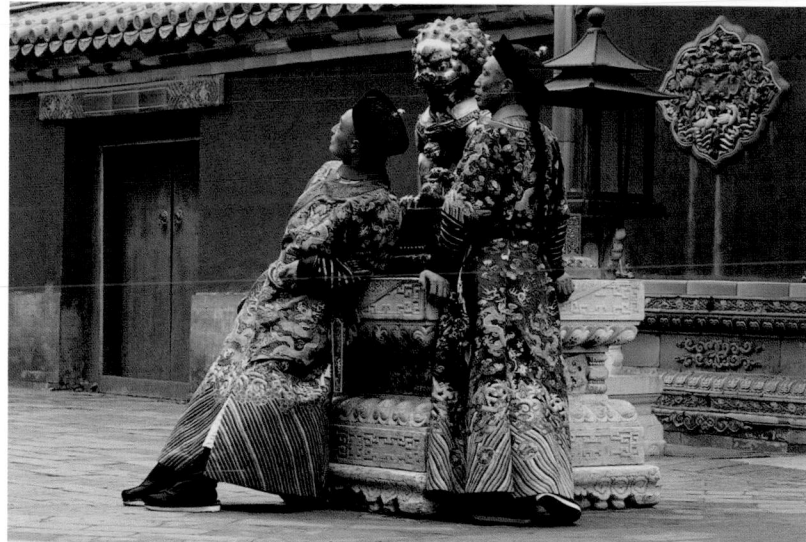

4

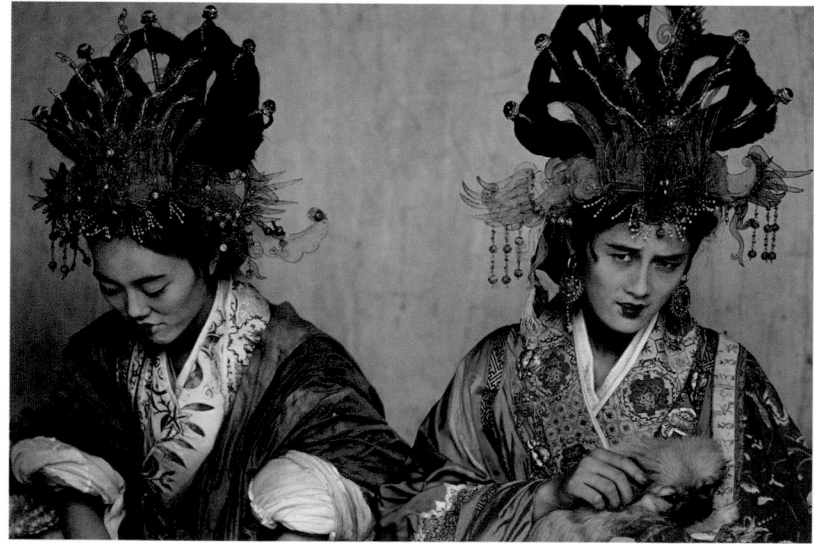

5

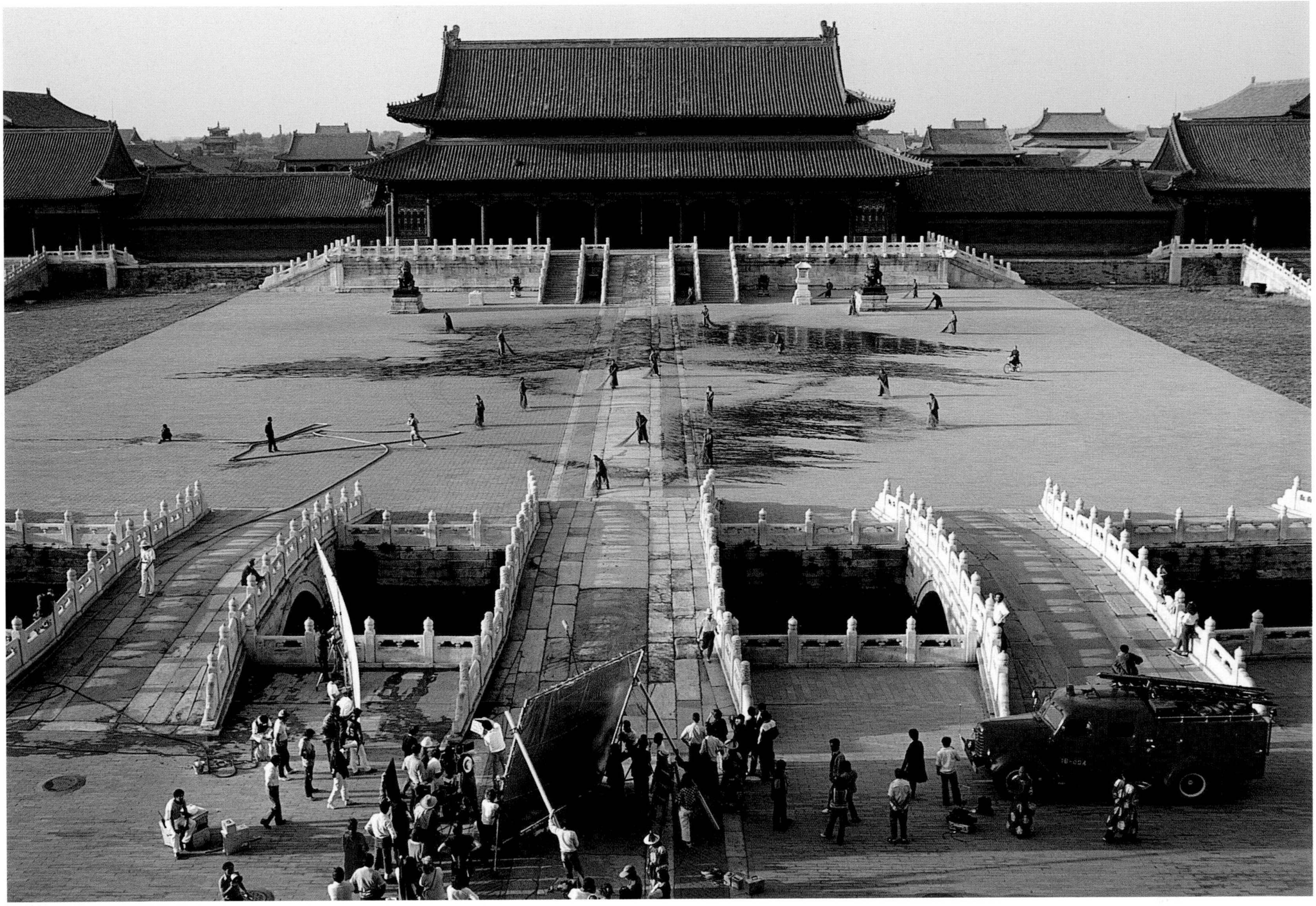

6

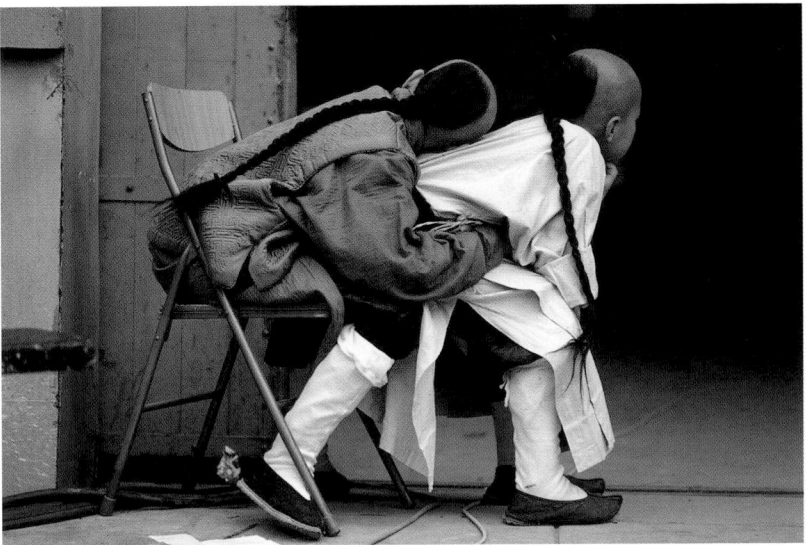

7

IN AUGUST 1986, maestro Bernardo Bertolucci led an international cast and crew into the Forbidden City to begin the filming of *The Last Emperor*. He brought with him actors from five countries, 120 technicians from Italy and Britain and 2 Italian chefs. The chefs arrived with two tonnes of pasta and several hundred kilos of Parmesan cheese – enough to cover four months of filming in Bei'jing, Da'lian and Chang'chun. Supported by the government, the film received unlimited access to locations and labour. A 150-strong Chinese crew from local film studios smoothed the way and played the lead role in organizing the 19,000 extras (including 2,000 PLA soldiers) in the epic crowd scenes. The film went on to sweep the 1988 awards season, including nine Oscars. [1] A 'bridesmaid' in the wedding scene. [2] 'Ladies-in-waiting' at the Summer Palace. [3] Bertolucci directing outside Wu'men (Meridian Gate) – the traditional entrance into the Imperial Palace. [4] 'Eunuchs' waiting for the next set-up. [5] 'Living statues' draped in metres of elaborate embroidery and heavy head-dresses struggle to stay cool in the blazing summer heat. [6] Filming outside the Gate of Supreme Harmony. [7] Young extras relaxing at the Bei'jing Film Studios.

179

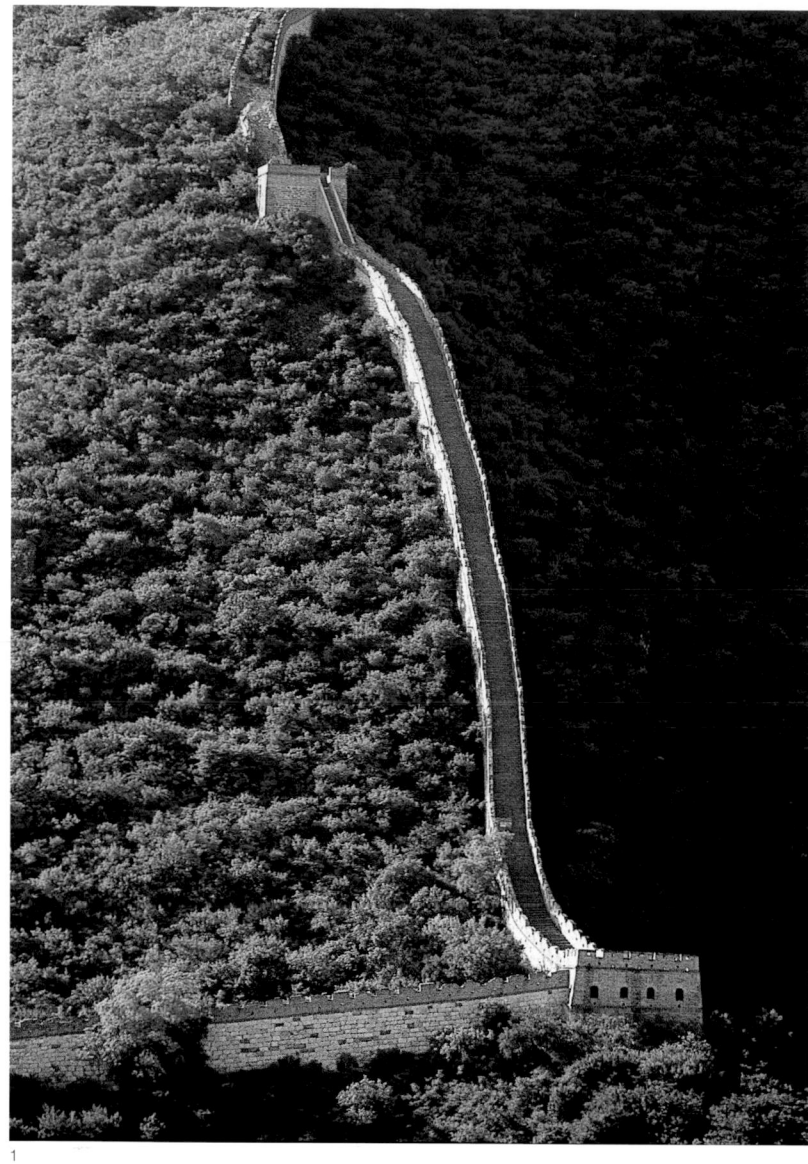

1

TRAFFIC DIVERSIONS AT THE CONSTRUCTION SITE of what will become the new terminal at the Bei'jing Capital Airport resulted in the road to Mu'tian'yu taking an eccentric turn. To get to the highway that heads northeast towards Huai'rou County, one had first to drive into the domestic terminal's Arrivals area and join a service road circling the immense construction site. Beyond this controlled mayhem, however, the landscape shifts abruptly from the frenetic race for the future to the calm and comfort of a more leisurely past. A tree-lined avenue reminiscent of the old airport road of my youth winds slowly upwards into pine-scented mountains, the scenery varying between tourist tat and [2] enchanting countryside. [1] It was late afternoon and there was not anyone on top of the wall at Mu'tian'yu to enjoy the dramatic views. The serpentine fortifications that wind up and down the precipitous Yan'shan Mountains were first built during the Northern Qi Dynasty (550–577 CE). The great Ming Dynasty general Xu Da, charged with strengthening the northern defences during the Hong Wu reign (1368–98), built the present walls and watch-towers on the original foundations. He extended the wall to join up with the passes of Shan'hai'guan to the east and Ju'yong'guan in the west, forming an uninterrupted line of defence around the capital and the imperial tombs.

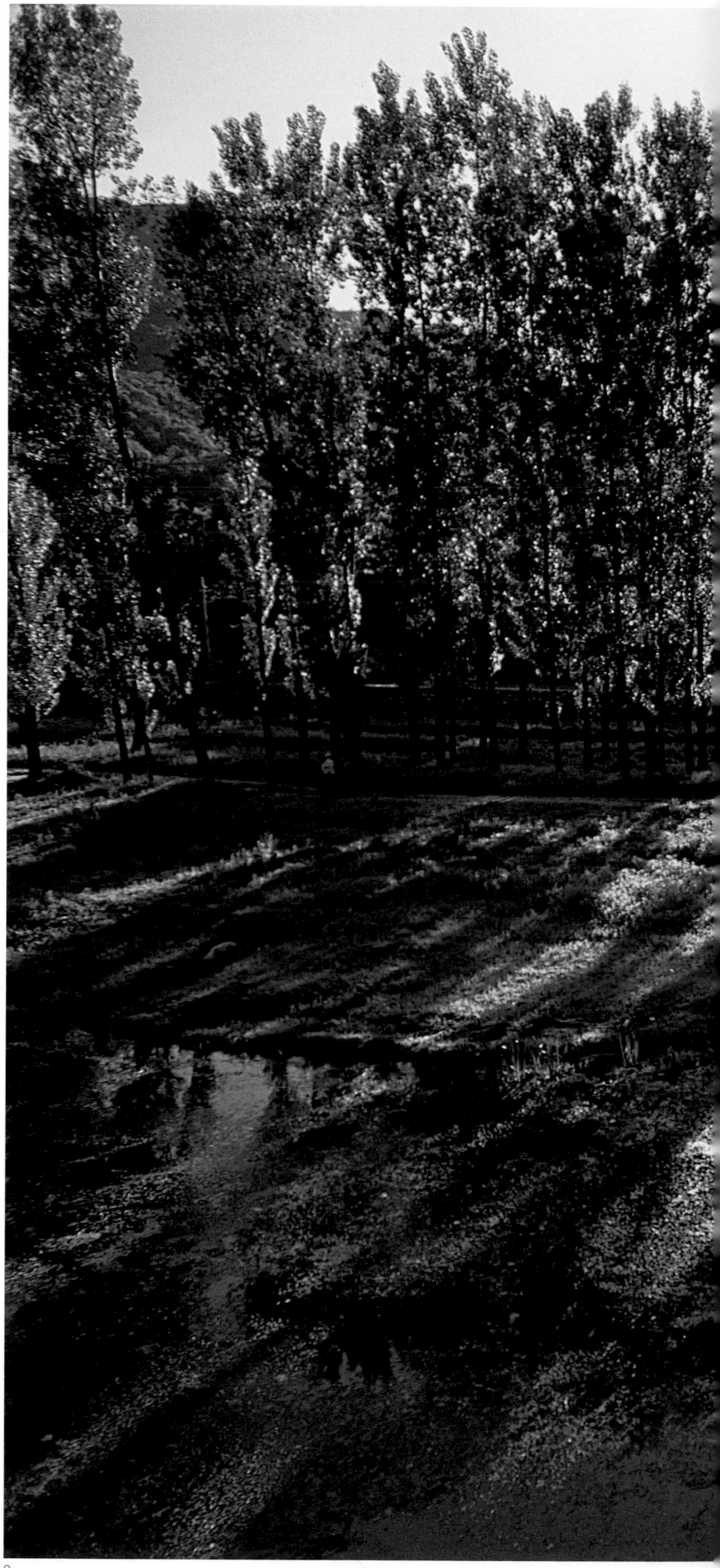

2

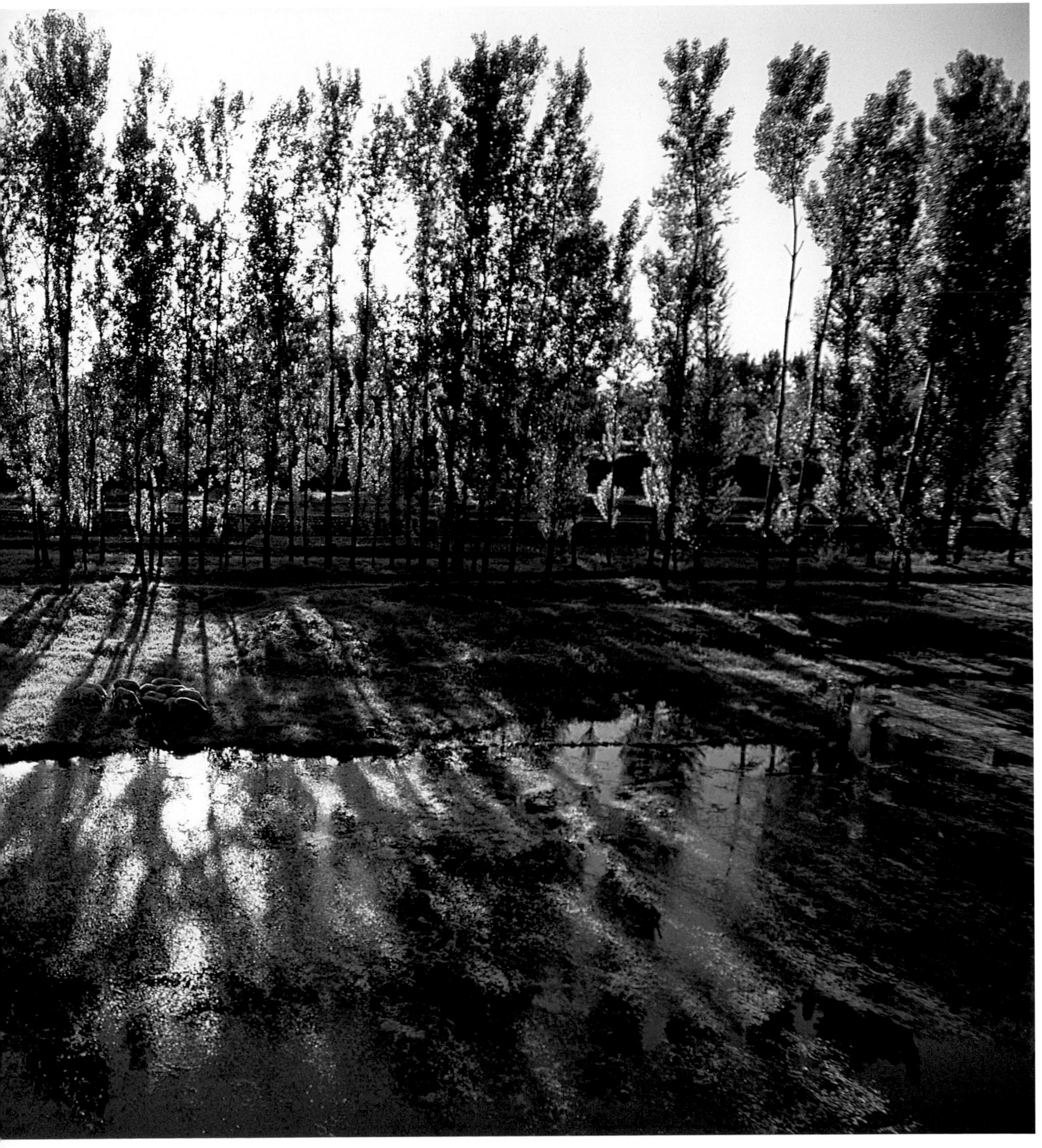

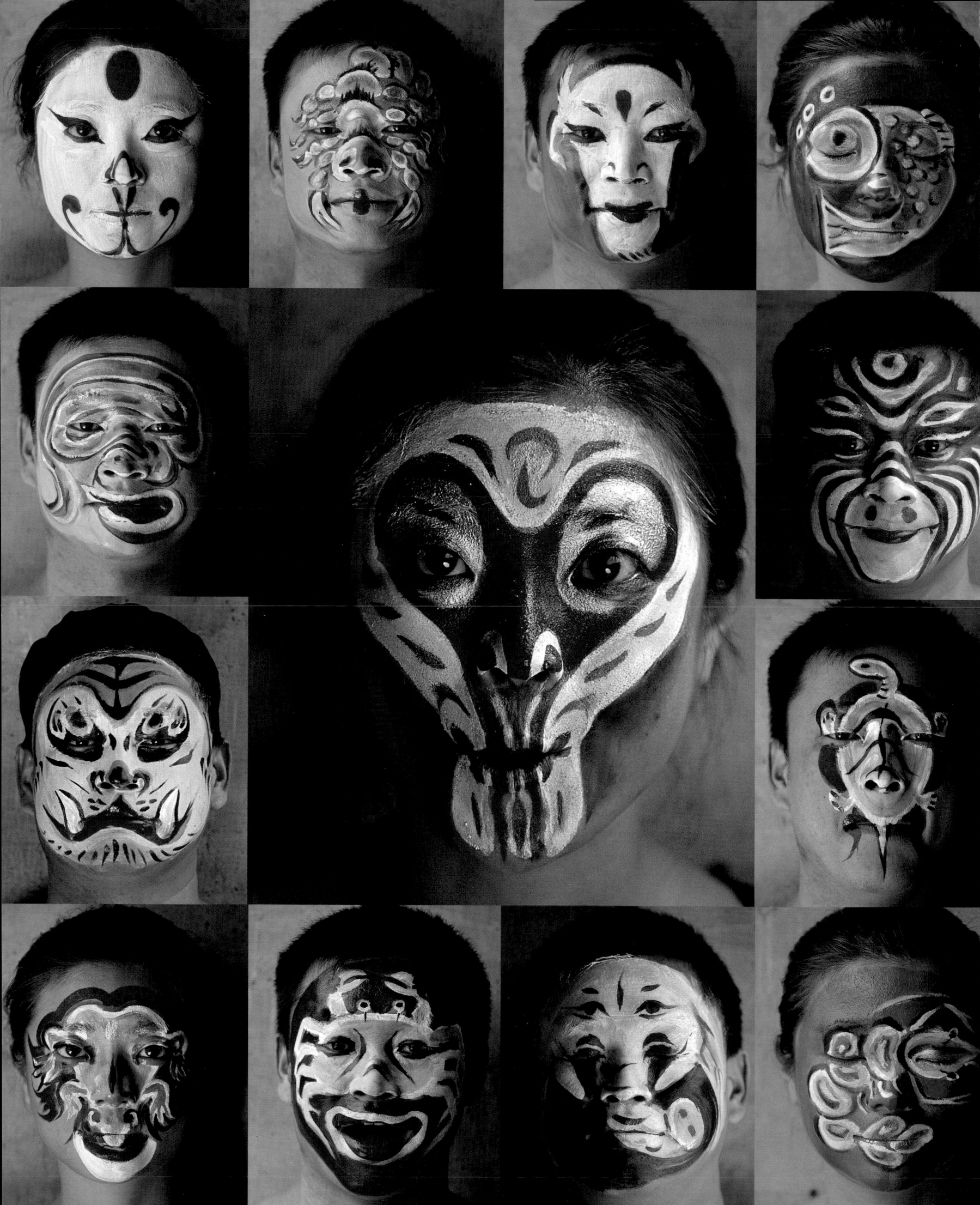

THE POWDER, INK & HEAVY MAKEUP STUDIO

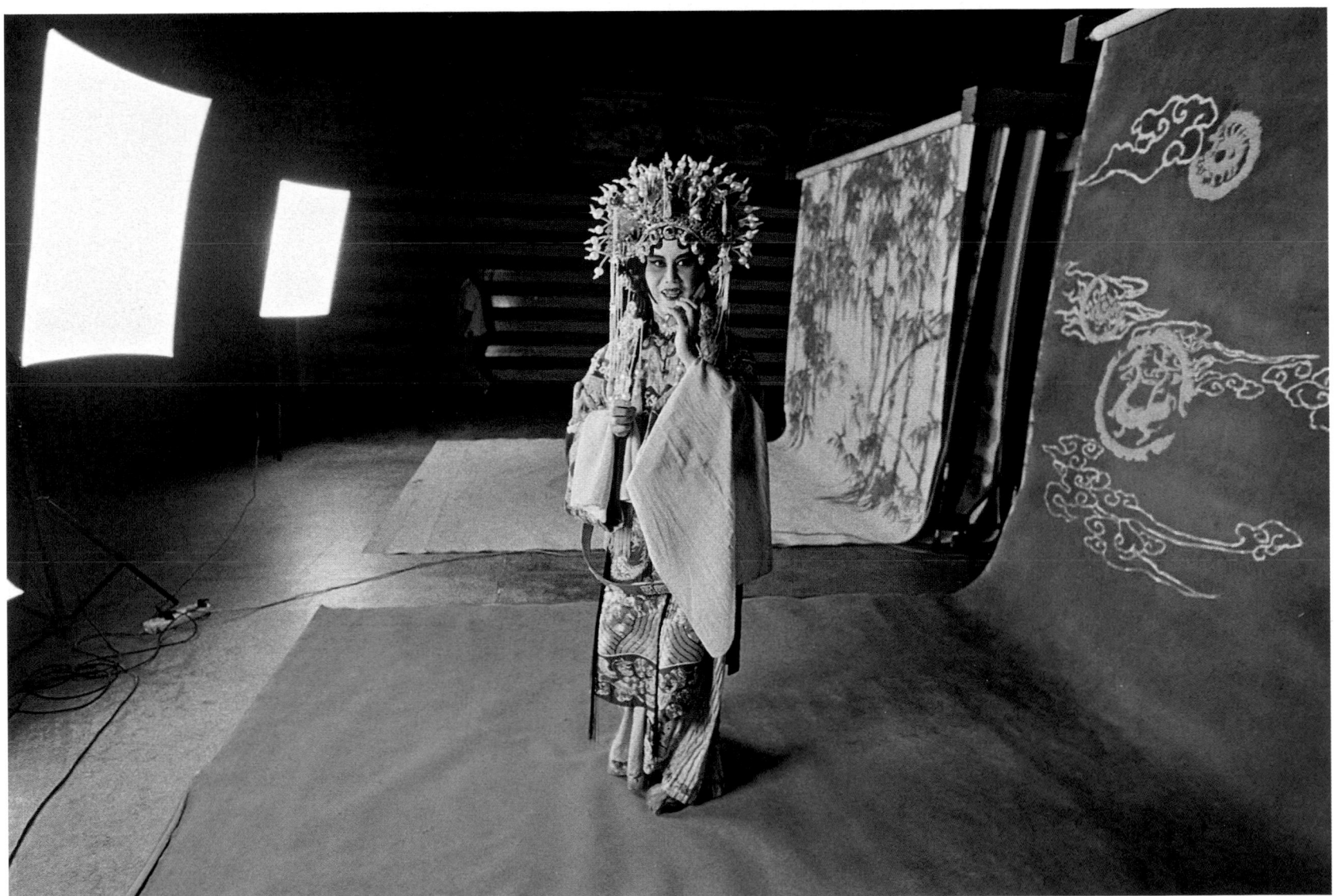

IN AN URBAN RENEWAL MOVEMENT reminiscent of the halcyon days of Manhattan's SoHo-NoHo district in the 1970s, the '798 factory' – an abandoned Soviet-era industrial complex that once manufactured key electronic components for China's first atomic bomb – was transformed in the 1990s into a thriving community of artists' studios and galleries. Penniless dreamers rubbed shoulders with the nouveau riche and wealthy expatriates in the trendy restaurants and bars, and the complex's success led numerous rundown factories surrounding Bei'jing to be renovated to house new businesses run by young capitalists. A compound along a nondescript backstreet in the capital's northeastern suburb is home to a photographic studio named "Powder, Ink and Heavy Makeup". They specialize in portraiture, with their team of makeup artists and stylists transforming clients into [ABOVE] famous Peking opera characters. I ask them to do some of the least-known Peking opera masks, the animals in Journey to the West. [LEFT, CLOCKWISE FROM TOP LEFT] Crane, Scorpion, Goat, Fish, Tiger, Turtle, Shrimp, Elephant, Crab, Frog, Pig, Snake, Monkey King.

NORTH BY NORTHEAST

TIAN'JIN MUNICIPALITY

LOCATION
Latitude 38°34'–40°15'N
Longtitude 116°43'–118°03'E

AREA 11,399 km² (4,400 sq miles)

GEOGRAPHY Tian'jin occupies both banks of the lower reaches of the Hai'he River some 50 km before it enters the Yellow Sea at Tang'gu. Bei'jing is around 120 km to the northwest, and the city serves as the capital's principal seaport. The region is generally flat and low-lying, with higher ground in the far north where the Yan'shan Mountains pass through the province.

CLIMATE The province's climate reflects its location between the influence of continental and maritime weather systems. The average January temperature is -1.7°C, rising to 26°C in July. The lowest recorded temperature is -20.3°C and the highest is 41.7°C. Annual average rainfall is 560 mm.

POPULATION 10.23 million (end 2004)

AGRICULTURE About 40 per cent of the municipality is farmland, growing mainly wheat, rice and maize. Fishing is important along the coast and on the local waterways and lakes.

MAIN INDUSTRIES Tian'jin is an important manufacturing centre, with heavy industries such as iron and steel, chemicals and engineering. Other sectors include textiles, food processing, paper, vehicles, rubber, electronics, high-technology equipment and carpets. The city is also an important trade and banking centre.

ANNUAL PER CAPITA INCOME (2005)
Disposable income of urban residents:
RMB 12,639 (US$1,544)
Net income of rural residents:
RMB 7,202 (US$899)

HISTORICAL AND SCENIC SITES
Temple of Great Compassion, Wang'hai'lou Church, Fort Dagukou, Qing Dynasty gun emplacements, Huangyaguan Great Wall.

FOOD Tian'jin food follows northern China's reliance on wheat flour to produce some of its most notable contributions to the national cuisine. The city is famous for its fried snacks, including dough twists, Erduoyan fried cakes, Goubuli steamed stuffed buns, pancakes and chestnuts roasted in sand with brown sugar.

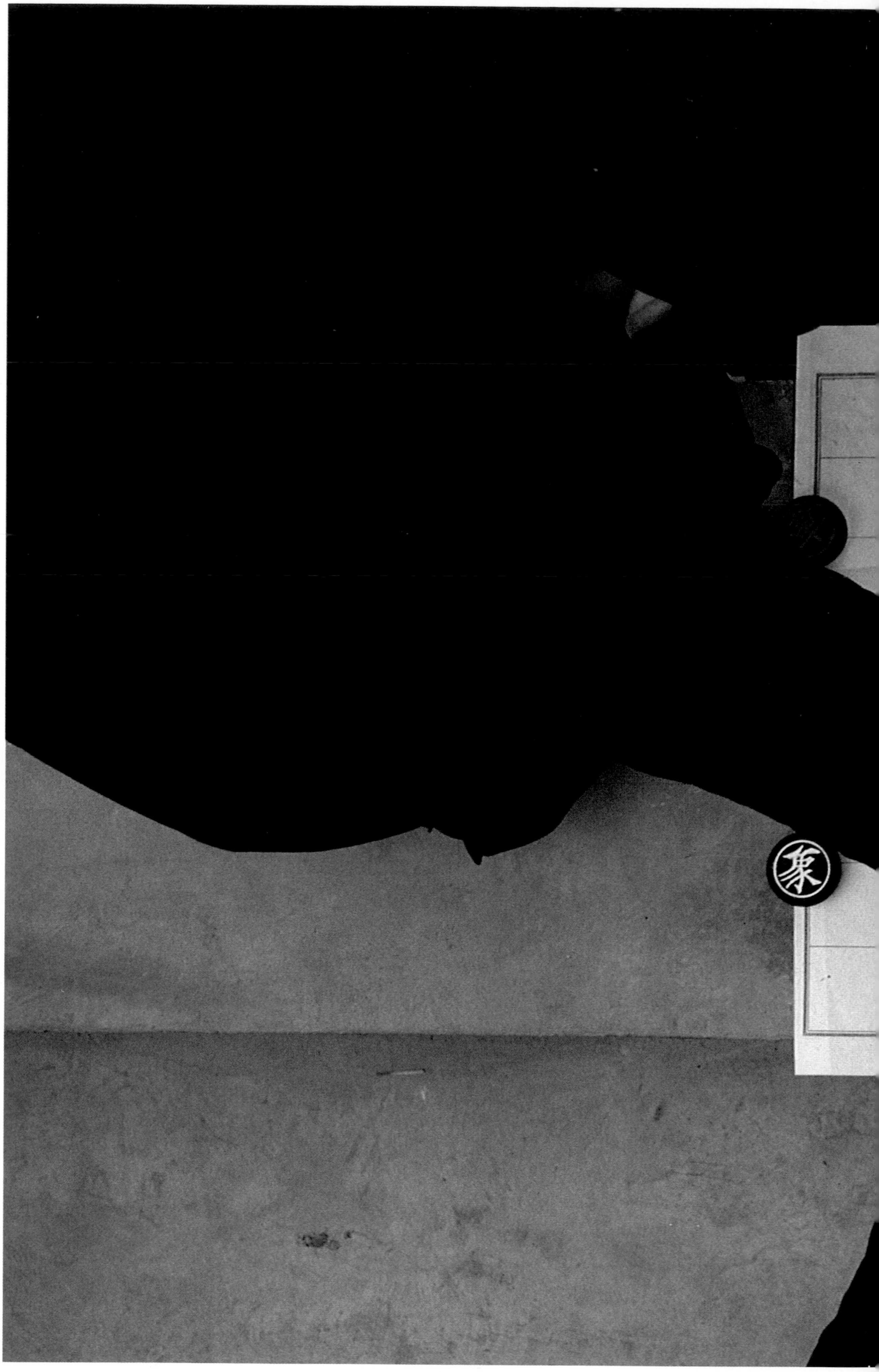

[RIGHT] A game of Chinese chess in the park.

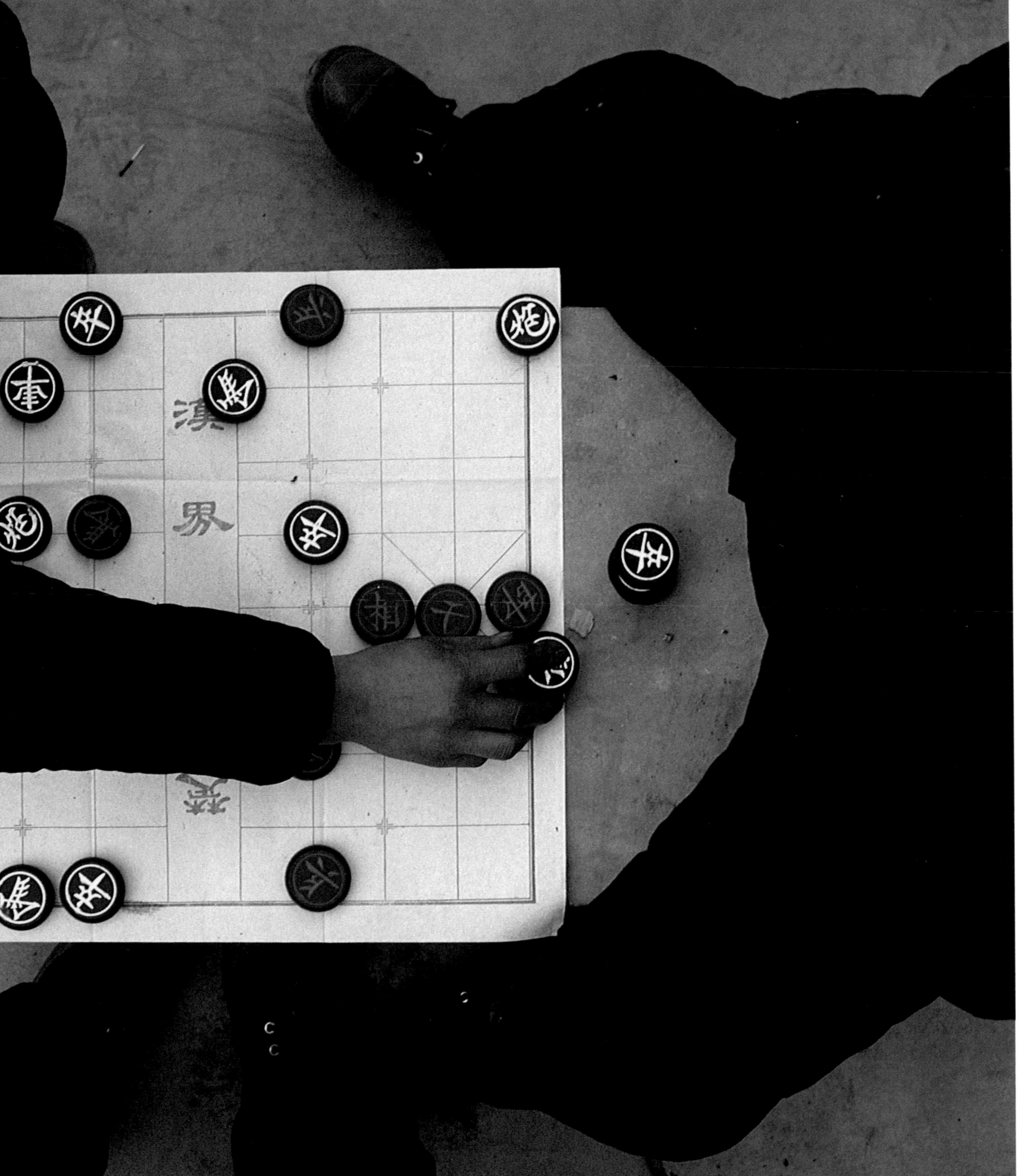

TIAN'JIN STREET SCENES

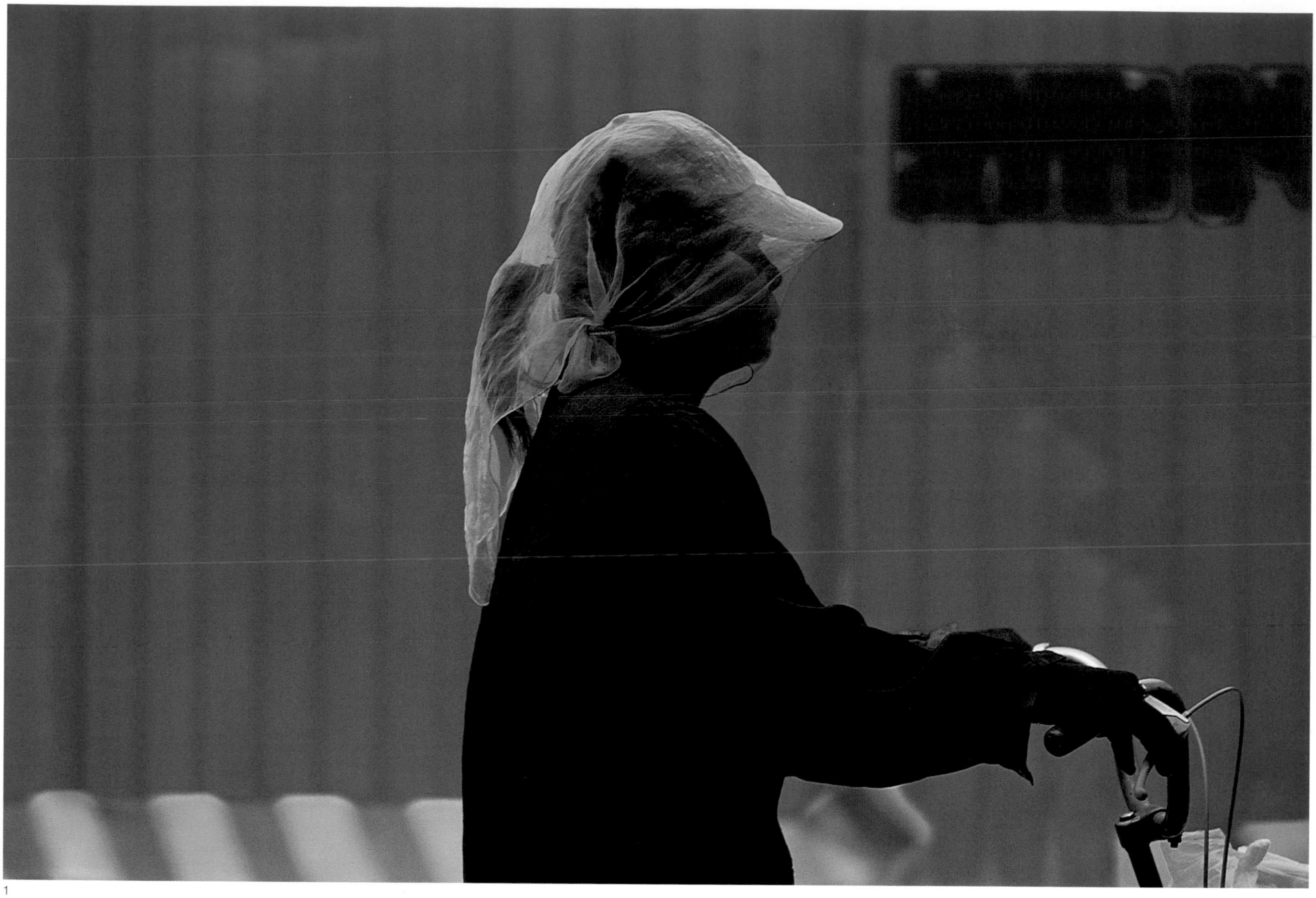

ZHU'GU (VERTICAL PORT) WAS ESTABLISHED AS A TRADING CENTRE during the Sui Dynasty (581–618 CE) at the point where the northern end of the Grand Canal enters the Bo'hai Gulf. Ming Emperor Yong'le renamed the town Tian'jin (Heaven's Ford) in 1404 after he forded the river here. The name first entered the world's consciousness with the Treaties of Tian'jin in 1858 during the Second Opium War, and from then until the 1949 communist victory, the city came under the domination of a Who's Who of colonial powers. Beginning with Britain and France, followed by Japan, Russia and Germany, all controlled their own concessions beyond the reach of Chinese laws. The Boxers seized Tian'jin and laid siege to the foreign concessions for a few weeks in 1900, bringing more mayhem for the long-suffering citizens. The Japanese ran the city between 1937 and 1945, and at the end of the Second War Tian'jin served as an American military base until 1947. With the massive Bin'hai New Area development now underway, the government hopes to turn Heaven's Ford into the Shang'hai and Shen'zhen of the North. [1-5] The streets of Tian'jin.

186

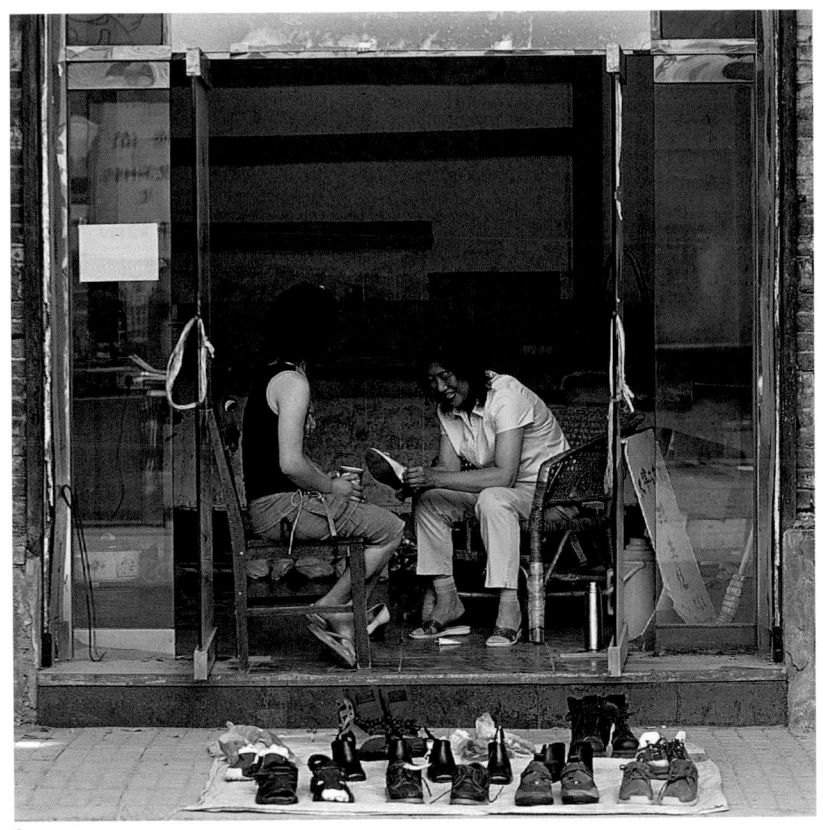

2

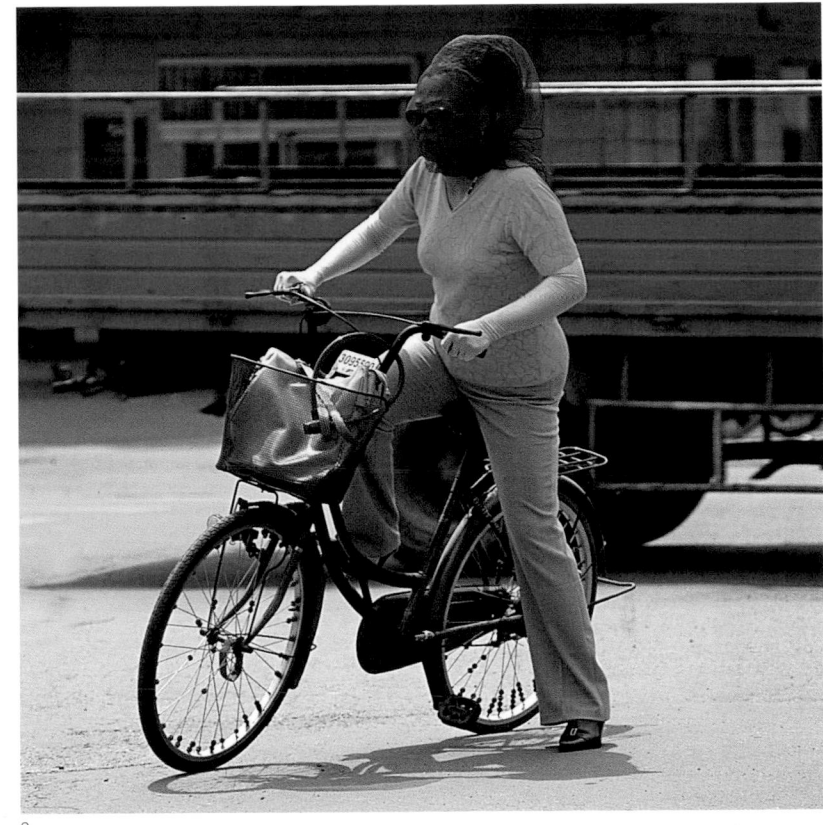

3

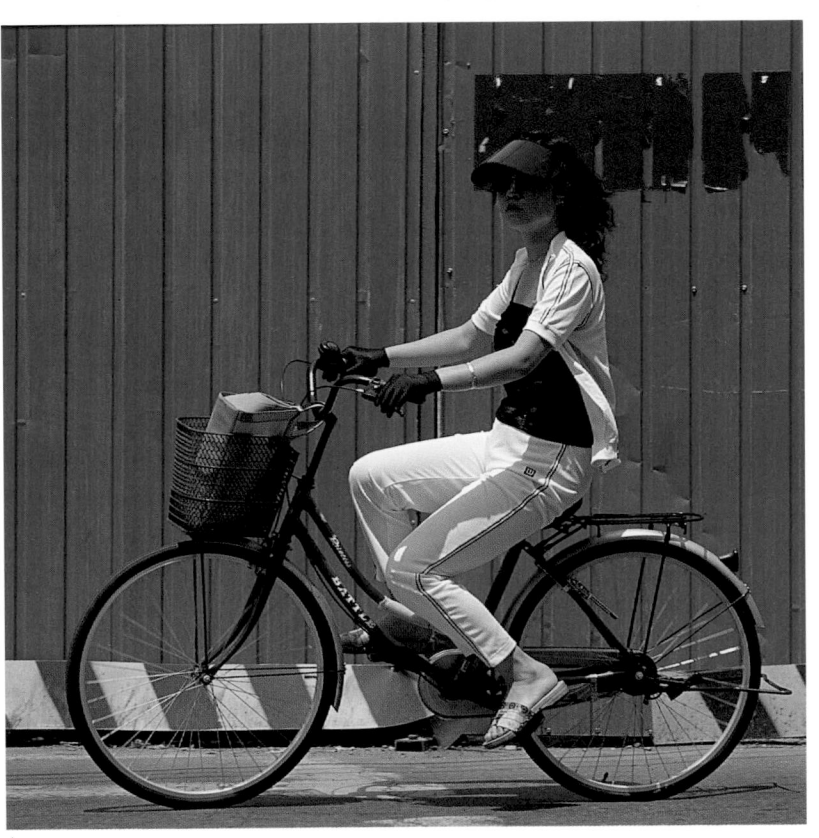

4

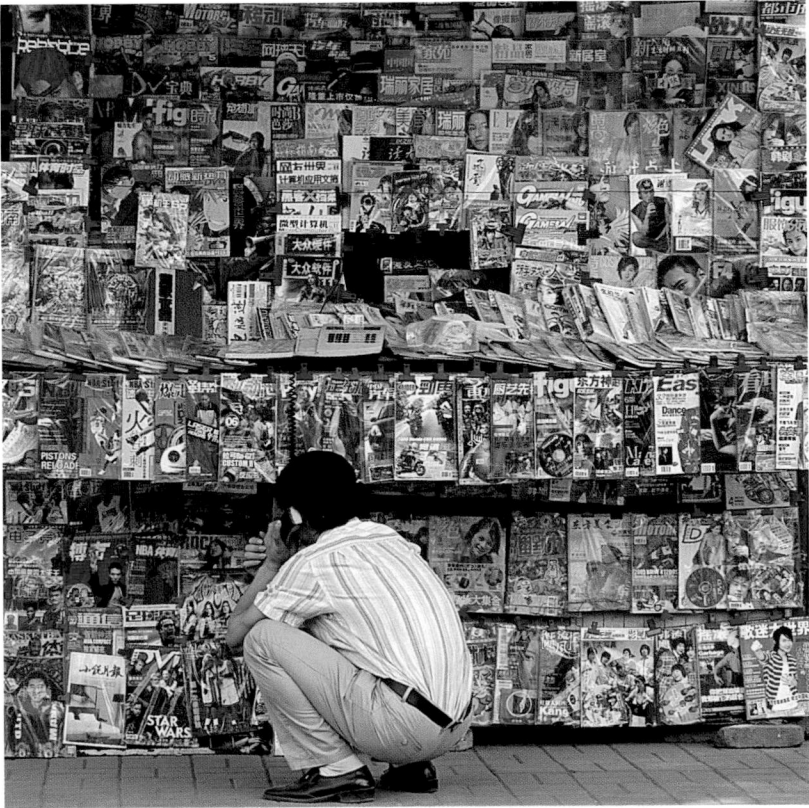

5

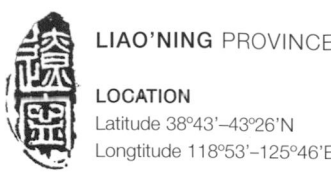

LIAO'NING PROVINCE

LOCATION
Latitude 38º43'–43º26'N
Longtitude 118º53'–125º46'E

AREA 151,295 km² (58,400 sq miles)

GEOGRAPHY The province is defined by the watershed of two major rivers and the flanking highlands. Central Liao'ning has been shaped by the Liao'he and Da'liao rivers and their numerous tributaries to produce mainly flat and fertile plains. The west is dominated by the Nulu'erhu Mountains, and the east, by the Chang'bai Shan and Qian Shan ranges, which extend into the Bo'hai Gulf to form the Liao'dong Peninsula. The highest point is Mount Huabozi at 1,336 m on the peninsula. Liao'ning's nearly 2,200 km coastline on the Yellow Sea and Bo'hai Gulf represents almost 12 per cent of China's total. The province shares a border with North Korea, demarcated by the Ya'lu River.

CLIMATE Liao'ning has a continental monsoon climate characterized by long winters and warm summers. January temperatures range from -15ºC to -5ºC, reaching 22ºC to 26ºC in July. The highest recorded temperature is 43ºC, and the lowest, -39.2ºC. Annual average rainfall is between 440 mm and 1,130 mm.

POPULATION 42.17 million (end 2004)

MAJOR CITIES Shen'yang (capital), Da'lian, An'shan, Liao'yang, Fu'shun, Dan'dong, Ying'kou

AGRICULTURE Main food crops are maize, sorghum and soybeans. The region around Da'lian produces 75 per cent of China's apples and peaches. Cash crops include cotton and forestry, while the province also supports a major fishery.

MAIN INDUSTRIES Liao'ning is one of China's most important industrial bases. The Liao'he oilfield is the country's third largest domestic source of oil and natural gas. Coal mining and iron ore deposits support a variety of industries, including steel making, shipbuilding, chemicals and electronics. The province is also a major source of electrical power for northeast China.

ANNUAL PER CAPITA INCOME (2005)
Disposable income of urban residents:
RMB 9,108 (US$1,137)
Net income of rural residents:
RMB 3,690 (US$460)

IMPORTANT HISTORICAL SITES
Shen'yang Imperial Palace, Northern and Eastern mausoleums, Russo-Japanese battlefields in Lu'shun, An'shan Jade Buddha, White Pagoda at Liao'yang.

FOOD Liao'ning cooking blends northern Chinese cuisine with foods and techniques introduced by Manchus, Russians, Japanese and Koreans. Noted dishes include Shen'yang Lao'bian dumplings, Mongolian pies and hotpots and smoked chicken.

[RIGHT] The Mao monument in Shen'yang.

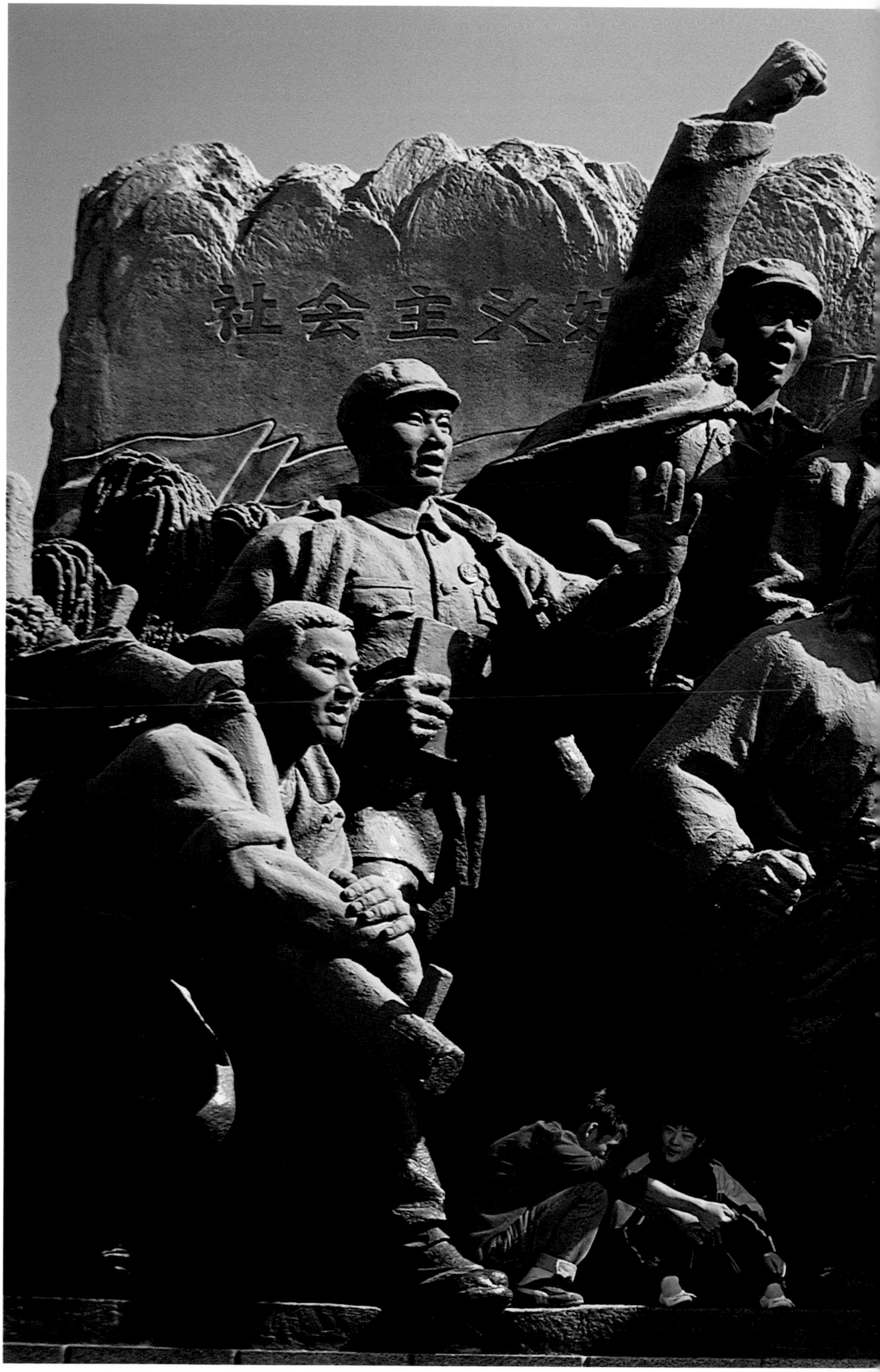

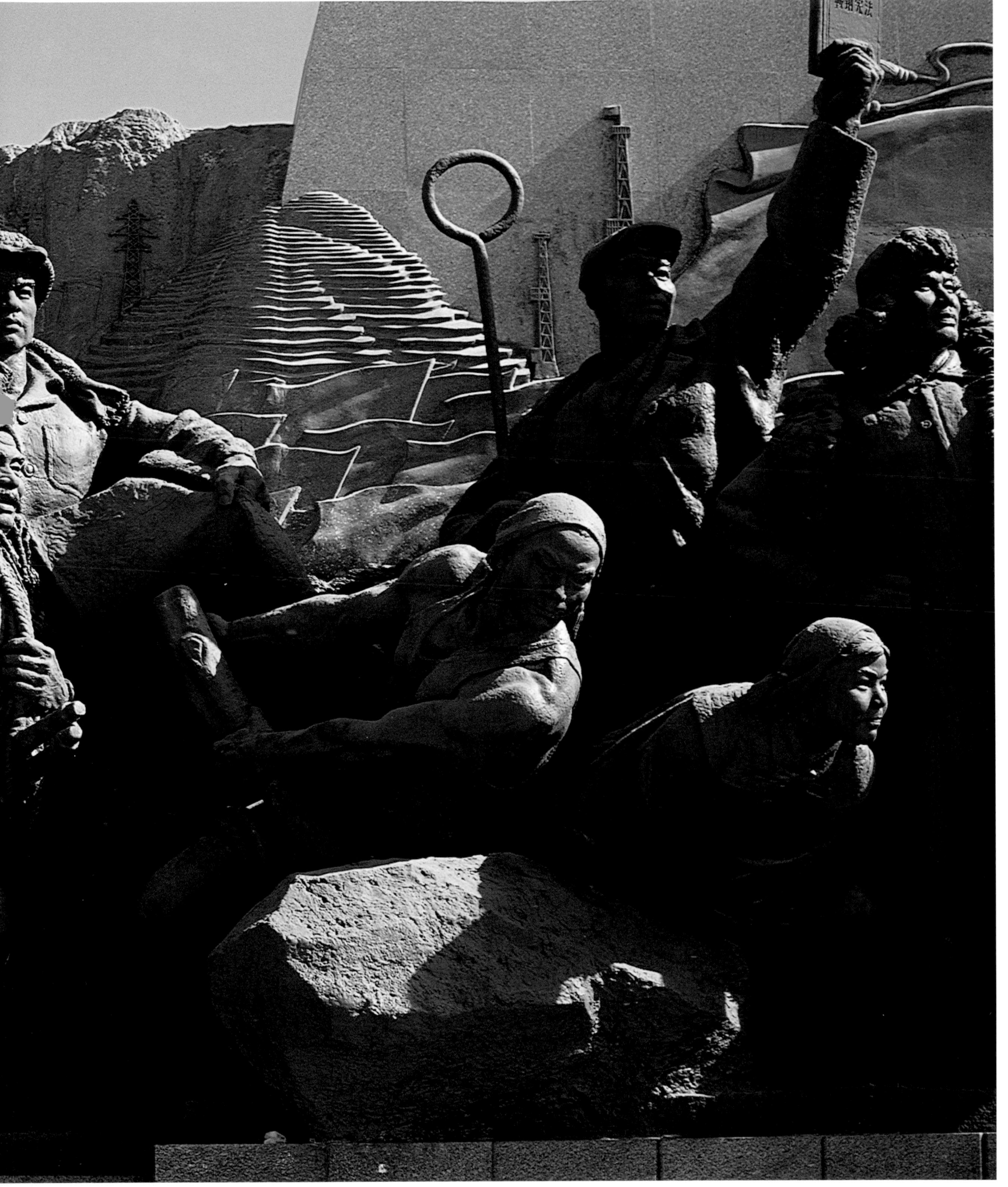

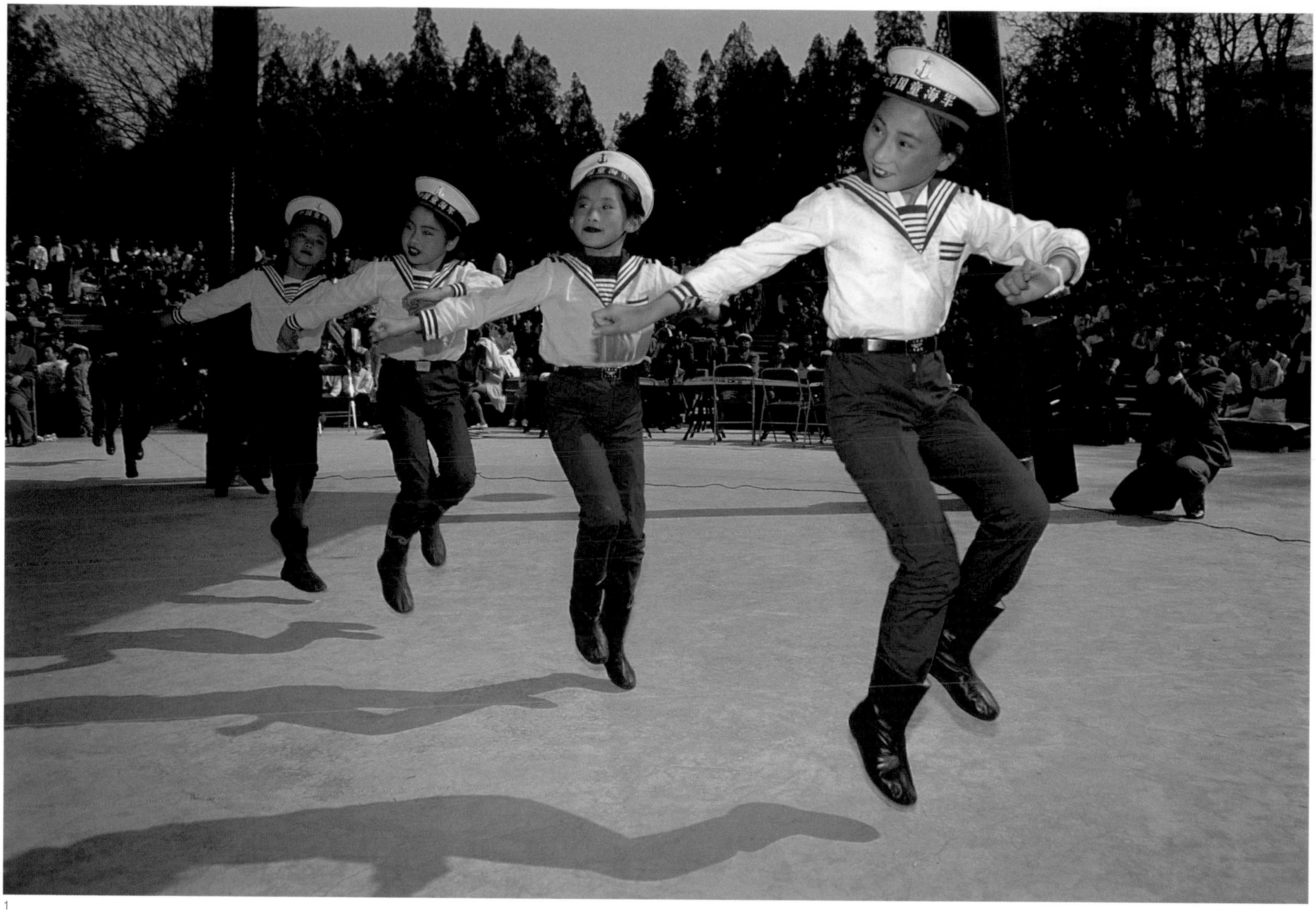

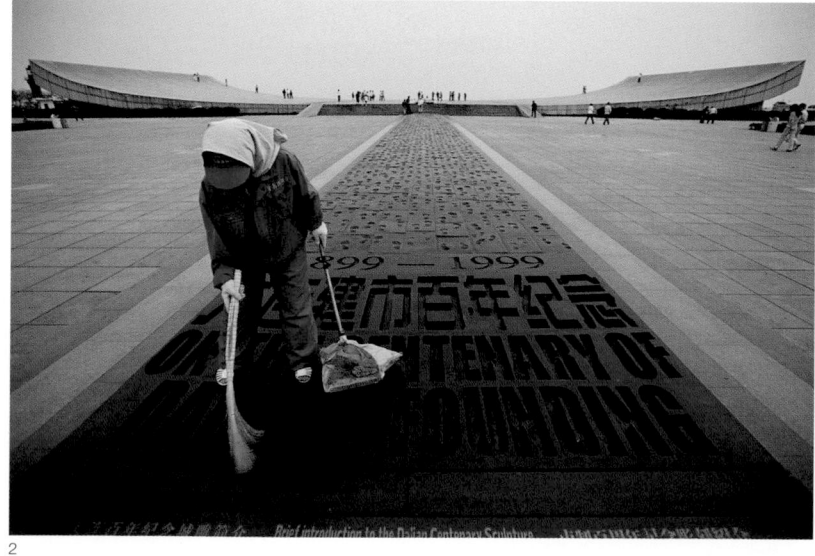

DA'LIAN HAS BEEN DUBBED THE 'HONG KONG OF THE NORTH' because of its present status as a major powerhouse in the booming Chinese economy. But the two cities have more in common than that. Both came into being as a result of the Opium Wars in the 19th Century, leaving them unencumbered by the burden of ancient history. Both were ruled by colonial powers for much of their existence – Da'lian by Tsarist Russia, Imperial Japan and finally the Soviet Union until 1955; Hong Kong by Britain until 1997. This experience and the absence of distant memories have left both cities adaptable and cosmopolitan. But while Hong Kong sizzles with the nervous energy it creates, the lack of a definitive cultural identity seems to have breathed a lightness of being into the citizens of Da'lian. While Hong Kong revels in its ever-changing and spectacular skyline, Da'lian has chosen to leave the Paris-obsessed Russian architects' creations alone, allowing its wide tree-lined avenues to continue radiating from elegant plazas all the way down to the open sea. [1] A school performance in Lao'dong Park. [2] The Centenary Monument in Xing'hai Square. [3] One of the city's beautiful women troopers.

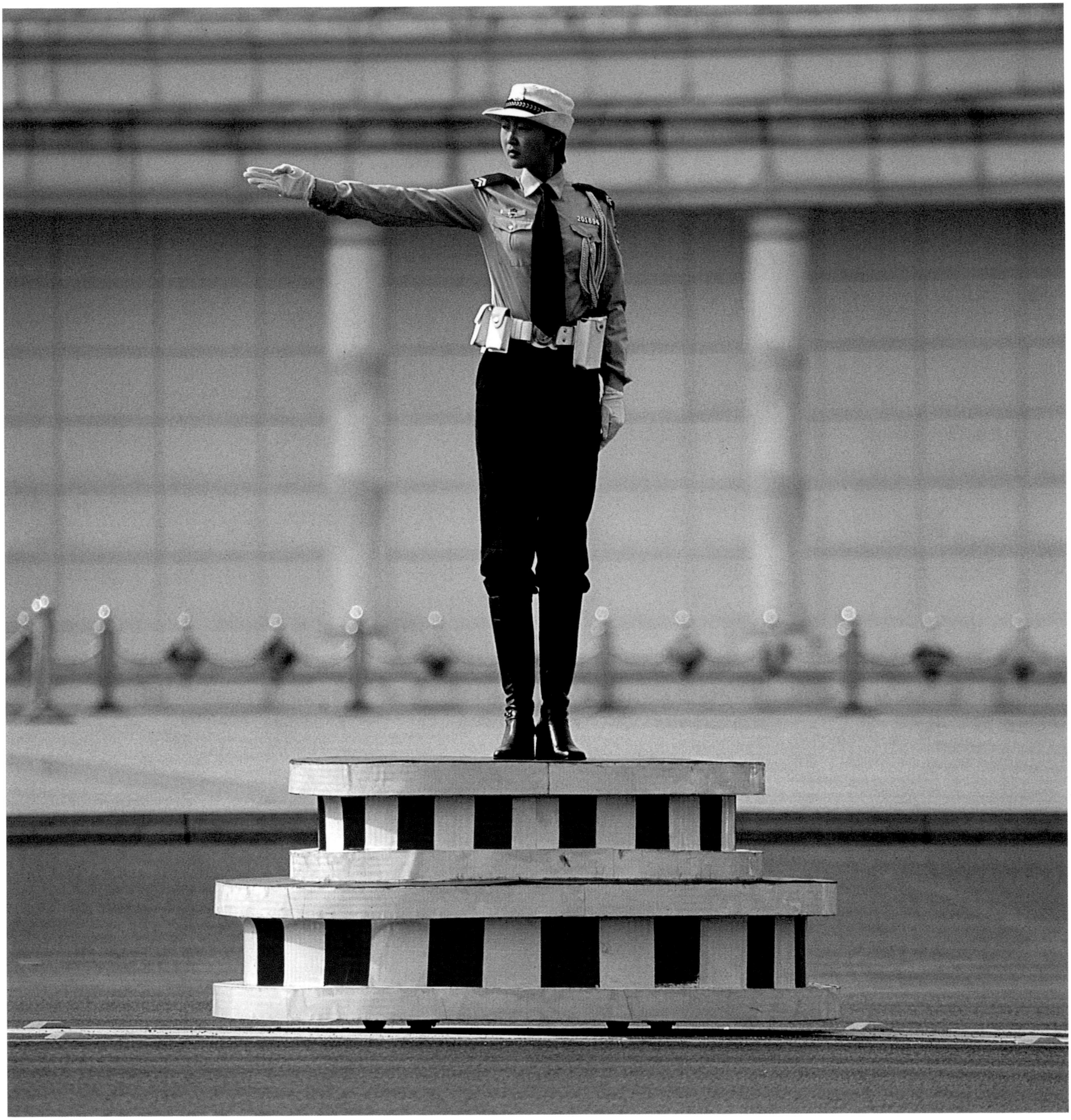

THE LU'SHUN–DA'LIAN COAST

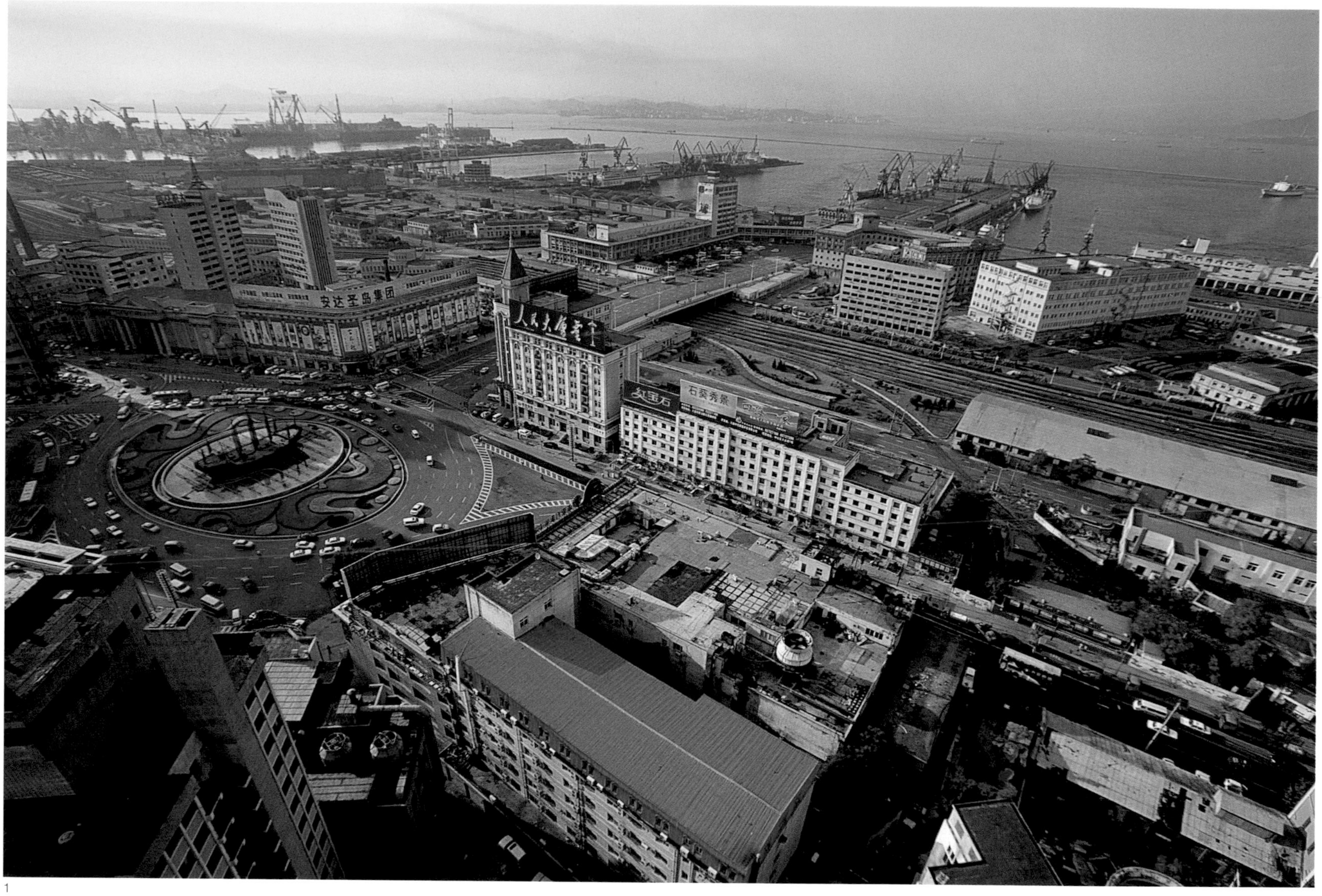

FROM ITS HUMBLE ORIGINS as the smuggler's haven of Ni'wa'kou (Muddy Bay), Da'lian has risen from the ashes of six wars to become [1] one of China's most prosperous cities and largest trading ports. The narrow isthmus at the tip of Liao'dong Peninsula that separates the Bo'hai Sea and the Yellow Sea has always been considered the gateway to the riches of Manchuria. The British first occupied the settlement in1858, the Qing Dynasty got it back in 1880, Japan occupied it in 1895, then the Russians 'leased' the peninsula and built the city of Dalny (Da'lian) and Port Arthur (Lu'shun) on it. During the Russo-Japanese War (1904–05) Port Arthur was surrendered to Japan after an 11-month siege. The Japanese took over the 'lease' and expanded the two cities they called Dairen and Ryojun that became part of Manchuko in 1932. At the end of the Second World War in 1945 the Russians returned as the Soviets – and refused to leave until 1955. [2] A Chinese tour group staring out at Lu'shun'kou (Port Arthur). [3] [4] Harvesting seaweed on the Bo'hai coast.

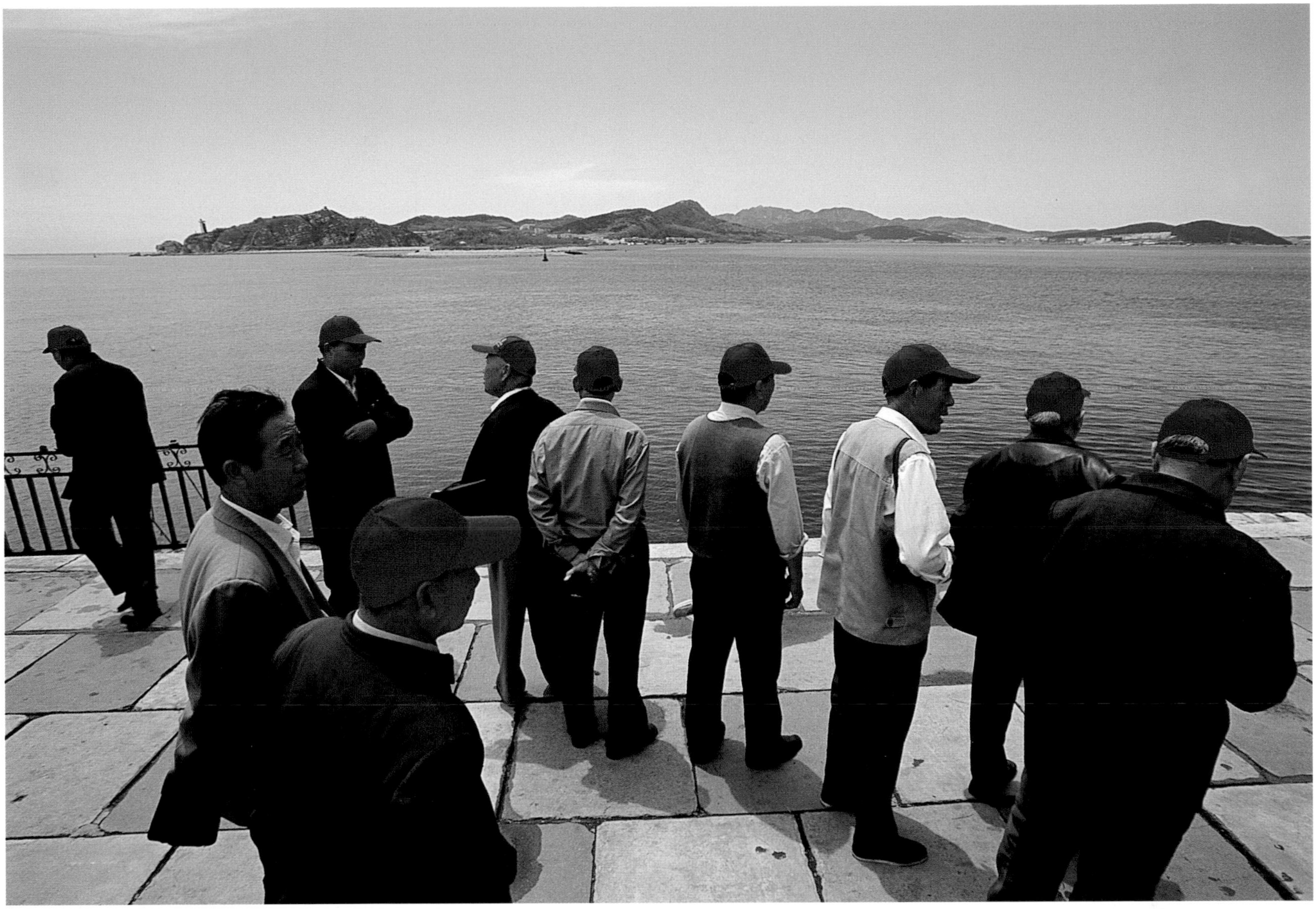

2

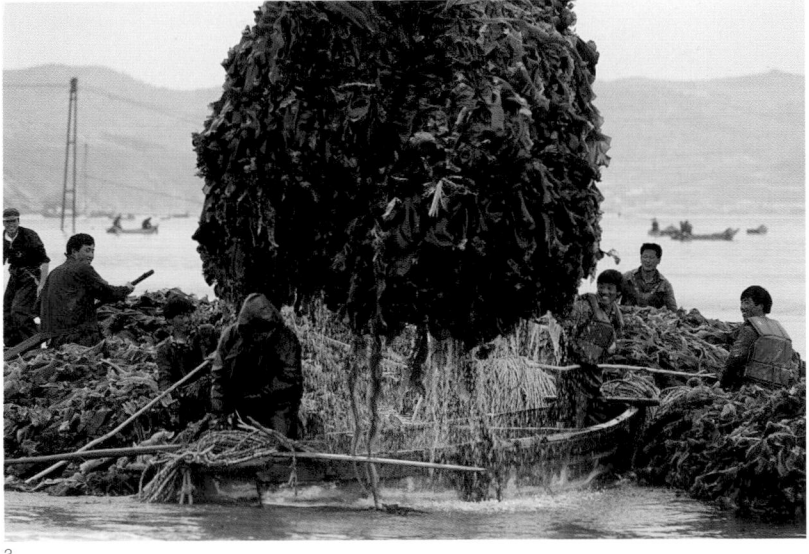

3

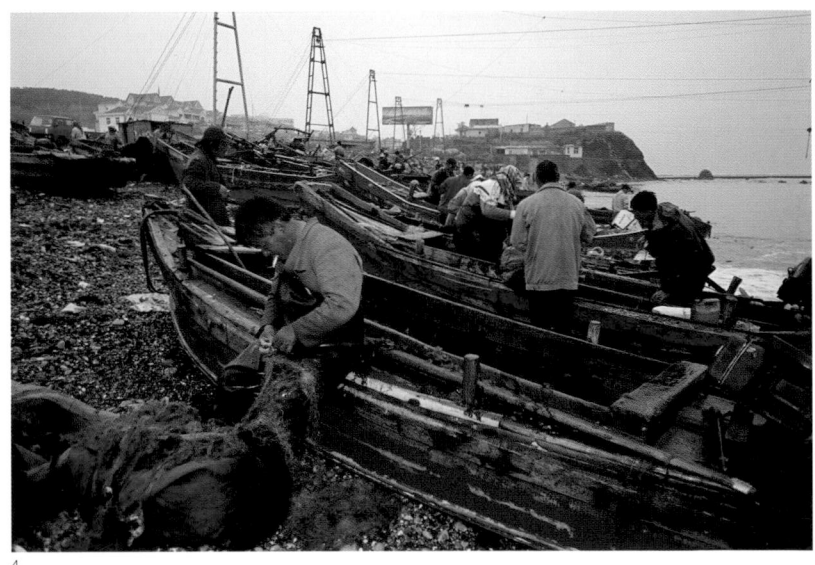

4

1

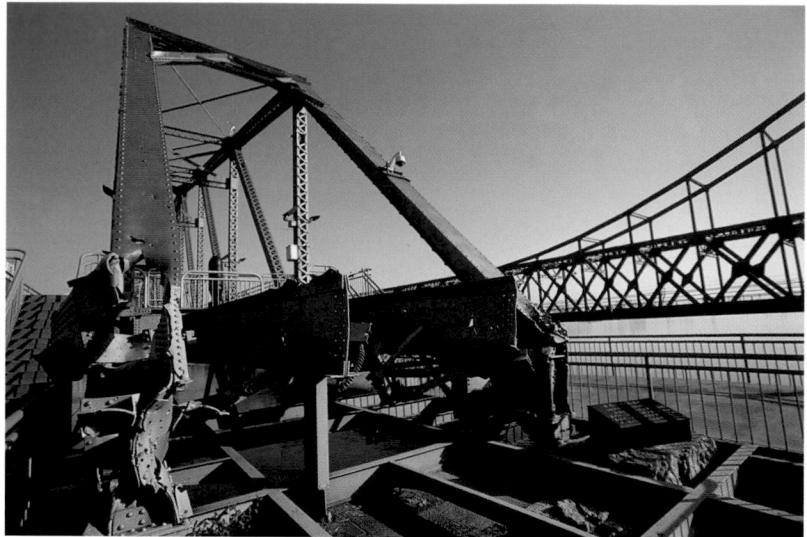

2

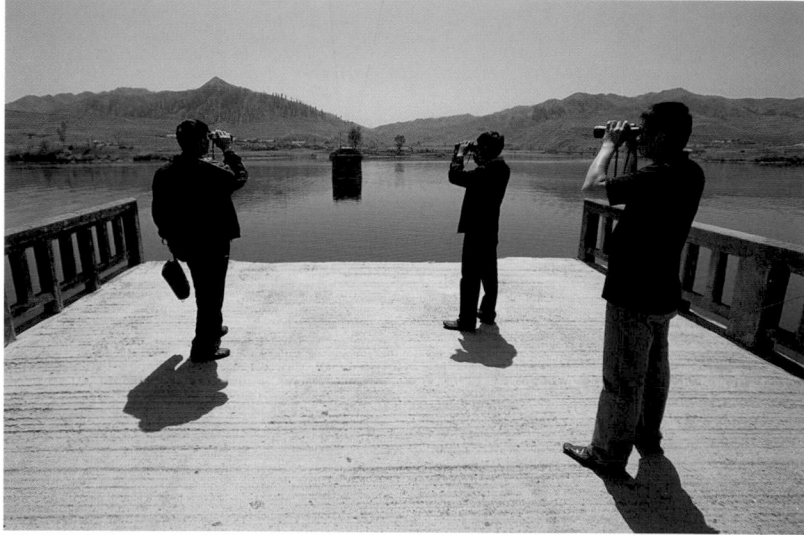

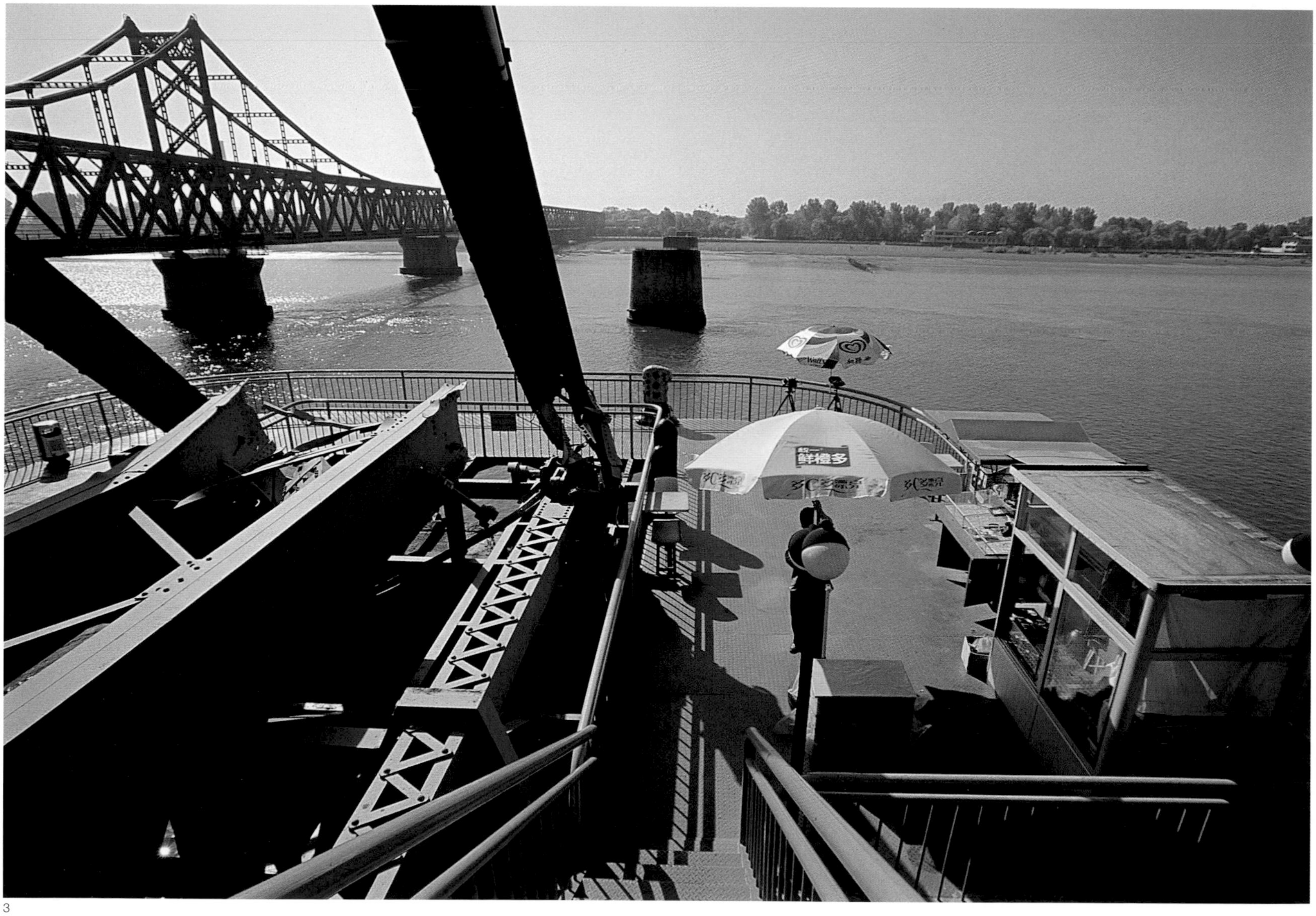

3

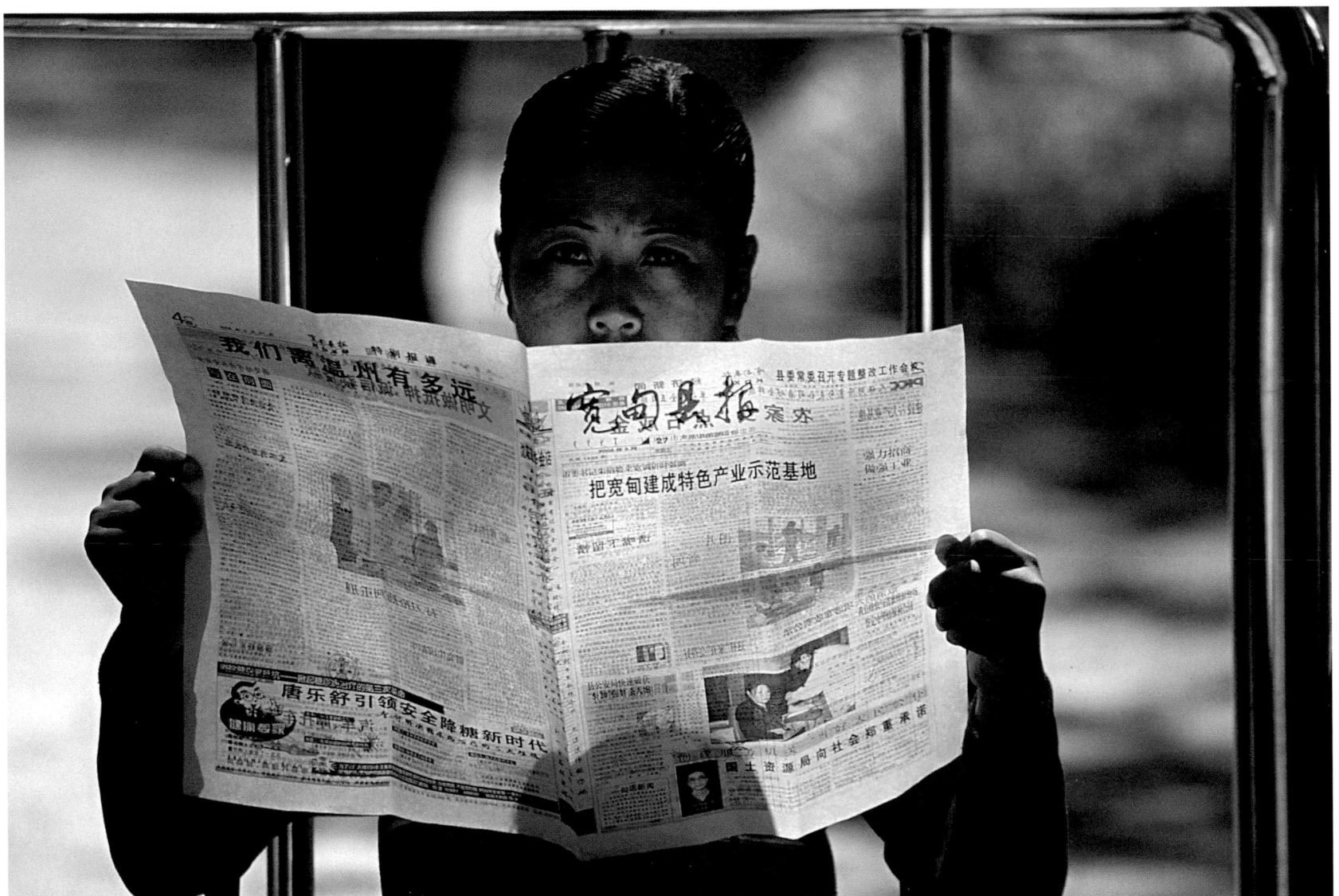

4

IT RAINED AROUND SUNSET. We drove into Dan'dong after dark with the gleaming tarmac hissing under our wheels, glistening with reflections of the multi-coloured neon signs of MSG palaces like Pearl Bay Seafood and Arirang Korean Barbecue. The gaudy strip along the Ya'lu'jiang River looked like something out of *Blade Runner*. Groups of tourists and locals promenaded along the embankment, a mile-long strip of waterfront lit 'bright as a white night'. Across the river, North Korea was pitch black. [1] [3] There was nothing much to see except for twisted steel from the tip of the broken bridge where Chinese troops and supplies once poured into North Korea during a senseless war. Some claim the US Air Force had 'accidentally' severed the long bridge in a strafing attack in 1950, but from where I stood it looked like darned good precision bombing to me. [2] Further north along the Ya'lu'jiang in Kuan'dian village is the other broken bridge, built for the Japanese invasion in 1942 and destroyed by American bombs in 1951. [4] The ticket collector at the He'kou Broken Bridge.

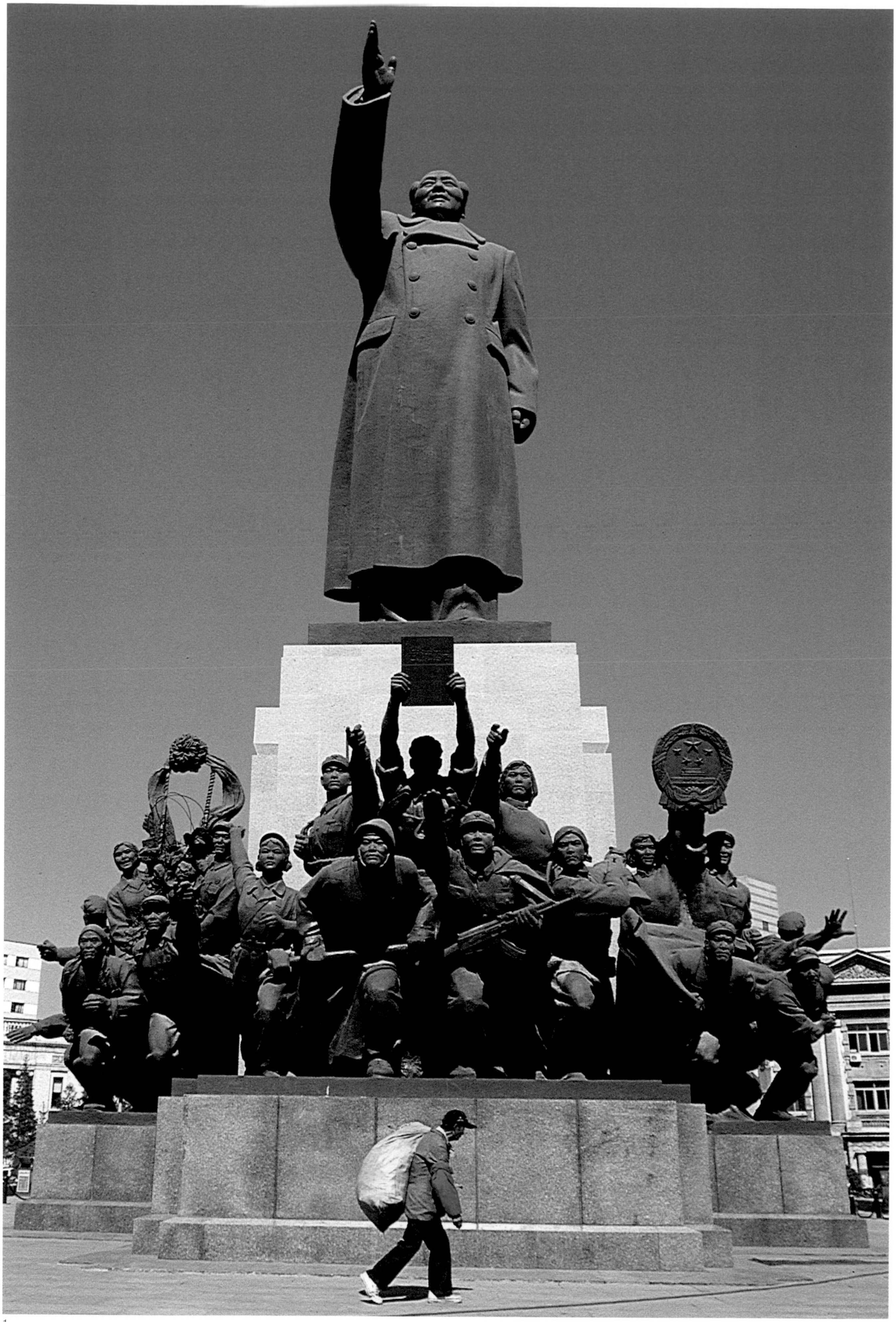

1

THE KEY TO THE EMPIRE

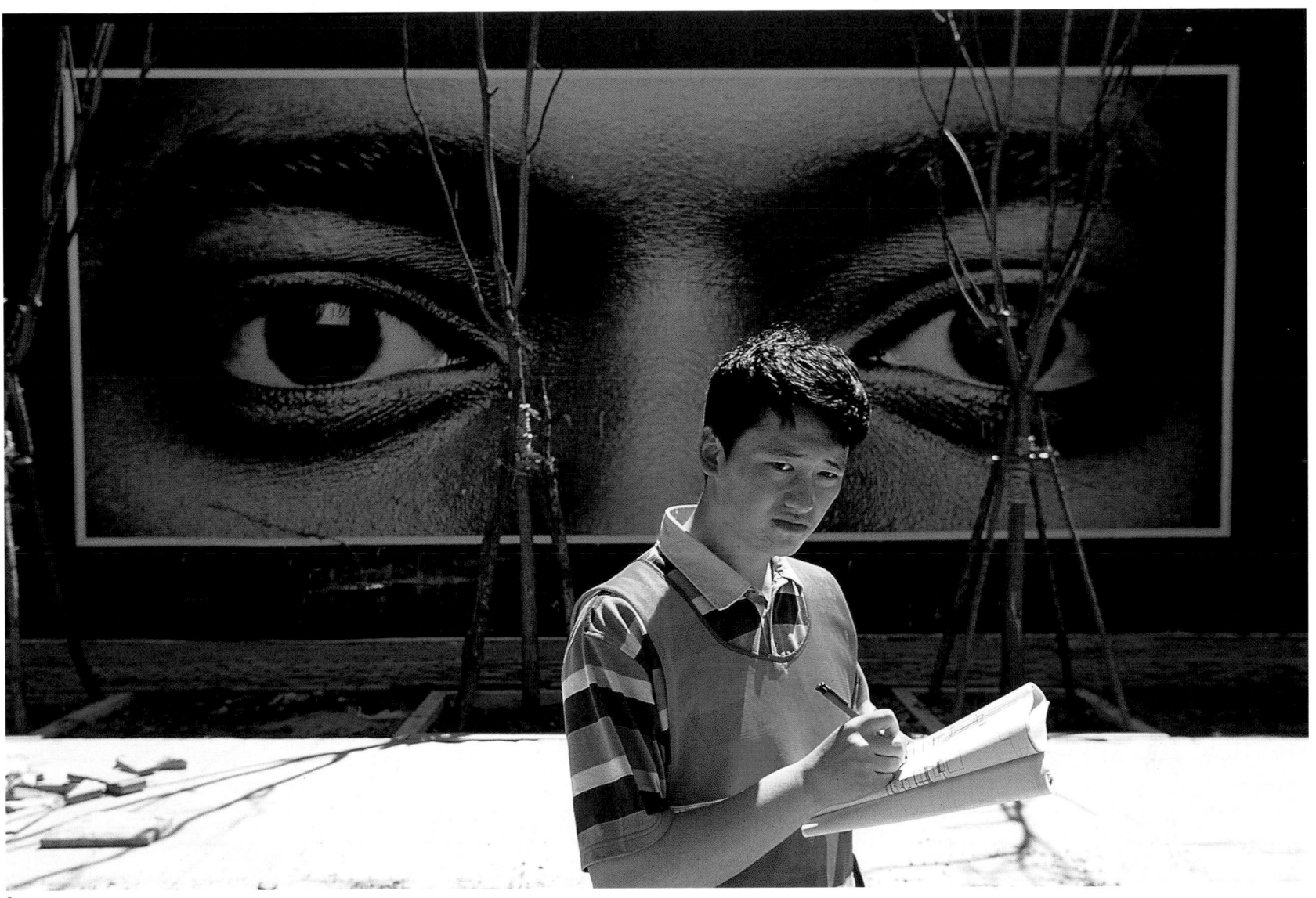

2

ARCHAEOLOGICAL EVIDENCE SUGGESTS Shen'yang was first settled 7,200 years ago, but the city did not rise to prominence until the Manchu leader Nurhachi moved his capital there in 1625. He began construction of a mini-Forbidden City, with his eyes firmly set on the real thing in Bei'jing. His son completed the complex in 1636 and renamed the city Mukden, meaning 'to rise'. He fulfilled his father's dream of conquering China and was crowned Emperor Shun'zhi of the Qing Dynasty in the mini-Imperial Palace before crossing the Great Wall to his new capital in Bei'jing. As the Qing Dynasty faded into irrelevance towards the end of 19th Century, Shen'yang became a key battleground for those seeking to control Manchuria. They included the Russian Empire, Japan, Chinese warlords, the puppet Manchukuo, the Soviet Union, U.S.-backed nationalists and the Chinese communists, who took the city on 30th October 1948. As for Nurhachi before them, Shen'yang was the key to the conquest of China. [1] The spectacular Mao monument in Zhong'shan Square. [2] An engineer in front of a walled construction site in downtown Shen'yang.

NORTH BY NORTHEAST

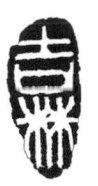

JI'LIN PROVINCE

LOCATION
Latitude 40º52'–46º18'N
Longtitude 121º38'–131º17'E

AREA 186,528 km² (72,000 sq miles)

GEOGRAPHY Over half Ji'lin is mountainous, with the remainder a mix of densely forested foothills and the grasslands of the Song'liao Plain. The Chang'bai Mountains dominate the southeast, where the province's highest point Bai'yun Peak reaches 2,691 m. Ji'lin is drained by the Ya'lu and Tumen rivers in the far southwest, which between them form the border between China and North Korea. The province also shares a short border with the Russian Far East.

CLIMATE Ji'lin has a temperate continental monsoonal climate, with long cold winters and short warm summers. Average January temperatures range from -20ºC to -11ºC, climbing to 8ºC to 23ºC in July. The highest recorded temperature is 40.6ºC and the lowest is -45ºC. Annual rainfall averages 350 mm to 1,000 mm.

POPULATION 27.16 million (end 2005)

MAJOR CITIES Chang'chun (capital), Ji'lin, Si'ping, Liao'yuan

AGRICULTURE The province is one of China's main corn- and wheat-growing regions. Other food crops include rice, fruit and beans. Cash crops include sugar beet, oilseeds, tobacco, jute, ginseng and medicinal herbs. The Chang'bai Mountains support a major forestry industry, while sheep and cattle are reared on the western grasslands.

MAIN INDUSTRIES Main industries include coal mining, oil refining, metallurgy, vehicle and railway rolling stock manufacture, chemicals, paper and fertilizer.

ANNUAL PER CAPITA INCOME (2005)
Disposable income of urban residents:
RMB 8,690 (US$1,118)
Net income of rural residents:
RMB 3,264 (US$407)

HISTORICAL AND SCENIC SITES
Chang'bai'shan Nature Reserve, the Tomb of General Yang Jing'yu, Wan'du, Liao Pagoda.

FOOD Ji'lin cooking combines the culinary traditions of Manchuria, Korea and Mongolia. The region's abundant stocks of wildlife, herbs and ginseng is also reflected in some of the province's more notable dishes, including venison, raw salmon, chicken and ginseng in an earthenware pot and the Manchurian Three-set Bowl Banquet.

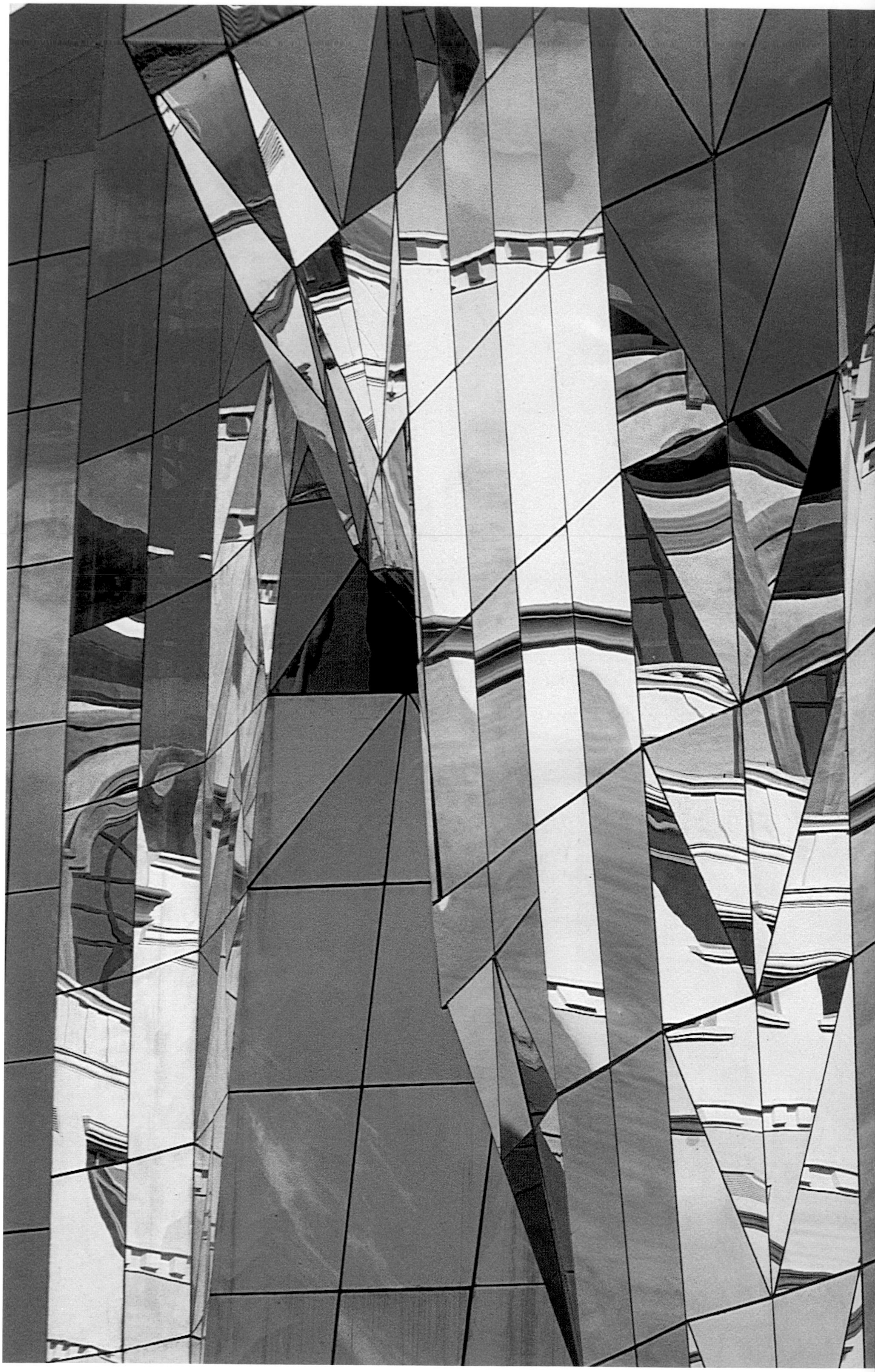

[RIGHT] Three park attendants chatting outside the Crystal Palace in the Chang'chun Film Century City.

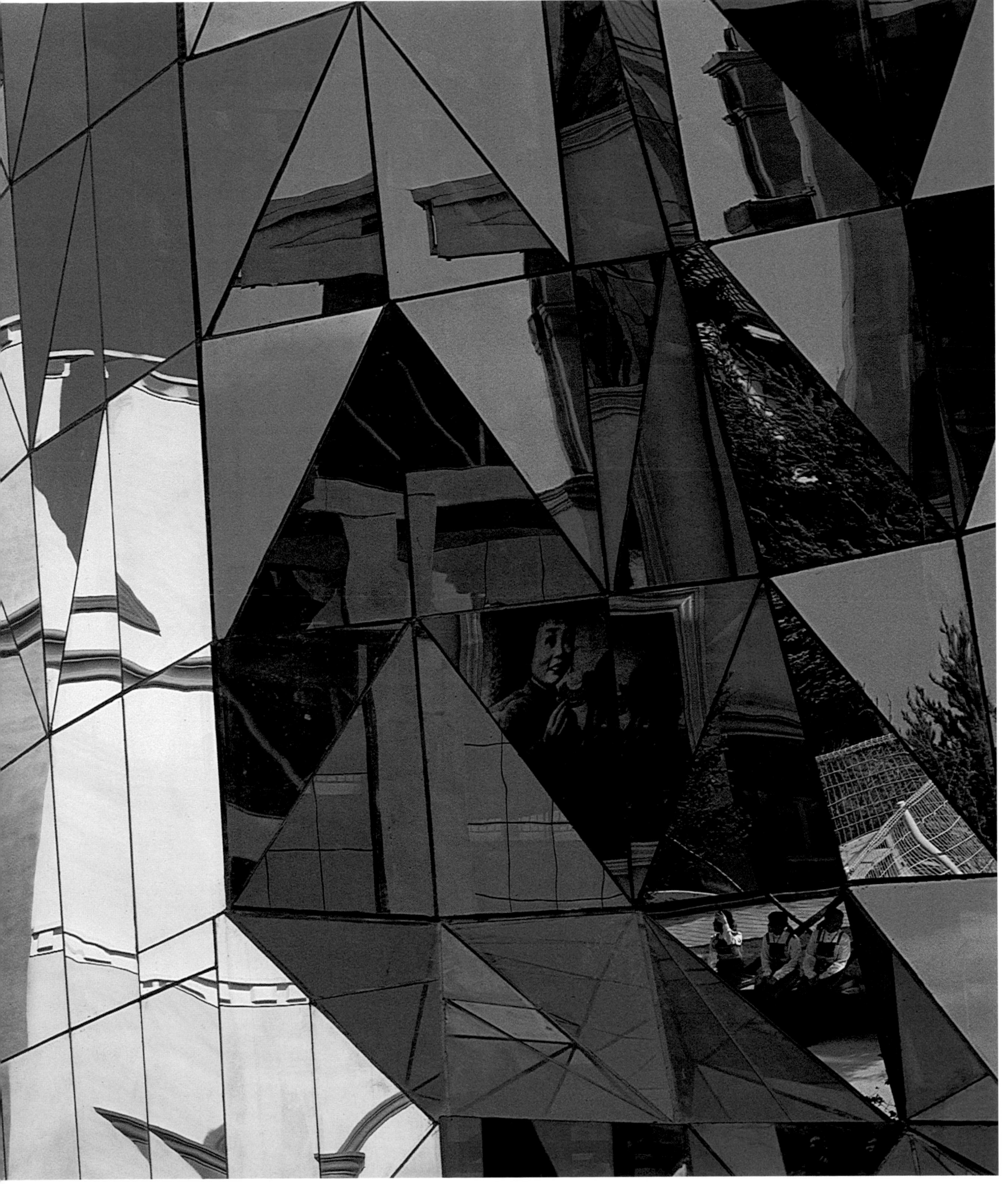

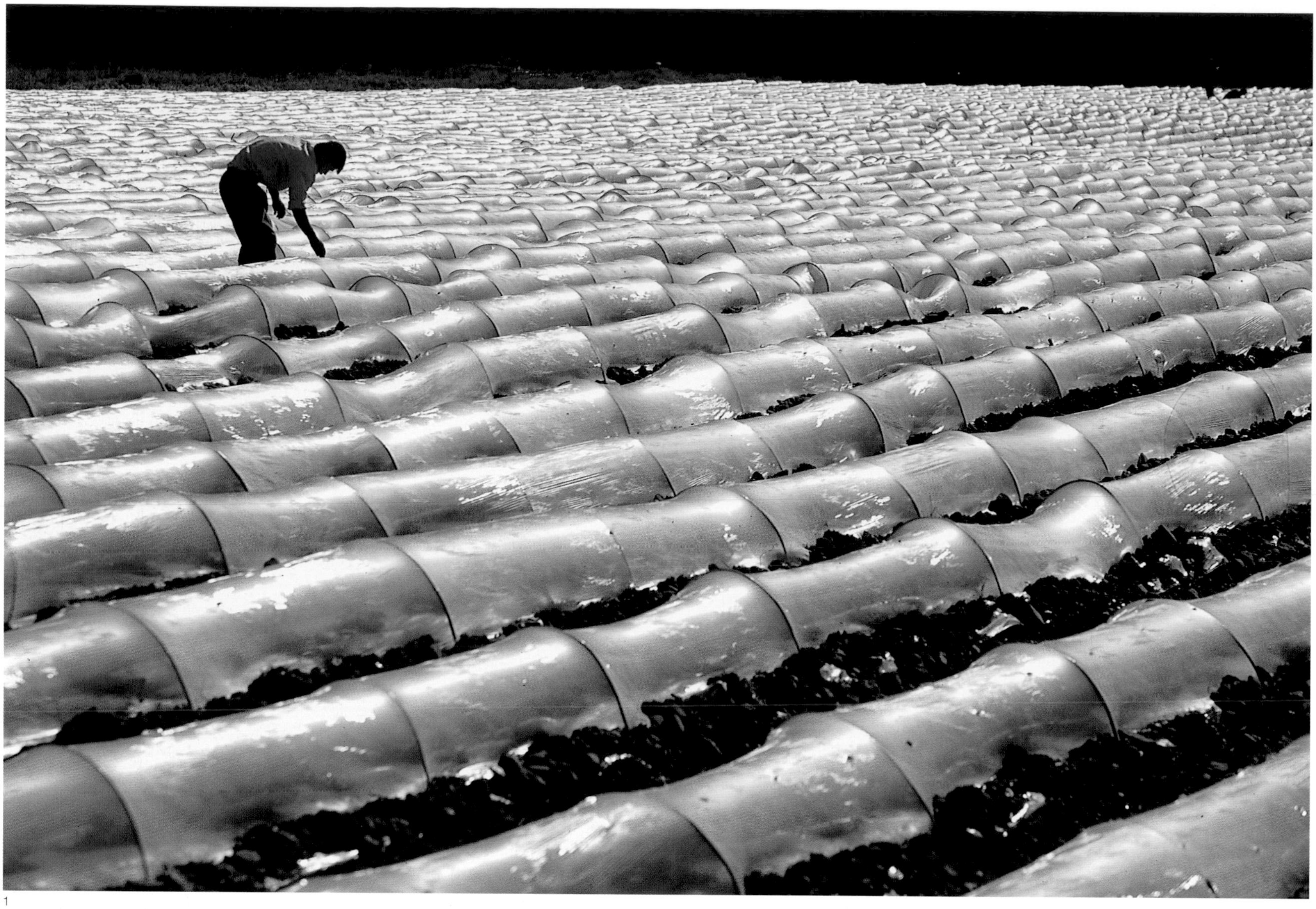

1

THE DRIVE THROUGH THE COUNTRYSIDE to Chang'chun (Eternal Spring), the capital of Ji'lin province, finally let me see with my own eyes what had made China's northeast so desirable to the would-be conquerors. [1] [2] The rolling plains of super-fertile black soil not only produce multiple harvests of anything you'd care to grow, but are also indicative of mineral deposits in the nearby hills. The Japanese installed Pu'yi, the last Qing emperor, as head of the puppet Manchukuo in 1931 with Chang'chun as its capital. The Soviet Union occupied Chang'chun between 1945 and 1956, introducing the industries they believed were needed to turn the city into the 'Detroit of China'. Today, the city's automobile industry produces about twenty per cent of all cars and trucks on China's roads. [3] A brand new Mazda assembly line, one of the many joint ventures with international automakers. [4] At the No.1 Automotive Factory, renowned for producing the 'Red Flag' limousines for the Chinese leadership, a new-model sedan bearing the famous brand rolls off the line – with an Audi engine. [5] In the parking lot of the factory, thousands of their other famous brand, the 'Liberation' truck, await delivery.

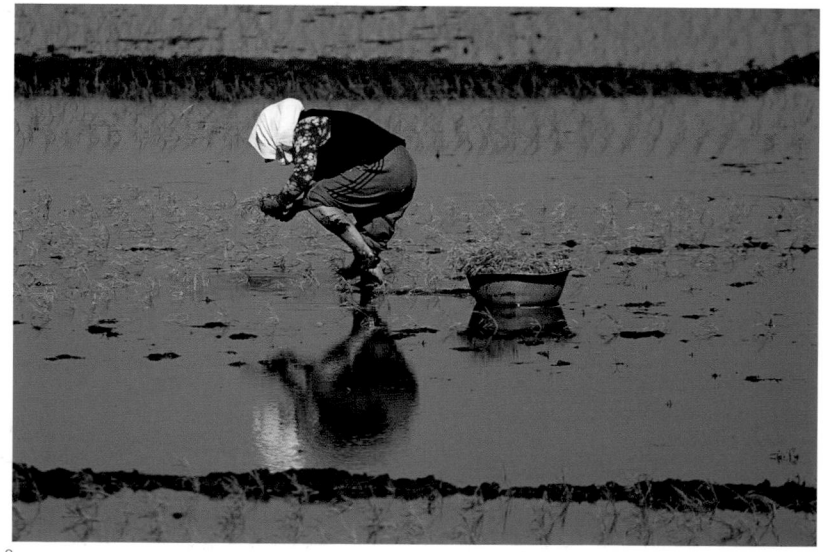

2

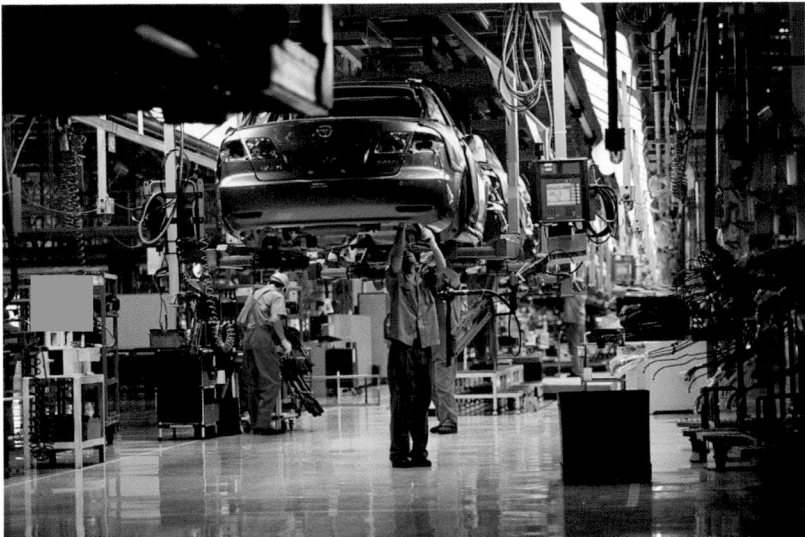

3

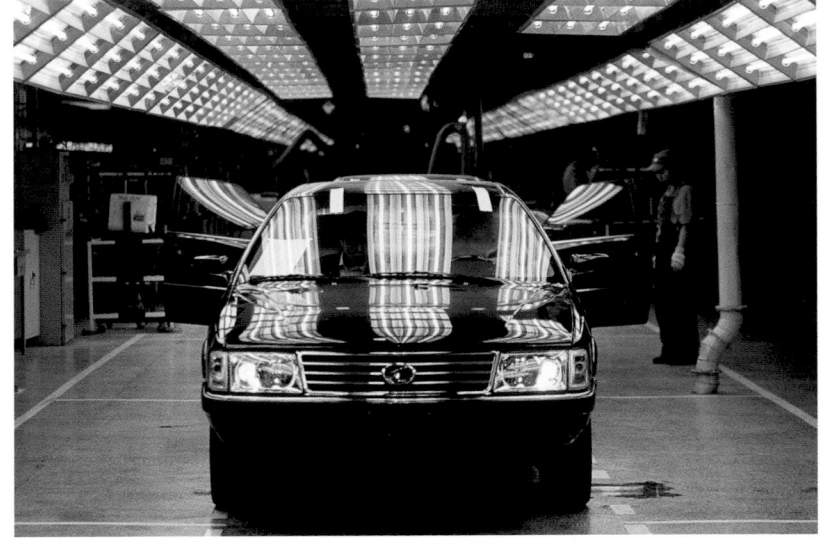

4

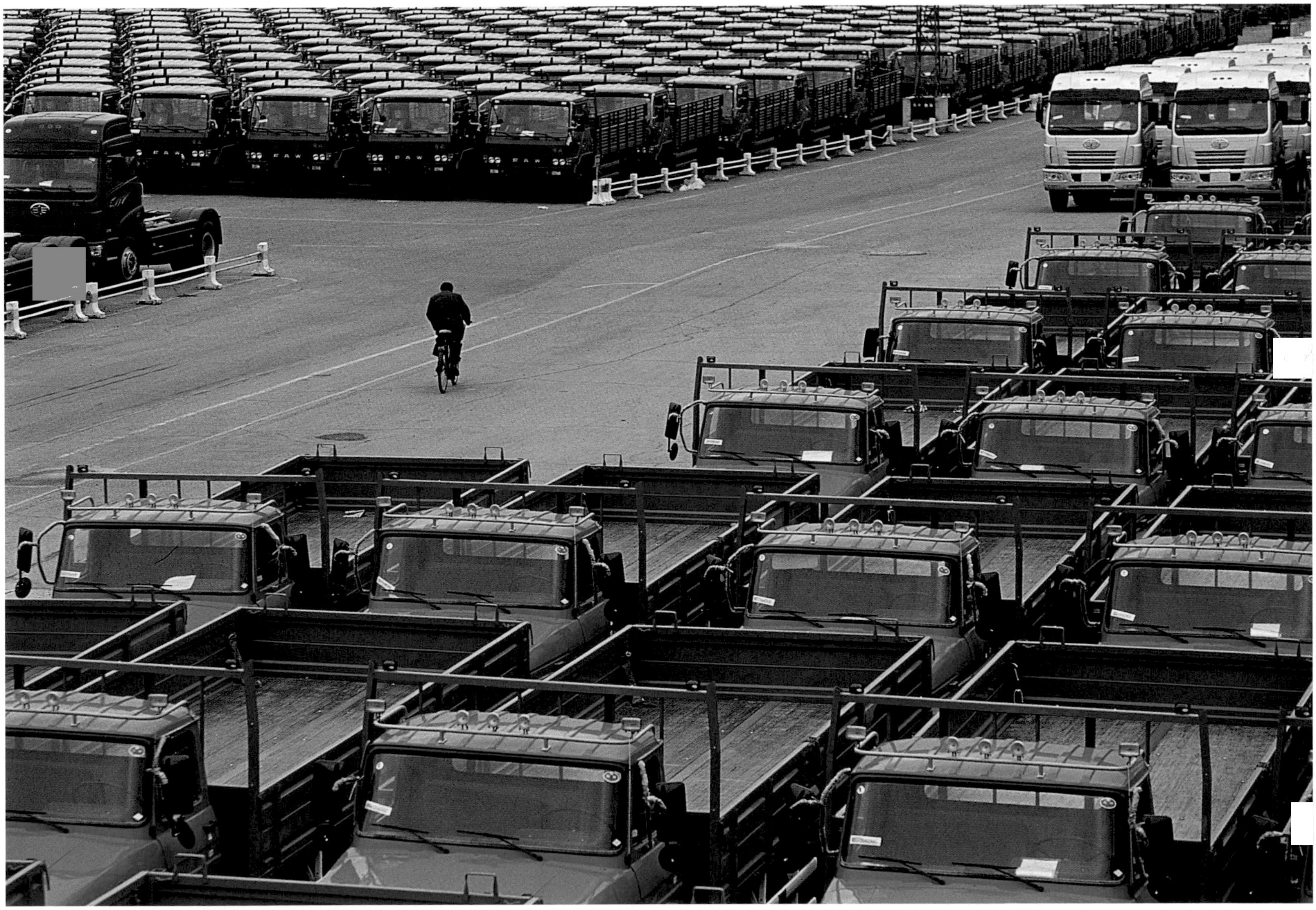

5

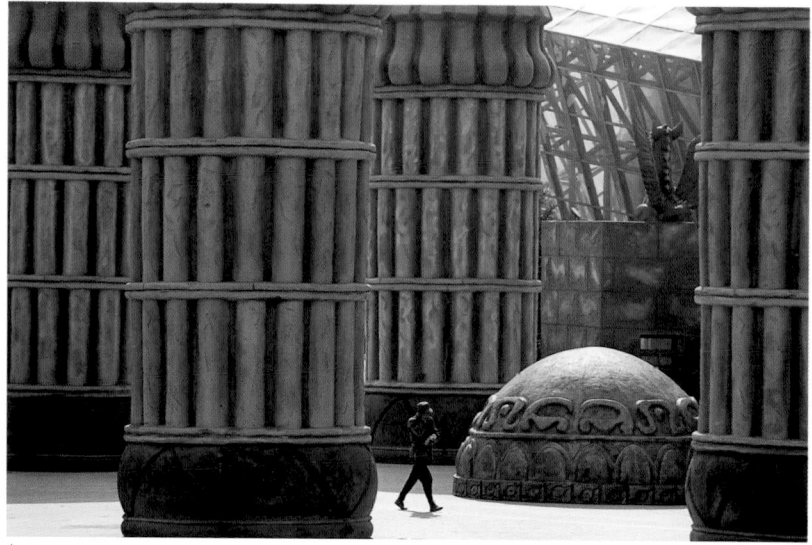

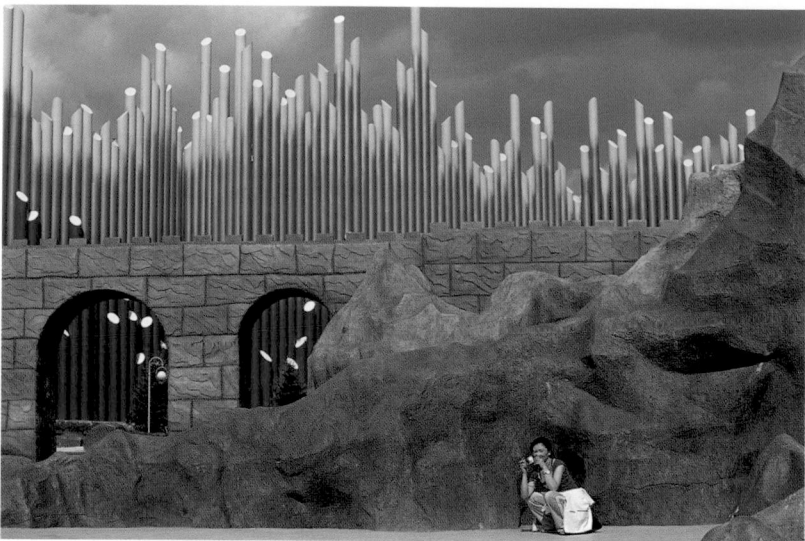

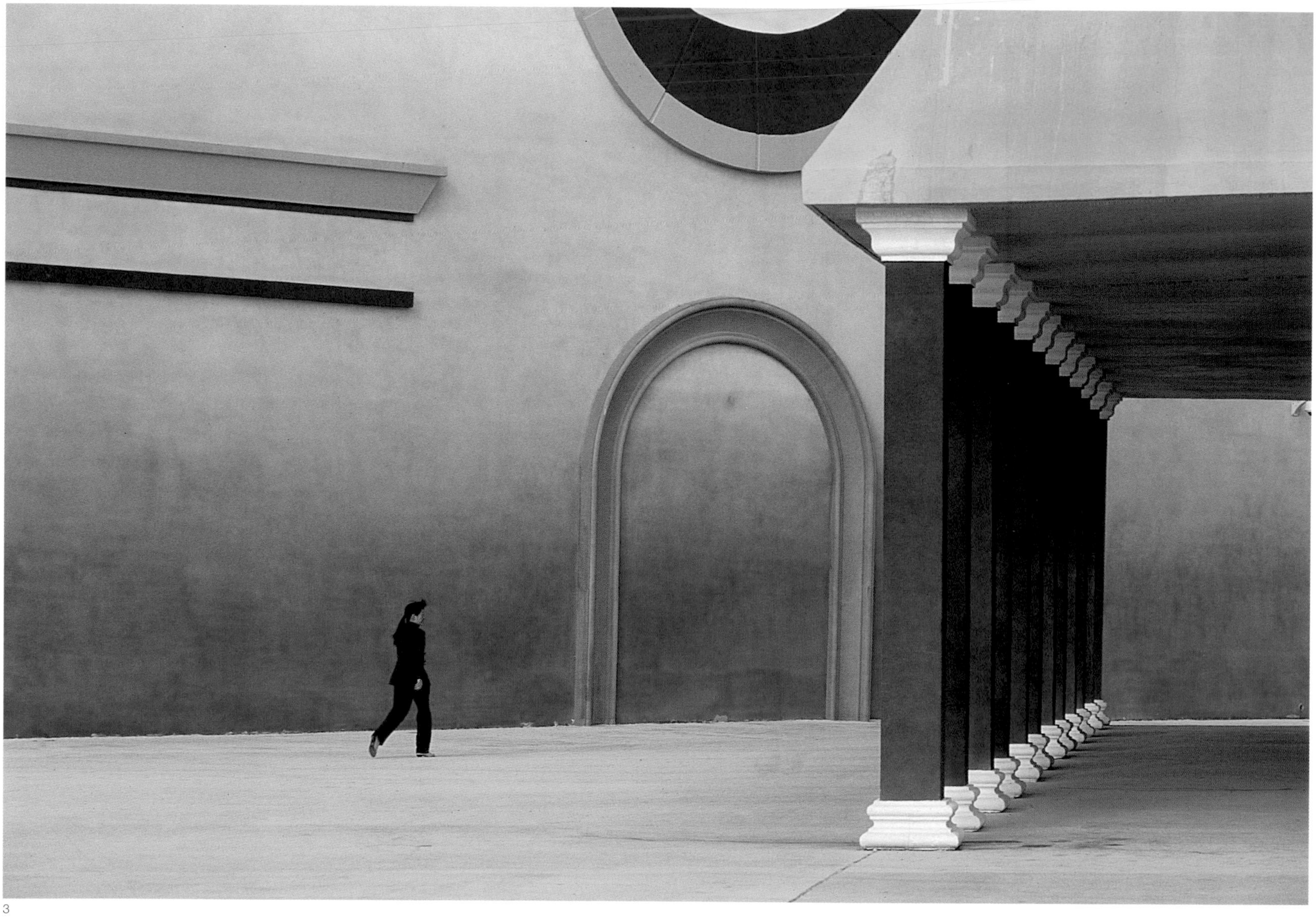

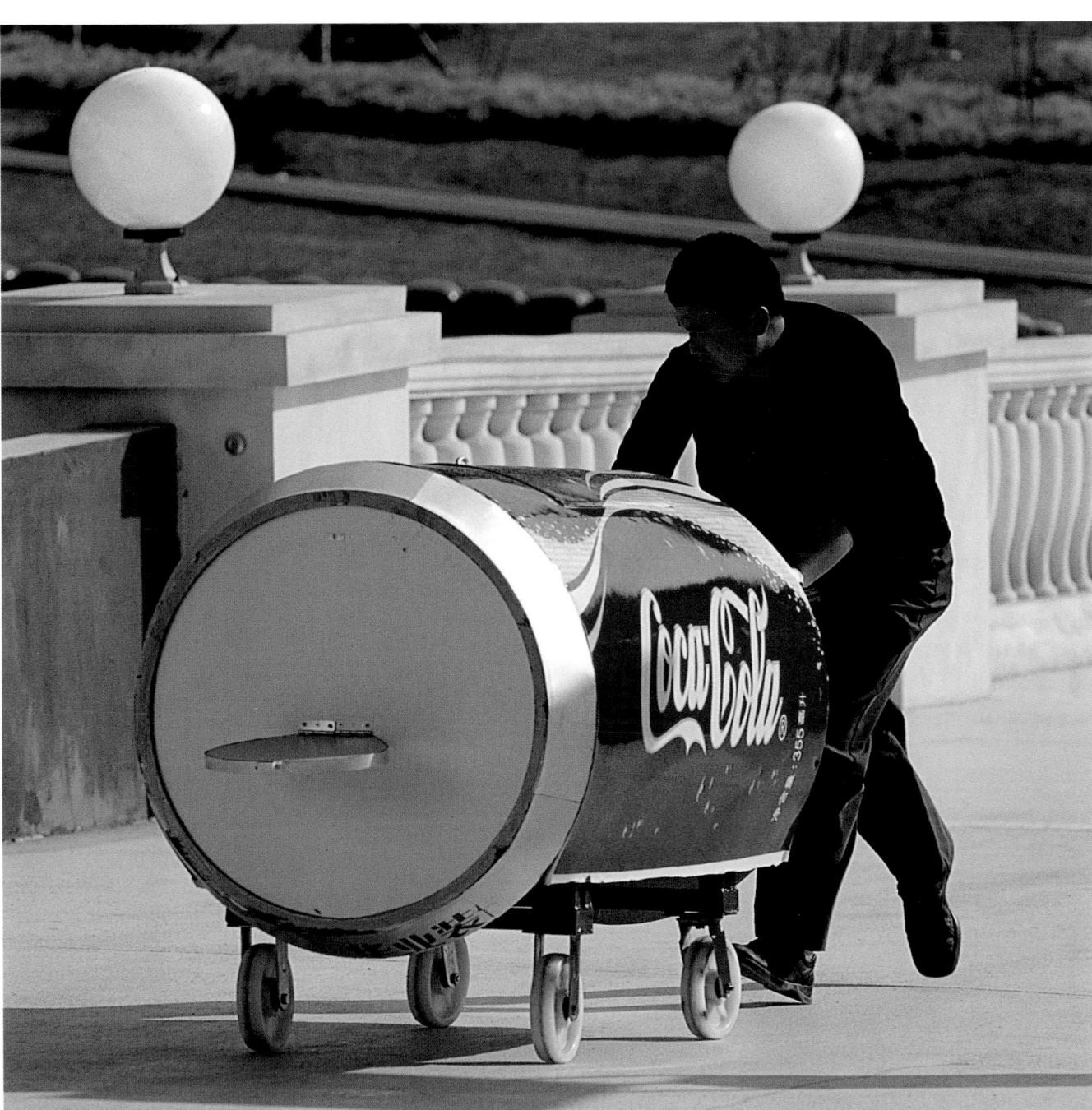

4

IN THE EARLY DAYS OF COMMUNIST RULE, the Chang'chun Film Studio produced some of the best Chinese feature films of that era. They were mostly 'revolutionary dramas with patriotic themes' (i.e. propaganda films); tales of struggling peasants, guerrilla heroes, or renditions of those Chinese classics deemed ideologically sound. Shot in lush black and white in a communist neo-realist style, they are classics of the Chinese cinema and gems of that genre. The studio went into a tailspin during the Cultural Revolution, when Madame Mao, a former starlet in Shang'hai, seized personal control of the country's performing arts. These days the local industry languishes as other more nimble production facilities across China take its place. Unable to meet the new challenges of modern film production, the studio sought to cash in on its past, a plan that went badly wrong. [1-4] The Chang'chun Film Century City is a monument to the folly of a half-baked dream, a Universal Studios without the rides and the production facilities. It is a giant waste of money, but it did offer a few good photo opportunities.

NORTH BY NORTHEAST

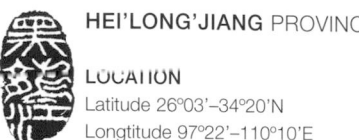

HEI'LONG'JIANG PROVINCE

LOCATION
Latitude 26º03'–34º20'N
Longtitude 97º22'–110º10'E

AREA 463,730 km² (179,000 sq miles)

GEOGRAPHY Hei'long'jiang province contains China's most northerly and easterly points. The Amur River on the province's eastern border demarcates the border with Russia. Much of it is dominated by the Khingan, Zhangguangcai, Laoye and Wanda mountain ranges, which reach up to 1,780 m and comprise around 70 per cent of the province's land mass. The interior is relatively flat and is watered by the Song'hua, Nen and Mu'dan rivers, all tributaries of the Amur.

CLIMATE The climate is sub-Arctic with long (September–April), harsh winters punctuated by frequent Siberian storms. Summers are short and cool. Temperatures in January range from -31ºC to -15ºC, climbing to 18–23ºC in July. The lowest recorded temperature is -52.3ºC and the highest is over 40ºC. Annual average rainfall is 500–600 mm.

POPULATION 38.2 million (end 2005)

MAJOR CITIES Ha'erbin (capital), Qi'qi'ha'er, Mu'dan'jiang, Jia'mu'si, Da'qing, Hei'he

AGRICULTURE The province is a major wheat producer. Other food crops are maize, millet, sorghum and soybeans. Cash crops include sugar beet, flax and sunflowers. The province is also China's leading milk-production centre.

MAIN INDUSTRIES The province produces almost 50 per cent of China's oil, much of it from the Da'qing fields. The Ji'xi and He'gang coal mining centres are among the largest in China, while Hei'long'jiang's abundant water supplies and high mountains have made the province the principal source of hydroelectric power for northeast China. The province is also an important industrial centre, specializing in heavy machinery. It also has the largest commercial forestry industry in the country.

ANNUAL PER CAPITA INCOME (2005)
Disposable income of urban residents:
RMB 8,273 (US$1,031)
Net income of rural residents:
RMB 3,221 (US$401)

HISTORICAL AND SCENIC SITES
Ha'erbin's Russian-influenced architecture and churches and its annual Ice Festival, winter sports, wildlife and eco-tourism.

FOOD Hei'long'jiang cooking has evolved around dishes derived from the province's mountains, rivers and seas. Long, hard winters encourage a high-carbohydrate diet based around dumplings, stews, sausages and potatoes. More elaborate dishes such as Crystal Sugar snow clams, green onions with Liao'ning sea cucumbers and Nurhachi golden meat are reserved for banquets.

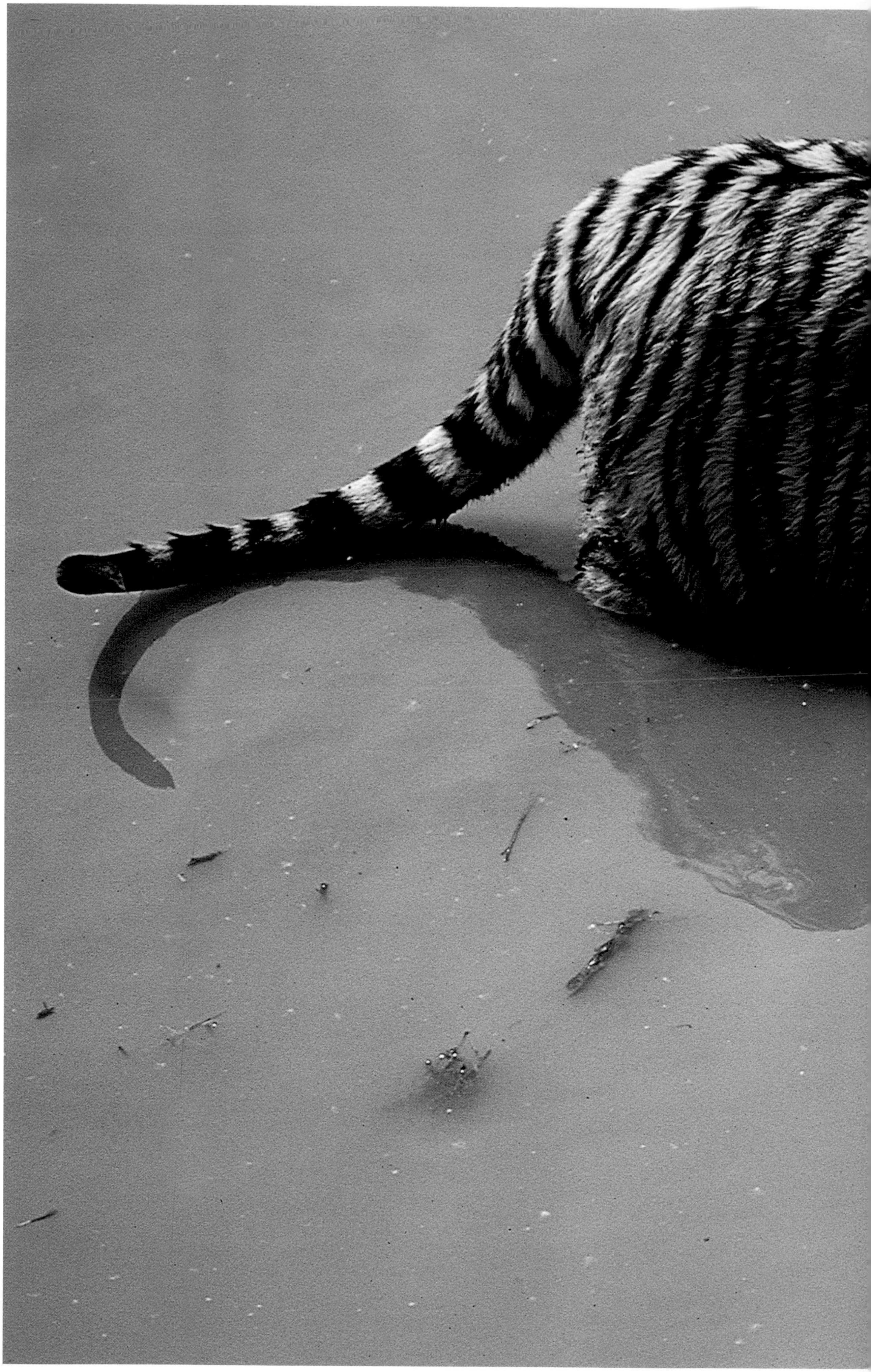

[RIGHT] The Northeast Siberian Tiger Park.

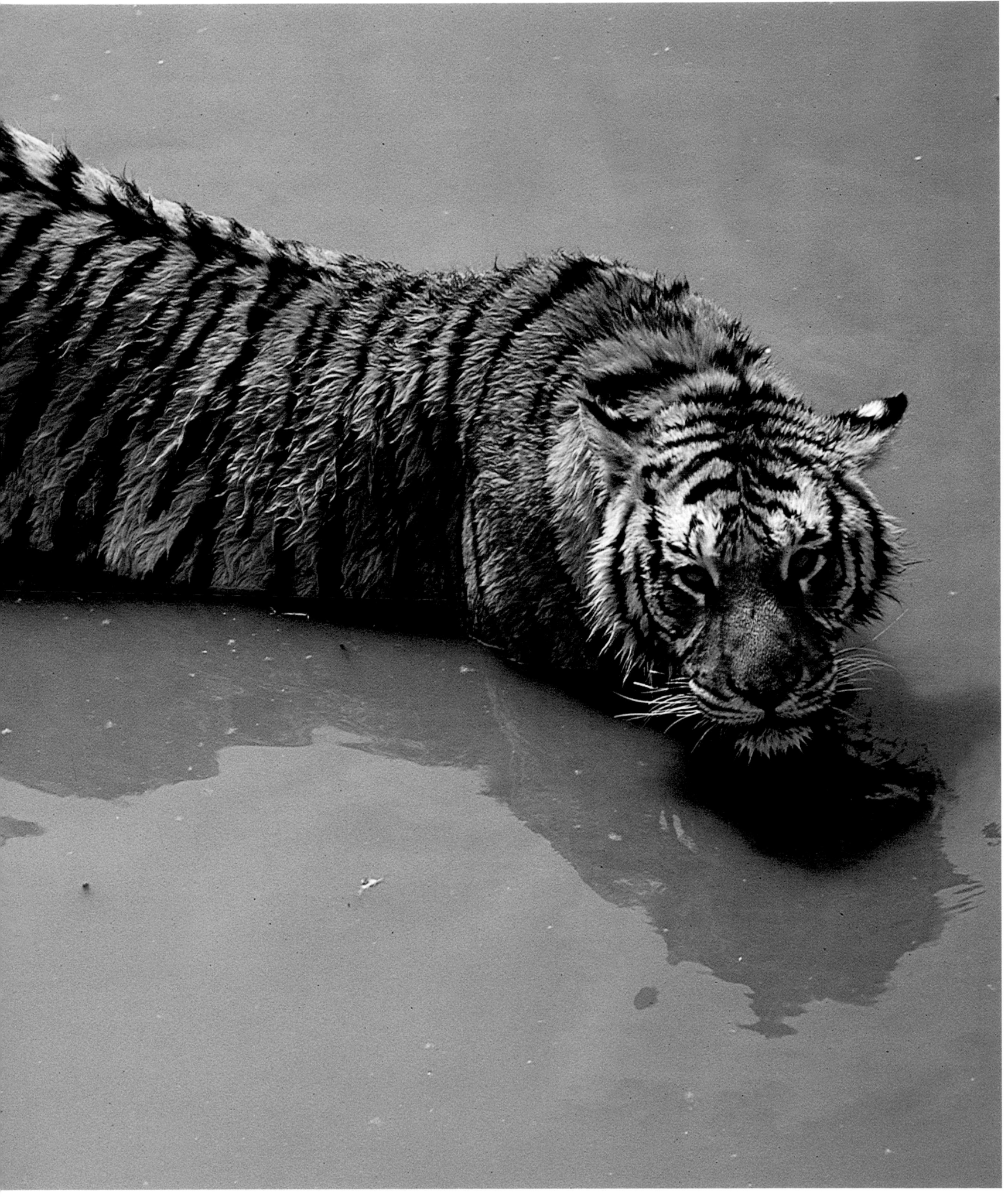

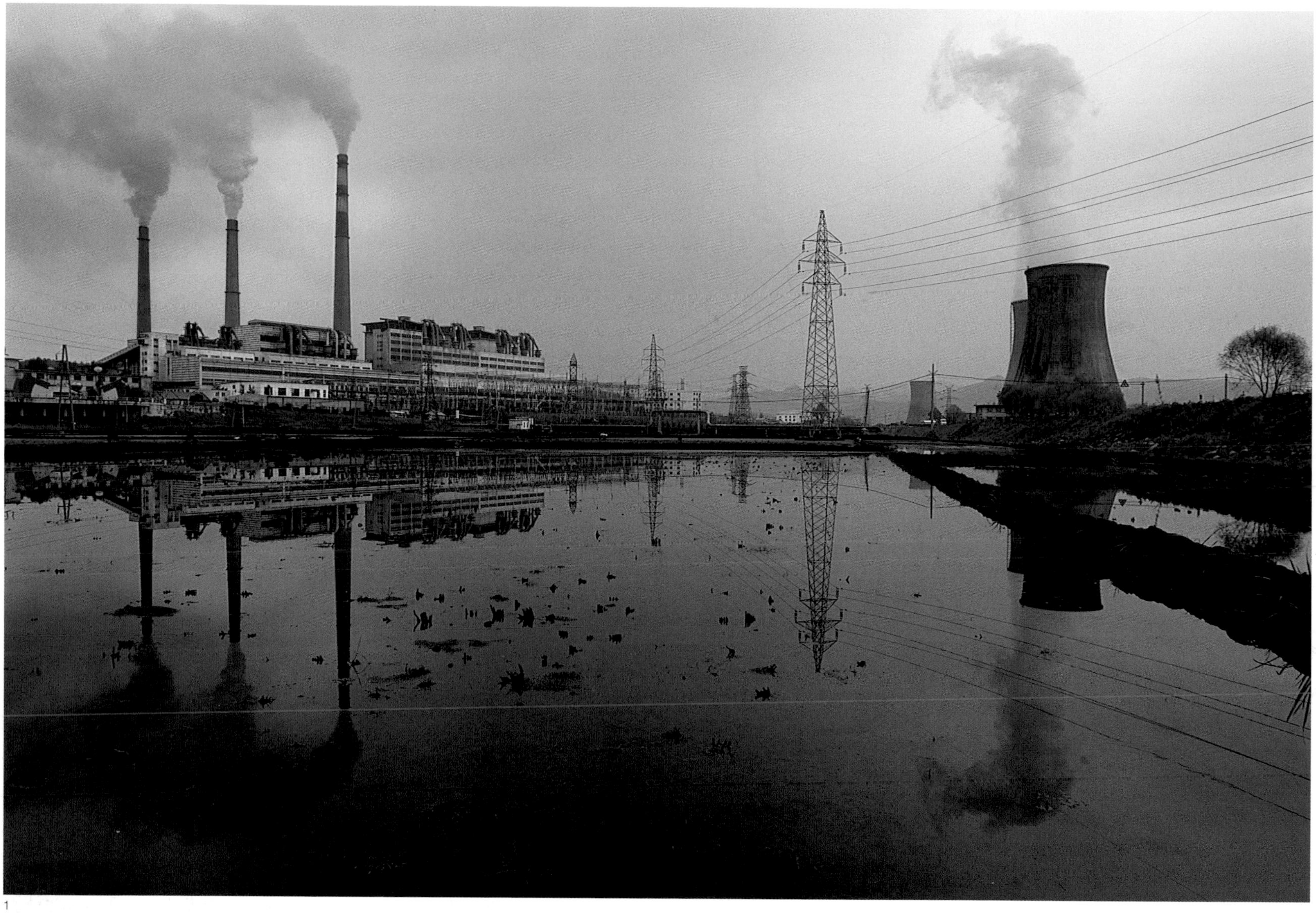

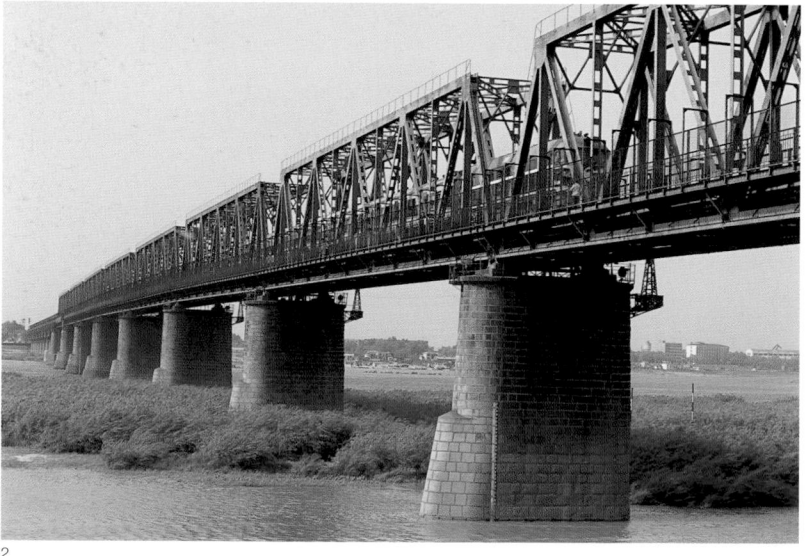

THE WORD HA'ERBIN means 'a place for drying fishing nets' in Manchu. While human settlement in the area dates back to the late Stone Age (2,200 BCE), the birth of the city came in 1898 when the Trans-Siberian and the Chinese Eastern Railways met at the original village. The arrival of Russian workers and foreign nationals from thirty-three countries, and the subsequent influx of White Russian émigrés and Russian Jews that followed the collapse of the Tsarist empire in 1918, laid the foundations for what became the political, economic, industrial and international trading centre of northeastern China. Also known as the 'Oriental St Petersberg', the capital of Hei'long'jiang (Black Dragon River) province remains a Russian city with Chinese characteristics. [1] Flooded paddy fields in front of a giant power plant outside Ha'erbin. [2] The railway bridge across the Song'hua River helps connect Da'lian to Moscow and Vladivostok. [3] Watch out, here comes the bride. [4] On Central Street, portraits of pop idols and movie stars seem to attract more customers for the street artists than self-portraits. [5] Saint Sophia Cathedral, one of ten Russian Orthodox churches that survived the Cultural Revolution.

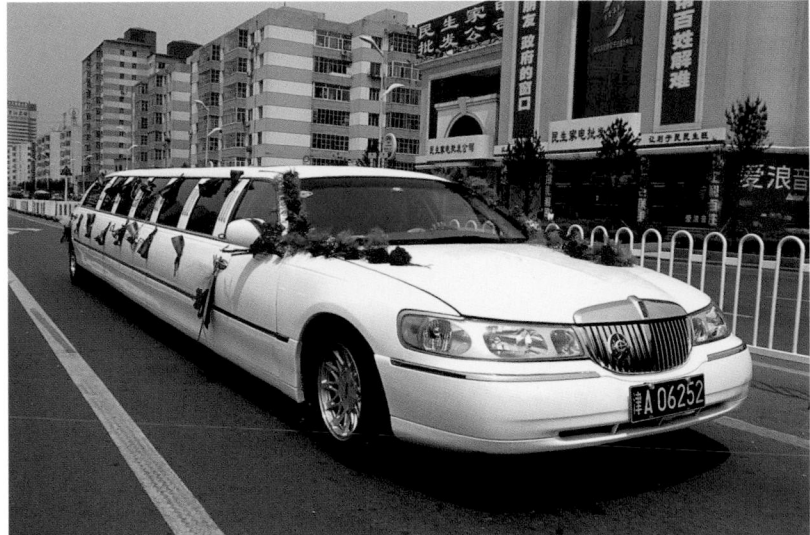

3

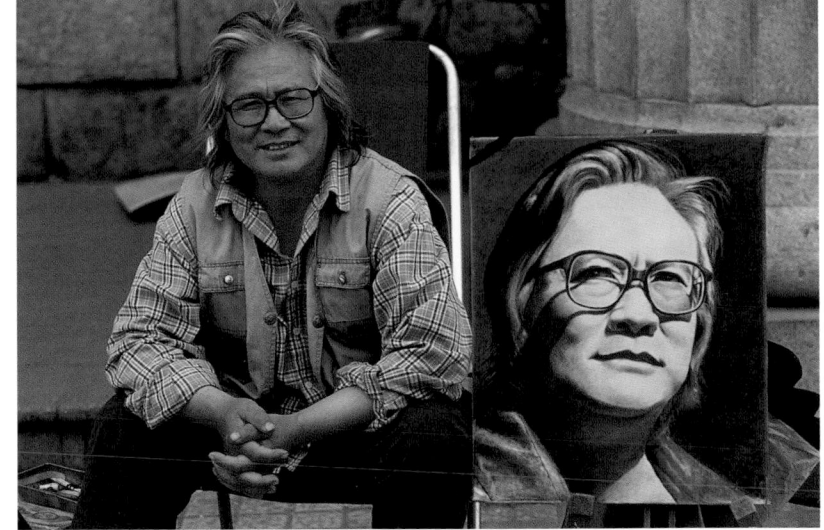

4

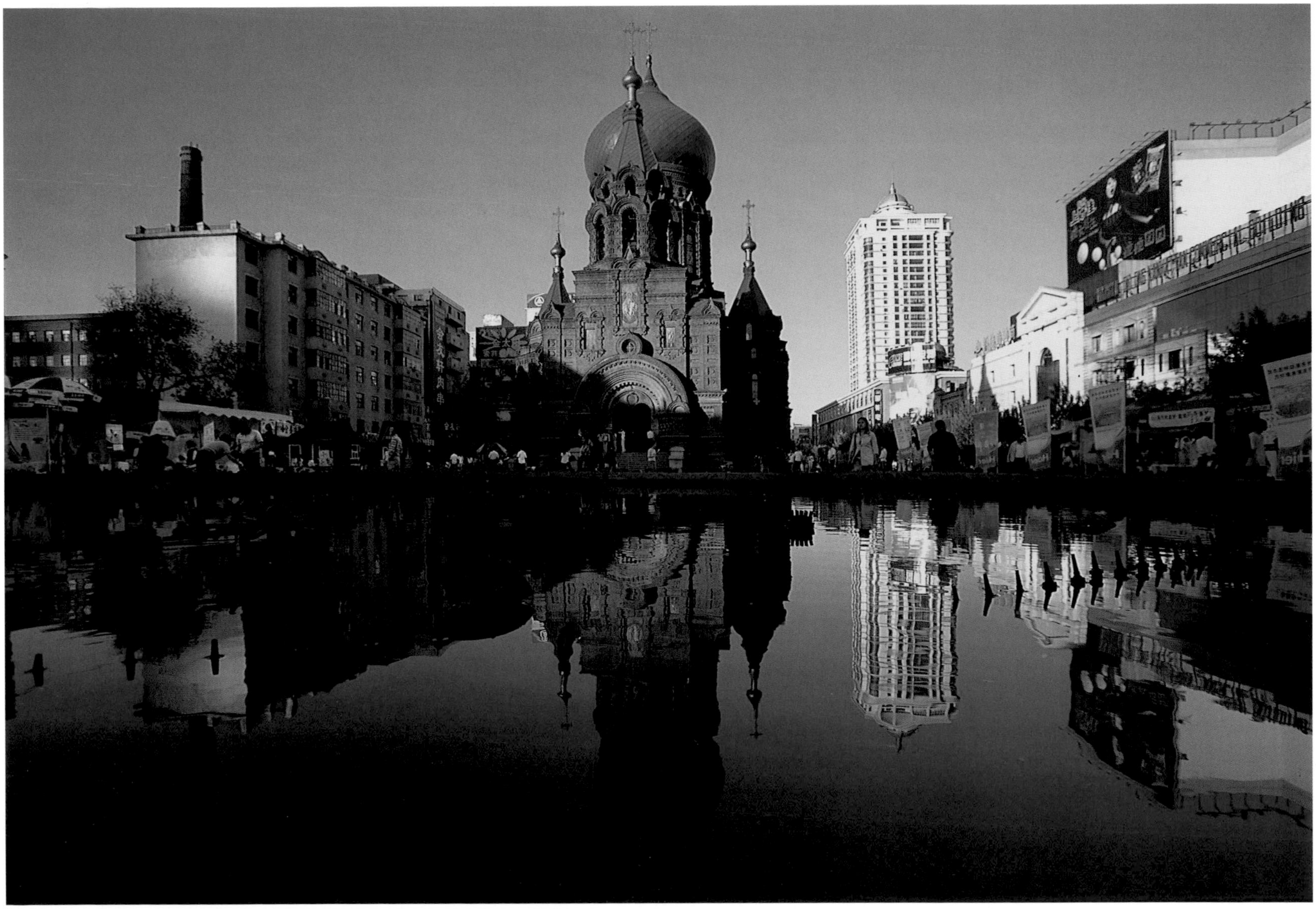

5

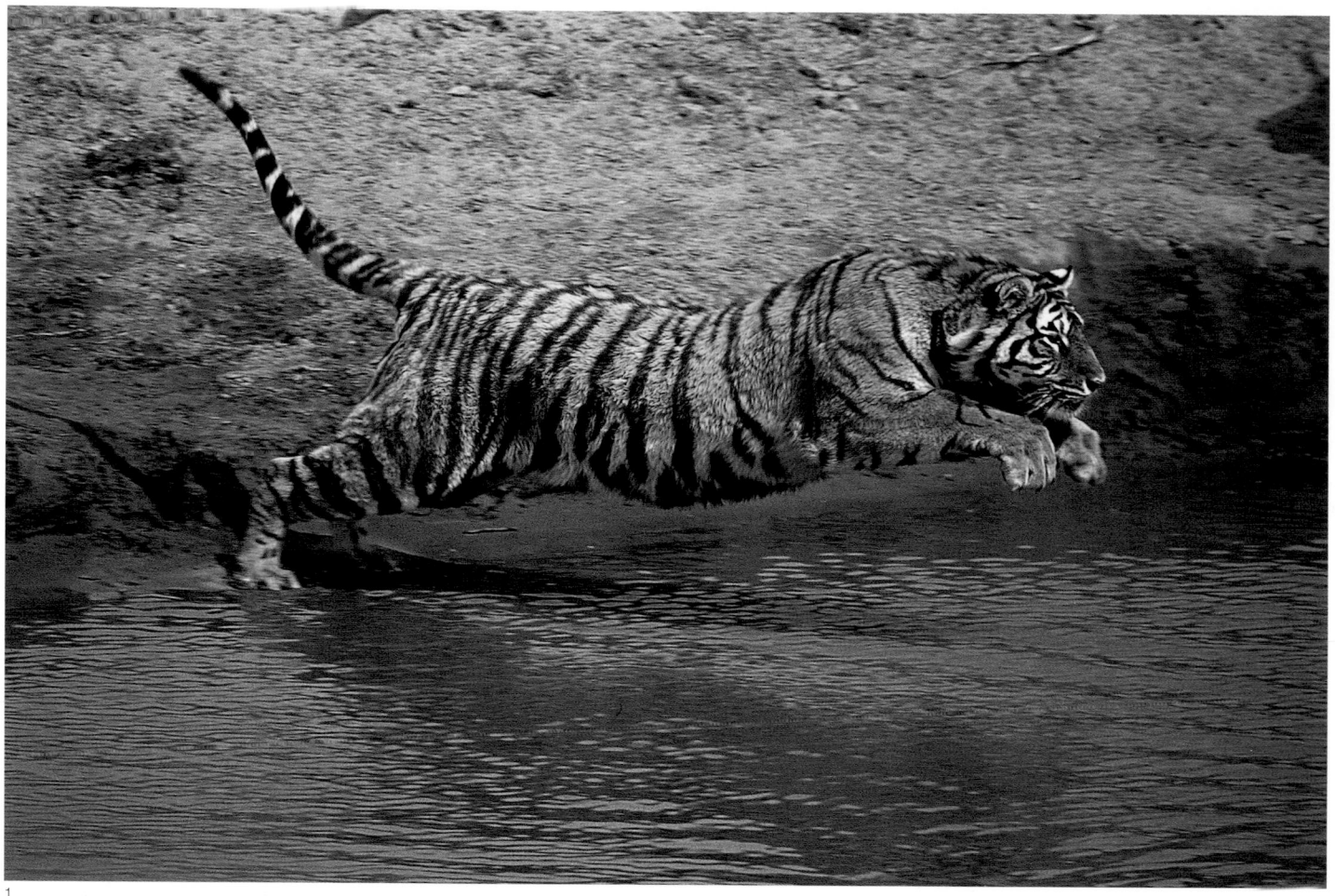

1

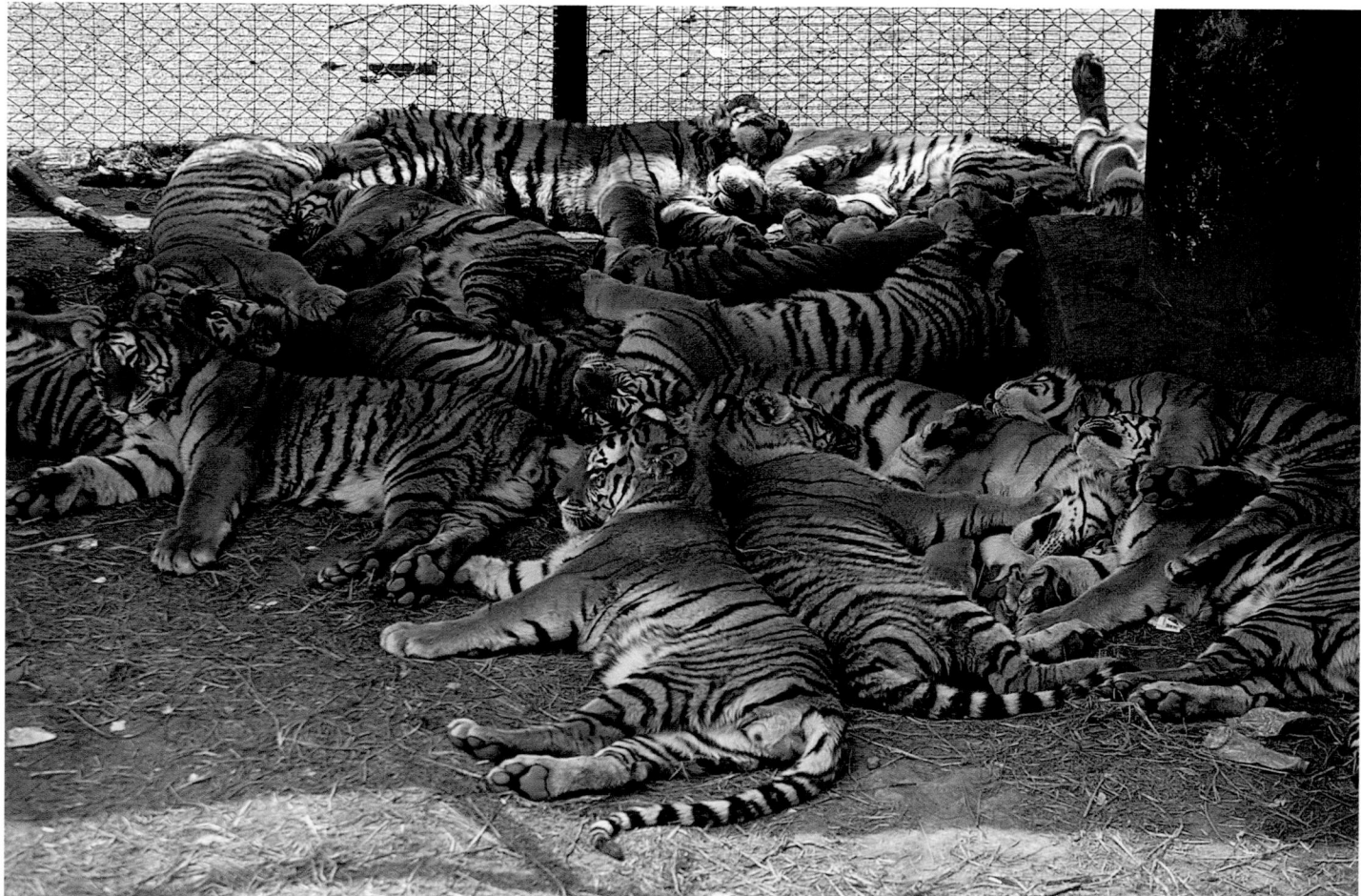

2

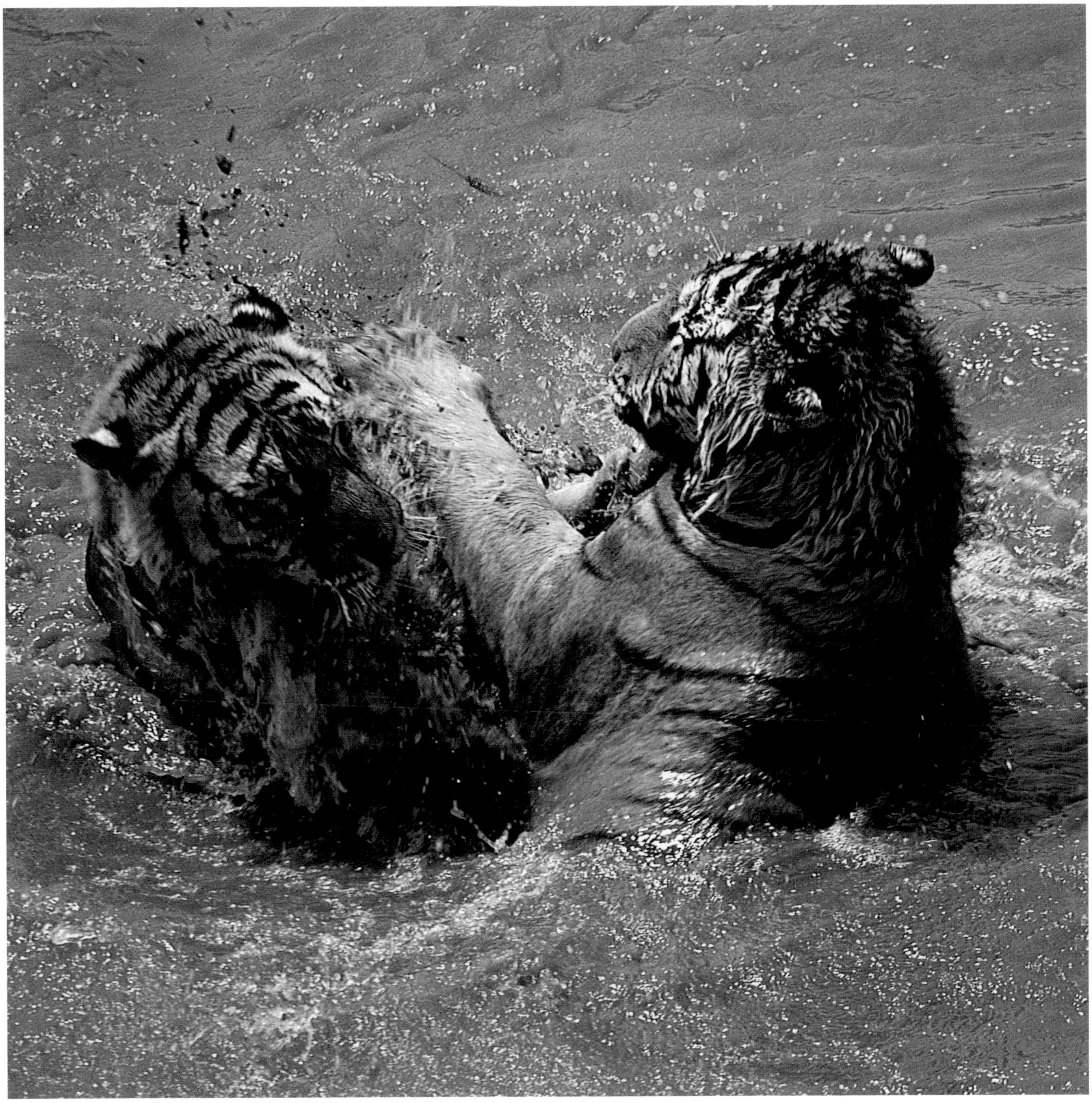

3

THE **SIBERIAN TIGER** is one of the most endangered animals in the world. Less than 600 are believed to be still roaming free in the wild, where they face starvation and the constant threat of poachers. The Chinese government set up a series of breeding centres in Hei'long'jiang province to try and restore the tiger population in captivity with the aim of eventually releasing them back into their natural habitat. On paper, the breeding programme has been hugely successful. From the eight animals they started with in 1986, the centre now has over 300 tigers under its care. [2] The animals are clearly well fed and cared for, if somewhat bored, but they looked magnificent nonetheless. [1] [3] There is abundant evidence for the argument that allowing the tigers to grow too accustomed to large numbers of tourists will greatly reduce the likelihood that they can ever be rehabilitated in the wild. But for ordinary people like myself, the park remains the only way to see these magnificent cats in action, even if they were only trying to catch a duck.

NORTH BY NORTHEAST

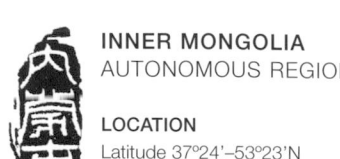

INNER MONGOLIA
AUTONOMOUS REGION

LOCATION
Latitude 37º24'–53º23'N
Longtitude 97º12'–126º04'E

AREA 1,178,755 km² (455,000 sq miles)

GEOGRAPHY Most of the region consists of high plateaus and deserts with a range of mountains to the east. The Gobi desert extends across the border into Mongolia, the Ordus desert lies to the south of the great bend in the Huang'he River (Yellow River) and the Badian Jaran desert to the west. The Hinggan Mountain range covers much of the east of the region, while the Yinshan and Langshan ranges dominate the interior. Mount Helan is the highest point in Inner Mongolia with an elevation of 3,556 m. The watersheds of the Amur and Liao Rivers shape the far east of the region, where they serve as the border with Russia.

CLIMATE The region has a temperate continental monsoonal climate, giving long cold winters and short warm summers. Inner Mongolia ranges from arid to semi-arid and semi-humid from west to east. January temperatures range form -30ºC to -10ºC, rising in July to 15-25ºC. The lowest temperature ever recorded is -60ºC and the highest is 43ºC. Annual rainfall is between 50 mm and 450 mm.

POPULATION 23.86 million (end 2005)

MAJOR CITIES Hohhot (capital), Bao'tou, Wu'hai, Chi'feng

AGRICULTURE Main food crops are wheat, rice, sorghum, millet, oats and corn. Cash crops include oilseeds, soybeans, and sugar beet. Livestock ensure the huge grasslands remain productive, although there are deepening concerns over the impact of desertification.

MAIN INDUSTRIES Industries centre on coal mining, iron and steel, power-generation, textiles and forestry.

ANNUAL PER CAPITA INCOME (2005)
Disposable income of urban residents:
RMB 9,137 (US$1,140)
Net income of rural residents:
RMB 2,989 (US$373)

HISTORICAL AND SCENIC SITES
Genghis Khan's Mausoleum, the Great Wall, Wu'dang Monastery, Easter Han Dynasty Tomb Murals, Hinggan Mountain Forests, Xiang'sha Gulf, the grasslands.

FOOD The region's cooking mixes Mongolian and Chinese styles, with a strong emphasis on meat and dairy products. Notable dishes include roast lamb, mutton hotpot, sour milk and cheese.

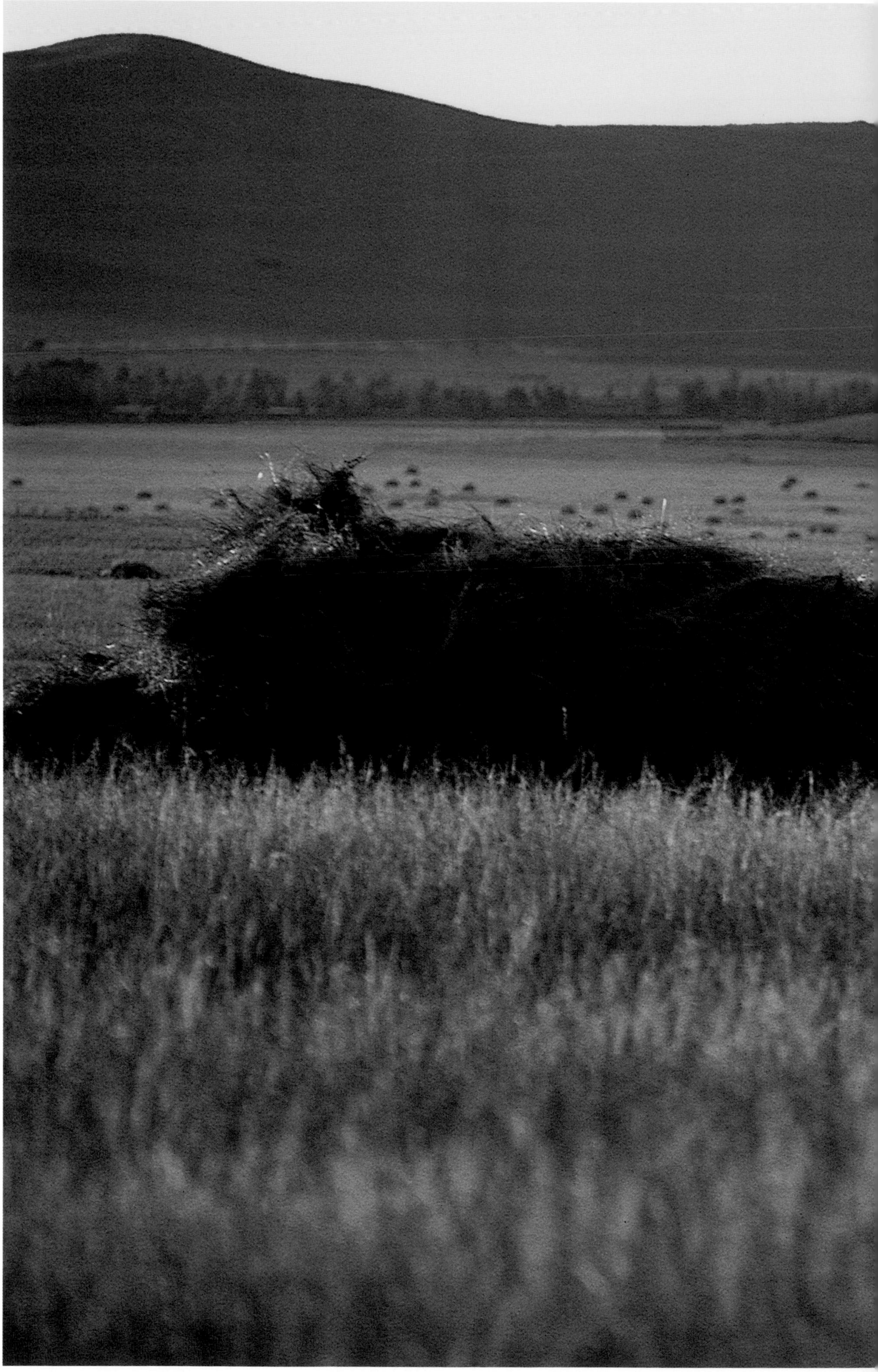

[RIGHT] The Monri'gele River Grassland.

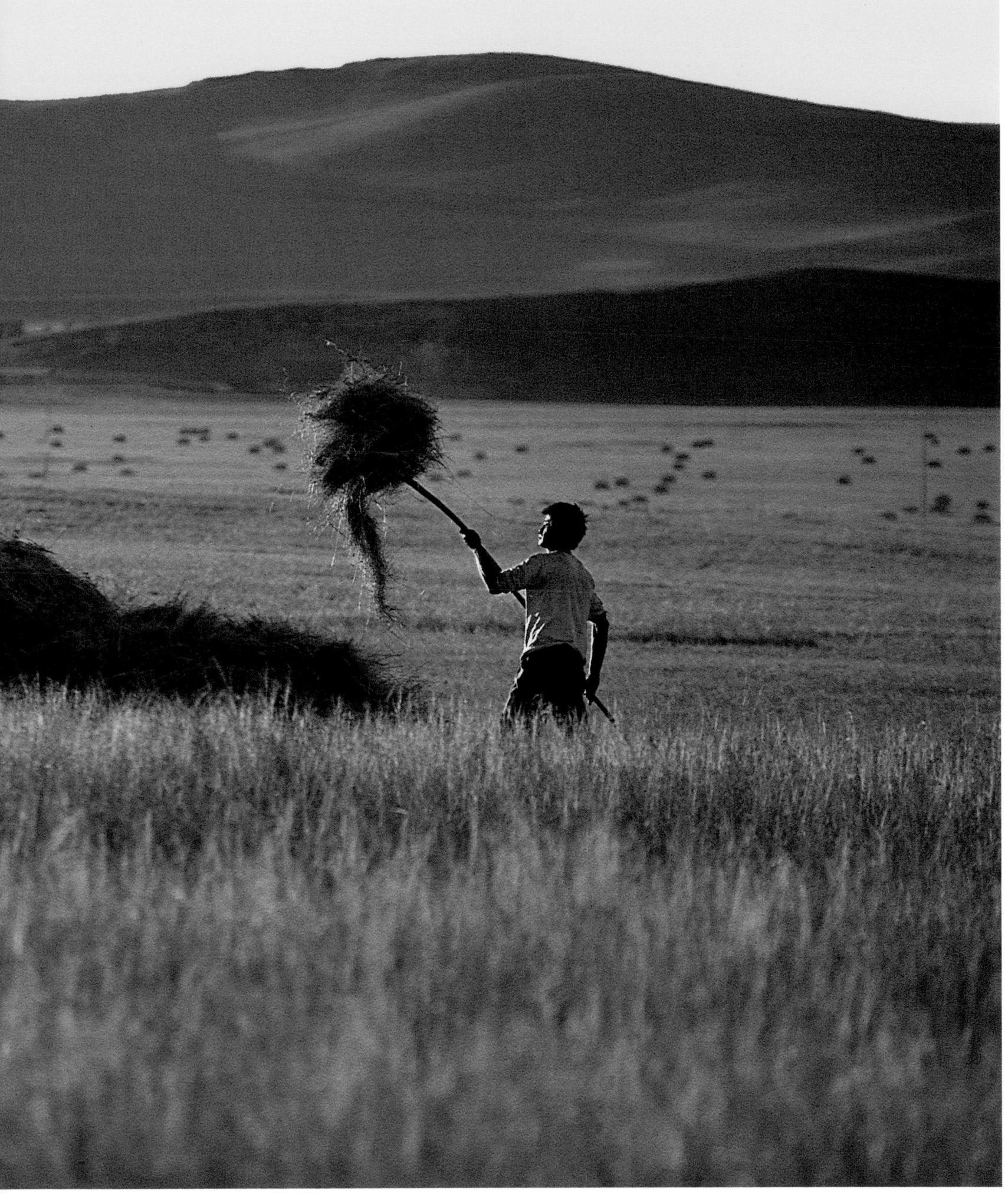

THE HULUN'BUIR PRAIRIE

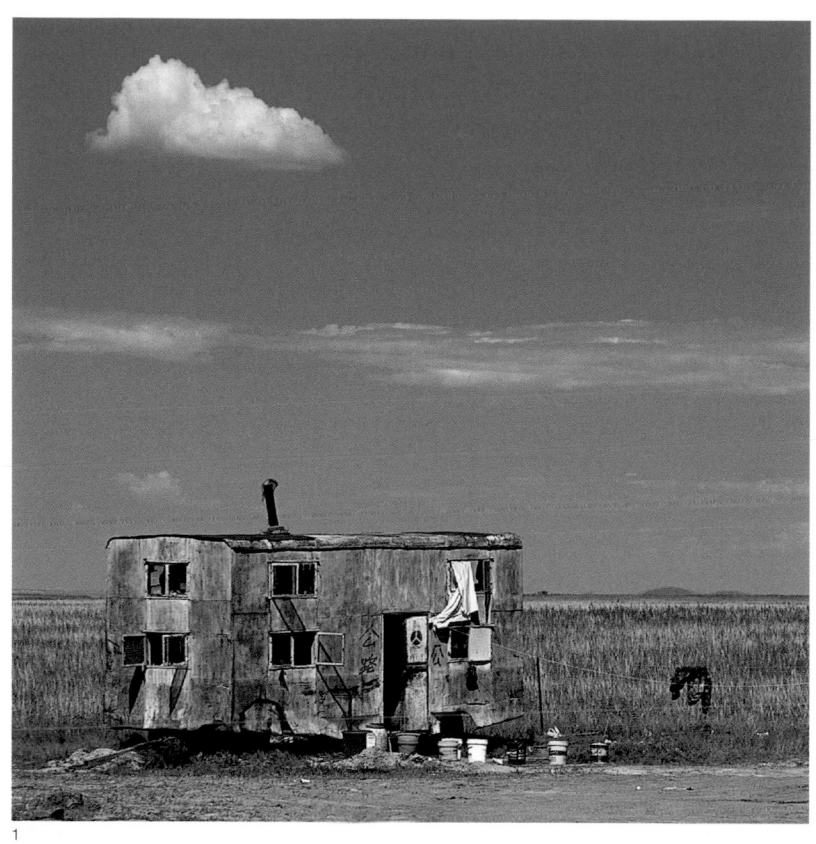

1

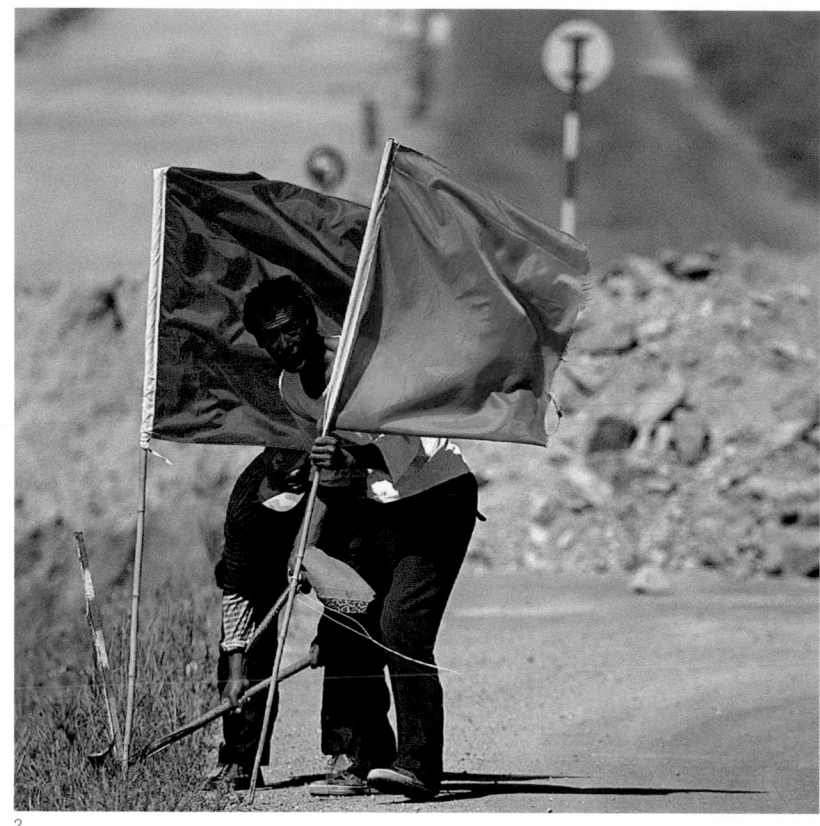

2

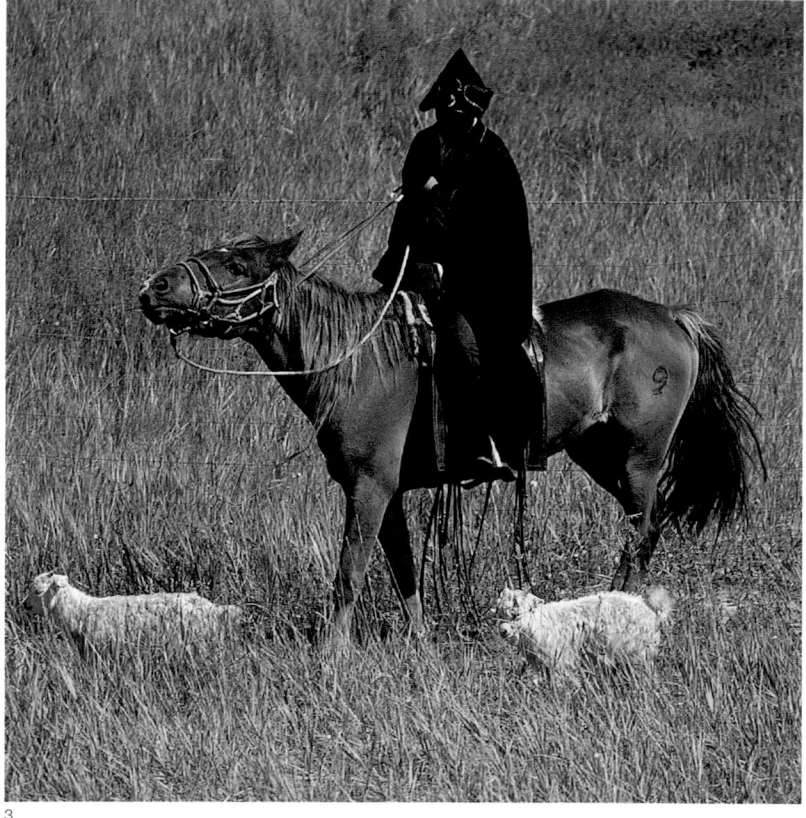

3

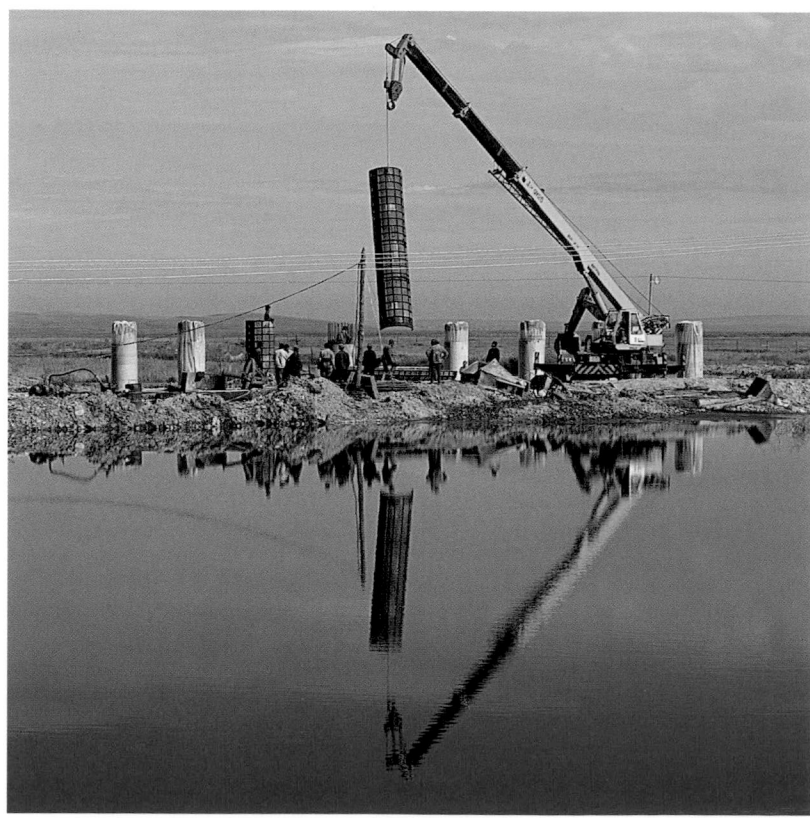

4

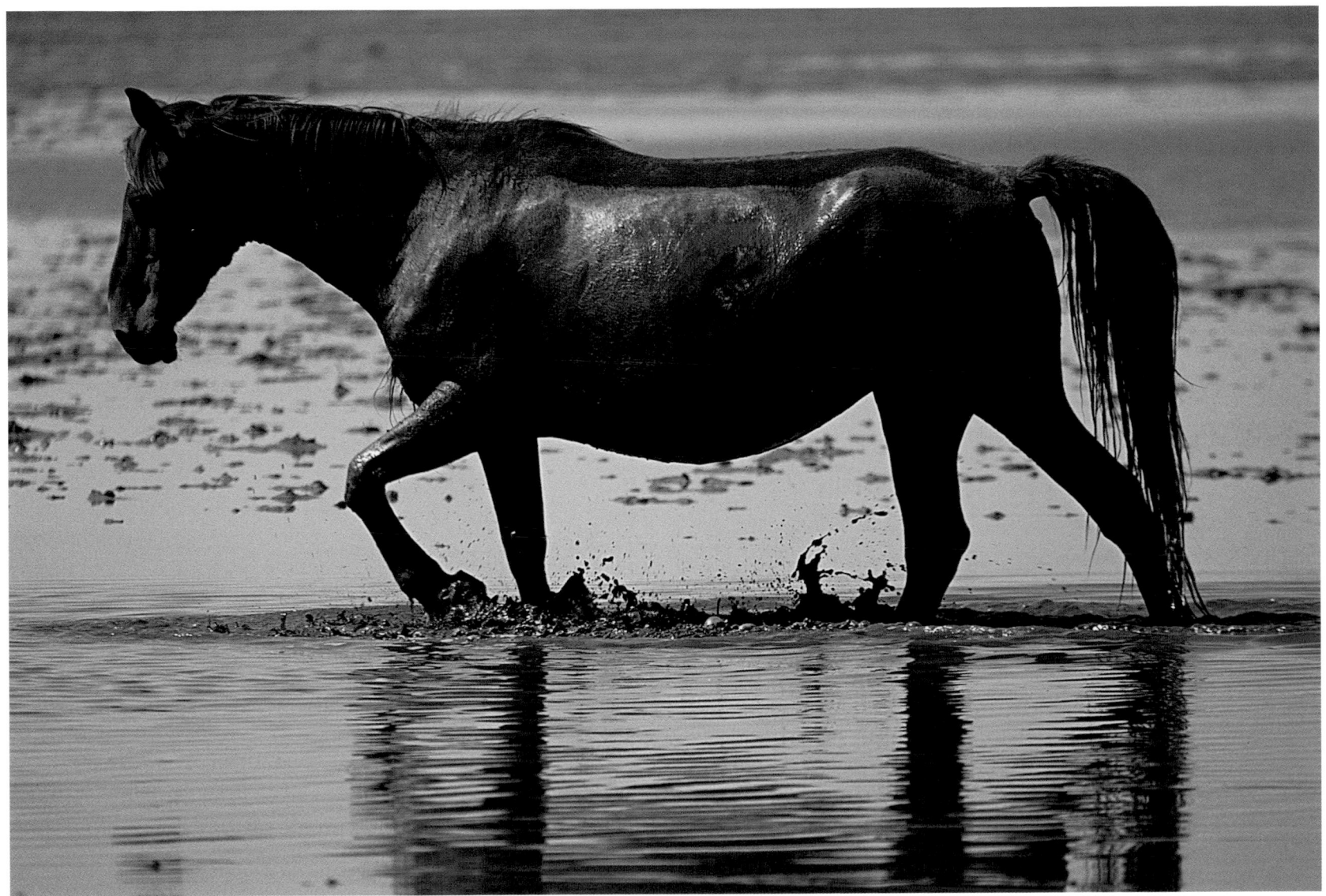

5

STARTING TO THE WEST OF BEI'JING, the southern border of Inner Mongolia Autonomous Region follows the contours of the Ming Dynasty Great Wall. The area contained in the 1.18-million-square-kilometre (457,000-square-mile) province was historically a loosely governed 'buffer zone' between China's Han agriculturalists and the numerous nomad tribes that roamed its prairies. It is a land of shifting boundaries over which control has frequently changed hands. The Hulun'buir Prairie, China's largest, occupies the northeastern tip of the region and has traditionally been considered part of Manchuria. Clouds of dust drift over the yellowing grass as the highway between Hai'laer and Man'zhou'li is expanded – a fresh cut along an old scar across the endless grassland. [1] A makeshift dormitory for the road builders. [2] Workers marking the detours. [3] Beside the highway, a Mongolian horsewoman rounds up the stragglers of her herd. [4] Concrete pilings being poured by a lake. [5] Genghis Khan's secret weapon – the Mongols conquered the largest empire in history with their cavalry, which rode as far as the gates of Vienna.

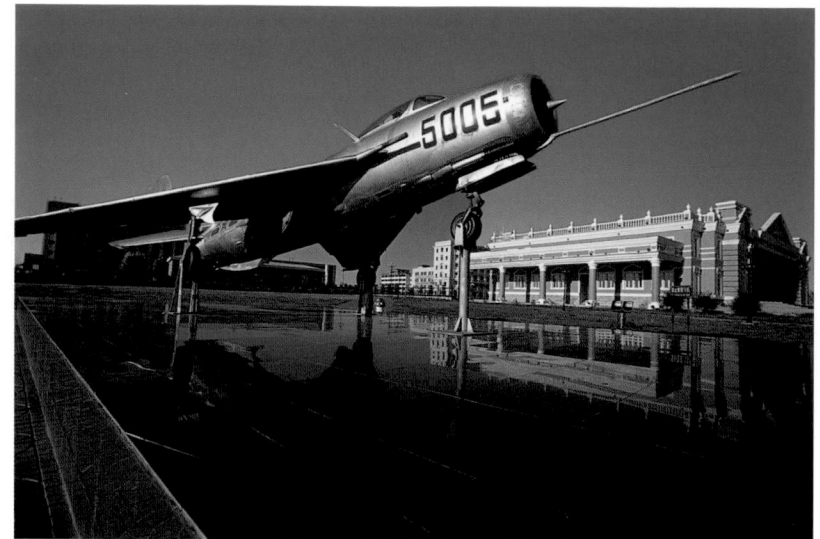

1

2

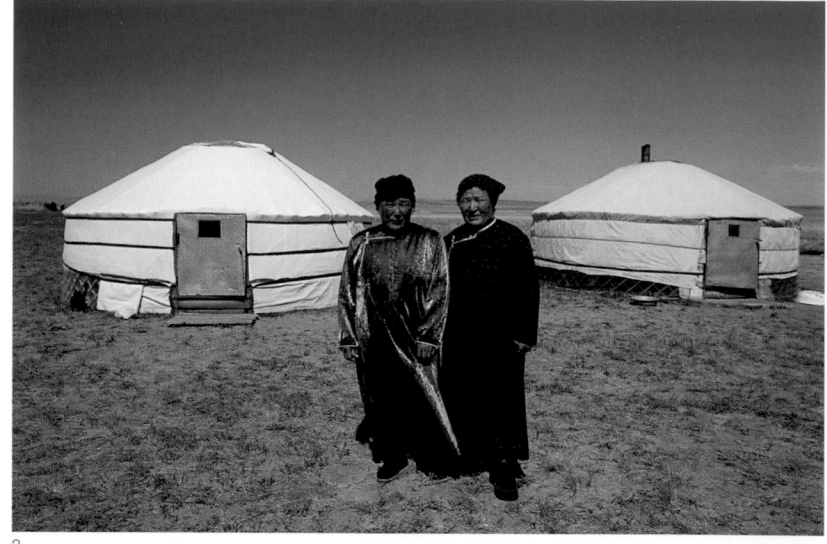

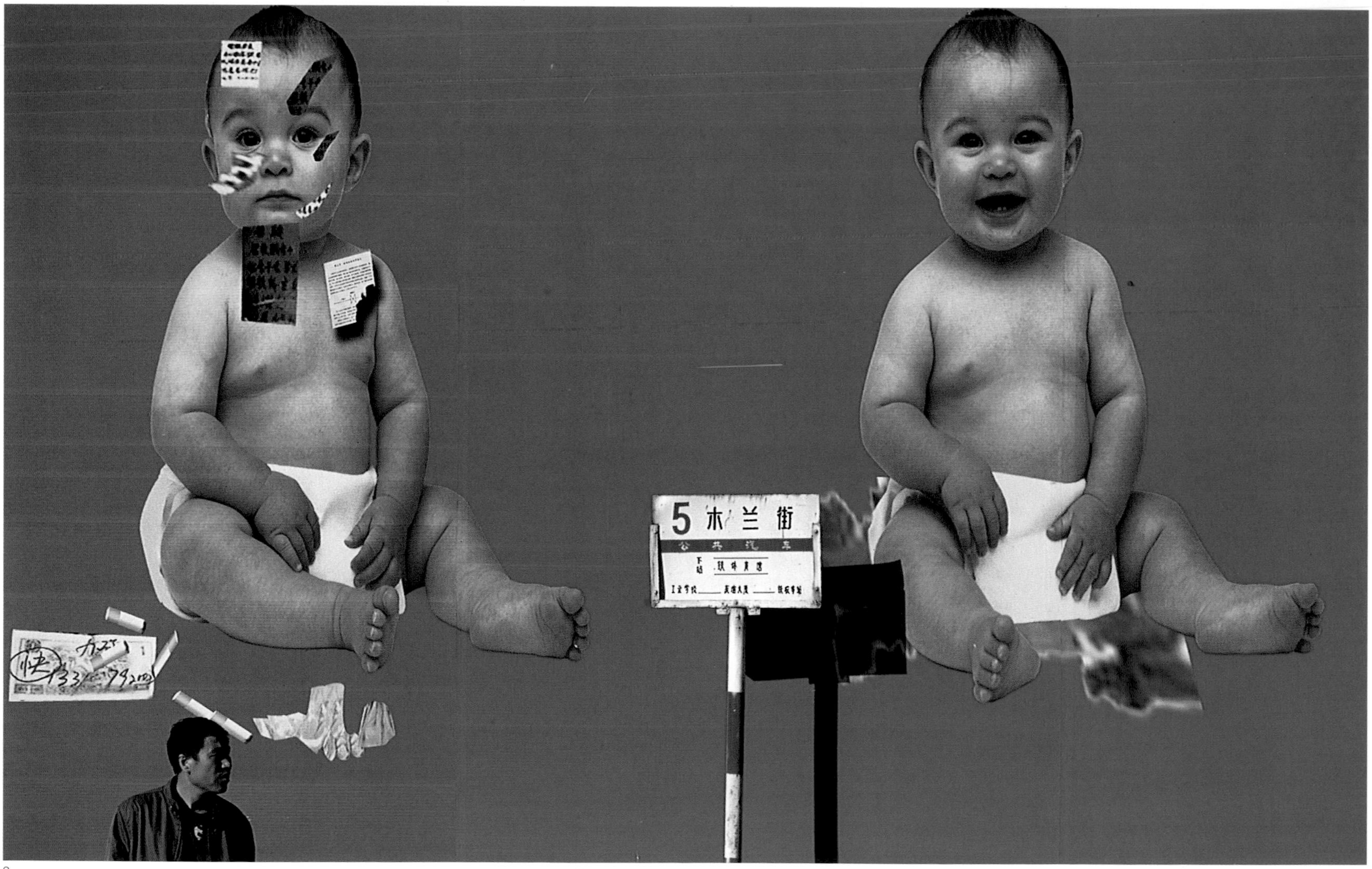

3

THE SIBERIAN FRONTIER

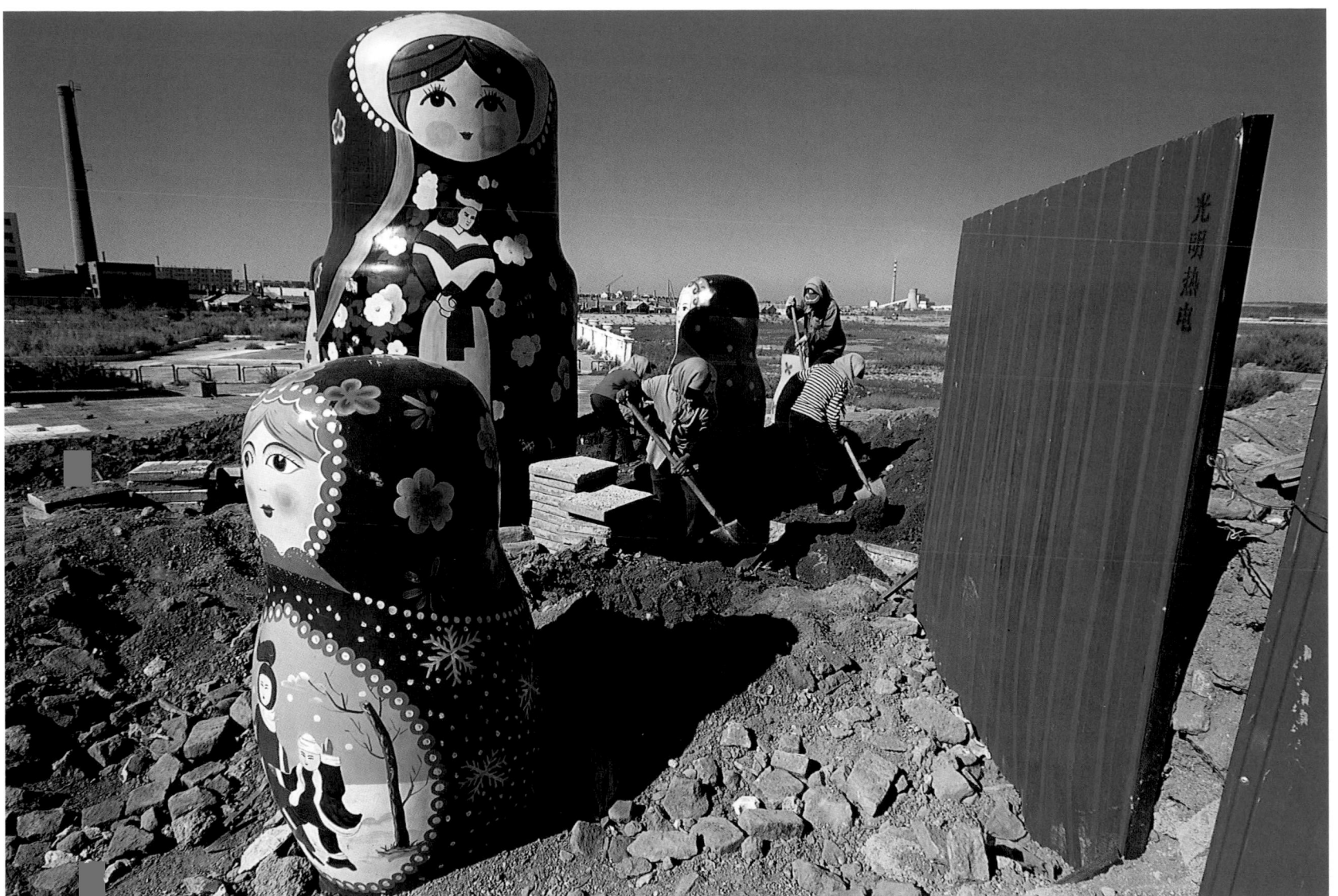

4

THE SEVEN-DAY, 9,288-kilometre (5,772-mile) journey between Moscow and Vladivostok on the Trans-Siberian Railway crosses the Chinese border at the small Inner Mongolian city of Man'zhou'li. A settlement grew up around the Manchzhuriya Station (Russian for Manchuria) during the construction of the railway between 1891 and 1916. The city benefited greatly from the breakup of the Soviet Union, with Russians flooding across the border to buy Chinese household items and electronic goods. The Man'zhou'li customs is now responsible for monitoring more than half the trade between Russia, Eastern Europe and China. [1] The Sino-Russian Frontier Trade Market next to the border crossing is the favourite destination for many Russian visitors. [2] Two sisters from a semi-nomadic Mongolian family outside their two yurts – the living room is on the left and the kitchen is on the right. [3] A rather strange poster promoting civic responsibility for keeping Inner Mongolia clean. [4] Drains and utilities pipes are being laid for a new development on the edge of the rapidly expanding city.

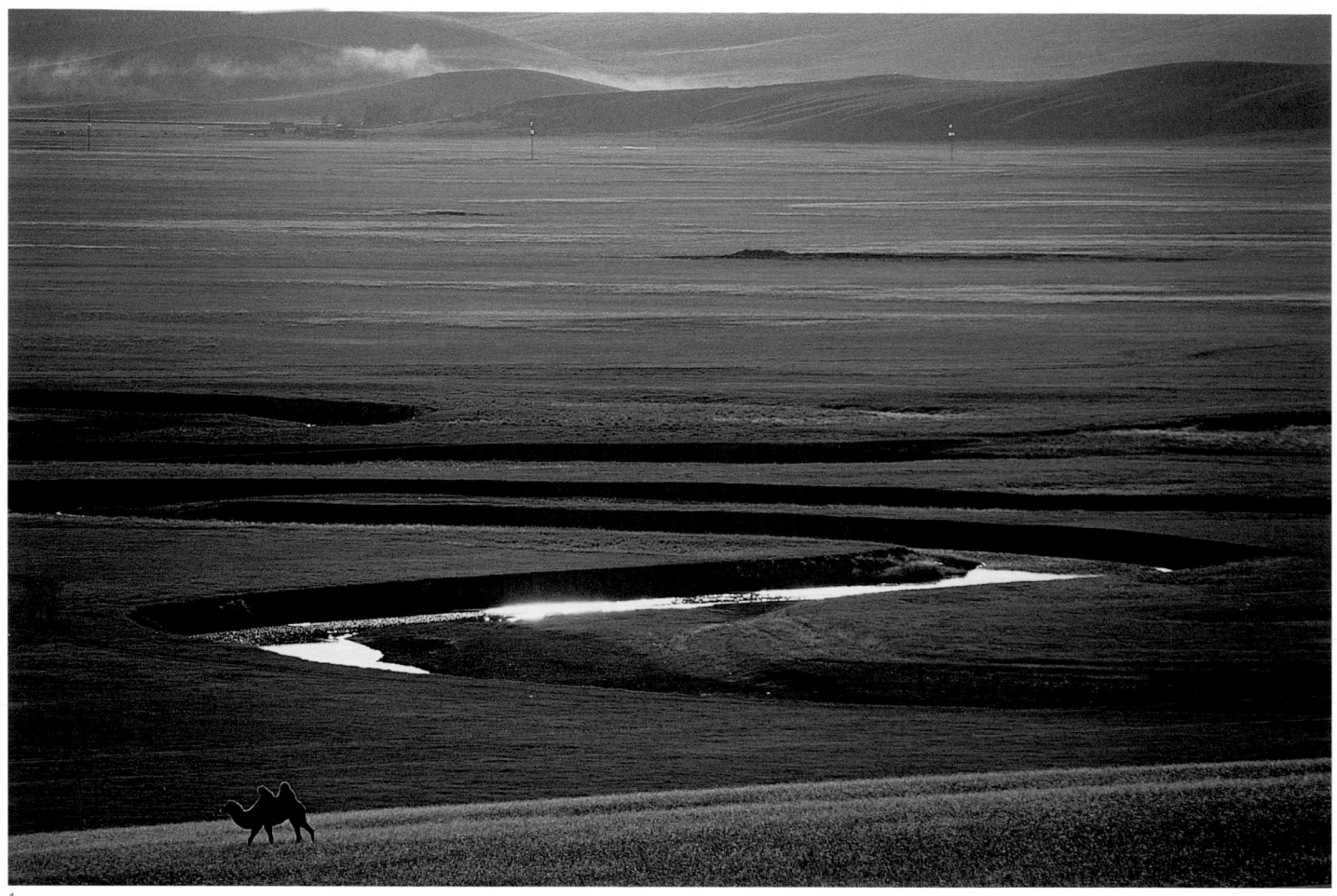

1

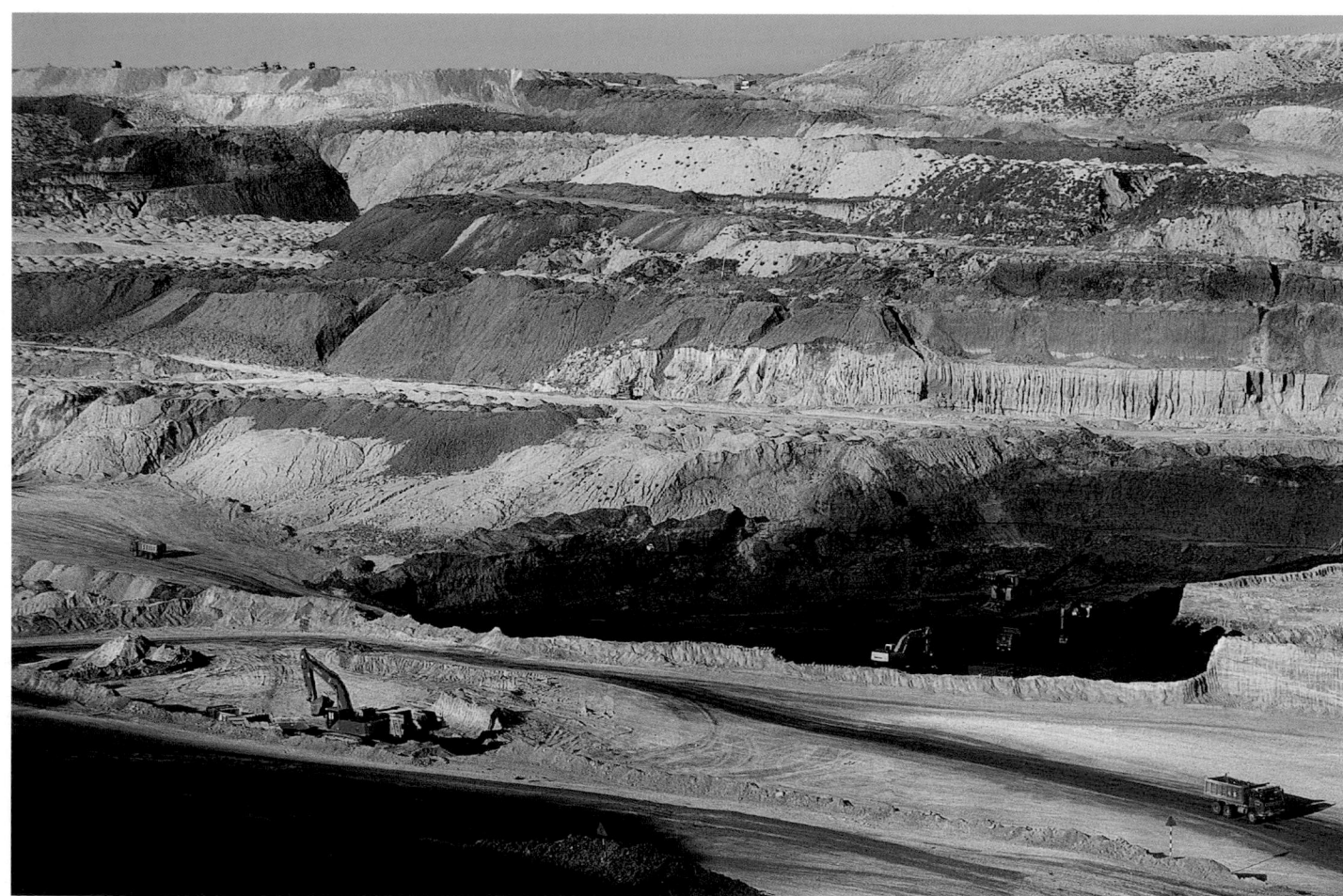

2

THE MORI'GELE RIVER GRASSLAND

3

A COMBINATION OF GLOBAL WARMING and human exploitation over the past 30 years has put the Hulun'buir grassland on the brink of disaster. Some forty per cent of the 32,278-square-mile (8.36 million hectare) prairie has been badly degraded by sandstorms, drought and the replacement of vast stretches of pasture by grain cultivation to meet China's insatiable demand for food. Hundreds of thousands of acres of new desert now cut into the region, encroaching on the 3,000 rivers and 500 lakes scattered across the grassland. Let's hope the local government's US$2 billion plan to try to arrest and reverse the situation is not too little, too late. Just outside Man'zhou'li the future of the prairie lies on either side of the highway. [1] The meadows along the zigzagging Mori'gele River are reputed to be the most beautiful grasslands in all Hulunbuir. [2] [3] Open-pit mining. The region's rich coal deposit was the original reason Man'zhou'li became the key station on the Trans-Siberian Railway. Inner Mongolia now wants to double its annual coal output to 500 million tons by 2010.

NORTH BY NORTHEAST

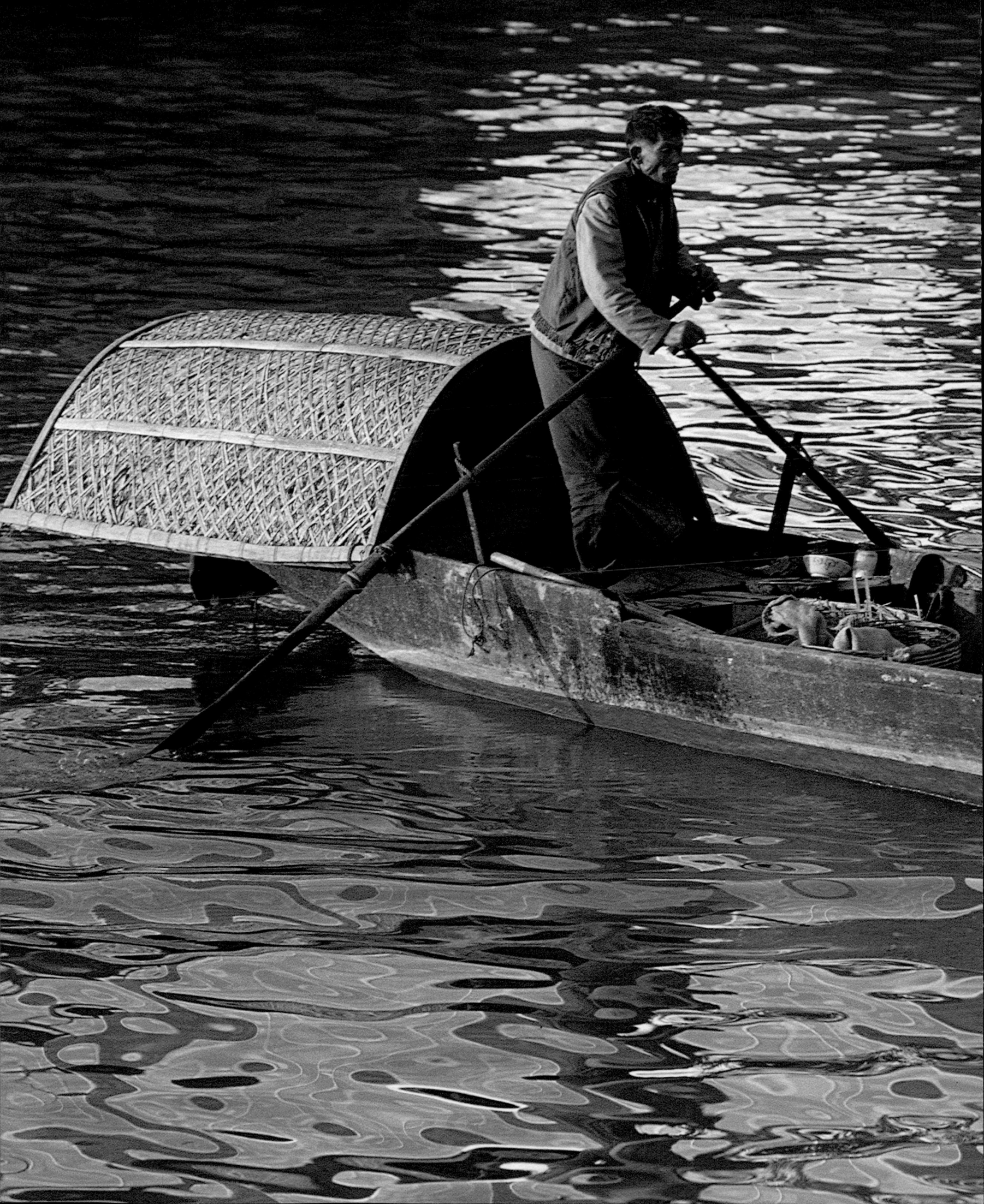

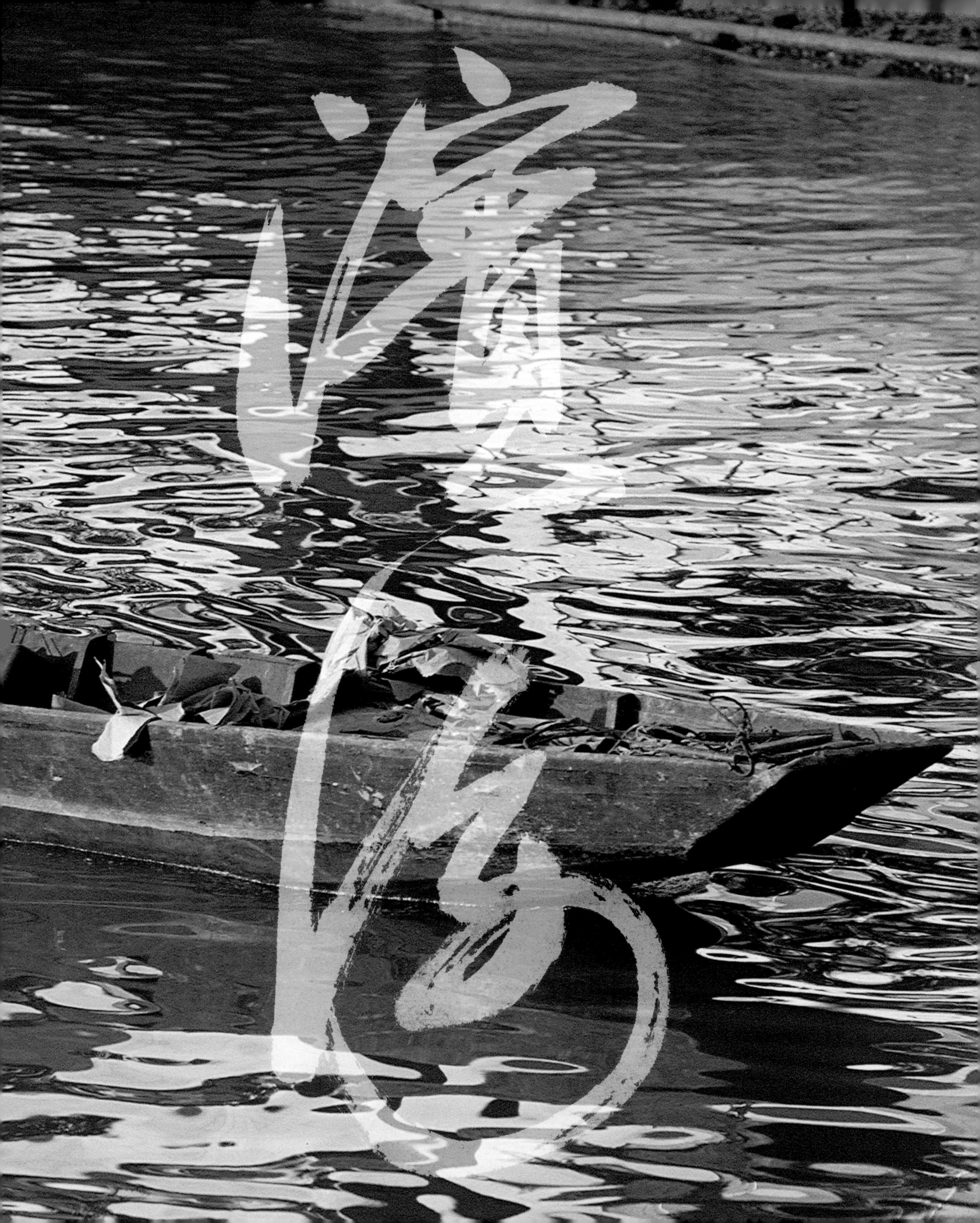

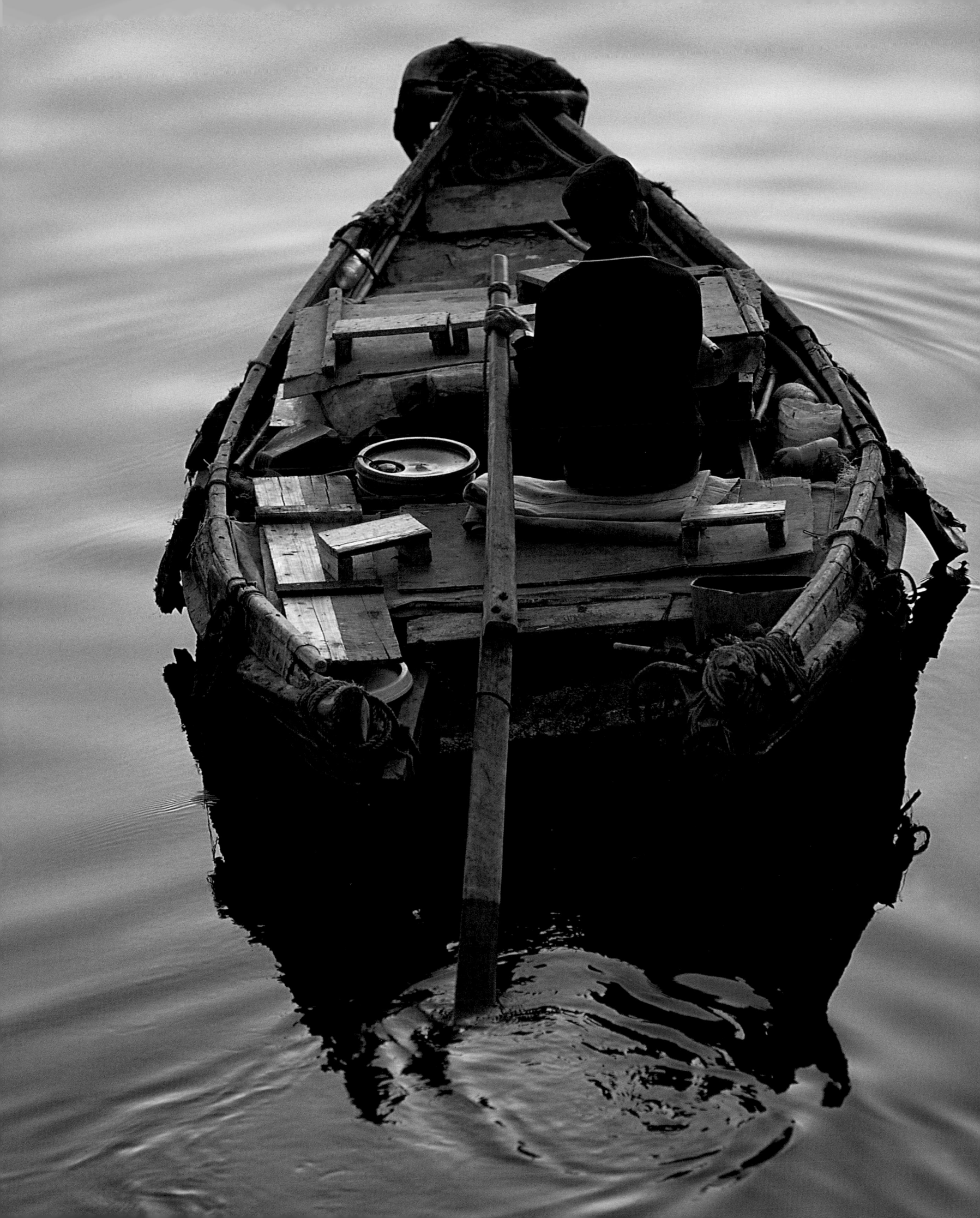

ON THE WATERFRONT

From the moment I step onto the platform of the Maglev (magnetic levitation) train station in Shang'hai's Pu'dong International Airport and see the brass stands with red velvet ropes lined up along the exposed track channel, I know something is amiss. This is, after all, the platform of the fastest passenger train on the planet, not the box office of an old-fashioned theatre or entrance to a bouncer-protected nightclub. One simply expects a slightly more formidable barrier, like a glass wall with sliding doors that can prevent passengers from falling or jumping into the open ditch with the high-voltage tracks. As I wait for the train on the grungy red VIP carpet, my mind drifts back to the faraway place where this all began.

"Getting Rich is Glorious..." Paramount leader Deng Xiao'ping uttered those immortal words back in 1984 during the Lunar New Year celebrations for the Year of the Rat. And with just those four words, the 'Little Emperor' changed the course of history by unleashing the pent-up energy, resourcefulness and skills, along with the greed and desires, of 1.3 billion people. He was on an unofficial inspection tour of Shen'zhen – one of the first Special Economic Zones in his 'Socialism with Chinese characteristics' experiment, just across the barbed-wire fence that separates the capitalists' haven of Hong Kong from its sickly communist neighbour. Twenty-three years on, the once-drowsy village of Shen'zhen has transformed itself into a soulless, sleazy metropolis, with its own stock exchange and two million migrant workers from all over China, working in the SEZ that has become, along with Shang'hai and Bei'jing, one of the top three high-tech manufacturing bases in the country. The city has also become an icon of Deng's revolution, a symbol for its economic successes and for all the collateral damage that has littered the road to riches since the launch of what some now call his 'Totalitarian Capitalism' movement.

One cannot help but wonder, as China faces the inevitability of becoming a major power and the world's largest economy, whether Deng foresaw this eventual outcome when he first set his reforms in motion. Could he have known that a mere 10 years after his death China would have a trillion US dollars of foreign exchange reserves, or that it would become a major player in a new Great Game? Had he anticipated the extraordinary transformation of the country and its social and environmental consequences? Did he expect the new policy to cause socialism itself to disappear almost completely, to be replaced by an oligarchy of party elites – leading to rampant corruption and creating an almost insurmountable income gap between the rich and the poor? With at least eight billionaires and 300,000 millionaires at one end of the scale, and the peasants of the interior who earn less than 2,000 RMB (US$250) a year at the other? What must have been clear to him from the start was that the primary driving force for his new 'open-door' policy would be coming from the eastern seaboard, where nearly all of China's contacts with the Western world had taken place since the 19th Century.

Since the time of legends, this region along China's 12,000-kilometre (7,456-mile) coastline, from the tip of Shan'dong Peninsula in the Yellow Sea down to the Pearl River Delta that drains into the South China Sea, has been the stage upon which some of the most epic dramas and gut-wrenching tragedies of the Middle Kingdom have unfolded. The water's edge is where the 'great men' of Chinese history came to dream big dreams as they stared out at the distant horizon; and where the ordinary people came to escape from the chaos and mayhem triggered by the great men's dreams.

[LEFT] A sampan on the San'ya River, Hai'nan Island. [PRECEDING PAGES] Sunrise on the Chun'shan River in Guang'dong province.

One of the earliest of these 'great men' was the first emperor Qin Shi'huang, who, having conquered and united China, set out to conquer death itself. Taoist holy man Xu Fu was dispatched to find the 'Isles of the Immortals in the Eastern Seas', where the herb of immortality was thought to grow. Starting in 219 BCE, three expeditions set sail from the Yellow Sea coast, including a fleet carrying 6,000 young virgins – 3,000 men and 3,000 women – plus artisans of many disciplines and a variety of grains. Another one transported an entire army. The emperor died in 210 BCE and the priest never returned from his final voyage. Some believe that Xu Fu is Jimmu Tenno, the founder of the Japanese empire, while others think that the Chinese fleet crossed the Pacific and landed in Central America, where it played an important role in the Mayan civilization.

Khubilai Khan, who ruled over the largest empire in Chinese history during the Yuan Dynasty, dreamt about conquering Japan from these same shores. After the debacle of the first invasion in 1274, where he lost the bulk of 900 ships, 40,000 men and 15,000 horses to a freak winter typhoon, Khubilai assembled an armada of 4,500 ships, manned by 60,000 sailors, to transport 100,000 soldiers for his second invasion of Japan. But once again, after initial successes against the samurai warriors, the Mongol soldiers withdrew to their ships, and the fleet was hit by a summer typhoon off Kyushu. One hundred thousand men perished in the raging sea and few ships survived the rocky coast to tell the tale. The military disasters of the mighty Mongols gave birth to the Japanese term *Kamikaze* – the Divine Wind.

Then came the moment, a very brief moment of twenty-eight years in China's 4,000-year-history, when Chinese junks ruled the seven seas. During the reign of emperor Yong'le in the Ming Dynasty, the eunuch admiral Zheng He (1371–1433), one of the Muslim minority from Yun'nan, undertook seven legendary voyages between 1405 and 1433, setting sail from the port of Liu'he in Tai'tsang county, on the coast of Jiang'su province, with fleets of more than 300 ships crewed by 28,000 men. These giant Chinese junks were known as *bao chuan* (treasure ships) for the precious cargos of fine silks and delicate porcelains they carried. The sixty large ships were each 122 metres (400 feet) long, with the tallest of their nine masts measuring over 91 metres (300 feet) high; they were supported and supplied by 255 smaller vessels that included warships and water tankers. The fleet sailed all around the South China Sea and Indian Ocean, reaching Aden at the mouth of the Red Sea on its fourth voyage in 1413, from which an auxiliary fleet sailed on to Jeddah for a pilgrimage to Mecca. And in 1417, on the fifth voyage, the fleet sailed down the east coast of Africa from the tip of the Horn in Somalia down to the Mozambique Channel, landing in Malindi in Kenya eighty years before Vasco da Gama's fleet of three 26-metre (85-foot) long caravels stopped there on their way to India.

With the death of the emperor, Zheng He lost his patron, the vermillion gates of Yong'le's Forbidden City slammed shut to overseas adventures, and the mighty fleet simply vanished into the mists of history. Ironically, it was the success of the 'treasure fleets', which brought back embassies and tributes from the far side of the world, that had convinced the court that the Middle Kingdom was the centre of the universe – an illusion that gave rise to the superiority complex and delusions of invincibility that have been the mindset of the Forbidden City residents ever since. This fatal policy formulated by the eunuchs who dominated the Ming court caused endless sorrow and pain for the Chinese people in the centuries that followed. From the moment China abandoned its technological edge and relinquished its domination of the maritime trade routes, the pendulum of history began swinging the other way.

The Portuguese arrived on the coast of Guang'dong in 1514, and by 1557 they had gained a permanent settlement in Macau. The Spaniards established a base in Tai'wan in 1626, only to be usurped by the Dutch in 1642. The British arrived in 1637, just as the Ming Dynasty faded to make way for the rise of the Manchurian Qing Dynasty. The Manchus, being foreigners themselves, were quite open-minded about foreign trade and influences at first, as they embarked on their aggressive campaign of enlarging the empire's territory to include Korea, Mongolia, Xin'jiang and Tibet. But their powers waned in the 19th Century, thanks to the changing dynamics of a new world order imposed by the Industrial Revolution. Xenophobia set in and they retreated back into the Forbidden City and the warm comfort of self-delusion, proposing even that England's George III should pay homage to the Chinese court. The era of incursions by 'foreign devils' into China through the porous and largely unprotected coastline continued unabated. The difficulties of economic trade culminated in the Opium Wars, which resulted in the 'Unequal Treaties' that opened up the China coast like the soft belly of a fish for all the colonial powers to carve up and fight over.

The irony is that these foreign settlements, forced upon the Qing court at gunpoint, became cradles of the revolution. Contact with foreigners and new political ideas ignited the passion for change within many young Chinese revolutionaries; Dr Sun Yat'sen led his first uprising in Guang'zhou, while the International Settlement in Shang'hai provided a safe haven for the formation of the Chinese Communist Party in 1921. It was the invaders, too, that gave birth to New China's most dynamic and prosperous cities. From the German concession of Qing'dao, to Nan'jing and Shang'hai, to the British colony of Hong Kong, the imperial navies of the colonial powers have today been replaced by fleets of container ships and cargo planes transporting everything from sophisticated computers to plastic buckets into the far corners of the global village, as China emerges as the largest manufacturer of consumer goods in the world.

Within four minutes of 'takeoff', the Maglev, floating on a one-centimetre cushion of air above the magnetic field, hits its top speed of 431 kph (267 mph). As the large red numbers on the digital display flicker between 430 and 431 kph, excited Japanese tourists jump out of their wobbly plastic seats and rush to the front of the carriage to take pictures, but there is no time for them to flash the 'V' sign and pose with the display screen, for within thirty seconds, the speed starts to decline and soon we are on the platform of Long'yang Road station at the end of the 7 minute and 20 second ride. As I go down the escalator, I am convinced that a large chunk of the over US$1.2 billion spent on the thirty-kilometre line has disappeared into somebody's numbered account overseas: the cheap moulded-plastic seats in the VIP carriage have removed all doubts. Once outside the station, I understand why it is nicknamed 'the fastest train to nowhere': so far, no one has been able to explain why an airport express train terminates in a nondescript suburb of Pu'dong instead of at the centre of the new financial district by Huang'pu'jiang. As I sit in traffic inside my taxi, which will eventually take another hour and a half to reach my hotel off the Bund, I wonder what the point of the Maglev train is, besides being able to say "We have the fastest passenger train on the planet, and it goes nowhere, fast."

On September 24th 2006, Shang'hai's Communist Party chief and member of the Politburo Chen Liang'yu was dismissed, accused of corruption on a massive scale.

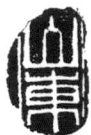

SHAN'DONG PROVINCE

LOCATION
Latitude 34°25'–38°23'N
Longtitude 114°36'–112°43'E

AREA 156,000 km² (60,231 sq miles)

GEOGRAPHY The province is dominated by fertile plains fed by the Huang'he River (Yellow River), its tributaries and consorts and anchored by two distinct mountainous areas. Much of Shan'dong's north and west are part of the North China Plain while the centre is formed by the Tai'shan, Lu'shan and Meng'shan mountains. Mount Tai'shan, at 1,545m, is the highest point in the province. The Shan'dong Peninsula extends eastwards to separate the Bo'hai Gulf and the Yellow Sea.

CLIMATE Shandong has a temperate climate, with dry, cold winters and warm, humid summers. Temperatures in January are between -5°C and 1°C, rising to 24–28°C in July. The lowest recorded temperature is -20°C and the highest is 43°C. Average annual rainfall is between 550 mm and 950 mm.

POPULATION 91.8 million (end 2004)

MAJOR CITIES Ji'nan (capital), Yan'tai, Qing'dao, Qu'fu

AGRICULTURE The province is one of China's main agricultural regions, growing food crops such as wheat, sorghum, maize and fruit. Cash crops include cotton, oilseeds, tobacco, hemp, silkworms and medicinal herbs. Shan'dong's fishery is China's largest single source of local prawns, shellfish, abalone and sea slugs.

MAIN INDUSTRIES Shan'dong is the third main industrial production centre in China. Major industries include coal mining and oil production from the Sheng'li and Zhong'yuan fields, petrochemicals, textiles and garments, steel, food processing and brewing.

ANNUAL PER CAPITA INCOME (2005)
Disposable income of urban residents:
RMB 10,744 (US$1,341)
Cash income of rural residents:
RMB 3,930 (US$490)

HISTORICAL AND SCENIC SITES
Mount Tai'shan, Cemetery of Confucius (both UNESCO World Heritage Sites), Mount Lao'shan, Ling'zi, Peng'lai and Rong'cheng.

FOOD Shan'dong cuisine is one of the oldest in China, tracing its origins to the Spring and Autumn Period 2,500 years ago. Proximity to the ocean and great rivers is reflected in the province's notable dishes, such as sweet and sour carp, sea cucumbers stewed with shallots, braised shark's fin with shredded chicken and steamed buns.

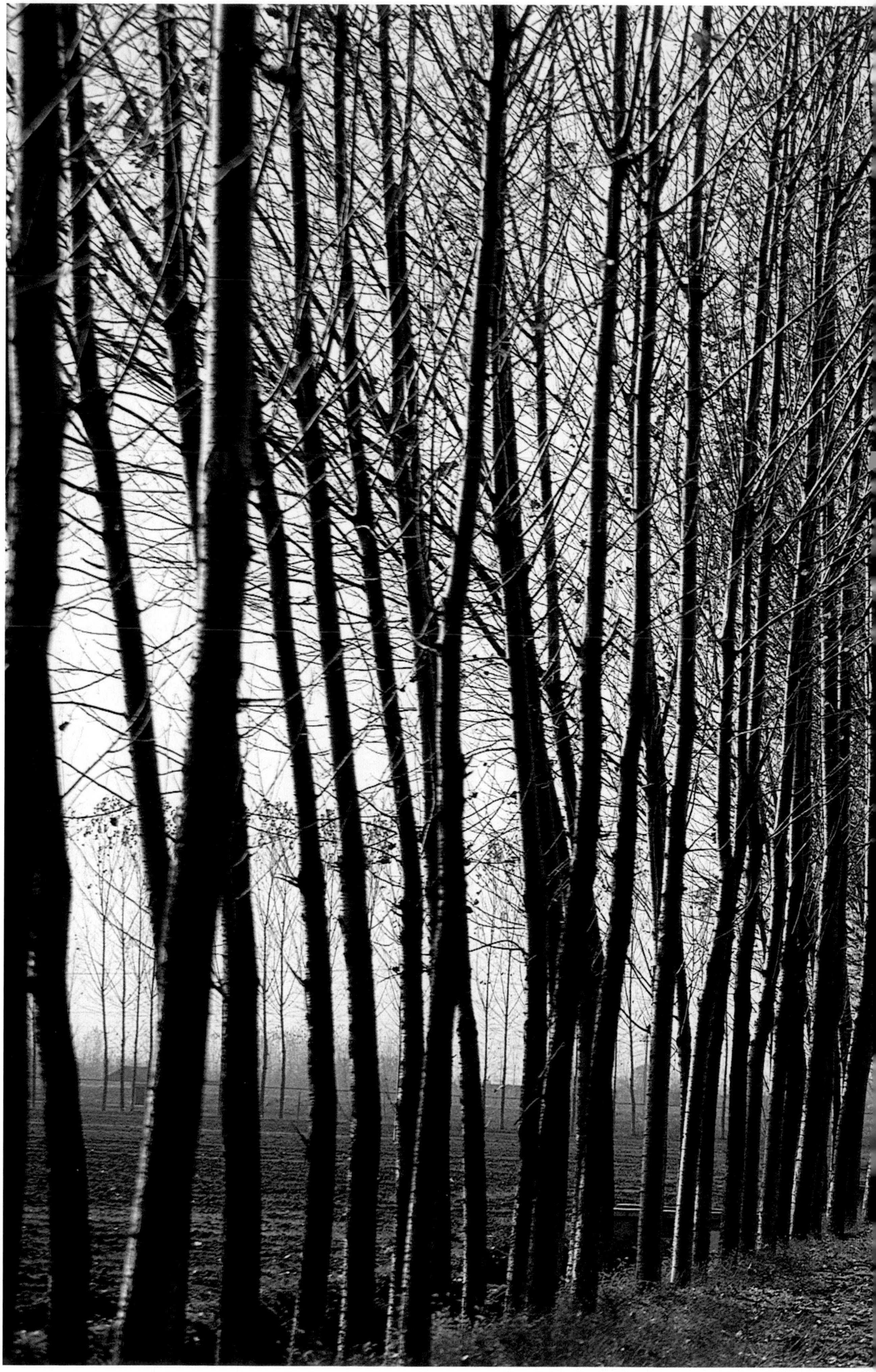

[RIGHT] A tree-lined avenue near Qu'fu in the Shan'dong countryside.

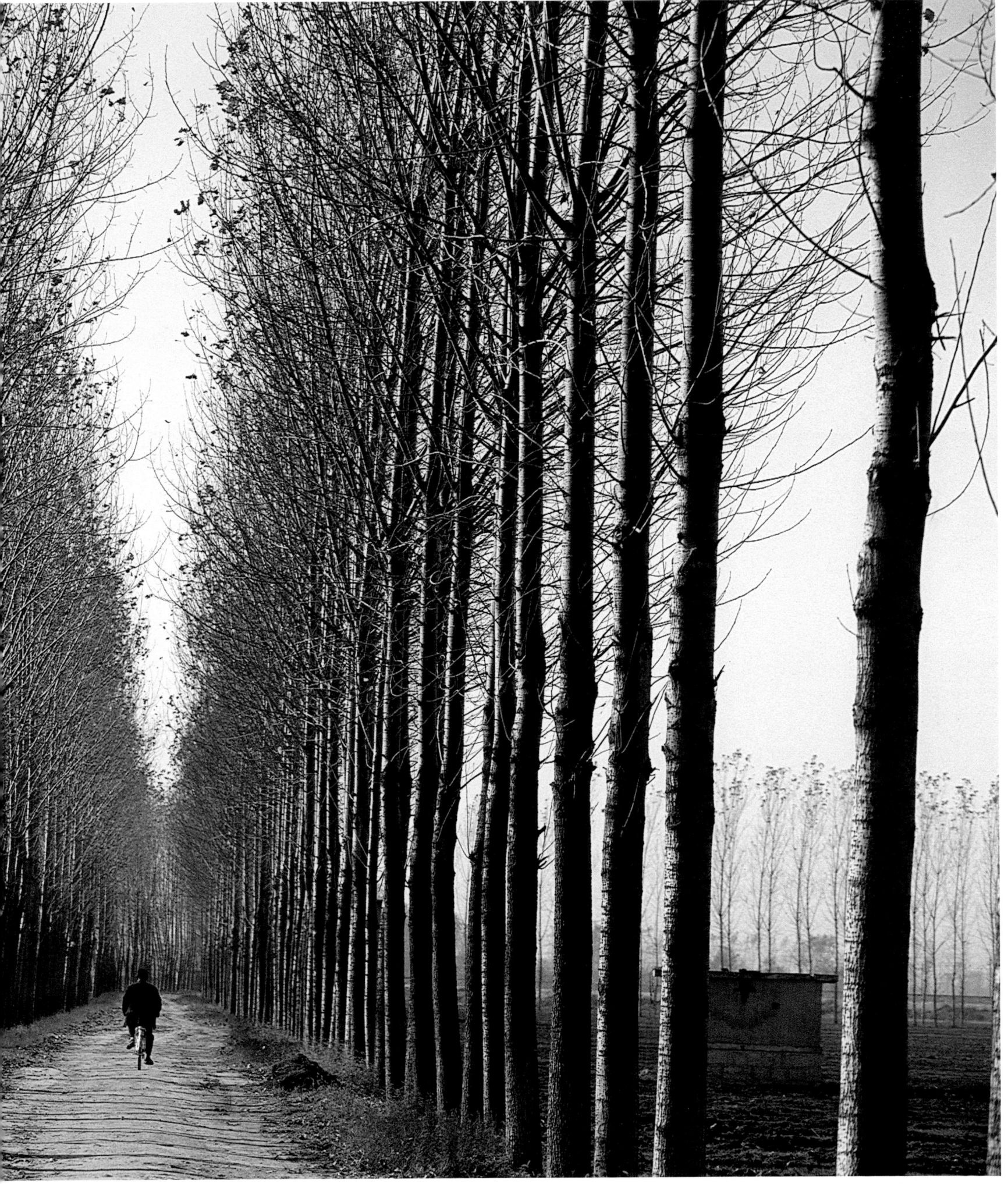

SERENE MOUNTAIN & GREEN ISLAND

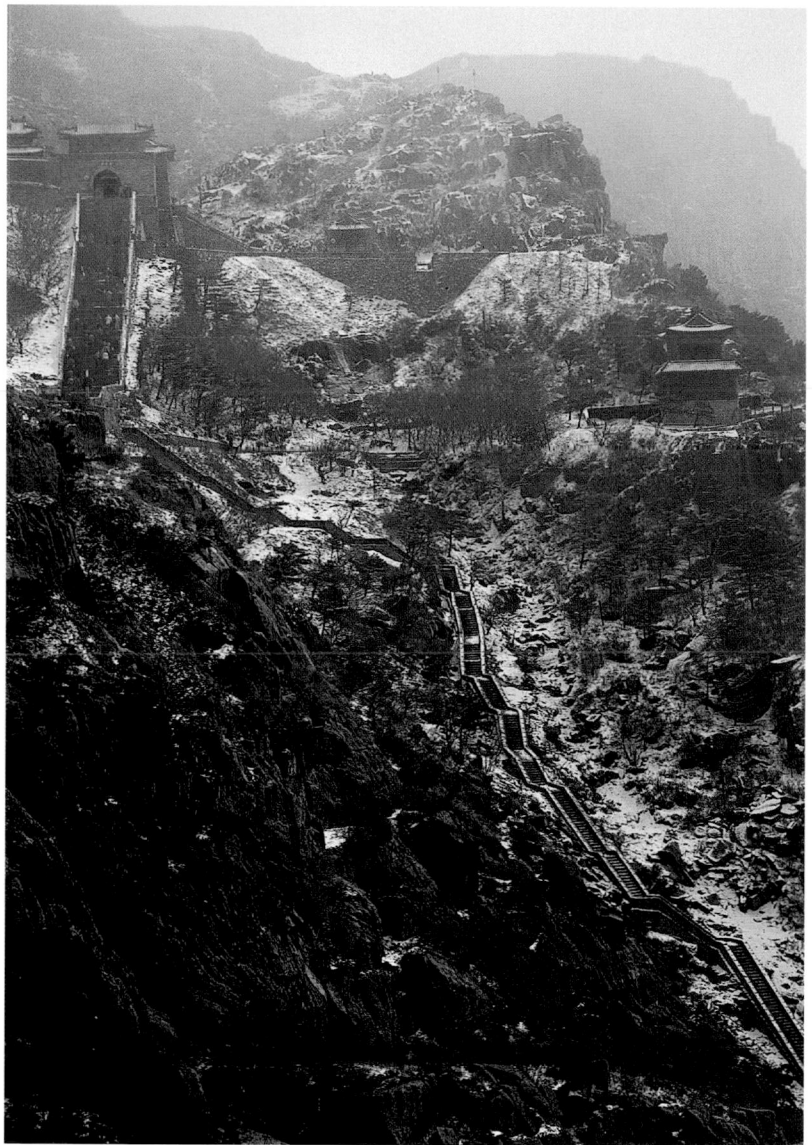

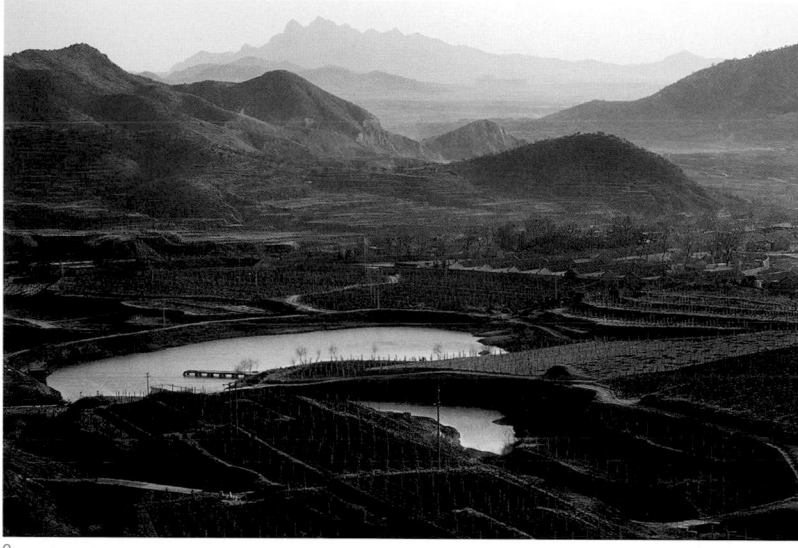

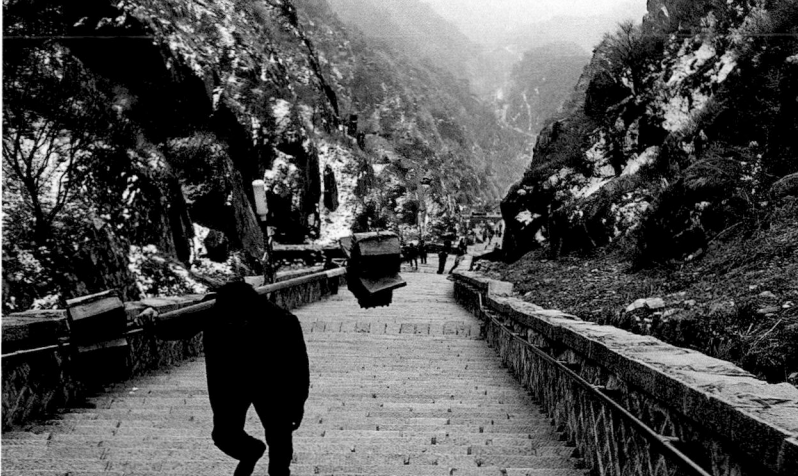

1

2

3

ON THE WATERFRONT

OF THE FIVE SACRED TAOIST MOUNTAINS of China, Tai'shan (Serene Mountain) is the most venerated because of the ancient belief that the sun lives there. The 1,545-metre (5,068-foot) summit has traditionally been the site of imperial sacrifices where the rulers of China (including Mao) prayed for the blessings of heaven and earth. [1] Though the 7.5-kilometre (4.6-mile) climb to the top is neither for the faint-hearted nor for heavy smokers, [3] labourers scale the 'stairway to heaven' several times a day transporting material for the temple complex around the peak. Qing'dao (Green Island) is one of the most beautiful and livable cities in China, though its charm grew out of a bitter colonial past. [4] [5] The fishing village by the Yellow Sea on the Shan'dong Peninsula was ceded to Imperial Germany in 1898 on a 99-year-lease. Japan seized the port in 1914, but 15 years was long enough for the Germans to leave behind their architecture and the legendary Qing'dao beer; an 'alcoholic' legacy now being challenged by [2] new vineyards and a burgeoning wine industry.

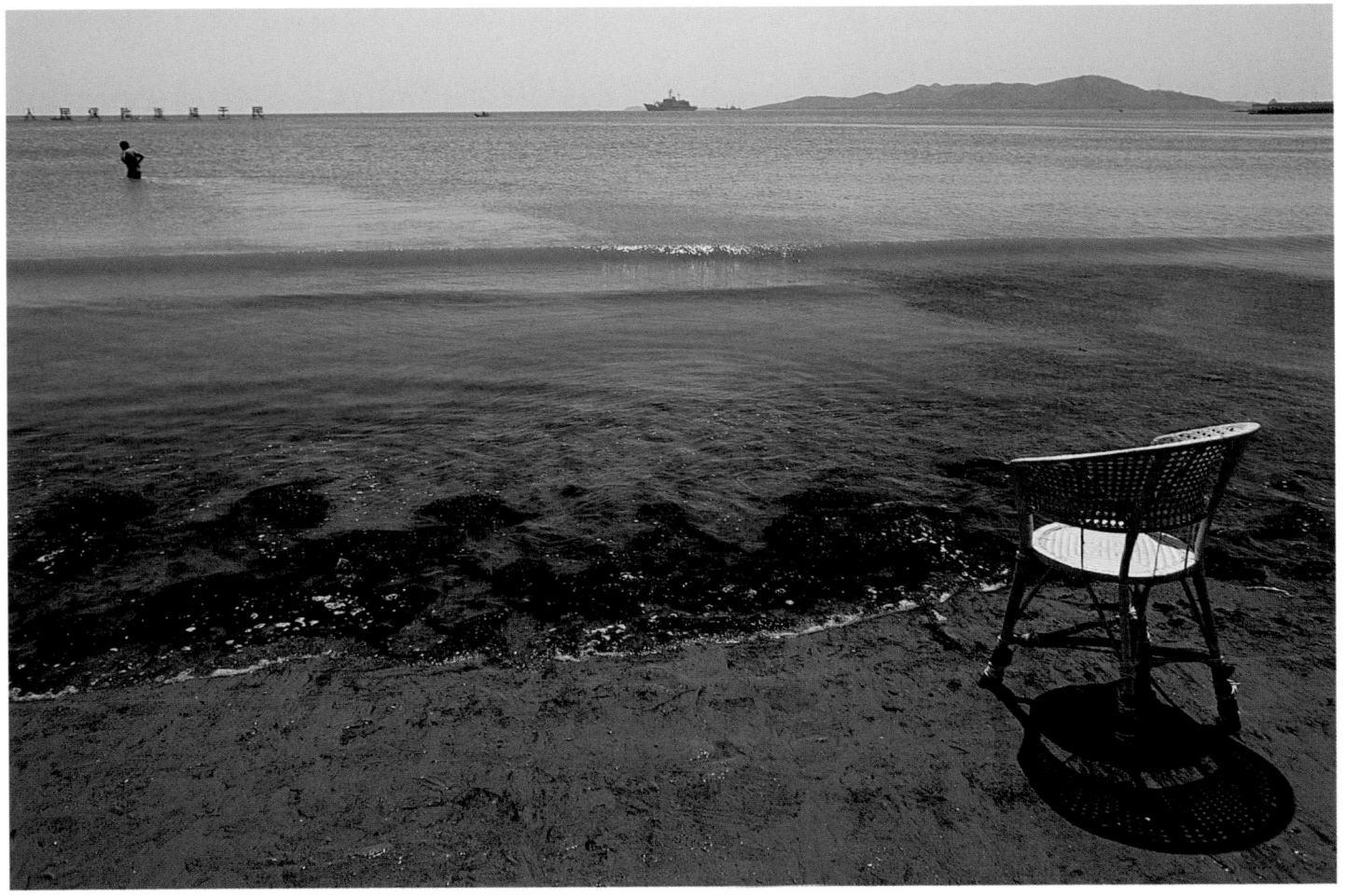

4

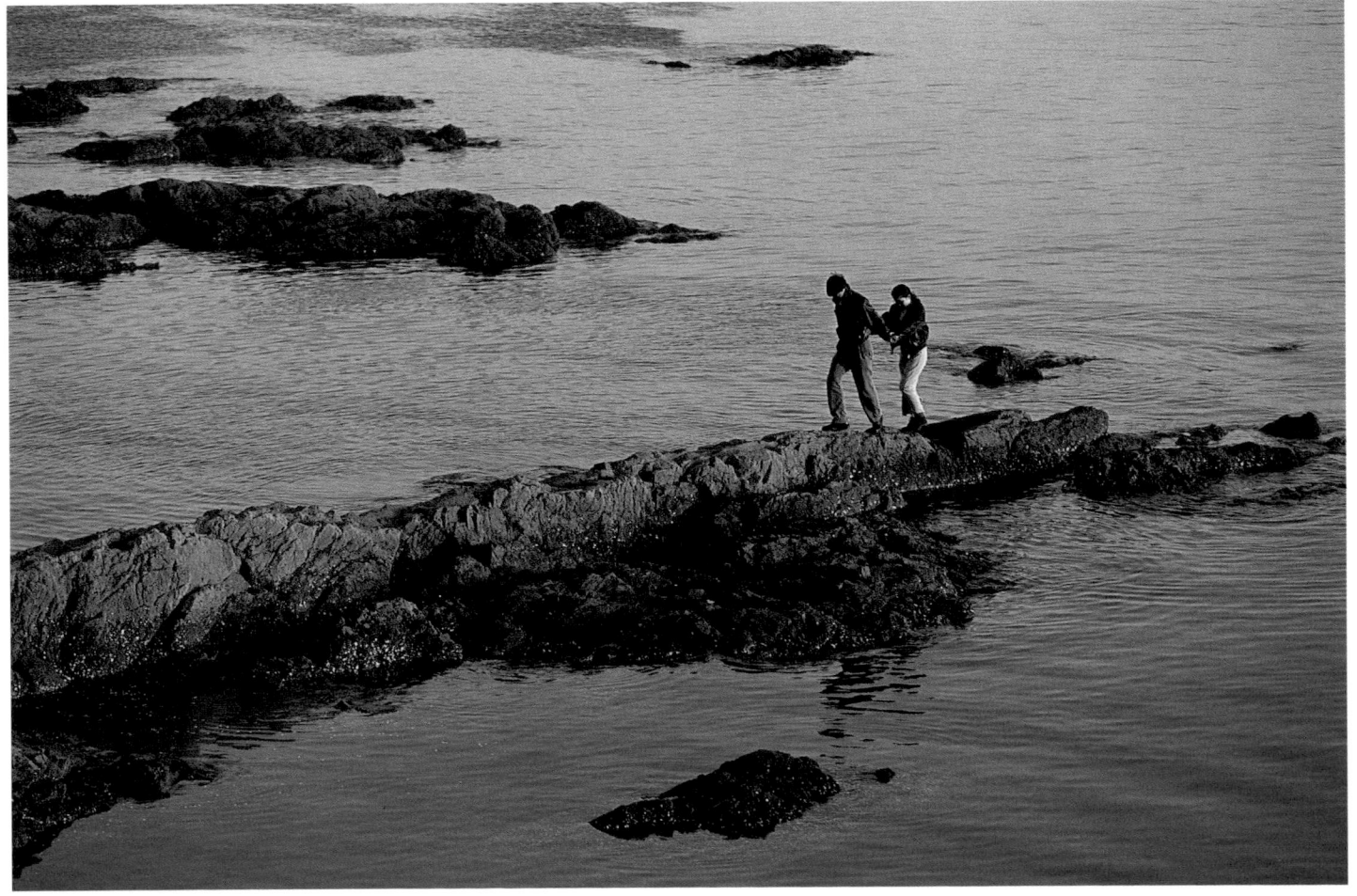

5

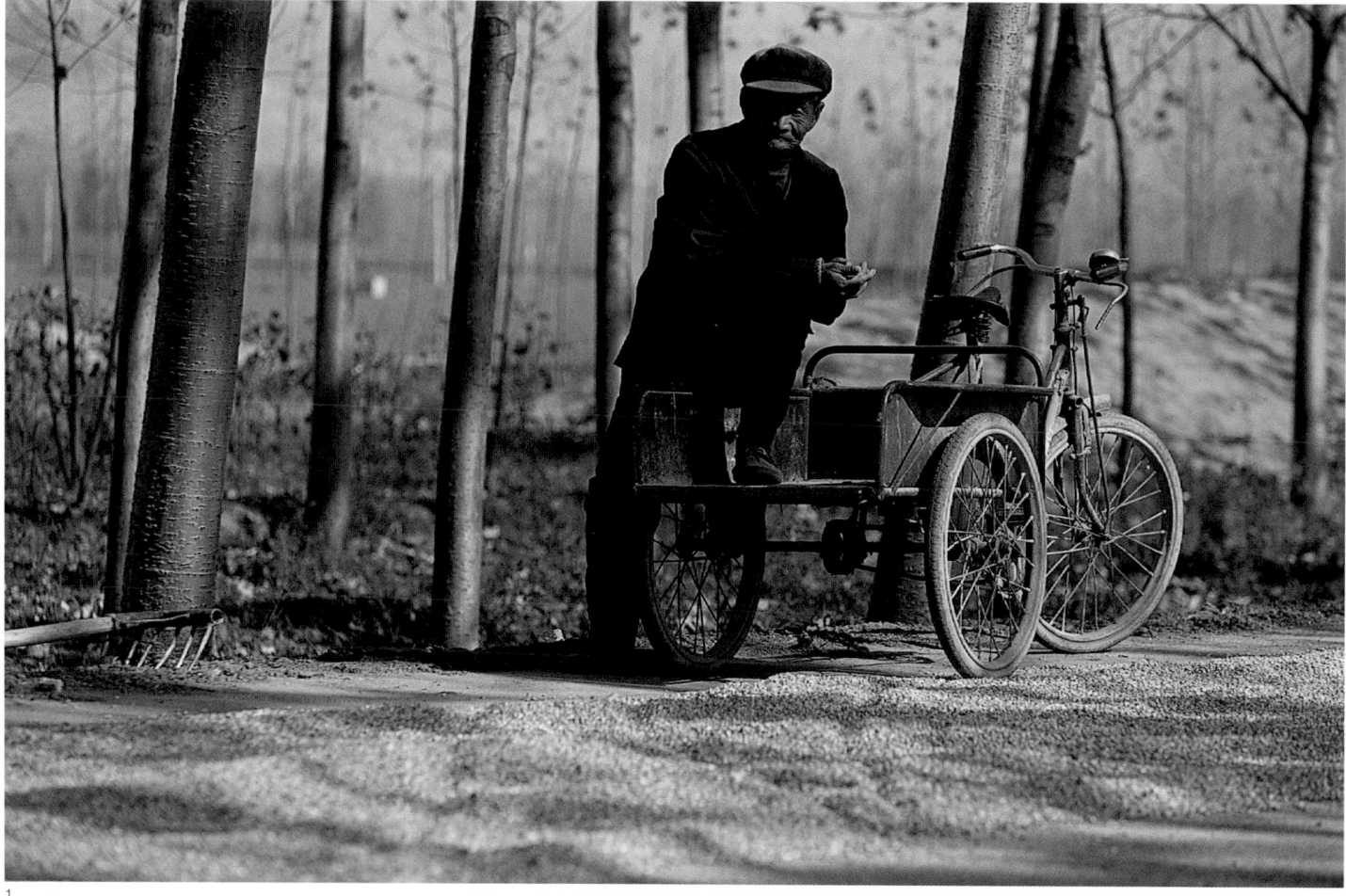

1

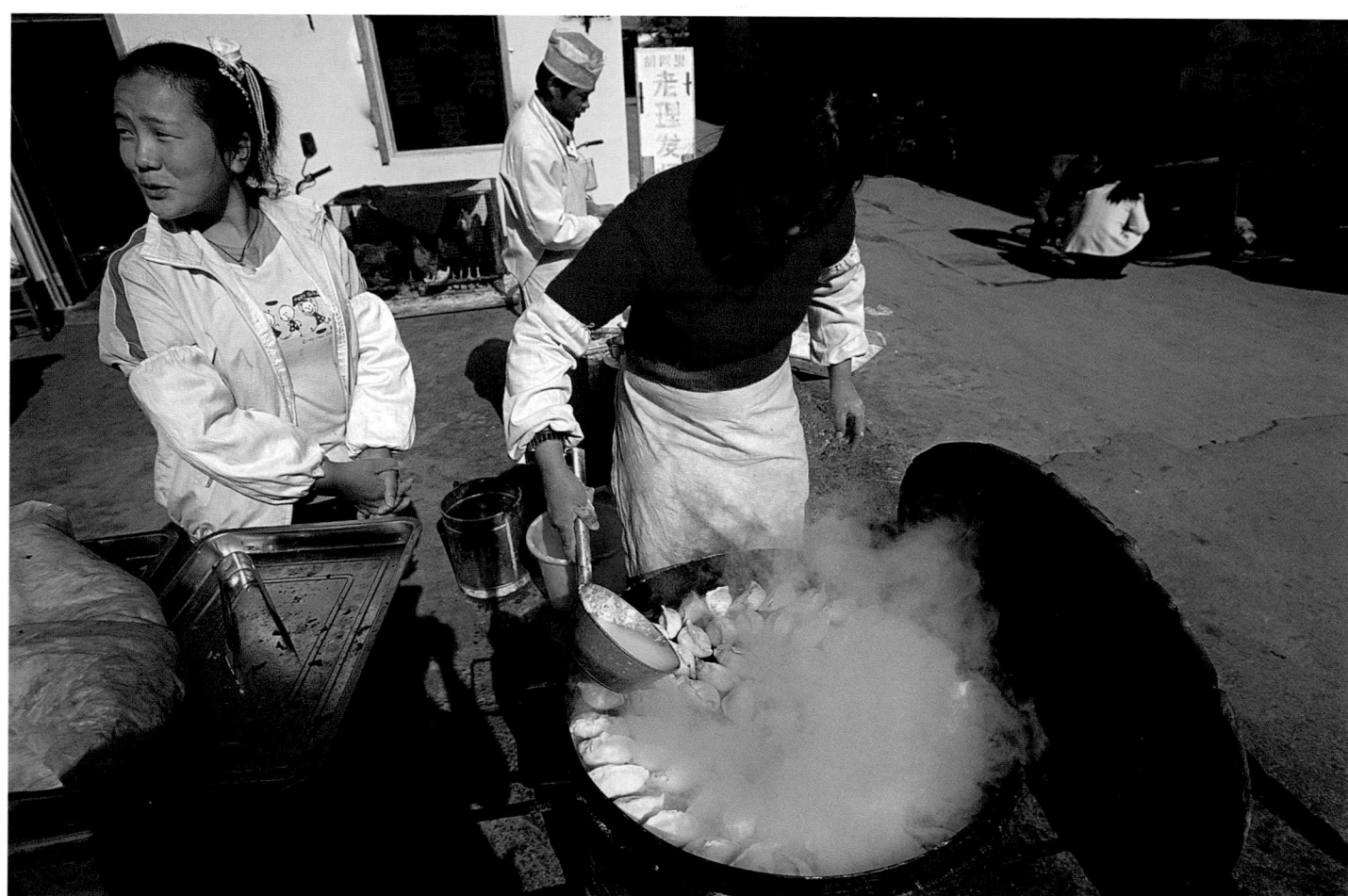

2

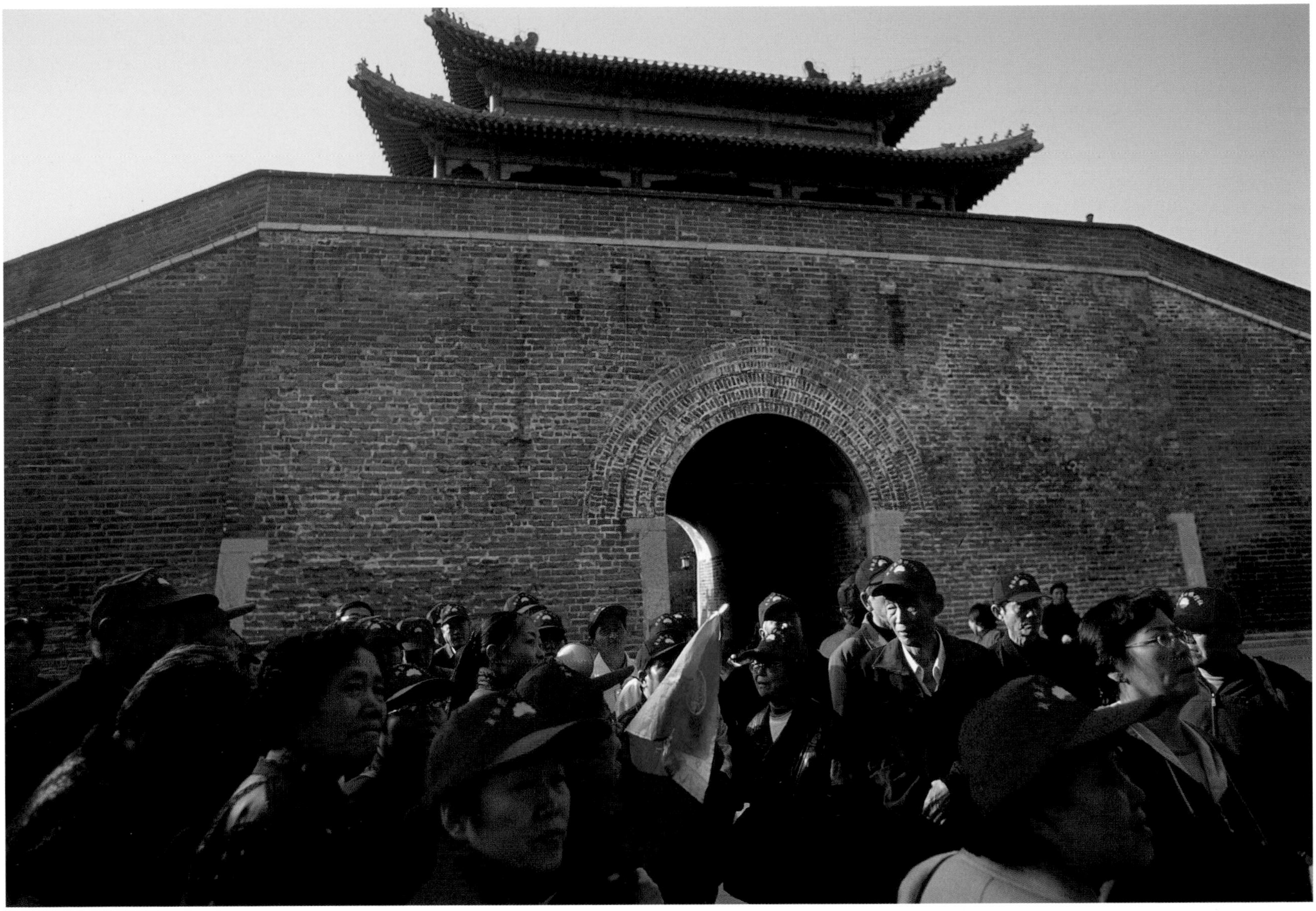

3

LEGEND HAS IT that Confucius was born inside a cave in the foothills of Ni'shan Mountains, 30 kilometres (18 miles) southeast of Qu'fu. [1] I had visited his alleged birthplace many years ago, but on my recent return trip found that although the countryside had changed little, the valley had been flooded and Master Kong's 'birthplace' now lay beneath the waters of a reservoir. [3] [4] As the founder of arguably the most important school of philosophical and political thought in Chinese history, Confucius' ancestral temple in Qu'fu is suitably grand and well maintained. The damage inflicted by the Cultural Revolution, so evident 20 years ago, has been restored for the booming tourist trade. His largely humanistic teachings, collected in *The Analects of Confucius*, have been the pillar of Chinese government policies for two millennia. They continue to exert an influence on governments, with Singapore frequently cited as an ideal Confucian state. To the West Confucius remains the symbol of Chinese wisdom, where some of his less esoteric thoughts are readily accepted and digested in the form of Fortune cookies. [2] On the outskirts of town a fresh batch of delicious dumplings goes into the pan.

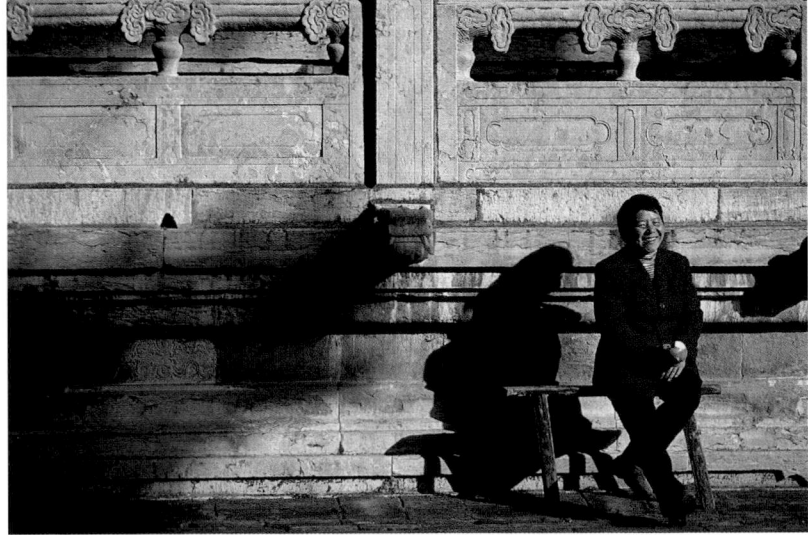

4

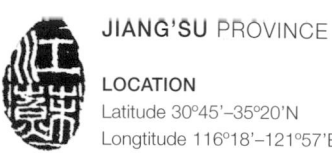

JIANG'SU PROVINCE

LOCATION
Latitude 30°45'–35°20'N
Longtitude 116°18'–121°57'E

AREA 106,190 km² (41,000 sq miles)

GEOGRAPHY Jiang'su's location in the
Yang'tze River delta ensures much of the
province is flat and low-lying. Average elevations
range from 10 m to 60 m , with the highest
point of 625 m at the summit of Mount Yun'tai.
The Yang'tze cuts the province in half, while the
Grand Canal provides a direct route from
Nan'jing to Su'zhou. Lakes Tai'hu and Hong'ze
respectively dominate the province's northern
and southern regions. Jiang'su has a 1,000-km
coastline on the Yellow Sea.

CLIMATE Jiang'su is monsoonal, spanning
the sub-tropical and warm-temperate climatic
zones. Average temperatures in January are
between -4°C and -2°C, reaching 26–30°C in
July. The highest recorded temperature is
41.1°C and the lowest is -23.1°C. There are
frequent 'plum rains' between spring and
summer, with typhoons in late summer and
early autumn. Annual average rainfall is
botwoon 800 mm and 1,200 mm.

POPULATION 74.75 million (end 2005)

MAJOR CITIES Nan'jing (capital), Su'zhou,
Wu'xi, Yang'zhou, Zhen'jiang, Xu'zhou,
Lian'yun'gang

AGRICULTURE Main food crops are rice,
wheat, maize and sorghum. Cash crops
include cotton, soybeans, oilseeds, ambary
hemp and tea. The Tai'hu Lake region is a
major silk production area, and the province's
extensive lakes and waterways support a large
freshwater fishery.

MAIN INDUSTRIES Heavy industries
include oil refining, chemical production and
construction materials. Other industries involve
textiles, food processing and production of
high-technology products and equipment.

ANNUAL PER CAPITA INCOME (2005)
Disposable income of urban residents:
RMB12,319 (US$1,538)
Net income of rural residents:
RMB 5,276 (US$659)

HISTORICAL AND SCENIC SITES
Purple Mountain, Sun Yat'sen Mausoleum,
Ming Dynasty city wall and gates in the major
cities, Lake Xuan'wu, Nan'jing's Confucius
Temple, Su'zhou's classical gardens, Han'shan
Temple and Hu'qiu Hill, Yang'zhou's Thin West
Lake and Yan'ziji's Swallow Rock.

FOOD Jiang'su cuisine is divided into two
sub-groups: Huai'yang and Su'zhou. Both make
much use of sea and freshwater fish and
crustaceans, with Su'zhou favouring a little more
sweetness in its recipes. Noted dishes include
Butterfish in creamy juice, stewed crab with
clear soup, Squirrel fish, Liang'xi crisp eel.

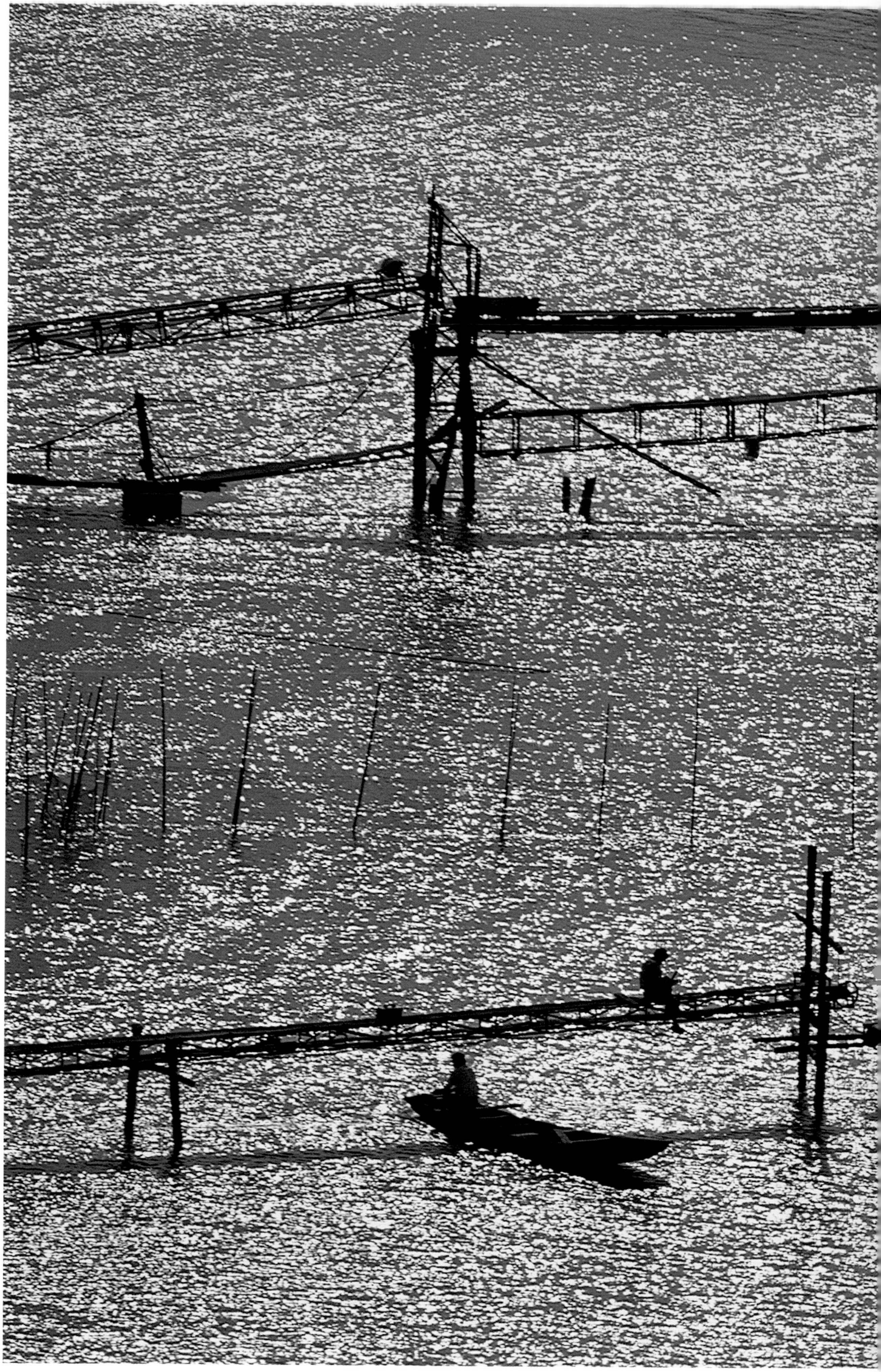

[RIGHT] The Yang'tze River shoreline in Nan'jing.

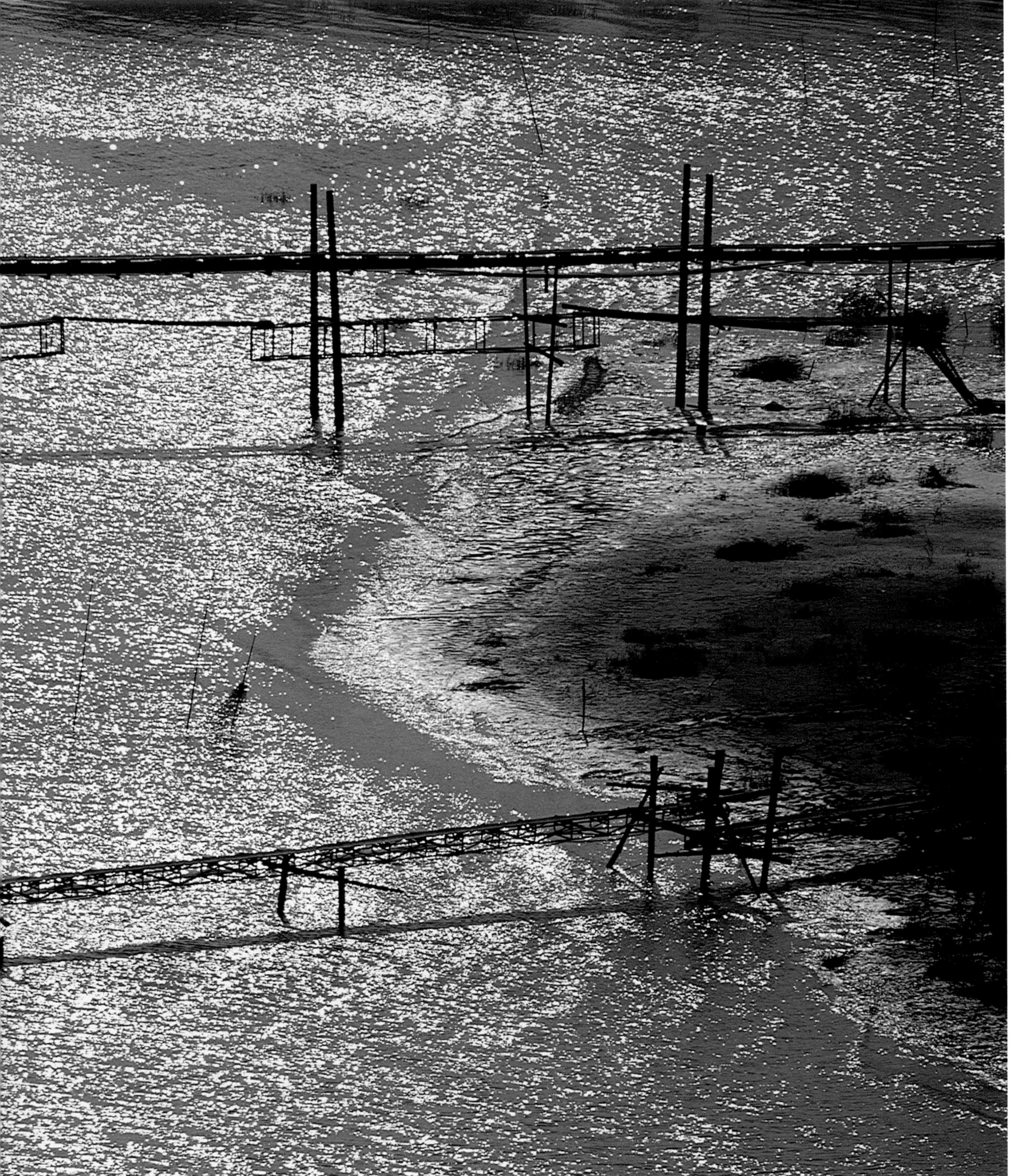

1

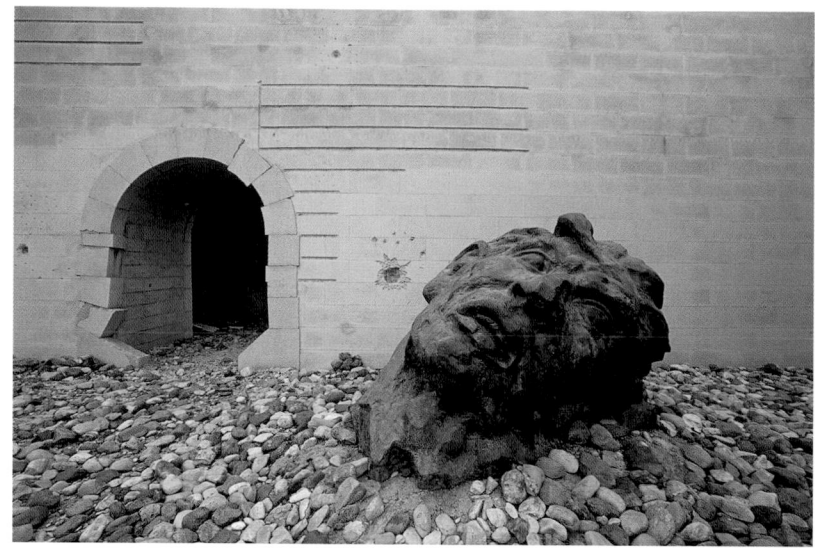

2

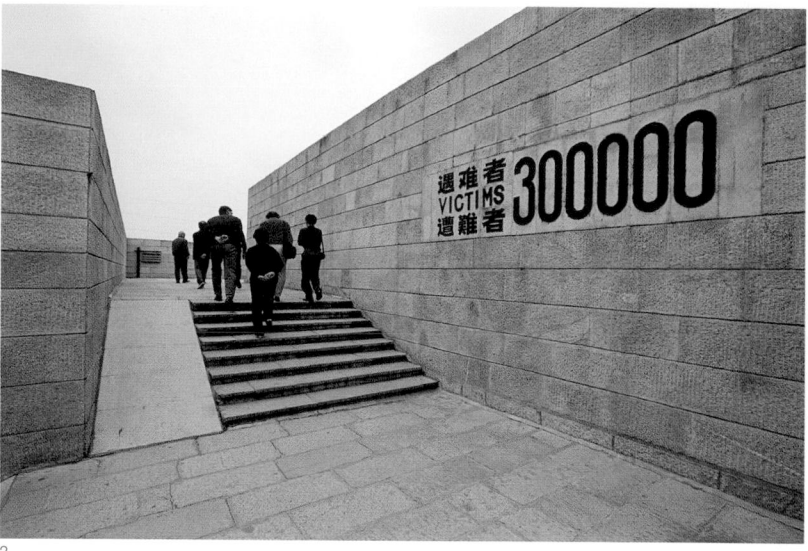

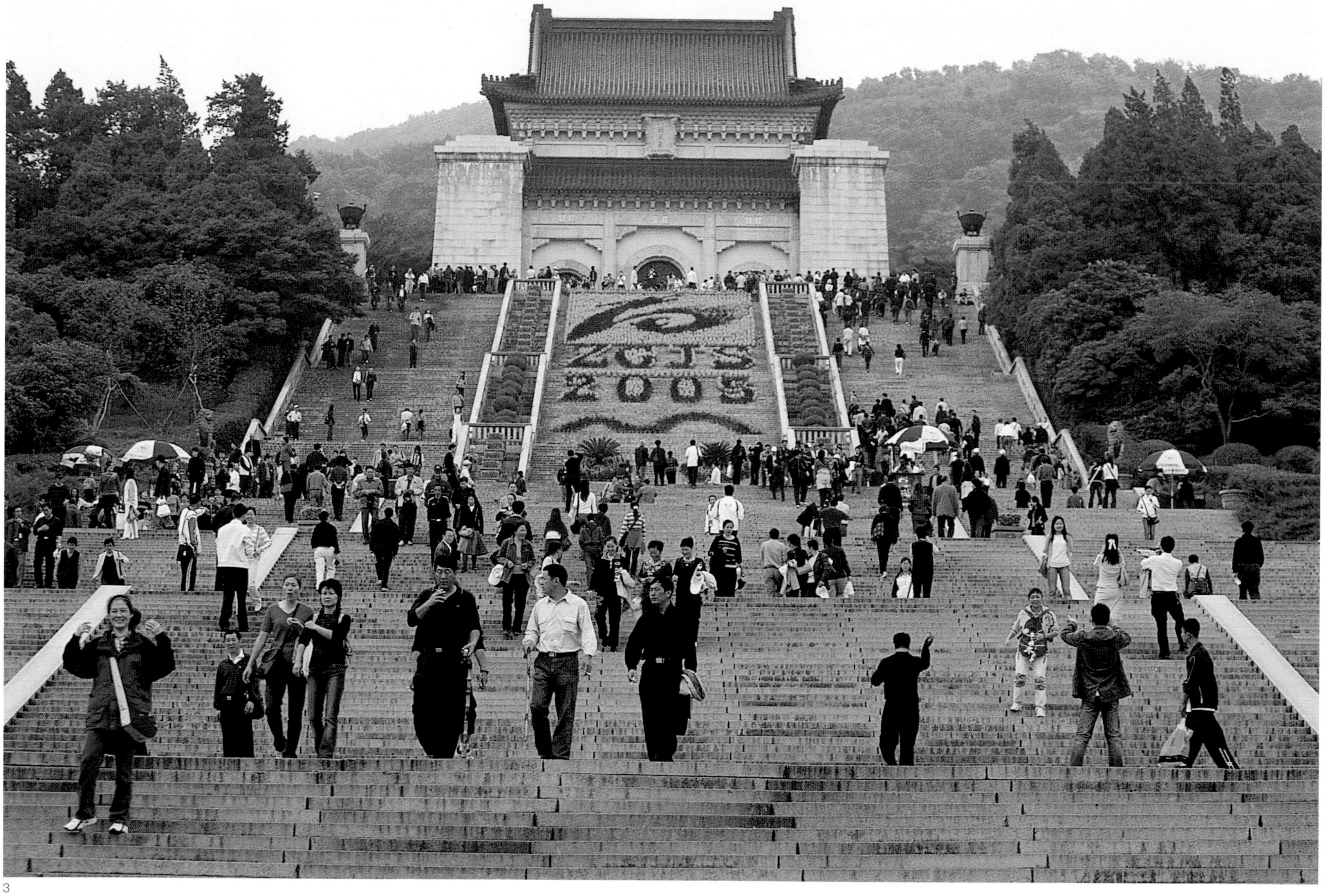

3

MEMORIALS OF COURAGE AND SHAME

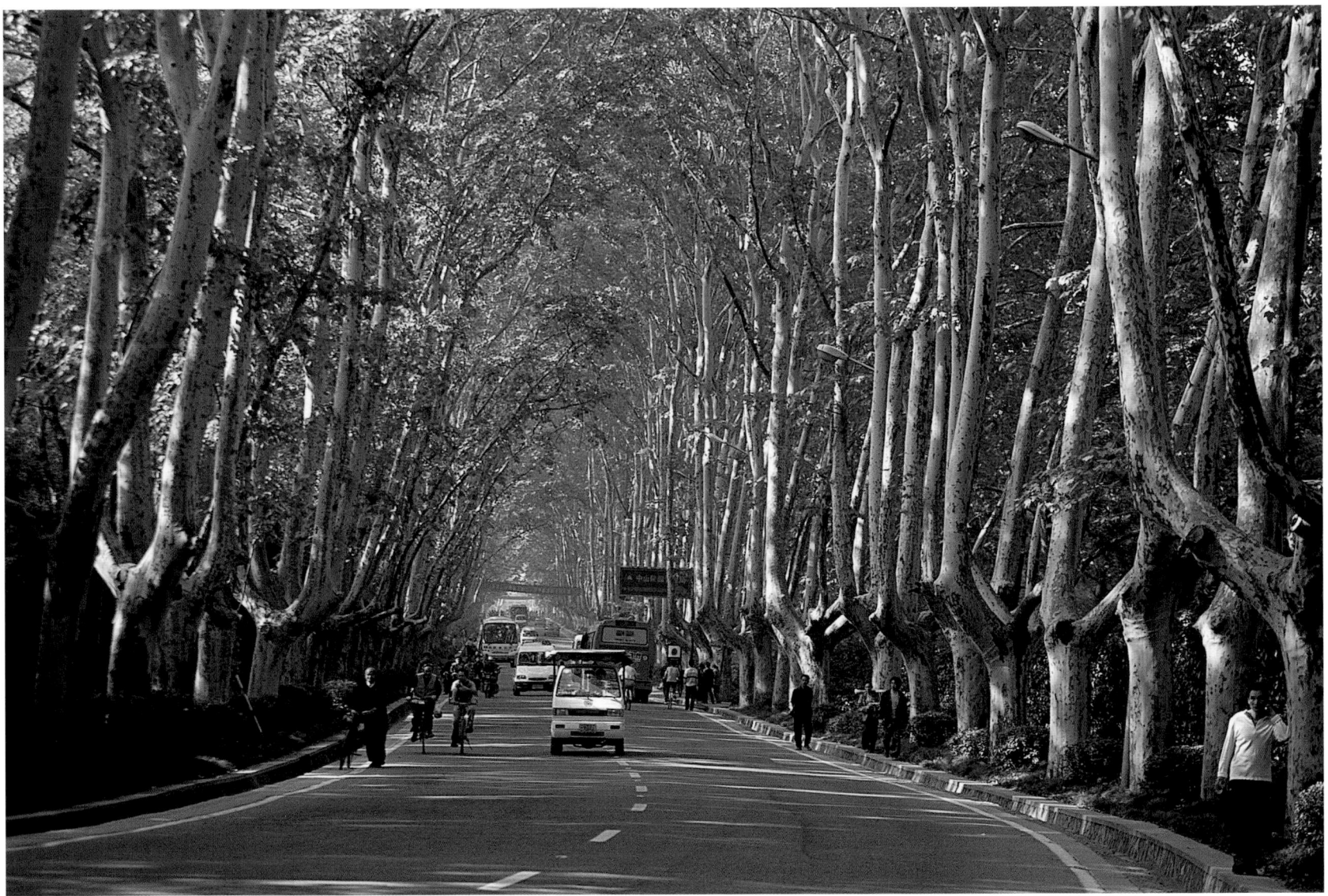

4

ON 10TH OCTOBER 1911, Nan'jing became the capital of the Republic of China when a provisional government of disparate anti-Qing forces was formed with Dr Sun Yat'sen (alias Sun Zhong'shan) as its president. As author of the *Three People's Principles* – Nationalism, Democracy and Equality for the People, which became the ideological pillar and battle cry for the revolution, Sun is revered by both Communists and Republicans as the Father of Modern China. He died in 1925 without coming close to achieving any of his three guiding principles for the new nation. Millions of tourists and pilgrims each year travel the [4] Chinese plane tree-lined avenue to the Sun Yat'sen Mausoleum, where [3] a monumental staircase leads up to Zhong'shan Ling (Middle Mountain Mausoleum). Of all the atrocities committed by the Japanese army in China, the 'Rape of Nan'jing' will always stand out as one of the most shameful episodes of the invasion. [1] [2] The Memorial Hall of the Nan'jing Massacre commemorates the 300,000 defenseless victims who, abandoned by their fleeing government, were slaughtered during a six-week bloodbath in 1937.

ON THE WATERFRONT

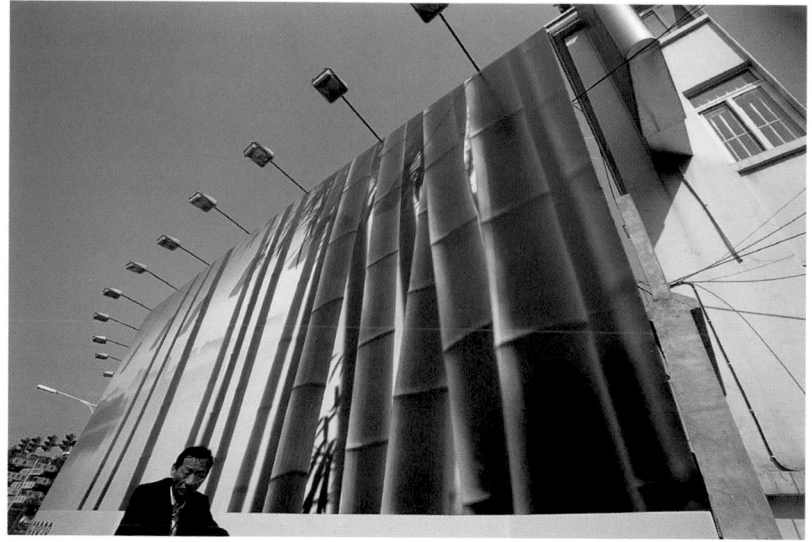

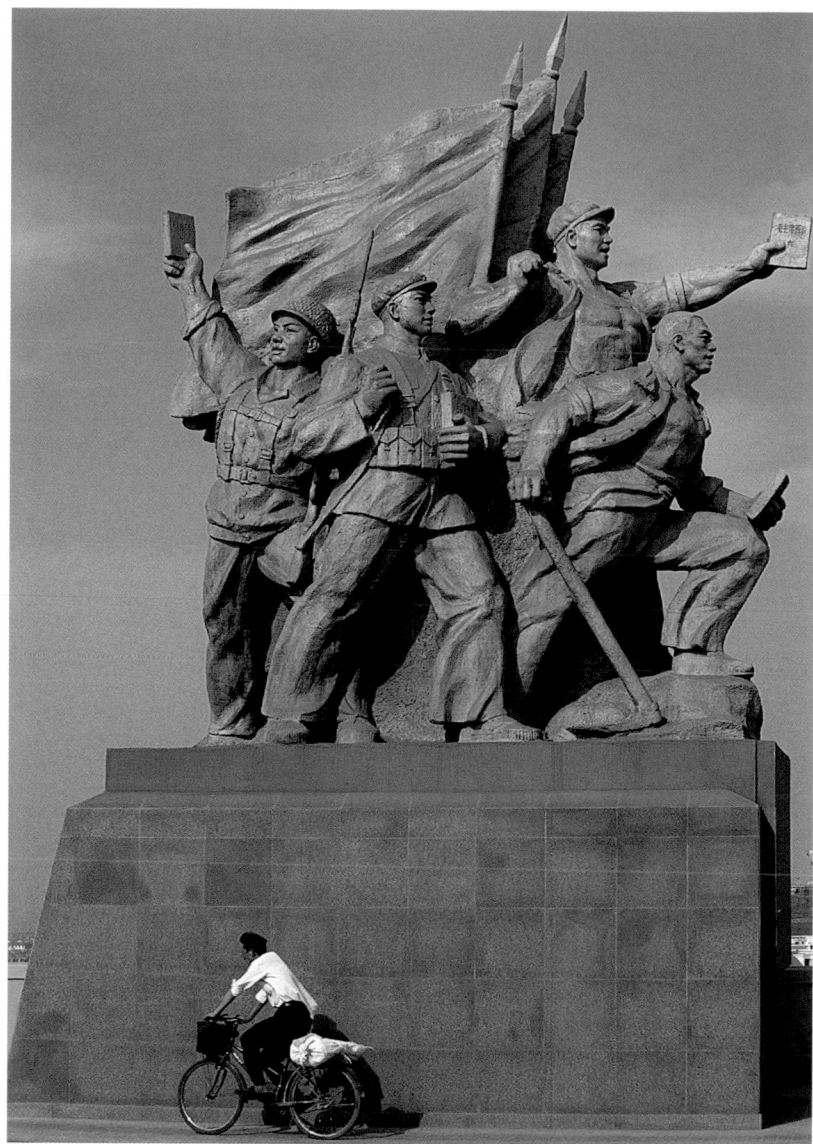

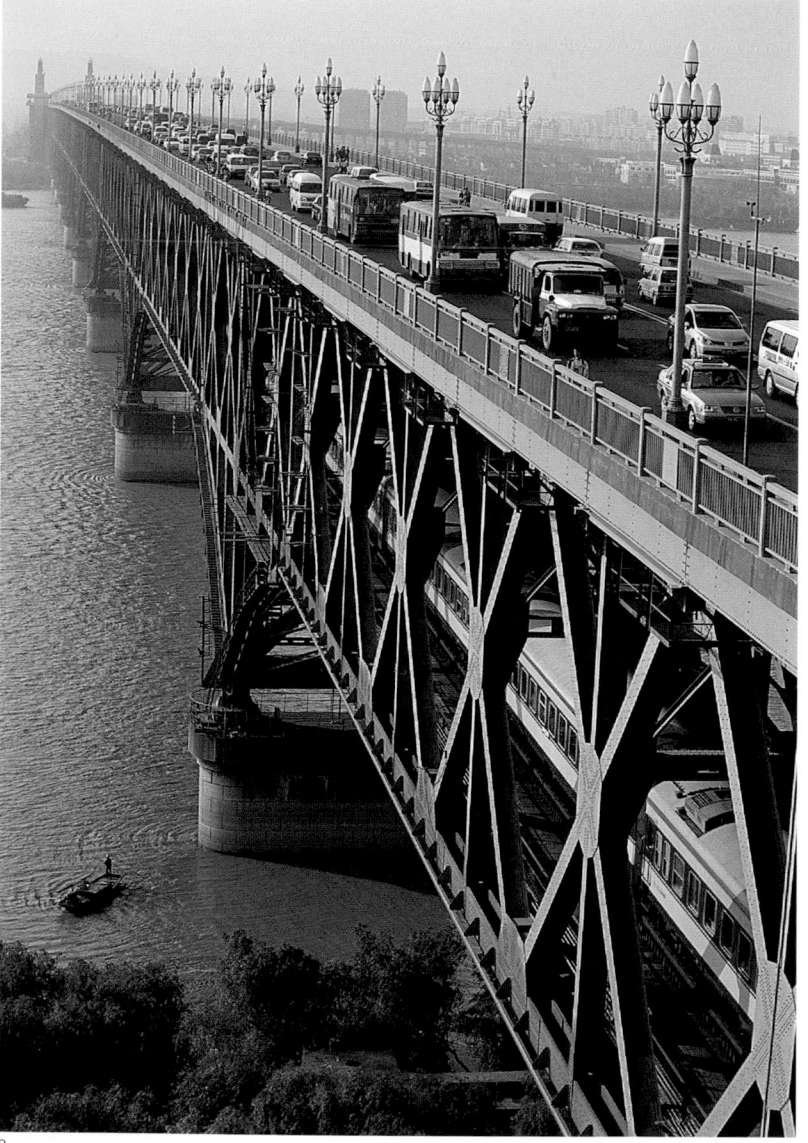

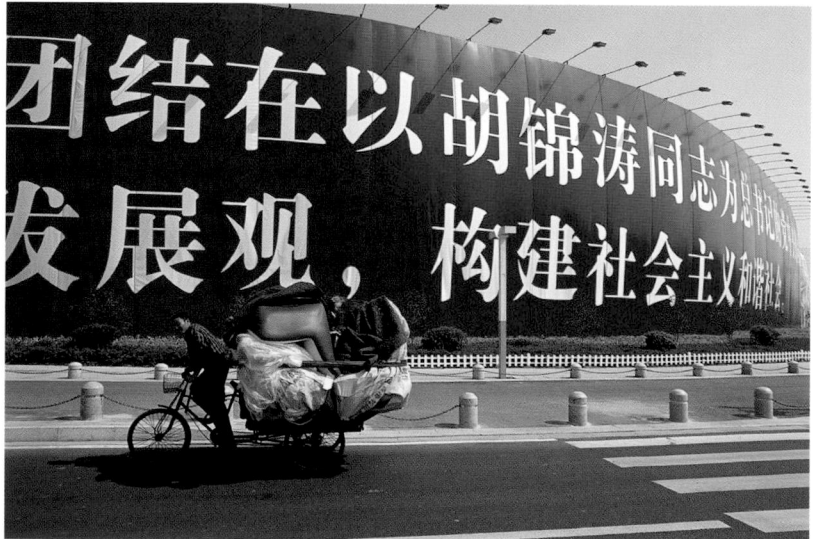

THE SOUTHERN CAPITAL

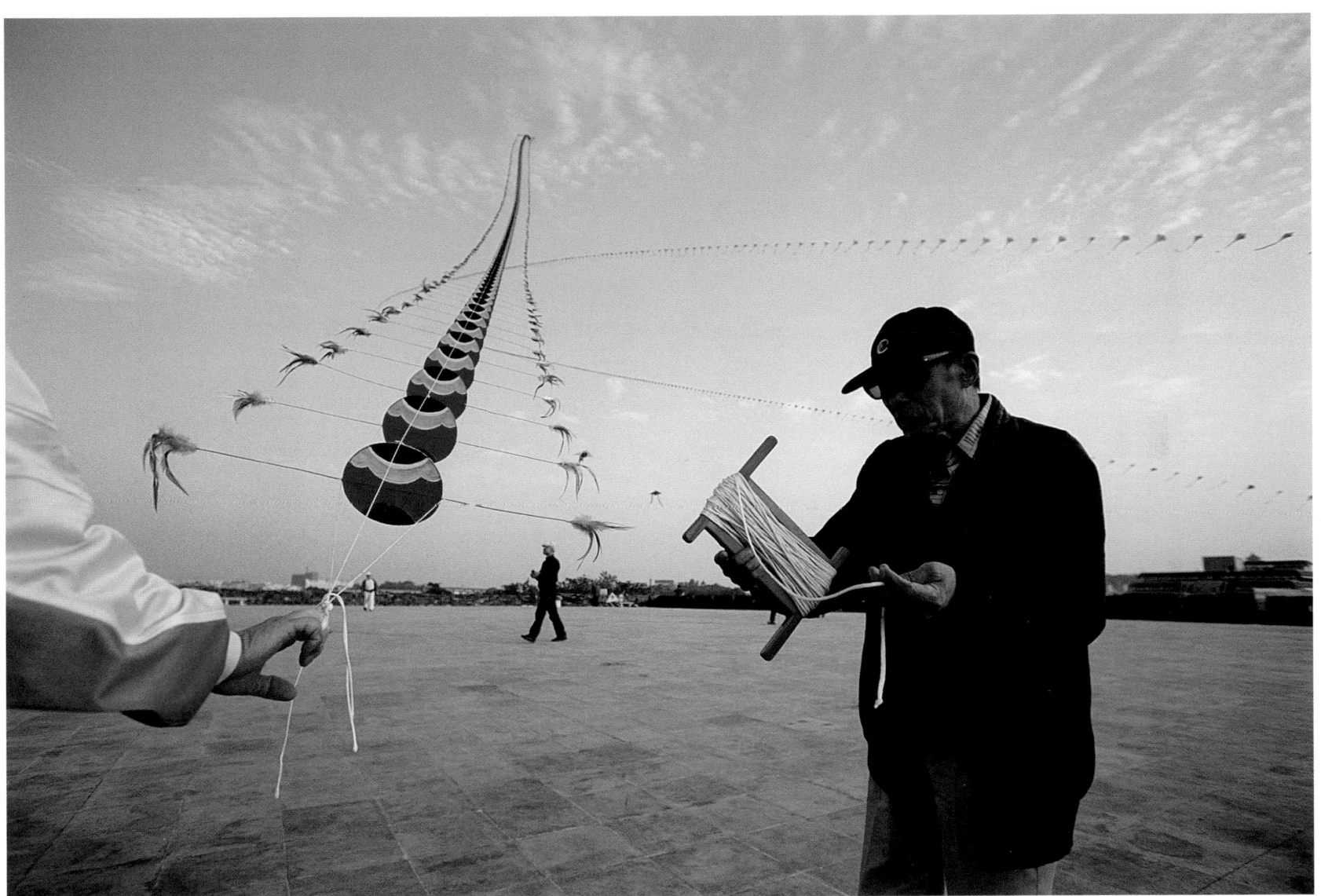

5

APART FROM ITS HEYDAY between 1356 and 1420, when it served as the Ming Dynasty's inaugural capital, Nan'jing's history since the time of the Warring States (453–221 BCE) has been a series of tragic encounters with conquering armies and natural disasters. The 1842 Treaty of Nan'jing that ceded Hong Kong to Britain opened the door to a century of foreign incursions and internal chaos. After 1949 the city's strategic location on the lower reaches of the Yang'tze River led the communist government to turn Nan'jing into one of the country's most important industrial and transportation centres. The Soviet engineers who originally designed [2] [3] the Yang'tze River Bridge left with the blueprints when relations between the two communist giants soured in the 1960s. Completion of the bridge by Chinese engineers became an important propaganda tool and symbol of self-reliance for the new Red China. Propaganda remains an important part of life in the city, whether it is [1] selling real estate or [4] slogans of President Hu Jin'tao's 'Harmonious Society' campaign. [5] Nan'jing residents flying kites on top of Zhong'hua Gate.

ON THE WATERFRONT

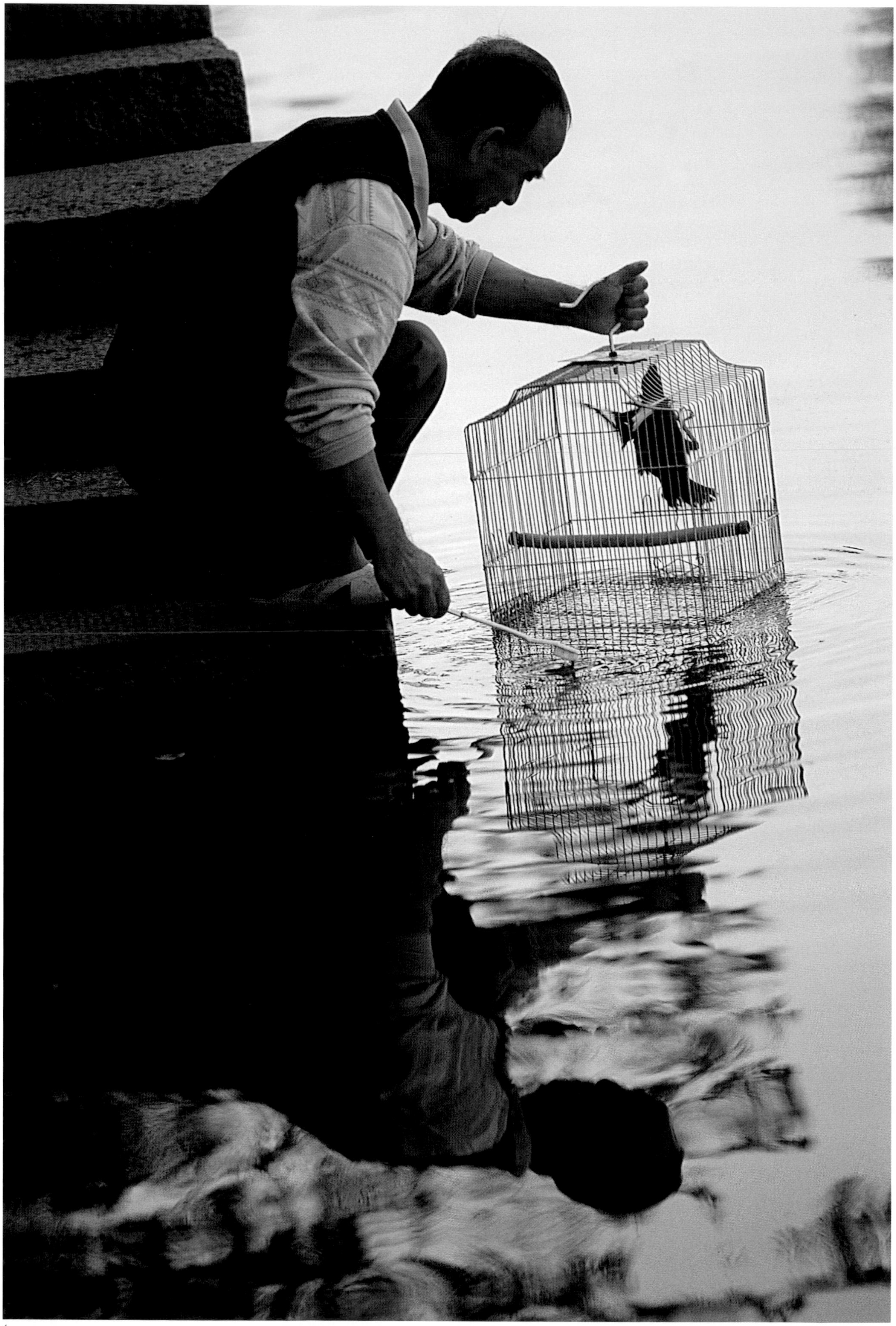

1

ANOTHER VENICE OF THE ORIENT

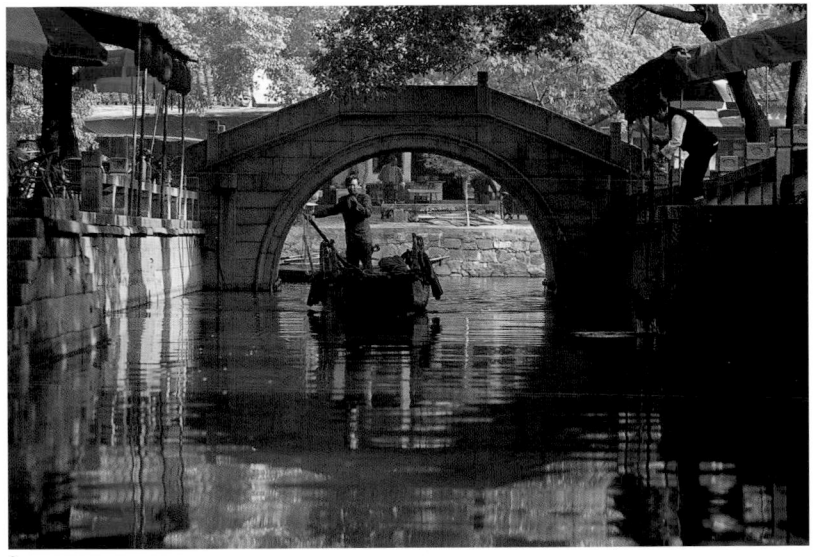

2

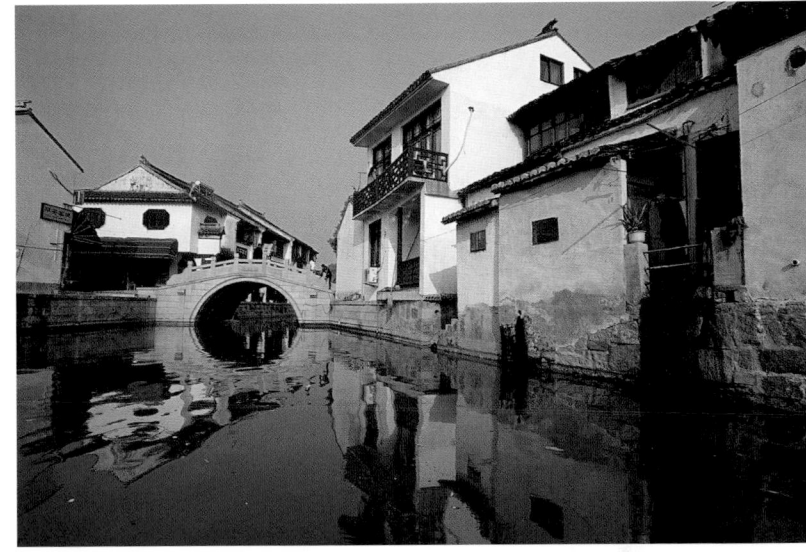

3

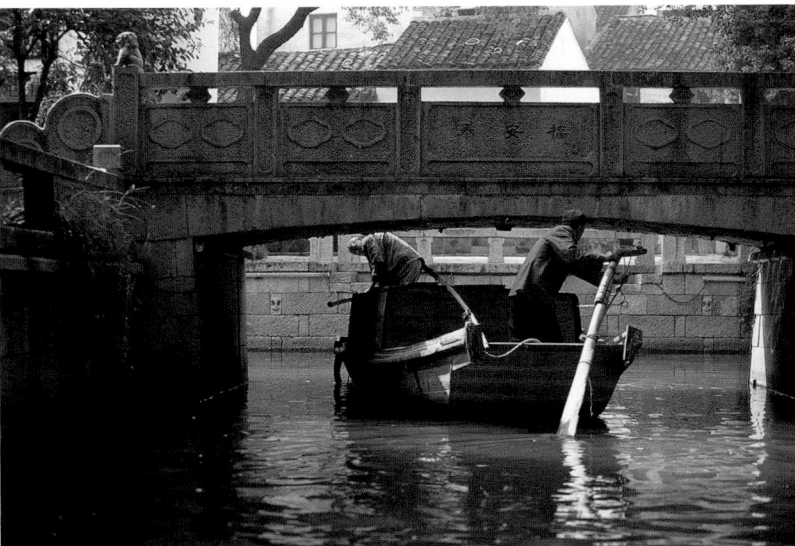

4

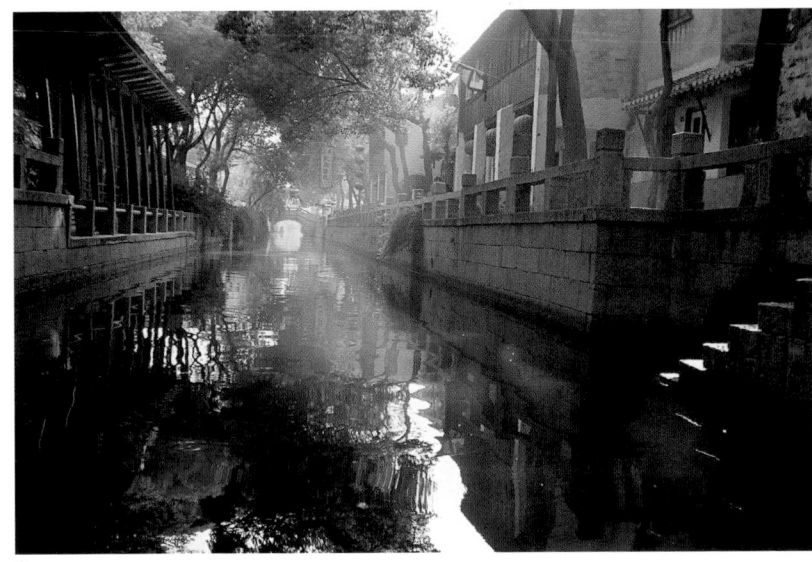

5

THE REGION AROUND SU'ZHOU along the tributaries of the Grand Canal is famous for its scenic 'water towns'. These communities, built around narrow waterways connected by ancient bridges, once served as distribution hubs between the main trade route and the interior. With the surge in domestic tourism, local governments are rushing to clean up and 'develop' these long-neglected villages, all vying for the title of Venice of the Orient. Perhaps predictably, in the haste to cash in on the tourist dollar most of the once-sleepy towns have been overdeveloped and turned into gaudy amusement parks. One exception is the thousand-year-old village of Tong'li, which manages to retain some of the romance of the bygone era despite being only 18 kilometres (11 miles) from Su'zhou and on the main tourist route. [1] It was a rude awakening for the bird whose owner decided to clean its cage in the canal. [2] [3] [5] At dawn, one can catch a glimpse of the 'authentic' Tong'li before the tour buses arrive. [4] One of the two-man teams charged with keeping the canals spotless.

ON THE WATERFRONT

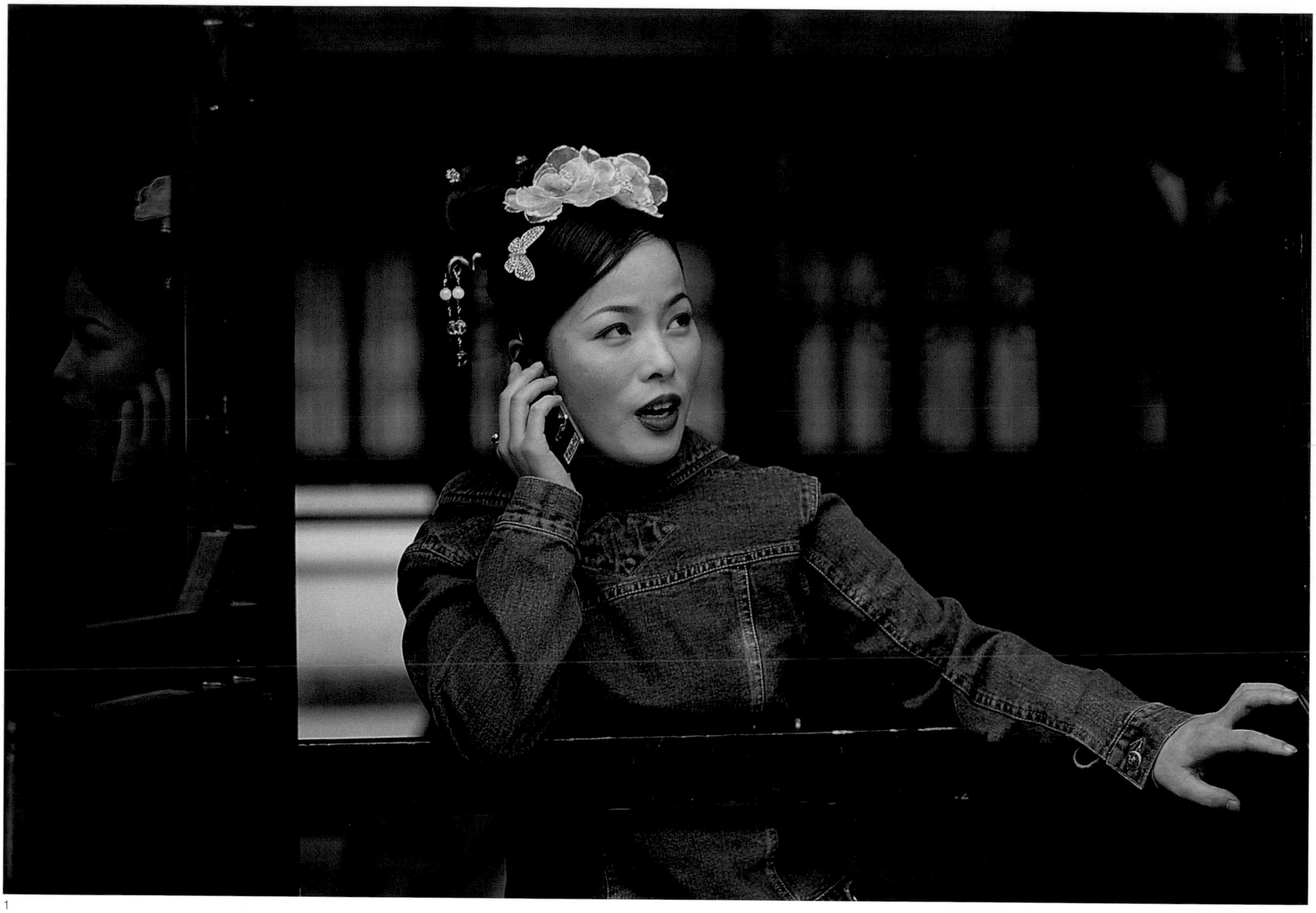

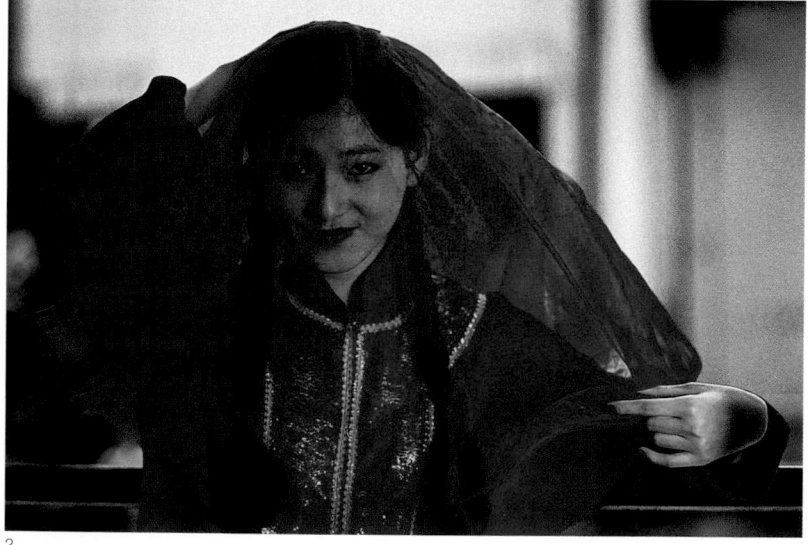

"PARADISE IS IN HEAVEN, ON EARTH WE HAVE SU-HANG." So goes the Chinese saying that eulogizes the beauty of Su'zhou and Hang'zhou. Both cities came to prominence in the 7th Century as key trading centres along the Grand Canal. Their fortunes and stature grew through successive dynasties as the capital moved successively northwards away from Xi'an, which increased its reliance on the canal system for providing basic needs. Both cities are important manufacturing centres for high-quality silk and porcelain, but Su'zhou is perhaps best known for its beautiful women and its gardens. Along with the imperial gardens of the Summer Palace and Cheng'de, two of the Four Great Classic Gardens of China are within miles of each other in Su'zhou. In the 'Garden for Lingering In' I found [1] a lovely musician chatting on her mobile phone during a break, and [2] a beautiful model posing for an advertisement in a traditional wedding costume. [4] [5] The Humble Administrator's Garden is an impeccably designed five-hectare compound built around 1513 as a retirement retreat for a Ming Dynasty Imperial Inspector. [3] [6] Aerial views from the top of the North Temple Pagoda, once the tallest tower south of the Yang'tze River.

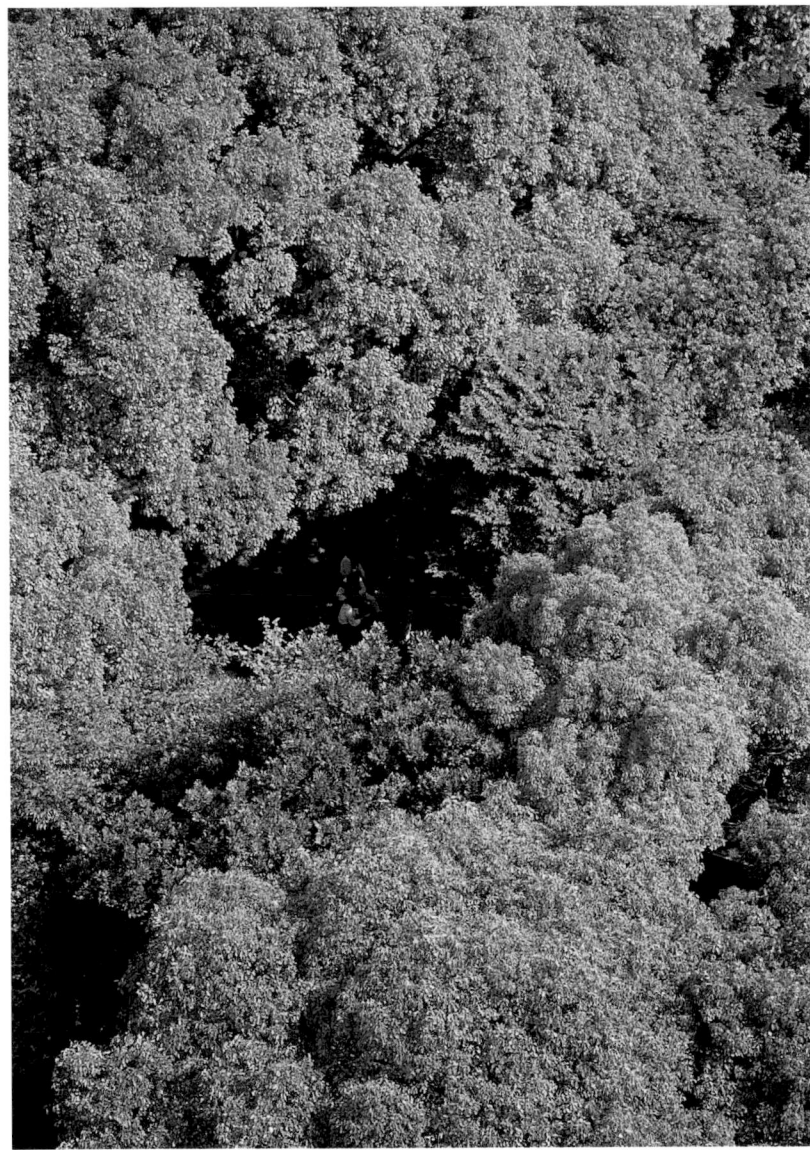

3

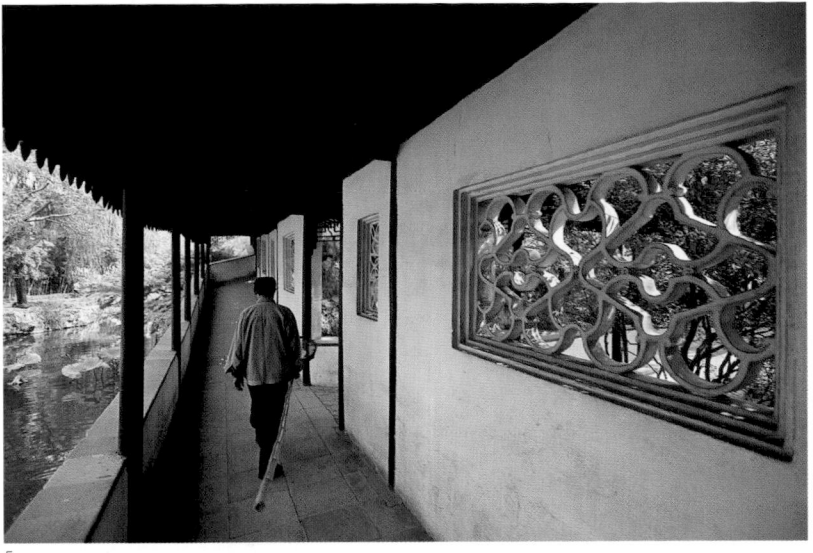

5

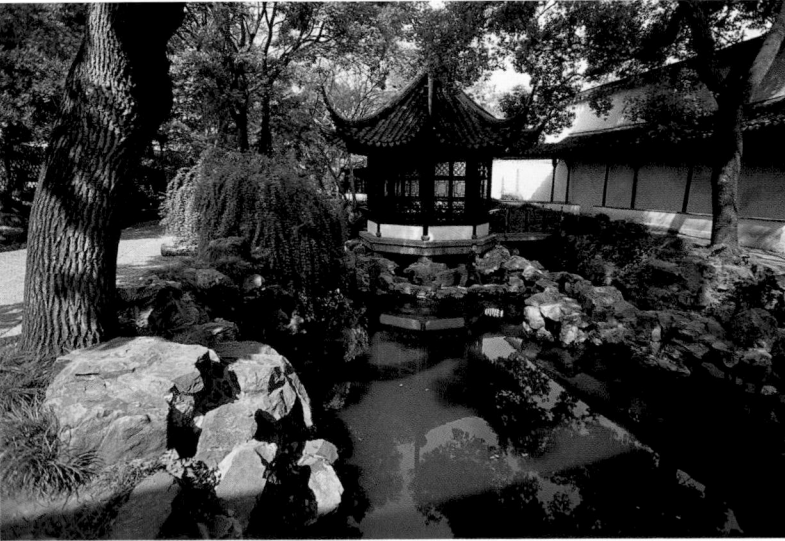

4

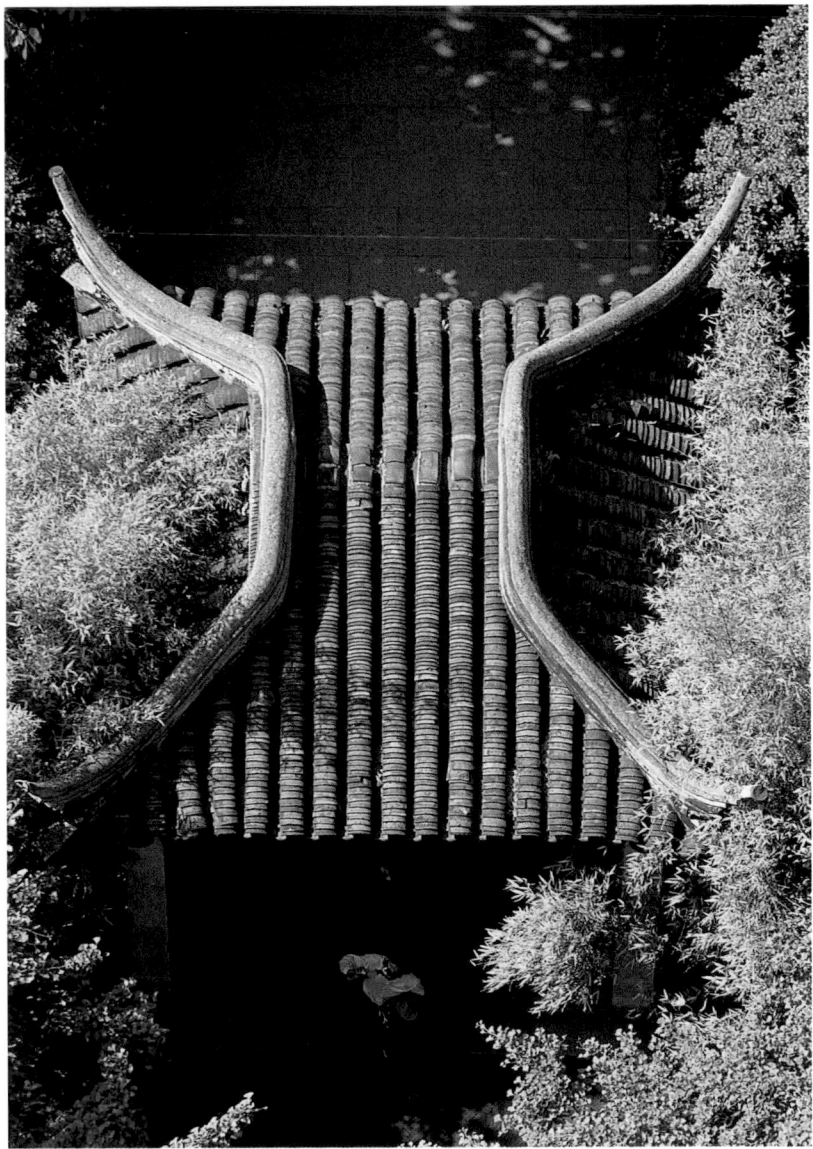

6

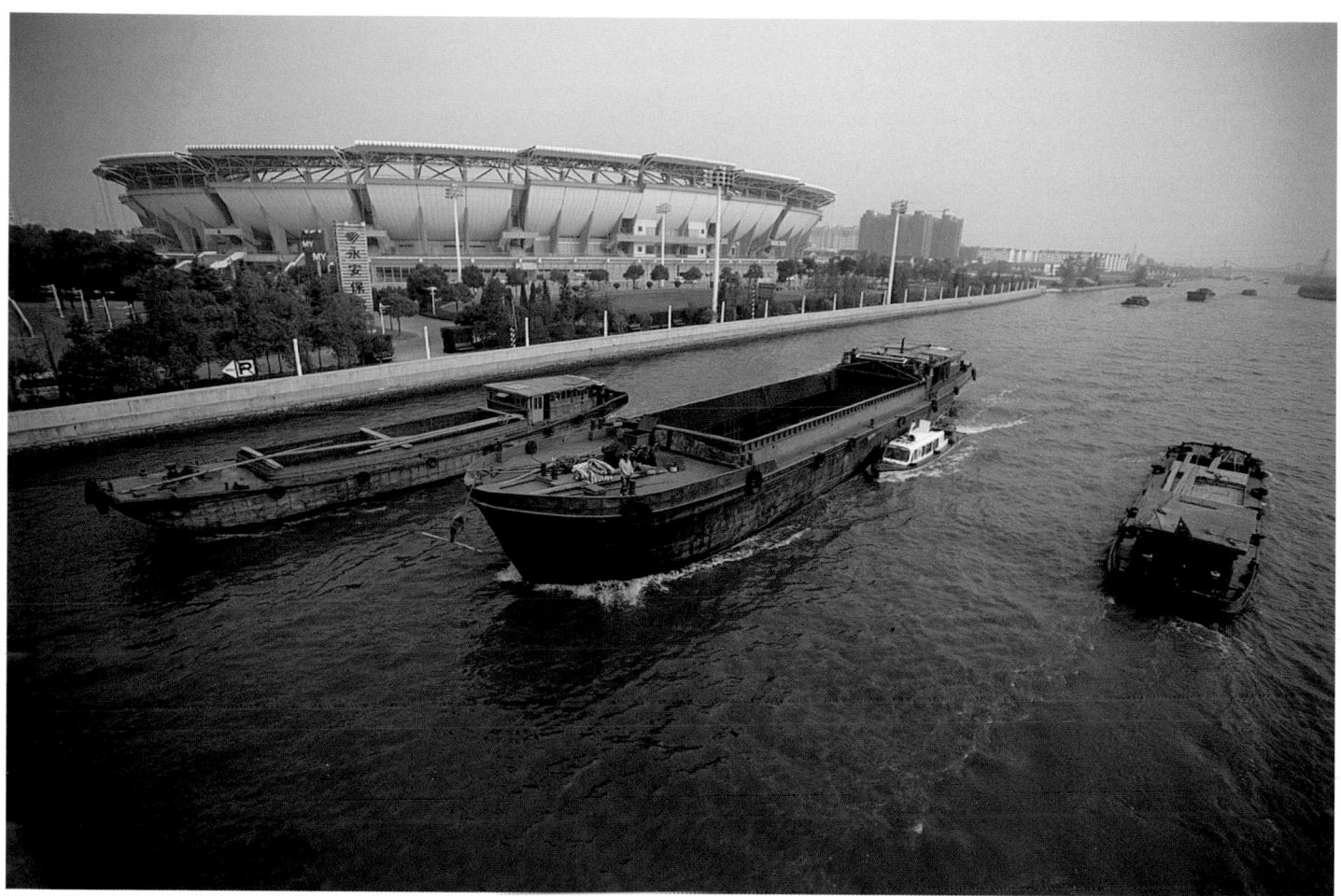

1

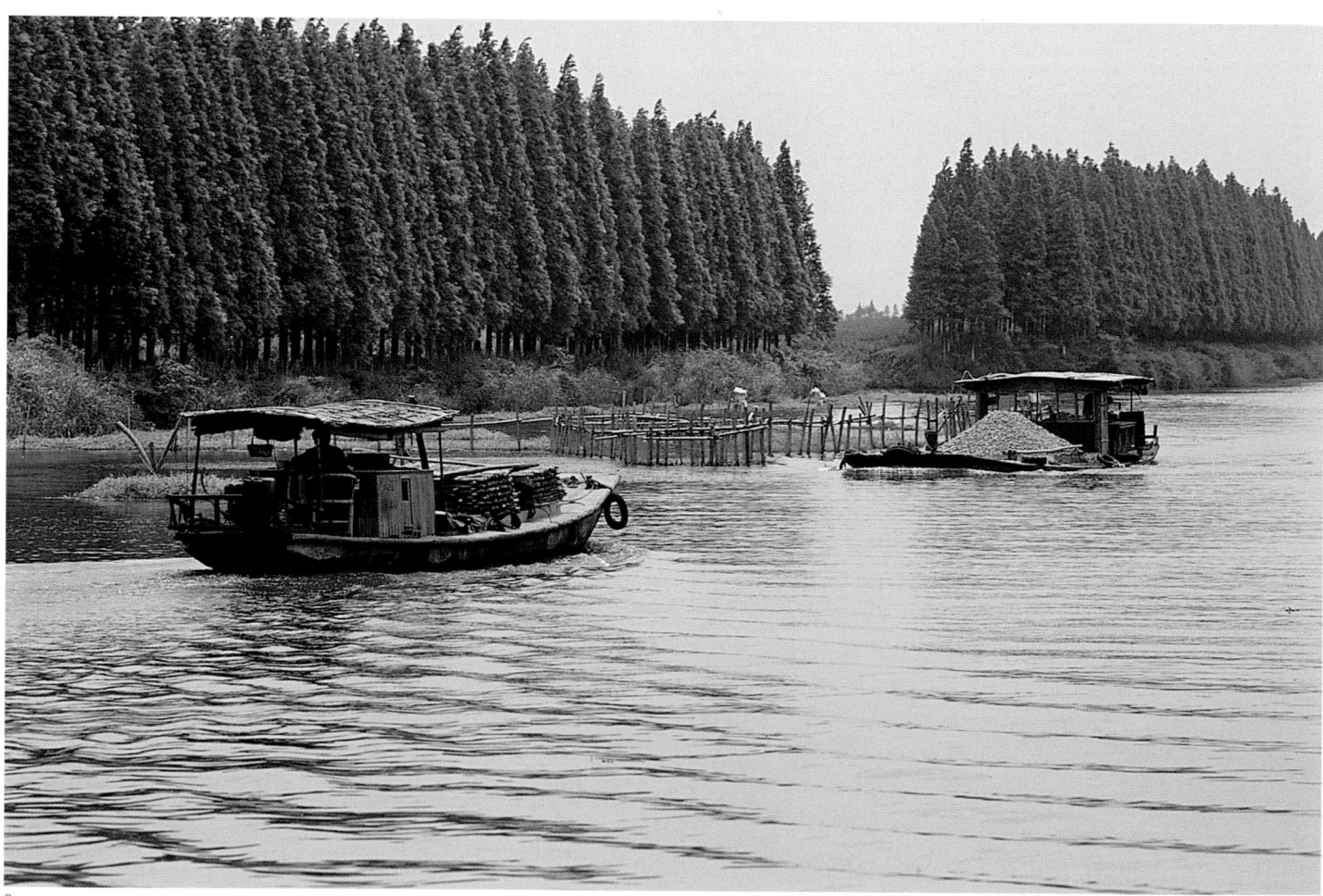

2

THE GRAND CANAL

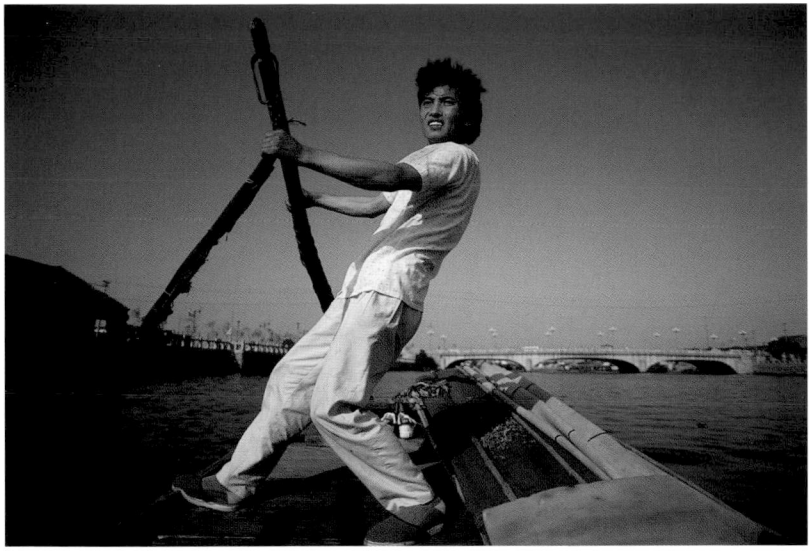

3

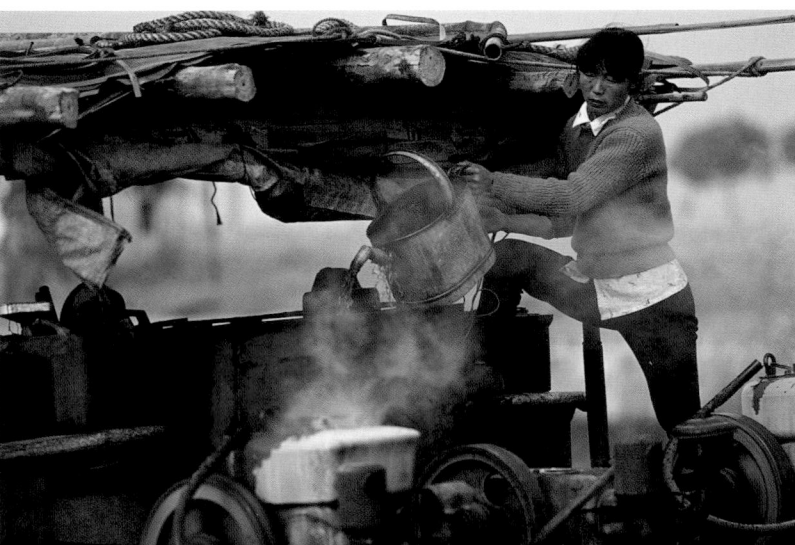

4

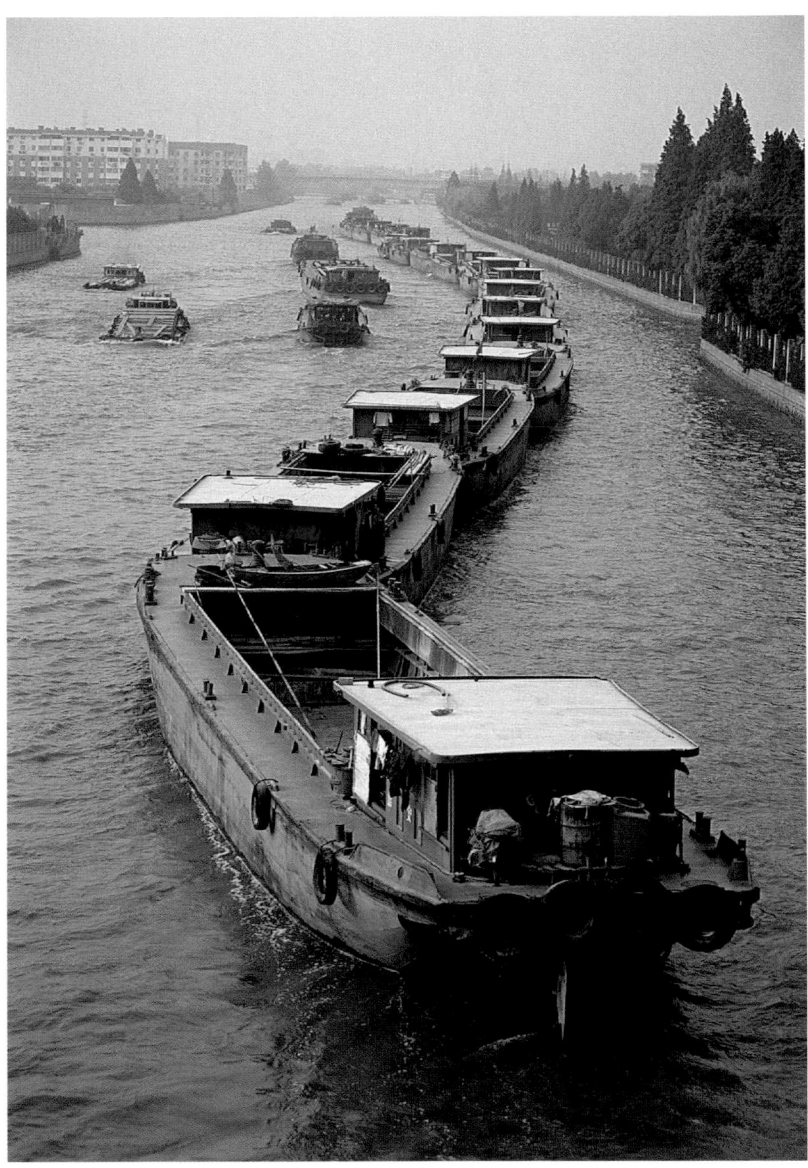

5

THE **DEVELOPMENT AND CONSTRUCTION** of the 1,800-kilometre (1,115-mile) Grand Canal, the largest man-made waterway in the world, took place in three main stages spanning 17 centuries. It began with a 85-kilometre (52-mile) long canal system built for military purposes between 486 and 495 BCE during the tumultuous Spring–Autumn period of the Eastern Chou Dynasty. The main excavation work was done between 605 and 609 CE in the Sui Dynasty, when Emperor Yang'guang is said to have conscripted five million able-bodied men to complete the task of connecting the Yang'tze, Qian'tang'jiang and Huai'he rivers with the Yellow River by linking the lakes and tributaries between them with canals to create a single navigable south-north waterway. Stage three came during the Yuen Dynasty (1271–1368) when the canal was extended north to Bei'jing, connecting the population of Khubilai Khan's new capital to Hang'zhou and the rice-growing region of the Yang'tze River. The southern section of the canal is generally deep, wide and flat and is still very much in use. [1] [5] Canal traffic cuts through the middle of Su'zhou's new city on its way south [2] [3] [4] to Hang'zhou.

ON THE WATERFRONT

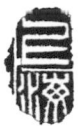

SHANG'HAI MUNICIPALITY

LOCATION
Latitude 31°14'N
Longtitude 121°29'E

AREA 6,341 km² (2,448 sq miles)

GEOGRAPHY Shang'hai's original Pu'xi district is located on the west bank of the Huang'pu River, some 15 km inland from where the Yang'zte River meets the East China Sea. A new financial and administrative centre has been built at Pu'dong on the eastern bank over the past 20 years. The city is low-lying with an average elevation of 4 m above sea level.

CLIMATE Shang'hai has four distinct seasons, with long cool winters and long hot summers. Average January temperatures range between 2°C and 7°C, rising in July to 24–32°C. The lowest recorded temperature is -10°C and the highest is 41°C. Average annual rainfall is around 1,300 mm – 50 per cent of it during the summer typhoon season.

POPULATION 13.52 million (end 2004)

AGRICULTURE Farming in Shang'hai's immediate hinterland is dominated by market gardens producing fresh vegetables and commodities for the city. Other food crops include rice and wheat. Cash crops include cotton and oilseeds. There are also major sea and freshwater fisheries.

MAIN INDUSTRIES Shang'hai is China's principal industrial city. Heavy industries include steelworks, shipbuilding, oil and gas, petrochemicals, plastics and machinery. Other sectors include textiles, electronics, electrical and mechanical engineering, aircraft, vehicles, pharmaceuticals and publishing. The trend since the 1980s has been to move away from manufacturing and towards non-polluting industries and services.

ANNUAL PER CAPITA INCOME (2005)
Disposable income of urban residents:
RMB 18,645 (US$2,326)
Net income of rural residents:
RMB 8,342 (US$1.041)

HISTORICAL AND SCENIC SITES
The Bund, Long'hua Temple, Yu'yuan Gardens, Jade Buddha Temple, Jing An Temple, Lu Xun Memorial, the houses of Sun Yat'sen, Chiang Kai-shek and Qing Dynasty Viceroy General Li Hong'zhang, rivertowns of Zhu'jia'jiao and Zhou'shi.

FOOD Shang'hai's role as a port and commercial centre has created a cuisine that blends styles from throughout China and beyond. Local distinctive features include the widespread use of alcohol and sugar in cooking, notably in 'drunken' seafoods and the liberal use of sweetened soy sauce. Notable dishes include beggar's chicken, soup dumplings, Ten Varieties hotpot, soused shrimp, '1,000-year-old' eggs and steamed buns.

[RIGHT] The Science Museum in Shang'hai.

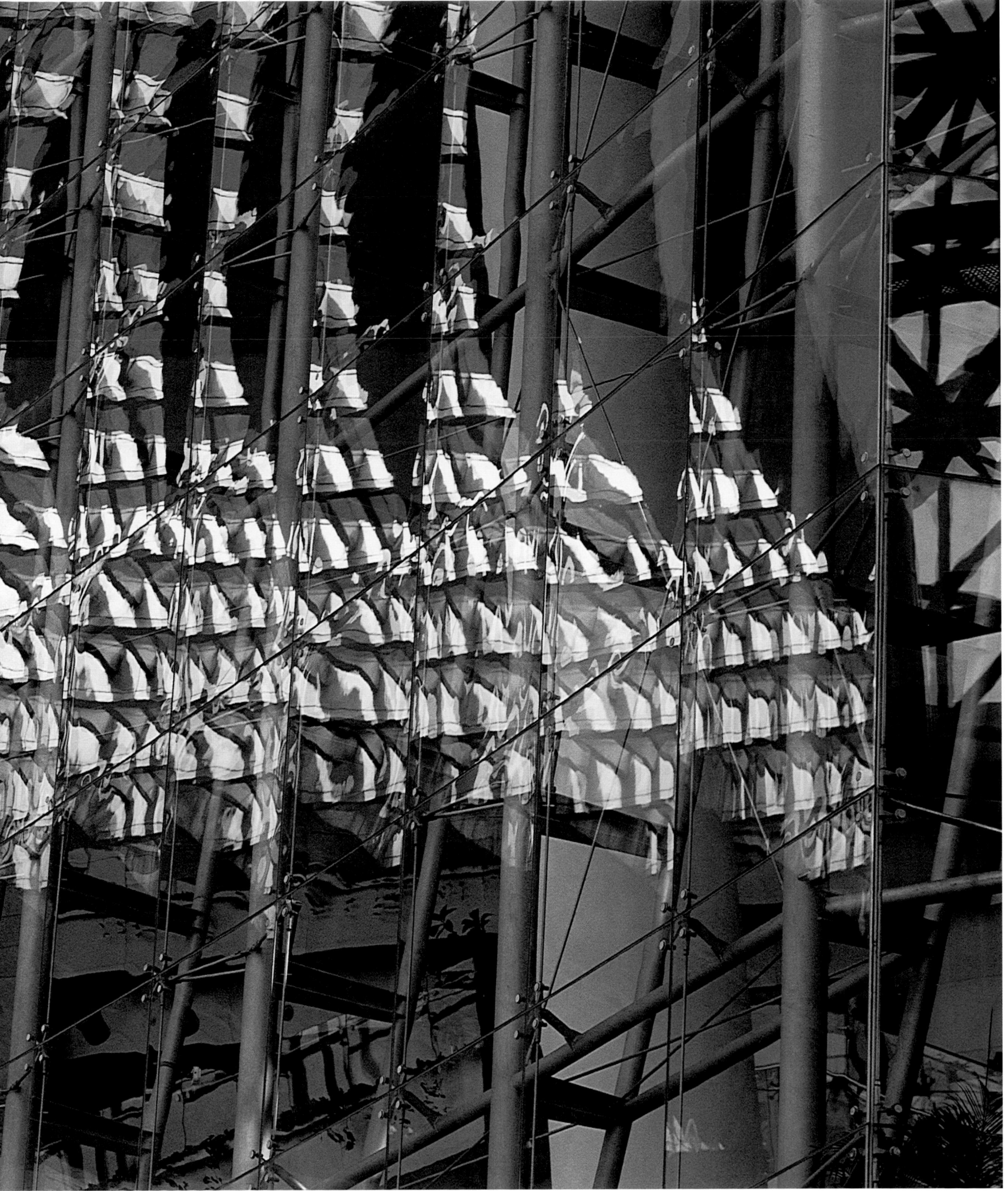

1

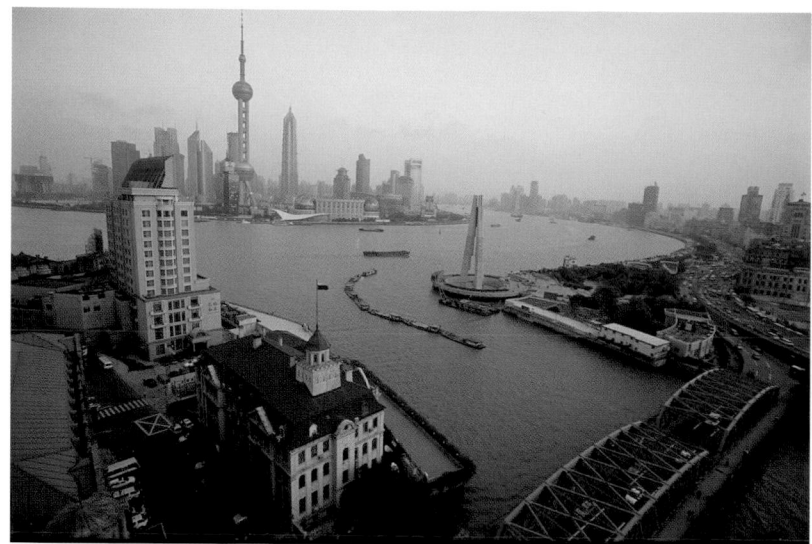

2

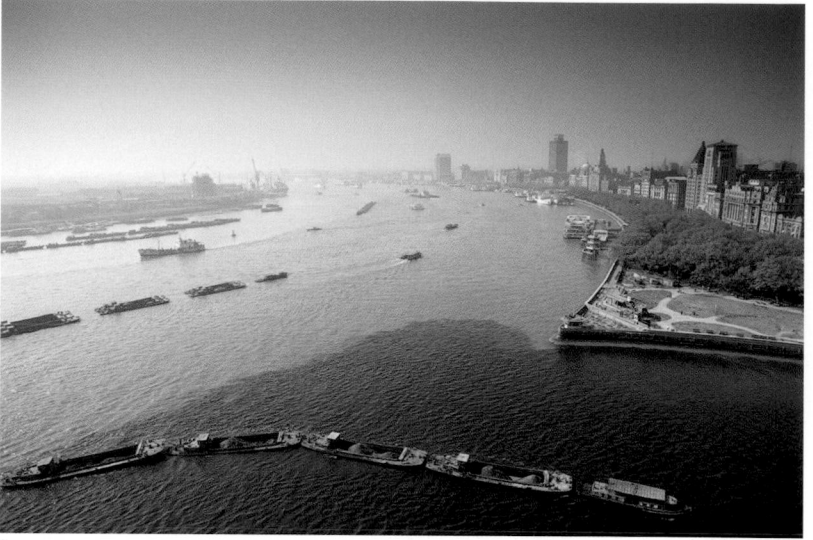

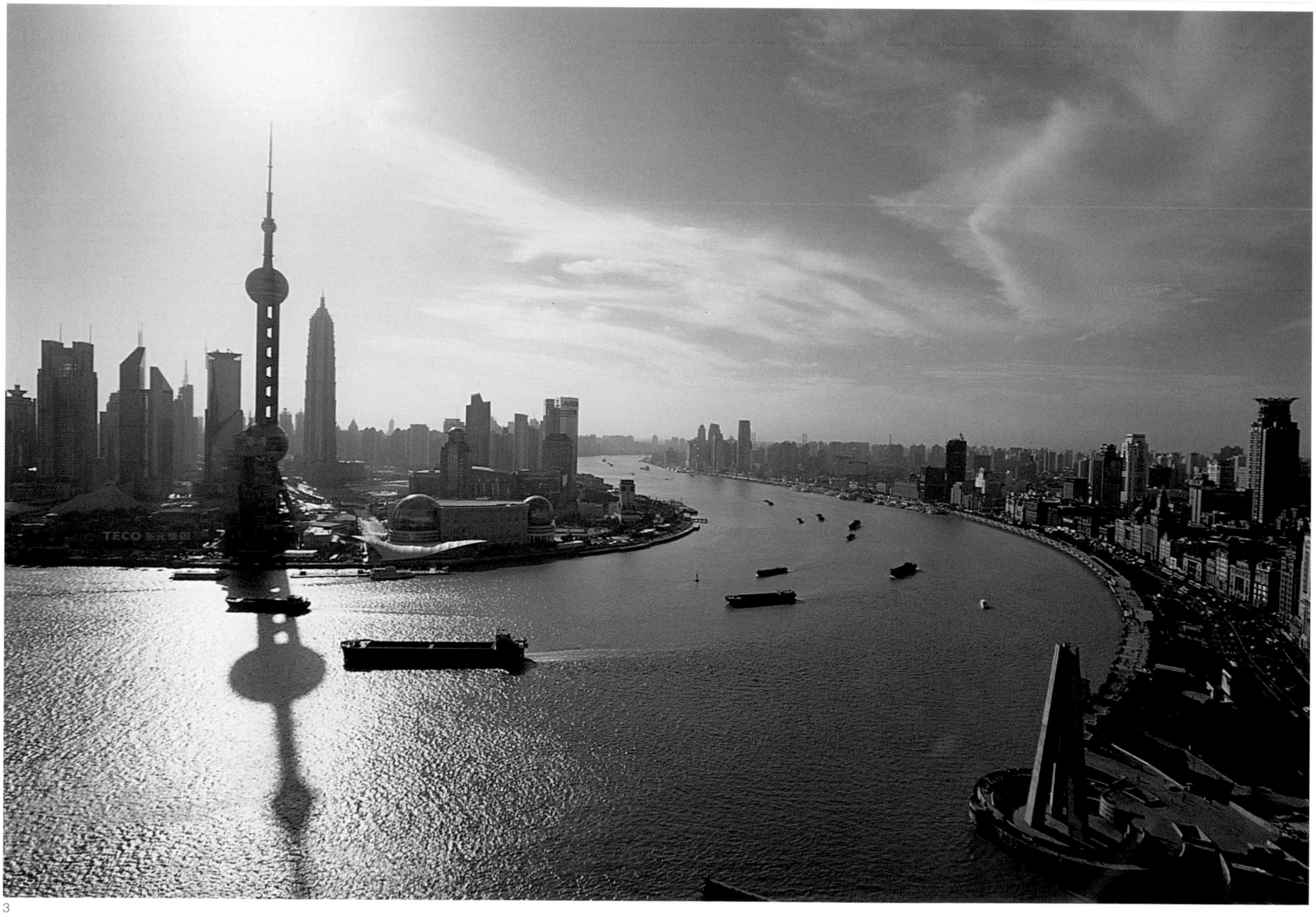

3

HUANG'PU'JIANG RIVER

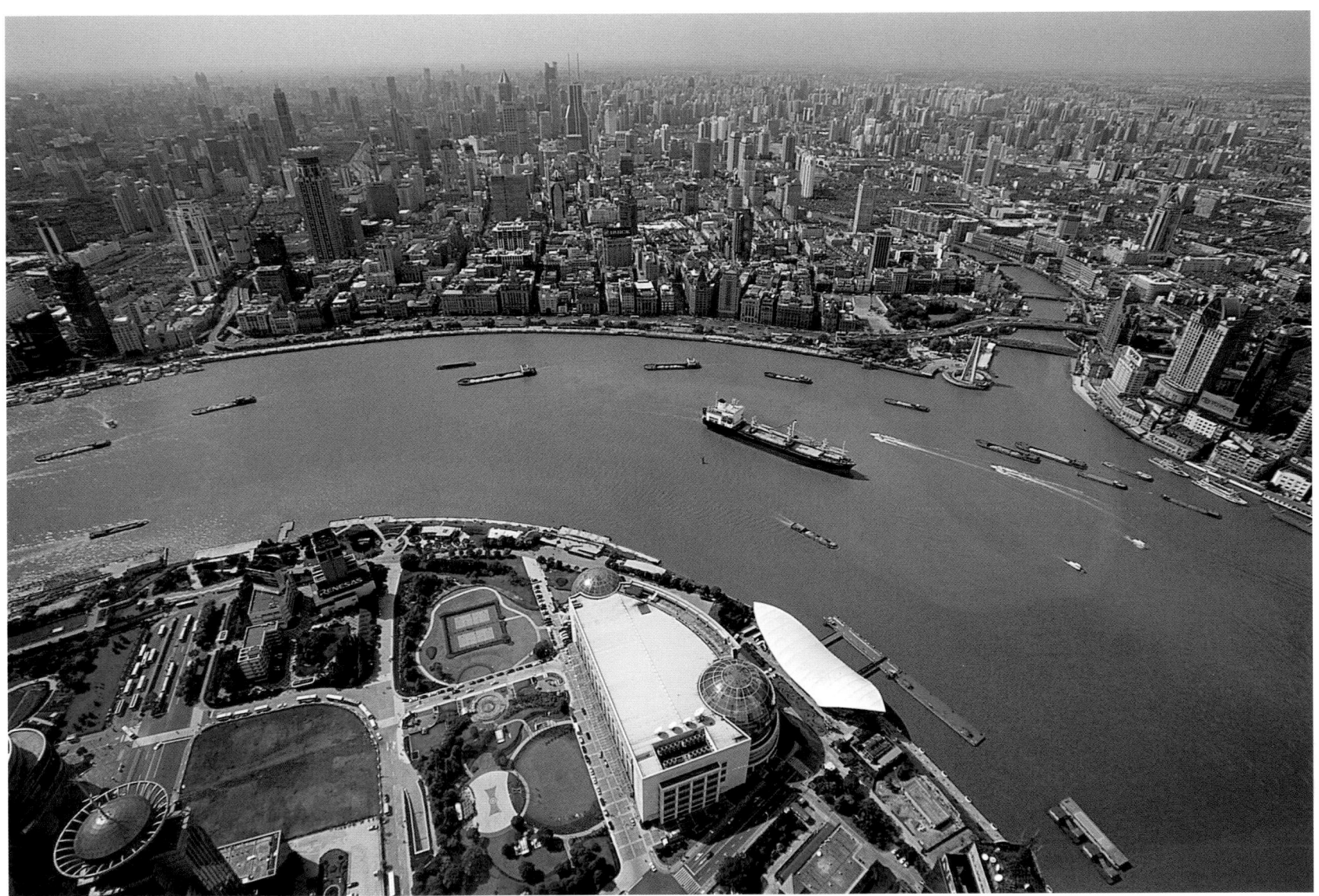

4

THE NAME SHANG'HAI ZHEN, meaning 'Market-town by the Sea', was first recorded in the Song Dynasty (960–1279), suggesting that Shang'hai may have been 'pushed' inland and away from the coast by centuries of silt deposits in the Yang'tze River delta. Though the city has been a busy port since the 16th Century, primarily as a transshipment hub for trade with Japan, the Shang'hai we now know is an early 20th-century creation hewn from the restless egos of European merchants, and built on fortunes made from trading opium for tea and silk. The city grew up on the west bank of [2] [4] the Huang'pu'jiang River, which originates from the mouth of the Yang'tze River at Wu'song and drains into the East China Sea. With the massive development of Pu'dong (Huang'pu East) Special Economic Zone on the opposite bank in the 1990s, the 114-kilometre (71-mile) waterway has become a main artery of China's foreign trade as Shang'hai steps ahead of Singapore and Rotterdam to become the world's busiest port. [1] [3] The Huang'pu'jiang–Shang'hai skyline in October 2005.

ON THE WATERFRONT

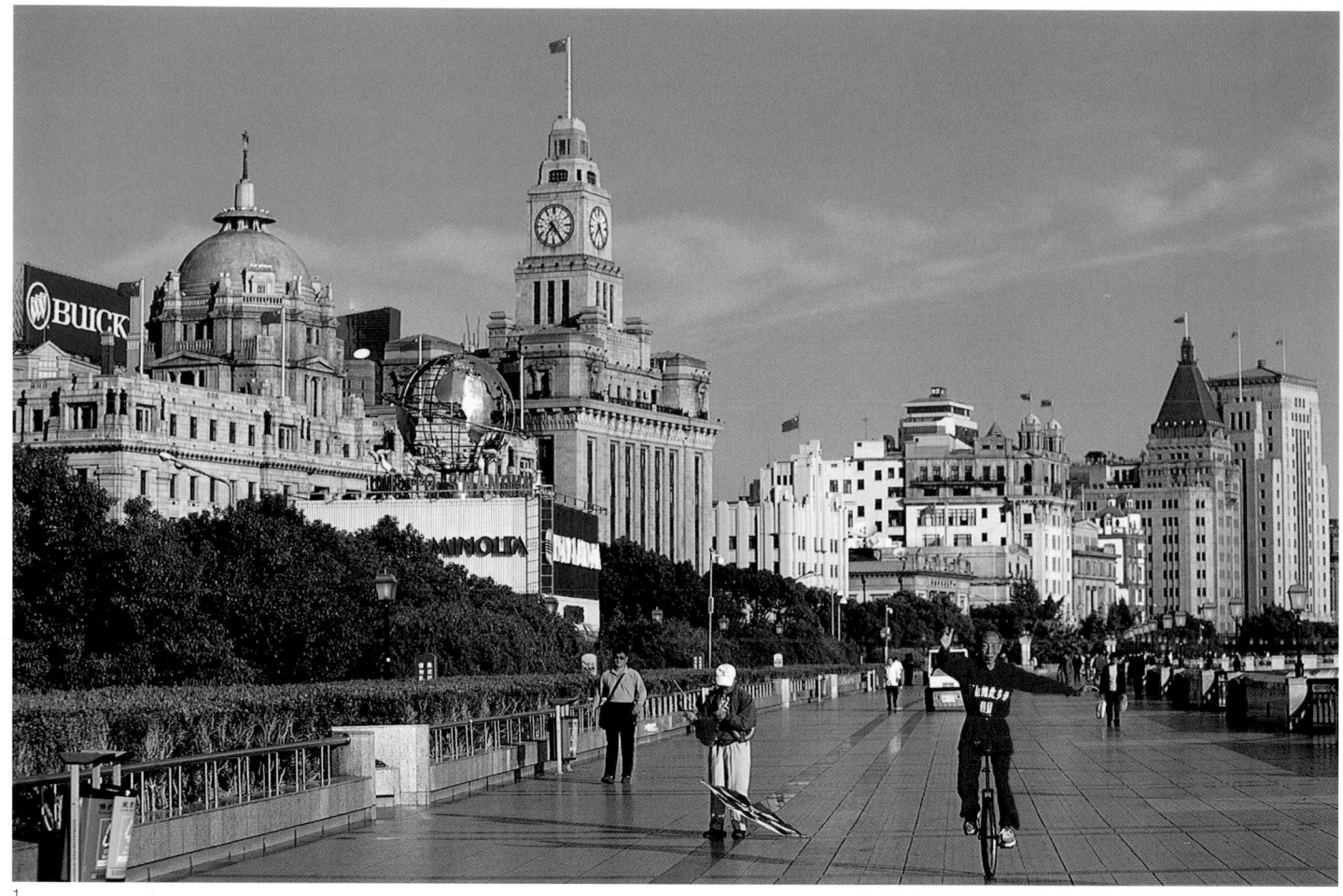

1

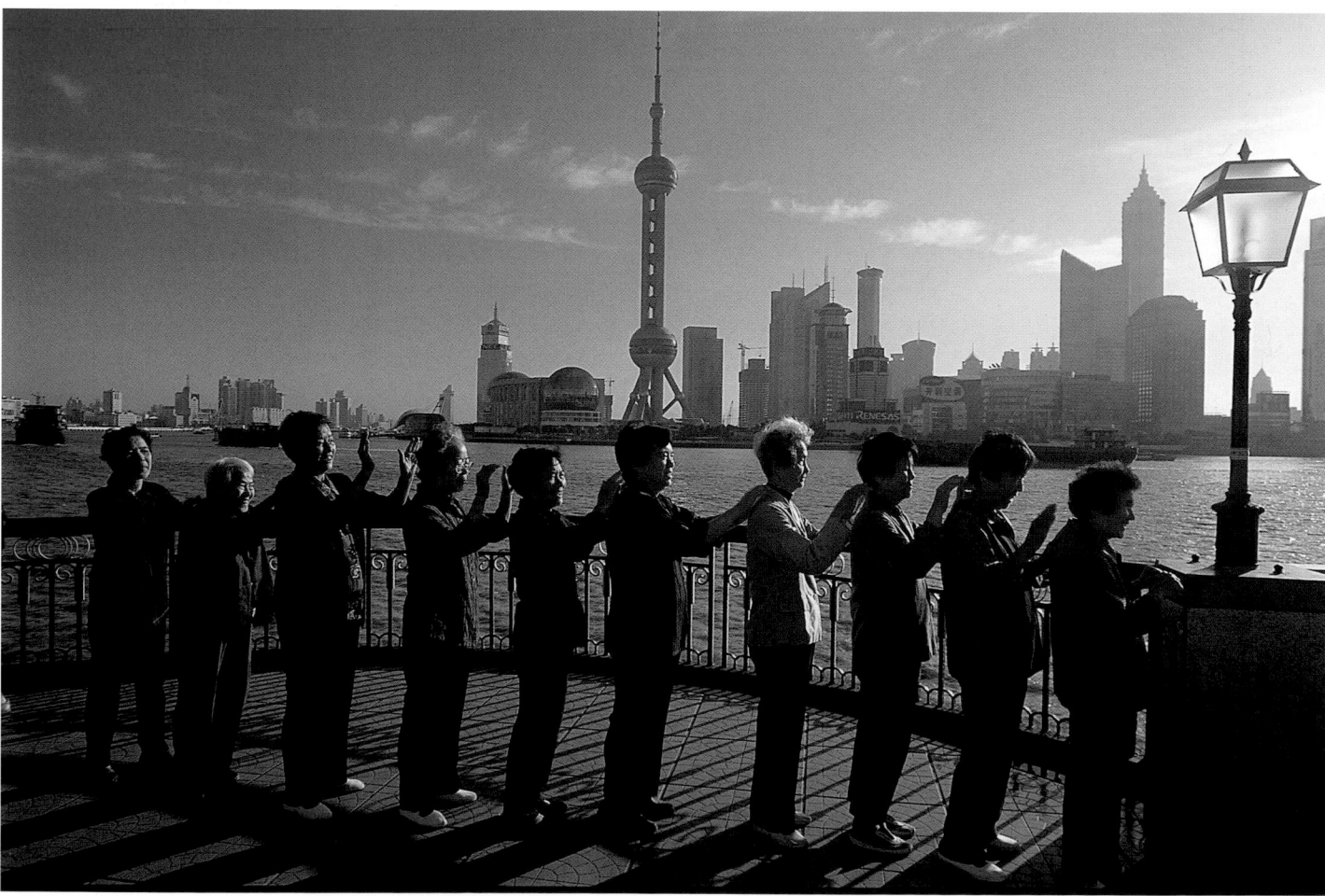

2

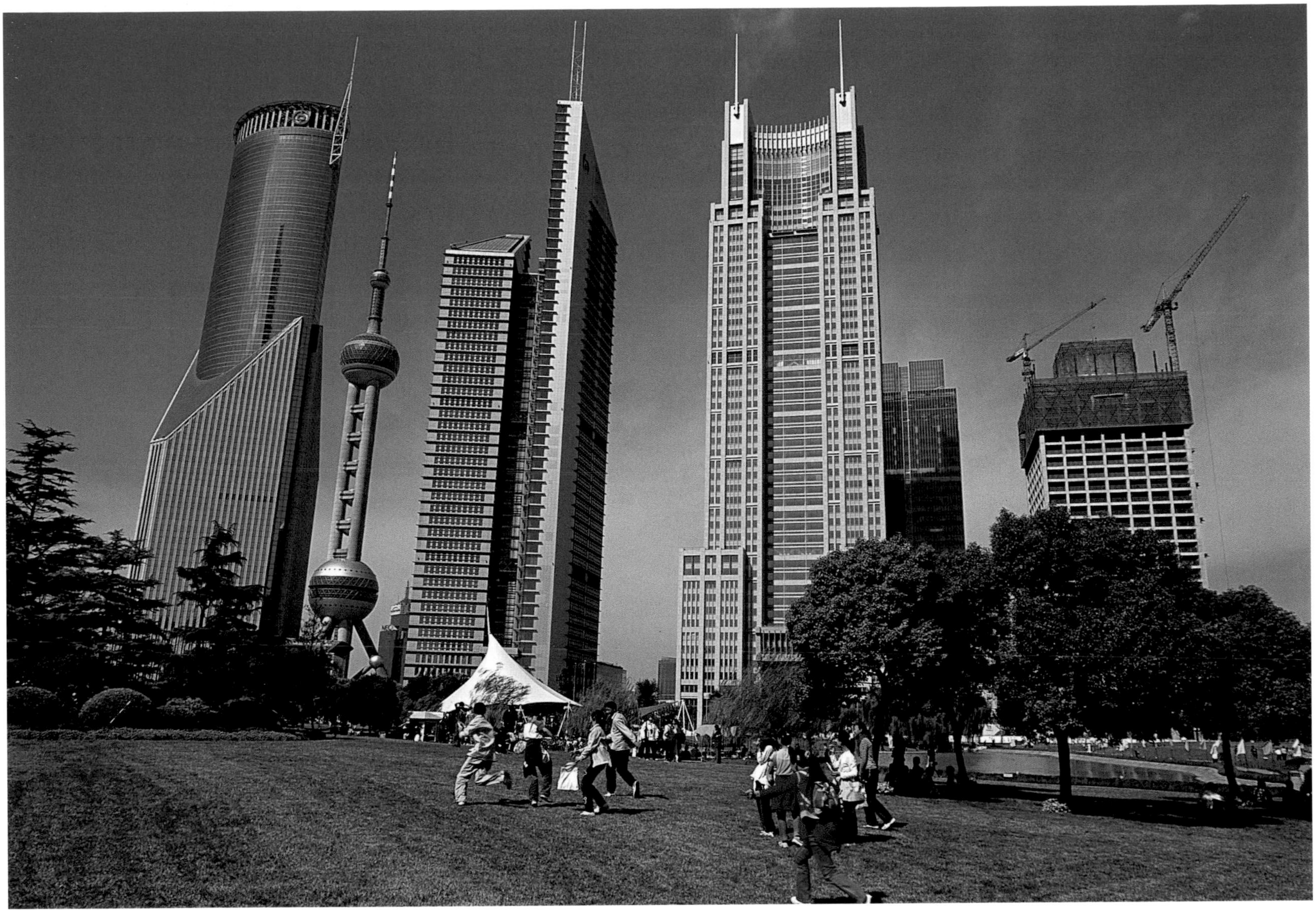

3

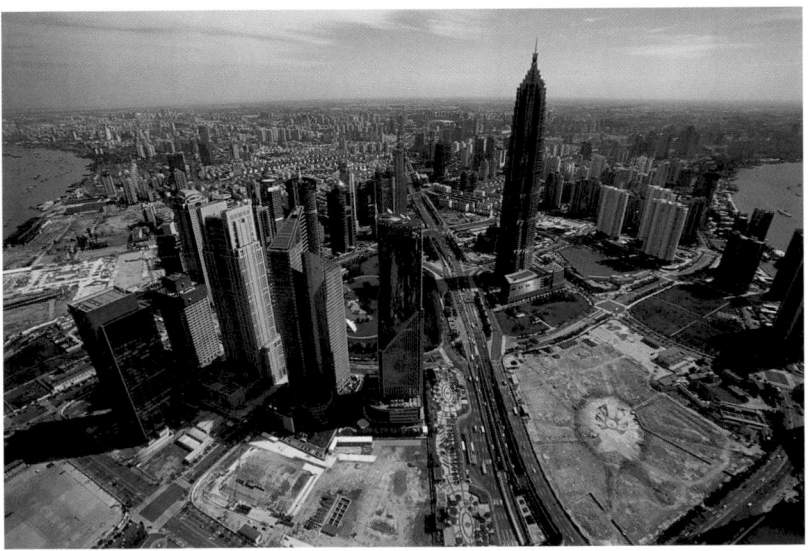

4

SHANG'HAI'S MODERN HISTORY began with the Opium Wars. The British arrived and established their first concession in 1842 after the Treaty of Nan'jing opened Canton, Xia'men, Fu'zhou, Ning'bo and Shang'hai to trade and foreign settlements on Chinese soil. The French, Americans and Japanese soon followed, and together recreated Shang'hai in their own image. By the 1930s, some 60,000 foreigners were living in the International Settlements. The Bund is probably their best creation and possibly the most famous mile-long (1,500-metre) stretch of waterfront property in China. The series of remarkable buildings are monuments to personal ambitions, individual achievements and commercial prowess projected by military might half-way around the world. They form the backdrop to the promenade along the Huang'pu'jiang River where [1] [2] residents gather to exercise at dawn and visitors come to drink in the atmosphere of a bygone era deep into the night. Across the river, [3] the flashy Lui'jia'zui commercial district may have been built with the same restless energy and brash confidence, but it lacks the romance of its older sister. [4] Pu'dong SEZ from the top of the 457-metre (1,500-foot) Oriental Pearl TV Tower.

1

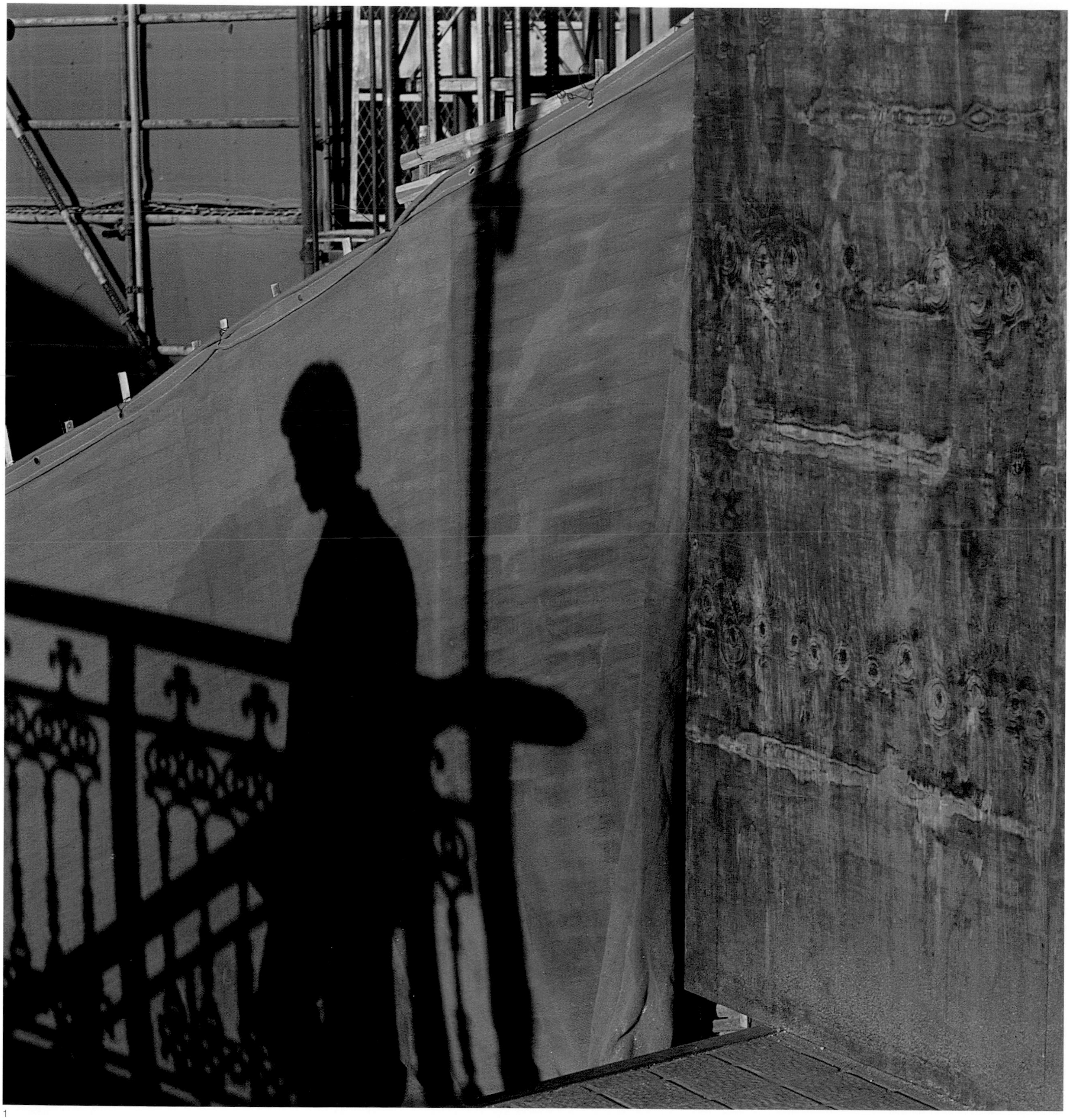

THE STREETS OF SHANG'HAI

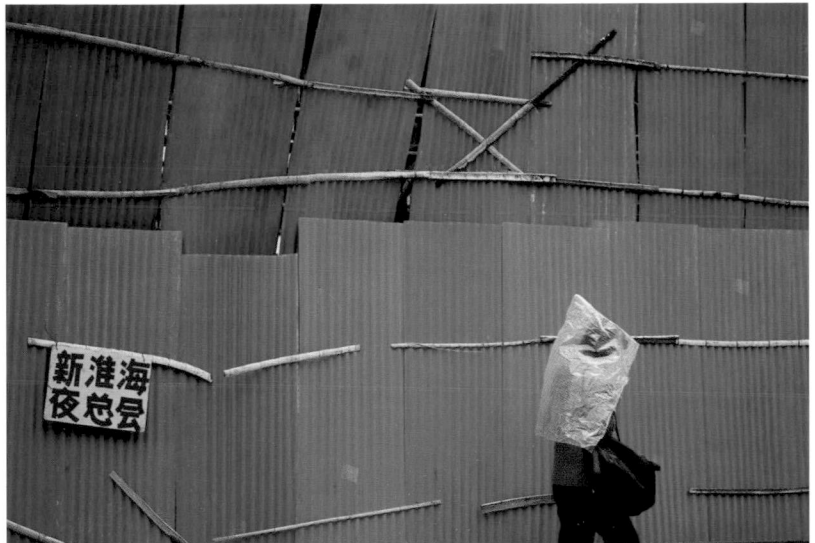

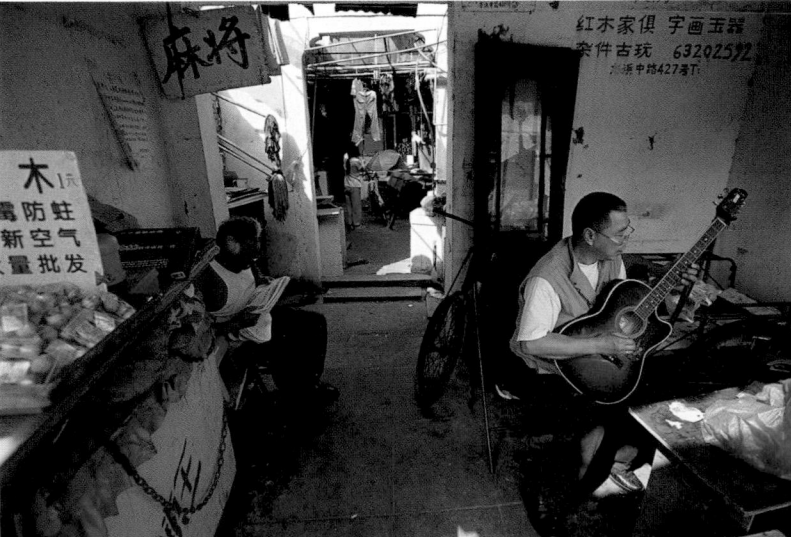

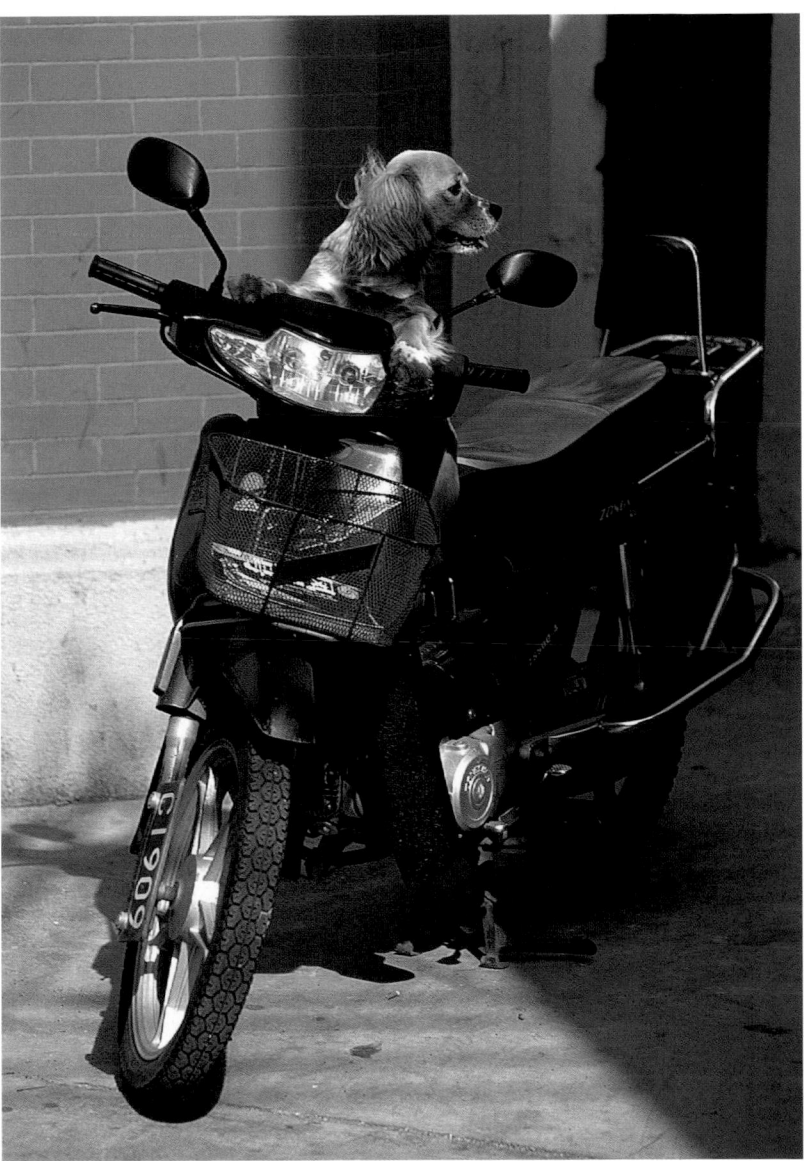

SHANG'HAI'S LOCATION at the mouth of the Yang'tze River delta makes it the gateway to China's riches along the river and its tributaries. This natural advantage first drew foreign traders to the port and it is what the city has fallen back on ever since. The settlement of foreigners from around the globe made Shang'hai the window through which new ideas and technologies could flow into China's often xenophobic and calcified society. Adversity forged strange symbiotic relationships between the foreigners and the local Chinese population. Together they succeeded in turning Shang'hai into a manufacturing powerhouse and international financial centre, even as the first half of the 20th Century saw the world convulsed and China plunged into utter chaos. At the dawn of a new century, expatriates – both Chinese and foreign – are arriving in droves to seek their fortunes in newly awakened Shang'hai. [1] [2] Construction sites are everywhere in a city-wide development boom. [3] An old shop in the Yu Gardens Bazaar. [4] Owning a 'barbarian' pet is a major status symbol in modern Shang'hai.

ON THE WATERFRONT

1

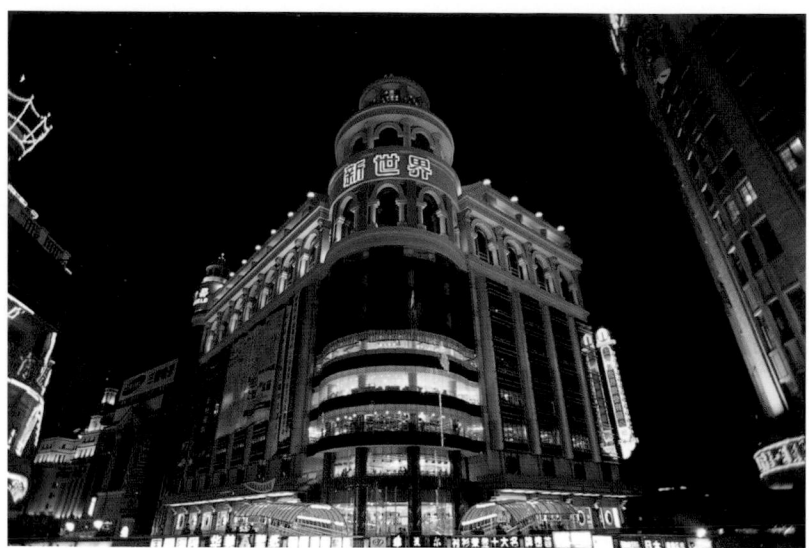

2

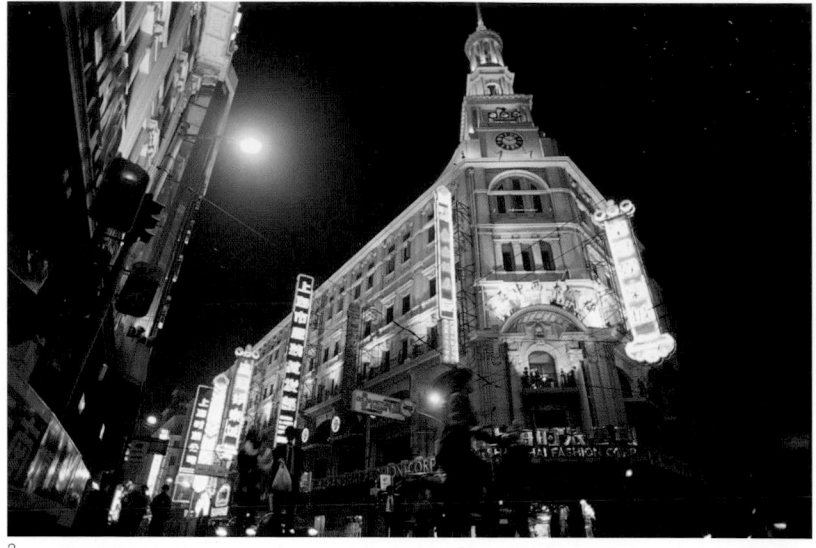

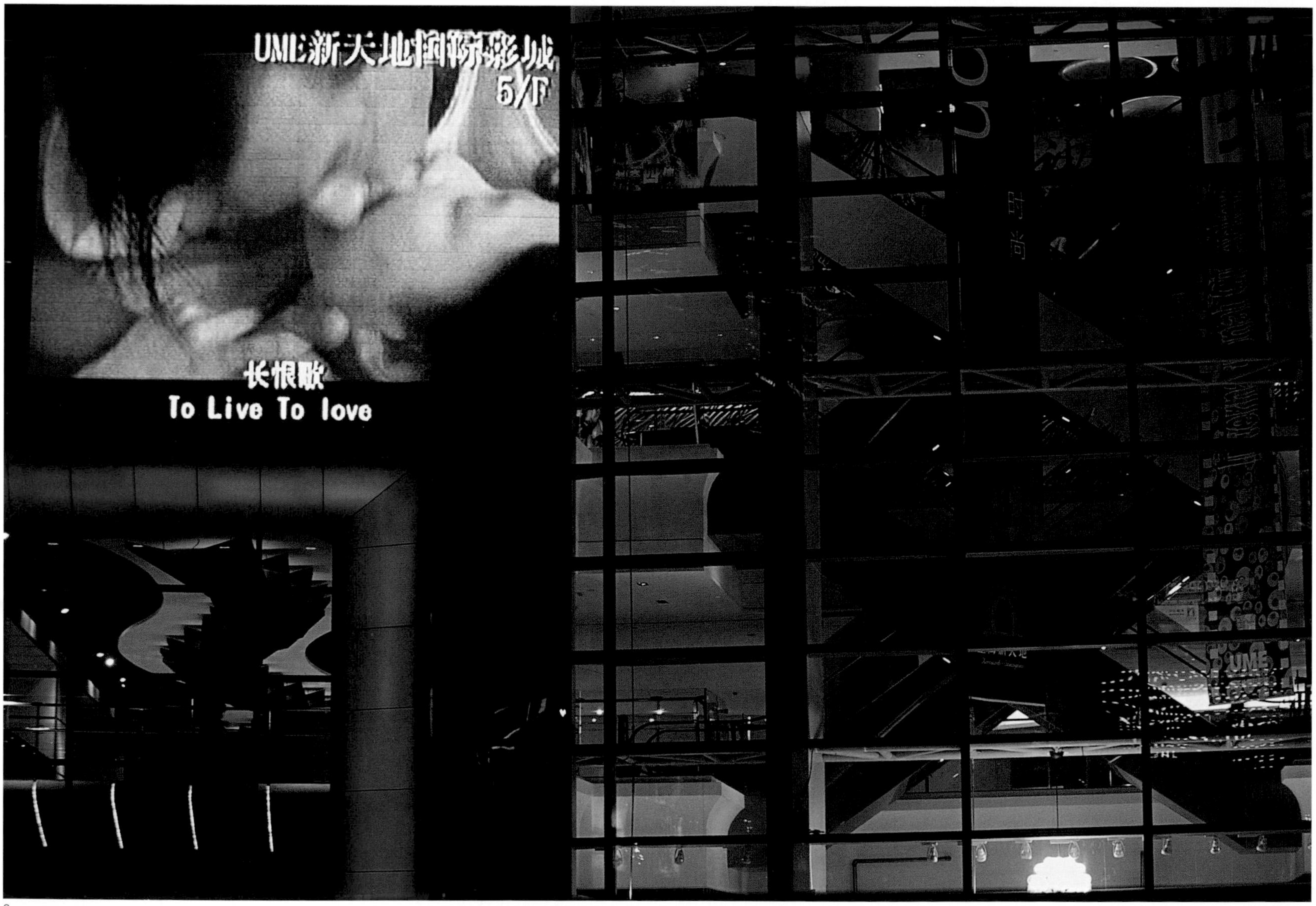

3

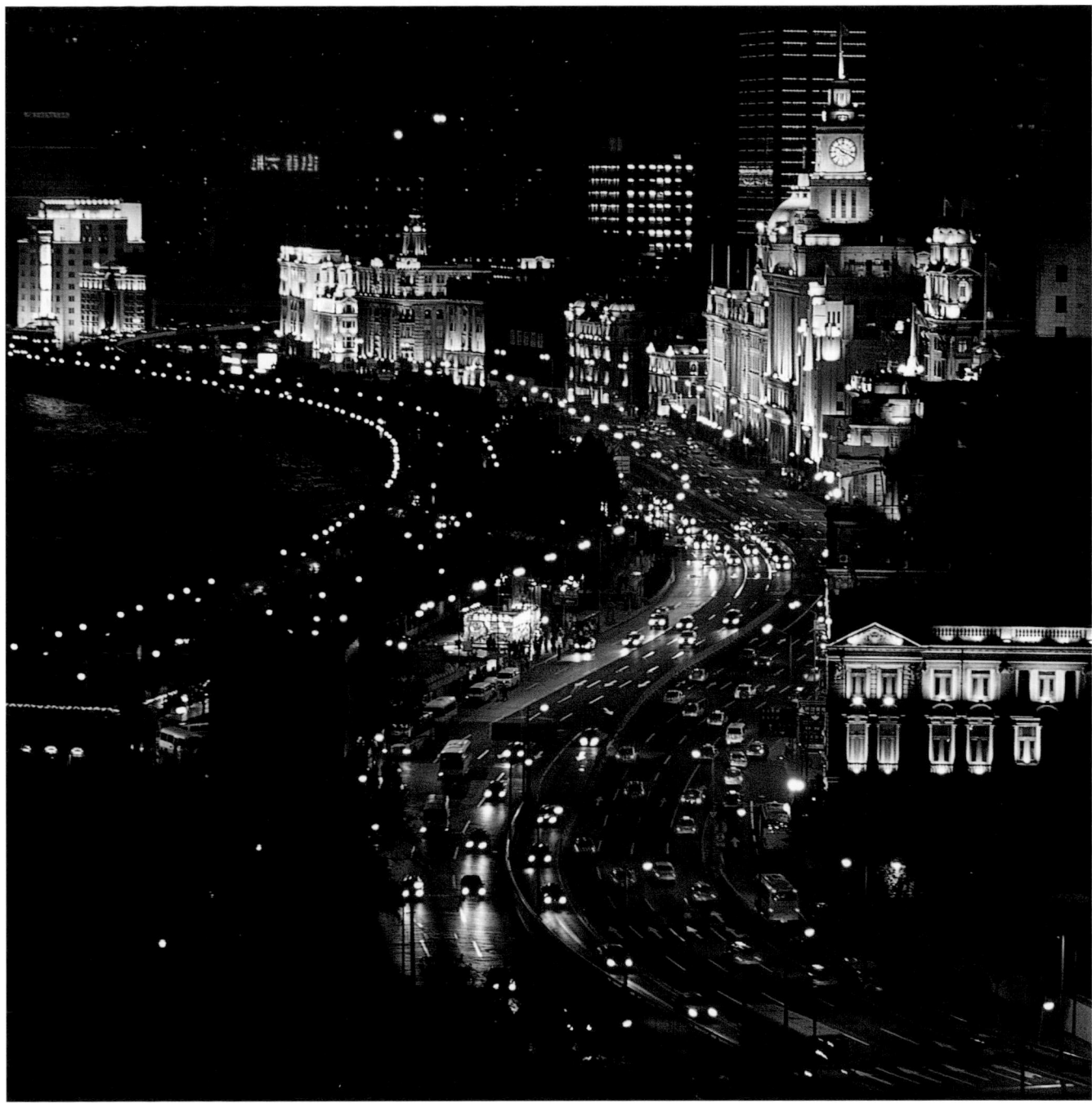

4

MANY ASIAN CITIES HAVE CLAIMED THE TITLES, but the original 'Pearl of the Orient' and 'Whore of Asia' is back with a vengeance. Beneath the thin veneer of glamour and respectability in this newly fashionable city, the whiff of decadence and corruption on its perfumed breath permeates the seductive nights. In the 1920s and 1930s Du Yue'sheng and his Green Gang ruled the night with opium, gambling and prostitution while also trading his 'services' to break workers' unions and treacherously exterminate the communists for political cover from Chang Kai'shek's Kuo'ming'tang government. Now international crime syndicates flood the city's trendy nightclubs and 'Relaxation Centres' with designer drugs and imported Russian blondes under the protection of corrupt party officials. All attempts to rehabilitate opium addicts and eradicate prostitution after 1949 have vanished into the night as Shang'hai charges ahead with blinding speed into a brilliant future, a counterpoint to the shadow of its notorious past. [1] [2] Nan'jing Road, haven of Shang'hai's shoppers, in the 1990s. [3] The new commercial and entertainment complex of Xin Tian'di (New World). [4] The Bund at night.

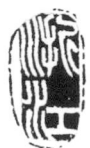

ZHE'JIANG PROVINCE

LOCATION
Latitude 27°01'–31°10'N
Longtitude 118°01'–123°08'E

AREA 103,600 km² (40,000 sq miles)

GEOGRAPHY Zhe'jiang is characterized by the highlands that comprise about 70 per cent of its total area. Elevations are higher in the southwest, where mountains such as the Wu'yi range are over 1,500 m. Mount Huang'ya'jian, at 1,921 m, is the province's highest peak. The northeast is a large, low, flat and fertile alluvial plain crisscrossed with waterways. Numerous rivers drain the province, notably the Fu'chun, the Wu, the Ling and the Qian'tang. The east is formed by a rugged coast, with hundreds of islands set in the East China Sea.

CLIMATE The sub-tropical climate brings short, cool winters and long, hot summers. Average January temperatures are between 2°C and 8°C, rising to 27–30°C in July. The lowest recorded temperature is -16°C and the highest is 42.1°C. Annual rainfall is between 1,000 mm and 1,900 mm. The province is subject to typhoons in late summer.

POPULATION 74.75 million (end 2005)

MAJOR CITIES Hang'zhou (capital), Wen'zhou, Jia'xing, Zhu'zi, Qu'zhou, Ning'bo, Hu'zhou

AGRICULTURE Major food crops are rice and wheat. Cash crops include jute, cotton, tea and silk. The northern plain is a centre of aquaculture in China, with the Zhoushan fishery the country's largest.

MAIN INDUSTRIES Manufacturing is dominated by mechanical and electrical engineering, textiles, chemicals and food processing. Zhe'jiang's development based on entrepreneurship within small businesses has made this one of China's richest provinces.

ANNUAL PER CAPITA INCOME (2005)
Disposable income of urban residents:
RMB 16,294 (US$2,032)
Net income of rural residents:
RMB 6,660 (US$ 831)

HISTORICAL AND SCENIC SITES
Bao'guo Temple, Pu'tuo Shan Mountain, Qi'ta Temple, Shao'xing, Tian'tai Shan, West Lake, Ling'yin Temple, the Grand Canal.

FOOD Zhe'jiang food is one of the Eight Great Cuisines of China. Dishes from Hang'zhou, many based on fish and seafood, are at the centre of the cuisine. Specialities include West Lake fish in sweet and sour sauce, fried shrimps with Long'jing tea leaves and whitefish with fermented glutinous rice.

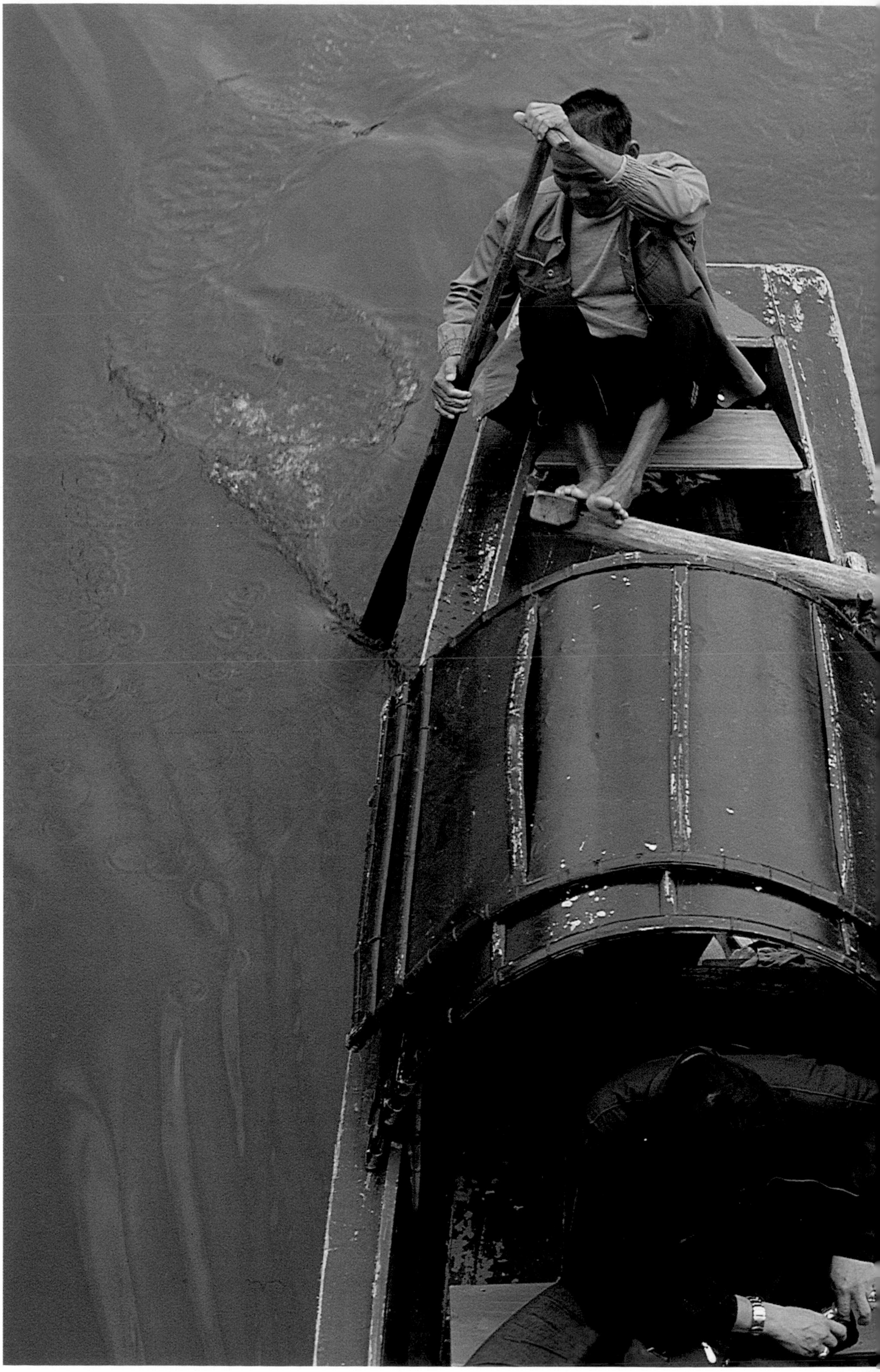

[RIGHT] A bare-foot boatman in Shao'xing.

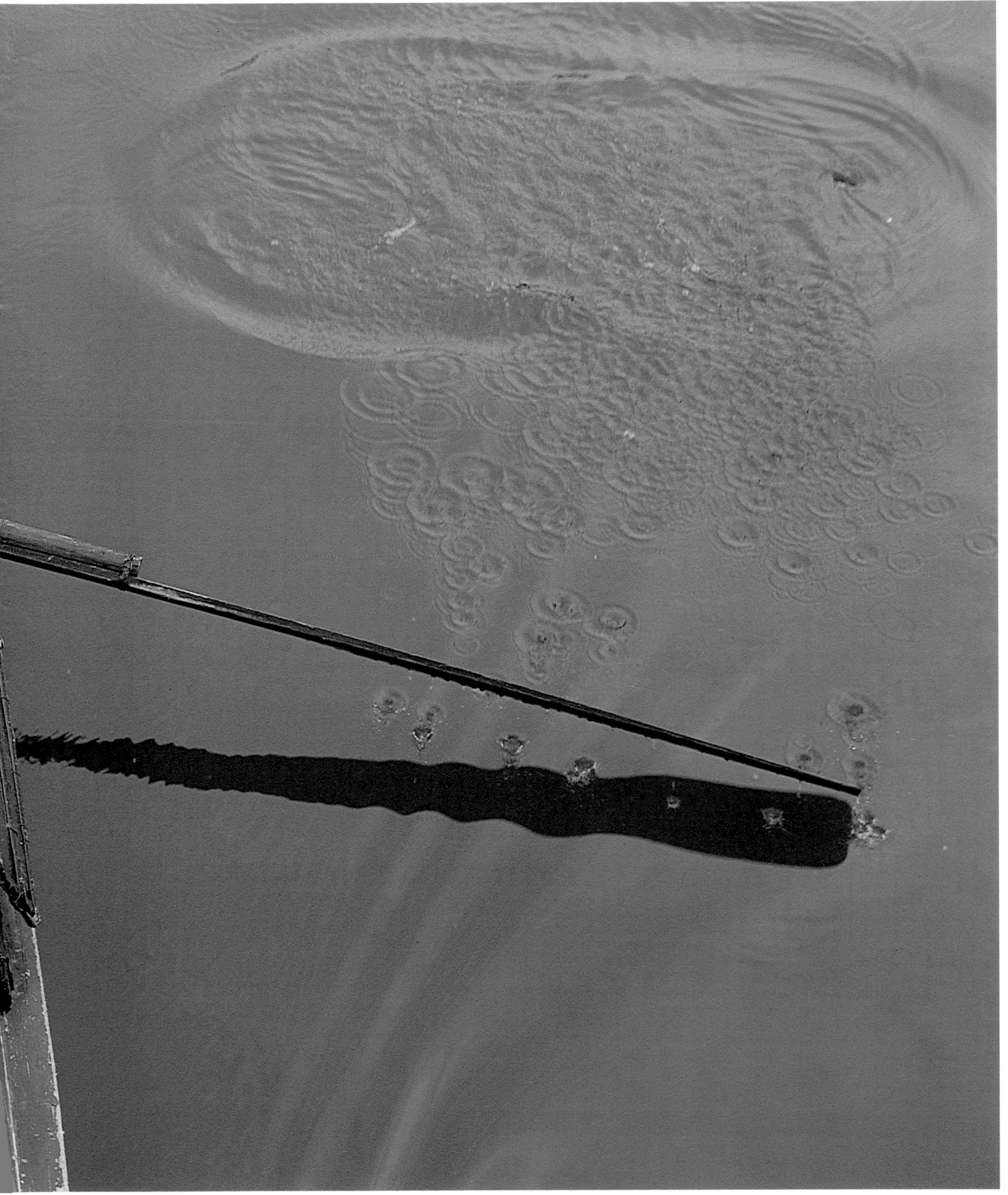

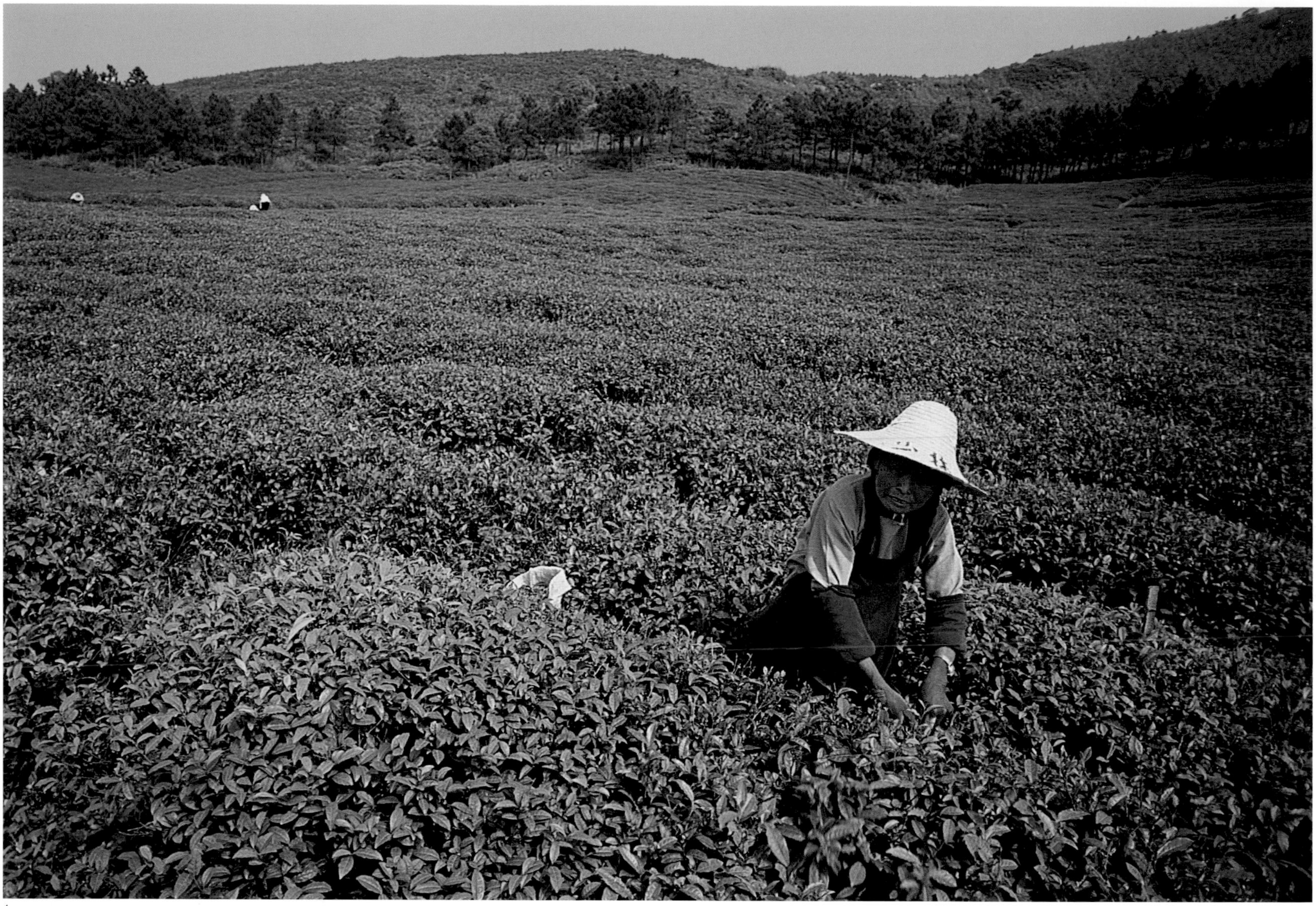

1

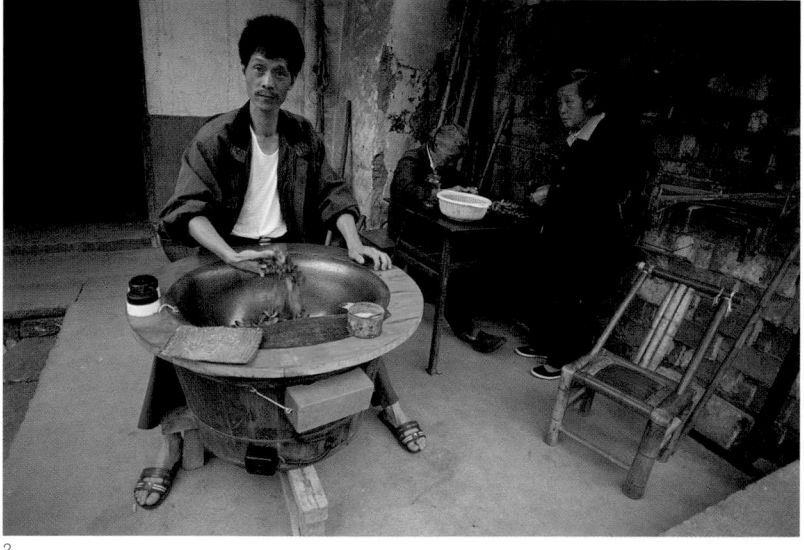

2

HANG'ZHOU'S MOMENT OF DESTINY came in 1126 when the Juc'hen of Manchuria crushed the Song Dynasty, seized Kai'feng and captured the emperor. The remnants of the Song court fled south across the Yang'tze River and established Hang'zhou as the capital of the Southern Song Dynasty. Franciscan friar Oderic of Pordendone, visiting Hang'zhou in 1320s, described it as "so great a city" crammed full of "houses ten to twelve storeys high, one above the other". Marco Polo was equally enthralled, calling it "the City of Heaven, the most magnificent in all the world". And he's from Venice! Sadly, the Tai'ping Rebellion reduced the old city to ashes when they laid siege to Hang'zhou in 1861. Xi'hu (Western Lake) is the symbol of Hang'zhou and was also Chairman Mao's favourite retreat. He had one of his concrete-bunker villas built here on a sprawling estate that offered panoramic views of the lake and a nuclear shelter in the hill behind. It is said the lake looks most magical when seen through a veil of mist, [3] [4] unfortunately, I've only ever seen it during torrential rain. [1] [2] The famous Dragon Well (Long'jing) tea is produced in the valley behind the western hills of the lake.

254

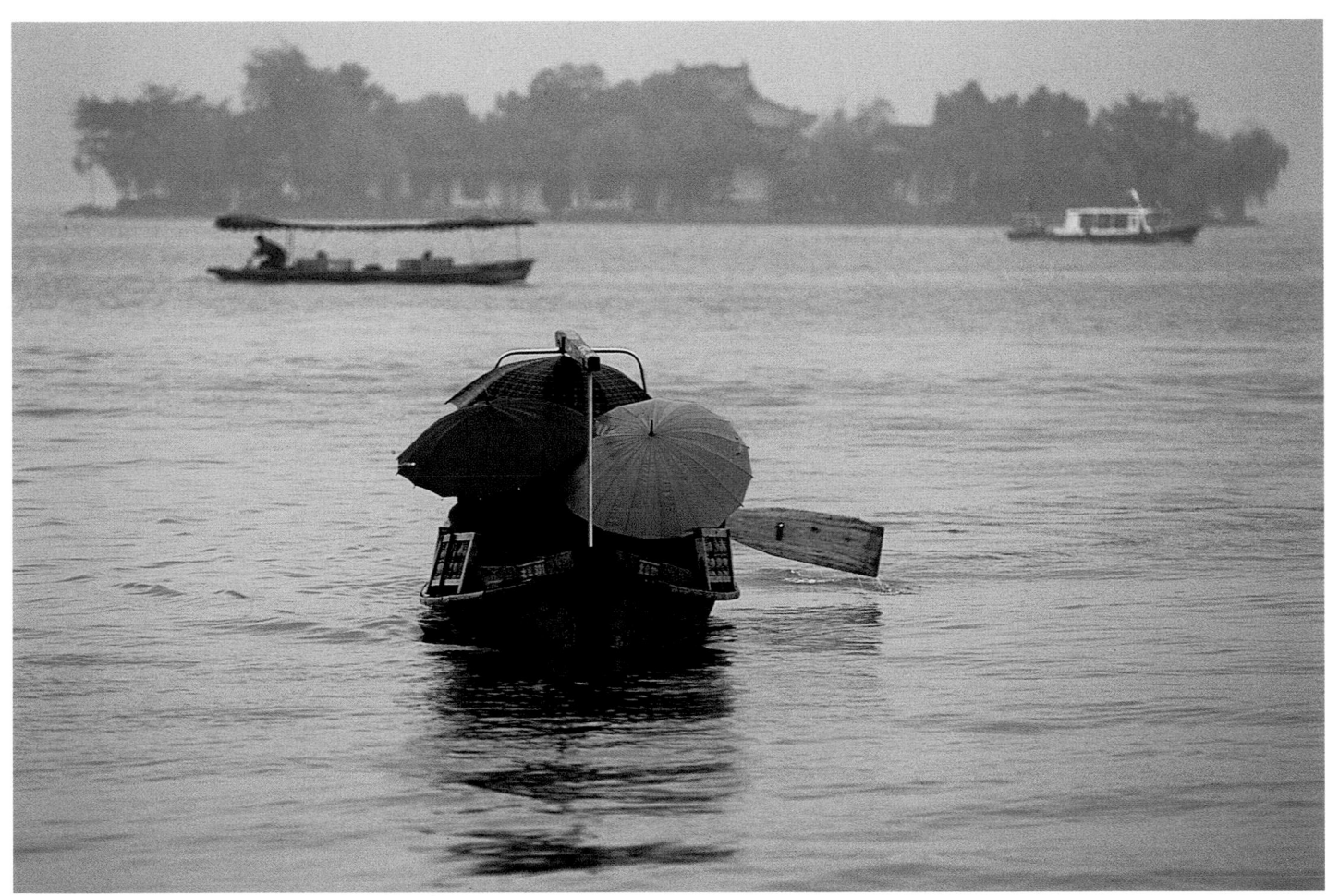

3

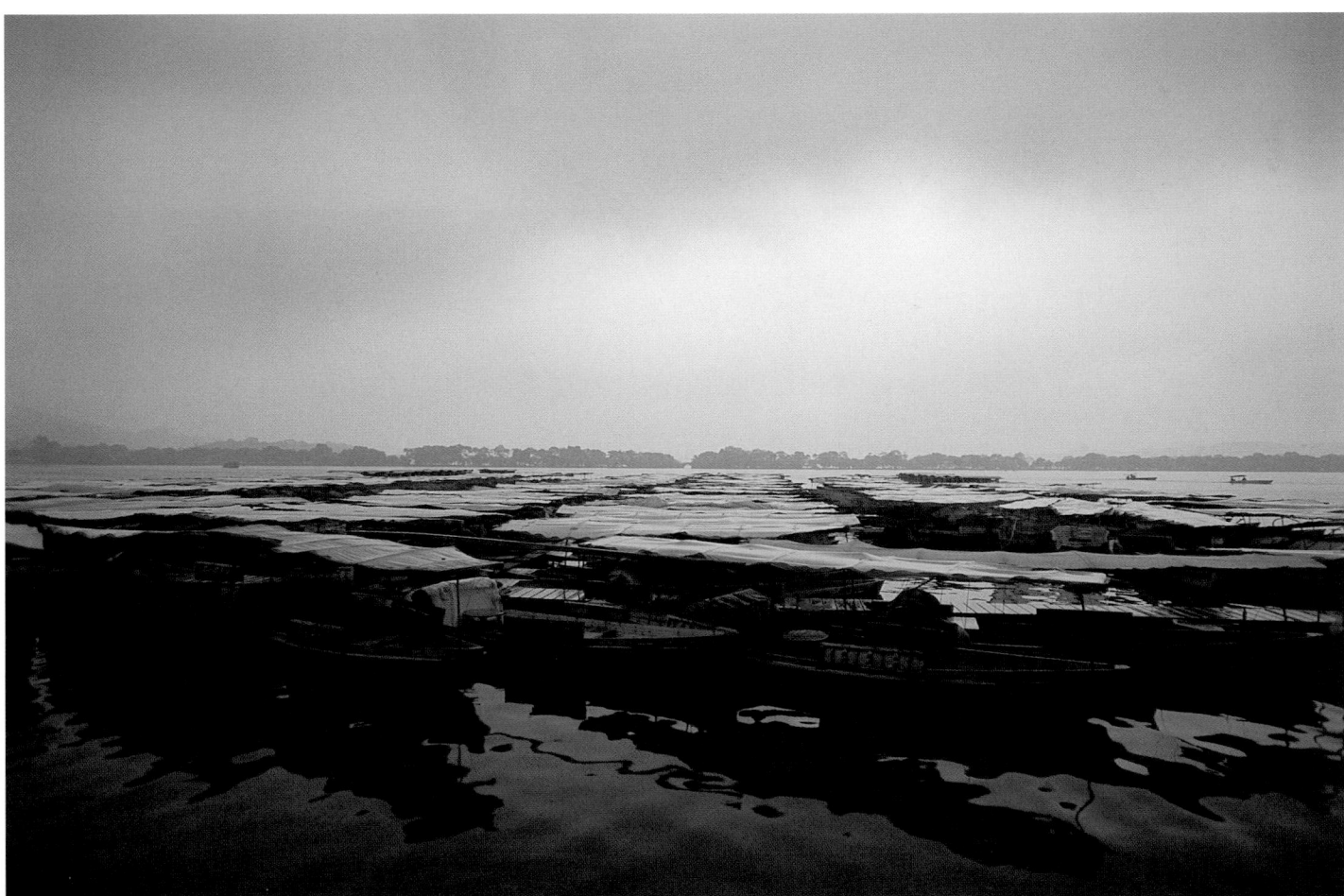

4

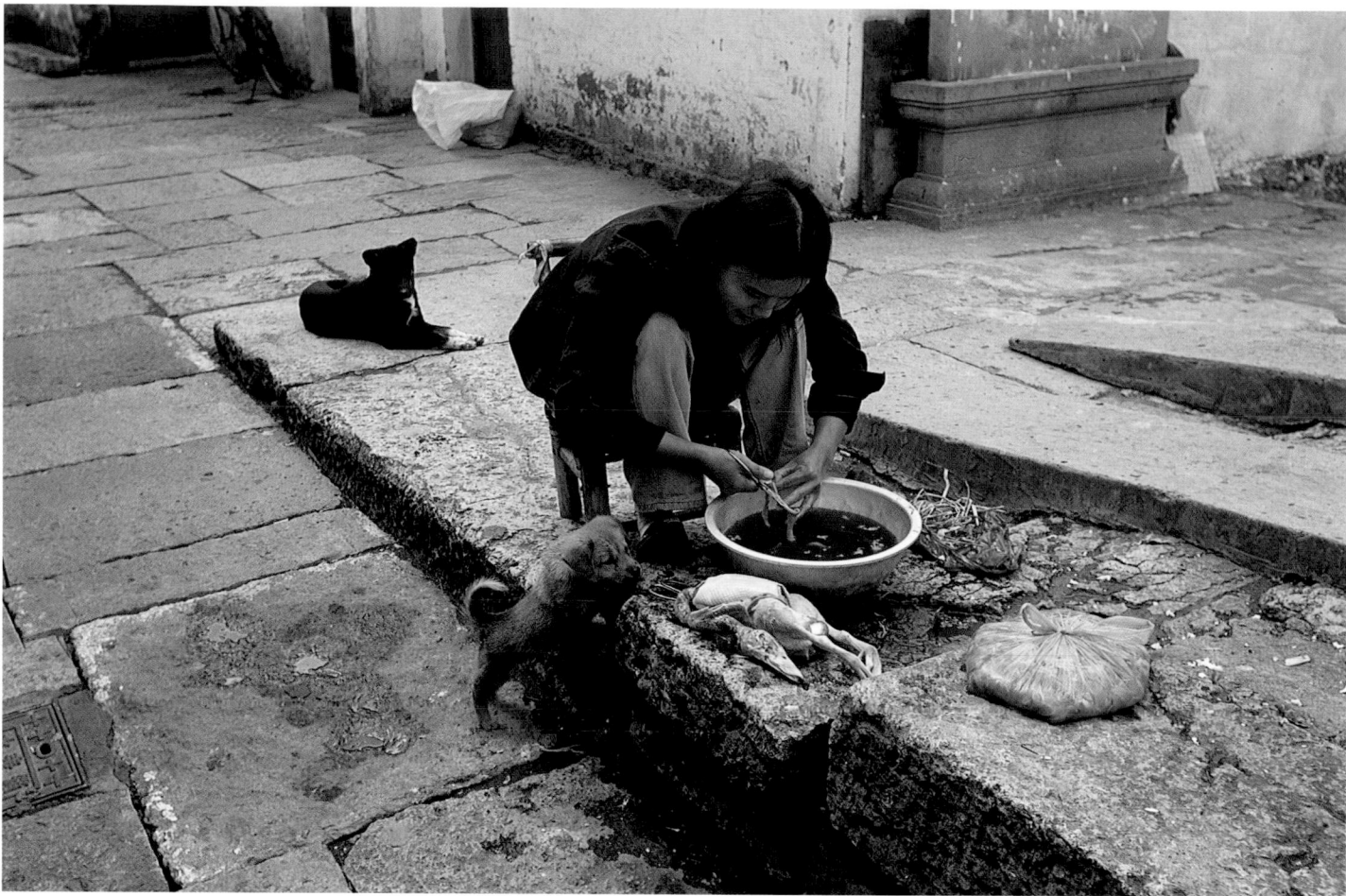

1

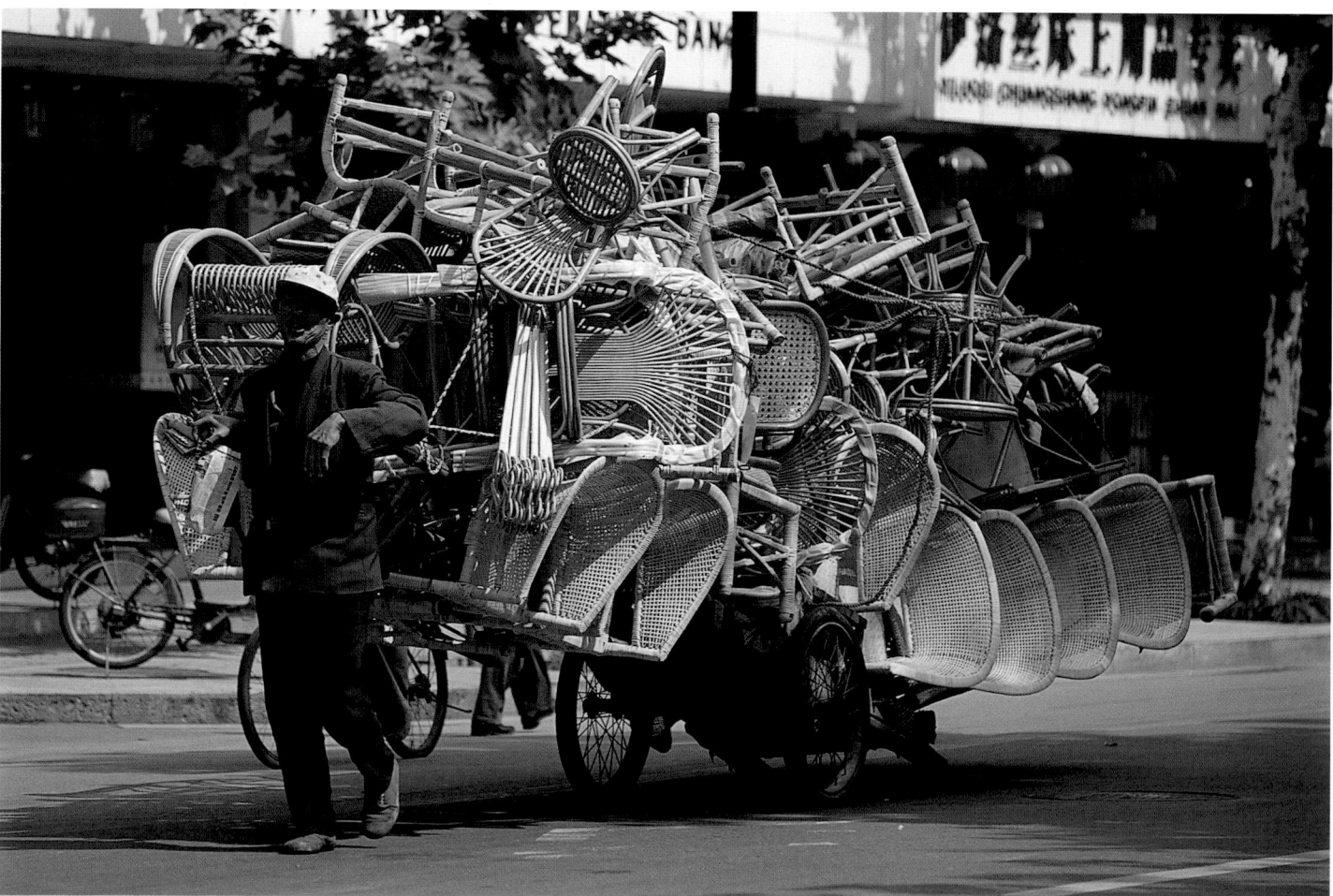

2

STREET OF SHAO'XING

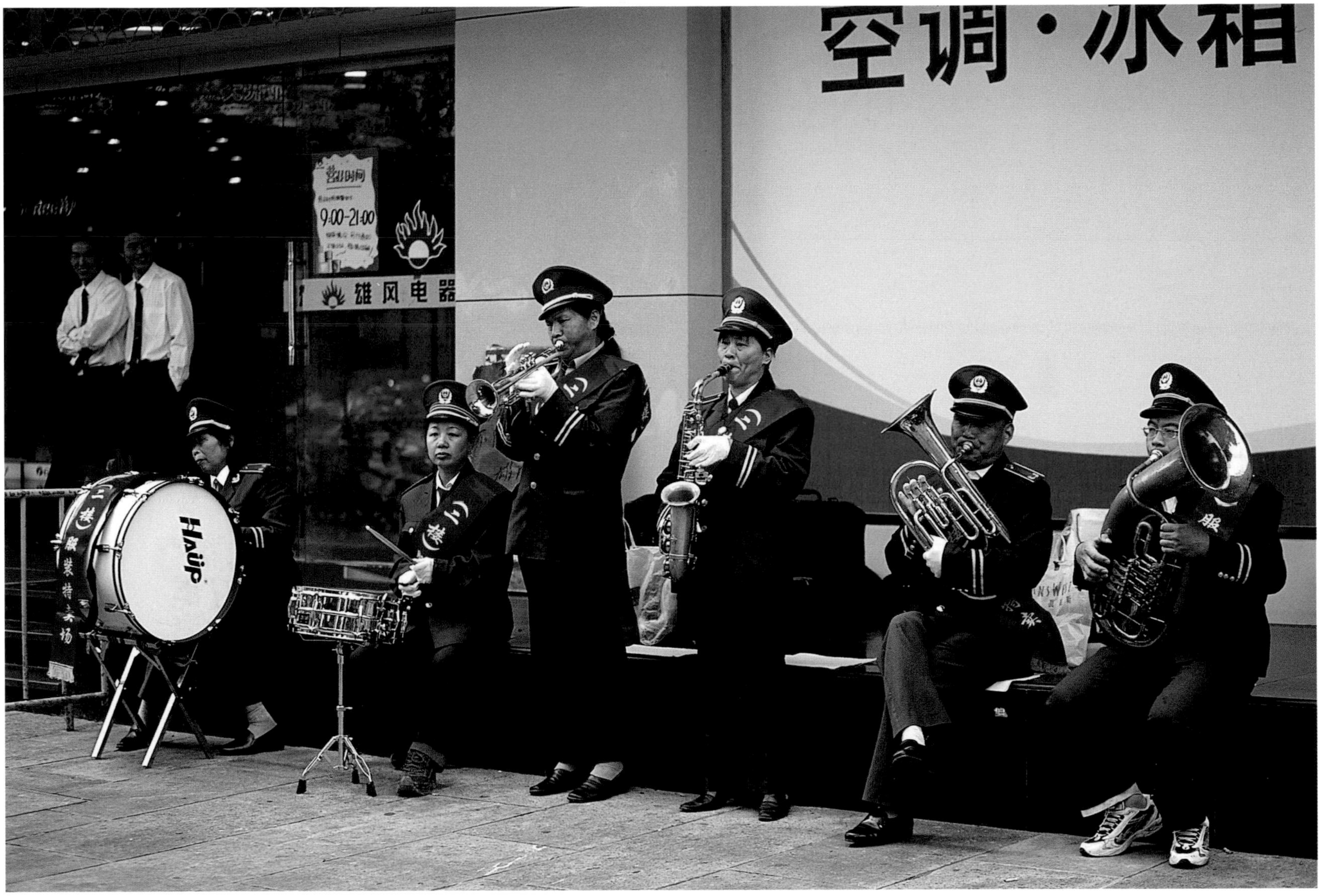

3

SHAO'XING IS FAMOUS FOR ITS RICE WINE, but the small 'water town' at the centre of northern Zhe'jiang's canal system is even better known as the birthplace of Lu Xun (1881–1936), the 'Father of Modern Chinese Literature'. Lu's first short story, *Diary of a Madman*, was published in 1918 as a scathing critique of Confucian feudalism, which he thought was "gnawing at the Chinese people like a cannibal". His most famous work, *The True Story (or Official Biography) of Ah Q* went further. The book created great controversy because its protagonist, Ah Q, was the embodiment of all the psychological hang-ups, philosophical confusions and character flaws of the Chinese race. Mao Ze'dong hailed Lu as "the commander of China's cultural revolution" while Chang Kai'shek tried to throw him into prison – his books remained banned in Taiwan until the late 1980s. I met some lovely people from the master's hometown, including [1] a woman preparing a duck dinner by the Ba'zi Bridge. [2] A rattan furniture salesman. [3] A local PLA marching band performing at a department store opening.

ON THE WATERFRONT

FU'JIAN PROVINCE

LOCATION
Latitude 23°31'–28°19'N
Longtitude 115°50'–120°44'E

AREA 124,352 km² (48,000 sq miles)

GEOGRAPHY Fu'jian is mainly mountainous with the higher peaks of the Wu'yi range forming the border with Jiang'xi province in the northwest. The highest point is the 2,157-m Huang'gang Peak in the Wu'yi Mountains. The province's coastal area, noted for its thousands of bays and small islands, extends from the East China Sea and Taiwan Strait to the South China Sea. The Min Jiang River and its tributaries cut through much of northern and central Fu'jian. Other rivers include the Jin'jiang and the Jiulong.

CLIMATE Fu'jian has a subtropical climate, with hot summers and mild winters. The average January temperatures are 7–10°C in the coastal regions and 6–8°C in the mountains. Average July temperatures are 26–29°C. The highest recorded temperature is 42.3°C and the lowest is -4.6°C. The province is subject to typhoons during the summer months. Average annual rainfall is 1,400–2,000 mm.

POPULATION 35.35 million (end 2005)

MAJOR CITIES Fu'zhou (capital), Xia'men, Quan'zhou, Zhang'zhou

AGRICULTURE Rice is the main crop, supplemented by sweet potatoes and wheat. Cash crops include sugarcane and rapeseed. Fu'jian is the leading producer of longan fruit in China and is also a major producer of lychees and tea. Seafood, notably shellfish, is an important export.

MAIN INDUSTRIES Fu'jian's industries include textiles, iron and steel, cement, ceramics, timber and woodworking, tea processing, sugar refining, salt panning and preserved fruits.

ANNUAL PER CAPITA INCOME (2005)
Disposable income of urban residents:
RMB 12,069 (US$1,505)
Net income of rural residents:
RMB 4,318 (US$538)

IMPORTANT HISTORICAL SITES
Nanputuo Temple, Mount Wu'yi, Kai'yuan Temple, Chong'wu Town, Hui'an, Nan'shan Temple, Zhang'zhou, the Mat'su pilgrimage centres, Yong'quan Temple.

FOOD Fu'jian cooking relies heavily on seafood and freshwater fish and is one of the Eight Great Cuisines of China. The most famous dish is Fo'tiao'qiang ('Buddha jumps over the wall'), a complex soup/stew that includes fin, sea cucumber, abalone and Shao'xing wine. Many famous teas originate from Fu'jian, including oolong and jasmine. The English word 'tea' is derived from the Xiamen dialect.

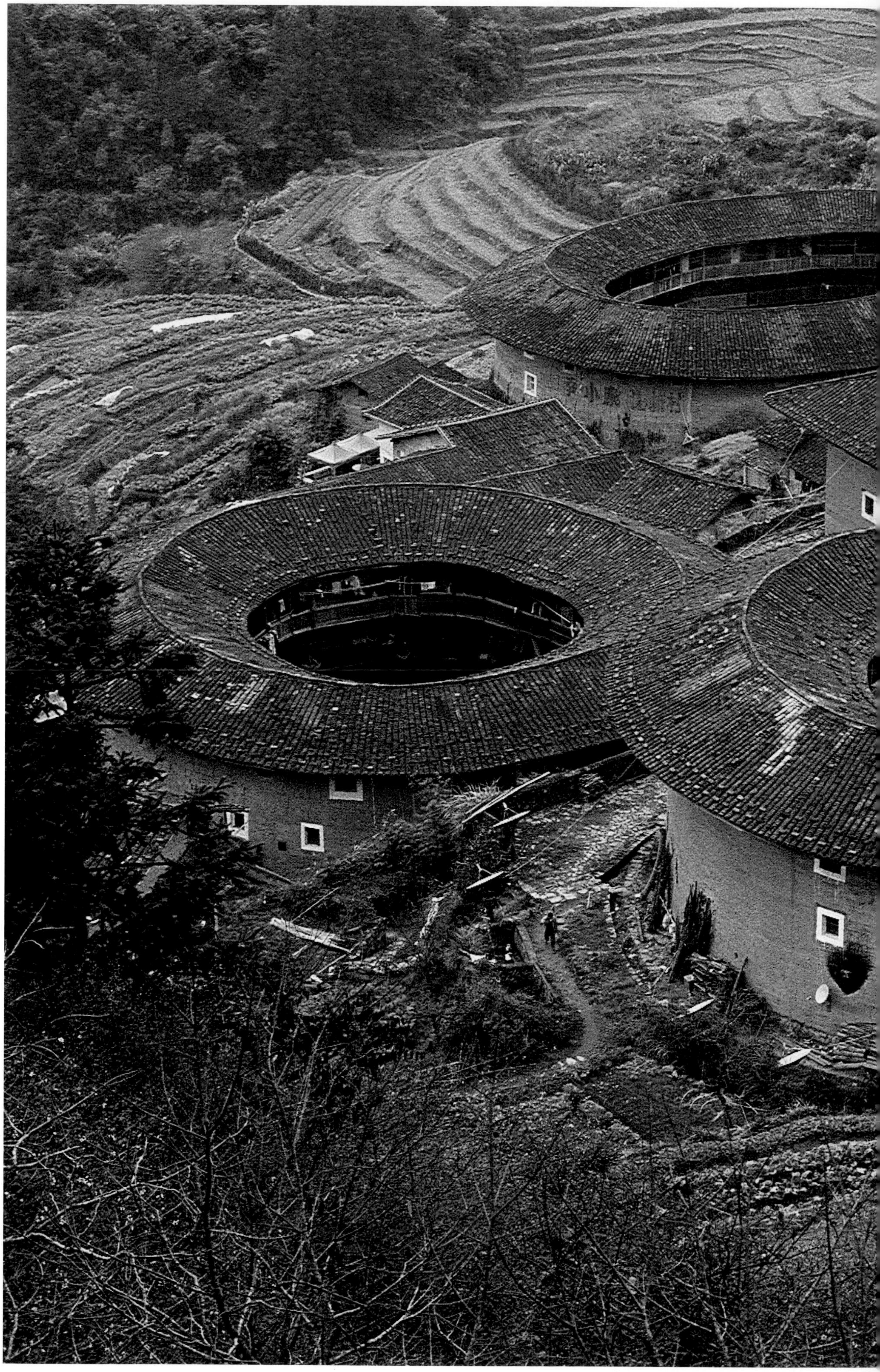

[RIGHT] A cluster of *tu'lou* in Yong'ding.

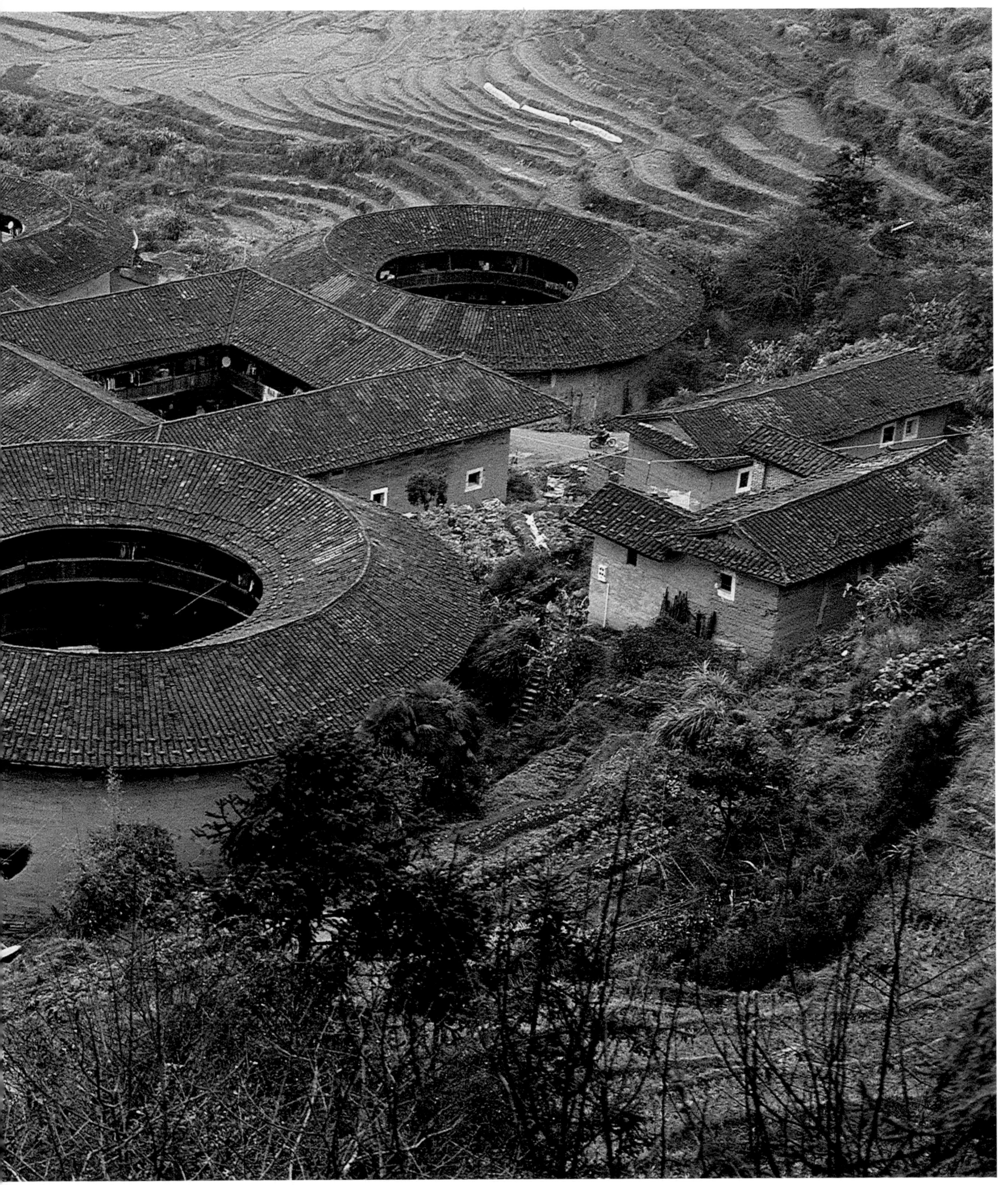

1

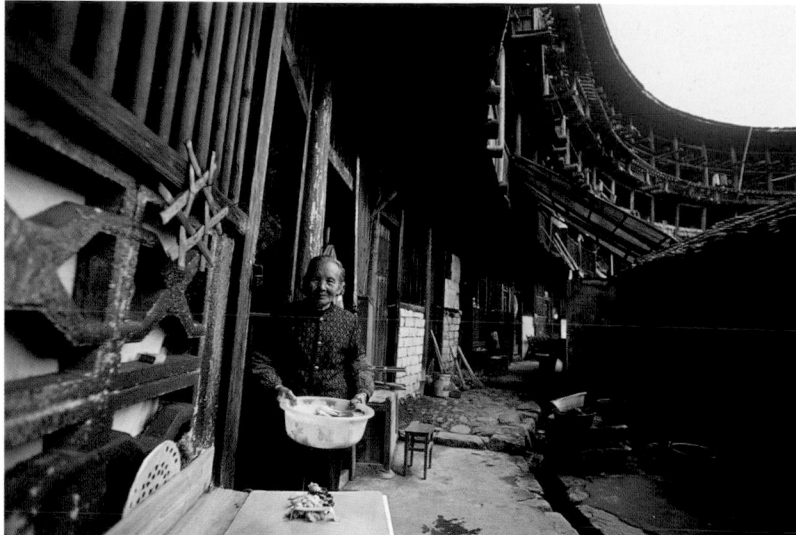

2

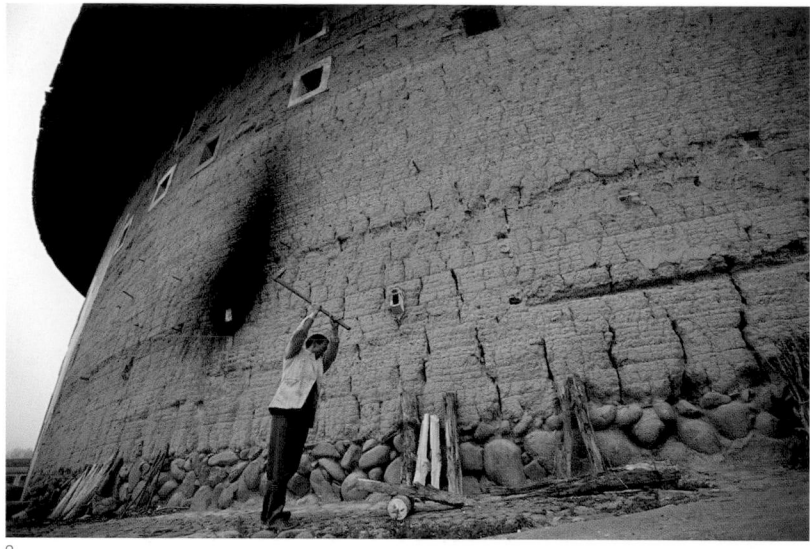

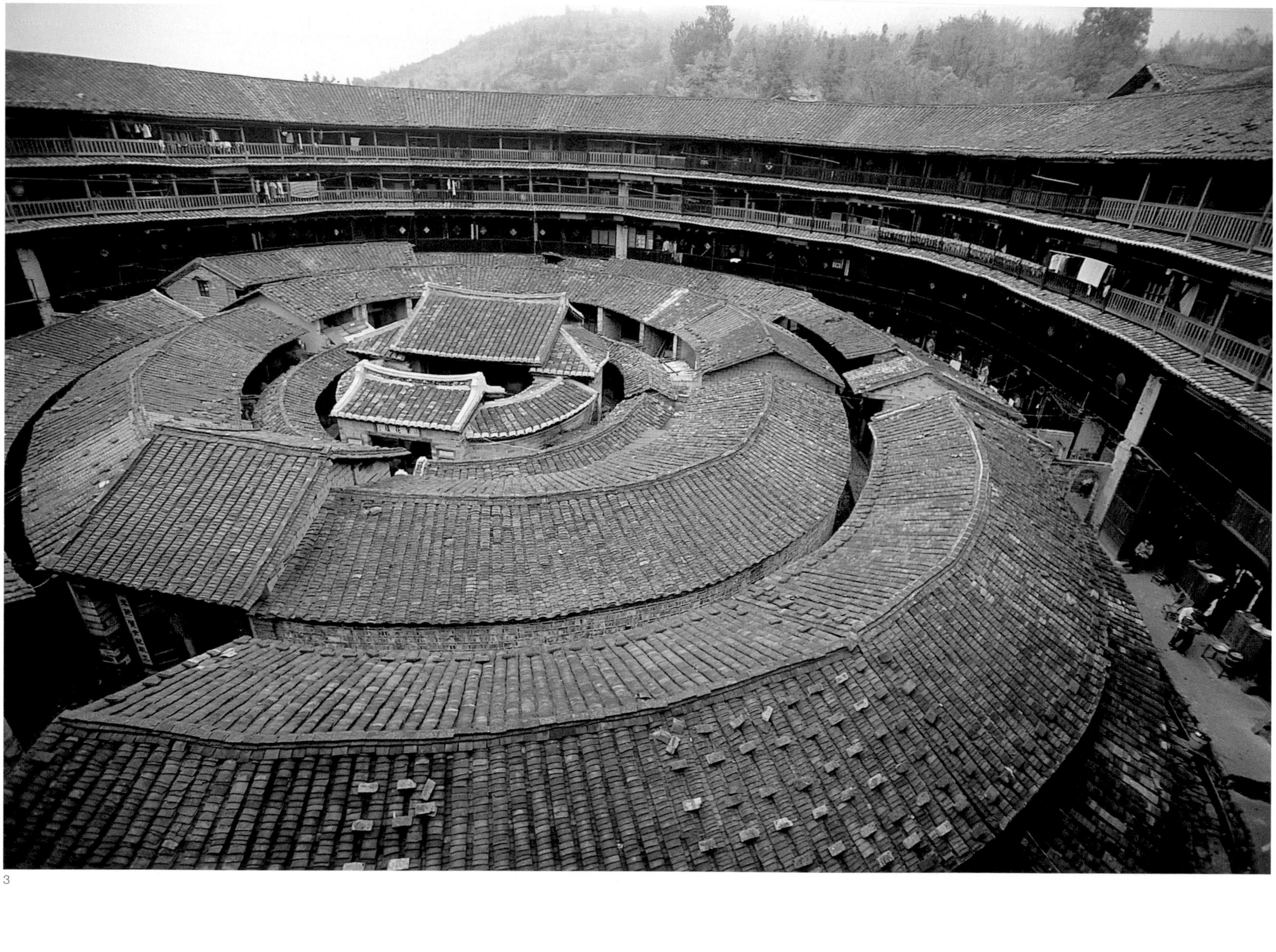

3

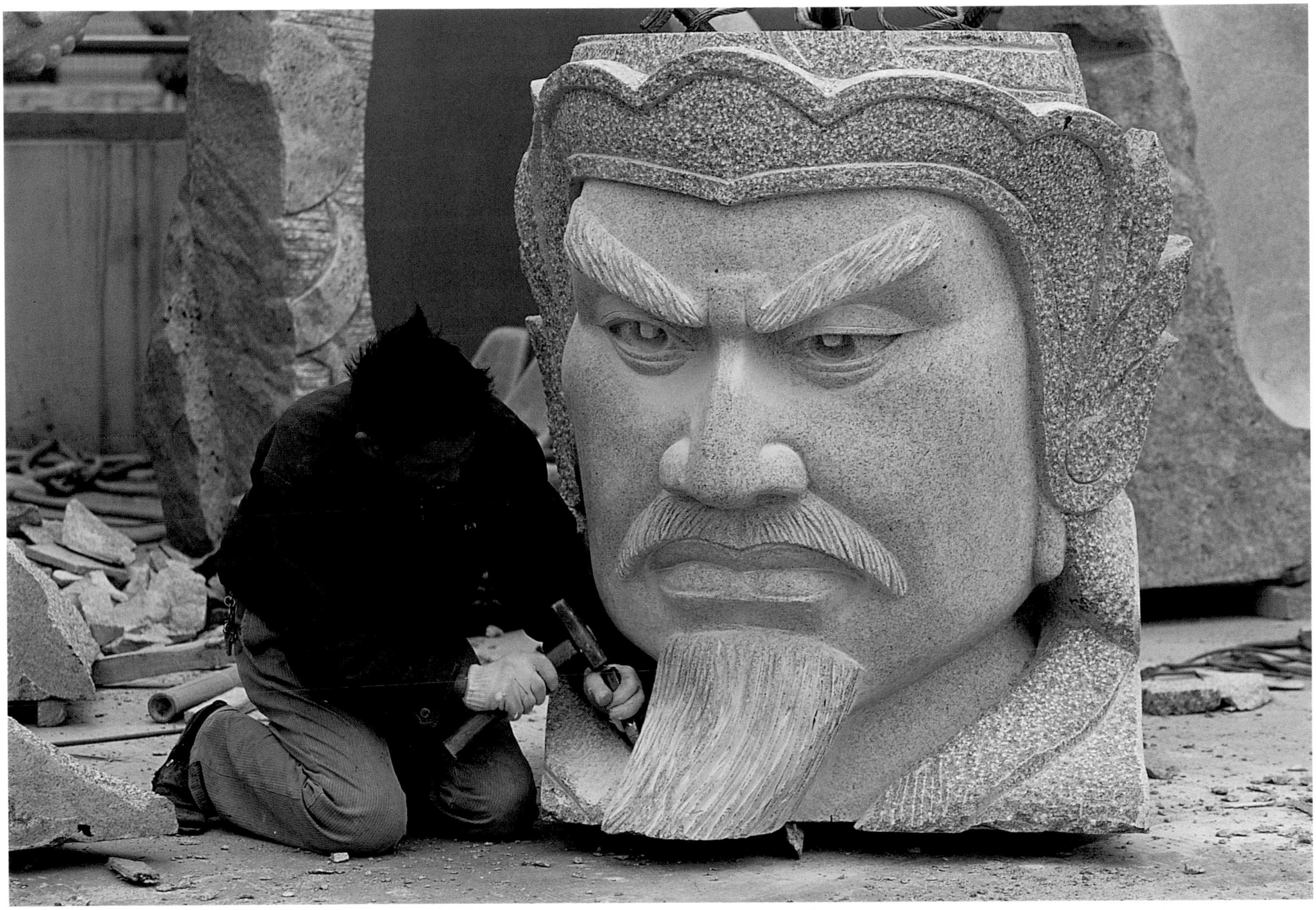

4

BETWEEN THE FALL OF THE TANG DYNASTY in 907 CE and the rise of the Song Dynasty in 960 CE, the Middle Kingdom was transformed into a combat zone as five dynasties and ten kingdoms fought each other constantly for domination. A massive exodus of refugees from the central plains began a diaspora of northern Han Chinese into the 'Barbaric South' that lasted a millennium. These migrants came to be known as Hak'ka (Guest Family) people. One group from He'nan province settled in the remote mountains of Fu'jian and built these [1] [2] [3] unique circular rammed-earth fortresses that can accommodate a clan of several hundred people. The *tu'lou* (earthen building) became known to the wider world in the 1980s after CIA analysts 'discovered' them in satellite surveillance photographs, prompting President Ronald Reagan to demand to know why China had built these 'new' missile silos across the Taiwan Straits. Ming Dynasty general Zheng Cheng'gong, who drove the Dutch out of Taiwan in 1661, is a heroic figure in the 'Reunification' propaganda war, with giant statues of him a common sight along the Fu'jian coast. [4] [5] At a stone factory in Quan'zhou another one is being given the final touches before delivery.

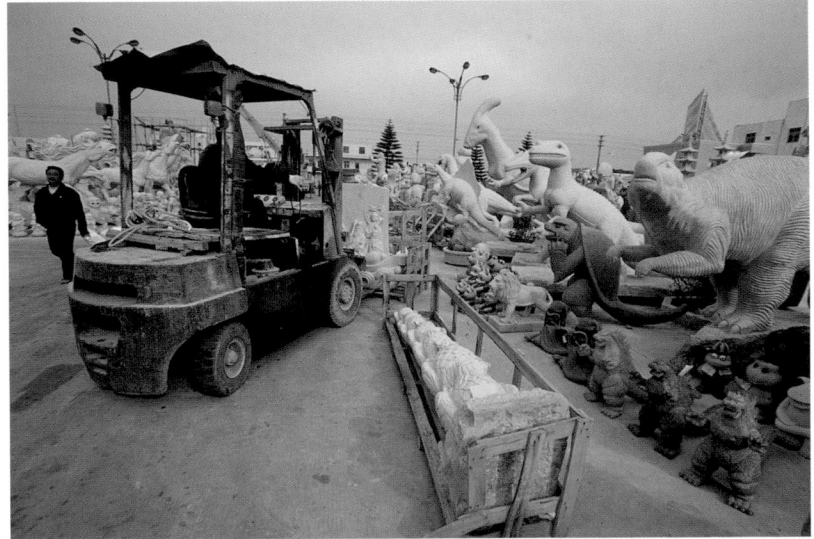

5

261

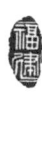

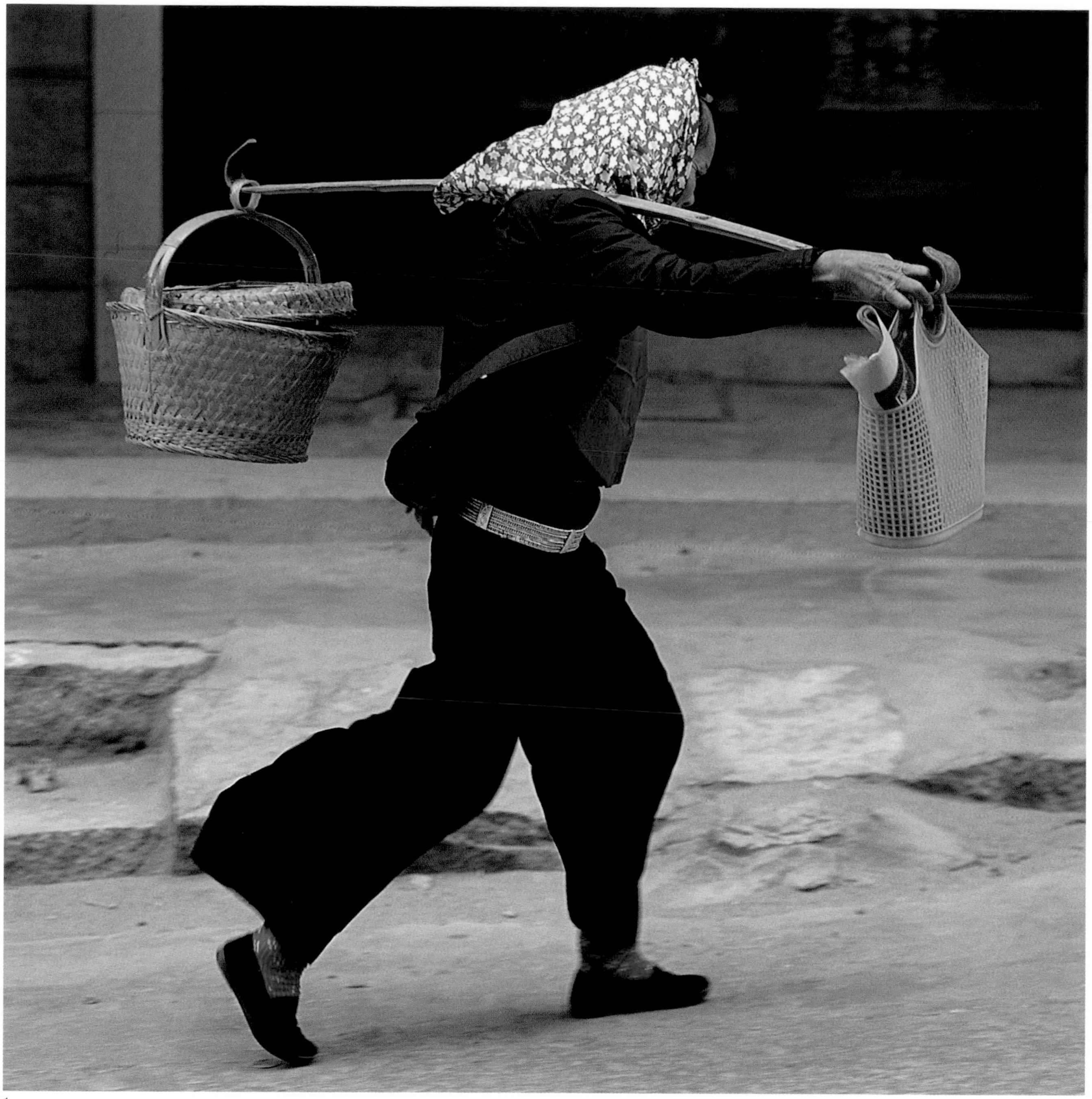

1

OTHER BRANCHES OF THE HAK'KA PEOPLE settled along the Fu'jian coast and became seafarers. From there they spread out across the South China Sea, over centuries establishing Han Chinese settlements in Southeast Asian ports along the Malay Peninsula and throughout Indonesia. Some of them came from Hui'an County [4] near the city of Quan'zhou, a key port on the maritime silk route during the Song and Yuen dynasties. The Hui'an women's distinctive style of dress has attracted the attention of anthropologists and fashion designers alike. Both agree Hui'an attire, which Fu'jian urbanites whimsically sum up as 'feudal head, democratic belly, economical shirt and generous trousers', illustrate how a 12th-century costume has been adapted to suit the needs of a new environment – manual labour in high winds and turbulent seas – without losing its essence. Regrettably, I was there in the winter and all the ladies were wrapped up against the cold [1] [2] [3], so I never saw the extra-short bare-midriff shirts – and only caught glimpses of the elaborate Song Dynasty style hair ornaments under their headscarves.

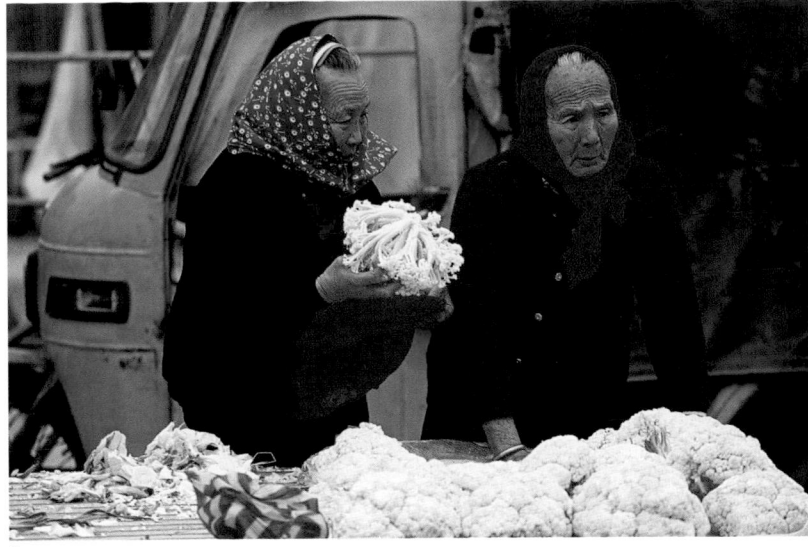

2

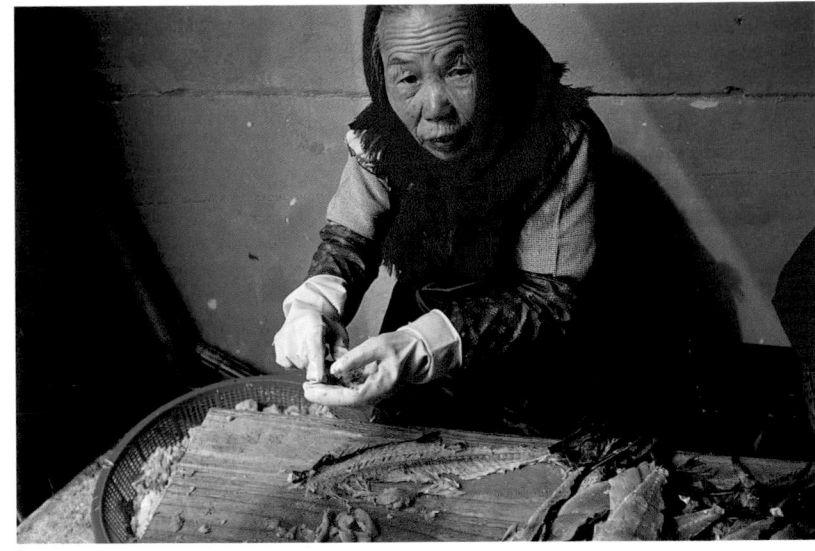

3

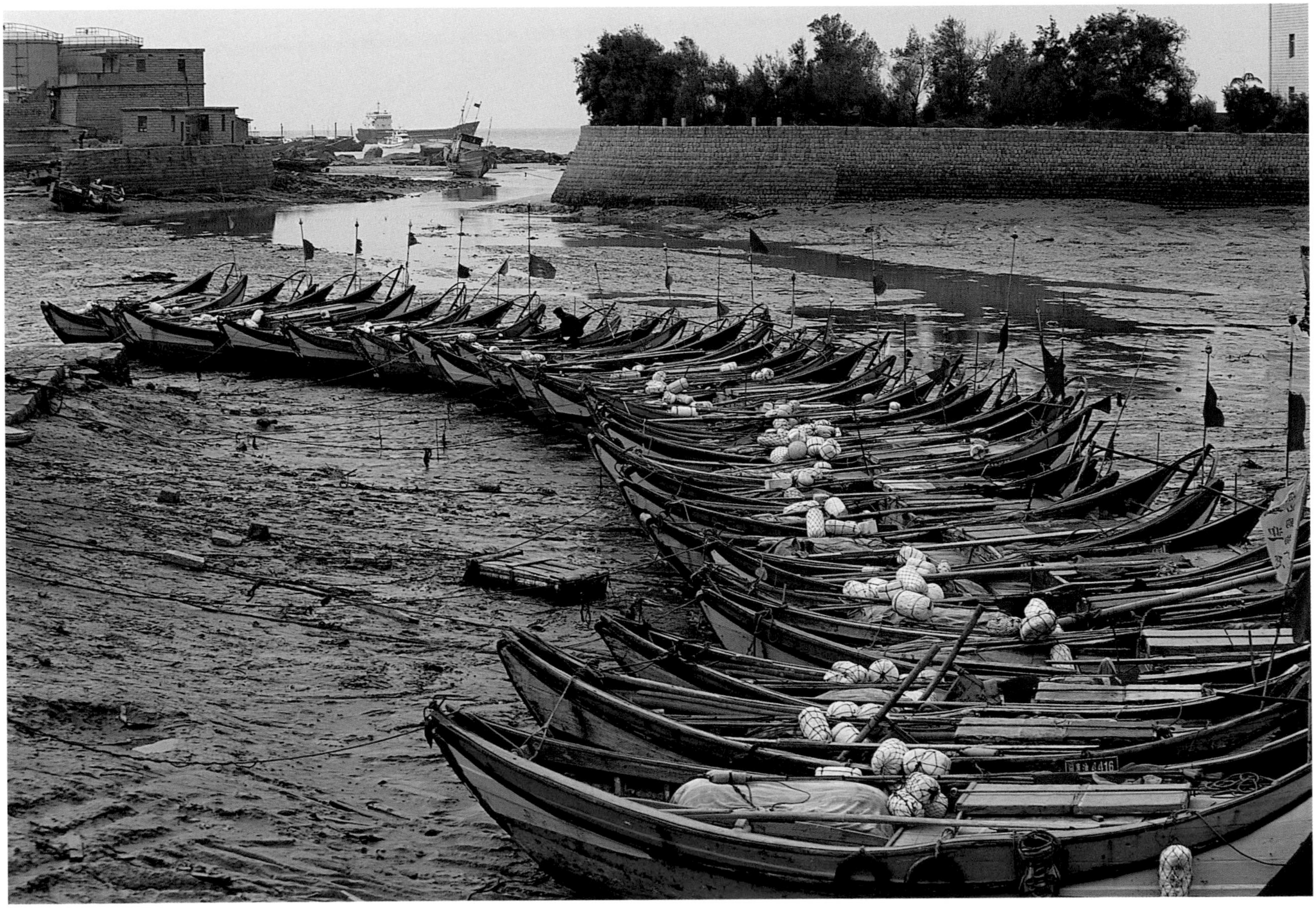

4

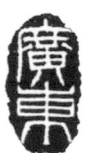

GUANG'DONG PROVINCE

LOCATION
Latitude 20º13'–25º31'N
Longtitude 109º9'–117º19'E

AREA 196,891 km² (76,000 sq miles)

GEOGRAPHY Guang'dong is a maritime province facing the South China Sea. The province's 3,370-km (2,095-mile) coastline provides safe harbours for hundreds of small fishing and trading communities. Southwest Guang'dong is anchored on the Lei'zhou Peninsula. Three major rivers converge in the Pearl (Zhu River) Delta: the East, North and West rivers link the province's hinterland with the sea. The province is separated by the Southern Mountain Range, which reaches 1,902 m at its highest point.

CLIMATE Guang'dong has a sub-tropical climate, characterized by hot and humid summers and mild winters. Average winter temperatures range from 12ºC to 20ºC and summer temperatures can reach 32ºC or higher. The lowest recorded temperature in the province is -3ºC and the highest is 40ºC. Annual average rainfall is between 1,500 mm and 2,000 mm.

POPULATION 91.94 million (end 2005)

MAJOR CITIES Guang'zhou (capital), Zhu'hai, Shen'zhen, Dong'guan, Fu'shan, Chao'zhou, Hui'zhou

AGRICULTURE Guang'dong is China's main source of sugarcane and a major rice and silk producer. Cash crops include hemp, tobacco, tea, tropical and sub-tropical fruits and peanuts. Guang'dong's fisheries account for about 20 per cent of China's catch.

MAIN INDUSTRIES Guang'dong is a major centre for the textile, apparel and electronics sectors. There are also a number of large oil refineries, timber and paper mills, food processing, printing, cement and fertilizer plants in the province.

ANNUAL PER CAPITA INCOME (2005)
Disposable income of the urban residents:
RMB 14,770 (US$1,842)
Net income of rural residents:
RMB 4,690 (US$585)

HISTORICAL AND SCENIC SITES
Sun Yat'sen's memorial hall, Six-Banyan Monastery, Tomb of the Nan'yue King, Huai'sheng Mosque, Bai'yun Mountain, Guang'xiao Temple.

FOOD Cantonese cooking is one of the Eight Great Cuisines of China. Typical dishes are clear, light, crisp and fresh with an emphasis on steaming and stir-frying. Notable dishes include dim sum, shrimp wonton soup and *char siu* (barbeque pork).

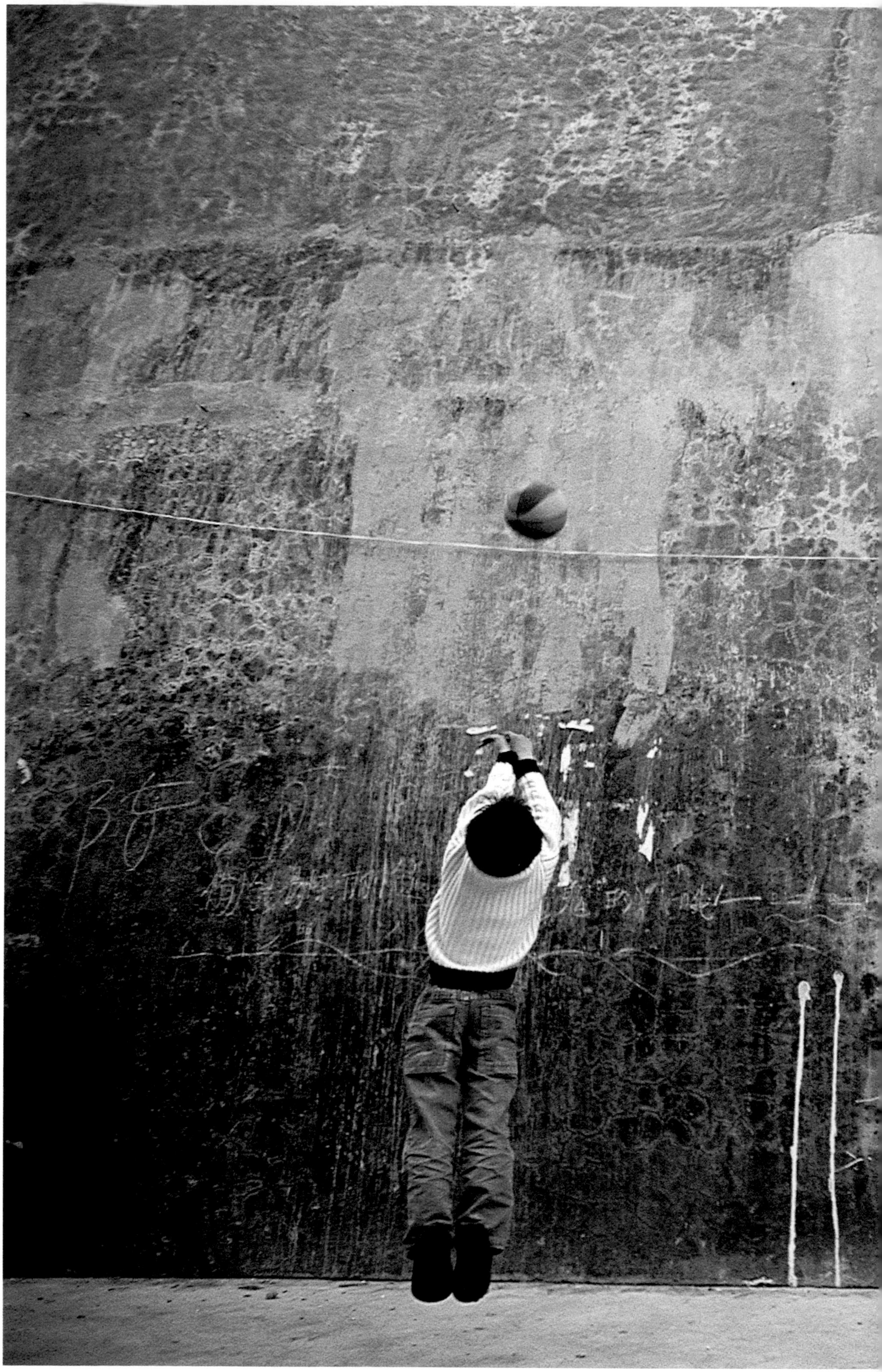

[RIGHT] A playground in the 600-year-old fortified town of Ping'hai.

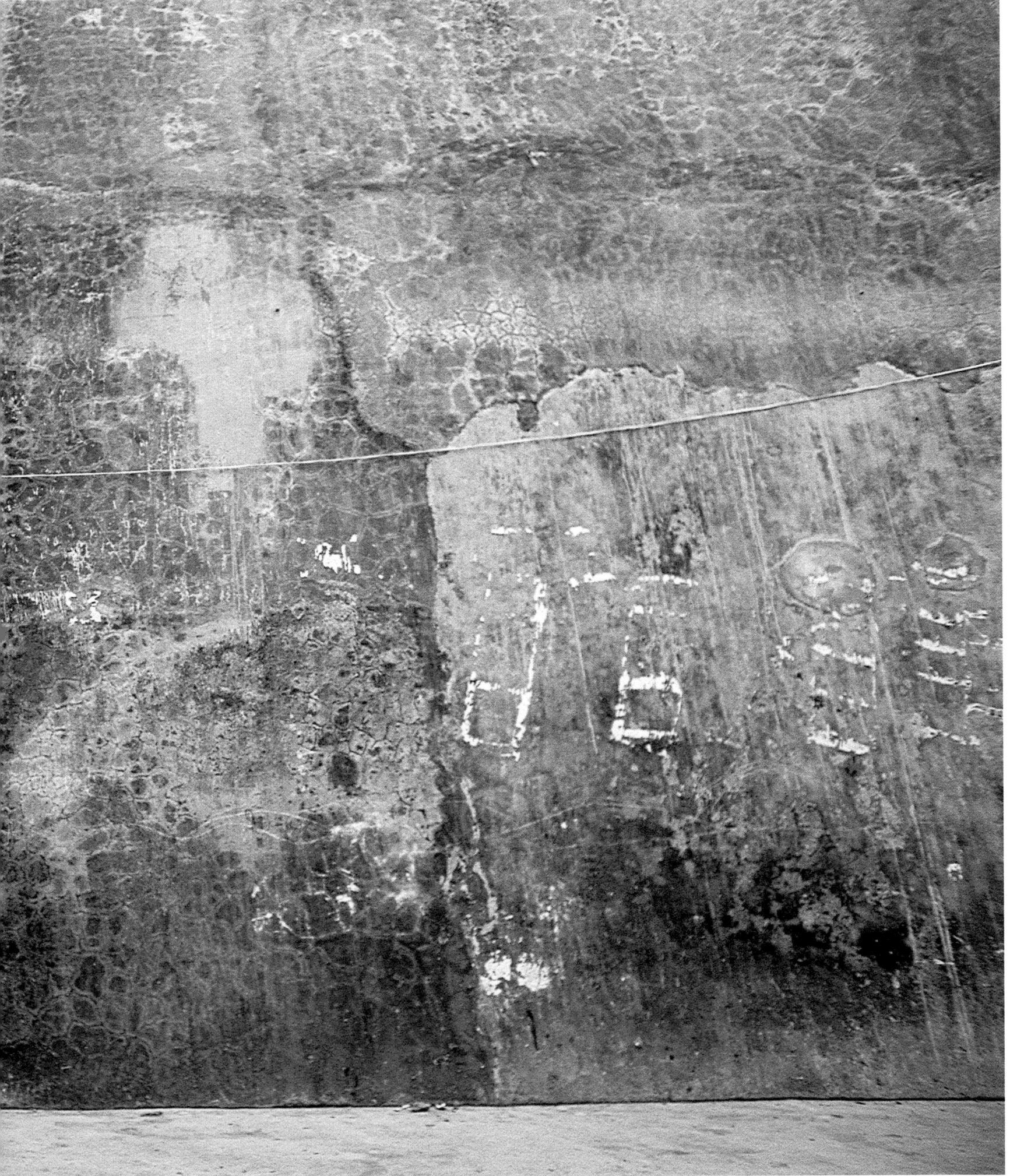

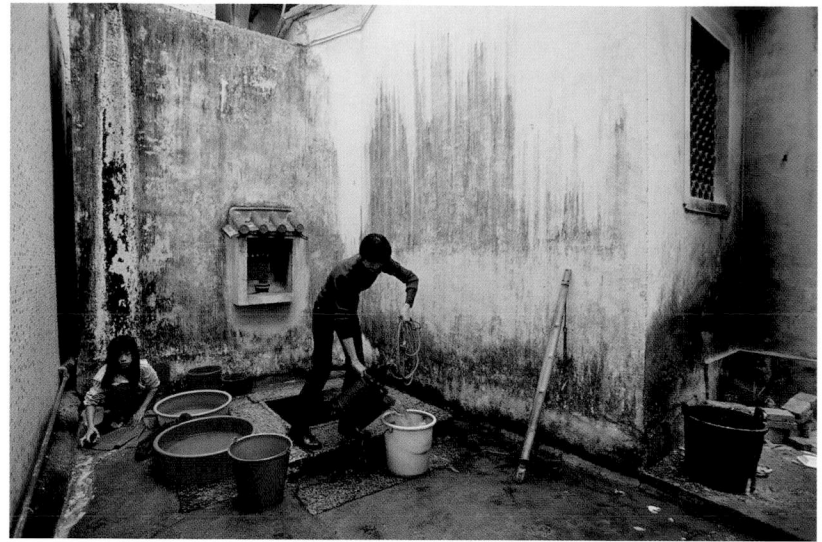

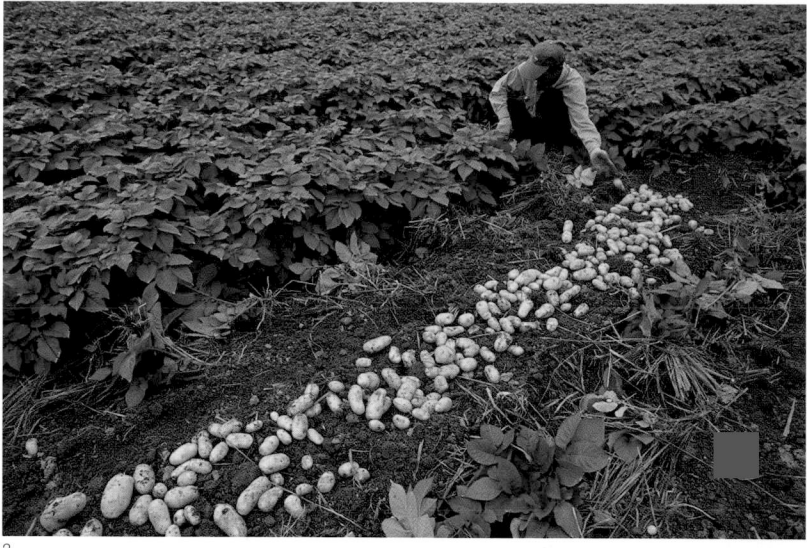

1

2

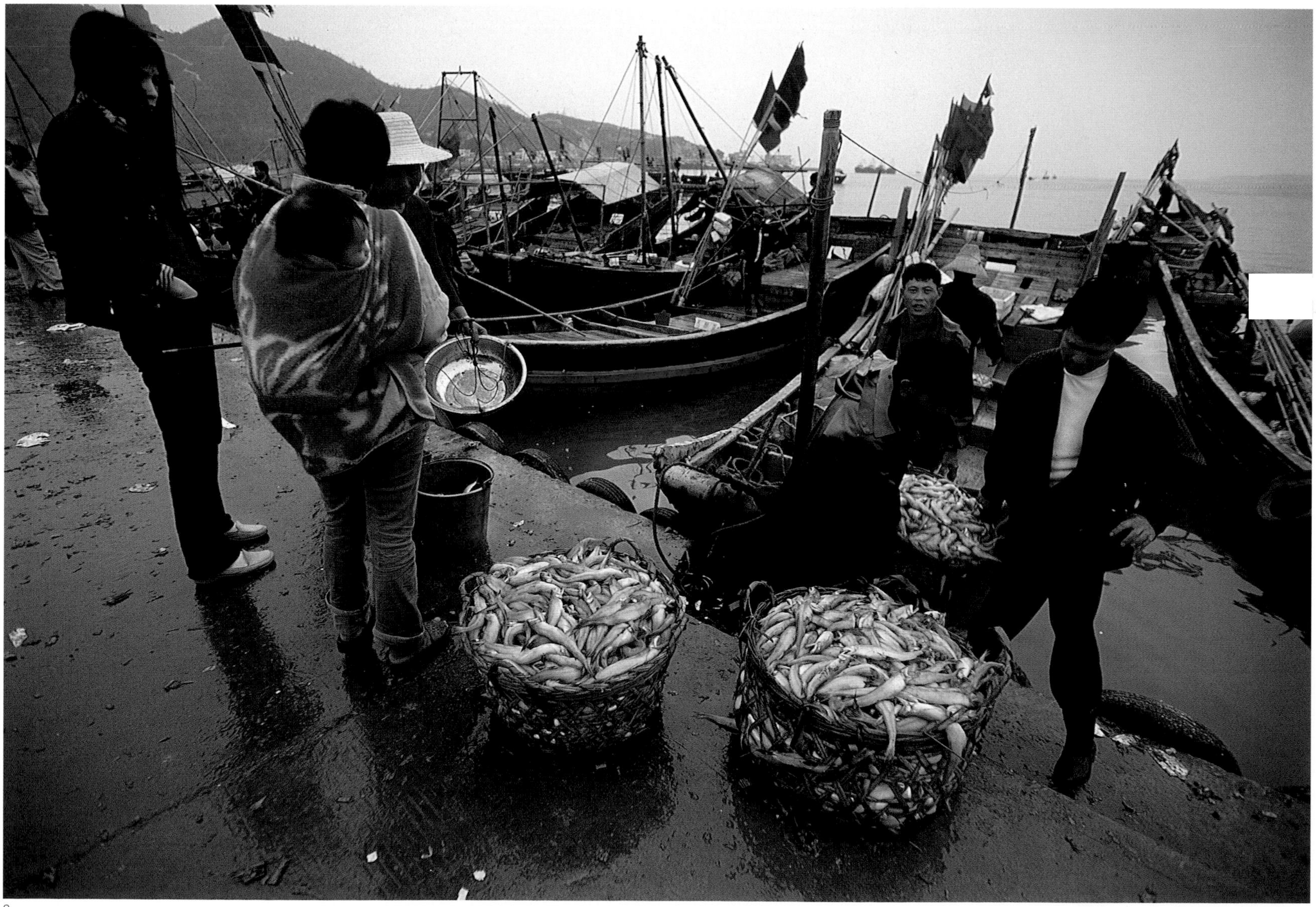

3

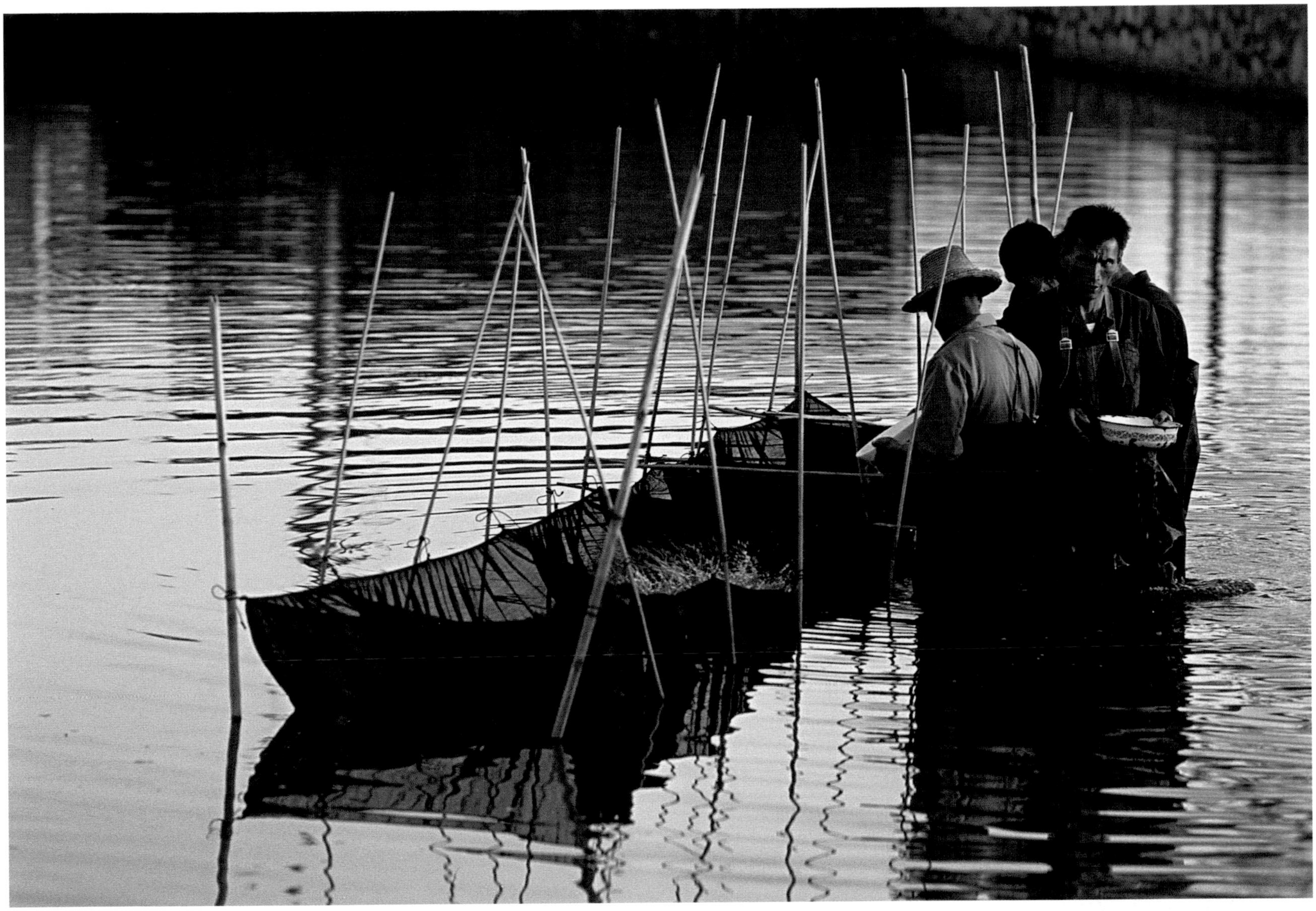

4

IF THE HE'XI CORRIDOR was the carriageway that led to the front gate of China, then the Pearl River Delta is the tradesman's entrance around the back. Roman merchants arrived in the area in the 2nd Century, and by the 7th Century Indian and Arab traders were regular visitors. The Portuguese became the first Europeans to gain a foothold on Chinese soil in Macau in 1557. But it was the British, who first reached the China coast in 1625 and finally 'acquired' Hong Kong in 1842, that had the most profound and lasting influence on the delta. Along with Guang'zhou, the 'Golden Triangle' is among China's fastest-growing regions. But one does not have to stray far into the countryside to see that not everyone is sharing in the benefits. [1] Despite Guang'dong's phenomenal growth, residents of Ping'hai – a fortress town established in 1385 to defend against bandits and pirates – still draw their water from communal wells. [2] Farmers outside Hou'men grow potatoes for an upmarket Hong Kong restaurant chain. [3] A Hou'men fishing fleet returns to port from the South China Sea. [4] A fish farm outside Zhong'shan. [5] An old lady lives alone in San'men'li Village.

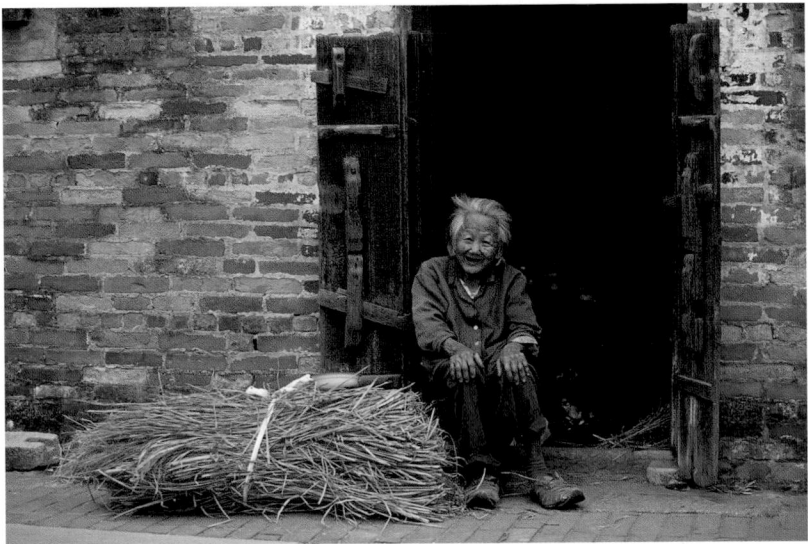

5

267

THE NEW OLD SUMMER PALACE

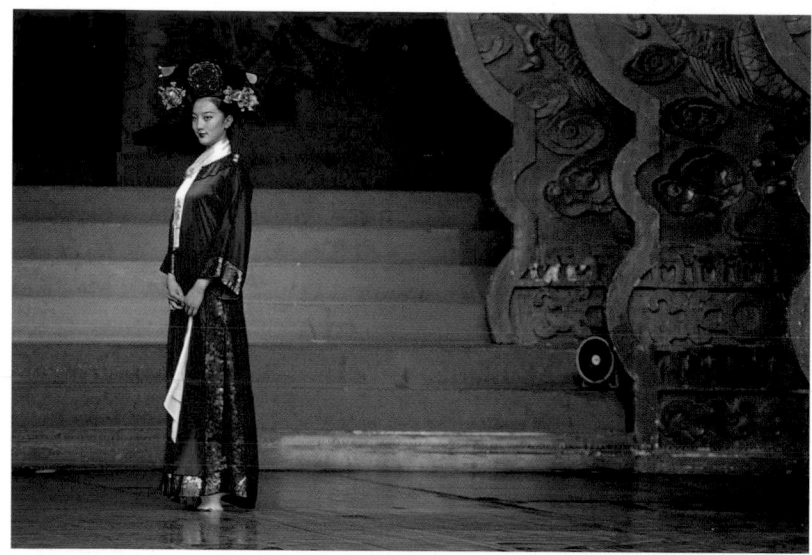

1

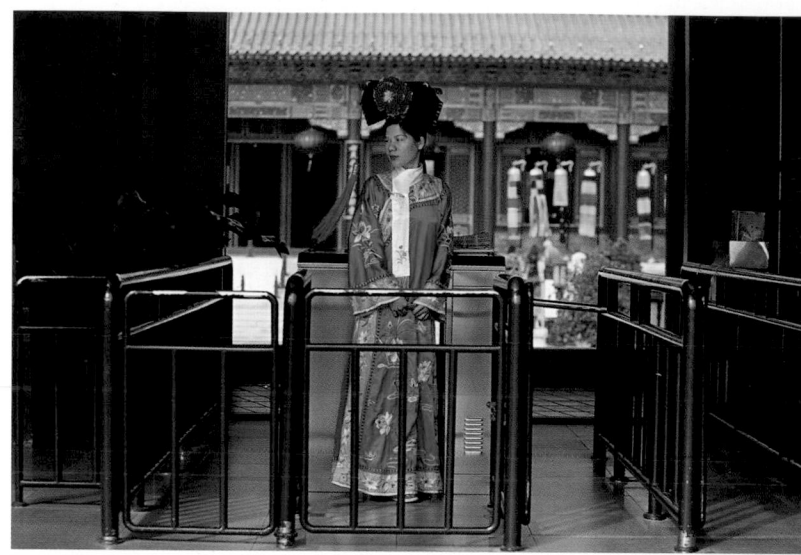

2

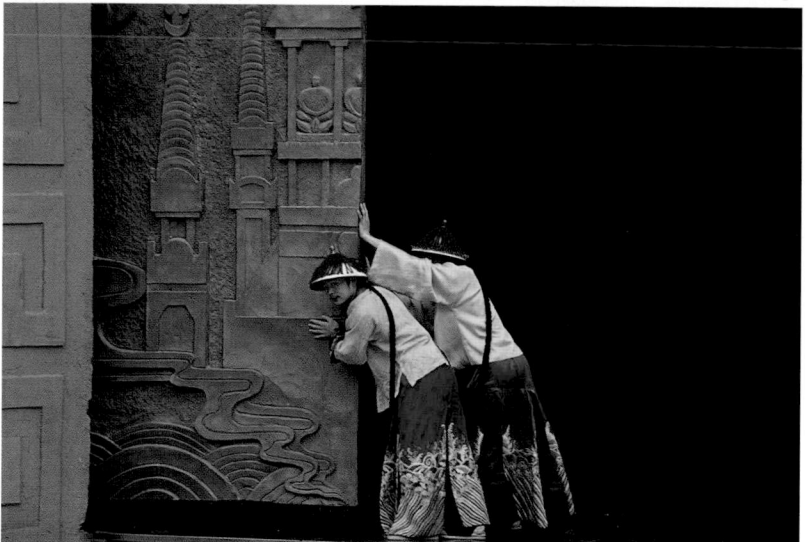

3

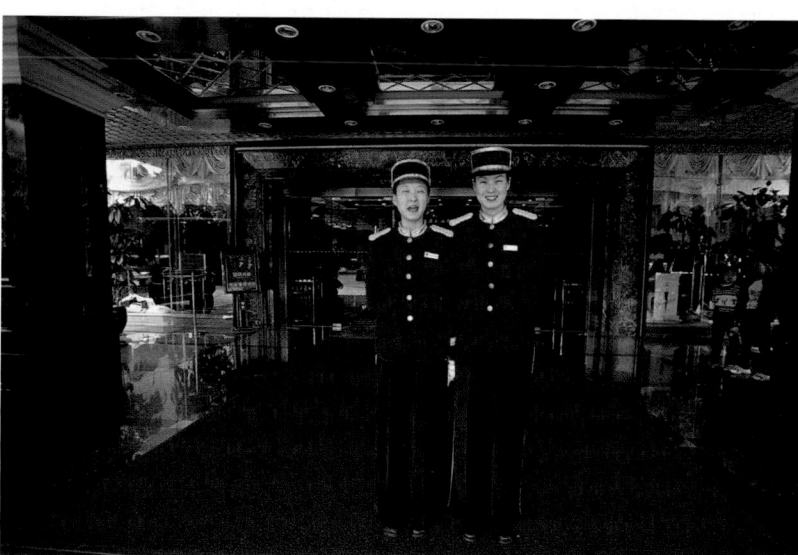

4

THE RANSACKING AND DESTRUCTION of Bei'jing's Yuan'ming Yuan (Old Summer Palace) by rampaging British and French troops in 1860 during the 2nd Opium War is, for most Chinese people, a shameful page in their country's history. But apparently not for the geniuses behind the 'New Yuan'ming Palace' in Zhu'hai. The idea of turning a national tragedy into a theme park adds a whole new dimension to the concept of kitsch. Once past the [2] ticket-collecting 'concubine' alluringly guarding the turnstiles, you can try your luck at the amphitheatre [3], where you risk being chosen to go on stage as the Qing Emperor for an interminable half-hour that will test your capacity for humiliation by playing the [1] 'Emperor picks a new consort' game in front of a 'live' audience. You can then wander over to the scaled-down replica of the 'European Palaces' [5] and watch a truly disturbing Las Vegas-style re-enactment of the wedding between Emperor Qian'long and his favourite concubine, the Uygur princess Xian'fei. [4] After this, it was a great relief to see the bell-girls back at the hotel.

ON THE WATERFRONT

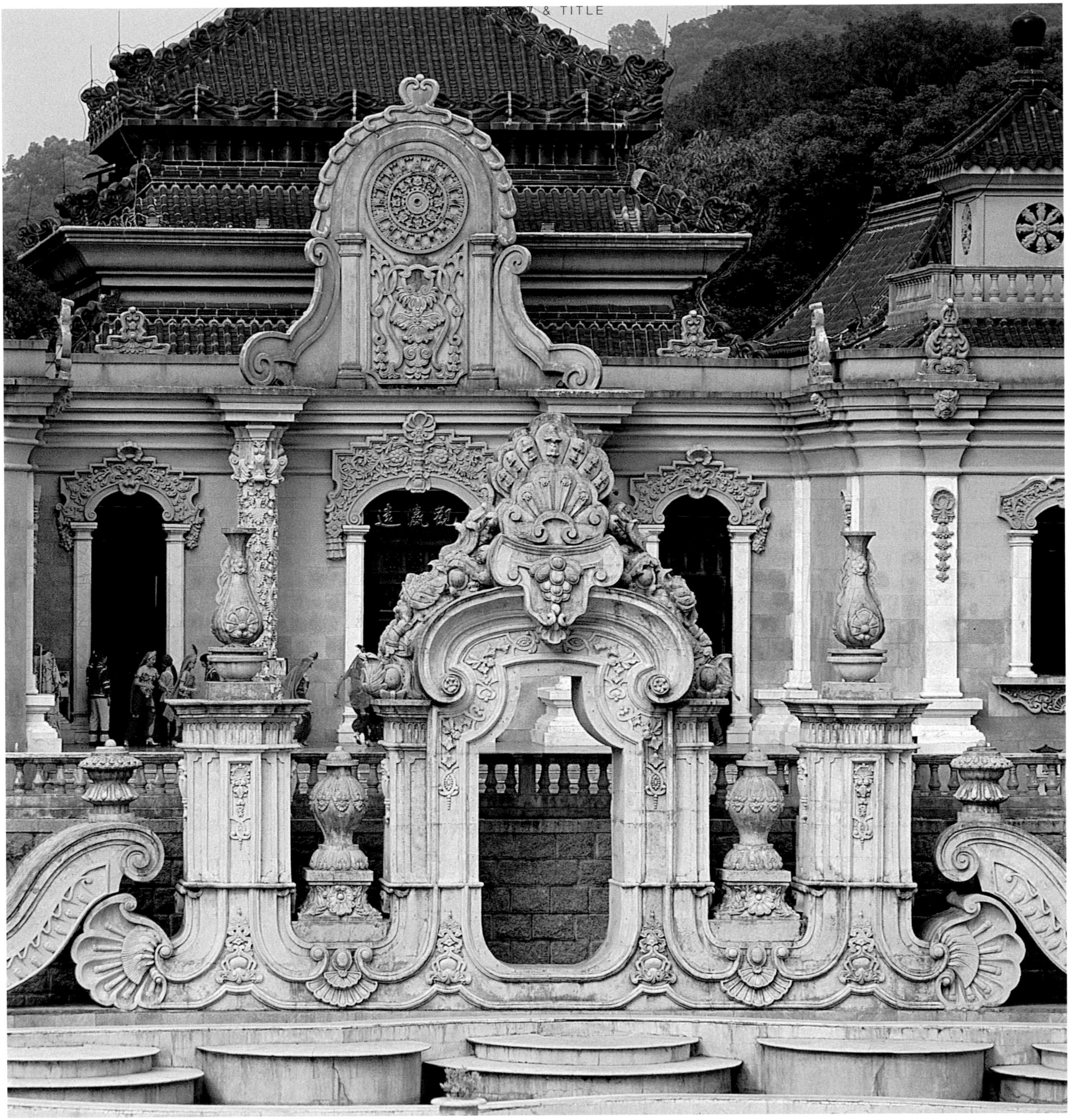

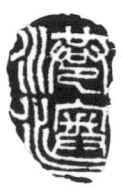

HONG KONG
Special Administrative Region (SAR)

LOCATION
Latitude 22°15'N
Longtitude 114°10'E

AREA 1,092 km² (422 sq miles)

GEOGRAPHY Hong Kong comprises 263 islands scattered between the Pearl River Delta and the South China Sea, the Kowloon Peninsula and the New Territories. The Shenzhen River separates Hong Kong from mainland China. Terrain in hilly to mountainous, with Tai Mo Shan at 958 m.the highest point in the SAR.

CLIMATE Sub-tropical and monsoonal, the weather is cool and dry in winter and hot, humid and wet through spring and summer. Hong Kong is subject to typhoons during summer and autumn. Average temperature in January is 16°C and in July it is 28°C. The highest recorded temperature is 40°C and the lowest is 0°C. Average annual rainfall is 2,225–3,000 mm.

POPULATION 6.9 million (2006 estimate)

AGRICULTURE Small quantities of rice and a variety of vegetables are grown in the SAR, but most food is imported from the mainland and elsewhere. The local fishery is unable to meet local demand.

MAIN INDUSTRIES Hong Kong is one of East Asia's leading service, trading and transshipment centres. The shipping, banking, insuranco, tourism, media and entertainment sectors dominate the economy. Light manufacturing centres on textiles and garments, plastics, electrical and electronic equipment, appliances, metal and rubber products, chemicals, watches, jewellery and toys.

ANNUAL PER CAPITA INCOME (2005)
Per capita GDP: US$24,080
Per capita GDP-PPP: US$32,292

HISTORICAL AND SCENIC SITES
Hong Kong is noted for its shopping and restaurants rather than its cultural or historical artifacts. The Peak on Hong Kong Island and Po Lin Monastery on Lantau Island are among the notable sites.

FOOD Hong Kong food is Cantonese cuisine. The dishes most closely associated with the territory include wonton noodles, *congee*, dim sum, charcoal-roasted goose, duck, pigeon or pork loin and shark's fin soup.

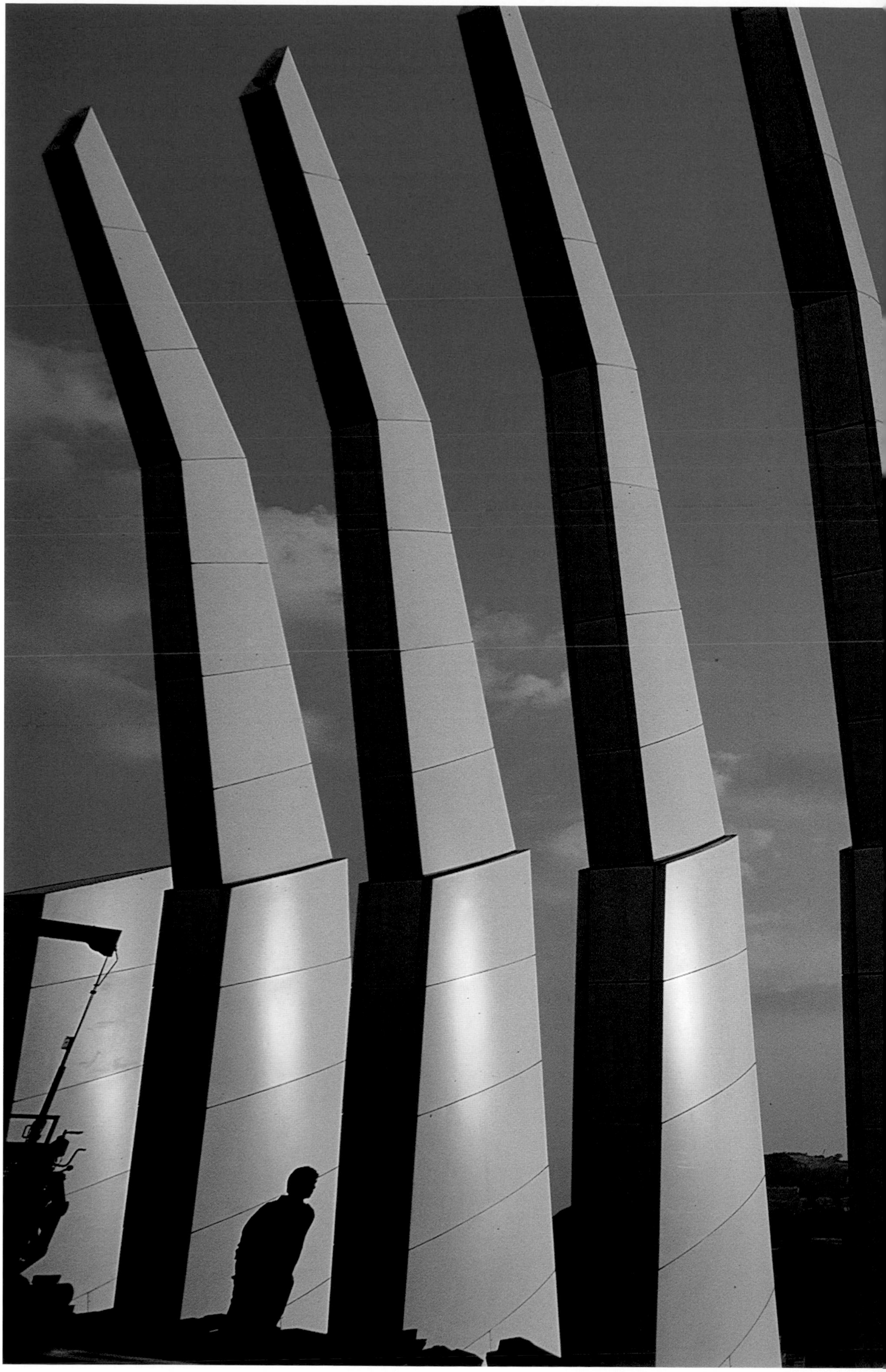

[RIGHT] The top of the International Financial Centre, the tallest building in Hong Kong, is level with the tram station on Victoria Peak.

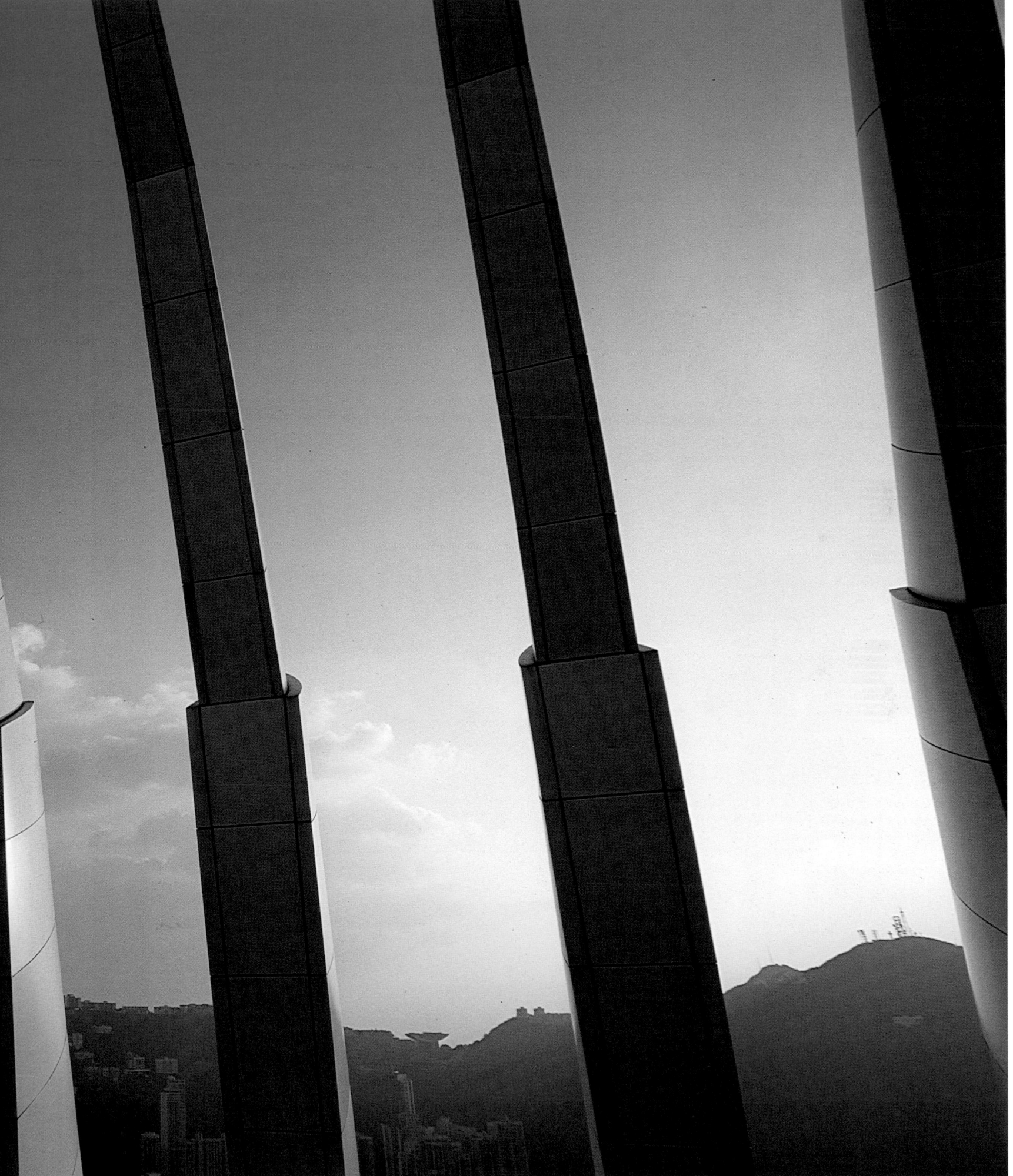

THE STEEL & GLASS JUNGLE

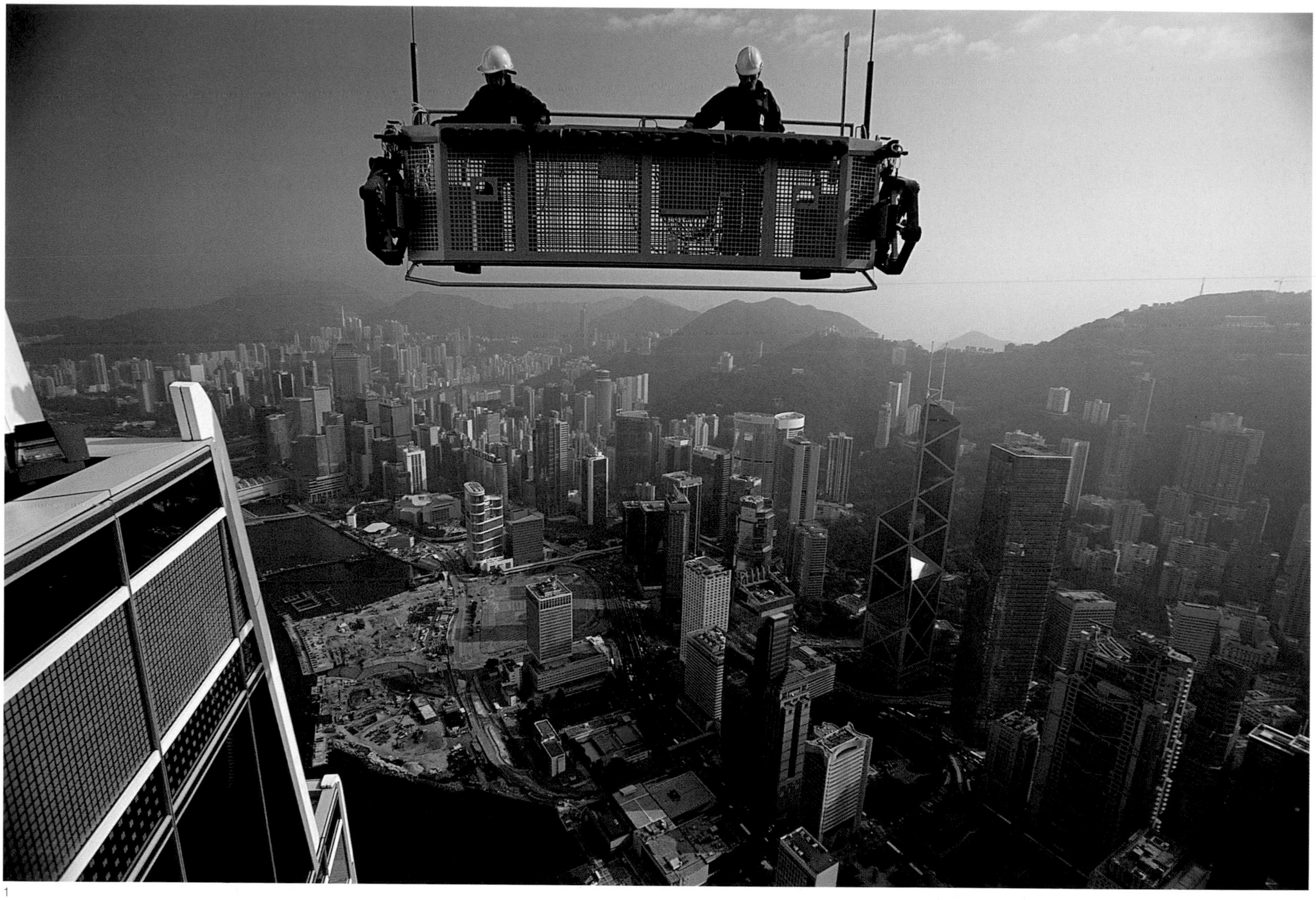

ON 1ST JULY 1997, in torrential rain worthy of the Great Flood, a nervous Hong Kong was handed back to China with the expiration of the 99-year lease on the New Territories. As a Special Administrative Region under the 'one country, two systems' banner, the former British colony is to remain unchanged for at least 50 years and enjoy a 'high degree of autonomy'. But right from the start it was clear the new 'puppet' legislature was not going to go to the bathroom without Bei'jing's permission, and some unnecessarily trying times during the late 1990s Asian financial crisis followed. Despite such setbacks, the unreliability of mainland China's legal and banking systems ensure – for now – Hong Kong's role as the major financial and banking centre for the China trade will endure and [1] [3] [4] its world-famous sky-line will continue to reach heights far beyond those aspired to [2] before the handover.

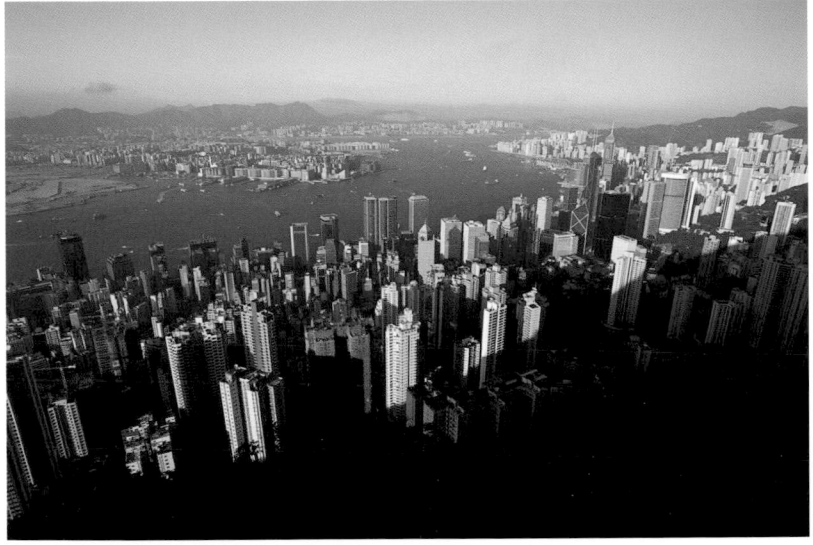

2

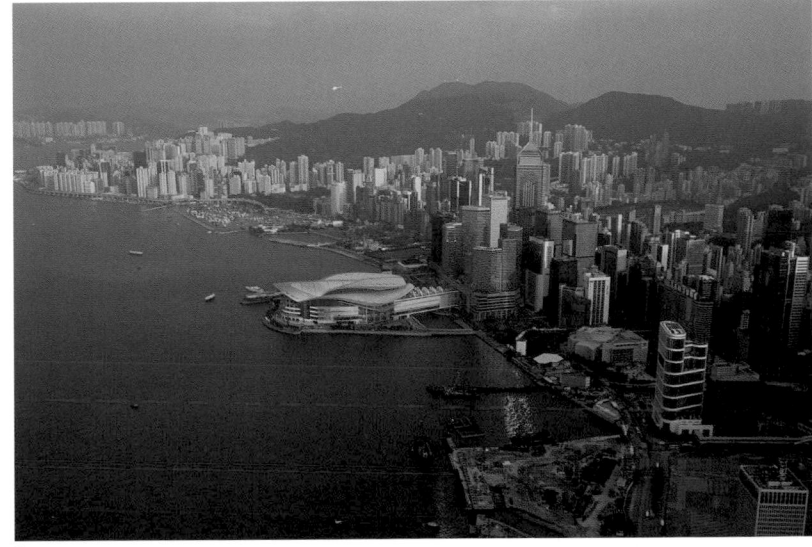

3

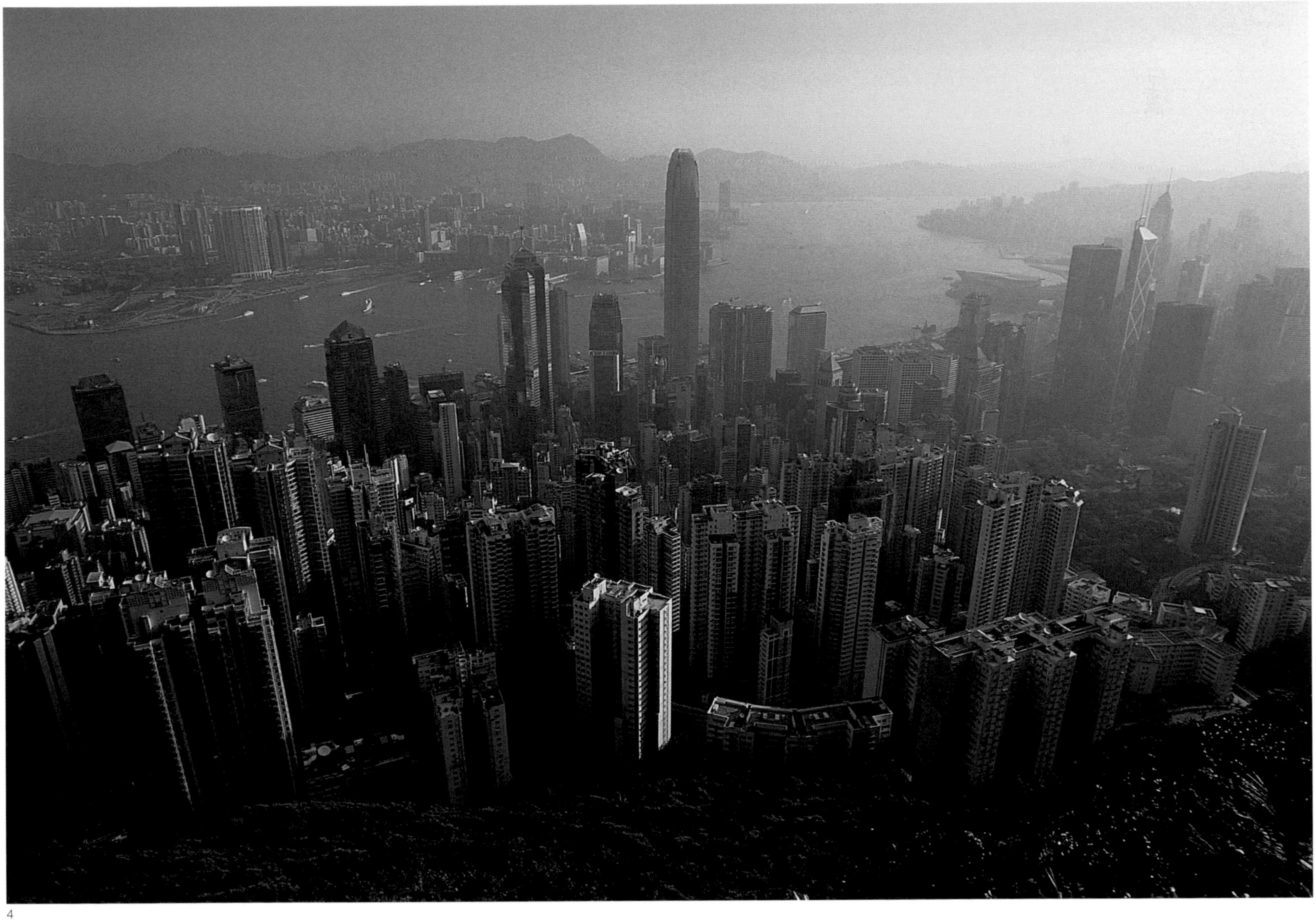

4

THE 'HONG'KIE' SPIRIT

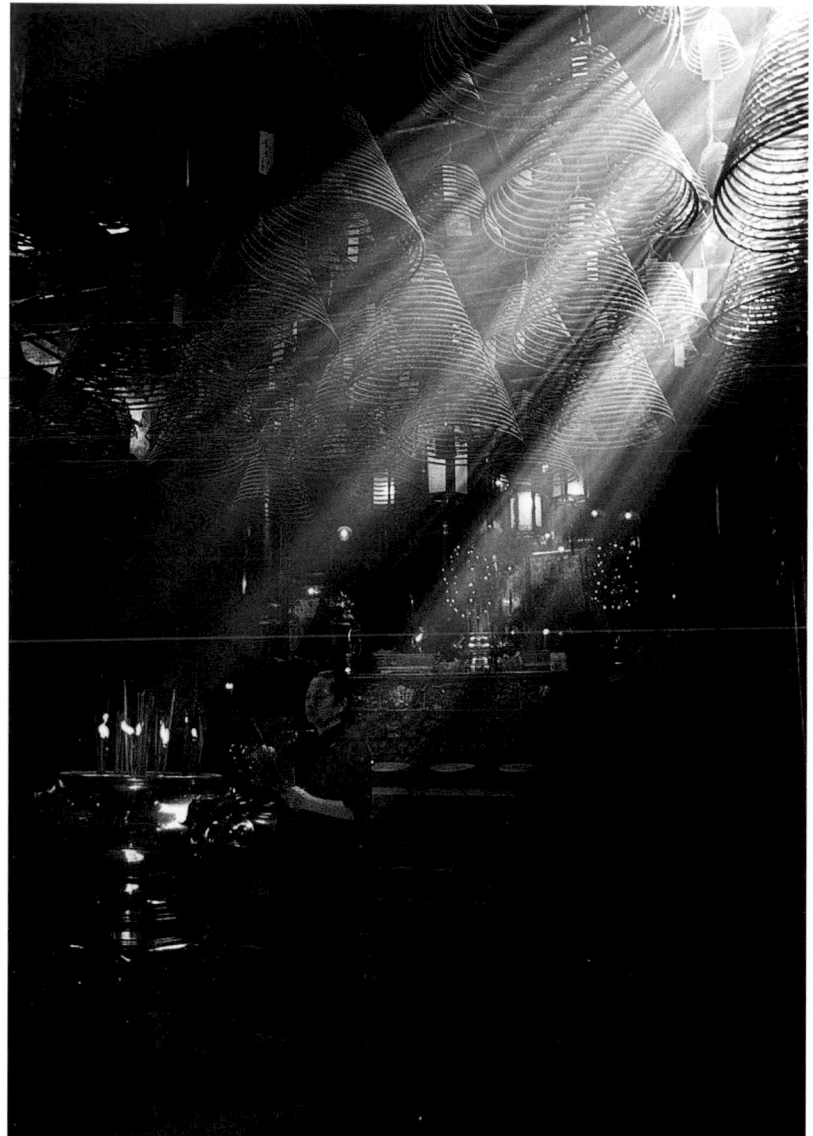

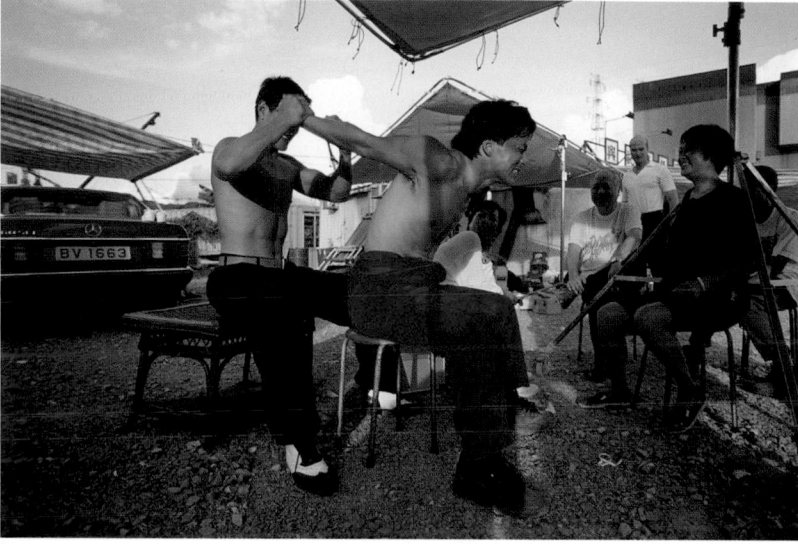

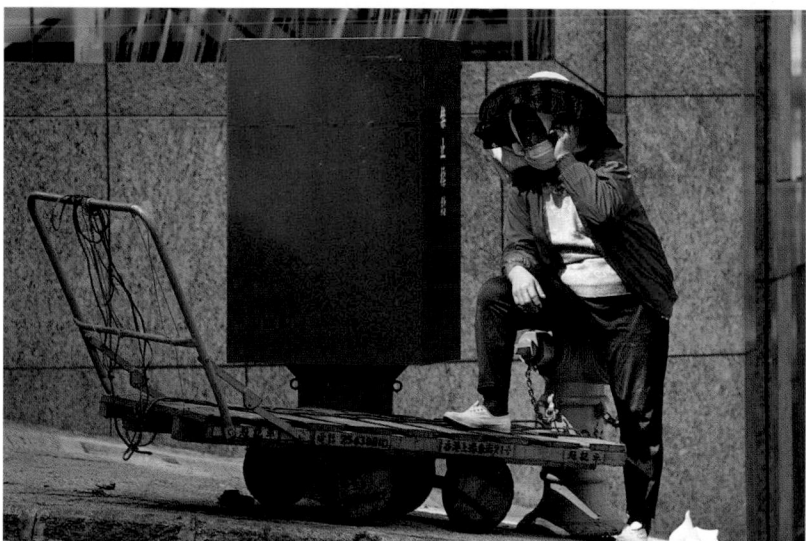

ON THE WATERFRONT

LAID-BACK SINGAPOREANS coined the mildly derogatory term 'Hong'kie' to describe the aggressive Hong Kong migrants encouraged to settle in their Confucian state ahead of the 1997 handover. The newcomers seemed restless to the point of exhaustion, with ambitions verging on madness. As a 'Hong'kie' myself I feel duty bound to define 'Hong'kieness' beyond its surface manifestations. At our best, we are hard working, resilient and ingenious. At our worst we are cunning, selfish and mercenary. But as a society of refugees we have all inherited the 'can do' spirit from those who had fled to the extreme edges of the empire with a single choice – either climb up or fall into the sea. [1] Praying for good fortune in Man Mo (Civil & Martial) Temple on Hollywood Road. [2] Jackie Chan is perhaps Hong Kong's most famous export and the embodiment of the 'Hong'kie' spirit. Seen here on set being 'treated' for an injury sustained during one of his trademark stunts. [3] A Hak'ka labourer on the phone to her broker? [4] A dance student at the Academy of Performing Arts.

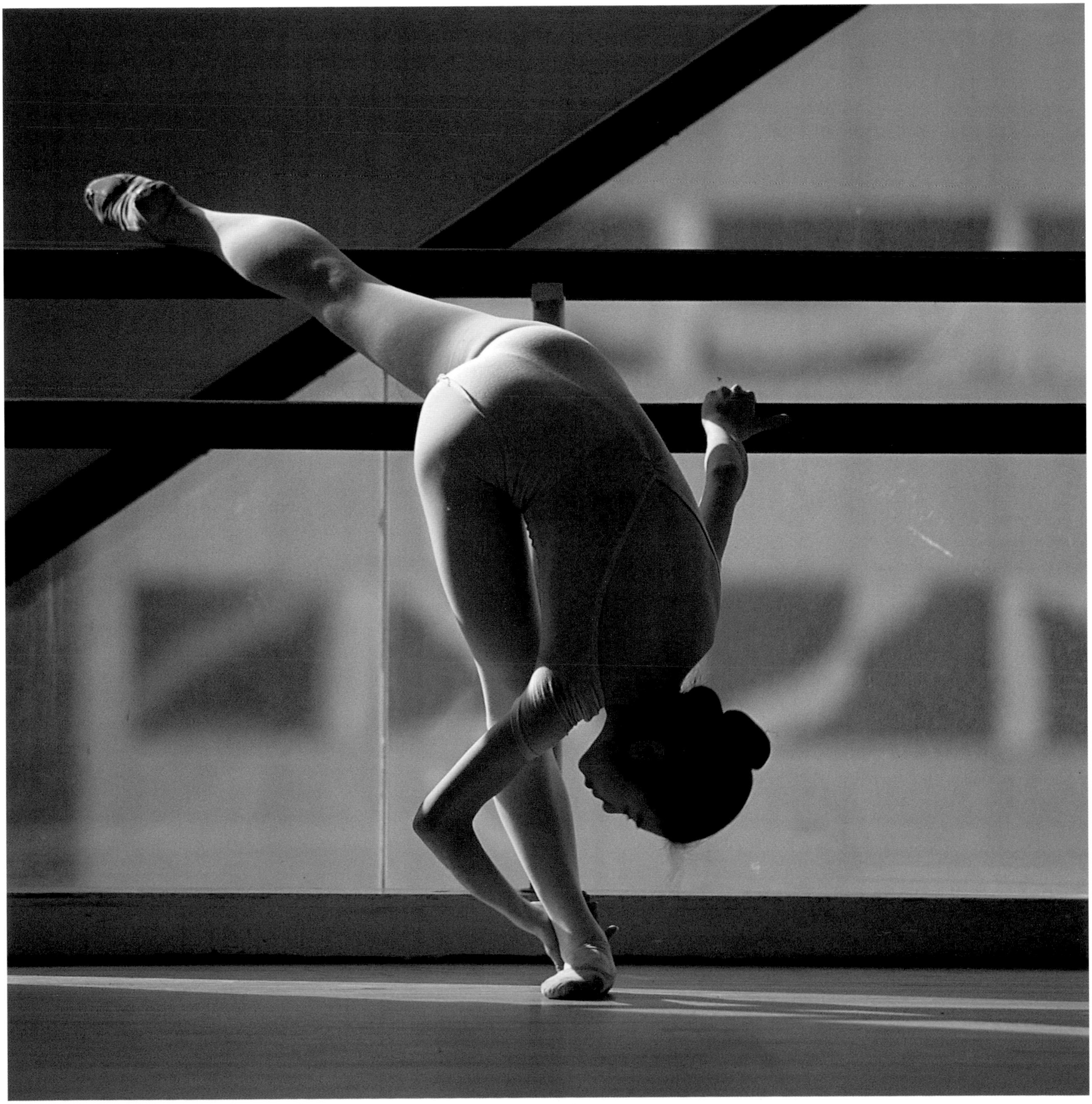

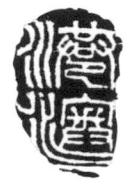

MACAU SPECIAL ADMINISTRATIVE REGION (SAR)

LOCATION
Latitude 22°06'–22°03'N
Longtitude 113°31'–13°35'E

AREA 27.5 km² (10.6 sq miles)

GEOGRAPHY Macau consists of a peninsula and the islands of Taipa and Coloane, linked to each other by bridges and a causeway. The peninsula is between the Zhujiang River estuary to the east and the Xijiang River in the west. The SAR borders China's Zhuhai Special Economic Zone and is 70 km southwest of Hong Kong. More than 60 per cent of Macau's landmass has been reclaimed, rendering much of the densely populated territory flat and low-lying. The highest point is Songshan at 91.07 m.

CLIMATE Macau's climate is sub-tropical with mild winters and hot, humid summers. January temperatures range between 10°C and 15°C, rising to 28–33°C in July. The highest recorded temperature is 38.9°C and the lowest is -1.8°C. Average annual rainfall is around 1,900 mm. Macau is subject to typhoons between July and November.

POPULATION 509,000 (end 2006 estimate)

AGRICULTURE Only 2 per cent of Macau's land area is cultivated, mainly by vegetable growers. Fishing concentrates on crabs and prawns for local consumption. Most food requirements are met by imports, primarily from China.

MAIN INDUSTRIES Macau's economy is based largely on tourism, notably gambling at its casinos. Other industries include textiles and garments, toys and electronics.

ANNUAL PER CAPITA INCOME (2005)
Per capita GDP: US$22,615
Average income: MOP$66,000 (US$8,250)

HISTORICAL AND SCENIC SITES
Ruins of Saint Paul's Cathedral, Barra Fort and Lighthouse, A-Ma Temple, Coloane Island.

FOOD Macanese cuisine is influenced by Cantonese, Portuguese, Malay, Indian, Brazilian and African cooking and ingredients. Noted dishes include feijoada bean and sausage stews from Brazil, grilled sardines from Portugal, African chicken from Mozambique and chilli prawns from the Malay Peninsula.

[RIGHT] A former Gurkha soldier dressed as a Roman centurion stands guard outside the new casino in Macau's Fisherman's Wharf.

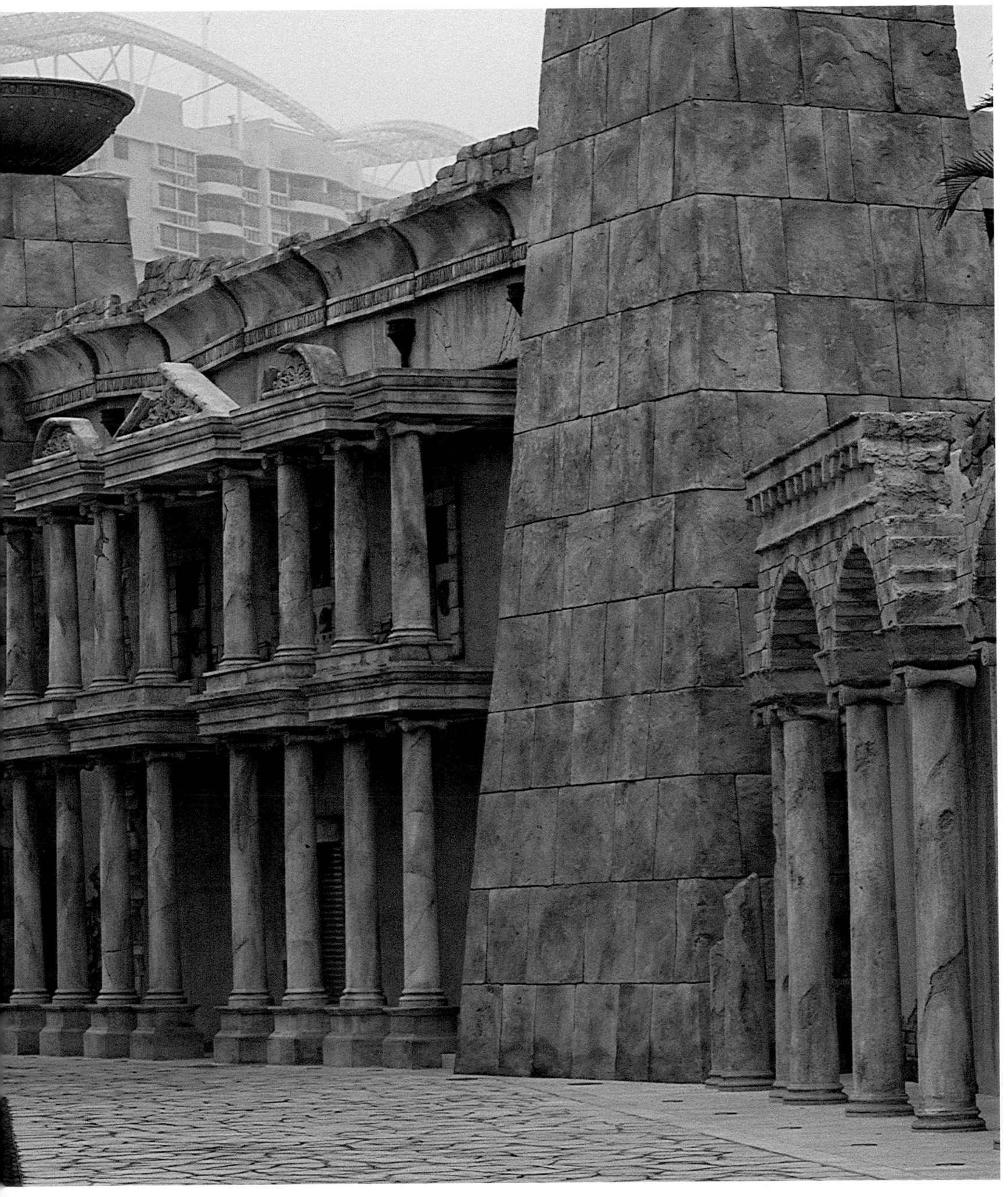

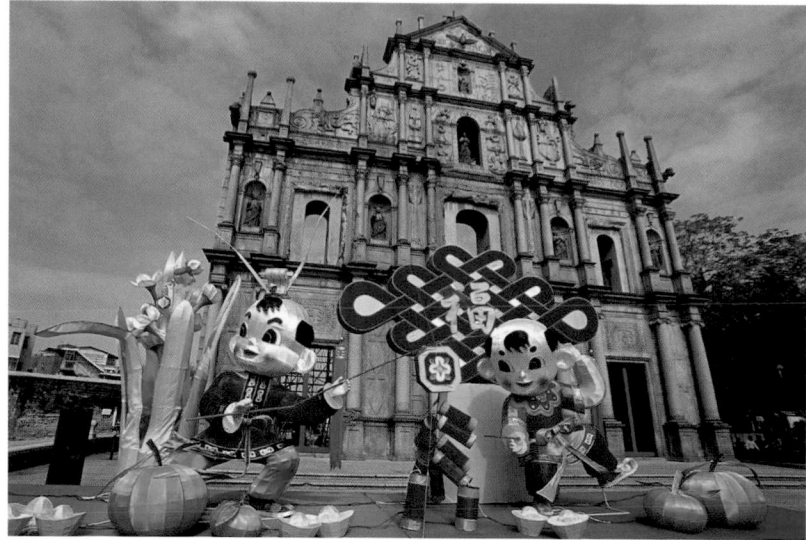

1

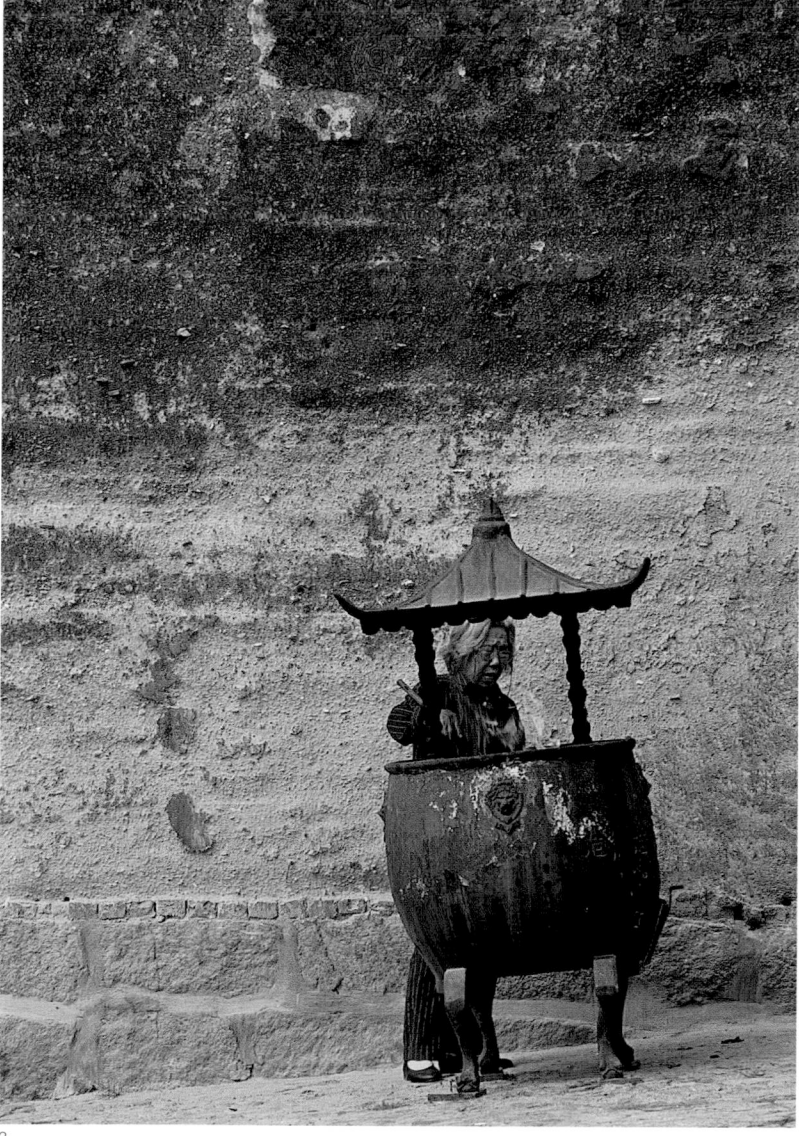

2

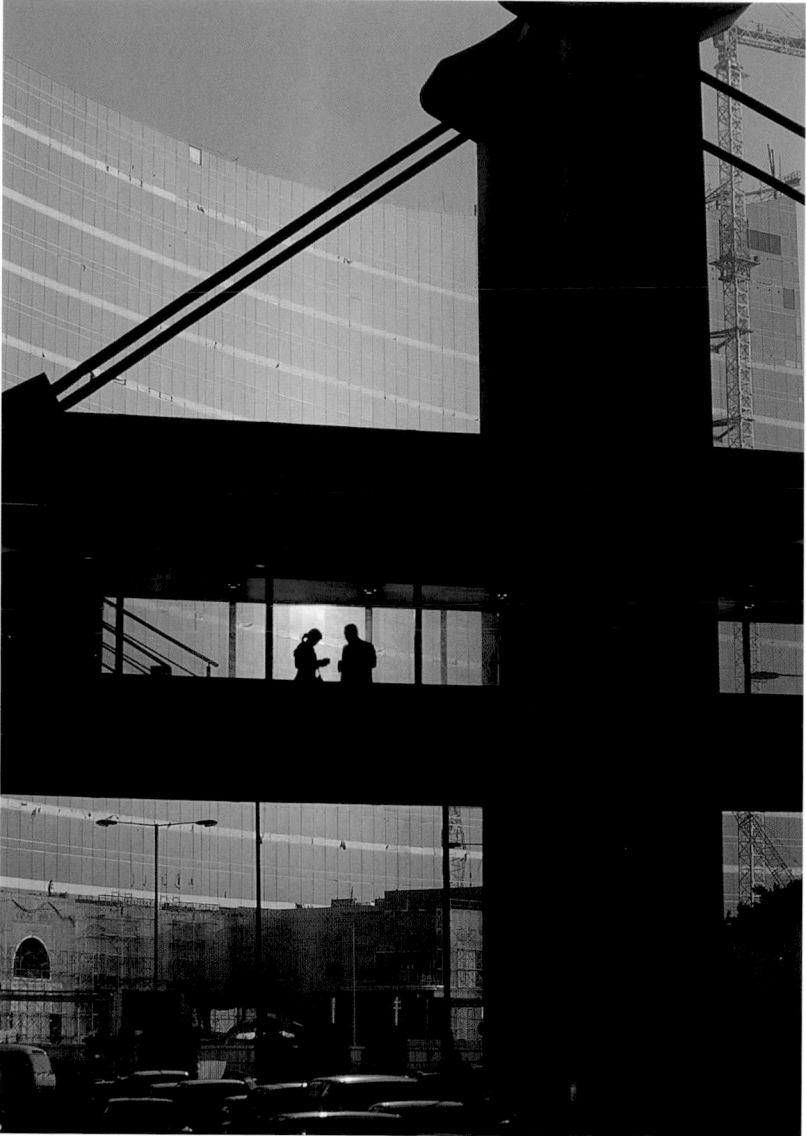

3

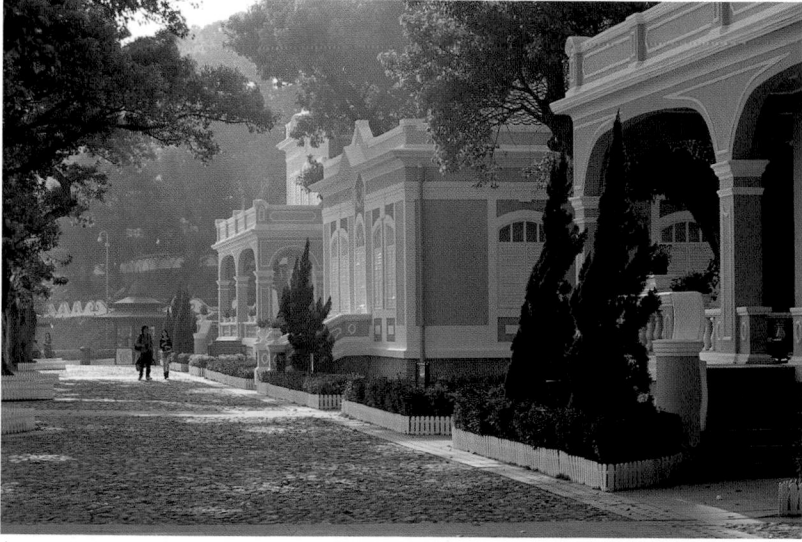

4

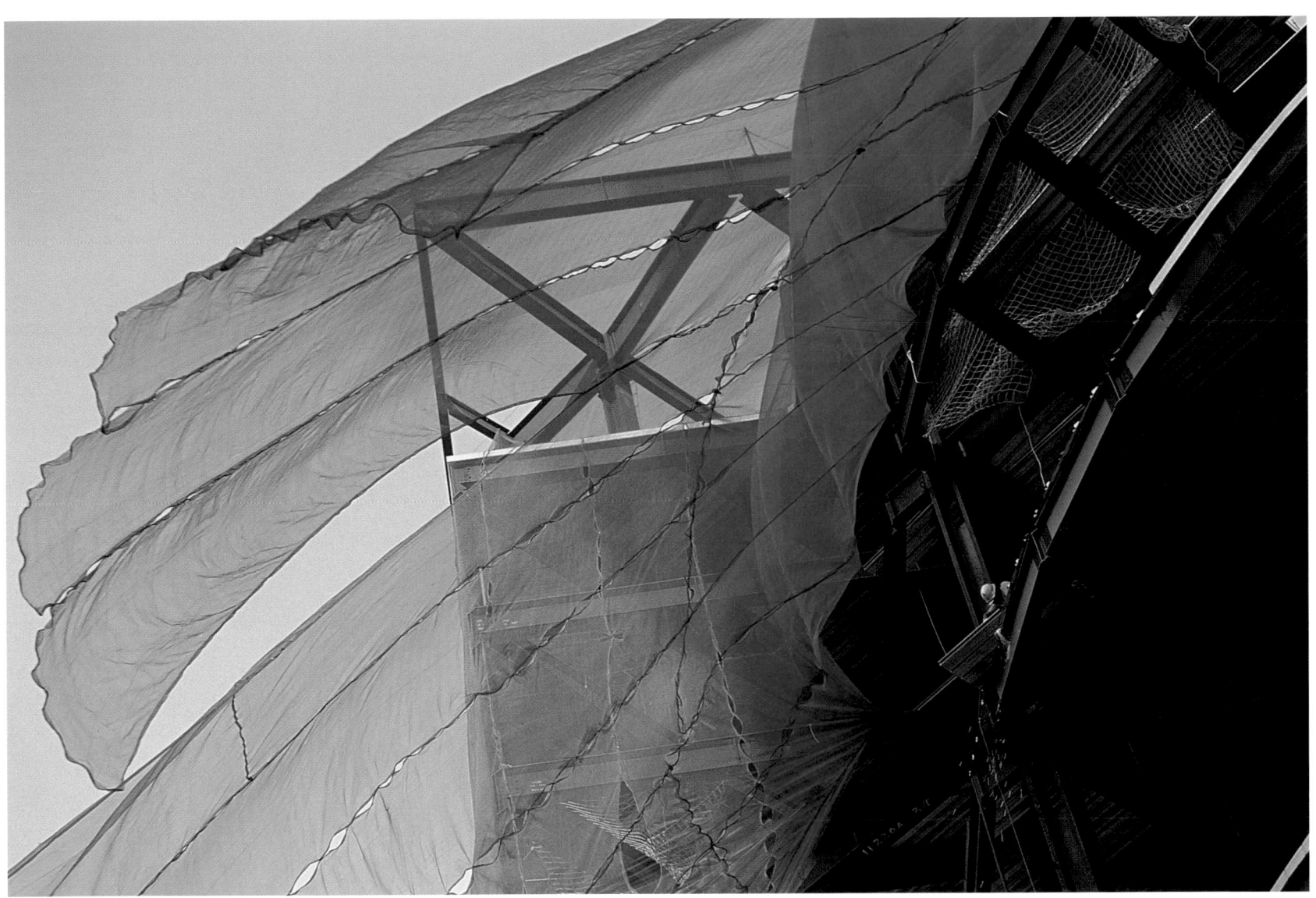

5

AFTER 442 YEARS UNDER PORTUGUESE RULE, the oldest European colony in Asia was returned to China in 1999. With the handover of sovereignty, the Ho family's monopoly on Macau's gambling industry also ended when Bei'jing decided to open up the Special Administrative Region to international gaming syndicates. Soon enormous Las Vegas-style casinos started popping up like mushrooms after a shower and private jets jostled for space at the new international airport. With millions of mainland gamblers pouring into the enclave, including more than a few government officials trying their luck with public funds, the city prospered beyond anyone's wildest expectations. At the end of 2006 Macau had overtaken Las Vegas as the world's biggest gambling centre. [1] Chinese New Year decorations in front of the icon of Macau – the façade of Sao Paulo church. [2] A quiet word during the downtown rush hour. [3] A small Chinese temple behind the ruins of Sao Paulo. [4] Restored Macanese houses on the old waterfront of Taipa Island. [5] 'Dr Ho Strikes Back' with the construction of a new flagship Lisboa Hotel Casino.

ON THE WATERFRONT

HAI'NAN PROVINCE

LOCATION
Latitude 3°58'–20°20'N
Longtitude 108°37'–117°50'E

AREA 33,940 km² (13,100 sq miles)

GEOGRAPHY Hai'nan is China's second largest island. Guang'dong's Lei'zhou Peninsula is to the north across the Qiong'zhou Strait, Bei'bu (Tonkin) Gulf is to the west and the South China Sea to the south and east. The highest elevation is Mount Wu'zhi (1,876 m). Major rivers include the Nan'du and its tributary Xin'wu in the north, the Chang'hua in the west and the Wan'quan in the east.

CLIMATE Hai'nan is in the tropical monsoonal zone, with the east coast subject to typhoons. The island does not have a recognizable winter, with average temperatures in January between 16°C and 23°C. Summers are hot, at 25–29°C in July. The highest recorded temperature is 41.1°C and the lowest is -1.4°C. Average annual rainfall is between 1,500 mm and 2,500 mm.

POPULATION 8.28 million (end 2005)

MAJOR CITIES Haikou (capital), Sanya

AGRICULTURE The main crops are rice, coconuts, palm oil, sisal, tropical fruit, coffee, tea, and sugarcane. Hai'nan is the only rubber-producing area in China, while forestry yields tropical hardwoods. The island's fisheries cover a huge area and are an important source of income for the province.

MAIN INDUSTRIES Hai'nan is rich in mineral resources, with important oil and natural gas fields in the Bei'bu (Tonkin) Gulf and 70 per cent of China's high-grade iron ore and titanium reserves also in the province. Tourism has also become a key element in Hai'nan's economy.

ANNUAL PER CAPITA INCOME (2005)
Disposable income of urban residents:
RMB 8,124 (US$1,014)
Net income of rural residents:
RMB 3,004 (US$375)

HISTORICAL AND SCENIC SITES
Wu'gong (Five Revered Officials) Temple, Lord Su's Temple, Dong'po Academy of Classical Learning, Tomb of Qiu Jun, Ya'zhou town, Xiu'ying Fort Barbette, beaches.

FOOD Hai'nanese food is heavily influenced by Cantonese cuisine while retaining traces of Vietnamese and Hak'ka cooking. The island's four best known dishes are Wen'cheng chicken, Jia'ji duck, Dong'shan goat and Hele crab. Wen'cheng chicken forms the basis of what has been called Singapore's national dish, Hai'nan chicken rice.

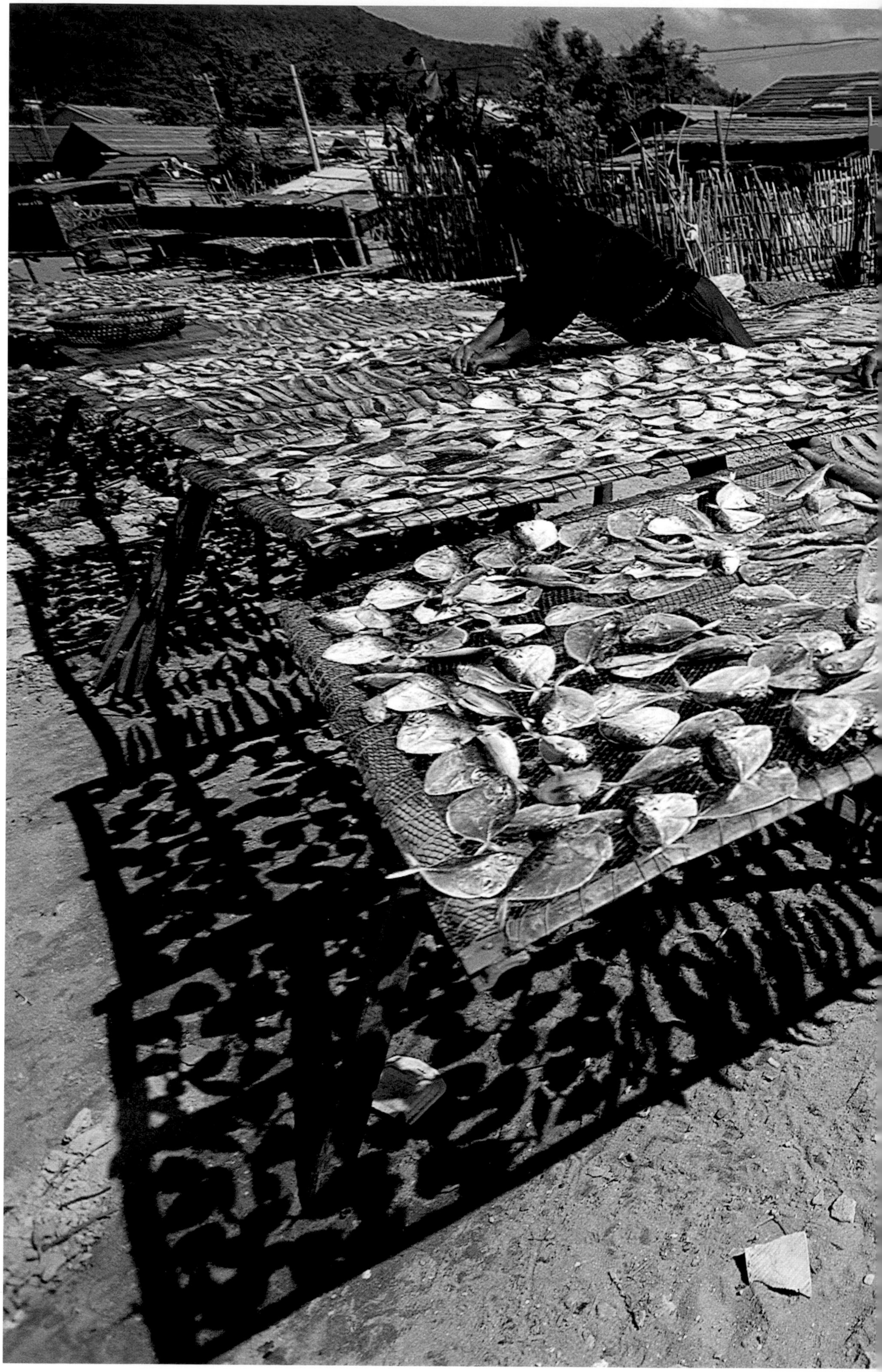

[RIGHT] Fish laid out to dry by the beach in Mei'lian Village on the west coast.

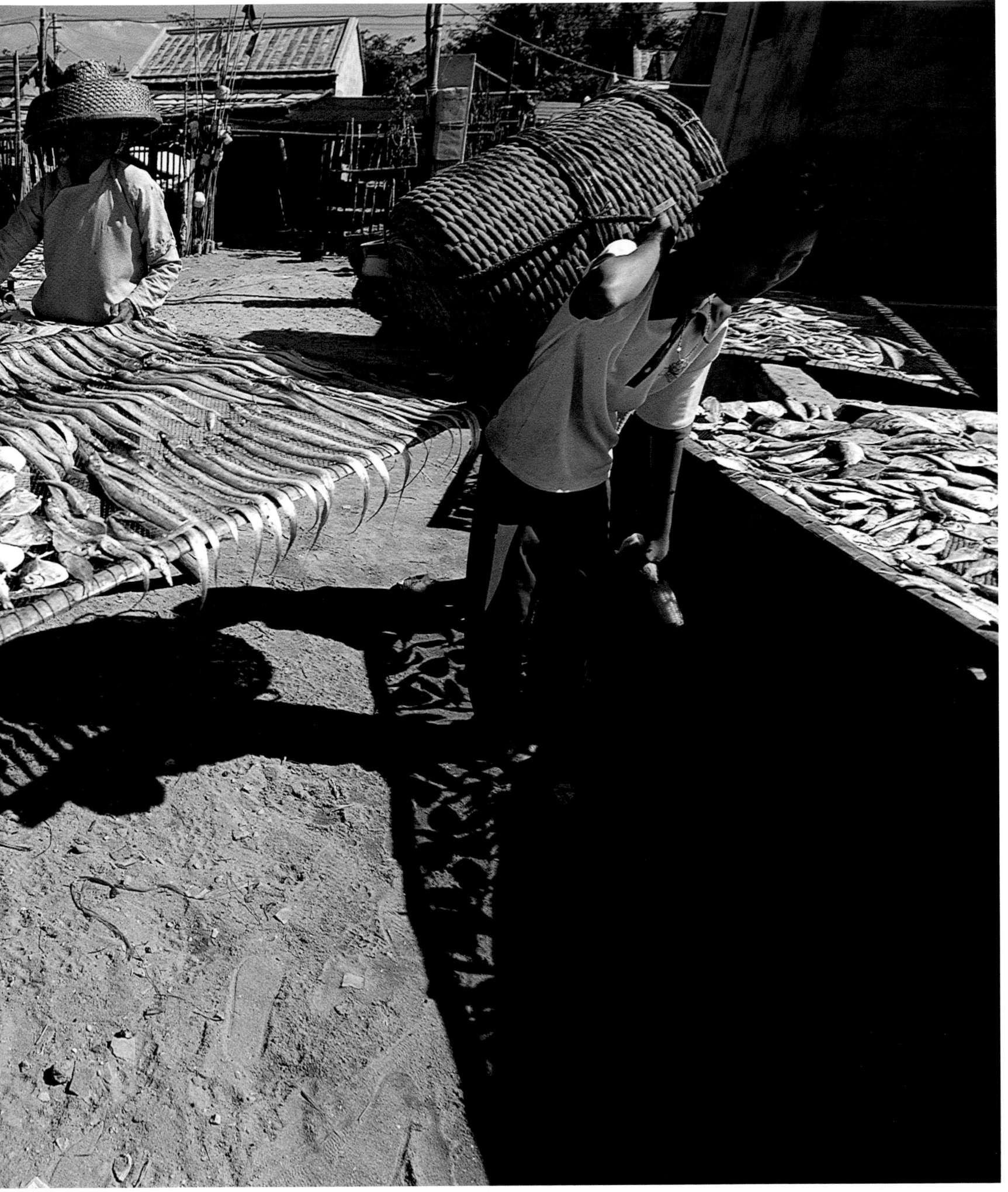

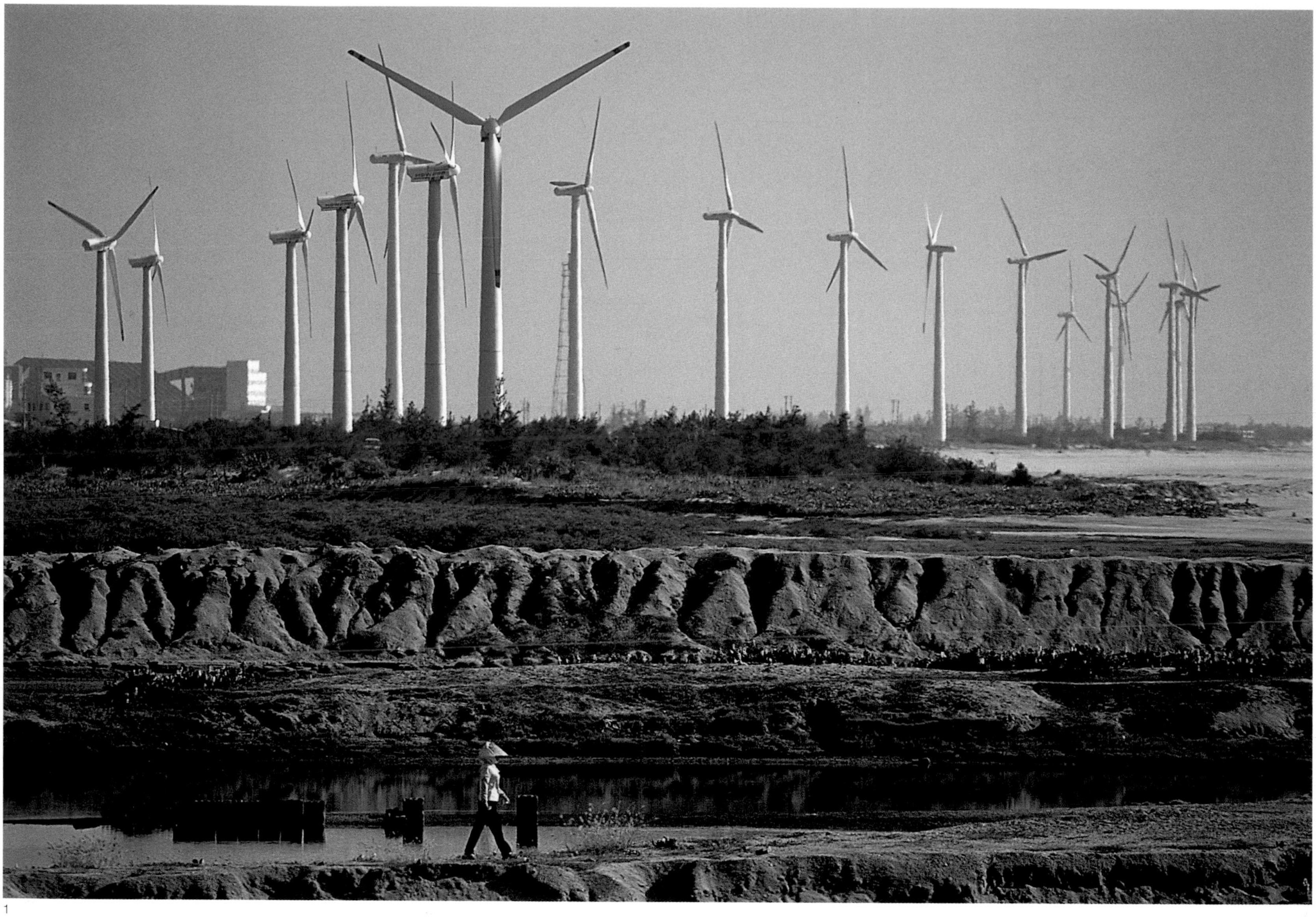

1

THE FACT THAT WEN'CHENG CHICKEN – a recipe that went on to become Singapore's national dish as Hai'nan chicken rice – is the only significant cultural contribution the island has ever made to the world, says a lot about China's largest island and smallest province. The central government tried to change that in 1988 by turning Hai'nan into a SEZ, pouring massive amounts of money into the island. But, as the famous Chinese saying goes, "the mountains are high and the emperor is far, far away" – which means "we are *way* beyond the law". The millions in investments did not result in new industries or improved infrastructure. Instead, Hai'nan is littered with abandoned half-built factories and earned notoriety for the biggest smuggling scandal in the history of communist China – sucking in customs, police, the military and other government departments. Such blatant corruption helped trigger Bei'jing's national and continuing campaign against graft. [1] The Hai'nan Dong'fang Wind Farm on the west coast. [2] An old fisherwoman in Mei'lian Village. [3] Mending nets with hands and feet. [4] A fisher-family having lunch on their houseboat. [5] Fishing boats in the typhoon shelter on the west side of San'ya River.

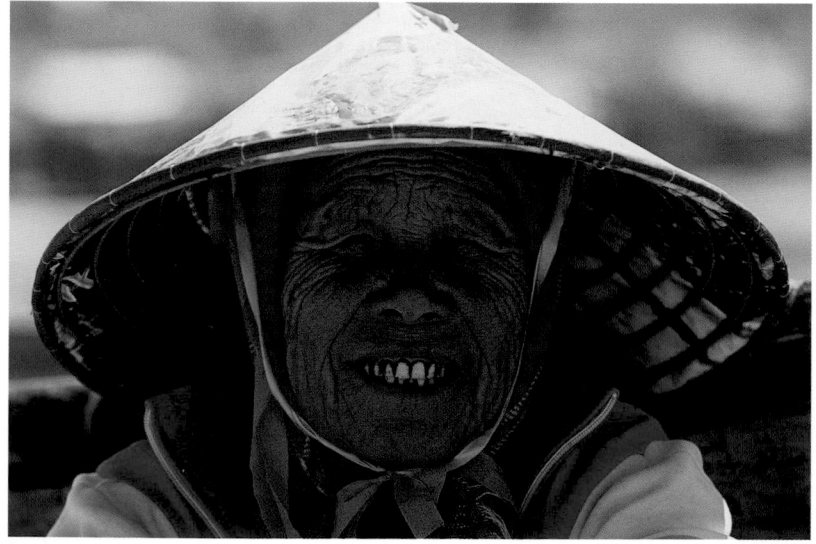

2

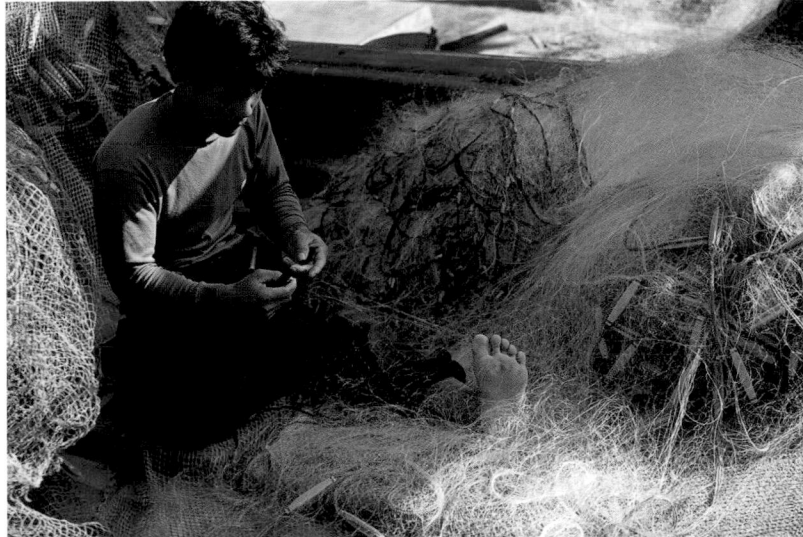

3

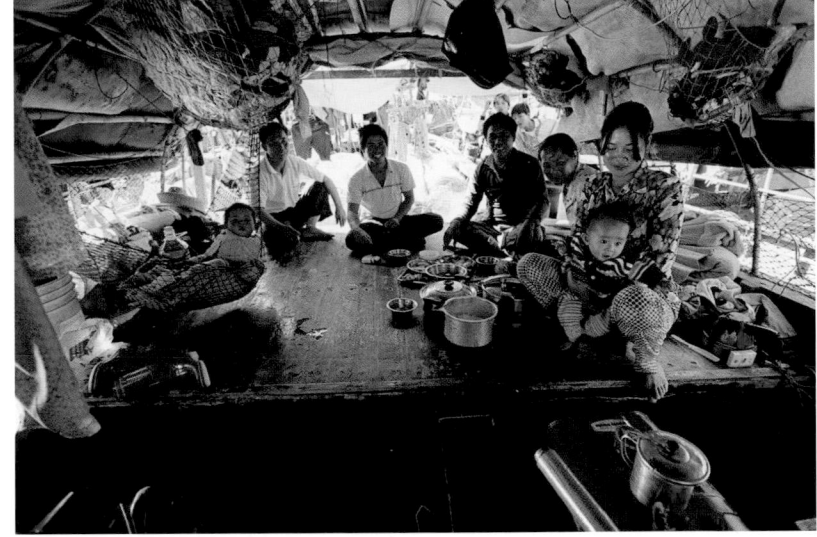

4

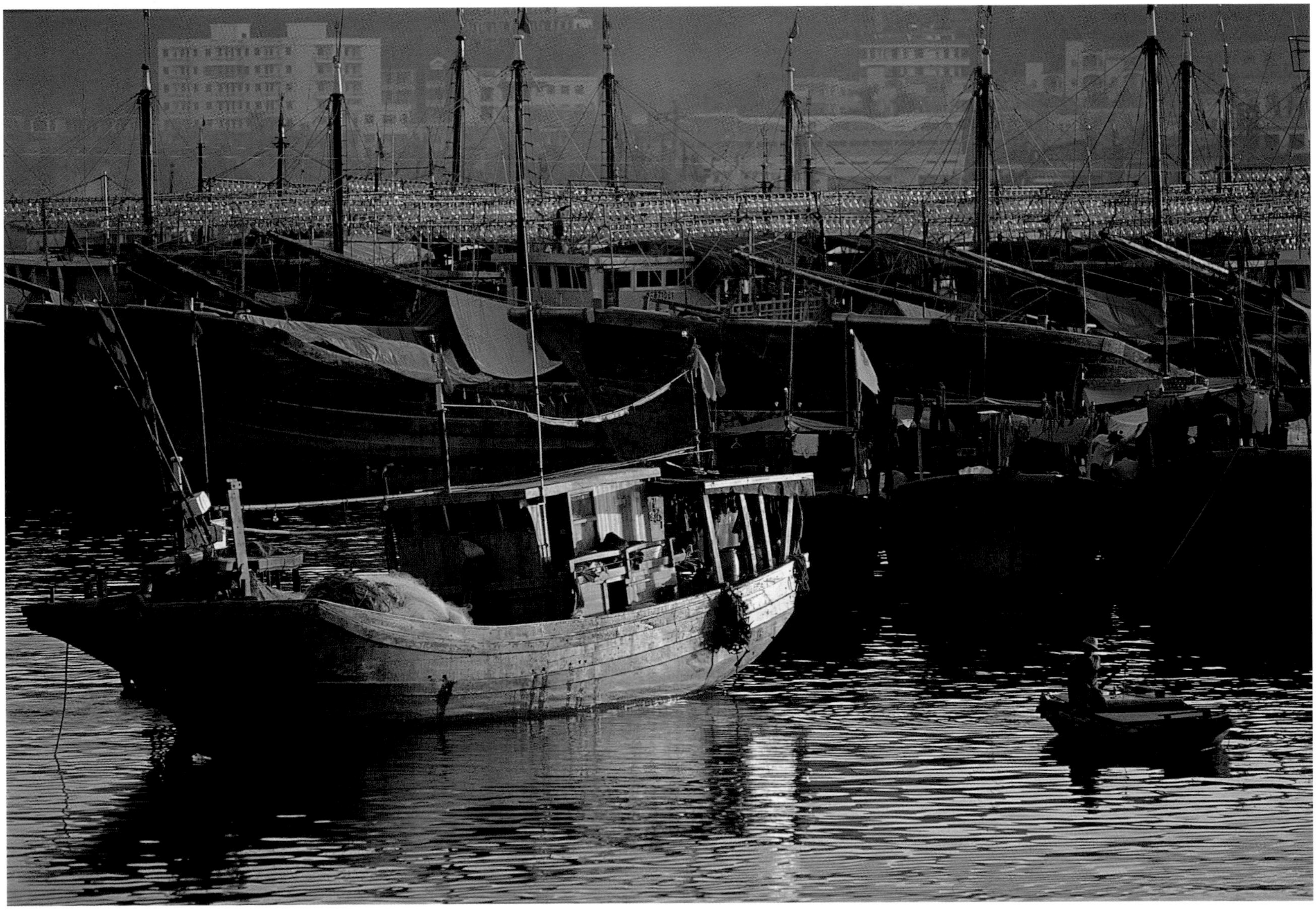

5

THE SNOWBIRDS' PARADISE

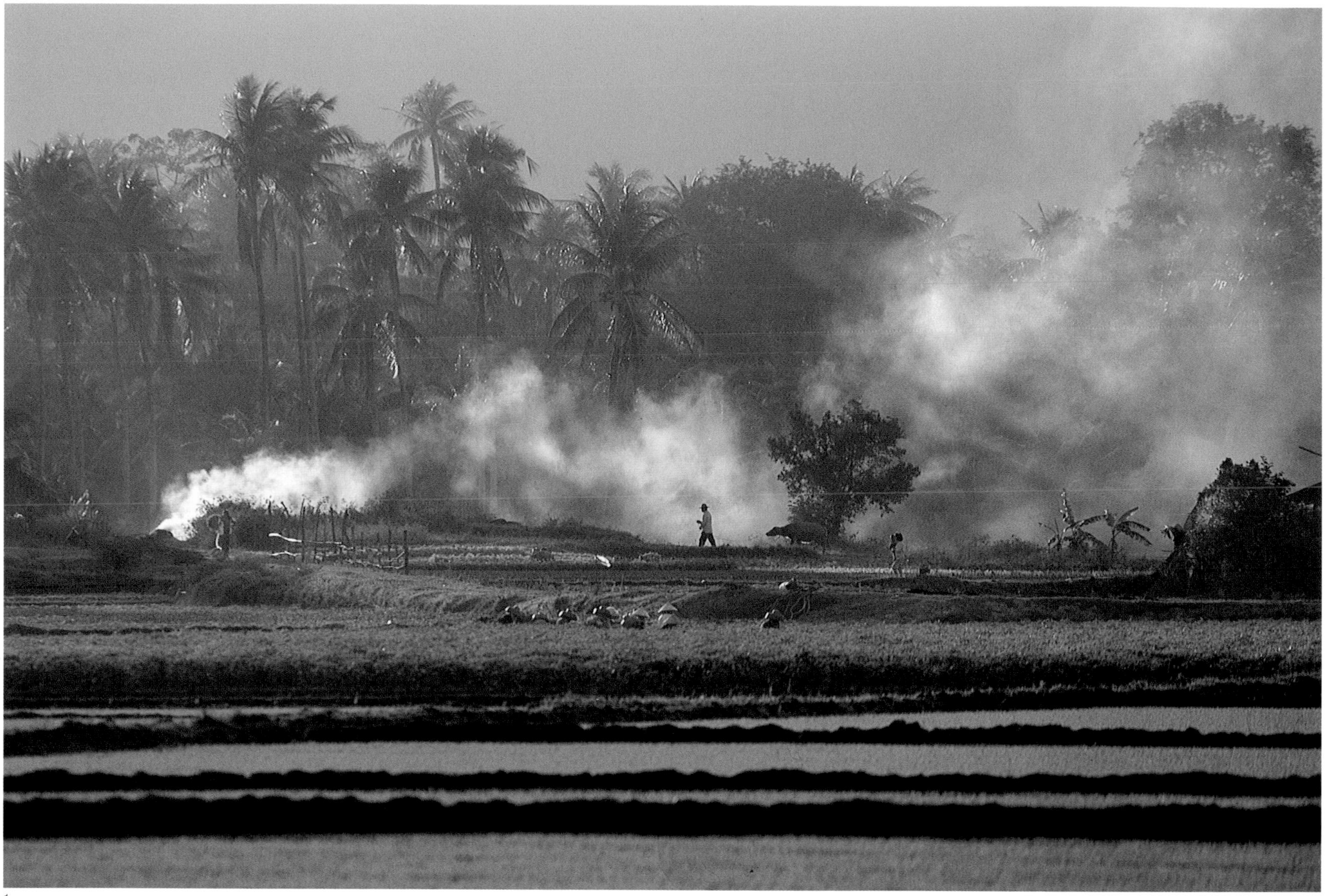

ON THE WATERFRONT

UNTIL RECENTLY, Hai'nan had nothing to offer its overlords in the north beyond serving as a distant and inhospitable place to exile one's enemies. Then someone decided that lying on a beach drinking cocktails with little umbrellas as the sun fried your skin constituted a good time. Along came the jet-set age, and the rest is history. Mass migrations of domestic and Russian tourists from frigid northern winters to the island's endless golden beaches and swaying palm trees now account for over 80 per cent of the province's economy. The tourist industry likes to call Hai'nan the 'Hawaii of the Orient', a slogan that has clearly clicked in the Russian Far-East. During the winter months, when temperature hovers around -30ºC (-22ºF) back home, daily Aeroflot charter flights from Vladivostok land in San'ya on the south coast. [2] [3] Here, Hai'nan's best beaches and largest tourist resorts await the Siberian 'refugees' with the promise of hot sun, cheap drinks and fresh seafood. [1] Meanwhile, in villages just beyond the resorts, local people carry on their daily lives in a separate existence.

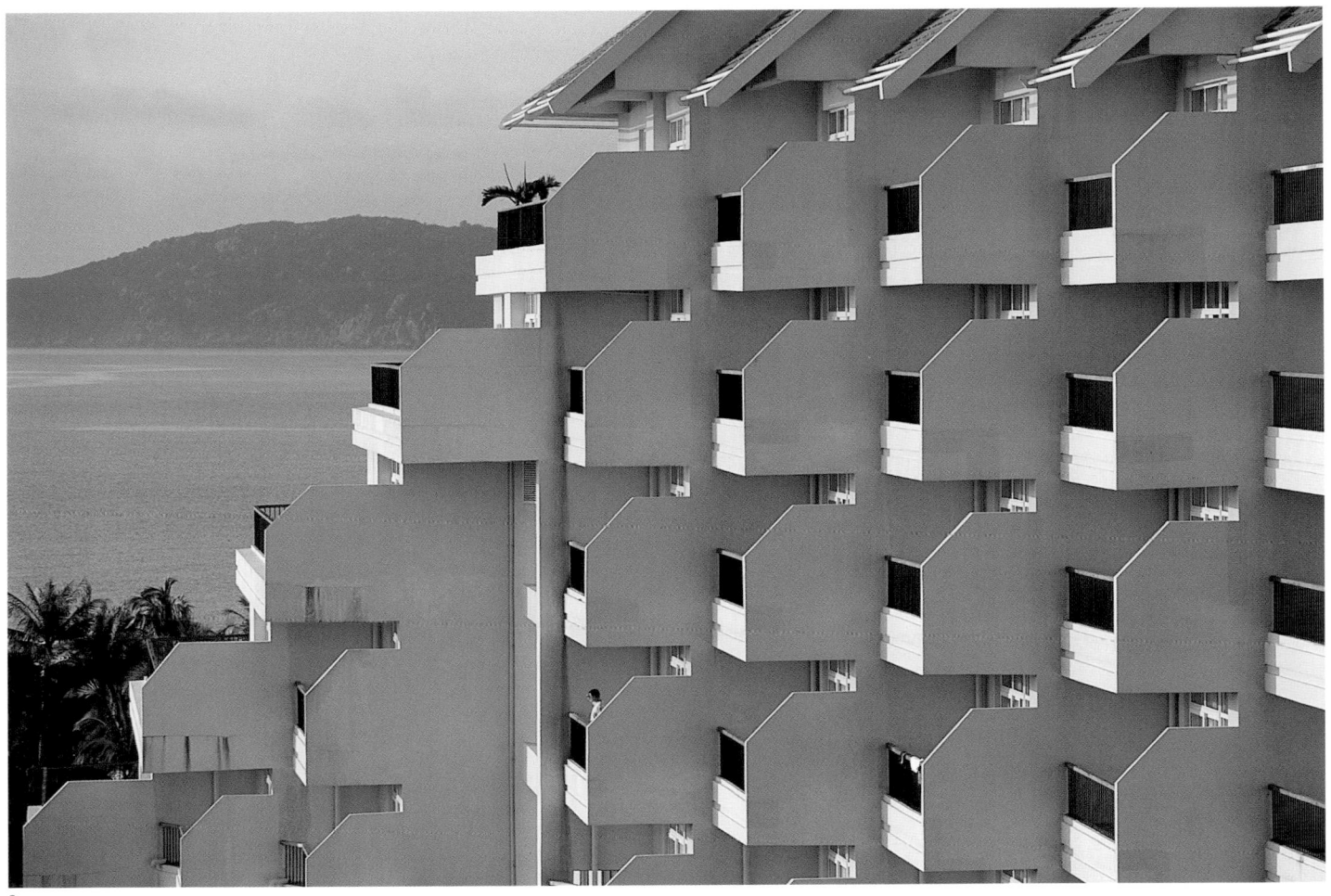

2

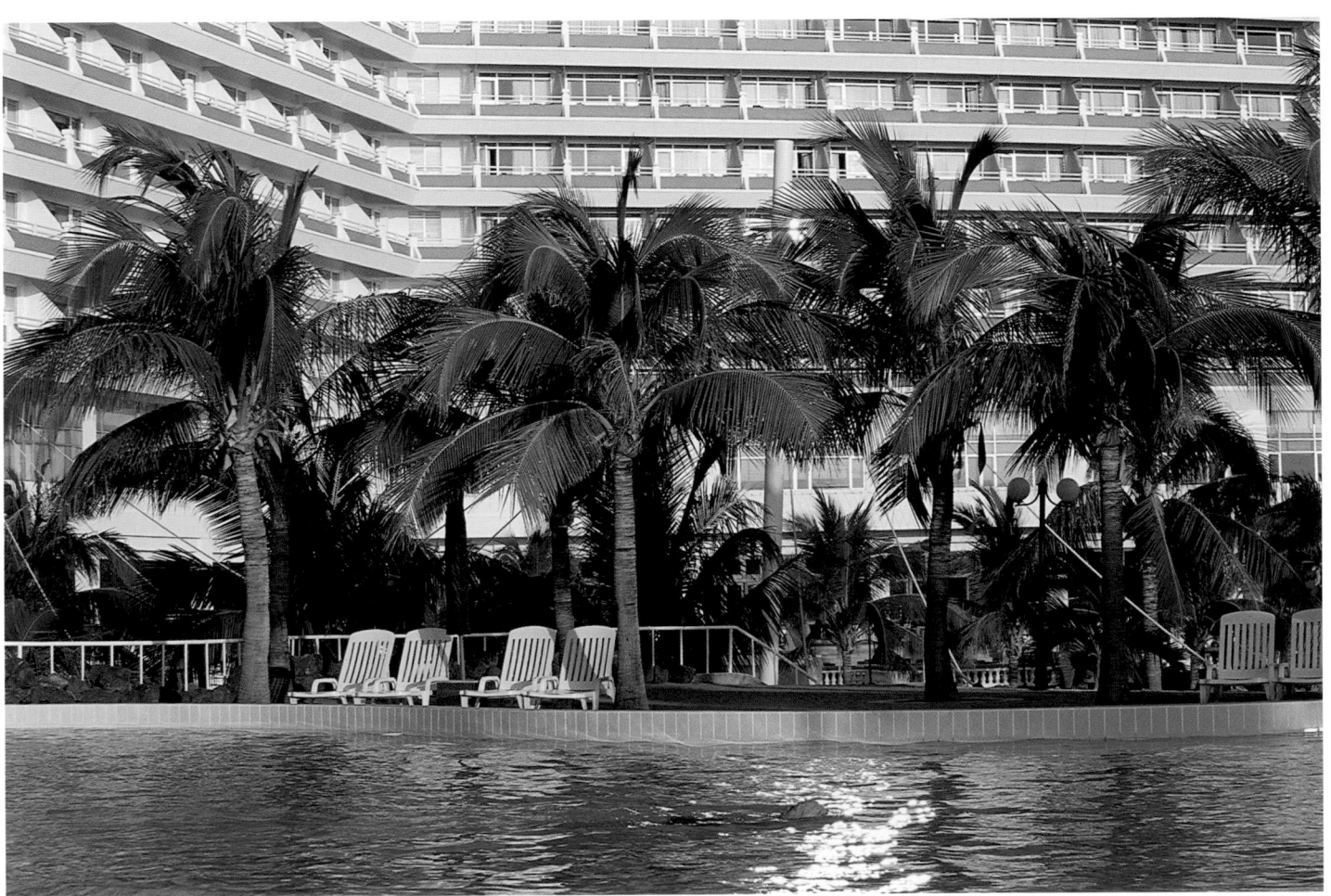

3

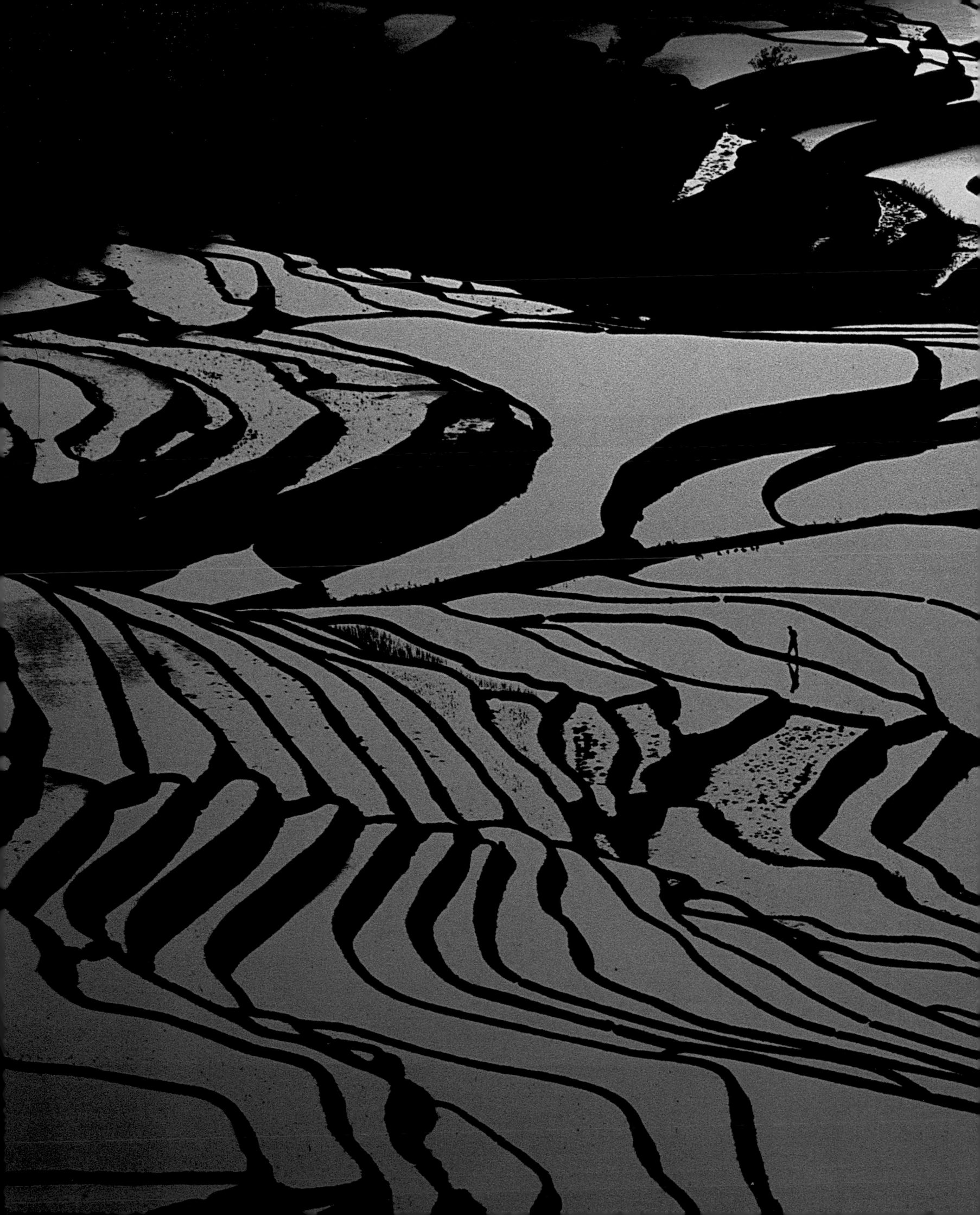

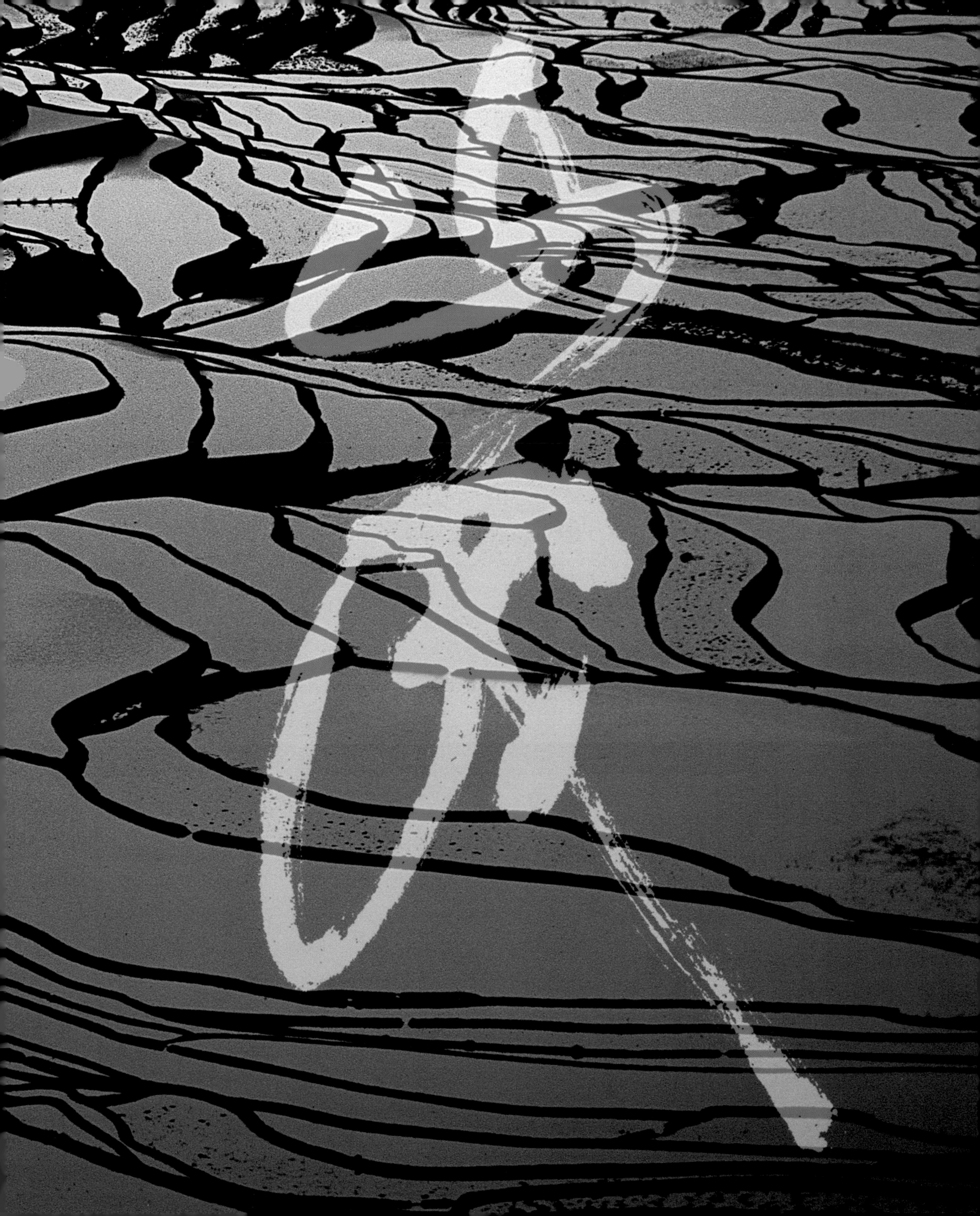

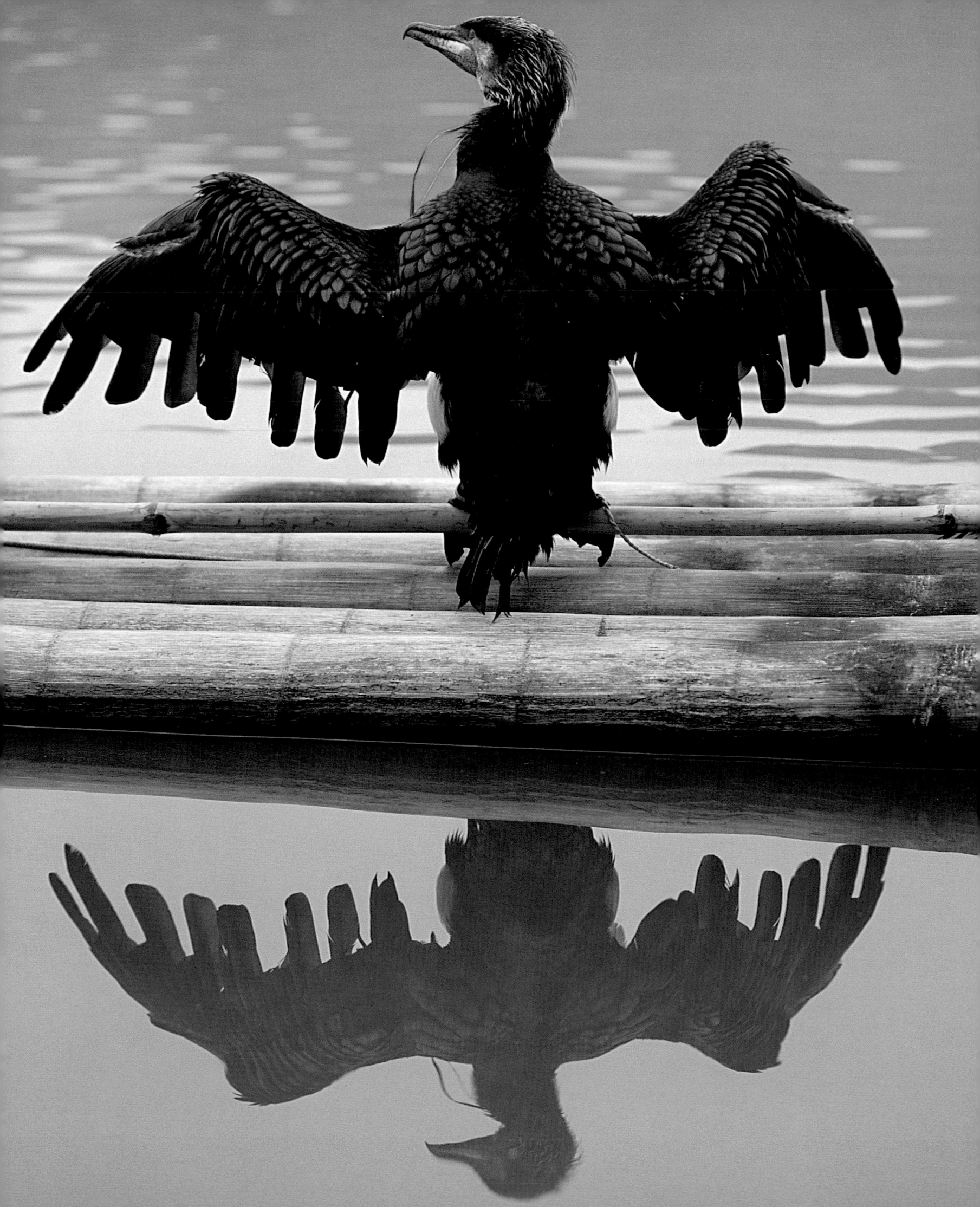

THE TRIBAL MOUNTAINS

A single long-stemmed red rose in a small elegant white porcelain vase greets me as I enter my room in the small town of Rong'jiang in the remote mountains of Gui'zhou. Because it is perched precariously on the edge of the desk, I instinctively move forward to rescue it and discover it is crudely made out of red velveteen paper. The long green stem is fashioned out of wire wrapped with the same material and two small plastic leaves stick out awkwardly from its sides. The vase, though one size too small for the tall 'flower', is quite beautiful, a fine example of the classical design that one sees in paintings and statues of Guan Yin, the Goddess of Mercy – usually cradled in her graceful hands, ready to sprinkle sacred water to heal the ills and sins of all mankind. But as I throw my cameras down on the bed and survey the room for the first time, I realize that no amount of holy water is going cure the grimness of room 209 of the Electric Power Hotel. For a start, no cleaning agent known to man or divinity will ever be able to remove the indescribable filth from the carpeting – which is a veritable living tapestry, a piece of performance art that has faithfully captured and retained the history of every spill, spit and stain since the hotel opened its doors for business. Though one might be tempted to appreciate it for its artistic merits, since it resembles a late De Kooning or an early Pollack in the faint light, only a total madman would consider walking on it with his bare feet.

Next I try to turn on some lights so I can unpack. A panel between the single beds proudly announces the options: Left Bed Lamp, Room Light, Front Light, Desk Lamp, Night Light, TV, Do Not Disturb, Right Bed Lamp. I try each one, but none of them work except for the 'Do Not Disturb' switch, which, when pressed, switches off the 'Left Bed Lamp' – the only light in the room that's working – and plunges the room into darkness. I try to switch on the giant, brand new *Konka* television set on the desk and, of course, nothing happens. A glance behind the desk reveals the TV plug lying on the floor next to a hole in the wall, where presumably there was once a socket.

There is a loud bang on my door as it bursts open and two men charge into my room, followed by Wilson, my local guide, shouting excitedly at each other in the totally incomprehensible dialect of regional Gui'zhou. Without greeting me, or even acknowledging my presence, they all pile into my tiny bathroom and disappear behind the lime green door. I poke my head in to see what is going on. A red light is flickering on and off on the side of the giant metallic green water tank strapped to one corner of the low ceiling. The two men, dressed in practically identical shapeless clothes in shades of dark brown, are busy sorting and pulling apart a mass of loose wires spilling out of a gaping hole in the tiled wall just above their heads.

Suddenly there is a lot of lifting of legs and cursing as water comes gushing out of the blue plastic concertina tubing that is dangling loose from the bottom of the sink and unattached to anything resembling plumbing. Sheets of water spread across the floor and drain around the mens' feet into the 'squatter' toilet, which is, who knows why, directly under the shower fitting. Judging by the amount of water coming through, the guest upstairs is evidently either doing his laundry or washing his dog in his sink. Finally, the little red light stays on and the men march out as unceremoniously as they had come, shaking their wet feet as they exit the room. Wilson proudly announces that hot water will be available in about an hour.

I stand outside the bathroom door for a long time, mesmerized by the black, watery footprints on the glistening floor and the absurdity of the scene I have just witnessed. Water continues to gush from under the sink, and I begin to wonder if all the sinks in the upper floors are draining into my toilet. "Whatever happened to the

[LEFT] A cormorant on Li Jiang River in Yang'shuo. [PRECEDING PAGES] Yuan'yang terrace fields in Yun'nan province.

original plumbing," I ask the sink, "did somebody steal it? Or was it just never installed?" I finally decide that rather than risk injury from falling accidentally into the toilet while attempting a shower, I shall remain unwashed for just one more night until we get to Kai'li, where a 'four-star' hotel awaits.

For an establishment that is owned by the local government electric company, there is precious little evidence of the stuff around. I've had to use my head-torch to find my way to the adjoining Electricity Restaurant because the lobby is almost pitch black but for the flickering light of a small television screen hidden under the reception counter, which is casting eerie shadows onto the half-buried face huddled inside a heavy PLA coat. I'm stunned by the revelation that the hotel is only two years old, given its advanced state of decay. Two waitresses in the restaurant reveal the secret of their artistic carpeting as they splash out with mops and buckets, smearing the dirt deeper into the carpeting of the corridor with masterly strokes. Later in the evening, as I walk gingerly over the abstract expressionist painting to my bed, wondering what other of God's little creatures I will be sharing it with, I come to the conclusion that this is the saddest hotel room I have ever been in in my life. It is sad not just because nothing works – after all, I have spent a good portion of my travelling life in tents and mud huts where there were no light switches or sinks at all. It is sad because it represents all that is wrong with the misguided craving for 'modernity' – which in the hearts and minds of small town cadres, equals 'mass tourism' and hence, fabulous riches. Millions upon millions in investment have been wasted on hotels like this one. Empty and rotting away silently without anyone even noticing, because they are completely alien to their environments in every possible way, and the tourist coaches were never going to make it this far up the mountain in the first place. In their mad dash to show that they are not backwards, they have inadvertently done exactly that.

Gui'zhou is one of the poorest provinces in China, and perhaps because of that unfortunate fact, it is one of the most fascinating and unspoiled places in the country. Unlike its neighbours in the tribal mountains, it has practically no tourist industry. Guang'xi to the east is blessed with the Translucent River (Li Jiang) with its surreal karst peaks and the tourist meccas of Gui'lin and Yang'shuo at either end of a spectacular cruise. Yun'nan to the west is regarded as one of the premier tourist destinations in the country, with snow-capped Himalayan mountains to the north and lush tropical jungles in the south. This mountainous region in southwestern China is home to at least thirty government-registered ethnic minorities and around 100 smaller unrecognized groups; it is also home to the oldest human remains (estimated to be 1.75 to 2.5 million years old) ever discovered in China, which were excavated from Yuan'mou in Yun'nan. Throughout history, this area has always been only marginally under the direct control of the empire in the north. Armies of the Qin Dynasty annexed Guang'xi in 214 BCE, while Gui'zhou became part of the Han empire between 206 BCE and 220 CE. But by the Tang Dynasty, between the 7th and 10th centuries, the powerful Nan'zhao kingdom rose up from Da'li and the Bai people ruled over an empire that extended across the plateau encompassing most of southwestern China and the upper-half of modern-day Vietnam, Laos, Thailand and Burma, from which they prospered through their control of the southern Silk Road trade routes to India and Southeast Asia. The smaller Kingdom of Da'li that came afterwards managed to resist imperial rule until the mid-13th Century, when it finally succumbed to the mighty Kubilai Khan's warriors and was absorbed into the Mongol empire. But the memory of the Nan'zhao kingdom is fast disappearing as mass tourism sets in. Its most significant relic, the former capital city of Da'li, is being 'renovated' to within an inch of its life. One evening recently, I found myself on Foreigners Street inside the renowned walled city, having a cappuccino in a sidewalk café called Tai Bai Pavillion where classical Indian music was drifting out from the restaurant inside. Not long after I sat down, 'techno-pop' of the heavy-handed kind came thumping out of the Tang Dynasty Bar & Grill across the street, while, a few doors down, a workman wielded a chainsaw with great fanfare as he worked overtime to try and finish the new bar on time. All the while, down on the street corner, an old man sat on a stool on the pavement, playing *Moon reflected in two springs*, the saddest and most heart-wrenching song in the repertoire of the *er'hu* – the ancient two-stringed fiddle – as backpackers and Chinese tour groups wandered through the cacophony under a bright full moon and the blinking of neon lights.

Culturally, the aboriginal people of Guang'xi, Gui'zhou and Yun'nan province share a common ancestry and heritage with the hill tribes of their southeast Asian neighbours on the other side of the Red River valley, sharing very similar languages, costumes, customs and traditions. Some of the natives of the provinces also share the enviable reputation as the only people in the world who have ever eaten the entire Chinese zodiac. From the years of the Monkey and Rat (large field mouse and domestic), to Tiger (the whole cat family) and Dragon (giant iguana-like lizards), all twelve animals are fair game; particularly the Snake and Dog, which are the specialties of the region. I remember walking past a restaurant in the outskirts of Kai'li, not far from the aptly named 'The Only (Wei'yi) Supermarket', where the owner was preparing his special clay-pot stews; and on the counter next to the stove was a very realistic plaster statue of a life-size German shepherd, with it pink tongue hanging out and a hand-written Chinese sign around its neck that read, 'Eat me, it's good for your health.'

In another hotel room somewhere in the tribal mountains, I found a brochure inside a leather folder which contained the following passage about the gardens of the hotel: 'The all flowers vomits the nice, in really the whole ecosystem whole humanities whole nature reside to stop the vivid environment of the portrayal. Tranquil and enjoyable quietly, the environment of the delightfully fresh the person, let you returning to return the nature, release true me.' My reason for quoting this unintentionally funny piece here is not because I want to ridicule the innocent translator, but rather as a demonstration of what happens when you translate a piece of Chinese writing character by character, leaving it in its original order. But we all remember how the litany of American slang words have made their way into the Oxford dictionary over the years and how the lexicon of eccentric Japanese–English phrases have found their way into popular culture on T-shirts and elsewhere. Who is to say then, given the probable rise of Chinese cultural influence alongside its growing economic and political clout, that the strange grammar we see today may not become some kind of hip Sci-fi 'newspeak', or maybe even a new breakthrough in literature for our children's children in a hundred years time. One thing is certain though, future generations of architecture students will *not* be going on a pilgrimage to Rong'jiang to see the Electric Power Hotel.

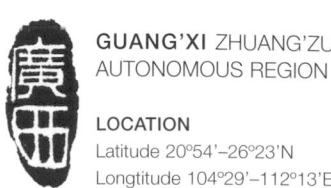

GUANG'XI ZHUANG'ZU AUTONOMOUS REGION

LOCATION
Latitude 20°54'–26°23'N
Longtitude 104°29'–112°13'E

AREA 220,150 km² (85,000 sq miles)

GEOGRAPHY Guang'xi is dominated by mountains. The Nan'ling Mountains and the shorter Hai'yang and Yue'cheng ranges demarcate the province's northeastern boundary. The Da'yao and Daming Mountains form the centre, the Du'yao and Feng'huang Mountains are to the north and the Yun'kai Mountains line the southeastern border. The province's average elevation is over 1,000 m, with the highest point at Mount Mao'er (2,141 m) in the Yue'cheng range. Guang'xi is drained by the navigable Xi River (West River) and its many tributaries.

CLIMATE Guang'xi is sub-tropical with mild winters and hot summers. Temperatures average 6°C to 15°C in January and 23–28°C in July. The lowest temperature on record is -6°C and the highest is 42°C. Average annual rainfall is between 1,250 mm and 1,750 mm.

POPULATION 49.25 million (end 2005)

MAJOR CITIES Nan'ning (capital), Bei'hai, Gui'lin, Liu'zhou

AGRICULTURE The main crops are rice, maize, sweet potatoes, wheat, sugarcane, peanuts, tobacco and kenaf (used in paper making). Guang'xi is in the double-crop agricultural belt, but only about 10 to 15 per cent of the land is cultivated because of the mountainous terrain. Fisheries in the Bei'bu (Tonkin) Gulf are rich in mackerel and squid.

MAIN INDUSTRIES Guang'xi is a major producer of manganese ore, coal, iron, tin and fluorspar. Crude oil has been discovered off-shore in the Bei'bu (Tonkin) Gulf. The industrial sector includes heavy manufacturing, oil refining, iron and steel making, fertilizer, cement, textile and paper production. The province also produces leather, pharmaceuticals and handicrafts. The climate, sea and scenery are the basis of an expanding tourist industry.

ANNUAL PER CAPITA INCOME (2005)
Disposable income of urban residents:
RMB 8,916 (US$1,112)
Net income of rural residents:
RMB 2,490 (US$310)

HISTORICAL AND SCENIC SITES
Towns along the Li River, notably Gui'lin and Yang'shuo, set amidst spectacular karst landscapes popular in Chinese watercolours. Jing'jiang Princes City and Long'men Rice Terraces.

FOOD Guang'xi cooking is best known for its use of game, notably venison, snake, mountain tortoise and pigeon. Famous dishes include rice noodles with minted horse meat and braised dog meat in a clay pot.

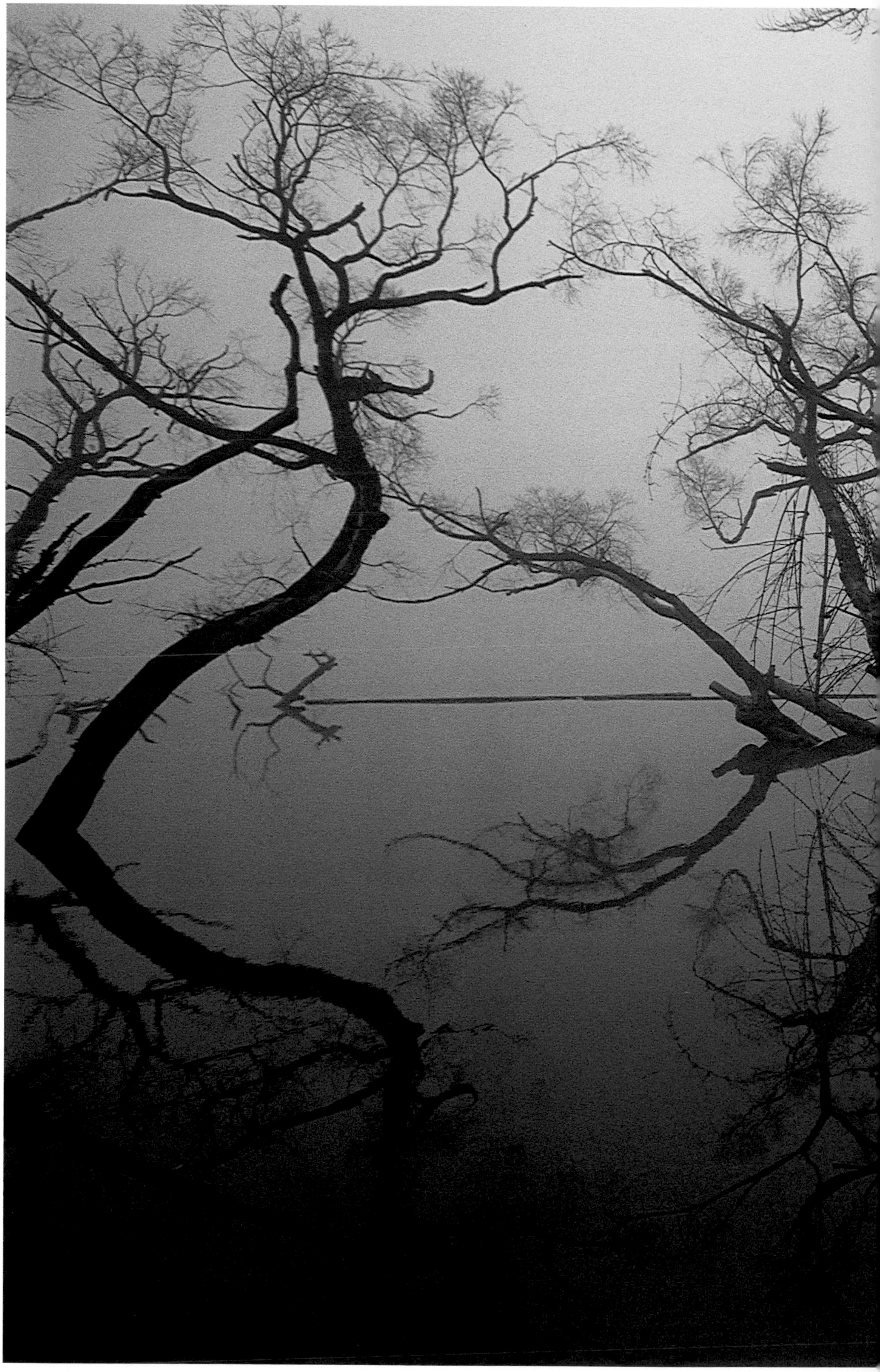

[RIGHT] A fisherman on the misty San'jiang River near the Gui'zhou border.

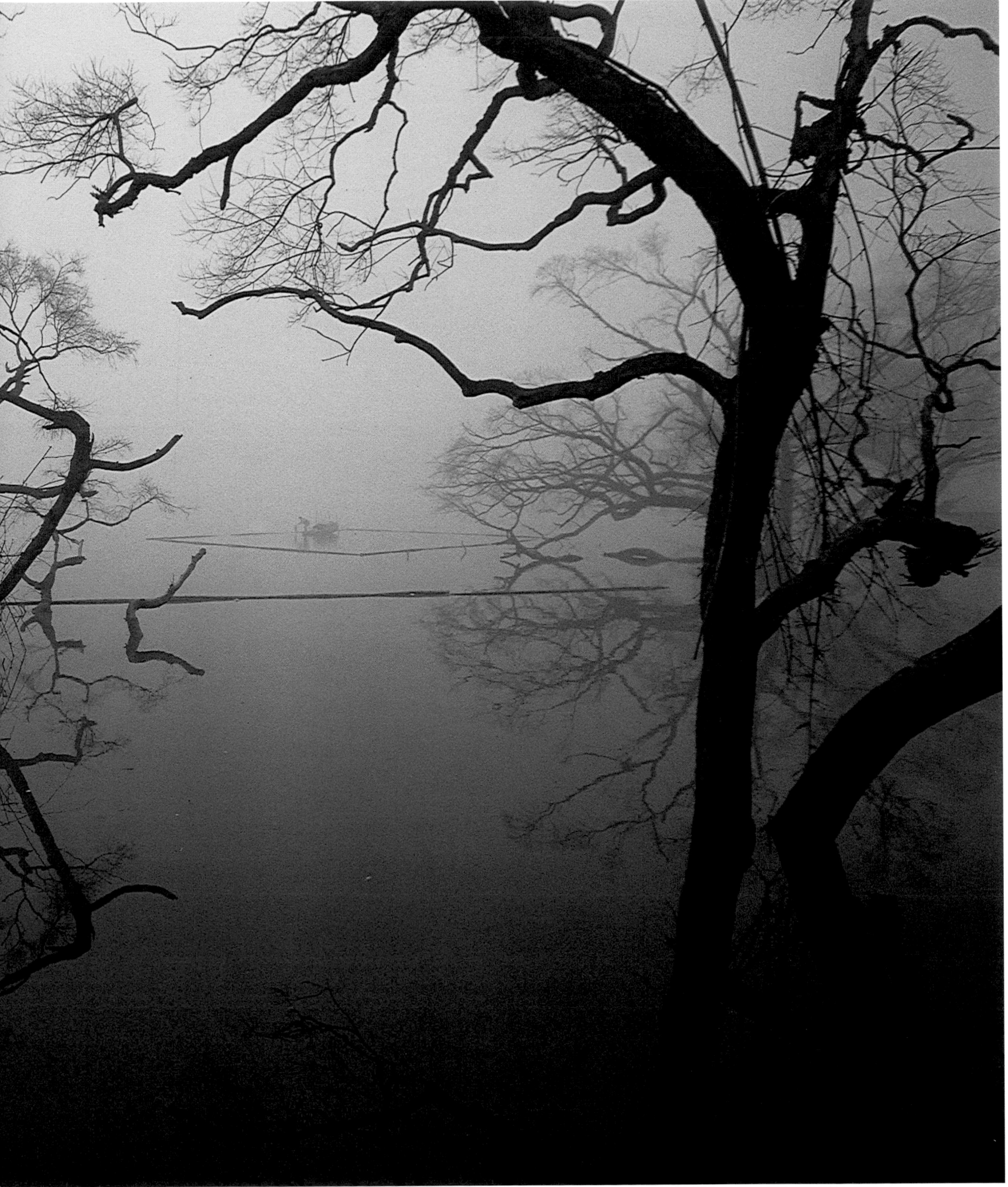

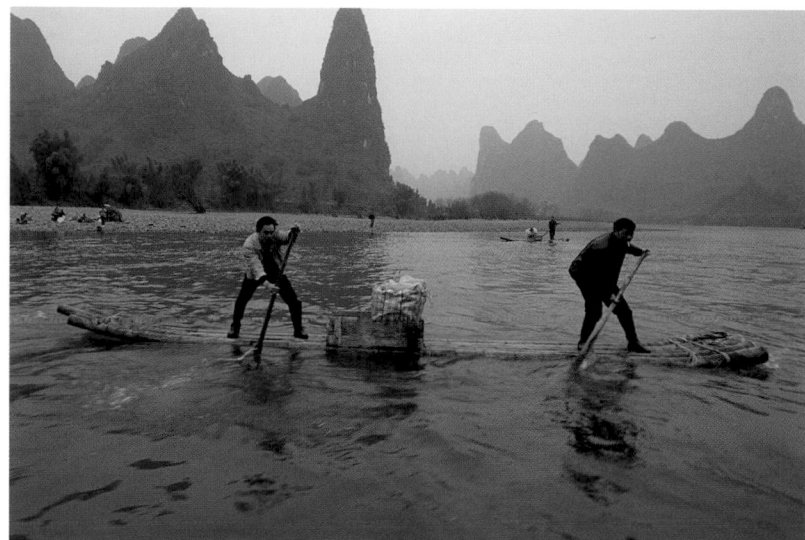

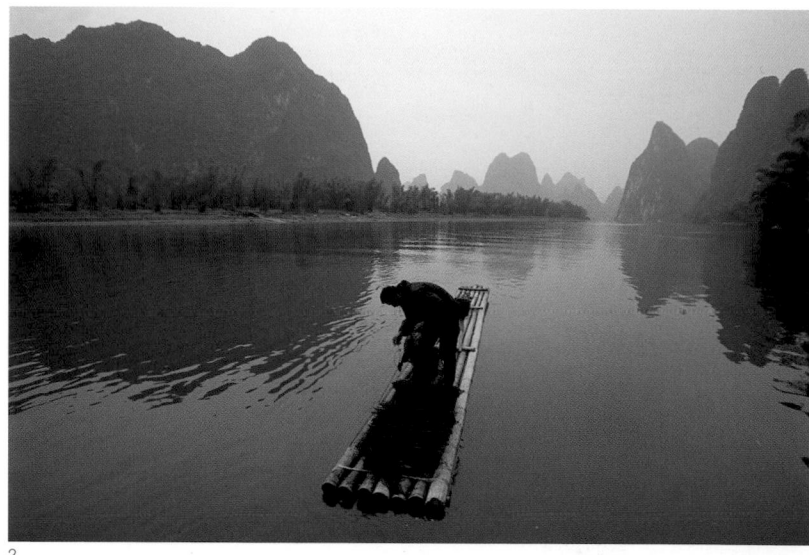

1

2

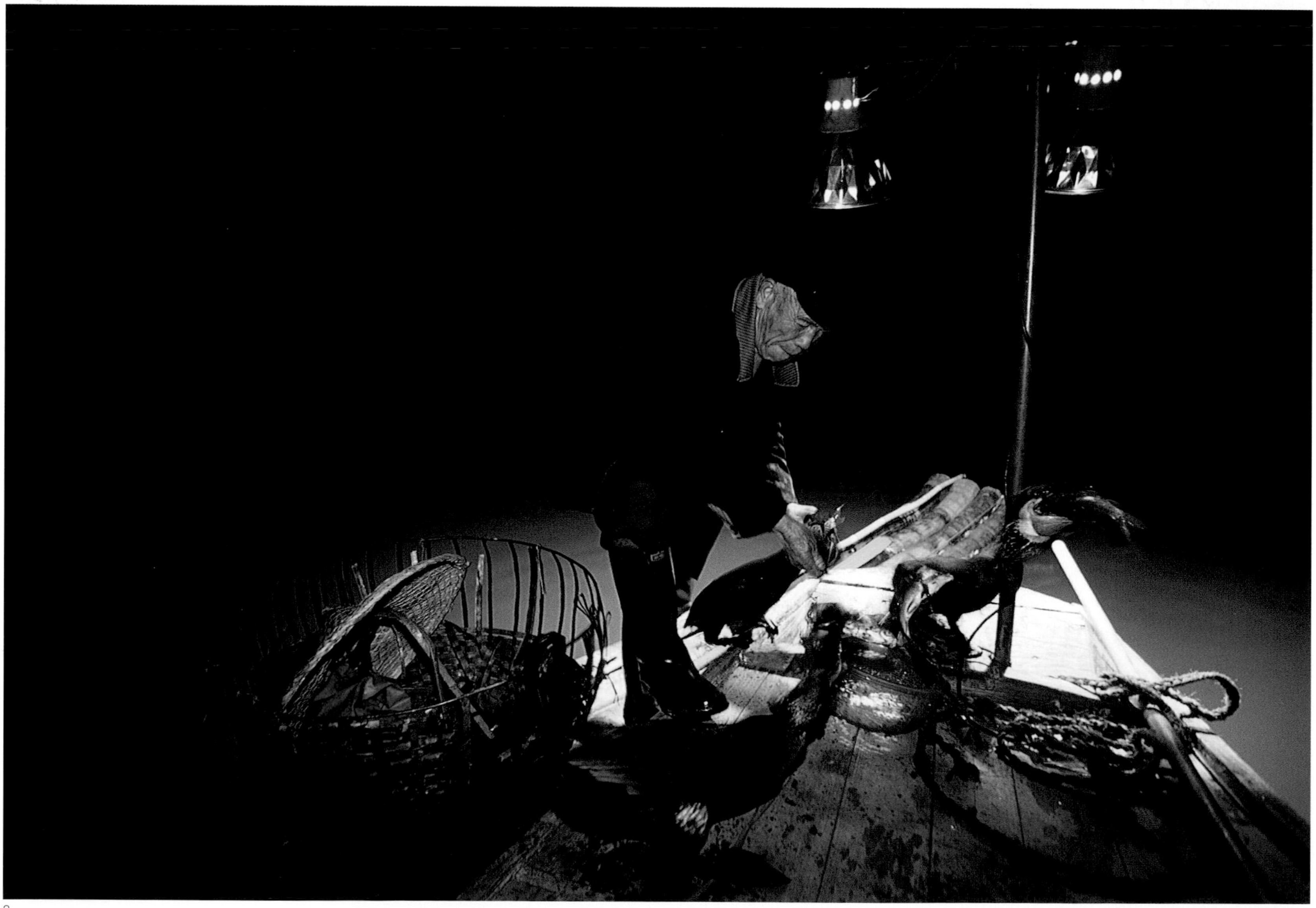

3

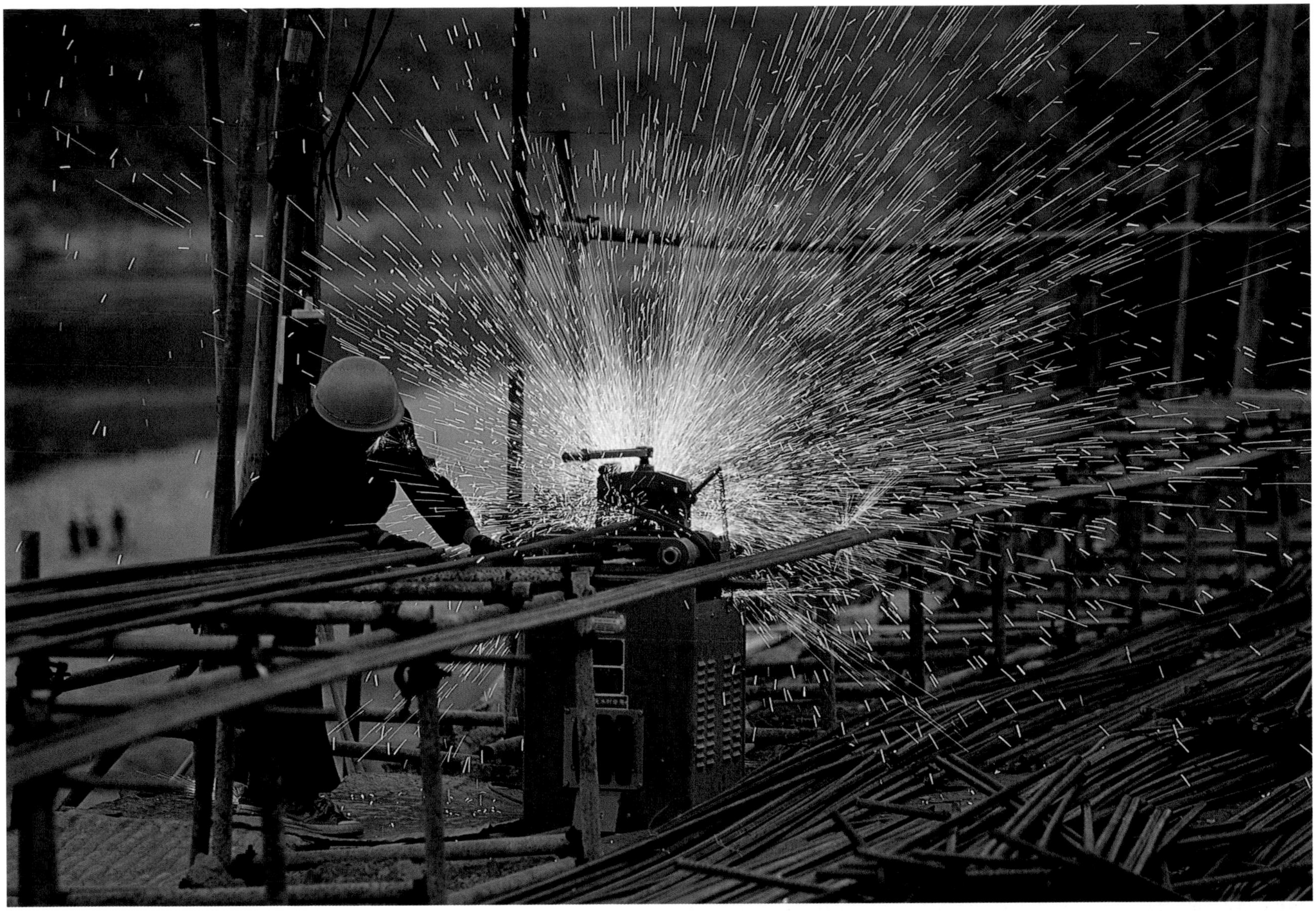

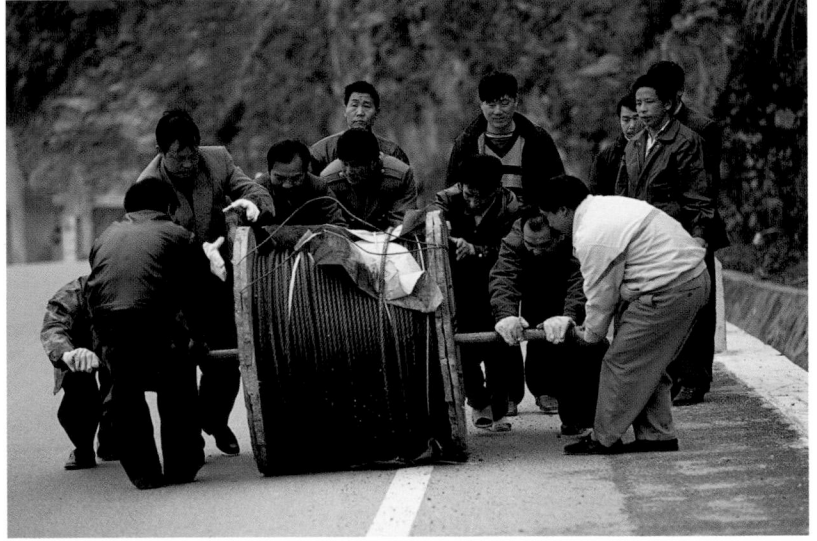

4

AFTER THE GREAT WALL IN BEI'JING and the Terracotta Army in Xi'an, the Li Jiang
(Translucent River) cruise between Gui'lin and Yang'shuo is probably China's most
famous tourist attraction. The surreal and wonderful shapes of the limestone karst
peaks along the banks of the meandering river have attracted poets and painters
to the area since the Sui Dynasty in the late 6th Century. Gui'lin is now inundated
with large tour groups all year round, while the once-charming village of Yang'shuo
65 kilometres (40 miles) downstream has become a backpackers' haven offering
cheap living in a beautiful setting. But once you step away from these well-trodden
paths and popular hangouts, the old magic that inspired generations of bards and
artists still lingers in the surrounding hills. [1] Hawkers laden with tacky souvenirs
paddle hard to hook their bamboo rafts onto passing tourist boats. [2] A fisherman
draws his nets in at one of the most scenic bends of the river. [3] Night fishing with
cormorants. [4] Construction site outside of Long'sheng where a new bridge across
the San'jiang River is being built. [5] How many drunken comrades does it take to
roll a steel cable drum up the hill?

5

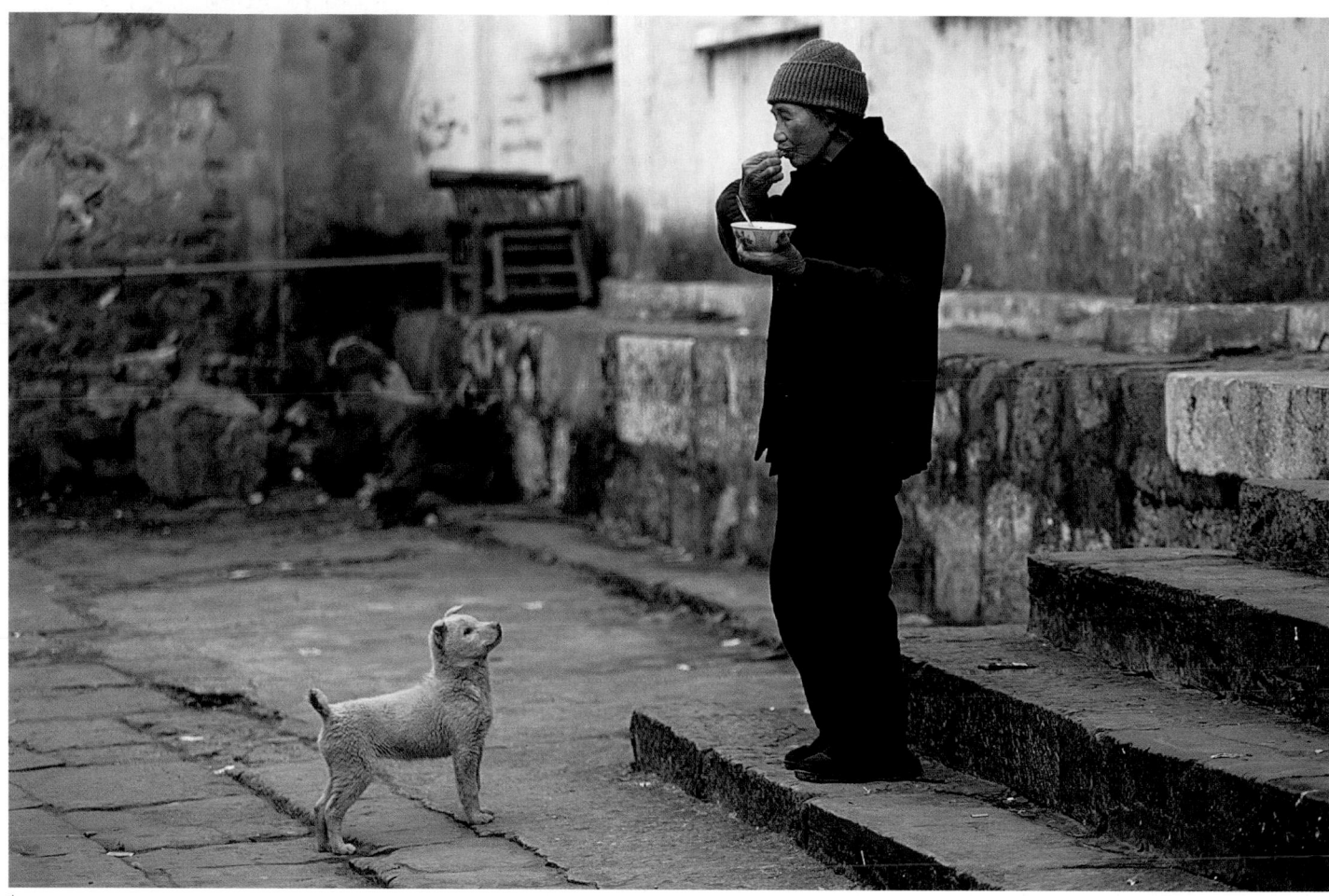

1

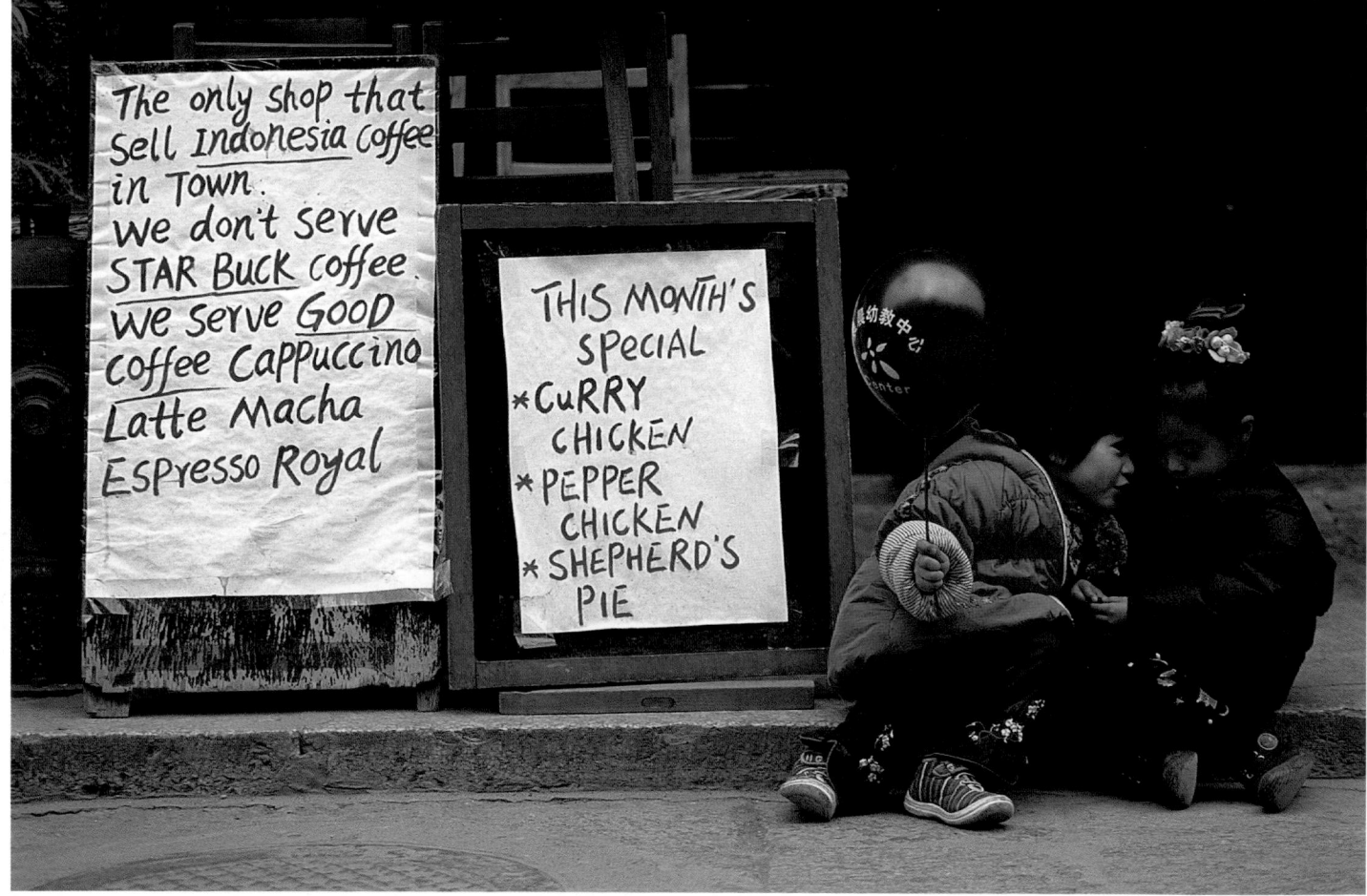

2

GLIMPSES OF GUANG'XI

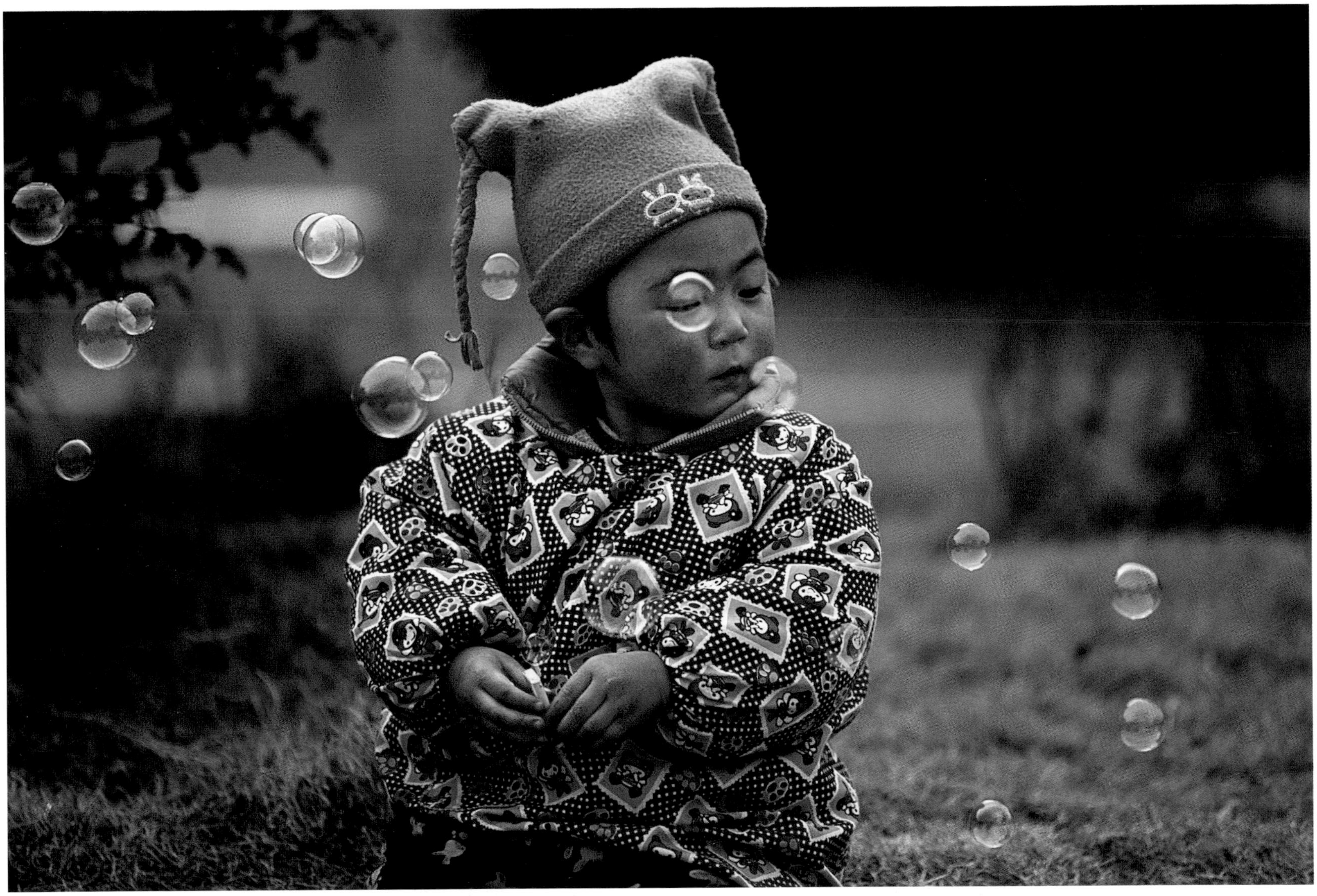

3

IN AROUND 200 BCE QIN SHI'HUANG, the first emperor of China, ordered the construction of the Ling dyke to connect the Pearl and the Yang'tze River systems by linking the Li Jiang and the Xiang rivers. [1] The old trading town of Da'xu, 20 kilometres (12 miles) southeast of Gui'lin, was a major transshipment hub on this trade route. It is now a ghost of its former self and pins its future hopes on the scraps from Gui'lin's overflowing tourist trade. Dissatisfied with its reputation as a 'backpackers' paradise', Yang'shuo is attempting to reinvent itself as a destination of culture and entertainment. The new Yu'xi Paradise hotel, is set in an enormous garden of massive contemporary sculptures, while a multi-media musical extravaganza based on the story of local folk heroine Liu San'jie (Third Sister Liu) by famous film director Zhang Yi'mou, who is due to produce the opening ceremonies of the 2008 Bei'jing Olympics, lights up the night sky over Li Jiang. [2] Two local children share a secret outside a café on 'Foreigners Street' in Yang'shuo. [3] In a Long'sheng park, baby sister contemplates her brother's string of successful bubbles.

THE TRIBAL MOUNTAINS

GUI'ZHOU PROVINCE

LOCATION
Latitude 24°07'–29°32'N
Longtitude 103°37'–109°32'E

AREA 170,940 km² (66,000 sq miles)

GEOGRAPHY Gui'zhou rises from relatively flat plains in the south before gaining an elevation of 1,107 m. The province is dominated by five mountains – Da'lou, Wu'ling, Wu'meng, Lao'wang and Miao'ling. Numerous deep river valleys and gorges drain the Wu, He and Yuan rivers.

CLIMATE Gui'zhou has a sub-tropical climate giving mild winters and hot and humid summers. January's temperatures range from 1°C to 10°C and July's reach 28°C. The lowest recorded temperature is -13°C and the highest is 36°C. Average annual rainfall is between 1,100 mm and 1,400 mm.

POPULATION 39.311 million (end 2005)

MAJOR CITIES Gui'yang (capital), An'shun, Cong'jiang, Zun'yi

AGRICULTURE Rice is the province's major crop. The same acreage is given to corn, but with about half the yield. Soybeans, wheat, oats, barley, sweet potatoes, sorghum and beans are raised for food. Cash crops include rapeseed, tobacco, tea, peanuts, oak leaf silk, sugarcane and indigo.

MAIN INDUSTRIES The province's industries are mainly centred on extractive sectors such as coal mining, oil-shale, limestone, gypsum and forestry.

ANNUAL PER CAPITA INCOME (2005)
Disposable income of urban residents:
RMB 8,147 (US$1,016)
Net income of rural residents:
RMB 1,877 (US$234)

HISTORICAL AND SCENIC SITES
The province is renowned for its many covered 'Wind and Rain' bridges built by the Dong minority people. Huang'guo'shu is China's largest waterfall.

FOOD Gui'zhou cooking is noted for being spicy and savoury. Special dishes include noodles with intestines, Ye'lang dough fish, dumplings made of glutinous rice flour and glutinous rice and meats cooked inside freshly cut bamboo. Mao'tai, China's most famous alcoholic drink, is made in the province.

[RIGHT] The Lu'sheng Spring Festival in Zhou'xi is one of the biggest Miao minority festivals of the year.

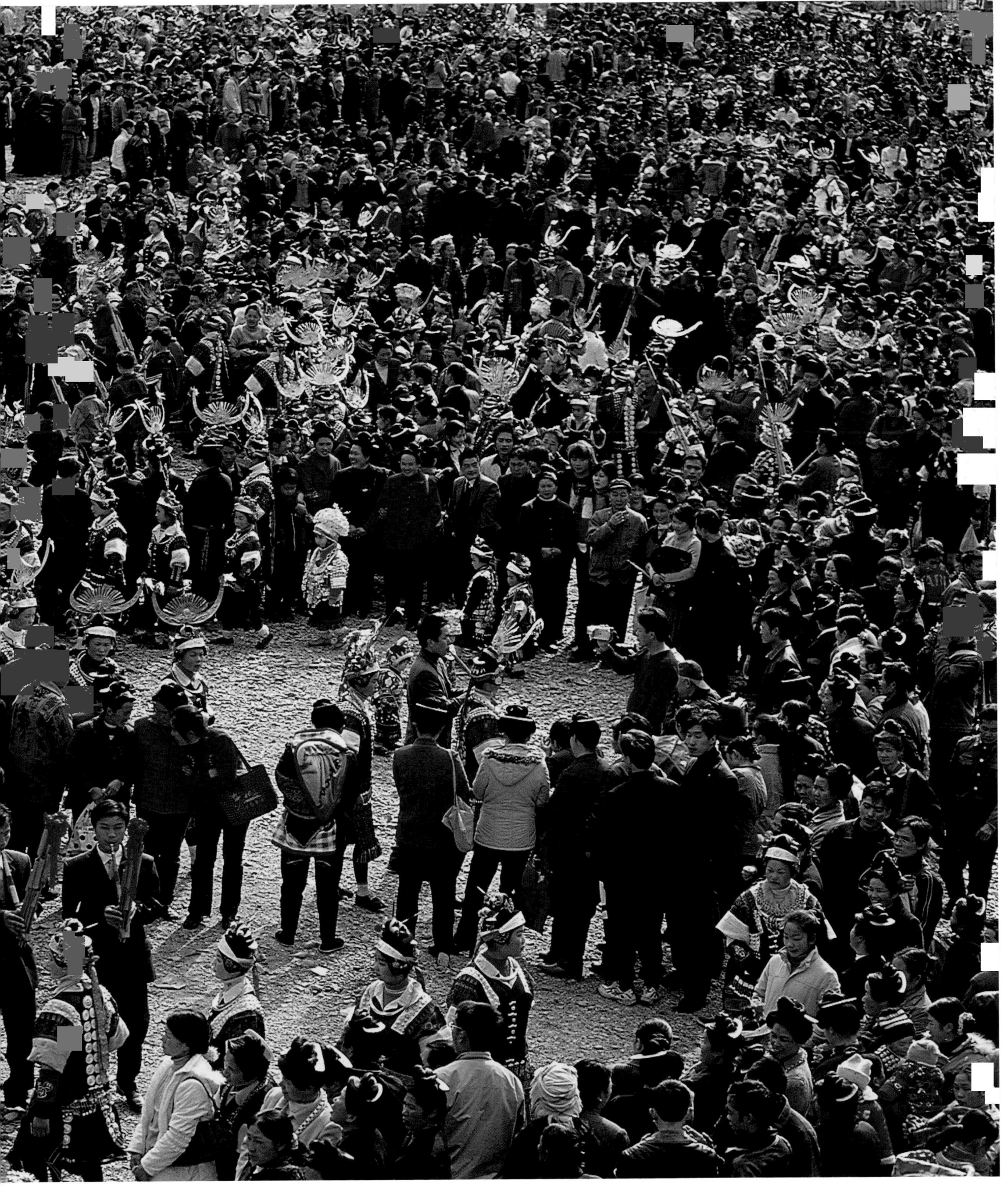

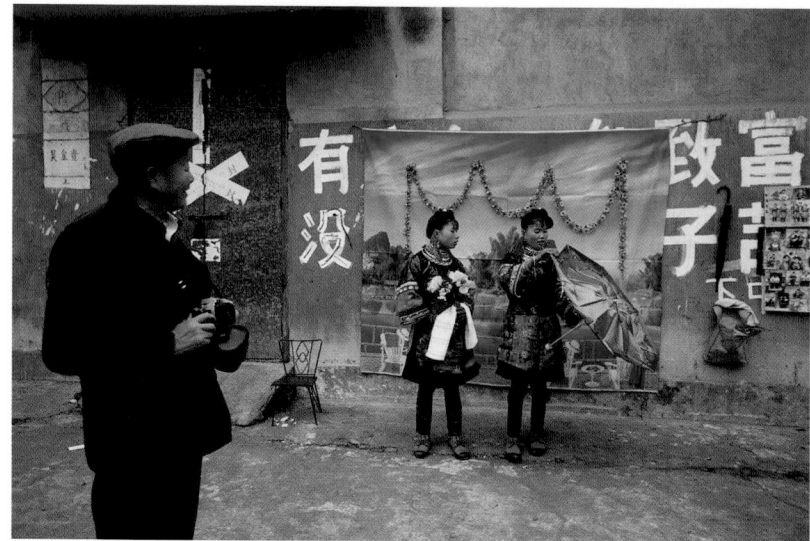

1

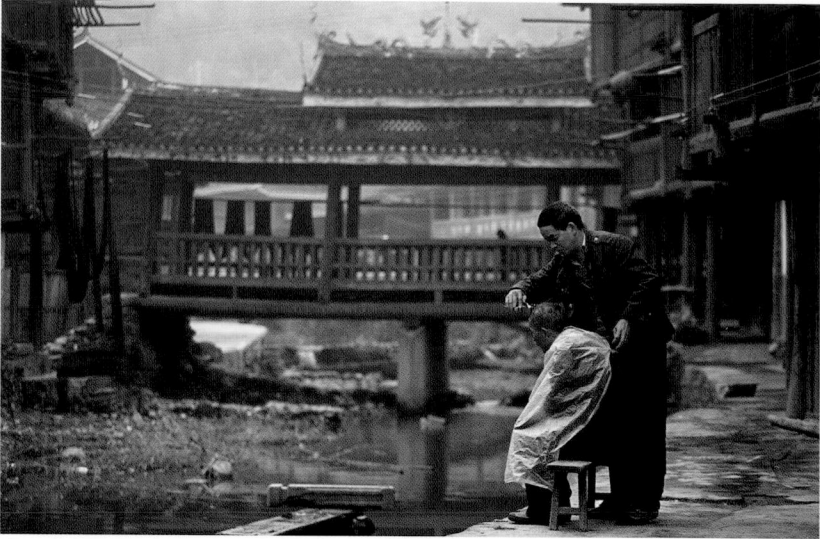

2

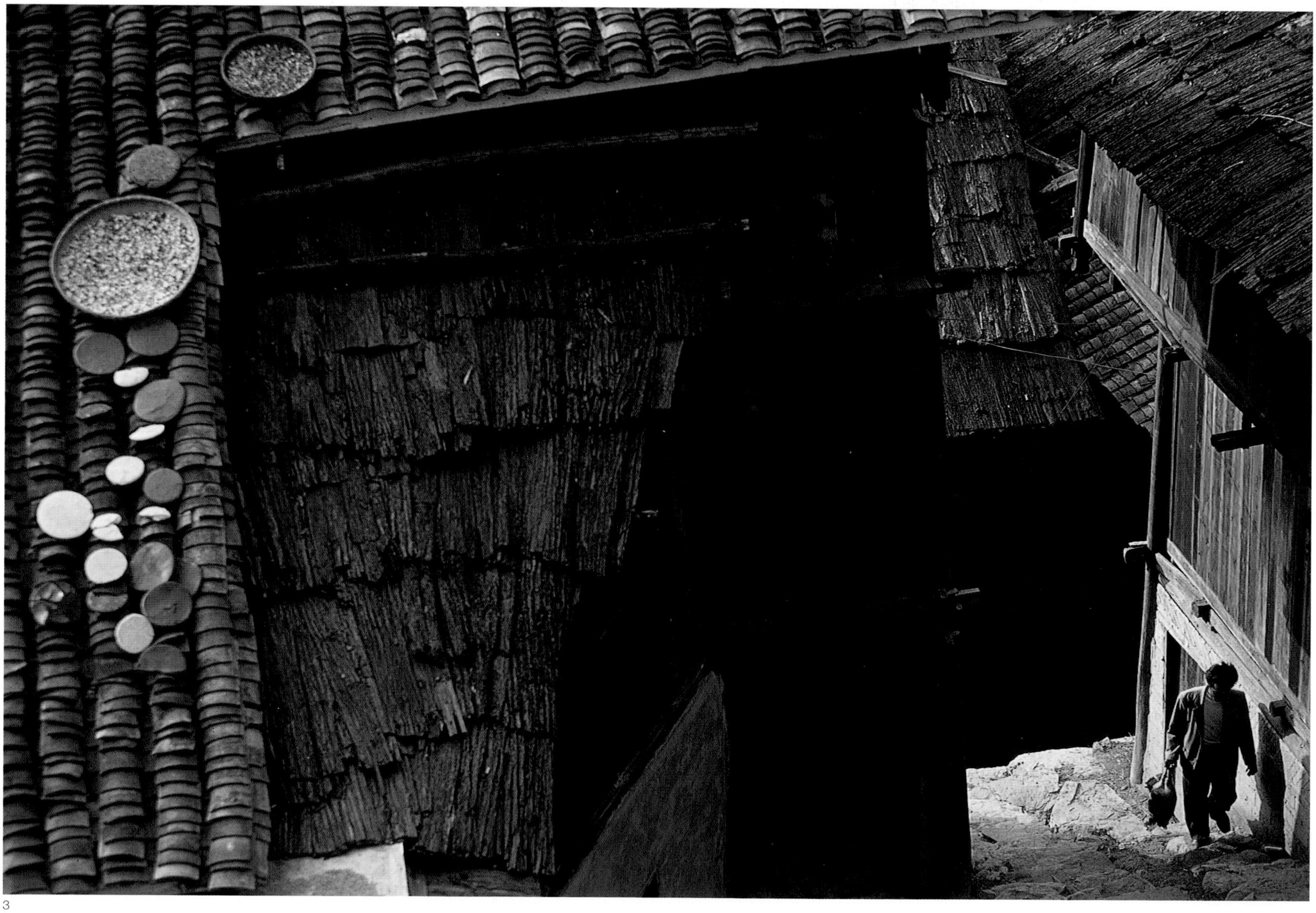

3

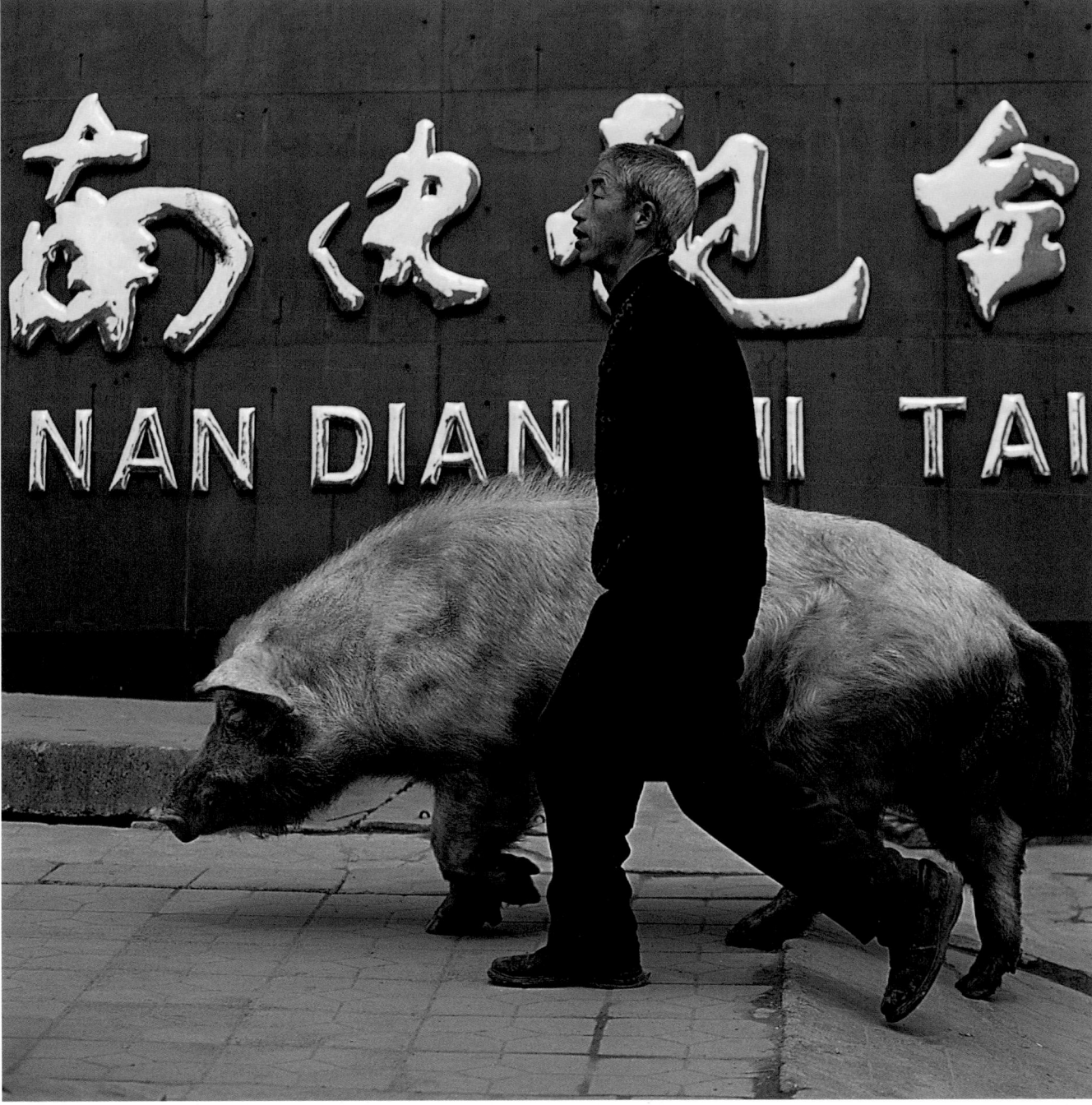

南伙电视台

NAN DIAN II TAI

4

IN THIS REMOTE MOUNTAINOUS REGION, festivals and weekly markets are vital to the survival and sanity of the isolated villagers as they provide the events and venues for social interaction, entertainment and trading goods and services. [1] Two Dong minority girls at the country fair in the town of Xia'jiang try out different props for the first 'studio' portraits of their lives by a professional photographer, who has set up shop outside a condemned building during the weekly market. [2] In the village of Zhoa'xing, a local barber plies his trade by the small 'Wind and Rain' bridge – so called because they were originally designed as shelters for villagers caught in sudden rainstorms. As the bridges have grown larger and more elaborate over time, they have become communal spaces where the villagers congregate. [3] In the hilltop villages of Tang'an'dong, brightly dyed rice cakes left over from the New Year celebrations are put out on the roof for the birds. [4] A man takes his pig for a walk along Kai'li's main street, passing the headquarters of the regional television station.

THE TRIBAL MOUNTAINS

THE MINORITIES OF GUI'ZHOU

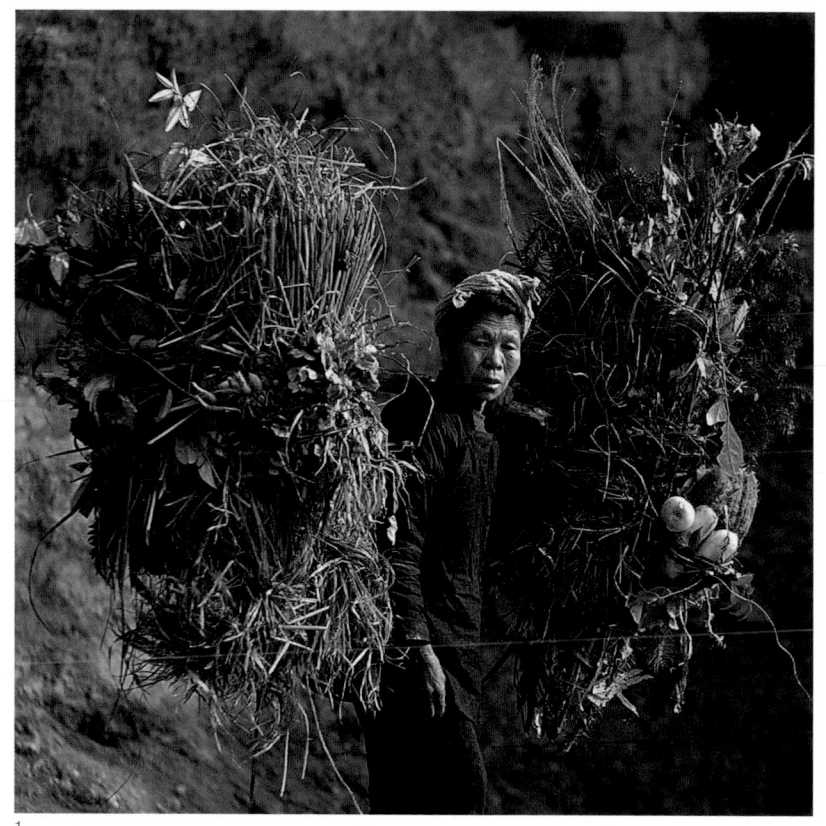

1

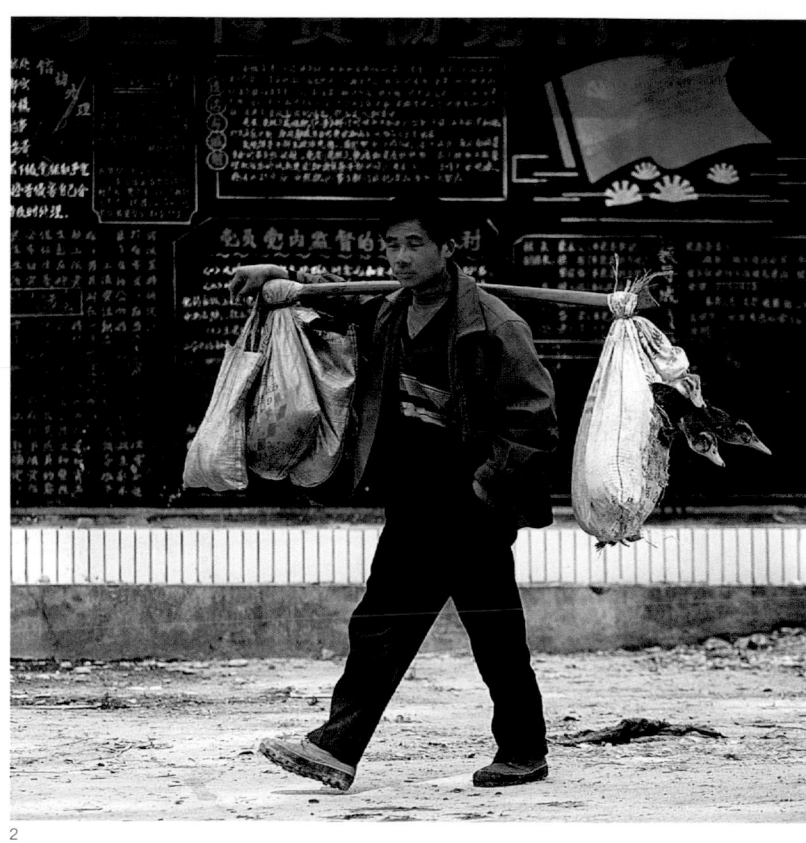

2

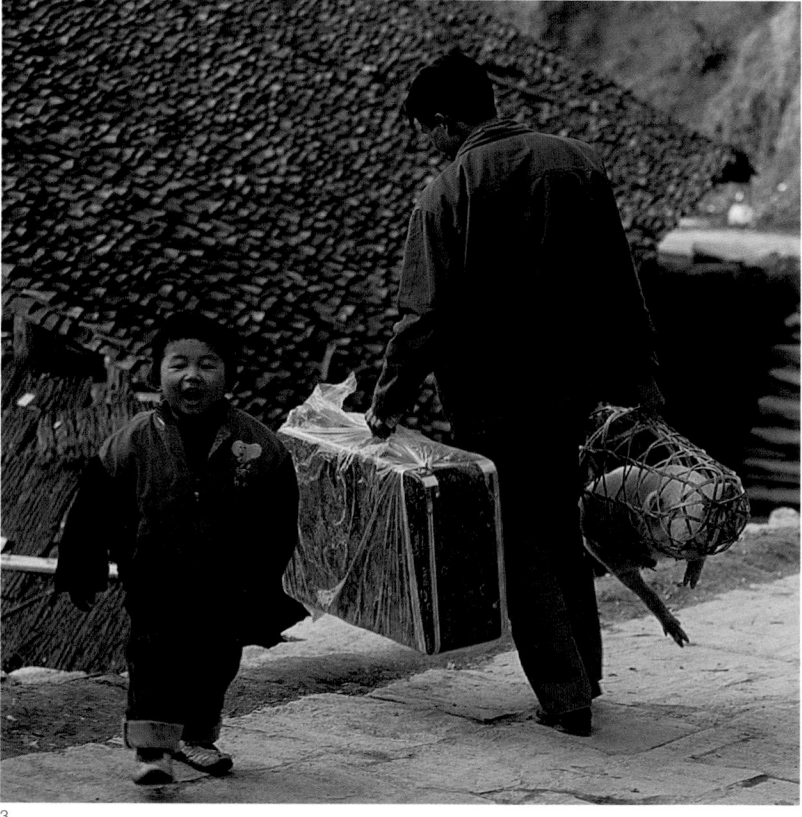

3

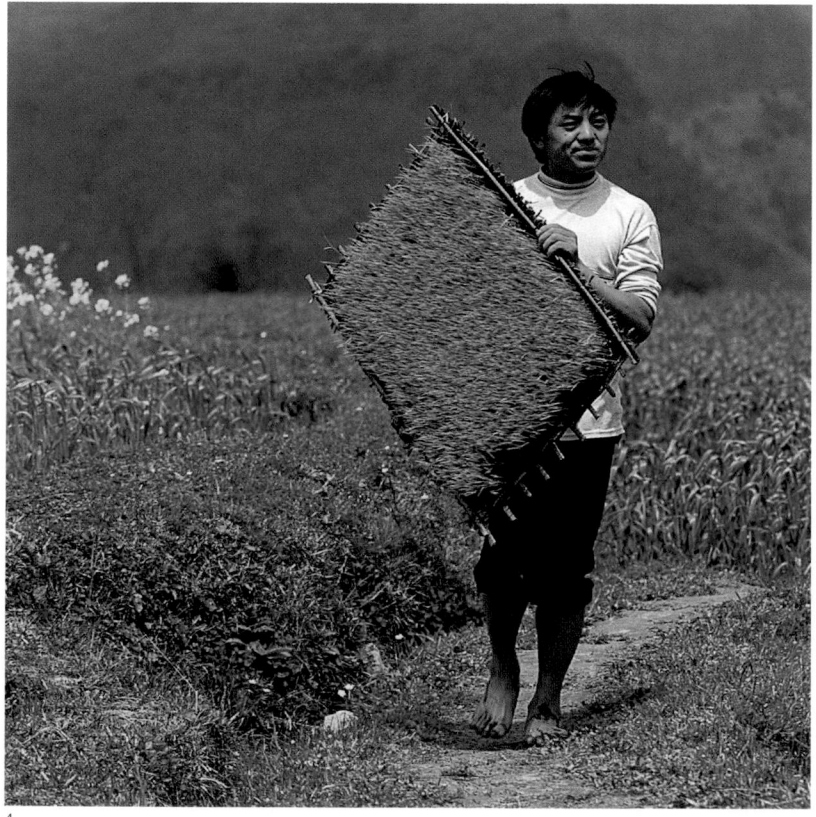

4

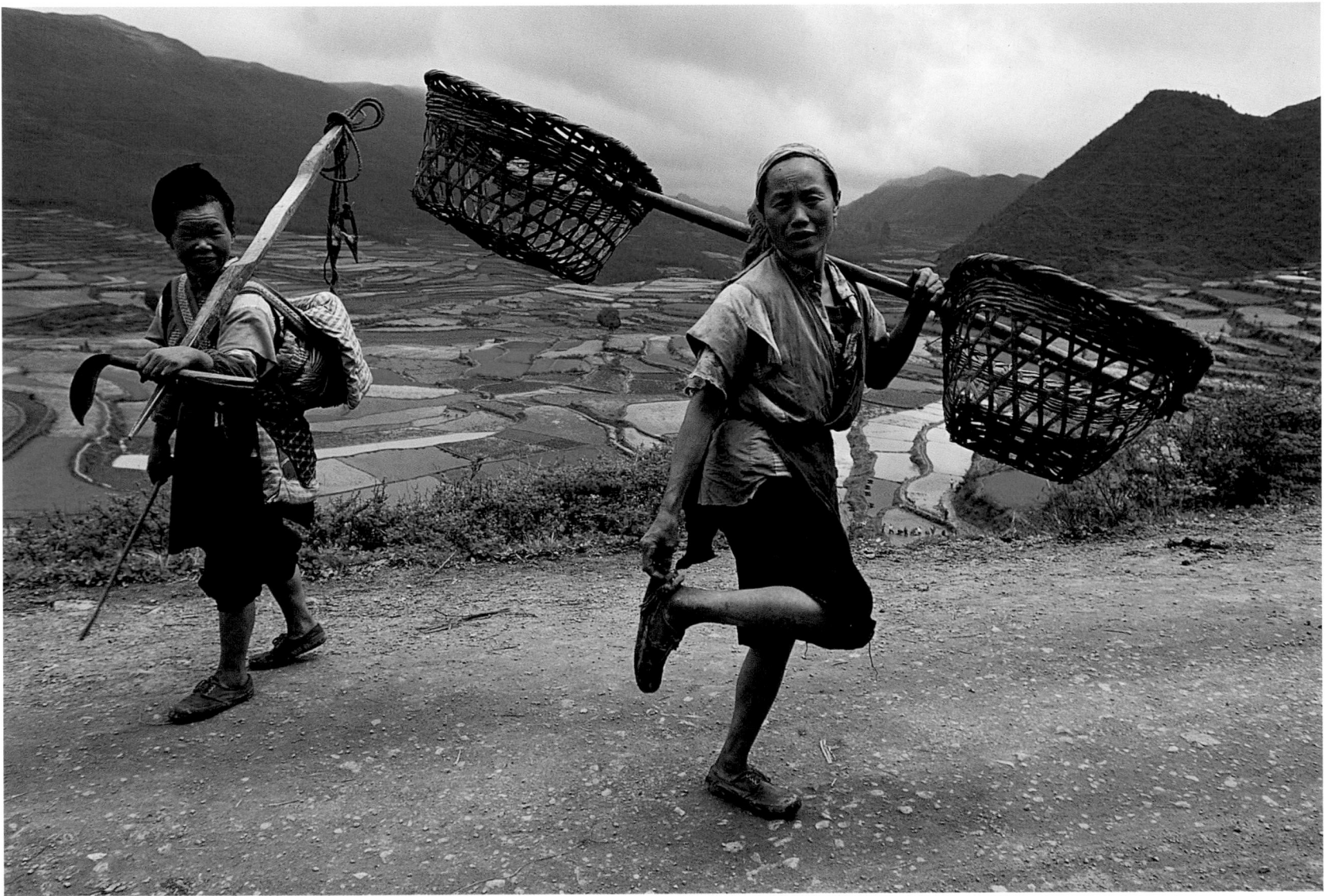

5

WITH INDUSTRIALIZATION AND NEW DEVELOPMENTS happening mostly in the north of the province, the lives of the Dong and Miao minority in this southeastern region remain hard and basically unchanged over the centuries. [1] A Tang'an'dong woman returns to her village at sunset after foraging in the mountains where she's gathered wild vegetables for her family and grass for the animals. [2] A farmer in search of buyers for his ducks walks past a wall of old-fashioned communist propaganda lining the main street of a small country town. [3] A family glad to be home with their new suitcase and a piglet after being away for the Chinese New Year holidays. [4] In the hills outside of Gui'yang it was rice-planting season in the Miao villages. A young farmer with a tray of rice seedlings makes his way towards the terraced fields where women knee deep in icy mud are engaged in the ancient ritual of cyclical renewal. [5] "Will you buy me a new pair of shoes?" asked the Miao woman on her way home from the fields.

THE TRIBAL MOUNTAINS

TWO WEDDINGS AND TWO FUNERALS

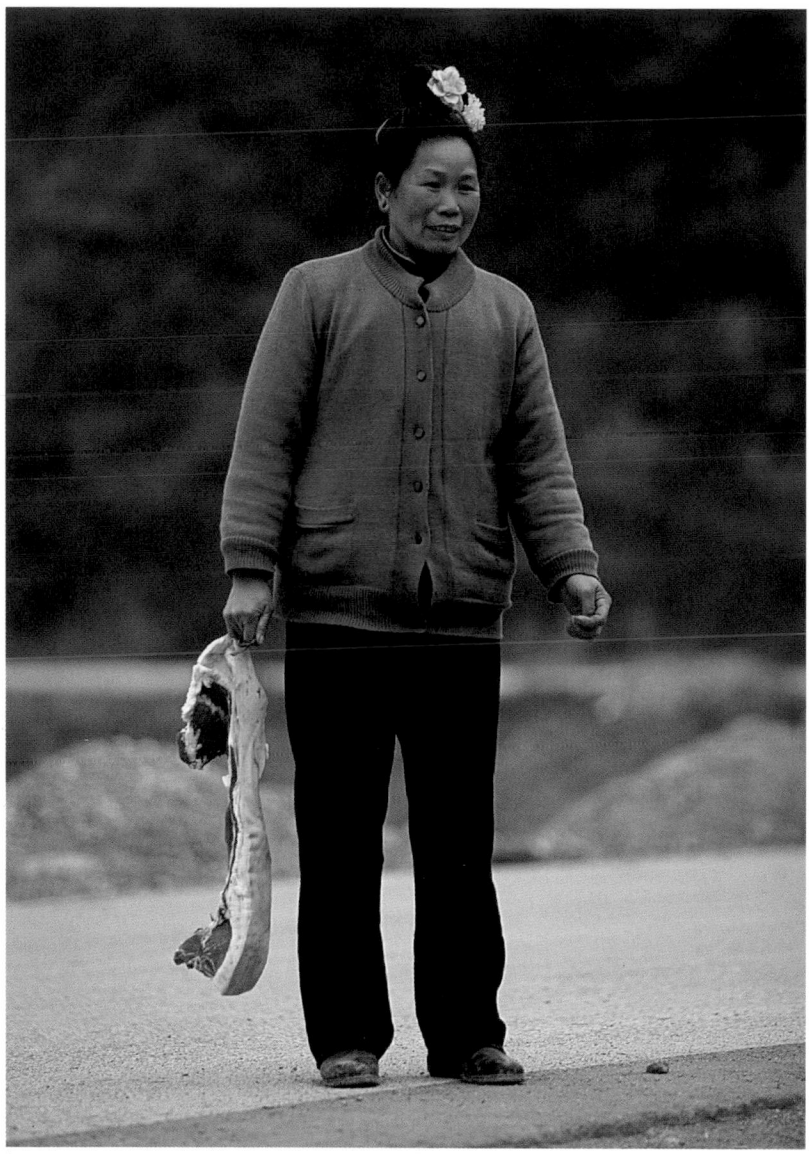

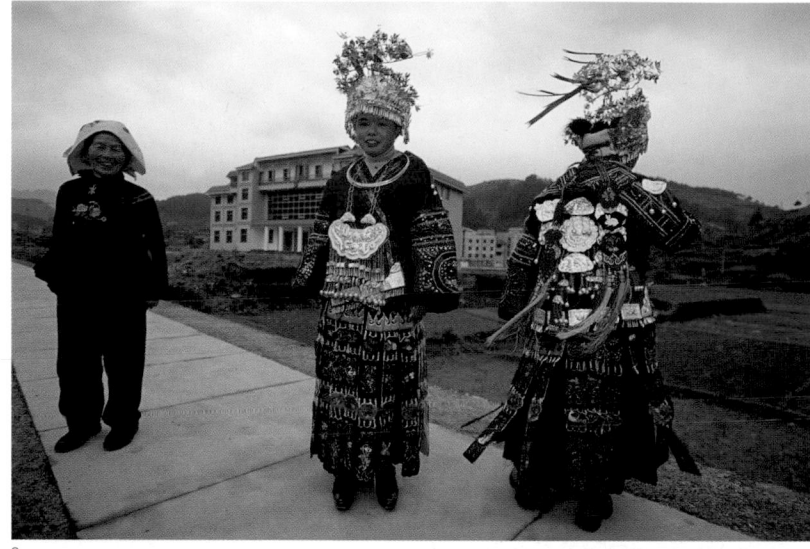

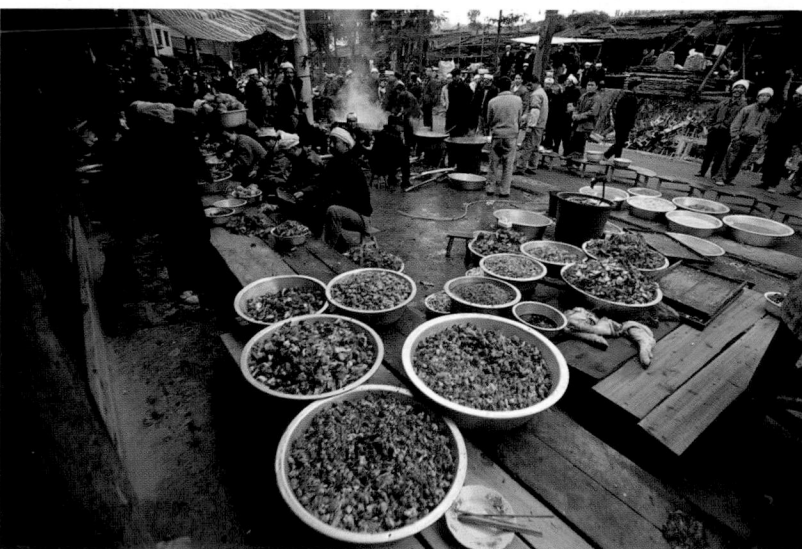

AS A PRIMARILY AGRARIAN SOCIETY, Gui'zhou's minorities take the Lunar Almanac very seriously and follow it almost to the letter – particularly in the area of 'what-not-to-do'. This explained why we ran into two weddings and two funerals as we passed through towns on the road between Rong'jiang to Kai'li on the 16th day of the Chinese New Year. According to the almanac, this is the first auspicious day of the year for such activities. In the first town [3] women sat chopping great mounds of vegetables beside the road as figures in white headscarves moved between huge columns of steam, [4] while a crowd of men worked up an appetite over a raucous guessing game. Further down the road, hundreds of people ate at tables set up for an enormous funeral banquet on either side of the main street. The teenage bride in the first wedding looked shell-shocked, but [2] the Miao bride and her maid-of-honour in the second seem quite happy. [1] A wedding guest leaves the party with the Chinese equivalent of a piece of the wedding cake.

THE TRIBAL MOUNTAINS

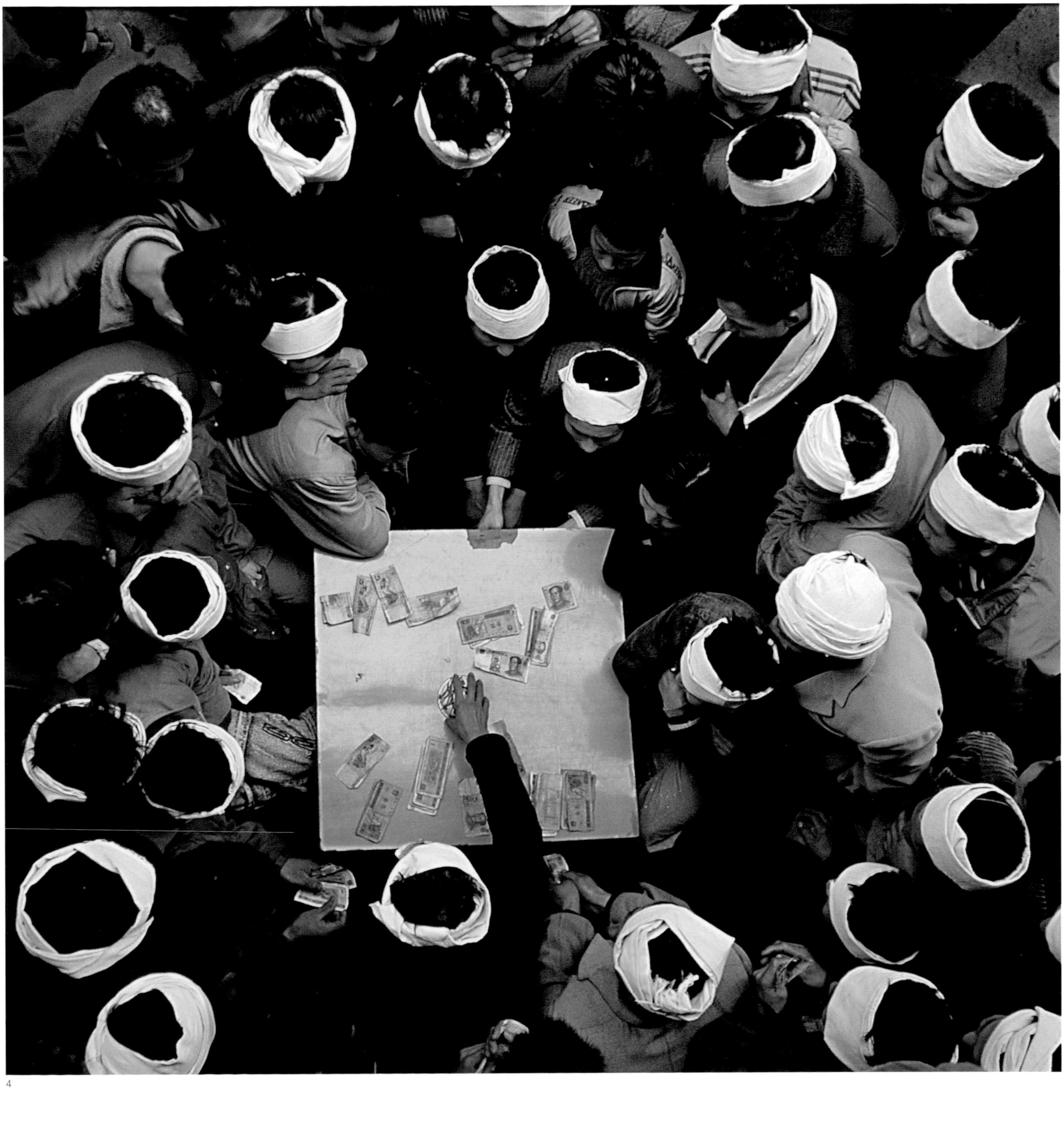

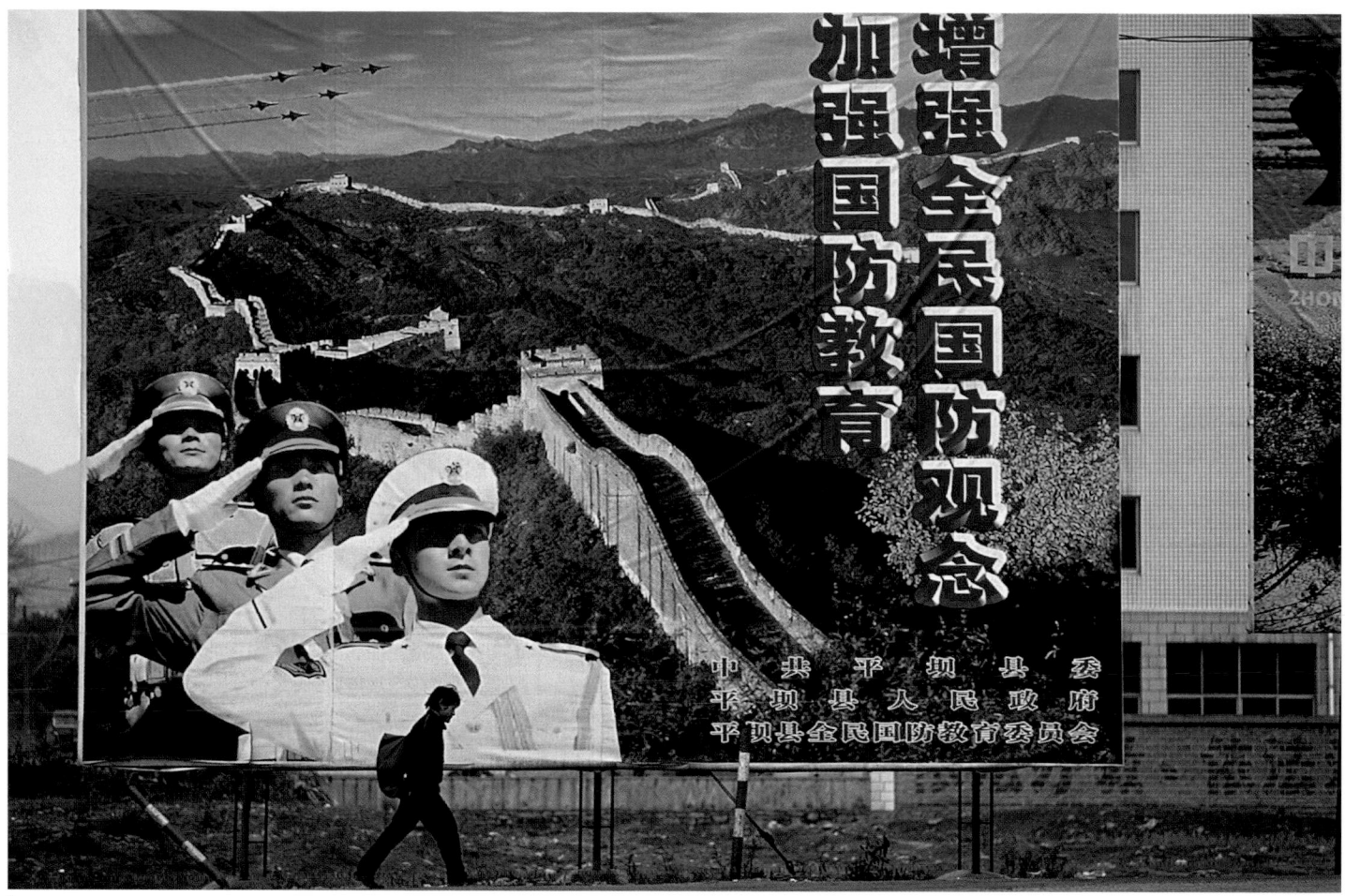

1

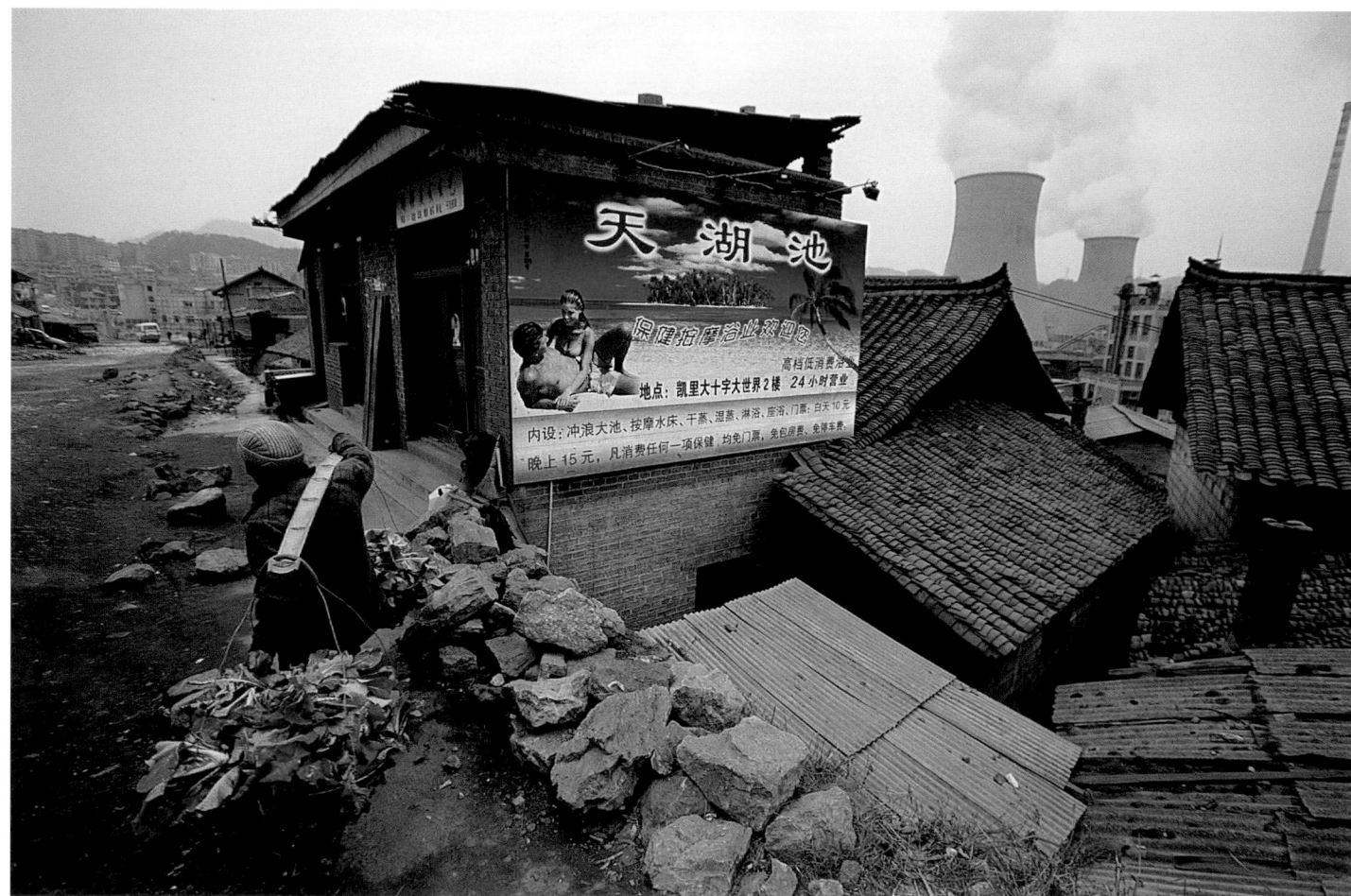

2

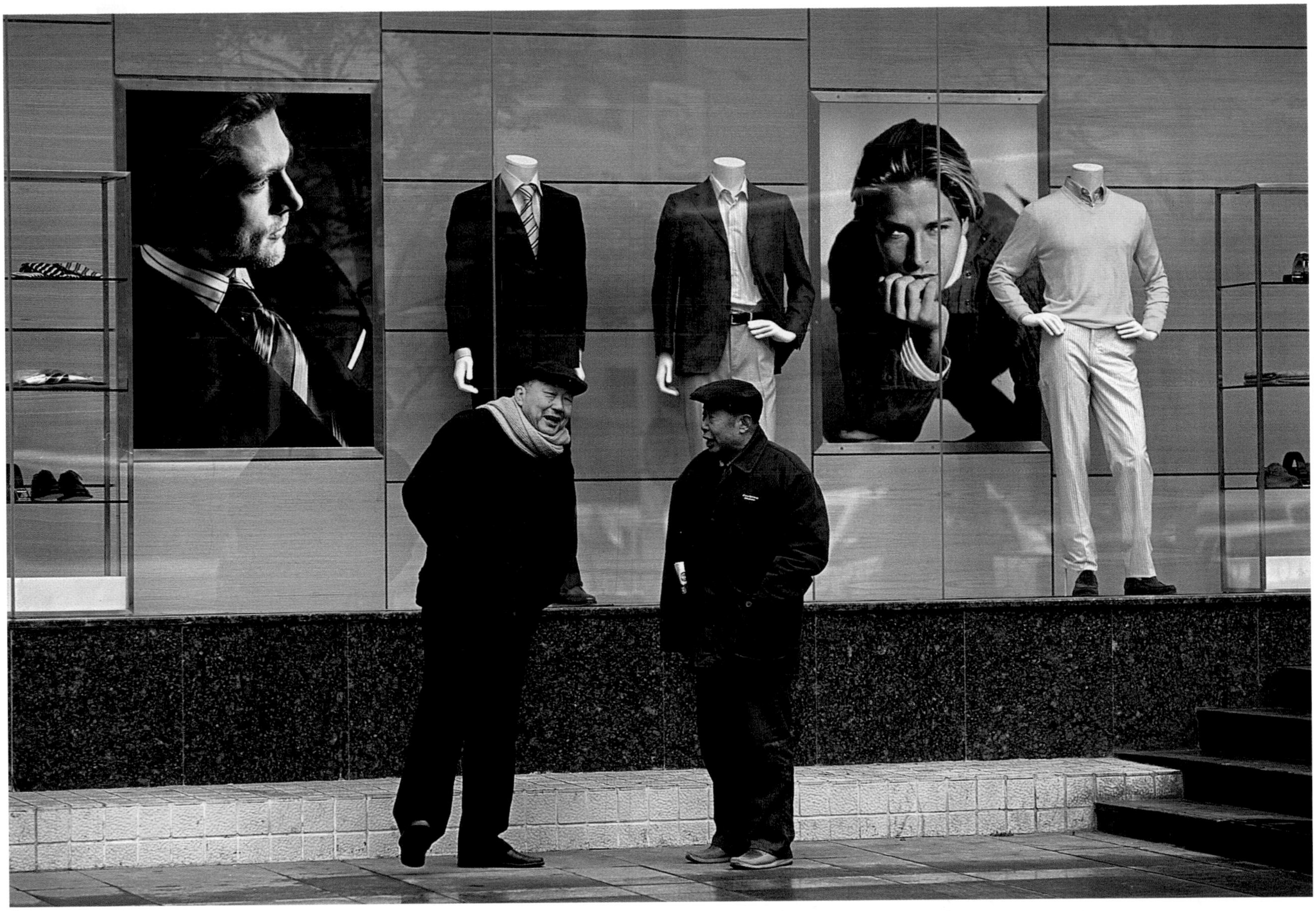

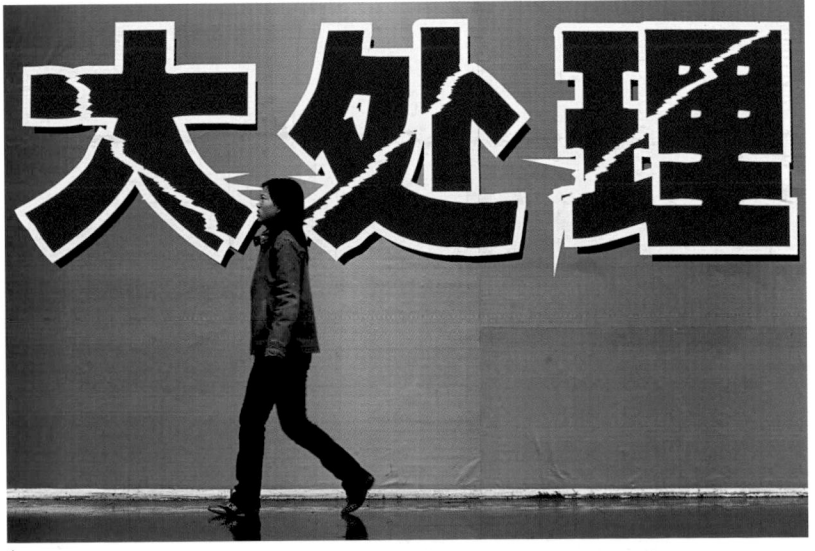

3

SINCE THE HAN DYNASTY at the beginning of 3rd Century, when the mountainous deep south became part of the Chinese empire, the Gui'zhou region has been mostly autonomous and largely ignored by the central government unless there was trouble. It remains one of China's poorest provinces to this day, with more than eight million people living below the poverty line. When communist guerrillas first passed through here on the Long March in 1934 the people were starving and, apart from the seldom-used rail ink to Guang'xi, they found no industry and little infrastructure. After 1949 the central government tried to open up the region by putting in railways, roads and industries – but these mainly benefited the northern urban centres and the Han majority who lived in them. For the under-educated young men and women who wish to escape the terraced hills and the harsh realities of subsistence farming, [1] joining the military is often their only option. [2] A farmer with fresh vegetables goes to market in the suburbs of Kai'li. [3] European fashion has not yet made any inroads into the consciousness of these two old comrades. [4] A 'giant' sale at a local department store in Gui'yang.

4

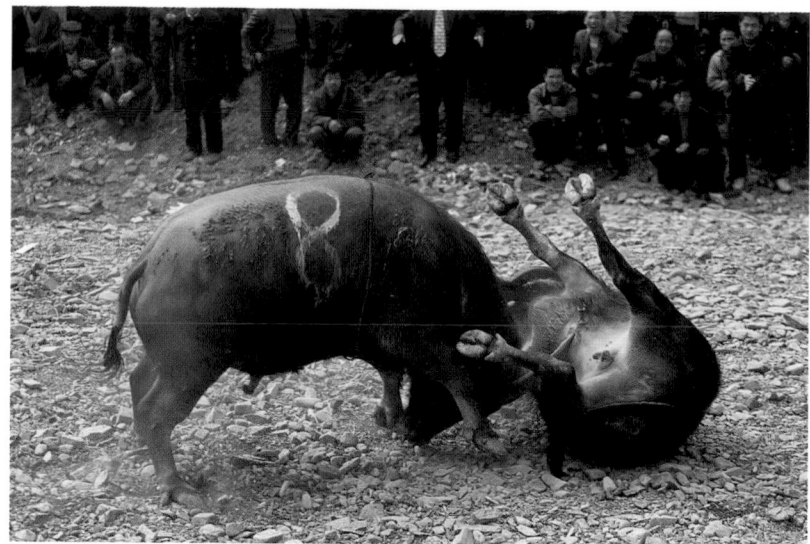

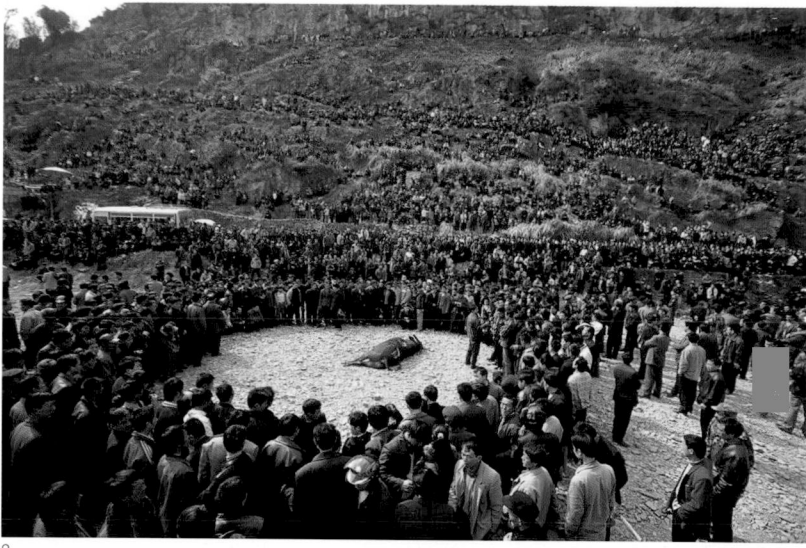

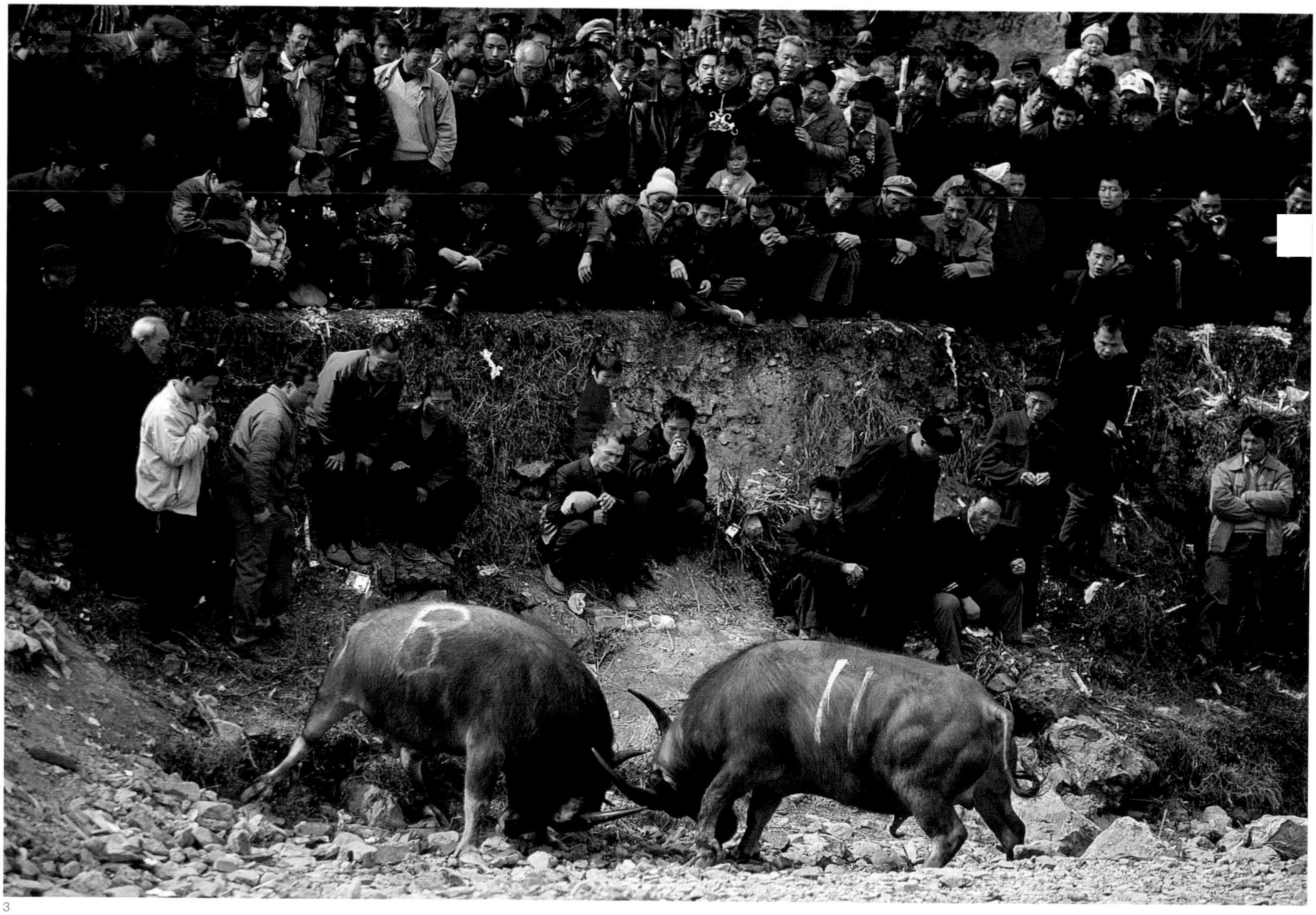

THE LU'SHENG FESTIVAL

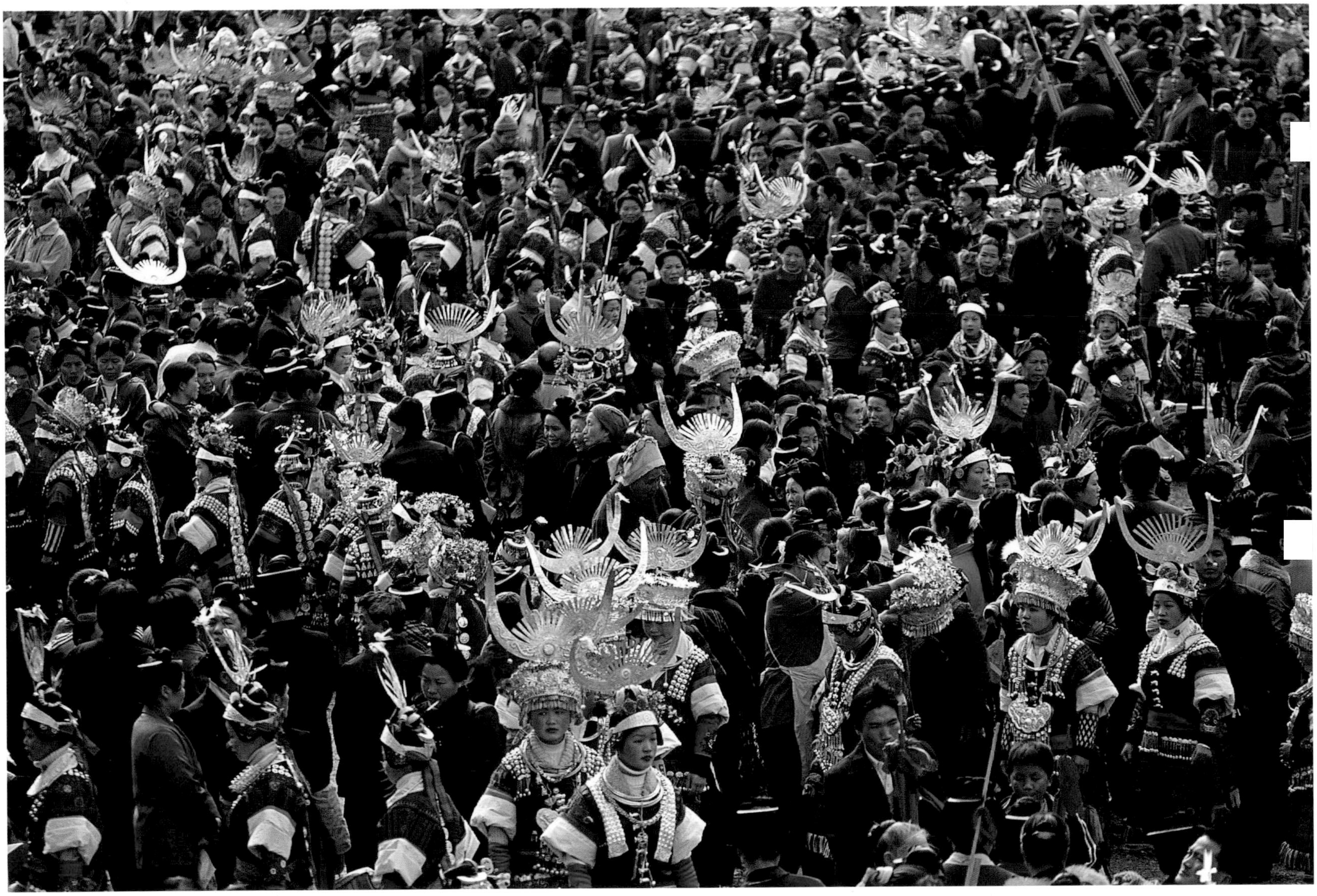

AT THE FIRST FULL MOON of the Lunar New Year, Miao people celebrate the arrival of spring with big festivals – and the Lu'sheng Festival in Zhou'xi is the biggest of them all. Hundreds of thousands of people flock to this remote village for the week-long party and to witness a spectacular mating ritual. [4] The dry riverbed shimmered like flowing silver lava as thousands of young girls, wearing fantastic multi-layered and intricately-designed silver headdresses adorned with giant stylised buffalo horns, sang and danced to the accompaniment of young men playing the *lu'sheng* (a bamboo reed instrument). [3] Buffalo fights are the other big attraction. Villages from many miles around pitch their strongest bull against their neighbours' champions in knockout competitions. One unfortunate bull was literally 'knocked out' in the first round by the previous year's champion. The two bulls were let loose 90 metres (100 yards) apart. They charged, their heads met and there was a loud, deep thud like a firecracker exploding under a pillow. [1] [2] One bull toppled over, never to rise again.

THE TRIBAL MOUNTAINS

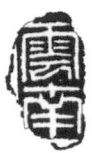

YUN'NAN PROVINCE

LOCATION
Latitude 21°08'–29°15'N
Longtitude 97°31'–106°11'E

AREA 419,600 km² (162,000 sq miles)

GEOGRAPHY The province forms part of the Yun'nan-Gui'zhou Plateau, which has an average elevation of around 2,000 m. Between the north and south of the province, the elevation falls from 6,700 m at Mount Meili near Tibet to 76 m on the Vietnam border. These sharp contrasts and Yun'nan's southerly location mean the province contains snowcapped mountains and lush rainforests. The Yang'tzo, Mc'kong, Salween and Red rivers flow through the province.

CLIMATE Yun'nan's varied terrain and elevation gives the province, north to south, three distinct climatic zones: temperate, sub-tropical and tropical. Mean annual temperatures range from 7°C in the mountainous northwest to 22°C in the southeastern Yuanjiang River valley. The lowest recorded temperature is -8.4°C and the highest is 42°C. Average rainfall is between 750 mm and 1,750 mm.

POPULATION 44.15 million (end 2004)

MAJOR CITIES Kun'ming (capital), Qu'jing, Ge'jiu, Xia'guan, Yu'xi.

AGRICULTURE Main food crops include rice, corn, wheat, sweet potatoes and soybeans. Cash crops include tea, sugarcane and cotton. The province is the centre of China's tobacco industry. There is a major hardwood forestry in the southwest.

MAIN INDUSTRIES The province is a major mining centre, producing iron and bauxite ores, coal, copper, gold, zinc, tin, silver and other minerals. Hydroelectric power provides energy for these and other industries. Tourism produces more than 10 per cent of Yunnan's GDP.

ANNUAL PER CAPITA INCOME (2005)
Disposable income of urban residents:
RMB 9,250 (US$1,154)
Net income of rural residents:
RMB 2,042 (US$255)

HISTORICAL AND SCENIC SITES
Xia'guan, Jing'hong, Li'jiang, Stone Forest, Kun'ming's karst outcrops, Yuan'yang Rice Terraces.

FOOD Yun'nan cooking is a blend of the chilli-laced cuisine of neighbouring Si'chuan and the influence of migrations from other regions. Dishes reflect the province's climatic and natural diversity, featuring hams, poultry, eels, cheese, fungi and noodles.

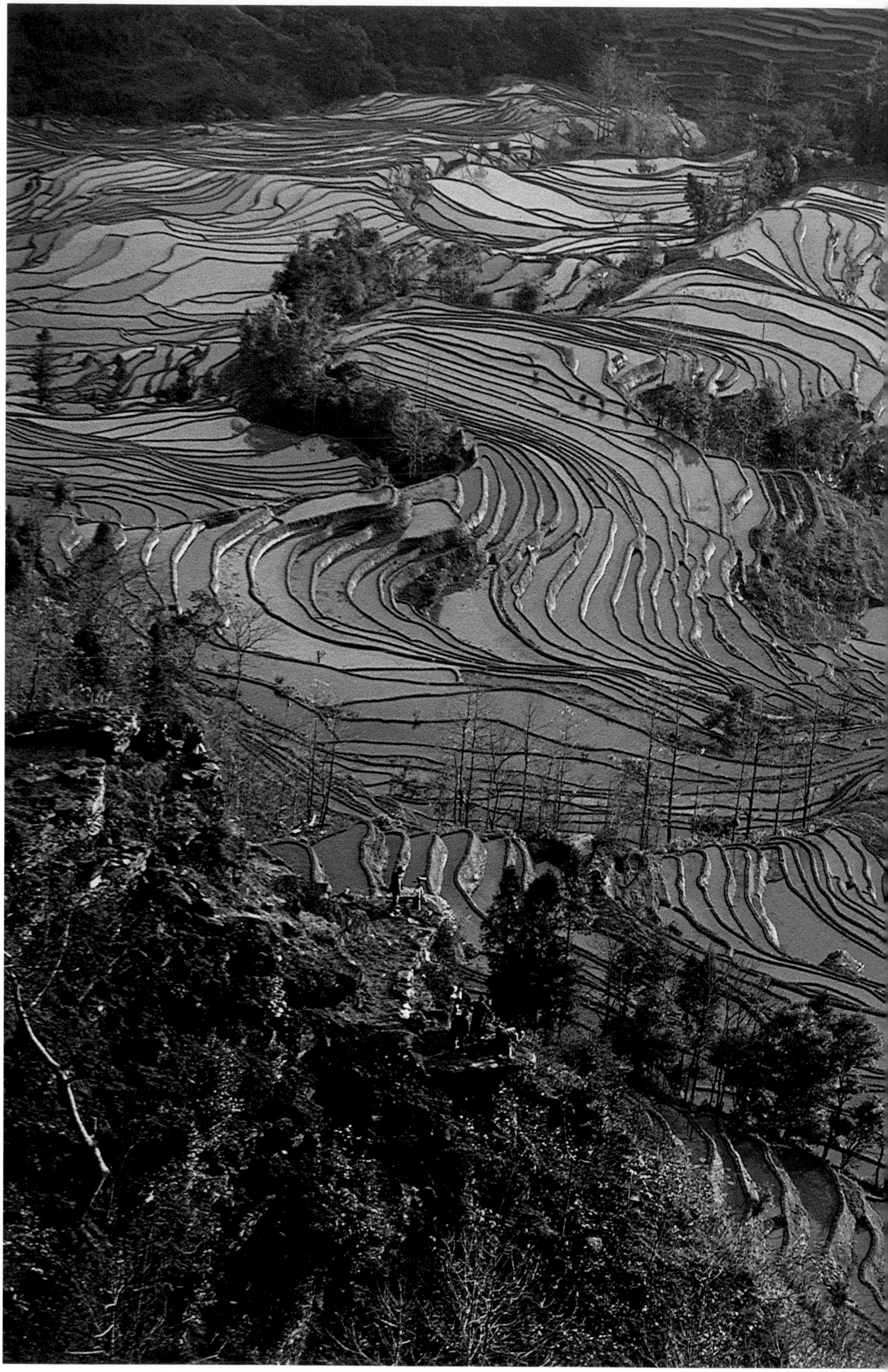

[RIGHT] The Tiger's Mouth terrace fields in Yuan'yang County.

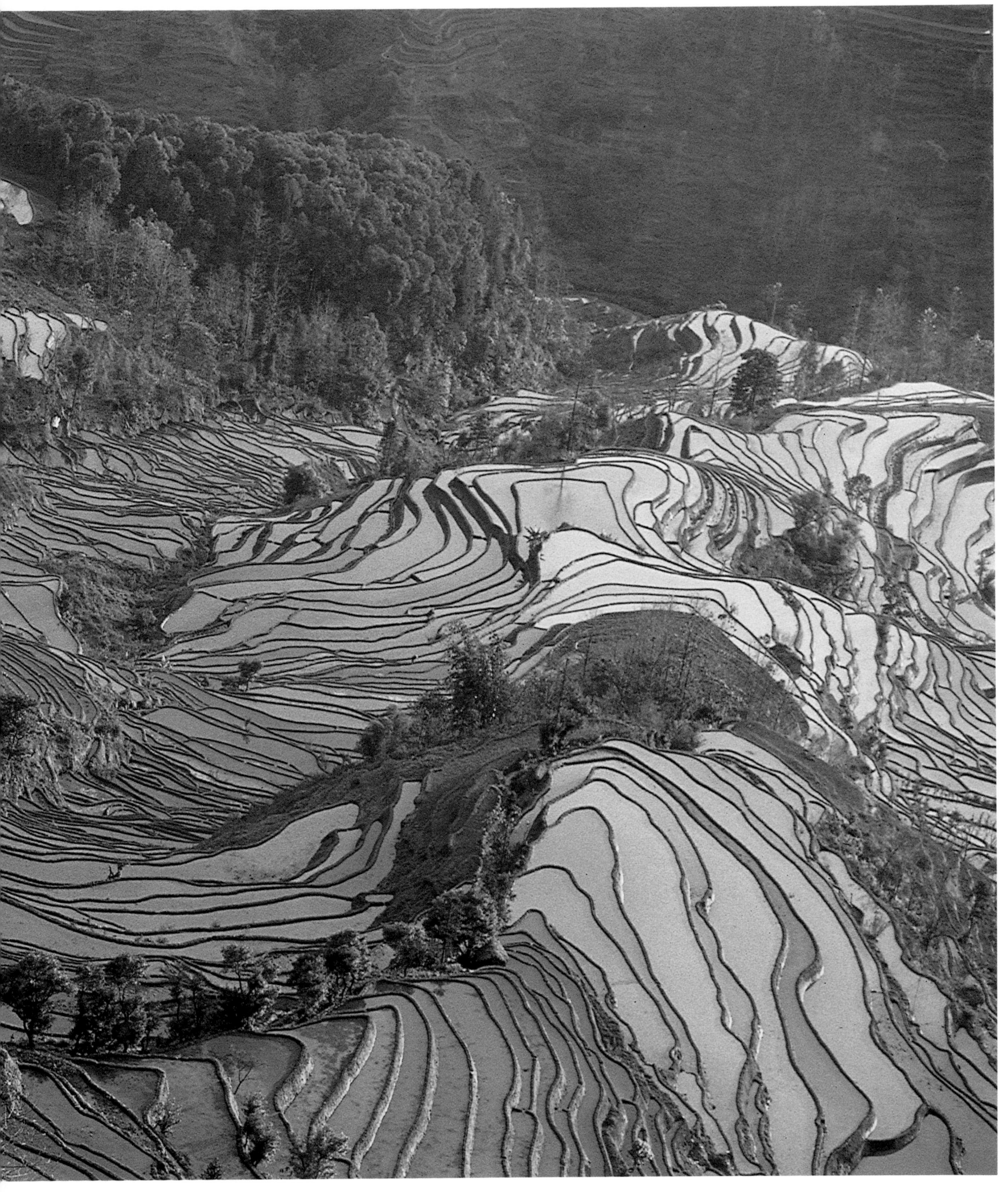

HA'NI TERRACES AT YUAN'YANG

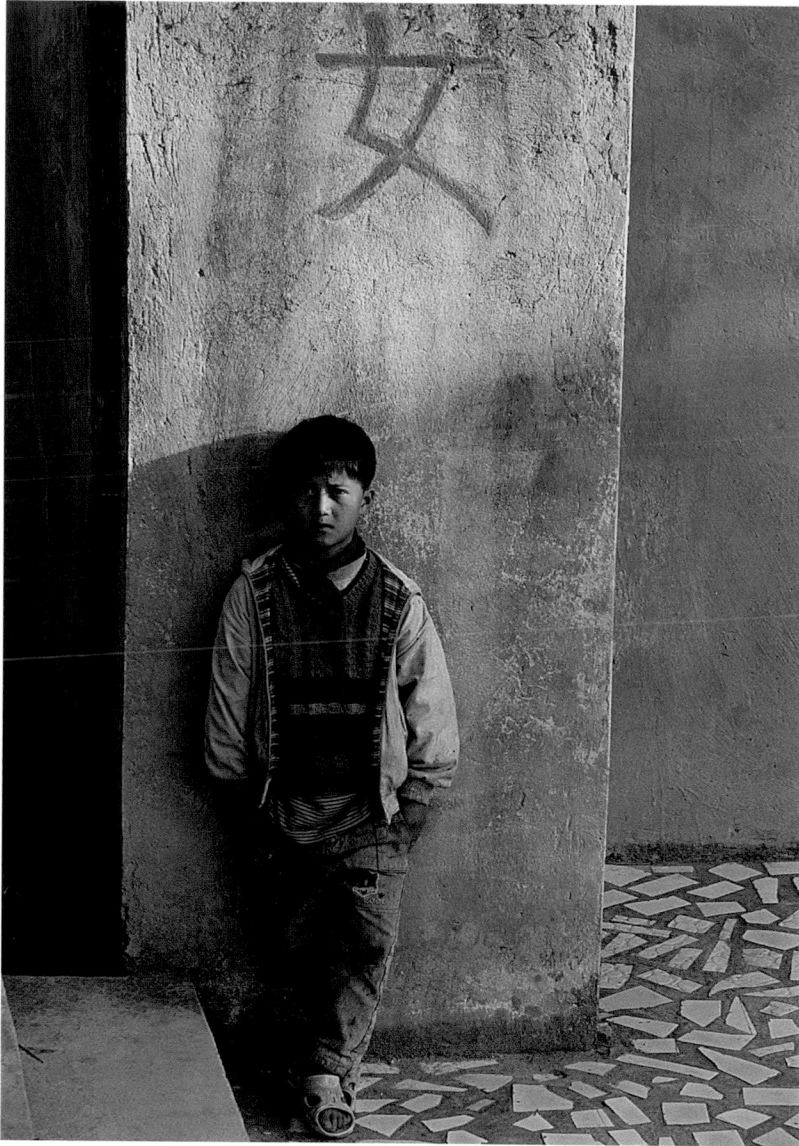

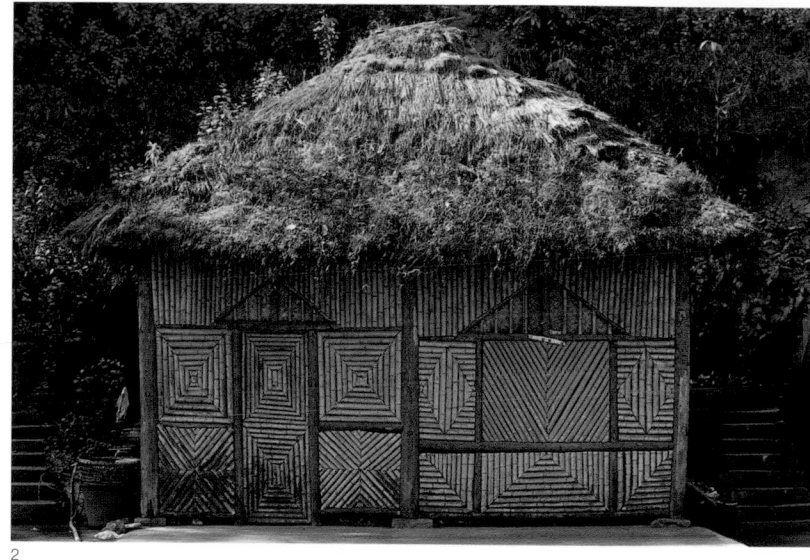

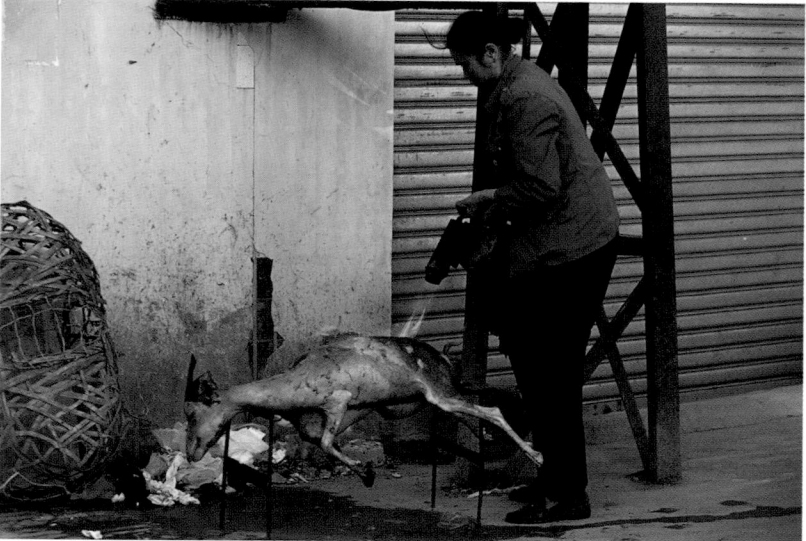

THE HA'NI MINORITY of Hong'he (Red River) region in the deep south of Yun'nan province near the Vietnam border have been carving ter-raced fields out of the mountains for at least 1,300 years. The remarkable design of these terraces, which produce both rice and fish, demonstrate a perfect agricultural system while also reflecting the agro-worship culture of the Ha'ni people based on their deep empathy for the land and a sublime belief that man and nature can live in harmony. In Yuan'yang County alone [4] [5] [6] there are more than 11,000 hectares (27,000 acres) of terraces. Some of these are 3,000 steps deep, reaching down from high mountain ridges to the depths of the valleys far into the distance. [1] A village boy hanging around outside the public ladies' facility at a terrace viewpoint. [2] The design of this local bamboo and grass hut is both whimsical and unique. [3] A lady with a blowtorch in Yuan'yang new town prepares an animal for the famous local dish of Clay-pot Lamb by burning off any obstinate hair still left on the carcass.

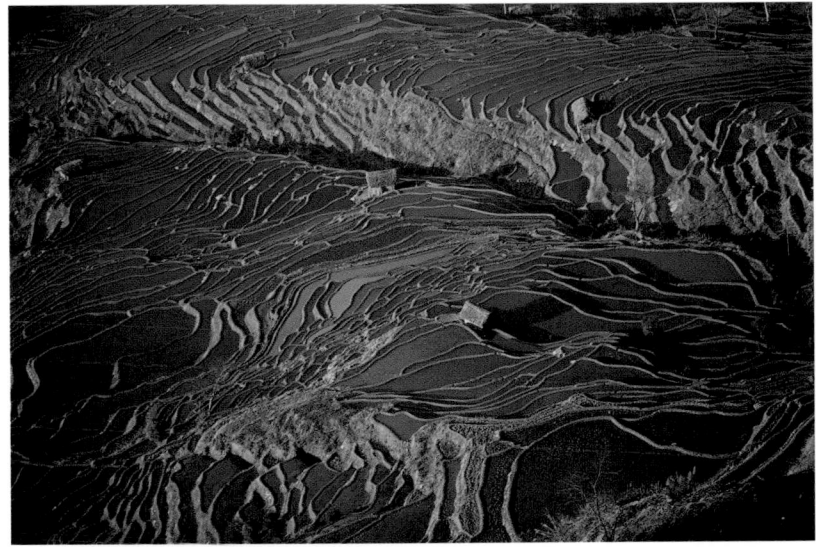
4

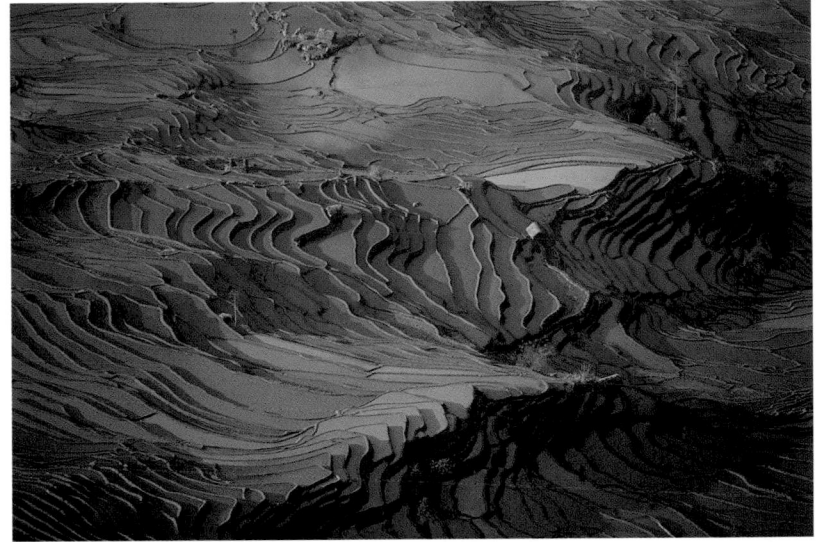
5

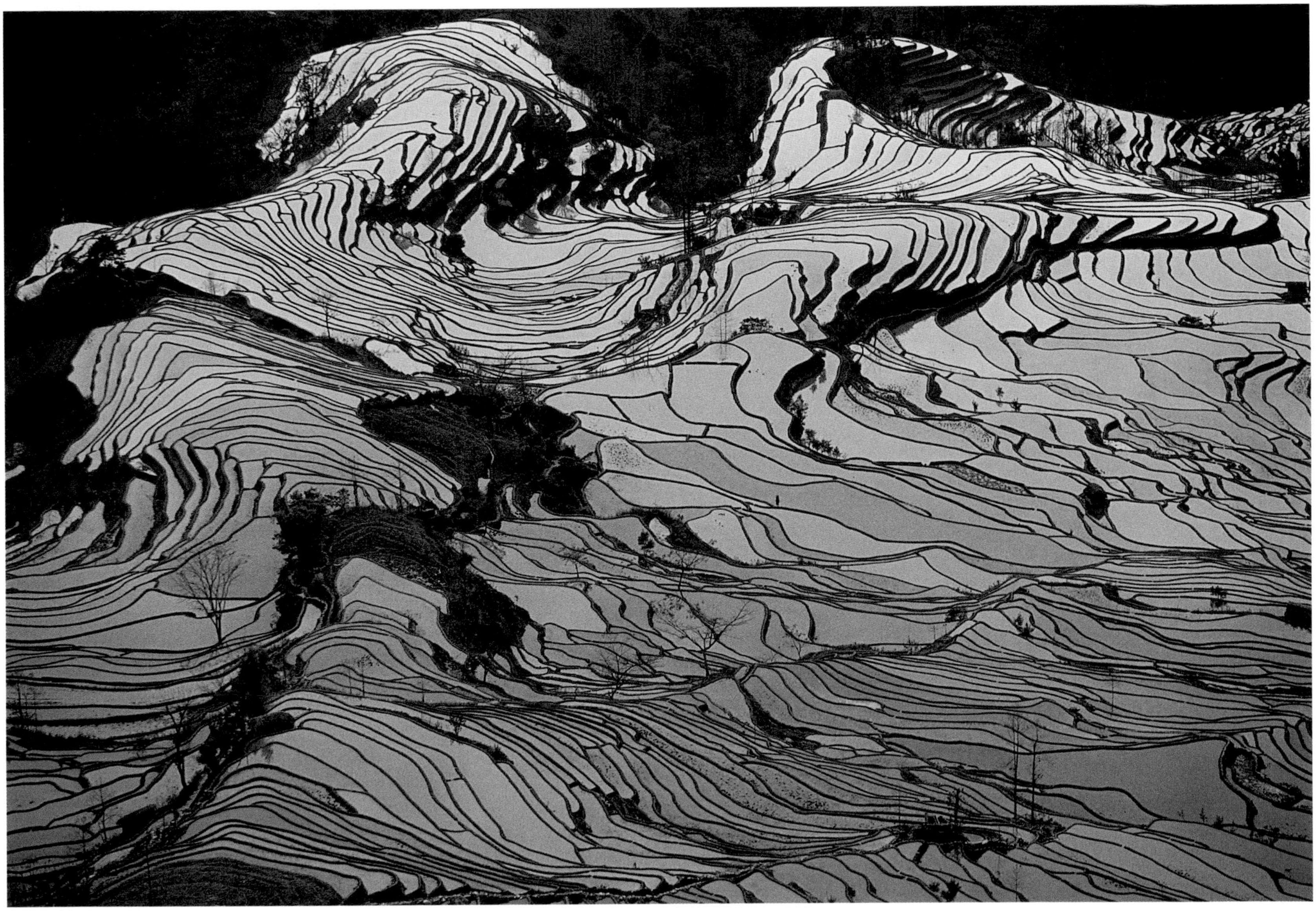

6

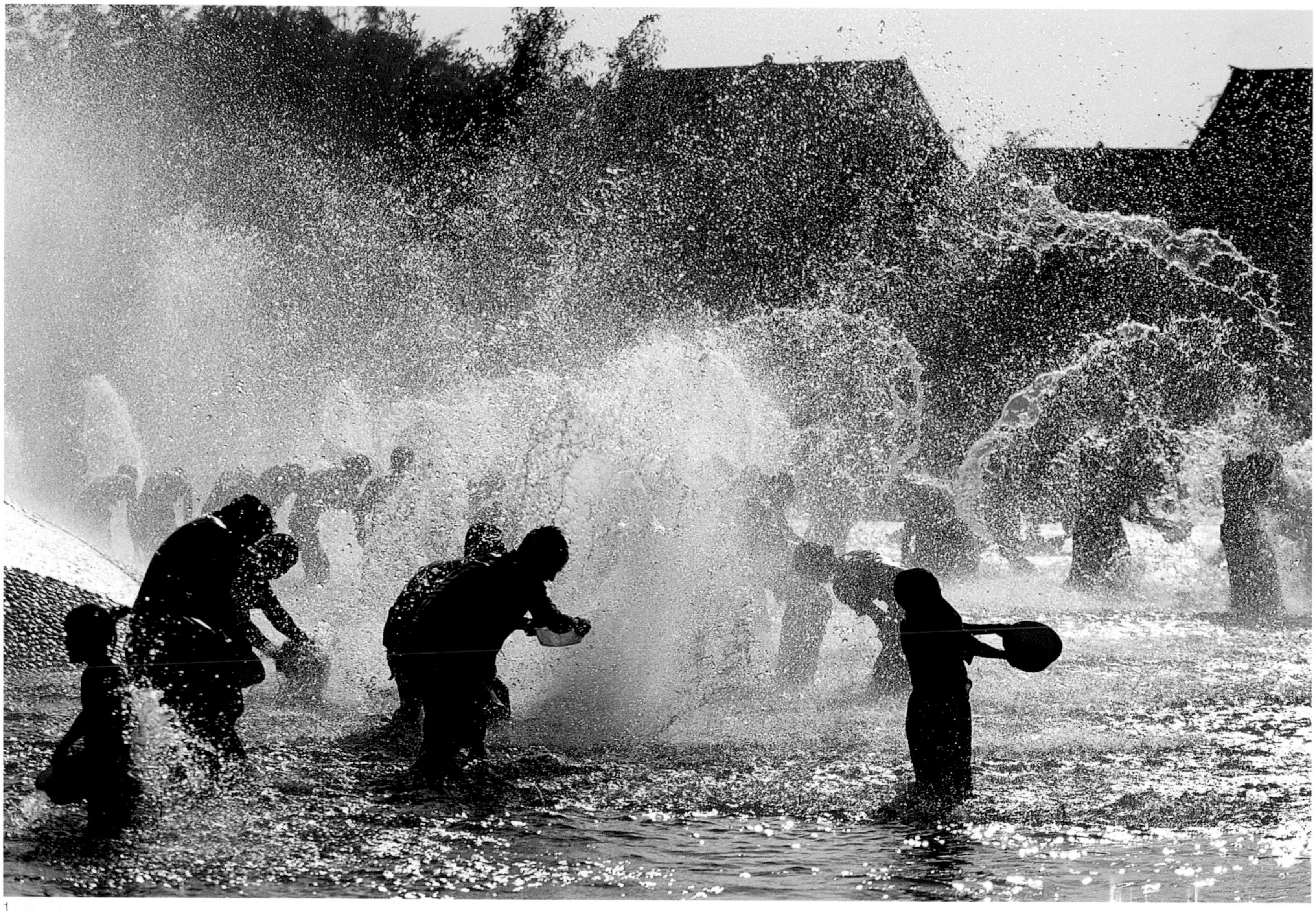

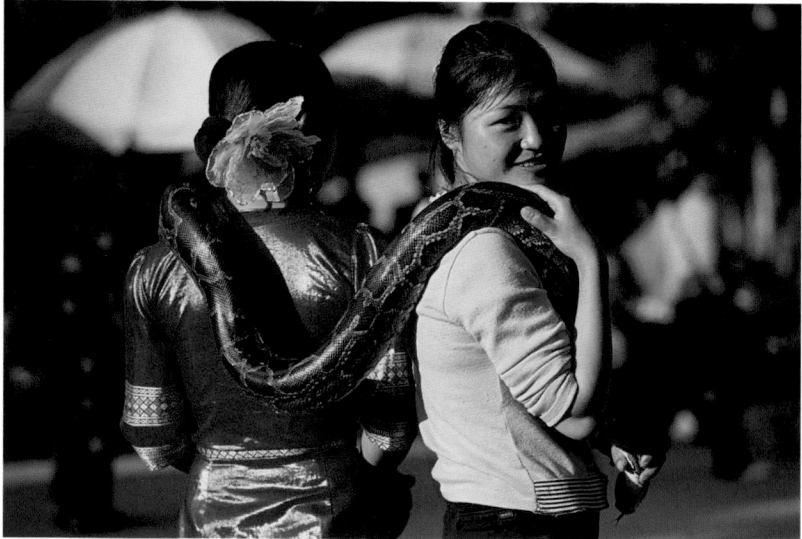

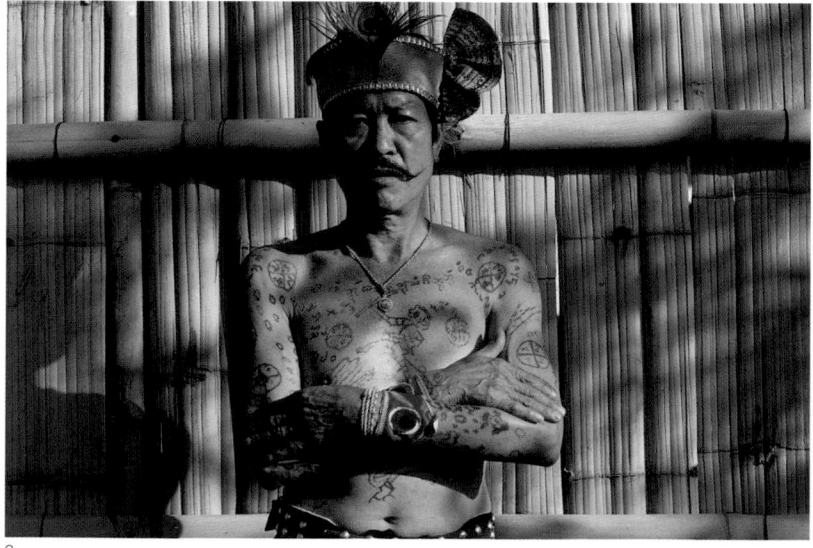

THE DAI MINORITY GARDEN IN XI'SHUANG'BANNA

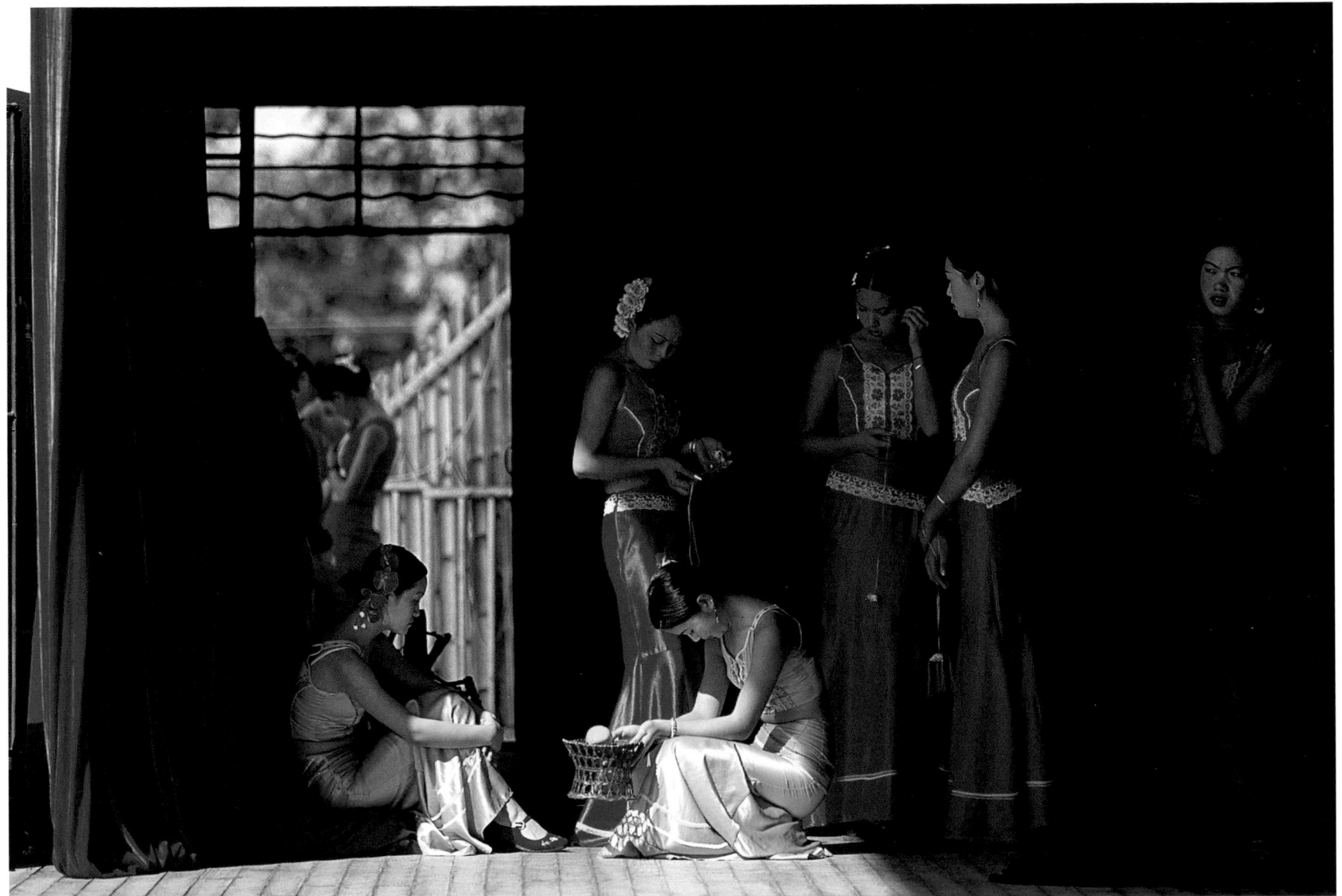

4

ADVERTISED AS THE 'FIRST ECOLOGICAL VILLAGE IN CHINA', the Dai Minority Garden is an attempt at marrying anthropology with tourism. The 'garden' was a product of the 'getting rich is glorious' era in the roaring 1980s. A parking lot and ticket booths were built outside five Dai minority villages in Gan'lan'ba. The 309 households with 1,487 inhabitants were instantly transformed into a cultural 'safari park' where visitors can spend the night in traditional stilt-houses, sample local delicacies and participate in the Dai's New Year celebration in [1] the 'annual' Water-Splashing Festival – which takes place in the main square twice a day. It's easy to feel indignant at such blatant exploitation of minority cultures, yet the place is beautiful, the people gentle and lovely and the food delicious. It's just ironic that the only way minorities can try and retain their cultural identity and heritage is by letting tour operators sell them – a process that will inevitably destroy them. [2] Dai girls with a python. [3] A Dai warrior. [4] Dai dancers waiting to go on stage for the 4:30 show.

THE TRIBAL MOUNTAINS

CHINA'S MINI-THAILAND ON THE ME'KONG

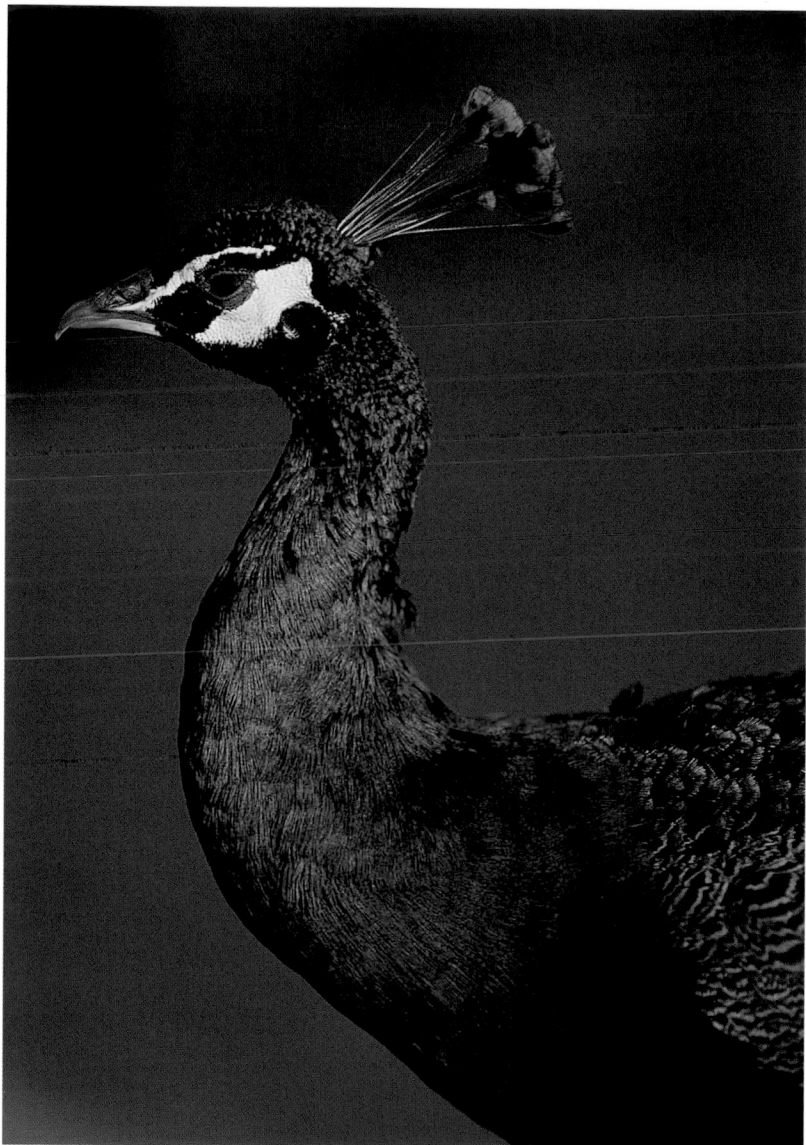

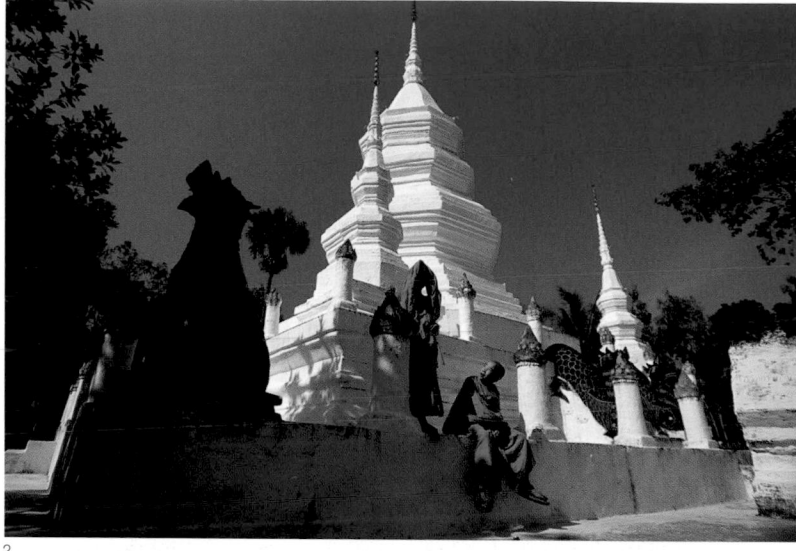

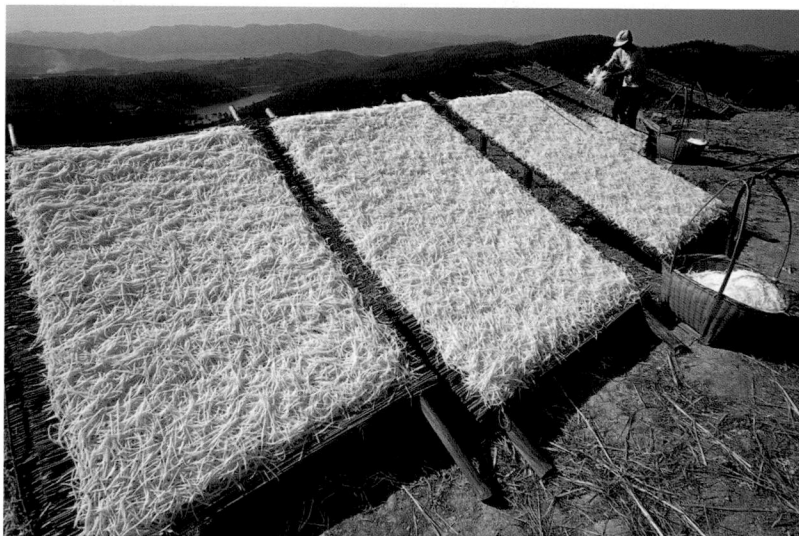

THE TRIBAL MOUNTAINS

OVER FIFTY MINORITY RACES LIVE IN CHINA, half of them in Yun'nan province, and at least eight of them reside in Xi'shuang'banna prefecture. They include the Yao, Li'su, Ha'ni and its cousins Ai'ni, Bu'lang, Ji'nuo, La'hu, Wa and the Dai (or Thai) people – who account for half of the 530,000 minorities' population. The Dais are part of the extensive family of hill tribes residing in northern Thailand, Laos and Burma. Their architecture and languages are very similar and they share the same religion – Hinayana Buddhism. [2] This scene from a temple in Jing'hong, the capital of Xi'shaung'banna, could easily have been taken in any one of the Southeast Asian countries across the border. [1] A peacock at the Dai Minority Garden. [3] Shredded white turnip is being dried on racks in preparation for pickling. A staple in the region, it is available in many different marinades [5] at shops that specialize in pickled vegetables in Jing'hong's produce market. [4] The Ji'nuo-minority headman of Da'gu (Big Drum) village offers us tea in his longhouse on top of the hill.

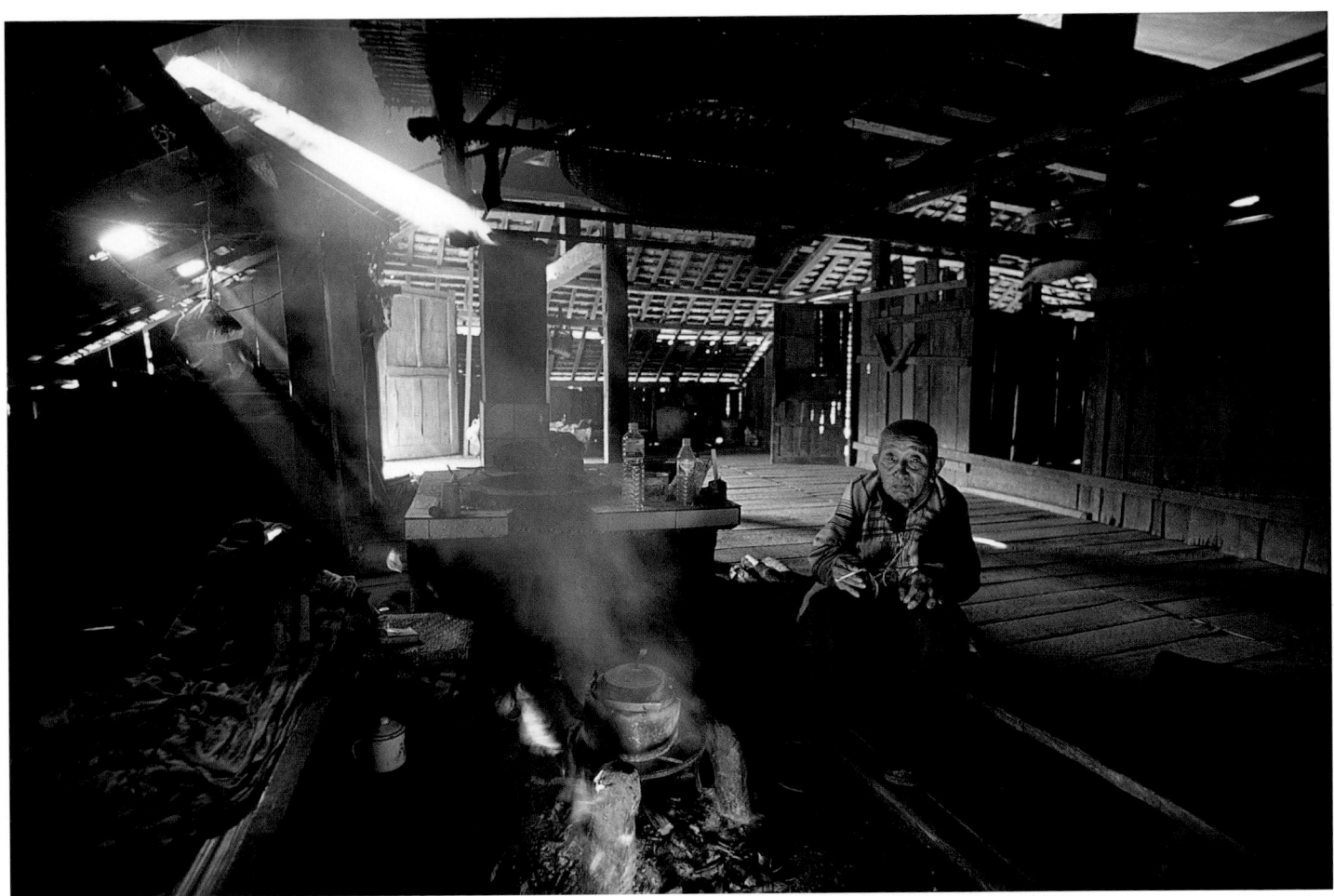

4

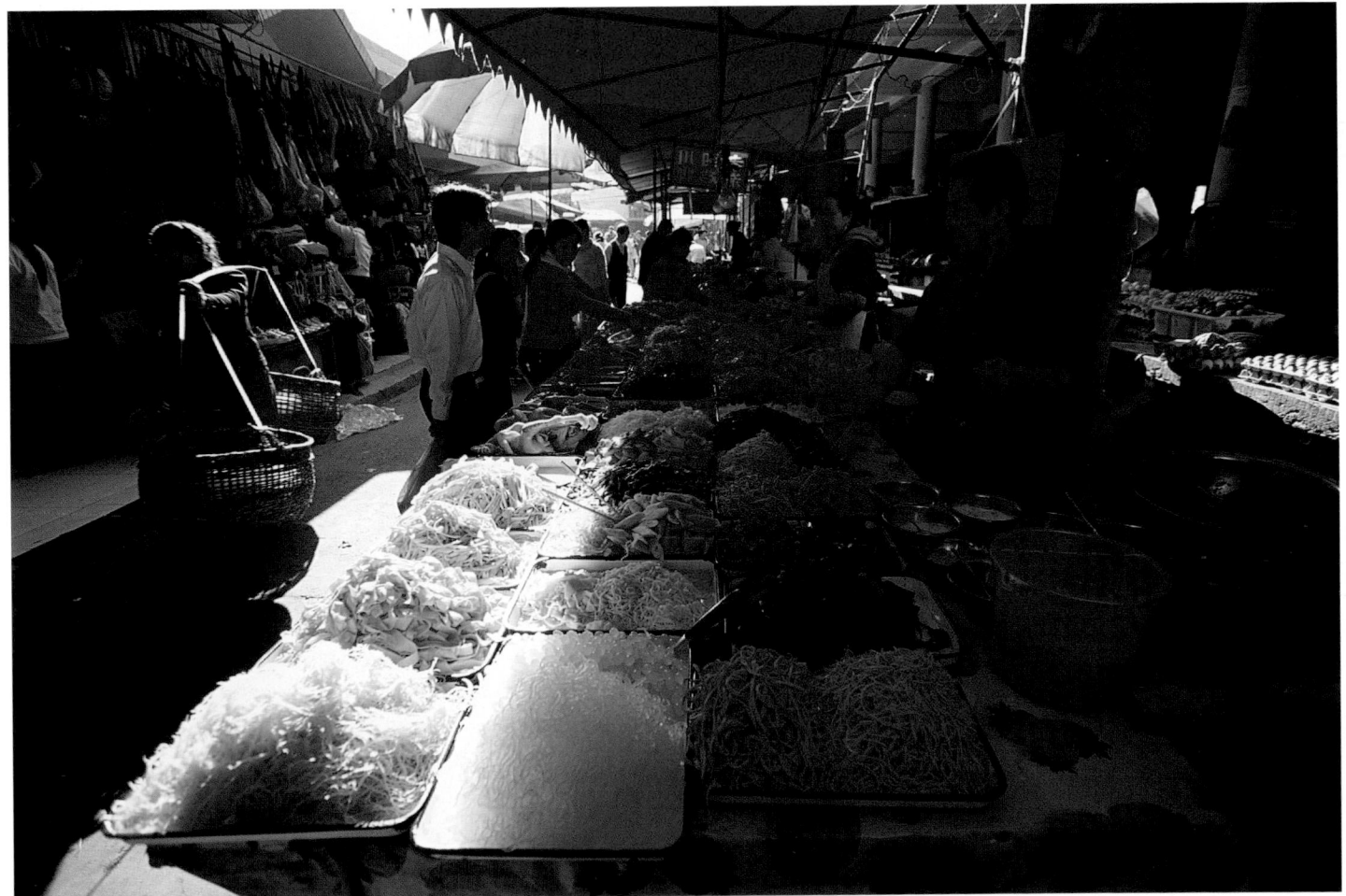

5

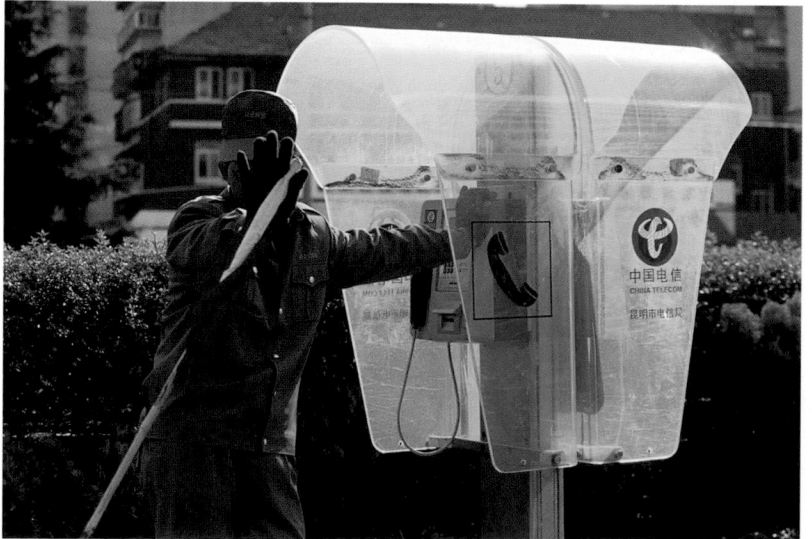

KUN'MING, THE CAPITAL OF YUN'NAN, is perhaps best known in the West as the northern terminus of the Burma Road. This 1,000-kilometre (620-mile) dirt track from Lashio in Burma allowed Anglo-American supplies to be shipped in to support the Chinese army's fight against the Japanese invasion during the Second World War. After the Japanese captured Lashio in 1942, allied aircraft flew from India over the Himalayan 'hump' to supply the Chinese nationalist and American 'Flying Tigers' fighter squadrons in Kun'ming. Chiang Kai'shek's army, however, had no intentions of fighting the Japanese and most of the shipments ended up on the black market – making some Kuo'min'tang generals and local warlords very, very rich. After 1949 the war-profiteers moved south across the Burmese border, where their armies took over the gems, jade and opium trade of the Golden Triangle. [1] An entire street of neon-lit advertisements selling "Breasts Enhancement" surgery in Kun'ming. [2] An unwilling subject in the City of Eternal Spring. [3] [4] [5] Official 'minorities tour guides' touch up their make-up before leading the hordes into the labyrinth of eroded limestone pillars known as Shi'lin – the Stone Forrest.

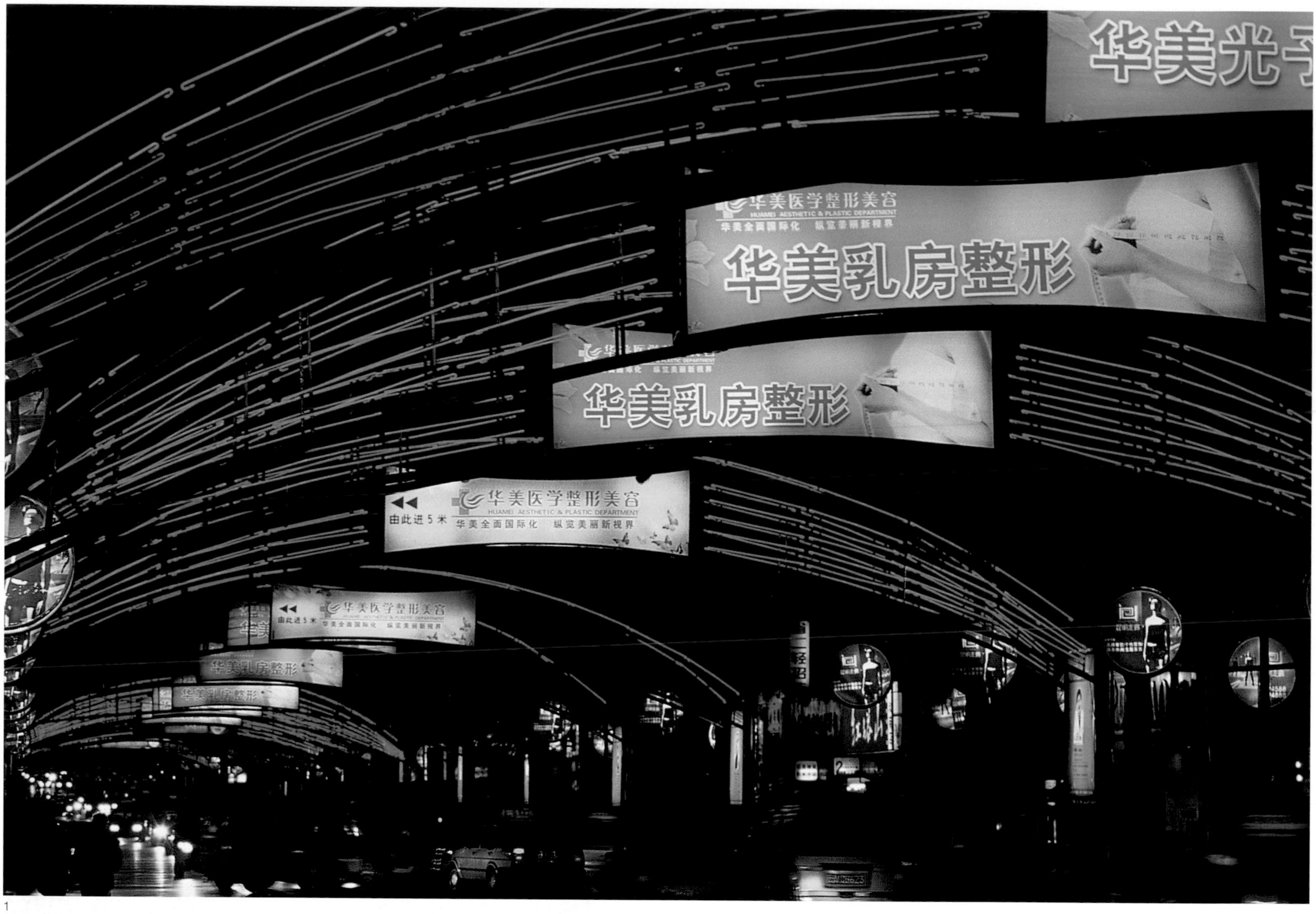

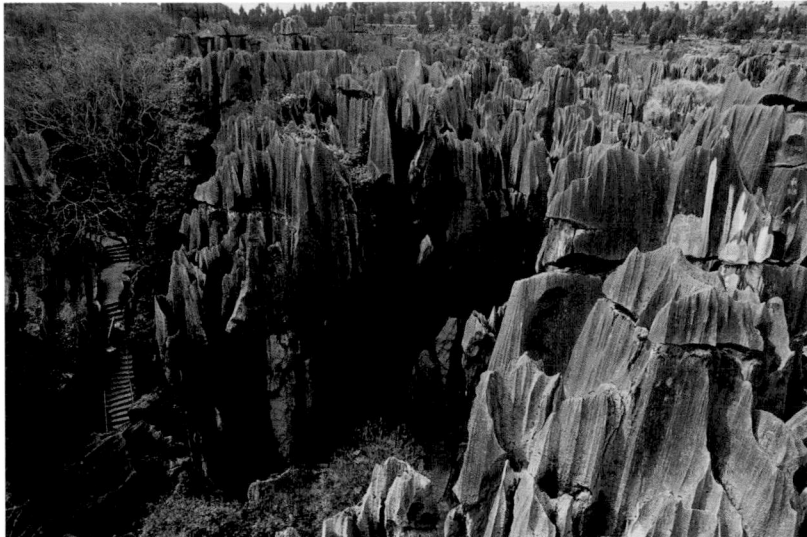

3

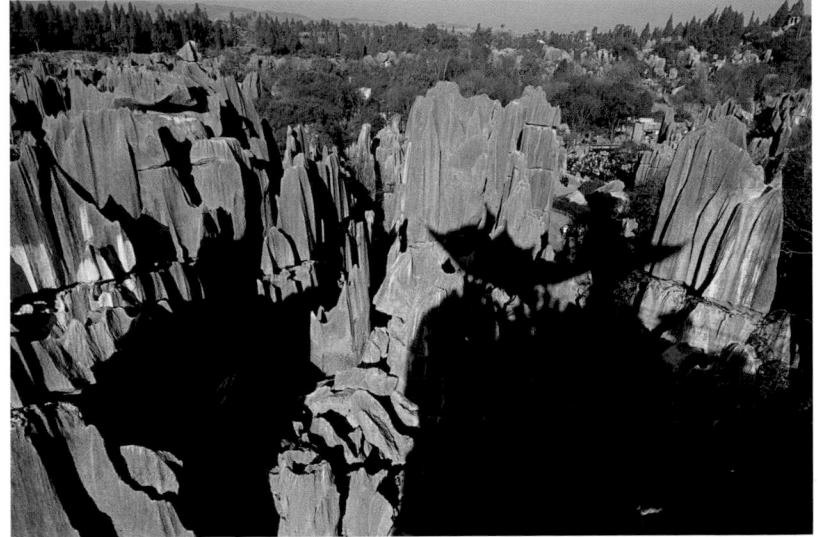

4

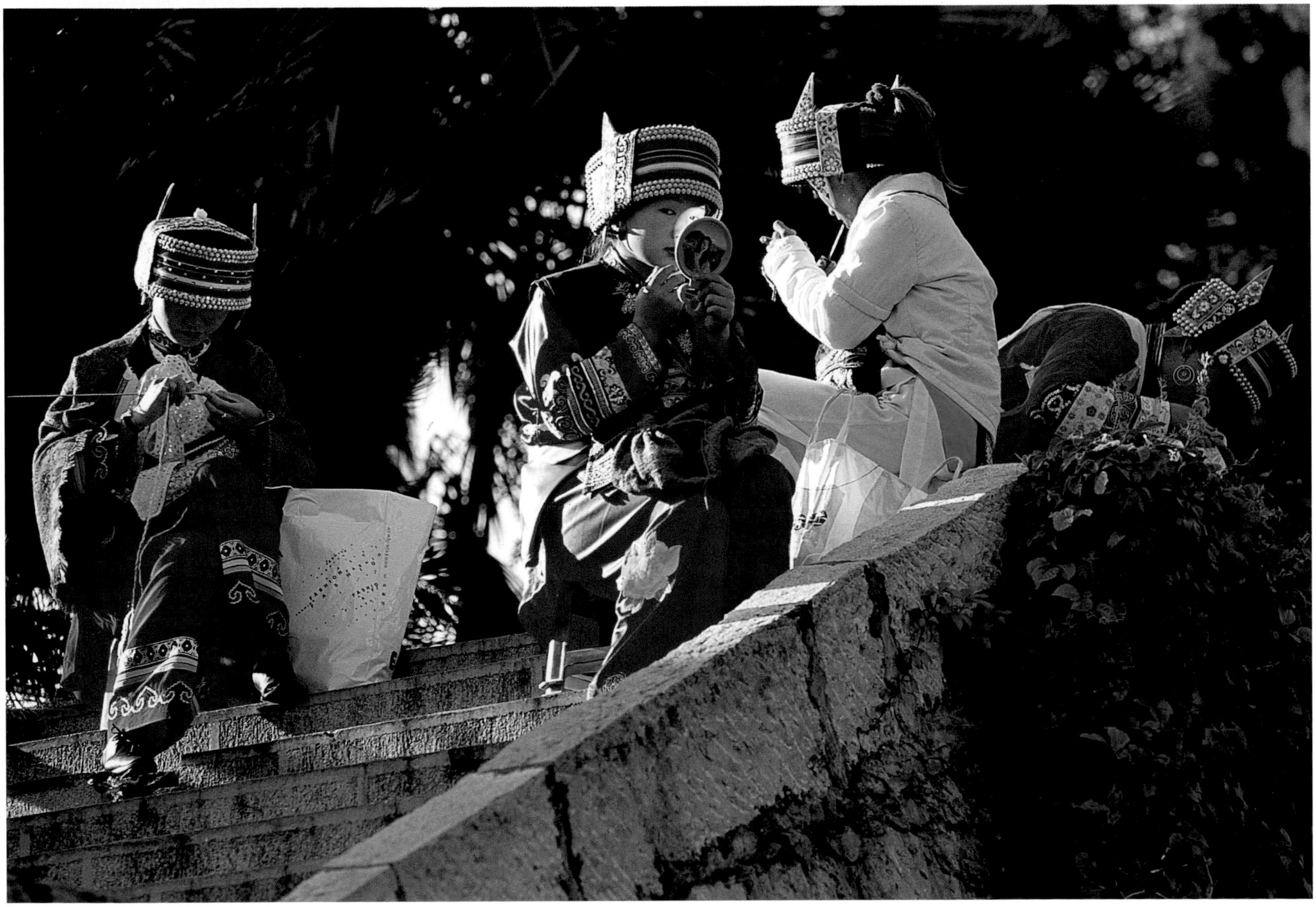

5

THE CITY OF MARBLE

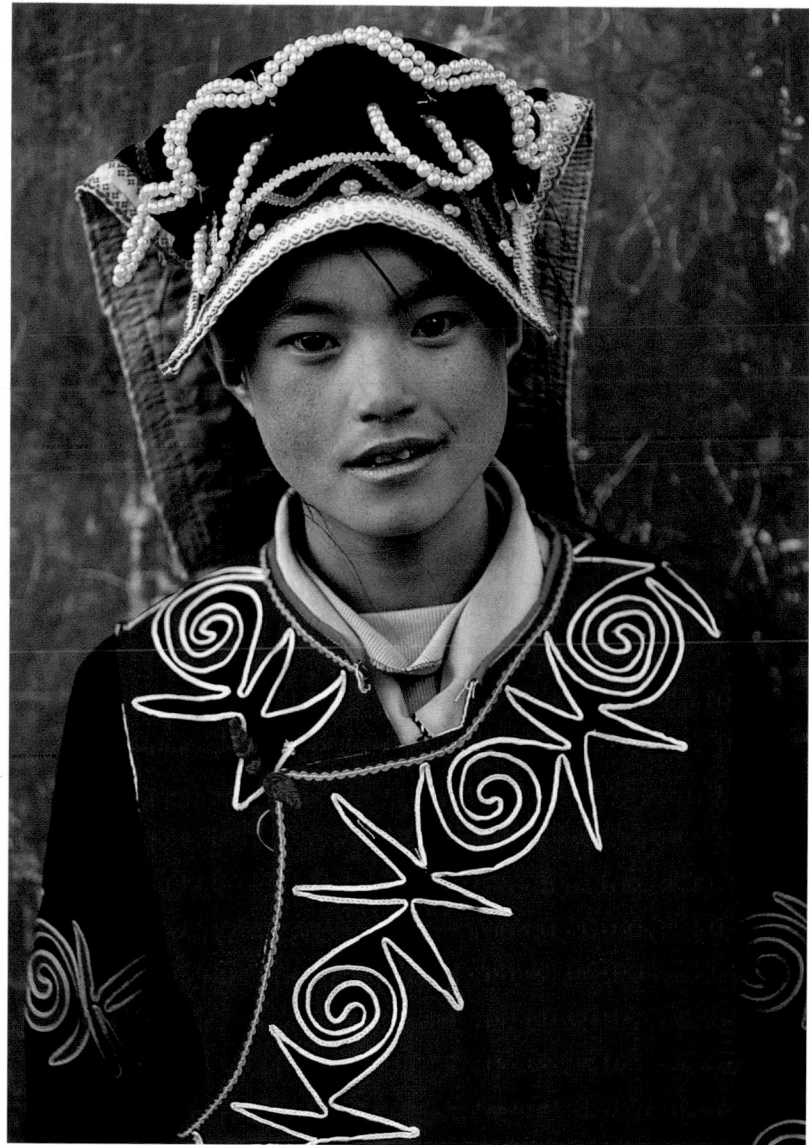

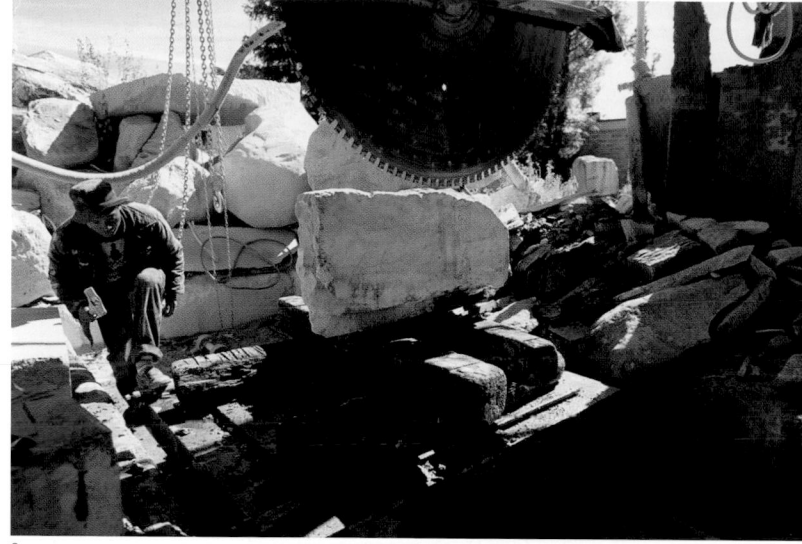

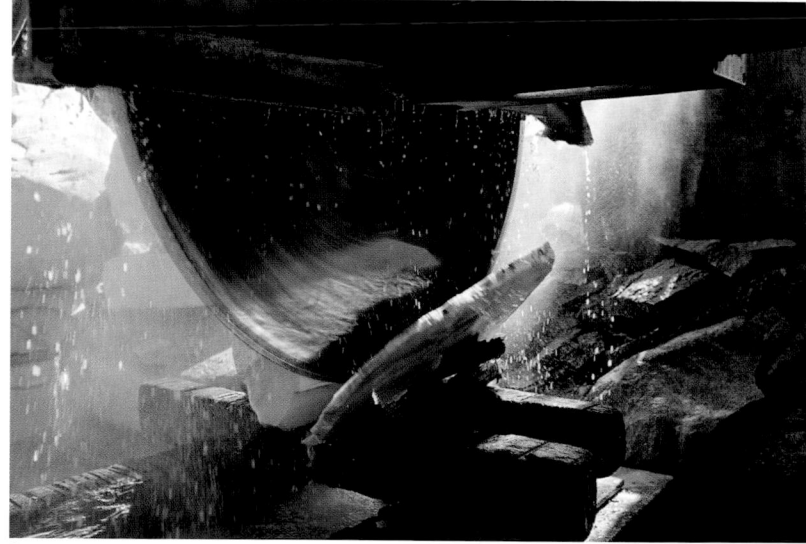

THE ANCIENT WALLED CITY OF DA'LI was the capital of the Nan'zhou Kingdom of Yun'nan between the 8th and mid-13th centuries, during which period the influence of the Bai people dominated southwest China and northern Burma. These influences can still be glimpsed today in [1] the traditional costumes and customs of the other minority groups in the region. [2] [3] The Chinese name for marble is 'Da'li stone' and the city has supplied its renowned polished marble pieces that resemble Chinese watercolours to, among others, the architects of the Forbidden City, the gardens of Su'zhou and Xi'an's mosques. [4] The San Ta Si (Three Pagodas Temple) nestles in the verdant foothills of the 4,000-metre (13,000-foot) Cang Shan (Jade Green Mountain) overlooking the giant ear-shaped Er'hai Lake. First erected in the mid-9th Century and flanked by two smaller ten-tier pagodas, [4] the sixteen-tier 70-metre (230-foot) Qian'xun Pagoda is reminiscent of the Big Goose Pagoda in Xi'an. Further along the mountain range, [5] local kilns produce the traditional grey bricks that are being used for the renovation of the old city.

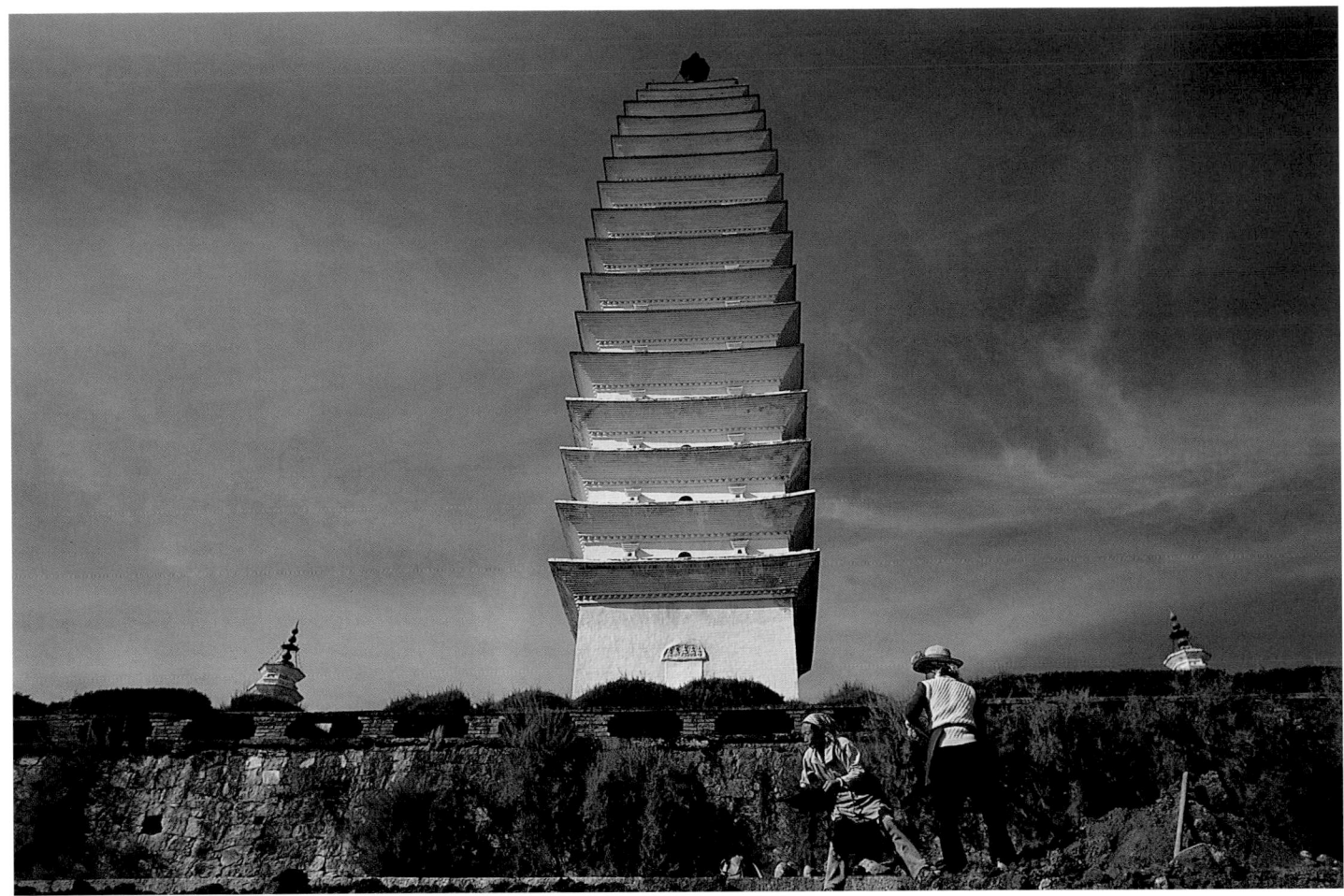

4

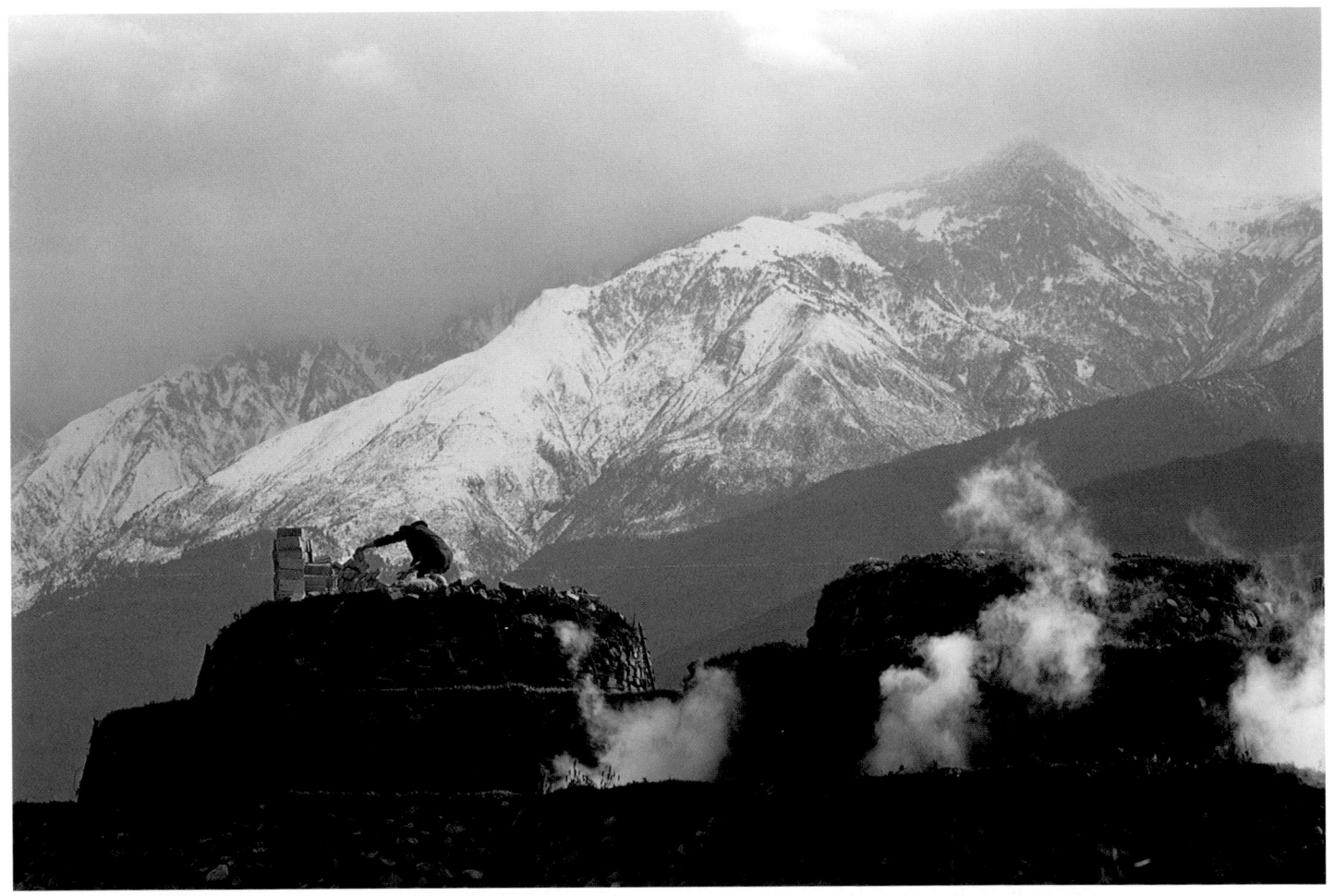

5

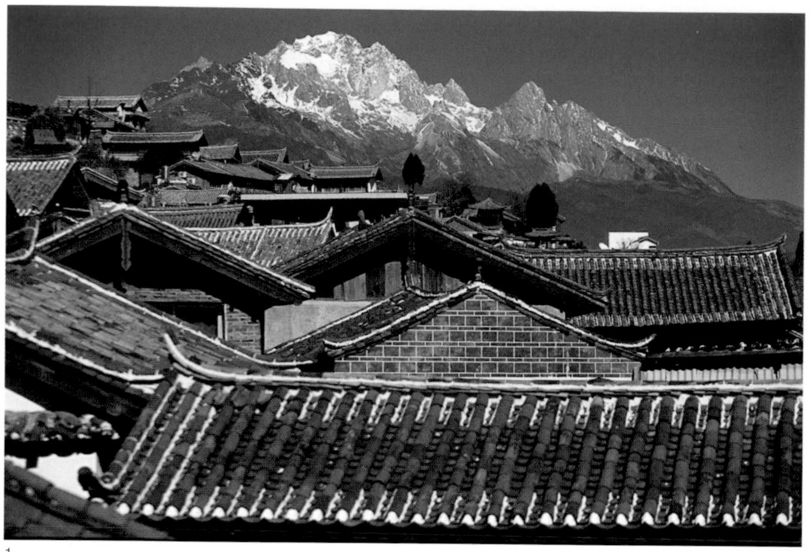

1

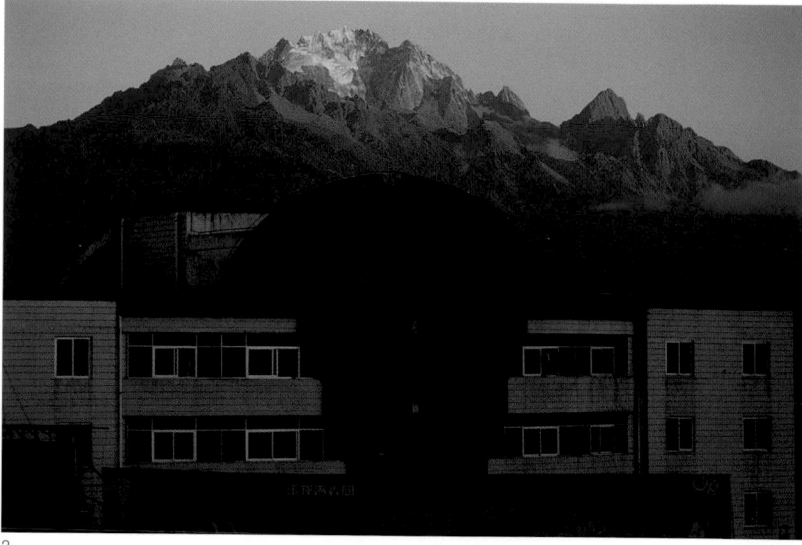

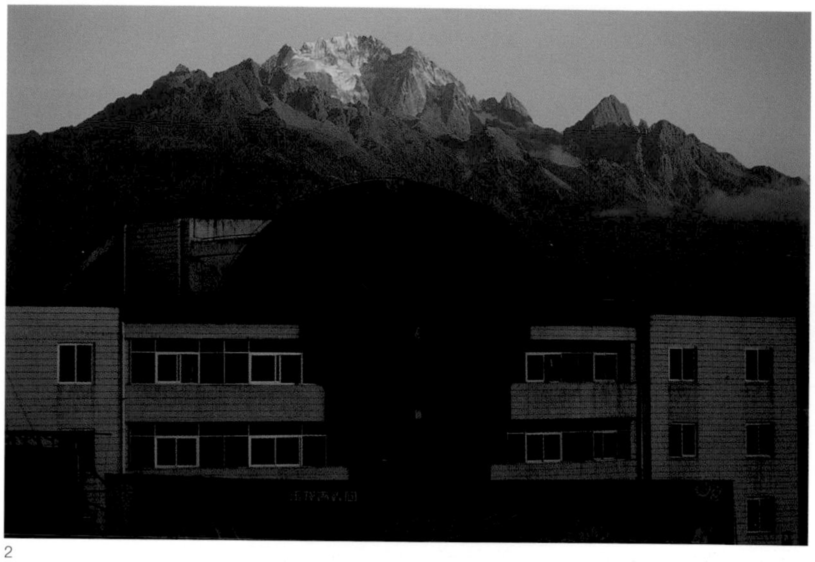

2

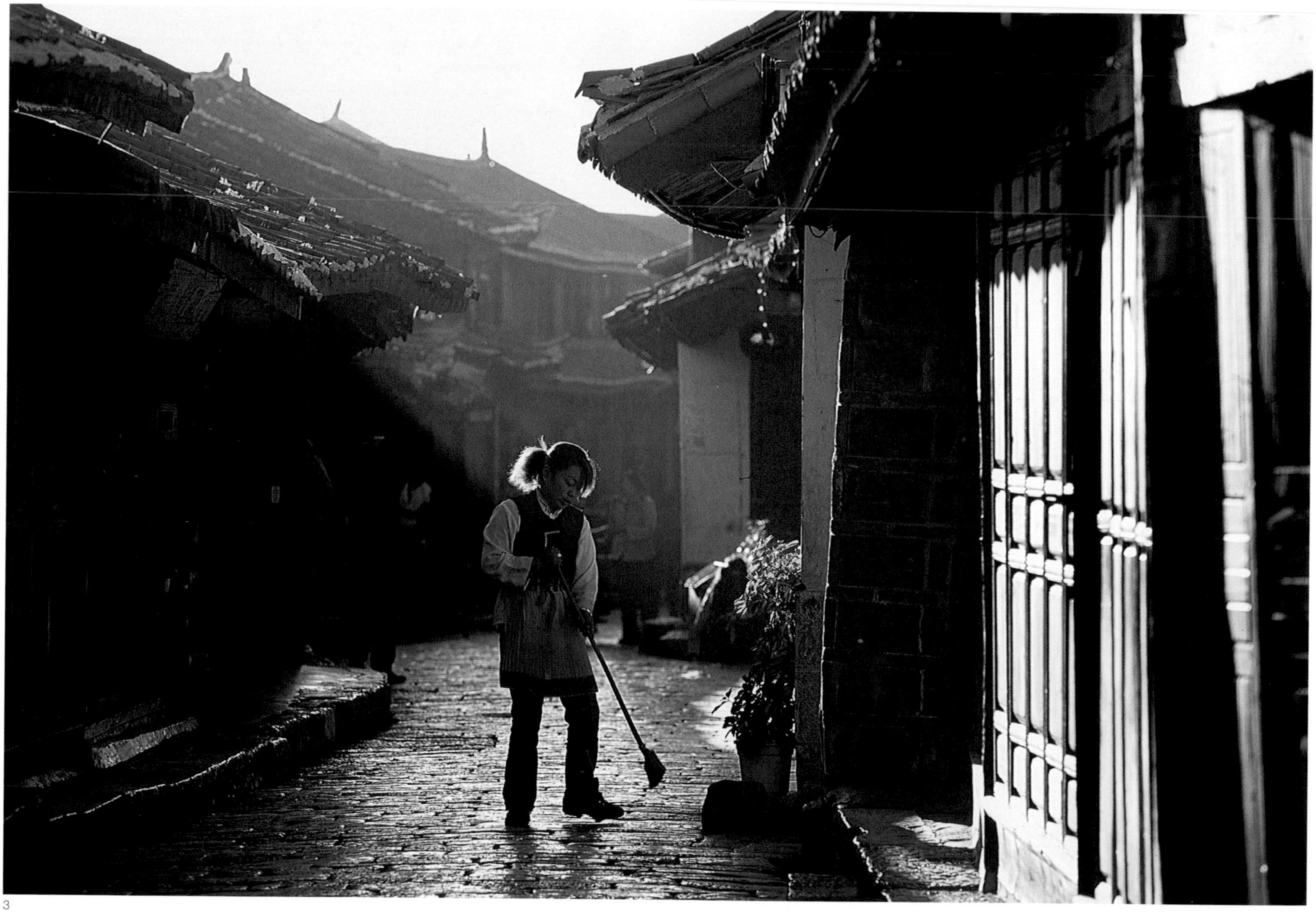

3

THE NA'XI HOMELAND

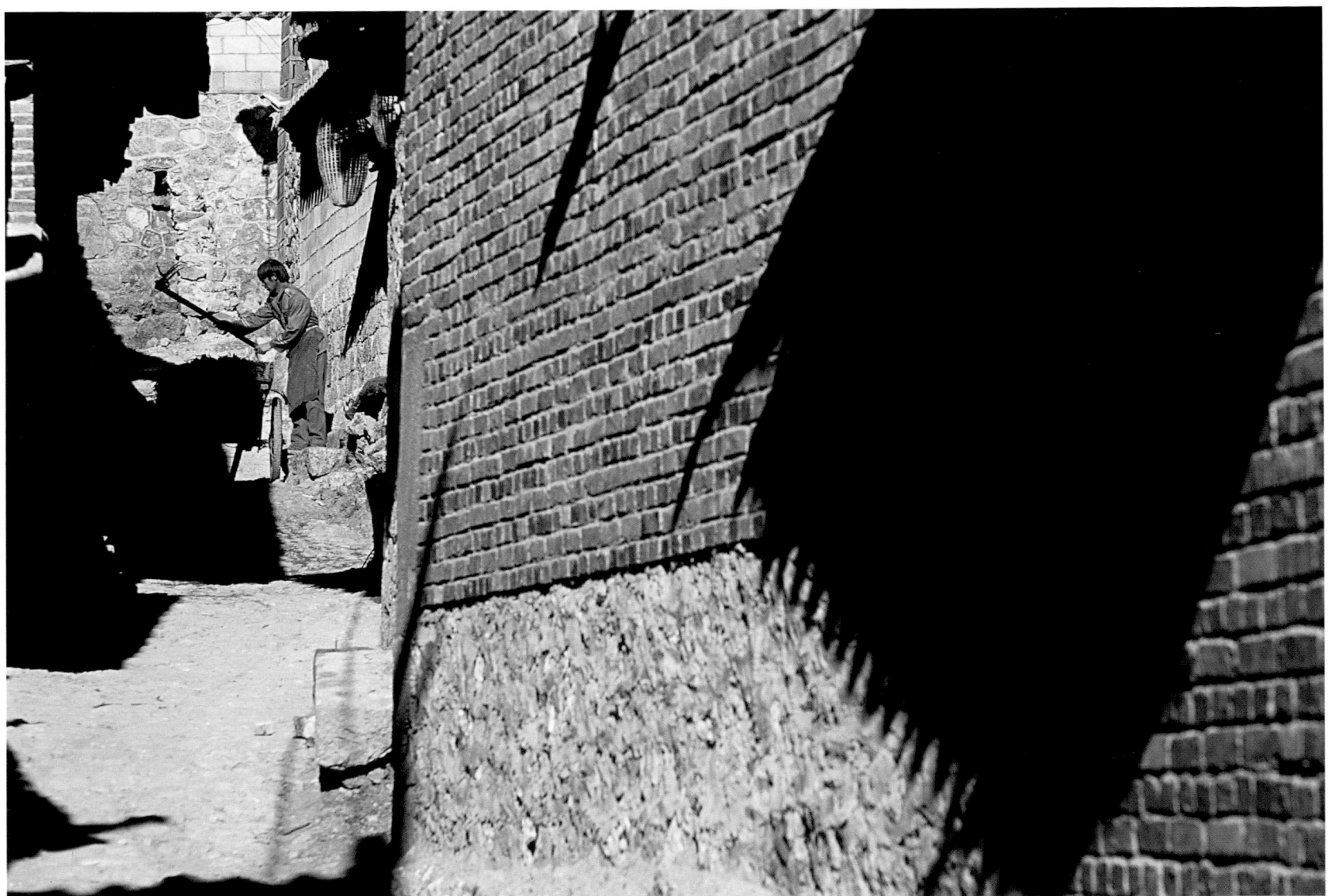

4

LI'JIANG (BEAUTIFUL RIVER), once a sleepy rundown town under the spectacular [1] [2] Yu'long Shan (Jade Dragon Mountain) at the eastern tail of the Himalayas, [3] now has over three million tourists traipsing through its cobble-stoned streets each year. The road from being the remote homeland for the Na'xi minority people where only a handful of scholars ventured to research their remarkable 1,000-year-old pictographs (the only ancient hieroglyphic language still in use), to becoming southwest China's most popular tourist destination was set by a massive 7.0 earthquake in 1966. The quake devastated the new town, killing 300 people and injuring 16,000. The old town, built by people who knew about earthquakes (50 major quakes over the past 130 years), mostly survived. Li'jiang went through a rebirth as the government poured money into rebuilding and expanding the infrastructure, while UNESCO contributed to the restoration of the old town. [4] A sanitation worker on his rounds in neighbouring Shu'he old town, a quieter and more authentic version of what Li'jiang once was.

THE TRIBAL MOUNTAINS

YANG'TZE RIVER'S U-TURN

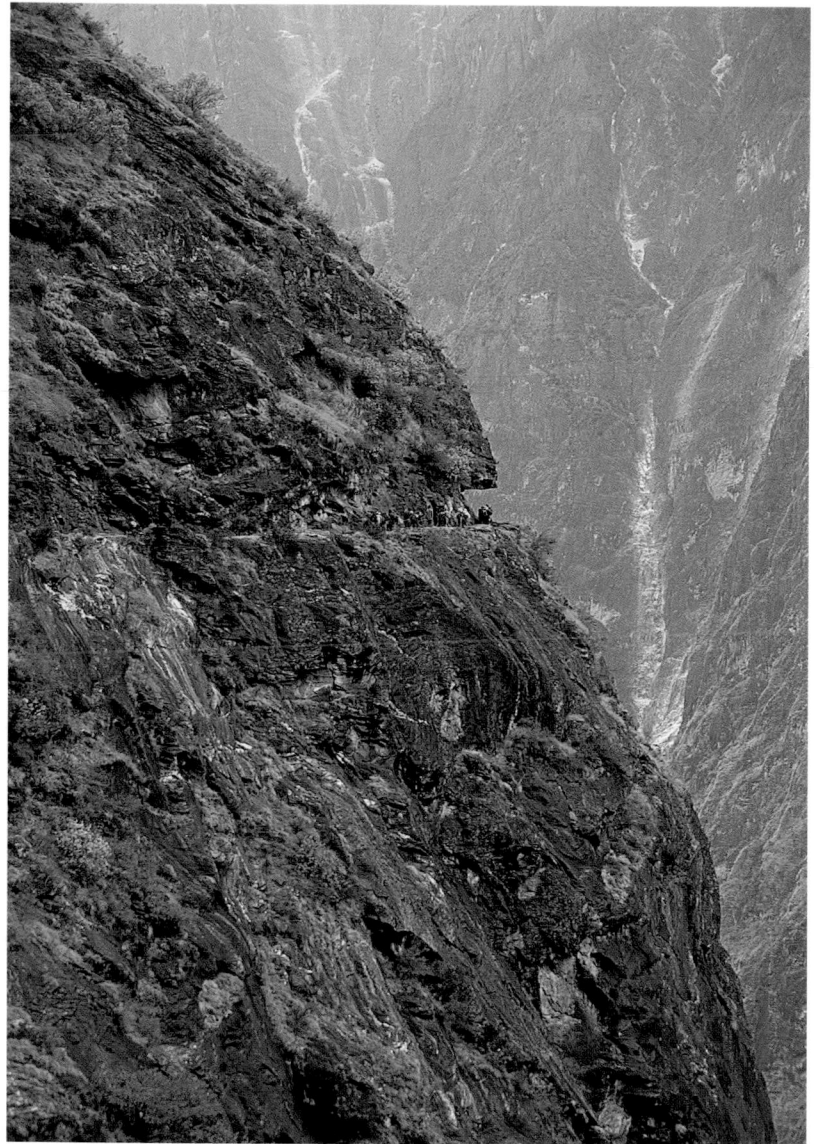

1

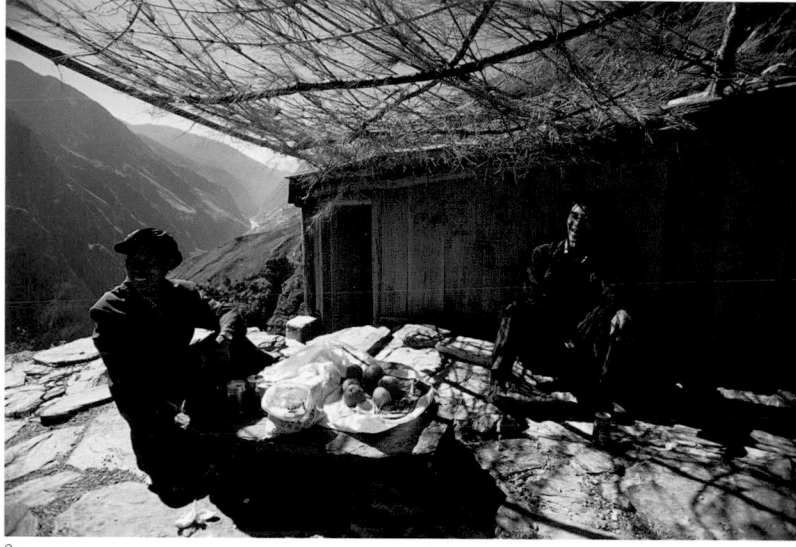

2

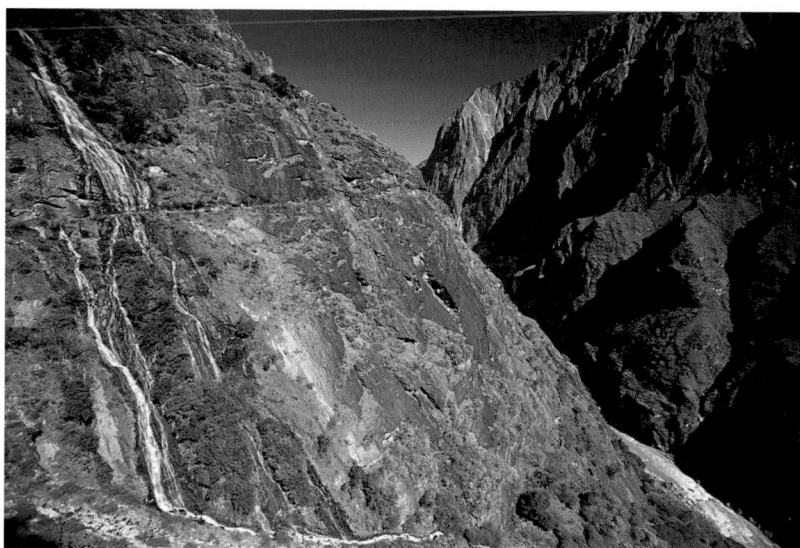

3

THE HU'TIAO XIA (Tiger Leaping Gorge) in the far northwestern corner of Yun'nan is only a tiny wrinkle on the eastern edge of the Himalayan range, but for the Chinese it is the wrinkle that spawned a civilization. For in Shi'gu (Stone Drum), at the start of the 3,960-metre (13,000-foot) deep ravine, the Yang'tze River parts ways with the other great rivers that rise in western Tibet to make a dramatic U-turn; pushing northeastwards through the thunderous rapids of the 16-kilometre (10-mile) long Hu'tiao Xia, while the other rivers flow south. The vast alluvial plain left behind on its long track towards the Yellow Sea became the cradle and rice bowl of the Middle Kingdom. [1] A team of horses treads carefully along the narrow slippery stone path carved into [3] the sheer mountain 1,220 metres (4,000 feet) above the river. The trail was part of the famous 'Tea and Horses Road', China's main southern trade route. [2] A rest stop on the mountaintop overlooking the northern end of the gorge. [4] A Yi minority woman with her grandson.

THE TRIBAL MOUNTAINS

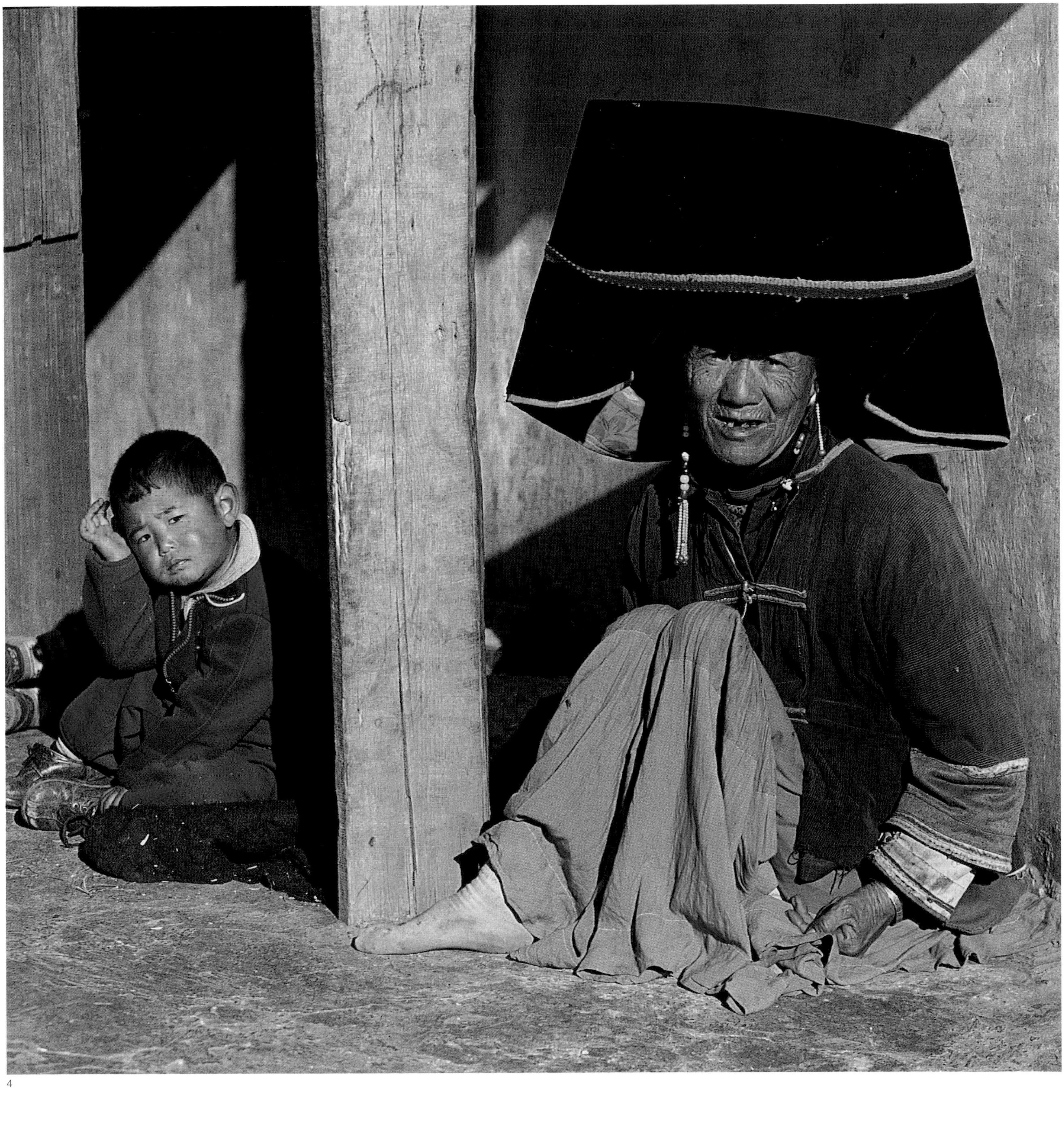

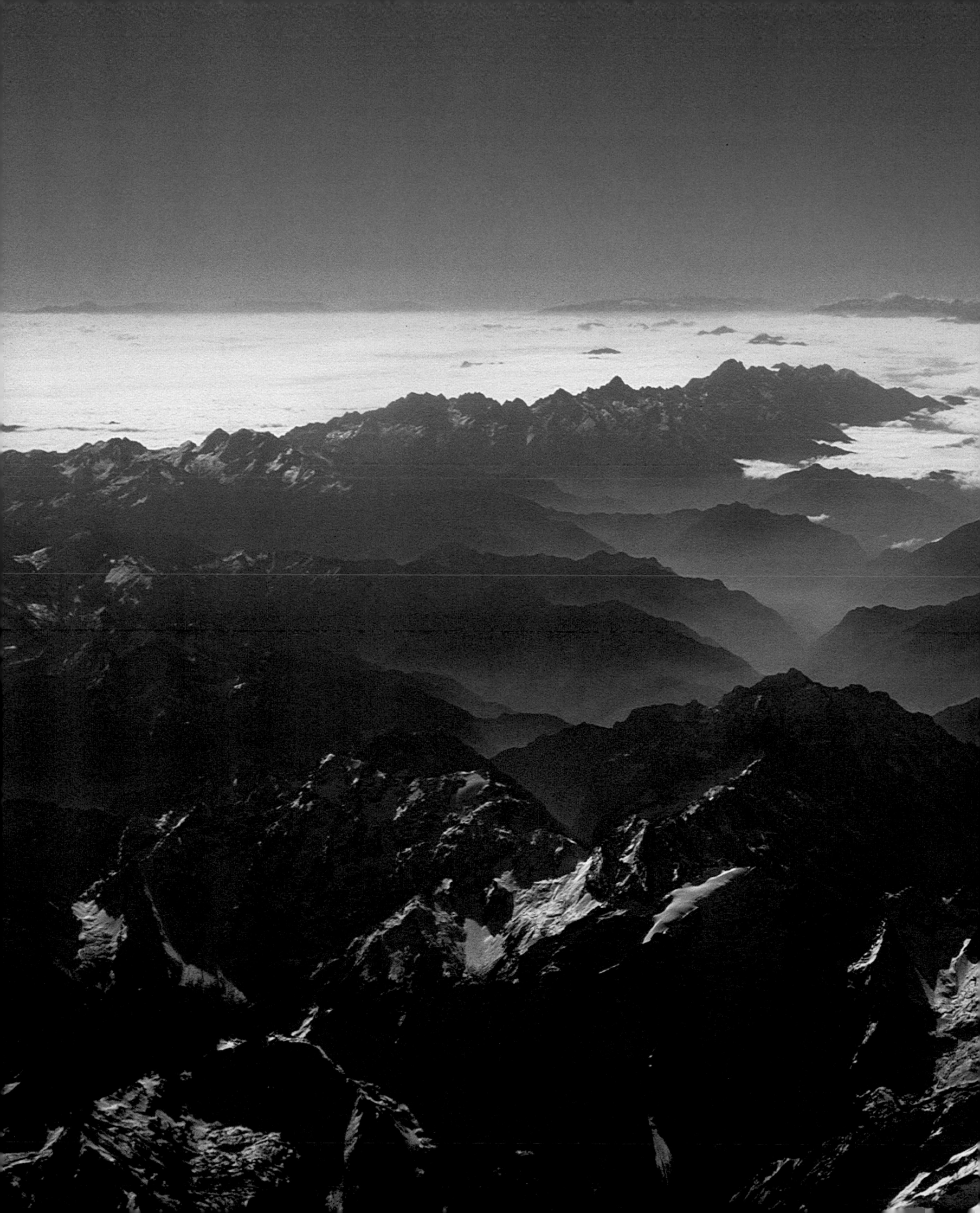

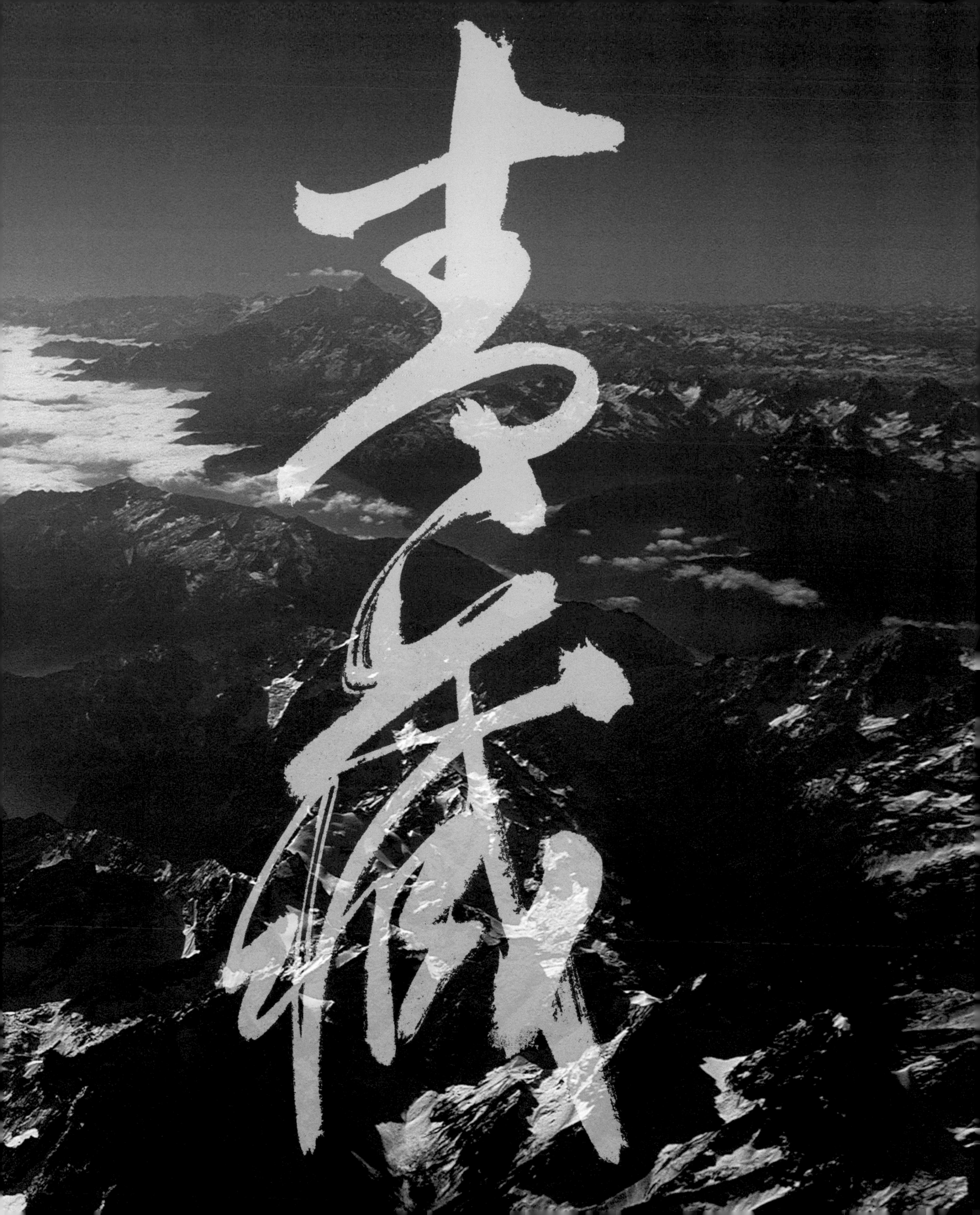

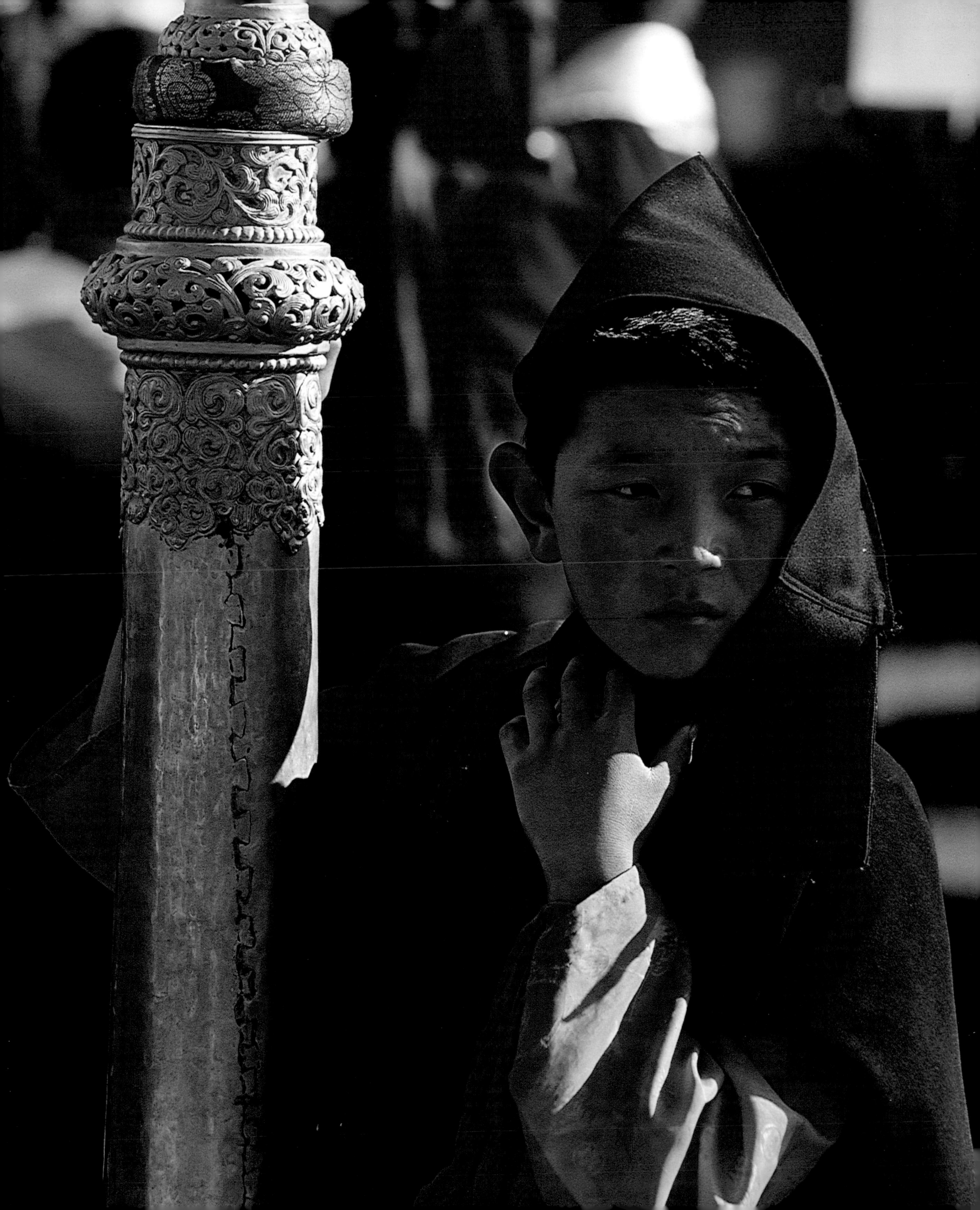

THE TIBETAN PLATEAU

A very nice girl at the China Air check-in desk in Cheng'du tells me that the flight I'm booked on, flight CA4447 to Lhasa, has been delayed indefinitely due to weather conditions en-route. But mysteriously she can put me onto another flight, an 'added flight', which is also delayed but will leave 35 minutes before the original scheduled departure time of flight CA4447. Will that be OK? I find the flight on the departures board and am surprised to see several other flights heading for Lhasa that afternoon, all within an hour of each other; all except for CA4447, of course, which seems destined for cancellation.

A large party in holiday mood boards our plane late, laughing and talking loudly and blissfully unaware that they have kept a plane full of people waiting for quite some time. They turn out to be government officials, a woman party-boss and her entourage from Shang'hai. So it appears that the 'weather conditions' our nice Air China lady spoke of had perhaps more to do with the political climate than the meteorological one. And all those extra flights to Lhasa have been put on to carry communist party officials from all over the country to the big celebration this week of the '50th Anniversary of the Founding of the Tibetan Autonomous Region', and in turn 'delayed' to wait for all the connecting flights coming in from different cities. It is also the reason why the annual Shoton festival, for which I had originally timed my visit – booking hotels and flights 6 months ahead of time, was pushed forward by a month to make room for this big shindig; a grim reminder that whatever the claims to the contrary, the people are here to serve the party. Well, at least they avoided using the word 'liberation' in the slogan for their jamboree; thank the Buddha for small mercies.

The last time I was on this flight I was coming the other way, en-route to Yun'nan after taking photographs for a book at Everest base camp. I spent almost the entire flight photographing the wondrous frozen landscape outside the window, trying to imagine the endless plateau as a wide-open ocean far below. I have read somewhere that 50 million years ago, the Indo-Australian and Eurasian plates collided and a new chunk of land, over 2.3 million square kilometres (1.4 million square miles) in size, was wrenched from the bowels of the ocean and thrown 5,000 metres (16,404 feet) up into the air. By the time the water had drained off its edges in a million waterfalls, what was left was the Tibetan Plateau, the highest plateau on the planet, with the peaks of vast mountain ranges breaking cloud cover at over 8,000 metres (26,240 feet) and gorges plunging deep into fertile river valleys. Within their shadows are wide-open stretches of bone-dry desert and rolling grassland dotted with brackish turquoise lakes, presumed to be the remnants of the Tethys Sea that once covered this land. The slab of fossilized clamshells, locked together in a chaotic embrace, which I had uncovered amongst the trinkets and faux-antiques in a souvenir shop by Qing'hai Lake and which now lean against a wall in my studio, may actually be a piece of evidence of that theory, or, perhaps more likely, somebody's dinner scraps glued together by cement and dirt, specially created for guileless tourists. The plateau is host to eight of the world's highest peaks, including the 8,848-metre (29,021-foot) Mount Everest (Qomolangma), the summit of the world. The water that flows down from their ranges is the source of all the major rivers of South and East Asia and affects the livelihood of over half of the world's population and the climate conditions of the regions in which they live. Two of the rivers that rise from the plateau, the Yang'tze (6,380 kilometres/3,964 miles; the longest river in Asia, from the north side of the Tanghla range) and the Yellow River (5,464 kilometres/3,395 miles; from the Qing'hai Plateau), constitute the lifeblood of Chinese civilization.

[LEFT] A young novice at the Yu'shu Horse Festival. [PRECEDING PAGES] The eastern edge of the Tibetan Plateau.

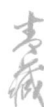

Over the years, I have seen the plateau from many angles, felt the intensity of the ultra-violet in different lights and breathed the rarified air in diverse locations. I have travelled around its edges, from the deep gorges of Yun'nan to the emerald mountains of Si'chuan and the loess terraces in Shaan'xi in the east, to the He'xi corridor along the Silk Road to the north, through the Pamirs and the Karakoram highway in the west, and across the 24,500-kilometre (15,225-mile) wide Himalaya in the south, where I trekked and drove through some of the most stunning and varied landscapes in India, Nepal, Bhutan and Assam. I have traversed the fertile plains of Qing'hai where massive herds graze and crossed the empty quarters of Tibet where not a soul can be seen. Wherever I have travelled I have met and befriended people who are strong and generous in spirit, and have come to admire the courage, humour and dignity with which they deal with the challenges presented by their harsh environment and difficult twists of fate. This present journey takes me into the spiritual heart of the plateau, to Kailash, the most sacred mountain in Asia. This, according to the cosmologies and creation myths shared by the Hindu, Jain, Bon and Buddhist religions, is Mount Meru, the birthplace and the centre of the world.

My driver and Tibetan guide are apologetic about having to go the long way from the airport into Lhasa, explaining that the new bridge into town has been closed to all traffic apart from authorized vehicles carrying official guests. But I have no complaints. The old scenic road looks wonderful with a very high Lhasa River lapping at its edge and I am just overjoyed to be back in Tibet. Entering the city, we drive past a convoy of buses full of performers in a variety of national costumes heading for Potala Square, apparently for a dress rehearsal that evening. The event seems to have complicated life for the guide and he apologizes again for not being able to get me into the Lhasa Hotel, the former Holiday Inn which is still the best hotel in town, because all the rooms have been reserved for the VIPs attending the celebrations. And, apparently, the local authorities have also cancelled all entry permits for foreign tourists for the duration, so the travel agency he belongs to is inundated with complaints and is having to reschedule all its clients.

For the next few days, as I slowly acclimatize to the altitude, and with Potala Square out of bounds to those without permits or tickets for the shows, I stay mostly in the old city, around the Barkhor (Eight Corners) of the Jokhang, the first Buddhist temple in Tibet. King Songsten originally built it for his new bride Princess Wen'cheng to house a sacred image of Buddha that was part of her dowry when they married in 641, to seal a peace treaty between the Kingdom of To'fan (Tibet) and the court of the Tang Emperor; this also became the official date for the introduction of Buddhism into Tibet. The temple, destroyed and rebuilt many times over the centuries, remains the spiritual heart of the Tibetan people to this day. And today they are dressing it up for the visiting bigwigs,hanging bright banners all over the façade, giving the old shrine the air of a painted courtesan. Small red Chinese-five-star flags stick out of every window all around the old city, reminding me of the time right after September 11th when all the minorities in the U.S., to show their patriotism (some out of fear), rushed to put up the Stars and Stripes outside their homes.

And as dignitaries continue to pour in in convoys that wreak havoc on local traffic, rumours of sharpshooters being placed in the Potala Palace for the leaders' safety during the ceremonies float freely in the air;

and it becomes impossible not to remember the invasion, the exile and the violent purges and wanton destructions in the intervening years – but those are well known tales that need not be rehashed here. So, early the next morning, armed with a large box of instant noodles and some tins, we abandon the capital to the occupation and set off west along the Yar'lung Tsangpo (Brahmaputra River) Valley in two fully loaded Landcruisers, to search for the heart and soul of Tibet.

The journey that follows, across the width of Tibet, is some of the toughest and most magical travelling of my life. From the top of a steep hill over the lush Yar'lung Valley where I marvel at the design of the 3-dimensional *mandala* that is Samye, the first Buddhist Monastery in Tibet, to Yamdrok-tso Lake, where my surprise on seeing the luminescent turquoise colour of its water is matched only by that of seeing the violet-blue colour of the beef our cook has brought along from Shigatse, boiling in a pot of water at a guesthouse in Zhong'ba. From the terrifying night spent in Pa'yang, where gangs of fearsome wild dogs rule the darkness, to the first sighting of the snow-capped Mount Kailash in the distance from a hilltop above Lake Manasarovar, the 'Lake of Consciousness and Enlightenment'. From the unexpected snowstorm that sweeps across the plain from the holy lake to Ta'erqin, enveloping us there the night before we set off on our trek to Kailash – a phenomenon that our Tibetan team blame squarely on the party of Hindu pilgrims who have just arrived – to the lingering doubts that gnaw at my already hard-pressed innards when Kailash remains stubbornly out of sight behind thick clouds pregnant with snow; and the elation towards the end when the sky suddenly opens up and reveals the mythical Mount Meru as we make our final approach. We camp by a stream in its shadow and photograph it at dawn, and in the blissful silence, I feel, for the first time in my life, the sensation of a physical connection with a mountain. By the time we have packed up and loaded the yaks, storm clouds are once again sweeping in to cover up the massive black rock. On our way out of the valley, after a long, strenuous trek that has brought me to the brink of collapse, a full circular rainbow appears around the sun directly overhead.

One night in Shigatse on our way back to Lhasa, we have dinner in an excellent Si'chuanese restaurant owned by friends of our Tibetan cook, a nice Chinese couple from Cheng'du. The husband comes by our table to say hello. "Om Mani Padme Hum," he says with a big smile, and I think, "How nice, he's using the *Jewel in the Lotus* mantra as a greeting." Not until our cook responds with, "All Money Go My Home…" and they laugh uproariously and shake hands do I realize that it is a running joke between them. The joke is perhaps apposite for the Tibetan Plateau itself. It covers over twenty per cent of China's land mass while supporting less than one per cent of its population, and the Bei'jing government is trying to change that ratio by encouraging mass migration into the region, often with cash and tax incentives. Already, out of the eight million people on the plateau, around 3.4 million are Chinese and Muslim immigrants, mostly residing in Qing'hai. Major new highways and the controversial 'Lhasa Express' – a 1,118-kilometre (695-mile) high-speed railway line between Golmad in Qing'hai and Lhasa are under construction, all scheduled to be completed by the spring of 2008, in time for the Bei'jing Olympics. It seems almost inevitable that the Tibetans will soon become a minority in their own land.

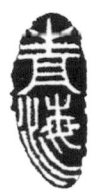

QING'HAI PROVINCE

LOCATION
Latitude 31º39'–39º19'N
Longtitude 89º35'–103º04'E

AREA 722,797 km² (279,073 sq miles)

GEOGRAPHY Qing'hai is set in high mountains on the edge of the Tibetan Plateau. More than 50 per cent of the province is between 4,000–5,000 m. Qing'hai divides into three regions: the Qi'lian Mountains to the northeast, the Qaidam Basin to the northwest and the Tibetan Plateau to the southwest. The Huang'he (Yellow) River rises in the centre of the province, while the Yang'tze and Me'kong rivers have their sources in the south. Qing'hai Lake in the northeast is the largest in China.

CLIMATE The province's location and altitude mean long, cold winters and short, cool summers. January temperatures range from -18.2ºC to -7ºC, rising to between 5ºC and 21ºC in July. The lowest recorded temperature is -46ºC and the highest, 35.9ºC. Qing'hai is also prone to strong winds and sandstorms. Average annual precipitation varies from 17.6 mm to 764.4 mm.

POPULATION 5.39 million (end 2004)

MAJOR CITIES Xi'ning (capital), Yu'shu, Gonghe, Delingha

AGRICULTURE Rearing livestock, including yak, camels, sheep and goats, on the province's grasslands is the principal farming activity. Wheat, potatoes and other vegetables are also grown.

MAIN INDUSTRIES Heavy and extractive industries include the oil and gas fields of the Qaidam Basin, mining and hydropower. Iron and steel plants have also been developed to take advantage of the abundant energy.

ANNUAL PER CAPITA INCOME (2005)
Disposable income of urban residents:
RMB 8,058 (US$1,006)
Net income of rural residents:
RMB 2,165 (US$270)

HISTORICAL AND SCENIC SITES
Great Mosque of Xi'ning, North Mountain Temple, Kumbum Monastery, Qing'hai Lake

FOOD Qing'hai cuisine is strongly influenced by the tastes and strictures of the Muslim Hui minority. Meat, flour and dairy produce feature prominently in local cooking. Typical dishes include roast lamb and mutton in numerous variations, fried carp, dry-stirred noodles, pastries and steamed buns.

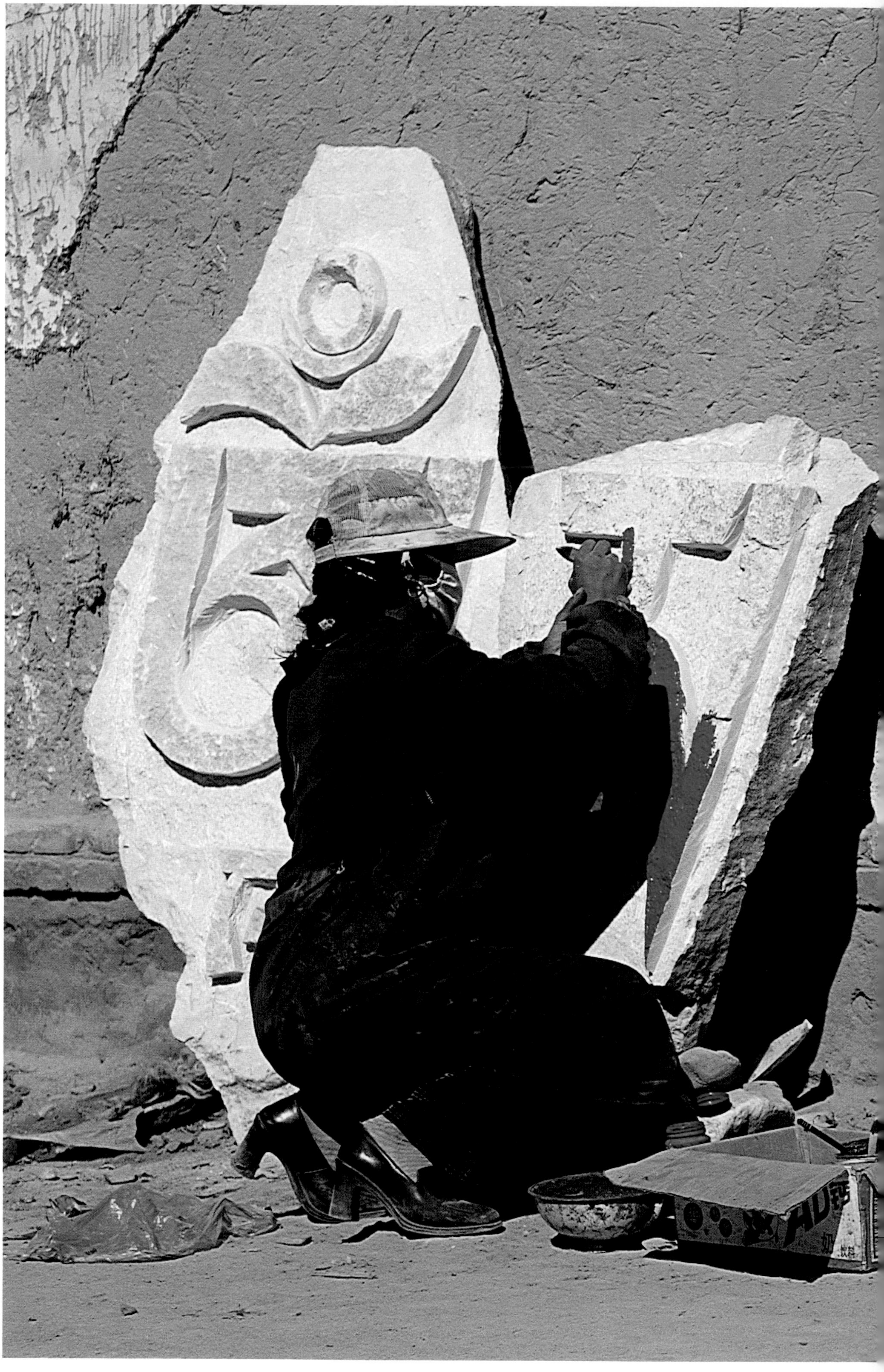

[RIGHT] 'Om Mani Padme Hum' – the *Jewel in the Lotus* mantra – carved in stone and being painted at the Gyanak Mani temple.

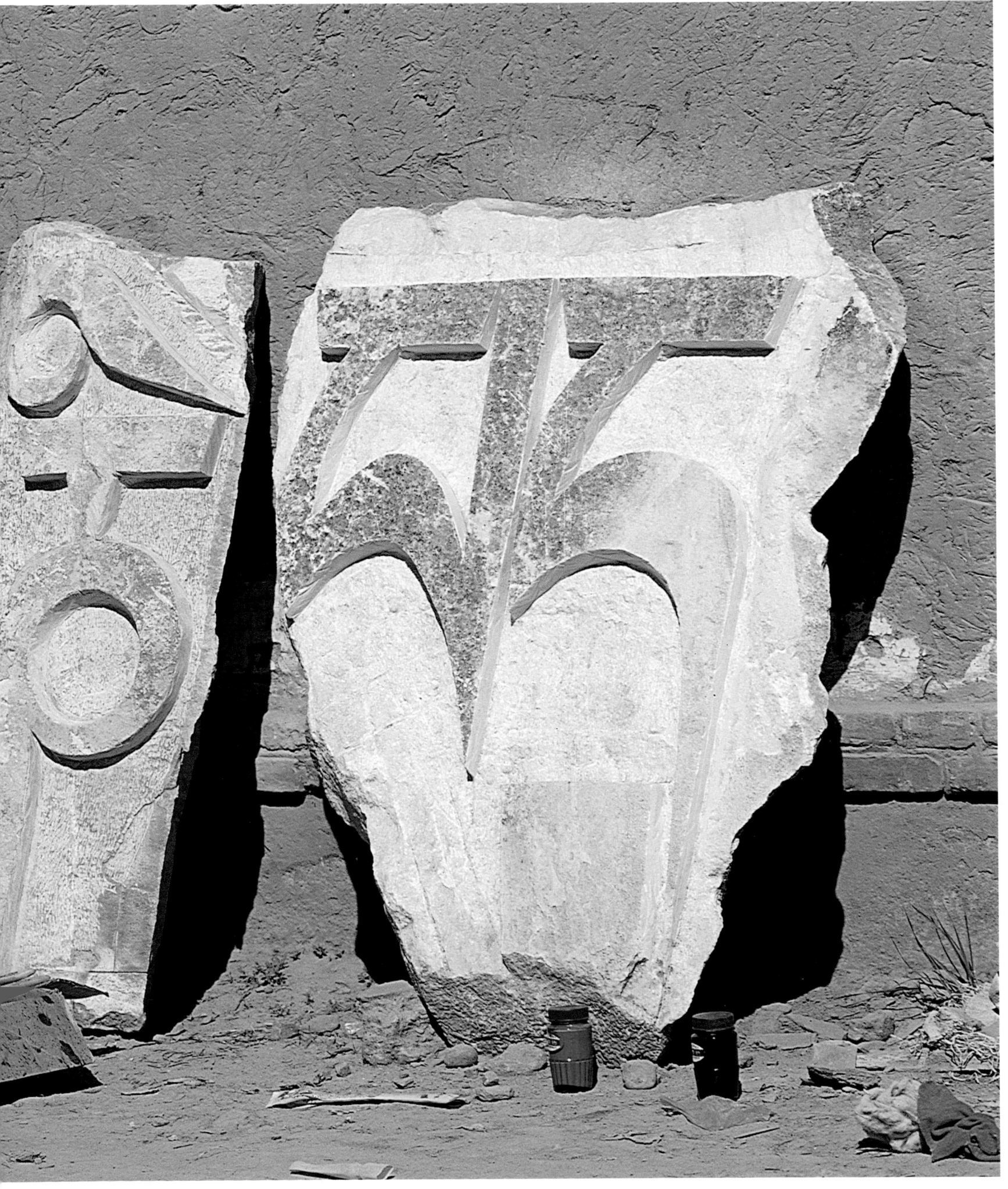

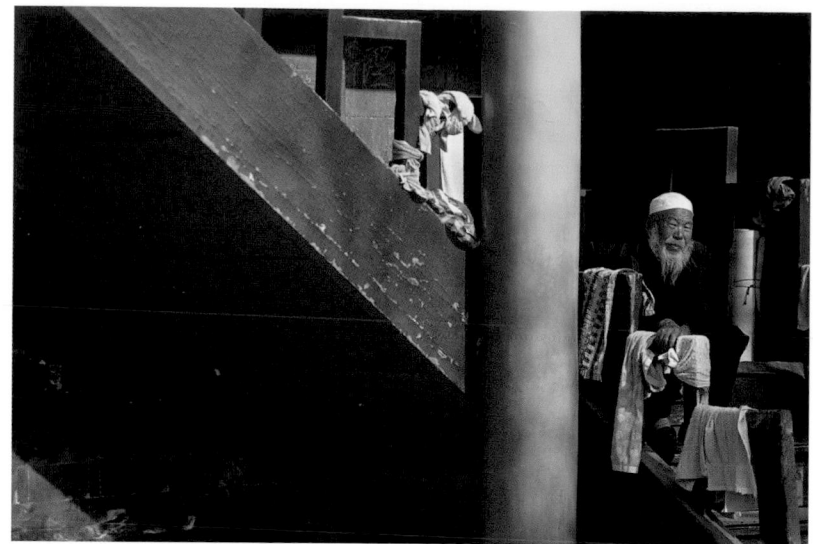

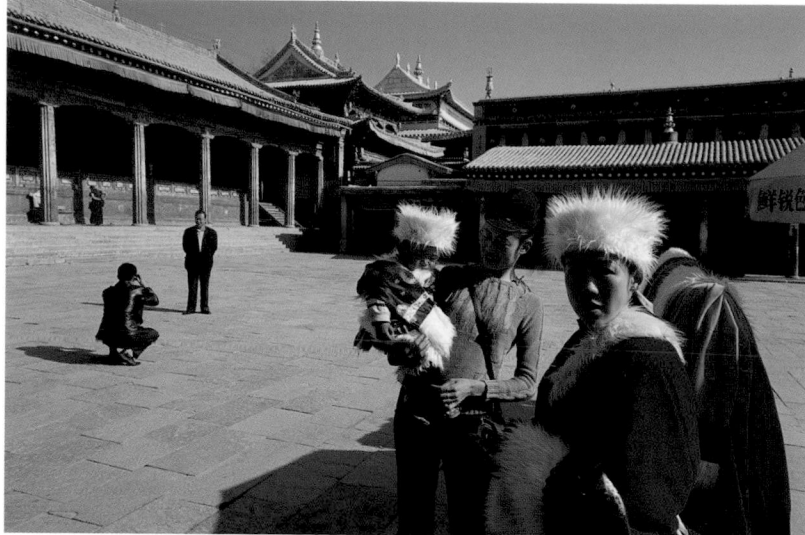

1

2

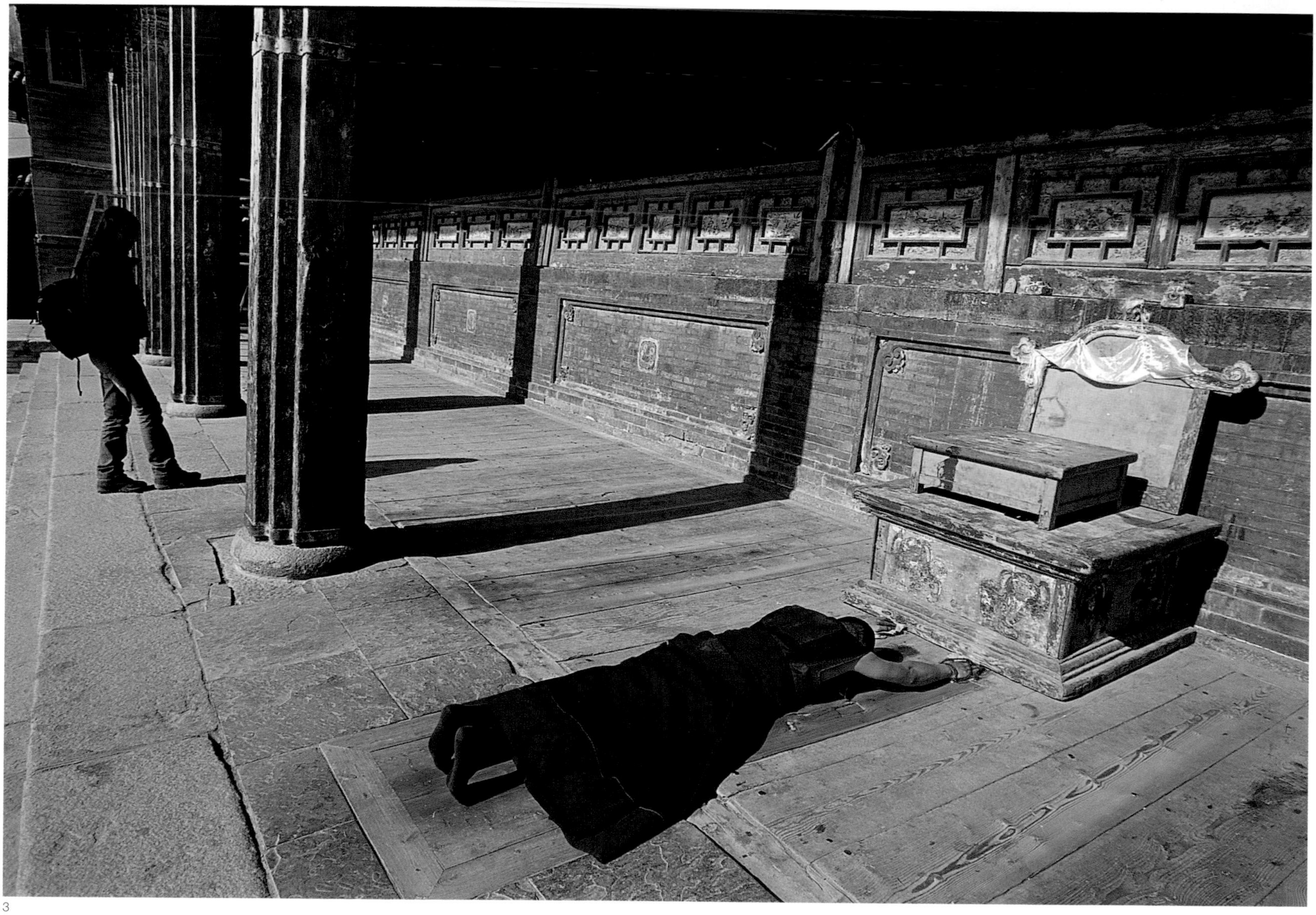

3

GATEWAY TO TIBET

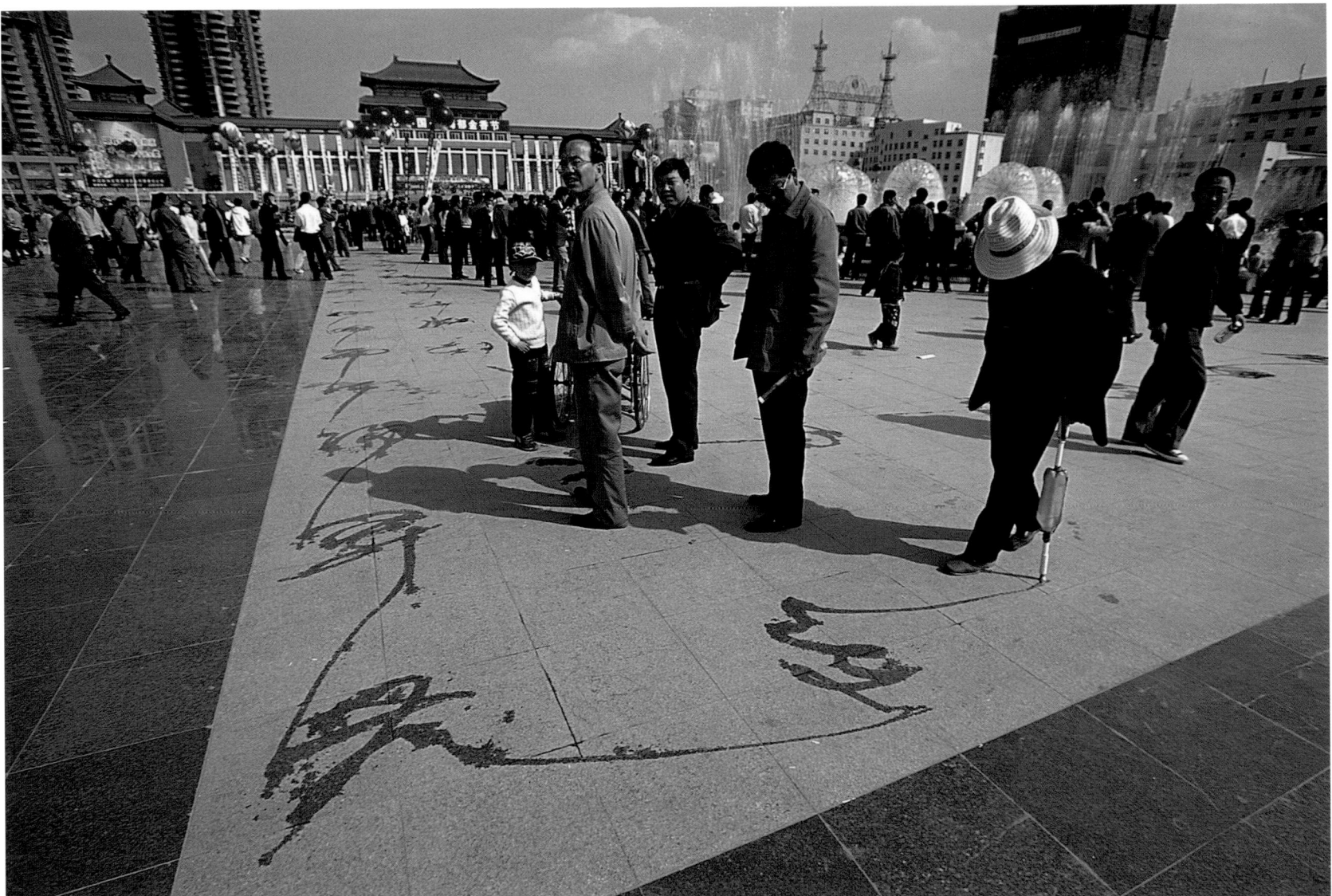

4

THE KUMBUM MONASTERY (Ta'er Si) was one of the great learning centres of the Gelugpa (Yellow Hat) school, playing a pivotal role in introducing Tibetan Buddhism to Mongolia and the Court of Genghis Khan. According to legend, when its founder Tsong'khapa was born in 1357, drops of blood from his umbilical cord fell on the ground. A sandalwood tree with Sanskrit symbols on its leaves and Buddha images on its bark grew on the sacred site. A temple was built around the tree, whose blossoms were said to fill the air with an ethereal scent. The temple grew over the centuries into a leading Buddhist university, contributing to the education of many Dalai Lamas and other revered teachers. Today [2] [3] Kumbum remains an important pilgrimage site and tourist attraction. [1] Muslim elder at the Grand Mosque of Xi'ning, one of the largest in Northern China. [4] A retiree practices 'water-calligraphy' at the Xi'ning People's Square. Many have used the art as a form of silent and 'invisible' protest against the authorities, where incriminating evidence simply evaporates into thin air.

THE TIBETAN PLATEAU

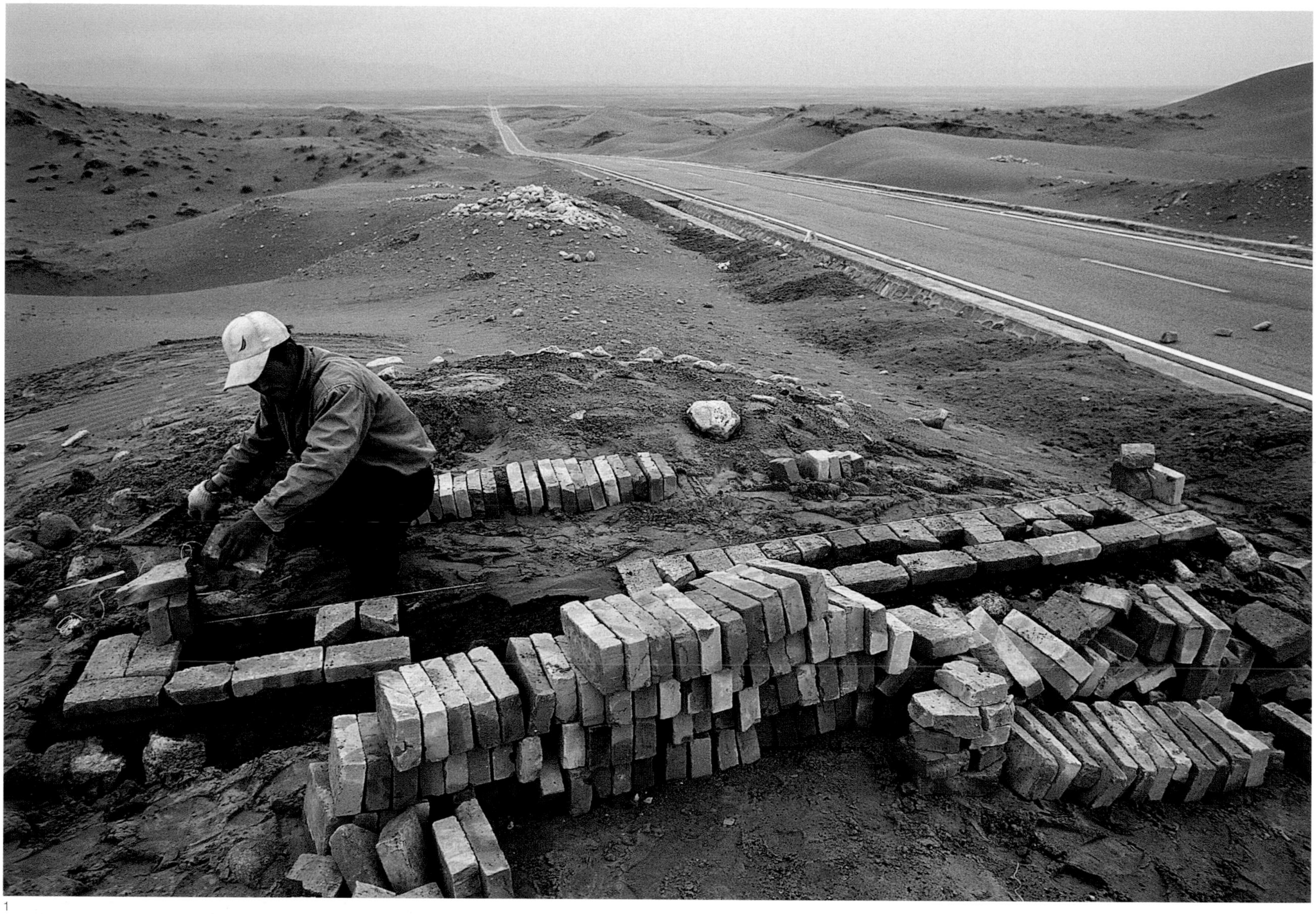

A POSTER IN THE HOTEL LOBBY in Xi'ning advertised luxury cruises around the 4,635-square-kilometre (1,790-square-mile) Kokonor Lake aboard a luxury liner. This turned out to be wildly optimistic. The road to the *Emerald Sea* was largely empty of traffic and people, apart from [1] a bricklayer building the base of an advertising billboard and [5] twin sisters waiting for a bus in the middle of nowhere. On this exceptionally bleak and grey day I found [2] the half-finished and abandoned seven-storey 'floating palace' quietly rusting on the shores of China's largest saltwater lake. The project had apparently been abandoned after high-powered environmentalists and scientists in Bei'jing expressed concerns over the impact of mass tourism on the lake's fragile ecosystems. There were few tourists on main street and [4] the 'photo-opportunity' yak had no customers. Even the restaurant that employed [3] [6] a bevy of hostesses to perform traditional Tibetan dances on the sidewalk to entice diners remained empty. I later learned that while I was lamenting the 'filthy' light along the shore, birds were dying from avian flu on Bird Island. The island is the lake's main tourist attraction and a breeding ground for hundreds of thousands of migratory birds.

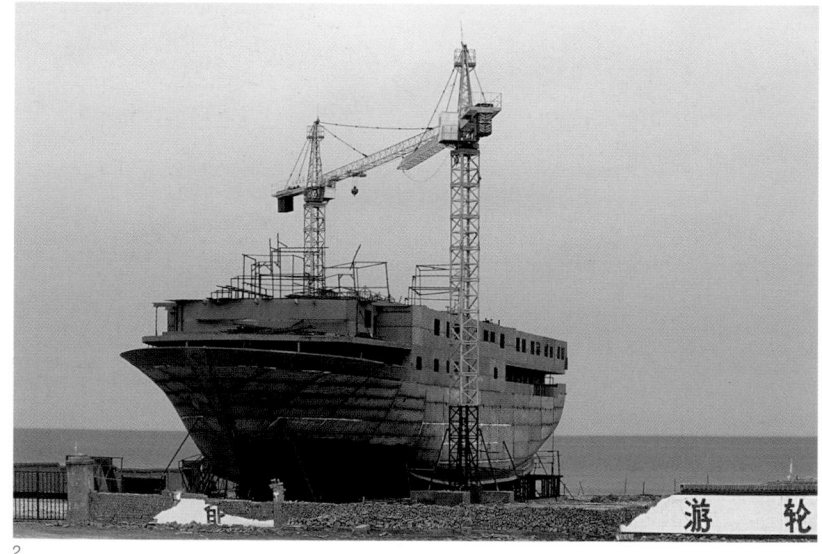

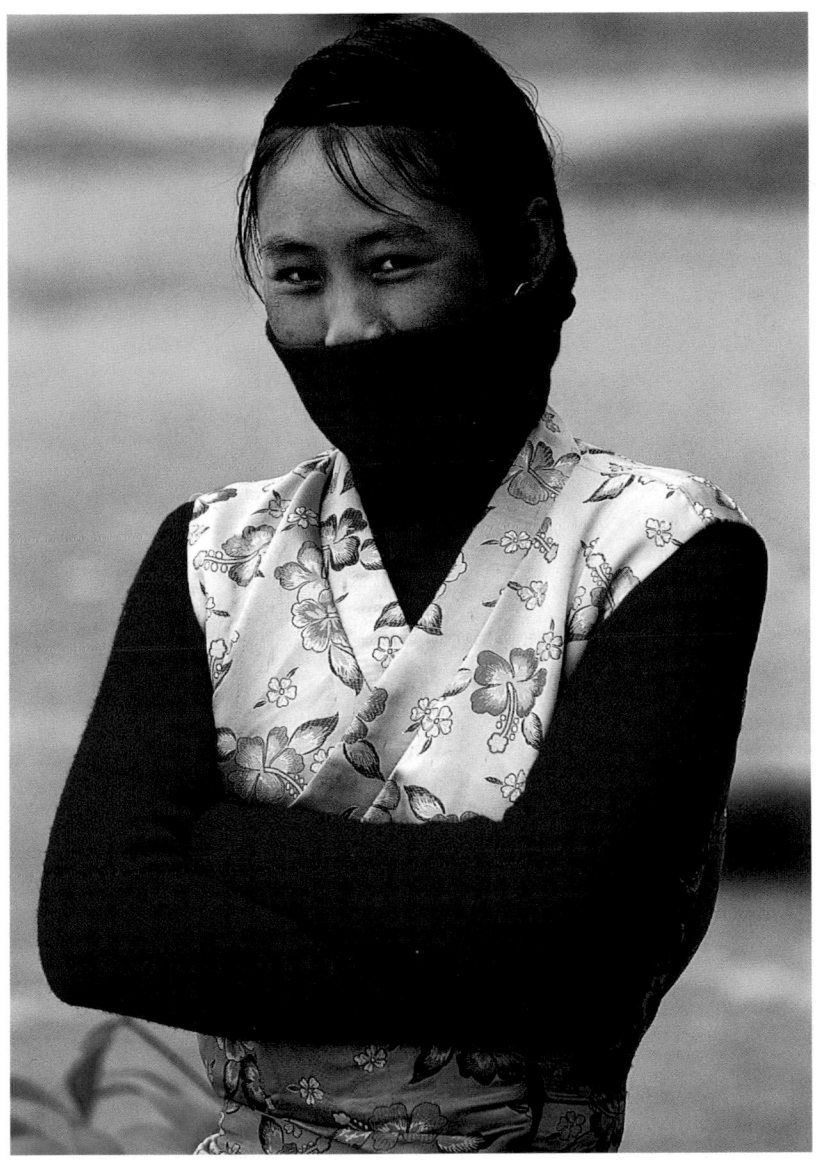

3

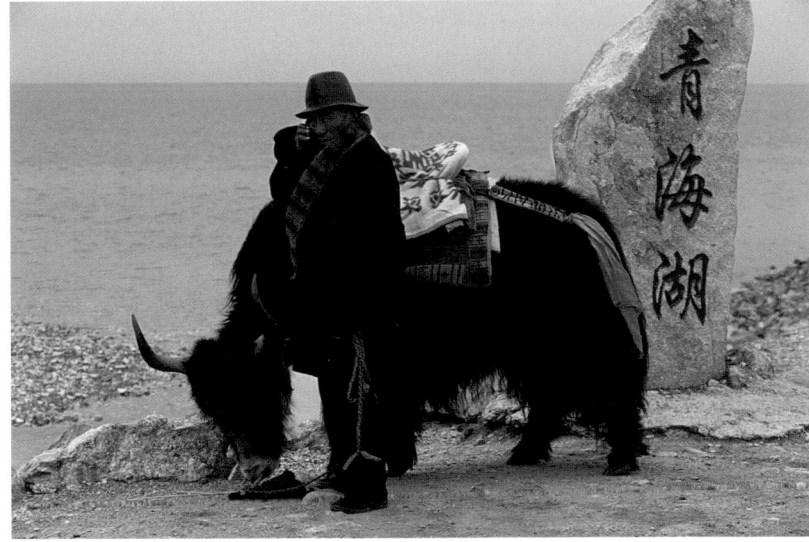

4

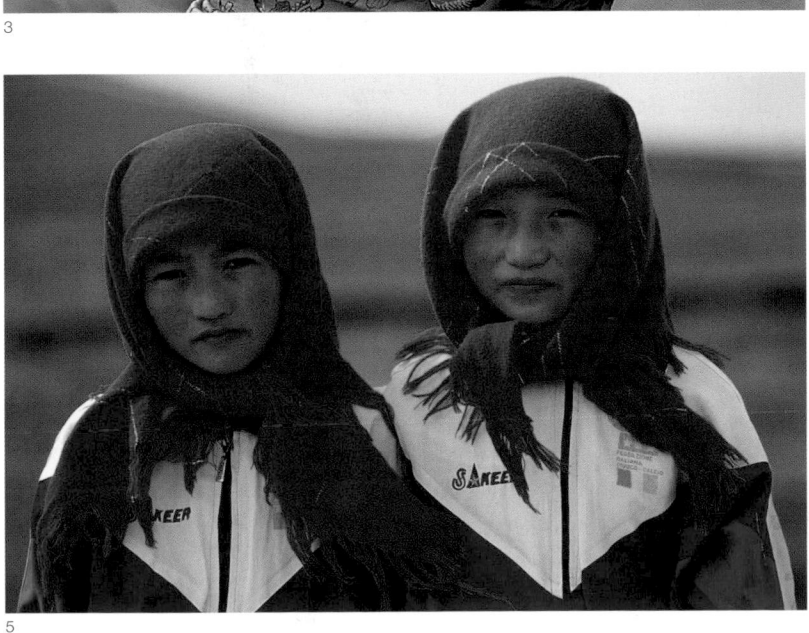

5

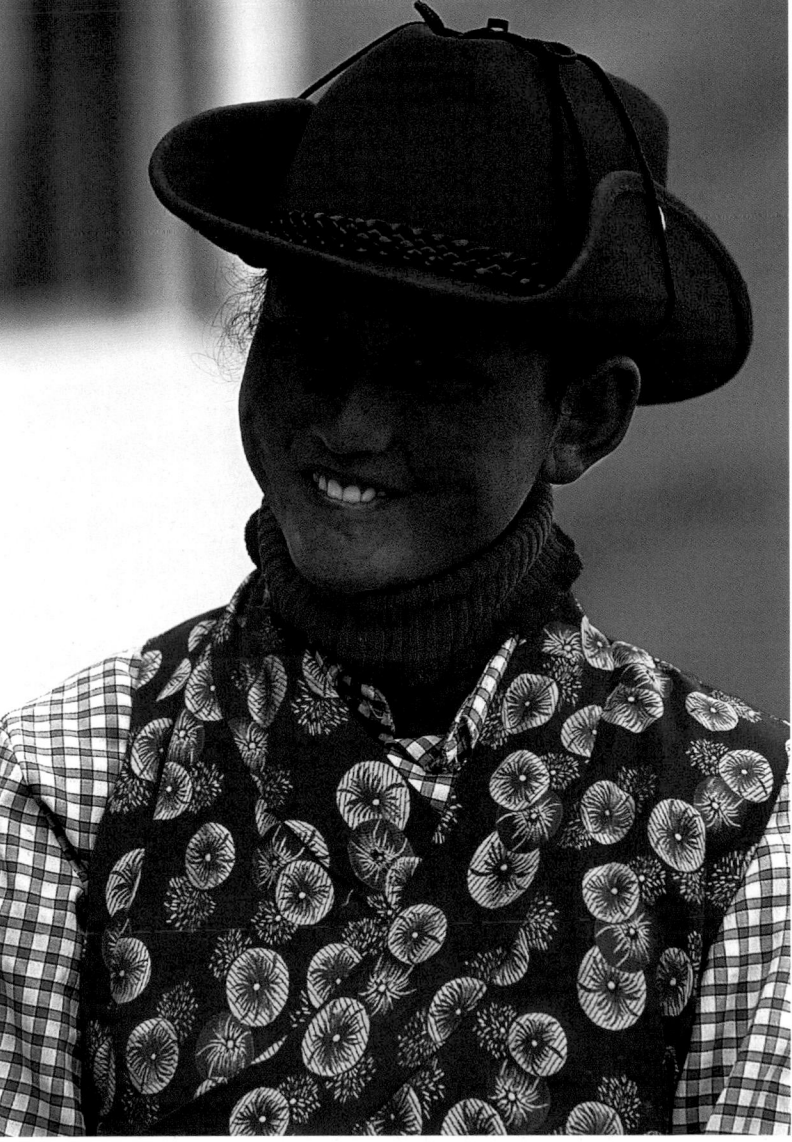

6

THE GYANAK MANI TEMPLE

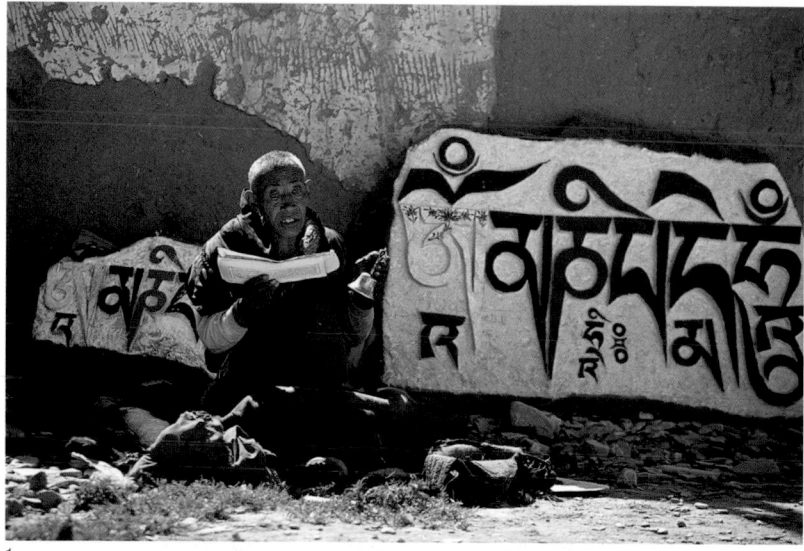

1

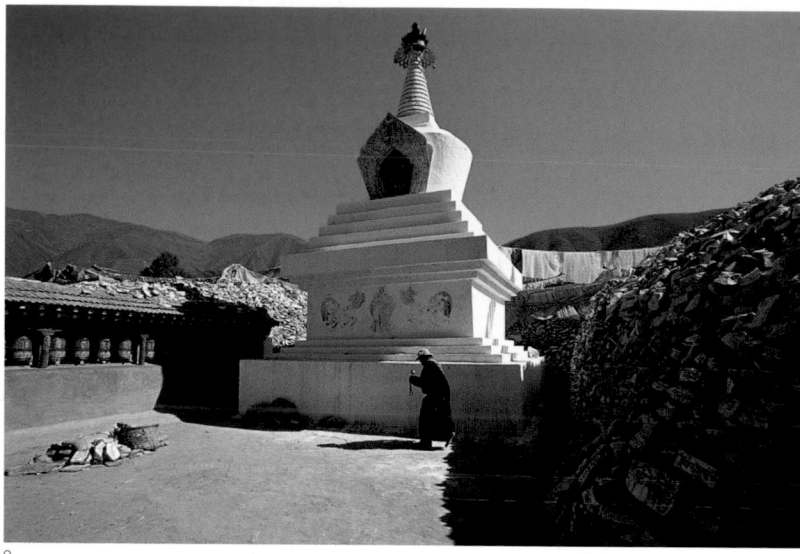

2

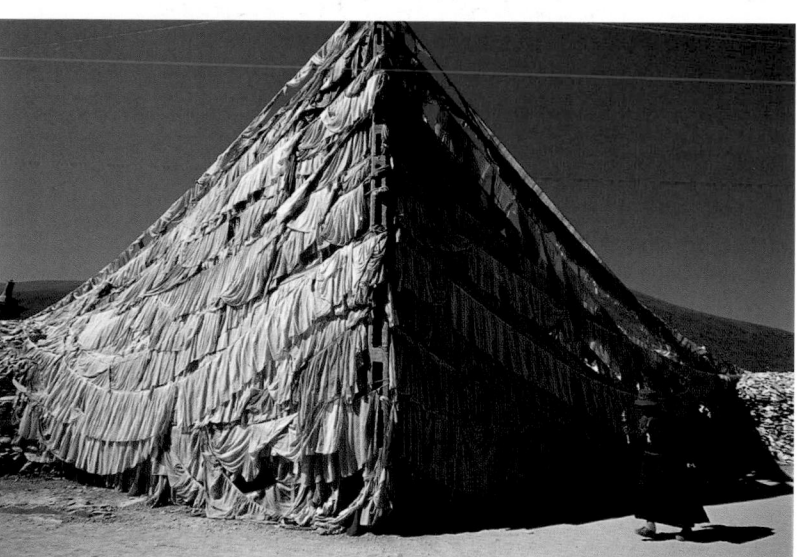

3

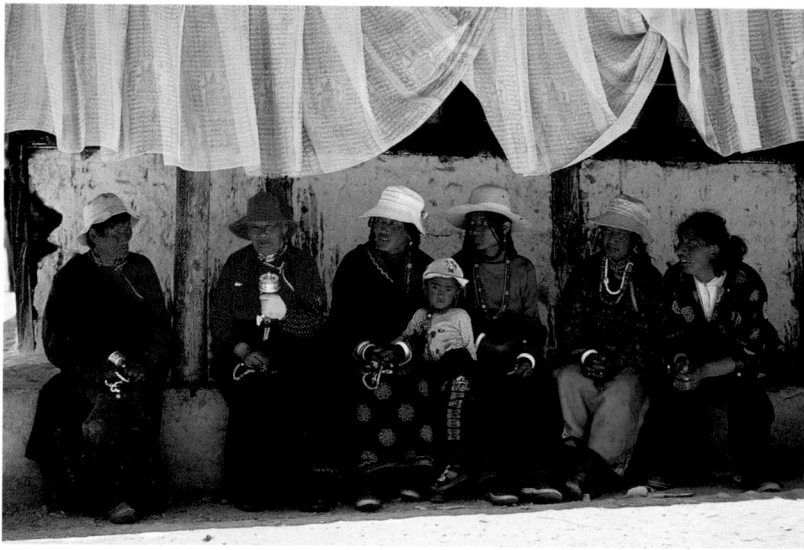

4

FROM A DISTANCE THE VAST TEMPLE GROUNDS OF THE GYANAK MANI at the head of the Jyekundo Valley look like the remains of a village after an air-strike. However, the rubble-strewn fields around the temple contain the largest collection of *mani* stones on the Tibetan plateau. Princess Wen'cheng, credited with converting the Tibetan royal court to Buddhism, passed this way 1,400 years ago on her way from Xi'an to Lhasa to marry King Songsten Gampo. Their union ensured peace between the Tang Empire and the powerful Tibetan Kingdom rising out of the Yar'lung Valley. For centuries pilgrims from across the plateau have left carved or painted stones here. Ranging from the monumental to the minute, all are covered with mantras and some are even inscribed with entire passages of scriptures and the likenesses of saints. [1] A wandering monk reciting the scriptures. Pilgrims walk through [2] the alleys between the mountains of *mani* stones and [3] the prayer-flag towers. [4] A nomad family takes a rest from their *kora* outside the main temple. [5] A lady pilgrim from Amdo.

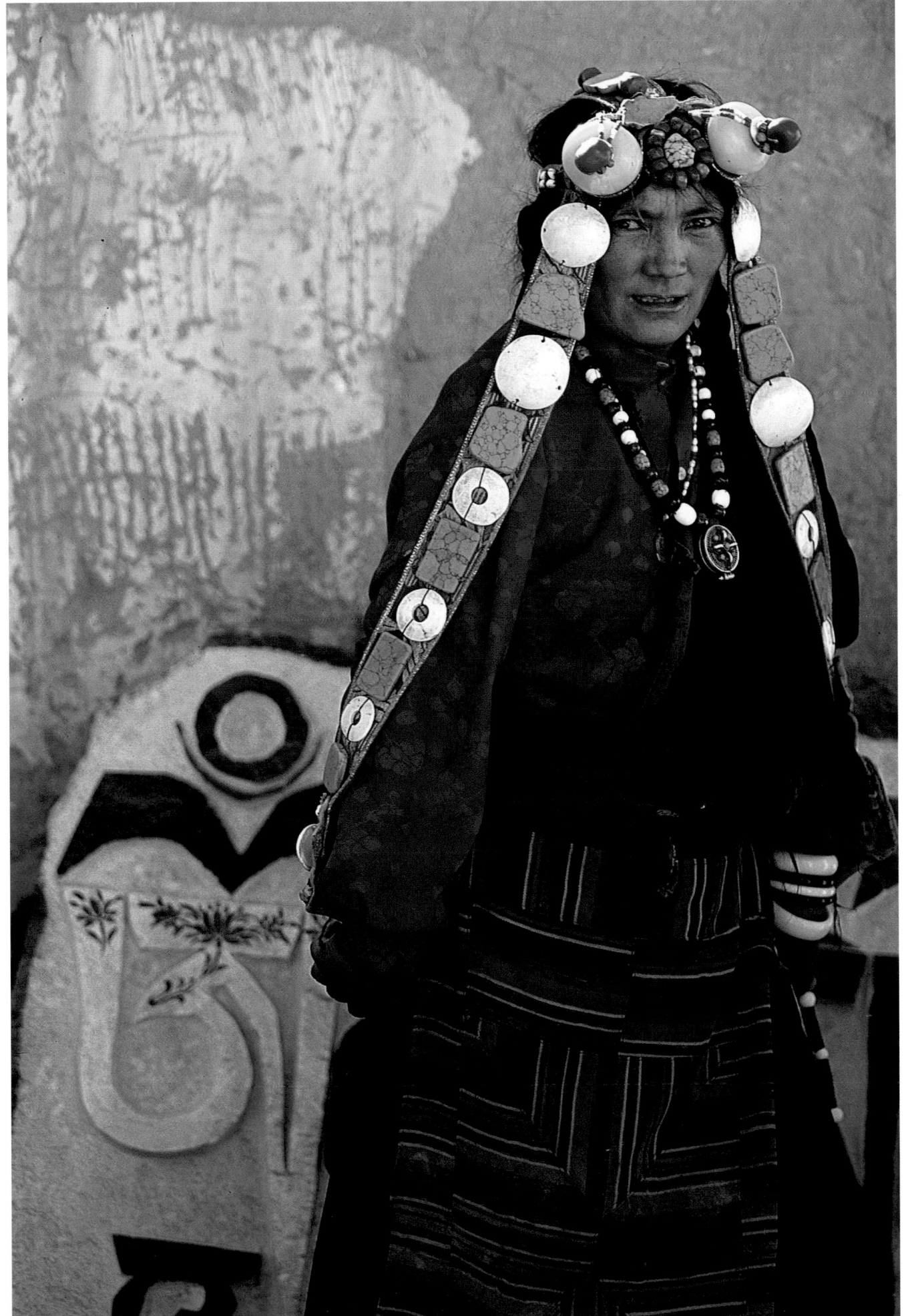

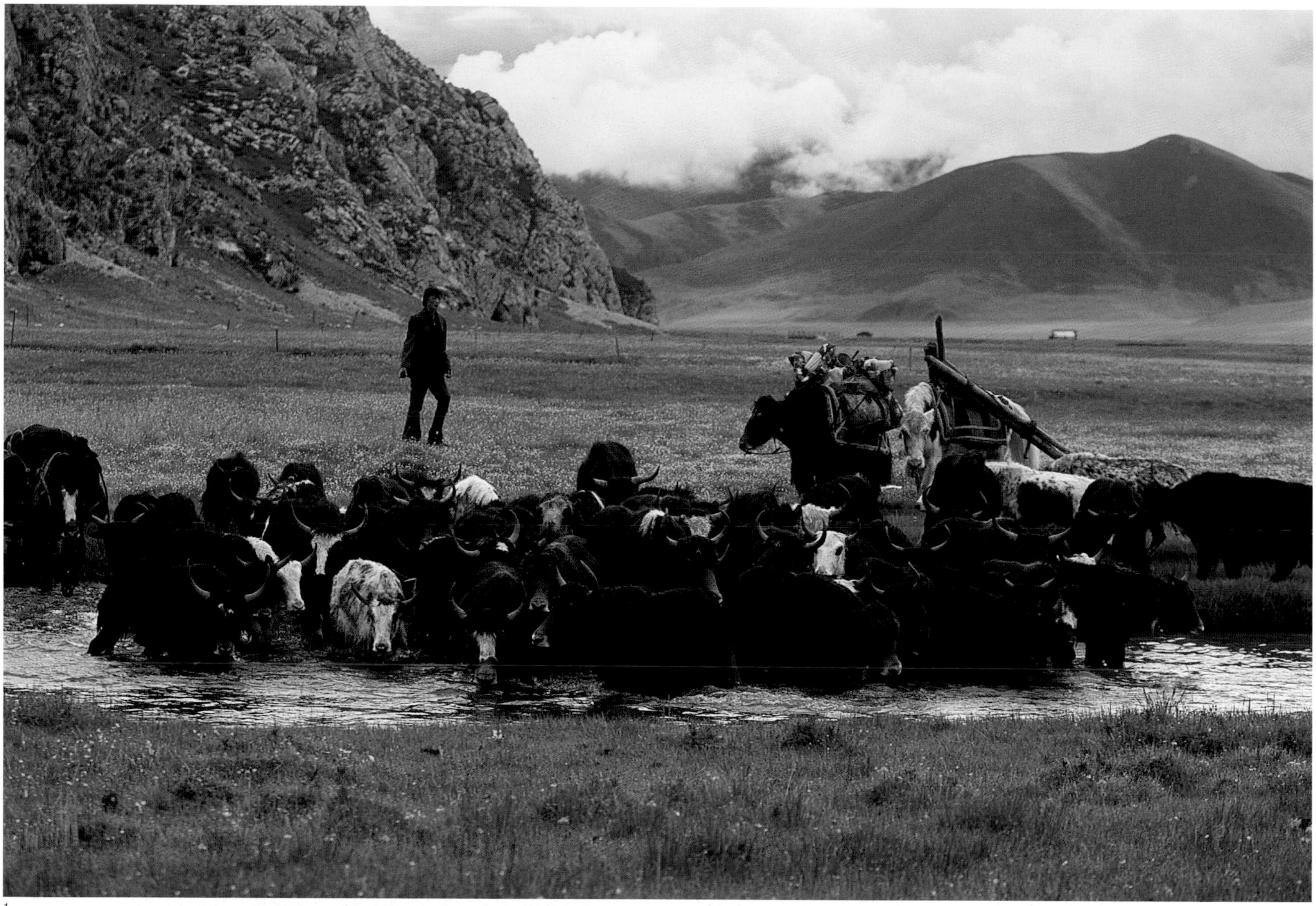

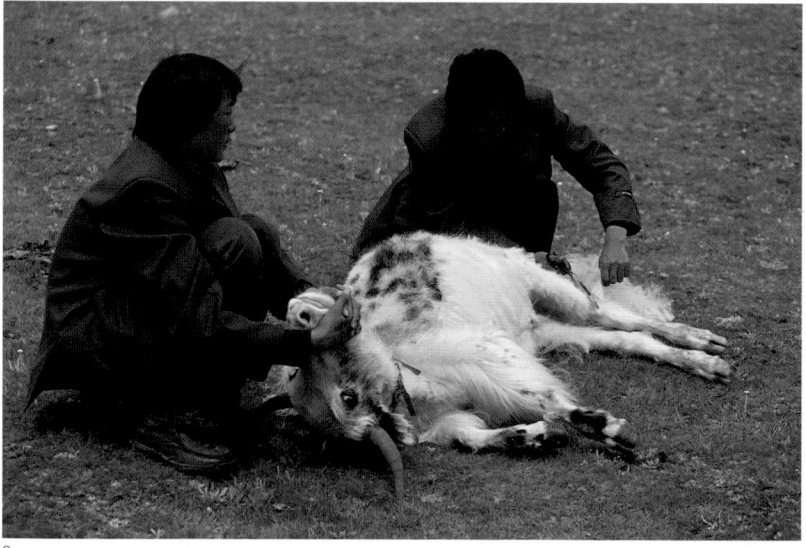

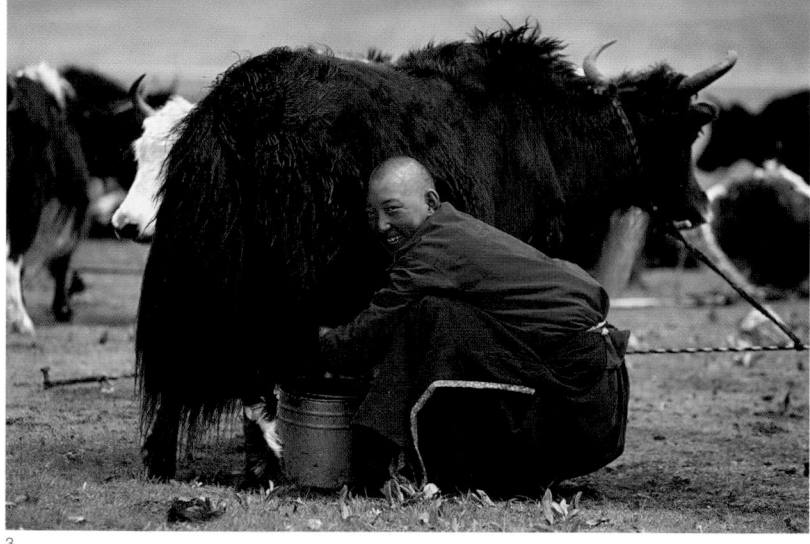

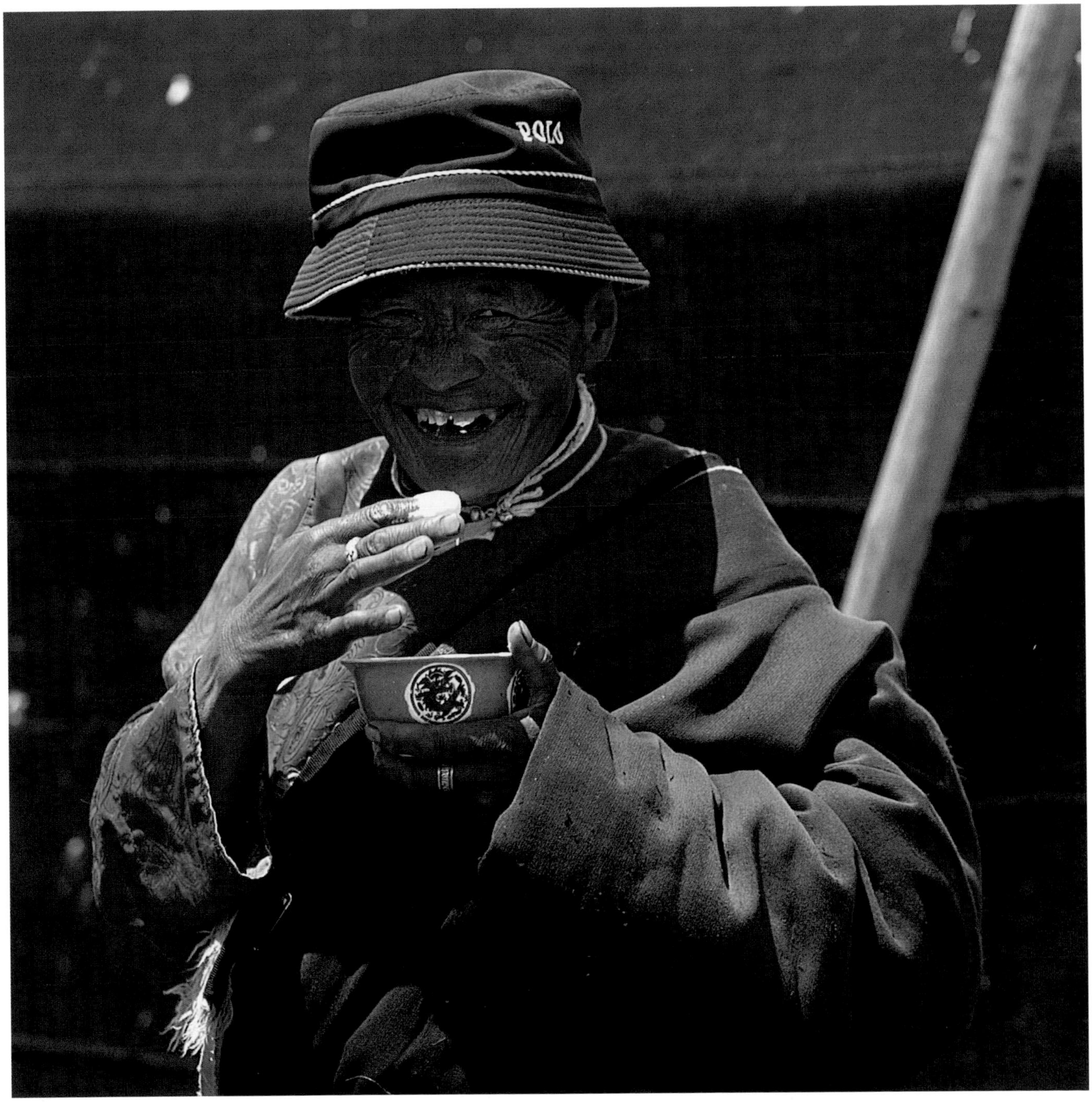

4

THE VAST AND SPARSELY POPULATED QING'HAI PROVINCE has historically been the often final destination for enemies of the Emperor. During the Cold War the name conjured images of desolate gulags where 'enemies of the people' mined uranium in the frozen windswept hills, many of them never to be heard from again. It is easy to forget today, amid the rise of 'capitalism with Chinese characteristics', that the province is still known as the 'prison state', and also serves as the centre of the country's nuclear weapons industry. More romantically, Qing'hai is also the source of three of Asia's great rivers – the Yang'tze, the Me'kong and the Yellow River – and the natural wonders and cultural heritage that trace their banks. The semi-nomadic family we came upon is a good example of how traditional life goes on despite Qing'hai's reputation. [1] Herding yaks across a stream with a few precisely thrown rocks and the occasional whistle. [2] A calf gets a trim from the brothers while [3] their sister, a nun, milks the yaks and [4] 'grandma' samples the fresh yogurt.

341

THE TIBETAN PLATEAU

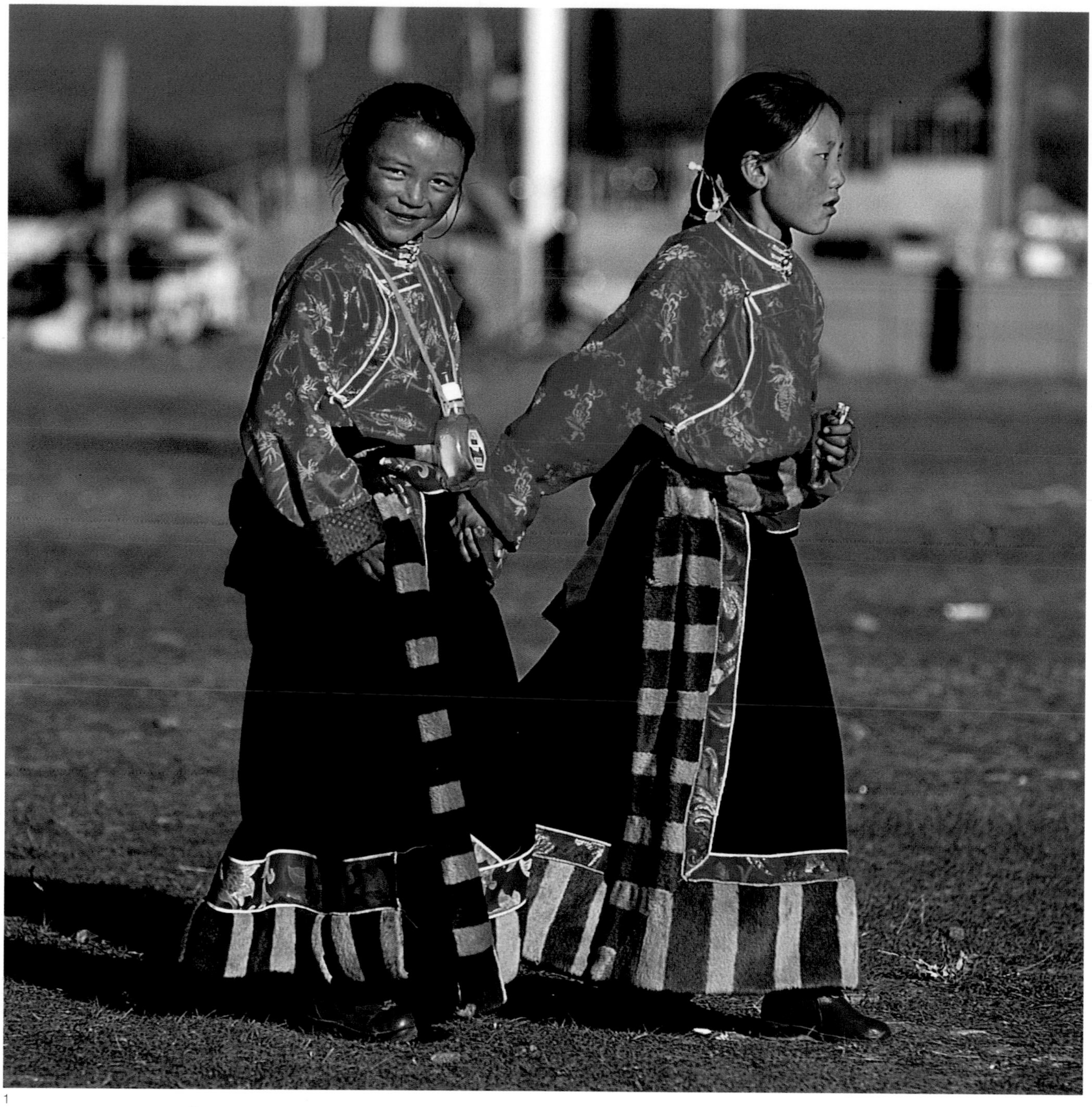

1

THE TOWN OF YU'SHU (Jade Tree), also known as Jyekundo, is the administrative centre of six counties in southern Qing'hai bordering Tibet and is *literally* a thousand miles from everywhere. The town grew around the famous hilltop monastery of Jyekundo Dondrubling and has historically served as an important trading centre on the north-south caravan route between Xi'ning and Lhasa. Yu'shu's annual summer festival attracts tens of thousands of Tibetan nomads from the Kham homeland of traditional Tibet. A tent city rises from the town's parade ground, spreading up onto the emerald hills along the riverbanks. There are funfairs for the children and markets for trading everything from yak cheese and furs to Caterpillar fungus (*cordyceps sinensis*), a rare and much sought-after Himalayan plant seen by many Tibetans as a cure-all medication. [1] Two little girls on their way to the funfair. [2] [4] The high priests, dressed in their finest ceremonial robes, approach the parade ground to bless the festival's opening ceremony. [3] Folk dancing performance. [5] The MTV generation brings mobile communication to the tent city.

THE TIBETAN PLATEAU

342

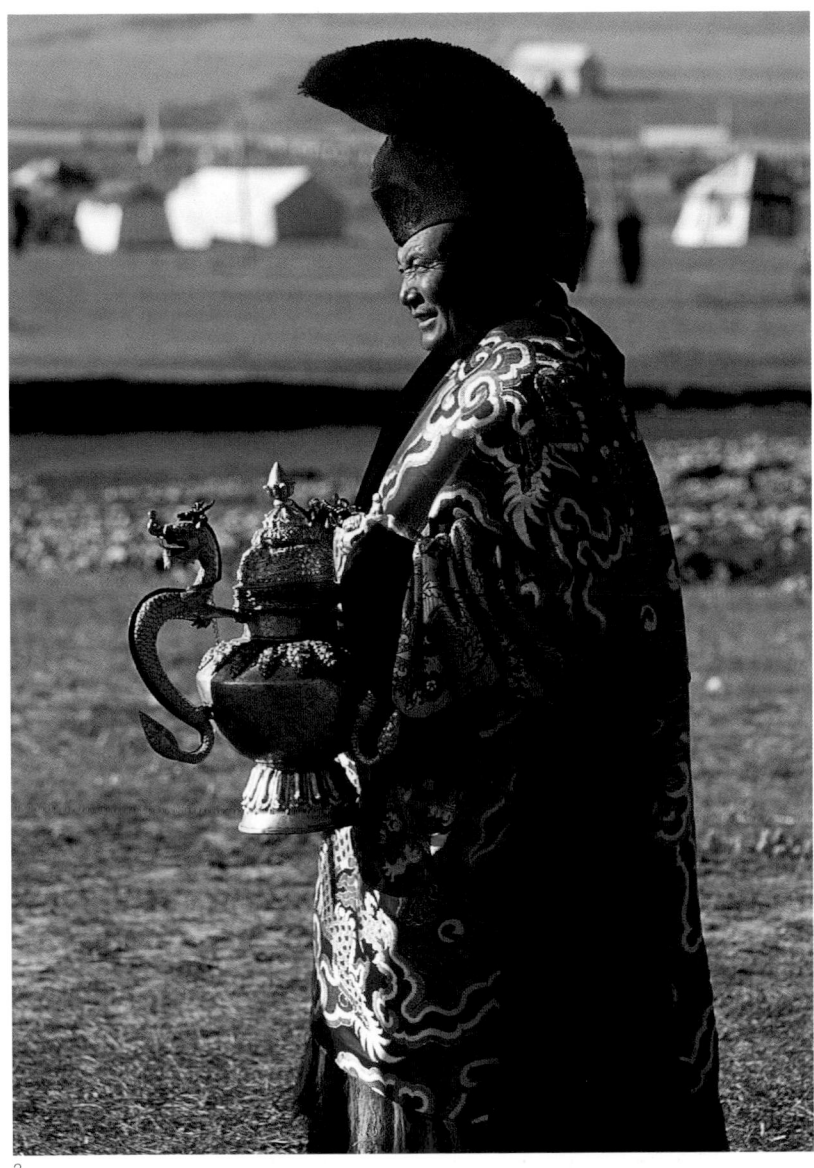

2

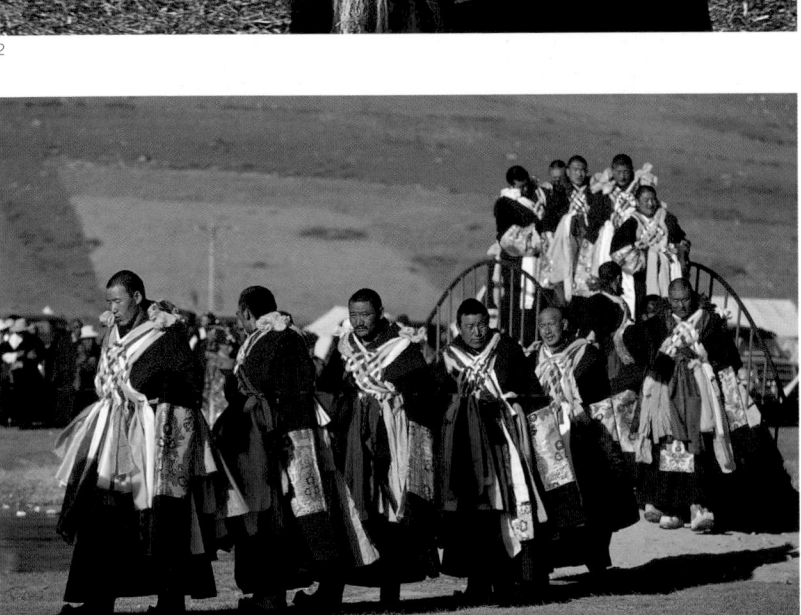

3

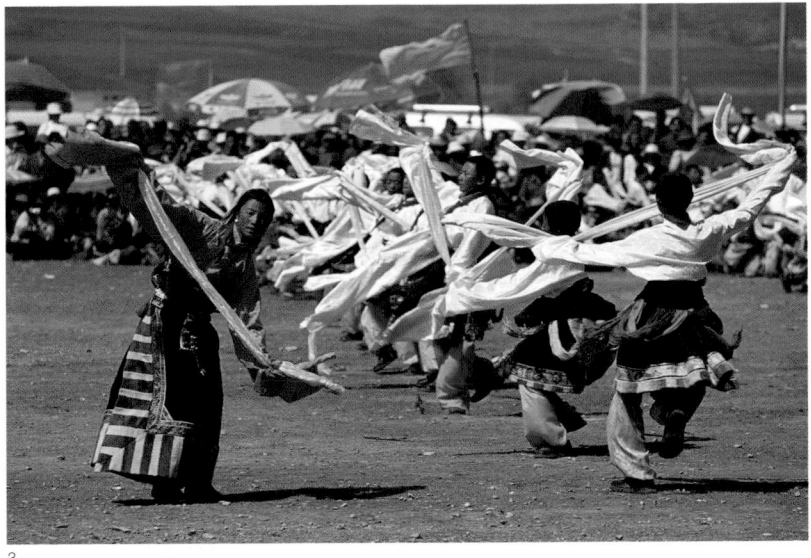

4

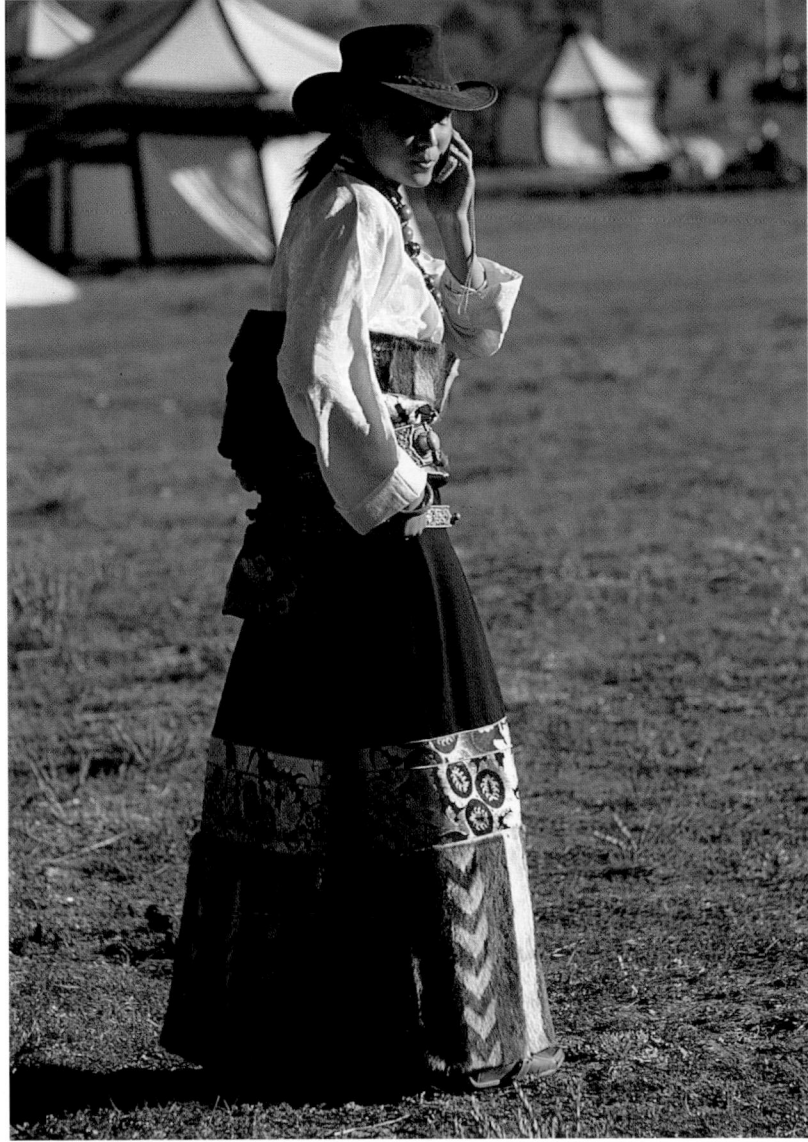

5

THE YU'SHU SUMMER HORSE FESTIVAL

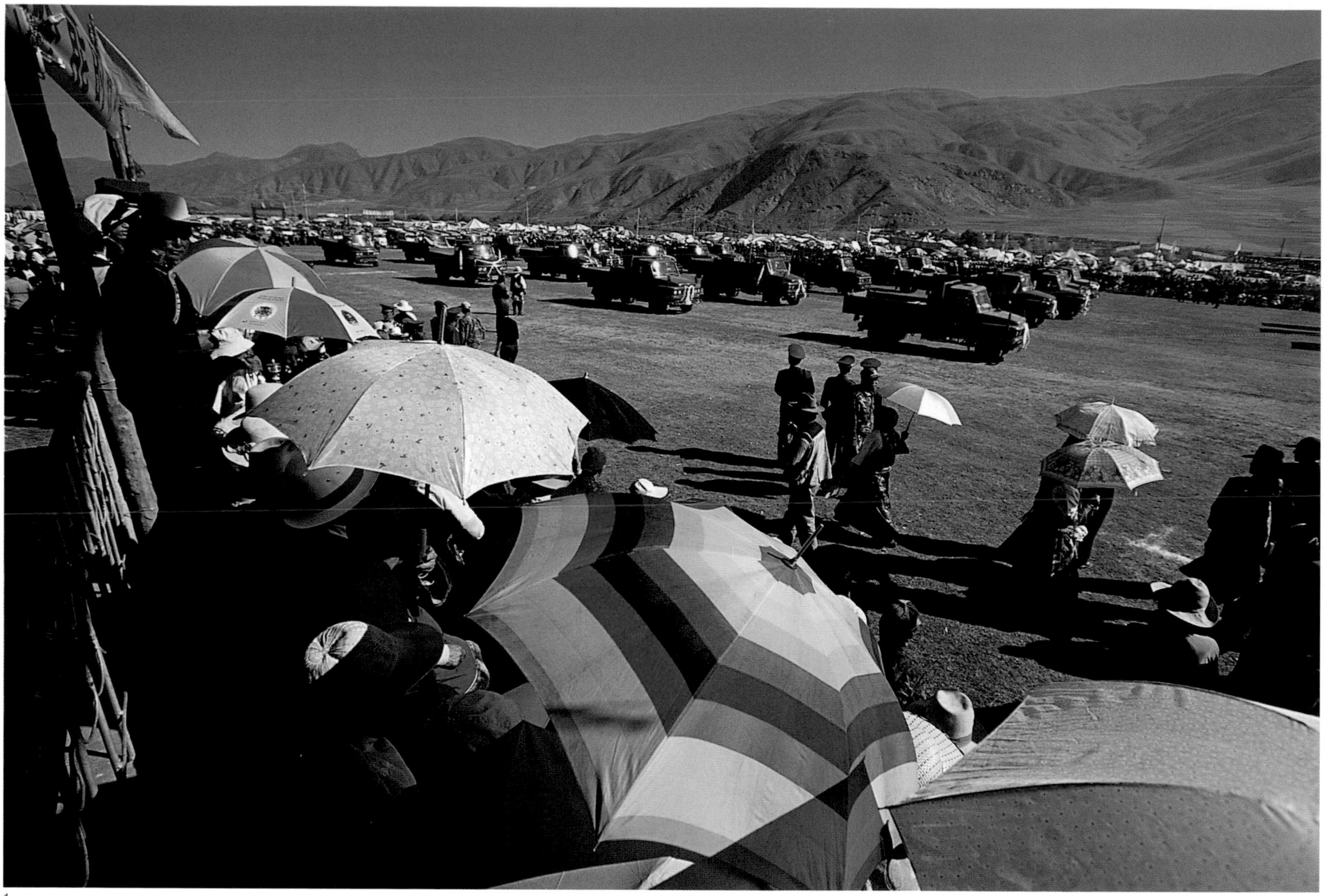

A SEA OF EYE-PIERCING COLOURS shimmers in the parade ground set inside a valley of vibrant green mountains atop the 4,420-metre (14,500-foot) high plateau. Tens of thousands of dancers and spectators in traditional costumes – a riot of bright reds, pinks, blues and yellows set off by amber, coral and turquoise jewellery braided into their long black hair – competed for attention inside the hallucinatory backdrop magnified by intense mountain light rich in UV rays and thin on oxygen. [1] The opening ceremonies strongly resembled a set-piece communist 'May Day' parade. Columns of lumbering blue trucks and rattling tractors garlanded with flowers, ribbons and communist-slogan banners drove past to the applause of a politely enthusiastic crowd. The parade was led by a phalanx of high-powered motorcycles ridden by Tibetan horsemen turned Hell's Angels for the occasion. These men later demonstrated their amazing horsemanship by [2] [5] shooting at tiny targets and [3] sweeping up as many silk *katas* as possible while galloping at high speed. [4] One overzealous competitor managed to literally ride his horse into the ground.

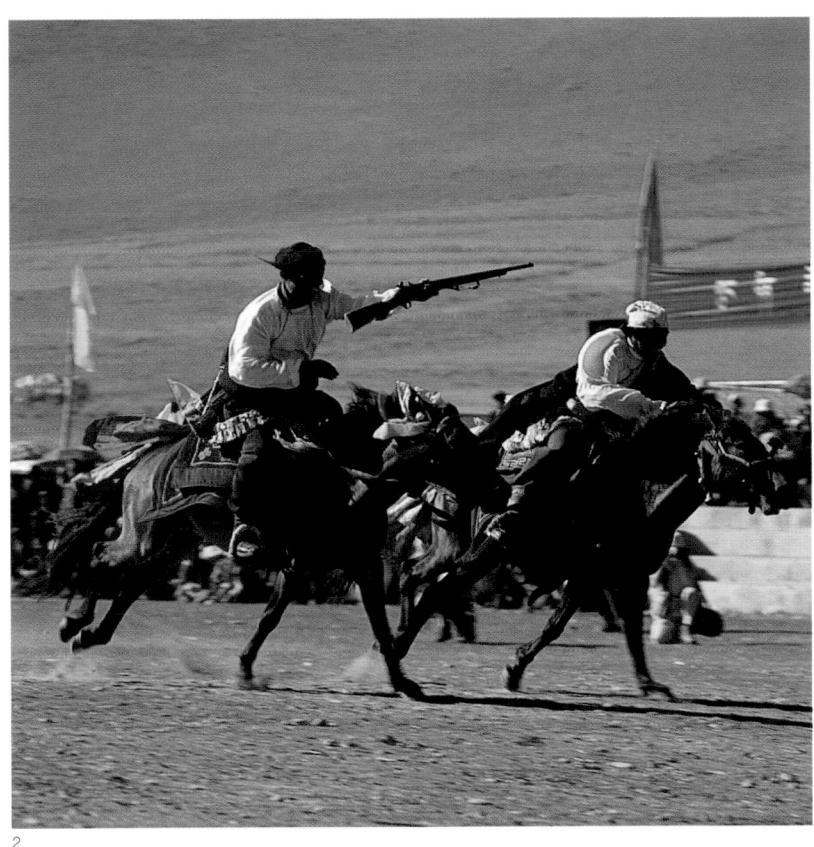

2

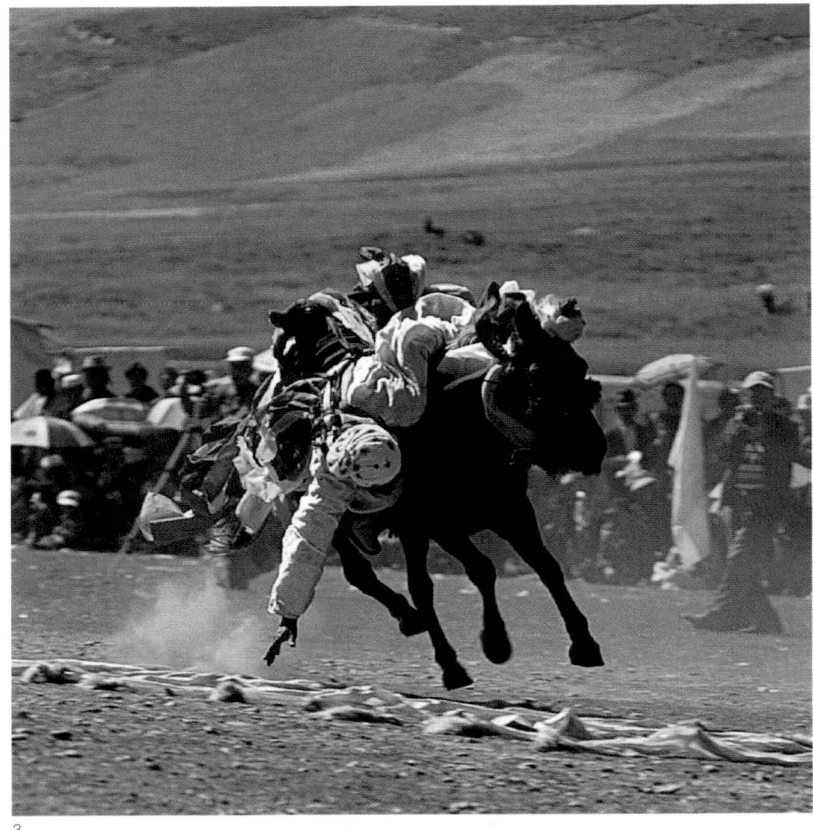

3

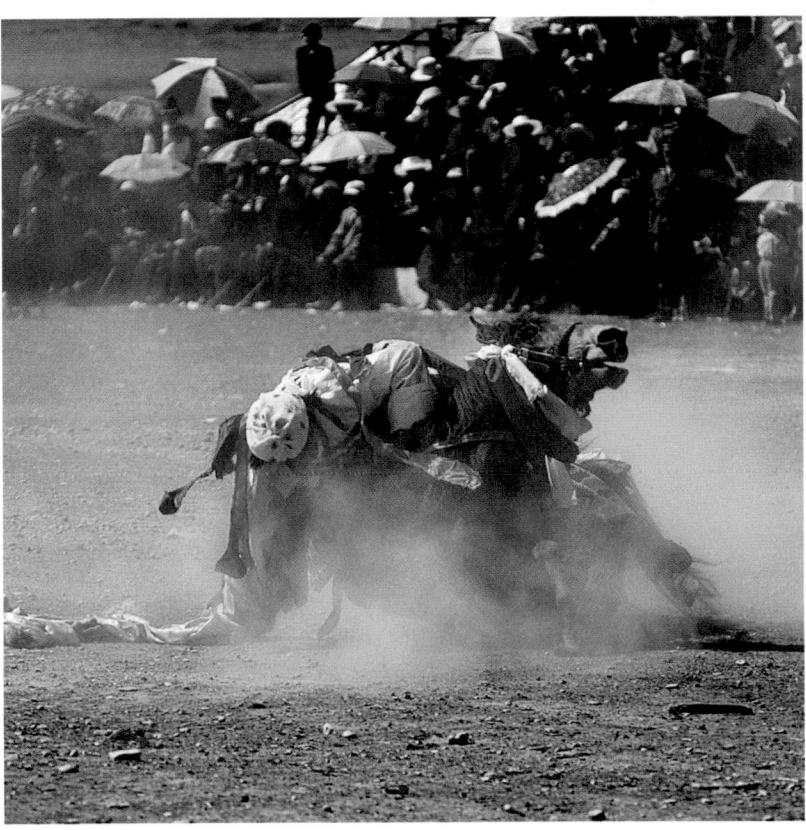

4

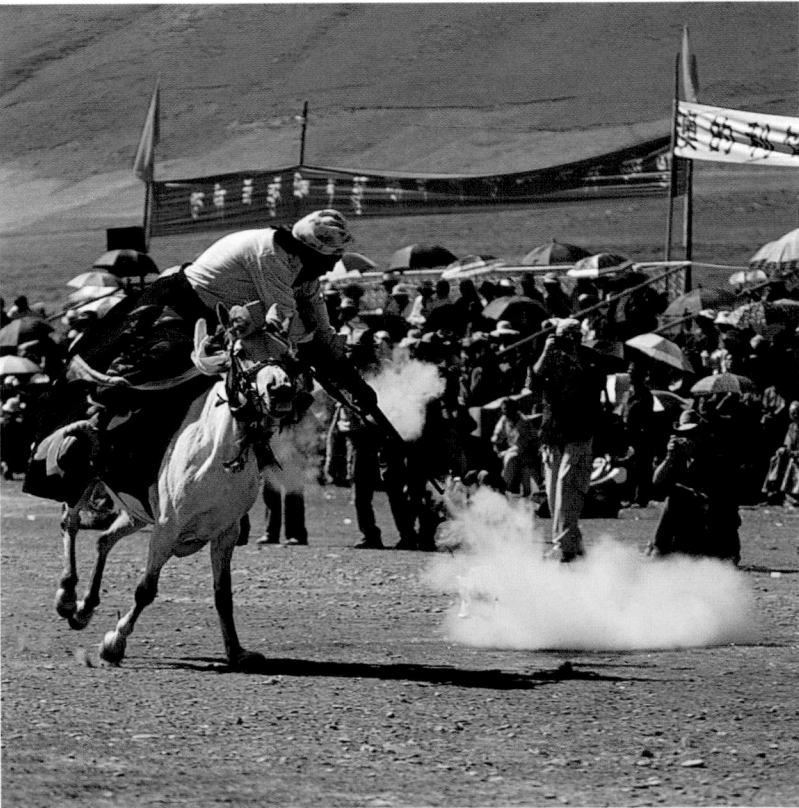

5

TIBET
AUTONOMOUS REGION

LOCATION
Latitude 26°52'–36°32'N
Longtitude 78°24'–99°06'E

AREA 1,221,700 km² (471,700 sq miles²)

GEOGRAPHY Tibet comprises high-altitude plateau lands and mountains. The average elevation is around 4,000 m. The Himalayas form the region's southern boundary, with the Karakoram range to the west and the Kun'lun mountains to the north. Four mountains exceed altitudes of 8,000 m and a further 38 rise to 7,000 m. Tibet is also the source for the Yang'tze and Brahmaputra rivers.

CLIMATE Tibet has two distinctive climates. The Northern Tibet Plateau has an average annual temperature of -2ºC and is covered with snow for half of the year. The valleys in Southern Tibet are temperate and humid. The average January temperature in Lhasa in the country's south is around -16ºC, rising to 29ºC in July. Even in summer, variations can be extreme as daytime highs of around 30ºC are matched by sub-zero temperatures at night. The lowest recorded temperature is -44.6ºC and the highest, 32.2ºC. Average annual rainfall is between 300 and 1,000 mm.

POPULATION 2.74 million (end 2004)

MAJOR CITIES Lhasa (capital), Shigatse, Shan'nan, Nakchu, Ngari, Nyingchi, Zhang'mu

AGRICULTURE The only extensive agricultural region is the Yar'lung Tsangpo Valley, where barley, wheat, potatoes, millet and turnips are grown. Other areas can sustain yak, sheep and goat grazing.

MAIN INDUSTRIES Tourism is the main non-agricultural industry in Tibet. Extensive mineral resources exist, although few have been exploited. The Yangbajain geothermal field near Lhasa is a cheap source of local energy, but has no export potential.

ANNUAL PER CAPITA INCOME (2005)
Disposable income of urban residents:
RMB 8,411 (US$1,050)
Net income of rural residents:
RMB 2,075 (US$259)

IMPORTANT HISTORICAL SITES
Potala Palace, Jokhang Temple, Tashilunpo Monastery, Kumbum, Mount Everest, Yamdrok Yumtso Lake, Lake Manasarovar, Mount Kailash, Yar'lung Tsangpo Gorge.

FOOD Tibetan food reflects the region's agricultural resources. Dishes include *tsampa* (roasted barley flour), *momo* (steamed or fried dumplings), *thukpa* (noodle soup with meat and sometimes vegetables), *soja* (butter tea) and many variations on mutton, lamb and yak meat.

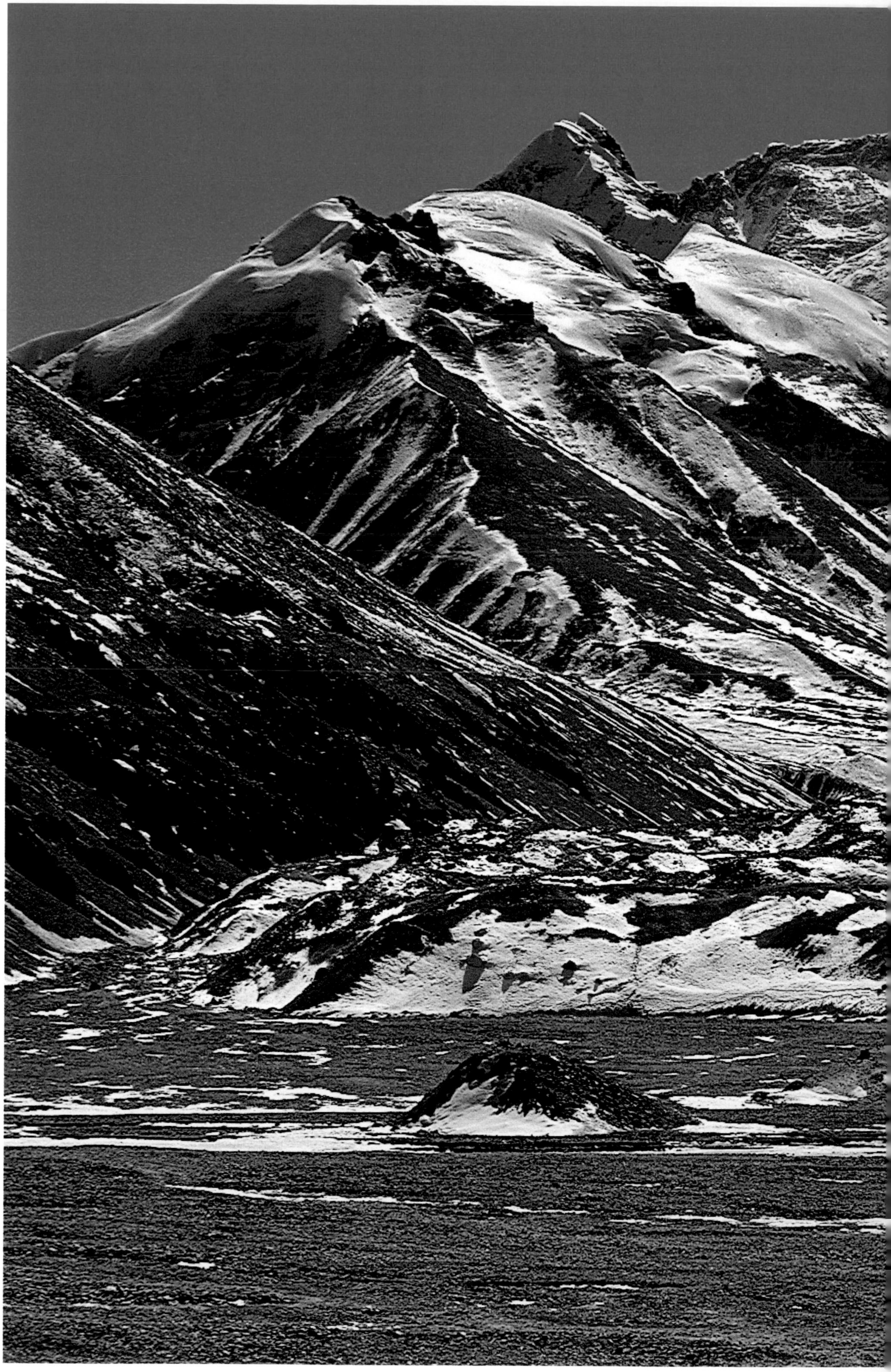

[RIGHT] The north face of Qomolangma – 'Mother Goddess of the Earth' – from the Everest base camp at Rongbuk.

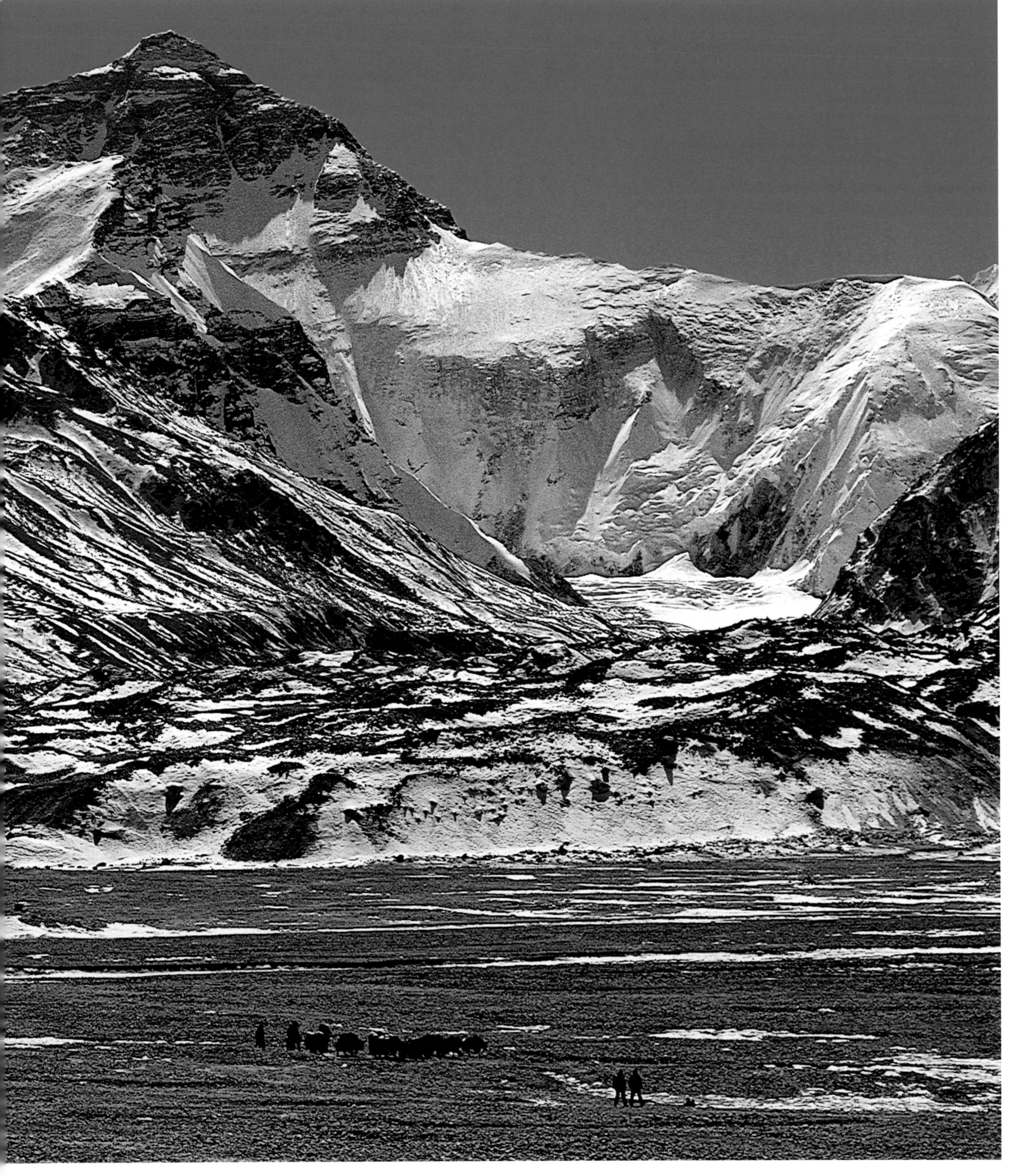

1

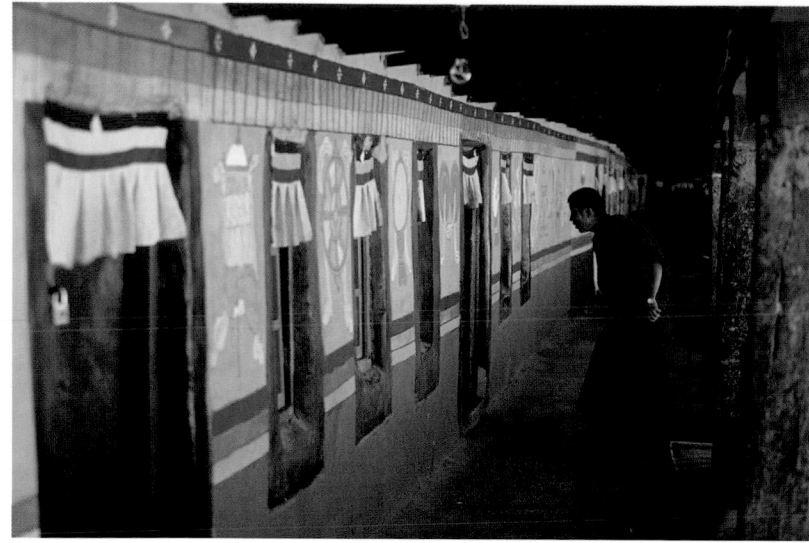

2

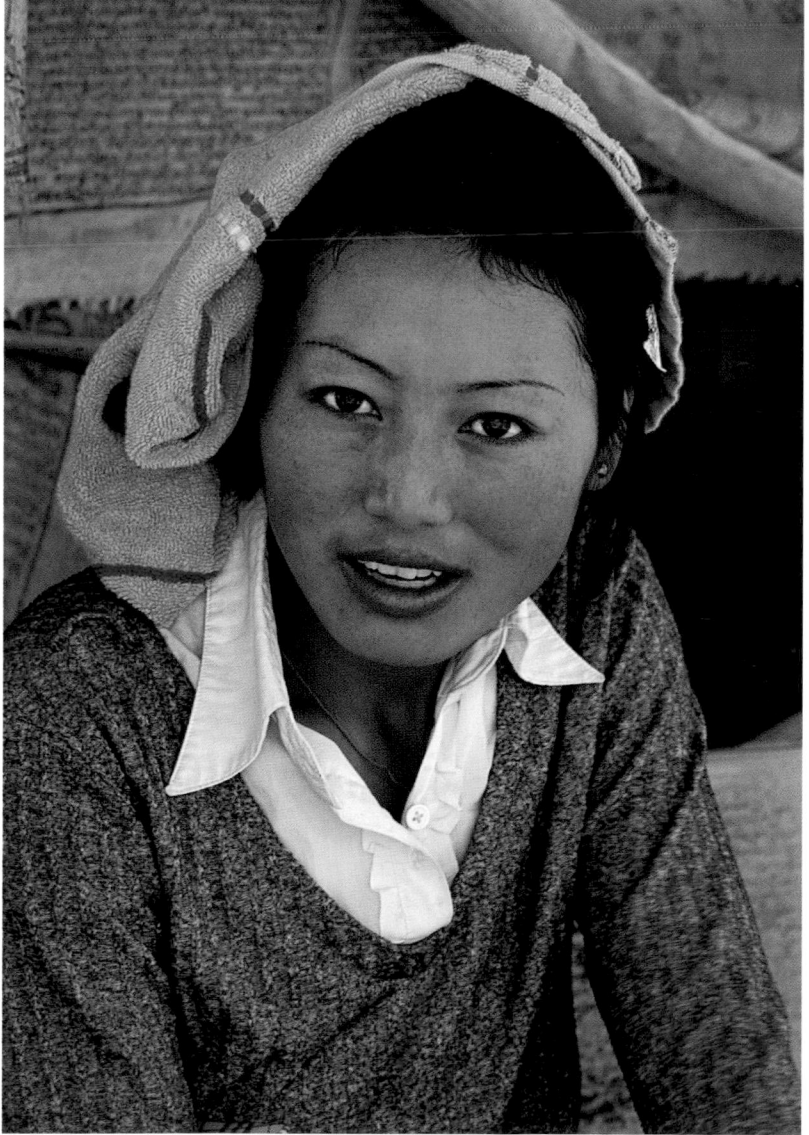

3

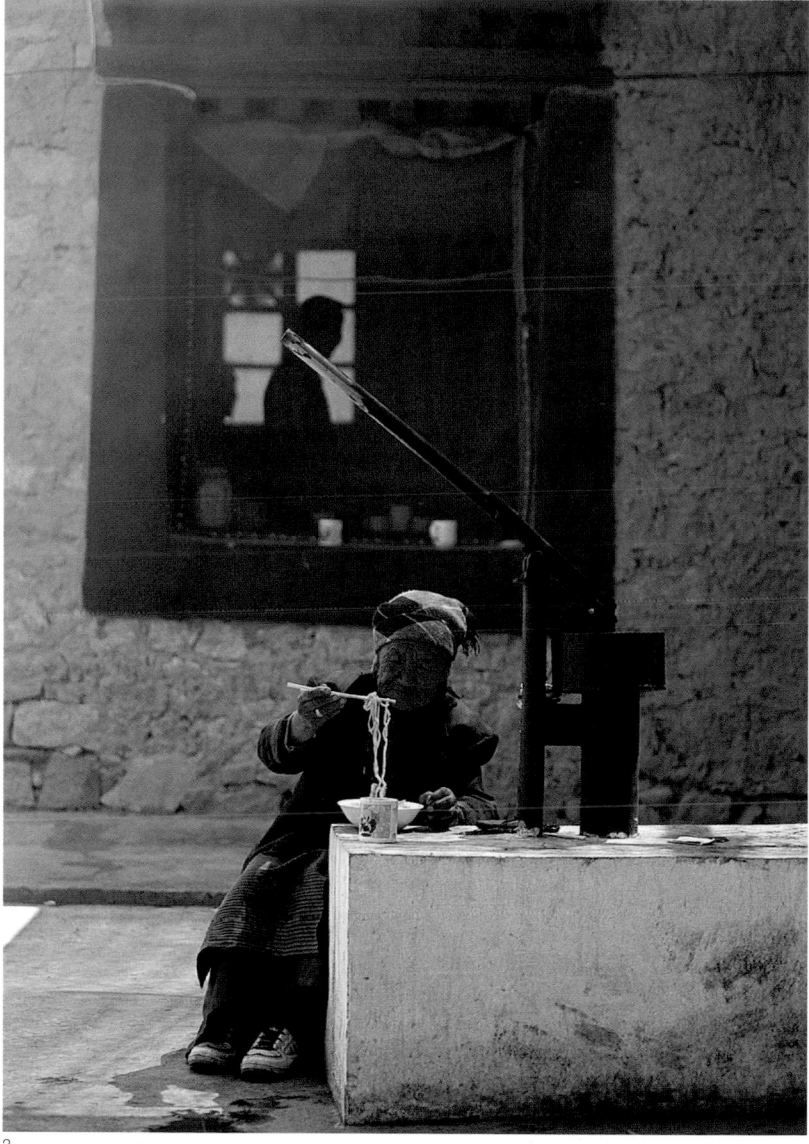

4

YAR'LUNG TSANGPO VALLEY

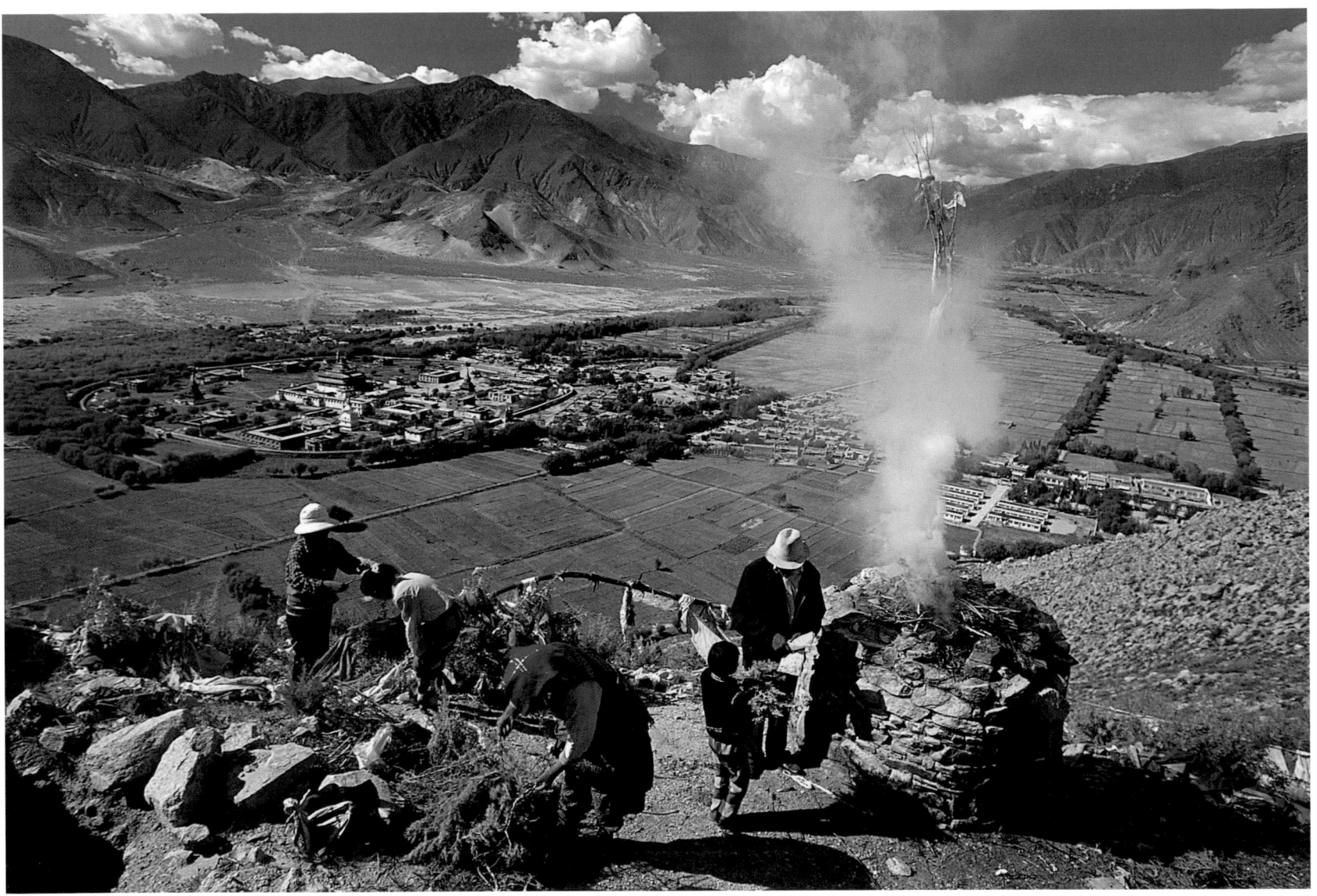

5

SAMYE, SITUATED IN THE LUSH VALLEY on the north bank of the Yar'lung Tsangpo (Brahmaputra) River, was Tibet's first Buddhist monastery. The temple was completed in 779 BCE, marking the official establishment of Buddhism in the country and the end of the native Bon religion's influence at court. King Khri-Srong invited the Indian *Mahayana* scholar Santiraksita and Padma'sambhava ('the Lotus-born'), a Tantric mystic from Swat (Pakistan) to advise on the building of the monastery. One legend is that Samye, meaning 'unimaginable,' refers to the magical feat performed by Padma'sambhava when he presented the monastery's design as a hologram in the palm of his hand. Another version says Santiraksita designed the monastery but was forced to quit when 'demons' plagued the construction. Padma'sambhava, a master in taming demonic forces, defeated the demons at Hepo Ri and completed the monastery, while Santiraksita became its first Abbot. [3] [5] Pilgrims on the hill overlooking Samye monastery, designed as a three-dimensional *mandala*. [1] The monks' living quarters. [2] A pilgrim eats noodles in the monastery cafeteria. [4] Traditional grain processing in a Yar'lung village.

THE TIBETAN PLATEAU

THE POTALA PALACE IS THE ICONIC SYMBOL OF TIBET and a constant reminder of the absence of the country's spiritual leader, the exiled Dalai Lama. Built on the foundation of King Songsten Gampo's 7th-century palace, construction of the nine-storey White Palace began in 1645 with 7,000 workers and 1,500 artisans. Dalai Lama V moved the seat of government to the summit of Mount Marpo'ri (Red Hill) from the Drepung Monastery in 1649 and the project was completed in 1653. According to one account, the Red Palace was designed by Dalai Lama V to be his own funerary *chorten*, and its construction was well underway by the time of his passing in 1682. Desi Sangye Gyatso, the regent who ruled Tibet between 1679 and 1703, concealed his death for 12 years, until after the central structure was completed. The Potala has since served as the winter home for subsequent Dalai Lamas, with the inner 'red' section of the palace containing the chapels and tombs of eight of the spiritual leaders. Now a government-run museum, the 1,000-room, 13-storey structure was one of the tallest buildings in the world before the introduction of skyscrapers. [1] [2] [3] Different faces of the Potala Palace.

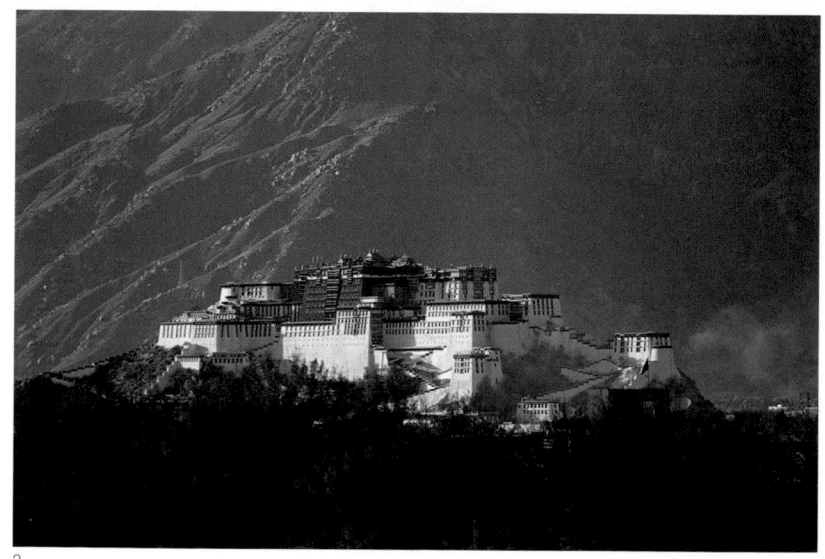

SUBJECT & TITLE

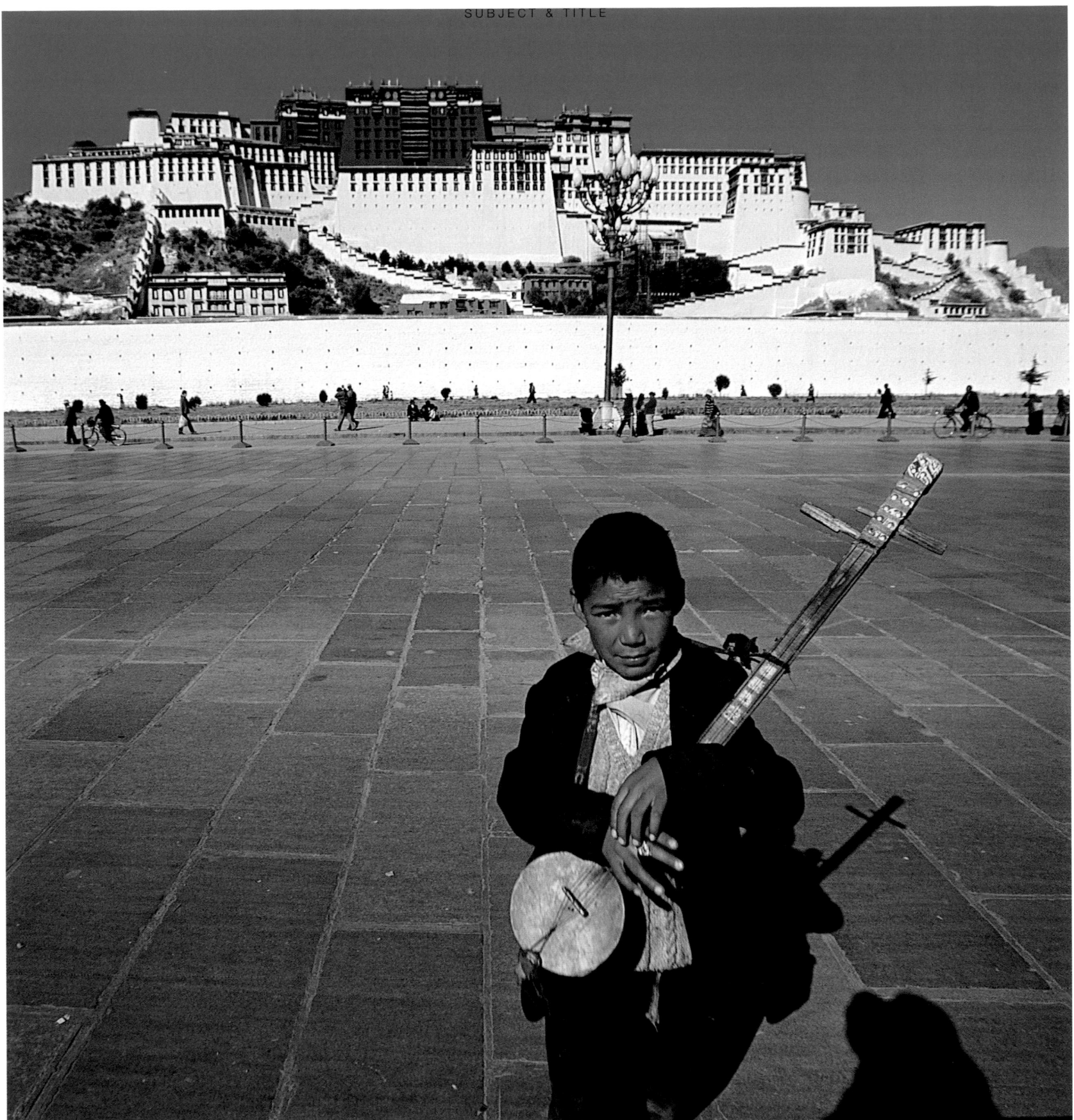

3

351

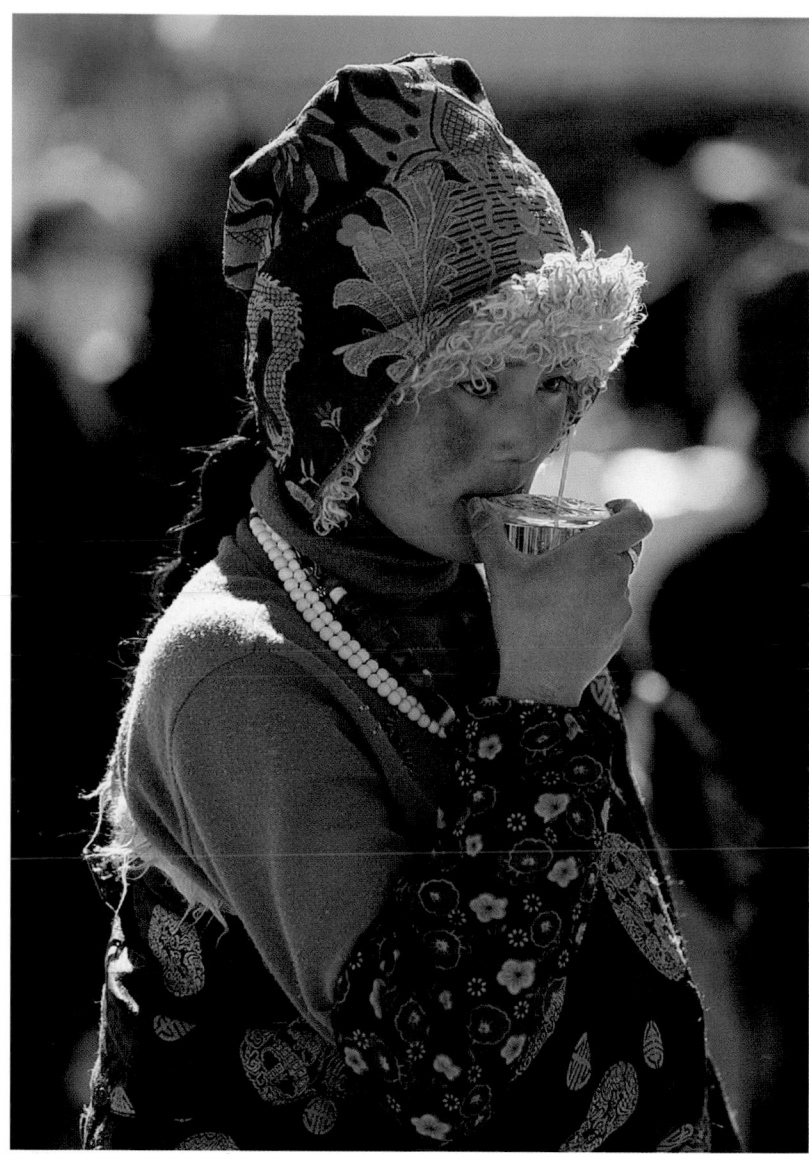

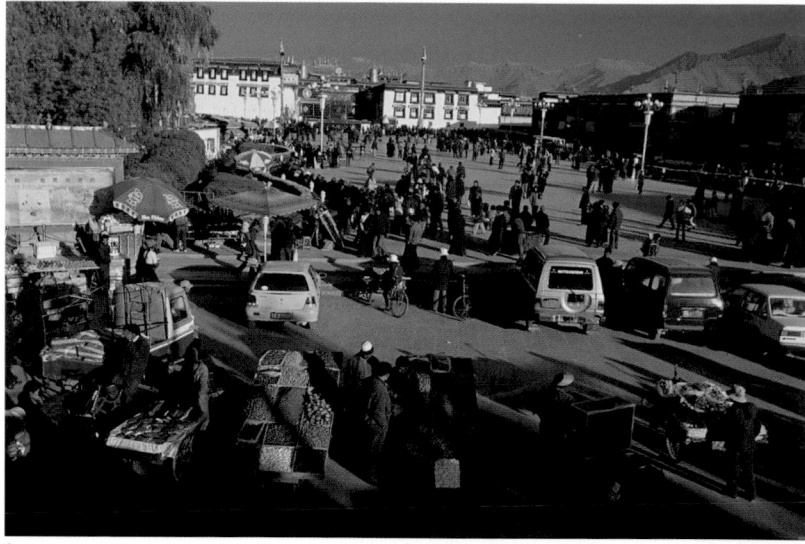

1

2

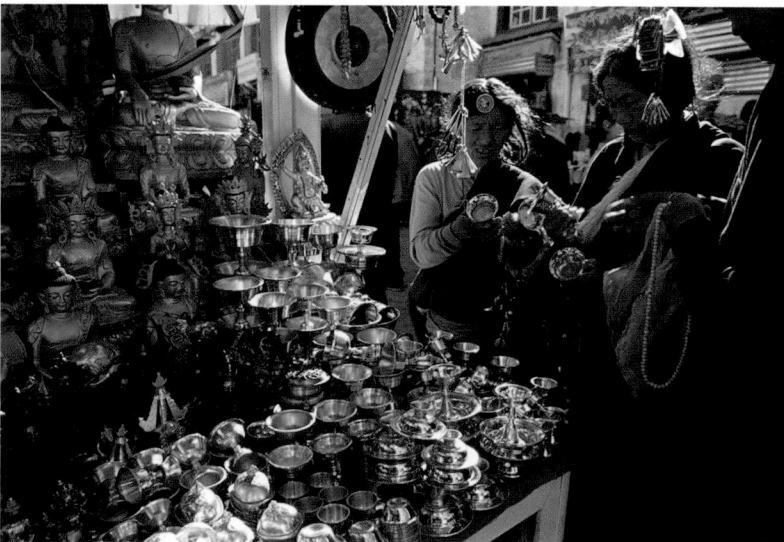

3

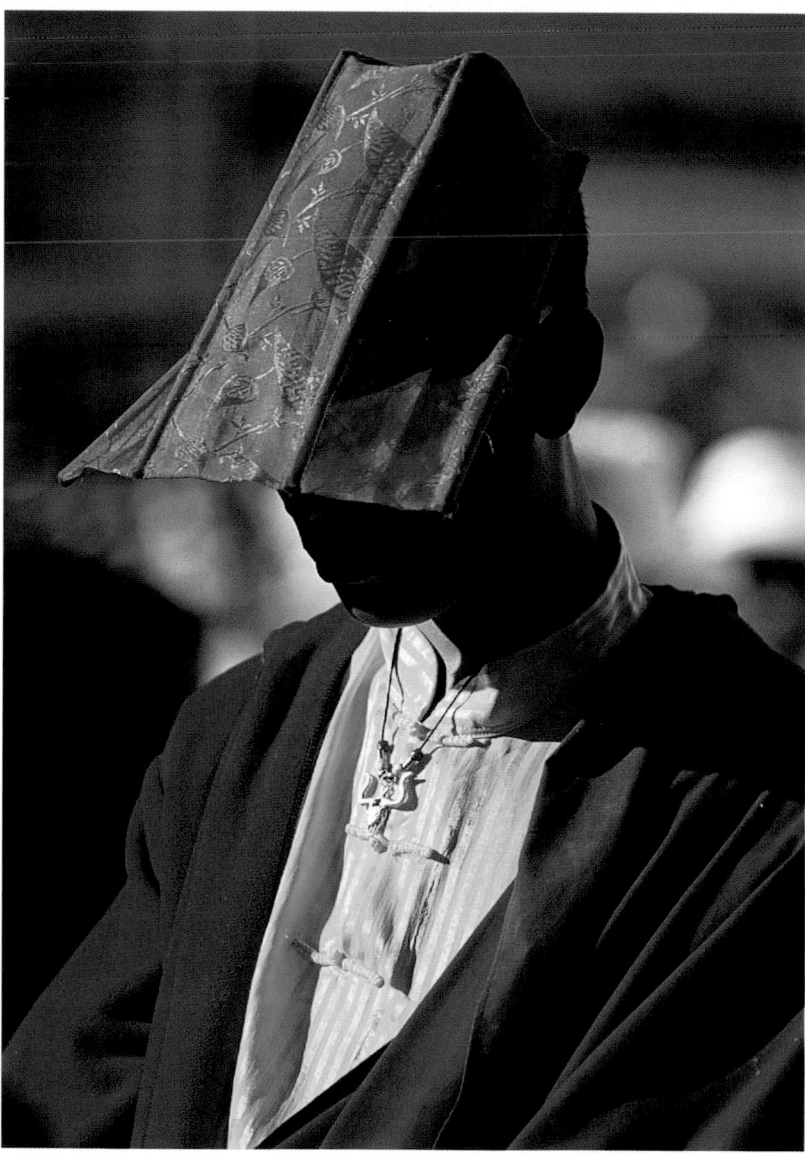

4

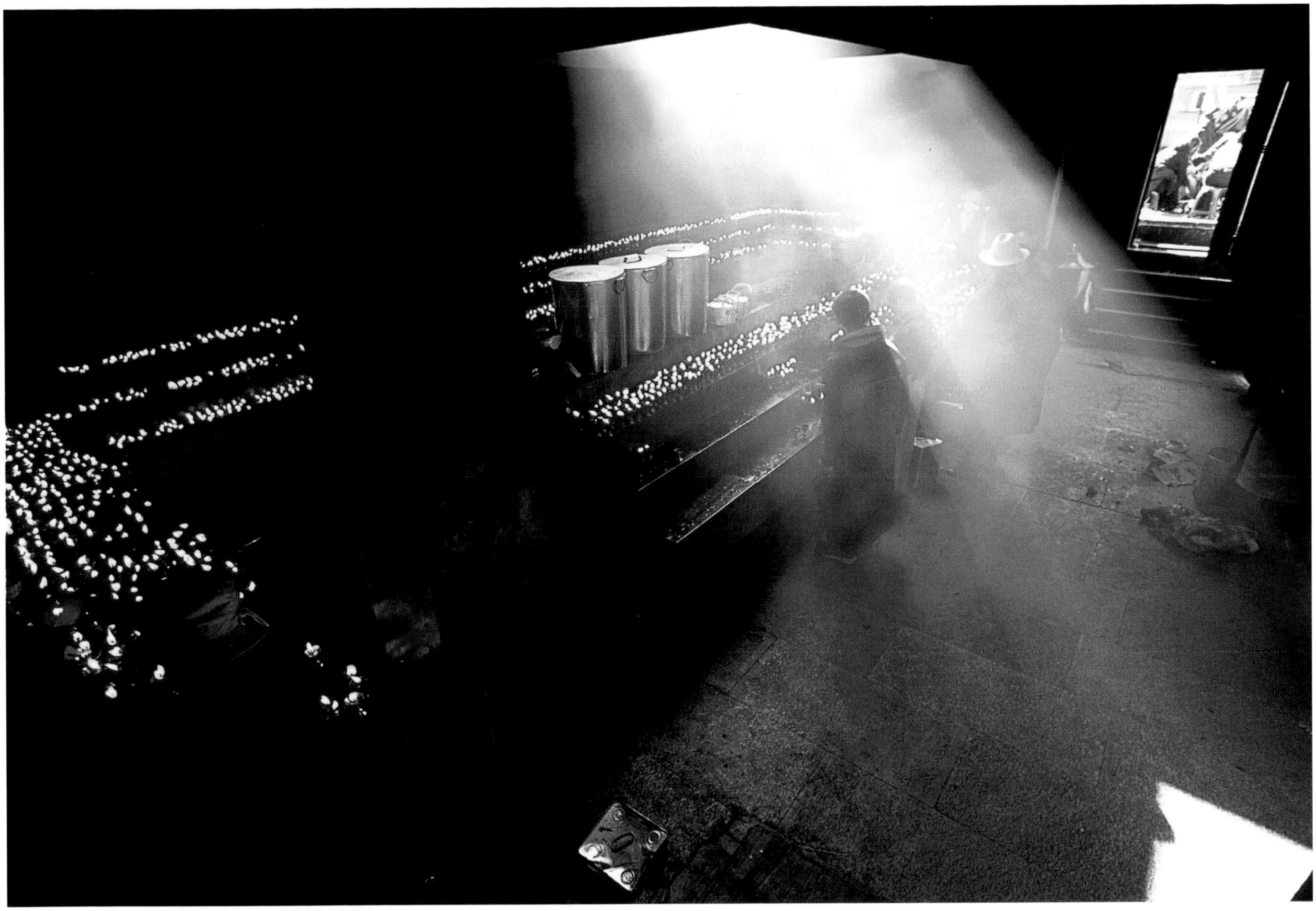

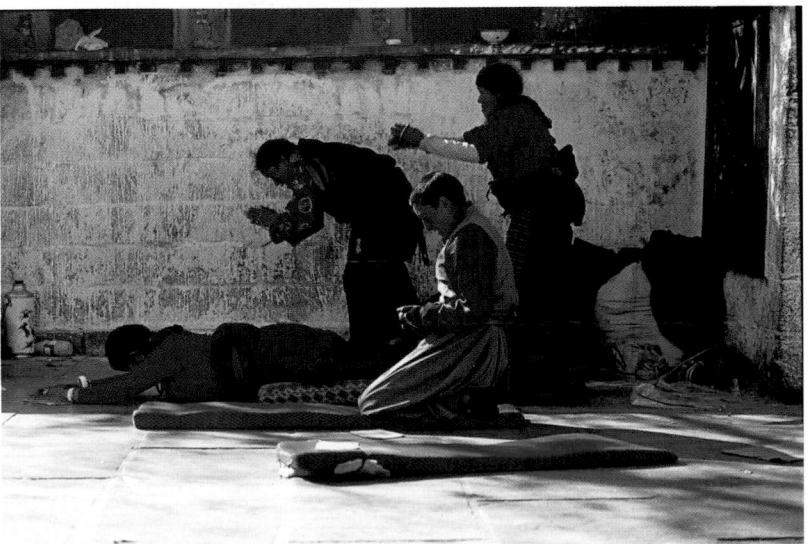

ACCORDING TO LEGEND, when the Chinese princess Wen'cheng arrived in Lhasa, a chariot bearing the statue of Jowo Sakyamuni – a representation of the Buddha at age 12 and now the most sacred image in Tibet – became hopelessly stuck in the mud on the shores of Othang Lake. Wen'cheng's soothsayers' explanation for the inauspicious omen was that a demon ogress lived beneath Tibet, determined to resist the introduction of the new religion. The solution was to build a protective *mandala* of 108 Buddhist temples across Tibetan territory to subdue the demon. The Jokhang was built between 638–647 CE over the heart of the ogress. It is the centre from which the geomantic sphere radiates, and remains the spiritual heart of the Tibetan people today. [1] A nomad girl outside Tibet's most sacred shrine. [2] The Jokhang plaza. [3] Religious paraphernalia stalls line the Barkhor ('Eight Corners') around the temple. [4] An increasing number of fake 'monks' loiter around the Jokhang asking tourists for money to rebuild their imaginary monasteries. A swaggering demeanor, glossy outfit and sparkly jewellery betrayed this young man's true identity. [5] Butter lamps in the spirit house by the main entrance. [6] Three stages of a full prostration.

THE NAM'TSO LAKE

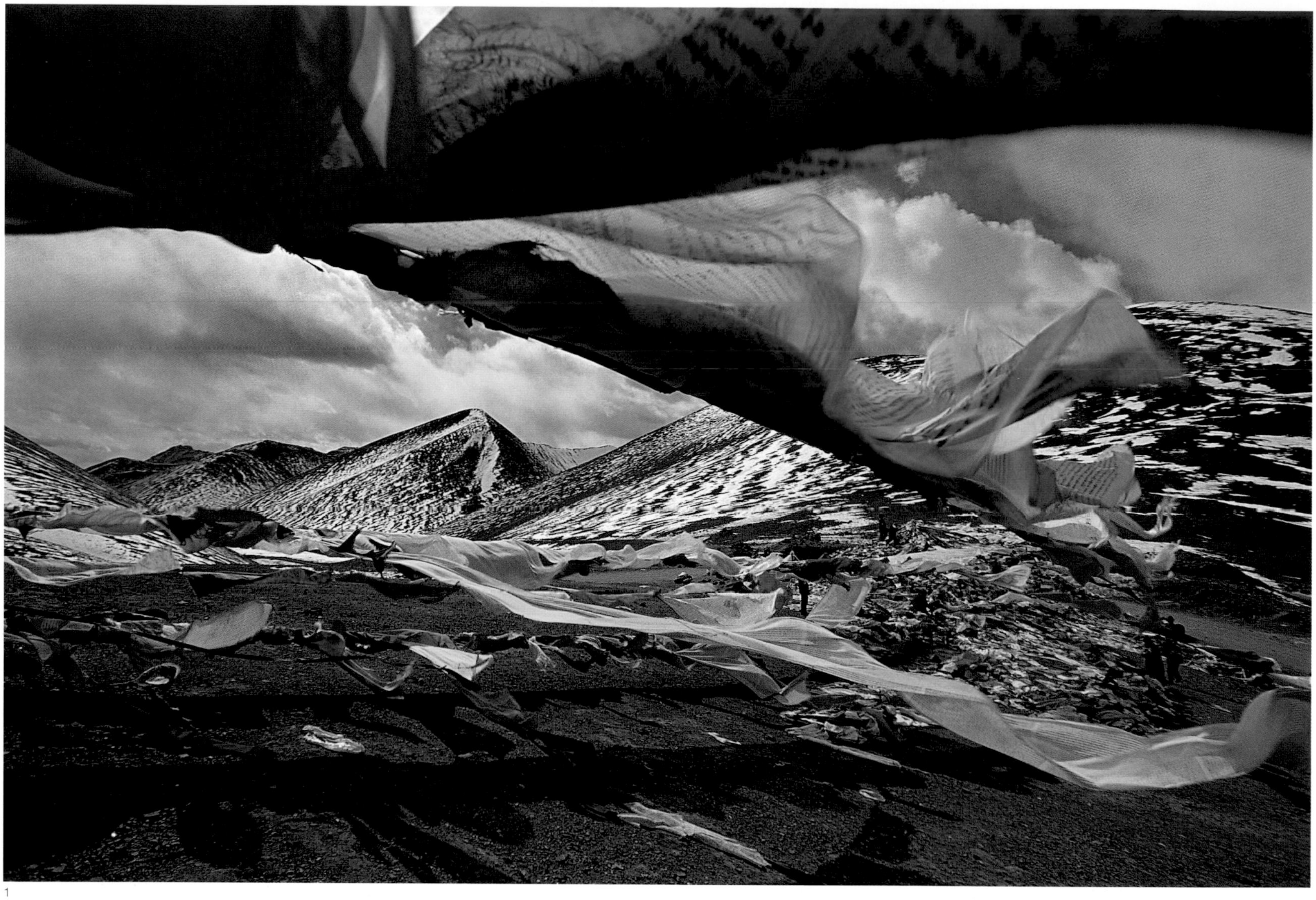

WE HEADED NORTHWEST OUT OF LHASA for the 190-kilometre (120-mile) drive up to Nam'tso Lake with a snowstorm nipping at our heels. By the time we crossed [1] the 5,090-metre (16,700-foot) Lhachen'la Pass at the head of the Nam'tso Chukmo Valley, the howling wind had reached a sustained shriek. There was no sign of the famed ethereal turquoise water of China's second largest saltwater lake, only a turbulent sheet of slate under a tempestuous sky. We parked near [2] the cave hermitage of Tashi'dor, which houses a chapel for the Bon deity Nyenchen Tanglha. He is guardian and namesake of the snow-dusted mountain range that encompasses the lake, and as protector of Mount Marpo'ri (Red Hill), he is the landlord of the Potala Palace. The icy wind felt like it was biting my face off, but the pilgrims appeared completely unconcerned by such conditions. Leaning hard into the wind, they made their *kora* around the holy lake, some performing full prostrations on the frozen ground where [3] fallen strings of prayer flags flutter on the *mani* stones along the shoreline.

THE TIBETAN PLATEAU

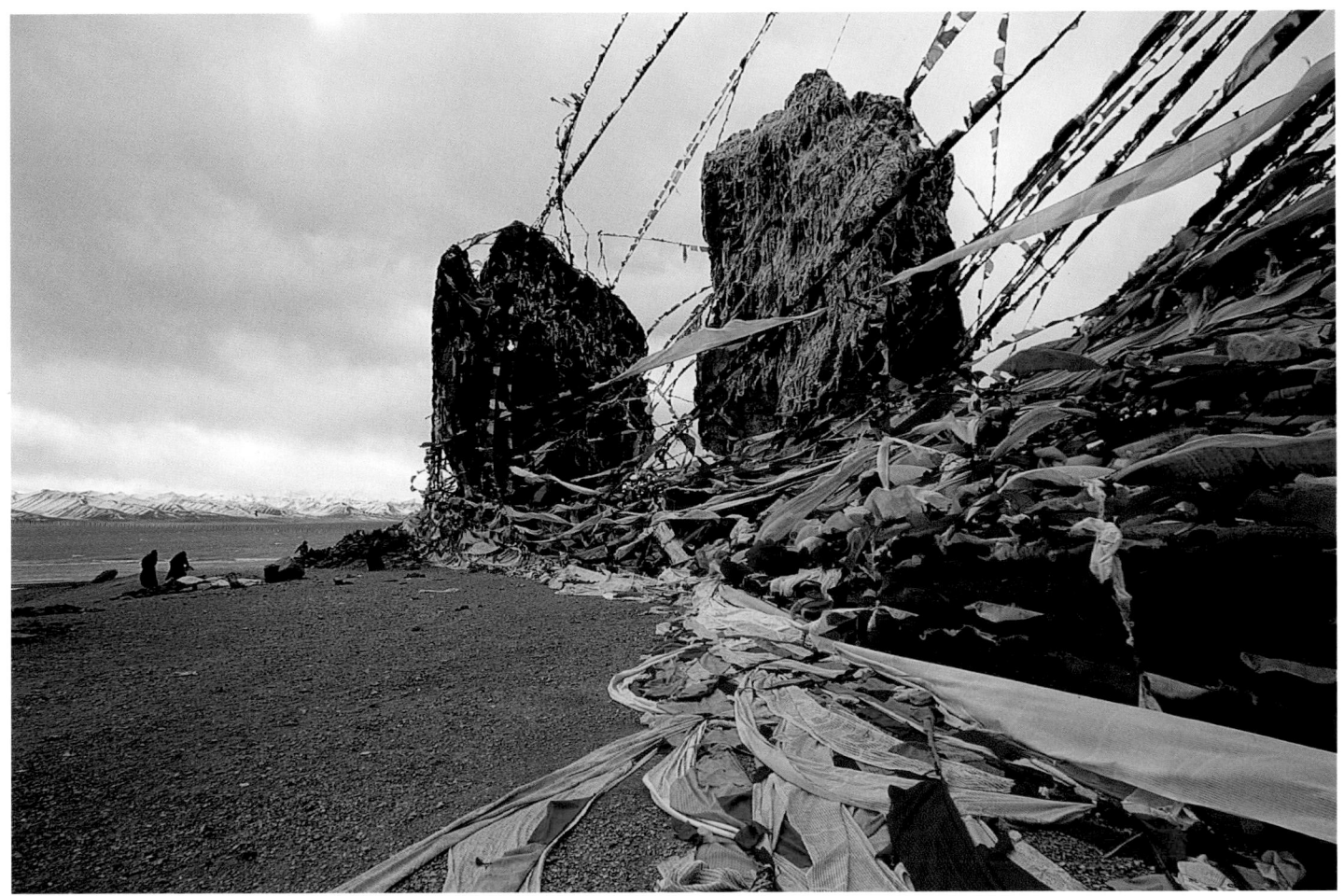

2

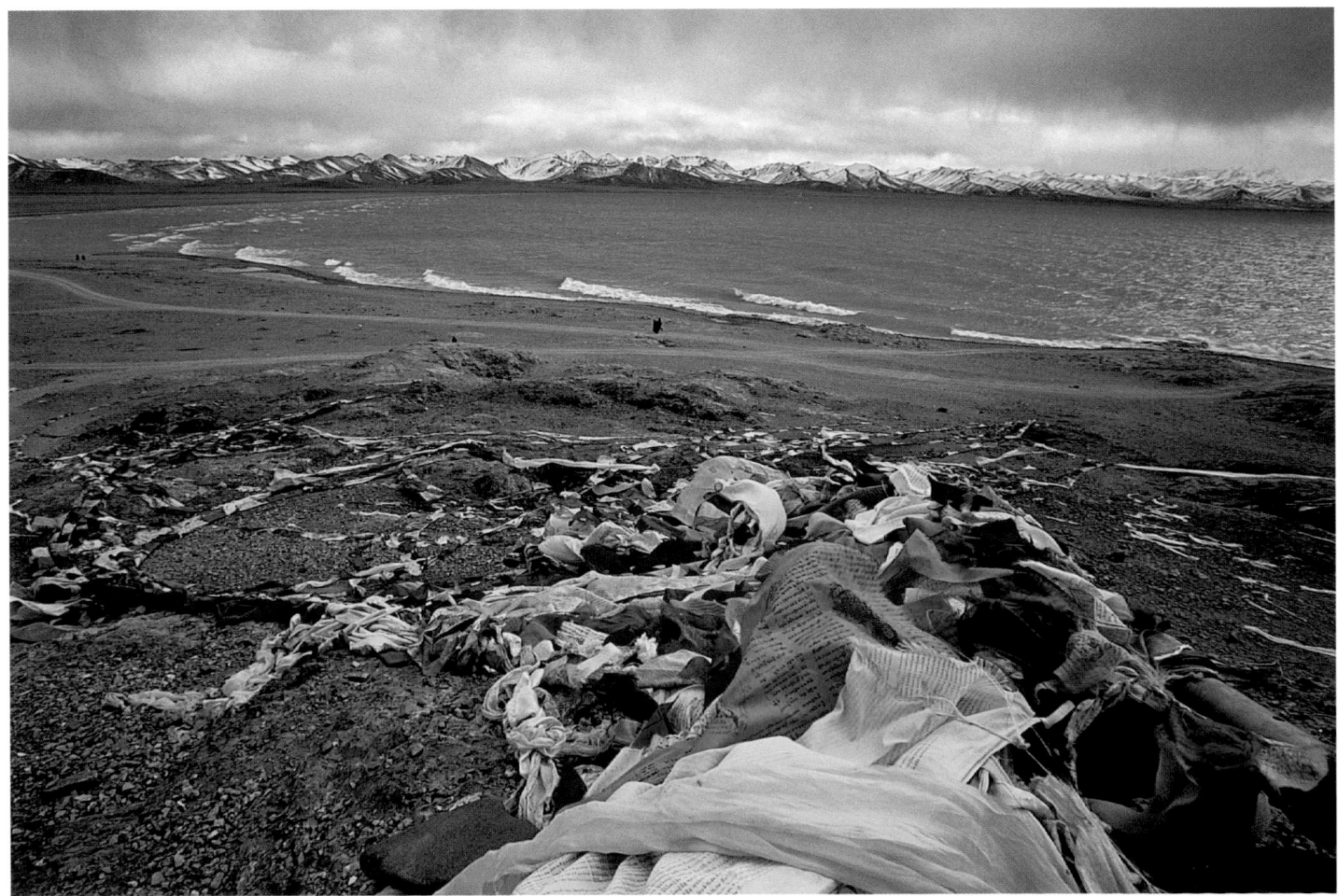

3

THE TIBETAN PLATEAU

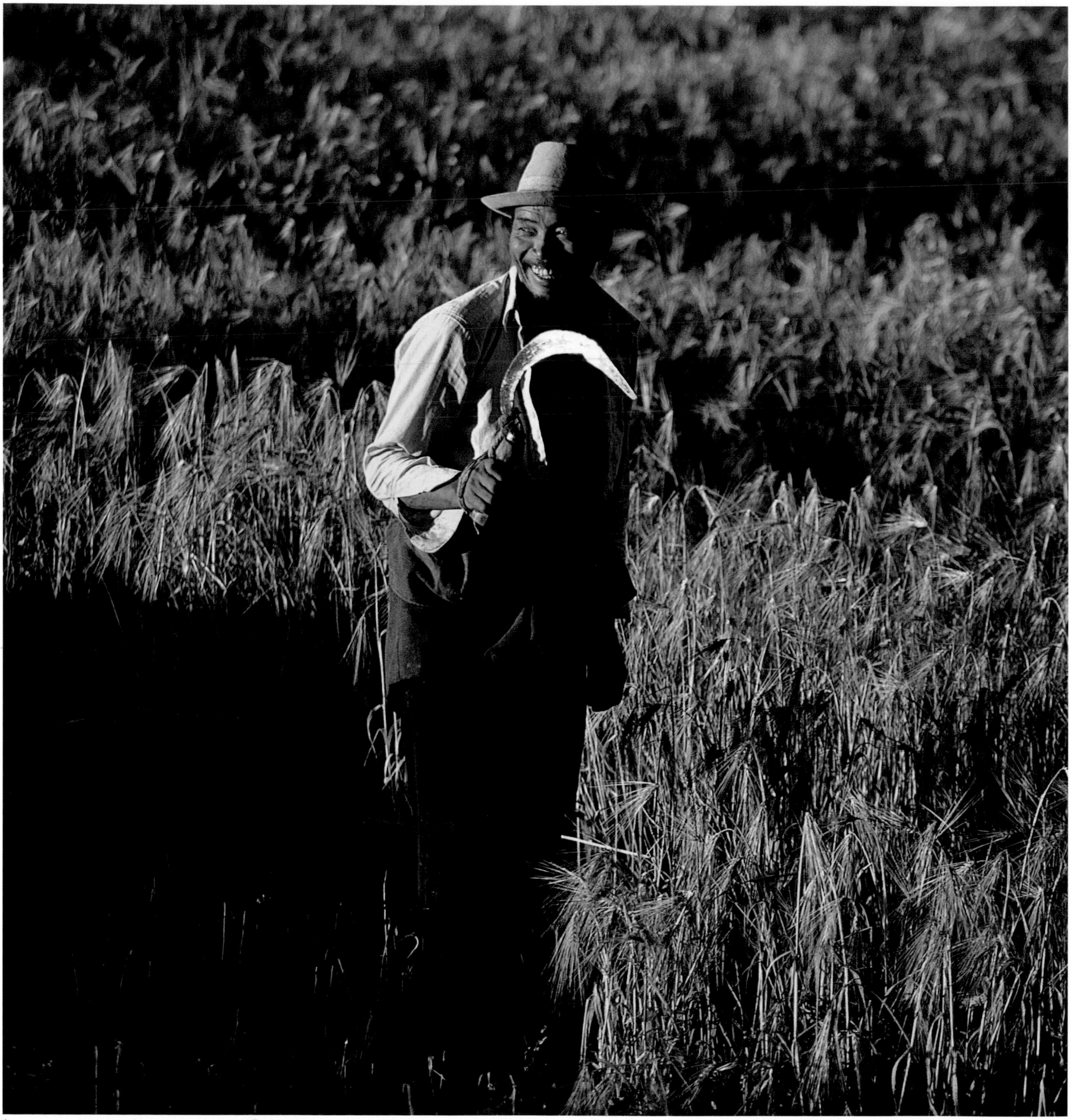

1

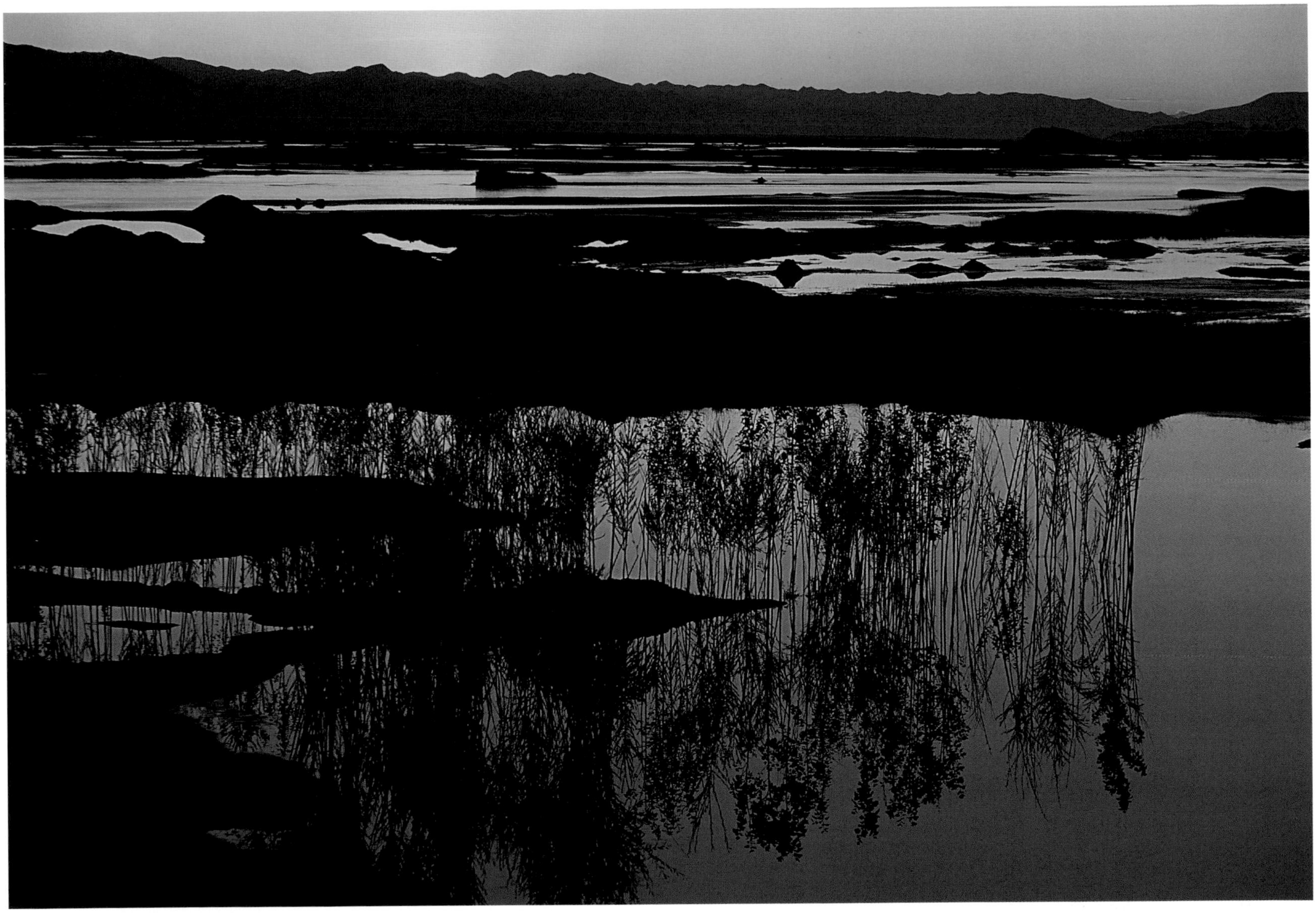

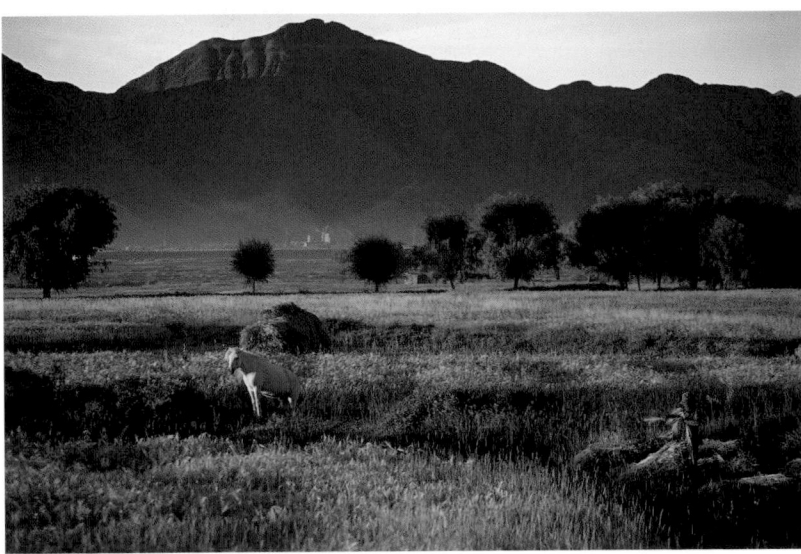

2

3

IN THE SHADOW OF SOME OF THE HIGHEST MOUNTAINS on earth, Asia's great river systems have carved broad fertile valleys through the Tibetan Plateau. A sizeable farming community works this land, growing staples like barley and buckwheat and a wide variety of fruit and vegetables. One of the most productive regions is the Yar'lung Valley, fed by the Brahmaputra River (Yar'lung Tsangpo), which rises in the western Himalayas. Tibetans were traditionally able to produce surplus grain they could store for years in the dry mountain climate. Large-scale famine was unknown until the Chinese communists 'liberated' Tibetans from 'feudalism'. More than fifty years of high taxes, persecution and purges have destroyed the carefully balanced cycle of production, creating chronic food shortage. Conditions have improved in recent years due to China's economic boom and more reasoned policies, but the ability of the indigenous people of the plateau to be self-sufficient has almost certainly been lost for ever. [1] [3] A golden harvest outside of Shigatse where the peasants chant as they work and a white horse looks on. [2] The Yar'lung River at dawn.

FRIENDSHIP HIGHWAY TO HEAVEN

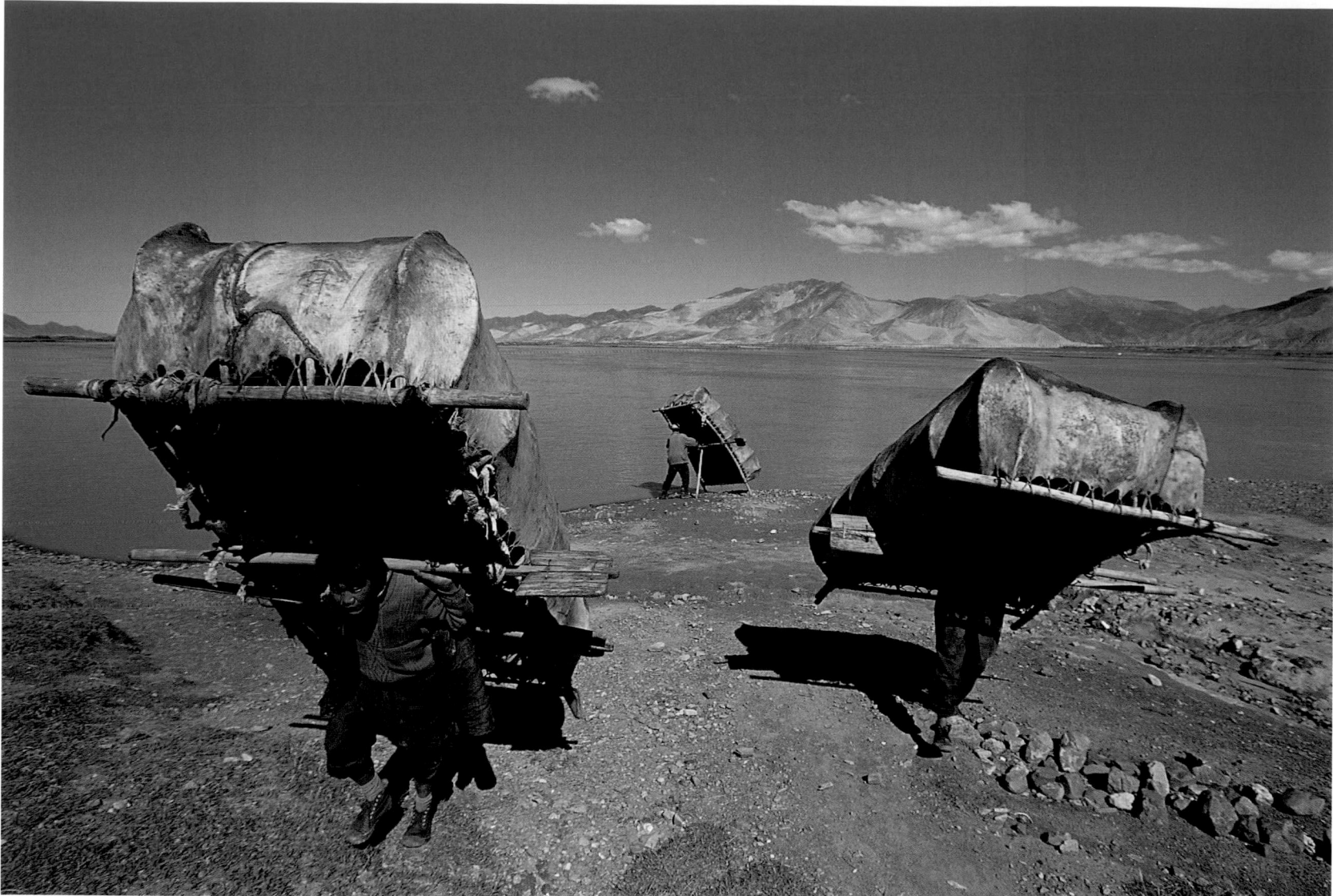

1

THE FRIENDSHIP HIGHWAY connects Lhasa to Kathmandu at Kodari on the Tibetan-Nepalese border. Travelling this road across the Himalayan range is among the most scenic – and literally breathtaking – journeys on earth. The new northern section between Lhasa and Shigatse may have introduced the concept of 'speed' to local travel, but local boatmen still use [1] traditional yak-skin rafts to carry people, goods and livestock across the river. Similar craft would have ferried Francis Younghusband's force of 1,000 troops, 10,000 servants and 4,000 yaks across the river when they marched on Lhasa in 1903 to resolve a dispute between Tibet and British India. Younghusband besieged [4] the fortress monastery of Gangtse Dzong for eight months while waiting for emissaries from Lhasa who never arrived. The old southern road heads up [3] the Kamba-la Pass over the Holy Lake of Yamdruk'tso (Lake of Swans), where a souvenir vendor naps against the magnificent backdrop. [2] In the small town of Langkang'tze on the other side of the lake a young construction worker finds her lunch break interrupted by unwanted attention.

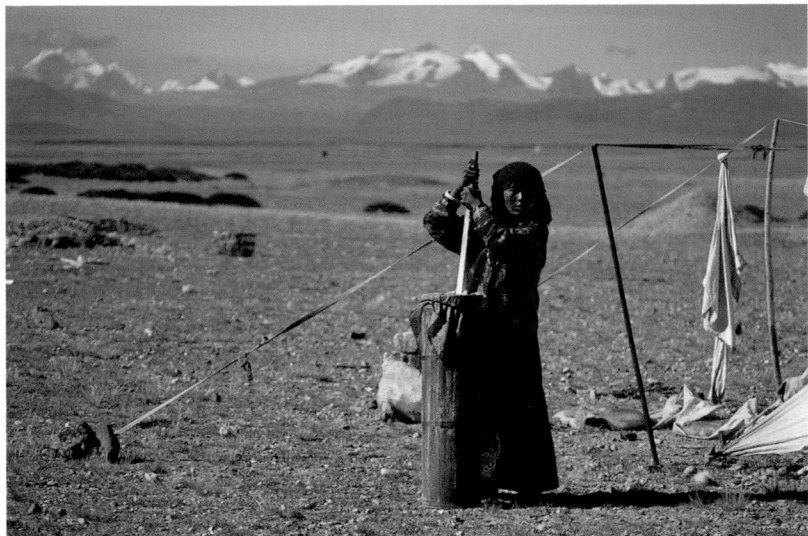

2

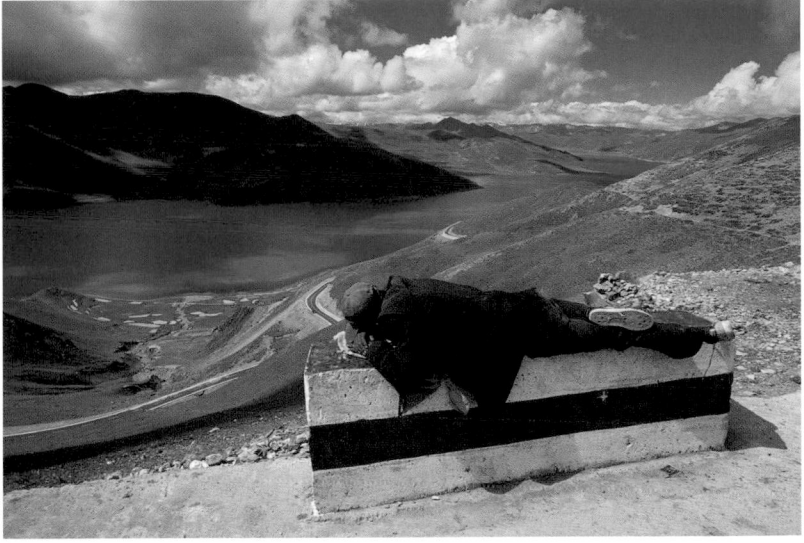

3

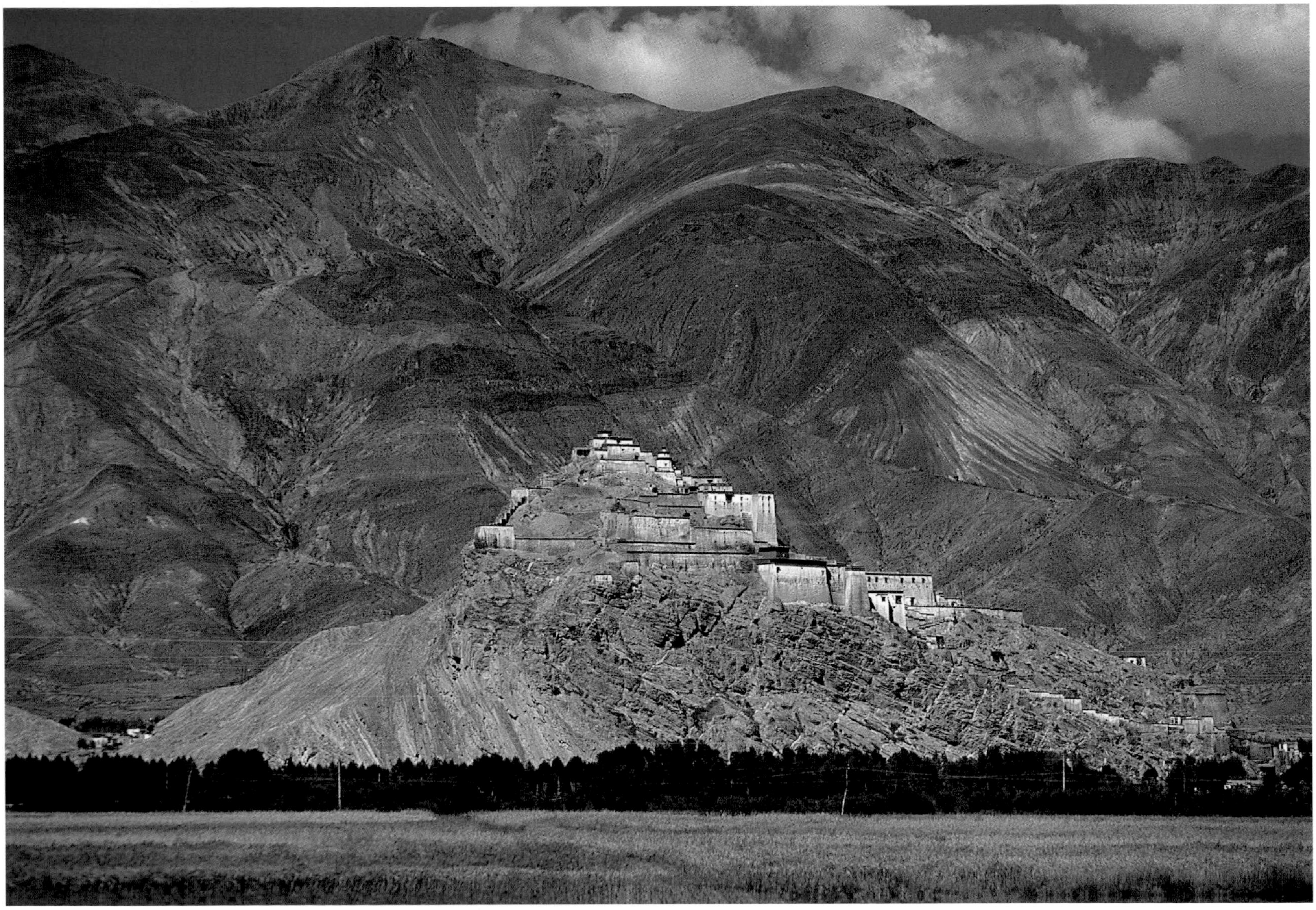

4

THE TASHILUNPO MONASTERY

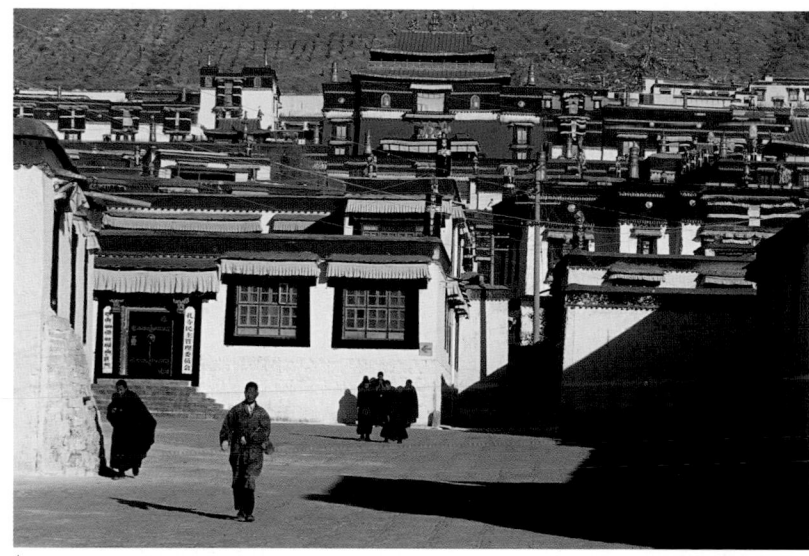

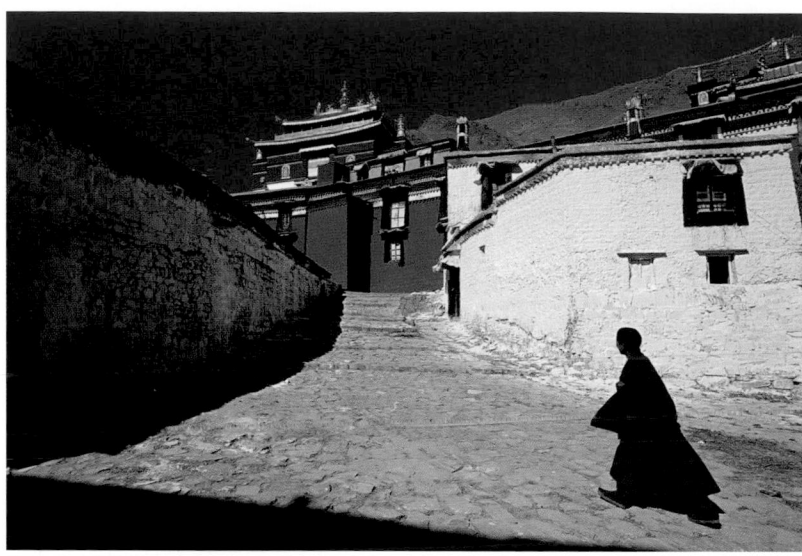

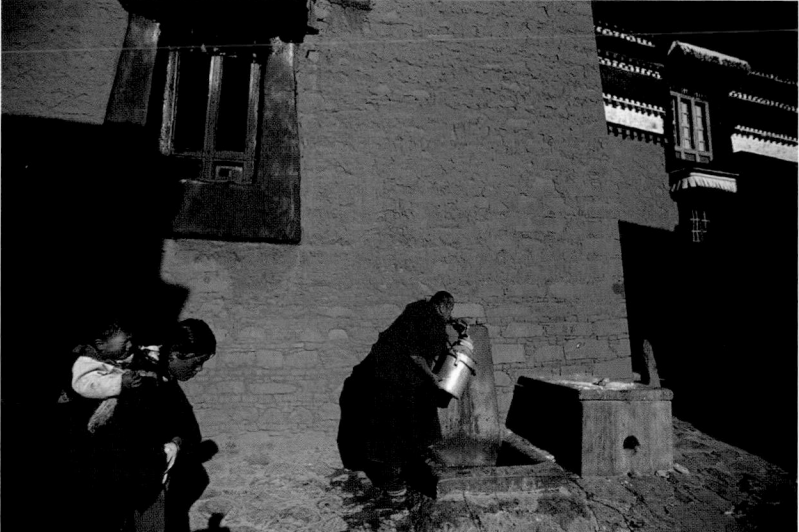

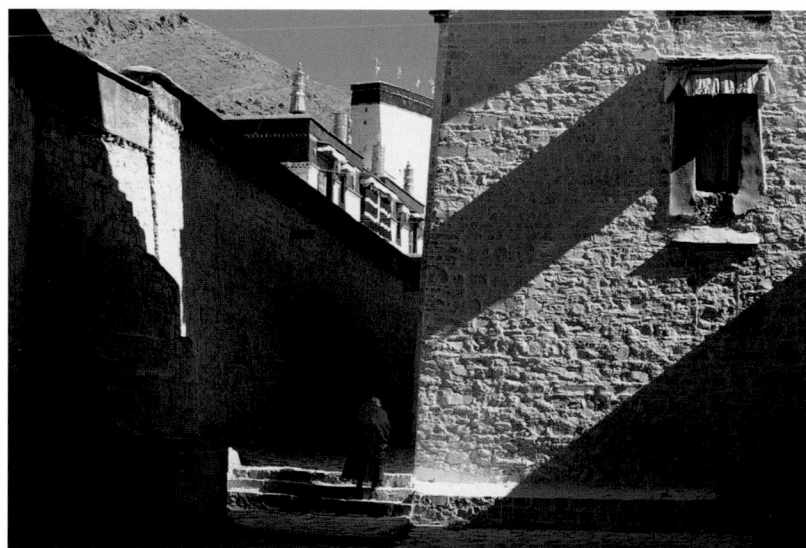

TASHILUNPO IS THE SEAT OF THE PANCHEN LAMA, the second most influential lineage in the Gelugpa (Yellow Hats) order after the Dalai Lama. The monastery has been at the centre of political intrigue and religious and regional rivalries between Lhasa and Shigatse since its foundation in 1447. Ironically perhaps, the Dalai Lama V created the Panchen Lama by deifying his teacher, the Abbot of Tashilunpo. The 'sibling rivalry' between God King and Great Teacher has long been exploited by foreign powers, including Mongols, Manchus, British, Russians and finally the Chinese in their efforts to influence Tibetan politics. Tashilunpo was the only major monastery on the Tibetan Plateau to escape the ravages of China's Cultural Revolution partly because the tenth Panchen Lama was essentially a political prisoner who grew up in Bei'jing. [1] Approaching Tashilunpo. [2] A novice on his way to the Assembly Hall. [3] A monk collects water outside the Chapel of Jampa, which houses the immense statue of Maitreya – the Future Buddha. [4] Whitewashed towers in the monks' quarters. [5] A pilgrim with a large ceremonial oil jug.

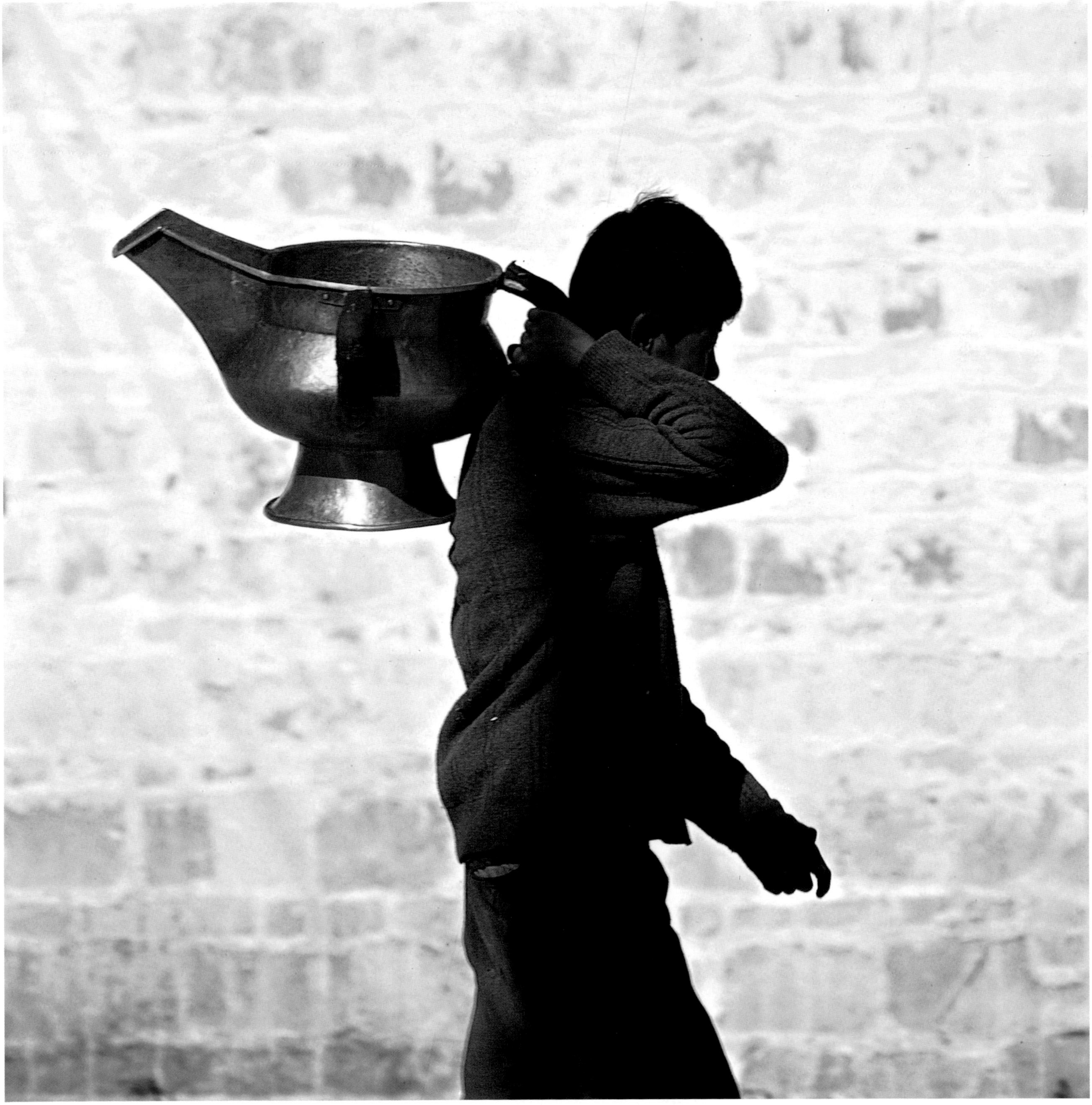

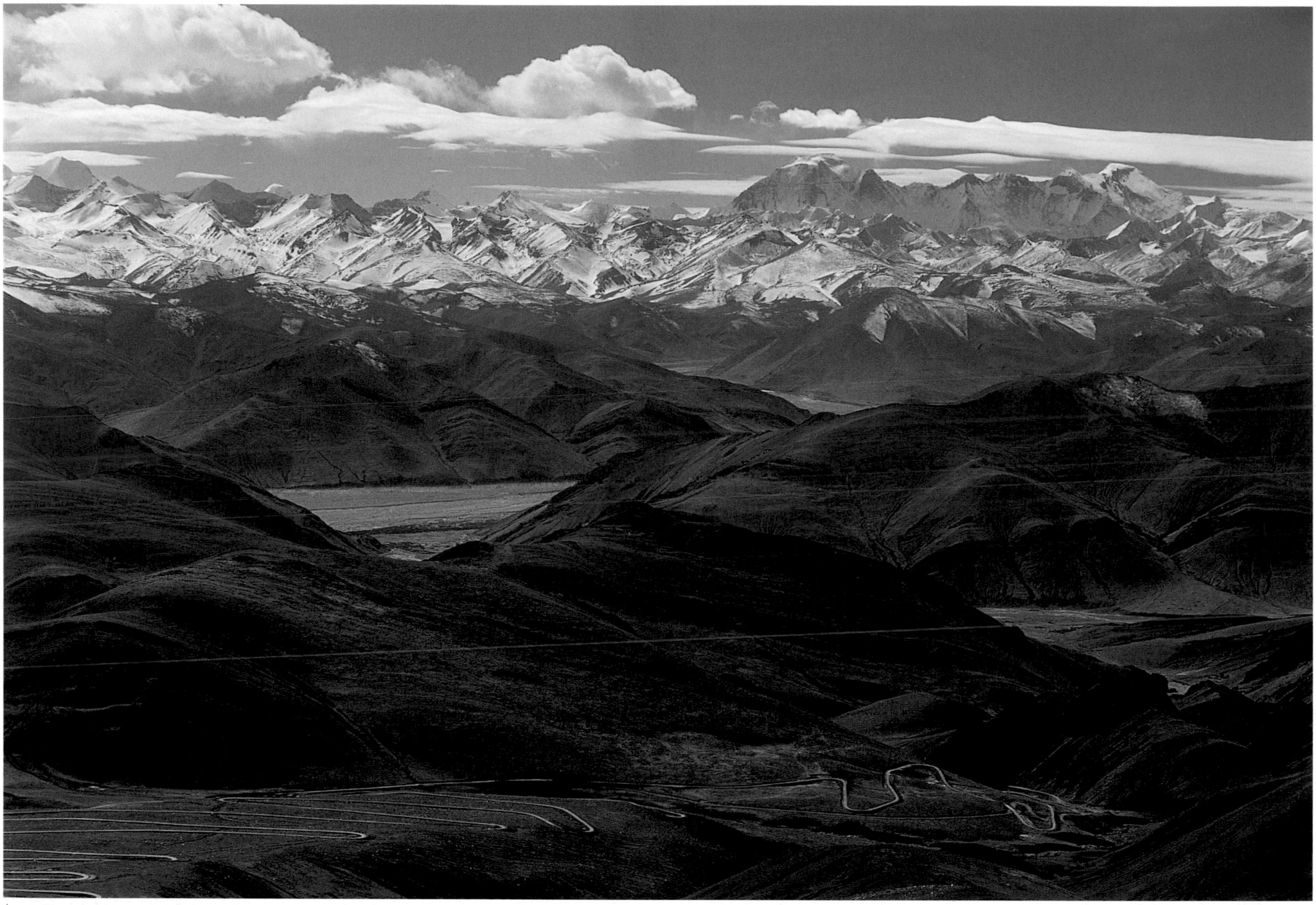

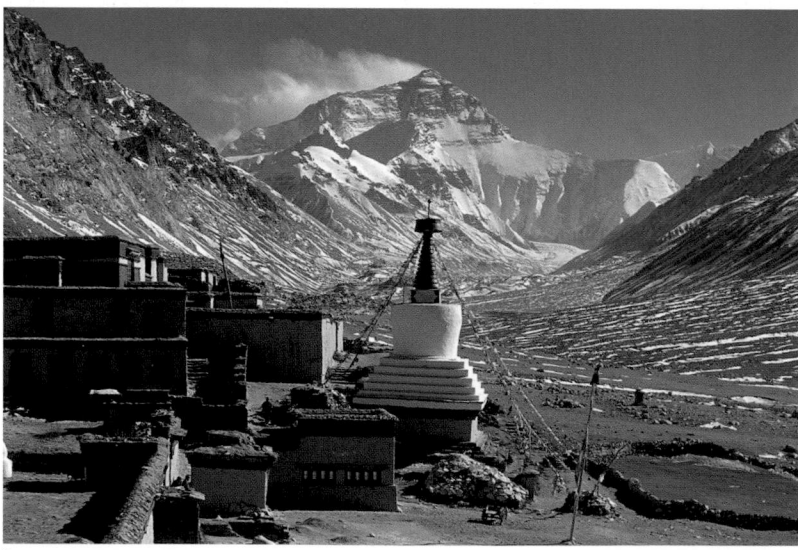

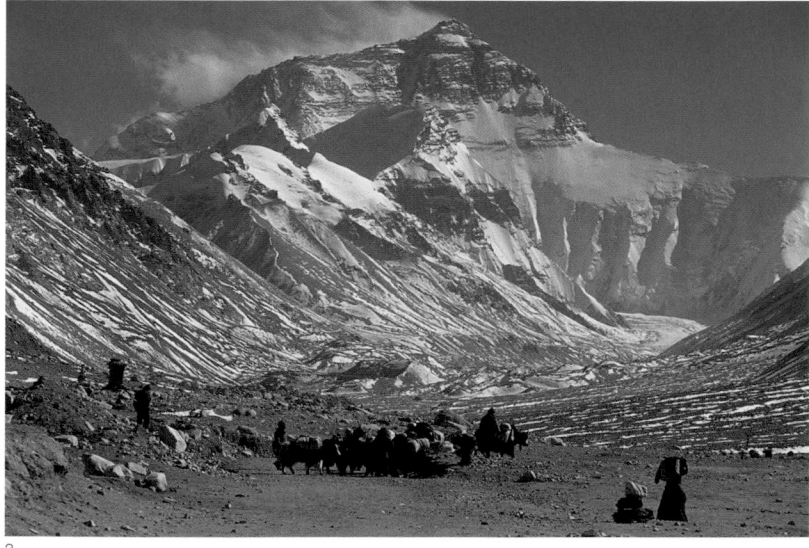

THE NORTH FACE OF PEAK XV

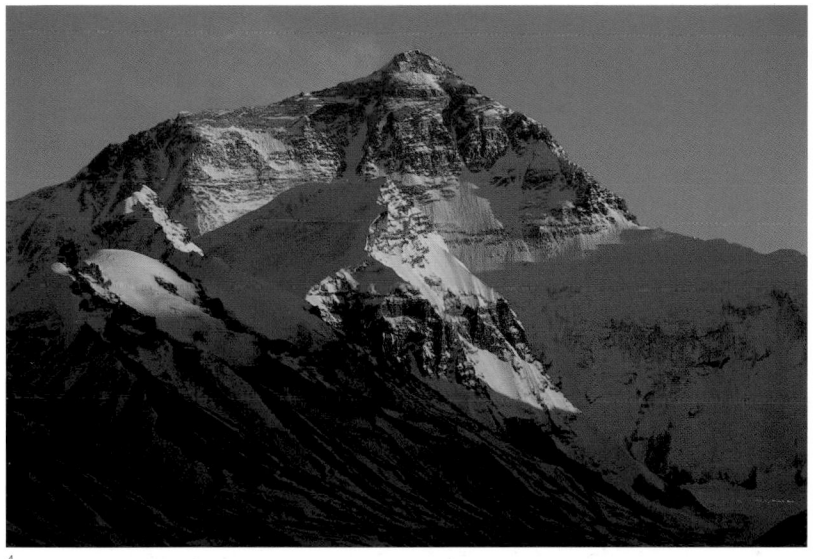

4

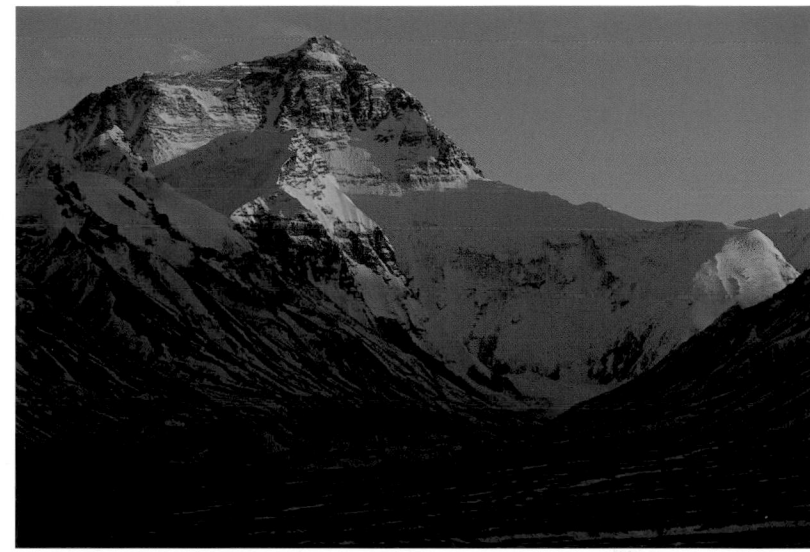

5

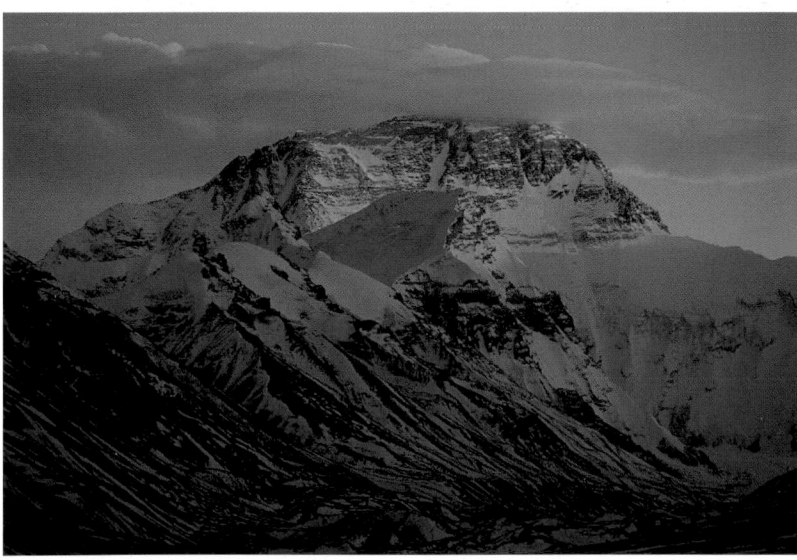

6

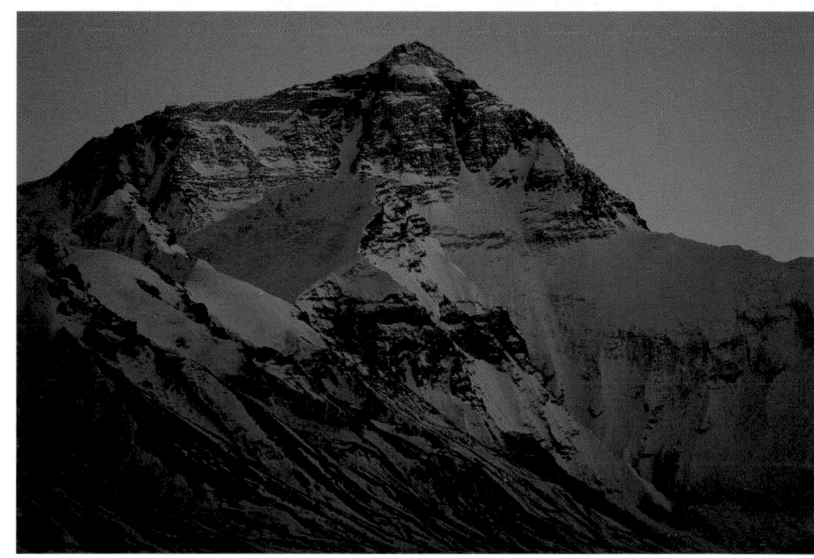

7

GEORGE MALLORY FAMOUSLY REPLIED "because it is there…" when asked why he wanted to climb Mount Everest. Although the mystery as to whether he and his partner Andrew Irvine reached the summit of Everest twenty years ahead of Norgay and Edmund Hillary before vanishing into the Himalayan snows in 1933 may never be resolved, his quip remains a standard retort for unanswerable actions. As I surveyed the mountain, with strings of fluorescent prayer flags fluttering wildly in a blistering wind and the Rongbuk Glacier stretching into the distance, my thought was not "I want to climb that." Rather, it was, "I need a cigarette, a cup of tea – and a bowl of noodles would be nice…" [1] The Himalayan range from Pang'la Pass, where four giant peaks – Xixabangma Feng, Cho Oyo, Lhotse and the Makalu (all over 8,000 metres high) encircle the roof of the world, Qomolangma (Mount Everest) like protective deities. [2] Rongphu is the highest monastery on earth. [3] Nomads moving through Rongbuk Pass. [4-7] North face of Qomolangma – Goddess Mother of the Universe, or the Princess Cow.

THE TIBETAN PLATEAU

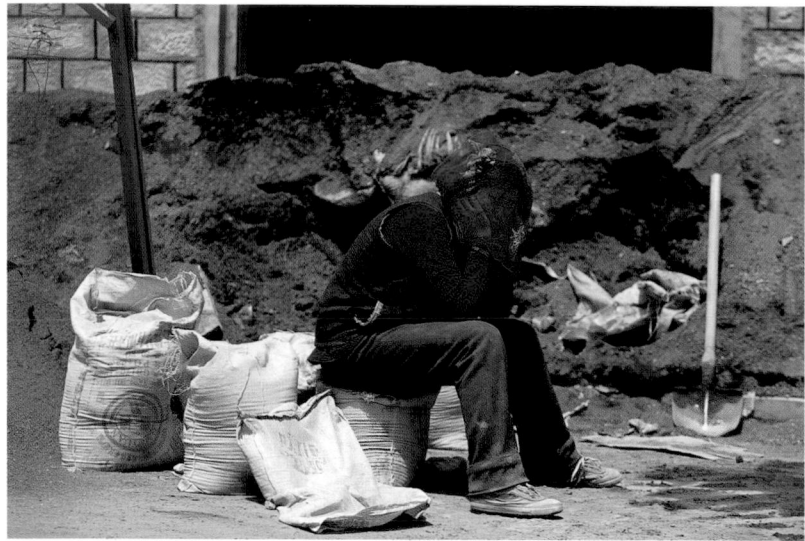

1

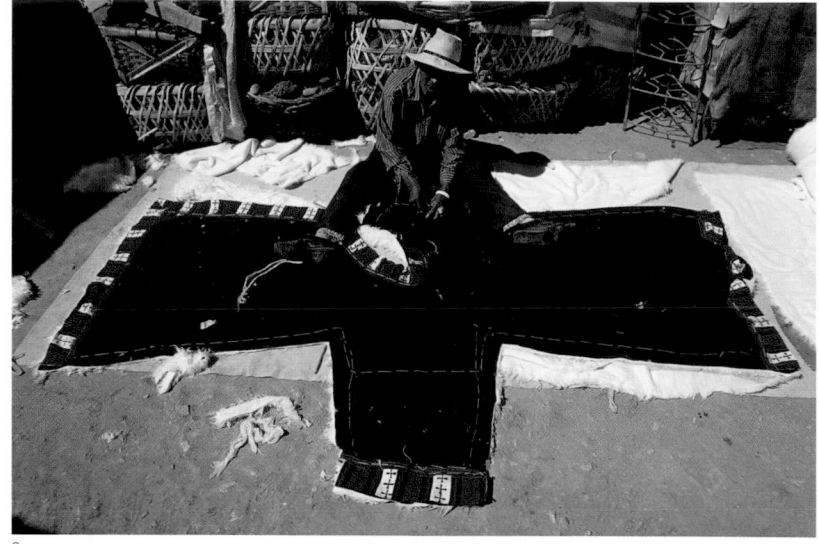

2

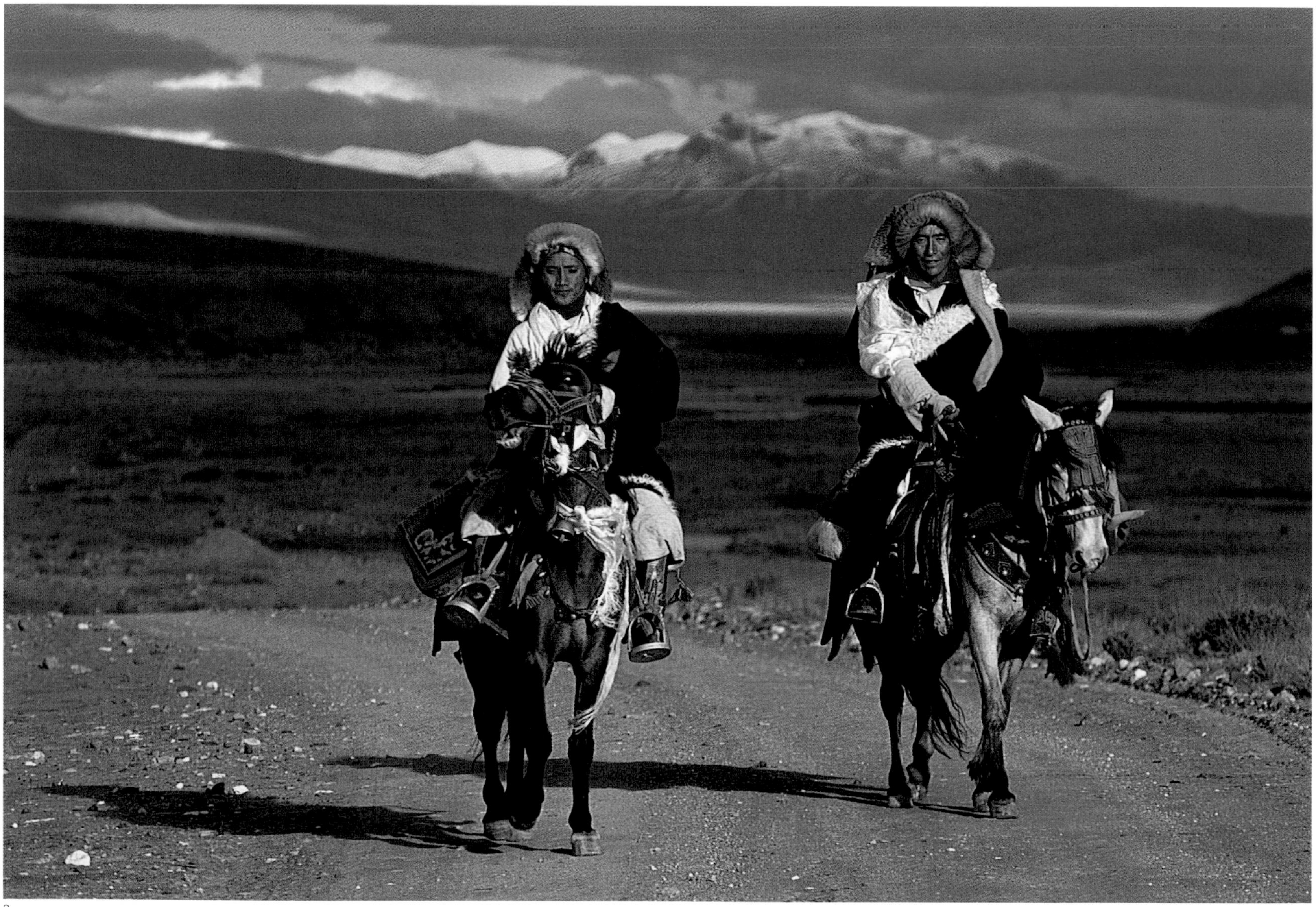

3

ROAD TO THE LAKE OF CONSCIOUSNESS

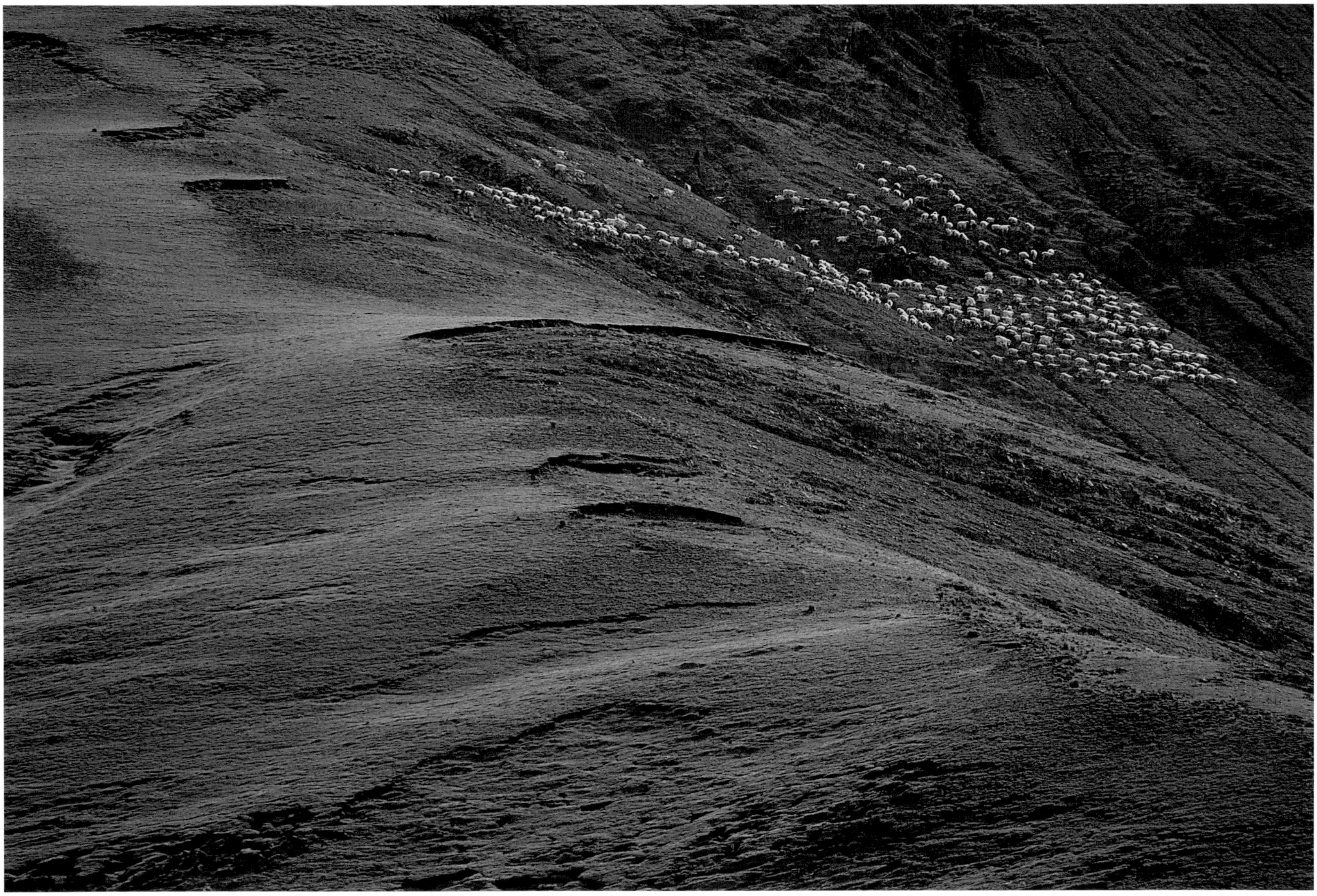

4

THE AIR WAS THIN, the journey long and the road rough. The view beyond the windscreen was harsh and stunning. [1] On the road between Saga and Pa'yang, we came across a nomad family whose teenage daughter was churning yak butter outside their tent, with the great Himalayan range along the Nepalese frontier in the background. It wasn't until we drew closer that I realized the brutal reality beneath the picturesque scene. The whole family, and many others in the region, suffered from arthritis. They asked for medicine, but I had nothing to offer except for a few aspirins. [2] In the small township of Huo'er, a tailor fashions a Tibetan robe. [3] At dusk, horsemen from western Tibet ride towards Lake Manasarovar – 'the ocean of milk manifested from the mind of Brahman'. [4] At first, all I saw here was a mass of tiny white dots, like rice scattered across the mottled green baize of an old pool table. They turned out to be flocks of sheep being driven down to lower pastures away from the approaching winter snows.

THE TIBETAN PLATEAU

365

THE MOUNT KAILASH KORA

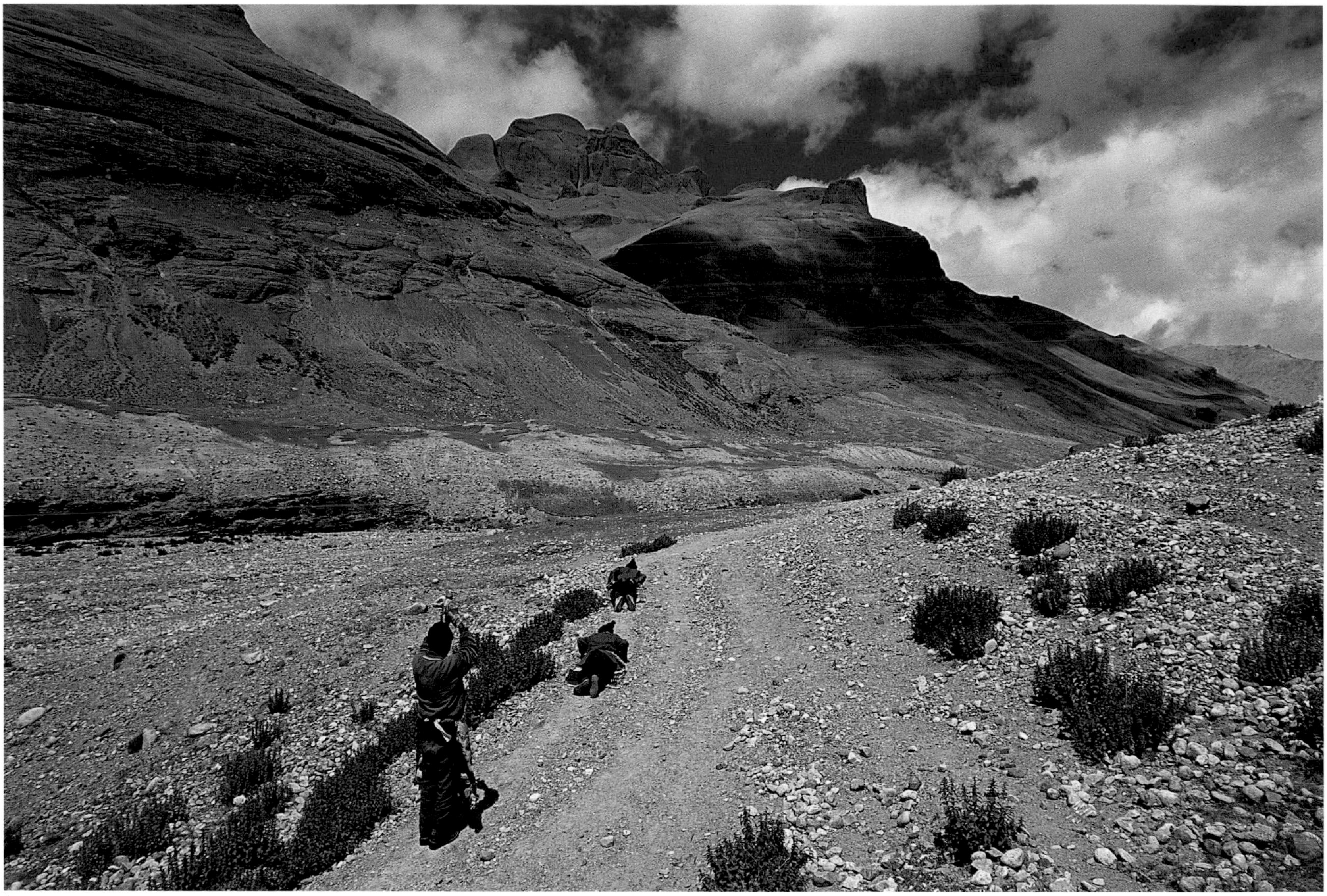

1

THE EVENING BEFORE OUR TREK TO MOUNT KAILASH, the sky turned black at sunset. The hills over Lake Manasarovar glowed in the dark along a thin slither of horizon as a snowstorm swept across the plains to envelop us in Dar'chen. We set off before dawn, with snow on the ground and a sky heavy with bad omens; my Tibetan guides blamed the bad weather squarely on the Hindu pilgrims who had arrived the previous night. The south face of the holy mountain remained behind clouds as we entered the valley from the Darpoche – the Great Prayer Flagpole, a major landmark of the Kailash *kora*. Several hours later, the clouds suddenly lifted to reveal the western face of Kailash, where we caught up with [1] three pilgrims undertaking a 'full-prostration *kora*' around the mountain, which they estimated would take them a month to complete. [2] Tibetan pilgrims. [3] As we neared the Drirapuk Temple beneath the north face of the mountain, we confronted the grim reality of human pollution. [4] A nomad family on the *kora* with all their worldly possessions.

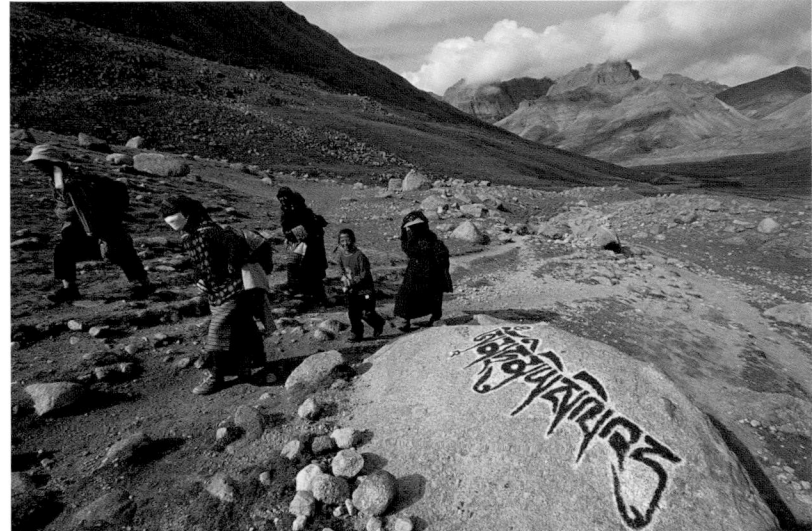

2

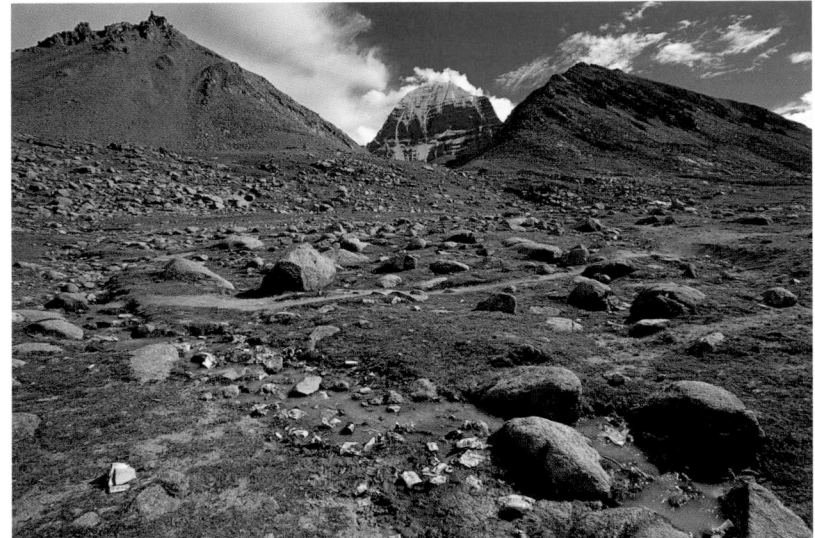

3

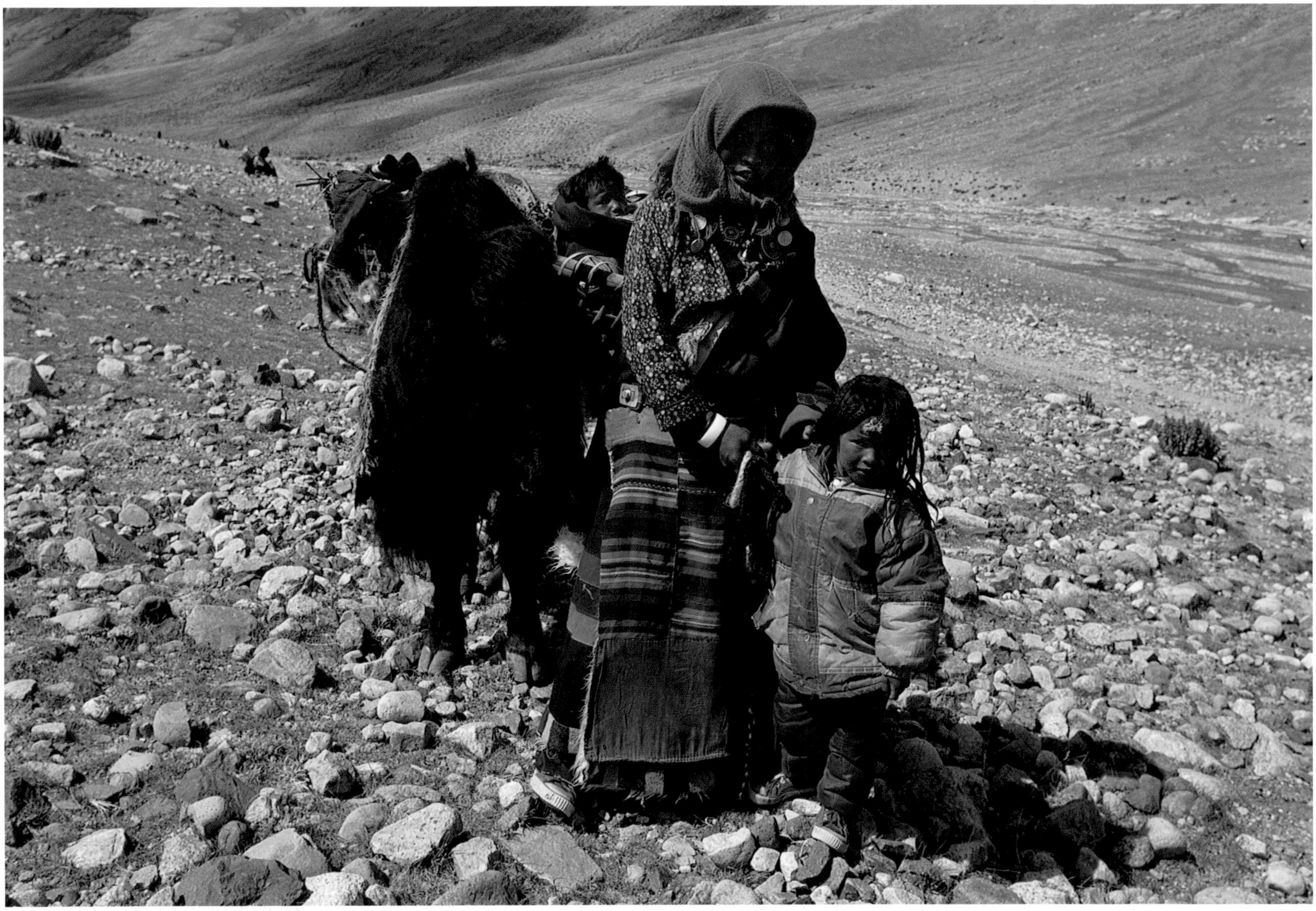

4

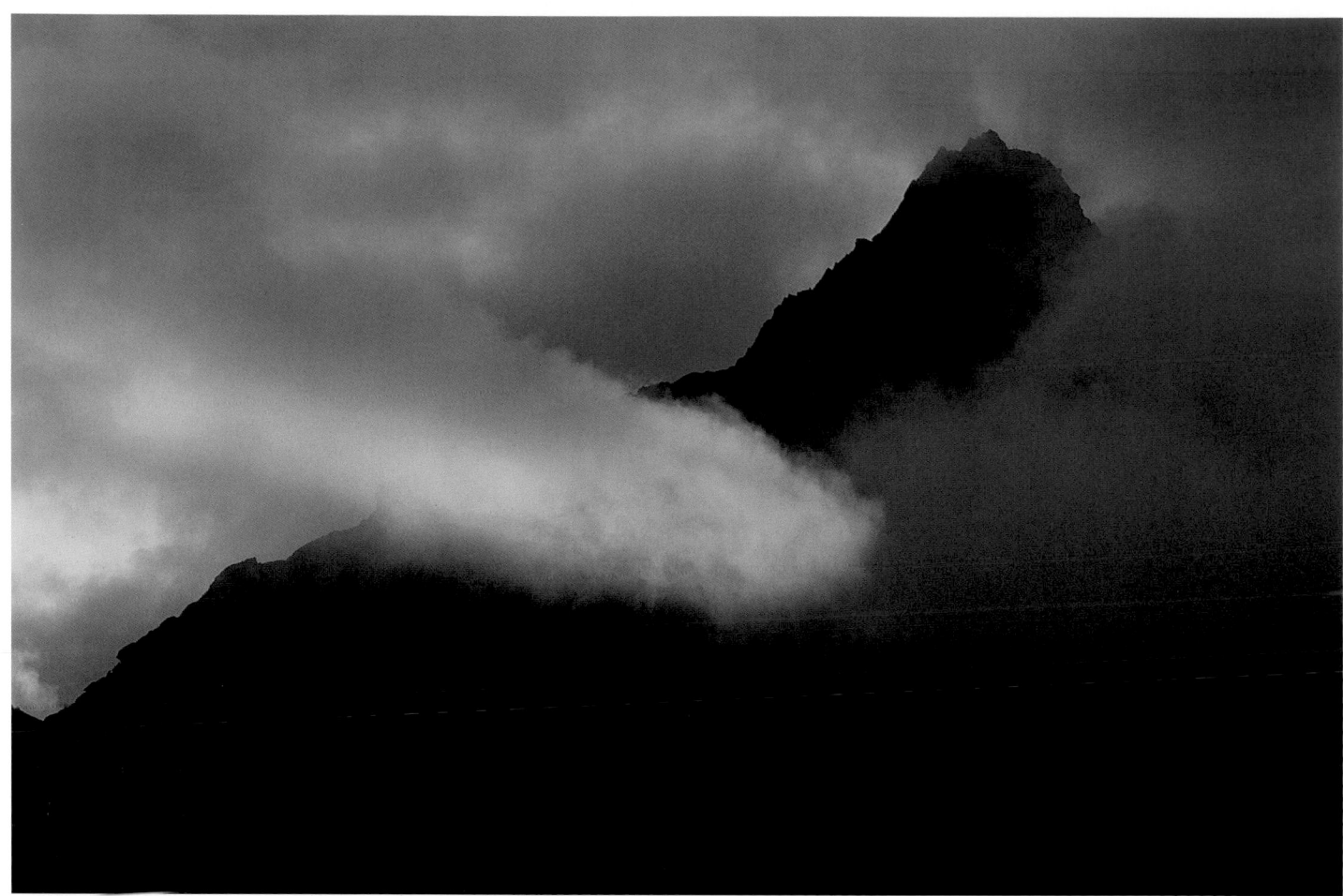

1

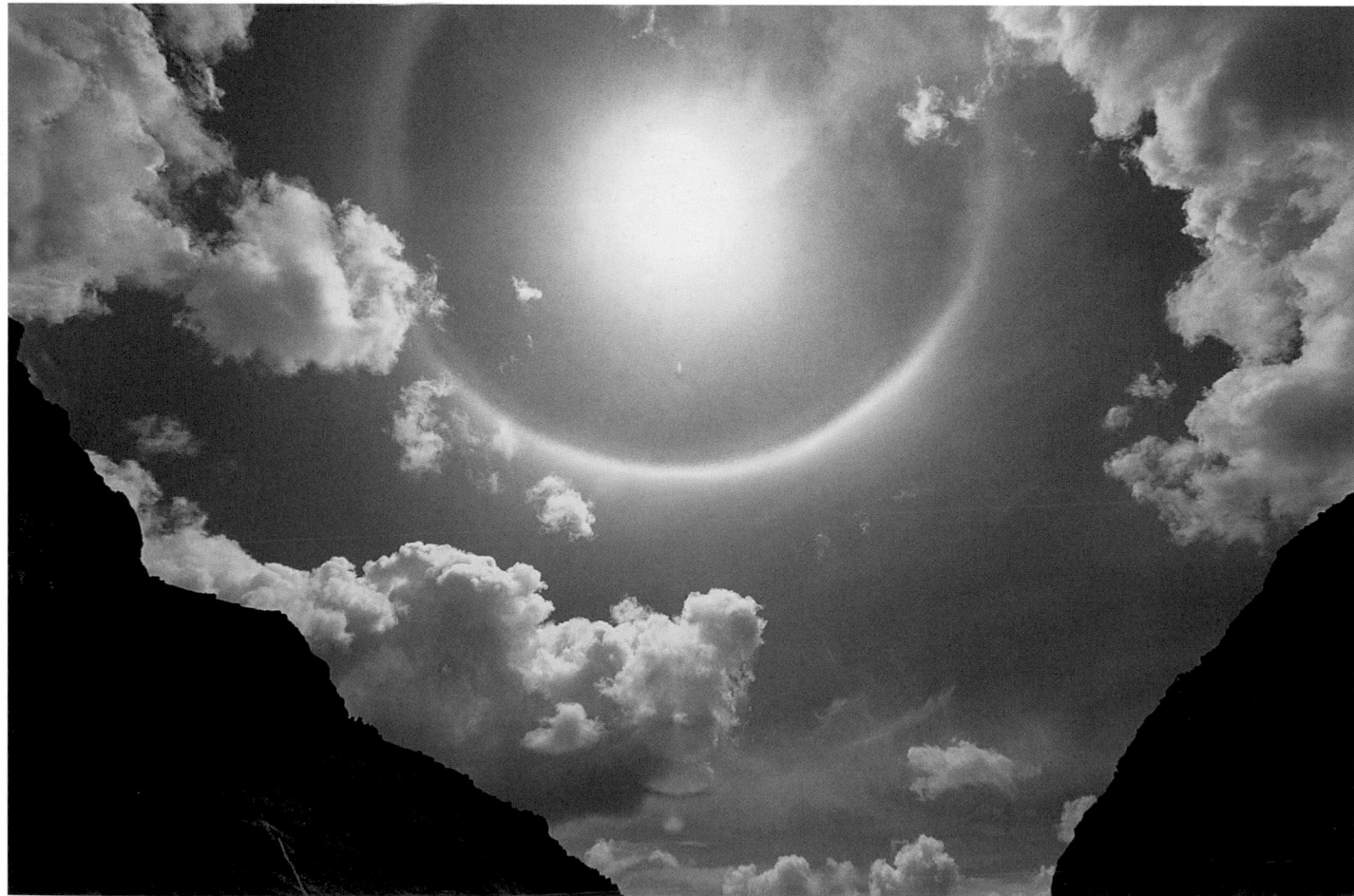

2

THE MYTHICAL MOUNT MERU

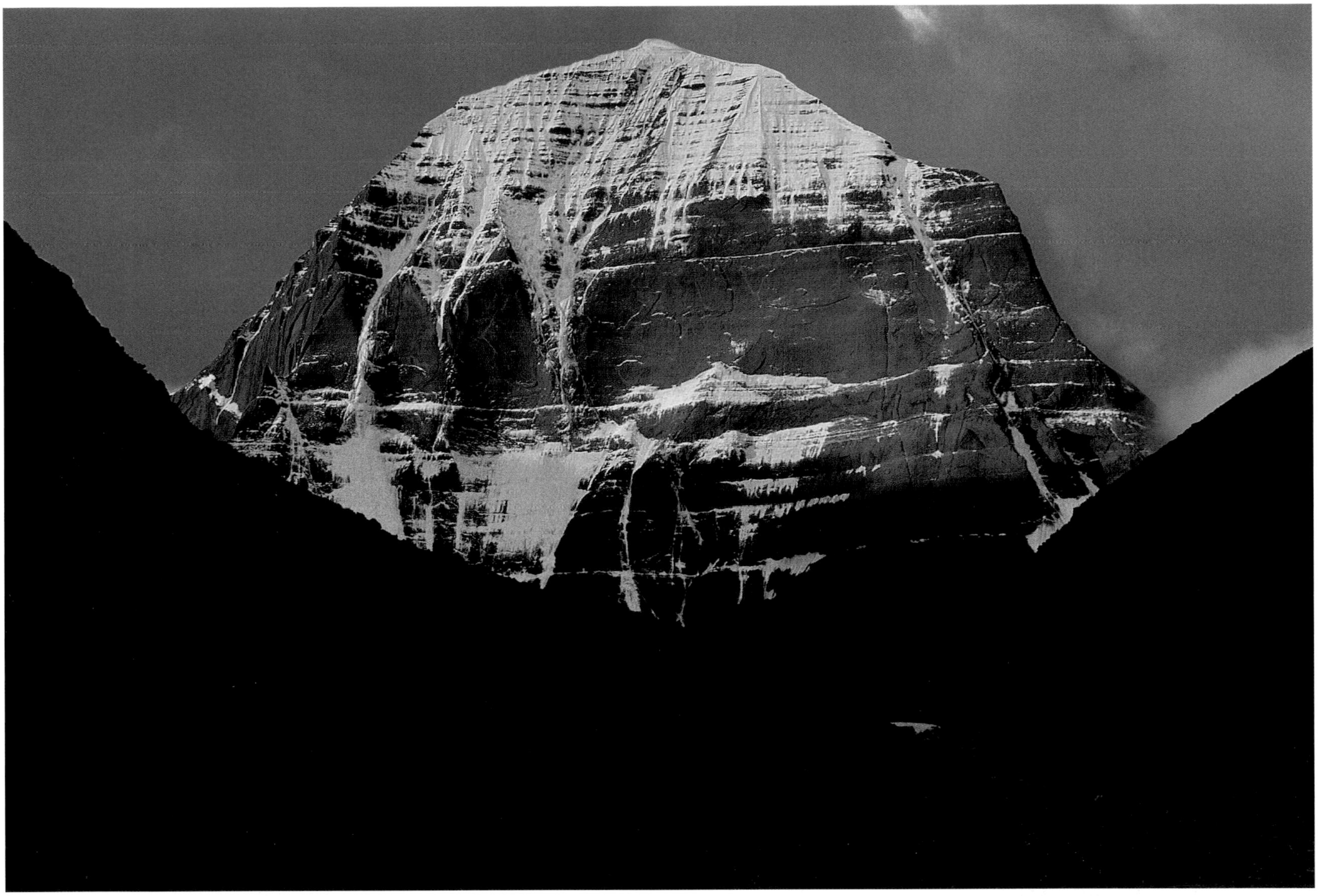

3

KAILASH IS THE MOST SACRED MOUNTAIN IN ASIA. According to the cosmologies and creation myths shared by the Hindu, Jain, Bon and Buddhist religions, it is the mythical Mount Meru, birthplace and the centre of the universe, the abode of the gods. It is a magical place where myth and truth seem to merge seamlessly. The four sheer vertical faces of the monumental 4,714-metre (15,465-foot) black rock correspond to the cardinal points on the compass, with a great river rising in each direction around it. The Indus flows to the north, eventually reaching the Arabian Sea. The Kanali flows south to become a tributary of the Ganges. The Brahmaputra flows east along the length of the Himalayas. The Sutlej debouches from Lake Mansarovar to head west into Pakistan. These rivers and their tributaries provide water to support the livelihood of countless millions of people across the sub-continent. [1] Clouds moving in towards Kailash. [2] A full rainbow appeared overhead as I staggered out of the valley at the end of the trek. [3] The north face of Mount Kailash.

THE TIBETAN PLATEAU

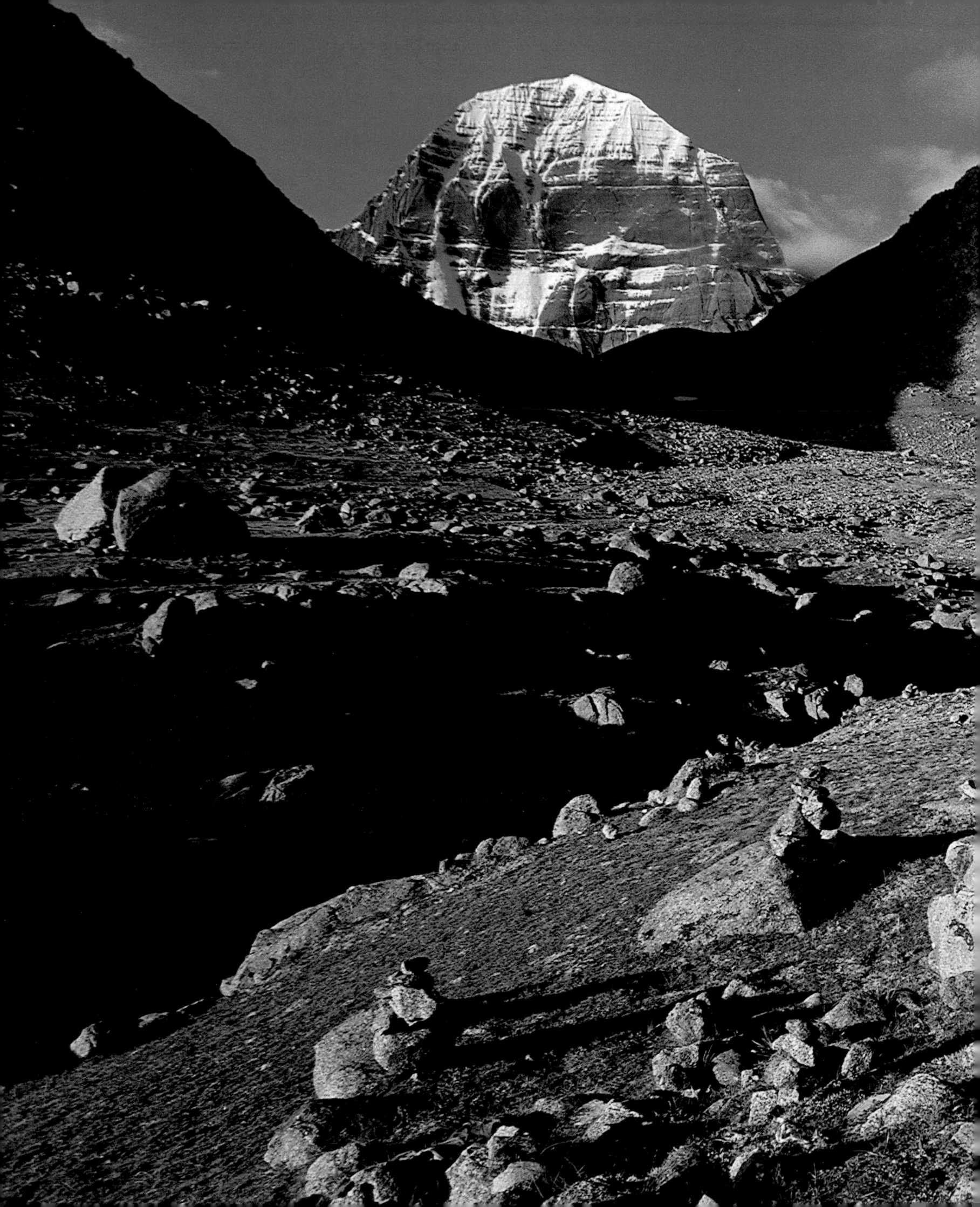

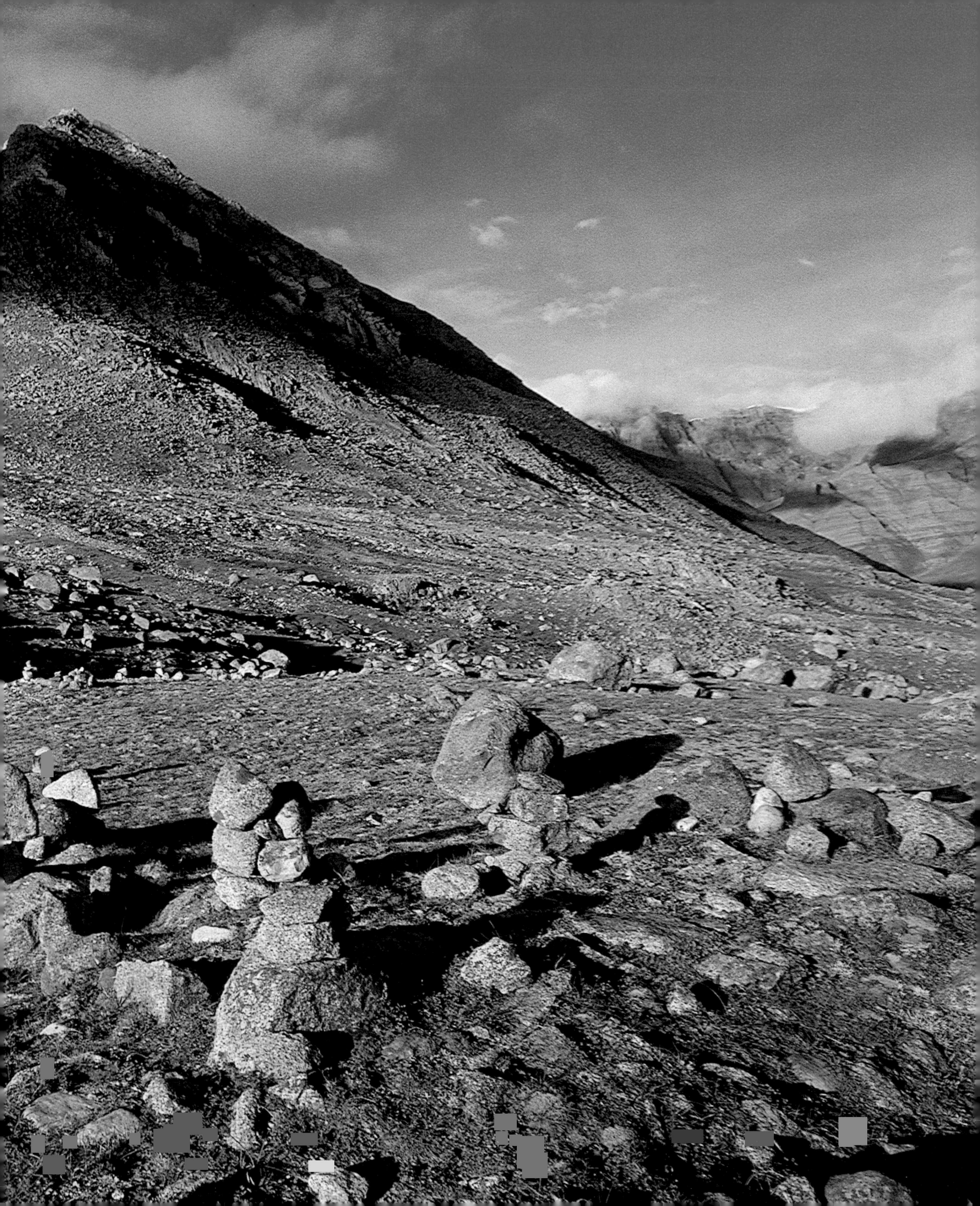

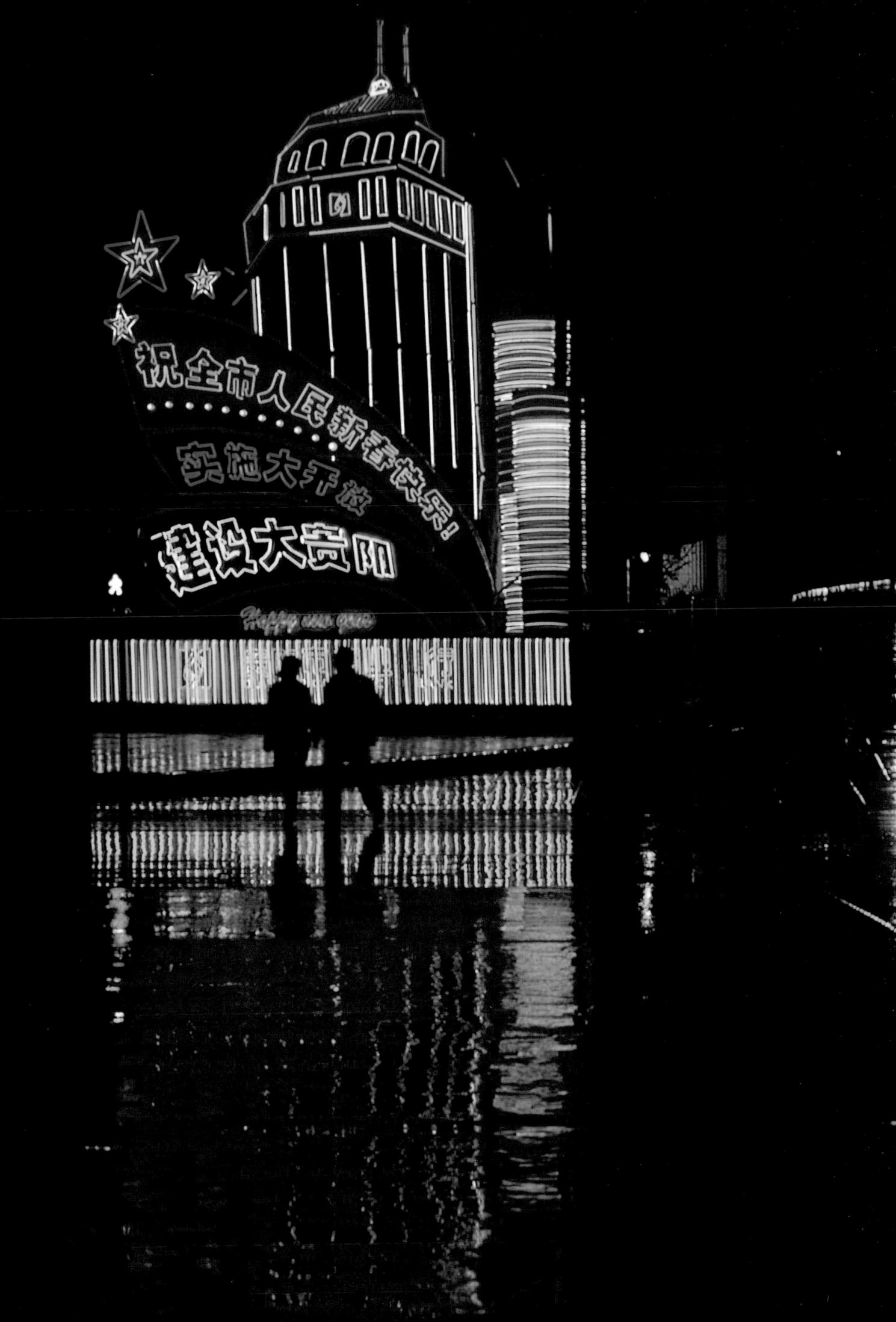

THE GREAT GAME AND THE DRY MARTINI
OR
BIG TREE ATTRACTS WIND

The vodka-martini slides down smoothly and slips into a stream of consciousness that is reserved exclusively for the club. For the past twenty-odd years since my return to Hong Kong, the Main Bar of the FCC (Foreign Correspondents Club) has been my refuge from the merciless and the insane. It is my home away from home now. Each time I return after weeks of photography on the mainland, it is the second place I come to after I've dropped off my bags, the first stop being Mak's for a bowl of wonton noodles.

I do not normally indulge in martinis at 4:30 in the afternoon, but today is special. I have just come back from the last journey for this project and I am in the mood to celebrate. Even if it's just with the bartenders, since there is no one else here at this hour except for the solicitors in 'Lawyers' Corner' at the far end of the bar who are still finishing their lunch. My band of alcoholic brothers, with whom I indulge in conversations and debates in which no subject is out of bounds, no conspiracy theory too wild, and no joke too vile or politically incorrect, will not start drifting in until after six, so I'm in for a very long night. But that's just fine because I could do with a bit of solitude before getting royally plastered.

After all the years of gestation and thirteen months of relentless travelling, I have managed to see almost all the places in China I've always dreamt of seeing. Though I didn't always manage to capture it all on film, I have been there and experienced it and most importantly, I have finally done it. I have stared the dragon in the face without blinking, and, hopefully, exorcized the beast from my system for good. Feeling exhausted and drained but relieved and elated at the same time, I order up another martini, very dry with a twist, with Polish vodka this time.

Perhaps because I have misspent so much of my adult life here, draped over the bar or hunched over a pool table in the basement, I love everything about the club. Even its undeserved reputation as being the place where 'women with a past meet men without a future' makes me feel comfortable and secure, it's like a womb with a full bar. I like the fact that I had read about the 'urinals with a harbour view' in the old club at Sutherland House in John Le Carré's The *Honourable Schoolboy* long before I ever relieved myself there. I love the idea that after a night of serious drinking, I can bare my soul and reveal my darkest secrets to practical strangers at the bar, knowing that they won't remember a thing in the morning. Above all, I love the fact that it has been a bastion for the free press in China since its inception in Chong'qing in 1943, when a handful of foreign journalists formed the club to fight the Chang Kai'shek government for their right to tell the truth about the Japanese war. From its Shang'hai days, when two members were almost executed by the Kuo'min'tang in 1949 for reporting the imminent victory of the communists, to its 'good ol' days' as the premier watering hole for journalists and photographers covering the Vietnam War, right up until today, where it remains the place in post-handover Hong Kong where people can speak their minds, and sometimes tell the truth.

I remember one particularly long session that went on until well after the bartenders went home at 2 am. It was the night former Secretary of State Colin Powell did his 'Cuban Missile Crisis' act at the UN, holding up a phiall of a 'deadly chemical substance' that could have been anything, and showing photographs of 'Mobile Biological Weapons Labs' that later turned out to be vehicles producing helium for weather balloons. The news item was endlessly repeating itself on the overhead screen tuned to CNN as a debate raged on at the bar as to whether the U.S. would invade Iraq. A few seats away from our increasingly noisy group, a large man sat alone in silence,

[LEFT] Rainy night in Gui'yang, Gui'zhou province. [PRECEDING PAGES] Mount Kailash.

slumped over the bar sipping his drink and staring at the extra whiskies he'd ordered at the last call, which were lined up in front of him like ceremonial guards. Suddenly he stood up, stumbled and almost fell off his stool. We glanced over just as he said, in a heavy Aussie accent, "You idiots can argue about this all you want, the war is going to happen whether you like it or not…" He drained his drink before continuing, slurring his words, "It's going to start at the end of February, because we've booked satellite time…" He steadied himself as he turned to leave, "I've just sent my boys to Kuwait today…" His voice trailed off as tears welled up in his eyes. He turned away from us and staggered out of the bar, leaving his extra whiskies behind.

Though he was off by a few weeks, I still think about that man sometimes, especially at times like this when I am sitting quietly at the bar alone, rummaging through the darker crevasses of my memories. I wonder whether it is morally reprehensible that we finished the whiskies he left behind when the man was clearly in such pain. But more often, I think of him because he opened my eyes to the fact that in the information age, the Military Industrial Complex, whose 'acquisition of unwarranted influence' President Eisenhower warned America about in his 1961 speech before he left office, must now be updated to read the Military Media Industrial Empire.

On the column behind me hangs a framed *TIME* magazine cover from June 19th 1989, with the iconic photograph of a Bei'jing man with his groceries trying to stop the tanks on Chang'an Avenue. The headline reads "Revolt Against Communism – China, Poland, USSR". It reminds me of the many discussions we've had about how that event cast a permanent shadow over the way the world viewed China, and how it fundamentally changed the nature of news coverage by putting the '24–7' news cycle on the map. Amongst my friends who covered the Tian'an'men 'incident', some argued that the massacre could have and should have been avoided, and the moment it should have ended was when the students called off the hunger strike after Zhou Zi'yang's tearful plea in the early hours of May 19th – if only the naïve student leaders had been willing to relinquish their '15 minutes of fame' in front of a worldwide audience. Others believe it was the influence of Tai'wan, Hong Kong and the CIA, pointing to the millions of dollars that were pouring into Tian'an'men Square towards the end and the swift evacuation of student leaders to America through Triad smuggling networks afterwards as evidence. The opposing camp thought that the *High Noon* showdown was inevitable, because that was what all the parties involved had wanted – the students, the media, the covert forces and particularly Deng Xiao'ping, who was determined to cleanse his humiliation with blood, and demonstrate to the world that the people must 'tremble and obey' the emperor's edicts. One thing we all agreed on was that it told the world in no uncertain terms that China was not going to loose the shackles of its Confucian-imperial past and change into a western-style democracy overnight.

"Another one, Mr Pao?" A voice from the friendly face behind the bar lifts me out of my reverie. I nod absently as I turn around to look at the picture of the man with the tanks again, remembering vividly the anger and outrage I felt back then. My bitterness has evaporated with time; in its place is a deep sadness for the victims and a quiet resignation at the futility of pitching human frailty against the tide of history. Everyone involved felt they were doing what they *had* to do. Unfortunately, they were all wrong. My friends who knew me back then are often amazed by the sea change in my attitude towards China since I started this book. I have gone being from a detractor who mistrusted everything about the place a few years ago to becoming practically a cheerleader, regaling them with tales of

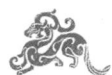

encounters with wonderful people and special local dishes in astonishing far-off places, away from the hustle and pollution of the cities that they all know. I have been most impressed by how hard the ordinary people work in this country, how frugal they are in the way they live, and how generous they are to total strangers like me. And how, like the proletariat the world over, their greatest desire is for their children to have a better life than they did. But my friends seem to prefer the stories about the despicable parasites on the other end of the human spectrum.

Even though I know there is nothing I can do about the environmental degradation, the unemployment, the income gap, the corruption and crime, the people's fashion sense, and the host of other problems facing China, I have become almost obsessive about worrying for its future. I worry that the country has become too rich – with enough foreign exchange reserves to buy all the gold bricks in the bank vaults of the world twice over. I worry whether the government will spend this new-found wealth wisely or catch the 'more money than sense' disease and spend it all on trophy projects like the biggest this or the tallest that. Or worse, hand the riches over to PLA generals, sucking China into an arms race with America, just like the Soviet Union during the Cold War. But maybe they will spend it on developing renewable energy to replace those evil-smelling, toxic, coal-fired plants, or on rescuing the badly depleted environment, or on improving the lot of the peasants. Perhaps now is the time to finally fulfill the party's long-neglected promise of giving the land back to the farmers who till it; for most experts agree that private land ownership is the most important reform that the current and future regimes must tackle if China is to avoid the violent upheaval of another 'peasant revolution'.

I worry about the new Great Game. Ever since the first battle between bands of cavemen for the possession of a campfire, mankind has been fighting over natural resources and the territories that contain them. In the 21st Century, energy, in the form of fossil fuel, is what everyone is after, and the stakes are slightly higher than the risk of being hit on the head with a dinosaur bone. America's foreign policy, based on the neo-conservative's central doctrine, formulated after the fall of the Berlin wall and the collapse of the 'Evil Empire', seeks to ensure that the USA remains the sole superpower on the planet. And the attempt to stop any other country from trying to become one by any means possible – by force if necessary – has led to American adventurism abroad. Their conduct in the Iraq war has left the World's Only Superpower with few friends, and all its neighbours in the global village suspicious of its true intentions. With America stuck in this quagmire of its own making and its prestige at an all-time low, China has been dragged from the delivery room kicking and screaming, a 'premature superpower' in an incubator, thrust onto the centre-stage before an audience hungry for a new act. It is a role that China is not fully prepared for and may not even desire – because of the conventional wisdom encompassed in the old Chinese saying, that 'Big tree attracts wind'.

Most of all, I worry that I worry so much about the country that until recently I knew so little about, and for which I felt nothing apart from animosity and a vague curiosity – indeed, one that I once hated with a passion. Just then, I feel the dragon rising up inside me, but instead of the fear and loathing I always used to feel whenever it stirred, there is a great warmth enveloping my being as it takes flight, and a mysterious sensation of peace with the beast within – or is it just the martinis kicking in?

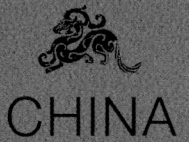

CHINA	ASIA	EUROPE	OTHER
9,000–8,000 BCE			
Pottery produced in Xianrendong.	Wheat harvested, sheep domesticated in Middle East.	Glaciers retreat as the Ice Age ends.	Cultivation of grains, beans, peppers in Peru.
7,999–5,000 BCE			
Farm communities develop, animals domesticated and rice cultivation starts along the Yang'tze River.	Irrigation in Mesopotamia leads to creation of first city (Sumer).	Copper and gold metalworking.	Cattle domesticated in the Sahara region of North Africa.
4,999–3,000 BCE			
Jade imported from what is now Siberia and used in ornaments.	Wheel developed in Mesopotamia (Iraq).	Draught animals pull simple plough. First wheeled vehicles.	First sailing boats developed in Egypt on the River Nile.

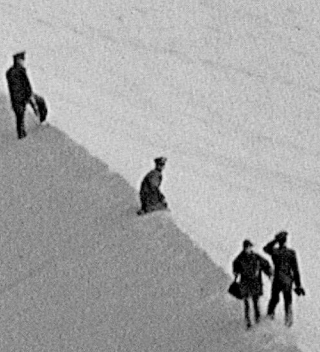

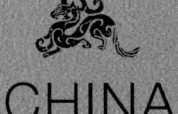

CHINA ASIA EUROPE OTHER

2,999–1,000 BCE

Silk weaving starts. Bronze, inks, lacquers, wheel-thrown pottery developed.

Rise and fall of the Indus civilization.

600–1450 Rise and fall of Minoan civilisation.

2575–1650 Pyramids built in Egypt.

1666–1045 Shang Dynasty, China's first fully documented period of imperial rule.

1650 Hittite empire destroys Babylon.

1030 Kingdom of Israel founded.

1600 Stonehenge completed in southern Britain.

2200 Temple of the Fox in Peru – the earliest man-made structure in the Americas.

1325 Tutankhamun buried in the Valley of the Kings.

999 BCE–1 CE

Chinese script fully developed, iron plough invented.

612 Defeat of the Assyrian empire by Babylon.

600 Rise of the Etruscan states in Italy.

950 Early Mayan civilization (Central America).

551–479 Confucius

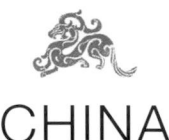

CHINA   ASIA   EUROPE   OTHER

999 BCE–1 CE

China

Silk Road between China and the West opens.

221–210 Qin Shi Huangdi, first emperor of China.

221 Work begins on the Great Wall.

206 Beginning of Han Dynasty.

Asia

566–486 Siddartha Gautama, founder of Buddhism.

490 Athenians defeat the Persians at Battle of Marathon.

480 Greeks defeat the Persians at Salamis.

63 Rome occupies Judah (Israel).

Europe

256–223 Alexander the Great conquers Egypt, campaigns as far east as India.

Other

30 Queen Cleopatra commits suicide in Egypt.

1–200 CE

China

50 New Han Dynasty introduces Buddhism.

150 Paper invented by Cai Lun.

200 Stern-mounted rudder, watertight compartments, multiple masts for shipping in use.

200 Hydraulic power, chain pumps widely introduced.

Asia

33 Jesus Christ crucified.

66–73 Revolt against Rome in Judah leads to diaspora (dispersal of the Jews).

100 Indonesian mariners reach coast of East Africa.

150 First recorded Sanskrit inscription in India.

Europe

43 Roman occupation of Britain.

116–117 Roman power at its zenith.

180 Death of Emperor Marcus Aurelius marks start of decline of Roman empire.

Other

90–168 Egyptian mathematician and astronomer Ptolemy lays foundations of modern mapmaking.

150 Pyramid of the Sun, the largest pre-colonial building in the Americas, completed at Teotihuacan (Mexico).

201–400 CE

China

220 Han Dynasty replaced by the Three Kingdoms and Jin Dynasty.

300 Porcelain in production. Magnetic compass and stirrup developed.

Asia

300 Creation of Yamato state in Japan.

320 Foundation of Gupta empire in Northern India.

Europe

330 Rome divides into two empires with new centre in Constantinople.

380 Christianity becomes the official religion of the Roman empire.

Other

100 Anasazi culture, marked by adobe buildings, basic farming and weaving, develops in southwestern United States.

300–400 Beginning of cattle herding in Southern Africa.

401–600 CE

China

500 The Indian monk Bodhidharma credited with introducing Zen Buddhism to China.

553 Silkworms smuggled to Europe, damaging trade.

Asia

500 India's Gupta empire destroyed by Huns.

500 Indian mathematicians introduce concept of 'zero'.

540 Buddhism reaches Japan.

570 Mohammad, the Prophet of Islam, born in Mecca.

Europe

410 Visigoths sack Rome, signalling end to the empire.

450 Angle, Saxon and Jute invasions of Britain.

Other

500 Polynesian migration from Southeast Asia reaches Hawaii and other western Pacific islands.

601–800 CE

China

610 Grand Canal between Yang'tze and Chang'an completed.

618 Tang Dynasty begins.

751 Defeat by Arab armies at Talas (Central Asia) marks centuries of military decline.

700 Gunpowder, firearms and rockets developed for warfare.

Asia

622 Mohammad and his followers leave Mecca for Medina (the Hijrah) an event that begins the Muslim conquests and serves as the start of the Islamic calendar.

632 Mohammad dies.

650 Koran written. Islam separates into Sunni and Shia strands.

645–784 Japan adopts Chinese system of government. Nara becomes country's first capital.

Europe

700 Muslim armies occupy much of Spain.

742–814 Charlemagne, founder of the Holy Roman Empire, begins unification of Europe in France, Germany.

732 Charles Martel halts Islamic expansion into Europe at the French city of Tours.

787 Viking raids against Britain begin.

Other

600 High point of the Mayan empire (Central America).

633–642 Muslim Arab armies conquer Egypt, Palestine, Mesopotamia, the North African coast, parts of the Persian and Byzantine Empires.

801–1000 CE

China

800 Block printing developed.

845 Buddhism banned in favour of Confucianism.

868 First printed book, Jingang Jing (Diamond Sutra), produced.

Asia

800 Angkor (Cambodia) and Borobudur (Java) temple complexes built.

820 Persian mathematician develops algebraic system.

Europe

850–1000 Viking influence stretches from Constantinople to North America.

Other

787–809 Harun al-Rashid, Caliph of Baghdad, whose reign forms the basis for *The Book of 1,001 Nights*.

800 Arab and Persian navigators establish trading posts down the East African coast.

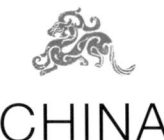

CHINA   ASIA   EUROPE   OTHER

801–1000 CE

907 Tang Dynasty collapses, leading to years of warfare.

960 Song Dynasty restores unity.

970 Paper money introduced, creating inflation and bankrupting the state.

893 Japan's emperor orders end to commercial relations with China.

939 Ngo Quyen drives the Chinese from Vietnam to become first head of the new country.

849–899 Alfred the Great becomes the first English king after defeating the Danes.

975 Modern mathematical symbols introduced to Europe by the Arabs.

850 Coffee discovered in Ethiopia.

900 Settlement of New Zealand by Maori people.

900 Mayan civilization of Central America suddenly declines as climate changes.

1001–1200 CE

1041 Use of moveable clay printing type developed.

1127 Southern Song Dynasty established in Hangzhou.

1000 The Tale of Genji, considered by many to be the first ever novel, written in Japan.

1095–99 First Crusade by Christian armies to Palestine.

1054 Christian Church divides between Rome (Catholic) and Byzantium (Orthodox).

1066 Rise of Norman power, including the invasion of Britain.

1000 Viking Lief Erickson reaches North America at Newfoundland.

1201–1400 CE

1211–1368 Mongol invasion and occupation lead to creation of the Yuan Dynasty. Mongol occupation marks one of China's most creative periods as orthodoxy is replaced by invention and self-expression.

1274–95 Marco Polo's visit increases European interest in China.

1300–1400 Luo Guanzhong writes Romance of the Three Kingdoms and The Water Margin.

1368 Ming armies drive the Mongol Yuan Dynasty from China.

1206 Series of Muslim invasions culminates in creation of Delhi Sultanate.

1221 First Mongol invasion of India by Genghis Khan.

1281 Mongol invasion of Jaoan thwarted by a typhoon (kamikaze, a 'divine wind').

1300 Ottoman empire founded in Turkey.

1332 Black Death (bubonic plague) begins in India.

1398 Mongol leader Tamerlane destroys Delhi.

1100 First universities established.

1215 Magna Carta transfers power in England from monarch to aristocracy.

1242 Mongol armies end invasion of Europe.

1250 The longbow, the most powerful weapon before firearms, is developed in Britian.

1290 Spectacles invented in Italy.

1347–51 Black Death kills a third of Europe's population.

1387 Chaucer's Canterbury Tales.

1200 Foundation of the iron-age Great Zimbabwe civilization.

1201 Earthquake kills more than 1 million people in Egypt, Eastern Mediterranean.

1206 Genghis Khan founds the Mongol empire.

1300 Inca empire begins to dominate the central Andes.

1327 Aztecs establish Mexico City.

1401–1600 CE

1405–33 Zheng He's seven voyages to India, Africa, Middle East.

1406 Construction of Forbidden City in Bei'jing begins.

1460 First overseas exports of Ming porcelain.

1488 Work on rebuilding the Great Wall begins.

1516 Portuguese establish the first European trading post in China at Macau.

1590 Journey to the West published.

1430 Khmer empire destroyed by Thais, Angkor Wat abandoned.

1492 Portuguese navigator Vasco de Gama arrives in India.

1542 Portuguese navigator Antonio da Mota is the first European to enter Japan.

1570 Japan opens Nagasaki to foreign trade.

1571 Ottoman fleet destroyed by Christians at Lepanto, marking the end of Muslim expansion.

1456 The Gutenberg Bible, the first book produced in Europe using movable type, is printed.

1492 Muslins and Jews expelled from Spain following the Reconquista.

1517 Martin Luther publishes anti-Catholic theses that will lead to the creation of Protestantism.

1519 Death of Leonardo da Vinci.

1560 Tobacco imported into Europe.

1564 William Shakespeare born.

1575 European copies of Chinese porcelain made in Italy.

1440–50 Incas build Cuzco and Machu Picchu in Peru.

1492 Christopher Colombus sails from Spain to North America.

1521 Spanish solider Hernanado Cortez destroys Azetc empire in Mexico.

1522 Portuguese expedition completes first circumnavigation of the world.

1530 Start of the trans-Atlantic slave trade.

1601–1800 CE

1637 English trading post established in Canton (Guangzhou).

1644 Manchus overthrow the Ming, and establish the Qing, Dynasty

1600 East India Company founded in London

1600–30 Beginning of Edo period in Japan and country's withdrawal from the wider world.

1609 First shipment of Chinese tea arrives in Europe.

1642–47 English Civil War.

1649 Execution of Charles I in London.

1607 Jamestown colony established in Virginia as the first permanent English settlement in North America.

1616 Dutch sailors under Dirk Hartog became the first Europeans to land in Australia.

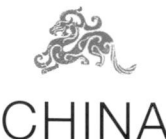

CHINA   ASIA   EUROPE   OTHER

1601–1800 CE

1683 Formosa (Taiwan) annexed by China.

1685 All Chinese ports opened to foreign trade.

1729 Emperor Yongzheng bans opium smoking.

1735 China signs Treaty of Kiakhta with Russia to settle borders.

1736–96 Reign of Emperor Qianlong, zenith of Manchu empire.

1750 Manchus seize Lhasa and occupy Tibet.

1750 Cao Xuequin writes *Dream of the Red Chamber*.

1784 The United States begin to trade directly with China.

1793 British envoy Lord McCartney fails to establish formal ties with China.

1796–1804 Anti-Manchu 'White Lotus' rebellion contributed to erosion of the Qing Dynasty's authority.

1619–24 Dutch establish monopoly over the Southeast Asian spice trade.

1685 First British outpost in Southeast Asia established in Sumatra.

1707 Death of Emperor Aurangzeb marks start of collapse of India's Moghul empire.

1739 Persian ruler Nadir Shah sacks Delhi, removing the Peacock Throne and much of the Mughals' remaining wealth.

1757 Battle of Plassey, north of Kolkata, marks the start of British rule in India.

1767 Burmese armies invade Siam, destroying its capital at Ayudhya.

1782–85 Chakri Dynasty founded in Siam by Rama I; Burmese driven out and new capital built in Bangkok.

1652–54 First Anglo-Dutch War.

1665–66 Great Plague and Fire of London.

1682–1725 Reign of Peter the Great in Russia.

1683 Ottoman Turks defeated at the siege of Vienna, ending Muslim threat to Europe.

1701–13 Europe engulfed in War of Spanish Succession.

1756–63 Seven Years War between Britain, Prussia and France, Austria and Russia.

1779–95 French Revolution.

1783 First recorded manned flight successfully carried out by a hot air balloon built by the Montgolfier brothers in France.

1792–1815 Revolutionary and Napoleonic Wars between France, Britain and much of the rest of Europe.

1620 'Pilgrim Fathers' establish colony in Massachusetts.

1638 First printing press established in North America.

1651 Dutch found Cape Town in South Africa.

1661 Slavery of African migrants legalized in Virginia.

1664 British seize New Amsterdam from Dutch, and rename it New York.

1701 Start of the West African Asante kingdom.

1754–63 Anglo-French war in North America.

1775–83 American War of Independence.

1787 First steam boat tested on the Delaware river in the United States by John Fitch.

1788 First British convicts sent to Australia.

1795 British seize Cape Town from Dutch.

1801–2008 CE

1839–42 Ban on opium leads to war with Britain, and annexation of Hong Kong.

1850–64 Anti-Manchu Taiping Rebellion lasts 30 years, leaving 30 million dead.

1860 Anglo-French forces occupy and sack Bei'jing.

1894-95 Japan defeats China and occupies Taiwan.

1900 Anti-Western Boxer Rebellion in Bei'jing leads to increased foreign domination.

1911–12 Sun Yat'sen topples Qing Dynasty, leading to creation of a republic.

1921 Communist Party of China formed.

1934–35 Over 100,000 communist troops retreat from nationalist forces in the 12,500-km 'Long March' from Jiang'xi to Shaan'xi province. Barely 25 per cent survive.

1936–37 Japan invades China; communist and nationalist forces unite to confront the occupiers.

1945 World War II ends, Japan withdraws forces from China.

1826 British extend influence on Malay peninsula by combining Malacca, Penang, Singapore as Straits Settlements.

1853 U.S. Navy warships arrive in Japan to enforce demands that the country open up to foreign trade.

1854 U.S. and Japan sign first trade agreement.

1857–58 Indian Mutiny leads Britain to impose direct rule.

1858 French troops land in Tourane (Danang) in modern Vietnam.

1869 Opening of the Suez canal shortens distance between Europe and Asia.

1885-86 Burma becomes a province of British India.

1885 Indian National Congress is founded to challenge British rule.

1887 French Indochina formed from Annam, Tonkin, Cochin, China and Cambodia.

1892–98 Insurrection against Spanish colonial power in the Philippines.

1804 Napoleon crowned emperor of France.

1815 Napoleon defeated at Battle of Waterloo, sent into exile.

1827 Nicephore Niepce of France produces first photograph.

1848 Publication of Marx and Engel's *Communist Manifesto*.

1853-56 Crimean War between Russia and Britain, France and Turkey.

1871 Unification of Germany.

1890 German and French investors and manufacturers start modern car industry.

1895 France's Lumiere brothers invent the firm projector and the cinema.

1895 Guglielmo Marconi pioneers wireless telegraphy in Italy.

1904 Entente Cordiale signed between France and Britain, ending centuries of conflict between the two nations.

1905 Revolutionary uprising suppressed in Russia.

1914–18 First World War.

1812–14 U.S. war with Britain.

1831–36 Charles Darwin's scientific voyage to the Pacific aboard the *Beagle*.

1844 Samuel Morse sends first telegraph message.

1859 First oil well drilled at Titusville, Pennsylvania.

1861–65 American Civil War.

1876 Alexander Graham Bell patents the telephone.

1877 Thomas Edison makes the first phonograph (gramophone) recording.

1880–81 First Boer War between British and Transvaal Boers in South Africa.

1884–85 Berlin Conference signalled European occupation of much of Africa.

1888 George Eastman introduces the Kodak hand-held portable box camera.

1899–1902 Second Boer War ends with South Africa under British rule.

1902 Cuba becomes independent under U.S. protection.

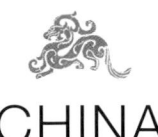

CHINA   ASIA   EUROPE   OTHER

1801–2008 CE

CHINA

1949 Communist forces defeat nationalist Kuomintang and proclaim People's Republic of China with Mao Ze'dong as its leader.

1950–53 China joins North Korea in fighting UN forces on Korean peninsula.

1958 Mao launches 'Great Leap Forward' economic plan based on collectivization of agriculture and labour-intensive industry. The plan fails, leading to mass starvation.

1962 Chinese and Indian forces clash along their disputed Himalayan border in Ladakh and Assam.

1966–76 Mao's 'Cultural Revolution', intended to rekindle China's radical spirit, creates long-lasting economic, political and social chaos.

1970 China launches first satellite, which remains in orbit for 26 days transmitting the revolutionary song 'The East Is Red'.

1976–77 Mao dies and is succeeded by Deng Xiaoping, who emphasises economic development over political purity.

1979 Diplomatic ties with United States established.

1986–90 Deng's 'Open-door policy' encourages foreign investment, the creation of a market economy and a private sector.

1989 Troops fire on demonstrators in Bei'jing's Tian'an'men Square after weeks of peaceful protests, killing at least 200. China is diplomatically isolated for some years after the killings

1997 Hong Kong reverts to China after more than 150 years of British colonial rule.

1999 Macau, the last European colony in Asia, reverts to China after more than 440 years of Portuguese colonial rule.

1999 Test launch of the first unmanned space capsule.

2003 China's first manned space flight, by astronaut Yang Liwei.

2005 Second manned space flight, with two astronauts circling Earth in the Shenzhou VI space capsule.

2008 Beijing Olympics.

ASIA

1898 U.S. ceded Philippines after defeating Spain in the Spanish-American War.

1899–1902 Insurrection in the Philippines against U.S. occupation.

1904–05 Japan defeats Russia at Port Arthur, Tsushima.

1910 Japan annexes Korea.

1931 Japan invades Manchuria and installs puppet regime.

1932 Siam's monarchy replaced by parliamentary government.

1941 Japan attacks U.S. and British bases and colonies in Hawaii and Southeast Asia without warning. Pacific War begins.

1945 U.S. drops atomic bombs on Japanese cities of Hiroshima and Nagasaki, ending World War II.

1945 Indonesian nationalists declare independence from Dutch.

1945 Communists declare Vietnam independence from France.

1946 Philippines granted full independence from U.S.

1947 Britain partitions the sub-continent between India and Pakistan and withdraws.

1948 Burma gains independence from Britain.

1951 Japan signs peace treaty with the U.S. and other nations.

1954 France withdraws from Vietnam, leaving country divided.

1957 Malaya becomes independent from Britain.

1964 U.S. launches bombing offensive against North Vietnam, builds up ground forces.

1975 North Vietnam defeats South Vietnam, country unified.

1997–98 Asian financial crisis causes deep economic damage.

2004 At least 230,000 dead and missing in Southeast Asia, India and Sri Lanka after earthquake triggers tsunami.

EUROPE

1917 Russian government toppled by Bolsheviks.

1918 Russia and Germany sign peace treaty. Tsar and family killed by communists.

1922 Italy's Fascist leader Mussolini forms government.

1922–91 Union of Soviet Socialist Republics.

1929 World stock market crash leads to mass unemployment.

1933 Nazi Party leader Adolf Hitler becomes German Chancellor.

1936–39 Spanish Civil War.

1938 Germany annexes Austria and Sudetenland.

1939–45 Second World War.

1949 Germany divided into two zones.

1949 First modern computer operational at Manchester University.

1956 Hungarians opposed to presence of Soviet forces staged uprising in which thousands died.

1957 Formation of European Economic Community (EEC).

1957 Soviet Union launches the first man-made satellite, Sputnik I.

1961 Construction of the Berlin Wall.

1968 Around 500,000 Warsaw Pact troops invade Czechoslovakia to prevent the country leaving Soviet orbit.

1986 Reactor at the Ukraine's Chernobyl nuclear power station explods, sending a radioactive plume across Europe.

1989 Berlin Wall torn down.

1991 Soviet Union replaced by Commonwealth of Independent States, comprising most former Soviet republics.

2001 China and Russia sign Friendship treaty.

2002 Russia and U.S. agree to radically reduce their nuclear missile arsenals.

2004 191 people killed by bombs on Madrid trains.

2005 52 people killed in bomb attacks on London's transport system.

OTHER

1903 First powered flight conducted by Orville Wright in North Carolina.

1905 Albert Einstein publishes his theory on relativity.

1908 Henry Ford makes first Model T car using production-line techniques.

1914 Opening of Panama Canal accelerates trade between U.S. and Asia.

1926 U.S. physicist Robert Goddard tests the first liquid-fueled rocket, reaching an altitude of 14 metres.

1927 Television demonstrated by Philo Farnsworth.

1942 German scientists test the V2 rocket, the first ballistic missile.

1942 First atomic reaction produced under controlled conditions in Chicago.

1945 Atomic bomb tested at Los Alamos, New Mexico. Within months, two bombs dropped in Japan, ending World War II.

1951 First commercial computer, the UNIVAC 1, made in the US.

1956 U.S. forces Britain and France to withdraw from Egypt after their attempt to recover the Suez Canal.

1959 Fidel Castro overthrows the U.S.-backed Cuban government.

1962 Algeria gains independence from France.

1967 Israel launches attacks against its Arab neighbours, seizing large areas of Jordan, Egypt and Syria.

1969 U.S. Astronaut Neil Armstrong walks on the moon.

1973 Egypt attacks Israel in Sinai, inflicting serious losses before being repulsed.

1975 Microsoft formed to write computer software.

1980–88 Iran-Iraq War.

1982–83 Britain recovers Falklands Islands from Argentinean invaders.

1991 First Gulf War expels Iraqi forces from Kuwait.

2001 Terrorist attacks in U.S. kill almost 3,000 people.

2003– Second Gulf War and occupation of Iraq.

ACKNOWLEDGEMENTS

This is by far the most ambitious project I have ever attempted, and among all the people who contributed to making this book there are three without whom it would have simply remained just another idea.

My grateful thanks must go first to Michael Dover, my publisher and editor who was quick to see the project's potential and committed his unwavering support from the start. In particular, Michael brought home to me that the book should be accessible to a wide audience and not just those already familiar with China's extraordinary culture, diversity and sheer physical beauty. Above all, thank you for your patience and for believing that I could and should write the text – despite my struggle with tenses and the more arcane rules governing the use of the English language. And I hope I have not shattered your illusions about my 'literary voice'.

If Michael provided the intellectual and visionary energy I required to get started then Nina Huang'fan, my producer in Beijing, provided much of the raw power I needed to get the book finished. I first worked with Huang'fan on Michael Palin's *Himalaya* TV series, and, from the very beginning of this project, her invaluable research added substance to my dreams. Her meticulous planning and extensive network of contacts throughout China ensured we could meet our ambitious goals within budget and on time. Her long-distance contributions to the book's design and text were also vital, and the procurement of the calligraphy for the chapters and 'chops' for the provinces, as well as the research and collecting of material for my writing – were all done with maximum efficiency and minimum fuss. Thank you, my dear friend, for your total commitment to the project, for which I will be forever grateful. I hope that you will be happy with what I've done with *our* book.

It is difficult to find the words, literary or otherwise, to adequately express my gratitude to Michael Palin – my great friend and patron, to whom I owe my career. Michael has literally shown me the world through his insatiable appetite for new horizons. He has dragged me from my comfortable couch and transformed me into a moderately adventurous tourist. Thank you Mike for choosing to take your 'gap year' at just the right time so that I could also pursue my dream project; for being positive and encouraging about my first attempt at stringing 'words' instead of 'snaps' together and for the wisdom and generosity that gave me the confidence to finish the job. The next round of martinis is on me.

My grateful thanks must also go to my Cheung Chau Gang – to my old friend and neighbour Gavin Greenwood, who has so expertly composed the Timeline and Provincial Openings and helped to edit the captions. And to my goddaughter Stella Lai, associate designer and computer wizard, for her keen eye and fast fingers. I look forward to the day, which I know will be very soon, when I can just hand you a stack of pictures with the knowledge that you will come back with a beautiful book.

I thank all at Weidenfeld & Nicolson in London, particularly Debbie Woska for her fine editing and Fiona McIntosh for supervising the production. Also to Newsele in Milano for the excellent colour reproductions, and to Dario Martinelli and his team at Printer Trento for once again producing the final book with dedication and finesse. *Grazie mille.*

Thanks to Steve Abbott and Paul Bird at Mayday Management for handling the finances, and to my old friend and agent Peter Bennett-Jones who took time from running his empire to protect me from the big bad world of commerce. Thank you all.

On a more personal note, I thank my parents and my family for their support – particularly Pat, Sonia and Ed for tolerating my relentless travel schedule.

Finally, to all the people in China who helped us on this journey. *Xie-xie* from my heart and from my soul.

Basil Pao 2007

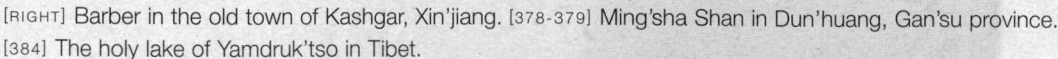

[RIGHT] Barber in the old town of Kashgar, Xin'jiang. [378-379] Ming'sha Shan in Dun'huang, Gan'su province. [384] The holy lake of Yamdruk'tso in Tibet.

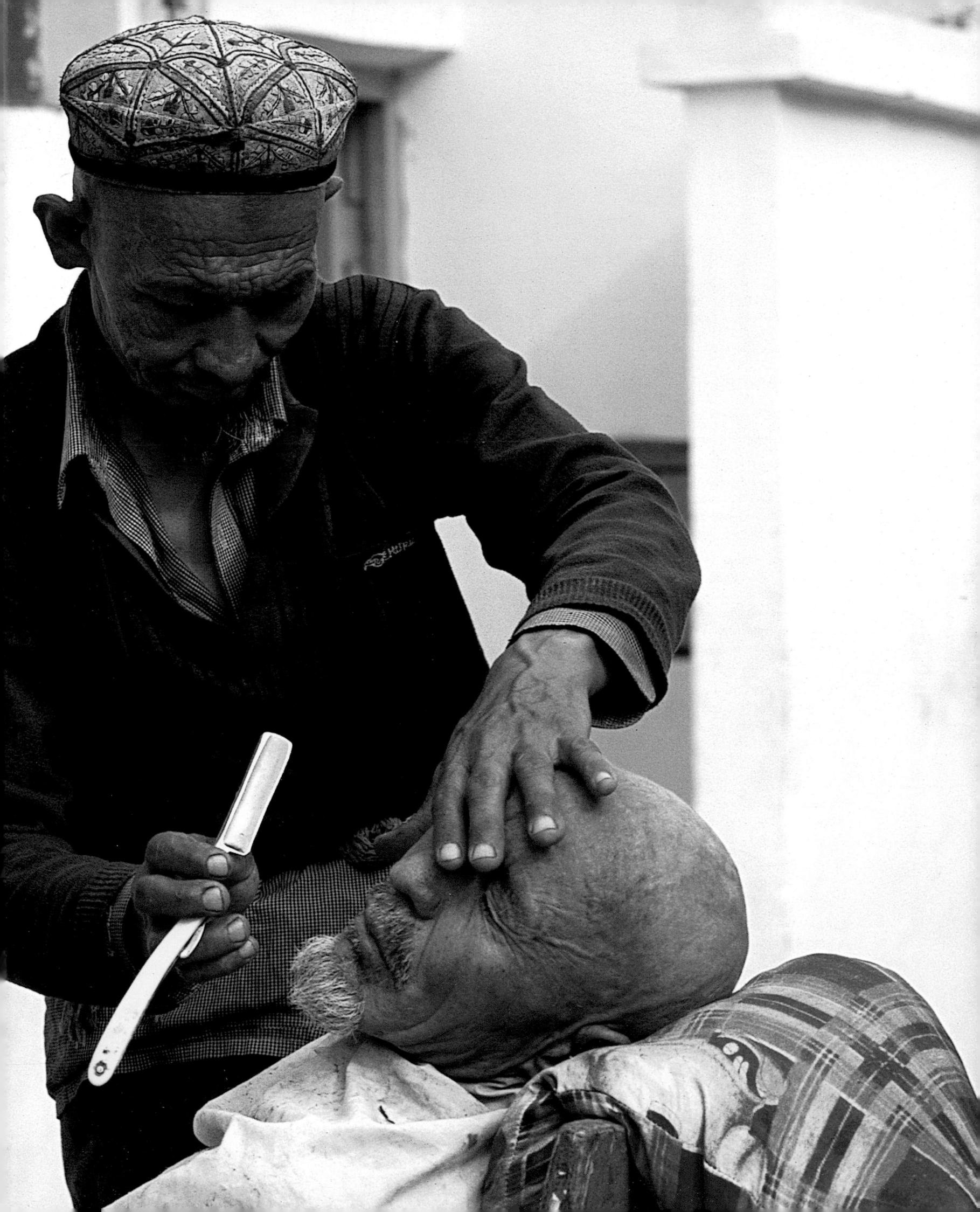

You rule a kingdom by ordinary deeds,
You conduct a war by exceptional actions,
But you rule the world by letting it alone.
And how do I know this?
By what lies within.

The more prohibitions and taboos, the poorer the people will be.
The sharper the weapons are, the greater the chaos and confusion will be.
The cleverer the people are, the bigger the craze for waste will be.
The more laws and regulations, the more thieves and robbers will rise.

Therefore the sage says:
If I do not issue commands, the people will behave themselves.
If I do not preach and remain silent, the people will find serenity.
If I do not meddle, the people will prosper by themselves.
If I do not impose my desires, the people will return to simplicity.

Chapter 57 of *Tao Teh Ching* by Lao Tzu

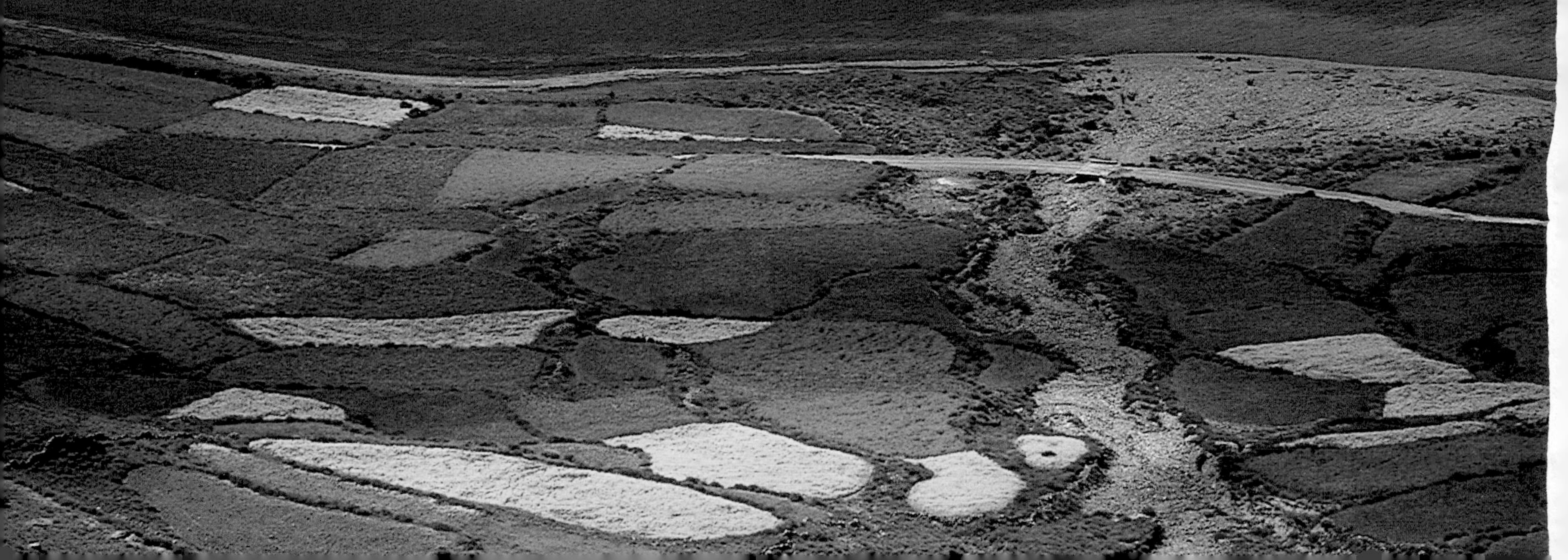